W9-BEF-919

FIELDS OF
READING

Motives for Writing

SEVENTH EDITION

FIELDS OF READING
Motives for Writing

NANCY R. COMLEY
Queens College, CUNY

DAVID HAMILTON
University of Iowa

CARL H. KLAUS
University of Iowa

ROBERT SCHOLES
Brown University

NANCY SOMMERS
Harvard University

BEDFORD/ST. MARTIN'S   Boston ◆ New York

For Bedford/St. Martin's

Developmental Editor: Bennett Morrison
Production Editor: Sarah Ludwig
Production Supervisor: Jennifer Wetzel
Marketing Manager: Brian Wheel
Art Director: Lucy Krikorian
Copy Editor: Rosemary Winfield
Photo Research: Joan Scafarello
Cover Design: Lucy Krikorian
Cover Art: David Hockney, *The Road Across the Wolds*, 1997, Oil on Canvas, 48×60", © David Hockney
Composition: Macmillan Indian Limited, Bangalore, India
Printing and Binding: Haddon Craftsmen, Inc., an R.R. Donnelley & Sons Company

President: Joan E. Feinberg
Editorial Director: Denise B. Wydra
Editor in Chief: Nancy Perry
Director of Marketing: Karen Melton Soeltz
Director of Editing, Design, and Production: Marcia Cohen
Managing Editor: Erica T. Appel

Library of Congress Control Number: 2003107547

Copyright © 2004 by Bedford/St. Martin's
All rights reserved. No part of this book may be reproduced, stored in a retrieval system, or transmitted in any form or by any means, electronic, mechanical, photocopying, recording, or otherwise, except as may be expressly permitted by the applicable copyright statutes or in writing by the Publisher.

Manufactured in the United States of America.

9 8 7 6 5 4
f e d c b a

For information, write: Bedford/St. Martin's, 75 Arlington Street, Boston, MA 02116   (617-399-4000)

ISBN: 0-312-40471-9

Acknowledgments and copyrights appear at the back of the book on pages 785–789, which constitute an extension of the copyright page.

It is a violation of the law to reproduce these selections by any means whatsoever without the written permission of the copyright holder.

Preface

The title *Fields of Reading: Motives for Writing* identifies our goal of providing students with tools to establish and develop their own motives for writing throughout their college and professional lives. This seventh edition of *Fields of Reading* contains eighty-five readings from a broad range of academic, professional, and literary writing, organized around four main purposes for writing: Reflecting, Reporting, Explaining, and Arguing. In focusing on purpose, we give students and instructors the opportunity to explore the complex relationships among writers and readers that vary according to "what" and "why" people write and read.

Highlights of the Seventh Edition

Flexible Organization. The four broad rhetorical categories—Reflecting, Reporting, Explaining, and Arguing—represent essential kinds of reading and writing in virtually every academic or professional area. In every field, individuals consider past experience (reflecting), convey information (reporting), make sense of knowledge (explaining), and debate controversial ideas and issues (arguing). Within each of the four categories, we have grouped the selections by academic field: Arts and Humanities, Social Sciences and Public Affairs, and Sciences and Technologies. We hope that this dual organization will assist instructors in discovering and assigning selections for a variety of classroom purposes.

New Reading Selections. Of the seventy-six prose selections, twenty-nine are new to the seventh edition. These pieces represent a diverse array of well-known thinkers, critics, and scholars writing on timely and interesting topics—such as Barry Commoner writing about genetic engineering and the Human Genome Project; Adam Gopnik writing on the terrorist attacks of September 11, 2001; and Judith Ortiz Cofer writing about race, culture, and her physical self. Also included among the selections are nine poems — six of them new — that were chosen as models of rhetorical effectiveness and grouped under the same rhetorical and cross-curricular categories as their prose counterparts.

New Photographs and Illustrations. For this edition, we researched the first publication of every reading in the collection to determine whether it included informationally pertinent photographs or illustrations. Based on that research, we have included the original photographs and illustrations for fifteen of the readings. These photos and illustrations provide students the context to experience the readings closer to the way they were originally intended.

Thematic Connections. For instructors who prefer to teach the selections by theme, we have grouped all of the selections by thematically related clusters. Any selection can be taught in terms of its themes or area of interest by using the updated Thematic Table of Contents, which includes clusters on such topics as Interpreting the Body, Myths and Rituals, and Understanding the Physical World. As a result, students will have ample opportunity to read and consider different perspectives on a single issue or explore a particular issue in depth. The Making Connections questions following selections also encourage students to explore thematic relationships between readings.

New Casebook on working in America. Building on the notion of thematic connections between readings, a new group of readings brings together C. Wright Mills, Vivian Gomick, Barbara Ehrenreich, Eric Schlosser, and Philip Levine on the topic of work. This thematic casebook at the end of the collection allows students to focus intensely on a single topic. Students can use the Making Connections questions to examine the different ways each author treats the subject, and they are encouraged to enter the discussion with their own writing and research.

Introduction to the Reading and Writing Process. Beginning with the introduction to the book, *Fields of Reading* helps students to write in responses to readings and to perform their own research. The introduction explains and illustrates the interrelationship between the reading and writing processes, primarily through an examination of a specially commissioned essay by Patricia Hampl. In "Reviewing Anne Frank," Hampl reflects on her own response to a particular writing assignment, a book review for the *New York Times*. In doing so, she both illustrates her own writing process and demonstrates that even accomplished writers struggle with some of the same challenges student writers face. We have also reprinted in this section Hampl's published review, "The Whole Anne Frank." These introductory materials, like the rest of the book, are meant to present reading and writing not in abstract terms, but through discussion and examples that vividly demonstrate what is actually involved in each activity.

Help with Evaluating and Using Sources. Within the introduction, we have included guidelines for acknowledging sources, including the broad issues of how to evaluate potential source materials and how to use them within a piece of writing. This section focuses particularly on sources drawn from the Web, because those pose the greatest pitfalls for students who might be uncertain of how to judge the relative work of online material and incorporate it appropriately, with proper acknowledgment, in their own writing.

Extensive Critical Apparatus. Much of our critical apparatus focuses on the rhetorical concepts and techniques that apply to reading and writing across the curriculum as introduced in the section "For Students." The detailed introductions to each of the four main sections, Reflecting, Reporting, Explaining, and Arguing (which are illustrated from passages from the anthologized readings), define the type of writing featured in that section and discuss its use in differing fields and situations. The introductions also identify and explain the rhetorical methods used to achieve each type of writing's aims, for example, how description and narration are basic to reporting or how analogy, comparison and contrast, definition, and illustration are basic to explaining. All the rhetorical aims and modes covered in the introductions are also referenced in the Rhetorical Index. The headnote for each piece identifies and, wherever necessary, explains the professional fields of its author and the rhetorical context or source of its original publication. Likewise, the questions following each selection call for reading and writing that relate form and style to purpose, subject, and academic field.

Acknowledgments

For their detailed reactions to the sixth edition of *Fields of Reading* and suggestions for improving the seventh edition, we are grateful to the following reviewers: Nancy G. Barron, Northern Arizona University; Mary Bly, University of California—Davis; Peter Bricklebank, New York University; Diane Canow, Central Missouri State University; James H. Clemmer, Austin Peay State University; John Coakley, New Jersey Institute of Technology; Pamela Demory, University of California—Davis; Sean

Egan, Queens College; Shawn Fagundes-Hansen, Sacramento City College; Susan Fanetti, Saint Louis University; Julie Funderburk, University of North Carolina — Greensboro; Lisa Gim, Fitchburg State College; Janis E. Haswell, Texas A&M University — Corpus Christi; Loren Hecht, Northern Illinois University; Ivan D. McDaniel, Tulane University; Joseph Millichap, Western Kentucky University, Nathan K. Nelson, Ferris State University; Angelia M. Northrip, Southwest Missouri State University; Kathleen J. O'Shea, Monroe Community College; Annie Papreck, Saint Louis University; Teri Pastore, Portland Community College; Diane Quantic, Wichita State University; Laima Sruoginis, University of Southern Maine; William K. Storey, Millsaps College; Margaret L. Wick, The College of Wooster; John R. Woznicki, Georgian Court College; and Katherine Wright, Northern Illinois University. Finally, we would like to thank our Development Editor, Ben Morrison, as well as the other staff members of Bedford/St. Martin's for their help and encouragement, in particular Joan Feinberg, President; Nancy Perry, Editor-in-Chief; Kristy Bredin, Editorial Assistant; Erica Appel, Managing Editor; and Sarah Ludwig, Project Editor.

                                                                    N. R. C.
                                                                       D. H.
                                                                    C. H. K.
                                                                       R. S.
                                                                       N. S.

Contents

Social Sciences and Public Affairs   86

Social Sciences and Public Affairs   379

Sciences and Technologies   467

ARGUING   517

Thematic Contents

VALUES AND BELIEFS

CULTURES IN COLLISION AND CONTACT

RACE AND RACISM

THE EXPERIENCES OF WOMEN

INTERPRETING THE BODY

VIOLENCE AND WAR

LIFE AND DEATH

OBSERVING THE NATURAL WORLD

UNDERSTANDING THE PHYSICAL WORLD

HUMAN PORTRAITS

TEACHING, LEARNING, AND SCHOOLING

HEALTH, DISEASE, AND MEDICINE

INTERPRETING THE PAST

ANNE FRANK: HER PLACE IN HISTORY

THE ATOMIC BOMBING OF JAPAN

INTERPRETING CURRENT AFFAIRS AND CONTEMPORARY HUMAN EXPERIENCE

CASEBOOK

INTERPRETING THE ARTS AND POPULAR CULTURE

MYTHS AND RITUALS

For Students

Fields of Reading: Motives for Writing, seventh edition, is intended to help you develop the abilities in reading and writing that you will need as you move from one course to another, one field of study to another, throughout your college career. In some senses, of course, all areas of study expect the same things of you—namely, close and careful reading as well as clear and exact writing, with an attentiveness above all to information and ideas. But the particular kinds of information, ideas, and concerns that distinguish each field of study also call for somewhat different reading and writing abilities. A book review for a literature course, for example, requires a different form and style from a lab report in physics. So we have tried to give you a sampling of the varied fields of writing you are likely to encounter in the academic world.

Most undergraduate schools are organized around some version of the traditional division of studies into "the humanities," "the social sciences," and "the sciences." The humanities generally include fields of learning that are thought of as having a cultural orientation, such as language, literature, history, philosophy, and religion. The social sciences, which include such fields as anthropology, economics, education, political science, psychology, and sociology, deal with social institutions and the behavior of their individual members. The sciences include fields of knowledge that are concerned with the natural and physical world, such as astronomy, botany, chemistry, physics, and zoology.

These traditional divisions of study are closely affiliated with applied areas of study and work that also exist in the professional world. The humanities, for example, are closely allied with the arts; the social sciences, with public affairs such as business and government; and the sciences, with technology. These divisions and clusterings of fields—Arts and Humanities, Social Sciences and Public Affairs, Sciences and Technologies—are so broadly applicable that we have used them as one of the organizing principles in our table of contents.

Like any set of categories, these divisions are a convenient, but by no means foolproof, system of classification. Although the system can help you to understand the academic world, it does not reflect the exact state of affairs in every specialized field at every college and university. Specialists in a particular field sometimes migrate from one area of learning to another, from the social sciences to the sciences, for example, according to the orientation of their research in a particular project. Or specialists from several fields may form an interdisciplinary area of research, such as environmental studies, which involves a wide range of academic disciplines — botany, chemistry, economics, philosophy, political science, and zoology. So the writing that results from these projects often can be categorized in more than one broad area of learning.

The writing we have collected in *Fields of Reading* can be understood not only in terms of the area of learning that it represents, but also in terms of the particular purpose it is meant to achieve. Every piece of writing, of course, is the product of an author's personal and professional motives, so in a sense the purposes for writing are as varied and ultimately mysterious as are authors themselves. But setting aside the mysteries of human nature, it is possible to identify and define a set of different purposes for writing, which we refer to as Reflecting, Reporting, Explaining, and Arguing, one or another of which predominates in most academic and professional writing. Therefore, we have used this set of purposes as the major organizing principle in our table of contents.

By Reflecting, we mean a kind of writing in which authors are concerned with recalling and thinking about their past experience, for personal experience is often an especially valuable source of knowledge and learning. By Reporting, we mean writing that is concerned primarily with conveying factual information about some particular aspect of the world, past or present. By Explaining, we mean writing that is concerned primarily with making sense of information or shedding light on a particular subject. By Arguing, we mean writing that is given to debating controversial explanations, values, or beliefs. Like our other categories, these are convenient, but not rigid, modes of classification. So they need to be used tactfully, with an awareness that to some degree they are bound to overlap. Most pieces of explanation, for example, will at some point involve reporting, if only to convey the information or subject to be explained. And most pieces of argument will call for some explanation, if only to make clear the issues that are at odds with one another. But generally you will find one or another of these purposes to be dominant in any particular piece of writing.

We think that an awareness of these basic purposes can be especially helpful both in the process of reading and in the process of writing, no matter what academic or professional field is involved. We have introduced each section of our collection with an essay on Reflecting, Reporting, Explaining, or Arguing. In these essays you will find detailed definitions and examples of each purpose, as well as explanations and illustrations of how to carry it out in differing fields and situations. Each selection is accompanied by a brief headnote, explanatory footnotes where necessary, and questions for you to think about in your reading and writing. In addition, each selection is also followed by questions to help you make connections among related readings in this collection.

Immediately following this preface, you will find an introduction to reading and writing. In the first section, we show an actual example of how one writer goes through the process of composing a piece of writing; in Reading and Rereading, we discuss various ways to read and understand the pieces in this book or any other material you might encounter in your studies; and in Using and Acknowledging Sources, we discuss how to evaluate, incorporate, and document source materials and why such acknowledgment is important in every field of study. This introduction, like the headnotes, questions, and sectional introductions, is meant to help you become a thoughtful and responsible reader and writer. The rest is up to your instructor, your classmates, and you.

Introduction: Why Write?

No matter what your field of study, you will need to read and write. Often you will need not just to read but to read critically, not just to write but to write clearly, sometimes with argumentative force. This book brings together many readings with those goals in mind. Among the readings, you will find quite a few that discussion will make richer. You should also find some that prompt you to write, perhaps even without an assignment. In putting together this collection, we have sought out readings that we have found provocative as readers and as teachers. Although we realize that a textbook is intended for the classroom and study, it is not an enemy of pleasure. If you carry it with you on vacation or keep it by your bed, we will be pleased and not entirely shocked.

We assume that reading and writing are the daily concerns of your course, skills to be developed in interaction with your classmates and instructor rather than taught from a book's introduction. Nevertheless, in this introduction we offer a few observations that readers and writers might do well to keep in mind. By emphasizing the situation of writers and writing, we focus on what we take to be the deeper intention of your course. Along the way, however, we touch frequently on reading, too, since they are inevitably linked.

Writing as Conversation

Scholars and professional writers take part in extended discussions, which we can think of as conversations. For example, suppose a new discovery is made about the prehistory of humankind, how ancient our species is, or when humans first migrated to the Americas. Any such discovery provokes discussion, modification, and dissent, all of which take place, back and forth, in the specialized publications of the field. Or suppose a less academic situation — a book review or a business report. In these examples

1

as well, writing follows from much that has been said and written before, at the very least a book to be reviewed in the one case and a business situation with its own history — part oral, part written, and to some extent observable — in the other. Our motivation for writing often stems from wanting to join in a discussion about such matters and to offer our own understandings of things.

In a short essay titled "Reviewing Anne Frank" (p. 4), the writer Patricia Hampl reflects on how she once joined in such a discussion. Her essay is about writing a book review (which is reproduced on p. 22). "Literature is a conversation," she says, and her review will play a part in one conversation. Quickly, therefore, Hampl conveys an image of herself as a reader. She has read the book under review. As she reveals in her essay, she has reviewed several other books before this one, and along the way, she has read numerous other reviews. How else would she know what a review is, much less have an idea of how to make hers in some way unusual?

In addition to hints about her reading, Hampl's essay allows us to consider her motivation to write. It is difficult to write well without motivation, and Hampl's motivation is complicated. She is moved by the book under review, a new edition of *The Diary of a Young Girl* by Anne Frank, and she wants to express that emotion. Our best writing usually follows from taking a personal interest in our topic, which Hampl has certainly done. But writing a review for a leading paper like the *New York Times* will also influence her standing in the literary community, which may play a part. Moreover, the *Times* will pay her for her work — no insignificant matter. Most of all, however, Hampl conveys a sense of urgency about the book. If money or standing were primary, she could have sought out other assignments rather than accepting this one.

For most student writers, the motivation for writing is normally a mixture of the same sorts of things: grades, class standing, and convictions about our subjects parallel the motivations Hampl brought to her work. Clearly, the last of these is the most important. When the first two are primary, the writer is simply doing a job. When the latter takes over, the writer becomes more of a presence in the writing and begins to express him- or herself.

Hampl found herself caught up in the story of Anne Frank, and she began her review, "The Whole Anne Frank" (p. 22), with two matter-of-fact paragraphs:

> On Tuesday, March 28, 1944, Gerrit Bolkestein, Education Minister of the Dutch Government in exile, delivered a radio message from London urging his war-weary countrymen to collect "vast quantities of simple, everyday material," as part of the historical record of the Nazi occupation.
>
> "History cannot be written on the basis of official decisions and documents alone," he said. "If our descendants are to understand fully what we as a nation have had to endure and overcome during

these years, then what we really need are ordinary documents — a diary, letters."

Stories in Our Writing

Straightforward as they may appear, these few sentences imply a story—stories within stories for that matter. Minister Bolkestein was aware that he was living through a significant historical moment. He foresaw composing a record of that moment that would stand as history, a history derived from a collection of "ordinary documents." He imagined future readers who would need to understand what the Dutch people had endured. Their understanding would be shaped by the stories such documents could offer. And as we will see, his words stimulated one writer, Anne Frank, to think of her diary differently.

But his words also played a role in the secondary story of Hampl's writing her review. In her essay "Reviewing Anne Frank" (p. 4), Hampl's story begins as she accepts the assignment to review the "Definitive Edition" of Anne Frank's *Diary*, a later, more complete edition than the one first published in 1947. Although Hampl's attitude toward reviewing books is positive and she thinks of it as a "pleasure" akin to the pleasure of reading, she found this assignment more "daunting" than any other. She struggled to begin, and when she finally managed that, she launched herself by way of Bolkestein's remarks.

One story, then, signaled by the two short paragraphs above, is the opportunity Hampl seized to enter into a "conversation" when she agreed to review Anne Frank's book. Her agreement meant that she would participate in a larger public discussion. Every time you take up an essay assignment, you too are entering into a discussion of some sort. If we are speaking only to ourselves, readers will be unlikely to sympathize with us much. If instead we discover a way to join a conversation already begun, we are much more likely to be heard. Thus the importance of another story hinted at here, one having to do with the beginning Hampl found in Bolkestein's message. In those remarks she found a point of entrance that would lift her away from speaking to herself and make it much more likely that she would connect, through her writing, with us.

Let us turn now to Hampl and to her story.

REVIEWING ANNE FRANK

Patricia Hampl

Book reviewing is generally regarded as humble literary work, the bread-and-butter labor of the writing life, far removed from the expressive glories of poetry or fiction. At worst, reviewing is classed as hackwork. Not by me, though. For some reason, I have always harbored an idealistic, even a romantic, affection for reviewing. This romance may be rooted in the fact that my first published work, in my college newspaper when I was nineteen, was a book review—of a new book of poems called *Ariel* by someone named Sylvia Plath.

Although the job demands that a reviewer note the successes and failures in a book, reviewing has never struck me as having much to do with assigning scores or handing out demerits. The reviewer's job—and pleasure—is akin to any reader's. It is the pleasure of talk. Fundamentally, literature is a conversation, strangely intimate, conducted between writer and reader—countless writers, unknown readers. If nobody *talks* about books, if they are not discussed or somehow contended with, literature ceases to be a conversation, ceases to be dynamic. Most of all, it ceases to be intimate. It degenerates into the author's monologue or just a private mutter. Without the reader's response, a book would go silent, like a struck bell that gives no resonance. Reviews are the other half of a conversation that the author of a book begins. Without them, literature would be oddly mute in spite of all those words on all those pages.

But I have never had an assignment as daunting as the one given me to review the new "Definitive Edition" of Anne Frank's *Diary*. For many reasons, the *Diary* is a book like no other. For one thing, virtually every other book I have reviewed has just come off the press. A reviewer is usually a kind of first reader, an explorer describing a new book, like a new country, to the people who have yet to travel there. But who does not know about Anne Frank and her heartbreaking diary? It was first published almost fifty years ago and has been translated into virtually every language in the world that sustains a book culture. Most readers know this book, like very few others, from childhood, and they carry it into adulthood. Even if they haven't read it, people know the story and the essential personality of its extraordinary author. Besides the familiarity of the book, who on earth would claim to "review" Anne Frank? The book seems to defy the very enterprise of book reviewing. I suppose that the emotion ruling me as I approached my task was a paralyzing shyness: who was I to write about this beloved and historic icon of the Holocaust?

In the face of all this, my first act was to procrastinate as long as I could. I did everything to keep from writing the review. I was very good at this. I read the book slowly, I underlined passages that struck me, I took notes, jotting down lines from the *Diary*, some of them passages I remembered with surprising sharpness from girlhood when I had first read the book, some of them new to me. The more I felt the power of the book, the more hopeless I felt. I missed the first deadline and called my editor, begging for an extension. Granted! A reprieve.

Then I procrastinated some more. I developed a sudden urgency about cleaning my oven and sorting out my sock drawer. I called friends, made lunch dates (I never go out to lunch when I'm working). I asked my friends what *they* thought about Anne Frank. I had a ferocious resistance to writing the review. I found yet another way to avoid writing that I could at least call "research": I dug up an essay about Anne Frank by the poet John Berryman, which I remembered having read or having heard about years before. I took notes on *that*.

I was genuinely fascinated, moved even, by the Berryman essay, "The Development of Anne Frank," which I saw from a note in the text had been written in 1967. I had been Berryman's student at the University of Minnesota that very year, taking two courses in "Humanities of the Western World" from him in a packed, overheated room with fifty or sixty other undergraduates. I found myself thinking about this great poet, my old teacher, about the fierce way he had talked about literature, his uncanny ability to bring a roomful of undergraduates to tears just by reading aloud the farewell scene between Hector and Andromache in the *Iliad*. I thought with sorrow of his suicide only a few years after that, how he had jumped to his death from a bridge I walked across every day. I couldn't remember his ever saying anything about Anne Frank, but reading his essay about her all these years later brought him powerfully back to me, the force of his inquiring mind, his determination to understand what was at stake in her book. I still hadn't written a word.

But maybe at last my mind had wandered not away from the task at hand, but right into it. Though I ended up referring briefly to a remark in Berryman's essay when I wrote my own review (a kind of private homage to him), it wasn't so much what his essay said that began to unlock my own timidity. Rather, it was the tone I felt in his essay, a voice that was so poised on *trying to understand* that it had no room for the kind of hand-wringing and worry that I was indulging in myself.

Berryman began by telling how he had first come across Anne Frank's *Diary*—in 1952 when the first installment of the translated text appeared in *Commentary* magazine. "I read it with amazement," he says in his essay. He was so galvanized by the writing that, he says, "The next day, when I went to town to see my analyst, I stopped in the magazine's offices . . . to see if proofs of the *Diary's* continuation were available, and they were." Then, "like millions of people later," he wrote, "I was bowled over with pity and horror and admiration for the astounding doomed little girl."

But he didn't stop with this emotional anchor. He demanded, right from the start, that he think as well as feel. "But what I *thought* was: a sane person. A sane person, in the twentieth century." I recognized that he had found the tip of his subject: how had such extraordinary sanity come to be

developed in the crushing circumstances of Anne Frank's life? It wasn't necessary to know the details of Berryman's own tragic end to feel his urgency
in searching for "a sane person in the twentieth century."

I liked the naturalness of this beginning, the casualness of his saying he   10
was "bowled over." I liked how, having established his feeling, he refused
to dwell on it but pushed on to a thought. I could feel a mind at work —
and more than that, I felt a story unfolding. He was writing a *story*, I suddenly thought, the story of his relation to this book. The *ideas* were like
characters in the story that he kept looking at from one angle and then
another, to make sense of them, to come to a conclusion, much the way a
story must bring its characters to some resolving, if mysterious, finale.

Strangely enough, it was at this point (if I remember correctly) that I
made my first mark on paper, my first stab at my own response to Anne
Frank. I wrote the first three paragraphs of the review, more or less as they
stand now, quite easily, as if there had been no procrastination, no moan-
ing and groaning at all for several weeks of fretful nonwriting. After reading Berryman's essay, I knew what to do — at least for three paragraphs.

The connections between his essay and my review are not obvious. No
one, reading his opening about being bowled over and then mine, which is
a straightforward piece of historical information, would imagine that I had
finally been nudged off the dime by Berryman's essay. His tone is personal
and immediate. Mine is distanced (I don't make use of the first-person pronoun anywhere in my entire review) and rests its authority on certain historical facts I am able to present to the reader.

I got the hint about the Dutch education minister's clandestine radio message from the foreword to the "Definitive Edition," but I tracked down the
exact quotation of the speech from another source at the library. If I wasn't
going to allow myself the kind of authority and presence that Berryman had
with the use of the personal pronoun, I needed to achieve that sense of immediacy another way. Direct quotation, I knew instinctively, would enliven this
bit of historical information.

I tried to make Anne Frank's knowledge of the minister's radio message
part of this story — as indeed it really was. I wanted the reader to see history happening as it happened for Anne Frank herself. That is why I began
the review in a narrative, storylike way: "On Tuesday, March 28, 1944,
Gerrit Bolkestein, Education Minister of the Dutch Government in exile,
delivered a radio message from London . . ." To bolster the authority of this
information in every way possible — and thereby bolster my own authority
as the writer of the piece — I even checked at the library to find out what
day of the week March 28 fell on in the year 1944 so that, casually, I could
note that it was a Tuesday. I wanted to seduce the reader with the authority of simple facts. Words *are* small, but each one can count for a lot. And
maybe I wasn't attempting to "seduce" my readers, but to assure them.

It is odd — even to me — that reading Berryman's very personal (though   15
certainly highly intellectual and closely analytical) essay should have shown
me the way into my own piece about Anne Frank. I had a number of

constraints that hadn't hampered him. For one thing, I had much less space: my editor had allotted me a certain number of words and no more. Berryman had written an essay, a much more open form; I was writing a review.

Still, many reviewers rightly use the first-person voice, and Berryman certainly had won me over partly because of his very immediate presence in his own essay. So why did I steer away from that voice? I think I understood, after reading Berryman, the different task I had before me, especially given my space limitations and my audience in a newspaper. I wasn't coming upon Anne Frank's *Diary* as it came out in proofs for the first time. I was responding to a definitive edition of a book that has long been a classic of postwar literature. I did not need to present myself as having been moved by the *Diary*: History had provided several generations of such readers. But I benefited from the freedom of Berryman's prose, the genuineness of his inquiry. It was a model for me — not a model of style, but of intention.

Also, while I had been procrastinating by having lunch with my friends, one of my companions mentioned that there had been (and continues to be) an ugly and quite demented attempt to deny the authenticity of the *Diary*. Like many anti-Holocaust theories, this one tried to prove that while there might have been a little girl named Anne Frank who had died during the war of "natural causes" (or in some versions had not died but been "lost" or who was herself a fabrication), this child had never written a diary. *The Diary of a Young Girl*, these conspiracy theorists claimed, had been written by adults engaged in a "Jewish plot" — by Anne Frank's father (whose presence as the sole survivor of his murdered family this plot does not account for) or by others.

It was all quite mad, and like all such attempts to deny the truth of history, it was very disturbing and obviously fired by racial hatred. I wanted to be sure nothing I wrote could even remotely be used for such evil. The reason these allegations about the *Diary* had won any attention at all hinged on the fact that there were indeed several versions of Anne Frank's diaries. I studied the distinctions among the various texts carefully and attempted to present them briefly but clearly by making reference to the "Critical Edition," which had been published in 1986. I wanted to refute these very allegations, crazy and repugnant as they were, and to use my review, in part, to alert readers to false claims made in this regard.

Reading Berryman's essay had made me especially aware of the time that had passed between his first response to the book in 1952, hardly seven years after Anne Frank's death in Bergen-Belsen, and my reading of the 1995 "Definitive Edition" when she would have been sixty-six. I felt my task was to mediate time and history, at least in a modest way. I had to give readers some of the basic biographical information that for most readers, I knew would be unnecessary, but I also had to place the book in its public history.

With this in mind, I made reference at the end of the review to its age — fifty years old — and to Philip Roth's use of Anne Frank as a fictional character in his novel *The Ghost Writer*. I wanted to show how Anne Frank has entered our lives as a permanent presence, that to invoke her name is to invoke a person we know and who shall always be missing because her presence in her book has made her so alive it is "unthinkable and disorienting," as I say in my review, that she should have been snuffed out.

I remember feeling a kind of relief (not satisfaction, but the more unburdened feeling that the word *relief* suggests) when I stumbled on the word *disorienting*. I felt that this had something to do with the enduring grief and regret that mention of Anne Frank brings forward within us. I felt that my sense of being "disoriented" by her death was related to Berryman's relief in finding a "sane person in the twentieth century." We *should* be disoriented by such hellish hatred: I was writing my review, after all, as children were dying from similar sectarian hatred in Bosnia. I, too, needed to find a sane person in the twentieth century.

Finally, I wanted to remind people of the extraordinary person Anne Frank was, the splendid writer, the utterly natural girl-woman, and the gifted thinker. All my notes paid off, just as my luncheon with my friend had: I had many passages that I was able to use to present Anne Frank to readers not only as the icon of a murdered child, but as a strong and vital writer. I came away from my reading of the *Diary* convinced absolutely that had she lived, Anne Frank would have written many books and that we would know her not only as the author of her diary.

When I was a girl first reading the *Diary*, I had treasured it because of how Anne fought and contended with her mother, just as I did, how she battled to become a person — the very thing Berryman honored most in her, too. I *needed* Anne Frank then, not because she was the child who died and put a face on the six million murdered (I was not yet capable of taking in that historical fact), but because, like me, she was determined to live, to grow up to be herself and no one else. She was, simply, my friend. I don't think I was able to keep in mind that she was dead. I went to her *Diary* as she went to Kitty, for a friendship not to be found anywhere else but in books. As Anne Frank wrote to Kitty in a letter in her red plaid notebook, "Paper is more patient than people." It is the secret motto not only of a passionate teenager, but of any writer.

About two weeks after my review was published, I received a small white envelope, addressed in a careful hand in blue ink, forwarded to me from the *New York Times,* which had received it. There was no return address, but the envelope was postmarked New York. A fan letter, I thought with a brief flutter of vanity.

Inside was a single sheet, my name written again with the careful blue ink, and below that a crazy quilt of black headlines apparently photocopied from various articles in newspapers and periodicals. All of them claimed in their smudged, exclamatory way, to have evidence of the "Anne Frank Zionist Plot" or the "Frank Lies." The headlines were all broken off and crammed into one another; bits and pieces of the articles to which they belonged overlapped. There wasn't a complete sentence on the entire mashed and deranged page.

But there it was: the small insane mind responding spasmodically to the expansive sane person the poet John Berryman had been so relieved to discover, the same sane person so many girls recognize as their truest friend as they move into the uncharted territory of womanhood. I stood there holding that piece of paper (it literally felt *dirty*, perhaps because of the smudged typefaces, which looked like old-fashioned pornography), disoriented all over again.

And then I did the only thing possible: I burned it. Somehow it required burning, not just tossing out. I burned it in the kitchen sink and washed away the ashes. I still don't know what it will take to convince me of the world's capacity to hate life, that this dark instinct does exist. Anne Frank, I reminded myself, knew this hard truth as a child. And she refused to cave in to it even as she acknowledged it. I was glad I had acknowledged this when I quoted her: "I hear the approaching thunder that, one day, will destroy us too, I feel the suffering of millions." The conversation she began with Kitty, her imaginary correspondent to whom she addressed her diary, was founded on a discipline of compassion. Even in acknowledging her own likely death, she felt not only for herself, but felt "the suffering of millions."

This was the sane person who, Berryman says at the end of his essay, "remained able to weep with pity, in Auschwitz, for naked gypsy girls driven past to the crematory." She is the sane person we still seek at the end of the terrible twentieth century.

Entering the Conversation

Hampl's essay contains elements familiar to us all. She procrastinated. Daunted by the task, she found sock drawers to organize and sudden opportunities to lunch with friends. But she also read and reread the *Diary*, underlined useful passages, and thought ahead to her work.

One trustworthy motive for the writing to come was that Hampl cared deeply about this book, a "beloved and historic icon of the Holocaust" as she calls it. Hampl had known the *Diary* from childhood, and she assumed that this experience would be true for large numbers of her readers. Especially for women who grew up after World War II, *The Diary of a Young Girl* has gone beyond being an icon of the Holocaust and has succeeded as a poignant and persuasive account of growing up.

But Hampl's sense of the conversation before her is complicated. She not only knew and felt moved by the *Diary*, she knew and was "fascinated" by an essay on it written by a former teacher. Consequently, she felt as responsible to him as she did to Anne Frank.

Searching for a way to launch her own work, she not only immersed herself in the *Diary* but read and reread Berryman's essay. In the end, her response was shaped less by his specific ideas and more by the example he set of pursuing an idea with conviction, of letting his ideas become, as she observes, "characters" in the story of John Berryman thinking about Anne Frank. The spur, though, that brought her first words to the page came from a hint she found in the foreword to the "Definitive Edition."

This is a crucial moment in Hampl's story of her writing because it underscores her resourcefulness. Bolkestein's plea is not quoted in that foreword; it is only mentioned. Hampl had to track it down and find the exact quotation in the library, but she does not explain how she decided to do so. How did it occur to her that remarks heard over the radio, and unknown to her so far, would make a strong opening for her review? Hampl says she "wanted the reader to see history happening as it happened for Anne Frank herself," but where did this approach, so different from Berryman's, come from? Hampl does not address this question directly, although she does observe that she knew "instinctively" that "direct quotation . . . would enliven this bit of historical information."

We should take note of this moment because thoughts like these allow us to find our own approach as we join a conversation. Whereas Berryman came to his essay through a personal story (and, as Hampl also makes clear, through a very personal concern for the nature of sanity and madness), Hampl begins with historical information couched in direct quotation. Moreover, Hampl went one canny step further. Knowing the day of Bolkestein's address and finding the text of it, she decided to "bolster" her authority by providing the day of the week on which March 28 fell in 1944. This extra, unexpected step, uncovering the telling detail that clinches a part of her story, is a hallmark of a strong writer. It is the hallmark equally of the student who has gotten into her subject. Hampl wished to "seduce" her readers "with the authority of simple facts." Accordingly, she made the effort to locate and verify more than we may have thought was needed. Certainly, the day of the week is a detail we do not expect, which may be exactly why it attracts us.

In this example, we can see how writing tends to be embedded in larger stories and how when we trace those stories, we often find that they have everything to do with our motivation to write. Here then is one more story, a particularly telling one, that further shapes Hampl's review:

> In her diary the next day, Anne Frank mentions this broadcast, which she and her family heard on a clandestine radio in their Amsterdam hiding place. "Ten years after the war," she writes on March 29, "people would find it very amusing to read how we lived, what we ate and what we talked about as Jews in hiding."

Amusing, as Hampl is quick to observe, is hardly the word we would choose now, but looking past the tragedy of Frank's situation, we can see how she, too, was moved to contribute to a larger conversation and to think of herself less as a young woman with a diary than as a writer. Consequently, as Hampl observes in her review, Frank "immediately set about organizing the diary entries, giving the residents of the 'Secret Annex' pseudonyms like characters in a novel, rearranging passages for better narrative effect."

As you may already know, Anne Frank began her diary when she was given a small plaid notebook for her thirteenth birthday. Not long after, she took it with her into hiding. Very quickly, Frank invented a necessary friend, Kitty, who became her imagined reader. She began as almost all writers begin, in a private world, taking notes, keeping a journal meant only for an intimate audience, writing "letters" to "dear Kitty." Although one can hardly imagine a more intimate audience than a secret, imaginary playmate, over the two years of her writing Frank seems to grow in confidence and prepare herself more or less unconsciously for a larger audience. Thus we may conjecture that Bolkestein's plea came at an appropriate time for her, precisely when she was ready, even eager, to enlarge the world of her conversation. A more practiced writer by then, Frank began to think more expansively. "I'd like to publish a book," she remarks. (You can trace more of this story in the excerpt "At Home, at School, in Hiding" from *The Diary of a Young Girl* beginning on p. 171.)

Reviewing the Writing Process

Hampl's essay tells us a good deal about her writing process, one that is ongoing, acquiring clarity and focus in stages. Keeping in mind the significant steps of Hampl's process will help you prepare your own writing assignments. Note especially how revision happens by increments and at all stages.

Getting Started and Overcoming Procrastination

Hampl approached her review in "a paralyzing shyness" and with an urge to procrastinate through a long period of reading and taking notes. Some of those notes would prove useful; some would not. At this early stage, Hampl did not discriminate among them. Her reading and note taking led instead to more procrastination by way of luncheon dates and conversation with friends, which in turn led finally to something that Hampl was willing to call research.

Exploring a Topic and Gathering Information

Another writer, John Berryman, a poet and scholar and Hampl's former teacher, had also written about Anne Frank, so Hampl turned to his essay. She found herself fascinated by Berryman's work on their common subject. Suddenly Hampl had writing to react to, inspiring her to review her notes and distinguish the more valuable from the less. This was the first important step of her revising process: a general eagerness to write about the *Diary* was replaced by a more focused topic.

Finding a Beginning

As Hampl observes, her mind "had wandered not away from the task at hand, but right into it." She was drawn into "a story unfolding," that of Berryman's relation to the *Diary*. As Hampl recognized that "he had found the tip of his subject," she discovered that his example had "nudged" her "off the dime," and soon she had her own opening paragraphs.

Doing Additional Research

Having taken the hint from the foreword to the "Definitive Edition," Hampl went to the library to track down the exact quotation she wanted. No longer following Berryman, she followed her own lead. Now she understood better that she did not share Berryman's perspective. Instead, she developed two different motivations for writing her review.

First, she stressed a "kinship" she felt with Anne Frank's experience of becoming a young woman. This Anne Frank, whom Hampl had taken from the first to be a friend, was also a fine writer, one who would have published more books had she lived. This conviction reinforced Hampl's desire to write. But she needed to offer reason for it, even if her conviction lies beyond absolute proof. She did so by describing Frank's power as a writer, her writerly authority on a subject she and Hampl share — becoming a woman and a person. This culminated in Hampl's recognizing "the motto of a writer" in one of Frank's remarks, "Paper is more patient than people."

These are good reasons for Hampl to find "kinship" with her subject. Thus they reinforce her second motivation, that she give no aid to deniers of the Holocaust, people whom Hampl is ready to call evil. Her commitment to that task inspired further library research. Hampl couldn't just deny the accusations swirling about; she needed to assemble evidence against them, so she "studied the distinctions among the various texts carefully and attempted to present them briefly but clearly."

Producing a First Draft

You may have noticed that Hampl does not talk about her first or second draft as such. Although *draft* is a word that Hampl does not use, she describes thinking about her topic and writing. She discovered ideas about what she needed to know and went to the library or elsewhere to find out. All the while she took notes, which later became explanations in her draft. Hampl does not say how many hours or days this took. But we get the sense from reading her essay that she explained her discoveries and her thinking to herself by writing. When she had covered all that she felt compelled to say, she had a first draft.

Revising

Most writers today use word processors. Revision has never been easier; we can run through our writing again and again, making changes along the way without retyping the whole piece. However, with the use of word processors, writers leave less of a trail of their revisions than they once did, since the process is more continuous. In Hampl's essay, though, we can find several clues to her revision process.

First she tells us that after reading and thinking about Berryman she suddenly started to write and had her first three paragraphs all at once. Perhaps she touched them up a little, but those first paragraphs came quickly, and she was on her way. But what was the lag between that first start and the next? Where did the next impulse to proceed come from? Hampl's comment on Frank's word *amusing* follows in the review. Had a few minutes passed, a few hours, or a day before she wrote that next paragraph? As writers, we rarely set pen to paper or our fingers to the keyboard and just keep going. We write a bit, move back to the beginning, read through it all, and continue. Something in what we have written spurs the next thought. Whether we began with a list of topics, an outline, or just ideas in our head, as we write our writing makes its own suggestions. All good writers learn to be alert to those suggestions.

Later Hampl says, "I remember feeling a kind of relief (not satisfaction, but the more unburdened feeling that the word *relief* suggests) when I stumbled on the word *disorienting*." Did Hampl find the word she wanted in the first act of writing that sentence, or did it occur afterward, on one of her later passes through her work? We cannot know for certain. But her own yoking of *stumbling* with *relief* is a fine shorthand for what we look for in revision: a sense of where a problem lies and a glimpse, however stumbling it may seem, of how we may deal with that. Stumbling in this case is a kind of lucky lurching ahead. It is a discovery, and a happy one, as Hampl's word *relief* suggests. Such discoveries are the rewards of revision. They come from paying close attention to our first drafts, from reading and rereading them.

Finally, returning to the first sentence of Hampl's review ("On Tuesday, March 28, 1944, Gerrit Bolkestein, Education Minister of the Dutch Government in exile, delivered a radio message . . ."), note that the detail she secured last she placed first. First the day of the week, then the date, then Bolkestein's name and title. Hampl tells us that she first found reference to the quotation, then looked up the exact quotation, then thought to make its date as exact as possible. In her writing, however, she inverted that order because she found the order as phrased above the most satisfying. That decision is another sign of Hampl's revising as she works. Revision is much more than catching errors of grammar and spelling; it is primarily our efforts, first to discover how to say things better, then equally to identify what else we need to find out.

Drawing Conclusions

The conclusions reached by Frank, by Berryman, and then by Hampl are never "the conclusion," wrapped up once and for all. A vital subject can always be extended; further refinements and angles can always be found. In other words, in principle, serious work always remains "under revision."

Some revisions prove indefensible, as Hampl records by reference to the letter she received. Holocaust deniers apparently wish to argue that if Anne Frank was indeed a real person, she died of "natural causes." Their vicious approach thrives on a mean-spirited insistence on narrow literalism, and accounts of Anne Frank's death hand them a crumb to work with.

For example, an Academy Award–winning feature documentary, *Anne Frank Remembered* (1996), includes interviews with Dutch survivors of the Holocaust, several of whom knew Anne Frank. One survivor, Hanneli Goslar, speaks of meeting her at Bergen-Belsen and talking with her through a barbed wire fence. Another, Janny Brandes-Brilleslijper, the woman who first informed Otto Frank of his daughters' deaths only months after the end of the war, repeats that information for the camera, telling how the sisters died in misery of malnutrition and typhus, exposed to the cold in their bunks by the barracks door. Only the perverse would call their deaths "natural" — Anne and her sister Margot suffering the merciless conditions of Bergen-Belsen until they roll wasted from their bunks in their sleep — but Holocaust deniers do. They seize on illness as our normal understanding of "natural causes," ignore all other details about Bergen-Belsen, and insist that Anne Frank was simply sick.

Some arguments are best not joined, some conversations better refused than taken up. That is the choice Hampl makes, wisely it seems. Instead, she rids herself of the letter she received, for there is other, healthier work to do.

Reading and Rereading

If you have taken an interest in Patricia Hampl's story and in her example, you may have already done several things common to most writers. Having read her essay (p. 4) and this introduction's comments on it, you may have read Hampl's review (p. 22) or the excerpt from Frank's diary (p. 171). You may have gone to the library to look up the essay by Berryman that Hampl mentions or related works, or you may have logged on to the Internet to see what you could find. No doubt you haven't taken in everything all at once. More than likely, you have gone back over some of this material and reread it.

As writers, we read and reread as we prepare to write. Anything in which we take a serious interest deserves rereading. Hampl's essay, for example, describes how she read slowly, underlined passages, jotted down lines, and took notes.

It is often useful to read things twice: first skimming, or reading for an overview, and then settling down to a thorough second reading. Sometimes our readings blend together, and they aren't always limited to two. We read and reread and go back to at least parts of a piece again if it is important, looking for details that we may not have caught earlier. Quite naturally, our understanding of a work becomes more subtle as we become familiar with its overall contours. Sometimes that first reading isn't really skimming, but it begins to feel like skimming as, on rereading, we notice more and more.

First Readings

To get an overall picture of a piece, begin by reading it through from beginning to end, primarily to get a sense of the author's subject, purpose, and main ideas. This initial reading will help you get acquainted with the piece as a whole. Don't get bogged down in details, but don't hesitate to note or underline important (or puzzling) words, phrases, sentences, ideas, or points that seem important and to which you may wish to return. Once you have completed your initial reading, jot down a few sentences about its main subject, purpose, points, and pertinent information.

Annotating

After you've got the gist of the piece, reread and annotate it more thoroughly. Annotations consist of explanatory notes. For example, if the piece contains words, names, titles of works, or other bits of information that you are unfamiliar with, consult dictionaries, encyclopedias, and other reference works, and make notes that you can refer to in the future.

Summarizing

If you are serious about a piece and want to test your understanding of it, one way is to write a summary. By definition, a summary will leave out much. Writing a summary requires you to discriminate the more important information from the less important information. Hampl doesn't summarize either the *Diary* or Berryman's essay completely, but she does offer partial summaries of both. These isolate what she finds of significance. The best way to see what a summary reveals is for several people to write summaries of the same text and to compare them.

Here, for example, is a summary of Hampl's essay.

> Hampl's intention is to reflect on and explain the process of writing a review of the "Definitive Edition" of Anne Frank's *Diary* for the *New York Times*. First, Hampl describes feeling paralyzed and resistant to starting her assignment. She also relates how after procrastinating, she discovered another writer's work on the subject, which helped her find inspiration for her own work. Finally, Hampl discusses her motivation to write the review, which was rooted in her desire to remind her audience of the extraordinary person Anne Frank was, and of what talent she had as a writer.

Outlining

Not all readers outline their reading, but it can be helpful. Like a summary, an outline asks you to decide what is important in something you've read. Unlike a summary, an outline also asks you to show how one important item relates to another. Often, we want to know both why and how a conclusion was reached. That conclusion will depend on evidence, and the relation of the claim to the supporting evidence can be shown in an outline.

An outline always identifies superior and subordinate items. Depending on how formal you wish to make it, those items can be labeled with letters and numerals:

I. _____

   A. _____

      1. _____

         a. _____

B. _____

    1. _____

    2. _____

        a. _____

        b. _____

II. _____

One principle governs making any outline: superior items (claims) require subordinate items. The subordinate items are what we call support. You cannot make a claim without offering a reason for it. The more support you give your claims, the more willing readers will be to accept them. It's like building a firm foundation for a building. Arguments without this firm support will crumble.

In a very real sense, the lowercase letters and Arabic numerals are more important than the capital letters and Roman numerals. The smaller items hold the larger ones up. So if you want to think critically about an argument you have read, or if you want to avoid problems in arguments of your own, try making an outline. Be sure that the subordinate items go where they belong and that they provide secure support for your argument.

Toward the end of her essay, Hampl restates a claim that had been a strong motivation for her having written the review in the first place: "I wanted to remind people of the *extraordinary person* Anne Frank was, the *splendid writer*, the *utterly natural girl-woman*, and the *gifted thinker*." For Hampl, those last three terms add up to the first; they are what constitute an "extraordinary person," at least in this instance. Hence this outline:

A. Extraordinary person
    1. Splendid writer
    2. Utterly natural girl-woman
    3. Gifted thinker

Now it is Hampl's responsibility to come through with evidence in support of *1*, *2*, and *3*. You could outline that evidence as *a*, *b*, *c*, and so on and arrange it beneath the numerals.

Using and Acknowledging Sources

In most of the writing you will do, both during and after college, you will find yourself drawing on the ideas, information, and statements of others, interpreting this material, and combining it with your own experience,

observation, and thought to generate new ideas of your own. Some of this
material will come from your reading, some from lectures and class discussions, some from conversations and interviews. Our thinking does not take
place in a vacuum but is shaped by a wide array of influences and sources.
In this introduction, we have seen Hampl refer to Berryman and to the
Dutch minister of education. Anne Frank's *Diary*, of course, has been openly acknowledged throughout and quoted several times. We have also cited
a documentary film, for which we found specific information on the
Internet. These are several instances of writers acknowledging their sources,
specifically but informally.

To acknowledge your intellectual debts is by no means a confession
that your work is unoriginal or without merit. In fact, original work in
every field invariably builds on the prior work of researchers and thinkers.
Most pieces you find in this book, except for those that deal entirely with
personal experience, include some kind of acknowledgment or reference to
the ideas, information, or statements of others. By acknowledging their
sources, the writers of these pieces implicitly establish what is new or special in their own way of thinking. Academic writing — the kind of writing
you do in college and the kind of writing that most of your teachers do
when they make contributions to their professional fields — depends on
learning, on sources. Most of these sources are to be found in books and
periodicals, but many are to be found in other places — especially on the
Internet, to which the World Wide Web provides the easiest access.

What the Web Offers

The World Wide Web (or "the Web," as it is commonly known) is an
excellent resource for writers — if it is used properly. The Web is a vast network of information, much of which is not available in print or even on
microfilm, and you can reach this material without moving from your chair.
You can find online magazines and scholarly journals, groups discussing
topics you are investigating, reports from organizations and institutions:
words, pictures, music — it's all out there.

Even when the "same" text is available in a book, newspaper, or magazine, the Web version may offer advantages. The printed materials are easier
to hold, carry, and read, but the Web materials are easier to find and search.
If you don't take careful notes when you are reading a book, you may have
great difficulty finding an important passage when you are writing about that
book. With a digital text, however, whether on the Web or a disk, you can
easily locate almost any passage you remember by using a search engine, a
program that scans the Web looking for specific subject areas or specific
words and phrases. Many search engines will bring back not just the word
you are seeking but the whole context in which that word appears.

For example, one Web site, which your search engine can find, includes
the text of all of Jane Austen's novels in digital form. If you go to that site
and ask the search engine to find a particular word, such as "envy," it will

bring up every use of that word in all the novels, with the passage in which it occurs. If you are writing about Jane Austen, such a resource can be very helpful.

But if more information is available to you on the Web than in print, most Web resources have passed through less screening from editors and publishers than most books or magazine articles have. This means you have to be selective in what you use from the Web and cautious in how you use it.

Evaluating Web Sources   Many inexperienced users of the Web—including many students—do not use its resources effectively. They locate the name of an "expert," send the person an email, and ask for ideas they can use in writing papers or for a short summary of the person's knowledge that can be quoted in a paper to prove to a teacher that "research" has been done. But this is *not* research. Real experts seldom reply to such requests—they get too many—and false experts will lead a student astray. We know of a person who once had something he said about the 1962 Cuban missile crisis quoted on the Web. He has been getting emails ever since—asking him for his "expert" opinion—from students writing papers on that topic. But everything he knew was in the material already quoted on the Web.

The Web is full of material that can be used in research. But none of that material will do your thinking for you. The value of a paper depends on the critical intelligence you bring to bear on the material you collect. Here are some things to look for in evaluating potential sources from the Web:

1. Is the creator or sponsor of the site identified? Does this information—or its absence—tell you anything about the purpose of the site? Does it reveal any possible biases?

2. Can you use links or a search engine to find out more about the site's creator or sponsor? Does this person or group seem knowledgeable? Trustworthy?

3. Is there an indication of when the site was created or last updated? Does the information seem current?

Using Web Information   Of course, you can take notes about material on the Web just as you can about print sources, but most Web sites also allow you to select and copy material that you can then paste directly into your own writing. In some cases, using the "Save As" command, you can save a whole page to your drive. Digital research tools, like Research Assistant Hyperfolio, also are available, and they allow you to drag and drop entire Web pages into research folders on your computer. In using material from the Web, here are a few rules you should follow:

1. If you use any material from a Web page in writing an academic paper, you must include a source citation in a list of works cited, in an endnote or a footnote, or in another location required by the

documentation system you are using (see the next section, "Acknowledging Sources"). Web information is just like other information. You must give credit where credit is due.

2. Keep a record of the URL (Uniform Resource Locator) of the page from which you have taken the material, the date you accessed it, and any other information (such as the name of the site, its sponsor, or the author of the text) that might help someone locate the site again. Check the guidelines of your documentation system for what information is required.

3. If you paste another person's text into your own writing, you must indicate clearly that it is not your own material, either by putting it in quotation marks or by indenting it as you indent other long quotations. In either case, you need to cite your source. The Web makes it easy to cut and paste, so you need to take care in indicating where your material has come from.

4. Whether you just refer to information on the Web or actually copy it and paste it into your text, you must use it in your own argument. The bigger the item you paste, the more discussion and analysis you must develop. Don't fill your paper up with pasted material. Don't quote more than you need. And, remember, quoted material is most useful when you add something to or disagree with something in the quote. You are not looking for "answers" when you search the Web, but for material you can use in developing your *own* answers.

Acknowledging Sources

To get some idea of the various ways in which sources can be acknowledged, note the ways different writers in this book handle this task. The different methods are not just a question of differences among writers; different publications and disciplines have their own styles and standards. Within our collection, you will notice that some writers cite only the names of authors or interviewees or the titles of works from which they have gathered ideas or quoted statements. These citations are incorporated into the written discussion, as Hampl incorporates Berryman. You can see this technique used in Martin Luther King Jr.'s "Pilgrimage to Nonviolence" (p. 106). Other writers use footnotes or endnotes in which they provide the names of authors or interviewees, the titles of works, the dates of publication or of interviews, and specific page references, as you can see by looking at Theodore R. Sizer's "What High School Is" (p. 345), or Barbara Tuchman's "This Is the End of the World: The Black Death" (p. 217). Finally, instead of using footnotes, some writers provide author and page references in the text of their discussion and include more detailed publication data, such as titles and dates of publication, in a complete list of works cited at the end, as Monica M. Moore does in her "Nonverbal Courtship in Women" (p. 412).

These various forms of acknowledgment are usually determined by the different purposes and audiences for which the pieces were written. Personal essays, newspaper reports, and magazine articles, which are written for a general audience, tend to rely on a more casual and shorthand form of acknowledgment, citing only the author or title of the source and placing that acknowledgment in the midst of the discussion. Work written for a more specialized audience, such as academic research papers and scholarly articles or books, tends to rely on more detailed and systematic forms of acknowledgment, using either footnotes or a combination of references in the text with a complete list of works cited at the end. These specialized forms vary somewhat from one field to another, but papers in the arts and humanities tend to follow the guidelines set down by the Modern Language Association (MLA), and papers in the social sciences use the system of the American Psychological Association (APA). In the sciences and technologies, each discipline tends to have its own system. For further reference, consult the *MLA Handbook for Writers of Research Papers,* 6th ed. (New York: Modern Language Association of America, 2003), or the *Publication Manual of the American Psychological Association,* 5th ed. (Washington, D.C: American Psychological Association, 2001). The APA's latest guidelines for citing Web sources can be found at the association's Web site, <http://www.apastyle.org/elecref.html>.

As you can see, making proper acknowledgment of sources is both a matter of intellectual honesty and a social issue of many dimensions. Different groups agree on and enforce their own standards. That goes for your writing course as well. For the moment, your college or university or perhaps your writing class is the ultimate authority for you. Therefore, don't hesitate to look to your instructor for guidance. Most instructors have their specific preferences, but all will expect you to acknowledge your sources.

THE WHOLE ANNE FRANK

Patricia Hampl

On Tuesday, March 28, 1944, Gerrit Bolkestein, Education Minister of the Dutch Government in exile, delivered a radio message from London urging his war-weary countrymen to collect "vast quantities of simple, everyday material" as part of the historical record of the Nazi occupation.

"History cannot be written on the basis of official decisions and documents alone," he said. "If our descendants are to understand fully what we as a nation have had to endure and overcome during these years, then what we really need are ordinary documents — a diary, letters."

In her diary the next day, Anne Frank mentions this broadcast, which she and her family heard on a clandestine radio in their Amsterdam hiding place. "Ten years after the war," she writes on March 29, "people would find it very amusing to read how we lived, what we ate and what we talked about as Jews in hiding."

The word "amusing" reads strangely now, chillingly. But her extraordinary commitment to the immediacy of individual experience in the face of crushing circumstance is precisely what has made Anne Frank's *Diary* — since the first edition of the book appeared in the Netherlands in 1947 — the single most compelling personal account of the Holocaust (an account now augmented by this "Definitive Edition," published on the 50th anniversary of her death in Bergen-Belsen and containing entries not present in the earlier standard version).

Bolkestein's broadcast galvanized Anne Frank, or perhaps ignited an idea she already had: her diary, at first a private confidante, now struck her as a source for a book. "I'd like to publish a book called 'The Secret Annex,' " she writes on May 11, 1944. "It remains to be seen whether I'll succeed, but my diary can serve as the basis." She immediately set about organizing the diary entries, giving the residents of the "Secret Annex" pseudonyms like characters in a novel, rearranging passages for better narrative effect.

She was still engaged in this work when the hiding place was raided by the Gestapo on Aug. 4, 1944. Miep Gies, one of the office employees in the Frank spice and pectin firm who had been protecting the Jews hidden above the office, gathered all the diary notebooks and papers left in disarray by the Gestapo. She hid them in her desk for the rest of the war. After Anne's father, Otto Frank, returned to Amsterdam late in 1945, Miep Gies returned all the papers to him. He was the sole survivor of the eight people who had sheltered together for over two years in the annex.

Anne Frank had been keeping her diary since June 12, 1942, the day her parents gave her a red-and-white plaid notebook for her 13th birthday. Less than a month later the diary went with her into hiding.

From the first, she addressed the notebook as a trusted girlfriend: "I'll begin from the moment I got you, the moment I saw you lying on the table among my other birthday presents." A few days later this anonymous "you" becomes the imaginary "Kitty," and the entries turn into letters, giving the diary the intimacy and vivacity of a developing friendship. The growing relationship, of course, is with her own emerging self. As John Berryman said, the *Diary* has at its core a subject "even more mysterious and fundamental than St. Augustine's" in his classic "Confessions": namely, "the conversion of a child into a person."

Otto Frank, in preparing the first edition of the diary, was compelled, partly by his own sense of discretion and partly by the space limitations imposed on him by the original Dutch publisher, to limit the book. The restored entries, constituting, according to the publisher, 30 percent more material, do not alter our basic sense of Anne Frank, but they do give greater texture and nuance — and punch — to some of the hallmark concerns of the diary.

There are more searching passages about her erotic feelings and her   10
urgent curiosity about sexuality, more emphatic distancing from her dignified but apparently critical mother. None of these new entries, however, surpass the urgency shown in the standard version about the need to accomplish real work as a woman: "I can't imagine having to live like Mother, Mrs. van Daan and all the women who go about their work and are then forgotten," she writes on April 5, 1944. "I need to have something besides a husband and children to devote myself to! . . . I want to be useful or bring enjoyment to all people, even those I've never met. I want to go on living even after my death!"

The new material also includes sketches of short stories she was writing in the Secret Annex. The additions are not always whole entries or complete new letters to Kitty. Sometimes passages of only a few lines are set in a text already familiar. But the effect underscores the acuity of Anne Frank's eye, the keen relish of her descriptive powers. In one of her habitual reviews of the "inmates" of the annex, she regards the fussy dentist Dussel with the coolness of a practiced novelist: "One of my Sunday morning ordeals is having to lie in bed and look at Dussel's back when he's praying. . . . A praying Dussel is a terrible sight to behold."

Even her transports over her first kiss, with Peter van Daan, the son of the family sharing the Franks' hiding space, are subject to her mordant observation: "Oh, it was so wonderful. I could hardly talk, my pleasure was too intense; he caressed my cheek and arm, a bit clumsily." Only a born writer would snap that clear-eyed "a bit clumsily" into place, along with the body's first rhapsodic shiver of delight.

In 1986, a "Critical Edition" of the *Diary* was published that meticulously presented Anne's original diary (designated by its editors diary a), the version she was working on for her proposed book "The Secret Annex" (diary b), and the edition her father eventually published and which all the world has come to know (diary c). This monumental task included as well exhaustive scientific examination of the original documents to prove what should never have been questioned in the first place: that this is indeed the work of a girl named Anne Frank who lived and eventually died as she prophetically sensed she would: "I hear the approaching thunder that, one day, will destroy us too, I feel the suffering of millions."

The earlier "Critical Edition" is the book for research, but this "Definitive Edition," smoothly translated anew by Susan Massotty, is the reader's edition, unencumbered by notes, with only the barest afterword to conclude the story that Anne Frank was unable to finish herself.

The *Diary,* now 50 years old, remains astonishing and excruciating. It   15 is a work almost sick with terror and tension, even as it performs its miracle of lucidity. On Feb. 12, 1944, Anne Frank writes Kitty, "I feel as if I were about to explode. . . . I walk from one room to another, breathe through the crack in the window frame. . . . I think spring is inside me." The crack in the window frame was her purchase on the world: she put her nose to it and drew in life.

It is uncanny how, reading the *Diary,* one falls into escape fantasies for Anne Frank and the inhabitants of the Secret Annex. No wonder that in his 1979 novel "The Ghost Writer," Philip Roth sustains an entire section devoted to a detailed fabrication about how, after all, Anne Frank survived, how she came to America, how she lives among us still in disguise. It is unthinkable and disorienting to know that this life was crushed.

All that remains is this diary, evidence of her ferocious appetite for life. It gnaws at us still.

REFLECTING

Here in "Reflecting," as in other parts of this collection, you will encounter writing that touches on a wide range of topics—from a high school graduation in Arkansas to a sacred landmark in Oklahoma, from earth, air, fire, and water to inner-city playground politics. But you will also find that the writing in this particular section relies heavily on personal experiences. This personal element may strike you at first as being out of place in a college textbook. However, if you consider the matter just a bit, you will see that personal experiences are a basic source of knowledge and understanding. Think for a moment about someone you have known for a long time or about a long-remembered event in your life. Then think about what you have learned from being with that person or going through that event, and you will see that personal experience is, indeed, a valuable source of knowledge. You will probably also notice that in thinking about that person or event you rely heavily on your remembrance of things past—on your memory of particular words or deeds or gestures or scenes that are especially important to you. Your memory, after all, is the storehouse of your personal knowledge, and whenever you look into this storehouse, you will invariably find an image or impression of your past experience. So you should not be surprised to find the authors in this section looking into their own memories as they might look into a mirror. Ultimately, the activity of looking back is a hallmark of reflection because it involves writers in recalling and thinking about some aspect of their world in order to make sense of it for themselves and for others.

This essential quality of reflective writing can be seen in the following passage from George Orwell's "Shooting an Elephant":

> One day something happened which in a roundabout way was enlightening. It was a tiny incident in itself, but it gave me a better glimpse than I had had before of the real nature of imperialism—

the real motives for which despotic governments act. Early one morning the sub-inspector at a police station the other end of the town rang me up on the phone and said that an elephant was ravaging the bazaar. Would I please come and do something about it? I did not know what I could do, but I wanted to see what was happening and I got on to a pony and started out.

This passage, which comes from the third paragraph of Orwell's essay, clearly presents him as being in a reflective frame of mind. In the opening sentence, for example, he looks back to a specific event from his personal experiences in Burma — to "one day" when "something happened." And in the midst of looking back, he also makes clear that this event is important to him because "in a roundabout way" it "was enlightening." Again, in the second sentence, he looks back not only to the event, "a tiny incident in itself," but also to the understanding that he gained from the event — "a better glimpse than I had had before of the real nature of imperialism — the real motives for which despotic governments act." Having announced the general significance of this event, he then returns to looking back at the event itself, to recalling the particular things that happened that day: the phone call informing him "that an elephant was ravaging the bazaar," the request that he "come and do something about it," and his decision to get "on to a pony" in order "to see what was happening."

This alternation between recalling things and commenting on their significance is typical not only of Orwell's piece but of all the writing in this section. Sometimes the alternation takes place within a single sentence, as in the opening of the previous passage. Sometimes the alternation occurs between sentences or clusters of sentences, as in the following passage from Adam Gopnik's "The City and the Pillars":

> A little while later, a writer who happened to be downtown saw a flock of pigeons rise, high and fast, and thought, Why are the pigeons rising? It was only seconds before he realized that the pigeons had felt the wave of the concussion before he heard the sound. In the same way, the shock wave hit us before the sound, the image before our understanding. For the lucky ones, the day from then on was spent in a strange, calm, and soul-emptying back and forth between impossible images on television and the usual things on the street.
>
> Around noon, a lot of people crowded around a lamppost on Madison, right underneath a poster announcing the Wayne Thiebaud show at the Whitney: all those cakes, as if to signal the impotence of our abundance. The impotence of our abundance! In the uptown supermarkets, people began to shop. It was a hoarding instinct, of course, though oddly not brought on by any sense of panic; certainly no one on television or radio was suggesting people needed to hoard. Yet people had the instinct to do it, and, in any case, in

New York the instinct to hoard quickly seemed to shade over into the instinct to consume, shop for anything, shop because it might be a comfort. One woman emerged from a Gristede's on Lexington with a bottle of olive oil and said, "I had to get *something.*"

This passage comes, as you probably inferred, from a reflective report on the feel of the streets of New York City on the day the World Trade Center towers were attacked. The feel of those streets, or the writer's sense of the mood of the people on the streets that day, is a matter of interpretation based on what he observed. The actual points of observation are quite particular: pigeons rise; a shock wave precedes sound; "images" on television alternate with life "on the street"; pedestrians cluster beneath a poster; people begin to shop; a woman emerges from a store with a bottle of olive oil and more or less explains herself.

These observed details become the skeleton of the passage, one that is fleshed out by Gopnik's reading of those images. He sees the pigeons rise and interprets their behavior as the sound hits him too. The alternation then is from images that are "impossible" to life in its "usual" form. This "usual" activity he finds "strange, calm, and soul-emptying." The poster features "cakes," which "signal" for him "the impotence of our abundance." Gopnik is so struck by his phrase that he repeats it. Its last word seems to trigger his next thoughts since he begins then to interpret shopping, an observable activity, by renaming it. Is it an instinct to hoard? No, he decides, it is instead an "instinct to consume," which he sees also as behavior distinctive to New York.

As Gopnik ranges over his memories of that day, each image or idea that comes to mind is occasioned by a preceding memory or reflection or by some aspect of his immediate situation. Guiding him always is a sense of what is usual for New York. That sense of what is normal structures his reflections, which move by association and suggestion, with one thing leading to another. The cakes on the poster lead to ideas of consumption, abundance, and to a sense of impotence in relation to the destruction occurring downtown. Then, as if in confirmation of all that, Gopnik notices a shopper who feels compelled to acquire "olive oil" but who cannot explain her purchase, even to herself. This linked sequence of memories, images, bits of information, and ideas is typical of reflective writing. Equally typical is its tendency to interpret our behavior.

The alternation between recalling and interpreting will vary from writer to writer and from work to work, depending on the details of the experience and the author's reflective purpose. Nevertheless, every piece of reflective writing contains both kinds of material, for every reflective writer is concerned with sharing something memorable and also with showing why it is memorable. And as it happens, most memorable experiences, images, or bits of information stick in our minds because they give us, as Orwell says, "a better glimpse than [we] had had before of the real nature of" someone, something, or some aspect of the world. As a reader of reflective writing, you should always be attentive both to the details of an author's recollected experience and also to the "glimpse" that it gives the author, and you, into the "real nature" of things. And in your own reflective writing, you should make sure that you convey both dimensions of your experience — both what happened and what the events enabled you to see.

The Range of Reflective Writing

The range of reflective writing is in one sense limitless, for it necessarily includes the full range of things that make up our personal experience or the personal experience of anyone else in the world. Reflecting, in other words, may deal with anything that anyone has ever seen, heard, done, or thought about and considered memorable enough to write about. Though the range of reflective writing is extraordinarily broad, the subject of any particular piece is likely to be very specific, and as it happens, most pieces can be classified in terms of a few recurrent types of subject matter.

A single, memorable event is often the center of attention in reflective writing, as in Maya Angelou's "Graduation" or Orwell's "Shooting an Elephant." In reflecting on this kind of subject, the author will usually provide a meticulous detailing of the event itself and some background information that serves as a context for making sense of the event. In "Graduation," for example, Angelou tells about all the pregraduation excitement in her home, at school, and around town before turning to the graduation ceremony itself. And in "Shooting an Elephant," Orwell gives an overall description of his life as a colonial officer in Burma before he turns to the story about shooting the elephant. The event, in turn, is of interest not only in itself but also for what it reveals to the author (and the reader) about some significant aspect of experience. Thus for Angelou, graduation remains memorable because it helped her to see how African American people have been "sustained" by "Black known and unknown poets," and for Orwell, the shooting remains memorable because it helped him to see "the real nature of imperialism."

A notable person is a subject that often moves people to writing reflectively, as in N. Scott Momaday's "The Way to Rainy Mountain." In reflecting on a particular individual, writers may seek to discover and convey what they consider to be the most essential aspects of that person's character. They may survey a number of memorable incidents or images from the person's life. Momaday, for example, recalls the stories and legends that he heard from his grandmother, "the several postures that were peculiar to her," and her "long, rambling prayers."

Instead of concentrating on a particular person or event, reflective writing may center on a specific problem or significant issue in the past experience of an author, as in Frederick Douglass's "Learning to Read and Write" or Martin Luther King Jr.'s "Pilgrimage to Nonviolence." A piece with this kind of subject is likely to touch on a number of people and events and to encompass a substantial period of time, in the process of recalling and reflecting on the problem with which it is concerned. Douglass, for example, covers seven years of his life in his piece about the problem of learning to read and write, and King recalls events and issues throughout his life that led him to espouse the principles of nonviolent resistance. In each case, the breadth of coverage serves to reveal the scope and complexity of the problem, as well as the author's special understanding of it.

As you can see from just this brief survey of possibilities, reflective writing may deal with a single event, several events, or a whole lifetime of events. It may be as restricted in its attention as a close-up or as all-encompassing as a wide-angle shot. But no matter how little or how much experience it takes into account, reflective writing is always decisively focused through the author's persistent attempt to make sense of the past, to push memory to the point of understanding the significance of experience.

Methods of Reflecting

Your experience is unique, as is your memory, so in a sense you know the best methods to follow whenever you are of a mind to reflect on something that interests you. But once you have recalled something in detail and made sense of it for yourself, you are still faced with the problem of how to present it to readers in a way that will also make sense to them. Given the fact that your readers will probably not be familiar with your experience, you will need to be careful in selecting and organizing your material so that you provide a clearly detailed account of it. By the same token, you will need to emphasize aspects or elements of your experience that will enable readers to understand their significance. Usually, you will find that your choice of subject suggests a corresponding method of presenting it clearly and meaningfully to your readers.

If your reflections are focused on a single, circumscribed event, you will probably find it most appropriate to use a narrative presentation, telling your readers what happened in a relatively straightforward chronological order. Though you cover the event from beginning to end, your narrative should be carefully designed to emphasize the details that you consider most striking and significant. In "Shooting an Elephant," for example, Orwell devotes the largest segment in his piece to covering the very, very brief period of a few moments when he finds himself on the verge of having to shoot the elephant despite his strong desire not to do so. In fact, he devotes one-third of his essay to these few moments of inner conflict because they bring about one of his major insights — "that when the white man turns tyrant it is his own freedom that he destroys." So in telling about a memorable event of your own, you should deliberately pace your story to make it build toward some kind of climax or surprise or decisive incident, which in turn leads to a moment of insight for you (and your readers).

If your reflections are focused on a particular person, you will probably find it necessary to use both narrative and descriptive methods of presentation, telling about several events in order to make clear to readers the character and thought of the person in question. Though you rely heavily on narration, you will not be able to cover incidents in as much detail as if you were focusing on a single event. Instead, you will find it necessary to isolate only the most striking and significant details from each incident you choose to recall. Momaday, for instance, relates his grandmother's background by way of the history of the Kiowa. But to describe her individual character, he isolates particular details—her postures, her praying, her dress—that are carefully chosen to resonate with the "ancient awe" that Momaday says was "in her" and with which he regards her. So, too, in writing about an individual whom you have known, you should carefully select and arrange the details that you recall to make them convey a clear and compelling impression of that person's character.

If your reflections are focused on a particular problem or issue in your past experience, you will probably need to combine narrative, descriptive, and explanatory methods of presentation, bringing together your recollections of numerous events and persons to reveal the nature and significance of the problem. Although you will survey the problem chronologically from beginning to end, you will also need to organize your narrative so that it highlights the essential aspects, elements, or facets of the problem. For example, in "Pilgrimage to Nonviolence," King immediately focuses on the "new and sometimes complex doctrinal lands" through which he traveled. And from this point on, he recalls the various theological and philosophical ideas with which he struggled in formulating his belief in nonviolence. So in writing about a particular problem of your own, your recollections should be deliberately selected and organized to highlight your special understanding of the issue.

No matter what specific combination of methods you use in your reflective writing, you will probably find, as do most writers, that a striking recollection is the most effective way to interest your readers and that a significant observation about experience is the most rewarding means to send them on their way. In the following selections, you will get to see how a wide variety of writers use language to produce some very striking and significant pieces of reflection.

Arts and Humanities

GRADUATION

Maya Angelou

*In six volumes of autobiography, including her most recent, A Song
Flung Up to Heaven (2002), Maya Angelou (b. 1928) has written
vividly of her struggles to achieve success as an actor, a dancer, a
songwriter, a teacher, and a poet. An active worker in the civil
rights movement of the 1960s, Angelou continues to focus much of
her writing on racial and cultural issues. The following selection is
from* I Know Why the Caged Bird Sings *(1969), in which she
writes, "I speak to the Black experience, but I am always talking
about the human condition."*

The children in Stamps[1] trembled visibly with anticipation. Some
adults were excited too, but to be certain the whole young population had
come down with graduation epidemic. Large classes were graduating
from both the grammar school and the high school. Even those who were
years removed from their own day of glorious release were anxious to
help with preparations as a kind of dry run. The junior students who
were moving into the vacating classes' chairs were tradition-bound to
show their talents for leadership and management. They strutted through
the school and around the campus exerting pressure on the lower grades.
Their authority was so new that occasionally if they pressed a little too
hard it had to be overlooked. After all, next term was coming, and it
never hurt a sixth grader to have a play sister in the eighth grade, or a
tenth-year student to be able to call a twelfth grader Bubba. So all was
endured in a spirit of shared understanding. But the graduating classes
themselves were the nobility. Like travelers with exotic destinations on

---

[1]*Stamps:* A town in Arkansas. [Eds.]

their minds, the graduates were remarkably forgetful. They came to school without their books, or tablets or even pencils. Volunteers fell over themselves to secure replacements for the missing equipment. When accepted, the willing workers might or might not be thanked, and it was of no importance to the pregraduation rites. Even teachers were respectful of the now quiet and aging seniors, and tended to speak to them, if not as equals, as beings only slightly lower than themselves. After tests were returned and grades given, the student body, which acted like an extended family, knew who did well, who excelled, and what piteous ones had failed.

Unlike the white high school, Lafayette County Training School distinguished itself by having neither lawn, nor hedges, nor tennis court, nor climbing ivy. Its two buildings (main classrooms, the grade school and home economics) were set on a dirt hill with no fence to limit either its boundaries or those of bordering farms. There was a large expanse to the left of the school which was used alternately as a baseball diamond or basketball court. Rusty hoops on swaying poles represented the permanent recreational equipment, although bats and balls could be borrowed from the P.E. teacher if the borrower was qualified and if the diamond wasn't occupied.

Over this rocky area relieved by a few shady tall persimmon trees the graduating class walked. The girls often held hands and no longer bothered to speak to the lower students. There was a sadness about them, as if this old world was not their home and they were bound for higher ground. The boys, on the other hand, had become more friendly, more outgoing. A decided change from the closed attitude they projected while studying for finals. Now they seemed not ready to give up the old school, the familiar paths and classrooms. Only a small percentage would be continuing on to college—one of the South's A & M (agricultural and mechanical) schools, which trained Negro youths to be carpenters, farmers, handymen, masons, maids, cooks and baby nurses. Their future rode heavily on their shoulders, and blinded them to the collective joy that had pervaded the lives of the boys and girls in the grammar school graduating class.

Parents who could afford it had ordered new shoes and ready-made clothes for themselves from Sears and Roebuck or Montgomery Ward. They also engaged the best seamstresses to make the floating graduating dresses and to cut down secondhand pants which would be pressed to a military slickness for the important event.

Oh, it was important, all right. Whitefolks would attend the ceremony, 5 and two or three would speak of God and home, and the Southern way of life, and Mrs. Parsons, the principal's wife, would play the graduation march while the lower-grade graduates paraded down the aisles and took their seats below the platform. The high school seniors would wait in empty classrooms to make their dramatic entrance.

In the Store I was the person of the moment. The birthday girl. The center. Bailey[2] had graduated the year before, although to do so he had had to forfeit all pleasures to make up for his time lost in Baton Rouge.

My class was wearing butter-yellow piqué dresses, and Momma launched out on mine. She smocked the yoke into tiny crisscrossing puckers, then shirred the rest of the bodice. Her dark fingers ducked in and out of the lemony cloth as she embroidered raised daisies around the hem. Before she considered herself finished she had added a crocheted cuff on the puff sleeves, and a point crocheted collar.

I was going to be lovely. A walking model of all the various styles of fine hand sewing and it didn't worry me that I was only twelve years old and merely graduating from the eighth grade. Besides, many teachers in Arkansas Negro schools had only that diploma and were licensed to impart wisdom.

The days had become longer and more noticeable. The faded beige of former times had been replaced with strong and sure colors. I began to see my classmates' clothes, their skin tones, and the dust that waved off pussy willows. Clouds that lazed across the sky were objects of great concern to me. Their shiftier shapes might have held a message that in my new happiness and with a little bit of time I'd soon decipher. During that period I looked at the arch of heaven so religiously my neck kept a steady ache. I had taken to smiling more often, and my jaws hurt from the unaccustomed activity. Between the two physical sore spots, I suppose I could have been uncomfortable, but that was not the case. As a member of the winning team (the graduating class of 1940) I had outdistanced unpleasant sensations by miles. I was headed for the freedom of open fields.

Youth and social approval allied themselves with me and we trammeled memories of slights and insults. The wind of our swift passage remodeled my features. Lost tears were pounded to mud and then to dust. Years of withdrawal were brushed aside and left behind, as hanging ropes of parasitic moss. 10

My work alone had awarded me a top place and I was going to be one of the first called in the graduating ceremonies. On the classroom blackboard, as well as on the bulletin board in the auditorium, there were blue stars and white stars and red stars. No absences, no tardinesses, and my academic work was among the best of the year. I could say the preamble to the Constitution even faster than Bailey. We timed ourselves often: "WethepeopleoftheUnitedStatesinordertoformamoreperfectunion. . . ." I had memorized the Presidents of the United States from Washington to Roosevelt in chronological as well as alphabetical order.

My hair pleased me too. Gradually the black mass had lengthened and thickened, so that it kept at last to its braided pattern, and I didn't have to yank my scalp off when I tried to comb it.

---

[2]*Bailey:* The author's brother. [Eds.]

Louise and I had rehearsed the exercises until we tired out ourselves. Henry Reed was class valedictorian. He was a small, very black boy with hooded eyes, a long, broad nose and an oddly shaped head. I had admired him for years because each term he and I vied for the best grades in our class. Most often he bested me, but instead of being disappointed I was pleased that we shared top places between us. Like many Southern Black children, he lived with his grandmother, who was as strict as Momma and as kind as she knew how to be. He was courteous, respectful and soft-spoken to elders, but on the playground he chose to play the roughest games. I admired him. Anyone, I reckoned, sufficiently afraid or sufficiently dull could be polite. But to be able to operate at a top level with both adults and children was admirable.

His valedictory speech was entitled "To Be or Not to Be." The rigid tenth-grade teacher had helped him write it. He'd been working on the dramatic stresses for months.

The weeks until graduation were filled with heady activities. A group   15
of small children were to be presented in a play about buttercups and daisies and bunny rabbits. They could be heard throughout the building practicing their hops and their little songs that sounded like silver bells. The older girls (nongraduates, of course) were assigned the task of making refreshments for the night's festivities. A tangy scent of ginger, cinnamon, nutmeg and chocolate wafted around the home economics building as the budding cooks made samples for themselves and their teachers.

In every corner of the workshop, axes and saws split fresh timber as the woodshop boys made sets and stage scenery. Only the graduates were left out of the general bustle. We were free to sit in the library at the back of the building or look in quite detachedly, naturally, on the measures being taken for our event.

Even the minister preached on graduation the Sunday before. His subject was, "Let your light so shine that men will see your good works and praise your Father, Who is in Heaven." Although the sermon was purported to be addressed to us, he used the occasion to speak to backsliders, gamblers and general ne'er-do-wells. But since he had called our names at the beginning of the service we were mollified.

Among Negroes the tradition was to give presents to children going only from one grade to another. How much more important this was when the person was graduating at the top of the class. Uncle Willie and Momma had sent away for a Mickey Mouse watch like Bailey's. Louise gave me four embroidered handkerchiefs. (I gave her crocheted doilies.) Mrs. Sneed, the minister's wife, made me an undershirt to wear for graduation, and nearly every customer gave me a nickel or maybe even a dime with the instruction "Keep on moving to higher ground," or some such encouragement.

Amazingly the great day finally dawned and I was out of bed before I knew it. I threw open the back door to see it more clearly, but Momma said, "Sister, come away from that door and put your robe on."

I hoped the memory of that morning would never leave me. Sunlight   20
was itself young, and the day had none of the insistence maturity would

bring it in a few hours. In my robe and barefoot in the backyard, under cover of going to see about my new beans, I gave myself up to the gentle warmth and thanked God that no matter what evil I had done in my life He had allowed me to live to see this day. Somewhere in my fatalism I had expected to die, accidentally, and never have the chance to walk up the stairs in the auditorium and gracefully receive my hard-earned diploma. Out of God's merciful bosom I had won reprieve.

Bailey came out in his robe and gave me a box wrapped in Christmas paper. He said he had saved his money for months to pay for it. It felt like a box of chocolates, but I knew Bailey wouldn't save money to buy candy when we had all we could want under our noses.

He was as proud of the gift as I. It was a soft-leather-bound copy of a collection of poems by Edgar Allan Poe, or, as Bailey and I called him, "Eap." I turned to "Annabel Lee" and we walked up and down the garden rows, the cool dirt between our toes, reciting the beautifully sad lines.

Momma made a Sunday breakfast although it was only Friday. After we finished the blessing, I opened my eyes to find the watch on my plate. It was a dream of a day. Everything went smoothly and to my credit. I didn't have to be reminded or scolded for anything. Near evening I was too jittery to attend to chores, so Bailey volunteered to do all before his bath.

Days before, we had made a sign for the Store, and as we turned out the lights Momma hung the cardboard over the doorknob. It read clearly: CLOSED. GRADUATION.

My dress fitted perfectly and everyone said that I looked like a sunbeam 25 in it. On the hill, going toward the school, Bailey walked behind with Uncle Willie, who muttered, "Go on, Ju." He wanted him to walk ahead with us because it embarrassed him to have to walk so slowly. Bailey said he'd let the ladies walk together, and the men would bring up the rear. We all laughed, nicely.

Little children dashed by out of the dark like fireflies. Their crepe-paper dresses and butterfly wings were not made for running and we heard more than one rip, dryly, and the regretful "uh uh" that followed.

The school blazed without gaiety. The windows seemed cold and unfriendly from the lower hill. A sense of ill-fated timing crept over me, and if Momma hadn't reached for my hand I would have drifted back to Bailey and Uncle Willie, and possibly beyond. She made a few slow jokes about my feet getting cold, and tugged me along to the now-strange building.

Around the front steps, assurance came back. There were my fellow "greats," the graduating class. Hair brushed back, legs oiled, new dresses and pressed pleats, fresh pocket handkerchiefs and little handbags, all home-sewn. Oh, we were up to snuff, all right. I joined my comrades and didn't even see my family go in to find seats in the crowded auditorium.

The school band struck up a march and all classes filed in as had been rehearsed. We stood in front of our seats, as assigned, and on a signal from the choir director, we sat. No sooner had this been accomplished than the band started to play the national anthem. We rose again and sang the song, after which we recited the pledge of allegiance. We remained standing for a brief minute before the choir director and the principal signaled to us, rather desperately I thought, to take our seats. The command was so unusual that our carefully rehearsed and smooth-running machine was thrown off. For a full minute we fumbled for our chairs and bumped into each other awkwardly. Habits change or solidify under pressure, so in our state of nervous tension we had been ready to follow our usual assembly pattern: the American national anthem, then the pledge of allegiance, then the song every Black person I knew called the Negro National Anthem. All done in the same key, with the same passion and most often standing on the same foot.

Finding my seat at last, I was overcome with a presentiment of worse   30 things to come. Something unrehearsed, unplanned, was going to happen, and we were going to be made to look bad. I distinctly remember being explicit in the choice of pronoun. It was "we," the graduating class, the unit, that concerned me then.

The principal welcomed "parents and friends" and asked the Baptist minister to lead us in prayer. His invocation was brief and punchy, and for a second I thought we were getting on the high road to right action. When the principal came back to the dais, however, his voice had changed. Sounds always affected me profoundly and the principal's voice was one of my favorites. During assembly it melted and lowed weakly into the audience. It had not been in my plan to listen to him, but my curiosity was piqued and I straightened up to give him my attention.

He was talking about Booker T. Washington, our "late great leader," who said we can be as close as the fingers on the hand, etc. . . . Then he said a few vague things about friendship and the friendship of kindly people to those less fortunate than themselves. With that his voice nearly faded, thin, away. Like a river diminishing to a stream and then to a trickle. But he cleared his throat and said, "Our speaker tonight, who is also our friend, came from Texarkana to deliver the commencement address, but due to the irregularity of the train schedule, he's going to, as they say, 'speak and run.'" He said that we understood and wanted the man to know that we were most grateful for the time he was able to give us and then something about how we were willing always to adjust to another's program, and without more ado — "I give you Mr. Edward Donleavy."

Not one but two white men came through the door off-stage. The shorter one walked to the speaker's platform, and the tall one moved to the center seat and sat down. But that was our principal's seat, and already occupied. The dislodged gentleman bounced around for a long breath or two before the Baptist minister gave him his chair, then with more dignity than the situation deserved, the minister walked off the stage.

Donleavy looked at the audience once (on reflection, I'm sure that he wanted only to reassure himself that we were really there), adjusted his glasses and began to read from a sheaf of papers.

He was glad "to be here and to see the work going on just as it was in   35 the other schools."

At the first "Amen" from the audience I willed the offender to immediate death by choking on the word. But Amens and Yes, sir's began to fall around the room like rain through a ragged umbrella.

He told us of the wonderful changes we children in Stamps had in store. The Central School (naturally, the white school was Central) had already been granted improvements that would be in use in the fall. A well-known artist was coming from Little Rock to teach art to them. They were going to have the newest microscopes and chemistry equipment for their laboratory. Mr. Donleavy didn't leave us long in the dark over who made these improvements available to Central High. Nor were we to be ignored in the general betterment scheme he had in mind.

He said that he had pointed out to people at a very high level that one of the first-line football tacklers at Arkansas Agricultural and Mechanical College had graduated from good old Lafayette County Training School. Here fewer Amen's were heard. Those few that did break through lay dully in the air with the heaviness of habit.

He went on to praise us. He went on to say how he had bragged that "one of the best basketball players at Fisk sank his first ball right here at Lafayette County Training School."

The white kids were going to have a chance to become Galileos and 40
Madame Curies and Edisons and Gauguins, and our boys (the girls weren't even in on it) would try to be Jesse Owenses and Joe Louises.

Owens and the Brown Bomber were great heroes in our world, but what school official in the white-goddom of Little Rock had the right to decide that those two men must be our only heroes? Who decided that for Henry Reed to become a scientist he had to work like George Washington Carver, as a bootblack, to buy a lousy microscope? Bailey was obviously always going to be too small to be an athlete, so which concrete angel glued to what county seat had decided that if my brother wanted to become a lawyer he had to first pay penance for his skin by picking cotton and hoeing corn and studying correspondence books at night for twenty years?

The man's dead words fell like bricks around the auditorium and too many settled in my belly. Constrained by hard-learned manners I couldn't look behind me, but to my left and right the proud graduating class of 1940 had dropped their heads. Every girl in my row had found something new to do with her handkerchief. Some folded the tiny squares into love knots, some into triangles, but most were wadding them, then pressing them flat on their yellow laps.

On the dais, the ancient tragedy was being replayed. Professor Parsons sat, a sculptor's reject, rigid. His large, heavy body seemed devoid of will or willingness, and his eyes said he was no longer with us. The other teachers examined the flag (which was draped stage right) or their notes, or the windows which opened on our now-famous playing diamond.

Graduation, the hush-hush magic time of frills and gifts and congratulations and diplomas, was finished for me before my name was called. The accomplishment was nothing. The meticulous maps, drawn in three

colors of ink, learning and spelling decasyllabic words, memorizing the
whole of *The Rape of Lucrece*[3] — it was for nothing. Donleavy had
exposed us.

We were maids and farmers, handymen and washerwomen, and any-   45
thing higher that we aspired to was farcical and presumptuous.

Then I wished that Gabriel Prosser[4] and Nat Turner[5] had killed all whitefolks in their beds and that Abraham Lincoln had been assassinated before
the signing of the Emancipation Proclamation, and that Harriet Tubman[6]
had been killed by that blow on her head and Christopher Columbus had
drowned in the *Santa Maria*.

It was awful to be a Negro and have no control over my life. It was
brutal to be young and already trained to sit quietly and listen to charges
brought against my color with no chance of defense. We should all be
dead. I thought I should like to see us all dead, one on top of the other. A
pyramid of flesh with the whitefolks on the bottom, as the broad base,
then the Indians with their silly tomahawks and teepees and wigwams and
treaties, the Negroes with their mops and recipes and cotton sacks and
spirituals sticking out of their mouths. The Dutch children should all stumble in their wooden shoes and break their necks. The French should choke
to death on the Louisiana Purchase (1803) while silkworms ate all the
Chinese with their stupid pigtails. As a species, we were an abomination.
All of us.

Donleavy was running for election, and assured our parents that if he
won we could count on having the only colored paved playing field in that
part of Arkansas. Also — he never looked up to acknowledge the grunts of
acceptance — also, we were bound to get some new equipment for the home
economics building and the workshop.

He finished, and since there was no need to give any more than the
most perfunctory thank-you's, he nodded to the men on the stage, and the
tall white man who was never introduced joined him at the door. They left
with the attitude that now they were off to something really important.
(The graduation ceremonies at Lafayette County Training School had been
a mere preliminary.)

The ugliness they left was palpable. An uninvited guest who wouldn't   50
leave. The choir was summoned and sang a modern arrangement of

-----

[3]*The Rape of Lucrece*: A 1,855-line narrative poem by William Shakespeare.
[Eds.]

[4]*Gabriel Prosser* (c. 1775–1800): A leader of a thwarted slave rebellion in
Virginia in 1800. [Eds.]

[5]*Nat Turner* (1800–1831): The leader of about sixty slaves who killed about
fifty-five white Virginians in 1831. [Eds.]

[6]*Harriet Tubman* (c. 1820–1913): A Maryland slave who escaped to
Pennsylvania in 1850 and who conducted approximately 300 persons to freedom
on the Underground Railroad and worked as an abolitionist. [Eds.]

"Onward, Christian Soldiers," with new words pertaining to graduates seeking their place in the world. But it didn't work. Elouise, the daughter of the Baptist minister, recited "Invictus,"[7] and I could have cried at the impertinence of "I am the master of my fate, I am the captain of my soul."

My name had lost its ring of familiarity and I had to be nudged to go and receive my diploma. All my preparations had fled. I neither marched up to the stage like a conquering Amazon, nor did I look in the audience for Bailey's nod of approval. Marguerite Johnson, I heard the name again, my honors were read, there were noises in the audience of appreciation, and I took my place on the stage as rehearsed.

I thought about colors I hated: ecru, puce, lavender, beige and black.

There was shuffling and rustling around me, then Henry Reed was giving his valedictory address, "To Be or Not to Be." Hadn't he heard the whitefolks? We couldn't *be,* so the question was a waste of time. Henry's voice came out clear and strong. I feared to look at him. Hadn't he got the message? There was no "nobler in the mind" for Negroes because the world didn't think we had minds, and they let us know it. "Outrageous fortune"? Now, that was a joke. When the ceremony was over I had to tell Henry Reed some things. That is, if I still cared. Not "rub," Henry, "erase." "Ah, there's the erase." Us.

Henry had been a good student in elocution. His voice rose on tides of promise and fell on waves of warnings. The English teacher had helped him to create a sermon winging through Hamlet's soliloquy. To be a man, a doer, a builder, a leader, or to be a tool, an unfunny joke, a crusher of funky toadstools. I marveled that Henry could go through with the speech as if we had a choice.

I had been listening and silently rebutting each sentence with my eyes   55
closed; then there was a hush, which in an audience warns that something unplanned is happening. I looked up and saw Henry Reed, the conservative, the proper, the A student, turn his back to the audience and turn to us (the proud graduating class of 1940) and sing, nearly speaking,

> "Lift ev'ry voice and sing
> Till earth and heaven ring
> Ring with the harmonies of Liberty . . ."

It was the poem written by James Weldon Johnson. It was the music composed by J. Rosamond Johnson. It was the Negro National Anthem. Out of habit we were singing it.

Our mothers and fathers stood in the dark hall and joined the hymn of encouragement. A kindergarten teacher led the small children onto the stage and the buttercups and daisies and bunny rabbits marked time and

---

[7] *"Invictus":* A poem by the English poet William Ernest Henley (1849–1903). Its inspirational conclusion is quoted here. [Eds.]

tried to follow:

> "Stony the road we trod
> Bitter the chastening rod
> Felt in the days when hope, unborn, had died.
> Yet with a steady beat
> Have not our weary feet
> Come to the place for which our fathers sighed?"

Each child I knew had learned that song with his ABC's and along with "Jesus Loves Me This I Know." But I personally had never heard it before. Never heard the words, despite the thousands of times I had sung them. Never thought they had anything to do with me.

On the other hand, the words of Patrick Henry had made such an impression on me that I had been able to stretch myself tall and trembling and say, "I know not what course others may take, but as for me, give me liberty or give me death."

And now I heard, really for the first time:

> "We have come over a way that with tears
> has been watered,
> We have come, treading our path through
> the blood of the slaughtered."

While echoes of the song shivered in the air, Henry Reed bowed his   60
head, said "Thank you," and returned to his place in the line. The tears that slipped down many faces were not wiped away in shame.

We were on top again. As always, again. We survived. The depths had been icy and dark, but now a bright sun spoke to our souls. I was no longer simply a member of the proud graduating class of 1940; I was a proud member of the wonderful, beautiful Negro race.

Oh, Black known and unknown poets, how often have your auctioned pains sustained us? Who will compute the only nights made less lonely by your songs, or the empty pots made less tragic by your tales?

If we were a people much given to revealing secrets, we might raise monuments and sacrifice to the memories of our poets, but slavery cured us of that weakness. It may be enough, however, to have it said that we survive in exact relationship to the dedication of our poets (include preachers, musicians and blues singers).

QUESTIONS

1. Why was grammar and high school graduation such an important event in Stamps, Arkansas? Note the rituals and preparations associated with this event. How do they compare with those that accompanied your own junior high or high school graduation?

2. At the beginning of the graduation ceremony, Angelou was "overcome with a presentiment of worse things to come. Something unrehearsed, unplanned, was going to happen" (paragraph 30). What "unrehearsed, unplanned" event does occur? How does Angelou convey to the reader the meaning of this event?

3. Toward the end of the essay we are told, "I was no longer simply a member of the proud graduating class of 1940; I was a proud member of the wonderful, beautiful Negro race" (paragraph 61). How did the experience of the graduation change Angelou's way of thinking about herself and her people?

4. Understanding the structure of this essay is important for understanding the meaning of the essay. How does Angelou organize her material, and how does this organization reflect her purpose? Why do you think Angelou changes her point of view from third person in the first five paragraphs to first person in the rest of the essay?

5. Think of an event in your life that didn't turn out as you expected. What were your expectations for this event? What was the reality? Write an essay in which you show the significance of this event by contrasting how you planned for the event with how it actually turned out.

6. We all have had experiences that have changed the directions of our lives. These experiences may be momentous, such as moving from one country to another or losing a parent, or they may be experiences that did not loom large at the time but that changed the way you thought about things, such as finding that your parents disapproved of your best friend because of her race. Recall such a turning point in your life, and give readers a sense of what your life was like before the event and how it changed after the event.

MAKING CONNECTIONS

1. Compare the points of view taken by Angelou and Alice Walker (p. 42). How does the "presence" of the valedictorian in Angelou's essay influence the point of view she takes?

2. Two things link this essay with George Orwell's "Shooting an Elephant" (p. 114): each essay turns on an unexpected event, and each event prompts reflections on political domination. The two essays are from dissimilar points of view, but both Orwell in the Indian village and Mr. Donleavy at the Stamps graduation ceremonies are outsiders. Write an essay in which you compare and contrast these two events.

BEAUTY
When the Other Dancer Is the Self

Alice Walker

Born in Eatonton, Georgia, in 1944, Alice Walker is the youngest of eight children. Her father was a sharecropper, and her mother was a maid. A graduate of Sarah Lawrence College, Walker has been an active worker for civil rights. She has been a fellow of the Radcliffe Institute, a contributing and consulting editor for Ms. *magazine, and a teacher of literature and writing at a number of colleges and universities. She has published poetry, essays, short stories, and five novels:* The Third Life of Grange Copeland *(1970),* Meridian *(1976),* The Color Purple *(1982), for which she won the Pulitzer Prize,* The Temple of My Familiar *(1989), and* By the Light of My Father's Smile *(1998). "Beauty: When the Other Dancer Is the Self" appeared first in* Ms. *magazine and later in a collection of essays,* In Search of Our Mothers' Gardens *(1983). When asked why she writes, Walker said, "I'm really paying homage to people I love, the people who are thought to be dumb and backward but who were the ones who first taught me to see beauty."*

It is a bright summer day in 1947. My father, a fat, funny man with beautiful eyes and a subversive wit, is trying to decide which of his eight children he will take with him to the county fair. My mother, of course, will not go. She is knocked out from getting most of us ready: I hold my neck stiff against the pressure of her knuckles as she hastily completes the braiding and then beribboning of my hair.

My father is the driver for the rich old white lady up the road. Her name is Miss Mey. She owns all the land for miles around, as well as the house in which we live. All I remember about her is that she once offered to pay my mother thirty-five cents for cleaning her house, raking up piles of her magnolia leaves, and washing her family's clothes, and that my mother — she of no money, eight children, and a chronic earache — refused it. But I do not think of this in 1947. I am two and a half years old. I want to go everywhere my daddy goes. I am excited at the prospect of riding in a car. Someone has told me fairs are fun. That there is room in the car for only three of us doesn't faze me at all. Whirling happily in my starchy frock, showing off my biscuit-polished patent-leather shoes and lavender socks, tossing my head in a way that makes my ribbons bounce, I stand, hands on hips, before my father. "Take me, Daddy," I say with assurance; "I'm the prettiest!"

Later, it does not surprise me to find myself in Miss Mey's shiny black car, sharing the back seat with the other lucky ones. Does not surprise me that I thoroughly enjoy the fair. At home that night I tell the unlucky ones all I can remember about the merry-go-round, the man who eats live chickens, and the teddy bears, until they say: that's enough, baby Alice. Shut up now, and go to sleep.

It is Easter Sunday, 1950. I am dressed in a green, flocked, scalloped-hem dress (handmade by my adoring sister, Ruth) that has its own smooth satin petticoat and tiny hot-pink roses tucked into each scallop. My shoes, new T-strap patent leather, again highly biscuit-polished. I am six years old and have learned one of the longest Easter speeches to be heard that day, totally unlike the speech I said when I was two: "Easter lilies / pure and white / blossom in / the morning light." When I rise to give my speech I do so on a great wave of love and pride and expectation. People in the church stop rustling their new crinolines. They seem to hold their breath. I can tell they admire my dress, but it is my spirit, bordering on sassiness (woman-ishness), they secretly applaud.

"That girl's a little *mess*," they whisper to each other, pleased.   5

Naturally I say my speech without stammer or pause, unlike those who stutter, stammer, or worst of all, forget. This is before the word "beautiful" exists in people's vocabulary, but "Oh, isn't she the *cutest* thing!" frequently floats my way. "And got so much sense!" they gratefully add . . . for which thoughtful addition I thank them to this day.

It was great fun being cute. But then, one day, it ended.

I am eight years old and a tomboy. I have a cowboy hat, cowboy boots, checkered shirt and pants, all red. My playmates are my brothers, two and four years older than I. Their colors are black and green, the only difference in the way we are dressed. On Saturday nights we all go to the picture show, even my mother; Westerns are her favorite kind of movie. Back home, "on the ranch," we pretend we are Tom Mix, Hopalong Cassidy, Lash LaRue (we've even named one of our dogs Lash LaRue); we chase each other for hours rustling cattle, being outlaws, delivering damsels from distress. Then my parents decide to buy my brothers guns. These are not "real" guns. They shoot "BBs," copper pellets my brothers say will kill birds. Because I am a girl, I do not get a gun. Instantly I am relegated to the position of Indian. Now there appears a great distance between us. They shoot and shoot at everything with their new guns. I try to keep up with my bow and arrows.

One day while I am standing on top of our makeshift "garage" — pieces of tin nailed across some poles — holding my bow and arrow and looking out toward the fields, I feel an incredible blow in my right eye. I look down just in time to see my brother lower his gun.

Both brothers rush to my side. My eye stings, and I cover it with my   10
hand. "If you tell," they say, "we will get a whipping. You don't want that to happen, do you?" I do not. "Here is a piece of wire," says the older brother, picking it up from the roof; "say you stepped on one end of it and the other

flew up and hit you." The pain is beginning to start. "Yes," I say. "Yes, I will say that is what happened." If I do not say this is what happened, I know my brothers will find ways to make me wish I had. But now I will say anything that gets me to my mother.

Confronted by our parents we stick to the lie agreed upon. They place me on a bench on the porch and I close my left eye while they examine the right. There is a tree growing from underneath the porch that climbs past the railing to the roof. It is the last thing my right eye sees. I watch as its trunk, its branches, and then its leaves are blotted out by the rising blood.

I am in shock. First there is intense fever, which my father tries to break using lily leaves bound around my head. Then there are chills: my mother tries to get me to eat soup. Eventually, I do not know how, my parents learn what has happened. A week after the "accident" they take me to see a doctor. "Why did you wait so long to come?" he asks, looking into my eye and shaking his head. "Eyes are sympathetic," he says. "If one is blind, the other will likely become blind too."

This comment of the doctor's terrifies me. But it is really how I look that bothers me most. Where the BB pellet struck there is a glob of whitish scar tissue, a hideous cataract, on my eye. Now when I stare at people — a favorite pastime, up to now — they will stare back. Not at the "cute" little girl, but at her scar. For six years I do not stare at anyone, because I do not raise my head.

Years later, in the throes of a mid-life crisis, I ask my mother and sister whether I changed after the "accident." "No," they say, puzzled. "What do you mean?"

What do I mean?   15

I am eight, and, for the first time, doing poorly in school, where I have been something of a whiz since I was four. We have just moved to the place where the "accident" occurred. We do not know any of the people around us because this is a different county. The only time I see the friends I knew is when we go back to our old church. The new school is the former state penitentiary. It is a large stone building, cold and drafty, crammed to overflowing with boisterous, ill-disciplined children. On the third floor there is a huge circular imprint of some partition that has been torn out.

"What used to be here?" I ask a sullen girl next to me on our way past it to lunch.

"The electric chair," says she.

At night I have nightmares about the electric chair, and about all the people reputedly "fried" in it. I am afraid of the school, where all the students seem to be budding criminals.

"What's the matter with your eye?" they ask, critically.   20

When I don't answer (I cannot decide whether it was an "accident" or not), they shove me, insist on a fight.

My brother, the one who created the story about the wire, comes to my rescue. But then brags so much about "protecting" me, I become sick.

After months of torture at the school, my parents decide to send me back to our old community, to my old school. I live with my grandparents and the teacher they board. But there is no room for Phoebe, my cat. By the time my grandparents decide there *is* room, and I ask for my cat, she cannot be found. Miss Yarborough, the boarding teacher, takes me under her wing, and begins to teach me to play the piano. But soon she marries an African — a "prince," she says — and is whisked away to his continent.

At my old school there is at least one teacher who loves me. She is the teacher who "knew me before I was born" and bought my first baby clothes. It is she who makes life bearable. It is her presence that finally helps me turn on the one child at the school who continually calls me "one-eyed bitch." One day I simply grab him by his coat and beat him until I am satisfied. It is my teacher who tells me my mother is ill.

My mother is lying in bed in the middle of the day, something I have   25
never seen. She is in too much pain to speak. She has an abscess in her ear. I stand looking down on her, knowing that if she dies, I cannot live. She is being treated with warm oils and hot bricks held against her cheek. Finally a doctor comes. But I must go back to my grandparents' house. The weeks pass but I am hardly aware of it. All I know is that my mother might die, my father is not so jolly, my brothers still have their guns, and I am the one sent away from home.

"You did not change," they say.

Did I imagine the anguish of never looking up?

I am twelve. When relatives come to visit I hide in my room. My cousin Brenda, just my age, whose father works in the post office and whose mother is a nurse, comes to find me. "Hello," she says. And then she asks, looking at my recent school picture, which I did not want taken, and on which the "glob," as I think of it, is clearly visible, "You still can't see out of that eye?"

"No," I say, and flop back on the bed over my book.

That night, as I do almost every night, I abuse my eye. I rant and rave   30
at it, in front of the mirror. I plead with it to clear up before morning. I tell it I hate and despise it. I do not pray for sight. I pray for beauty.

"You did not change," they say.

I am fourteen and baby-sitting for my brother Bill, who lives in Boston. He is my favorite brother and there is a strong bond between us. Understanding my feelings of shame and ugliness he and his wife take me to a local hospital, where the "glob" is removed by a doctor named O. Henry. There is still a small bluish crater where scar tissue was, but the ugly white stuff is gone. Almost immediately I become a different person from the girl who does not raise her head. Or so I think. Now that I've raised my head I win the boyfriend of my dreams. Now that I've raised my head I have plenty of friends. Now that I've raised my head classwork comes from my lips faultlessly as Easter speeches did, and I leave high school as valedictorian, most popular student, and *queen*, hardly believing my luck. Ironically, the girl who was voted most beautiful in our class (and was) was later shot twice through the chest by a male companion, using a "real" gun, while she was pregnant. But that's another story in itself. Or is it?

"You did not change," they say.

It is now thirty years since the "accident." A beautiful journalist comes to visit and to interview me. She is going to write a cover story for her magazine that focuses on my latest book. "Decide how you want to look on the cover," she says. "Glamorous, whatever."

Never mind "glamorous," it is the "whatever" that I hear. Suddenly all I   35
can think of is whether I will get enough sleep the night before the photography session: if I don't, my eye will be tired and wander, as blind eyes will.

At night in bed with my lover I think up reasons why I should not appear on the cover of a magazine. "My meanest critics will say I've sold out," I say. "My family will now realize I write scandalous books."

"But what's the real reason you don't want to do this?" he asks.

"Because in all probability," I say in a rush, "my eye won't be straight."

"It will be straight enough," he says. Then, "Besides, I thought you'd made your peace with that."

And I suddenly remember that I have.   40

I remember:

I am talking to my brother Jimmy, asking if he remembers anything unusual about the day I was shot. He does not know I consider that day the last time my father, with his sweet home remedy of cool lily leaves, chose me, and that I suffered and raged inside because of this. "Well," he says, "all I remember is standing by the side of the highway with Daddy, trying to flag down a car. A white man stopped, but when Daddy said he needed somebody to take his little girl to the doctor, he drove off."

I remember:

I am in the desert for the first time. I fall totally in love with it. I am so overwhelmed by its beauty, I confront for the first time, consciously, the meaning of the doctor's words years ago: "Eyes are sympathetic. If one is blind, the other will likely become blind too." I realize I have dashed about the world madly, looking at this, looking at that, storing up images against the fading of the light. *But I might have missed seeing the desert!* The shock of that possibility — and gratitude for over twenty-five years of sight — sends me literally to my knees. Poem after poem comes — which is perhaps how poets pray.

ON SIGHT

I am so thankful I have seen
The Desert
And the creatures in the desert
And the desert Itself.

The desert has its own moon
Which I have seen
With my own eye.

There is no flag on it.

Trees of the desert have arms
All of which are always up
That is because the moon is up
The sun is up
Also the sky
The stars
Clouds
None with flags.

If there *were* flags, I doubt
the trees would point.
Would you?

But mostly, I remember this: 45

I am twenty-seven, and my baby daughter is almost three. Since her birth I have worried about her discovery that her mother's eyes are different from other people's. Will she be embarrassed? I think. What will she say? Every day she watches a television program called "Big Blue Marble." It begins with a picture of the earth as it appears from the moon. It is bluish, a little battered-looking, but full of light, with whitish clouds swirling around it. Every time I see it I weep with love, as if it is a picture of Grandma's house. One day when I am putting Rebecca down for her nap, she suddenly focuses on my eye. Something inside me cringes, gets ready to try to protect myself. All children are cruel about physical differences, I know from experience, and that they don't always mean to be is another matter. I assume Rebecca will be the same.

But no-o-o-o. She studies my face intently as we stand, her inside and me outside her crib. She even holds my face maternally between her dimpled little hands. Then, looking every bit as serious and lawyerlike as her father, she says, as if it may just possibly have slipped my attention: "Mommy, there's a *world* in your eye." (As in, "Don't be alarmed, or do anything crazy.") And then, gently, but with great interest: "Mommy, where did you *get* that world in your eye?"

For the most part, the pain left then. (So what, if my brothers grew up to buy even more powerful pellet guns for their sons and to carry real guns themselves. So what, if a young "Morehouse man"[1] once nearly fell off the

---

[1]*Morehouse man:* A student at Morehouse College, a traditionally black college for men in Atlanta, Georgia. [Eds.]

steps of Trevor Arnett Library because he thought my eyes were blue.) Crying and laughing I ran to the bathroom, while Rebecca mumbled and sang herself off to sleep. Yes indeed, I realized, looking into the mirror. There *was* a world in my eye. And I saw that it was possible to love it: that in fact, for all it had taught me of shame and anger and inner vision, I *did* love it. Even to see it drifting out of orbit in boredom, or rolling up out of fatigue, not to mention floating back at attention in excitement (bearing witness, a friend has called it), deeply suitable to my personality, and even characteristic of me.

That night I dream I am dancing to Stevie Wonder's song "Always" (the name of the song is really "As," but I hear it as "Always"). As I dance, whirling and joyous, happier than I've ever been in my life, another bright-faced dancer joins me. We dance and kiss each other and hold each other through the night. The other dancer has obviously come through all right, as I have done. She is beautiful, whole and free. And she is also me.

QUESTIONS

1. Walker's essay moves forward in time through abrupt though steadily progressive descriptions of episodes. What effect on the reader does this structure produce? Why do you suppose Walker chose this form instead of providing transitions from one episode to the next?
2. Consider Walker's method of contrasting other people's memories with her own. What effect is created by the repetition of "You did not change"?
3. Consider Walker's choices of episodes or examples of beauty. How does each one work toward developing a definition of beauty?
4. In what ways does this essay play with the possible meanings of the familiar adage, "Beauty is in the eye of the beholder"?
5. One theme of this essay could be that of coming to terms with a disfigurement or with an imagined loss of physical beauty. Recall an event (or accident) in your own life that changed your perception of yourself. Write a reflective narrative in which you use Walker's method of chronologically arranged episodes, including reflections on the time before the change, the change itself, and episodes following the change. Like Walker, you may want to contrast (or compare) your memories with those of others.
6. Recall a memorable event that occurred a year or more ago. It might be an event in your family's life or a public event at which you and your friends were present. Write down your memories of the event, and then interview your family or friends and write down their recollections. Compare the various memories of the event. Come to a conclusion about the differences or similarities you find and perhaps about the selectivity of memory.

MAKING CONNECTIONS

Walker's daughter's exclamation, "Mommy, there's a *world* in your eye" (paragraph 47), is a transcendent moment. It is also a metaphor. Other writers in this section could also be said to have a world in their eye. For example, Carl Sagan's description of how insight depends on a degree of restriction (p. 150) is closely related to Walker's theme. Select another essay from this "Reflecting" section, and show how Walker's reflections on her blind eye can help us understand the discoveries that the writer of the other essay is making.

MIRRORS

Lucy Grealy

Lucy Grealy (1963–2002), an award-winning poet, attended the Iowa Writer's Workshop and was a fellow at the Bunting Institute of Radcliffe. At the age of nine, Grealy had cancer of the jaw, and the right side of her jaw was removed. In the following essay, which first appeared in Harper's *and which received the National Magazine Award, Grealy writes about the thirty operations she had in twenty years to try to reconstruct her face. In both this selection and her book,* Autobiography of a Face *(1994), Grealy reflects on the obsessions and perceptions of physical beauty that dominate our culture. Her last book was the essay collection* As Seen on TV: Provocations *(2000). She died at the age of thirty-nine, an apparent suicide.*

There was a long period of time, almost a year, during which I never looked in a mirror. It wasn't easy; just as you only notice how often people eat on television when you yourself are on a diet, I'd never suspected just how omnipresent were our own images. I began as an amateur, avoiding merely mirrors, but by the end of the year I found myself with a professional knowledge of the reflected image, its numerous tricks and wiles, how it can spring up at any moment: a glass tabletop, a well-polished door handle, a darkened window, a pair of sunglasses, a restaurant's otherwise magnificent brass-plated coffee machine sitting innocently by the cash register.

I hadn't simply woken up one morning deciding not to look at myself as part of some personal experiment, as my friend Sally had attempted once before me: She'd lasted about three days before finally giving in to the need "to make sure I was still there." For Sally, not looking in the mirror meant enacting a conscious decision against a constant desire that, at the end of her three days, she still was at a loss to define as either solely habit or instinct. For me, however, the act of not looking was insidious. It was nihilistic, an insurgence too chaotic even to know if it was directed at the world or at myself.

At the time I was living alone in Scotland, surviving financially because of my eligibility for the dole, the vernacular for Britain's social security benefits. When I first arrived in Aberdeen I didn't know anyone, had no idea just how I was going to live, yet I went anyway because I'd met a plastic surgeon there who said he could help me. I had been living in London, working temp jobs. Before that I'd been in Berlin, and ostensibly had come to London only to earn money for a few weeks before returning to Germany. Exactly why I had this experience in London I don't know, but in my first week there I received more nasty comments about my face than I had in the past three years of living in

Iowa, New York, and Germany. These comments, all from men and all odiously sexual, hurt and disoriented me so much I didn't think twice about a friendly suggestion to go see a plastic surgeon. I'd already had more than a dozen operations in the States, yet my insurance ran out and so did my hope that any real difference could be made. Here, however, was a surgeon who had some new techniques, and here was a government willing to foot the bill: I didn't feel I could pass up yet another chance to "fix" my face, which I confusedly thought concurrent with "fixing" my self, my soul, my life.

Sixteen years earlier, when I was nine and living in America, I came home from school one day with a toothache. Several weeks and misdiagnoses later surgeons removed most of the right side of my jaw as part of an attempt to prevent the cancer they found there from spreading. No one properly explained the operation to me and I awoke in a cocoon of pain that prevented me from moving or speaking. Tubes ran in and out of my body and because I couldn't ask, I made up my own explanations for their existence.

Up until this time I'd been having a great time in the hospital. For starters   5 it was in "The City," a place of traffic and noise and dangers and, best of all, elevators. Never having been in an elevator before, I thrilled not just at the ride itself, but also at the game of nonchalance played out in front of the other elevator-savvy children who stepped on and off without thought.

Second, I was free from school. In theory a school existed on the third floor for children well enough to attend, but my friend Derek and I quickly discovered that the volunteer who came each day after lunch to pick us up was a sucker for a few well-timed groans, and once we learned to play straight man for each other there was little trouble getting out of it. We made sure the nurses kept thinking we had gone off to school, leaving us free for a few brief hours to wander the mazelike halls of the ancient hospital. A favorite spot was the emergency waiting room; they had good magazines and sometimes you got to see someone covered in blood come through the door. Derek tried to convince me that a certain intersection in the subbasement was an ideal place to watch for bodies heading toward the morgue, but the one time we did actually see one get wheeled by beneath its clichéd white sheet, we silently allowed each other to save face by suddenly deciding it was so much more fun to steal get-well cards from the gift shop than hang out in a cold basement. Once we stole the cards we sent them out randomly to other kids on the ward, signing them "Love and Kisses, Michael Jackson." Our theory was to watch them open up what they would think was a card from a famous star, but no one ever actually fell for it; by then we were well pegged as troublemakers.

There was something else going on too, something I didn't know how to articulate. Adults treated me in a mysterious manner. They asked me to do things: lie still for X rays, not cry for needles, things that, although not easy, never seemed equal to the praise I received in return. Reinforced to me again and again was how I was "a brave girl" for not crying, "a good girl" for not complaining, and soon I began defining myself this way, equating strength with silence.

Then the chemotherapy began. In the early seventies chemo was even cruder than it is now, the basic premise of it to poison the patient right up until the very brink of their own death. Up until this point I almost never cried, almost always received some sort of praise and attention in return for this, got what I considered the better part of the deal. But now, now it was like a practical joke that had gotten out of hand. Chemotherapy was a nightmare and I wanted it to stop, I didn't want to be brave any more. Yet I had so grown used to defining myself as "brave," i.e., silent, that even more terrifying was the thought of losing this sense of myself, certain that if I broke down this would be seen as despicable in the eyes of both my parents and doctors.

Mostly the task of taking me into the city for the injections fell upon my mother, though sometimes my father had to take me. Overwhelmed by the sight of the vomiting and weeping, my father developed the routine of "going to get the car," meaning that he left the office before the actual injection on the premise that then he could have the car ready and waiting when it was all over. Ashamed of my suffering, I felt relief when he was finally out of the room. When my mother was with me she stayed in the room, yet this only made the distance even more tangible, an almost palpable distance built on the intensity of our desperate longing to be anywhere else, anywhere at all. She explained that it was wrong to cry before the needle went in; afterward was one thing, but before, that was mere fear, and hadn't I already demonstrated my bravery earlier? Every week, every Friday, or "d-day" as we called it, for two and a half years I climbed up onto that too-big doctor's table and told myself not to cry, and every week I failed. The injections were really two large syringes, filled with chemicals so caustic to the vein that each had to be administered only very slowly. The whole process took about four minutes; I had to remain very still throughout it. Dry retching began in the first fifteen seconds, then the throb behind my eyes gave everything a yellow-green aura, and the bone-deep pain of alternating extreme hot and cold flashes made me tremble, yet still I had to sit motionless and not move my arm. No one spoke to me, not the doctor who was a paradigm of the cold-fish physician, not the nurse who told my mother I reacted much more violently than many of the other children, and not my mother, who, surely overwhelmed by the sight of her child's suffering, thought the best thing to do was remind me to be brave, to try and not cry. All the while I hated myself for having wept before the needle went in, convinced that the nurse and my mother were right, that I was "overdoing it," that the throwing up was psychosomatic, that my mother was angry with me for not being good or brave enough. So involved with controlling my guilt and shame, the problem of physical pain seemed easy by comparison.

Yet each week, usually two or three days after the injection, there 10 came the first flicker of feeling better, the always forgotten and gratefully rediscovered understanding that simply to be well in my body was the greatest thing I could ask for. I thought other people felt this gratitude, this appreciation and physical joy all the time, and I felt cheated because I only was able to feel it once a week.

When you are only ten, which is when the chemotherapy began, two and a half years seems like your whole life, yet it did finally end. I remember the last day of chemotherapy very clearly for two reasons: one, because it was the only day on which I succeeded in not crying, and because later, in private, I cried harder than I had in years; I thought now I would no longer be "special," that without the arena of chemotherapy in which to prove myself no one would ever love me, that I would fade unnoticed into the background. This idea about not being different didn't last very long. Before I thought people stared because I was bald. I wore a hat constantly, but this fooled no one, least of all myself.

During this time my mother worked in a nursing home in a Hasidic community. Hasidism dictates that married women cover their hair, and most commonly this is done with a wig. My mother's friends were all too willing to donate their discarded wigs, and soon the house filled with wigs. I never wore one of them, they frightened me even when my mother insisted I looked better in one of the few that actually fit, yet we didn't know how to say no to the women who kept graciously offering their wigs. The cats enjoyed sleeping on them and the dogs playing with them, and we grew used to having to pick a wig up off a chair we wanted to sit in. It never struck us as odd until one day a visitor commented wryly as he cleared a chair for himself, and suddenly a great wave of shame overcame me. I had nightmares about wigs, felt a flush if I even heard the word, and one night I put myself out of my misery by getting up after everyone was asleep, gathering all the wigs except for one the dogs were fond of and might miss, and which they had chewed anyway into something other than a wig. I hid all the rest in an old chest where they weren't found for almost a year.

But my hair eventually grew in, and it didn't take long before I understood that I looked different for other reasons. People stared at me in stores, other children made fun of me to the point where I came to expect it constantly, wherever I went. School became a battleground, and I came home at the end of each day exhausted with the effort of keeping my body so tense and hard that I was sure anything would bounce off of it.

I was living in an extreme situation, and because I did not particularly care for the world I was in, I lived in others, and because the world I did live in was a dangerous one, I incorporated this danger into my private life. I saw movies about and envied Indians, imagined myself one. Walking down the streets I walked down through the forest, my body ready for any opportunity to fight or flee one of the big cats I knew stalked the area. Vietnam and Cambodia were other places I walked through frequently, daily even as I made my way down the school hall, knowing a landmine or a sniper might give themselves away at any moment with the subtle, soft metal clicks I'd read about in the books I took from the library. When faced with a landmine, a mere insult about my face seemed a frivolous thing.

In the early years, when I was still on the chemo, I lived in worse places than Cambodia. Because I knew it was somehow inappropriate, I read only

15

in secret Primo Levi,[1] Elie Wiesel,[2] every book by a survivor I could find by myself without resorting to asking the librarian for. Auschwitz, Birkenau: I felt the senseless blows of the Capos and somehow knew that because at any moment we might be called upon to live for a week on one loaf of bread and some water called soup, the peanut butter sandwich I found on my plate was nothing less than a miracle, an utter and sheer miracle capable of making me literally weep with joy.

I decided I wanted to become a "deep" person. I wasn't exactly sure what this would entail, but I believed that if I could just find the right philosophy, think the right thoughts, my suffering would end. To try to understand the world I was in, I undertook to find out what was "real," and quickly began seeing reality as existing in the lowest common denominator, that suffering was the one and only dependable thing. But rather than spend all of my time despairing, though certainly I did plenty of that, I developed a form of defensive egomania: I felt I was the only one walking about in the world who understood what was really important. I looked upon people complaining about the most mundane things—nothing on TV, traffic jams, the price of new clothes—and felt both joy because I knew how unimportant those things really were and unenlightened feelings of superiority because other people didn't. Because I lived a fantasy life in which I had to be thankful for each cold, blanketless night I survived on the cramped wooden bunks, chemotherapy—the nausea, pain, and deep despair it brought—was a breeze, a stroll through the country in comparison. I was often miserable, but I knew that to feel warm instead of cold was its own kind of joy, that to eat was a reenactment of the grace of some god whom I could only dimly define, and that simply to be alive was a rare, ephemeral miracle. It was like reliving The Fall a dozen times a day: I was given these moments of grace and insight, only to be invariably followed by a clumsy tumble into narcissism.

As I got older, as I became a teenager, I began to feel very isolated. My nonidentical twin sister started going out with boys, and I started, my most tragic mistake of all, to listen to and believe the taunts thrown at me daily by the very boys she and the other girls were interested in. I was a dog, a monster, the ugliest girl they had ever seen. Of all the remarks the most damaging wasn't even directed at me, but was really an insult to Jerry, a boy I never saw because every day, between fourth and fifth periods when I was cornered by this particular group, I was too ashamed to lift my eyes off the floor. "Hey, look, it's Jerry's girlfriend," they yelled when they saw me, and I felt such shame, knowing that this was the deepest insult they could throw at Jerry.

---

[1]*Primo Levi* (1919–1987): An Italian chemist, novelist, poet, and memoirist. He survived one year at Auschwitz and wrote about his war and postwar experiences. His death was an apparent suicide. [Eds.]

[2]*Elie Wiesel* (b. 1928): A Romanian-born American writer and scholar who survived over a year at various concentration camps, including Auschwitz. His writings and work with persecuted groups earned him the Nobel Prize for Peace in 1986. [Eds.]

I became interested in horses and got a job at a run-down local stable. Having those horses to go to each day after school saved my life; I spent all of my time either with them or thinking about them. To keep myself thinking objectively I became an obsessive reader and an obsessive television watcher, anything to keep me away from the subjective. I convinced myself I was smarter than everyone else, that only I knew what mattered, what was important, but by the time I was sixteen this wasn't true, not by a long shot. Completely and utterly repressed, I was convinced that I never wanted a boyfriend, not ever, and wasn't it convenient for me, a blessing I even thought, that none would ever want me. I told myself I was free to concentrate on the "true reality" of life, whatever that was. My sister and her friends put on blue eye shadow, blow-dried their hair, and went to spend interminable hours in the local mall, and I looked down on them for this, knew they were misleading themselves and being overoccupied with the "mere surface" of living. I had thought like this when I was younger, but now it was different, now my philosophy was haunted by desires so frightening I was unable to even admit they existed.

It wasn't until I was in college that I finally allowed that maybe, just maybe, it might be nice to have a boyfriend. As a person I had, as they say, blossomed in college. I went to a small, liberal, predominantly female school and suddenly, after years of alienation in high school, discovered that there were other people I could enjoy talking to, people who thought me intelligent and talented. I was, however, still operating on the assumption that no one, not ever, would be physically attracted to me, and in a curious way this shaped my personality. I became forthright and honest and secure in the way only the truly self-confident are, those who do not expect to be rejected, and those like me, who do not even dare to ask and so also expect no rejection. I had come to know myself as a person, but it would be graduate school before I was literally, physically able to use my name and the word woman in the same sentence.

Throughout all of this I was undergoing reconstructive surgery in an attempt to rebuild my jaw. It started when I was fifteen, several years after the chemo ended. I had known for years I would have operations to fix my face, and sometimes at night I fantasized about how good my life would finally be then. One day I got a clue that maybe it would not be so easy. At fourteen I went first to an older plastic surgeon who explained the process of pedestals to me, and told me it would take ten years to fix my face. Ten years? Why even bother? I thought. I'll be ancient by then. I went to the library and looked up the pedestals he talked about. There were gruesome pictures of people with grotesque tubes of their own skin growing out of their bodies, tubes of skin that were harvested like some kind of crop and then rearranged in ways with results that did not look at all normal or acceptable to my eye. But then I met a younger surgeon, a man who was working on a new way of grafting that did not involve pedestals, and I became more hopeful and once again began awaiting the fixing of my face, of the day when I would be whole, content, loved.

20

Long-term plastic surgery is not like the movies. There is no one single operation that will change everything, and there is certainly no slow unwrapping of the gauze in order to view the final product. There is always swelling, sometimes grotesque, there are often bruises, and always there are scars. After each operation, too scared to simply go look in the mirror, I developed an oblique method comprised of several stages. First, I tried to catch my reflection in an overhead lamp: The roundness of the metal distorted my image just enough to obscure details and give no true sense of size or proportion. Then I slowly worked my way up to looking at the reflection in someone's eyeglasses, and from there I went to walking as briskly as possible by a mirror, glancing only quickly. I repeated this as many times as it would take me, passing the mirror slightly more slowly each time until finally I was able to stand still and confront myself.

The theory behind most reconstructive surgery is to take large chunks of muscle, skin, and bone and slap them into the roughly appropriate place, then slowly begin to carve this mess into some sort of shape. It involves long, major operations, countless lesser ones, a lot of pain, and many, many years. And also, it does not always work. With my young surgeon in New York, who was becoming not so young with each passing year, I had two or three soft tissue grafts, two skin grafts, a bone graft, and some dozen other operations to "revise" my face, yet when I left graduate school at the age of twenty-five I was still more or less in the same position I had started in: a deep hole in the right side of my face and a rapidly shrinking left side and chin, a result of the radiation I'd had as a child and the stress placed upon it by the other operations. I was caught in a cycle of having a big operation, one that would force me to look monstrous from the swelling for many months, then have the subsequent revision operations that improved my looks tremendously, and then slowly, over the period of a few months or a year, watch the graft reabsorb back into my body, slowly shrink down and leave me with nothing but the scarred donor site the graft had originally come from.

I had little or no conception of how I appeared to other people. As a child, Halloween was my favorite holiday because I could put on a mask and walk among the blessed for a few brief, sweet hours. Such freedom I felt, walking down the street, my face hidden: Through the imperfect oval holes I could peer out at other faces, masked or painted or not, and see on those faces nothing but the normal faces of childhood looking back at me, faces I mistakenly thought were the faces everyone else but me saw all the time, faces that were simply curious and ready for fun, not the faces I usually braced myself for, the cruel, lonely, vicious ones I spent every day other than Halloween waiting to round each corner. As I breathed in the condensed, plastic air I somehow thought that I was breathing in normality, that this joy and weightlessness were what the world was comprised of, and it was only my face that kept me from it, my face that was my own mask, my own tangible barrier that kept me from knowing the true identity of the joy I was sure everyone but me lived with intimately. How could they not know it? Not know that to be free of the fear of taunts and the burden of knowing no one would ever love you was all anyone could ever ask for? I was a pauper walking for a short while in the clothes of the prince, and when the day ended, I gave up my disguise with dismay.

I also came to love winter, when I could wrap the lower half of my face up in a scarf: I could speak to people and they would have no idea of who and what they were really speaking to. I developed the bad habits of letting my long hair hang in my face, and of always covering my chin and mouth with my hand, hoping it might be seen as a thoughtful, accidental gesture. My one concession to this came in college, when I cut my hair short, very short, in an attempt to stop hiding behind it. It was also an attempt, though I didn't see it as such at the time, to desex myself. I had long, blond hair, and I also had a thin figure. Sometimes, from a distance, men would see the thin blonde and whistle, something I dreaded more than anything else because I knew as they got closer their tone would inevitably change, they would stare openly or, worse, turn away quickly, and by cutting my hair I felt I might possibly avoid this, clear up any misconception anyone, however briefly, might have about my being attractive.

Once in college my patient friends repeated for me endlessly that most of it was in my mind, that, granted, I did not look like everyone else, but that didn't mean I looked bad. I am sure now that they were right some of the time. But with the constant surgery I was in a perpetual state of transfiguration. I rarely looked the same for more than six months at a time. So ashamed of my face, I was unable to even admit that this constant change affected me at all; I let everyone who wanted to know that it was only what was inside that mattered, that I had "grown used to" the surgery, that none of it bothered me at all. Just as I had done in childhood, I pretended nothing was wrong, and this was constantly mistaken by others for bravery. I spent a great deal of time looking in the mirror in private, positioning my head to show off my eyes and nose, which were not just normal, but quite pretty, as my still-patient friends told me often. But I could not bring myself to see them for more than a glimmer: I looked in the mirror and saw not the normal upper half of my face, but only the disfigured lower half. People still teased me. Not daily, not like when I was younger, but in ways that caused me more pain than ever before. Children stared at me and I learned to cross the street to avoid them; this bothered me but not as much as the insults I got from men. They weren't thrown at me because I was disfigured, they were thrown at me because I was a disfigured woman.

They came from boys, sometimes men, and almost always a group of them. Only two or three times have I ever been teased by a single person, and I can think of only one time when I was ever teased by a woman. Had I been a man, would I have had to walk down the street while a group of young women followed and denigrated my sexual worth?

Not surprisingly, I viewed sex as my salvation. I was sure that if only I could get someone to sleep with me it would mean I wasn't ugly, that I was an attractive person, a lovable person. It would not be hard to guess where this line of reasoning led me, which was into the beds of a few manipulative men who liked themselves even less than they liked me, and I in turn left each short-term affair hating myself, obscenely sure that if only I had been prettier it would have worked, he would have loved me and it would have been like those other love affairs I was certain "normal" women had all the time. Gradually I became unable to say "I'm depressed," but could only say "I'm ugly," because the two had become inextricably linked in my mind. Into that universal lie, that sad equation of "if only" which we are all prey to, I was sure that if only I had a normal face, then I would be happy.

What our brains know is one thing, yet what our hearts know is another matter entirely, and when I met this new surgeon in Scotland, I offhandedly explained to my friends back home "why not, it's free, isn't it?" unable to admit that I believed in the fixability of life all over again.

Originally, it was planned I would have something called a tissue expander, followed by a bone graft. A tissue expander is a small balloon placed under the skin and then slowly blown up over the course of several months, the object being to stretch out the skin and create room and cover for the new bone. It is a bizarre, nightmarish thing to do to your face, yet I was hopeful about the end results and I was also able to spend the three months the expansion took in the hospital. I've always felt safe in hospitals: It's the one place I feel justified, sure of myself, free from the need to explain the way I look. For this reason the first tissue expander was bearable, just, and the bone graft that followed it was a success, it did not melt away like the previous ones.

However, the stress put upon my original remaining jaw from the sur-   30
gery instigated a period of deterioration of that bone, and it became apparent that I was going to need the same operation I'd just had on the right side done to the left. I remember my surgeon telling me this at an outpatient clinic. I planned to be traveling down to London that same night on an overnight train, and I barely made it to the station on time, I was in such a fumbling state of despair. I could not imagine doing it all over again, and just as I had done all my life, I was searching and searching through my intellect for a way to make it okay, make it bearable, for a way to do it. I lay awake all night on that train, feeling the tracks slip quickly and oddly erotic below me, when I remembered an afternoon from my three months in the hospital. Boredom was a big problem those long afternoons, the days punctuated and landmarked by meals and television programs. Waiting for the afternoon tea to come, wondering desperately how I could make time pass, it suddenly occurred to me I didn't have to make time pass, that it would do it of its own accord, that I simply had to relax and take no action. Lying on the train, remembering that, I realized I had no obligation to make my situation okay, that I didn't have to explain it, understand it, that I could invoke the idea of negative capability and just simply let it happen. By the time the train pulled into King's Cross Station, I felt able to bear it yet again, not entirely sure what other choice I had.

But there was an element I didn't yet know about. I returned to Scotland to set up a date to go in and have the tissue expander put in, and was told quite casually that I'd only be in the hospital three or four days.

Wasn't I going to spend the whole expansion time in the hospital? I asked almost in a whisper. What's the point of that? You can just come in every day to the outpatient to have it expanded. Horrified by this, I was speechless. I would have to live and move about in the outside world with a giant balloon in my face? I can't remember what I did for the next few days before I went into the hospital, but I vaguely remember that these days involved a great deal of drinking alone in bars and at home.

I went in and had the operation and, just as they said, went home at the end of the week. The only thing I can truly say gave me any comfort during the months I lived with my tissue expander was my writing and Kafka. I started a novel and completely absorbed myself in it, writing for hours and hours every day. It was the only way I could walk down the street, to stand the stares I received, to think to myself "I'll bet none of them are writing a novel." It was that strange, old familiar form of egomania, directly related to my dismissive, conceited thoughts of adolescence. As for Kafka, who had always been one of my favorite writers even before the new fashion for him, he helped me in that I felt permission to feel alienated, and to have that alienation be okay, to make it bearable, noble even. In the way living in Cambodia helped me as a child, I walked the streets of my dark little Scottish city by the sea and knew without doubt that I was living in a story Kafka would have been proud to write.

This time period, however, was also the time I stopped looking in the mirror. I simply didn't want to know. Many times before in my life I have been repelled by the mirror, but the repulsion always took the form of a strange, obsessive attraction. Previously I spent many hours looking in the mirror, trying to see what it was that other people were seeing, a purpose I understand now was laughable, as I went to the mirror with an already clearly fixed, negative idea of what people saw. Once I even remember thinking how awful I looked in a mirror I was quickly passing in a shopping center, seeing perfectly all the flaws I knew were there, when I realized with a shock that I wasn't looking in a mirror, that I was looking through into a store at someone who had the same coat and haircut as me, someone who, when I looked closer, looked perfectly fine.

The one good thing about a tissue expander is that you look so bad with it in that no matter what you look like once it's finally removed, it has to be better. I had my bone graft and my fifth soft tissue graft and yes, even I had to admit I looked better. But I didn't look like me. Something was wrong: Was this the face I had waited through twenty years and almost thirty operations for? I somehow just couldn't make what I saw in the mirror correspond to the person I thought It was. It wasn't just that I felt ugly, I simply could not associate the image as belonging to me. My own image was the image of a stranger, and rather than try to understand this, I simply ignored it. I reverted quickly back to my tissue expander mode of not looking in the mirror, and quickly improved it to include not looking at any image of myself. I perfected the technique of brushing my teeth without a mirror, grew my hair in such a way that it would require only a quick simple brush,

and wore clothes that were simply and easily put on, no complex layers or
lines that might require even the most minor of visual adjustments.

On one level I understood that the image of my face was merely that,   35
an image, a surface that was not directly related to any true, deep definition
of the self. But I also knew that it is only through image that we experience
and make decisions about the everyday world, and I was not always able
to gather the strength to prefer the deeper world over the shallower one.
I looked for ways to relate the two, to find a bridge that would allow
me access to both, anything no matter how tenuous, rather than ride
out the constant swings between peace and anguish. The only direction I
had to go in to achieve this was simply to strive for a state of awareness and
self-honesty that sometimes, to this day, rewards me and sometimes
exhausts me.

Our whole lives are dominated, though it is not always so clearly trans-
latable, with the question "How do I look?" Take all the many nouns in our
lives: car; house; job; family; love; friends; and substitute the personal pronoun — it is not that we are all so self-obsessed, it is that all things eventually
relate back to ourselves, and it is our own sense of how we appear to the
world by which we chart our lives, how we navigate our personalities that
would otherwise be adrift in the ocean of other peoples' obsessions.

One particular afternoon I remember very lucidly, an afternoon, toward the end of my yearlong separation from the mirror. I was talking to
someone, an attractive man as it happened, and we were having a wonderful, engaging conversation. For some reason it flickered across my
mind to wonder what I looked like to him. What was he seeing when he
saw me? So many times I've asked this of myself, and always the answer
was a bad one, an ugly one. A warm, smart woman, yes, but still, an un-
attractive one. I sat there in the café and asked myself this old question
and, startlingly, for the first time in my life I had no answer readily prepared. I had literally not looked in a mirror for so long that I quite simply had no clue as to what I looked like. I looked at the man as he spoke;
my entire life I had been giving my negative image to people, handing it
to them and watching the negative way it was reflected back to me. But
now, because I had no idea what I was giving him, the only thing I had
to judge by was what he was giving me, which, as reluctant as I was to
admit it, was positive.

That afternoon in that café I had a moment of the freedom I had been
practicing for behind my Halloween mask as a child. But where as a child
I expected it to come as a result of gaining something, a new face, it came
to me then as the result of shedding something, of shedding my image. I
once thought that truth was an eternal, that once you understood something it was with you forever. I know now that this isn't so, that most
truths are inherently unretainable, that we have to work hard all our lives
to remember the most basic things. Society is no help; the images it gives
us again and again want us only to believe that we can most be ourselves
by looking like someone else, leaving our own faces behind to turn into

ghosts that will inevitably resent us and haunt us. It is no mistake that in movies and literature the dead sometimes know they are dead only after they can no longer see themselves in the mirror. As I sat there feeling the warmth of the cup against my palm this small observation seemed like a great revelation to me, and I wanted to tell the man I was with about it, but he was involved in his own topic and I did not want to interrupt him, so instead I looked with curiosity over to the window behind him, its night-darkened glass reflecting the whole café, to see if I could recognize myself.

QUESTIONS

1. What did Grealy learn about herself from her "yearlong separation from the mirror"?
2. Why did Grealy think that "fixing" her face would "fix" herself, her soul, her life? What is the significance of the word *fix*?
3. One of the features of this essay that makes it so compelling is Grealy's command of details. Locate details that you believe are effective, and think about their function. Try to rewrite some of Grealy's sentences to remove the details. What is lost? How do details link the author and the reader?
4. Grealy tells us, "Most truths are inherently unretainable," and "we have to work hard all our lives to remember the most basic things" (paragraph 38). What truths does Grealy refer to?
5. How does Grealy use her personal experience as evidence so that her essay becomes a larger story with greater relevance to others?
6. Grealy writes about the freedom she feels as a result of accepting the truth about her face. Such freedom, as Grealy shows, is never easily achieved. Reflect on a struggle or conflict in your own life, and write a brief essay on the "truths" that have emerged from your struggle.

MAKING CONNECTIONS

1. Both Alice Walker (p. 42) and Grealy struggle to accept their bodies and their appearance. In what ways are their struggles similar? In what ways are they different? What does this struggle achieve for each writer?
2. Do you agree with the observation that Alice Walker loses sight in order to gain sight and that Grealy loses face in order to gain face?

LEARNING TO READ AND WRITE

Frederick Douglass

Frederick Augustus Washington Bailey (1817–1895) was born to a slave mother on the Eastern Shore of Maryland. His father was a white man. After his escape from the South in 1838, he adopted the name of Douglass and worked to free other slaves and later (after the Civil War) to protect the rights of freed slaves. He was a newspaper editor, a lecturer, the United States minister to Haiti, and the author of several books about his life and times. The Narrative of the Life of Frederick Douglass: An American Slave *(1841), from which the following selection has been taken, is his best-known work.*

I lived in Master Hugh's family about seven years. During this time, I succeeded in learning to read and write. In accomplishing this, I was compelled to resort to various stratagems. I had no regular teacher. My mistress, who had kindly commenced to instruct me, had, in compliance with the advice and direction of her husband, not only ceased to instruct, but had set her face against my being instructed by any one else. It is due, however, to my mistress to say of her, that she did not adopt this course of treatment immediately. She at first lacked the depravity indispensable to shutting me up in mental darkness. It was at least necessary for her to have some training in the exercise of irresponsible power, to make her equal to the task of treating me as though I were a brute.

My mistress was, as I have said, a kind and tender-hearted woman; and in the simplicity of her soul she commenced, when I first went to live with her, to treat me as she supposed one human being ought to treat another. In entering upon the duties of a slaveholder, she did not seem to perceive that I sustained to her the relation of a mere chattel, and that for her to treat me as a human being was not only wrong, but dangerously so. Slavery proved as injurious to her as it did to me. When I went there, she was a pious, warm, and tender-hearted woman. There was no sorrow or suffering for which she had not a tear. She had bread for the hungry, clothes for the naked, and comfort for every mourner that came within her reach. Slavery soon proved its ability to divest her of these heavenly qualities. Under its influence, the tender heart became stone, and the lamblike disposition gave way to one of tiger-like fierceness. The first step in her downward course was in her ceasing to instruct me. She now commenced to practise her husband's precepts. She finally became even more violent in her opposition than her husband himself. She was not satisfied with simply doing as well as he had commanded; she seemed anxious to do better. Nothing seemed to make her more angry than to see me with a newspaper. She seemed to think that here lay the danger. I have had her rush at me with a face made all up of fury, and snatch from me a newspaper, in a manner that fully revealed her apprehension. She was an apt woman; and a little experience soon demonstrated, to her satisfaction, that education and slavery were incompatible with each other.

From this time I was most narrowly watched. If I was in a separate room any considerable length of time, I was sure to be suspected of having a book, and was at once called to give an account of myself. All this, however, was too late. The first step had been taken. Mistress, in teaching me the alphabet, had given me the *inch*, and no precaution could prevent me from taking the *ell*.[1]

The plan which I adopted, and the one by which I was most successful, was that of making friends of all the little white boys whom I met in the street. As many of these as I could, I converted into teachers. With their kindly aid, obtained at different times and in different places, I finally succeeded in learning to read. When I was sent on errands, I always took my book with me, and by doing one part of my errand quickly, I found time to get a lesson before my return. I used also to carry bread with me, enough of which was always in the house, and to which I was always welcome; for I was much better off in this regard than many of the poor white children in our neighborhood. This bread I used to bestow upon the hungry little urchins, who, in return, would give me that more valuable bread of knowledge. I am strongly tempted to give the names of two or three of those little boys, as a testimonial of the gratitude and affection I bear them; but prudence forbids; — not that it would injure me, but it might embarrass them; for it is almost an unpardonable offence to teach slaves to read in this Christian country. It is enough to say of the dear little fellows, that they lived on Philpot Street, very near Durgin and Bailey's ship-yard. I used to talk this matter of slavery over with them. I would sometimes say to them, I wished I could be as free as they would be when they got to be men. "You will be free as soon as you are twenty-one, *but I am a slave for life!* Have not I as good a right to be free as you have?" These words used to trouble them; they would express for me the liveliest sympathy, and console me with the hope that something would occur by which I might be free.

I was now about twelve years old, and the thought of being *a slave for life* began to bear heavily upon my heart. Just about this time, I got hold of a book entitled "The Columbian Orator."[2] Every opportunity I got, I used to read this book. Among much of other interesting matter, I found in it a dialogue between a master and his slave. The slave was represented as having

---

[1]*ell:* A unit of measurement, no longer used, equal to 45 inches. [Eds.]

[2]*The Columbian Orator:* A collection of speeches widely used in early nineteenth-century schools to teach argument and rhetoric. [Eds.]

run away from his master three times. The dialogue represented the conversation which took place between them, when the slave was retaken the third time. In this dialogue, the whole argument in behalf of slavery was brought forward by the master, all of which was disposed of by the slave. The slave was made to say some very smart as well as impressive things in reply to his master — things which had the desired though unexpected effect; for the conversation resulted in the voluntary emancipation of the slave on the part of the master.

In the same book, I met with one of Sheridan's mighty speeches on and in behalf of Catholic emancipation.[3] These were choice documents to me. I read them over and over again with unabated interest. They gave tongue to interesting thoughts of my own soul, which had frequently flashed through my mind, and died away for want of utterance. The moral which I gained from the dialogue was the power of truth over the conscience of even a slaveholder. What I got from Sheridan was a bold denunciation of slavery, and a powerful vindication of human rights. The reading of these documents enabled me to utter my thoughts, and to meet the arguments brought forward to sustain slavery; but while they relieved me of one difficulty, they brought on another even more painful than the one of which I was relieved. The more I read, the more I was led to abhor and detest my enslavers. I could regard them in no other light than a band of successful robbers, who had left their homes, and gone to Africa, and stolen us from our homes, and in a strange land reduced us to slavery. I loathed them as being the meanest as well as the most wicked of men. As I read and contemplated the subject, behold! that very discontentment which Master Hugh had predicted would follow my learning to read had already come, to torment and sting my soul to unutterable anguish. As I writhed under it, I would at times feel that learning to read had been a curse rather than a blessing. It had given me a view of my wretched condition, without the remedy. It opened my eyes to the horrible pit, but to no ladder upon which to get out. In moments of agony, I envied my fellow-slaves for their stupidity. I have often wished myself a beast. I preferred the condition of the meanest reptile to my own. Any thing, no matter what, to get rid of thinking! It was this everlasting thinking of my condition that tormented me. There was no getting rid of it. It was pressed upon me by every object within sight or hearing, animate or inanimate. The silver trump of freedom had roused my soul to eternal wakefulness. Freedom now appeared, to disappear no more forever. It was heard in every sound, and seen in every thing. It was ever present to torment me with a sense of my wretched condition. I saw nothing without seeing it, I heard nothing without hearing it, and felt nothing without feeling it. It looked from every star, it smiled in every calm, breathed in every wind, and moved in every storm.

---

[3]*Richard Brinsley Sheridan* (1751–1816): A British dramatist, orator, and politician. Roman Catholics were not allowed to vote in England until 1829. [Eds.]

I often found myself regretting my own existence, and wishing myself dead; and but for the hope of being free, I have no doubt but that I should have killed myself, or done something for which I should have been killed. While in this state of mind, I was eager to hear any one speak of slavery. I was a ready listener. Every little while, I could hear something about the abolitionists. It was some time before I found what the word meant. It was always used in such connections as to make it an interesting word to me. If a slave ran away and succeeded in getting clear, or if a slave killed his master, set fire to a barn, or did any thing very wrong in the mind of a slaveholder, it was spoken of as the fruit of *abolition*. Hearing the word in this connection very often, I set about learning what it meant. The dictionary afforded me little or no help. I found it was "the act of abolishing"; but then I did not know what was to be abolished. Here I was perplexed. I did not dare to ask any one about its meaning, for I was satisfied that it was something they wanted me to know very little about. After a patient waiting, I got one of our city papers, containing an account of the number of petitions from the north, praying for the abolition of slavery in the District of Columbia, and of the slave trade between the States. From this time I understood the words *abolition* and *abolitionist*, and always drew near when that word was spoken, expecting to hear something of importance to myself and fellow-slaves. The light broke in upon me by degrees. I went one day down on the wharf of Mr. Waters; and seeing two Irishmen unloading a scow of stone, I went, unasked, and helped them. When we had finished, one of them came to me and asked me if I were a slave. I told him I was. He asked, "Are ye a slave for life?" I told him that I was. The good Irishman seemed to be deeply affected by the statement. He said to the other that it was a pity so fine a little fellow as myself should be a slave for life. He said it was a shame to hold me. They both advised me to run away to the north; that I should find friends there, and that I should be free. I pretended not to be interested in what they said, and treated them as if I did not understand them; for I feared they might be treacherous. White men have been known to encourage slaves to escape, and then, to get the reward, catch them and return them to their masters. I was afraid that these seemingly good men might use me so; but I nevertheless remembered their advice, and from that time I resolved to run away. I looked forward to a time at which it would be safe for me to escape. I was too young to think of doing so immediately; besides, I wished to learn how to write, as I might have occasion to write my own pass. I consoled myself with the hope that I should one day find a good chance. Meanwhile, I would learn to write.

The idea as to how I might learn to write was suggested to me by being in Durgin and Bailey's ship-yard, and frequently seeing the ship carpenters, after hewing, and getting a piece of timber ready for use, write on the timber the name of that part of the ship for which it was intended. When a piece of timber was intended for the larboard side, it would be marked thus— "L." When a piece was for the starboard side, it would be marked thus— "S." A piece for the larboard side forward, would be marked thus— "L. F." When

a piece was for starboard side forward, it would be marked thus—
"S. F." For larboard aft, it would be marked thus—"L. A." For starboard
aft, it would be marked thus—"S. A." I soon learned the names of these letters, and for what they were intended when placed upon a piece of timber in
the ship-yard. I immediately commenced copying them, and in a short time
was able to make the four letters named. After that, when I met with any boy
who I knew could write, I would tell him I could write as well as he. The next
word would be, "I don't believe you. Let me see you try it." I would then
make the letters which I had been so fortunate as to learn, and ask him to
beat that. In this way I got a good many lessons in writing, which it is quite
possible I should never have gotten in any other way. During this time, my
copy-book was the board fence, brick wall, and pavement; my pen and ink
was a lump of chalk. With these, I learned mainly how to write. I then commenced and continued copying the Italics in Webster's Spelling Book, until I
could make them all without looking on the book. By this time, my little
Master Thomas had gone to school, and learned how to write, and had written over a number of copy-books. These had been brought home, and shown
to some of our near neighbors, and then laid aside. My mistress used to go
to class meeting at the Wilk Street meetinghouse every Monday afternoon,
and leave me to take care of the house. When left thus, I used to spend the
time in writing in the spaces left in Master Thomas's copy-book, copying
what he had written. I continued to do this until I could write a hand very
similar to that of Master Thomas. Thus, after a long, tedious effort for years,
I finally succeeded in learning how to write.

QUESTIONS

1. As its title proclaims, Douglass's book is a narrative, the story of his life.
   So, too, is this selection a narrative, the story of his learning to read and
   write. Identify the main events of this story, and list them in chronological order.
2. Douglass is documenting some of the events in his life in this selection,
   but certain events are not simply reported. Instead, they are described so
   that we may see, hear, and feel what was experienced by the people who
   were present during each event. Which events are described most fully
   in this narrative? How does Douglass seek to engage our interest and
   direct our feelings through such scenes?
3. In this selection from his memoir and in the entire book, Douglass is
   engaged in evaluating an institution—slavery—and arguing a case
   against it. Can you locate the points in the text where reflecting gives way
   to argumentation? How does Douglass support his argument against
   slavery? What contributes to his persuasiveness?
4. The situation of Roman Catholics and by inference the Irish is a subtheme
   in this essay. You can trace it by locating every mention of Catholicism

and the Irish in the text. How does this theme relate to African American slavery? Locate *The Columbian Orator* in your library, or find out more about Sheridan and why he argued on behalf of "Catholic emancipation" (paragraph 6).
5. A subnarrative in this text tells the story of Master Hugh's wife, the "mistress" of the household in which Douglass learned to read and write. Retell *her* story in your own words. Consider how her story relates to Douglass's own story and how it relates to Douglass's larger argument about slavery.
6. Put yourself in the place of Master Hugh's wife, and retell all events in her words and from her point of view. To do so, you will have to decide both what she might have come to know about all these events and how she would feel about them. You will also have to decide when she is writing. Is she keeping a diary during this time (the early 1830s), or is she looking back from the perspective of later years? Has she been moved to write by reading Douglass's own book, which appeared in 1841? If so, how old would she be then, and what would she think about these past events? Would she be angry, bitter, repentant, embarrassed, indulgent, scornful, or what?

MAKING CONNECTIONS

1. What are the most common themes of the African American writers in this section — Maya Angelou (p. 31), Alice Walker (p. 42), and Douglass? On what issues, when they write about writing, do they have the most in common with the authors represented here who are white?
2. For Maya Angelou (p. 31), Alice Walker (p. 42), and Frederick Douglass, events of childhood and youth are particularly important. Compare how at least two of these writers viewed events when they were young, how they present their younger selves or viewpoints, and how they connect childhood experience to adult knowledge.

MOTHER TONGUE

Amy Tan

Born in 1952 in Oakland, California, Amy Tan is the daughter of immigrants who fled China's Communist revolution in the late 1940s. Her Chinese name, An-Mei, means "blessing from America." Tan has remarked that she once tried to distance herself from her ethnicity, but writing her first novel, The Joy Luck Club *(1989), helped her discover "how very Chinese I was." Known as a gifted storyteller, Tan has written three other novels,* The Kitchen God's Wife *(1991),* The Hundred Secret Senses *(1995), and* The Bonesetter's Daughter *(2001), as well as two children's books. The following essay, in which Tan reflects on her experience as a bilingual child speaking both Chinese and English, was originally published in* The Threepenny Review *in 1990.*

I am not a scholar of English or literature. I cannot give you much more than personal opinions on the English language and its variations in this country or others.

I am a writer. And by that definition, I am someone who has always loved language. I am fascinated by language in daily life. I spend a great deal of my time thinking about the power of language — the way it can evoke an emotion, a visual image, a complex idea, or a simple truth. Language is the tool of my trade. And I use them all — all the Englishes I grew up with.

Recently, I was made keenly aware of the different Englishes I do use. I was giving a talk to a large group of people, the same talk I had already given to half a dozen other groups. The nature of the talk was about my writing, my life, and my book *The Joy Luck Club.* The talk was going along well enough, until I remembered one major difference that made the whole talk sound wrong. My mother was in the room. And it was perhaps the first time she had heard me give a lengthy speech, using the kind of English I have never used with her. I was saying things like "The intersection of memory upon imagination" and "There is an aspect of my fiction that relates to thus-and-thus" — a speech filled with carefully wrought grammatical phrases, burdened, it suddenly seemed to me, with nominalized forms, past perfect tenses, conditional phrases, all the forms of standard English that I had learned in school and through books, the forms of English I did not use at home with my mother.

Just last week, I was walking down the street with my mother, and I again found myself conscious of the English I was using, the English I do use with her. We were talking about the price of new and used furniture and

I heard myself saying this: "Not waste money that way." My husband was with us as well, and he didn't notice any switch in my English. And then I realized why. It's because over the twenty years we've been together I've often used that same kind of English with him, and sometimes he even uses it with me. It has become our language of intimacy, a different sort of English that relates to family talk, the language I grew up with.

So you'll have some idea of what this family talk I heard sounds like, 5 I'll quote what my mother said during a recent conversation which I video-taped and then transcribed. During this conversation, my mother was talking about a political gangster in Shanghai who had the same last name as her family's, Du, and how the gangster in his early years wanted to be adopted by her family, which was rich by comparison. Later, the gangster became more powerful, far richer than my mother's family, and one day showed up at my mother's wedding to pay his respects. Here's what she said in part:

"Du Yusong having business like fruit stand. Like off the street kind. He is Du like Du Zong — but not Tsung-ming Island people. The local people call putong, the river east side, he belong to that side local people. That man want to ask Du Zong father take him in like become own family. Du Zong father wasn't look down on him, but didn't take seriously, until that man big like become a mafia. Now important person, very hard to inviting him. Chinese way, came only to show respect, don't stay for dinner. Respect for making big celebration, he shows up. Mean gives lots of respect. Chinese custom. Chinese social life that way. If too important won't have to stay too long. He come to my wedding. I didn't see, I heard it. I gone to boy's side, they have YMCA dinner. Chinese age I was nineteen."

You should know that my mother's expressive command of English belies how much she actually understands. She reads the *Forbes* report, listens to *Wall Street Week*, converses daily with her stockbroker, reads all of Shirley MacLaine's[1] books with ease — all kinds of things I can't begin to understand. Yet some of my friends tell me they understand 50 percent of what my mother says. Some say they understand 80 to 90 percent. Some say they understand none of it, as if she were speaking pure Chinese. But to me, my mother's English is perfectly clear, perfectly natural. It's my mother tongue. Her language, as I hear it, is vivid, direct, full of observation and imagery. That was the language that helped shape the way I saw things, expressed things, made sense of the world.

Lately, I've been giving more thought to the kind of English my mother speaks. Like others, I have described it to people as "broken" or "fractured" English. But I wince when I say that. It has always bothered me that I can

---

[1]*Shirley MacLaine* (b. 1934): An American actor, dancer, and writer. She has written her memoirs and several books on spirituality and self-help.

think of no way to describe it other than "broken," as if it were damaged and needed to be fixed, as if it lacked a certain wholeness and soundness. I've heard other terms used, "limited English," for example. But they seem just as bad, as if everything is limited, including people's perceptions of the limited English speaker.

I know this for a fact, because when I was growing up, my mother's "limited" English limited *my* perception of her. I was ashamed of her English. I believed that her English reflected the quality of what she had to say. That is, because she expressed them imperfectly her thoughts were imperfect. And I had plenty of empirical evidence to support me: the fact that people in department stores, at banks, and at restaurants did not take her seriously, did not give her good service, pretended not to understand her, or even acted as if they did not hear her.

My mother has long realized the limitations of her English as well.   10
When I was fifteen, she used to have me call people on the phone to pretend I was she. In this guise, I was forced to ask for information or even to complain and yell at people who had been rude to her. One time it was a call to her stockbroker in New York. She had cashed out her small portfolio and it just so happened we were going to go to New York the next week, our very first trip outside California. I had to get on the phone and say in an adolescent voice that was not very convincing, "This is Mrs. Tan."

And my mother was standing in the back whispering loudly, "Why he don't send me check, already two weeks late. So mad he lie to me, losing me money."

And then I said in perfect English, "Yes, I'm getting rather concerned. You had agreed to send the check two weeks ago, but it hasn't arrived."

Then she began to talk more loudly. "What he want, I come to New York tell him front of his boss, you cheating me?" And I was trying to calm her down, make her be quiet, while telling the stockbroker, "I can't tolerate any more excuses. If I don't receive the check immediately, I am going to have to speak to your manager when I'm in New York next week." And sure enough, the following week there we were in front of this astonished stockbroker, and I was sitting there red-faced and quiet, and my mother, the real Mrs. Tan, was shouting at his boss in her impeccable broken English.

We used a similar routine just five days ago, for a situation that was far less humorous. My mother had gone to the hospital for an appointment, to find out about a benign brain tumor a CAT scan had revealed a month ago. She said she had spoken very good English, her best English, no mistakes. Still, she said, the hospital did not apologize when they said they had lost the CAT scan and she had come for nothing. She said they did not seem to have any sympathy when she told them she was anxious to know the exact diagnosis, since her husband and son had both died of brain tumors. She said they would not give her any more information until the next time and she would have to make another appointment for that. So she said she would not leave until the doctor called her daughter. She wouldn't budge. And when the doctor finally called her daughter, me, who spoke in perfect English—lo and behold—we had assurances the CAT scan would be found, promises that a conference call on Monday would be held, and apologies for any suffering my mother had gone through for a most regrettable mistake.

I think my mother's English almost had an effect on limiting my possibilities in life as well. Sociologists and linguists probably will tell you that a person's developing language skills are more influenced by peers. But I do think that the language spoken in the family, especially in immigrant families which are more insular, plays a large role in shaping the language of the child. And I believe that it affected my results on achievement tests, IQ tests, and the SAT. While my English skills were never judged as poor, compared to math, English could not be considered my strong suit. In grade school I did moderately well, getting perhaps B's, sometimes B-pluses, in English and scoring perhaps in the sixtieth or seventieth percentile on achievement tests. But those scores were not good enough to override the opinion that my true abilities lay in math and science, because in those areas I achieved A's and scored in the ninetieth percentile or higher. 15

This was understandable. Math is precise; there is only one correct answer. Whereas, for me at least, the answers on English tests were always a judgment call, a matter of opinion and personal experience. Those tests were constructed around items like fill-in-the-blank sentence completion, such as "Even though Tom was _____, Mary thought he was _____." And the correct answer always seemed to be the most bland combinations of thoughts, for example, "Even though Tom was shy, Mary thought he was charming," with the grammatical structure "even though" limiting the correct answer to some sort of semantic opposites, so you wouldn't get answers like "Even though Tom was foolish, Mary thought he was ridiculous." Well, according to my mother, there were very few limitations as to what Tom could have been and what Mary might have thought of him. So I never did well on tests like that.

The same was true with word analogies, pairs of words in which you were supposed to find some sort of logical, semantic relationship—for example, "*Sunset* is to *nightfall* as _____ is to _____ ." And here you would be presented with a list of four possible pairs, one of which showed the same kind of relationship: *red* is to *stoplight, bus* is to *arrival, chills* is to *fever, yawn* is to *boring.* Well, I could never think that way. I knew what the tests were asking, but I could not block out of my mind the images already created by the first pair, "*sunset* is to *nightfall*"—and I would see a burst of colors against a darkening sky, the moon rising, the lowering of a curtain of stars. And all the other pairs of words—*red, bus, stoplight, boring*—just threw up a mass of confusing images, making it impossible for me to sort out something as logical as saying: "A sunset precedes nightfall" is the same as "a chill precedes a fever." The only way I would have gotten that answer right would have been to imagine an associative situation, for example, my being disobedient and staying out past sunset, catching a chill at night, which turns into feverish pneumonia as punishment, which indeed did happen to me.

I have been thinking about all this lately, about my mother's English, about achievement tests. Because lately I've been asked, as a writer, why there are not more Asian Americans represented in American literature. Why are there few Asian Americans enrolled in creative writing programs? Why do so many Chinese students go into engineering? Well, these are broad sociological questions I can't begin to answer. But I have noticed in surveys — in fact, just last week — that Asian students, as a whole, always do significantly better on math achievement tests than in English. And this makes me think that there are other Asian American students whose English spoken in the home might also be described as "broken" or "limited." And perhaps they also have teachers who are steering them away from writing and into math and science, which is what happened to me.

Fortunately, I happen to be rebellious in nature and enjoy the challenge of disproving assumptions made about me. I became an English major my first year in college, after being enrolled as premed. I started writing nonfiction as a freelancer the week after I was told by my former boss that writing was my worst skill and I should hone my talents toward account management.

But it wasn't until 1985 that I finally began to write fiction. And at first   20
I wrote using what I thought to be wittily crafted sentences, sentences that would finally prove I had mastery over the English language. Here's an example from the first draft of a story that later made its way into *The Joy Luck Club,* but without this line: "That was my mental quandary in its nascent state." A terrible line, which I can barely pronounce.

Fortunately, for reasons I won't get into today, I later decided I should envision a reader for the stories I would write. And the reader I decided upon was my mother, because these were stories about mothers. So with this reader in mind — and in fact she did read my early drafts — I began to write stories using all the Englishes I grew up with: the English I spoke to my mother, which for lack of a better term might be described as "simple"; the English she used with me, which for lack of a better term might be described as "broken"; my translation of her Chinese, which could certainly be described as "watered down"; and what I imagined to be her translation of her Chinese if she could speak in perfect English, her internal language, and for that I sought to preserve the essence, but neither an English nor a Chinese structure. I wanted to capture what language ability tests can never reveal: her intent, her passion, her imagery, the rhythms of her speech and the nature of her thoughts.

Apart from what any critic had to say about my writing, I knew I had succeeded where it counted when my mother finished reading my book and gave me her verdict: "So easy to read."

QUESTIONS

1. Why does Tan begin her essay with the disclaimer, "I am not a scholar of English or literature. I cannot give you much more than personal opinions on the English language and its variations in this country or others"? What advantage does this disclaimer offer Tan?
2. What are the different "Englishes" with which Tan grew up? Find an example of each "English." What did Tan need to learn about each?
3. Tan tells us that, as a writer, she cares about the way language "can evoke an emotion, a visual image, a complex idea, or a simple truth" (paragraph 2). Look closely at Tan's language. Find passages in her essay where her language is evocative. Where does Tan surprise you with her choice of words or her ability to use language to evoke emotion or imagery?
4. What did Tan learn about her "mother tongue"?
5. Think about your own mother tongue. In what ways does it reflect how you see and make sense of the world? What have you had to understand, accept, or reject about your mother tongue?
6. Tan writes that, "the language spoken in the family, especially in immigrant families . . . , plays a large role in shaping the language of the child" (paragraph 15). Write an essay in which you reflect on the role of language in your family.

MAKING CONNECTIONS

What kind of conversation can you imagine between Tan and George Orwell, author of "Politics and the English Language" (p. 114)? How, for instance, would Tan respond to Orwell's claim that thought can corrupt language as much as language can corrupt thought?

A Narrator Leaps Past Journalism

Vivian Gornick

Vivian Gornick (b. 1935) grew up in New York City and received degrees from the City College of New York and New York University. She was a staff writer with the Village Voice *from 1969 to 1977 and published her first book,* Essays in Feminism, *in 1978. Her other books include* Fierce Attachment: A Memoir *(1987), about her relationship with her mother;* Approaching Eye Level: Personal Essays *(1987); and* The Situation and the Story: The Art of Personal Narrative *(2001). A critic in the* Yale Review *said of her work that "Gornick tunes your ear to prose that thinks for itself, that makes you want to read it out loud for pleasure." The following essay was originally published as a "Writers on Writing" column in the* New York Times.

I began my working life in the 1970s as a writer of what was then called personal journalism, a hybrid term meaning part personal essay, part social criticism. On the barricades for radical feminism, it has seemed natural to me from the minute I approached the typewriter to use myself — to use my own response to a circumstance or an event — as a means of making some larger sense of things.

At the time, of course, that was a shared instinct. Many other writers felt similarly compelled. The personal had become political, and the headlines metaphoric. Immediate experience signified. But from the beginning, I saw the dangers of this kind of writing — people rushing into print with no clear idea of the relation between narrator and subject, falling quickly into confessionalism or therapy on the page or naked self-absorption — and I resolved to work hard at avoiding its pitfalls. The reliable reporter, I vowed, would keep the narrator trustworthy.

One day a book editor approached me with an idea that struck a note of response. I had confided to her the tale of an intimate friendship I'd made with an Egyptian whose childhood in Cairo had strongly resembled my own in the Bronx, and now I was being invited to go to Egypt to write about middle-class Cairenes. I said yes with easy pleasure, assuming that I would do in Cairo what I had been doing in New York. That is, I'd put myself down in the middle of the city, meet the people, use my own fears and prejudices to let them become themselves, and then I'd write as I always wrote.

But Cairo was not New York, and personal journalism turned out not exactly the right job description. The city — dark, nervous, tender; intelligent, ignorant, fearful — invaded me, and I saw myself swamped by thoughts and feelings I couldn't bring into line. When I had been a working journalist, politics had provided me with a situation, and polemics had given me my story.

Now, in Egypt, I found myself confused by a writing impulse whose   5
requirements I could not penetrate but whose power I felt jerked around by. What, exactly, was the situation here? And where was the story? Above all, where was my familiar, polemical narrator? I seemed to have lost her without having found a suitable replacement. At the time I didn't understand that it wasn't personal journalism I was trying to write; it was personal narrative. It would be years before I sat down at the desk with sufficient command of the distinction to control the material, to serve the situation and tell the kind of story I now wanted to tell.

A dozen years after Egypt I set out to write a memoir about my mother, myself, and a woman who lived next door to us when I was a child. Here, for the first time, I struggled to isolate the story (the thing I had come to say) from the situation (the plot, the context, the circumstance) and to puzzle out a narrator who would serve.

I soon discovered that if I wanted to speak truthfully in this memoir — that is, without cynicism or sentiment — I had to find a tone of voice normally not mine. The one I habitually lived with wouldn't do at all: it whined, it grated, it accused; above all, it accused. Then there was the matter of syntax: my own ordinary, everyday sentence — fragmented, interjecting, overriding — also wouldn't do; it had to be altered, modified, brought under control.

And then I could see, as soon as I began writing, that I needed to pull back — way back — from these people and these events to find the place where the story could draw a deep breath and take its own measure. In short, a useful point of view, one that would permit greater freedom of association — for that of course is what I have been describing — had to be brought along. What I didn't see, and for a long while, was that this point of view could only emerge from a narrator who was me and at the same time not me.

I began to correct for myself. The process was slow, painful, and riddled with self-doubt. But one day I had her. I had a narrator on the page who was telling the story that I alone, in my everyday person, would not have been able to tell. Devotion to this narrator — this persona — became, while I was writing the book, an absorption that in time went unequaled. I longed each day to meet again with her. It was not only that I admired her style, her generosity, her detachment (such a respite from the me that was me); she had become the instrument of my illumination. She could tell the truth as I alone could not.

I reread the greats in the personal essay, the ones we think of as open,   10
honest, confiding — Montaigne, Hazlitt, Orwell, Didion — and now I saw that it wasn't their confessing voices I was responding to, it was their brilliantly created personae, their persuasive truth speakers: Orwell's obsessed democrat, Hazlitt's irascible neurotic, Didion's anxiety-ridden Californian.

Each delivers that wholeness of being in a narrator that the reader experiences as reliable; the one we can trust will take us on a journey, make the piece arrive, bring us out into a clearing where the sense of things is larger than it was before.

Living as I now did with the idea of the nonfiction persona, I began to think better than I had before about the commonplace need, alive in all of us, to make large sense of things in the very moment, even as experience is overtaking us. Everywhere I turned in those days, I found an excuse for the observation that we pull from ourselves the narrator who will shape better than we alone can the inchoate flow of events into which we are continually being plunged.

I remember I once went on a rafting trip down the Rio Grande with the man who was then my husband and a friend of ours. The river was hot and wild; sad, brilliant, remote; closed in by canyon walls, desert banks, snakes, and flash floods; on one side Texas, the other Mexico. A week after we'd been there, snipers on the Mexico side killed two people also floating on a raft.

Later we each wrote about the trip. My husband focused brightly on the "river rats" who were our guides, our friend soberly on the misery of illegal immigrants, I morbidly on what strangers my husband and I had become. Reading these pieces side by side was in itself an experience. We had all used the river, the heat, the remoteness to frame our stories. Beyond that, how alone each of us had been, sitting there together on that raft, carving out of our separating anxieties the narrator who, in the midst of all that beauty and oppressiveness, would keep us company and tell us what we were living through.

It mimics one of the earliest of narrative impulses, this kind of writing: 15 to pull from one's own boring, agitated self the one who will make large sense of things; the persona — possessed of a tone, a syntax, a perspective not wholly one's own — who will find the story riding the tide that we, in our unmediated state, otherwise drown in.

That is what it means to become interested in one's own existence as a means of transforming event into writing experience.

QUESTIONS

1. What is the significance of Gornick's title? Why do you suppose she chooses the word *narrator* rather than *author* or *writer*? Why the phrase "leaps past" rather than "moves beyond"?

2. In paragraph 5, Gornick makes a distinction between "personal journalism" and "personal narrative," which she evidently believes to have been crucial in her development as a writer. What does she consider to be the most important differences between these two kinds of writing? Why do you suppose it took her so long to achieve "sufficient command of the distinction to control the material"?

3. In paragraph 8, she claims that "a useful point of view . . . could only emerge from a narrator who was me and at the same time not me." What does she mean by "a useful point of view"? How is it possible for a narrator to be "me and at the same time not me"? Why is such a paradoxical narrator more "useful" to the kind of writing that Gornick aims to produce? How might you create such a narrator for your own writing — that is, how could you be you and at the same time not you?

4. Gornick's essay itself might be considered a "personal narrative," since it tells a story about her development as a writer. How would you characterize the narrator, the persona, who tells Gornick's story? In what respects do you think the narrator is Gornick and at the same time is not her?

5. Think of an incident or experience that you consider to be important in your development as a writer, and then produce two different versions of your story. In one version, tell the story in your own personal voice in a way that feels most natural and comfortable to you. In the other version, tell the story using a narrator who is you and at the same time not you. How did your story and your writing change in the second version? Which version do you prefer and why?

MAKING CONNECTIONS

1. Read Gornick's "Working in the Catskills" (p. 753), and consider how closely she follows her own ideas about personal narrative. How does she come across as a narrator in that piece? How does her narrative manner in the piece about working compare with her narrative manner in this piece on writing? In which piece do you find her to be a more appealing and engaging person? Why?

2. Compare Gornick's ideas about "personal narrative" with Joan Didion's "On Keeping a Notebook" (p. 328). Since both authors are concerned with personal writing, how do you account for their differing ideas and emphases?

THE CITY AND THE PILLARS: TAKING A LONG WALK HOME

Adam Gopnik

Born in 1956 in Philadelphia, Adam Gopnik moved to Montreal, Canada, at the age of ten. There he graduated from McGill University, where his parents were on the faculty, and later he received a master's degree in art history from the Institute of Fine Arts in New York City. He has published monographs on artists as well as exhibition catalogs, but he is best known for his many contributions to The New Yorker, *where he has been a staff writer and editor since the mid-1980s. His book* Paris to the Moon *(2000) was based on his time as Paris correspondent for the magazine. The following recollection of the events of September 11, 2001, originally appeared in* The New Yorker.

On the morning of the day they did it, the city was as beautiful as it had ever been. Central Park had never seemed so gleaming and luxuriant — the leaves just beginning to fall, and the light on the leaves left on the trees somehow making them at once golden and bright green. A bird-watcher in the Ramble made a list of the birds he saw there, from the northern flicker and the red-eyed vireo to the rose-breasted grosbeak and the Baltimore oriole. "Quite a few migrants around today," he noted happily.

In some schools, it was the first day, and children went off as they do on the first day, with the certainty that, this year, we will have fun again. The protective bubble that for the past decade or so had settled over the city, with a bubble's transparency and bright highlights, still seemed to be in place above us. We always knew that that bubble would burst, but we imagined it bursting as bubbles do: no one will be hurt, we thought, or they will be hurt only as people are hurt when bubbles burst, a little soap in your mouth. It seemed safely in place for another day as the children walked to school. The stockbroker fathers delivered — no, inserted — their kids into school as they always do, racing downtown, their cell phones already at work, like cartoons waiting for their usual morning caption: "Exasperated at 8 A.M."

A little while later, a writer who happened to be downtown saw a flock of pigeons rise, high and fast, and thought, Why are the pigeons rising? It was only seconds before he realized that the pigeons had felt the wave of the concussion before he heard the sound. In the same way, the shock wave hit us before the sound, the image before our understanding. For the lucky ones, the day from then on was spent in a strange, calm, and soul-emptying back and forth between the impossible images on television and the usual things on the street.

Around noon, a lot of people crowded around a lamppost on Madison, right underneath a poster announcing the Wayne Thiebaud show at the Whitney: all those cakes, as if to signal the impotence of our abundance. The impotence of our abundance! In the uptown supermarkets, people began to shop. It was a hoarding instinct, of course, though oddly not brought on by any sense of panic; certainly no one on television or radio was suggesting that people needed to hoard. Yet people had the instinct to do it, and, in any case, in New York the instinct to hoard quickly seemed to shade over into the instinct to consume, shop for anything, shop because it might be a comfort. One woman emerged from a Gristede's on Lexington with a bottle of olive oil and said, "I had to get *something*." Mostly people bought water — bottled water, French and Italian — and many people, waiting in the long lines, had Armageddon baskets: the Manhattan version, carts filled with steaks, Häagen-Dazs, and butter. Many of the carts held the goods of the bubble decade, hothouse goods: flavored balsamics and cappellini and arugula. There was no logic to it, as one man pointed out in that testy, superior, patient tone: "If trucks can't get through, the Army will take over and give everybody K rations or some crazy thing; if they do, this won't matter." Someone asked him what was he doing uptown? He had been down there, got out before the building collapsed, and walked up.

People seemed not so much to suspend the rituals of normalcy as to   5
carry on with them in a kind of bemusement — as though to reject the image on the screen, as though to say, That's there, we're here, they're not here yet, *it's* not here yet. "Everything turns away quite leisurely from the disaster," Auden wrote, about a painting of Icarus falling from the sky; now we know why they turned away — they saw the boy falling from the sky, sure enough, but they did not know what to do about it. If we do the things we know how to do, New Yorkers thought, then what has happened will matter less.

The streets and parks were thinned of people, but New York is so dense — an experiment in density, really, as Venice is an experiment in water — that the thinning just produced the normal density of Philadelphia or Baltimore. It added to the odd calm. "You wouldn't put it in a book," a young man with an accent said to a girl in the Park, and then he added, "Do you like to ski?" Giorgio Armani was in the Park — Giorgio Armani? Yes, right behind the Metropolitan Museum, with his entourage, beautiful Italian boys and girls in tight white T-shirts. "*Cinema*," he kept saying, his hands moving back and forth like an, accordion player's. "*Cinema*."

Even urban geography is destiny, and New York, a long thin island, cuts downtown off from uptown, west side off from east. (And a kind of moral miniaturization is always at work, as we try unconsciously to seal ourselves from the disaster: people in Europe say "America attacked" and people in America say "New York attacked" and people in New York think, Downtown attacked.) For the financial community, this was the

Somme; it was impossible not to know someone inside that building, or thrown from it. Whole companies, tiny civilizations, an entire Zip Code vanished. Yet those of us outside that world, hovering in midtown, were connected to the people dying in the towers only by New York's uniquely straight lines of sight — you looked right down Fifth Avenue and saw that strange, still neat package of white smoke.

The city has never been so clearly, so surreally, sectioned as it became on Wednesday and Thursday. From uptown all the way down to Fourteenth Street, life is almost entirely normal — fewer cars, perhaps, one note quieter on the street, but children and moms and hot-dog venders on nearly every corner. In the flower district, the wholesalers unpack autumn branches from the boxes they arrived in this morning. "That came over the bridge?" someone asks, surprised at the thought of a truck driver waiting patiently for hours just to bring in blossoming autumn branches. The vender nods.

At Fourteenth Street, one suddenly enters the zone of the missing, of mourning not yet acknowledged. It is, in a way, almost helpful to walk in that strange new village, since the concussion wave of fear that has been sucking us in since Tuesday is replaced with an outward ripple of grief and need, something human to hold on to. The stanchions and walls are plastered with homemade color-Xerox posters, smiling snapshots above, a text below, searching for the missing: "Roger Mark Rasweiler. Missing. One WTC, 100th floor." "We Need Your Help: Giovanna 'Gennie' Gambale." "We're Looking for Kevin M. Williams, 104th Fl, WTC." "Have You Seen Him? Robert 'Bob' Dewitt." "Ed Feldman — Call Ross." "Millan Rustillo — Missing WTC." Every lost face is smiling, caught at Disney World or Miami Beach, on vacation. Every poster lovingly notes the missing person's height and weight to the last ounce and inch. "Clown tattoo on right shoulder," one says. On two different posters there is an apologetic note along with the holiday snap: "Was Not Wearing Sunglasses on Tuesday."

Those are the ones who've gone missing. On television, the reporters   10
keep talking about the World Trade Center as a powerful symbol of American financial power. And yet it was, in large part, the back office of Wall Street. As Eric Darton showed in his fine social history of the towers, they were less a symbol of America's financial might than a symbol of the Port Authority's old inferiority complex. It was not the citadel of capitalism but, according to the real order of things in the capitalist world, just a come-on — a desperate scheme dreamed up in the late fifties to bring businesses back downtown. In later years, of course, downtown New York became the center of world trade, for reasons that basically had nothing to do with the World Trade Center, so that now Morgan Stanley and Cantor Fitzgerald were there, but for a long time it was also a big state office building, where you went to get a document stamped or a license renewed. No one loved it save children, who took to it because it was iconically so simple, so tall and two. When a child tried to draw New York, he would draw the simplest available icons: two rectangles and an airplane going by them.

Near Washington Square, the streets empty out, and the square itself is beautiful again. "I saw it coming," a bicycle messenger says. "I thought it was going to take off the top of that building." He points to the little Venetian-style campanile on Washington Square South. The Village seems like a village. In a restaurant on Washington Place at ten-thirty, the sous-chefs are quietly prepping for lunch, with the chairs still on all the tables and the front door open and unguarded. "We're going to try and do dinner today," one of the chefs says. A grown woman rides a scooter down the middle of LaGuardia Place. Several café owners, or workers, go through the familiar act of hosing down the sidewalk. With the light pall of smoke hanging over everything, this everyday job becomes somehow cheering, cleansing. If you enter one of the open cafés and order a meal, the familiar dialogue — "And a green salad with that." "You mean a side salad?" "Yeah, that'd be fine. . . . What kind of dressing do you have?" — feels reassuring, too, another calming routine.

Houston Street is the dividing line, the place where the world begins to end. In SoHo, there is almost no one on the street. No one is allowed on the streets except residents, and they are hidden in their lofts. Nothing is visible, except the cloud of white smoke and soot that blows from the dense stillness below Canal. An art critic and a museum curator watched the explosions from right here. "It was a sound like two trucks crashing on Canal, no louder than that, than something coming by terribly fast, and the building was struck," the critic said. "I thought, This is it, mate, the nuclear attack, I'm going to die. I was peaceful about it, though. But then the flame subsided, and then the building fell." The critic and the curator watched it fall together. Decades had passed in that neighborhood where people insisted that now everything was spectacle, nothing had meaning. Now there was a spectacle, and it *meant*.

The smell, which fills the empty streets of SoHo from Houston to Canal, blew uptown on Wednesday night, and is not entirely horrible from a reasonable distance — almost like the smell of smoked mozzarella, a smell of the bubble time. Closer in, it becomes acrid, and unbreathable. The white particulate smoke seems to wreathe the empty streets — to wrap right around them. The authorities call this the "frozen zone." In the "Narrative of A. Gordon Pym," spookiest and most cryptic of Poe's writings, a man approaches the extremity of existence, the pole beneath the Southern Pole. "The whole ashy material fell now continually around us," he records in his diary, "and in vast quantities. The range of vapor to the southward had arisen prodigiously in the horizon, and began to assume more distinctness of form. I can liken it to nothing but a limitless cataract, rolling silently into the sea from some immense and far-distant rampart in the heaven. The gigantic curtain ranged along the whole extent of the southern horizon. It emitted no sound." Poe, whose house around here was torn down not long ago, is a realist now.

More than any other city, New York exists at once as a city of symbols and associations, literary and artistic, and as a city of real things. This is an emotional truth, of course — New York is a city of wacky dreams and of disillusioning realities. But it is also a plain, straightforward architectural truth, a visual truth, a material truth. The city looks one way from a distance, a skyline full of symbols, inviting pilgrims and Visigoths, and another way up close, a city full of people. The Empire State and Chrysler Buildings exist as symbols of thirties materialism and as abstract ideas of skyscrapers and as big dowdy office buildings — a sign and then a thing and then a sign and then a thing and then a sign, going back and forth all the time. (It is possible to transact business in the Empire State Building, and only then nudge yourself and think, Oh, yeah, this is the Empire State Building.) The World Trade Center existed both as a thrilling double exclamation point at the end of the island and as a rotten place to have to go and get your card stamped, your registration renewed.

The pleasure of living in New York has always been the pleasure of   15
living in both cities at once: the symbolic city of symbolic statements (this is big, I am rich, get me) and the everyday city of necessities, MetroCards and coffee shops and long waits and longer trudges. On the afternoon of that day, the symbolic city, the city that the men in the planes had attacked, seemed much less important than the real city, where the people in the towers lived. The bubble is gone, but the city beneath — naked now in a new way, not startling but vulnerable — seemed somehow to increase in our affection, our allegiance. On the day they did it, New Yorkers walked the streets without, really, any sense of "purpose" or "pride" but with the kind of tender necessary patriotism that lies in just persisting.

New York, E. B. White wrote in 1949, holds a steady, irresistible charm for perverted dreamers of destruction, because it seems so impossible. "The intimation of mortality is part of New York now," he went on to write, "in the sound of jets overhead." We have heard the jets now, and we will probably never be able to regard the city with quite the same exasperated, ironic affection we had for it before. Yet on the evening of the day, one couldn't walk through Central Park, or down Seventh Avenue, or across an empty but hardly sinister Times Square — past the light on the trees, or the kids on their scooters, or the people sitting worried in the outdoor restaurants with menus, frowning, as New Yorkers always do, as though they had never seen a menu before — without feeling a surprising rush of devotion to the actual New York, Our Lady of the Subways, New York as it is. It is the symbolic city that draws us here, and the real city that keeps us. It seems hard but important to believe that that city will go on, because we now know what it would be like to lose it, and it feels like losing life itself.

QUESTIONS

1. Though this essay is concerned with events that took place in New York City on September 11, 2001, Gopnik never mentions that date in his piece, nor does he ever explicitly refer to the hijacked commercial

airplanes that terrorists used to attack the World Trade Center. Why do you suppose that he avoids any specific references to such important facts? How were you affected, for example, by his vague beginning: "On the morning of the day they did it . . ."?

2. Gopnik's piece begins with six paragraphs that provide a straightforward recollection of the morning of September 11, 2001, in various parts of the city. But his recollections of that day do not extend beyond this first section. Examine each of the essay's three other sections to determine each section's basic form, content, purpose, and contribution to the overall significance of Gopnik's reflections.

3. In paragraph 2, Gopnik goes on at length about "the protective bubble that for the past decade or so had settled over the city." What do you think the image of the bubble refers to? In what sense was the bubble "protective"? How do you suppose that people "knew the bubble would burst"? Note all the other references to the bubble in the remainder of the paragraph, and consider how they contribute to the significance of Gopnik's reflections.

4. In his title, Gopnik refers to the World Trade Center buildings as "pillars," whereas later he refers to them as "a thrilling double exclamation point" (paragraph 14). What do you think Gopnik is trying to convey about the buildings by each of these symbolic images? In what other ways does Gopnik describe and symbolize the World Trade Center buildings? Why do you suppose that he uses so many different images to describe them?

5. Where were you on "the day they did it," and what images and thoughts passed through your mind on that day and the days that immediately followed the terrorist attacks? Write an essay in which you convey your reflections, making sure to anchor them in specific images and details that bear witness to your own recollections of that day.

6. Think of a memorable building in your home town, on your college campus, or in some place that you've visited, and write an essay describing and evoking that building to convey it as both an actual and a symbolic place.

MAKING CONNECTIONS

Compare Gopnik's piece on September 11 with Serge Schmemann's "U.S. Attacked" (p. 247). Which one do you find more informative? Which one do you find more evocative? Which one do you find more thoughtful? How do you account for the differences in each case?

BECAUSE I COULD NOT STOP FOR DEATH—

Emily Dickinson

One of America's most orginal and admired poets, Emily Dickinson (1830–1886) was completely unknown to a wide audience in her own lifetime. Only about ten of her more than seventeen hundred existing poems were published prior to her death (probably without her permission), and the first volume of her work was not published until 1890. The definitive collection did not appear until 1955. Born in Amherst, Massachusetts, Dickinson spent her entire life there except for the year that she lived at school when she was in her teens. A reclusive woman who dressed only in white, she never married and for the last quarter century of her life rarely saw anyone outside her immediate family, although she maintained an extensive written correspondence. Her poems broke many of the conventions of the poetry of her day — particularly the poetry of women, who were expected to focus on homely or religious themes. Dickinson abandoned organized religion at an early age, but an intense personal spirituality is reflected in her poetry: "Because I Could Not Stop for Death — " is one of her best-known works.

Because I could not stop for Death—
He kindly stopped for me—
The Carriage held but just Ourselves—
And Immortality.

We slowly drove—He knew no haste   5
And I had put away
My labor and my leisure too,
For His Civility—

We passed the School, where Children strove
At Recess—in the Ring—   10
We passed the Fields of Gazing Grain—
We passed the Setting Sun—

Or rather—He passed Us—
The Dews drew quivering and chill—
For only Gossamer, my Gown—   15
My Tippet—only Tulle—

We paused before a House that seemed
A Swelling of the Ground—
The Roof was scarcely visible—
The Cornice—in the Ground—   20

Since then—'tis Centuries—and yet
Feels shorter than the Day
I first surmised the Horses' Heads
Were toward Eternity—

QUESTIONS

1. Death is so often depicted as a grim reaper that Dickinson's description of him in this poem is quite unusual. Notice the key words that she uses to describe death, and consider why she chooses to depict him so favorably. In what way(s) would her depiction of death be altered by changing its gender from "he" to "she"? Read the poem to yourself, changing all the pronoun references, to see how it sounds.
2. Given Dickinson's favorable description of death, why do you suppose that she could not stop for him? What do you think she means to imply by her opening remark?
3. In the remainder of the poem, Dickinson describes a carriage ride that she took with death and immortality. Notice each of the things that she reports herself as having seen from the beginning to the end of the carriage ride, and consider her reasons for taking note of each in the order that she reports them. Why do you suppose that she chooses to describe her encounter with death as if it were a carriage ride?
4. How could it possibly be that centuries have passed since the day of her ride? How could it possibly be that she had an encounter with death and survived it? Why do you suppose that she says nothing about immortality beyond her mention of it as another passenger in the carriage?
5. Imagine yourself having an encounter with death. Then write a piece in which you remember what death was like and what took place during your encounter.
6. Have you ever observed the death of a person or an animal? If so, write an essay in which you remember what happened, as well as your thoughts and feelings on that occasion.

MAKING CONNECTIONS

Dickinson, like Elisabeth Kübler-Ross in "On the Fear of Death" (p. 405), is concerned with the process by which a person comes to terms with the inevitability of death. Compare the processes outlined in each work, noting what you consider to be the most important similarities and differences.

Social Sciences and Public Affairs

THE WAY TO RAINY MOUNTAIN

N. Scott Momaday

N. Scott Momaday was born in Lawton, Oklahoma, in 1934. His father is a Kiowa, and his mother is part Cherokee. After attending schools on Navajo, Apache, and Pueblo reservations, Momaday graduated from the University of New Mexico and earned his doctorate at Stanford University. His works include two poetry collections, Angle of Geese and Other Poems *(1974) and* The Gourd Dancer *(1976); a memoir,* The Names *(1976); and an essay compilation,* A Man Made of Words *(1997). In 1969 his novel* House Made of Dawn *won the Pulitzer Prize. When asked about his writing, Momaday said, "When I was growing up on the reservations of the Southwest, I saw people who were deeply involved in their traditional life, in the memories of their blood. They had, as far as I can see, a certain strength and beauty that I find missing in the modern world. I like to celebrate that involvement in my writing." The following essay appeared first in the* Reporter *magazine in 1967 and later as the introduction to* The Way to Rainy Mountain *(1969), a collection of Kiowa legends.*

A single knoll rises out of the plain in Oklahoma, north and west of the Wichita range. For my people, the Kiowas, it is an old landmark, and they gave it the name Rainy Mountain. The hardest weather in the world is there. Winter brings blizzards, hot tornadic winds arise in the spring, and in summer the prairie is an anvil's edge. The grass turns brittle and brown, and it cracks beneath your feet. There are green belts along the rivers and creeks, linear groves of hickory and pecan, willow and witch hazel. At a distance in July or August the steaming foliage seems almost to writhe in fire.

Great green and yellow grasshoppers are everywhere in the tall grass, popping up like corn to sting the flesh, and tortoises crawl about on the red earth, going nowhere in the plenty of time. Loneliness is an aspect of the land. All things in the plain are isolate; there is no confusion of objects in the eye, but *one* hill or *one* tree or *one* man. To look upon that landscape in the early morning, with the sun at your back, is to lose the sense of proportion. Your imagination comes to life, and this, you think, is where Creation was begun.

I returned to Rainy Mountain in July. My grandmother had died in the spring, and I wanted to be at her grave. She had lived to be very old and at last infirm. Her only living daughter was with her when she died, and I was told that in death her face was that of a child.

I like to think of her as a child. When she was born, the Kiowas were living the last great moment of their history. For more than a hundred years they had controlled the open range from the Smoky Hill River to the Red, from the headwaters of the Canadian to the fork of the Arkansas and Cimarron. In alliance with the Comanches, they had ruled the whole of the Southern Plains. War was their sacred business, and they were the finest horsemen the world has ever known. But warfare for the Kiowas was preeminently a matter of disposition rather than of survival, and they never understood the grim, unrelenting advance of the U.S. Cavalry. When at last, divided and ill provisioned, they were driven onto the Staked Plains in the cold of autumn, they fell into panic. In Palo Duro Canyon they abandoned their crucial stores to pillage and had nothing then but their lives. In order to save themselves, they surrendered to the soldiers at Fort Sill and were imprisoned in the old stone corral that now stands as a military museum. My grandmother was spared the humiliation of those high gray walls by eight or ten years, but she must have known from birth the affliction of defeat, the dark brooding of old warriors.

Her name was Aho, and she belonged to the last culture to evolve in North America. Her forebears came down from the high country in western Montana nearly three centuries ago. They were a mountain people, a mysterious tribe of hunters whose language has never been classified in any major group. In the late seventeenth century they began a long migration to the south and east. It was a journey toward the dawn, and it led to a golden age. Along the way the Kiowas were befriended by the Crows, who gave them the culture and religion of the Plains. They acquired horses, and their ancient nomadic spirit was suddenly free of the ground. They acquired Tai-me, the sacred sun-dance doll, from that moment the object and symbol of their worship, and so shared in the divinity of the sun. Not least, they acquired the sense of destiny, therefore courage and pride. When they entered upon the Southern Plains they had been transformed. No longer were they slaves to the simple necessity of survival; they were a lordly and dangerous society of fighters and thieves, hunters and priests of the sun. According to their origin myth, they entered the world through a hollow

log. From one point of view, their migration was the fruit of an old prophecy, for indeed they emerged from a sunless world.

Though my grandmother lived out her long life in the shadow of Rainy   5
Mountain, the immense landscape of the continental interior lay like memory in her blood. She could tell of the Crows, whom she had never seen, and
of the Black Hills, where she had never been. I wanted to see in reality what
she had seen more perfectly in the mind's eye, and drove fifteen hundred
miles to begin my pilgrimage.

A dark mist lay over the Black Hills, and the land was like iron. At the
top of a ridge I caught sight of Devil's Tower upthrust against the gray sky
as if in the birth of time the core of the earth had broken through its crust
and the motion of the world was begun. There are things in nature that
engender an awful quiet in the heart of man; Devil's Tower is one of them.
Two centuries ago, because of their need to explain it, the Kiowas made a
legend at the base of the rock. My grandmother said:

"Eight children were there at play, seven sisters and their brother.
Suddenly the boy was struck dumb; he trembled and began to run upon his
hands and feet. His fingers became claws, and his body was covered with
fur. There was a bear where the boy had been. The sisters were terrified;
they ran, and the bear after them. They came to the stump of a great tree,
and the tree spoke to them. It bade them climb upon it, and as they did so,
it began to rise into the air. The bear came to kill them, but they were just
beyond its reach. It reared against the tree and scored the bark all around
with its claws. The seven sisters were borne into the sky, and they became
the stars of the Big Dipper." From that moment, and so long as the legend
lives, the Kiowas have kinsmen in the night sky. Whatever they were in the
mountains, they could be no more. However tenuous their well-being, however much they had suffered and would suffer again, they had found a way
out of the wilderness.

My grandmother had a reverence for the sun, a holy regard that now is
all but gone out of mankind. There was a wariness in her, and an ancient
awe. She was a Christian in her later years, but she had come a long way
about, and she never forgot her birthright. As a child she had been to the sun
dances; she had taken part in that annual rite, and by it she had learned the
restoration of her people in the presence of Tai-me. She was about seven
when the last Kiowa sun dance was held in 1887 on the Washita River above
Rainy Mountain Creek. The buffalo were gone. In order to consummate
the ancient sacrifice — to impale the head of a buffalo bull upon the Tai-me
tree — a delegation of old men journeyed into Texas, there to beg and barter
for an animal from the Goodnight herd. She was ten when the Kiowas came
together for the last time as a living sun-dance culture. They could find no
buffalo; they had to hang an old hide from the sacred tree. Before the dance
could begin, a company of soldiers rode out from Fort Sill under orders to
disperse the tribe. Forbidden without cause the essential act of their faith,
having seen the wild herds slaughtered and left to rot upon the ground, the

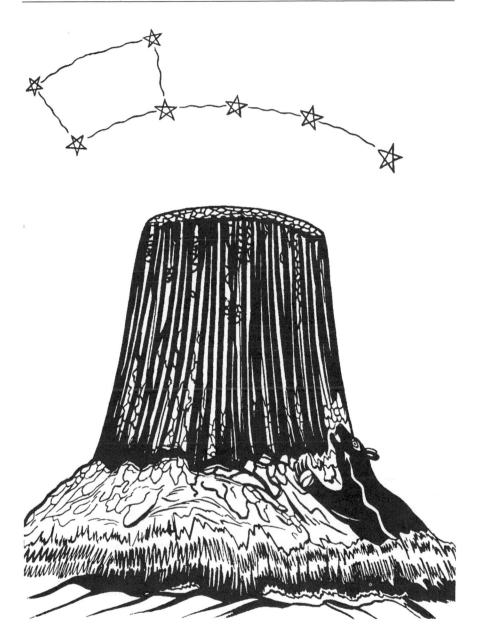

Illustration of Devil's Tower by Al Momaday, N. Scott Momaday's father. [Eds.]

Kiowas backed away forever from the tree. That was July 20, 1890, at the great bend of the Washita. My grandmother was there. Without bitterness, and for as long as she lived, she bore a vision of deicide.[1]

Now that I can have her only in memory, I see my grandmother in the several postures that were peculiar to her: standing at the wood stove on a winter morning and turning meat in a great iron skillet; sitting at the south window, bent above her beadwork, and afterwards, when her vision failed, looking down for a long time into the fold of her hands; going out upon a cane, very slowly as she did when the weight of age came upon her; praying. I remember her most often at prayer. She made long, rambling prayers out of suffering and hope, having seen many things. I was never sure that I had the right to hear, so exclusive were they of all mere custom and company. The last time I saw her she prayed standing by the side of the bed at night, naked to the waist, the light of a kerosene lamp moving upon her dark skin. Her long black hair, always drawn and braided in the day, lay upon her shoulders and against her breasts like a shawl. I do not speak Kiowa, and I never understood her prayers, but there was something inherently sad in the sound, some merest hesitation upon the syllables of sorrow. She began in a high and descending pitch, exhausting her breath to silence; then again and again — and always the same intensity of effort, of something that is, and is not, like urgency in the human voice. Transported so in the dancing light among the shadows of her room, she seemed beyond the reach of time. But that was illusion; I think I knew then that I should not see her again.

Houses are like sentinels in the plain, old keepers of the weather watch.   10
There, in a very little while, wood takes on the appearance of great age. All colors wear soon away in the wind and rain, and then the wood is burned gray and the grain appears and the nails turn red with rust. The window panes are black and opaque; you imagine there is nothing within, and indeed there are many ghosts, bones given up to the land. They stand here and there against the sky, and you approach them for a longer time than you expect. They belong in the distance; it is their domain.

Once there was a lot of sound in my grandmother's house, a lot of coming and going, feasting and talk. The summers there were full of excitement and reunion. The Kiowas are a summer people; they abide the cold and keep to themselves, but when the season turns and the land becomes warm and vital they cannot hold still; an old love of going returns upon them. The aged visitors who came to my grandmother's house when I was a child were made of lean and leather, and they bore themselves upright. They wore great black hats and bright ample shirts that shook in the wind. They rubbed fat upon their hair and wound their braids with strips of colored cloth. Some of them painted their faces and carried the scars of old and cherished enmities. They were an old council of warlords, come to remind and be reminded of who

---

[1]*deicide:* The killing of a deity or god. [Eds.]

they were. Their wives and daughters served them well. The women might indulge themselves; gossip was at once the mark and compensation of their servitude. They made loud and elaborate talk among themselves, full of jest and gesture, fright and false alarm. They went abroad in fringed and flowered shawls, bright beadwork and German silver. They were at home in the kitchen, and they prepared meals that were banquets.

There were frequent prayer meetings, and nocturnal feasts. When I was a child I played with my cousins outside, where the lamplight fell upon the ground and the singing of the old people rose up around us and carried away into the darkness. There were a lot of good things to eat, a lot of laughter and surprise. And afterwards, when the quiet returned, I lay down with my grandmother and could hear the frogs away by the river and feel the motion of the air.

Now there is a funereal silence in the rooms, the endless wake of some final word. The walls have closed in upon my grandmother's house. When I returned to it in mourning, I saw for the first time in my life how small it was. It was late at night, and there was a white moon, nearly full. I sat for a long time on the stone steps by the kitchen door. From there I could see out across the land; I could see the long row of trees by the creek, the low light upon the rolling plains, and the stars of the Big Dipper. Once I looked at the moon and caught sight of a strange thing. A cricket had perched upon the handrail, only a few inches away. My line of vision was such that the creature filled the moon like a fossil. It had gone there, I thought, to live and die, for there, of all places, was its small definition made whole and eternal. A warm wind rose up and purled like the longing within me.

The next morning, I awoke at dawn and went out on the dirt road to Rainy Mountain. It was already hot, and the grasshoppers began to fill the air. Still, it was early in the morning, and birds sang out of the shadows. The long yellow grass on the mountain shone in the bright light, and a scissortail hied above the land. There, where it ought to be, at the end of a long and legendary way, was my grandmother's grave. She had at last succeeded to that holy ground. Here and there on the dark stones were ancestral names. Looking back once, I saw the mountain and came away.

QUESTIONS

1. What is this essay about? Explain whether it is a history of the Kiowas, a biography of Momaday's grandmother, or a narrative of his journey.
2. Trace the movement in time in this essay. How much takes place in the present, the recent past, the distant past, or legendary time? What effect does such movement create?
3. How much of the essay reports events, and how much of the essay represents a sense of place or of people through description of what Momaday sees and feels? Trace the pattern of reporting and representing, and consider Momaday's purpose in such an approach to his subject.

4. The first paragraph ends by drawing the reader into the writer's point of view: "Your imagination comes to life, and this, you think, is where Creation was begun." Given the description of the Oklahoma landscape that precedes this in the paragraph, how do you react to Momaday's summarizing statement? Why? What other passages in the essay evoke a sense of place?

5. Visit a place that has historical significance. It may be a place where you or members of your family lived in the past, or it may be a place of local or national historical significance. Describe the place as it appears now, and report on events that took place there in the past. What, if any, evidence do you find in the present of those events that took place in the past?

6. If you have a grandparent or an older friend living nearby, ask this person about his or her history. What does this person remember about the past that is no longer in the present? Are there objects — pictures, clothing, medals, and so on — that can speak to you of your subject's past life? Reflect on the person's present life as well as on those events from the past that seem most memorable. Write an essay in which you represent your subject's life by concentrating on the place where he or she lives and the surrounding objects that help you to understand the past and present life.

MAKING CONNECTIONS

1. Compare Momaday's essay to Alice Walker's (p. 42), focusing on the way each essay moves through time. How do these essayists differ in their conception and representation of time, and how do those differences relate to their individual purposes as writers?

2. Compare Momaday's description of Devil's Tower (paragraph 6), with his grandmother's retelling of the Kiowa legend about it (paragraph 7), and the illustration of it done by Momaday's father. What's gained and what's lost in the illustration? What's gained and what's lost in the words alone?

THE STORY OF MY BODY

Judith Ortiz Cofer

Born in rural Puerto Rico, Judith Ortiz Cofer (b. 1952) moved to the United States in 1954 and spent most of her girlhood in Paterson, New Jersey. She took frequent trips to her native island to visit with family there. A graduate of Augusta College with a master's degree from Florida Atlantic University, she joined the faculty of the University of Georgia in 1984 and is now Franklin Professor of Creative Writing there. Her first book was a poetry collection, Perigrina *(1986), and it was followed by* Silent Dancing: A Partial Remembrance of a Puerto Rican Childhood *(1990),* The Latin Deli *(1993),* As Island Like You: Stories of the Barrio *(1998),* The Year of Our Revolution: Selected and New Prose and Poetry *(1998), and* Woman in Front of the Sun: On Becoming a Writer *(2000), among others. She once recalled, "Writing began for me as fascination with a language I was not born into. I first perceived of language, especially the English language, as a barrier, a challenge to be met with the same kind of closed-eye bravado that prompted me to jump into the deep end of the pool before taking my first swimming lesson. . . . I managed to surface and breathe the air of the real world, just as I took in words my first year in America — breathlessly, and yes, almost desperately, for I needed to be able to communicate almost as much as I needed to breathe."*

Migration is the story of my body.
— VÍCTOR HERNÁNDEZ CRUZ

Skin

I was born a white girl in Puerto Rico but became a brown girl when I came to live in the United States. My Puerto Rican relatives called me tall; at the American school, some of my rougher classmates called me Skinny Bones, and the Shrimp because I was the smallest member of my classes all through grammer school until high school, when the midget Gladys was given the honorary post of front row center for class pictures and score-keeper, bench warmer, in P.E. I reached my full stature of five feet in sixth grade.

I started out life as a pretty baby and learned to be a pretty girl from a pretty mother. Then at ten years of age I suffered one of the worst cases of chicken pox I have ever heard of. My entire body, including the inside of my ears and in between my toes, was covered with pustules which in a fit of panic at my appearance I scratched off my face, leaving permanent scars. A cruel school nurse told me I would always have them — tiny cuts that looked as if a mad cat had plunged its claws deep into my skin. I grew my hair long and hid behind it for the first years of my adolescence. This was when I learned to be invisible.

Color

In the animal world it indicates danger: the most colorful creatures are often the most poisonous. Color is also a way to attract and seduce a mate. In the human world color triggers many more complex and often deadly reactions. As a Puerto Rican girl born of "white" parents, I spent the first years of my life hearing people refer to me as *blanca*, white. My mother insisted that I protect myself from the intense island sun because I was more prone to sunburn than some of my darker, *trigueño* playmates. People were always commenting within my hearing about how my black hair contrasted so nicely with my "pale" skin. I did not think of the color of my skin consciously except when I heard the adults talking about complexion. It seems to me that the subject is much more common in the conversation of mixed-race peoples than in mainstream United States society, where it is a touchy and sometimes even embarrassing topic to discuss, except in a political context. In Puerto Rico I heard many conversations about skin color. A pregnant woman could say, "I hope my baby doesn't turn out *prieto*" (slang for "dark" or "black") "like my husband's grandmother, although she was a good-looking *negra* in her time." I am a combination of both, being olive-skinned — lighter than my mother yet darker than my fair-skinned father. In America, I am a person of color, obviously a Latina. On the Island I have been called everything from a *paloma blanca*, after the song (by a black suitor), to *la gringa*.

My first experience of color prejudice occurred in a supermarket in Paterson, New Jersey. It was Chrismastime, and I was eight or nine years old. There was a display of toys in the store where I went two or three times a day to buy things for my mother, who never made lists but sent for milk, cigarettes, a can of this or that, as she remembered from hour to hour. I enjoyed being trusted with money and walking half a city block to the new, modern grocery store. It was owned by three good-looking Italian brothers. I liked the younger one with the crew-cut blond hair. The two older ones watched me and the other Puerto Rican kids as if they thought we were going to steal something. The oldest one would sometimes even try to hurry me with my purchases, although part of my pleasure in these expeditions came from looking at everything in the well-stocked aisles. I was also teaching myself to read English by sounding out the labels in packages: L&M cigarettes, Borden's homogenized milk, Red Devil potted ham, Nestle's

chocolate mix, Quaker oats, Bustelo coffee, Wonder bread, Colgate tooth-
paste, Ivory soap, and Goya (makers of products used in Puerto Rican dishes) everything—these are some of the brand names that taught me nouns.
Several times this man had come up to me, wearing his blood-stained butcher's apron, and towering over me had asked in a harsh voice whether there
was something he could help me find. On the way out I would glance at the
younger brother who ran one of the registers and he would often smile and
wink at me.

It was the mean brother who first referred to me as "colored." It was a 5
few days before Christmas, and my parents had already told my brother
and me that since we were in Los Estados now, we would get our presents
on December 25 instead of Los Reyes, Three Kings Day, when gifts are
exchanged in Puerto Rico. We were to give them a wish list that they would
take to Santa Claus, who apparently lived in the Macy's store downtown —
at least that's where we had caught a glimpse of him when we went shopping. Since my parents were timid about entering the fancy store, we did not
approach the huge man in the red suit. I was not interested in sitting on a
stranger's lap anyway. But I did covet Susie, the talking schoolteacher doll
that was displayed in the center aisle of the Italian brothers' supermarket.
She talked when you pulled a string on her back. Susie had a limited repertoire of three sentences: I think she could say: "Hello, I'm Susie
Schoolteacher," "Two plus two is four," and one other thing I cannot
remember. The day the older brother chased me away, I was reaching to
touch Susie's blonde curls. I had been told many times, as most children
have, not to touch anything in a store that I was not buying. But I had been
looking at Susie for weeks. In my mind, she was my doll. After all, I had
put her on my Christmas wish list. The moment is frozen in my mind as if
there were a photograph of it on file. It was not a turning point, a disaster,
or an earthshaking revelation. It was simply the first time I considered—if
naively—the meaning of skin color in human relations.

I reached to touch Susie's hair. It seems to me that I had to get on tiptoe, since the toys were stacked on a table and she sat like a princess on
top of the fancy box she came in. Then I heard the booming "Hey, kid,
what do you think you're doing!" spoken very loudly from the meat counter. I felt caught, although I knew I was not doing anything criminal. I
remember not looking at the man, but standing there, feeling humiliated
because I knew everyone in the store must have heard him yell at me. I felt
him approach, and when I knew he was behind me, I turned around to face
the bloody butcher's apron. His large chest was at my eye level. He blocked
my way. I started to run out of the place, but even as I reached the door
I heard him shout after me: "Don't come in here unless you gonna buy
something. You PR kids put your dirty hands on stuff. You always look
dirty. But maybe dirty brown is your natural color." I heard him laugh and
someone else too in the back. Outside in the sunlight I looked at my hands.
My nails needed a little cleaning as they always did, since I liked to paint
with watercolors, but I took a bath every night. I thought the man was

dirtier than I was in his stained apron. He was also always sweaty—it showed in big yellow circles under his shirtsleeves. I sat on the front steps of the apartment building where we lived and looked closely at my hands, which showed the only skin I could see, since it was bitter cold and I was wearing my quilted play coat, dungarees, and a knitted navy cap of my father's. I was not pink like my friend Charlene and her sister Kathy, who had blue eyes and light brown hair. My skin is the color of the coffee my grandmother made, which was half milk, *leche con café* rather than *café con leche*. My mother is the opposite mix. She has a lot of café in her color. I could not understand how my skin looked like dirt to the super-market man.

I went in and washed my hands thoroughly with soap and hot water, and borrowing my mother's nail file, I cleaned the crusted watercolors from underneath my nails. I was pleased with the results. My skin was the same color as before, but I knew I was clean. Clean enough to run my fingers through Susie's fine gold hair when she came home to me.

Size

My mother is barely four feet eleven inches in height, which is average for women in her family. When I grew to five feet by age twelve, she was amazed and began to use the word tall to describe me, as in "Since you are tall, this dress will look good on you." As with the color of my skin, I didn't consciously think about my height or size until other people made an issue of it. It is around the preadolescent years that in America the games childen play for fun become fierce competitions where everyone is out to "prove" they are better than others. It was in the playground and sports fields that my size-related problems began. No matter how familiar the story is, every child who is the last chosen for a team knows the torment of waiting to be called up. At the Paterson, New Jersey, public schools that I attended, the volleyball or softball game was the metaphor for the battlefield of life to the inner city kids—the black kids versus the Puerto Rican kids, the whites ver-sus the blacks versus the Puerto Rican kids; and I was 4F, skinny, short, bespectacled, and apparently impervious to the blood thirst that drove many of my classmates to play ball as if their lives depended on it. Perhaps they did. I would rather be reading a book than sweating, grunting, and running the risk of pain and injury. I simply did not see the point in com-petitive sports. My main form of exercise then was walking to the library, many city blocks away from my barrio.

Still, I wanted to be wanted. I wanted to be chosen for the teams. Physical education was compulsory, a class where you were actually given a grade. On my mainly all A report card, the C for compassion I always received from the P.E. teachers shamed me the same as a bad grade in a real class. Invariably, my father would say: "How can you make a low grade for *playing games*?" He did not understand. Even if I had managed to make a hit (it never happened) or get the ball over that ridiculously high net, I already had a reputation as a "shrimp," a hopeless nonathlete. It was an area where the girls who didn't like me for one reason or another—mainly because I did better than they on academic subjects—could lord it over me; the playing field was the place where even the smallest girl could make me feel powerless and inferior. I instinctively understood the politics even then; how the *not* choosing me until the teacher forced one of the team captains to call my name was a coup of sorts—there, you little show-off, tomorrow you can beat us in spelling and geography, but this afternoon you are the loser. Or perhaps those were only my own bitter thoughts as I sat or stood in the sidelines while the big girls were grabbed like fish and I, the little brown tadpole, was ignored until Teacher looked over in my general direction and shouted, "Call Ortiz," or, worse, "Somebody's *got* to take her."

No wonder I read Wonder Woman comics and had Legion of Super   10
Heroes daydreams. Although I wanted to think of myself as "intellectual," my body was demanding that I notice it. I saw the little swelling around my once-flat nipples, the fine hairs growing in secret places; but my knees were still bigger than my thighs, and I always wore long- or half-sleeve blouses to hide my bony upper arms. I wanted flesh on my bones—a thick layer of it. I saw a new product advertised on TV. Wate-On. They showed skinny men and women before and after taking the stuff, and it was a transformation like the ninety-seven-pound-weakling-turned-into-Charles-Atlas ads that I saw on the back covers of my comic books. The Wate-On was very expensive. I tried to explain my need for it in Spanish to my mother, but it didn't translate very well, even to my ears—and she said with a tone of finality, eat more of my good food and you'll get fat—anybody can get fat. Right. Except me. I was going to have to join a circus someday as Skinny Bones, the woman without flesh.

Wonder Woman was stacked. She had a cleavage framed by the spread wings of a golden eagle and a muscular body that has become fashionable with women only recently. But since I wanted a body that would serve me in P.E., hers was my ideal. The breasts were an indulgence I allowed myself. Perhaps the daydreams of bigger girls were more glamorous, since our ambitions are filtered through our needs, but I wanted first a powerful body. I daydreamed of leaping up above the gray landscape of the city to where the sky was clear and blue, and in anger and self-pity, I fantasized about scooping my enemies up by their hair from the playing fields and dumping them on a barren asteroid. I would put the P.E. teachers each on their own rock in space too, where they would be the loneliest people in the universe, since I knew they had no "inner resources," no imagination, and in outer space, there would be no air for them to fill their deflated volleyballs with. In my mind all P.E. teachers have blended into one large spiky-haired woman with a whistle on a string around her neck and a volleyball under one arm. My Wonder Woman fantasies of revenge were a source of comfort to me in my early career as a shrimp.

I was saved from more years of P.E. torment by the fact that in my sophomore year of high school I transferred to a school where the midget,

Gladys, was the focal point of interest for the people who must rank according to size. Because her height was considered a handicap, there was an unspoken rule about mentioning size around Gladys, but of course, there was no need to say anything. Gladys knew her place: front row center in class photographs. I gladly moved to the left or to the right of her, as far as I could without leaving the picture completely.

Looks

Many photographs were taken of me as a baby by my mother to send to my father, who was stationed overseas during the first two years of my life. With the army in Panama when I was born, he later traveled often on tours of duty with the navy. I was a healthy, pretty baby. Recently, I read that people are drawn to big-eyed round-faced creatures, like puppies, kittens, and certain other mammals and marsupials, koalas, for example, and, of course, infants. I was all eyes, since my head and body, even as I grew older, remained thin and small-boned. As a young child I got a lot of attention from my relatives and many other people we met in our barrio. My mother's beauty may have had something to do with how much attention we got from strangers in stores and on the street. I can imagine it. In the pictures I have seen of us together, she is a stunning young woman by Latino standards: long, curly black hair, and round curves in a compact frame. From her I learned how to move, smile, and talk like an attractive woman. I remember going into a bodega for our groceries and being given candy by the proprietor as a reward for being *bonita*, pretty.

I can see in the photographs, and I also remember, that I was dressed in the pretty clothes, the stiff, frilly dresses, with layers of crinolines underneath, the glossy patent leather shoes, and, on special occasions, the skull-hugging little hats and the white gloves that were popular in the late fifties and early sixties. My mother was proud of my looks, although I was a bit too thin. She could dress me up like a doll and take me by the hand to visit relatives, or go to the Spanish mass at the Catholic church, and show me off. How was I to know that she and the others who called me "pretty" were representatives of an aesthetic that would not apply when I went out into the mainstream world of school?

In my Paterson, New Jersey, public schools there were still quite a few 15 white children, although the demographics of the city were changing rapidly. The original waves of Italian and Irish immigrants, silk-mill workers, and laborers in the cloth industries had been "assimilated." Their children were now the middle-class parents of my peers. Many of them moved their children to the Catholic schools that proliferated enough to have leagues of basketball teams. The names I recall hearing still ring in my ears: Don Bosco High versus St. Mary's High, St. Joseph's versus St. John's. Later I too would be transferred to the safer environment of a Catholic school. But I started school at Public School Number 11. I came there from Puerto Rico, thinking myself a pretty girl, and found that the hierarchy for popularity was as follows: pretty white girl, pretty Jewish girl, pretty Puerto Rican girl, pretty black girl. Drop the last two categories; teachers were too busy to have more than one favorite per class, and it was simply understood that if there was a big part in the school play, or any competition where the main qualification was "presentability" (such as escorting a school visitor to or from the principal's office), the classroom's public address speaker would be requesting the pretty and/or nice-looking white boy or girl. By the time I was in the sixth grade, I was sometimes called by the principal to represent my class because I dressed neatly (I knew this from a progress report sent to my mother, which I translated to her) and because all the "presentable" white girls had moved to the Catholic schools (I later surmised this part). But I was still not one of the popular girls with the boys. I remember one incident where I stepped out into the playground in my baggy gym shorts and one Puerto Rican boy said to the other: "What do you think?" The other one answered: "Her face is OK, but look at the toothpick legs." The next best thing to a compliment I got was when my favorite male teacher, while handing out the class pictures, commented that with my long neck and delicate features I resembled the movie star Audrey Hepburn. But the Puerto Rican boys had learned to respond to a fuller figure: long necks and a perfect little nose were not what they looked for in a girl. That is when I decided I was a "brain." I did not settle into the role easily. I was nearly devastated by what the chicken pox episode had done to my self-image. But I looked into the mirror less often after I was told that I would always have scars on my face, and I hid behind my long black hair and my books.

After the problems at the public school got to the point where even nonconfrontational little me got beaten up several times, my parents enrolled me at St. Joseph's High School. I was then a minority of one among the Italian and Irish kids. But I found several good friends there—other girls who took their studies seriously. We did our homework together and talked about the Jackies. The Jackies were two popular girls, one blonde and the other red-haired, who had women's bodies. Their curves showed even in the blue jumper uniforms with straps that we all wore. The blonde Jackie would often let one of the straps fall off her shoulder, and although she, like all of us, wore a white blouse underneath, all the boys stared at her arm. My friends and I talked about this and practiced letting our straps fall off our shoulders. But it wasn't the same without breasts or hips.

My final two and a half years of high school were spent in Augusta, Georgia, where my parents moved our family in search of a more peaceful environment. There we became part of a little community of our army-connected relatives and friends. School was yet another matter. I was enrolled in a huge school of nearly two thousand students that had just that year been forced to integrate. There were two black girls and there was me. I did extremely well academically. As to my social life, it was, for the most part, uneventful—yet it is in my memory blighted by one incident. In my junior year, I became wildly infatuated with a pretty white boy. I'll call him

Ted. Oh, he was pretty: yellow hair that fell over his forehead, a smile to die for—and he was a great dancer. I watched him at Teen Town, the youth center at the base where all the military brats gathered on Saturday nights. My father had retired from the navy, and we had all our base privileges—one other reason we had moved to Augusta. Ted looked like an angel to me. I worked on him for a year before he asked me out. This meant maneuvering to be within the periphery of his vision at every possible occasion. I took the long way to my classes in school just to pass by his locker, I went to football games, which I detested, and I danced (I too was a good dancer) in front of him at Teen Town—this took some fancy footwork, since it involved subtly moving my partner toward the right spot on the dance floor. When Ted finally approached me, "A Million to One" was playing on the jukebox, and when he took me into his arms, the odds suddenly turned in my favor. He asked me to go to a school dance the following Saturday. I said yes, breathlessly. I said yes, but there were obstacles to surmount at home. My father did not allow me to date casually. I was allowed to go to major events like a prom or a concert with a boy who had been properly screened. There was such a boy in my life, a neighbor who wanted to be a Baptist missionary and was practicing his anthropological skills on my family. If I was desperate to go somewhere and needed a date, I'd resort to Gary. This is the type of religious nut that Gary was: when the school bus did not show up one day, he put his hands over his face and prayed to Christ to get us a way to get to school. Within ten minutes a mother in a station wagon, on her way to town, stopped to ask why we weren't in school. Gary informed her that the Lord had sent her just in time to find us a way to get there in time for roll call. He assumed that I was impressed. Gary was even good-looking in a bland sort of way, but he kissed me with his lips tightly pressed together. I think Gary probably ended up marrying a native woman from wherever he may have gone to preach the Gospel according to Paul. She probably believes that all white men pray to God for transportation and kiss with their mouths closed. But it was Ted's mouth, his whole beautiful self, that concerned me in those days. I knew my father would say no to our date, but I planned to run away from home if necessary. I told my mother how important this date was. I cajoled and pleaded with her from Sunday to Wednesday. She listened to my arguments and must have heard the note of desperation in my voice. She said very gently to me: "You better be ready for disappointment." I did not ask what she meant. I did not want her fears for me to taint my happiness. I asked her to tell my father about my date. Thursday at breakfast my father looked at me across the table with his eyebrows together. My mother looked at him with her mouth set in a straight line. I looked down at my bowl of cereal. Nobody said anything. Friday I tried on every dress in my closet. Ted would be picking me up at six on Saturday: dinner and then the sock hop at school. Friday night I was in my room doing my nails or something else in preparation for Saturday (I know I groomed myself nonstop all week) when the telephone rang. I ran to get it. It was Ted. His voice sounded funny when he said my name, so funny that I felt compelled to ask: "Is something wrong?" Ted blurted it all out without a preamble. His father had asked who he was going out with. Ted had told him my name. "Ortiz? That's Spanish, isn't it?" the father had asked. Ted had told him yes, then shown him my picture in the yearbook. Ted's father had shaken his head. No. Ted would not be taking me out. Ted's father had known Puerto Ricans in the army. He had lived in New York City while studying architecture and had seen how the spics lived. Like rats. Ted repeated his father's words to me as if I should understand *his* predicament when I heard why he was breaking our date. I don't remember what I said before hanging up. I do recall the darkness of my room that sleepless night and the heaviness of my blanket in which I wrapped myself like a shroud. And I remember my parents' respect for my pain and their gentleness toward me that weekend. My mother did not say "I warned you," and I was grateful for her understanding silence.

In college, I suddenly became an "exotic" woman to the men who had survived the popularity wars in high school, who were now practicing to be worldly: they had to act liberal in their politics, in their lifestyles, and in the women they went out with. I dated heavily for a while, then married young. I had discovered that I needed stability more than social life. I had brains for sure and some talent in writing. These facts were a constant in my life. My skin color, my size, and my appearance were variables — things that were judged according to my current self-image, the aesthetic values of the times, the places I was in, and the people I met. My studies, later my writing, the respect of people who saw me as an individual person they cared about, these were the criteria for my sense of self-worth that I would concentrate on in my adult life.

QUESTIONS

1. According to its title, this piece purportedly tells a story, but it is divided into subtitled sections ("Skin," "Color," "Size," "Looks") like an article or essay. In what sense(s) does it tell a story, and how would you define the plot of that story? Does it have a clear beginning, middle, and end? In what ways might it be considered an essay?
2. Consider the significance of the epigraph that Cofer chose for her essay. In what ways is "migration" equivalent to the story of her body? How does the act of migration or the idea of migration pertain to the story of her body? How does it contribute to the meaning of her story?
3. Though the title of this piece implies that it will tell a single story, Cofer actually tells several stories in these reflections. In what ways do these multiple stories add up to a single story? What is the overarching theme of that story?
4. Cofer devotes separate sections to "Skin," "Color," "Size," and "Looks," even though they are concerned with overlapping, perhaps even synonymous aspects of her appearance. What is the distinctive slant of each

section that accounts for its title and its separateness? Why do you suppose she begins with "Skin" and ends with "Looks"? Why "Color"
before "Size" rather than vice versa?
5. Adapting Cofer's organizational approach to your own situation, write
a piece about the story of your body. Feel free to use her categories (in
whatever order you wish), or invent categories of your own. You might
also try to find (or create) a suitable epigraph for your piece or adapt
hers to suit your story.

MAKING CONNECTIONS

Given the title of her piece, Cofer invites us to see her as a storyteller — a
narrator, to use Vivian Gornick's term in "A Narrator Leaps Past
Journalism" (p. 74). How effective does Cofer seem to be in making "large
sense of things," which Gornick considers to be an important responsibility of a personal narrator? How does she come across in her storytelling?
How does Cofer's storytelling behavior compare or contrast to her behavior as a young child and later as a high school student?

THEME FOR ENGLISH B

Langston Hughes

Langston Hughes (1902–1967) grew up in Lawrence, Kansas, and Columbus, Ohio, and began writing at an early age, publishing his first poems when he was in high school. At twenty-one, he enrolled at Columbia University in New York City, but he left after his first year (he would later graduate from Lincoln University in Jefferson City, Missouri). In New York, Hughes came under the influence of the writers who were part of what came to be called the Harlem Renaissance, and he turned his poetic talents to the distinctive rhythms and concerns of the African American community. His first collection, The Weary Blues, *was published in 1926. Hughes went on to become one of the premier voices in American letters through his poems, short stories, novels, essays, articles, plays, and screenplays. He also translated the works of black poets from around the world. The following poem appeared in* Montage of a Dream Deferred *(1951).*

The instructor said,

> Go home and write
> a page tonight.
> And let that page come out of you—
> Then, it will be true.   5

I wonder if it's that simple?
I am twenty-two, colored, born in Winston-Salem.
I went to school there, then Durham, then here
to this college on the hill above Harlem.
I am the only colored student in my class.   10
The steps from the hill lead down into Harlem,
through a park, then I cross St. Nicholas,
Eighth Avenue, Seventh, and I come to the Y,
the Harlem Branch Y, where I take the elevator
up to my room, sit down, and write this page: 15

It's not easy to know what is true for you or me
at twenty-two, my age. But I guess I'm what
I feel and see and hear, Harlem, I hear you:
hear you, hear me—we two—you, me, talk on this page.
(I hear New York, too). Me—who?   20
Well, I like to eat, sleep, drink, and be in love.

I like to work, read, learn, and understand life.
I like a pipe for a Christmas present,
or records —Bessie,[1] bop, or Bach.
I guess being colored doesn't make me *not* like   25
the same things other folks like who are other races.
So will my page be colored that I write?
Being me, it will not be white.
But it will be
a part of you, instructor.   30
You are white—
yet a part of me, as I am a part of you.
That's American.
Sometimes perhaps you don't want to be a part of me.
Nor do I often want to be a part of you.   35
But we are, that's true!
As I learn from you,
I guess you learn from me—
although you're older—and white—

and somewhat more free.   40

This is my page for English B.

QUESTIONS

1. This poem presents itself as having been written to meet a composition assignment requiring students to write a page, "And let that page come out of you" (line 4). What do you think the instructor meant by urging his students to "let that page come out of you"? In what respects do you think that letting something "come out of you" might be similar to reflective writing? In what ways do you think it's different?

2. In line 19, the student says "we two—you, me talk on this page." Who is he referring to when he says "we two"? How is it possible for two voices to speak on a single page? In what ways does the style of Hughes's poem seem to be like "talk"? How does the form of the poem seem to be like "talk"? In what ways do you think talking on a page might be similar to reflective writing? In what ways do you think it's different?

––––––––––

[1]*Bessie:* Bessie Smith (1898?–1937), an American blues singer, considered by some to be the greatest of the classic blues singers of the 1920s. [Eds.]

3. How do the various thoughts and feelings of the poem seem to "come out of" the student? How do the flow and organization of thoughts seem to "come out of" the student?
4. Notice how the student repeatedly focuses on "being colored" (line 25) and the questions that raises for him as a student, a writer, and a person, especially in relation to his white instructor. Outline his train of thought to see if you can discover the reflective process by which he moves from the uncertainty of line 6 to the more confident tone of his concluding lines.

MAKING CONNECTIONS

1. Compare Hughes's reflections on "being the only colored student" in an all-white class, taught by a white instructor, to Judith Ortiz Cofer's experience of "being olive-skinned" in the high schools she attended in New Jersey and Georgia (p. 93). In what respects do the two writers' reactions and reflections seem to be similar? How do they differ?
2. Frederick Douglass also writes about learning to write (p. 62). Imagine a conversation between Douglass and Hughes about each other's report of this experience. How might they respond to each other's recollections and reflections about learning to write?

PILGRIMAGE TO NONVIOLENCE

Martin Luther King Jr.

The son of a minister, Martin Luther King Jr. (1929–1968) was ordained a Baptist minister in his father's church in Atlanta, Georgia, at the age of eighteen. He sprang into prominence in 1955 when he called a citywide boycott of the segregated bus system in Montgomery, Alabama, and he continued to be the most prominent civil rights activist in America until his assassination on April 4, 1968. During those tumultuous years, he was jailed at least fourteen times and endured countless threats against his life, but he persevered in his fight against racial discrimination, using a synthesis of the nonviolent philosophy of Mahatma Gandhi and Jesus's Sermon on the Mount. The 1964 Nobel Peace Prize was only one of the many awards he received, and his several books are characterized as much by their eloquent prose style as by their moral fervor. "Pilgrimage to Nonviolence" originally appeared in the magazine Christian Century *and was revised and updated for a collection of his sermons,* Strength to Love *(1963), the source of the following text.*

In my senior year in theological seminary, I engaged in the exciting reading of various theological theories. Having been raised in a rather strict fundamentalist tradition, I was occasionally shocked when my intellectual journey carried me through new and sometimes complex doctrinal lands, but the pilgrimage was always stimulating, gave me a new appreciation for objective appraisal and critical analysis, and knocked me out of my dogmatic slumber.

Liberalism provided me with an intellectual satisfaction that I had never found in fundamentalism. I became so enamored of the insights of liberalism that I almost fell into the trap of accepting uncritically everything it encompassed. I was absolutely convinced of the natural goodness of man and the natural power of human reason.

I

A basic change in my thinking came when I began to question some of the theories that had been associated with so-called liberal theology. Of course, there are aspects of liberalism that I hope to cherish always: its devotion to the search for truth, its insistence on an open and analytical mind, and its refusal to abandon the best lights of reason. The contribution of liberalism to the philosophical-historical criticism of biblical literature has been of immeasurable value and should be defended with religious and scientific passion.

But I began to question the liberal doctrine of man. The more I observed the tragedies of history and man's shameful inclination to choose the low road, the more I came to see the depths and strength of sin. My reading of the works of Reinhold Niebuhr made me aware of the complexity of human motives and the reality of sin on every level of man's existence.[1] Moreover, I came to recognize the complexity of man's social involvement and the glaring reality of collective evil. I realized that liberalism had been all too sentimental concerning human nature and that it leaned toward a false idealism.

I also came to see the superficial optimism of liberalism concerning human nature overlooked the fact that reason is darkened by sin. The more I thought about human nature, the more I saw how our tragic inclination for sin encourages us to rationalize our actions. Liberalism failed to show that reason by itself is little more than an instrument to justify man's defensive ways of thinking. Reason, devoid of the purifying power of faith, can never free itself from distortions and rationalizations.   5

Although I rejected some aspects of liberalism, I never came to an all-out acceptance of neo-orthodoxy. While I saw neo-orthodoxy as a helpful corrective for a sentimental liberalism, I felt that it did not provide an adequate answer to basic questions. If liberalism was too optimistic concerning human nature, neo-orthodoxy was too pessimistic. Not only on the question of man, but also on other vital issues, the revolt of neo-orthodoxy went too far. In its attempt to preserve the transcendence of God, which had been neglected by an overstress of his immanence in liberalism, neo-orthodoxy went to the extreme of stressing a God who was hidden, unknown, and "wholly other." In its revolt against overemphasis on the power of reason in liberalism, neo-orthodoxy fell into a mood of antirationalism and semifundamentalism, stressing a narrow uncritical biblicism. This approach, I felt, was inadequate both for the church and for personal life.

So although liberalism left me unsatisfied on the question of the nature of man, I found no refuge in neo-orthodoxy. I am now convinced that the truth about man is found neither in liberalism nor in neo-orthodoxy. Each represents a partial truth. A large segment of Protestant liberalism defined man only in terms of his essential nature, his capacity for good; neo-orthodoxy tended to define man only in terms of his existential nature, his capacity for evil. An adequate understanding of man is found neither in the thesis of liberalism nor in the antithesis of neo-orthodoxy, but in a synthesis which reconciles the truths of both.

---

[1]*Reinhold Niebuhr* (1892–1971): An American theologian, social activist, and noted writer on social and religious issues. [Eds.]

During the intervening years I have gained a new appreciation for the philosophy of existentialism. My first contact with the philosophy came through my reading of Kierkegaard and Nietzsche.[2] Later I turned to a study of Jaspers, Heidegger, and Sartre.[3] These thinkers stimulated my thinking; while questioning each, I nevertheless learned a great deal through a study of them. When I finally engaged in a serious study of the writings of Paul Tillich,[4] I became convinced that existentialism, in spite of the fact that it had become all too fashionable, had grasped certain basic truths about man and his condition that could not be permanently overlooked.

An understanding of the "finite freedom" of man is one of the permanent contributions of existentialism, and its perception of the anxiety and conflict produced in man's personal and social life by the perilous and ambiguous structure of existence is especially meaningful for our time. A common denominator in atheistic or theistic existentialism is that man's existential situation is estranged from his essential nature. In their revolt against Hegel's essentialism,[5] all existentialists contend that the world is fragmented. History is a series of unreconciled conflicts, and man's existence is filled with anxiety and threatened with meaninglessness. While the ultimate Christian answer is not found in any of these existential assertions, there is much here by which the theologian may describe the true state of man's existence.

Although most of my formal study has been in systematic theology and philosophy, I have become more and more interested in social ethics. During my early teens I was deeply concerned by the problem of racial injustice. I considered segregation both rationally inexplicable and morally unjustifiable. I could never accept my having to sit in the back of a bus or in the segregated section of a train. The first time that I was seated behind a curtain in a dining car I felt as though the curtain had been dropped on my selfhood. I also learned that the inseparable twin of racial injustice is economic injustice. I saw how the systems of segregation exploited both the Negro and the poor whites. These early experiences made me deeply conscious of the varieties of injustice in our society.

10

---

[2]*Søren Kierkegaard* (1813–1855): A Danish religious and aesthetic philosopher, concerned especially with the role of the individual. *Friedrich Nietzsche* (1844–1900): A German philosopher and moralist who sought a heroic, creative rejuvenation for a Western civilization that he considered decadent. [Eds.]

[3]*Karl Jaspers* (1883–1969): A German philosopher. *Martin Heidegger* (1889–1976): A German philosopher. *Jean-Paul Sartre* (1905–1980): A French philosopher and novelist. All three were existentialists, concerned with the existence and responsibility of the individual in an unknowable universe. [Eds.]

[4]*Paul Tillich* (1886–1965): A German-born American philosopher and theologian whose writings drew on psychology and existentialism. [Eds.]

[5]*Georg Friedrich Hegel* (1770–1831): A German philosopher best known for his theory of the dialectic (thesis versus antithesis produces synthesis). [Eds.]

II

Not until I entered theological seminary, however, did I begin a serious intellectual quest for a method that would eliminate social evil. I was immediately influenced by the social gospel. In the early 1950s I read Walter Rauschenbusch's *Christianity and the Social Crisis,* a book which left an indelible imprint on my thinking. Of course, there were points at which I differed with Rauschenbusch. I felt that he was a victim of the nineteenth-century "cult of inevitable progress," which led him to an unwarranted optimism concerning human nature. Moreover, he came perilously close to identifying the Kingdom of God with a particular social and economic system, a temptation to which the church must never surrender. But in spite of these shortcomings, Rauschenbusch gave to American Protestantism a sense of social responsibility that it should never lose. The gospel at its best deals with the whole man, not only his soul but also his body, not only his spiritual well-being but also his material well-being. A religion that professes a concern for the souls of men and is not equally concerned about the slums that damn them, the economic conditions that strangle them, and the social conditions that cripple them, is a spiritually moribund religion.

After reading Rauschenbusch, I turned to a serious study of the social and ethical theories of the great philosophers. During this period I had almost despaired of the power of love to solve social problems. The turn-the-other-cheek and the love-your-enemies philosophies are valid, I felt, only when individuals are in conflict with other individuals; when racial groups and nations are in conflict, a more realistic approach is necessary.

Then I was introduced to the life and teachings of Mahatma Gandhi.[6] As I read his works I became deeply fascinated by his campaigns of nonviolent resistance. The whole Gandhian concept of *satyagraha* (*satya* is truth which equals love and *graha* is force; *satyagraha* thus means truth-force or love-force) was profoundly significant to me. As I delved deeper into the philosophy of Gandhi, my skepticism concerning the power of love gradually diminished, and I came to see for the first time that the Christian doctrine of love, operating through the Gandhian method of nonviolence, is one of the most potent weapons available to an oppressed people in their struggle for freedom. At that time, however, I acquired only an intellectual understanding and appreciation of the position, and I had no firm determination to organize it in a socially effective situation.

When I went to Montgomery, Alabama, as a pastor in 1954, I had not the slightest idea that I would later become involved in a crisis in which nonviolent resistance would be applicable. After I had lived in the community about a year, the bus boycott began. The Negro people of Montgomery, exhausted by the humiliating experience that they had constantly faced on the buses, expressed in a massive act of noncooperation their determination

---

[6]*Mahatma Gandhi* (1869–1948): A Hindu nationalist and spiritual leader. [Eds.]

to be free. They came to see that it was ultimately more honorable to walk the streets in dignity than to ride the buses in humiliation. At the beginning of the protest, the people called on me to serve as their spokesman. In accepting this responsibility, my mind, consciously or unconsciously, was driven back to the Sermon on the Mount and the Gandhian method of nonviolent resistance. This principle became the guiding light of our movement. Christ furnished the spirit and motivation and Gandhi furnished the method.

The experience in Montgomery did more to clarify my thinking in regard   15 to the question of nonviolence than all of the books that I had read. As the days unfolded, I became more and more convinced of the power of nonviolence. Nonviolence became more than a method to which I gave intellectual assent; it became a commitment to a way of life. Many issues I had not cleared up intellectually concerning nonviolence were now resolved within the sphere of practical action.

My privilege of traveling to India had a great impact on me personally, for it was invigorating to see firsthand the amazing results of a nonviolent struggle to achieve independence. The aftermath of hatred and bitterness that usually follows a violent campaign was found nowhere in India, and a mutual friendship, based on complete equality, existed between the Indian and British people within the Commonwealth.

I would not wish to give the impression that nonviolence will accomplish miracles overnight. Men are not easily moved from their mental ruts or purged of their prejudiced and irrational feelings. When the underprivileged demand freedom, the privileged at first react with bitterness and resistance. Even when the demands are couched in nonviolent terms, the initial response is substantially the same. I am sure that many of our white brothers in Montgomery and throughout the South are still bitter toward the Negro leaders, even though these leaders have sought to follow a way of love and nonviolence. But the nonviolent approach does something to the hearts and souls of those committed to it. It gives them new self-respect. It calls up resources of strength and courage that they did not know they had. Finally, it so stirs the conscience of the opponent that reconciliation becomes a reality.

III

More recently I have come to see the need for the method of nonviolence in international relations. Although I was not yet convinced of its efficacy in conflicts between nations, I felt that while war could never be a positive good, it could serve as a negative good by preventing the spread and growth of an evil force. War, horrible as it is, might be preferable to surrender to a totalitarian system. But I now believe that the potential destructiveness of modern weapons totally rules out the possibility of war ever again achieving a negative good. If we assume that mankind has a right to survive, then we must find an alternative to war and destruction. In our day of space vehicles and guided ballistic missiles, the choice is either non-violence or nonexistence.

I am no doctrinaire pacifist, but I have tried to embrace a realistic paci-fism which finds the pacifist position as the lesser evil in the circumstances. I do not claim to be free from the moral dilemmas that the Christian non-pacifist confronts, but I am convinced that the church cannot be silent while mankind faces the threat of nuclear annihilation. If the church is true to her mission, she must call for an end to the arms race.

Some of my personal sufferings over the last few years have also served   20
to shape my thinking. I always hesitate to mention these experiences for fear of conveying the wrong impression. A person who constantly calls attention to his trials and sufferings is in danger of developing a martyr complex and impressing others that he is consciously seeking sympathy. It is possible for one to be self-centered in his self-sacrifice. So I am always reluctant to refer to my personal sacrifices. But I feel somewhat justified in mentioning them in this essay because of the influence they have had upon my thought.

Due to my involvement in the struggle for the freedom of my people, I have known very few quiet days in the last few years. I have been impris-oned in Alabama and Georgia jails twelve times. My home has been bombed twice. A day seldom passes that my family and I are not the recipients of threats of death. I have been the victim of a near-fatal stabbing. So in a real sense I have been battered by the storms of persecution. I must admit that at times I have felt that I could no longer bear such a heavy burden, and have been tempted to retreat to a more quiet and serene life. But every time such a temptation appeared, something came to strengthen and sustain my deter-mination. I have learned now that the Master's burden is light precisely when we take his yoke upon us.

My personal trials have also taught me the value of unmerited suffering. As my sufferings mounted I soon realized that there were two ways in which I could respond to my situation—either to react with bitterness or seek to transform the suffering into a creative force. I decided to follow the latter course. Recognizing the necessity for suffering, I have tried to make of it a virtue, if only to save myself from bitterness, I have attempted to see my per-sonal ordeals as an opportunity to transfigure myself and heal the people involved in the tragic situation which now obtains. I have lived these last few years with the conviction that unearned suffering is redemptive. There are some who still find the Cross a stumbling block, others consider it foolish-ness, but I am more convinced than ever before that it is the power of God unto social and individual salvation. So like the Apostle Paul I can now humbly, yet proudly, say, "I bear in my body the marks of the Lord Jesus."

The agonizing moments through which I have passed during the last few years have also drawn me closer to God. More than ever before I am convinced of the reality of a personal God. True, I have always believed in the personality of God. But in the past the idea of a personal God was lit-tle more than a metaphysical category that I found theologically and philo-sophically satisfying. Now it is a living reality that has been validated in the experiences of everyday life. God has been profoundly real to me in recent years. In the midst of outer dangers I have felt an inner calm. In the midst of lonely days and dreary nights I have heard an inner voice saying, "Lo, I will be with you." When the chains of fear and the manacles of frustration have all but stymied my efforts, I have felt the power of God transforming the fatigue of despair into the buoyancy of hope. I am convinced that the universe is under the control of a loving purpose, and that in the struggle for righteousness man has cosmic companionship. Behind the harsh appearances of the world there is a benign power. To say that this God is personal is not to make him a finite object beside other objects or attribute to him the limitations of human personality; it is to take what is finest and noblest in our consciousness and affirm its perfect existence in him. It is certainly true that human personality is limited, but personality as such involves no necessary limitations. It means simply self-consciousness and self-direction. So in the truest sense of the word, God is a living God. In him there is feeling and will, responsive to the deepest yearnings of the human heart: *this* God both evokes and answers prayer.

The past decade has been a most exciting one. In spite of the tensions and uncertainties of this period something profoundly meaningful is taking place. Old systems of exploitation and oppression are passing away; new systems of justice and equality are being born. In a real sense this is a great time to be alive. Therefore, I am not yet discouraged about the future. Granted that the easygoing optimism of yesterday is impossible. Granted that we face a world crisis which leaves us standing so often amid the surging murmur of life's restless sea. But every crisis has both its dangers and its opportunities. It can spell either salvation or doom. In a dark, confused world the Kingdom of God may yet reign in the hearts of men.

QUESTIONS

1. King found the extremes of liberalism on one hand and neo-orthodoxy on the other both unsatisfactory. Why?
2. Existentialism (paragraph 8) and Walter Rauschenbusch's social gospel (paragraph 11) proved more useful to King than liberalism or neo-orthodoxy. How did these concepts help shape his outlook?
3. King is interested in religious and philosophical theories not for their own sake but for their usefulness in the social world. How do Mahatma Gandhi's example (paragraphs 13 and 16) and King's own experience in Montgomery (paragraphs 14, 15, and 17) illustrate this concern?
4. How did King's personal faith in God aid in his struggles and sufferings? Is his dream of a better society totally dependent on the existence of this "benign power" (paragraph 23)?
5. King's intellectual development is described as a pilgrimage from a simple fundamentalist attitude through conflicting theological and philosophical

concepts to an intensified belief in a benign God and a commitment to international nonviolence. How is his final set of beliefs superior to his original one? Has he convinced you of the validity of his beliefs?

6. King writes for a general audience rather than one with theological and philosophical training. How successful is King at clarifying religious and philosophical concepts for the general reader? Point out examples that show how he treats such concepts.

7. Again and again King employs the classical rhetorical strategy of concession: the opposition's viewpoint is stated and partially accepted before King gives his own viewpoint. Locate two or three instances of this strategy, and explain how it aids a reader's understanding (if not acceptance) of King's views.

8. King's essay reflects on how he came to accept the method of nonviolence. Have you, over time, changed your thoughts or methods of approaching an issue or problem? Has someone you know well done this? If so, write an essay reflecting on the events central to this change and their significance.

9. King's hopes for a better world were expressed in the early 1960s. Based on your knowledge of history since then, write an essay in which you justify or disqualify King's guarded optimism.

MAKING CONNECTIONS

1. Like several other writers in this section, King reflects on a turning point in his life. Consider his essay in relation to two or three others, such as those by Maya Angelou (p. 31), Alice Walker (p. 42), George Orwell (p. 114), or Zoë Tracy Hardy (p. 126). Compare and contrast the ways these writers present their turning points. How does each present the crucial moment or event, and how does each show its meaning?

2. One way a writer convinces us is by the authority we sense in the person as he or she writes. What details in King's essay contribute to our sense of him as an authoritative person, a writer we are inclined to believe? What do you find of similar persuasiveness in the essays of Maya Angelou (p. 31), Judith Ortiz Cofer (p. 93), George Orwell (p. 114), or Zoë Tracy Hardy (p. 126)?

SHOOTING AN ELEPHANT

George Orwell

George Orwell (1903–1950) was the pen name of Eric Blair, the son of a British customs officer serving in Bengal, India. As a boy he was sent home to prestigious English schools, where he learned to dislike the rich and powerful. After finishing preparatory school at Eton College, he returned to Asia to serve as an officer of the British police in India and Burma, where he became disillusioned with imperialism. He later studied conditions among the urban poor and the coal miners of Wigan, a city in northwestern England, which strengthened his socialist beliefs. He was wounded in the Spanish civil war, defending the lost cause of the left against the fascists. Under the name Orwell, he wrote accounts of all of these experiences as well as the anti-Stalinist fable Animal Farm *and the novel* 1984. *In the following essay, first published in 1936, Orwell attacks the politics of imperialism.*

In Moulmein, in Lower Burma, I was hated by large numbers of people—the only time in my life that I have been important enough for this to happen to me. I was sub-divisional police officer of the town, and in an aimless, petty kind of way anti-European feeling was very bitter. No one had the guts to raise a riot, but if a European woman went through the bazaars alone somebody would probably spit betel juice over her dress. As a police officer I was an obvious target and was baited whenever it seemed safe to do so. When a nimble Burman tripped me up on the football field and the referee (another Burman) looked the other way, the crowd yelled with hideous laughter. This happened more than once. In the end the sneering yellow faces of young men that met me everywhere, the insults hooted after me when I was at a safe distance, got badly on my nerves. The young Buddhist priests were the worst of all. There were several thousands of them in the town and none of them seemed to have anything to do except stand on street corners and jeer at Europeans.

All this was perplexing and upsetting. For at that time I had already made up my mind that imperialism was an evil thing and the sooner I chucked up my job and got out of it the better. Theoretically—and secretly, of course—I was all for the Burmese and all against their oppressors, the British. As for the job I was doing, I hated it more bitterly than I can perhaps make clear. In a job like that you see the dirty work of Empire at close quarters. The wretched prisoners huddling in the stinking cages of the lock-ups, the grey, cowed faces of the long-term convicts, the scarred buttocks of the men who had been flogged with bamboos—all these oppressed me with

114

an intolerable sense of guilt. But I could get nothing into perspective. I was young and ill-educated and I had had to think out my problems in the utter silence that is imposed on every Englishman in the East. I did not even know that the British Empire is dying, still less did I know that it is a great deal better than the younger empires that are going to supplant it. All I knew was that I was stuck between my hatred of the empire I served and my rage against the evil-spirited little beasts who tried to make my job impossible. With one part of my mind I thought of the British Raj[1] as an unbreakable tyranny, as something clamped down, in *saecula saeculorum*,[2] upon the will of prostrate peoples; with another part I thought that the greatest joy in the world would be to drive a bayonet into a Buddhist priest's guts. Feelings like these are the normal by-product of imperialism; ask any Anglo-Indian official, if you can catch him off duty.

One day something happened which in a roundabout way was enlightening. It was a tiny incident in itself, but it gave me a better glimpse than I had had before of the real nature of imperialism—the real motives for which despotic governments act. Early one morning the sub-inspector at a police station at the other end of the town rang me up on the phone and said that an elephant was ravaging the bazaar. Would I please come and do something about it? I did not know what I could do, but I wanted to see what was happening and I got on to a pony and started out. I took my rifle, an old .44 Winchester and much too small to kill an elephant, but I thought the noise might be useful *in terrorem*.[3] Various Burmans stopped me on the way and told me about the elephant's doings. It was not, of course, a wild elephant, but a tame one which had gone "must."[4] It had been chained up, as tame elephants always are when their attack of "must" is due, but on the previous night it had broken its chain and escaped. Its mahout,[5] the only person who could manage it when it was in that state, had set out in pursuit, but had taken the wrong direction and was now twelve hours' journey away, and in the morning the elephant had suddenly reappeared in town. The Burmese population had no weapons and were quite helpless against it. It had already destroyed somebody's bamboo hut, killed a cow and raided some fruit-stalls and devoured the stock; also it had met the municipal rubbish van and, when the driver jumped out and took to his heels, had turned the van over and inflicted violences upon it.

The Burmese sub-inspector and some Indian constables were waiting for me in the quarter where the elephant had been seen. It was a very poor quarter, a labyrinth of squalid bamboo huts, thatched with palm-leaf, winding all over a steep hillside. I remember that it was a cloudy, stuffy morning at the beginning of the rains. We began questioning the people as to where

---

[1]*British Raj:* British rule in India and Burma. [Eds.]
[2]*saecula saeculorum:* Forever and ever. [Eds.]
[3]*in terrorem:* For fright. [Eds.]
[4]*"must":* The frenzied state of the bull elephant in sexual excitement. [Eds.]
[5]*mahout:* An elephant's keeper. [Eds.]

the elephant had gone and, as usual, failed to get any definite information. That is invariably the case in the East; a story always sounds clear enough at a distance, but the nearer you get to the scene of events the vaguer it becomes. Some of the people said that the elephant had gone in one direction, some said that he had gone in another, some professed not even to have heard of any elephant. I had almost made up my mind that the whole story was a pack of lies, when we heard yells a little distance away. There was a loud, scandalized cry of "Go away, child! Go away this instant!" and an old woman with a switch in her hand came round the corner of a hut, violently shooing away a crowd of naked children. Some more women followed, clicking their tongues and exclaiming; evidently there was something that the children ought not to have seen. I rounded the hut and saw a man's dead body sprawling in the mud. He was an Indian, a black Dravidian coolie,[6] almost naked, and he could not have been dead many minutes. The people said that the elephant had come suddenly upon him round the corner of the hut, caught him with its trunk, put its foot on his back and ground him into the earth. This was the rainy season and the ground was soft, and his face had scored a trench a foot deep and a couple of yards long. He was lying on his belly with arms crucified and head sharply twisted to one side. His face was coated with mud, the eyes wide open, the teeth bared and grinning with an expression of unendurable agony. (Never tell me, by the way, that the dead look peaceful. Most of the corpses I have seen looked devilish.) The friction of the great beast's foot had stripped the skin from his back as neatly as one skins a rabbit. As soon as I saw the dead man I sent an orderly to a friend's house nearby to borrow an elephant rifle. I had already sent back the pony, not wanting it to go mad with fright and throw me if it smelt the elephant.

The orderly came back in a few minutes with a rifle and five cartridges,   5 and meanwhile some Burmans had arrived and told us that the elephant was in the paddy fields below, only a few hundred yards away. As I started forward practically the whole population of the quarter flocked out of the houses and followed me. They had seen the rifle and were all shouting excitedly that I was going to shoot the elephant. They had not shown much interest in the elephant when he was merely ravaging their homes, but it was different now that he was to be shot. It was a bit of fun to them, as it would be to an English crowd; besides they wanted the meat. It made me vaguely uneasy. I had no intention of shooting the elephant—I had merely sent for the rifle to defend myself if necessary—and it is always unnerving to have a crowd following you. I marched down the hill, looking and feeling a fool, with the rifle over my shoulder and an ever-growing army of people jostling at my heels. At the bottom, when you got away from the huts, there was a metalled road and beyond that a miry waste of paddy fields a

---

[6]*Dravidian coolie: Dravidian* refers to a large ethnic group from south and central India. A *coolie* is an unskilled laborer. [Eds.]

thousand yards across, not yet ploughed but soggy from the first rains and dotted with coarse grass. The elephant was standing eight yards from the road, his left side towards us. He took not the slightest notice of the crowd's approach. He was tearing up bunches of grass, beating them against his knees to clean them and stuffing them into his mouth.

I had halted on the road. As soon as I saw the elephant I knew with perfect certainty that I ought not to shoot him. It is a serious matter to shoot a working elephant — it is comparable to destroying a huge and costly piece of machinery — and obviously one ought not to do it if it can possibly be avoided. And at that distance, peacefully eating, the elephant looked no more dangerous than a cow. I thought then and I think now that his attack of "must" was already passing off; in which case he would merely wander harmlessly about until the mahout came back and caught him. Moreover, I did not in the least want to shoot him. I decided that I would watch him for a little while to make sure that he did not turn savage again, and then go home.

But at that moment I glanced around at the crowd that had followed me. It was an immense crowd, two thousand at the least and growing every minute. It blocked the road for a long distance on either side. I looked at the sea of yellow faces above the garish clothes — faces all happy and excited all over this bit of fun, all certain that the elephant was going to be shot. They were watching me as they would watch a conjurer about to perform a trick. They did not like me, but with the magical rifle in my hands I was momentarily worth watching. And suddenly I realized that I should have to shoot the elephant after all. The people expected it of me and I had got to do it; I could feel their two thousand wills pressing me forward, irresistibly. And it was at this moment, as I stood there with the rifle in my hands, that I first grasped the hollowness, the futility of the white man's dominion in the East. Here was I, the white man with his gun, standing in front of the unarmed native crowd — seemingly the leading actor of the piece; but in reality I was only an absurd puppet pushed to and fro by the will of those yellow faces behind. I perceived in this moment that when the white man turns tyrant it is his own freedom that he destroys. He becomes a sort of hollow, posing dummy, the conventionalized figure of a sahib. For it is the condition of his rule that he shall spend his life in trying to impress the "natives," and so in every crisis he has got to do what the "natives" expect of him. He wears a mask, and his face grows to fit it. I had got to shoot the elephant. I had committed myself to doing it when I sent for the rifle. A sahib has got to act like a sahib; he has got to appear resolute, to know his own mind and do definite things. To come all that way, rifle in hand, with two thousand people marching at my heels, and then to trail feebly away, having done nothing — no, that was impossible. The crowd would laugh at me. And my whole life, every white man's life in the East, was one long struggle not to be laughed at.

But I did not want to shoot the elephant. I watched him beating his bunch of grass against his knees, with that preoccupied grandmotherly air that elephants have. It seemed to me that it would be murder to shoot him.

At that age I was not squeamish about killing animals, but I had never shot an elephant and never wanted to. (Somehow it always seems worse to kill a *large* animal.) Besides, there was the beast's owner to be considered. Alive, the elephant was worth at least a hundred pounds; dead, he would only be worth the value of his tusks, five pounds, possibly. But I had got to act quickly. I turned to some experienced-looking Burmans who had been there when we arrived, and asked them how the elephant had been behaving. They all said the same thing: he took no notice of you if you left him alone, but he might charge if you went too close to him.

It was perfectly clear to me what I ought to do. I ought to walk up to within, say, twenty-five yards of the elephant and test his behavior. If he charged, I could shoot; if he took no notice of me, it would be safe to leave him until the mahout came back. But also I knew that I was going to do no such thing. I was a poor shot with a rifle and the ground was soft mud into which one would sink at every step. If the elephant charged and I missed him, I should have about as much chance as a toad under a steam-roller. But even then I was not thinking particularly of my own skin, only of the watchful yellow faces behind. For at the moment, with the crowd watching me, I was not afraid in the ordinary sense, as I would have been if I had been alone. A white man mustn't be frightened in front of "natives"; and so, in general, he isn't frightened. The sole thought in my mind was that if anything went wrong those two thousand Burmans would see me pursued, caught, trampled on and reduced to a grinning corpse like that Indian up the hill. And if that happened it was quite probable that some of them would laugh. That would never do. There was only one alternative. I shoved the cartridges into the magazine and lay down on the road to get a better aim.

The crowd grew very still, and a deep, low, happy sigh, as of people who see the theatre curtain go up at last, breathed from innumerable throats. They were going to have their bit of fun after all. The rifle was a beautiful German thing with cross-hair sights. I did not then know that in shooting an elephant one would shoot to cut an imaginary bar running from ear-hole to ear-hole. I ought, therefore, as the elephant was sideways on, to have aimed straight at his ear-hole; actually I aimed several inches in front of this, thinking the brain would be further forward. 10

When I pulled the trigger I did not hear the bang or feel the kick — one never does when a shot goes home — but I heard the devilish roar of glee that went up from the crowd. In that instant, in too short a time, one would have thought, even for the bullet to get there, a mysterious, terrible change had come over the elephant. He neither stirred nor fell, but every line of his body had altered. He looked suddenly stricken, shrunken, immensely old, as though the frightful impact of the bullet had paralyzed him without knocking him down. At last, after what seemed a long time — it might have been five seconds, I dare say — he sagged flabbily to his knees. His mouth slobbered. An enormous senility seemed to have settled upon him. One could have imagined him thousands of years old. I fired again into the same spot. At the second shot he did not collapse but climbed with desperate slowness to his feet and stood weakly upright, with legs sagging and head drooping. I fired a third time. That was the shot that did for him. You could see the agony of it jolt his whole body and knock the last remnant of strength from his legs. But in falling he seemed for a moment to rise, for as his hind legs collapsed beneath him he seemed to tower upward like a huge rock toppling, his trunk reaching skywards like a tree. He trumpeted, for the first and only time. And then down he came, his belly towards me, with a crash that seemed to shake the ground even where I lay.

I got up. The Burmans were already racing past me across the mud. It was obvious that the elephant would never rise again, but he was not dead. He was breathing very rhythmically with long rattling gasps, his great mound of a side painfully rising and falling. His mouth was wide open—I could see far down into caverns of pale pink throat. I waited for a long time for him to die, but his breathing did not weaken. Finally I fired my two remaining shots into the spot where I thought his heart must be. The thick blood welled out of him like red velvet, but still he did not die. His body did not even jerk when the shots hit him, the tortured breathing continued without a pause. He was dying, very slowly and in great agony, but in some world remote from me where not even a bullet could damage him further. I felt that I had got to put an end to that dreadful noise. It seemed dreadful to see the great beast lying there, powerless to move and yet powerless to die, and not even to be able to finish him. I sent back for my small rifle and poured shot after shot into his heart and down his throat. They seemed to make no impression. The tortured gasps continued as steadily as the ticking of a clock.

In the end I could not stand it any longer and went away. I heard later that it took him half an hour to die. Burmans were bringing dahs[7] and baskets even before I left, and I was told they had stripped his body almost to the bones by the afternoon.

Afterwards, of course, there were endless discussions about the shooting of the elephant. The owner was furious, but he was only an Indian and could do nothing. Besides, legally I had done the right thing, for a mad elephant has to be killed, like a mad dog, if its owner fails to control it. Among the Europeans opinion was divided. The older men said I was right, the younger men said it was a damn shame to shoot an elephant for killing a coolie, because an elephant was worth more than any damn Coringhee coolie. And afterwards I was very glad that the coolie had been killed; it put me legally in the right and it gave me a sufficient pretext for shooting the elephant. I often wondered whether any of the others grasped that I had done it solely to avoid looking a fool.

---

[7]*dahs:* Large knives. [Eds.]

QUESTIONS

1. Describe Orwell's mixed feelings about serving as a police officer in Burma.
2. How do the natives "force" Orwell to shoot the elephant against his better judgment? How does he relate this personal episode to the larger problems of British imperialism?
3. What is Orwell's final reaction to his deed? How literally can we take his statement that he "was very glad that the coolie had been killed" (paragraph 14)?
4. From the opening sentence Orwell displays a remarkable candor concerning his feelings. How does this personal, candid tone add to or detract from the strength of the essay?
5. Orwell's recollection of shooting the elephant is shaped to support a specific point or thesis. Where does Orwell state this thesis? Is this placement effective?
6. In what ways does this essay read more like a short story than an expository essay? How effective is Orwell's use of narrative and personal experience?
7. Orwell often wrote with a political purpose, with a "desire to push the world in a certain direction, to alter other people's idea of the kind of society that they should strive after," as he said in his essay "Why I Write." To what extent does the "tiny incident" in this essay illuminate "the real nature of imperialism" (paragraph 3)? Does Orwell succeed in altering your idea of imperialism?
8. Using Orwell's essay as a model, write a reflection in which the narration of "a tiny incident" illuminates a larger social or political problem.

MAKING CONNECTIONS

The selections by Lucy Grealy (p. 50) and Adam Gopnik (p. 78) in this section read somewhat like short stories, as does Orwell's essay. Compare the narrative designs of two of these writers, and discuss the usefulness of storytelling in reflective writing.

TOOLS OF TORTURE: AN ESSAY ON BEAUTY AND PAIN

Phyllis Rose

Born in 1942 in New York City, Phyllis Rose holds degrees from Radcliffe College, Yale University, and Harvard University, and is currently a professor of English at Harvard University. She is the author of A Woman of Letters: A Life of Virginia Woolf *(1978),* Never Say Goodbye: Essays *(1991), and* The Year of Reading Proust *(1997), as well as the editor of* The Norton Book of Women's Lives *(1993). Rose contributes frequently to periodicals such as* The Atlantic Monthly *and* The New York Review of Books, *and she also serves on the editorial board of* The American Scholar. *Rose has said, "I love the essay form because I very often don't know when I start on a subject where I'm going to end up. I find out what I think." This essay was first published in* The Atlantic Monthly *in October 1986.*

In a gallery off the rue Dauphine, near the *parfumerie* where I get my massage, I happened upon an exhibit of medieval torture instruments. It made me think that pain must be as great a challenge to the human imagination as pleasure. Otherwise there's no accounting for the number of torture instruments. One would be quite enough. The simple pincer, let's say, which rips out flesh. Or the head crusher, which breaks first your tooth sockets, then your skull. But in addition I saw tongs, thumbscrews, a rack, a ladder, ropes and pulleys, a grill, a garrote, a Spanish horse, a Judas cradle, an iron maiden, a cage, a gag, a strappado, a stretching table, a saw, a wheel, a twisting stork, an inquisitor's chair, a breast breaker, and a scourge. You don't need complicated machinery to cause incredible pain. If you want to saw your victim down the middle, for example, all you need is a slightly bigger than usual saw. If you hold the victim upside down so the blood stays in his head, hold his legs apart, and start sawing at the groin, you can get as far as the navel before he loses consciousness.

Even in the Middle Ages, before electricity, there were many things you could do to torment a person. You could tie him up in an iron belt that held the arms and legs up to the chest and left no point of rest, so that all his muscles went into spasm within minutes and he was driven mad within hours. This was the twisting stork, a benign-looking object. You could stretch him out backward over a thin piece of wood so that his whole body weight rested on his spine, which pressed against the sharp wood. Then you could stop up his nostrils and force water into his stomach through his mouth. Then, if you wanted to finish him off, you and your helper could jump on his stomach, causing internal hemorrhage. This torture was called the rack. If you wanted to burn someone to death without hearing him scream, you could use a tongue lock, a metal rod between the jaw and collarbone that prevented him from opening his mouth. You could put a person in a chair with spikes on the seat and arms, tie him down against the spikes, and beat him, so that every time he flinched from the beating he drove his own flesh deeper onto the spikes. This was the inquisitor's chair. If you wanted to make it worse, you could heat the spikes. You could suspend a person over a pointed wooden pyramid and whenever he started to fall asleep, you could drop him onto the point. If you were Ippolito Marsili, the inventor of this torture, known as the Judas Cradle, you could tell yourself you had invented something humane, a torture that worked without burning flesh or breaking bones. For the torture here was supposed to be sleep deprivation.

The secret of torture, like the secret of French cuisine, is that nothing is unthinkable. The human body is like a foodstuff, to be grilled, pounded, filleted. Every opening exists to be stuffed, all flesh to be carved off the bone. You take an ordinary wheel, a heavy wooden wheel with spokes. You lay the victim on the ground with blocks of wood at strategic points under his shoulders, legs, and arms. You use the wheel to break every bone in his body. Next you tie his body onto the wheel. With all its bones broken, it will be pliable. However, the victim will not be dead. If you want to kill him, you hoist the wheel aloft on the end of a pole and leave him to starve. Who would have thought to do this with a man and a wheel? But, then, who would have thought to take the disgusting snail, force it to render its ooze, stuff it in its own shell with garlic butter, bake it, and eat it?

Not long ago I had a facial — only in part because I thought I needed one. It was research into the nature and function of pleasure. In a dark booth at the back of the beauty salon, the aesthetician put me on a table and applied a series of ointments to my face, some cool, some warmed. After a while she put something into my hand, cold and metallic. "Don't be afraid, madame," she said. "It is an electrode. It will not hurt you. The other end is attached to two metal cylinders, which I roll over your face. They break down the electricity barrier on your skin and allow the moisturizers to penetrate deeply." I didn't believe this hocus-pocus. I didn't believe in the electricity barrier or in the ability of these rollers to break it down. But it all felt very good. The cold metal on my face was a pleasant change from the soft warmth of the aesthetician's fingers. Still, since Algeria it's hard to hear the word "electrode" without fear. So when she left me for a few minutes with a moist, refreshing cheesecloth over my face, I thought, What if the goal of her expertise had been pain, not moisture? What if the electrodes had been electrodes in the Algerian sense? What if the cheesecloth mask were dipped in acid?

In Paris, where the body is so pampered, torture seems particularly   5
sinister, not because it's hard to understand but because — as the dark side of sensuality — it seems so easy. Beauty care is among the glories of Paris.

Soins esthétiques[1] include makeup, facials, massages (both relaxing and reducing), depilations (partial and complete), manicures, pedicures, and tanning, in addition to the usual run of *soins* for the hair: cutting, brushing, setting, waving, styling, blowing, coloring, and streaking. In Paris the state of your skin, hair, and nerves is taken seriously, and there is little of the puritanical thinking that tries to pursuade us that beauty comes from within. Nor do the French think, as Americans do, that beauty should be offhand and low-maintenance. Spending time and money on *soins esthétiques* is appropriate and necessary, not self-indulgent. Should that loving attention to the body turn malevolent, you have torture. You have the procedure — the aesthetic, as it were — of torture, the explanation for the rich diversity of torture instruments, but you do not have the cause.

Historically torture has been a tool of legal systems, used to get information needed for a trial or, more directly, to determine guilt or innocence. In the Middle Ages confession was considered the best of all proofs, and torture was the way to produce a confession. In other words, torture didn't come into existence to give vent to human sadism. It is not always private and perverse but sometimes social and institutional, vetted by the government and, of course, the Church. (There have been few bigger fans of torture than Christianity and Islam.) Righteousness, as much as viciousness, produces torture. There aren't squads of sadists beating down the doors to the torture chambers begging for jobs. Rather, as a recent book on torture by Edward Peters says, the institution of torture creates sadists; the weight of a culture, Peters suggests, is necessary to recruit torturers. You have to convince people that they are working for a great goal in order to get them to overcome their repugnance to the task of causing physical pain to another person. Usually the great goal is the preservation of society, and the victim is presented to the torturer as being in some way out to destroy it.

From another point of view, what's horrifying is how easily you can persuade someone that he is working for the common good. Perhaps the most appalling psychological experiment of modern times, by Stanley Milgram, showed that ordinary, decent people in New Haven, Connecticut, could be brought to the point of inflicting (as they thought) severe electric shocks on other people in obedience to an authority and in pursuit of a goal, the advancement of knowledge, of which they approved. Milgram used — some would say abused — the prestige of science and the university to make his point, but his point is chilling nonetheless. We can cluck over torture, but the evidence at least suggests that with intelligent handling most of us could be brought to do it ourselves.

In the Middle Ages, Milgram's experiment would have had no point. It would have shocked no one that people were capable of cruelty in the interest of something they believed in. That was as it should be. Only recently in

---

[1]*Soins esthétiques:* Literally beauty cares; that is, beauty treatments or cosmetic aids. [Eds.]

the history of human thought has the avoidance of cruelty moved to the forefront of ethics. "Putting cruelty first," as Judith Shklar says in *Ordinary Vices,* is comparatively new. The belief that the "pursuit of happiness" is one of man's inalienable rights, the idea that "cruel and unusual punishment" is an evil in itself, the Benthamite[2] notion that behavior should be guided by what will produce the greatest happiness for the greatest number—all these principles are only two centuries old. They were born with the eighteenth-century democratic revolutions. And in two hundred years they have not been universally accepted. Wherever people believe strongly in some cause, they will justify torture—not just the Nazis, but the French in Algeria.

Many people who wouldn't hurt a fly have annexed to fashion the imagery of torture—the thongs and spikes and metal studs—hence reducing it to the frivolous and transitory. Because torture has been in the mainstream and not on the margins of history, nothing could be healthier. For torture to be merely kinky would be a big advance. Exhibitions like the one I saw in Paris, which presented itself as educational, may be guilty of pandering to the tastes they deplore. Solemnity may be the wrong tone. If taking one's goals too seriously is the danger, the best discouragement of torture may be a radical hedonism that denies that any goal is worth the means, that refuses to allow the nobly abstract to seduce us from the sweetness of the concrete. Give people a good croissant and a good cup of coffee in the morning. Give them an occasional facial and a plate of escargots. Marie Antoinette picked a bad moment to say "Let them eat cake," but I've often thought she was on the right track.

All of which brings me back to Paris, for Paris exists in the imagination   10
of much of the world as the capital of pleasure—of fun, food, art, folly, seduction, gallantry, and beauty. Paris is civilization's reminder to itself that nothing leads you less wrong than your awareness of your own pleasure and a genial desire to spread it around. In that sense the myth of Paris constitutes a moral touchstone, standing for the selfish frivolity that helps keep priorities straight.

QUESTIONS

1. In the first two paragraphs of her essay, Rose lists more than thirty different tools of torture, and as she moves further into her list, she explains how each tool works and what kinds of torture it produces. Why do you think she goes into such elaborate detail? Why doesn't she confine herself to the tools she discusses in the first paragraph? How did you feel as you read these two paragraphs?

---

[2]*Benthamite:* One who believes in the social policies of the nineteenth century English philosopher Jeremy Bentham, who propounded the idea of the greatest good for the greatest number of people. [Eds.]

2. When Rose considers some tools of pleasure at the beauty salon, she also devotes two paragraphs (4 and 5) to her discussion, but the list of things she considers is shorter than her list of torture devices. Why do you suppose she is less detailed about pleasure?

3. Rose's reflections seem to be based in part on a supposition that tools of beauty (or pleasure) and tools of torture are the flip side of each other. What evidence and reasoning does she offer for this idea? In paragraph 9, she also seems to suggest that a widespread love of pleasure might be sufficient to put an end to torture. What evidence and reasoning does she offer for this idea?

4. In paragraphs 6 through 8, Rose is primarily concerned with exploring the origins and motivations for torture. What key points does she make in each paragraph, and what evidence does she offer in each case?

5. In paragraph 1, Rose names several tools of torture without explaining how they work. Research two or three of these tools, and then write an essay that compares and contrasts their origin, design, and effectiveness.

6. Though Rose focuses on medieval tools of torture, such tools also have been used more recently. Investigate two or three tools used in the twentieth century, and write an essay comparing and contrasting them to medieval tools of torture.

MAKING CONNECTIONS

How do Rose's ideas about the causes of sadistic behavior compare with those of Stanley Milgriam (p. 379), whom she discusses in her essay?

WHAT DID YOU DO IN THE WAR, GRANDMA?
A Flashback to August 1945

Zoë Tracy Hardy

Born in 1927 and raised in the Midwest, Zoë Tracy Hardy was one of millions of young women who worked in defense plants during World War II. Considered at first to be surrogates for male workers, these women — sometimes called "Rosie the Riveters" — soon were building bombers that their supervisors declared "equal in the construction [to] those turned out by experienced workmen in the plant's other departments," as a news feature at the time stated. After the eventful summer described in the following essay, Hardy finished college, married, and began teaching college English in Arizona, Guam, and Colorado. This essay first appeared in the August 1985 issue of Ms. *magazine — exactly forty years after the end of World War II.*

It was unseasonably cool that day in May, 1945, when I left my mother and father and kid brother in eastern Iowa and took the bus all the way to Omaha to help finish the war. I was 18, and had just completed my first year at the University of Iowa without distinction. The war in Europe had ended in April; the war against the Japanese still raged. I wanted to go where something *real* was being done to end this bitter war that had always been part of my adolescence.

I arrived in Omaha at midnight. The YWCA, where I promised my family I would get a room, was closed until 7 A.M., so I curled up in a cracked maroon leather chair in the crowded, smoky waiting room of the bus station.

In the morning I set off on foot for the YWCA, dragging a heavy suitcase and carrying my favorite hat trimmed in daisies in a large round hatbox. An hour of lugging and resting brought me to the Y, a great Victorian house of dark brick, where I paid two weeks in advance (most of my money) for board and a single room next to a bathroom that I would share with eight other girls. I surrendered my red and blue food-ration stamp books and my sugar coupons to the cook who would keep them as long as I stayed there.

I had eaten nothing but a wartime candy bar since breakfast at home the day before, but breakfast at the Y was already over. So, queasy and light-headed, I went back out into the cold spring day to find my job. I set out for the downtown office of the Glenn L. Martin Company. It was at their plant south of the city that thousands of workers, in around-the-clock shifts, built the famous B-29 bombers, the great Superfortresses, which the papers said would end the war.

I filled out an application and thought about the women welders and riveters and those who operated machine presses to help put the Superfortresses together. I grew shakier by the minute, more and more certain I was unqualified for any job here.

My interview was short. The personnel man was unconcerned about my total lack of skills. If I passed the physical, I could have a job in the Reproduction Department, where the blueprints were handled.

Upstairs in a gold-walled banquet room furnished with examination tables and hospital screens, a nurse sat me on a stool to draw a blood sample from my arm. I watched my blood rolling slowly into the needle. The gold walls wilted in the distance, and I slumped forward in a dead faint.

A grandfatherly doctor waved ammonia under my nose, and said if I would go to a café down the street and eat the complete 50-cent breakfast, I had the job.

The first week in the Reproduction Department, I learned to cut and fold enormous blueprints as they rolled from a machine that looked like a giant washing machine wringer. Then I was moved to a tall, metal contraption with a lurid light glowing from its interior. An ammonia guzzler, it spewed out smelly copies of specifications so hot my finger-tips burned when I touched them. I called it the dragon, and when I filled it with ammonia, the fumes reminded me of gold walls dissolving before my eyes. I took all my breaks outdoors, even when it was raining.

My boss, Mr. Johnson,[1] was a sandy-haired man of about 40, who spoke pleasantly when he came around to say hello and to check our work. Elsie, his secretary, a cool redhead, seldom spoke to any of us and spent most of her time in the darkroom developing negatives and reproducing photographs.

One of my coworkers in Reproduction was Mildred, a tall dishwater blond with a horsey, intelligent face. She was the first woman I'd ever met with an earthy unbridled tongue.

When I first arrived, Mildred warned me always to knock on the darkroom door before going in because Mr. Johnson and Elsie did a lot of screwing in there. I didn't believe her, I thought we were supposed to knock to give Elsie time to protect her negatives from the sudden light. "Besides," I said, "there isn't room to lie down in there." Mildred laughed until tears squeezed from the corners of her eyes. "You poor kid," she said. "Don't you *know* you don't have to lie down?"

I was stunned. "But it's easier if you do," I protested, defensive about my sex education. My mother, somewhat ahead of her time, had always

---

[1]All names but the author's have been changed.

been explicit in her explanations, and I had read "Lecture 14," an idyllic description of lovemaking being passed around among freshman girls in every dormitory in the country.

"Sitting, standing, any quick way you can in time of war," Mildred winked wickedly. She was as virginal as I, but what she said reminded us of the steady dearth of any day-to-day presence of young men in our lives.

We were convinced that the war would be over by autumn. We were   15
stepping up the napalm and incendiary bombing of the Japanese islands, the British were now coming to our aid in the Pacific, and the Japanese Navy was being reduced to nothing in some of the most spectacular sea battles in history.

Sometimes, after lunch, I went into the assembly areas to see how the skeletons of the B-29s were growing from our blueprints. At first there were enormous stark ribs surrounded by scaffolding two and three stories high. A few days later there was aluminum flesh over the ribs and wings sprouting from stubs on the fuselage. Women in overalls and turbans, safety glasses, and steel-toed shoes scrambled around the wings with riveting guns and welding torches, fitting fuel tanks in place. Instructions were shouted at them by hoarse, paunchy old men in hard hats. I cheered myself by thinking how we were pouring it on, a multitude of us together creating this great bird to end the war.

Away from the plant, however, optimism sometimes failed me. My room at the Y was bleak. I wrote letters to my unofficial fiancé and to other young men in the service who had been friends and classmates. Once in a while I attempted to study, thinking I would redeem my mediocre year at the university.

During those moments when I sensed real homesickness lying in wait, I would plan something to do with Betty and Celia, friends from high school, who had moved to Omaha "for the duration" and had jobs as secretaries for a large moving and storage company. Their small apartment was upstairs in an old frame house in Benson, a northwest suburb. Celia and Betty and I cooked, exchanged news from servicemen we all knew and talked about plans for the end of the war. Betty was engaged to her high school sweetheart, a soldier who had been wounded in Germany and who might be coming home soon. We guessed she would be the first one of us to be married, and we speculated, in the careful euphemisms of "well-brought-up girls," about her impending introduction to sex.

By the first of July, work and the pace of life had lost momentum. The war news seemed to repeat itself without advancing, as day after day battles were fought around jungly Pacific islands that all seemed identical and unreal.

At the plant, I was moved from the dragon to a desk job, a promotion   20
of sorts. I sat on a high stool in a cubicle of pigeonholed cabinets and filed blueprints, specs, and deviations in the proper holes. While I was working, I saw no one and couldn't talk to anybody.

In mid-July Betty got married. Counsel from our elders was always to wait — wait until things settle down after the war. Harold, still recuperating from shrapnel wounds, asked Betty not to wait.

Celia and I attended the ceremony on a sizzling afternoon in a musty Presbyterian church. Harold was very serious, gaunt-faced and thin in his loose-hanging Army uniform. Betty, a fair-skinned, blue-eyed brunet in a white street dress, looked pale and solemn. After the short ceremony, they left the church in a borrowed car. Someone had given them enough gasoline stamps for a honeymoon trip to a far-off cabin on the shore of a piney Minnesota lake.

Celia and I speculated on Betty's introduction to lovemaking. I had "Lecture 14" in mind and hoped she would like lovemaking, especially way off in Minnesota, far from the sweltering city and the war. Celia thought it didn't matter much whether a girl liked it or not, as long as other important parts of marriage got off to a good start.

That weekend Celia and I took a walk in a park and watched a grandfather carefully pump a seesaw up and down for his small grandson. We saw a short, middle-aged sailor walking with a sad-faced young woman who towered over him. "A whore," Celia said. "Probably one of those from the Hotel Bianca." Celia had been in Omaha longer than I and knew more of its secrets.

I wanted, right then, to see someone young and male and healthy cross   25
the grass under the trees, someone without wounds and without a cap, someone with thick disheveled hair that hadn't been militarily peeled down to the green skin on the back of his skull. Someone wearing tennis shorts to show strong, hair-matted legs, and a shirt with an open neck and short sleeves revealing smooth, hard muscles and tanned skin. Someone who would pull me out of this gloom with a wide spontaneous smile as he passed.

In the next few days, the tempo of the summer changed subtly. From friends stationed in the Pacific, I began to get letters free from rectangular holes where military censors had snipped out "sensitive" words. Our Navy was getting ready to surround the Japanese islands with a starvation blockade, and our B-29s had bombed the industrial heart of the country. We were dropping leaflets warning the Japanese people that we would incinerate hundreds of thousands of them by firebombing 11 of their major cities. Rumors rippled through the plant back in Omaha. The Japanese Empire would collapse in a matter of weeks, at most.

One Friday night, with Celia's help, I moved out of the Y to Celia's apartment in Benson. We moved by streetcar. Celia carried my towels and my full laundry bag in big rolls, one under each arm, and wore my straw picture hat with the daisies, which bobbled wildly on top of her head. My hatbox was crammed with extra underwear and the war letters I was determined to save. When we climbed aboard the front end of the streetcar, I dropped the hatbox, spilled an armload of books down the aisle, and banged my suitcase into the knees of an elderly man who was trying to help me retrieve them.

We began to laugh, at everything, at nothing, and were still laughing when we hauled everything off the car and down one block to the apartment, the daisies all the while wheeling recklessly on Celia's head.

It was a good move. Summer nights were cooler near the country, and so quiet I could hear the crickets. The other upstairs apartment was occupied by Celia's older sister, Andrea, and her husband, Bob, who hadn't been drafted.

Late in July, an unusual thing happened at the plant. Mr. Johnson asked   30 us to work double shifts for a few days. The situation was urgent, he said, and he wanted 100 percent cooperation from the Reproduction Department, even if it meant coming to work when we felt sick or postponing something that was personally important to us.

The next morning no one from the day shift was missing, and the place was full of people from the graveyard shift. Some of the time I worked in my cubicle counting out special blueprints and deviations. The rest of the time I helped the crews sweating over the blueprint machine cut out prints that contained odd lines and numbers that I had never seen before. Their shapes were different, too, and there was no place for them in the numbered pigeonholes of my cubicle. Some prints were small, about four inches square. Mildred said they were so cute she might tuck one in her shoe and smuggle it home as a souvenir even if it meant going to the federal pen if she got caught.

During those days I learned to nap on streetcars. I had to get up at 4:30, bolt down breakfast, and catch the first car to rumble out of the darkness at 5:15. The double shift wasn't over until 11:30, so I got home about one in the morning.

The frenzy at the plant ended as suddenly as it had begun. Dazed with fatigue, I slept through most of a weekend and hoped we had pushed ourselves to some limit that would lift us over the last hump of the war.

On Monday the familiar single shift was not quite the same. We didn't know what we had done, but an undercurrent of anticipation ran through the department because of those double shifts — and the news. The papers told of factories that were already gearing up to turn out refrigerators, radios, and automobiles instead of bombs and planes.

In Reproduction, the pace began to slacken. Five hundred thirty-six   35 B-29s, planes we had put together on the Nebraska prairie, had firebombed the principal islands of the Japanese Empire: Hokkaido, Honshu, Kyushu, Shikoku. We had reduced to ashes more than 15 square miles of the heart of Tokyo. The battered and burned Japanese were so near defeat that there couldn't be much left for us to do. With surprising enthusiasm, I began to plan for my return to college.

Going home on the streetcar the first Tuesday afternoon in August, I heard about a puzzling new weapon. Some excited people at the end of the car were jabbering about it, saying the Japanese would be forced to surrender in a matter of hours.

When I got home, Andrea, her round bespectacled face flushed, met me at the head of the stairs. "Oh, come and listen to the radio — it's a new bomb — it's almost over!"

I sat down in her living room and listened. There was news, then music, then expanded news. Over and over the newscaster reported that the United

States had unlocked a secret of the universe and unleashed a cosmic force — from splitting atoms of uranium — on the industrial seaport of Hiroshima. Most of the city had been leveled to the ground, and many of its inhabitants disintegrated to dust in an instant by a single bomb. "Our scientists have changed the history of the world," the newscaster said. He sounded as if he could not believe it himself.

We ate dinner from our laps and continued to listen as the news pounded on for an hour, then two, then three. I tried, at last, to *think* about it. In high school physics we had already learned that scientists were close to splitting an atom. We imagined that a cupful of the tremendous energy from such a phenomenon might run a car back and forth across the entire country dozens of times. I could visualize that. But I could not imagine how such energy put into a small bomb would cause the kind of destruction described on the radio.

About nine, I walked over to McCollum's grocery store to buy an   40
evening paper. The headline said we had harnessed atomic power. I skimmed through a front page story. Science had ushered us into a strange new world, and President Truman had made two things clear: the bomb had created a monster that could wipe out civilization; and some protection against this monster would have to be found before its secret could be given to the world.

Back out in the dark street, I hesitated. For the first time I could remember, I felt a rush of terror at being out in the night alone.

When I got back to the apartment, I made a pot of coffee and sat down at the kitchen table to read the rest of the paper. President Truman had said: "The force from which the sun draws its power has been loosed against those who brought war to the Far East. . . . If they do not now accept our terms they may expect a rain of ruin from the air the like of which has never been seen on this earth." New and more powerful bombs were now being developed.

I read everything, looking for some speculation from someone about how we were going to live in this new world. There was nothing. About midnight Andrea knocked on my open door to get my attention. She stood there a moment in her nightgown and curlers looking at me rather oddly. She asked if I was all right.

I said yes, just trying to soak it all in.

Gently she told me I had better go to bed and think about how soon   45
the war would be over.

The next day Reproduction was nearly demolished by the spirit of celebration. The *Enola Gay,* the plane that had dropped the bomb, was one of ours. By Thursday morning the United States had dropped a second atomic bomb, an even bigger one, on an industrial city, Nagasaki, and the Russians had declared war on Japan.

At the end of the day, Mr. Johnson asked us to listen to the radio for announcements about when to return to work, then shook hands all around. "You've all done more than you know to help win the war," he said.

We said tentative good-byes. I went home and over to McCollum's for an evening paper. An Army Strategic Air Forces expert said that there was no comparison between the fire caused by the atomic bomb and that of a normal conflagration. And there were other stories about radiation, like X-rays, that might cripple and poison living things for hours, weeks, maybe years, until they died.

I went to bed late and had nightmares full of flames and strange dry gale winds. The next noon I got up, exhausted, and called Mildred. She said they were still saying not to report to work until further notice. "It's gonna bore our tails off," she moaned. "I don't know how long we can sit around here just playing hearts." I could hear girls laughing in the background.

"Mildred," I blurted anxiously, "do you think we should have done this   50
thing?"

"Why not? Better us than somebody else, kid."

I reminded her that we knew the Japanese were finished weeks ago and asked her if it wasn't sort of like kicking a dead horse — brutally.

"Look," she said. "The war is really over even if the bigwigs haven't said so yet. What more do you want?"

The evening paper finally offered a glimmer of relief. One large headline said that serious questions about the morality of *Americans* using such a weapon were being raised by some civilians of note and some churchmen. I went to bed early and lay listening to the crickets and thinking about everyone coming home — unofficial fiancés, husbands, fathers, brothers — all filling the empty spaces between kids and women and old men, putting a balance in our lives we hadn't known in years.

Yet the bomb haunted me. I was still awake when the windowpanes   55
lightened up at daybreak.

It was all over on August 14, 1945. Unconditional surrender.

For hours at a time, the bomb's importance receded in the excitement of that day. Streetcar bells clanged up and down the streets; we heard sirens, whistles, church bells. A newscaster described downtown Omaha as a free-for-all. Perfect strangers were hugging each other in the streets; some were dancing. Churches had thrown open their doors, and people were streaming in and out, offering prayers of thanksgiving. Taverns were giving away free drinks.

Andrew wanted us to have a little whiskey, even though we were under age, because there would never be another day like this as long as we lived. I hated the first taste of it, but as we chattered away, inventing wild, gratifying futures, I welcomed the muffler it wrapped around the ugliness of the bomb.

In the morning Mildred called to say our jobs were over and that we should report to the plant to turn in our badges and get final paychecks. She had just talked to Mr. Johnson, who told her that those funny blueprints we had made during double shift had something to do with the bomb.

"Well, honey," she said, "I don't understand atomic energy, but old   60
jazzy Johnson said we had to work like that to get the *Enola Gay* and the *thing* to go together."

I held my breath, waiting for Mildred to say she was kidding, as usual. Ordinary 19- and 20-year-old girls were not, not in the United States of America, required to work night and day to help launch scientific monsters that would catapult us all into a precarious "strange new world"—forever. But I knew in my bones that Mildred, forthright arrow-straight Mildred, was only telling me what I had already, unwillingly, guessed.

After a long silence she said, "Well, kid, give me your address in Iowa, and I'll send you a Christmas card for auld lang syne."

I wanted to cry as we exchanged addresses. I liked Mildred. I hated the gap that I now sensed would always be between me and people like her.

"It's been nice talking dirty to you all summer," she said.

"Thanks." I hung up, slipped down the stairs, and walked past the   65
streetcar line out into the country.

The whole countryside was sundrenched, fragrant with sweet clover and newly mown alfalfa. I leaned against a fence post and tried to think.

The President had said we had unleashed the great secret of the universe in this way, to shorten the war and save American lives. Our commitment to defeat the Japanese was always clear to me. They had attacked us first. But we had already firebombed much of the Japanese Empire to char. That seemed decisive enough, and terrible enough.

If he had asked me whether I would work very hard to help bring this horror into being, knowing it would shorten the war but put the world into jeopardy for all time, how would I have answered?

I would have said, "No. With all due respect, Sir, how could such a thing make a just end to our just cause?"

But the question had never been asked of us. And I stood now, in the   70
warm sun, gripping a splintery fence post, outraged by our final insignificance—all of us who had worked together in absolute trust to end the war.

An old cow stood near the fence switching her tail. I looked at her great, uncomprehending brown eyes and began to sob.

After a while I walked back to the apartment, mentally packing my suitcase and tying up my hatbox of war letters. I knew it was going to be very hard, from now on, for the whole world to take care of itself.

I wanted very much to go home.

Questions

1. How does Hardy's attitude toward the war change in this essay? What event causes her to reevaluate her attitude?
2. Describe Hardy's feelings about the introduction of atomic power into her world. Are they optimistic or pessimistic?
3. "You've all done more than you know to help win the war," Hardy's boss tells her (paragraph 47). How does she react to the fact that she was not informed of the purpose of her work? How does her reaction differ from that of her coworker, Mildred?

4. As Hardy's attitude toward war changes, her attitude toward sex changes as well. Trace this change in attitude. What connection, if any, do you see between the two?

5. Is this essay merely a personal reminiscence, or does the author have a larger purpose? Explain what you think her purpose is.

6. This essay was published nearly twenty years ago and nearly forty years after the events it describes. Are Hardy's fears and speculations (on atomic power, on the authority of the government, on sex) dated in any way, or are they still relevant today? Explain your answer.

7. Have you, like Hardy, ever wondered about the larger social implications of any job that you've held or that a friend or parent holds? Write an essay like Hardy's reflecting on that job and describing how your attitude changed as you placed the job in a larger context.

MAKING CONNECTIONS

Could Hardy's essay be described as a "pilgrimage" to a particular intellectual or political position, somewhat like Martin Luther King Jr.'s "Pilgrimage to Nonviolence" (p. 106)? How fair would that retitling be to Hardy's essay? What aspects of pilgrimage do you find in it?

Sciences and Technologies

A MASK ON THE FACE OF DEATH

Richard Selzer

Richard Selzer (b. 1928) is the son of a general practitioner father and a singer mother, both of whom wanted their son to follow in their footsteps. At ten he began sneaking into his father's office to look at his medical textbooks, where he discovered "the rich alliterative language of medicine — words such as cerebellum which, when said aloud, melt in the mouth and drip from the end of the tongue like chocolate." After his father's death, he decided to become a doctor and was for many years a professor of surgery at Yale Medical School. Only after working as a doctor for many decades did he begin to write. About the similarities between surgery and writing he says, "In surgery, it is the body that is being opened up and put back together. In writing it is the whole world that is taken in for repairs, then put back in working order piece by piece." His articles have appeared in Vanity Fair, Harper's, Esquire, *and* The New York Times Magazine. *His books include the short story collections* Rituals of Surgery *(1974) and* The Doctor Stories *(1998); the essay collections* Mortal Lessons *(1976),* Raising the Dead *(1994), and* The Exact Location of the Soul *(2001); and an autobiography,* Down from Troy *(1992). This essay appeared in* Life *in 1988.*

It is ten o'clock at night as we drive up to the Copacabana, a dilapidated brothel on the rue Dessalines in the red-light district of Port-au-Prince. My guide is a young Haitian, Jean-Bernard. Ten years before, J-B tells me, at the age of fourteen, "like every good Haitian boy" he had been brought here by his older cousins for his *rite de passage*. From the car to the entrance, we are accosted by a half dozen men and women for sex. We enter, go down a long hall that breaks upon a cavernous room with a stone floor. The cubicles of the prostitutes, I am told, are in an attached wing of the building. Save for a red-purple glow from small lights on the walls, the place is unlit. Dark shapes float by, each with a blindingly white stripe of teeth. Latin music is blaring. We take seats at the table farthest from the door. Just outside, there is the rhythmic lapping of the Caribbean Sea. About twenty men are seated at the tables or lean against the walls. Brightly dressed women, singly or in twos or threes, stroll about, now and then exchanging banter with the men. It is as though we have been deposited in act two of Bizet's *Carmen*. If this place isn't Lillas Pastia's tavern, what is it?

Within minutes, three light-skinned young women arrive at our table. They are very beautiful and young and lively. Let them be Carmen, Mercedes and Frasquita.

"I want the old one," says Frasquita, ruffling my hair. The women laugh uproariously.

"Don't bother looking any further," says Mercedes. "We are the prettiest ones."

"We only want to talk," I tell her.   5

"Aaah, aaah," she crows. "*Massissi*. You are *massissi*." It is the contemptuous Creole term for homosexual. If we want only to talk, we must be gay. Mercedes and Carmen are slender, each weighing one hundred pounds or less. Frasquita is tall and hefty. They are dressed for work: red taffeta, purple chiffon and black sequins. Among them a thousand gold bracelets and earrings multiply every speck of light. Their bare shoulders are like animated lamps gleaming in the shadowy room. Since there is as yet no business, the women agree to sit with us. J-B orders beer and cigarettes. We pay each woman $10.

"Where are you from?" I begin.

"We are Dominican."

"Do you miss your country?"

"Oh, yes, we do." Six eyes go muzzy with longing. "Our country is   10
the most beautiful in the world. No country is like the Dominican. And it doesn't stink like this one."

"Then why don't you work there? Why come to Haiti?"

"Santo Domingo has too many whores. All beautiful, like us. All light-skinned. The Haitian men like to sleep with light women."

"Why is that?"

"Because always, the whites have all the power and the money. The black men can imagine they do, too, when they have us in bed."

Eleven o'clock. I look around the room that is still sparsely peopled   15
with men.

"It isn't getting any busier," I say. Frasquita glances over her shoulder. Her eyes drill the darkness.

"It is still early," she says.

"Could it be that the men are afraid of getting sick?" Frasquita is offended.

"Sick! They do not get sick from us. We are healthy, strong. Every week we go for a checkup. Besides, we know how to tell if we are getting sick."

"I mean sick with AIDS." The word sets off a hurricane of taffeta, chif-   20
fon and gold jewelry. They are all gesticulation and fury. It is Carmen who
speaks.

"AIDS!" Her lips curl about the syllable. "There is no such thing. It is a
false disease invented by the American government to take advantage of the
poor countries. The American President hates poor people, so now he makes
up AIDS to take away the little we have." The others nod vehemently.

"*Mira, mon cher.* Look, my dear," Carmen continues. "One day the
police came here. Believe me, they are worse than the *tonton macoutes* with
their submachine guns. They rounded up one hundred and five of us and
they took our blood. That was a year ago. None of us have died, you see?
We are all still here. *Mira,* we sleep with all the men and we are not sick."

"But aren't there some of you who have lost weight and have diarrhea?"

"One or two, maybe. But they don't eat. That is why they are weak."

"Only the men die," says Mercedes. "They stop eating, so they die. It   25
is hard to kill a woman."

"Do you eat well?"

"Oh, yes, don't worry, we do. We eat like poor people, but we eat."
There is a sudden scream from Frasquita. She points to a large rat that has
emerged from beneath our table.

"My God!" she exclaims. "It is big like a pig." They burst into laughter. For a moment the women fall silent. There is only the restlessness of
their many bracelets. I give them each another $10.

"Are many of the men here bisexual?"

"Too many. They do it for money. Afterward, they come to us."   30
Carmen lights a cigarette and looks down at the small lace handkerchief she
has been folding and unfolding with immense precision on the table. All at
once she turns it over as though it were the ace of spades.

"*Mira, blanc . . .* look, white man," she says in a voice suddenly full
of foreboding. Her skin seems to darken to coincide with the tone of her
voice.

"*Mira,* soon many Dominican women will die in Haiti!"

"Die of what?"

She shrugs. "It is what they do to us."

"Carmen," I say, "if you knew that you had AIDS, that your blood was   35
bad, would you still sleep with men?" Abruptly, she throws back her head
and laughs. It is the same laughter with which Frasquita had greeted the rat
at our feet. She stands and the others follow.

"*Méchant!* You wicked man," she says. Then, with terrible solemnity,
"You don't know anything."

"But you are killing the Haitian men," I say.

"As for that," she says, "everyone is killing everyone else." All at once,
I want to know everything about these three—their childhood, their
dreams, what they do in the afternoon, what they eat for lunch.

"Don't leave," I say. "Stay a little more." Again, I reach for my wallet.
But they are gone, taking all the light in the room with them—Mercedes and

Carmen to sit at another table where three men have been waiting. Frasquita is strolling about the room. Now and then, as if captured by the music, she breaks into a few dance steps, snapping her fingers, singing to herself.

Midnight. And the Copacabana is filling up. Now it is like any other seedy nightclub where men and women go hunting. We get up to leave. In the center a couple are dancing a *méringue*. He is the most graceful dancer I have ever watched; she, the most voluptuous. Together they seem to be riding the back of the music as it gallops to a precisely sexual beat. Closer up, I see that the man is short of breath, sweating. All at once, he collapses into a chair. The woman bends over him, coaxing, teasing, but he is through. A young man with a long polished stick blocks my way.

"I come with you?" he asks. "Very good time. You say yes? Ten dollars? Five?"

I have been invited by Dr. Jean William Pape to attend the AIDS clinic of which he is the director. Nothing from the outside of the low white-washed structure would suggest it as a medical facility. Inside, it is divided into many small cubicles and a labyrinth of corridors. At nine A.M. the hall-ways are already full of emaciated silent men and women, some sitting on the few benches, the rest leaning against the walls. The only sounds are sub-dued moans of discomfort interspersed with coughs. How they eat us with their eyes as we pass.

The room where Pape and I work is perhaps ten feet by ten. It contains a desk, two chairs and a narrow wooden table that is covered with a sheet that will not be changed during the day. The patients are called in one at a time, asked how they feel and whether there is any change in their symptoms, then examined on the table. If the patient is new to the clinic, he or she is questioned about sexual activities.

A twenty-seven-year-old man whose given name is Miracle enters. He is wobbly, panting, like a groggy boxer who has let down his arms and is waiting for the last punch. He is neatly dressed and wears, despite the heat, a heavy woolen cap. When he removes it, I see that his hair is thin, dull reddish and straight. It is one of the signs of AIDS in Haiti, Pape tells me. The man's skin is covered with a dry itchy rash. Throughout the interview and examination he scratches himself slowly, absentmindedly. The rash is called prurigo. It is another symptom of AIDS in Haiti. This man has had diarrhea for six months. The laboratory reports that the diarrhea is due to an organism called cryptosporidium, for which there is no treatment. The telltale rattling of the tuberculous moisture in his chest is audible without a stethoscope. He is like a leaky cistern that bubbles and froths. And, clearly, exhausted.

"Where do you live?" I ask.

"Kenscoff." A village in the hills above Port-au-Prince.

"How did you come here today?"

"I came on the *tap-tap*." It is the name given to the small buses that swarm the city, each one extravagantly decorated with religious slogans, icons, flowers, animals, all painted in psychedelic colors. I have never seen a *tap-tap* that was not covered with passengers as well, riding outside and hanging on. The vehicles are little masterpieces of contagion, if not of AIDS then of the multitude of germs which Haitian flesh is heir to. Miracle is given a prescription for a supply of Sera, which is something like Gatorade, and told to return in a month.

"*Mangé kou bêf*," says the doctor in farewell. "Eat like an ox." What can he mean? The man has no food or money to buy any. Even had he food, he has not the appetite to eat or the ability to retain it. To each departing patient the doctor will say the same words — "*Mangé kou bêf*." I see that it is his way of offering a hopeful goodbye.

"Will he live until his next appointment?" I ask.   50

"No." Miracle leaves to catch the *tap-tap* for Kenscoff.

Next is a woman of twenty-six who enters holding her right hand to her forehead in a kind of permanent salute. In fact, she is shielding her eye from view. This is her third visit to the clinic. I see that she is still quite well nourished.

"Now, you'll see something beautiful, tremendous," the doctor says. Once seated upon the table, she is told to lower her hand. When she does, I see that her right eye and its eyelid are replaced by a huge fungating ulcerated tumor, a side product of her AIDS. As she turns her head, the cluster of lymph glands in her neck to which the tumor has spread is thrown into relief. Two years ago she received a blood transfusion at a time when the country's main blood bank was grossly contaminated with AIDS. It has since been closed down. The only blood available in Haiti is a small supply procured from the Red Cross.

"Can you give me medicine?" the woman wails.

"No."   55

"Can you cut it away?"

"No."

"Is there radiation therapy?" I ask.

"No."

"Chemotherapy?" The doctor looks at me in what some might call   60
weary amusement. I see that there is nothing to do. She has come here because there is nowhere else to go.

"What will she do?"

"Tomorrow or the next day or the day after that she will climb up into the mountains to seek relief from the *houngan*, the voodoo priest, just as her slave ancestors did two hundred years ago."

Then comes a frail man in his thirties, with a strangely spiritualized face, like a child's. Pus runs from one ear onto his cheek, where it has dried and caked. He has trouble remembering, he tells us. In fact, he seems confused. It is from toxoplasmosis of the brain, an effect of his AIDS. This man is bisexual. Two years ago he engaged in oral sex with foreign men for money. As I palpate the swollen glands of his neck, a mosquito flies between our faces. I swat at it, miss. Just before coming to Haiti I had read that the AIDS virus had been isolated from a certain mosquito. The doctor senses my thought.

"Not to worry," he says. "So far as we know there has never been a case transmitted by insects."

"Yes," I say. "I see."   65

And so it goes until the last, the thirty-sixth AIDS patient has been seen. At the end of the day I am invited to wash my hands before leaving. I go down a long hall to a sink. I turn on the faucets but there is no water.

"But what about *you?*" I ask the doctor. "You are at great personal risk here—the tuberculosis, the other infections, no water to wash . . ." He shrugs, smiles faintly and lifts his hands palm upward.

We are driving up a serpiginous steep road into the barren mountains above Port-au-Prince. Even in the bright sunshine the countryside has the bloodless color of exhaustion and indifference. Our destination is the Baptist Mission Hospital, where many cases of AIDS have been reported. Along the road there are slow straggles of schoolchildren in blue uniforms who stretch out their hands as we pass and call out, "Give me something." Already a crowd of outpatients has gathered at the entrance to the mission compound. A tour of the premises reveals that in contrast to the aridity outside the gates, this is an enclave of productivity, lush with fruit trees and poinsettia.

The hospital is clean and smells of creosote. Of the forty beds, less than a third are occupied. In one male ward of twelve beds, there are two patients. The chief physician tells us that last year he saw ten cases of AIDS each week. Lately the number has decreased to four or five.

"Why is that?" we want to know.   70

"Because we do not admit them to the hospital, so they have learned not to come here."

"Why don't you admit them?"

"Because we would have nothing but AIDS here then. So we send them away."

"But I see that you have very few patients in bed."

"That is also true."   75

"Where do the AIDS patients go?"

"Some go to the clinic in Port-au-Prince or the general hospital in the city. Others go home to die or to the voodoo priest."

"Do the people with AIDS know what they have before they come here?"

"Oh, yes, they know very well, and they know there is nothing to be done for them."

Outside, the crowd of people is dispersing toward the gate. The clinic   80
has been canceled for the day. No one knows why. We are conducted to the office of the reigning American pastor. He is a tall, handsome Midwesterner with an ecclesiastical smile.

"It is voodoo that is the devil here." He warms to his subject. "It is a demonic religion, a cancer on Haiti. Voodoo is worse than AIDS. And it is one of the reasons for the epidemic. Did you know that in order for a man to become a *houngan* he must perform anal sodomy on another man? No, of course you didn't. And it doesn't stop there. The *houngans* tell the men that in order to appease the spirits they too must do the same thing. So you have ritualized homosexuality. That's what is spreading the AIDS." The pastor tells us of a nun who witnessed two acts of sodomy in a provincial hospital where she came upon a man sexually assaulting a houseboy and another man mounting a male patient in his bed.

"Fornication," he says. "It is Sodom and Gomorrah all over again, so what can you expect from these people?" Outside his office we are shown a cage of terrified, cowering monkeys to whom he coos affectionately. It is clear that he loves them. At the car, we shake hands.

"By the way," the pastor says, "what is your religion? Perhaps I am a kinsman?"

"While I am in Haiti," I tell him, "it will be voodoo or it will be nothing at all."

Abruptly, the smile breaks. It is as though a crack had suddenly   85
appeared in the face of an idol.

From the mission we go to the general hospital. In the heart of Port-au-Prince, it is the exact antithesis of the immaculate facility we have just left—filthy, crowded, hectic and staffed entirely by young interns and residents. Though it is associated with a medical school, I do not see any members of the faculty. We are shown around by Jocelyne, a young intern in a scrub suit. Each bed in three large wards is occupied. On the floor about the beds, hunkered in the posture of the innocent poor, are family members of the patients. In the corridor that constitutes the emergency room, someone lies on a stretcher receiving an intravenous infusion. She is hardly more than a cadaver.

"Where are the doctors in charge?" I ask Jocelyne. She looks at me questioningly.

"We are in charge."

"I mean your teachers, the faculty."

"They do not come here."   90

"What is wrong with that woman?"

"She has had diarrhea for three months. Now she is dehydrated." I ask the woman to open her mouth. Her throat is covered with the white plaques of thrush, a fungus infection associated with AIDS.

"How many AIDS patients do you see here?"

"Three or four a day. We send them home. Sometimes the families abandon them, then we must admit them to the hospital. Every day, then, a relative comes to see if the patient has died. They want to take the body. That is important to them. But they know very well that AIDS is contagious and they are afraid to keep them at home. Even so, once or twice a week the truck comes to take away the bodies. Many are children. They are buried in mass graves."

"Where do the wealthy patients go?"   95

"There is a private hospital called Canapé Vert. Or else they go to Miami. Most of them, rich and poor, do not go to the hospital. Most are never diagnosed."

"How do you know these people have AIDS?"

"We don't know sometimes. The blood test is inaccurate. There are many false positives and false negatives. Fifteen percent of those with the disease have negative blood tests. We go by their infections—tuberculosis, diarrhea, fungi, herpes, skin rashes. It is not hard to tell."

"Do they know what they have?"

"Yes. They understand at once and they are prepared to die."   100

"Do the patients know how AIDS is transmitted?"

"They know, but they do not like to talk about it. It is taboo. Their memories do not seem to reach back to the true origins of their disaster. It is understandable, is it not?"

"Whatever you write, don't hurt us any more than we have already been hurt." It is a young Haitian journalist with whom I am drinking a rum punch. He means that any further linkage of AIDS and Haiti in the media would complete the economic destruction of the country. The damage was done early in the epidemic when the Centers for Disease Control in Atlanta added Haitians to the three other high-risk groups—hemophiliacs, intravenous drug users and homosexual and bisexual men. In fact, Haitians are no more susceptible to AIDS than anyone else. Although the CDC removed Haitians from special scrutiny in 1985, the lucrative tourism on which so much of the country's economy was based was crippled. Along with tourism went much of the foreign business investment. Worst of all was the injury to the national pride. Suddenly Haiti was indicted as the source of AIDS in the western hemisphere.

What caused the misunderstanding was the discovery of a large number of Haitian men living in Miami with AIDS antibodies in their blood. They denied absolutely they were homosexuals. But the CDC investigators did not know that homosexuality is the strongest taboo in Haiti and that no man would ever admit to it. Bisexuality, however, is not uncommon. Many married men and heterosexually oriented males will occasionally seek out other men for sex. Further, many, if not most, Haitian men visit female prostitutes from time to time. It is not difficult to see that once the virus was set loose in Haiti, the spread would be swift through both genders.

Exactly how the virus of AIDS arrived is not known. Could it have been   105
brought home by the Cuban soldiers stationed in Angola and thence to Haiti, about fifty miles away? Could it have been passed on by the thousands of Haitians living in exile in Zaire, who later returned home or immigrated to the United States? Could it have come from the American and Canadian homosexual tourists, and, yes, even some U.S. diplomats who have traveled to the island to have sex with impoverished Haitian men all too willing to sell themselves to feed their families? Throughout the international gay community Haiti was known as a good place to go for sex.

On a private tip from an official at the Ministry of Tourism, J-B and I drive to a town some fifty miles from Port-au-Prince. The hotel is owned by two Frenchmen who are out of the country, one of the staff tells us. He is a man of about thirty and clearly he is desperately ill. Tottering, short of breath, he shows us about the empty hotel. The furnishings are opulent and extreme — tiger skins on the wall, a live leopard in the garden, a bedroom containing a giant bathtub with gold faucets. Is it the heat of the day or the heat of my imagination that makes these walls echo with the painful cries of pederasty?

The hotel where we are staying is in Pétionville, the fashionable suburb of Port-au-Prince. It is the height of the season but there are no tourists, only a dozen or so French and American businessmen. The swimming pool is used once or twice a day by a single person. Otherwise, the water remains undisturbed until dusk, when the fruit bats come down to drink in midswoop. The hotel keeper is an American. He is eager to set me straight on Haiti.

"What did and should attract foreign investment is a combination of reliable weather, an honest and friendly populace, low wages and multilingual managers."

"What spoiled it?"

"Political instability and a bad American press about AIDS." He pauses, then adds: "To which I hope you won't be contributing."   110

"What about just telling the truth?" I suggest.

"Look," he says, "there is no more danger of catching AIDS in Haiti than in New York or Santo Domingo. It is not where you are but what you do that counts." Agreeing, I ask if he had any idea that much of the tourism in Haiti during the past few decades was based on sex.

"No idea whatsoever. It was only recently that we discovered that that was the case."

"How is it that you hoteliers, restaurant owners and the Ministry of Tourism did not know what *tout*[1] Haiti knew?"

"Look. All I know is that this is a middle-class, family-oriented hotel.   115
We don't allow guests to bring women, or for that matter men, into their rooms. If they did, we'd ask them to leave immediately."

At five A.M. the next day the telephone rings in my room. A Creole-accented male voice.

"Is the lady still with you, sir?"

"There is no lady here."

"In your room, sir, the lady I allowed to go up with a package?"

"There is no lady here, I tell you."   120

At seven A.M. I stop at the front desk. The clerk is a young man.

"Was it you who called my room at five o'clock?"

---

[1] *tout*: All. [Eds.]

"Sorry," he says with a smile. "It was a mistake, sir. I meant to ring the room next door to yours." Still smiling, he holds up his shushing finger.

Next to Dr. Pape, director of the AIDS clinic, Bernard Liautaud, a dermatologist, is the most knowledgeable Haitian physician on the subject of the epidemic. Together, the two men have published a dozen articles on AIDS in international medical journals. In our meeting they present me with statistics:

- There are more than one thousand documented cases of AIDS in Haiti, and as many as one hundred thousand carriers of the virus.

- Eighty-seven percent of AIDS is now transmitted heterosexually. While it is true that the virus was introduced via the bisexual community, that route has decreased to 10 percent or less.

- Sixty percent of the wives or husbands of AIDS patients tested positive for the antibody.

- Fifty percent of the prostitutes tested in the Port-au-Prince area are infected.

- Eighty percent of the men with AIDS have had contact with prostitutes.

- The projected number of active cases in four years is ten thousand. (Since my last visit, the Haitian Medical Association broke its silence on the epidemic by warning that one million of the country's six million people could be carriers by 1992.)

The two doctors have more to tell. "The crossing over of the plague   125
from the homosexual to the heterosexual community will follow in the United States within two years. This, despite the hesitation to say so by those who fear to sow panic among your population. In Haiti, because bisexuality is more common, there was an early crossover into the general population. The trend, inevitably, is the same in the two countries."

"What is there to do, then?"

"Only education, just as in America. But here the Haitians reject the use of condoms. Only the men who are too sick to have sex are celibate."

"What is to be the end of it?"

"When enough heterosexuals of the middle and upper classes die, perhaps there will be the panic necessary for the people to change their sexual lifestyles."

This evening I leave Haiti. For two weeks I have fastened myself to this   130
lovely fragile land like an ear pressed to the ground. It is a country to break a traveler's heart. It occurs to me that I have not seen a single jogger. Such a public expenditure of energy while everywhere else strength is ebbing— it would be obscene. In my final hours, I go to the Cathédrale of Sainte Trinité, the inner walls of which are covered with murals by Haiti's most

renowned artists. Here are all the familiar Bible stories depicted in naïveté and piety, and all in such an exuberance of color as to tax the capacity of the retina to receive it, as though all the vitality of Haiti had been turned to paint and brushed upon these walls. How to explain this efflorescence at a time when all else is lassitude and inertia? Perhaps one day the plague will be rendered in poetry, music, painting, but not now. Not now.

QUESTIONS

1. Summarize the scene at the Copacabana. Which details are memorable? Why does Selzer spend so much time with Carmen, Mercedes, and Frasquita? Why are their attitudes toward AIDS so important?
2. Selzer writes at great length about his visit to the AIDS clinic directed by Dr. Jean William Pape. What does Selzer learn from observing patients at this clinic? What does Selzer learn about AIDS from the doctor at work?
3. A young Haitian journalist tells Selzer, "Whatever you write, don't hurt us any more than we have already been hurt" (paragraph 103). What is the significance of this request? After reading Selzer's essay, do you think Selzer has honored this request?
4. In the final paragraph of the essay, Selzer writes, "For two weeks I have fastened myself to this lovely fragile land like an ear pressed to the ground. It is a country to break a traveler's heart." What has Selzer learned about the politics of AIDS from his journey to Haiti?
5. Look at the various scenes and vignettes Selzer offers his readers. How does he connect these different scenes? How does this structure succeed in presenting his reflections?
6. What have you learned about the politics of AIDS from reading Selzer's essay? Write an essay reflecting on Selzer's essay.
7. Selzer offers his reflections as a way of justifying his strong feelings about AIDS. In other words, his reflections become a kind of argument. How would you make a more objective argument for his position?

MAKING CONNECTIONS

Selzer and Adam Gopnik (p. 78) both write as spectators of, rather than as participants in, the events they report. Compare and contrast the ways they develop their reflections within such a perspective.

LENSES

Annie Dillard

Annie Dillard (b. 1945) grew up in Pittsburgh, Pennsylvania, and earned degrees at Hollins College in Virginia's Roanoke Valley. Her first published book of prose, A Tinker at Pilgrim Creek *(1974), in which she focuses an intent eye on her rural Virginia surroundings, won the Pulitzer Prize. Dillard's other books include* Holy the Firm *(1978), a meditation on religion and spirituality;* Living by Fiction *(1982), a work of literary analysis;* An American Childhood *(1989), a memoir;* The Living *(1992), a novel;* For the Time Being *(1999), an inquiry into the place of God in a world marked by cruelty; and several volumes of poetry. "I am no scientist," she has said of herself. "I am a wanderer with a background in theology and a penchant for quirky facts. . . . I consider nature's facts — its beautiful and grotesque forms and events — in terms of the import to thought and their impetus to the spirit." The following essay appeared in* Teaching a Stone to Talk: Expeditions and Encounters *(1982).*

You get used to looking through lenses; it is an acquired skill. When you first look through binoculars, for instance, you can't see a thing. You look at the inside of the barrel; you blink and watch your eyelashes; you play with the focus knob till one eye is purblind.

The microscope is even worse. You are supposed to keep both eyes open as you look through its single eyepiece. I spent my childhood in Pittsburgh trying to master this trick: seeing through one eye, with both eyes open. The microscope also teaches you to move your hands wrong, to shove the glass slide to the right if you are following a creature who is swimming off to the left — as if you were operating a tiller, or backing a trailer, or performing any other of those paradoxical maneuvers which require either sure instincts or a grasp of elementary physics, neither of which I possess.

A child's microscope set comes with a little five-watt lamp. You place this dim light in front of the microscope's mirror; the mirror bounces the light up through the slide, through the magnifying lenses, and into your eye. The only reason you do not see everything in silhouette is that microscopic things are so small they are translucent. The animals and plants in a drop of pond water pass light like pale stained glass; they seem so soaked in water and light that their opacity has leached away.

The translucent strands of algae you see under a microscope — Spirogyra, Oscillatoria, Cladophora — move of their own accord, no one knows how or why. You watch these swaying yellow, green, and brown strands of algae half mesmerized; you sink into the microscope's field forgetful, oblivious, as if it were all a dream of your deepest brain. Occasionally a zippy rotifer comes barreling through, black and white, and in a tremendous hurry.

My rotifers and daphniae and amoebae were in an especially tremendous hurry because they were drying up. I burnt out or broke my little five-watt bulb right away. To replace it, I rigged an old table lamp laid on its side; the table lamp carried a seventy-five-watt bulb. I was about twelve, immortal and invulnerable, and did not know what I was doing; neither did anyone else. My parents let me set up my laboratory in the basement, where they wouldn't have to smell the urine I collected in test tubes and kept in the vain hope it would grow something horrible. So in full, solitary ignorance I spent evenings in the basement staring into a seventy-five-watt bulb magnified three hundred times and focused into my eye. It is a wonder I can see at all. My eyeball itself would start drying up; I blinked and blinked.

But the pond water creatures fared worse. I dropped them on a slide, floated a cover slip over them, and laid the slide on the microscope's stage, which the seventy-five-watt bulb had heated like a grill. At once the drop of pond water started to evaporate. Its edges shrank. The creatures swam among algae in a diminishing pool. I liked this part. The heat worked for me as a centrifuge, to concentrate the biomass. I had about five minutes to watch the members of a very dense population, excited by the heat, go about their business until — as I fancied sadly — they all caught on to their situation and started making out wills.

I was, then, not only watching the much-vaunted wonders in a drop of pond water; I was also, with mingled sadism and sympathy, setting up a limitless series of apocalypses. I set up and staged hundreds of ends-of-the-world and watched, enthralled, as they played themselves out. Over and over again, the last trump sounded, the final scroll unrolled, and the known world drained, dried, and vanished. When all the creatures lay motionless, boiled and fried in the positions they had when the last of their water dried completely, I washed the slide in the sink and started over with a fresh drop. How I loved that deep, wet world where the colored algae waved in the water and the rotifers swam!

But oddly, this a story about swans. It is not even a story; it is a description of swans. This description of swans includes the sky over a pond, a pair of binoculars, and a mortal adult who had long since moved out of the Pittsburgh basement.

In the Roanoke valley of Virginia, rimmed by the Blue Ridge Mountains to the east and the Allegheny Mountains to the west, is a little semi-agricultural area called Daleville. In Daleville, set among fallow fields and wooded ridges, is Daleville Pond. It is a big pond, maybe ten acres; it holds a lot of sky. I used to haunt the place because I loved it; I still do. In winter it had that airy scruffiness of deciduous lands; you greet the daylight and the open space, and spend the evening picking burrs out of your pants.

One Valentine's Day, in the afternoon, I was crouched among dried   10
reeds at the edge of Daleville Pond. Across the pond from where I crouched
was a low forested mountain ridge. In every other direction I saw only sky,
sky crossed by the reeds which blew before my face whichever way I
turned.

I was looking through binoculars at a pair of whistling swans.
Whistling swans! It is impossible to say how excited I was to see whistling
swans in Daleville, Virginia. The two were a pair, mated for life, migrating
north and west from the Atlantic coast to the high arctic. They had paused
to feed at Daleville Pond. I had flushed them, and now they were flying and
circling the pond. I crouched in the reeds so they would not be afraid to
come back to the water.

Through binoculars I followed the swans, swinging where they flew. All
their feathers were white; their eyes were black. Their wingspan was six
feet; they were bigger than I was. They flew in unison, one behind the other;
they made pass after pass at the pond. I watched them change from white
swans in front of the mountain to black swans in front of the sky. In clock-
wise ellipses they flew, necks long and relaxed, alternately beating their
wide wings and gliding.

As I rotated on my heels to keep the black frame of the lenses around
them, I lost all sense of space. If I lowered the binoculars I was always
amazed to learn in which direction I faced — dazed, the way you emerge
awed from a movie and try to reconstruct, bit by bit, a real world, in order
to discover where in it you might have parked the car.

I lived in that circle of light, in great speed and utter silence. When the
swans passed before the sun they were distant — two black threads, two live
stitches. But they kept coming, smoothly, and the sky deepened to blue
behind them and they took on light. They gathered dimension as they
neared, and I could see their ardent, straining eyes. Then I could hear the
brittle blur of their wings, the blur which faded as they circled on, and the
sky brightened to yellow behind them and the swans flattened and darkened and diminished as they flew. Once I lost them behind the mountain
ridge; when they emerged they were flying suddenly very high, and it was
like music changing key.

I was lost. The reeds in front of me, swaying and out of focus in the   15
binoculars' circular field, were translucent. The reeds were strands of color
passing light like cells in water. They were those yellow and green and
brown strands of pond algae I had watched so long in a light-soaked field.
My eyes burned; I was watching algae wave in a shrinking drop; they
crossed each other and parted wetly. And suddenly into the field swam two
whistling swans, two tiny whistling swans. They swam as fast as rotifers:
two whistling swans, infinitesimal, beating their tiny wet wings, perfectly
formed.

QUESTIONS

1. At the beginning of her essay, Dillard says that "looking through lenses. . . . is an acquired skill," and she then proceeds to discuss the challenges of learning to use both a microscope and binoculars. In what ways are these instruments similar? In what ways are they different?

2. At the beginning of paragraph 8, midway through her piece, Dillard says "But oddly, this is a story about swans." Why, then, does she wait so long to mention the swans? Why doesn't she begin with the swans? What, if anything, does her prior account of looking through a microscope at "the animals and plants in a drop of pond water" contribute to her description of the swans?

3. Compare and contrast Dillard's childhood behavior while looking through a microscope with her adult behavior while looking through binoculars. In which case does she appear to be most scientific?

4. Throughout her essay, Dillard frequently relies on analogies to clarify the nature of her perceptual experience. But in her final paragraph, she moves beyond analogies to claim that the reeds she watched through her binoculars are identical to the algae she had previously looked at through her microscope. In what ways are these two experiences identical? In what ways are they not? Why do you suppose that she makes so much of these identities in her final paragraph?

5. Write a piece remembering and reflecting on the most frustrating or most satisfying experience you've ever had looking through a microscope or a pair of binoculars. What were you trying to look at, and how did your microscope or binoculars help or hinder you?

MAKING CONNECTIONS

Dillard and Scott Russell Sanders (p. 156) both take stock of their youthful and adult approaches to scientific matters. Why do they bother to remember and reflect on their youthful scientific activities? How do their youthful activities prepare them for approaching scientific matters as adults? How do their youthful activities differ from their later scientific activities?

CAN WE KNOW THE UNIVERSE?
Reflections on a Grain of Salt

Carl Sagan

Carl Sagan (1934–1996) was renowned both as a scientist and a writer. For his work with the National Aeronautics and Space Administration's Mariner, Viking, *and* Voyager *expeditions, he was awarded NASA's Medals for Exceptional Scientific Achievement and for Distinguished Public Service. Sagan produced the* Cosmos *television series for public television and received the Peabody Award in 1981. He received the Pulitzer Prize in literature, for his book* The Dragons of Eden *(1977). Among his later works are* Comet *(1985),* Contact *(1985, a novel with Ann Druyan),* Shadows of Forgotten Ancestors *(1992), and* Billions and Billions: Thoughts on Life and Death at the Brink of the Millennium *(1997). The following selection is from* Broca's Brain: Reflections on the Romance of Science *(1979).*

Nothing is rich but the inexhaustible wealth
of nature. She shows us only surfaces,
but she is a million fathoms deep.
— RALPH WALDO EMERSON

Science is a way of thinking much more than it is a body of knowledge. Its goal is to find out how the world works, to seek what regularities there may be, to penetrate to the connections of things—from subnuclear particles, which may be the constituents of all matter, to living organisms, the human social community, and thence to the cosmos as a whole. Our intuition is by no means an infallible guide. Our perceptions may be distorted by training and prejudice or merely because of the limitations of our sense organs, which, of course, perceive directly but a small fraction of the phenomena of the world. Even so straightforward a question as whether in the absence of friction a pound of lead falls faster than a gram of fluff was answered incorrectly by Aristotle and almost everyone else before the time of Galileo. Science is based on experiment, on a willingness to challenge old dogma, on an openness to see the universe as it really is. Accordingly, science sometimes requires courage—at the very least the courage to question the conventional wisdom.

Beyond this the main trick of science is to *really* think of something: the shape of clouds and their occasional sharp bottom edges at the same altitude everywhere in the sky; the formation of a dewdrop on a leaf; the origin of a name or a word—Shakespeare, say, or "philanthropic"; the reason for human social customs—the incest taboo, for example; how it is that a lens in sunlight can make paper burn; how a "walking stick" got to look so much like a twig; why the Moon seems to follow us as we walk; what prevents us from digging a hole down to the center of the Earth; what the definition is of "down" on a spherical Earth; how it is possible for the body to convert yesterday's lunch into today's muscle and sinew; or how far is up—does the universe go on forever, or if it does not, is there any meaning to the question of what lies on the other side? Some of these questions are pretty easy. Others, especially the last, are mysteries to which no one even today knows the answer. They are natural questions to ask. Every culture has posed such questions in one way or another. Almost always the proposed answers are in the nature of "Just So Stories," attempted explanations divorced from experiment, or even from careful comparative observations.

But the scientific cast of mind examines the world critically as if many alternative worlds might exist, as if other things might be here which are not. Then we are forced to ask why what we see is present and not something else. Why are the Sun and the Moon and the planets spheres? Why not pyramids, or cubes, or dodecahedra? Why not irregular, jumbly shapes? Why so symmetrical, worlds? If you spend any time spinning hypotheses, checking to see whether they make sense, whether they conform to what else we know, thinking of tests you can pose to substantiate or deflate your hypotheses, you will find yourself doing science. And as you come to practice this habit of thought more and more you will get better and better at it. To penetrate into the heart of the thing—even a little thing, a blade of grass, as Walt Whitman said—is to experience a kind of exhilaration that, it may be, only human beings of all the beings on this planet can feel. We are an intelligent species and the use of our intelligence quite properly gives us pleasure. In this respect the brain is like a muscle. When we think well, we feel good. Understanding is a kind of ecstasy.

But to what extent can we *really* know the universe around us? Sometimes this question is posed by people who hope the answer will be in the negative, who are fearful of a universe in which everything might one day be known. And sometimes we hear pronouncements from scientists who confidently state that everything worth knowing will soon be known—or even is already known—and who paint pictures of a Dionysian or Polynesian age in which the zest for intellectual discovery has withered, to be replaced by a kind of subdued languor, the lotus eaters drinking fermented coconut milk or some other mild hallucinogen. In addition to maligning both the Polynesians, who were intrepid explorers (and whose brief respite in paradise is now sadly ending), as well as the inducements to intellectual discovery provided by some hallucinogens, this contention turns out to be trivially mistaken.

Let us approach a much more modest question: not whether we can   5
know the universe or the Milky Way Galaxy or a star or a world. Can we know, ultimately and in detail, a grain of salt? Consider one microgram of

table salt, a speck just barely large enough for someone with keen eyesight to make out without a microscope. In that grain of salt there are about 10^{16} sodium and chlorine atoms. This is a 1 followed by 16 zeros, 10 million billion atoms. If we wish to know a grain of salt, we must know at least the three-dimensional positions of each of these atoms. (In fact, there is much more to be known—for example, the nature of the forces between the atoms—but we are making only a modest calculation.) Now, is this number more or less than the number of things which the brain can know?

How much *can* the brain know? There are perhaps 10^{11} neurons in the brain, the circuit elements and switches that are responsible in their electrical and chemical activity for the functioning of our minds. A typical brain neuron has perhaps a thousand little wires, called dendrites, which connect it with its fellows. If, as seems likely, every bit of information in the brain corresponds to one of these connections, the total number of things knowable by the brain is no more than 10^{14}, one hundred trillion. But this number is only one percent of the number of atoms in our speck of salt.

So in this sense the universe is intractable, astonishingly immune to any human attempt at full knowledge. We cannot on this level understand a grain of salt, much less the universe.

But let us look more deeply at our microgram of salt. Salt happens to be a crystal in which, except for defects in the structure of the crystal lattice, the position of every sodium and chlorine atom is predetermined. If we could shrink ourselves into this crystalline world, we could see rank upon rank of atoms in an ordered array, a regularly alternating structure—sodium, chlorine, sodium, chlorine, specifying the sheet of atoms we are standing on and all the sheets above us and below us. An absolutely pure crystal of salt could have the position of every atom specified by something like 10 bits of information.[1] This would not strain the information-carrying capacity of the brain.

If the universe had natural laws that governed its behavior to the same degree of regularity that determines a crystal of salt, then, of course, the universe would be knowable. Even if there were many such laws, each of considerable complexity, human beings might have the capacity to understand them all. Even if such knowledge exceeded the information-carrying capacity of the brain, we might store the additional information outside our bodies—in books, for example, or in computer memories—and still, in some sense, know the universe.

Human beings are, understandably, highly motivated to find regularities, natural laws. The search for rules, the only possible way to understand such a vast and complex universe, is called science. The universe forces   10

----

[1]Chlorine is a deadly poison gas employed on European battlefields in World War I. Sodium is a corrosive metal which burns upon contact with water. Together they make a placid and unpoisonous material, table salt. Why each of these substances has the properties it does is a subject called chemistry, which requires more than 10 bits of information to understand.

those who live in it to understand it. Those creatures who find everyday experience a muddled jumble of events with no predictability, no regularity, are in grave peril. The universe belongs to those who, at least to some degree, have figured it out.

It is an astonishing fact that there *are* laws of nature, rules that summarize conveniently—not just qualitatively but quantitatively—how the world works. We might imagine a universe in which there are no such laws, in which the 10^{80} elementary particles that make up a universe like our own behave with utter and uncompromising abandon. To understand such a universe we would need a brain at least as massive as the universe. It seems unlikely that such a universe could have life and intelligence, because beings and brains require some degree of internal stability and order. But even if in a much more random universe there were such beings with an intelligence much greater than our own, there could not be much knowledge, passion or joy.

Fortunately for us, we live in a universe that has at least important parts that are knowable. Our common-sense experience and our evolutionary history have prepared us to understand something of the workaday world. When we go into other realms, however, common sense and ordinary intuition turn out to be highly unreliable guides. It is stunning that as we go close to the speed of light our mass increases indefinitely, we shrink toward zero thickness in the direction of motion, and time for us comes as near to stopping as we would like. Many people think that this is silly, and every week or two I get a letter from someone who complains to me about it. But it is a virtually certain consequence not just of experiment but also of Albert Einstein's brilliant analysis of space and time called the Special Theory of Relativity. It does not matter that these effects seem unreasonable to us. We are not in the habit of traveling close to the speed of light. The testimony of our common sense is suspect at high velocities.

Or consider an isolated molecule composed of two atoms shaped something like a dumbbell—a molecule of salt, it might be. Such a molecule rotates about an axis through the line connecting the two atoms. But in the world of quantum mechanics, the realm of the very small, not all orientations of our dumbbell molecule are possible. It might be that the molecule could be oriented in a horizontal position, say, or in a vertical position, but not at many angles in between. Some rotational positions are forbidden. Forbidden by what? By the laws of nature. The universe is built in such a way as to limit, or quantize, rotation. We do not experience this directly in everyday life; we would find it startling as well as awkward in sitting-up exercises, to find arms outstretched from the sides or pointed up to the skies permitted but many intermediate positions forbidden. We do not live in the world of the small, on the scale of 10^{-13} centimeters, in the realm where there are twelve zeros between the decimal place and the one. Our common-sense intuitions do not count. What does count is experiment—in this case observations from the far infrared spectra of molecules. They show molecular rotation to be quantized.

The idea that the world places restrictions on what humans might do is frustrating. Why *shouldn't* we be able to have intermediate rotational positions? Why *can't* we travel faster than the speed of light? But so far as we can tell, this is the way the universe is constructed. Such prohibitions not only press us toward a little humility; they also make the world more knowable. Every restriction corresponds to a law of nature, a regularization of the universe. The more restrictions there are on what matter and energy can do, the more knowledge human beings can attain. Whether in some sense the universe is ultimately knowable depends not only on how many natural laws there are that encompass widely divergent phenomena, but also on whether we have the openness and the intellectual capacity to understand such laws. Our formulations of the regularities of nature are surely dependent on how the brain is built, but also, and to a significant degree, on how the universe is built.

For myself, I like a universe that includes much that is unknown and,   15
at the same time, much that is knowable. A universe in which everything is known would be static and dull, as boring as the heaven of some weakminded theologians. A universe that is unknowable is no fit place for a thinking being. The ideal universe for us is one very much like the universe we inhabit. And I would guess that this is not really much of a coincidence.

QUESTIONS

1. How are *science* and *scientific thinking* defined in the first three paragraphs? What is Sagan's purpose in defining these terms? What does this tell you about Sagan's conception of his audience?
2. Sagan's mode of reflection might be considered less personal than others in this section in that he is reflecting on an idea rather than on an event in his life. How does Sagan keep his tone from becoming abstract? What elements of the personal are present in this essay?
3. Sagan cites scientists who believe that "everything worth knowing will soon be known" (paragraph 4). How does the evidence in this essay challenge that assumption?
4. We might consider paragraph 15 to be Sagan's most personal statement in his reflections on the universe: he likes "a universe that includes much that is unknown and, at the same time, much that is knowable." Why is this balance important to Sagan? Do you agree with his closing statements? Explain.
5. Consider the statement, "The more restrictions there are on what matter and energy can do, the more knowledge human beings can attain" (paragraph 14). Describe an example in your own experience (or another's) when you learned that rules or laws were helpful in ensuring your personal freedom.

6. In paragraph 3 Sagan concludes, "Understanding is a kind of ecstasy." Describe a time in your life when you understood something for the first time — when, as they say, the light went on in your head, shining on a difficult problem and bringing about a realization. Could your feelings at the time be considered ecstatic, or did you experience some other emotion?
7. What sort of universe would you consider ideal? What would you like to know about the universe that is now unknown to you? Explain.

MAKING CONNECTIONS

1. A number of the writers in this section offer their reflections to justify a belief or a strong feeling about a subject. In other words, their reflections become a kind of argument. Grealy (p. 50), Douglas (p. 42), Gornick (p. 74), King (p. 106), and Orwell (p. 114) come to mind as well as Sagan. How convincing is the argument in each case? How has the writer used purely personal responses to make a persuasive case? How would you go about developing a more objective argument for one of their positions? What would be the difference in effect?
2. Does Sagan's concern for "passion" and "joy" (paragraph 11) surprise you? Where else, especially in the writings by scientists in this section, do you find evidence of the same concerns? Citing several examples from essayists you have read, write an essay on the role of passion and joy in the work of scientists and other writers.

EARTH, AIR, FIRE, AND WATER

Scott Russell Sanders

Born in Memphis, Tennessee, in 1945, Scott Russell Sanders grew up in rural Ohio. He earned a scholarship to Brown University and completed a Ph.D. at Cambridge University before joining the faculty at Indiana University, where he is currently a distinguished professor of English. Sanders's numerous publications include novels, short story collections, and seven works for children, but he is probably best known for his essays and memoirs. Among these are the collections The Paradise of Bombs *(1987), which won the Associated Writing Programs Award in Creative Nonfiction;* Staying Put: Making Home in a Restless World *(1993), which won the Ohioana Book Award;* Writing from the Center *(1995), which won the Great Lakes Book Award;* The Country of Language *(1999), a brief reflection on experiences that have shaped his work as a writer; and* The Force of Spirit *(2000), meditations on the sacred in everyday life. Sanders has said of his work, "I have to be wrought up about something, and also deeply puzzled about it, before I'm moved to address it in an essay. So in my writing I'm always pushing outward on the boundaries of bewilderment." The following essay appeared in* Writing from the Center.

With money earned from helping neighbors gather hay in my thirteenth summer, I bought a colored poster of the periodic table, which I taped to the wall beside my bed. Before sleep each night, while my friends were listening to the rock-and-roll top forty or learning baseball statistics, I memorized the names and symbols and atomic weights of the elements. All of us were looking for some principle of order in the dizzy world. As my friends brooded on Elvis or Willie or Stan the Man, I murmured "actinium, krypton, zinc," trying to hold the alphabet of the universe in my head.

Chemists knew of 103 primary substances back then, from lowly hydrogen to weighty lawrencium. The makers of the poster allowed for future discoveries by leaving a few blank spaces at the bottom. And sure enough, in the fall of 1964, when I was a college sophomore, my physics professor announced that the Russians had produced element 104 in one of their accelerators. I penciled this news onto my periodic table, which I had mounted on the wall beside my dormitory bed, as a counterpoint of sorts to the pin-ups beside my roommate's bed. Within the next decade, along came numbers 105 and 106, but by then I had moved on in my search for order and was no longer keeping track.

What fascinated me, during those years of sleeping with the elements, was the idea that all the dazzling variety of things, from starfish to stars, had been concocted from a hundred or so ingredients. Physics taught me a breathtakingly simpler view, that the elements were not primary after all, but were themselves composed from a handful of particles, such as protons and electrons, and these in turn were composed of even simpler entities fancifully named quarks, mere eddies in the cosmic flow.

Except for the change in vocabulary, this claim that the universe is made from a single underlying stuff was anticipated by Heraclitus twenty-five centuries ago, in his famous aphorism: "It ever was, and is, and shall be, ever-living fire, in measures being kindled and in measures going out." Other Greeks put forward rival candidates for the original substance. "All is water," Thales maintained, "and the world is full of gods." All is air, Anaximenes believed; no, no, Xenophanes insisted, all is earth. Then along came Empedocles, in the fifth century B.C., to reconcile these views by proposing that the cosmos is made not from any one substance but from all four, giving us the familiar quartet of earth, air, fire, and water.

The elements themselves do not change, Empedocles argued, but they are stirred into ever changing combinations by Love and Strife, the one force drawing them together, the other driving them apart. These contrary forces are still recognizable in our notions of attraction and repulsion, positive and negative charge, particles and antiparticles. One of the central questions in cosmology these days is whether the universe will continue to expand forever, or whether it will eventually reverse direction and rush back toward the center. Empedocles might have posed the same question by asking which influence will triumph in the long run, strife or love. 5

As a devotee of the periodic table, I was at first inclined to scoff at the old-timers for believing that a mere quartet of elements could account for the world's variety. However, when I considered that only four kinds of taste buds — salt, bitter, sour, and sweet — allow us to enjoy an infinity of flavors, that all the DNA for the billions of creatures on earth is constructed from a series of four bases, and that all the motion in the universe may be attributed to four interacting forces, the ancient scheme no longer seemed so far-fetched.

Our science offers a much more complicated and, we trust, more accurate view of the cosmos than anything the Greeks imagined, yet we still rely on their twin concepts of malleable substance and shaping force. The more deeply we probe into matter, the less solid it appears; even if you could find a small enough hammer, you could not tap an electron. But at the everyday level of chairs and chocolate, the stuff of the world seems tangible enough, scraping our knees and teasing our tongues. Although we find it more plausible to divide that everyday stuff into a hundred-odd elements instead of four, in thinking of elements at all we are following a very old habit of mind.

For two thousand years, from the heyday of Greece through the Renaissance, sophisticated thinkers as well as ordinary folks throughout

Europe and the Middle East imagined the world to be compounded of earth and air and fire and water. The four elements permeated the thinking of the early Hebrews, Egyptians, and Persians. Aristotle elaborated the scheme by arguing that everything below the moon is composed of the four elements, and therefore perishable, while everything beyond the moon is forged of an imperishable material he called "aether," from the Greek word for "eternal."

The Stoics maintained that fire came first, then air, water, and earth, and they predicted that sooner or later all will be consumed back into fire and the cycle will repeat. Modern cosmology envisions a similar possibility, an accordion universe, expanding from the Big Bang, collapsing back toward a Big Crunch, then expanding once more, on and on forever. Physicists no longer believe, with Aristotle, that any portion of this turbulent universe is immune to change; instead, they have replaced the material aether with a conceptual one, for they assume that behind the fleeting phenomena are permanent laws.

From the Stoics, the system of four elements was passed down by way   10
of the Gnostics and Arab philosophers to the medieval alchemists, and from the alchemists to poets and visionaries right up into our own time. The old theory never really told us what the universe is made of, but rather how it moves, the way and feel of things. Earth is stubborn, conservative, and slow, with a long memory. Water is elusive and humble, seeking the low places. Air is a trickster, fickle and shifty. Fire is fierce, quick, greedy, and bold.

Over the centuries, these four characters have played leading roles in stories told by countless peoples. So Earth is the dry land that God separated from the watery beginnings. It is the mud brought up from the bottom of the primal sea by muskrat or loon, to offer solid ground where creatures with legs might walk. It is the dust from which we come and the dust to which we return. Water is the formless potential out of which creation emerged. It is the ocean of unconsciousness enveloping the islands of consciousness. Water bathes us at birth and again at death, and in between it washes away sin. It is by turns the elixir of life or the renewing rain or the devastating flood. Air is the wind that blows where it wills. It is the voice sounding in the depths of matter, the word made flesh. It is breath, which the Romans called *spiritus*, a divine thread drawn through every living creature. And Fire is the transformer, cooking meat, frightening beasts, warming huts, forging tools, melting, shaping. It is cleansing and punishing, flaming up from the sacred bush and lashing out from the furnaces of hell. Fire is a power given by the gods or stolen from them for the benefit of a bare forked animal. It is cosmic energy, lighting the stars, lurking in the atom, smoldering in every cell.

Turned over and over in our collective imagination, each element came to be associated with a color, a season, a number, a heavenly body, a point of the compass, a human temperament—earth is melancholic, air is sanguine, fire is choleric, water is phlegmatic—and each one accumulated an aura of metaphors. Late in the eighteenth century, while the French chemist Lavoisier was extending the list of elements to thirty-three, William Blake could write in *The Marriage of Heaven and Hell* about "The eyes of fire, the nostrils of air, the mouth of water, the beard of earth," and expect to be understood. Even today, when you pick up a bowl that has been turned on a potter's wheel, you hold the four elements in your palm, the clay shaped by wet fingers and dried in air and hardened in fire. And when you sit beside a lake — dirt or stone beneath you and waves lapping at your feet and wind blowing in your face and the sun beating down — you are still keeping company with the old quartet.

Why did this theory spread so far and endure so long? Perhaps any people with a written language would eventually surmise that the world is made from a small number of ingredients just as words are made from a small number of characters. If the universe is an expression of the Logos, as the Greeks believed and as John's Gospel taught Christians to believe, then the elements may be understood as the alphabet of that grand utterance. But why four? Why not three or nineteen or fifty-six? Indeed, why do so many categories of thought come in sets of four — seasons, humors, cardinal directions, parts of music, ages of life? Why do so many symbols embody the four-sided square or the four-armed cross?

After long study of the alchemists and Gnostics, Jung concluded that a four-fold scheme appeals to us because it stands for our intuition of wholeness. "The idea of those old philosophers was that God manifested himself first in the creation of the four elements," Jung wrote in *Psychology and Religion.* "The four symbolizes the parts, qualities and aspects of the One." That root idea has been preserved in modern science, but with regard to forces rather than substances. Since Einstein, physicists have been pursuing the hypothesis that the four known forces — gravity, electro-magnetism, weak and strong versions of the nuclear force — are descended from a single primordial energy, just as Heraclitus believed; and much current research is devoted to showing how, in the first moment after the Big Bang, the One broke down into Four. You can trace the old yearning for a vision of the whole through the pages of *A Brief History of Time,* where Stephen Hawking claims that by joining the four primordial forces into a single theory, we might achieve a complete model of the universe, and thereby come to "know the mind of God."

Although nowadays many scientists would be uncomfortable with   15
Hawking's use of religious language, the great interpreters of nature have consistently used it, from the early Greeks to the alchemists, on through Aquinas, Galileo, Newton, Darwin, and Einstein, for they believed that in deciphering the laws of the universe they were articulating a divine intelligence. "Between matter as we observe it in the laboratory and mind as we observe it in our consciousness," writes the physicist Freeman Dyson, "there seems to be only a difference in degree but not in kind. If God exists and is accessible to us, then his mind and ours may likewise differ from each other only in degree and not in kind." Whatever language we use to describe it, the quest for a unifying vision is at the heart of religion and science alike.

Jung discovered from his own dreams and those of his patients, and from icons and myths the world over, that four-fold designs such as crosses and squares—especially those linked to the circular figures he called mandalas—symbolize the search for a center, outwardly in the cosmos and inwardly in the psyche: "The wholeness of the celestial circle and the squareness of the earth, uniting the four principles or elements or psychical qualities, express completeness and union. Thus the mandala has the dignity of a 'reconciling symbol.'" In this way, according to Jung, "the reconciliation of God and man is expressed in the symbol of Christ or of the cross." When the Romans inscribed "Jesus of Nazareth, King of the Jews" atop the cross at Calvary, they meant the title mockingly. But for the Jews who looked on, the initial letters in those Latin words would have spelled out the sacred tetragram INRI, representing the Hebrew words for earth, air, fire, and water. Thus a sign of mockery in the language of the oppressors was a sign of mystical union in the language of the oppressed.

I realize now that for me the periodic table was a mandala of sorts, a reconciling symbol, with its neat grid of boxes, its promise of order behind the world's apparent disarray. Gazing at the poster, memorizing the numbers and letters, I sought to hold the universe in mind, as though by grasping that outward order I could bind together a self that seemed always about to scatter like smoke. What I dimly understood, even as a teenager, was that the inner and outer searches were the same. I sensed that my chief business, beyond the daily scramble, was to discover what I could of the source and true dimensions of Creation, for in doing so I would discover the ground of this flighty, flickering self.

The challenge for each of us, not only the physicist and philosopher, is to grasp the slippery world. How do you divide up this vast panorama into thinkable chunks? How do you speak of the parts without betraying the whole? The danger, for every sort of thinker, is a hardening of the categories; the danger is that we will take our metaphors literally, as though, by pinning our labels on the universe—ego and id, yin and yang, quarks and quanta, God and Son and Holy Ghost, the four elements or the hundred and four—we imagine that we have snared the universe itself. Any description of the world is a net thrown over a flood; no matter how fine the mesh, the world leaks through.

With that caution, and with due respect for the periodic table, let me return briefly to the lake I mentioned earlier—Wind Lake in northern Minnesota, to be precise—for that is where I found myself not long ago, listening to the music of the ancient quartet.

Late in July, I was canoeing in the Boundary Waters Wilderness with my daughter Eva and several friends. At our last campsite, on an island in Wind Lake, Eva showed me a spot along the shore that was hidden from the trail by a screen of hemlocks and birches, where an outcropping of dark volcanic rock thrust into the tea-green waves. Nearly as old as the continent, the stone had been smelted and harrowed and cracked, and every fissure

20

brimmed with life—clovers and lichens, pale runners of strawberries, ferns the size of a baby's hand, fur of moss, spiky grass, spider and frog.

On a cloudswept afternoon that would give way at dusk to a full moon, I went off to sit by myself in that vibrant spot. Sore from a week of paddling, I stretched out my legs, braced my arms behind, and leaned back. Time ticked on, slowed down, then stopped. I grew still. Presently, like voices rising, the elements revealed themselves. The rock beneath me felt like worn bone—and there was earth. A stiff wind shoved kingdom after kingdom of clouds along the horizon—and there was air. The sun glared through every gap, drawing flames into my hands and face—and there was fire. Mist from waves beating on the stone cooled my skin—and there was water.

Now, I separate the four voices in order to speak of the moment at all. While I was sitting on the lip of Wind Lake, immersed in that music, I did not feel any division. I knew an utter fullness and wholeness that turns clumsy when spoken.

In our various alphabets we keep gesturing toward the One behind the Many. We are always speaking about the unsayable in terms of what we can touch and taste and see. That is the best we can do, as brief-lived creatures with only a few doorways of perception and a small but curious brain. Given our history, it is hard to believe we were not put here to *think* about this place, to ask questions, to gaze back at the source, as though to complete a circuit of intelligence. No single alphabet can express the full range of our knowledge. For designing a new molecule or describing the intimate behavior of atoms, the periodic table is far superior to the old quartet of elements. But for speaking about those moments when all our senses chime and we feel the harmony of the whole, the music of earth, air, fire, and water is still compelling.

QUESTIONS

1. In paragraph 7, Sanders declares that "Our science offers a much more complicated and, we trust, more accurate view of the cosmos than anything the Greeks imagined." Given such an assertion, why does he devote so much attention to the ancient Greek view of the world as being composed of four elements? In what respect(s) is that ancient system appealing and useful to Sanders?
2. According to Sanders, what are the limitations of that ancient fourfold system? According to your own study and experience, what are the limitations of that system?
3. In paragraph 18, Sanders says that "the danger, for every sort of thinker, is a hardening of the categories." In what ways does Sanders seem to avoid that danger in his essay? In what ways, if any, do you think he has fallen prey to that danger? Aside from "hardening of the categories," what other dangers are important for "every sort of thinker" to avoid?

4. In paragraph 22, Sanders tells about a moment on Wind Lake, when he "did not feel any division" of things: "I knew an utter fullness and wholeness that turns clumsy when spoken." But in the final sentence of the essay, he seems to contradict himself by claiming that "when all our senses chime and we feel the harmony of the whole, the music of earth, air, fire, and water is still compelling." In what ways are these statements at odds with each other? In what ways are they consistent with each other?

5. Write an essay in which you reflect on the four elements in terms of your own life. Does this view help you to make sense of things that you've witnessed or experienced? Choose a few memorable incidents from your life to illustrate your piece.

6. Perhaps you have a different view of the basic elements. You might think that there are slightly less or slightly more — three or five, say, rather than four. If so, write an essay in which you identify the basic elements in your worldview and explain how they differ from one another, how they interact with one another, and why your system is preferable to the Greeks' four-element system.

MAKING CONNECTIONS

Sanders and Carl Sagan (p. 150) both attempt to use familiar aspects of experience to comprehend the nature of the world. Whose approach do you find more appealing? Whose do you find more comprehensive? Whose do you consider to be more scientific? Why?

REPORTING

Here in "Reporting" you will find writing that reflects a wide array of academic and professional situations—a naturalist describing the tool-using behavior of chimpanzees, a brain surgeon detailing the progress of a delicate operation, a historian telling about the plague that swept through medieval Europe, a reporter describing the September 11, 2001, attacks on the World Trade Center and the Pentagon. Informative writing is basic to every field of endeavor, and the writers in this section seek to fulfill that basic need by reporting material drawn from various sources: interviews, articles, books, public records, and firsthand observation. Working from such varied sources, these writers aim to provide detailed and reliable accounts of things—to give the background of a case, to convey the look and smell and feel of a place, to describe the appearance and behavior of people, to tell the story of recent or ancient events.

Though reporting depends on a careful gathering of information, it is by no means a mechanical and routine activity that consists simply of getting some facts and writing them up. Newspaper editors and criminal investigators often say that they want "just the facts," but they know that somehow the facts are substantially shaped by the point of view of the person who is gathering and reporting them. By *point of view*, we mean both the physical and the mental standpoints from which a person observes or investigates something. Each of us, after all, stands at a particular point in space and time, as well as in thought and feeling, whenever we look at any subject. And where we stand in relation to the subject will determine the particular aspects of it that we perceive and bring out in an account.

The influence that point of view exerts on reporting can be seen in the following passage from Gordon Grice's essay "Slice of Life" (p. 298):

It may be hard to grasp what had become of Jernigan, but it's easy to see. His image is on thousands of Web sites. I first saw it at a computer terminal in a university library in Oklahoma. I watched

Jernigan's upright body approach and pass through the plane of the computer screen, a smooth progression of glistening cross-sections. When I chose another angle, I could move from head to foot, the image kaleidoscoping — a blossoming of brain, a constriction of neck, a widening into the trunk packed with organs, a sudden bifurcation at the pelvis, and on down to the surprisingly dainty toes. (paragraph 10)

A condemned man, Jernigan had donated his body to science, and scientists at the National Library of Medicine transformed nearly two thousand cross-section slices of the body into digital images so that his anatomy could be studied on the screen. He now can be viewed straight on, as you might have met him face to face, or top down, from the crown of his head. Neither representation of Jernigan is truer than the other, although the images are so different that you might mistake the top-down image for a flower, a shrub, or another animal entirely.

Or consider this passage from *The Diary of Anne Frank* (p. 171), in which Frank describes an extra assignment given her in school as punishment for being a "chatterbox":

I thought and thought, and suddenly I had an idea. I wrote the three pages Mr. Keesing had assigned me and was satisfied. I argued that talking is a female trait and that I would do my best to keep it under control, but that I would never be able to break myself of the habit, since my mother talked as much as I did, if not more, and that there's not much you can do about inherited traits. (paragraph 19)

Here two points of view are in conflict. From her teacher's point of view, Frank should keep still. She counters, however, with a defense of her behavior. "Mr. Keesing," she says, "had a good laugh at my arguments" (paragraph 20), but soon her talking prompts a second essay titled "An Incorrigible Chatterbox" and then a third essay titled "'Quack, Quack, Quack,' said Mistress Chatterback":

The class roared. I had to laugh too, though I'd nearly exhausted my ingenuity on the topic of chatterboxes. It was time to come up with something else, something original. My friend Sanne, who's good at poetry, offered to help me write the essay from beginning to end in verse. I jumped for joy. Keesing was trying to play a joke on me with this ridiculous subject, but I'd make sure the joke was on him.

I finished my poem, and it was beautiful! It was about a mother duck and a father swan with three baby ducklings who were bitten to death by the father because they quacked too much. Luckily, Keesing took the joke the right way. He read the poem to the class, adding his own comments, and to several other classes as well. (paragraphs 21–22)

REPORTING 165

Keesing and Frank are in a kind of contest. Keesing sees his assignments as a punishment that will correct Frank's behavior. Frank sees them as a challenge and takes each assignment as an opportunity to turn the tables on Keesing.

Toward the end of the same selection, in a short passage with an entirely different tone, Frank describes the morning on which she and her family set off for their hiding place, fully aware of how she looks, feels, and could look to others. She is aware, that is, of her own point of view while fully able to anticipate the antagonistic point of view of others:

> The four of us were wrapped in so many layers of clothes it looked as if we were going off to spend the night in a refrigerator, and all that just so we could take more clothes with us. No Jew in our situation would dare leave the house with a suitcase full of clothes. I was wearing two undershirts, three pairs of underpants, a dress, and over that a skirt, a jacket, a raincoat, two pairs of stockings, heavy shoes, a cap, a scarf and lots more. (paragraph 57)

The point of view that a writer takes will have an enormous effect on the writing. Sometimes a point of view will be straightforward, quite literally, as is Grice's first view of the front of Jernigan's body. Sometimes it will be odd, even whimsical, as when Grice views the same body from head down to feet. A point of view taken can be playful, as when Frank responds to discipline as if it is a contest. Just as quickly, point of view can turn solemn, as when she describes, briefly and evocatively, her first steps of going into hiding.

Many reports are based on firsthand observation, as is Jane van Lawick-Goodall's report on chimpanzees (p. 237) and Richard Selzer's "The Discus Thrower" (p. 263). The careful descriptions of these authors' observations establish, quite literally, their points of view. In much scholarship, in contrast, footnotes contribute to the reader's point of view, as do other sources, which are all carefully acknowledged. A writer who wishes to persuade readers of the accuracy of a report that cannot be based on direct observation — a report like Barbara Tuchman's study of the Black Death during the late Middle Ages, for example (p. 217) — will be sure to ground it on authoritative historical sources.

Among the most compelling aspects of point of view are that, by definition, it belongs uniquely to the writer, is intensely local, and is impossible for another writer to duplicate exactly. So first through the good-humored combativeness of Anne Frank's behavior and then through the particularity of her ordeal of going into hiding, we come to feel for Anne Frank. In parallel fashion, we understand Richard Selzer to be one particular doctor, in a particular hospital ward, confronting a singular patient. Even a scholar like Barbara Tuchman, who relies on numerous written primary and secondary sources, has her own way of reading, synthesizing, and interpreting the information that she discovers. At the same time, the most authoritative point of view is one that seems to know everything, from every angle — the *omniscient* point of view. "In the beginning," the Bible's Book of Genesis says, "God created the heaven and the earth." W. H. Auden's poem, "The Unknown Citizen" (p. 261), adopts a version of this omniscience when he claims that his information comes from the "Bureau of Statistics" (line 1), and readers quickly recognize that his tone is somewhat satirical, especially since the level of omniscience demonstrated in the poem is something that cannot really be acquired.

News reports, however — especially lead stories that claim the headline on the first page of the paper — seek something like omniscience by synthesizing and summarizing diverse bits of information that will have come from several sources. So it is with Serge Schmemann's report, dated September 12, 2001, of the attacks of the day before (p. 247). He was not in a position to witness all four planes or to observe their flight plans, their terrible conclusions in three different locations, the conditions on board any of them, the subsequent collapse of the towers, the deaths of many rescue workers, and the movements of President George Bush throughout the day. Schmemann had to collect all this information and write from an imagined point of view that could seem to see and organize it all.

Once you try to imagine the various perspectives from which anything can be observed or investigated, you will see that no one person can possibly uncover everything there is to know about a subject. Schmemann's assignment was to come as close as possible to covering everything about September 11, 2001, but he certainly knew, as we all understand, that his report would be seen to be incomplete as soon as the next day. For this reason as a writer, you need to be as clear as possible about your own point of view and to understand its limitations. As a reader, you should always identify the point of view from which an author gathered the information included in a piece so that you may judge for yourself both its strengths and weaknesses. By the same token, in your own reporting you should carefully decide on the point of view that you already have or plan to use in observing or gathering information about something. Once you begin to pay deliberate attention to point of view, you will come to see that it is closely related to the various purposes for which people gather and report information in writing.

The Range of Reportorial Writing

The purpose of reporting is in one sense straightforward and self-evident, particularly when it is defined in terms of its commonly accepted value to readers. Whether it involves a firsthand account of some recent happening or the documented record of a long-past sequence of events, reportorial writing informs readers about the various subjects that may interest them but that they cannot possibly observe or investigate on their own. You may never get to see chimpanzees in their native African habitats, but you can get a glimpse of their behavior through the firsthand account of Jane van Lawick-Goodall. So, too, you will probably never have occasion to make your way through the many public records and personal reports of the bubonic plague that beset Europe in the mid-fourteenth century, but you can get a synoptic view of the plague from Barbara Tuchman's account, which is based on a thorough investigation of those sources. Reporting expands the range of its readers' perceptions and knowledge beyond the limits of their own immediate experience. From the outlook of readers, then, the function of reporting does seem to be very clear-cut.

But if we shift our focus and look at reporting in terms of the purposes to which it is evidently put by writers, it often turns out to serve a more complex function than might at first be supposed. An example of this complexity can be seen in the following passage from van Lawick-Goodall's account (p. 237):

> Suddenly I stopped, for I saw a slight movement in the long grass about sixty yards away. Quickly focusing my binoculars I saw that it was a single chimpanzee, and just then he turned in my direction. I recognized David Graybeard.
>
> Cautiously I moved around so that I could see what he was doing. He was squatting beside the red earth mound of a termite nest, and as I watched I saw him carefully push a long grass stem down into a hole in the mound. After a moment he withdrew it and picked something from the end with his mouth. (paragraphs 22–23)

This passage seems on the whole to be a very neutral bit of scientific reporting that details van Lawick-Goodall's observation of a particular chimpanzee probing for food in a termite nest. The only unusual aspect of the report is her naming of the creature, which has the unscientific effect of personifying the animal. Otherwise, she is careful in the opening part of the description to establish the physical point of view from which she observed the chimpanzee. And at the end of the passage she is equally careful not to identify or even conjecture about "something" beyond her range of detailed vision. As it turns out, however, this passage is a record not only of her observations but also of a pivotal moment in the story of how she came to make an important discovery about chimpanzees — that they are tool users — and thus how she came to regard their behavior as being much closer to that of human beings than had previously been supposed. So she climaxes her previous description of the chimpanzee with this sentence:

> I was too far away to make out what he was eating, but it was obvious that he was actually using a grass stem as a tool. (paragraph 23)

Here as elsewhere, then, her reporting is thoughtfully worded and structured to make a strong case for her ideas about chimpanzee and human behavior. Thus, she evidently intends her report to be both informative and persuasive.

A different set of purposes can be seen in yet another firsthand account —this time of a medical patient, as observed by his doctor, Richard Selzer (p. 263):

> From the doorway of Room 542 the man in the bed seems deeply tanned. Blue eyes and close-cropped white hair give him the appearance

of vigor and good health. But I know that his skin is not brown from the
sun. It is rusted, rather, in the last stage of containing the vile repose
within. And the blue eyes are frosted, looking inward like the windows
of a snowbound cottage. This man is blind. This man is also legless —
the right leg missing from midthigh down, the left from just below the
knee. It gives him the look of a bonsai, roots and branches pruned into
the dwarfed facsimile of a great tree. (paragraph 2)

In this passage, Selzer seeks to describe both the seemingly healthy visual
appearance of the patient and his decaying physical condition. Thus he
begins by reporting visual details, such as the "deeply tanned" skin as well
as the "blue eyes and close-cropped white hair," that convey "the appearance of vigor and good health." Then in the sentences that follow, Selzer
relies heavily on figurative language, on a striking sequence of metaphors
and similes, each of which reverses the initial impression so as to convey the
drastically impaired condition of the patient. The patient's skin turns out to
be "rusted," his eyes "frosted," and his body like "the dwarfed facsimile of
a great tree." Yet it is also clear from these and other bits of figurative language in the passage that Selzer is trying to convey not only the dire physical condition of his patient but also his own intense personal feelings about
him. Clearly, he intends his report to be provocative as well as informative.

As is apparent from just this handful of selections, writers invariably
seem to use reporting for a combination of purposes — to provide information, to convey their attitudes, beliefs, or ideas about it, and to influence
the views of their readers. This joining of purposes is hardly surprising,
given the factors involved in any decision to report on something. After all,
whenever we make a report, we do so presumably because we believe that
the subject of our report is important enough for others to be told about it.
And presumably we believe the subject to be important because of what we
have come to know and think about it. So when we are faced with deciding what information to report and how to report it, we inevitably base our
decisions on these ideas. At every point in the process of planning and writing a report, we act on the basis of our particular motives and priorities for
conveying information about the subject. And how could we do otherwise?
How else could van Lawick-Goodall have decided what information to
report out of all she must have observed during her first few months in
Africa? How else could Selzer have decided what to emphasize out of all the
information that he must have gathered from the time he first met his
patient until the time of the patient's death? Without specific purposes to
control our reporting, our records of events would be as long as the events
themselves.

Reporting, as you can see, necessarily serves a widely varied range of
purposes — as varied as the writers and their subjects. Thus, whenever you
read a piece of reportorial writing, you should always try to discover for
yourself what appear to be its guiding purposes by examining its structure,
its phrasing, and its wording, much as we have earlier in this discussion.

And once you have identified the purpose, you should then consider how it has influenced the selection, arrangement, and weighting of information in the report. When you turn to doing your own writing, you should be equally careful in determining your purposes for reporting as well as in organizing your report so as to put the information in a form that is true to what you know and think about the subject.

Methods of Reporting

In planning a piece of reportorial writing, you should be sure to keep in mind both your ideas about the subject and also the needs of your readers. Given that most of your readers will probably not be familiar with your information, you should be careful in selecting and organizing it to provide a clear and orderly report. Usually, you will find that the nature of your information suggests a corresponding method of presenting it most clearly and conveniently to your readers.

If the information concerns a single, detailed event or covers a set of events spread over time, the most effective method probably is narration — in the form of storytelling — in a more or less chronological order. This is the basic form that van Lawick-Goodall uses, and it proves to be a clear and persuasive form for gradually unfolding her discovery about the behavior of chimpanzees. If the information concerns a particular place or scene or spectacle, the most convenient method is description — presenting your information in a clear-cut spatial order to help your reader visualize both the overall scene and its important details. This is the method that Selzer uses in describing his patient's condition and in detailing the patient's posture and his hospital room. If your assignment were to synthesize what is known, up to that moment, about a complex public event, as was the case with Schmemann's report on the 9/11 attacks, you would need to look at a wider series of events. You might begin as he did, with the observable facts in New York and then introduce, as he did, other sources of information — flight schedules taken from the public record, Attorney General Ashcroft's announcements to reporters, the reported cell phone call from Barbara Olson, who was trapped on one of the flights, Mayor Giuliani's briefings to the press, White House announcements, and more. You would indicate the source of each piece of news, and by so doing, you would suggest the point of view from which it comes.

Although narration, description, topical summation, and other forms of reporting are often treated separately for purposes of identification, they usually end up working in combination with one another. Narratives, after all, involve events, people, and places, so they naturally should include descriptive passages. Similarly, descriptions of places frequently entail stories about events taking place in them, so it is not surprising that they include bits of narration. And given the synoptic nature of topical summations, they are likely to involve both descriptive and narrative elements. In writing, as in most other activities, form should follow function, rather than being forced to fit arbitrary rules of behavior.

Once you have settled on a basic form, you should then devise a way of managing—of selecting, arranging, and proportioning—your information within that form to achieve your purposes most effectively. To carry out this task, you will need to review all the material you have gathered to determine what you consider to be the most important information to report. Some bits or kinds of information inevitably will strike you as more significant than others, and these are the ones that you should feature in your report. Likewise, you will probably find that some information is simply not important enough even to be mentioned. Van Lawick-Goodall, for example, produces a striking account of her first few months in Africa because she focuses primarily on her observation of chimpanzees, subordinating all the other material she reports to her discoveries about their behavior. Thus, only on a couple of occasions does she include observations about the behavior of animals other than chimpanzees—in particular about the timidities of a bushbuck and a leopard. And she includes these observations only to point up by contrast the distinctively sociable behavior of chimpanzees. For the same reason, she proportions her coverage of several chimpanzee episodes to give the greatest amount of detail to the one that provides the most compelling indication of their advanced intelligence —namely, the final episode, which shows the chimpanzees to be tool users and makers, behaviors previously attributed only to human beings.

To help achieve your purposes, you should also give special thought to deciding on the perspective from which you present your information to the reader. Do you want to present the material in the first or third person? Do you want to be present in the piece, as are van Lawick-Goodall and Frank? Or do you want to be invisible, like Schmemann in his *New York Times* report, or W. H. Auden in his poem, "The Unknown Citizen" (p. 261)? To some extent, of course, your answer to these questions will depend on whether you gathered the information through your own firsthand observations and want to convey your firsthand reactions to your observations, as van Lawick-Goodall and Selzer do in their pieces. But there are no hard-and-fast rules on this score. You might look at "A Delicate Operation" by Roy C. Selby Jr. (p. 267). Although Selby must have written this piece on the basis of firsthand experience, he tells the story in the third person, removing himself almost completely from it except for such distant-sounding references to himself as "the surgeon." Selby is important to the information in this report, yet he evidently decided to deemphasize himself in writing the report. Ultimately, then, the nature of a report is substantially determined not only by *what* a writer gathers from various sources but also by *how* a writer presents the information.

In the reports that follow in this section, you will have an opportunity to see various ways of presenting things in writing. In later sections, you will see how reporting combines with other kinds of writing—explaining and arguing.

Arts and Humanities

AT HOME, AT SCHOOL, IN HIDING

Anne Frank

*Anne Frank (1929–1945) was born in Germany and lived there
until 1933, when her family moved to Holland to avoid the anti-
Jewish laws and other anti-Jewish conditions that were then taking hold in Nazi Germany. But the oppressiveness of those
conditions spread to Holland after the Nazi occupation in the
summer of 1940, as Frank reports in the following excerpt from
her diary. She started her diary on June 12, 1942, and continued
keeping it until August 1, 1944. Three days after the last entry,
the Frank family and a few employees who had been hiding with
them from the Nazis since July 1942 were arrested and taken to
a concentration camp in Auschwitz, Poland. In October 1944,
Anne and her sister, Margot, were moved to a concentration camp
at Bergen-Belsen, Germany, where Anne died of typhoid fever in
late February or early March 1945, a month or so before the
camp was liberated by British troops. Her father, Otto Frank, was
the only member of the family to survive the Holocaust, and in
1947 he produced a condensed version of the diary, which had
been hidden for safekeeping by two of his secretaries. The following excerpt is from the "Definitive Edition," published in
1995, which includes all of the material that Anne Frank had
imagined herself using in "a novel" or some other kind of account
about "how we lived, what we ate and what we talked about as
Jews in hiding." Her thoughts about making her story known
came to mind after she heard a radio broadcast in March 1944
about a planned postwar collection of diaries and letters dealing
with the war.*

SATURDAY, JUNE 20, 1942

Writing in a diary is a really strange experience for someone like me. Not only because I've never written anything before, but also because it seems to me that later on neither I nor anyone else will be interested in the musings of a thirteen-year-old schoolgirl. Oh well, it doesn't matter. I feel like writing, and I have an even greater need to get all kinds of things off my chest.

"Paper has more patience than people." I thought of this saying on one of those days when I was feeling a little depressed and was sitting at home with my chin in my hands, bored and listless, wondering whether to stay in or go out. I finally stayed where I was, brooding. Yes, paper *does* have more patience, and since I'm not planning to let anyone else read this stiff-backed notebook grandly referred to as a "diary," unless I should ever find a real friend, it probably won't make a bit of difference.

Now I'm back to the point that prompted me to keep a diary in the first place: I don't have a friend.

Let me put it more clearly, since no one will believe that a thirteen-year-old girl is completely alone in the world. And I'm not. I have loving parents and a sixteen-year-old sister, and there are about thirty people I can call friends. I have a throng of admirers who can't keep their adoring eyes off me and who sometimes have to resort to using a broken pocket mirror to try and catch a glimpse of me in the classroom. I have a family, loving aunts and a good home. No, on the surface I seem to have everything, except my one true friend. All I think about when I'm with friends is having a good time. I can't bring myself to talk about anything but ordinary everyday things. We don't seem to be able to get any closer, and that's the problem. Maybe it's my fault that we don't confide in each other. In any case, that's just how things are, and unfortunately they're not liable to change. This is why I've started the diary.

To enhance the image of this long-awaited friend in my imagination, I   5
don't want to jot down the facts in this diary the way most people would do, but I want the diary to be my friend, and I'm going to call this friend *Kitty*.

Since no one would understand a word of my stories to Kitty if I were to plunge right in, I'd better provide a brief sketch of my life, much as I dislike doing so.

My father, the most adorable father I've ever seen, didn't marry my mother until he was thirty-six and she was twenty-five. My sister Margot was born in Frankfurt am Main in Germany in 1926. I was born on June 12, 1929. I lived in Frankfurt until I was four. Because we're Jewish, my father immigrated to Holland in 1933, when he became the Managing Director of the Dutch Opekta Company, which manufactures products used in making jam. My mother, Edith Holländer Frank, went with him to Holland in September, while Margot and I were sent to Aachen to stay with our grandmother. Margot went to Holland in December, and I followed in February, when I was plunked down on the table as a birthday present for Margot.

I started right away at the Montessori nursery school. I stayed there until I was six, at which time I started first grade. In sixth grade my teacher was Mrs. Kuperus, the principal. At the end of the year we were both in tears as we said a heartbreaking farewell, because I'd been accepted at the Jewish Lyceum, where Margot also went to school.

Our lives were not without anxiety, since our relatives in Germany were suffering under Hitler's anti-Jewish laws. After the pogroms[1] in 1938 my two uncles (my mother's brothers) fled Germany, finding safe refuge in North America. My elderly grandmother came to live with us. She was seventy-three years old at the time.

After May 1940 the good times were few and far between: first there was   10 the war, then the capitulation and then the arrival of the Germans, which is when the trouble started for the Jews. Our freedom was severely restricted by a series of anti-Jewish decrees: Jews were required to wear a yellow star; Jews were required to turn in their bicycles; Jews were forbidden to use streetcars; Jews were forbidden to ride in cars, even their own; Jews were required to do their shopping between 3 and 5 P.M.; Jews were required to frequent only Jewish-owned barbershops and beauty parlors; Jews were forbidden to be out on the streets between 8 P.M. and 6 A.M.; Jews were forbidden to attend theaters, movies or any other forms of entertainment; Jews were forbidden to use swimming pools, tennis courts, hockey fields or any other athletic fields; Jews were forbidden to go rowing; Jews were forbidden to take part in any athletic activity in public; Jews were forbidden to sit in their gardens or those of their friends after 8 P.M.; Jews were forbidden to visit Christians in their homes; Jews were required to attend Jewish schools, etc. You couldn't do this and you couldn't do that, but life went on. Jacque always said to me, "I don't dare do anything anymore, 'cause I'm afraid it's not allowed."

In the summer of 1941 Grandma got sick and had to have an operation, so my birthday passed with little celebration. In the summer of 1940 we didn't do much for my birthday either, since the fighting had just ended in Holland. Grandma died in January 1942. No one knows how often *I* think of her and still love her. This birthday celebration in 1942 was intended to make up for the others, and Grandma's candle was lit along with the rest.

The four of us are still doing well, and that brings me to the present date of June 20, 1942, and the solemn dedication of my diary.

SATURDAY, JUNE 20, 1942

Dearest Kitty!

Let me get started right away; it's nice and quiet now. Father and Mother are out and Margot has gone to play Ping-Pong with some other young people at her friend Trees's. I've been playing a lot of Ping-Pong myself lately. So much that five of us girls have formed a club. It's called "The Little Dipper Minus Two." A really silly name, but it's based on a mistake. We wanted to give our club a special name; and because there were five of us, we came up

---

[1]*pogroms:* Violence against Jews and Jewish homes, businesses, and synagogues. [Eds.]

with the idea of the Little Dipper. We thought it consisted of five stars, but we turned out to be wrong. It has seven, like the Big Dipper, which explains the "Minus Two." Ilse Wagner has a Ping-Pong set, and the Wagners let us play in their big dining room whenever we want. Since we five Ping-Pong players like ice cream, especially in the summer, and since you get hot playing Ping-Pong, our games usually end with a visit to the nearest ice-cream parlor that allows Jews: either Oasis or Delphi. We've long since stopped hunting around for our purses or money — most of the time it's so busy in Oasis that we manage to find a few generous young men of our acquaintance or an admirer to offer us more ice cream than we could eat in a week.

You're probably a little surprised to hear me talking about admirers at such a tender age. Unfortunately, or not, as the case may be, this vice seems to be rampant at our school. As soon as a boy asks if he can bicycle home with me and we get to talking, nine times out of ten I can be sure he'll become enamored on the spot and won't let me out of his sight for a second. His ardor eventually cools, especially since I ignore his passionate glances and pedal blithely on my way. If it gets so bad that they start rambling on about "asking Father's permission," I swerve slightly on my bike, my schoolbag falls, and the young man feels obliged to get off his bike and hand me the bag, by which time I've switched the conversation to another topic. These are the most innocent types. Of course, there are those who blow you kisses or try to take hold of your arm, but they're definitely knocking on the wrong door. I get off my bike and either refuse to make further use of their company or act as if I'm insulted and tell them in no uncertain terms to go on home without me.

There you are. We've now laid the basis for our friendship. Until   15
tomorrow.

Yours, Anne

SUNDAY, JUNE 21, 1942

Dearest Kitty,

Our entire class is quaking in its boots. The reason, of course, is the upcoming meeting in which the teachers decide who'll be promoted to the next grade and who'll be kept back. Half the class is making bets. G. Z. and I laugh ourselves sick at the two boys behind us, C. N. and Jacques Kocernoot, who have staked their entire vacation savings on their bet. From morning to night, it's "You're going to pass," "No, I'm not," "Yes, you are," "No, I'm not." Even G.'s pleading glances and my angry outbursts can't calm them down. If you ask me, there are so many dummies that about a quarter of the class should be kept back, but teachers are the most unpredictable creatures on earth. Maybe this time they'll be unpredictable in the right direction for a change.

I'm not so worried about my girlfriends and myself. We'll make it. The only subject I'm not sure about is math. Anyway, all we can do is wait. Until then, we keep telling each other not to lose heart.

I get along pretty well with all my teachers. There are nine of them, seven men and two women. Mr. Keesing, the old fogey who teaches math, was mad at me for the longest time because I talked so much. After several warnings, he assigned me extra homework. An essay on the subject "A Chatterbox." A chatterbox, what can you write about that? I'd worry about that later, I decided. I jotted down the assignment in my notebook, tucked it in my bag and tried to keep quiet.

That evening, after I'd finished the rest of my homework, the note about the essay caught my eye. I began thinking about the subject while chewing the tip of my fountain pen. Anyone could ramble on and leave big spaces between the words, but the trick was to come up with convincing arguments to prove the necessity of talking. I thought and thought, and suddenly I had an idea. I wrote the three pages Mr. Keesing had assigned me and was satisfied. I argued that talking is a female trait and that I would do my best to keep it under control, but that I would never be able to break myself of the habit, since my mother talked as much as I did, if not more, and that there's not much you can do about inherited traits.

Mr. Keesing had a good laugh at my arguments, but when I proceeded   20
to talk my way through the next class, he assigned me a second essay. This time it was supposed to be on "An Incorrigible Chatterbox." I handed it in, and Mr. Keesing had nothing to complain about for two whole classes. However, during the third class he'd finally had enough. "Anne Frank, as punishment for talking in class, write an essay entitled '"Quack, Quack, Quack," Said Mistress Chatterback.'"

The class roared. I had to laugh too, though I'd nearly exhausted my ingenuity on the topic of chatterboxes. It was time to come up with something else, something original. My friend Sanne, who's good at poetry, offered to help me write the essay from beginning to end in verse. I jumped for joy. Keesing was trying to play a joke on me with this ridiculous subject, but I'd make sure the joke was on him.

I finished my poem, and it was beautiful! It was about a mother duck and a father swan with three baby ducklings who were bitten to death by the father because they quacked too much. Luckily, Keesing took the joke the right way. He read the poem to the class, adding his own comments, and to several other classes as well. Since then I've been allowed to talk and haven't been assigned any extra homework. On the contrary, Keesing's always making jokes these days.

Yours, Anne

WEDNESDAY, JULY 1, 1942

Dearest Kitty,

   Until today I honestly couldn't find the time to write you. I was with friends all day Thursday, we had company on Friday, and that's how it went until today.

   Hello and I have gotten to know each other very well this past week, and he's told me a lot about his life. He comes from Gelsenkirchen and is living with his grandparents. His parents are in Belgium, but there's no way he can get there. Hello used to have a girlfriend named Ursul. I know her too. She's perfectly sweet and perfectly boring. Ever since he met me, Hello has realized that he's been falling asleep at Ursul's side. So I'm kind of a pep tonic. You never know what you're good for!

Jacque spent Saturday night here. Sunday afternoon she was at   25
Hanneli's, and I was bored stiff.

Hello was supposed to come over that evening, but he called around six. I answered the phone, and he said, "This is Helmuth Silberberg. May I please speak to Anne?"

"Oh, Hello. This is Anne."

"Oh, hi, Anne. How are you?"

"Fine, thanks."

"I just wanted to say I'm sorry but I can't come tonight, though I would   30
like to have a word with you. Is it all right if I come by and pick you up in about ten minutes?"

"Yes, that's fine. Bye-bye!"

"Okay, I'll be right over. Bye-bye!"

I hung up, quickly changed my clothes and fixed my hair. I was so nervous I leaned out the window to watch for him. He finally showed up. Miracle of miracles, I didn't rush down the stairs, but waited quietly until he rang the bell. I went down to open the door, and he got right to the point.

"Anne, my grandmother thinks you're too young for me to be seeing you on a regular basis. She says I should be going to the Lowenbachs', but you probably know that I'm not going out with Ursul anymore."

"No, I didn't know. What happened? Did you two have a fight?"   35

"No, nothing like that. I told Ursul that we weren't suited to each other and so it was better for us not to go together anymore, but that she was welcome at my house and I hoped I would be welcome at hers. Actually, I thought Ursul was hanging around with another boy, and I treated her as if she were. But that wasn't true. And then my uncle said I should apologize to her, but of course I didn't feel like it, and that's why I broke up with her. But that was just one of the reasons.

"Now my grandmother wants me to see Ursul and not you, but I don't agree and I'm not going to. Sometimes old people have really old-fashioned ideas, but that doesn't mean I have to go along with them. I need my grandparents, but in a certain sense they need me too. From now on I'll be free on Wednesday evenings. You see, my grandparents made me sign up for a wood-carving class, but actually I go to a club organized by the Zionists.[2] My grandparents don't want me to go, because they're anti-Zionists. I'm not a fanatic Zionist, but it interests me. Anyway, it's been such a mess lately that I'm planning to quit. So next Wednesday will be my last meeting. That

---

[2]*Zionists:* Followers of an international movement to segregate the Jewish people as a state and to establish a Jewish state in Palestine, modern-day Israel. [Eds.]

means I can see you Wednesday evening, Saturday afternoon, Saturday evening, Sunday afternoon and maybe even more."

"But if your grandparents don't want you to, you shouldn't go behind their backs."

"All's fair in love and war."

Just then we passed Blankevoort's Bookstore and there was Peter Schiff   40
with two other boys; it was the first time he'd said hello to me in ages, and it really made me feel good.

Monday evening Hello came over to meet Father and Mother. I had bought a cake and some candy, and we had tea and cookies, the works, but neither Hello nor I felt like sitting stiffly on our chairs. So we went out for a walk, and he didn't deliver me to my door until ten past eight. Father was furious. He said it was very wrong of me not to get home on time. I had to promise to be home by ten to eight in the future. I've been asked to Hello's on Saturday.

Wilma told me that one night when Hello was at her house, she asked him, "Who do you like best, Ursul or Anne?"

He said, "It's none of your business."

But as he was leaving (they hadn't talked to each other the rest of the evening), he said, "Well, I like Anne better, but don't tell anyone. Bye!" And whoosh . . . he was out the door.

In everything he says or does, I can see that Hello is in love with me, and   45
it's kind of nice for a change. Margot would say that Hello is eminently suitable. I think so too, but he's more than that. Mother is also full of praise: "A good-looking boy. Nice and polite." I'm glad he's so popular with everyone. Except with my girlfriends. He thinks they're very childish, and he's right about that. Jacque still teases me about him, but I'm not in love with him. Not really. It's all right for me to have boys as friends. Nobody minds.

Mother is always asking me who I'm going to marry when I grow up, but I bet she'll never guess it's Peter, because I talked her out of that idea myself, without batting an eyelash. I love Peter as I've never loved anyone, and I tell myself he's only going around with all those other girls to hide his feelings for me. Maybe he thinks Hello and I are in love with each other, which we're not. He's just a friend, or as Mother puts it, a beau.

Yours, Anne

WEDNESDAY, JULY 8, 1942

Dearest Kitty,

It seems like years since Sunday morning. So much has happened it's as if the whole world had suddenly turned upside down. But as you can see, Kitty, I'm still alive, and that's the main thing, Father says. I'm alive all right, but don't ask where or how. You probably don't understand a word I'm saying today, so I'll begin by telling you what happened Sunday afternoon.

At three o'clock (Hello had left but was supposed to come back later), the doorbell rang. I didn't hear it, since I was out on the balcony, lazily reading in the sun. A little while later Margot appeared in the kitchen doorway looking very agitated. "Father has received a call-up notice from the SS,"[3] she whispered. "Mother has gone to see Mr. van Daan" (Mr. van Daan is Father's business partner and a good friend.)

I was stunned. A call-up: everyone knows what that means. Visions of concentration camps and lonely cells raced through my head. How could we let Father go to such a fate? "Of course he's not going," declared Margot as we waited for Mother in the living room. "Mother's gone to Mr. van Daan to ask whether we can move to our hiding place tomorrow. The van Daans are going with us. There will be seven of us altogether." Silence. We couldn't speak. The thought of Father off visiting someone in the Jewish Hospital and completely unaware of what was happening, the long wait for Mother, the heat, the suspense—all this reduced us to silence.

Suddenly the doorbell rang again. "That's Hello," I said.   50

"Don't open the door!" exclaimed Margot to stop me. But it wasn't necessary, since we heard Mother and Mr. van Daan downstairs talking to Hello, and then the two of them came inside and shut the door behind them. Every time the bell rang, either Margot or I had to tiptoe downstairs to see if it was Father, and we didn't let anyone else in. Margot and I were sent from the room, as Mr. van Daan wanted to talk to Mother alone.

When she and I were sitting in our bedroom, Margot told me that the call-up was not for Father, but for her. At this second shock, I began to cry. Margot is sixteen—apparently they want to send girls her age away on their own. But thank goodness she won't be going; Mother had said so herself, which must be what Father had meant when he talked to me about our going into hiding. Hiding . . . where would we hide? In the city? In the country? In a house? In a shack? When, where, how . . . ? These were questions I wasn't allowed to ask, but they still kept running through my mind.

Margot and I started packing our most important belongings into a schoolbag. The first thing I stuck in was this diary, and then curlers, handkerchiefs, schoolbooks, a comb and some old letters. Preoccupied by the thought of going into hiding, I stuck the craziest things in the bag, but I'm not sorry. Memories mean more to me than dresses.

Father finally came home around five o'clock, and we called Mr. Kleiman to ask if he could come by that evening. Mr. van Daan left and went to get Miep. Miep arrived and promised to return later that night, taking with her a bag full of shoes, dresses, jackets, underwear and stockings. After that it was quiet in our apartment; none of us felt like eating. It was still hot, and everything was very strange.

We had rented our big upstairs room to a Mr. Goldschmidt, a divorced   55
man in his thirties, who apparently had nothing to do that evening, since despite all our polite hints he hung around until ten o'clock.

---

[3]SS: The Schutzstaffel (German). By 1942, the SS, under the leadership of Heinrich Himmel, was the principal instrument of internal rule in Germany. Some SS units were put in charge of Germany's concentration camps. [Eds.]

Miep and Jan Gies came at eleven. Miep, who's worked for Father's company since 1933, has become a close friend, and so has her husband Jan. Once again, shoes, stockings, books and underwear disappeared into Miep's bag and Jan's deep pockets. At eleven-thirty they too disappeared.

I was exhausted, and even though I knew it'd be my last night in my own bed, I fell asleep right away and didn't wake up until Mother called me at five-thirty the next morning. Fortunately, it wasn't as hot as Sunday; a warm rain fell throughout the day. The four of us were wrapped in so many layers of clothes it looked as if we were going off to spend the night in a refrigerator, and all that just so we could take more clothes with us. No Jew in our situation would dare leave the house with a suitcase full of clothes. I was wearing two undershirts, three pairs of underpants, a dress, and over that a skirt, a jacket, a raincoat, two pairs of stockings, heavy shoes, a cap, a scarf and lots more. I was suffocating even before we left the house, but no one bothered to ask me how I felt.

Margot stuffed her schoolbag with schoolbooks, went to get her bicycle and, with Miep leading the way, rode off into the great unknown. At any rate, that's how I thought of it, since I still didn't know where our hiding place was.

At seven-thirty we too closed the door behind us; Moortje, my cat, was the only living creature I said good-bye to. According to a note we left for Mr. Goldschmidt, she was to be taken to the neighbors, who would give her a good home.

The stripped beds, the breakfast things on the table, the pound of meat   60
for the cat in the kitchen—all of these created the impression that we'd left in a hurry. But we weren't interested in impressions. We just wanted to get out of there, to get away and reach our destination in safety. Nothing else mattered.

More tomorrow.

Yours, Anne

QUESTIONS

1. In the first entry for June 20, Frank writes at length about wanting her diary to be a very special kind of friend. What kind of friend does she have in mind? How would you characterize Frank's friendship with Kitty as it develops over the several entries included in this excerpt?

2. How are your impressions of the friendship (and of Frank) affected by the fact that she sometimes goes several days without writing anything in her diary?

3. What kind of person does Frank appear to be from the information she reports and the stories she tells about her family? About anti-Jewish decrees? About her boyfriends? About her experiences at school?

4. What kind of person does Frank appear to be from the thoughts and feelings she expresses about these different aspects of her life? Does she

come across differently (or similarly) when she is writing about these different aspects of her life?

5. In what respects does Frank's life as a thirteen-year-old seem most different from yours when you were thirteen? In what respects does it seem most similar to yours when you were that age? In what ways do you identify with Frank? In what ways do you find her experience so different as to greatly distance you from her?

6. Given what you discover about Frank's day-to-day life with her friends and at school, what do you consider to be the most important similarities and differences between young adolescent life then and now?

7. Compare and contrast the anti-Jewish decrees that Frank reports with racist decrees that you have read about in South Africa, the United States, and other countries around the world.

8. Keep a diary for several weeks in which you try to make a detailed report of the different aspects of your life in a form that you might be willing to share with a close friend (real or imaginary) as well as with a large body of readers.

MAKING CONNECTIONS

1. What similarities do you find between the lives of the women that Amanda Coyne describes in "The Long Good-Bye: Mother's Day in Federal Prison" (p. 189) or the women in the San Francisco County Jail described by Christina Boufis (p. 198) and Frank's reaction to her own imprisonment?

2. To what extent does Patricia Hampl's "Reviewing Anne Frank" (p. 4) influence how you read Frank herself in this selection?

HATSUYO NAKAMURA

John Hersey

John Hersey (1914–1993) was born in Tientsin, China, where his father was a YMCA administrator and his mother a missionary. After graduating from Yale in 1936, Hersey was a war correspondent in China and Japan. When the United States entered World War II, Hersey covered the war in the South Pacific, the Mediterranean, and Moscow. In 1945, he won the Pulitzer Prize for his novel A Bell for Adano. *In 1946,* Hiroshima, *a book about the effects of the atomic bomb on the lives of six people, was widely acclaimed. Almost forty years later, Hersey returned to Japan to find out what the lives of those six people had been like. Their stories form the final chapter of the 1985 edition of* Hiroshima. *The selection presented here first appeared in* The New Yorker, *as did the first edition of* Hiroshima. *A prolific writer of fiction and nonfiction, Hersey believes that "journalism allows its readers to witness history; fiction gives its readers an opportunity to live it."*

In August, 1946, a year after the bombing of Hiroshima, Hatsuyo Nakamura was weak and destitute. Her husband, a tailor, had been taken into the Army and had been killed at Singapore on the day of the city's capture, February 15, 1942. She lost her mother, a brother, and a sister to the atomic bomb. Her son and two daughters—ten, eight, and five years old—were buried in rubble when the blast of the bomb flung her house down. In a frenzy, she dug them out alive. A month after the bombing, she came down with radiation sickness; she lost most of her hair and lay in bed for weeks with a high fever in the house of her sister-in-law in the suburb of Kabe, worrying all the time about how to support her children. She was too poor to go to a doctor. Gradually, the worst of the symptoms abated, but she remained feeble; the slightest exertion wore her out.

She was near the end of her resources. Fleeing from her house through the fires on the day of the bombing, she had saved nothing but a rucksack of emergency clothing, a blanket, an umbrella, and a suitcase of things she had stored in her air-raid shelter; she had much earlier evacuated a few kimonos to Kabe in fear of a bombing. Around the time her hair started to grow in again, her brother-in-law went back to the ruins of her house and recovered her late husband's Sankoku sewing machine, which needed repairs. And though she had lost the certificates of a few bonds and other meager wartime savings, she had luckily copied off their numbers before the bombing and taken the record to Kabe, so she was eventually able to cash them in. This money enabled her to rent for fifty yen a month—the equivalent then of less than fifteen cents — a small wooden shack built by a carpenter in the Nobori-cho neighborhood, near the site of her former home. In this way, she could free herself from the charity of her in-laws and begin a courageous struggle, which would last for many years, to keep her children and herself alive.

The hut had a dirt floor and was dark inside, but it was a home of sorts. Raking back some rubble next to it, she planted a garden. From the debris of collapsed houses she scavenged cooking utensils and a few dishes. She had the Sankoku fixed and began to take in some sewing, and from time to time she did cleaning and laundry and washed dishes for neighbors who were some-what better off than she was. But she got so tired that she had to take two days' rest for every three days she worked, and if she was obliged for some reason to work for a whole week she then had to rest for three or four days. She soon ran through her savings and was forced to sell her best kimono.

At that precarious time, she fell ill. Her belly began to swell up, and she had diarrhea and so much pain she could no longer work at all. A doctor who lived nearby came to see her and told her she had roundworm, and he said, incorrectly, "If it bites your intestine, you'll die." In those days, there was a shortage of chemical fertilizers in Japan, so farmers were using night soil, and as a consequence many people began to harbor parasites, which were not fatal in themselves but were seriously debilitating to those who had had radiation sickness. The doctor treated Nakamura-san (as he would have addressed her) with santonin, a somewhat dangerous medicine derived from certain varieties of artemisia.[1] To pay the doctor, she was forced to sell her last valuable possession, her husband's sewing machine. She came to think of that as marking the lowest and saddest moment of her whole life.

In referring to those who went through the Hiroshima and Nagasaki   5
bombings, the Japanese tended to shy away from the term "survivors," because in its focus on being alive it might suggest some slight to the sacred dead. The class of people to which Nakamura-san belonged came, therefore, to be called by a more neutral name, "hibakusha" — literally, "explosion-affected persons." For more than a decade after the bombings, the hibakusha lived in an economic limbo, apparently because the Japanese gov-ernment did not want to find itself saddled with anything like moral respon-sibility for heinous acts of the victorious United States. Although it soon became clear that many hibakusha suffered consequences of their exposure to the bombs which were quite different in nature and degree from those of survivors even of the ghastly fire bombings in Tokyo and elsewhere, the gov-ernment made no special provision for their relief — until, ironically, after the storm of rage that swept across Japan when the twenty-three crewmen of a fishing vessel, the Lucky Dragon No. 5, and its cargo of tuna were irra-diated by the American test of a hydrogen bomb at Bikini in 1954. It took three years even then for a relief law for the hibakusha to pass the Diet.

---

[1]*artemisia:* A genus of herbs and shrubs, including sagebrush and wormwood, distinguished by strong-smelling foliage. [Eds.]

Though Nakamura-san could not know it, she thus had a bleak period ahead of her. In Hiroshima, the early postwar years were, besides, a time, especially painful for poor people like her, of disorder, hunger, greed, thievery, black markets. Non-hibakusha employers developed a prejudice against the survivors as word got around that they were prone to all sorts of ailments, and that even those like Nakamura-san, who were not cruelly maimed and had not developed any serious overt symptoms, were unreliable workers, since most of them seemed to suffer, as she did, from the mysterious but real malaise that came to be known as one kind of lasting "A-bomb sickness": a nagging weakness and weariness, dizziness now and then, digestive troubles, all aggravated by a feeling of oppression, a sense of doom, for it was said that unspeakable diseases might at any time plant nasty flowers in their bodies, and even in those of their descendants.

As Nakamura-san struggled to get from day to day, she had no time for attitudinizing about the bomb or anything else. She was sustained, curiously, by a kind of passivity, summed up in a phrase she herself sometimes used — "*Shikata ga-nai*," meaning, loosely, "It can't be helped." She was not religious, but she lived in a culture long colored by the Buddhist belief that resignation might lead to clear vision; she had shared with other citizens a deep feeling of powerlessness in the face of a state authority that had been divinely strong ever since the Meiji Restoration,[2] in 1868; and the hell she had witnessed and the terrible aftermath unfolding around her reached so far beyond human understanding that it was impossible to think of them as the work of resentable human beings, such as the pilot of the *Enola Gay*,[3] or President Truman,[4] or the scientists who had made the bomb — or even, nearer at hand, the Japanese militarists who had helped to bring on the war. The bombing almost seemed a natural disaster — one that it had simply been her bad luck, her fate (which must be accepted), to suffer.

When she had been wormed and felt slightly better, she made an arrangement to deliver bread for a baker named Takahashi, whose bakery was in Nobori-cho. On days when she had the strength to do it, she would take orders for bread from retail shops in her neighborhood, and the next morning she would pick up the requisite number of loaves and carry them in baskets and boxes through the streets to the stores. It was exhausting work, for which she earned the equivalent of about fifty cents a day. She had to take frequent rest days.

After some time, when she was feeling a bit stronger, she took up another kind of peddling. She would get up in the dark and trundle a borrowed two-wheeled pushcart for two hours across the city to a section called Eba,

---

[2]*Meiji Restoration:* A revolution in Japan that restored imperial rule in 1868 under young Emperor Meiji and transformed the country from a feudal state into a modern state. [Eds.]

[3]*Enola Gay:* The U.S. Army Air Force's B-29 bomber that dropped an atomic bomb on Hiroshima. [Eds.]

[4]*Harry S Truman* (1884–1972): The president of the United States who gave the order to use the atomic bomb in Japan. [Eds.]

at the mouth of one of the seven estuarial rivers that branch from the Ota River through Hiroshima. There, at daylight, fishermen would cast their leaded skirt-like nets for sardines, and she would help them to gather up the catch when they hauled it in. Then she would push the cart back to Nobori-cho and sell the fish for them from door to door. She earned just enough for food.

A couple of years later, she found work that was better suited to her need   10 for occasional rest, because within certain limits she could do it on her own time. This was a job of collecting money for deliveries of the Hiroshima paper, the *Chugoku Shimbun*, which most people in the city read. She had to cover a big territory, and often her clients were not at home or pleaded that they couldn't pay just then, so she would have to go back again and again. She earned the equivalent of about twenty dollars a month at this job. Every day, her will power and her weariness seemed to fight to an uneasy draw.

In 1951, after years of this drudgery, it was Nakamura-san's good luck, her fate (which must be accepted), to become eligible to move into a better house. Two years earlier, a Quaker professor of dendrology from the University of Washington named Floyd W. Schmoe, driven, apparently, by deep urges for expiation and reconciliation, had come to Hiroshima, assembled a team of carpenters, and, with his own hands and theirs, begun building a series of Japanese-style houses for victims of the bomb; in all, his team eventually built twenty-one. It was to one of these houses that Nakamura-san had the good fortune to be assigned. The Japanese measure their houses by multiples of the area of the floor-covering *tsubo* mat, a little less than four square yards, and the Dr. Shum-o houses, as the Hiroshimans called them, had two rooms of six mats each. This was a big step up for the Nakamuras. This home was redolent of new wood and clean matting. The rent, payable to the city government, was the equivalent of about a dollar a month.

Despite the family's poverty, the children seemed to be growing normally. Yaeko and Myeko, the two daughters, were anemic, but all three had so far escaped any of the more serious complications that so many young hibakusha were suffering. Yaeko, now fourteen, and Myeko, eleven, were in middle school. The boy, Toshio, ready to enter high school, was going to have to earn money to attend it, so he took up delivering papers to the places from which his mother was collecting. These were some distance from their Dr. Shum-o house, and they had to commute at odd hours by streetcar.

The old hut in Nobori-cho stood empty for a time, and, while continuing with her newspaper collections, Nakamura-san converted it into a small street shop for children, selling sweet potatoes, which she roasted, and *dagashi*, or little candies and rice cakes, and cheap toys, which she bought from a wholesaler.

All along, she had been collecting for papers from a small company, Suyama Chemical, that made mothballs sold under the trade name Paragen. A friend of hers worked there, and one day she suggested to Nakamura-san that she join the company, helping wrap the product in its packages. The owner, Nakamura-san learned, was a compassionate man, who did not share the bias of many employers against hibakusha; he had several on his staff of twenty women wrappers. Nakamura-san objected that she couldn't work more than a few days at a time; the friend persuaded her that Suyama would understand that.

So she began. Dressed in company uniforms, the women stood, some- 15 what bent over, on either side of a couple of conveyor belts, working as fast as possible to wrap two kinds of Paragen in cellophane. Paragen had a dizzying odor, and at first it made one's eyes smart. Its substance, powdered paradichlorobenzene, had been compressed into lozenge-shaped mothballs and into larger spheres, the size of small oranges, to be hung in Japanese-style toilets, where their rank pseudomedicinal smell would offset the unpleasantness of non-flushing facilities.

Nakamura-san was paid, as a beginner, a hundred and seventy yen — then less than fifty cents — a day. At first, the work was confusing, terribly tiring, and a bit sickening. Her boss worried about her paleness. She had to take many days off. But little by little she became used to the factory. She made friends. There was a family atmosphere. She got raises. In the two ten-minute breaks, morning and afternoon, when the moving belt stopped, there was a birdsong of gossip and laughter, in which she joined. It appeared that all along there had been, deep in her temperament, a core of cheerfulness, which must have fueled her long fight against A bomb lassitude, something warmer and more vivifying than mere submission, than saying "*Shikata ga-nai.*" The other women took to her; she was constantly doing them small favors. They began calling her, affectionately, *Oba-san* — roughly, "Auntie."

She worked at Suyama for thirteen years. Though her energy still paid its dues, from time to time, to the A-bomb syndrome, the searing experiences of that day in 1945 seemed gradually to be receding from the front of her mind.

The Lucky Dragon No. 5 episode took place the year after Nakamura-san started working for Suyama Chemical. In the ensuing fever of outrage in the country, the provision of adequate medical care for the victims of the Hiroshima and Nagasaki bombs finally became a political issue. Almost every year since 1946, on the anniversary of the Hiroshima bombing, a Peace Memorial Meeting had been held in a park that the city planners had set aside, during the city's rebuilding, as a center of remembrance, and on August 6, 1955, delegates from all over the world gathered there for the first World Conference Against Atomic and Hydrogen Bombs. On its second day, a number of hibakusha tearfully testified to the government's neglect of their plight. Japanese political parties took up the cause, and in 1957 the Diet at last passed the A-Bomb Victims Medical Care Law. This law and its subsequent modifications defined four classes of people who would be eligible for support: those who had been in the city limits on the day of the bombing; those who had entered an area within two kilometers of the hypocenter in the first fourteen days after it; those who had come into physical contact with bomb victims, in administering first aid or in disposing of their bodies; and those who had been embryos in the wombs of women in any of the first three categories. These hibakusha were entitled to receive so-called health books, which would entitle them to free medical treatment. Later revisions of the law provided for monthly allowances to victims suffering from various aftereffects.

Like a great many hibakusha, Nakamura-san had kept away from all the agitation, and, in fact, also like many other survivors, she did not even bother to get a health book for a couple of years after they were issued. She had been too poor to keep going to doctors, so she had got into the habit of coping alone, as best she could, with her physical difficulties. Besides, she shared with some other survivors a suspicion of ulterior motives on the part of the political-minded people who took part in the annual ceremonies and conferences.

Nakamura-san's son, Toshio, right after his graduation from high   20
school, went to work for the bus division of the Japanese National Railways. He was in the administrative offices, working first on timetables, later in accounting. When he was in his midtwenties, a marriage was arranged for him, through a relative who knew the bride's family. He built an addition to the Dr. Shum-o house, moved in, and began to contribute to his mother's support. He made her a present of a new sewing machine.

Yaeko, the older daughter, left Hiroshima when she was fifteen, right after graduating from middle school, to help an ailing aunt who ran a *ryo-kan*, a Japanese-style inn. There, in due course, she fell in love with a man who ate at the inn's restaurant, and she made a love marriage.

After graduating from high school, Myeko, the most susceptible of the three children to the A-bomb syndrome, eventually became an expert typist and took up instructing at typing schools. In time, a marriage was arranged for her.

Like their mother, all three children avoided pro-hibakusha and anti-nuclear agitation.

In 1966, Nakamura-san, having reached the age of fifty-five, retired from Suyama Chemical. At the end, she was being paid thirty thousand yen, or about eighty-five dollars, a month. Her children were no longer dependent on her, and Toshio was ready to take on a son's responsibility for his aging mother. She felt at home in her body now; she rested when she needed to, and she had no worries about the cost of medical care, for she had finally picked up Health Book No. 1023993. It was time for her to enjoy life. For her pleasure in being able to give gifts, she took up embroidery and the dressing of traditional *kimekomi* dolls, which are supposed to bring good luck. Wearing a bright kimono, she went once a week to dance at the Study Group of Japanese Folk Music. In set movements, with expressive gestures, her hands now and then tucking up the long folds of the kimono sleeves, and with head held high, she danced, moving as if floating, with thirty agreeable women to a song of celebration of entrance into a house:

> May your family flourish
> For a thousand generations,
> For eight thousand generations.

A year or so after Nakamura-san retired, she was invited by an organi-   25
zation called the Bereaved Families' Association to take a train trip with
about a hundred other war widows to visit the Yasukuni Shrine, in Tokyo.
This holy place, established in 1869, was dedicated to the spirits of all the
Japanese who had died in wars against foreign powers, and could be thought
roughly analogous, in terms of its symbolism for the nation, to the Arlington
National Cemetery—with the difference that souls, not bodies, were hal-
lowed there. The shrine was considered by many Japanese to be a focus of a
still smoldering Japanese militarism, but Nakamura-san, who had never seen
her husband's ashes and had held on to a belief that he would return to her
someday, was oblivious of all that. She found the visit baffling. Besides the
Hiroshima hundred, there were huge crowds of women from other cities on
the shrine grounds. It was impossible for her to summon up a sense of her
dead husband's presence, and she returned home in an uneasy state of mind.

Japan was booming. Things were still rather tight for the Nakamuras, and
Toshio had to work very long hours, but the old days of bitter struggle began
to seem remote. In 1975, one of the laws providing support to the hibakusha
was revised, and Nakamura-san began to receive a so-called health-protection
allowance of six thousand yen, then about twenty dollars, a month; this would
gradually be increased to more than twice that amount. She also received a
pension, toward which she had contributed at Suyama, of twenty thousand
yen, or about sixty-five dollars, a month; and for several years she had been
receiving a war widow's pension of another twenty thousand yen a month.
With the economic upswing, prices had, of course, risen steeply (in a few years
Tokyo would become the most expensive city in the world), but Toshio managed to buy a small Mitsubishi car, and occasionally he got up before dawn
and rode a train for two hours to play golf with business associates. Yaeko's
husband ran a shop for sales and service of air-conditioners and heaters, and
Myeko's husband ran a newsstand and candy shop near the railroad station.
    In May each year, around the time of the Emperor's birthday, when the
trees along broad Peace Boulevard were at their feathery best and banked
azaleas were everywhere in bloom, Hiroshima celebrated a flower festival.
Entertainment booths lined the boulevard, and there were long parades,
with floats and bands and thousands of marchers. This year, Nakamura-san
danced with the women of the folk-dance association, six dancers in each
of sixty rows. They danced to "Oiwai-Ondo," a song of happiness, lifting
their arms in gestures of joy and clapping in rhythms of threes:

> Green pine trees, cranes and turtles . . .
> You must tell a story of your hard times
> And laugh twice.

The bombing had been four decades ago. How far away it seemed!
    The sun blazed that day. The measured steps and the constant lifting of
the arms for hours at a time were tiring. In midafternoon, Nakamura-san

suddenly felt woozy. The next thing she knew, she was being lifted, to her great embarrassment and in spite of begging to be let alone, into an ambulance. At the hospital, she said she was fine; all she wanted was to go home. She was allowed to leave.

QUESTIONS

1. What does Hatsuyo Nakamura's story tell us about the larger group of atomic-bomb survivors?
2. Why do you think Hersey chose Hatsuyo Nakamura as a subject to report on? How is she presented to us? How are we meant to feel about her?
3. In composing his article, Hersey presumably interviewed Hatsuyo Nakamura and reports from her point of view. At what points does he augment her story? For example, look at paragraph 5. What material in the article probably comes from Nakamura? What material probably comes from other sources?
4. How has Hersey arranged his material? He has covered forty years of Hatsuyo Nakamura's life in twenty-nine paragraphs. Make a list of the events he chose to report. At what points does he condense large blocks of time?
5. Interview a relative or someone else who participated in World War II or in some other war, such as Vietnam. How did the war change that person's life? What events does he or she consider most important in the intervening years?
6. Most Americans of certain ages remember days of critical national events —the attack on Pearl Harbor, the Kennedy and King assassinations, the space shuttle disasters, and so on. Interview several people about one such day, finding out where they were when they first learned of the event, how they reacted, what long-term impact they felt, and how they view that day now. Use the information from your interviews to write a report.

MAKING CONNECTIONS

1. Imagine an encounter between Nakamura and either Zoë Tracy Hardy ("What Did You Do in the War, Grandma? A Flashback to August 1945," p. 126), or William L. Laurence ("Atomic Bombing of Nagasaki Told by a Flight Member" p. 229). What might these people say to one another? Write the dialogue for a possible conversation between them.
2. One characteristic of reports is to be tentative or even oblique in drawing conclusions. Compare Hersey's report to one by Richard Selzer (p. 263), or Roy C. Selby Jr. (p. 267), and assess their differing methods of coming to a conclusion. What would you say the points are of the two reports you chose to compare?

THE LONG GOOD-BYE
Mother's Day in Federal Prison

Amanda Coyne

Amanda Coyne (b. 1966) was born in Colorado and subsequently migrated with her family from Alaska to ten other states as her father's "relentless pursuit of better employment" led him to hold such titles as fry cook, janitor, librarian, college professor, magazine editor, and presidential speechwriter. Coyne describes her own life as having thus far been "similarly kinetic and varied." "Between traveling, experimenting with religion, countercultural lifestyles, and writing," she has been employed as a waitress, nursing home assistant, teacher, public relations associate, and public policy analyst. A graduate of the University of Iowa, Coyne is currently a staff writer with the Anchorage Press *in Alaska. The following essay, which appeared in* Harper's *(May 1997), was her first publication.*

You can spot the convict-moms here in the visiting room by the way they hold and touch their children and by the single flower that is perched in front of them—a rose, a tulip, a daffodil. Many of these mothers have untied the bow that attaches the flower to its silver-and-red cellophane wrapper and are using one of the many empty soda cans at hand as a vase. They sit proudly before their flower-in-a-Coke-can, amid Hershey bar wrappers, half-eaten Ding Dongs, and empty paper coffee cups. Occasionally, a mother will pick up her present and bring it to her nose when one of the bearers of the single flower—her child—asks if she likes it. And the mother will respond the way that mothers always have and always will respond when presented with a gift on this day. "Oh, I just love it. It's perfect. I'll put it in the middle of my Bible." Or, "I'll put it on my desk, right next to your school picture." And always: "It's the best one here."

But most of what is being smelled today is the children themselves. While the other adults are plunking coins into the vending machines, the mothers take deep whiffs from the backs of their children's necks, or kiss and smell the backs of their knees, or take off their shoes and tickle their feet and then pull them close to their noses. They hold them tight and take in their own second scent—the scent assuring them that these are still their children and that they still belong to them.

The visitors are allowed to bring in pockets full of coins, and today that Mother's Day flower, and I know from previous visits to my older sister here at the Federal Prison Camp for women in Pekin, Illinois, that there is always an aberrant urge to gather immediately around the vending machines. The

189

Jennifer, Prisoner number 07235-029.

sandwiches are stale, the coffee weak, the candy bars the ones we always pass up in a convenience store. But after we hand the children over to their mothers, we gravitate toward those machines. Like milling in the kitchen at a party. We all do it, and nobody knows why. Polite conversation ensues around the microwave while the popcorn is popping and the processed-chicken sandwiches are being heated. We ask one another where we are from, how long a drive we had. An occasional whistle through the teeth, a shake of the head. "My, my, long way from home, huh?" "Staying at the Super 8 right up the road. Not a bad place." "Stayed at the Econo Lodge last time. Wasn't a good place at all." Never asking the questions we really want to ask: "What's she in for?" "How much time's she got left?" You never ask in the waiting room of a doctor's office either. Eventually, all of us—fathers, mothers, sisters, brothers, a few boyfriends, and very few husbands—return to the queen of the day, sitting at a fold-out table loaded with snacks, prepared for five or so hours of attempted normal conversation.

Most of the inmates are elaborately dressed, many in prison-crafted dresses and sweaters in bright blues and pinks. They wear meticulously applied makeup in corresponding hues, and their hair is replete with loops and curls—hair that only women with the time have the time for. Some of the better seamstresses have crocheted vests and purses to match their outfits. Although the world outside would never accuse these women of making haute-couture fashion statements, the fathers and the sons and the boyfriends and the very few husbands think they look beautiful, and they tell them so repeatedly. And I can imagine the hours spent preparing for this visit—hours of needles and hooks clicking over brightly colored yards of yarn. The hours of discussing, dissecting, and bragging about these visitors—especially the men. Hours spent in the other world behind the door where we're not allowed, sharing lipsticks and mascaras, and unraveling the occasional hair-tangled hot roller, and the brushing out and lifting and teasing . . . and the giggles that abruptly change into tears without warning—things that define any female-only world. Even, or especially, if that world is a female federal prison camp.

While my sister Jennifer is with her son in the playroom, an inmate's   5
mother comes over to introduce herself to my younger sister, Charity, my brother, John, and me. She tells us about visiting her daughter in a higher-security prison before she was transferred here. The woman looks old and tired, and her shoulders sag under the weight of her recently acquired bitterness.

"Pit of fire," she says, shaking her head. "Like a pit of fire straight from hell. Never seen anything like it. Like something out of an old movie about prisons." Her voice is getting louder and she looks at each of us with pleading eyes. "My *daughter* was there. Don't even get me started on that place. Women die there."

John and Charity and I silently exchange glances.

"My daughter would come to the visiting room with a black eye and I'd think, 'All she did was sit in the car while her boyfriend ran into the house.' She didn't even touch the stuff. Never even handled it."

She continues to stare at us, each in turn. "Ten years. That boyfriend talked and he got three years. She didn't know anything. Had nothing to tell them. They gave her ten years. They called it conspiracy. Conspiracy? Aren't there real criminals out there?" She asks this with hands out-stretched, waiting for an answer that none of us can give her.

The woman's daughter, the conspirator, is chasing her son through the   10
maze of chairs and tables and through the other children. She's a twenty-four-year-old blonde, whom I'll call Stephanie, with Dorothy Hamill[1] hair and matching dimples. She looks like any girl you might see in any shopping mall in middle America. She catches her chocolate-brown son and tickles him, and they laugh and trip and fall together onto the floor and laugh harder.

Had it not been for that wait in the car, this scene would be taking place at home, in a duplex Stephanie would rent while trying to finish her two-year degree in dental hygiene or respiratory therapy at the local community college. The duplex would be spotless, with a blown-up picture of her and her son over the couch and ceramic unicorns and horses occupying the shelves of the entertainment center. She would make sure that her son went to school every day with stylishly floppy pants, scrubbed teeth, and a good breakfast in his belly. Because of their difference in skin color, there would be occasional tension—caused by the strange looks from strangers, teachers, other mothers, and the bullies on the playground, who would chant

---

[1]*Dorothy Hamill:* The 1976 Olympic gold medal–winning figure skater whose "wedge" haircut became wildly popular in the United States. [Eds.]

after they knocked him down, "Your Momma's white, your Momma's white." But if she were home, their weekends and evenings would be spent together transcending those looks and healing those bruises. Now, however, their time is spent eating visiting-room junk food and his school days are spent fighting the boys in the playground who chant, "Your Momma's in prison, your Momma's in prison."

He will be ten when his mother is released, the same age my nephew will be when his mother is let out. But Jennifer, my sister, was able to spend the first five years of Toby's life with him. Stephanie had Ellie after she was incarcerated. They let her hold him for eighteen hours, then sent her back to prison. She has done the "tour," and her son is a well-traveled six-year-old. He has spent weekends visiting his mother in prisons in Kentucky, Texas, Connecticut (the Pit of Fire), and now at last here, the camp— minimum security, Pekin, Illinois.

Ellie looks older than his age. But his shoulders do not droop like his grandmother's. On the contrary, his bitterness lifts them and his chin higher than a child's should be, and the childlike, wide-eyed curiosity has been replaced by defiance. You can see his emerging hostility as he and his mother play together. She tells him to pick up the toy that he threw, say, or to put the deck of cards away. His face turns sullen, but she persists. She takes him by the shoulders and looks him in the eye, and he uses one of his hands to swat at her. She grabs the hand and he swats with the other. Eventually, she pulls him toward her and smells the top of his head, and she picks up the cards or the toy herself. After all, it is Mother's Day and she sees him so rarely. But her acquiescence makes him angrier, and he stalks out of the playroom with his shoulders thrown back.

Toby, my brother and sister and I assure one another, will not have these resentments. He is better taken care of than most. He is living with relatives in Wisconsin. Good, solid, middle-class, churchgoing relatives. And when he visits us, his aunts and his uncle, we take him out for adventures where we walk down the alley of a city and pretend that we are being chased by the "bad guys." We buy him fast food, and his uncle, John, keeps him up well past his bedtime enthralling him with stories of the monkeys he met in India. A perfect mix, we try to convince one another. Until we take him to see his mother and on the drive back he asks the question that most confuses him, and no doubt all the other children who spend much of their lives in prison visiting rooms: "Is my Mommy a bad guy?" It is the question that most seriously disorders his five-year-old need to clearly separate right from wrong. And because our own need is perhaps just as great, it is the question that haunts us as well.

Now, however, the answer is relatively simple. In a few years, it won't be. In a few years we will have to explain mandatory minimums, and the war on drugs, and the murky conspiracy laws, and the enormous amount of money and time that federal agents pump into imprisoning low-level drug dealers and those who happen to be their friends and their lovers. In a few years he might have the reasoning skills to ask why so many armed robbers and rapists and child-molesters and, indeed, murderers are

15

punished less severely than his mother. When he is older, we will somehow have to explain to him the difference between federal crimes, which don't allow for parole, and state crimes, which do. We will have to explain that his mother was taken from him for five years not because she was a drug dealer but because she made four phone calls for someone she loved.

But we also know it is vitally important that we explain all this without betraying our bitterness. We understand the danger of abstract anger, of being disillusioned with your country, and, most of all, we do not want him to inherit that legacy. We would still like him to be raised as we were, with the idea that we live in the best country in the world with the best legal system in the world—a legal system carefully designed to be immune to political mood swings and public hysteria; a system that promises to fit the punishment to the crime. We want him to be a good citizen. We want him to have absolute faith that he lives in a fair country, a country that watches over and protects its most vulnerable citizens: its women and children.

So for now we simply say, "Toby, your mother isn't bad, she just did a bad thing. Like when you put rocks in the lawn mower's gas tank. You weren't bad then, you just did a bad thing."

Once, after being given this weak explanation, he said, "I wish I could have done something really bad, like my Mommy. So I could go to prison too and be with her."

We notice a circle forming on one side of the visiting room. A little boy stands in its center. He is perhaps nine years old, sporting a burnt-orange three-piece suit and pompadour hair. He stands with his legs slightly apart, eyes half-shut, and sways back and forth, flashing his cuffs and snapping his fingers while singing:

> . . . *Doesn't like crap games with barons and earls.*
> *Won't go to Harlem in ermine and pearls.*
> *Won't dish the dirt with the rest of the girls.*
> *That's why the lady is a tramp.*

He has a beautiful voice and it sounds vaguely familiar. One of the visitors informs me excitedly that the boy is the youngest Frank Sinatra impersonator and that he has been on television even. The boy finishes his performance and the room breaks into applause. He takes a sweeping bow, claps his miniature hands together, and points both little index fingers at the audience. "More. Later. Folks." He spins on his heels and returns to the table where his mother awaits him, proudly glowing. "Don't mess with the hair, Mom," we overhear. "That little boy's slick," my brother says with true admiration.

Sitting a few tables down from the youngest Frank Sinatra is a table of Mexican-Americans. The young ones are in white dresses or button-down oxfords with matching ties. They form a strange formal contrast to the rest of the rowdy group. They sit silently, solemnly listening to the white-haired woman, who holds one of the table's two roses. I walk past and listen to the grandmother lecture her family. She speaks of values, of getting up early every day, of going to work. She looks at one of the young boys and points a finger at him. "School is the most important thing. *Nada más importante.*[2] You get up and you go to school and you study, and you can make lots of money. You can be big. You can be huge. Study, study, study."

The young boy nods his head. "Yes, *abuelita.*[3] Yes, *abuelita,*" he says.

The owner of the other flower is holding one of the group's three infants. She has him spread before her. She coos and kisses his toes and nuzzles his stomach.

When I ask Jennifer about them, she tells me that it is a "mother and daughter combo." There are a few of them here, these combos, and I notice that they have the largest number of visitors and that the older inmate, the grandmother, inevitably sits at the head of the table. Even here, it seems, the hierarchical family structure remains intact. One could take a picture, replace the fast-food wrappers with chicken and potatoes, and these families could be at any restaurant in the country, could be sitting at any dining room table, paying homage on this day to the one who brought them into the world.

Back at our table, a black-haired, Middle Eastern woman dressed in loose cottons and cloth shoes is whispering to my brother with a sense of urgency that makes me look toward my sister Charity with questioning eyes and a tilt of my head. Charity simply shrugs and resumes her conversation with a nineteen-year-old ex–New York University student — another conspirator. Eight years.

Prison, it seems, has done little to squelch the teenager's rebellious nature. She has recently been released from solitary confinement. She wears new retro-bellbottom jeans and black shoes with big clunky heels. Her hair is short, clipped perfectly ragged and dyed white — all except the roots, which are a stylish black. She has beautiful pale skin and beautiful red lips. She looks like any midwestern coed trying to escape her origins by claiming New York's East Village as home. She steals the bleach from the laundry room, I learn later, in order to maintain that fashionable white hue. But stealing the bleach is not what landed her in the hole. She committed the inexcusable act of defacing federal property. She took one of her government-issue T-shirts and wrote in permanent black magic marker, "I have been in your system. I have examined your system." And when she turned around it read, "I find it very much in need of repair."

But Charity has more important things to discuss with the girl than rebelling against the system. They are talking fashion. They talk prints versus plains, spring shoes, and spring dresses. Charity informs the girl that sling-back, high-heeled sandals and pastels are all the rage. She makes a disgusted face and says, "Damn! Pinks and blues wash me out. I hate pastels. I don't *have* any pastels."

25

---

[2]*Nada más importante:* Nothing more important (Spanish). [Eds.]
[3]*Abuelita:* Auntie (Spanish). [Eds.]

This fashion blip seems to be putting the girl into a deep depression. And so Charity, attempting to lighten up the conversation, puts her nose toward the girl's neck.

"New Armani scent, Gio," my sister announces.

The girl perks up. She nods her head. She calls one of the other inmates over.   30

Charity performs the same ritual: "Coco Chanel." And again: "Paris, Yves St. Laurent."

The line gets longer, and the girls talk excitedly to one another. It seems that Charity's uncanny talent for divining brand-name perfumes is perhaps nowhere on earth more appreciated than here with these sensory-starved inmates.

As Charity continues to smell necks and call out names, I turn back to my brother and find that the woman who was speaking to him so intensely has gone. He stares pensively at the concrete wall ahead of him.

"What did she want?" I ask.

"She heard I was a sculptor. She wants me to make a bust, presented in   35 her name, for Qaddafi."

"A bust of what?"

"Of Qaddafi. She's from Libya. She was a freedom fighter. Her kids are farmed out to strangers here—foster homes. It's Qaddafi's twenty-eighth anniversary as dictator in September. She knows him. He's mad at her now, but she thinks that he'll get over it and get her kids back to Libya if she gives him a present."

"Obsession. Calvin Klein," I hear my sister pronounce. The girls cheer in unison.

I get up and search for the girl. I want to ask her about her crime. I look in the book room only to find the four-foot Frank Sinatra crooning "Somewhere over the Rainbow" to a group of spellbound children.

I ask Ponytail, one of the female guards, where the woman went.   40 "Rule," she informs me. "Cannot be in the visiting room if no visitor is present. Should not have been here. Had to go back to unit one." I have spoken to Ponytail a few times while visiting my sister and have yet to hear her use a possessive pronoun, a contraction, or a conjunction.

According to Jennifer, Ponytail has wanted to be a prison guard since she was a little girl. She is one of the few female guards here and she has been here the longest, mainly because the male guards are continuously being fired for "indiscretions" with the inmates. But Ponytail doesn't mess around. She is also the toughest guard here, particularly in regard to the federal rules governing exposed skin. She is disgusted by any portion of the leg showing above the required eight-inch shorts length. In summer, they say, she is constantly whipping out her measuring tape and writing up those who are even a fraction of an inch off.

Last summer posed a particular problem for Ponytail, though. It seems that the shorts sold in the commissary were only seven inches from crotch to seam. And because they were commissary-issued, Ponytail couldn't censor them. So, of course, all the women put away their own shorts in favor of the commissary's. This disturbed Ponytail — a condition that eventually, according to one of the girls, developed into a low-grade depression. "She walked around with that sad old tape in her hands all summer, throwing it from one hand to the other and looking at our legs. After a while, not one of us could get her even to crack a smile — not that she's a big smiler, but you can get those corners to turn sometimes. Then she started looking downright sad, you know real depressed like."

Ponytail makes sure that the girls get proper medical care. Also none of the male guards will mess with them when she's around. But even if those things weren't true, the girls would be fond of Ponytail. She is in a way just another woman in the system, and perhaps no other group of women realizes the absolute necessity for female solidarity. These inmates know with absolute certainty what women on the outside only suspect — that men still hold ultimate power over their bodies, their property, and their freedom.

So as a token of this solidarity, they all agreed to slip off their federal shorts and put on their own. Ponytail perked up, the measuring tape appeared again with a vengeance, and quite a few of the shorts owners spent much of their free time that summer cleaning out toilet bowls and wiping the scuffs off the gym floor.

It's now 3:00. Visiting ends at 3:30. The kids are getting cranky, and the 45
adults are both exhausted and wired from too many hours of conversation, too much coffee and candy. The fathers, mothers, sisters, brothers, and the few boyfriends, and the very few husbands are beginning to show signs of gathering the trash. The mothers of the infants are giving their heads one last whiff before tucking them and their paraphernalia into their respective carrying cases. The visitors meander toward the door, leaving the older children with their mothers for one last word. But the mothers never say what they want to say to their children. They say things like, "Do well in school," "Be nice to your sister," "Be good for Aunt Betty, or Grandma." They don't say, "I'm sorry I'm sorry I'm sorry. I love you more than anything else in the world and I think about you every minute and I worry about you with a pain that shoots straight to my heart, a pain so great I think I will just burst when I think of you alone, without me. I'm sorry."

We are standing in front of the double glass doors that lead to the outside world. My older sister holds her son, rocking him gently. They are both crying. We give her a look and she puts him down. Charity and I grasp each of his small hands, and the four of us walk through the doors. As we're walking out, my brother sings one of his banana songs to Toby.

"Take me out to the — " and Toby yells out, "Banana store!"
"Buy me some — "
"Bananas!!"
"I don't care if I ever come back. For it's root, root, root for the — " 50
"Monkey team!"

I turn back and see a line of women standing behind the glass wall. Some of them are crying, but many simply stare with dazed eyes. Stephanie is holding both of her son's hands in hers and speaking urgently to him. He is struggling, and his head is twisting violently back and forth. He frees one of his hands from her grasp, balls up his fist, and punches her in the face. Then he walks with purpose through the glass doors and out the exit. I look back at her. She is still in a crouched position. She stares, unblinking, through those doors. Her hands have left her face and are hanging on either side of her. I look away, but before I do, I see drops of blood drip from her nose, down her chin, and onto the shiny marble floor.

QUESTIONS

1. How would you describe Coyne's point of view in this piece? Detached or involved? Insider or outsider? How does her point of view affect your perception of the federal prison for women that she writes about in this piece?
2. Why do you think that Coyne focuses on Mother's Day at the prison? What kinds of details is she able to report that might not be observable on most other days at the prison? What kinds of details are likely to be missing (or obscured) on such a day as this?
3. Coyne has come to visit her sister Jennifer, but why do you suppose she tells so little about Jennifer compared to what she reports about the other prisoners, particularly Stephanie and the nineteen-year-old former New York University student? Why do you suppose that Coyne tells so much about Stephanie's child, Ellie, and the young Frank Sinatra impersonator but so little about Jennifer's child, Toby?
4. What do you infer from the special attention that Coyne gives to reporting on the actions of her sister Charity and the guard Ponytail?
5. Given the selection and arrangement of descriptive details about the people who figure in this account, what do you consider to be Coyne's major purposes in writing this piece?
6. Compare and contrast Coyne's piece on women's prisons and female prisoners to one or two other stories that you find on this subject in newspapers, in magazines, or on the Internet.
7. Spend a few hours investigating a prison in your community, and write a report highlighting the details that you think are most important in revealing the quality of life in that prison.

MAKING CONNECTIONS

Compare and contrast the way that worlds collide in the visiting room of the women's prison with the cultural collisions that Judith Ortiz Cofer describes in "The Story of My Body" (p. 93).

Teaching Literature at the County Jail

Christina Boufis

*Christina Boufis (b. 1961) grew up on Long Island and is a gradu-
ate of Barnard College. She received an M.A. in English language
and literature from the University of Virginia and a Ph.D. in
English literature and a certificate in Women's Studies from the
Graduate Center of the City University of New York. For the past
eight years, she has been an affiliated scholar at Stanford
University's Institute for Research on Women and Gender. She has
also taught writing at Stanford, the University of California at
Berkeley, and the San Francisco County Jail. She is the coeditor of*
On the Market: Surviving the Academic Job Search *(1997), and her
work has appeared in many popular and academic journals. She
has said that the following essay "was written out of necessity:
teaching at the jail was so overwhelming at first that I absolutely
had to write about it to get some distance from my students'
painful experiences and be able to go back the next day." This
essay first appeared in* The Common Review *(Fall 2001).*

There is no money for books, so I am photocopying Toni Morrison's
Sula[1] chapter by chapter. This is in defiance of all copyright laws, but I think
if she knew, Morrison would understand. Sometimes I even imagine her
walking into our classroom, and I wonder how she would react to what she
saw: twenty-five women dressed in fluorescent orange, reading her works out
loud. It's been almost four years since I began teaching at the San Francisco
County Jail, and I barely notice the bright orange uniforms anymore, or that
my class is far from the traditional university setting in which I once imagined myself. Instead, I see only the women and their individual faces.

I arrived in San Francisco in 1994, as a new county jail was being built.
That year also marked a turning point in California's history: it was the first
time the state's corrections budget exceeded that of the entire University of
California system. I didn't know this then; I knew only that I wanted to live
and work in the city of my choice rather than follow the vagaries of a bleak
academic job market. When I heard that a substitute teaching position in
high-school equivalency was available at the jail, I didn't hesitate. Although
I knew next to nothing about the subject, I had spent the last several years

---

[1]*Toni Morrison* (b. 1931): The winner of the 1993 Nobel Prize for literature.
Sula (1973) is one of her novels. [Eds.]

in graduate school reading about women in literature. I was eager to work with real ones.

Other than telling me that many women inmates have difficulty reading (most are at a fourth- to seventh-grade reading level, I later discovered) and that I should perhaps start with simple math exercises, my predecessor prepared me for little. He was in a great hurry, offered the class for as long as I would have it, and took off for Tahoe[2] without waiting for my answer. Obviously, he'd had enough.

But he gave me a parting gift: a copy of Alice Walker's *The Color Purple,*[3] stored in the top drawer of the classroom filing cabinet. "Sometimes, at the end of class, if they're quiet, I read it out loud to them," he explained. Though the class was held at San Francisco's newest county jail (nicknamed the "glamour slammer" for its seemingly posh facility), the building's school-like appearance belied the fact that the Sheriff's Department spent not a single cent on any of the educational or rehabilitative programs that went on inside. Thus there was no money for more copies of Walker's novel or anyone else's. The class I was teaching was funded by the local community college, which provided only GED[4] books.

I forgot all about *The Color Purple* my first harried, difficult day at the   5
jail. My shock at seeing the women, who appeared as a blur of orange, turned to alienation, then anger, as the class wore on. "Man, we're going to eat you alive," one woman repeatedly uttered. Others told me they didn't have to do any work and weren't going to. A few more crumpled up the math exercises I'd photocopied and told me they didn't know their multiplication tables.

But toward the end of class, one woman seemed to take pity on me and asked for "the book."

"What book?" I replied a little too eagerly.

"The book, the book," others chimed in as if it were obvious.

Another student pointed to the filing cabinet, and I remembered Walker's novel. There was some disagreement about where the previous instructor had left off, but the last ten minutes of class were spent in relative silence as I read and they listened. I wasn't happy with this as a pedagogical strategy — I'd much rather the students read for themselves — but I was thankful that it worked. The women nodded sympathetically to Celie's painful story and thanked me when they left for the day.

"Miss B, Miss B," calls Tanya, a woman who looks and acts much   10
younger than her nineteen years. It has been several months since the other instructor was let go and I was hired; my nickname is a sign of acceptance.

---

[2]*Tahoe:* Lake Tahoe, the largest alpine lake in North America. It is surrounded by the Sierra Nevadas on the California-Nevada border. [Eds.]

[3]*Alice Walker* (b. 1944): The best-selling writer of the Pulitzer Prize–winning novel *The Color Purple* (1982). [Eds.]

[4]*GED:* General equivalency diploma. [Eds.]

Tanya sits up front — the better to get my attention — and soon her pleas take on added urgency. "I need a pencil. I need some more paper." When she finishes with one demand, she moves on to the next. When she gets bored, which happens fairly quickly, she calls repeatedly for *Sula* as if she were a great personal friend. "Where's *Sula*? When do we get to *Sula*?"

I have kept up the practice that my predecessor initiated, spending the last half hour of class reading novels or plays aloud, but with a difference: the students do the reading. The women have come to depend on this promise. The strategy also helps with continuity in what I found to be an almost impossible teaching situation. Turnover is extremely high at county jails and likewise in my classroom. I can have from six to sixteen new students a day and I never know how long any of them will stay. Most serve sentences of less than a year, yet jail is a liminal time during which many wait indeterminately to be sentenced on to prison or parole. Release dates can come and go mysteriously without the promised freedom and no explanation for the delay. Life is thus more volatile in county jails than in prisons and the future more uncertain. Not surprisingly, jails are one of the least studied and understood institutions in the criminal justice system.

Such unsettledness can make anyone edgy, if not downright crazy. Although Tanya has difficulty keeping up with the novel, it doesn't seem to matter. What is important to her is the routine we have established in class, my assurance that we will read the work each day. From what I know of my students' backgrounds, even this modicum of stability was often missing from their lives. Many were homeless before incarceration; few had support from parents, friends, or partners. For Tanya and some of the others, *Sula* has become a talisman of security, something they can rely on in a constantly shifting world.

Tanya has difficulty understanding some of the language and following the plot, but many of the other women do not. They are quick to spot the fact that when Sula's brother, Plum, returns from the war he is a drug addict, though Morrison never states this directly. They can tell by several clues: Plum's weight loss and antisocial behavior, his sugary diet, and the "bent spoon black from steady cooking" found in his bedroom.

The following semester, I teach this same novel in my college writing   15
seminar at the University of California, Berkeley. My Berkeley students don't pick up on the drug connection. Most of them think that Plum uses the spoon to cook soup in his room, and they look at me with disbelief when I tell them otherwise.

My jail students seem able to spot danger everywhere, practically in the way an author uses a semicolon. Reading on O'Henry short story, they immediately inferred that one character was a prostitute, just from the author's description of an abandoned shoe. And if my Berkeley students are frustrated with Morrison for not providing explanations (for Sula's mother's missing leg, or Sula's role in a murder), the women at the jail shrug off such ambiguities. They assume that a character can do an evil act, such as not rescuing someone from drowning, and not be evil herself. My Berkeley students want to know what I think the work ultimately means, and they are frustrated with Morrison for being evasive. My jail students seem to rest more easily in uncertainty, knowing that life itself does not provide answers.

I can sympathize with both sets of student reactions (I clearly remember being an undergraduate eager to understand the depths of literature), yet the more I discover about my students at the jail, both individually and statistically, the more I appreciate their acute and emotionally sensitive readings. Studies vary, but several show that as many as 90 percent of incarcerated women have been sexually, emotionally, or physically abused. Like their imprisoned sisters elsewhere, most of my students are mothers, women of color, and the sole supporters of young children. They are also most likely in jail on drug charges, primarily for possessing minor amounts of crack cocaine. Before the 1980s "war on drugs" legislation mandated jail time for possessing crack cocaine — but none for possessing the same amount of its more expensive cousin, powder cocaine (a drug used predominantly by whites) — these women would have had rehabilitation or community-based programs as options. Not anymore.

The longer I worked at the jail, the more my curiosity was piqued by what I learned and the more I wanted to help. Years of reading Victorian novels had left me with a strong sense of social reform; I believed I could make a difference teaching at the jail, more so than at other places. And I still believe this despite the fact that I have seen hundreds of women get released from jail and come back again — often the same ones, and often more times than I can count.

Tanya is released before we finish reading *Sula*, and I promise to send the remaining chapters to the address she's given. She tells me that when she gets out, she is going to get her son back, get a job, and turn her life around. I am surprised when she mentions her baby; she looks so much like a child and in need of mothering herself.

We finish Morrison's novel, but it is anticlimactic. No one seems particularly interested in discussing the themes, nor is anyone as thrilled as I hoped they'd be when I announce that our next novel will be Zora Neale Hurston's *Their Eyes Were Watching God*.[5] The class seems subdued and sad. Perhaps this is due to Tanya's absence: although so many students come and go, Tanya has been a steady presence, and her noisy but good-natured complaints have punctuated our days.

I try to get one new student to do some work. She is much older, perhaps around fifty-five, and near toothless. "My mind is on burying my son, not on this schoolwork," she tells me, shaking her head. "It ain't right that they should put me in here when I ain't been in a classroom for thirty years. And I just buried my son. It don't make no sense."

20

[5]*Zora Neale Hurston* (1891–1960): A writer and folklorist. *Their Eyes Were Watching God* (1937) is her most popular novel. [Eds.]

I don't know what to say. Educational programs are mandatory at this jail, but the policy makes little sense to me, too, at times.

The next day, the women are livelier, and we begin reading *Their Eyes*. They quickly pick up on the dialect, something I feared would be prohibitive. "That's country," says one woman. Instead of finding Hurston's phonetic spellings a hindrance to understanding, the women seem to relish sounding out the dialogue and laugh when they trip over words. One fairly new student, a white woman whose face is pockmarked with what looks like deep cigarette burns, stands up to give Hurston's novel a try. The other students are encouraging, telling her to go on when she stumbles, and even yelling at me when I correct a mispronunciation. "Let her do it, Miss B! She's getting it."

As the novel continues, the women become hooked on the story and wonder what will happen next. They recognize Joe Starks for the smooth talker he is and think that the main character, Janie, should have stayed with her first husband, Logan, instead of running off with the slick Joe. "Logan wasn't so bad," says one student who has been in and out of jail several times — this despite the fact that Logan had wanted to buy Janie a mule to plow the field, and the protagonist remarks that she cannot love her first husband. "Besides, he was trying to teach her an important lesson — how to work."

When we get to the part where Janie meets her true love, Tea Cake, who 25 takes her to a new world in the Florida Everglades, my students are quick to note that "he turned her out." I ask about the phrase and am told that it means to be introduced to new people and places, a whole new way of life.

"Is it a bad thing?"

"It doesn't have to be," one woman explains, "but it usually is. You're turned on to the life." That is, a life of drug use or prostitution.

I ask them to write essays about this, and I get back many that explain how they were turned out to drugs: on first dates, with boyfriends, cousins, even mothers.

When we get to the same scene in my Berkeley class, I say something about Tea Cake turning Janie out. My Cal students stare at me as if I've said something incredibly dumb. Some of them have heard the term before, but it doesn't resonate with meaning. We move on.

Tanya, I have heard, is back in jail. Out for less than a week before get- 30 ting rearrested, she likely did not get the photocopies I sent her. She was apparently caught selling drugs to an undercover cop on the same street corner where she was arrested before. I ask the program's administrator about the rumor I heard, and she confirms it. Tanya said she needed money for clothes and that's why she was selling. "It didn't occur to her to get a job," the administrator states. Yet, knowing her educational level, I wonder how easy it would have been for her to get one.

When Tanya comes back into class, she hugs me and asks me not to be mad at her. I'm not and I tell her so. I am always happy to see my former students again, even in jail; at least I know that they are alive and safe. But the rest of the class is unruly. It's a Monday, the day after visiting hours when the women are allowed a two-hour personal contact with their children. The aftermath of these visits is a palpable feeling of malaise. The women often can't concentrate, nor do they feel like doing anything but talking and complaining.

There are four new students, one of whom tells me she is going to prison in a few days and won't bother doing anything. "That crack took away my brain," says another. One young woman who always sits sullenly in the back spits out, "Why don't you take a day off? All the other classes are canceled today. How come ours isn't?"

I'm frustrated and tired of coercing them to work. So I pull out a passage from *Their Eyes*, where Janie talks about feeling like a rut in a road, beaten down, with the life all beneath the surface, and I tell them to respond in writing.

After much cajoling, they begin to write. One woman details the years she spent with a husband who, like Janie's Joe, always put her down. A new student calls me over and tells me she felt trampled this way when she was homeless. "I need more than one sheet of paper to tell this," she states. I agree.

My best student, Linnea, writes quickly, then hands me her essay to   35
read. "I felt I was in a rut when I found myself homeless, hooked on drugs and losing some of my hope," she writes. "I found myself doing things (sexually) that I never thought I would do for drugs. I would have sex in an alleyway, the back seat of an abandoned vehicle, and even out in the open park in front of crowds of people. I would eat out of trash cans. I would go days without bathing, or changing my clothes. . . . I would even try to sell drugs on a very, very small scale. I felt my life was becoming meaningless. . . . I now have a chance to regain my life by being here."

As painful as these stories often are, the women always want to share them by reading them out loud. They clap after each one and make supportive comments. "All you need now is Jesus," or "You're gonna make it, girl. I know it." I correct their punctuation ("Oh yeah, I forget how to use periods," says one student) but am often at a loss for words on the content.

From their essays and comments in class, I can piece together the world that many of my students come from. It's a world of broken promises — mothers who abandon them, boyfriends and fathers who rape them, partners who beat them — and one where home and school are fractured places at best. But despite some of the horrific experiences these women have had, there's a strong element of hope in their writing, a survivor's instinct that things can get better and life will turn around.

We are reading Toni Morrison's *The Bluest Eye*, a somber book about a girl, Pecola, who has internalized white standards of beauty and believes she would be loved if only she had blue eyes. One day, I tell my students that I sometimes feel self-conscious about my position: I'm a white woman teaching mostly African American literature to women of color. "Damn, Miss B, you worry too much," says one student. "Yeah," says another, "you think too hard." As unbelievable as it may sound, there is no racial tension among the women in the jail. Drugs, abuse, and poverty are the great levelers here, at least from what I've seen. It is these elements that transcend division by race, uniting my students with one another and the literature we read.

Similarly, Pecola's life is one of repeated rejection and abuse: she is raped by her father, neglected by her mother. This is by far my students' favorite work, and I suggest they write letters to the author. I vow to someday send them to Toni Morrison and apologize for photocopying her novels.

"Dear Toni," one woman writes, "I can really apperciate your book   40
cuz it gives without a doubt insight. . . . Also men abusing women it is a strong issue and your book brought strength to me as a woman of abuse." Despite the bleak outcome of the novel, the women find positive messages. "Dear Professor Morrison," writes another, "this book made me think about how we put off the beauty of are black people an put on the ugly, but I see the light now an when I leave jail I will keep my Lord with me black women like you makes me proud."

"To Toni Morrison," writes another, "I love the slang that you use it was kind of difficult getting it together but it was real. I love real stuff. . . . you are a dream come true."

"Dear Ms. Morrison. I really enjoyed reading 'The Bluest Eye.' . . . Even tho the cover states that the story is fiction, I truly believe that some little girl may have gone through this. It was a common thing. And Im sorry to say, that it still happens. . . . P.S. If you can please send me an autograph book I would really enjoy it. Thank you."

QUESTIONS

1. Boufis teaches in two different worlds. In each world, her students have their own kinds of knowledge, and for each audience, Boufis must shift her mode of teaching. What does she learn about teaching from her students in the county jail?
2. What does Boufis criticize about the criminal justice system in California? What do you think needs to be changed?
3. Boufis chooses to read books by African American women writers with her county jail students. If you are familiar with the books she mentions in this essay, what was your experience reading them? Why would you or would you not consider them good choices for these students?
4. Boufis starts teaching at the county jail as a substitute teacher, but she stays on as a regular teacher there. What reasons does she give for continuing to teach there?

5. What programs are available for prisoners in your local county jail? If there aren't any, what reasons are given for this lack? Write a report on what you learn.

MAKING CONNECTIONS

Compare Boufis's and Amanda Coyne's (p. 189) criticisms of harsh penalties for low-level drug dealing. Do some further research on this issue, and write a report of your findings.

TOIL AND TEMPTATION

Michael Kamber

*Born in Harpswell, Maine, in 1963, Michael Kamber has worked
as a New York City–based freelance writer and photographer since
the 1980s. In the early 1990s, Kamber traveled to the Caribbean to
cover social and political issues in Puerto Rico, the Dominican
Republic, and Haiti, where he reported on the terror killings following the overthrow of that country's dictator. He has written
extensively about Mexican immigrants in New York City, and in
September 2001, he traveled to Pakistan and Afghanistan to document in print and photographs the plight of long-term Afghan
refugees and the future of a post-Taliban Afghanistan. Kamber
writes for the* Village Voice, *and his photographs have appeared in
the* New York Times, Newsday, *and other news publications. He
has been nominated for a World Press Photo award, and his* Village
Voice *series on Mexican immigration won the Columbia University
School of Journalism's Mike Berger Award and was nominated for
a Pulitzer Prize. The following essay, which was collected in* The
Best American Nonrequired Reading *(2002), is excerpted from
Kamber's series on Mexican immigration.*

For seven days after his arrival from Mexico in mid-January, Antonio
Gonzalez spent his time alone in the apartment, watching Spanish-language
soaps and game shows, occasionally looking out the window at the snowy
Bronx streets or gazing at the 6 train as it clattered by on the el. Two years
earlier, his older brother, Juan Carlos, had learned the neighborhood by each
day venturing a block farther from the apartment, then returning home.
When he had mastered the surrounding streets, he traveled a stop on the
subway — then two, then three. But Antonio saw the police cars passing by
on the streets and, fearing deportation, he stayed inside. On the eighth day
the skies cleared, and he went to work at the car wash with his brother.

Antonio and Juan Carlos left before dawn, walking north along
Westchester Avenue,[1] past the candy store, restaurant, pizza parlor, real
estate office, and bodega, each business owned by immigrants: Indians,
Dominicans, Italians, Guyanese, and Puerto Ricans, respectively. Antonio
smiled as he passed the pizza parlor. A fifteen-year-old acquaintance from
Zapotitlán, Antonio's village of 4500 in southern Mexico, had vanished a

---

[1] *Westchester Avenue:* A major street running northeast through the Bronx, one
of the five boroughs of New York City. [Eds.]

year earlier, and a few nights ago Antonio had gone to buy a slice and found the young man there, sweeping bits of crusts and garlic salt from the floor.

At Westchester Square, the two brothers caught the X31 bus along Tremont and Williamsbridge Avenues to Eastchester, a north Bronx neighborhood remarkable for its dreary nondescriptness: block upon block of squat one-story brick buildings, stores selling auto parts and laminated furniture, a KFC, a Dunkin' Donuts, some gas stations.

At the car wash, no one tells Antonio how much he is being paid, and he does not ask. In lieu of training, he is handed a towel and told to join a dozen others — all compact, brown-skinned men like himself — who stand in the mist at the foot of the wash tunnel, eyes sandy from sleep, waiting for the cars to roll out. The men regard him coolly, saying nothing, but shout to one another in Spanish over the roar of the machinery — the blowers, spray jets, and huge flopping strands of soapy cloth that make sucking noises as they slap against the cars.

At 7 A.M., a sedan rolls out of the tunnel, and six men swarm the vehicle, quickly burnishing the exterior and wiping clean the windows from the inside. Thirty seconds later another vehicle is spit out, and Antonio joins the second group, trying to walk alongside the still-rolling car as the others do, wiping as they move.   5

The former slaughterhouse worker left school at thirteen. He has been a laborer for five years, frequently averaging seventy or more hours a week at jobs in Mexico. He has assumed that rubbing a car dry will be easy work, easy money. He is wrong. The teenager stoops, bends, and reaches for the elusive water droplets; an hour later his legs and back ache, and pain rockets through his arm as he drags the waterlogged towel over the cars for the thousandth time. The areas that he wipes are still damp, and the others take up his slack and grumble about the poor job he's doing. He is nervous and afraid to disappoint his brother, who has paid $1600 for Antonio's illegal passage to New York. He sees the boss watching him from inside the glass booth, motionless and grim-faced.

Another worker shows Antonio how to fold his towel to get better coverage, but Antonio repeatedly drops the towel as he tries to double it. Behind him, the cars are piling up in the tunnel, and he works quickly, just short of frantic. He has eleven hours and five hundred cars to go. Before the day is over, he is thinking that his journey to New York is a mistake. He is thinking that he will return home soon, to Zapotitlán, his village in the state of Puebla, where the majority of New York's Mexicans come from.

If Antonio does return, he will be a man very nearly alone, in the company of young children and the elderly. Fully one third of Antonio's village — including nearly all of the working-age males and 20 percent of the women — is in New York City. Firm figures are hard to come by for a community that is largely illegal, but in the last decade, New York City's Mexican population has grown between 300 and 600 percent — depending on which experts are consulted — to a total of at least 300,000. Dr. Robert

Smith, a Barnard College expert on Mexican immigration, calls the growth "astounding — the fastest of any group in the city." (So many Mexicans have left Puebla that they are called the Puebla York, in much the same way that New York City's Puerto Ricans are referred to as Nuyoricans, and Manhattan-based channel 47 hosts *Hechos Puebla*,[2] a weekly show on Puebla current events.)

Like Antonio, nearly all the newly arrived Mexicans have traded one life of labor and poverty for another. They are young men and women who in their homeland have run up against the walls created by class, lack of education, and the detritus of seventy-plus years of one-party rule. In Mexico, there is no future; in New York, there might be.

The residents of Zapotitlán began arriving in New York eighteen years   10
ago. A two-month investigation into the community reveals a clear majority who have fallen into a semi-permanent underclass: men and women here illegally, who trade seventy-hour workweeks for a handful of cash. A small but growing number of young men have drifted into drugs and gangs. But many others — maybe one in five — have found some degree of prosperity in New York, settling into comfortable middle-class lives and easing ties to their homeland. Still others have created a dual existence, maintaining families and even businesses in Zapotitlán. They fly home a few times a year, then travel back like thieves in the night, slipping past the Border Patrol into the Arizona desert. Of New York City's Mexican population as a whole, 75 percent are not upwardly mobile, as many as nine in ten are "illegal," and fully half the teens are not in school.

April 15 is opening day for the Liga Mexicana de Beisból, made up of sixteen teams, each representing a town in Puebla. (The baseball-crazy city of Tulcingo is fielding four separate teams.) Zapotitlán's team is making its league debut; they have new white uniforms, ordered from Mexico, bearing a cactus logo and the words *Club Zapotitlán*. On Sunday morning the players gather early at City Island[3] and win an error-filled first game, 8–4, using a pitcher who was chased through the Arizona desert by the Border Patrol scant weeks ago. His nineteen-year-old son, also here illegally, works in a Dominican bodega on Tremont Avenue; the pitcher has come to help make money to pay for the son's house, under construction in Zapotitlán. He has come, he says, because he wants his son home soon, "before he becomes Americanized."

In years past, Zapotitlán's players were dispersed throughout other clubs in the league, yet a hundred or more Zapotecos would show up for a game if they heard a few of their *paisanos*[4] were playing. "We love baseball," explains Angel Flores, one of Club Zapotitlán's founders. "But really we put the team together because the people from Zapotitlán need

---

[2]*Hechos Puebla:* Puebla Facts (Spanish). [Eds.]
[3]*City Island:* An island in Long Island Sound in the northeastern Bronx. [Eds.]
[4]*paisanos:* Countrymen. [Eds.]

a place to gather." Hundreds of people from the village are expected to show up for games this year, which will be followed by barbecues and socializing.

Angel has spent twelve and a half of the past thirteen years in New York working as a laborer. For several years he has worked as a painter for an Irish contractor in Yonkers. He has watched as the man has gone from a rented house and car to an ornate home, three rental properties, and three new cars. "There is a network," Angel explains. "My boss gets all his contracts from other Irishmen."

Yet Angel is not envious of the Irishman's success; Angel makes $130 a day, tax free, a princely sum by the standards of illegal Mexicans in New York. And he has his own network; he has managed to stack the work crew with five others from Zapotitlán — including the pitcher, who is his cousin. Angel's father was a miner in Mexico, and he brags softly about his siblings there: a nurse, a lawyer, an engineer. He is not envious of them either, he put each through college with money he earned in New York. He is an uneducated laborer, they are professionals, yet he has enabled their social mobility. His one complaint about New York? "The people from Zapotitlán, I don't see some of them for years," he says. From the Bronx, they are slowly dispersing into Queens and Brooklyn, like water seeping into the earth after the rains.

Luis Garcia, the first resident of Zapotitlán to arrive in New York, in 1983, settled near Willis Avenue, in the Bronx, down the block from where the 6 train stops under the 40th Precinct. Within a few years, dozens of friends and relatives were arriving with little more than his phone number, and they slept on his couch or on mattresses lined up on the floor. Gradually the community grew and relocated; some went out to Queens, and a few moved south to the burgeoning Mexican community in Sunset Park, Brooklyn. Most, however, stayed near the 6 train, following the el north along Westchester Avenue to Soundview and Castle Hill in the Bronx. They are there today, perhaps a thousand strong; at just one building, 690 Allerton Avenue, at the corner of White Plains Road, there are an estimated fifty families from Zapotitlán. (One of the few remaining Puerto Ricans in the building says, "You're looking for Mexicans? You came to the right place, and it's getting worse!") They find each other work, baby-sit one another's children. In a strange land, they take comfort in neighbors they have known since childhood.

And sometimes, in their insular community, they find love. In 1996, Alma Rosa, a tall, graceful teenager, placed second in the local beauty pageant in San Antonio, Mexico, a nearby village that makes Zapotitlán seem like a metropolis. Alfonso, the second oldest son of a middle-class family in Zapotitlán, found her there at the pageant, and the two began to date. Yet the young girl's family strongly disapproved of Alfonso, and they sent their nineteen-year-old daughter away, to San Bernardino, California, where there is a small colony of townspeople. Alfonso followed and searched northern California in vain for several weeks, eventually losing hope,

15

assuming she would be married if he ever found her. He left for New York to seek work. The following spring, at a gathering of people from Zapotitlán, he heard two men speak of her. She too had come to New York, and he called her that evening. The couple live today in a building full of Mexicans on Dean Street, in downtown Brooklyn, with their two small children and three of Alfonso's brothers.

About one fifth of the immigrants from Zapotitlán are women, and the percentage is growing steadily. In the Mexican community as a whole, the number of women arriving in New York is higher, probably approaching 40 percent. They are working in factories, cleaning houses, and having children. The birthrate among Mexican women rose 232 percent between 1989 and 1996; they now rank third among immigrant groups in New York City — higher than Chinese, South Asians, or Haitians. "Most of these [Mexican] women are very young, and they have a high fertility rate; it's a double whammy," says Peter Lobo of the New York City Department of Planning. "This is going to have a huge impact on New York City."

At the car wash, a week has passed. The pain in Antonio's body has lessened; he has learned how to handle the towel, how to flip the car doors open, wipe the seals with one quick motion, then snap the towel over his shoulder and quickly wipe the windows with a softer blue rag. His coworkers are not so intimidating now; the other Mexicans see that he will work and begin to talk and joke with him — the Salvadorans also, though they speak differently and seem harder men, having been through a war that Antonio knows nothing about. And then there are the tall, dark-skinned men, men unlike any he has seen in Mexico, whom he has assumed are *morenos*,[5] African Americans, but who turn out to be Africans, and at first he is confused by the distinction ("In the dark of the tunnel, you can see just their eyes," he says with some wonderment). Because they are African, they are very proud, he is told, and dislike taking orders. With the exception of a garrulous Nigerian who has learned to speak Spanish, the Africans are given jobs where they work alone.

Spend seventy-two hours a week wiping other people's cars, and resentment is a constant companion. Until recently, Antonio has known only Mexicans. Lunch and downtime at the car wash are filled with talk of money and race. Eastchester is a working- to middle-class neighborhood of West Indian and African American civil servants, secretaries, teachers, construction workers. Most work hard, many favor nice cars, and the line at the car wash is a parade of conspicuous consumption — Cadillacs, Lexuses, late-model SUVs. People come here because it is nearby, and because the "Super," which includes hot wax, polish, and wheels Armoralled,[6] costs $9,

---

[5]*morenos:* Dark-skinned people; here, African Americans or Africans. [Eds.]
[6]*Armoralled:* Polished with Armor All, a protective polish. [Eds.]

a savings of $3 over the other car wash, a half-mile down Baychester Avenue, where the white people go.

But the black people — especially the young black men — don't appreciate paying hard-earned money to have a bunch of illegals leave drops of water on their cars. If they feel they are not getting their money's worth, they wave their hands in the air and shout at the workers and then mock them: "No speek eengleesh." Antonio quickly learns the phrase "Yo, yo, yo" and an utterance that sounds to him like "fock" or "focking," which he believes to be a mean word. And noise is of particular concern. Antonio and Juan Carlos are soft-spoken and courteous. They would never raise their voices unless they were ready to fight. These black men raise their voices all the time.

The tips left by the black clientele run to silver and copper, with some dollar bills thrown in. At the end of a twelve-hour shift, Antonio takes home maybe $5 in tips. Down the hill, *los blancos*[7] leave $5 bills, and rumor has it the workers average $30 a day in tips. Times six days, that's good money. But here Antonio is stuck with the cheap *morenos* who shout at him, wear their clothes baggy, and lounge against the wall. "Where do they get their money?" he wants to know. To him, and to the other Mexicans, the young black men seem lazy and dangerous.

The first week there are days when it rains and there is no work, but soon Antonio is averaging seventy-two hours a week. His hourly rate remains a mystery to him. He is simply handed an envelope with $270 in cash at week's end, which he accepts without complaint. Juan Carlos is the senior laborer at the car wash. With a year and a half of experience, he makes $4 an hour. The others, he believes, make $3.75 an hour. It is straight time — nothing extra after forty hours. A laborer working at the legal minimum wage,[8] plus overtime, would be paid $497. The car wash has approximately twenty employees. By using workers without green cards, the owner, a Portuguese immigrant, is saving nearly a quarter of a million dollars a year.

Twenty years ago, Mexican workers had the second highest per capita income among Hispanics. Today they have the lowest. Their average earning power has dropped 50 percent, a result of the flood of illegal laborers like Antonio, who are readily exploited by tens of thousands of small businesses throughout the city — restaurants, delis, small factories, and building contractors who rely on their sub-minimum-wage labor to turn a profit.

But to Antonio, $300 a week is about $270 more than most men make in Mexico, where the minimum wage is $4 a day. After work one evening in mid-February, the two brothers walk down to the Western Union near Castle Hill Avenue. There, they send a money order for $300 to their

---

[7]*los blancos:* The whites. [Eds.]

[8]*minimum wage:* In 2002, the New York State minimum wage law provided that all employees must be paid at least $5.15 per hour. It made no provision for overtime or for withholding of federal, state, city, Social Security, or Medicare taxes.

mother in Mexico. It is their combined savings from three weeks of work. Theirs is a drop in the bucket: in 1996, the last year for which figures are available, $5.6 billion was sent home by Mexicans in the United States, making *remesas*[9] the third largest factor in the Mexican economy.

Of Antonio's townspeople here in New York, there is a shoe-store   25 owner in Queens who is building a gas station in the village; a busboy at a restaurant on Madison who is part owner of construction vehicles that are rented out in Zapotitlán for $2000 a month; a seventeen-year-old bodega worker on Tremont who makes $1200 a month and sends $1000 home to his mother — eating free food at his job and staying inside on his day off, lest he be tempted to spend money. They say that those who suffer the most in New York live the best when they return to Mexico.

When he left Zapotitlán for New York, Antonio stated that his dream was to build a kitchen for his mother. Upon receiving her son's money, she hires a local contractor to begin work on the addition, then abandons the project, to be completed another time. A few weeks later Antonio sends more money, and the mother of nine — who cannot read or write, but adds complex sums with lightning speed — buys several hundred dollars' worth of food and soda and opens a small store in the front room of her house.

By late February, Antonio has begun to feel secure in the Bronx. There is solace in the daily routine; he is no longer afraid of the police that pass by, and the dollar bills and coins are less confusing. Yet the frustration starts early each morning. At work, vacuum cleaner in hand, Antonio has learned to say, "Open the trunk." But the patrons frequently respond with a torrent of words, and he stands and listens helplessly. Buying coffee at the bodega is an ordeal; he gets nervous, procrastinates. What if the Puerto Rican woman is not working today? The other counter workers ask him questions that he does not understand. The customers stare as he grows flustered.

And Antonio begins to see the long-term limitations as well. The two brothers are living doubled up and being gouged on the rent, but cannot move; landlords won't rent to "illegals" with no credit history. Juan Carlos has a friend working at a midtown parking lot — a union job, $20 an hour, and they're hiring. But between Antonio and Juan Carlos, they have only one fake green card from Texas, with someone else's name on it. It will never do. So they stay at the car wash, surrounded by opulence and possibilities, caged by their illegal status and lack of English. A friend suggests English classes and Antonio laughs. "We leave the house before six in the morning and get home after eight at night — some nights we work until ten. When do we take the classes?" A week later he says, "We could just stay right here, buy from the Puerto Ricans, work with the Mexicans, stay right here." He means literally and figuratively, and he shakes his head. Right here is not going to be good enough.

---

[9]*remesas:* Remittances; money orders. [Eds.]

For the first generation who arrived from Zapotitlán, in the 1980s, right here wasn't good enough either. Lupe Gonzalez came across in 1987, in the trunk of a car with holes cut in the floor. The coyotes[10] gave him a straw through which he sucked fresh air as he bounced over the roads near San Diego. The eighteen-year-old entered the workforce as a messenger in midtown Manhattan — $100 a week plus tips. Yet the job suited him no more than the conservative lifestyle of his hometown. "I used to dress up in my sister's clothes and play with dolls when I was a child," explains Lupe. In 1991 he found a job as a hairdresser at a shop on a Bronx side street, near the Morrison Avenue stop on the 6 train. He slowly built up his clientele in the Hispanic neighborhood, and became best friends with two Puerto Rican stylists, who were also gay. "They taught me how to do my makeup, how to wear fake *tetas*[11] and high heels. They took me to the gay clubs and balls," he says, explaining his entry into New York's gay community.

Eight years ago, he put down $5000, bought the shop he worked in,   30
and renamed it Versace; in February of 2001, he opened a second, larger location, Style 2000. He now has five employees. On a recent April evening, the tall hairdresser with the lipstick and long hair formed elaborate curls with a hot comb in the crowded salon, the air filled with hairspray and merengue blasting from overhead speakers. The four chairs were full, and a crowd of people — Dominicans, Puerto Ricans, Mexicans, one Chinese woman — waited near the door for their hair to be cut.

As an openly gay man, a successful businessperson, a legal resident of the United States, and a fluent English speaker, Lupe is clearly an anomaly in the Mexican community, whose biggest holiday is December 12, the birthday of the Virgin of Guadalupe. One expects to hear painful stories of his exclusion among his fellow immigrants from Zapotitlán; there are none. "They wave at me on the street," he says. "They know that I'm one of the twelve sons and daughters of Delfino Gonzalez, from Zapotitlán. That's all that matters."

One Saturday night in late March, Los Tigres del Norte, a hugely popular Mexican *norteño*[12] band, comes to New York. Antonio and Juan Carlos are there, and as the band takes the stage, the audience erupts, waves of adulation washing over the musicians. They launch into a set of ballads about being from Mexico, having nothing there — no profession or future — and risking your life to cross the border illegally; about grueling workweeks and a life that is nothing more than "from home to work, from work to home." In the crowd there is a wave of emotion that Antonio has never felt before, a current very nearly electric. He is

---

[10]*coyotes:* People who transport Mexicans illegally across the U.S.-Mexican border. [Eds.]

[11]*tetas:* Breasts. [Eds.]

[12]*norteño:* A person from the northern region of Mexico; the type of music popular in that region. [Eds.]

surrounded by thousands of cheering, nearly hysterical countrymen who share his life, his pain, his frustration. Grown men — macho Mexican men — are weeping all around him.

The following Saturday night, the eighteen-year-old's destination is the notorious Chicano Club. Three thousand miles away, in small Mexican villages, women speak of this Bronx nightspot in hushed tones. Men speak of it with smiles on their faces. They speak of the Dominican and Puerto Rican women in high heels, skin-tight pants, and halter tops. You can hold them as close as you want — at least as long as the song is playing. You're paying for it: $2 a dance. Antonio, Juan Carlos, and two friends sit at a table, drinking rounds of Corona and watching the women in the smoke-filled room. A live band is pounding out *bachatas, cumbias,*[13] and covers of hits by Los Tigres. The music and bodies and laughter begin to run together. Money that could have been saved and sent to Mexico is spent on women and beer. It is the cost of feeling alive for a night. Antonio gets home about 4 A.M., sleeps for an hour, and leaves for work, exhausted, hung over, smelling of perfume, and feeling good.

Mexicans say that teenagers like Antonio lose their money and their innocence at the Chicano, but it is New York that takes these things. In Sunset Park, Brooklyn, Ignacio, a twenty-two-year-old man from Zapotitlán, knows the Chicano well — but he cannot go there, because it is in the Bronx, and people will kill him if they find him. A strikingly handsome, muscular man, he sits in a dreary apartment, roaches blazing trails over pinups of naked women on the walls. He sends $500 a month to his wife and three children in Zapotitlán. They live in a house overlooking the desert and the forests of giant saguaro cactus, in a place where, in the middle of the day, one hears total silence. His family is waiting patiently for his return. He is never going back. He cannot. He is addicted to New York.

Ignacio made his first trip to New York when he was seventeen. He 35 worked delivering pizzas for an Italian place on the Grand Concourse, in the Bronx. One day the teenager made the mistake of looking inside the pizza box. "When you come from Mexico, your eyes are closed," he says of his early days in the city. "Now my eyes are open." His is a complex story involving drug deliveries, vendettas, betrayals, attempted murders. The details do not matter. What matters is that he stands at night on Brooklyn street corners in a tight T-shirt and baggy pants. He has a gold chain, a .25 automatic, and some bags of coke. Much of the profit goes up his nose, and he works a day job washing dishes to support his habit and his children. His life in New York is a secret he keeps from his family. "They have this dream of who I am — why ruin that?" he asks. He's made a couple of trips back, gotten his wife pregnant twice more. But he could not stay around the friendly, trusting people of his hometown. "Their eyes are closed," he repeats dismissively.

---

[13]*bachatas, cumbias:* Dance and music forms. [Eds.]

Living in New York is costing more than Antonio expected, much more. Rent, food, and transit take up over half of the $1200 a month that he earns. Then there are clothes to be bought, weekly phone calls to Mexico, haircuts, nights out, Laundromats, a large fake gold watch from Canal Street: it has been more than a month since he sent money home. Juan Carlos commiserates: "I've been here two and a half years," he says. "All I have to show for it is a pizza oven in Mexico." Though he doesn't say so, he has also purchased the building materials for his family's new concrete house, and now Antonio has helped pay for the kitchen and for his mother's new store, modest though it may be. But it is true; for themselves, they have nothing. Juan Carlos's dream of the two brothers opening a *taqueria*[14] in Mexico seems to be years away. It is mid-April, however. Spring has come to the Bronx, and Antonio does not seem as fixated on his brother's dream as he once was. A Puerto Rican girl smiles at Antonio on a subway platform, he boldly asks for her number, and they talk on the phone. And there are more nights ahead at the Chicano Club, and at the nightspots that he has discovered along Roosevelt Avenue in Queens, where he danced for several hours one night with a pretty Peruvian woman.

At the car wash, his boss has seen that Antonio is good with his hands and is training him to compound paint, which entails running a large buffing wheel gently over the car's surface. Antonio has heard there is good money in this, that paint shops pay $500 or more a week for a good compound man. And he has heard that the boss may open another car wash, and that Juan Carlos will be manager if he can learn English. "Really, life in New York is pretty good," Antonio says one night, sitting on a park bench, Juan Carlos at his side. "All you need is a little money." Then he and his brother begin to discuss their latest plan, which is to save enough to bring their sixteen-year-old brother, Fernando, to the Bronx. He has already told them he wants to come.

QUESTIONS

1. How did Kamber put his story together? How much of this piece involved reporting from various locations? Whom did he interview? Which parts did he research from documents?
2. Why did he choose the title "Toil and Temptation"? What does he mean by *temptation*? Does he give equal weight to both, as his title suggests?
3. How many success stories are presented in this piece? What degrees of success are shown? How do you think that Antonio would define *success*?
4. If immigrants reside in your community, research their opportunities for employment and their success at being accepted in your community. Write a report of your findings.

---

[14]*taqueria:* A place for Mexican fast food, such as tacos and burritos. [Eds.]

5. Have you ever had a low-paying job like Antonio's, such as working at a fast-food place? If so, describe what you did on this job and how you felt about it. What do you know about workers such as busboys, cleaning people, and car wash workers? If you have never worked at this kind of job, interview someone about their work, and write a report on what you learned.

MAKING CONNECTIONS

Compare Antonio's experience with that of Barbara Ehrenreich or one of her subjects in "Nickel and Dimed: On (Not) Getting by in America" (p. 760) or with that of the Mexican day laborers in Eric Schlosser and Jon Lowenstein's "Making It Work" (p. 775). Do some research on Mexican workers in other communities, and compare their daily lives with Antonio's.

Social Sciences
and Public Affairs

"THIS IS THE END
OF THE WORLD"
The Black Death

Barbara Tuchman

*Barbara Wertheim Tuchman (1912–1989) wrote books on histori-
cal subjects ranging over six centuries — from the Middle Ages to
the Vietnam War. Her careful research and lively writing in books
like* The Guns of August *(1962),* A Distant Mirror *(1978),* The
March of Folly: From Troy to Vietnam *(1984), and* The First Salute
*(1988) pleased not only the general public but many professional
historians as well. She twice won the Pulitzer Prize.* A Distant
Mirror, *from which the following selection has been taken, was on
the* New York Times *best-seller list for more than nine months.*

In October 1347, two months after the fall of Calais, Genoese trading
ships put into the harbor of Messina in Sicily with dead and dying men at
the oars. The ships had come from the Black Sea port of Caffa (now
Feodosiya) in the Crimea, where the Genoese maintained a trading post.
The diseased sailors showed strange black swellings about the size of an egg
or an apple in the armpits and groin. The swellings oozed blood and pus
and were followed by spreading boils and black blotches on the skin from
internal bleeding. The sick suffered severe pain and died quickly within five
days of the first symptoms. As the disease spread, other symptoms of continuous fever and spitting of blood appeared instead of the swellings or
buboes. These victims coughed and sweated heavily and died even more
quickly, within three days or less, sometimes in 24 hours. In both types

everything that issued from the body—breath, sweat, blood from the buboes and lungs, bloody urine, and blood-blackened excrement—smelled foul. Depression and despair accompanied the physical symptoms, and before the end "death is seen seated on the face."

The disease was bubonic plague, present in two forms: one that infected the bloodstream, causing the buboes and internal bleeding, and was spread by contact; and a second, more virulent pneumonic type that infected the lungs and was spread by respiratory infection. The presence of both at once caused the high mortality and speed of contagion. So lethal was the disease that cases were known of persons going to bed well and dying before they woke, of doctors catching the illness at a bedside and dying before the patient. So rapidly did it spread from one to another that to a French physician, Simon de Covino, it seemed as if one sick person "could infect the whole world." The malignity of the pestilence appeared more terrible because its victims knew no prevention and no remedy.

The physical suffering of the disease and its aspects of evil mystery were expressed in a strange Welsh lament which saw "death coming into our midst like black smoke, a plague which cuts off the young, a rootless phantom which has no mercy for fair countenance. Woe is me of the shilling in the armpit! It is seething, terrible . . . a head that gives pain and causes a loud cry . . . a painful angry knob . . . Great is its seething like a burning cinder . . . a grievous thing of ashy color." Its eruption is ugly like the "seeds of black peas, broken fragments of brittle sea-coal . . . the early ornaments of black death, cinders of the peelings of the cockle weed, a mixed multitude, a black plague like halfpence, like berries. . . ."

Rumors of a terrible plague supposedly arising in China and spreading through Tartary (Central Asia) to India and Persia, Mesopotamia, Syria, Egypt, and all of Asia Minor had reached Europe in 1346. They told of a death toll so devastating that all of India was said to be depopulated, whole territories covered by dead bodies, other areas with no one left alive. As added up by Pope Clement VI at Avignon, the total of reported dead reached 23,840,000. In the absence of a concept of contagion, no serious alarm was felt in Europe until the trading ships brought their black burden of pestilence into Messina while other infected ships from the Levant carried it to Genoa and Venice.

By January 1348 it penetrated France via Marseille, and North Africa   5
via Tunis. Shipborne along coasts and navigable rivers, it spread westward from Marseille through the ports of Languedoc to Spain and northward up the Rhône to Avignon, where it arrived in March. It reached Narbonne, Montpellier, Carcassonne, and Toulouse between February and May, and at the same time in Italy spread to Rome and Florence and their hinterlands. Between June and August it reached Bordeaux, Lyon, and Paris, spread to Burgundy and Normandy, and crossed the Channel from Normandy into southern England. From Italy during the same summer it crossed the Alps into Switzerland and reached eastward to Hungary.

A detail from *The Triumph of Death*, a fresco by Francesco Traini in the
Camposanto, Pisa, Italy, c. 1350.

In a given area the plague accomplished its kill within four to six
months and then faded, except in the larger cities, where, rooting into the
close-quartered population, it abated during the winter, only to reappear in
spring and rage for another six months.

In 1349 it resumed in Paris, spread to Picardy, Flanders, and the Low
Countries, and from England to Scotland and Ireland as well as to Norway,
where a ghost ship with a cargo of wool and a dead crew drifted offshore
until it ran aground near Bergen. From there the plague passed into Sweden,
Denmark, Prussia, Iceland, and as far as Greenland. Leaving a strange
pocket of immunity in Bohemia, and Russia unattacked until 1351, it had
passed from most of Europe by mid-1350. Although the mortality rate was
erratic, ranging from one fifth in some places to nine tenths or almost total
elimination in others, the overall estimate of modern demographers has settled — for the area extending from India to Iceland — around the same figure expressed in Froissart's casual words: "a third of the world died." His
estimate, the common one at the time, was not an inspired guess but a borrowing of St. John's figure for mortality from plague in Revelation, the
favorite guide to human affairs of the Middle Ages.

A third of Europe would have meant about 20 million deaths. No one
knows in truth how many died. Contemporary reports were an awed impression, not an accurate count. In crowded Avignon, it was said, 400 died daily;
7,000 houses emptied by death were shut up; a single graveyard received
11,000 corpses in six weeks; half the city's inhabitants reportedly died,

including 9 cardinals or one third of the total, and 70 lesser prelates. Watching the endlessly passing death carts, chroniclers let normal exaggeration take wings and put the Avignon death toll at 62,000 and even at 120,000, although the city's total population was probably less than 50,000.

When graveyards filled up, bodies at Avignon were thrown into the Rhône until mass burial pits were dug for dumping the corpses. In London in such pits corpses piled up in layers until they overflowed. Everywhere reports speak of the sick dying too fast for the living to bury. Corpses were dragged out of homes and left in front of doorways. Morning light revealed new piles of bodies. In Florence the dead were gathered up by the Compagnia della Misericordia—founded in 1244 to care for the sick—whose members wore red robes and hoods masking the face except for the eyes. When their efforts failed, the dead lay putrid in the streets for days at a time. When no coffins were to be had, the bodies were laid on boards, two or three at once, to be carried to graveyards or common pits. Families dumped their own relatives into the pits, or buried them so hastily and thinly "that dogs dragged them forth and devoured their bodies."

Amid accumulating death and fear of contagion, people died without last   10
rites and were buried without prayers, a prospect that terrified the last hours of the stricken. A bishop in England gave permission to laymen to make confession to each other as was done by the Apostles, "or if no man is present then even to a woman," and if no priest could be found to administer extreme unction, "then faith must suffice." Clement VI found it necessary to grant remissions of sin to all who died of the plague because so many were unattended by priests. "And no bells tolled," wrote a chronicler of Siena, "and nobody wept no matter what his loss because almost everyone expected death. . . . And people said and believed, 'This is the end of the world.'"

In Paris, where the plague lasted through 1349, the reported death rate was 800 a day, in Pisa 500, in Vienna 500 to 600. The total dead in Paris numbered 50,000 or half the population. Florence, weakened by the famine of 1347, lost three to four fifths of its citizens, Venice two thirds, Hamburg and Bremen, though smaller in size, about the same proportion. Cities, as centers of transportation, were more likely to be affected than villages, although once a village was infected, its death rate was equally high. At Givry, a prosperous village in Burgundy of 1,200 to 1,500 people, the parish register records 615 deaths in the space of fourteen weeks, compared to an average of thirty deaths a year in the previous decade. In three villages of Cambridgeshire, manorial records show a death rate of 47 percent, 57 percent, and in one case 70 percent. When the last survivors, too few to carry on, moved away, a deserted village sank back into the wilderness and disappeared from the map altogether, leaving only a grass-covered ghostly outline to show where mortals once had lived.

In enclosed places such as monasteries and prisons, the infection of one person usually meant that of all, as happened in the Franciscan convents of Carcassonne and Marseille, where every inmate without exception died. Of the 140 Dominicans at Montpellier only seven survived. Petrarch's brother

Burial of plague victims, from *Annales de Gilles li Muisis* (The Annals of Gilles li Muisis, c. 1272–1352)

Gherardo, member of a Carthusian monastery, buried the prior and 34 fellow monks one by one, sometimes three a day, until he was left alone with his dog and fled to look for a place that would take him in. Watching every comrade die, men in such places could not but wonder whether the strange peril that filled the air had not been sent to exterminate the human race. In Kilkenny, Ireland, Brother John Clyn of the Friars Minor, another monk left alone among dead men, kept a record of what had happened lest "things which should be remembered perish with time and vanish from the memory of those who come after us." Sensing "the whole world, as it were, placed within the grasp of the Evil One," and waiting for death to visit him too, he wrote, "I leave parchment to continue this work, if perchance any man survive and any of the race of Adam escape this pestilence and carry on the work which I have begun." Brother John, as noted by another hand, died of the pestilence, but he foiled oblivion.

The largest cities of Europe, with populations of about 100,000, were Paris and Florence, Venice and Genoa. At the next level, with more than 50,000, were Ghent and Bruges in Flanders, Milan, Bologna, Rome, Naples, and Palermo, and Cologne. London hovered below 50,000, the only city in England except York with more than 10,000. At the level of 20,000 to 50,000 were Bordeaux, Toulouse, Montpellier, Marseille, and Lyon in France, Barcelona, Seville, and Toledo in Spain, Siena, Pisa, and other secondary cities in Italy, and the Hanseatic trading cities of the Empire. The plague raged through them all, killing anywhere from one third to two thirds of their inhabitants. Italy, with a total population of 10 to 11 million, probably suffered the heaviest toll. Following the Florentine bankruptcies, the crop failures and workers' riots of 1346–47, the revolt of Cola di Rienzi that plunged Rome into anarchy, the plague came as the peak of successive calamities. As if the world were indeed in the grasp of the Evil One, its first appearance on the European mainland in January 1348 coincided with a fearsome earthquake that carved a path of wreckage from Naples up to Venice. Houses collapsed, church towers toppled, villages were crushed, and the destruction reached as far as Germany and Greece. Emotional response, dulled by horrors, underwent a kind of atrophy epitomized by the chronicler who wrote, "And in these days was burying without sorrowe and wedding without friendschippe."

In Siena, where more than half the inhabitants died of the plague, work was abandoned on the great cathedral, planned to be the largest in the world, and never resumed, owing to loss of workers and master masons and "the melancholy and grief" of the survivors. The cathedral's truncated transept still stands in permanent witness to the sweep of death's scythe. Agnolo di Tura, a chronicler of Siena, recorded the fear of contagion that froze every other instinct. "Father abandoned child, wife husband, one brother another," he wrote, "for this plague seemed to strike through the breath and sight. And so they died. And no one could be found to bury the dead for money or friendship. . . . And I, Agnolo di Tura, called the Fat, buried my five children with my own hands, and so did many others likewise."

There were many to echo his account of inhumanity and few to balance   15
it, for the plague was not the kind of calamity that inspired mutual help. Its loathsomeness and deadliness did not herd people together in mutual distress, but only prompted their desire to escape each other. "Magistrates and notaries refused to come and make the wills of the dying," reported a Franciscan friar of Piazza in Sicily; what was worse, "even the priests did not come to hear their confessions." A clerk of the Archbishop of Canterbury reported the same of English priests who "turned away from the care of their benefices from fear of death." Cases of parents deserting children and children their parents were reported across Europe from Scotland to Russia. The calamity chilled the hearts of men, wrote Boccaccio in his famous account of the plague in Florence that serves as introduction to the *Decameron*. "One man shunned another . . . kinsfolk held aloof, brother was forsaken by brother, oftentimes husband by wife; nay, what is more, and scarcely to be believed, fathers and mothers were found to abandon their own children to their fate, untended, unvisited as if they had been strangers." Exaggeration and literary pessimism were common in the 14th century, but the Pope's physician, Guy de Chauliac, was a sober, careful observer who reported the same phenomenon: "A father did not visit his son, nor the son his father. Charity was dead."

Yet not entirely. In Paris, according to the chronicler Jean de Venette, the nuns of the Hotel Dieu or municipal hospital, "having no fear of death, tended the sick with all sweetness and humility." New nuns repeatedly took the places of those who died, until the majority "many times renewed by death now rest in peace with Christ as we may piously believe."

When the plague entered northern France in July 1348, it settled first in Normandy and, checked by winter, gave Picardy a deceptive interim until the next summer. Either in mourning or warning, black flags were flown from church towers of the worst-stricken villages of Normandy. "And in that time," wrote a monk of the abbey of Fourcarment, "the mortality was so great among the people of Normandy that those of Picardy mocked them." The same unneighborly reaction was reported of the Scots, separated by a winter's immunity from the English. Delighted to hear of the disease that was scourging the "southrons," they gathered forces for an invasion, "laughing at their enemies." Before they could move, the savage mortality fell upon them too, scattering some in death and the rest in panic to spread the infection as they fled.

In Picardy in the summer of 1349 the pestilence penetrated the castle of Coucy to kill Enguerrand's[1] mother, Catherine, and her new husband. Whether her nine-year-old son escaped by chance or was perhaps living elsewhere with one of his guardians is unrecorded. In nearby Amiens, tannery workers, responding quickly to losses in the labor force, combined to bargain for higher wages. In another place villagers were seen dancing to drums and trumpets, and on being asked the reason, answered that, seeing their neighbors die day by day while their village remained immune, they believed that they could keep the plague from entering "by the jollity that is in us. That is why we dance." Further north in Tournai on the border of Flanders, Gilles li Muisis, Abbot of St. Martin's, kept one of the epidemic's most vivid accounts. The passing bells rang all day and all night, he recorded, because sextons were anxious to obtain their fees while they could. Filled with the sound of mourning, the city became oppressed by fear, so that the authorities forbade the tolling of bells and the wearing of black and restricted funeral services to two mourners. The silencing of funeral bells and of criers' announcements of deaths was ordained by most cities. Siena imposed a fine on the wearing of mourning clothes by all except widows.

Flight was the chief recourse of those who could afford it or arrange it. The rich fled to their country places like Boccaccio's young patricians of Florence, who settled in a pastoral palace "removed on every side from the roads" with "wells of cool water and vaults of rare wines." The urban poor died in their burrows, "and only the stench of their bodies informed neighbors of their deaths." That the poor were more heavily afflicted than the rich was clearly remarked at the time, in the north as in the south. A Scottish chronicler, John of Fordun, stated flatly that the pest "attacked especially the meaner sort and common people—seldom the magnates." Simon de Covino of Montpellier made the same observation. He ascribed it to the misery and want and hard lives that made the poor more susceptible, which was half the truth. Close contact and lack of sanitation was the unrecognized other half. It was noticed too that the young died in greater proportion than the old;

---

[1]*Enguerrand de Coucy:* A French nobleman. Tuchman follows his life as a way of unifying her study of the fourteenth century. [Eds.]

Simon de Covino compared the disappearance of youth to the withering of flowers in the fields.

In the countryside peasants dropped dead on the roads, in the fields, in   20
their houses. Survivors in growing helplessness fell into apathy, leaving ripe wheat uncut and livestock untended. Oxen and asses, sheep and goats, pigs and chickens ran wild and they too, according to local reports, succumbed to the pest. English sheep, bearers of the precious wool, died throughout the country. The chronicler Henry Knighton, canon of Leicester Abbey, reported 5,000 dead in one field alone, "their bodies so corrupted by the plague that neither beast nor bird would touch them," and spreading an appalling stench. In the Austrian Alps wolves came down to prey upon sheep and then, "as if alarmed by some invisible warning, turned and fled back into the wilderness." In remote Dalmatia bolder wolves descended upon a plague-stricken city and attacked human survivors. For want of herdsmen, cattle strayed from place to place and died in hedgerows and ditches. Dogs and cats fell like the rest.

The dearth of labor held a fearful prospect because the 14th century lived close to the annual harvest both for food and for next year's seed. "So few servants and laborers were left," wrote Knighton, "that no one knew where to turn for help." The sense of a vanishing future created a kind of dementia of despair. A Bavarian chronicler of Neuberg on the Danube recorded that "Men and women . . . wandered around as if mad" and let their cattle stray "because no one had any inclination to concern themselves about the future." Fields went uncultivated, spring seed unsown. Second growth with nature's awful energy crept back over cleared land, dikes crumbled, salt water reinvaded and soured the lowlands. With so few hands remaining to restore the work of centuries, people felt, in Walsingham's words, that "the world could never again regain its former prosperity."

Though the death rate was higher among the anonymous poor, the known and the great died too. King Alfonso XI of Castile was the only reigning monarch killed by the pest, but his neighbor King Pedro of Aragon lost his wife, Queen Leonora, his daughter Marie, and a niece in the space of six months. John Cantacuzene, Emperor of Byzantium, lost his son. In France the lame Queen Jeanne and her daughter-in-law Bonne de Luxemburg, wife of the Dauphin, both died in 1349 in the same phase that took the life of Enguerrand's mother. Jeanne, Queen of Navarre, daughter of Louis X, was another victim. Edward III's second daughter, Joanna, who was on her way to marry Pedro, the heir of Castile, died in Bordeaux. Women appear to have been more vulnerable than men, perhaps because, being more housebound, they were more exposed to fleas. Boccaccio's mistress Fiammetta, illegitimate daughter of the King of Naples, died, as did Laura, the beloved—whether real or fictional—of Petrarch. Reaching out to us in the future, Petrarch cried, "Oh happy posterity who will not experience such abysmal woe and will look upon our testimony as a fable."

In Florence Giovanni Villani, the great historian of his time, died at 68 in the midst of an unfinished sentence: " . . . *e dure questo pistolenza fino a* . . . (in the midst of this pestilence there came to an end . . .)." Siena's master painters, the brothers Ambrogio and Pietro Lorenzetti, whose names never appear after 1348, presumably perished in the plague, as did Andrea Pisano, architect and sculptor of Florence. William of Ockham and the English mystic Richard Rolle of Hampole both disappear from mention after 1349. Francisco Datini, merchant of Prato, lost both his parents and two siblings. Curious sweeps of mortality afflicted certain bodies of merchants in London. All eight wardens of the Company of Cutters, all six wardens of the Hatters, and four wardens of the Goldsmiths died before July 1350. Sir John Pulteney, master draper and four times Mayor of London, was a victim, likewise Sir John Montgomery, Governor of Calais.

Among the clergy and doctors the mortality was naturally high because of the nature of their professions. Out of 24 physicians in Venice, 20 were said to have lost their lives in the plague, although, according to another account, some were believed to have fled or to have shut themselves up in their houses. At Montpellier, site of the leading medieval medical school, the physician Simon de Covino reported that, despite the great number of doctors, "hardly one of them escaped." In Avignon, Guy de Chauliac confessed that he performed his medical visits only because he dared not stay away for fear of infamy, but "I was in continual fear." He claimed to have contracted the disease but to have cured himself by his own treatment; if so, he was one of the few who recovered.

Clerical mortality varied with rank. Although the one-third toll of cardinals reflects the same proportion as the whole, this was probably due to their concentration in Avignon. In England, in strange and almost sinister procession, the Archbishop of Canterbury, John Stratford, died in August 1348, his appointed successor died in May 1349, and the next appointee three months later, all three within a year. Despite such weird vagaries, prelates in general managed to sustain a higher survival rate than the lesser clergy. Among bishops the deaths have been estimated at about one in twenty. The loss of priests, even if many avoided their fearful duty of attending the dying, was about the same as among the population as a whole.

Government officials, whose loss contributed to the general chaos, found, on the whole, no special shelter. In Siena four of the nine members of the governing oligarchy died, in France one third of the royal notaries, in Bristol 15 out of the 52 members of the Town Council or almost one third. Tax-collecting obviously suffered, with the result that Philip VI was unable to collect more than a fraction of the subsidy granted him by the Estates in the winter of 1347–48.

Lawlessness and debauchery accompanied the plague as they had during the great plague of Athens of 430 B.C., when according to Thucydides, men grew bold in the indulgence of pleasure: "For seeing how the rich died in a moment and those who had nothing immediately inherited their property, they reflected that life and riches were alike transitory and they resolved to enjoy themselves while they could." Human behavior is timeless. When St. John had his vision of plague in Revelation, he knew from

25

some experience or race memory that those who survived "repented not of the work of their hands. . . . Neither repented they of their murders, nor of their sorceries, nor of their fornication, nor of their thefts."

Notes

Although Tuchman's notes are labeled by page number, the numbers in this Notes section refer to the paragraphs in which the sources are mentioned. Tuchman does not use numbered footnotes. At the end of her book, she numbers her notes by page number and provides a source for each quotation and citation. Following her notes, she provides a bibliography that provides the full citation for every reference given in her notes.

1. "death is seen seated": Simon de Covino, q. Campbell, 80.
2. "could infect the whole world": q. Gasquet, 41.
3. Welsh lament: q. Ziegler, 190.
9. "dogs dragged them forth": Agnolo di Tura, q. Ziegler, 58.
10. "or if no man is present": Bishop of Bath and Wells, q. Ziegler, 125. "No Bells Tolled": Agnolo di Tura, q. Schevill, Siena, 211. The same observation was made by Gabriel de Muisis, notary of Piacenza, q. Crawfurd, 113.
11. Givry parish register: Renouard, 111. three villages of Cambridgeshire: Saltmarsh.
12. Petrarch's brother: Bishop, 273. Brother John Clyn: q. Ziegler, 195.
13. "And in these days": q. Deaux, 143, citing only "an old northern chronicle."
14. Agnolo Di Tura, "Father abandoned child": q. Ziegler, 58.
15. "Magistrates and notaries": q. Deaux, 49. English Priests Turned Away: Ziegler, 261. Parents Deserting Children: Hecker, 30. Guy De Chauliac, "A Father": q. Gasquet, 50–51.
16. nuns of the Hotel Dieu: *Chron. Jean de Venette*, 49.
17. Picards and Scots mock mortality of neighbors: Gasquet, 53, and Ziegler, 198.
18. Catherine de Coucy: *L'Art de vérifier*, 237. Amiens Tanners: Gasquet, 57. "By the Jollity That Is in Us": *Grandes Chrôns.*, VI, 486–87.
19. John of Fordun: q. Ziegler, 199. Simon de Covino on the poor: Gasquet, 42. on youth: Cazelles, *Peste*.
20. Knighton on sheep: q. Ziegler, 175. Wolves of Austria and Dalmatia: ibid., 84, 111. dogs and cats: Muisis, q. Gasquet, 44, 61.
21. Bavarian chronicler of Neuberg: q. Ziegler, 84. Walsingham, "the world could never": Denifle, 273.
22. "Oh happy posterity": q. Ziegler, 45.
23. Giovanni Villani, "*e dure questo*": q. Snell, 334.
24. physicians of Venice: Campbell, 98. Simon de Covino: ibid., 31. Guy de Chauliac, "I was in continual fear": q. Thompson *Ec. and Soc.*, 379.
27. Thucydides: q. Crawfurd, 30–31.

Bibliography

L'Art de vérifier les dates des faits historiques, par un Religieux de la Congregation de St.-Maur, vol. XII. Paris, 1818.
Bishop, Morris. *Petrarch and His World*. Indiana University Press, 1963.

Campbell, Anna M. *The Black Death and Men of Learning.* Columbia University Press, 1931.

Cazelles, Raymond. "*La Peste de 1348–49 en Langue d'oil: épidémie prolitarienne et enfantine.*" *Bull philologique et historique,* 1962, pp. 293–305.

Chronicle of Jean de Venette. Trans. Jean Birdsall. Ed. Richard A. Newhall. Columbia University Press, 1853.

Crawfurd, Raymond. *Plague and Pestilence in Literature and Art.* Oxford, 1914.

Deaux, George. *The Black Death, 1347.* London, 1969.

Denifle, Henri. *La Dèsolation des églises, monastères et hopitaux en France pendant la guerre de cent ans,* vol. I. Paris, 1899.

Gasquet, Francis Aidan, Abbot. *The Black Death of 1348 and 1349,* 2nd ed. London, 1908.

Grandes Chroniques de France, vol. VI (to 1380). Ed. Paulin Paris. Paris, 1838.

Hecker, J. F. C. *The Epidemics of the Middle Ages.* London, 1844.

Renouard, Yves. "*La Peste noirs de 1348–50.*" *Rev. de Paris,* March, 1950.

Saltmarsh, John. "Plague and Economic Decline in England in the Later Middle Ages," *Cambridge Historical Journal,* vol. VII, no. 1, 1941.

Schevill, Ferdinand. *Siena: The History of a Medieval Commune.* New York, 1909.

Snell, Frederick. *The Fourteenth Century.* Edinburgh, 1899.

Thompson, James Westfall. *Economic and Social History of Europe in the Later Middle Ages.* New York, 1931.

Ziegler, Philip. *The Black Death.* New York, 1969. (The best modern study.)

QUESTIONS

1. Try to imagine yourself in Tuchman's position. If you were assigned the task of reporting on the Black Plague in Europe, how would you go about it? What problems would you expect to encounter in the research and in the composition of your report?

2. The notes and bibliography reveal a broad scholarly base: Tuchman's research was clearly prodigious. But so were the problems of organization after the research had been done. Tuchman had to present her information to readers in a way that would be clear and interesting. How has she solved her problem? What overall patterns of organization do you find in this selection? Mark off subsections with topics of their own.

3. How does Tuchman organize her paragraphs? Consider paragraph 20, for example. What is the topic? What are the subtopics? Why does the paragraph begin and end as it does? Consider paragraph 22. How does the first sentence serve as a transition from the previous paragraph? How is the rest of the paragraph ordered? Does the next paragraph start a new topic or continue developing the topic announced at the beginning of paragraph 22?

4. Many paragraphs end with direct quotations. Examine some of these. What do they have in common? Why do you think Tuchman closes so many paragraphs in this way?

5. Much of this essay is devoted to the reporting of facts and figures. This could be very tedious, but Tuchman is an expert at avoiding dullness. How does she help the reader see and feel the awfulness of the plague? Locate specific examples in the text, and discuss their effectiveness.

6. Examine Tuchman's list of sources, and explain how she has used them. Does she quote directly from each source, or does she paraphrase it? Does she use a source to illustrate a point, as evidence for argument, or in some other way?

7. Taking Tuchman as a model, write a report on some other catastrophe, blending factual reporting with description of what it was like to be there. This will require both careful research and artful selection and arrangement of the fruits of that research.

8. Using Tuchman's notes to *A Distant Mirror* as a reference guide, find out more about some specific place or event mentioned by Tuchman. Write a report of your findings.

MAKING CONNECTIONS

Compare this account of the Black Death to the writing by William L. Laurence (p. 229) or Jane van Lawick-Goodall (p. 237) included in this section. Make your comparison in terms of the points of view established and sustained in the reports you compare. What is Tuchman's point of view toward her subject?

ATOMIC BOMBING OF NAGASAKI TOLD BY FLIGHT MEMBER

William L. Laurence

William L. Laurence (1888–1997) was born in Lithuania and came to the United States in 1905. He studied at Harvard and the Boston University Law School. His main interest, however, was always science, and after working at the New York World *for five years, Laurence went to the* New York Times *as a science reporter. During World War II, Laurence was the only reporter who knew about the top-secret testing of the atomic bomb. On August 9, 1945, he was permitted to fly with the mission to drop the second atomic bomb on Nagasaki. Three days earlier, more than one hundred thousand people had been killed in the Hiroshima bombing. Laurence won the Pulitzer Prize for this account of the bombing of Nagasaki. The article appeared in the* New York Times *on September 9, 1945.*

With the atomic-bomb mission to Japan, August 9 (Delayed) — We are on our way to bomb the mainland of Japan. Our flying contingent consists of three specially designed B-29 Superforts, and two of these carry no bombs. But our lead plane is on its way with another atomic bomb, the second in three days, concentrating in its active substance an explosive energy equivalent to twenty thousand and, under favorable conditions, forty thousand tons of TNT.

We have several chosen targets. One of these is the great industrial and shipping center of Nagasaki, on the western shore of Kyushu, one of the main islands of the Japanese homeland.

I watched the assembly of this man-made meteor during the past two days and was among the small group of scientists and Army and Navy representatives privileged to be present at the ritual of its loading in the Superfort last night, against a background of threatening black skies torn open at intervals by great lightning flashes.

It is a thing of beauty to behold, this "gadget." Into its design went millions of man-hours of what is without doubt the most concentrated intellectual effort in history. Never before had so much brain power been focused on a single problem.

This atomic bomb is different from the bomb used three days ago with such devastating results on Hiroshima.   5

I saw the atomic substance before it was placed inside the bomb. By itself it is not at all dangerous to handle. It is only under certain conditions, produced in the bomb assembly, that it can be made to yield up its energy, and even then it gives only a small fraction of its total contents — a fraction, however, large enough to produce the greatest explosion on earth.

The briefing at midnight revealed the extreme care and the tremendous amount of preparation that had been made to take care of every detail of the mission, to make certain that the atomic bomb fully served the purpose for which it was intended. Each target in turn was shown in detailed maps and in aerial photographs. Every detail of the course was rehearsed — navigation, altitude, weather, where to land in emergencies. It came out that the Navy had rescue craft, known as Dumbos and Superdumbos, stationed at various strategic points in the vicinity of the targets, ready to rescue the fliers in case they were forced to bail out.

The briefing period ended with a moving prayer by the chaplain. We then proceeded to the mess hall for the traditional early-morning breakfast before departure on a bombing mission.

A convoy of trucks took us to the supply building for the special equipment carried on combat missions. This included the Mae West,[1] a parachute, a lifeboat, an oxygen mask, a flak suit, and a survival vest. We still had a few hours before take-off time, but we all went to the flying field and stood around in little groups or sat in jeeps talking rather casually about our mission to the Empire, as the Japanese home islands are known hereabouts.

In command of our mission is Major Charles W. Sweeney, twenty-five, of 124 Hamilton Avenue, North Quincy, Massachusetts. His flagship, carrying the atomic bomb, is named *The Great Artiste,* but the name does not appear on the body of the great silver ship, with its unusually long, four-bladed, orange-tipped propellers. Instead, it carries the number 77, and someone remarks that it was "Red" Grange's winning number on the gridiron.

We took off at 3:50 this morning and headed northwest on a straight line for the Empire. The night was cloudy and threatening, with only a few stars here and there breaking through the overcast. The weather report had predicted storms ahead part of the way but clear sailing for the final and climactic stages of our odyssey.

We were about an hour away from our base when the storm broke. Our great ship took some heavy dips through the abysmal darkness around us, but it took these dips much more gracefully than a large commercial air liner, producing a sensation more in the nature of a glide than a "bump," like a great ocean liner riding the waves except that in this case the air waves were much higher and the rhythmic tempo of the glide was much faster.

I noticed a strange eerie light coming through the window high above the navigator's cabin, and as I peered through the dark all around us I saw a startling phenomenon. The whirling giant propellers had somehow

10

---

[1]*Mae West:* A personal flotation device or life jacket. Sailors named the device after the well-known film star. [Eds.]

become great luminous disks of blue flame. The same luminous blue flame appeared on the plexiglass windows in the nose of the ship, and on the tips of the giant wings. It looked as though we were riding the whirlwind through space on a chariot of blue fire.

It was, I surmised, a surcharge of static electricity that had accumulated on the tips of the propellers and on the di-electric material of the plastic windows. One's thoughts dwelt anxiously on the precious cargo in the invisible ship ahead of us. Was there any likelihood of danger that this heavy electric tension in the atmosphere all about us might set it off?

I expressed my fears to Captain Bock, who seems nonchalant and unper-   15
turbed at the controls. He quickly reassured me.

"It is a familiar phenomenon seen often on ships. I have seen it many times on bombing missions. It is known as St. Elmo's fire."

On we went through the night. We soon rode out the storm and our ship was once again sailing on a smooth course straight ahead, on a direct line to the Empire.

Our altimeter showed that we were traveling through space at a height of seventeen thousand feet. The thermometer registered an outside temperature of thirty-three degrees below zero Centigrade, about thirty below Fahrenheit. Inside our pressurized cabin the temperature was that of a comfortable air-conditioned room and a pressure corresponding to an altitude of eight thousand feet. Captain Bock cautioned me, however, to keep my oxygen mask handy in case of emergency. This, he explained, might mean either something going wrong with the pressure equipment inside the ship or a hole through the cabin by flak.

The first signs of dawn came shortly after five o'clock. Sergeant Curry, of Hoopeston, Illinois, who had been listening steadily on his earphones for radio reports, while maintaining a strict radio silence himself, greeted it by rising to his feet and gazing out the window.

"It's good to see the day," he told me. "I get a feeling of claustropho-   20
bia hemmed in this cabin at night."

He is a typical American youth, looking even younger than his twenty years. It takes no mind reader to read his thoughts.

"It's a long way from Hoopeston," I find myself remarking.

"Yep," he replies, as he busies himself decoding a message from outer space.

"Think this atomic bomb will end the war?" he asks hopefully.

"There is a very good chance that this one may do the trick," I assured   25
him, "but if not, then the next one or two surely will. Its power is such that no nation can stand up against it very long." This was not my own view. I had heard it expressed all around a few hours earlier, before we took off. To anyone who had seen this man-made fireball in action, as I had less than a month ago in the desert of New Mexico, this view did not sound overoptimistic.

By 5:50 it was really light outside. We had lost our lead ship, but Lieutenant Godfrey, our navigator, informs me that we had arranged for that contingency. We have an assembly point in the sky above the little island of Yakushima, southeast of Kyushu, at 9:10. We are to circle there and wait for the rest of our formation.

Our genial bombardier, Lieutenant Levy, comes over to invite me to take his front-row seat in the transparent nose of the ship, and I accept eagerly. From that vantage point in space, seventeen thousand feet above the Pacific, one gets a view of hundreds of miles on all sides, horizontally and vertically. At that height the vast ocean below and the sky above seem to merge into one great sphere.

I was on the inside of that firmament, riding above the giant mountains of white cumulus clouds, letting myself be suspended in infinite space. One hears the whirl of the motors behind one, but it soon becomes insignificant against the immensity all around and is before long swallowed by it. There comes a point where space also swallows time and one lives through eternal moments filled with an oppressive loneliness, as though all life had suddenly vanished from the earth and you are the only one left, a lone survivor traveling endlessly through interplanetary space.

My mind soon returns to the mission I am on. Somewhere beyond these vast mountains of white clouds ahead of me there lies Japan, the land of our enemy. In about four hours from now one of its cities, making weapons of war for use against us, will be wiped off the map by the greatest weapon ever made by man: In one tenth of a millionth of a second, a fraction of time immeasurable by any clock, a whirlwind from the skies will pulverize thousands of its buildings and tens of thousands of its inhabitants.

But at this moment no one yet knows which one of the several cities   30
chosen as targets is to be annihilated. The final choice lies with destiny. The winds over Japan will make the decision. If they carry heavy clouds over our primary target, the city will be saved, at least for the time being. None of its inhabitants will ever know that the wind of a benevolent destiny had passed over their heads. But that same wind will doom another city.

Our weather planes ahead of us are on their way to find out where the wind blows. Half an hour before target time we will know what the winds have decided.

Does one feel any pity or compassion for the poor devils about to die? Not when one thinks of Pearl Harbor[2] and of the Death March on Bataan.[3]

Captain Bock informs me that we are about to start our climb to bombing altitude.

――――――――――

[2]*Pearl Harbor:* The U.S. Navy base on the island of Oahu, Hawaii, that was attacked by the Japanese Imperial Navy on December 7, 1941. The surprise attack caused the death of 1,177 people and prompted the United States to enter World War II. [Eds.]

[3]*Death March on Bataan:* The forced march of American and Filipino defenders of the Bataan peninsula in the Philippines. The men were forced by their Japanese captors to march more than sixty miles with almost no food or water to a prisoner-of-war camp in Manila. Between 5,000 and 11,000 died before reaching the camp. [Eds.]

He manipulates a few knobs on his control panel to the right of him, and I alternately watch the white clouds and ocean below me and the altimeter on the bombardier's panel. We reached our altitude at nine o'clock. We were then over Japanese waters, close to their mainland. Lieutenant Godfrey motioned to me to look through his radar scope. Before me was the outline of our assembly point. We shall soon meet our lead ship and proceed to the final stage of our journey.

We reached Yakushima at 9:12 and there, about four thousand feet ahead   35
of us, was *The Great Artiste* with its precious load. I saw Lieutenant Godfrey and Sergeant Curry strap on their parachutes and I decided to do likewise.

We started circling. We saw little towns on the coastline, heedless of our presence. We kept on circling, waiting for the third ship in our formation.

It was 9:56 when we began heading for the coastline. Our weather scouts had sent us code messages, deciphered by Sergeant Curry, informing us that both the primary target as well as the secondary were clearly visible.

The winds of destiny seemed to favor certain Japanese cities that must remain nameless. We circled about them again and again and found no opening in the thick umbrella of clouds that covered them. Destiny chose Nagasaki as the ultimate target.

We had been circling for some time when we noticed black puffs of smoke coming through the white clouds directly at us. There were fifteen bursts of flak in rapid succession, all too low. Captain Bock changed his course. There soon followed eight more bursts of flak, right up to our altitude, but by this time they were too far to the left.

We flew southward down the channel and at 11:33 crossed the coast-   40
line and headed straight for Nagasaki, about one hundred miles to the west. Here again we circled until we found an opening in the clouds. It was 12:01 and the goal of our mission had arrived.

We heard the prearranged signal on our radio, put on our arc welder's glasses, and watched tensely the maneuverings of the strike ship about half a mile in front of us.

"There she goes!" someone said.

Out of the belly of *The Great Artiste* what looked like a black object went downward.

Captain Bock swung to get out of range; but even though we were turning away in the opposite direction, and despite the fact that it was broad daylight in our cabin, all of us became aware of a giant flash that broke through the dark barrier of our arc welder's lenses and flooded our cabin with intense light.

We removed our glasses after the first flash, but the light still lingered   45
on, a bluish-green light that illuminated the entire sky all around. A tremendous blast wave struck our ship and made it tremble from nose to tail. This was followed by four more blasts in rapid succession, each resounding like the boom of cannon fire hitting our plane from all directions.

Observers in the tail of our ship saw a giant ball of fire rise as though from the bowels of the earth, belching forth enormous white smoke rings.

Next they saw a giant pillar of purple fire, ten thousand feet high, shooting skyward with enormous speed.

By the time our ship had made another turn in the direction of the atomic explosion the pillar of purple fire had reached the level of our altitude. Only about forty-five seconds had passed. Awe-struck, we watched it shoot upward like a meteor coming from the earth instead of from outer space, becoming ever more alive as it climbed skyward through the white clouds. It was no longer smoke, or dust, or even a cloud of fire. It was a living thing, a new species of being, born right before our incredulous eyes.

At one stage of its evolution, covering millions of years in terms of seconds, the entity assumed the form of a giant square totem pole, with its base about three miles long, tapering off to about a mile at the top. Its bottom was brown, its center was amber, its top white. But it was a living totem pole, carved with many grotesque masks grimacing at the earth.

Then, just when it appeared as though the thing had settled down into a state of permanence, there came shooting out of the top a giant mushroom that increased the height of the pillar to a total of forty-five thousand feet. The mushroom top was even more alive than the pillar, seething and

Nagasaki: Damage wrought on second city to be hit by missile. Large factory, right, is a mass of torn steel and rubble. Bridges over canal at left are either demolished or unusable.

boiling in a white fury of creamy foam, sizzling upward and then descending earthward, a thousand Old Faithful geysers rolled into one.

It kept struggling in an elemental fury, like a creature in the act of break-   50
ing the bonds that held it down. In a few seconds it had freed itself from its gigantic stem and floated upward with tremendous speed, its momentum carrying it into the stratosphere to a height of about sixty thousand feet.

But no sooner did this happen when another mushroom, smaller in size than the first one, began emerging out of the pillar. It was as though the decapitated monster was growing a new head.

As the first mushroom floated off into the blue it changed its shape into a flowerlike form, its giant petals curving downward, creamy white outside, rose-colored inside. It still retained that shape when we last gazed at it from a distance of about two hundred miles. The boiling pillar of many colors could also be seen at that distance, a giant mountain of jumbled rainbows, in travail. Much living substance had gone into those rainbows. The quivering top of the pillar was protruding to a great height through the white clouds, giving the appearance of a monstrous prehistoric creature with a ruff around its neck, a fleecy ruff extending in all directions, as far as the eye could see.

QUESTIONS

1. What do we learn from this article about the crew members on the mission? Why has Laurence bothered to tell us about them?
2. Laurence's description of the bomb as "a thing of beauty" (paragraph 4) suggests that this eyewitness report is not wholly objective. What is Laurence's moral stance on this mission?
3. Consider Laurence's arrangement of time in his narrative. What effect do you think he wishes to create by switching back and forth between past tense and present tense?
4. Consider Laurence's description of the blast and its resulting cloud (paragraphs 44 through 52). His challenge as a reporter is to help his newspaper readers see this strange and awesome thing. What familiar images does he use to represent this unfamiliar sight? What do those images say — especially the last one — about Laurence's feelings as he watched the cloud transform itself?
5. Write an eyewitness report about an event that you participated in and that you consider important. Present the preparations or actions that led up to the event, and include information about the people who were involved. What imagery can you use to describe the glorious, funny, or chaotic event itself?
6. For a report on the basis for Laurence's attitude toward the bombings of Hiroshima and Nagasaki, look at as many newspapers as you can for August 6 through 10 in 1945. Be sure to look at the editorial pages as well as the front pages. If possible, also interview relatives and friends

who are old enough to remember the war or who might have fought in it. What attitudes toward the bomb and its use were expressed then? How do these compare or contrast with Laurence's attitude?

MAKING CONNECTIONS

1. Describe the differences in point of view taken toward this cataclysmic event by Laurence, John Hersey (p. 181), and Zoë Tracy Hardy (p. 126). How does each writer respond to this unparalleled story? Which responses do you find most unusual, most believable, most sympathetic? Why?
2. Imagine a meeting today between Laurence and Hatsuyo Nakamura from John Hersey's piece (p. 181). What might they say to one another? How might Laurence reflect today on his feelings more than fifty years ago? Imagine this meeting, and write a report of it. If you prefer, substitute Zoë Tracy Hardy (p. 126) for Hatsuyo Nakamura.

FIRST OBSERVATIONS

Jane van Lawick-Goodall

Jane van Lawick-Goodall (b. 1934), the British student of animal behavior, began her work as an assistant to Louis Leakey, an anthropologist and paleontologist whose studies focused on human origins. In 1960, with his help, she settled in Tanzania, East Africa, in the Gombe Stream Game Reserve to investigate the behavior of chimpanzees in their natural habitat. Her discoveries have been widely published in professional journals and in a number of books for more general audiences, including Through a Window: My Thirty Years with the Chimpanzees of Gombe *(1990) and* Reason for Hope: A Spiritual Journey *(1999). The selection reprinted here is taken from* In the Shadow of Man *(1971), a popular work in which she is careful to report her own behavior as well as that of her chimpanzee subjects.*

For about a month I spent most of each day either on the Peak or over-looking Mlinda Valley where the chimps, before or after stuffing themselves with figs, ate large quantities of small purple fruits that tasted, like so many of their foods, as bitter and astringent as sloes or crab apples. Piece by piece, I began to form my first somewhat crude picture of chimpanzee life.

The impression that I had gained when I watched the chimps at the msulula tree of temporary, constantly changing associations of individuals within the community was substantiated. Most often I saw small groups of four to eight moving about together. Sometimes I saw one or two chimpanzees leave such a group and wander off on their own or join up with a different association. On other occasions I watched two or three small groups joining to form a larger one.

Often, as one group crossed the grassy ridge separating the Kasekela Valley from the fig trees on the home valley, the male chimpanzee, or chimpanzees, of the party would break into a run, sometimes moving in an upright position, sometimes dragging a fallen branch, sometimes stamping or slapping the hard earth. These charging displays were always accompanied by loud pant-hoots and afterward the chimpanzee frequently would swing up into a tree overlooking the valley he was about to enter and sit quietly, peering down and obviously listening for a response from below. If there were chimps feeding in the fig trees they nearly always hooted back, as though in answer. Then the new arrivals would hurry down the steep slope and, with more calling and screaming, the two groups would meet in the fig trees. When groups of females and youngsters with no males present joined other feeding chimpanzees, usually there was none of this excitement; the

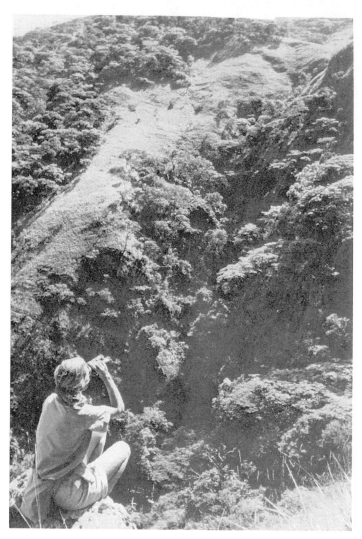

My best place on the Peak offered one of the best vantage points in the area.

newcomers merely climbed up into the trees, greeted some of those already there, and began to stuff themselves with figs.

While many details of their social behavior were hidden from me by the foliage, I did get occasional fascinating glimpses. I saw one female, newly arrived in a group, hurry up to a big male and hold her hand toward him. Almost regally he reached out, clasped her hand in his, drew it toward him, and kissed it with his lips. I saw two adult males embrace each other in greeting. I saw youngsters having wild games through the treetops, chasing around after each other or jumping again and again, one after the other, from a branch to a springy bough below. I watched small infants dangling happily by themselves for minutes on end, patting at their toes with one hand, rotating gently from side to side. Once two tiny infants pulled on opposite ends of a twig in a gentle tug-of-war. Often, during the heat of midday or after a long spell of feeding, I saw two or more adults grooming each other, carefully looking through the hair of their companions.

At that time of year the chimps usually went to bed late, making their nests when it was too dark to see properly through binoculars, but sometimes they nested earlier and I could watch them from the Peak. I found that every individual, except for infants who slept with their mothers, made his own nest each night. Generally this took about three minutes: the chimp chose a firm foundation such as an upright fork or crotch, or two horizontal branches. Then he reached out and bent over smaller branches onto this foundation, keeping each one in place with his feet. Finally he tucked in the small leafy twigs growing around the rim of his nest and lay down. Quite often a chimp sat up after a few minutes and picked a handful of leafy twigs, which he put under his head or some other part of his body before settling down again for the night. One young female I watched went on and on bending down branches until she had constructed a huge mound of greenery on which she finally curled up.

I climbed up into some of the nests after the chimpanzees had left them. Most of them were built in trees that for me were almost impossible to climb. I found that there was quite complicated interweaving of the branches in some of them. I found, too, that the nests were fouled with dung; and later, when I was able to get closer to the chimps, I saw how they were always

Chimpanzees make nests to sleep in.

careful to defecate and urinate over the edge of their nests, even in the middle of the night.

During that month I really came to know the country well, for I often went on expeditions from the Peak, sometimes to examine nests, more frequently to collect specimens of the chimpanzees' food plants, which Bernard Verdcourt had kindly offered to identify for me. Soon I could find my way around the sheer ravines and up and down the steep slopes of three valleys — the home valley, the Pocket, and Mlinda Valley — as well as a taxi driver finds his way about in the main streets and byways of London. It is a period I remember vividly, not only because I was beginning to accomplish something at last, but also because of the delight I felt in being completely by myself. For those who love to be alone with nature I need add nothing further; for those who do not, no words of mine could ever convey, even in part, the almost mystical awareness of beauty and eternity that accompanies certain treasured moments. And, though the beauty was always there, those moments came upon me unaware: when I was watching the pale flush preceding dawn; or looking up through the rustling leaves of some giant forest tree into the greens and browns and black shadows that occasionally ensnared a bright fleck of the blue sky; or when I stood, as darkness fell, with one hand on the still-warm trunk of a tree and looked at the sparkling of an early moon on the never still, sighing water of the lake.

One day, when I was sitting by the trickle of water in Buffalo Wood, pausing for a moment in the coolness before returning from a scramble in Mlinda Valley, I saw a female bushbuck moving slowly along the nearly dry streambed. Occasionally she paused to pick off some plant and crunch it. I kept absolutely still, and she was not aware of my presence until she was little more than ten yards away. Suddenly she tensed and stood staring at me, one small forefoot raised. Because I did not move, she did not know what I was — only that my outline was somehow strange. I saw her velvet nostrils dilate as she sniffed the air, but I was downwind and her nose gave her no answer. Slowly she came closer, and closer — one step at a time, her neck craned forward — always poised for instant flight. I can still scarcely believe that her nose actually touched my knee; yet if I close my eyes I can feel again, in imagination, the warmth of her breath and the silken impact of her skin. Unexpectedly I blinked and she was gone in a flash, bounding away with loud barks of alarm until the vegetation hid her completely from my view.

It was rather different when, as I was sitting on the Peak, I saw a leopard coming toward me, his tail held up straight. He was at a slightly lower level than I, and obviously had no idea I was there. Ever since arrival in Africa I had had an ingrained, illogical fear of leopards. Already, while working at the Gombe, I had several times nearly turned back when, crawling through some thick undergrowth, I had suddenly smelled the rank smell of cat. I had forced myself on, telling myself that my fear was foolish, that only wounded leopards charged humans with savage ferocity.

On this occasion, though, the leopard went out of sight as it started to   10
climb up the hill — the hill on the peak of which I sat. I quickly hastened to

climb a tree, but halfway there I realized that leopards can climb trees. So I uttered a sort of halfhearted squawk. The leopard, my logical mind told me, would be just as frightened of me if he knew I was there. Sure enough, there was a thudding of startled feet and then silence. I returned to the Peak, but the feeling of unseen eyes watching me was too much. I decided to watch for the chimps in Mlinda Valley. And, when I returned to the Peak several hours later, there, on the very rock which had been my seat, was a neat pile of leopard dung. He must have watched me go and then, very carefully, examined the place where such a frightening creature had been and tried to exterminate my alien scent with his own.

As the weeks went by the chimpanzees became less and less afraid. Quite often when I was on one of my food-collecting expeditions I came across chimpanzees unexpectedly, and after a time I found that some of them would tolerate my presence provided they were in fairly thick forest and I sat still and did not try to move closer than sixty to eighty yards. And so, during my second month of watching from the Peak, when I saw a group settle down to feed I sometimes moved closer and was thus able to make more detailed observations.

It was at this time that I began to recognize a number of different individuals. As soon as I was sure of knowing a chimpanzee if I saw it again, I named it. Some scientists feel that animals should be labeled by numbers—that to name them is anthropomorphic—but I have always been interested in the *differences* between individuals, and a name is not only more individual than a number but also far easier to remember. Most names were simply those which, for some reason or other, seemed to suit the individuals to whom I attached them. A few chimps were named because some facial expression or mannerism reminded me of human acquaintances.

The easiest individual to recognize was old Mr. McGregor. The crown of his head, his neck, and his shoulders were almost entirely devoid of hair, but a slight frill remained around his head rather like a monk's tonsure. He was an old male—perhaps between thirty and forty years of age (the longevity record of a captive chimp is forty-seven years). During the early months of my acquaintance with him, Mr. McGregor was somewhat belligerent. If I accidentally came across him at close quarters he would threaten me with an upward and backward jerk of his head and a shaking of branches before climbing down and vanishing from my sight. He reminded me, for some reason, of Beatrix Potter's old gardener in *The Tale of Peter Rabbit*.

Ancient Flo with her deformed, bulbous nose and ragged ears was equally easy to recognize. Her youngest offspring at that time were two-year-old Fifi, who still rode everywhere on her mother's back, and her juvenile son, Figan, who was always to be seen wandering around with his mother and little sister. He was then about six years old; it was approximately a year before he would attain puberty. Flo often traveled with another old mother, Olly. Olly's long face was also distinctive; the fluff of hair on the back of her head— though no other feature—reminded me of my aunt, Olwen. Olly, like Flo, was accompanied by two children, a daughter younger than Fifi, and an adolescent son about a year older than Figan.

Then there was William, who, I am certain, must have been Olly's   15
blood brother. I never saw any special signs of friendship between them, but their faces were amazingly alike. They both had long upper lips that wobbled when they suddenly turned their heads. William had the added distinction of several thin, deeply etched scar marks running down his upper lip from his nose.

Two of the other chimpanzees I knew well by sight at that time were David Graybeard and Goliath. Like David and Goliath in the Bible, these two individuals were closely associated in my mind because they were very often together. Goliath, even in those days of his prime, was not a giant, but he had a splendid physique and the springy movements of an athlete. He probably weighed about one hundred pounds. David Graybeard was less afraid of me from the start than were any of the other chimps. I was always pleased when I picked out his handsome face and well-marked silvery beard in a chimpanzee group, for with David to calm the others, I had a better chance of approaching to observe them more closely.

Before the end of my trial period in the field I made two really exciting discoveries — discoveries that made the previous months of frustration well worth while. And for both of them I had David Graybeard to thank.

One day I arrived on the Peak and found a small group of chimps just below me in the upper branches of a thick tree. As I watched I saw that one of them was holding a pink-looking object from which he was from time to time pulling pieces with his teeth. There was a female and a youngster and they were both reaching out toward the male, their hands actually touching his mouth. Presently the female picked up a piece of the pink thing and put it to her mouth: it was at this moment that I realized the chimps were eating meat.

After each bite of meat the male picked off some leaves with his lips and chewed them with the flesh. Often, when he had chewed for several minutes on this leafy wad, he spat out the remains into the waiting hands of the female. Suddenly he dropped a small piece of meat, and like a flash the youngster swung after it to the ground. Even as he reached to pick it up the undergrowth exploded and an adult bushpig charged toward him. Screaming, the juvenile leaped back into the tree. The pig remained in the open, snorting and moving backward and forward. Soon I made out the shapes of three small striped piglets. Obviously the chimps were eating a baby pig. The size was right and later, when I realized that the male was David Graybeard, I moved closer and saw that he was indeed eating piglet.

For three hours I watched the chimps feeding. David occasionally let   20
the female bite pieces from the carcass and once he actually detached a small piece of flesh and placed it in her outstretched hand. When he finally climbed down there was still meat left on the carcass; he carried it away in one hand, followed by the others.

Of course I was not sure, then, that David Graybeard had caught the pig for himself, but even so, it was tremendously exciting to know that these chimpanzees actually ate meat. Previously scientists had believed that although these apes might occasionally supplement their diet with a few insects or small rodents and the like they were primarily vegetarians and fruit eaters. No one had suspected that they might hunt larger mammals.

It was within two weeks of this observation that I saw something that excited me even more. By then it was October and the short rains had begun. The blackened slopes were softened by feathery new grass shoots and in some places the ground was carpeted by a variety of flowers. The Chimpanzees' Spring, I called it. I had had a frustrating morning, tramping up and down three valleys with never a sign or sound of a chimpanzee. Hauling myself up the steep slope of Mlinda Valley I headed for the Peak, not only weary but soaking wet from crawling through dense undergrowth. Suddenly I stopped, for I saw a slight movement in the long grass about sixty yards away. Quickly focusing my binoculars I saw that it was a single chimpanzee, and just then he turned in my direction. I recognized David Graybeard.

Cautiously I moved around so that I could see what he was doing. He was squatting beside the red earth mound of a termite nest, and as I watched I saw him carefully push a long grass stem down into a hole in the mound. After a moment he withdrew it and picked something from the end with his mouth. I was too far away to make out what he was eating, but it was obvious that he was actually using a grass stem as a tool.

I knew that on two occasions casual observers in West Africa had seen chimpanzees using objects as tools: one had broken open palm-nut kernels by using a rock as a hammer, and a group of chimps had been observed pushing sticks into an underground bees' nest and licking off the honey. Somehow I had never dreamed of seeing anything so exciting myself.

For an hour David feasted at the termite mound and then he wandered slowly away. When I was sure he had gone I went over to examine the mound. I found a few crushed insects strewn about, and a swarm of worker termites sealing the entrances of the nest passages into which David had obviously been poking his stems. I picked up one of his discarded tools and carefully pushed it into a hole myself. Immediately I felt the pull of several termites as they seized the grass, and when I pulled it out there were a number of worker termites and a few soldiers, with big red heads, clinging on with their mandibles. There they remained, sticking out at right angles to the stem with their legs waving in the air.

Before I left I trampled down some of the tall dry grass and constructed a rough hide—just a few palm fonds leaned up against the low branch of a tree and tied together at the top. I planned to wait there the next day. But it was another week before I was able to watch a chimpanzee "fishing" for termites again. Twice chimps arrived, but each time they saw me and moved off immediately. Once a swarm of fertile winged termites—the princes and princesses, as they are called—flew off on their nuptial flight,

25

their huge white wings fluttering frantically as they carried the insects high-er and higher. Later I realized that it is at this time of year, during the short rains, when the worker termites extend the passages of the nest to the sur-face, preparing for these emigrations. Several such swarms emerge between October and January. It is principally during these months that the chim-panzees feed on termites.

On the eighth day of my watch David Greybeard arrived again, togeth-er with Goliath, and the pair worked there for two hours. I could see much better: I observed how they scratched open the sealed-over passage entrances with a thumb or forefinger. I watched how they bit the end off their tools when they became bent, or used the other end, or discarded them in favor of new ones. Goliath once moved at least fifteen yards from the heap to select a firm-looking piece of vine, and both males often picked three or four stems while they were collecting tools, and put the spares beside them on the ground until they wanted them.

Most exciting of all, on several occasions they picked small leafy twigs and prepared them for use by stripping off the leaves. This was the first recorded example of a wild animal not merely *using* an object as a tool, but actually modifying an object and thus showing the crude beginnings of tool*making*.

Tool*making*—leaves are stripped from a stem to make a tool suitable for termite-fishing. In addition, the edges of a wide blade of grass may be stripped off in order to make an appropriate tool.

Previously man had been regarded as the only toolmaking animal. Indeed, one of the clauses commonly accepted in the definition of man was that he was a creature who "made tools to a regular and set pattern." The chimpanzees, obviously, had not made tools to any set pattern. Nevertheless, my early observations of their primitive toolmaking abilities convinced a number of scientists that it was necessary to redefine man in a more complex manner than before. Or else, as Louis Leakey put it, we should by definition have to accept the chimpanzee as Man.

QUESTIONS

1. This essay is principally an example of reporting; that is, it is a gathering of facts by a clearheaded, unbiased observer. Identify passages in the essay in which this kind of reporting takes place.
2. Although van Lawick-Goodall is a mostly neutral observer of chimpanzee behavior, neutrality is impossible in any absolute sense. For example, she writes with an eye always on comparisons of chimpanzee and human behaviors. Make a list of words from paragraphs 3 and 4 that reveal that particular bias.
3. Describe how van Lawick-Goodall's comparisons of chimpanzee and human behaviors become increasingly prominent as her essay continues.
4. Paraphrase the last discovery van Lawick-Goodall reports toward the end of her essay. What exactly was her contribution to science in this instance? What other activities, described earlier in the piece, make that discovery understandable, perhaps even unsurprising once we come to it?
5. What do you make of the choice outlined in paragraph 29? Which choice do you suppose the scientists made? Why?
6. Van Lawick-Goodall's scientific work resembles that of an anthropologist in that she goes into the field to observe the behavior of a social group. Even from this short piece we can learn a good deal about the practices and the way of life of such a worker in the field. Describe van Lawick-Goodall's life in the field, making whatever inferences you can from this single essay.
7. Amplify the description of van Lawick-Goodall's life in the field that you created for question 6 by reading articles about her and her work.
8. Place yourself somewhere, and observe behavior more or less as van Lawick-Goodall does. You might observe wildlife—pigeons, sparrows, crows, squirrels, or whatever is available—or you might observe some aspect of human behavior. If you choose the latter, look for behavior that is unfamiliar to you, such as that of children at play, workers on a job, or members of a social group very different from your own. Write a report detailing your observations.
9. After you have completed question 8, write a second, shorter report in which you comment on the nature of your task as an observer. Was it

difficult to watch? Was it difficult to decide what was meaningful behavior? Did you influence what you saw so that you could not be confident that the behavior was representative? Can you propose any improvement in your methodology?

10. One of the tools that van Lawick-Goodall lacks in her research is the ability to interview relevant parties. Imagine her interviewing Mr. McGregor, Goliath, and David Graybeard. What questions would she be likely to ask? What would you like to know about one of those individuals if you were able to interview him? Write out the interview that you can imagine.

MAKING CONNECTIONS

1. Both van Lawick-Goodall and John Yarbrough in Malcolm Gladwell's "The Naked Face" (p. 438) study a specific kind of animal in its natural habitat. How are their procedures similar? How are they different? What kinds of refinement do they venture in their studies as they proceed? How do their procedures influence both their findings and their presentation of those findings?

2. Compare and contrast van Lawick-Goodall's account of observing the chimpanzees with Amanda Coyne's observations of convict moms at the federal prison camp (p. 189). To what extent are both writers ethnographers, studying and describing behavior in a specific society?

U.S. ATTACKED
Hijacked Jets Destroy Twin Towers and Hit Pentagon in Day of Terror

Serge Schmemann

Serge Schmemann (b. 1945) spent his youth in Paris before attending Harvard University, where he received his bachelor's degree, and Columbia University, where he earned a master's degree in journalism. He then worked as a correspondent for the Associated Press wire service and later as a reporter for the New York Times, *serving as bureau chief in Bonn, Jerusalem, and Moscow. Currently deputy foreign editor at the* Times *as well as a member of the faculty at the Columbia School of Journalism, Schmemann was awarded a Pulitzer Prize in 1991 for coverage of the reunification of East and West Germany. In 1997, he published* Echos of a Native Land: Two Centuries of a Village, *about life in rural Russia. The following originally appeared in the* New York Times *on September 12, 2001.*

Hijackers rammed jetliners into each of New York's World Trade Center towers yesterday, toppling both in a hellish storm of ash, glass, smoke, and leaping victims, while a third jetliner crashed into the Pentagon in Virginia. There was no official count, but President Bush said thousands had perished, and in the immediate aftermath the calamity was already being ranked the worst and most audacious terror attack in American history.

The attacks seemed carefully coordinated. The hijacked planes were all en route to California, and therefore gorged with fuel, and their departures were spaced within an hour and 40 minutes. The first, American Airlines Flight 11, a Boeing 767 out of Boston for Los Angeles, crashed into the north tower at 8:48 A.M. Eighteen minutes later, United Airlines Flight 175, also headed from Boston to Los Angeles, plowed into the south tower.

Then an American Airlines Boeing 757, Flight 77, left Washington's Dulles International Airport bound for Los Angeles, but instead hit the western part of the Pentagon, the military headquarters where 24,000 people work, at 9:40 A.M. Finally, United Airlines Flight 93, a Boeing 757 flying from Newark to San Francisco, crashed near Pittsburgh, raising the possibility that its hijackers had failed in whatever their mission was.

There were indications that the hijackers on at least two of the planes were armed with knives. Attorney General John Ashcroft told reporters in the evening that the suspects on Flight 11 were armed that way. And Barbara Olson, a television commentator who was traveling on American

"All the News That's Fit to Print"

The New York Times

Late Edition

New York: Today, mainly, a few afternoon clouds. High 77. Tonight, slightly more humid. Low 65. Tomorrow, sun then clouds. High 81. Yesterday, high 81, low 63. Weather map, Page C19.

VOL. CL .. No. 51,874   Copyright © 2001 The New York Times   *NEW YORK, WEDNESDAY, SEPTEMBER 12, 2001*   75 CENTS

U.S. ATTACKED

HIJACKED JETS DESTROY TWIN TOWERS AND HIT PENTAGON IN DAY OF TERROR

A CREEPING HORROR

Buildings Burn and Fall as Onlookers Search for Elusive Safety

By N. R. KLEINFIELD

It kept getting worse.

The horror arrived in episodic bursts of chilling disbelief, signified first by trembling floors, sharp eruptions, cracked windows. There was the actual unfathomable realization of a gaping, flaming hole in first one of the tall towers, and then the same holing all over again in its twin. There was the merciless sight of bodies helplessly tumbling out, some of them in flames.

Finally, the mighty towers themselves were reduced to nothing. Dense plumes of smoke raced through the downtown avenues, coursing between the buildings, shaped like tornadoes on their sides.

Every sound was cause for alarm. A plane appeared overhead. Was another one coming? No, it was a fighter jet. But was it friend or enemy? People scrambled for their lives, but they didn't know where to go. Should they go north, south, east, west? Stay outside, go indoors? People had beneath cars and each other. Some contemplated jumping into the river.

For those trying to flee the very epicenter of the collapsing World Trade Center towers, the most horrid thought of all finally dawned on them: nowhere was safe.

For several panic-stricken hours yesterday morning, people in Lower Manhattan witnessed the inexpressible, the incomprehensible, the unthinkable. "I don't know what the gates of hell look like, but it's got to be like this," said John Maloney, a security director for an Internet firm in the trade center. "I'm a combat veteran, Vietnam, and I never saw anything like this."

The first warnings were small ones. Blocks away, Jim Farmer, a film composer, was having breakfast at a small restaurant near West Broadway. He heard the sound of a jet. An odd sound — too loud, it seemed, to be

Continued on Page A7

A Somber Bush Says Terrorism Cannot Prevail

By ELISABETH BUMILLER with DAVID E. SANGER

WASHINGTON, Sept. 11 — President Bush vowed tonight to retaliate against those responsible for today's attacks on New York and Washington, declaring that he would "make no distinction between the terrorists who committed these acts and those who harbor them."

"These acts of mass murder were intended to frighten our nation into chaos and retreat, but they have failed," the president said in his first speech to the nation from the Oval Office. "Our country is strong. Terrorist acts can shake the foundation of our biggest buildings, but they cannot touch the foundation of America."

His speech came after a day of trauma that seems destined to define his presidency. Seeking to at once calm the nation and declare his determination to exact retribution, he told a country numbed by repeated scenes of carnage that "these acts shattered steel, but they cannot dent the steel of American resolve."

Mr. Bush spoke only hours after returning from a zigzag course across the country, as his Secret Service and military security teams moved him from Florida, where he woke up this morning expecting to press for his education bill, to command posts in Louisiana and Nebraska before it was determined that attacks had probably ended and he could safely return to the capital. It was a sign of the catastrophic

Continued on Page A4

President Vows to Exact Punishment for 'Evil'

By SERGE SCHMEMANN

Hijackers rammed jetliners into each of New York's World Trade Center towers yesterday, toppling both in a hellish storm of ash, glass, smoke and leaping victims, while a third jetliner crashed into the Pentagon in Virginia. There was no official count, but President Bush said thousands had perished, and in the immediate aftermath the calamity was already being ranked the worst and most audacious terror attack in American history.

The attacks seemed carefully coordinated. The hijacked planes were all en route to California, and therefore packed with fuel, and their departures were spaced within an hour and 40 minutes. The first, American Airlines Flight 11, a Boeing 767 out of Boston for Los Angeles, crashed into the north tower at 8:48 a.m. Eighteen minutes later, United Airlines Flight 175, also headed from Boston to Los Angeles, plowed into the south tower.

Then an American Airlines Boeing 757, Flight 77, left Washington's Dulles International Airport bound for Los Angeles, but instead hit the western part of the Pentagon, the military headquarters where 24,000 people work, at 9:40 a.m. Finally, United Airlines Flight 93, a Boeing 737 flying from Newark to San Francisco, crashed near Pittsburgh, raising the possibility that its hijackers had failed in whatever their mission was.

SECOND PLANE United Airlines Flight 175 nearing the trade center's south tower.

There were indications that the hijackers on at least two of the planes were armed with knives. Attorney General John Ashcroft told reporters in the evening that the suspects on Flight 11 were armed that way. And Barbara Olson, a television commentator who was traveling on American Flight 77, managed to reach her husband, Solicitor General Theodore Olson, by cell phone and to tell him that the hijackers were armed with knives and a box cutter.

In all, 266 people perished in the four planes and several score more were known dead elsewhere. Numerous firefighters, police officers and other rescue workers who responded to the initial disaster in Lower Manhattan were killed or injured when the buildings collapsed. Hundreds were treated for cuts, broken bones, burns and smoke inhalation.

But the real carnage was concealed for now by the twisted, smoking, ash-choked carcasses of the twin towers, in which thousands of people used to work on a weekday. The collapse of the towers caused another World Trade Center building to fall 7 hours later, and several

Continued on Page A14

Awaiting the Aftershocks

Washington and Nation Plunge Into Fight With Enemy Hard to Identify and Punish

By R. W. APPLE Jr.

WASHINGTON, Sept. 11 — Today's devastating and astonishingly well-coordinated attacks on the World Trade Center towers in New York and on the Pentagon outside of Washington plunged the nation into a warlike struggle against an enemy that will be hard to identify with certainty and hard to punish with precision.

News Analysis

The whole nation — to a degree the whole world — shook as hijacked airliners plunged into buildings that symbolize the financial and military might of the United States. The sense of security and self-confidence that Americans take as their birthright suffered a grievous blow, from which recovery will be slow. The after-shocks will be nearly as bad, as hundreds and possibly thousands of people discover that friends or relatives died awful, fiery deaths.

Scenes of chaos and destruction evocative of the nightmare world of Hieronymus Bosch, with smoke and debris blotting out the sun, were carried by television into homes and workplaces across the nation. Echoing Franklin D. Roosevelt's description of the attack on Pearl Harbor as an event "which will live in infamy," Gov. George E. Pataki of New York, a Republican, spoke of an "incredible outrage" and Senator Charles E. Schumer of New York, a Democrat, spoke of "a dastardly attack."

But many words are inadequate vessels to contain the sense of shock and horror that people felt. As Washington struggled to regain a sense of equilibrium, with warplanes and heavily armed helicopters crossing overhead, past and present national security officials earnestly debated the possibility of a Congressional declaration of war — but against precisely whom, and in what exact circumstances? Warships were maneuvering to protect New York and Washington. The North American Air Defense Command, which had seemed to many a relic of the cold war, adopted a pos-

Continued on Page A24

MORE ON THE ATTACKS

RESCUERS BECOME VICTIMS Firefighters who rushed to the trade center were killed.   PAGE A3

SEARCH FOR SURVIVORS Some people trapped in the rubble for hours were rescued.   PAGE A3

OFFICIALS SUSPECT BIN LADEN Eavesdropping intercepts after the attacks were cited.   PAGE A20

TERRORISTS EXPLOIT WEAKNESS Investigators had criticized precautions against hijacking.   PAGE A17

CASUALTIES IN WASHINGTON An unknown number of people were killed at the Pentagon.   PAGE A11

FOR HOME DELIVERY CALL 1-800-NYTIMES

AMERICAN TARGETS A ball of fire exploded outward after the second of two jetliners slammed into the World Trade Center; less than two hours later, both of the 110-story towers were gone. Hijackers crashed a third airliner into the Pentagon, setting off a huge explosion and fire.

U.S. Attacked.

Flight 77, managed to reach her husband, Solicitor General Theodore Olson, by cell phone and to tell him that the hijackers were armed with knives and a box cutter.

In all, 266 people perished in the four planes and several score more were known dead elsewhere. Numerous firefighters, police officers, and other rescue workers who responded to the initial disaster in Lower Manhattan were killed or injured when the buildings collapsed. Hundreds were treated for cuts, broken bones, burns, and smoke inhalation.

But the real carnage was concealed for now by the twisted, smoking, ash-choked carcasses of the twin towers, in which thousands of people used to work on a weekday. The collapse of the towers caused another World Trade Center building to fall seven hours later, and several other buildings in the area were damaged or aflame.

"I have a sense it's a horrendous number of lives lost," said Mayor Rudolph W. Giuliani. "Right now we have to focus on saving as many lives as possible." The mayor warned that "the numbers are going to be very, very high." He added that the medical examiner's office will be ready "to deal with thousands and thousands of bodies if they have to."

For hours after the attacks, rescuers were stymied by other buildings that threatened to topple. But by 11 P.M., rescuers had been able to begin serious efforts to locate and remove survivors. Mr. Giuliani said two Port Authority police officers had been pulled from the ruins, and he said hope existed that more people could be saved. Earlier, police officer volunteers using dogs had found four bodies in the smoldering, stories-high pile of rubble where the towers had once stood and had taken them to a make-shift morgue in the lobby of an office building at Vesey and West Streets.

Within an hour of the attacks, the United States was on a war footing. The military was put on the highest state of alert, National Guard units were called out in Washington and New York, and two aircraft carriers were dispatched to New York harbor. President Bush remained aloft in Air Force One, following a secretive route and making only brief stopovers at Air Force bases in Louisiana and Nebraska before finally setting down in Washington at 7 P.M. His wife and daughters were evacuated to a secure, unidentified location. The White House, the Pentagon and the Capitol were evacuated, except for the Situation Room in the White House where Vice President Cheney remained in charge, giving the eerie impression of a national capital virtually stripped of its key institutions.

Nobody immediately claimed responsibility for the attacks. But the scale and sophistication of the operation, the extraordinary planning required for concerted hijackings by terrorists who had to be familiar with modern jetliners, and the history of major attacks on American targets in recent years led many officials and experts to point to Osama bin Laden, the Islamic militant believed to operate out of Afghanistan. Afghanistan's hard-line Taliban rulers rejected such suggestions, but officials took that as a defensive measure. Senator Orrin Hatch, Republican of Utah, told reporters that the United States had some evidence that people associated with Mr. bin Laden had sent out messages "actually saying over the airwaves, private airwaves at that, that they had hit two targets." In the evening, explosions were reported in Kabul, the Afghan capital. But officials at the Pentagon denied that the United States had attacked that city.

President Bush, facing his first major crisis in office, vowed that the United States would hunt down and punish those responsible for the "evil, despicable acts of terror," which, he said, took thousands of American lives. He said the United States would make no distinction between those who carried out the hijackings and those who harbored and supported them.

"These acts of mass murder were intended to frighten our nation into chaos and retreat, but they have failed," a somber president told the nation in an address from the Oval office shortly after 8:30 P.M. "The search is under way for those who are behind these evil acts," Mr. Bush said. "We will make no distinction between the terrorists who committed these acts and those who harbor them."

The repercussions of the attack swiftly spread across the nation. Air traffic across the United States was halted at least until today and international flights were diverted to Canada. Borders with Canada and Mexico were closed. Most federal buildings across the country were shut down. Major skyscrapers and a variety of other sites, ranging from Disney theme parks to the Golden Gate Bridge and United Nations headquarters in New York, were evacuated.

But it was in New York that the calamity achieved levels of horror and destruction known only in war. The largest city in the United States, the financial capital of the world, was virtually closed down. Transportation into Manhattan was halted, as was much of public transport within the city. Parts of Lower Manhattan were left without power, compelling Mayor Giuliani to order Battery Park City to be evacuated. Major stock exchanges closed. Primary elections for mayor and other city offices were cancelled. Thousands of workers, released from their offices in Lower Manhattan but with no way to get home except by foot, set off in vast streams, down the avenues and across the bridges under a beautiful, clear sky, accompanied by the unceasing serenade of sirens.

While doctors and nurses at hospitals across the city tended to hundreds of damaged people, a disquieting sense grew throughout the day at other triage centers and emergency rooms that there would, actually, be less work: the morgues were going to be busiest.   15

A sense of shock, grief, and solidarity spread rapidly through the city. There was the expectation that friends and relatives would be revealed among the victims. Schools prepared to let students stay overnight if they could not get home or if it emerged that there was no one to go home to. There was also the fear that it was not over: stores reported a run on basic goods. And there was the urge to help. Thousands of New Yorkers lined up outside hospitals to donate blood.

As in great crises past, people exchanged stories of where they were when they heard the news. "There is a controlled professionalism, but also a sense of shock," said Mark G. Ackerman, an official at the St. Vincent Medical Center. "Obviously New York and all of us have experienced a trauma that is unparalleled." "I invite New Yorkers to join in prayer," said Cardinal Edward M. Egan as he emerged from the emergency room of St. Vincent's in blue hospital garb. "This is a tragedy that this great city can handle. I am amazed at the goodness of our police and our firefighters and our hospital people."

All communications creaked under the load of the sudden emergency. Mobile phones became all but useless, intercity lines were clogged and major Internet servers reported overloads.

The area around the World Trade Center resembled a desert after a terrible sandstorm. Parts of buildings, crushed vehicles, and the shoes, purses, umbrellas, and baby carriages of those who fled lay covered with thick, gray ash, through which weeping people wandered in search of safety, each with a story of pure horror.

Imez Graham, 40, and Dee Howard, 37, both of whom worked on the   20
61st floor of the north tower, were walking up Chambers Street, covered in soot to their gracefully woven dreadlocks caked in soot, barefoot. They had spent an hour walking down the stairs after the first explosion. They were taken to an ambulance, when the building collapsed. They jumped out and began to walk home. "They need me; I've got to get home," Ms. Howard said. Where was that? "As far away from here as possible." In Chinatown, a woman offered them a pair of dainty Chinese sandals. Nearby, construction workers offered to hose the soot off passing people.

The twin pillars of the World Trade Center were among the best-known landmarks in New York, 110-floor unadorned blocks that dominated any approach to Manhattan. It is probably that renown, and the thousands of people who normally work there each weekday, that led Islamic militants to target the towers for destruction already in 1993, then by parking vans loaded with explosives in the basement.

There is no way to know how many people were at work shortly before 9 A.M. when the first jetliners sliced into the north tower, also known as One World Trade Center. CNN and other television networks were quick to focus their cameras on the disaster, enabling untold numbers of viewers to witness the second jetliner as it banked into the south tower 18 minutes later, blowing a cloud of flame and debris out the other side.

Even more viewers were tuned in by 9:50 A.M. when the south tower suddenly vanished in swirling billows of ash, collapsing in on itself. Then at 10:29 A.M. the north tower followed. A choking grey cloud billowed out, blocking out the bright sunshine and chasing thousands of panicked workers through the canyons of Lower Manhattan. Plumes continued to rise high over the city late into the night.

"The screaming was just horrendous," recalled Carol Webster, an official of the Nyack College Alliance Seminary who had just emerged from the

PATH trains when the carnage began. "Every time there would be another explosion, people would start screaming and thronging again."

The scenes of horror were indelible; people who left from the broken   25
towers, people who fought for pay phones, people white with soot and red with blood. "We saw people jumping from the tower as the fire was going on," said Steve Baker, 27. "The sky went black, all this stuff came onto us, we ran."

The timing was murderous for the armada of rescue vehicles that gathered after the planes crashed, and were caught under the collapsing buildings. Many rescue workers were reported killed or injured, and the anticipation that Building Seven would soon follow led to a suspension of operations. The firefighters union said that at least 200 of its members had died. Mayor Giuliani, along with the police and fire commissioners and the director of emergency management, was forced to abandon a temporary command center at 75 Barclay Street, a block from the World Trade Center, and the mayor emerged with his gray suit covered with ash.

In the evening, officials reported that Buildings Five and Seven of the World Trade Center had also collapsed, and buildings all around the complex had their windows blown out. The Rector Street subway station collapsed, and the walkway at West Street was gone.

World leaders hastened to condemn the attacks, including Palestinian leader Yasir Arafat and Libya's Muammar el-Qaddafi. European leaders began quiet discussions last night about how they might assist the United States in striking back, and Russia's president, Vladimir Putin, joined in expressing support for a retaliatory strike. But in the West Bank city of Nablus, rejoicing Palestinians, who have been locked in a bitter struggle with Israel for almost a year, went into the streets to chant, "God is great!" and to distribute candies to celebrate the attacks.

Many governments took their own precautions against attack. Israel evacuated many of its embassies abroad, and nonessential staffers at NATO headquarters in Brussels were ordered home. In Afghanistan, the ruling Taliban argued that Mr. bin Laden could not have been responsible for the attacks. "What happened in the United States was not a job of ordinary people," an official, Abdul Hai Mutmaen, told Reuters. "It could have been the work of governments. Osama bin Laden cannot do this work."

Apart from the major question of who was responsible, a host of other   30
questions were certain to be at the forefront in coming days and weeks. One was the timing — why September 11? The date seemed to have no obvious meaning. One of the men convicted in the bombing of the United States Embassy in Nairobi in 1998, in which 213 were killed, was originally scheduled for sentencing on September 12. But the sentencing of the man, Mohamed Rasheed Daoud al-'Owhali, had been put off to mid-October. It was possible that Mr. Al-'Owhali and the others convicted with him were close witnesses to the bombings, since terror suspects typically await sentencing at the Metropolitan Correctional Center in Lower Manhattan. Officials have not confirmed that the convicted Nairobi bombers are there.

Many questions would also be raised about how hijackers managed to seize four jets with all the modern safeguards in place. Initial information was sketchy, although a passenger on the United Airlines jetliner that crashed in Pennsylvania managed to make a cellular phone call from the toilet. "We are being hijacked, we are being hijacked," the man shouted at 9:58 A.M. As he was speaking, the plane crashed about eight miles east of Jennerstown, killing all 45 aboard.

For all the questions, what was clear was that the World Trade Center would take its place among the great calamities of American history, a day of infamy like Pearl Harbor, Oklahoma City, Lockerbie. The very absence of the towers would become a symbol after their domination of the New York skyline for 25 years. Though initial reviews were mixed when the towers were dedicated in 1976, they came into their own as landmarks with passing years. King Kong climbed one tower in a remake of the movie classic. In April, the Port Authority of New York and New Jersey, which ran the World Trade Center through its first 30 years, leased the complex for $3.2 billion to a group led by Larry A. Silverstein, a developer, and Westfield America Inc. In recent years, the complex has filled up with tenants and revenues have increased. In addition to the towers — designed by the architect Minoru Yamasaki, each 1,350 feet tall — the complex included four other buildings, two of which were also gone, for a total of 12 million square feet of rentable office space.

Morning of Mayhem

By 8 A.M. yesterday morning, a chain of events had been set in motion that, two hours later, would erase the World Trade Center towers from the New York City skyline, rip open the west wall of the Pentagon, drop four planes from the sky and kill an uncounted number of people. Following is a look at how events unfolded.

7:55 A.M.	American Airlines Flight 11 leaves Boston bound for Los Angeles.
8:00 A.M.	United Airlines Flight 93 leaves Newark bound for San Francisco.
8:10 A.M.	American Airlines Flight 77 departs Washington bound for Los Angeles.
8:15 A.M.	United Airlines Flight 175 departs Boston bound for Los Angeles.
8:48 A.M.	Flight 11 hits the north tower of the World Trade Center.
9:00 A.M.	President Bush, who is in Sarasota, Fla. is informed of the attacks.
9:06 A.M.	Flight 175 strikes the south tower of the World Trade Center.

9:15 A.M.   President Bush makes statement condemning terrorist attacks.

9:18 A.M.   The F. A. A. shuts down all New York City airports.

9:21 A.M.   All bridges and tunnels into Manhattan are closed.

9:40 A.M.   Flight 77 hits the Pentagon.

The F. A. A. grounds all flights.

9:50 A.M.   South tower of the World Trade Center collapses.

10:00 A.M. President Bush leaves Sarasota. The White House is evacuated.

10:10 A.M. Flight 93 crashes in Somerset County, 80 miles southeast of Pittsburgh. A portion of the Pentagon collapses.

10:28 A.M. North tower of the World Trade Center collapses.

11:05 A.M. U. N. headquarters in New York is fully evacuated.

12:04 P.M. Los Angeles International airport is closed and evacuated.

12:15 P.M. San Francisco International Airport is closed and evacuated.

1:05 P.M.   President Bush speaks from Barksdale Air Force Base in Louisiana.

1:45 P.M.   Pentagon announces that warships and aircraft carriers will take up positions in the New York and Washington areas.

QUESTIONS

1. There were four separate articles on page 1 of the *New York Times* on September 12, 2001. Schmemann's, the lead article, gave an overview of the events of September 11. How does he arrange his story? Does he rely on a chronological arrangement, or does he make other choices? If so, describe them.
2. How many sources does the writer draw on for this piece? What kinds of sources are they? Why do Imez Graham and Dee Howard appear in this article (paragraph 20)?
3. Reporters are supposed to be objective. How well does Schmemann meet this criterion? What examples of evaluative language can you find? For example, he refers to the wrecked towers as "carcasses" (paragraph 6). What is the effect of such language?
4. Look at the first pages of other newspapers printed on September 12, 2001, in the United States or other countries. Do they simply reprint Schmemann's story from the *Times*, or do they use other material? How do these other writers present the events?
5. Look at the front page of a newspaper from December 8, 1941, the day after the Japanese attack on Pearl Harbor, Hawaii. How does the

presentation of that disaster compare with this lead article from September 12, 2001?

6. Many books and articles appeared after the events of September 11. Examine at least six, and write a report on one that you think is the most effective, giving the reasons for your choice.

MAKING CONNECTIONS

1. Compare Schmemann's report with that of another disaster, William L. Laurence's "Atomic Bombing of Nagasaki Told by Flight Member" (p. 229), which also appeared in the *New York Times*. Both writers witnessed an event, though one was a more active participant.

2. Compare Adam Gopnik's reflective treatment of the events of September 11 (p. 78) with Schmemann's re-creation of its immediate impact. Where do the two overlap, such as in stressing similar feelings or moments of that day? Discuss which treatment you find most effective, and why.

EDGY FIRST COLLEGE ASSIGNMENT: STUDY THE KORAN

Patrik Jonsson

Born in Sweden in 1969, Patrik Jonsson immigrated to the United States with his family when he was eight, living first in Georgia and later in New Hampshire. He got his first newspaper job after graduating from high school and has worked for the Portsmouth (N.H.) Press, *the* Portsmouth Herald, *and the* Deming (N.M.) Headlight. *Currently a freelance reporter, Jonsson has contributed to the* Boston Globe, *and, based in Raleigh, North Carolina, he covers the southern region for the* Christian Science Monitor. *Of the following piece, written for the* Monitor *in the summer of 2002, Jonsson said, "The Koran piece was one of the most interesting I've done. The debate really seemed to strike at the heart of some hard-to-untangle emotions Americans are experiencing after 9/11, while trying to figure out just exactly how to deal with the often-ambiguous duality of what the Koran teaches."*

Brynn Hardman was all set to sit back and glide through some Danielle Steel on Atlantic Beach this summer. Just graduated from high school in Raleigh, North Carolina, she was looking forward to a bit of light fare before hitting the heavy tomes of freshman year. Instead, the tanned teen is immersed in the curlicue phrasings of what would have been her personal last choice for beachside reading: the Koran.[1]

Ms. Hardman and 3,500 other soon-to-be freshmen at the University of North Carolina in Chapel Hill have a controversial assignment: to delve into excerpts of a text invoked by the September 11 terrorists. Only two pages into *Approaching the Qur'an*, by Michael Sells, Hardman says the book is "an awful choice."

For the past three years, UNC freshmen have been handed summer reading tasks on topics such as the growth of Civil War reenactments and the Vietnam War. But this year's choice raises a question other campuses are likely to face as the United States wages its war on terrorism: How far should a public school go in educating students about religion when the faith in question sits at the center of present-day conflicts — and is closely linked in many students' minds to terror?

---

[1]*Koran (or Qur'an):* The sacred book of Islam. Muslims believe it contains the actual word of God (Allah) as transmitted by the angel Gabriel to the prophet Mohammad.

"The timing couldn't be worse," says Jody Hardman, a public school teacher who's on campus with her daughter for an orientation session. "At a time when we're told we can't say 'under God' during the pledge, here's a public school assigning the Koran." Last week, three students and a conservative Christian organization took their discontent a step further and filed a lawsuit.

UNC officials say they have not only the prerogative but the responsibility to open students' eyes to the Muslim religion and culture. Indeed, pundits here on campus say UNC's experiment should be a call to other institutions to follow suit — for the good of the country. But critics say this bulwark of liberal thought — a campus where antiwar signs went up even before bombs had begun falling over Afghanistan — has crossed the line by forcing students to read the book. The controversy simply fuels UNC's reputation of chief gadfly here, smack in the heart of Baptist country. People with religious objections can opt out by writing an essay explaining why, but they still must attend a group discussion when they arrive in mid-August.

"The question is, what's the big role of the university here?" says Carl Ernst, the religious-studies professor who recommended the book to a selection committee of faculty, staff, and students. "[Critics] assume the choice represents advocacy, but we just want to advance knowledge," he says. "This will not explain the terrorist attacks of last September, but this will be a first step toward understanding something important about Islamic spirituality and to see its adherents as human beings."

So far, no other university has gone so far as to mandate the reading of the Koran, although many schools have seen renewed interest in religious and international studies after September 11.

No Proselytizing Here

For many people, a quick perusal of *Approaching the Qur'an* would dispel the idea that this assignment is a scheme to proselytize. Instead, the book about the "early revelations," which includes a CD of sung prayer, delves into the mystery and poetry of the spoken Koran. It explores how the text has wended its way into the hearts of 1 billion people and deep into the framework of politics and culture in the East. "The purpose of this book is neither to refute nor to promote the Qur'anic message," Mr. Sells writes. "Rather, the goal is to allow those who do not have access to the Qur'an in its recited, Arabic form to encounter one of the most influential texts in human history in a manner that is accessible."

For the parents of freshman Jennifer DeCurtis of Asheville, North Carolina, the choice of a book that focuses on a major world religion is appropriate — even during a war with religious overtones. "I think it will open their thinking up to what Islam is really all about," says dad David DeCurtis. "And I think that's an appropriate role for a school like UNC." Some parents, on the other hand, have refused to let their children attend because of the assignment. Other parents and alumni have called the chancellor to complain.

What's more, the ACLU[2] has vowed to oversee some of the discussion   10
groups, which will be led by about 180 faculty volunteers who were trained
this summer. School officials say the program will "pass the smell test." But
they won't comment on the lawsuit, which was filed by three freshmen of various religious backgrounds and the Virginia-based Family Policy Network.

John Sanders, a fellow at the conservative John Locke Foundation in
Raleigh, North Carolina, which has long questioned a variety of university
actions, says he wouldn't have a problem if the school was merely urging
teenagers to read the text before they come to school. It's the requirement
that rubs. "We're at war, after all," says Mr. Sanders. "This isn't akin to
teaching the Bible. We do need to understand them, yes, but it's not the best
thing to cram this down people's throats right now."

Still, Fred Eckel, faculty adviser for the Campus Crusade for Christ,
says that studying a variety of religious texts may not be a bad idea, especially since the school already has an energetic religious-studies department.
"As a person who supports prayer in schools, it makes no sense to object
to the use of other religious texts in the classroom, as long as the discussions are appropriate," Professor Eckel says. "It's a positive thing to discuss
issues in the Koran, and it may also further discussions that need to be
going on within the Christian community."

For Professor Ernst, the choice to bring the Koran to Baptist country isn't
so revolutionary. He points to the narrative of Omar Ibin Sayyid, a Muslim
brought here as a slave from Africa in the eighteenth century and the subject
of an exhibit soon to go up at the Ackland Museum on campus. "Studies suggest that about 15 percent of slaves were indeed Muslims," he says.

What's more, many of North Carolina's cities — which have attracted
Middle Easterners seeking jobs and education — are now dotted with
mosques. One local Muslim was arrested during the post-September 11
investigations last fall, and a national newsweekly recently documented that
at least one "American Al Qaeda" made his home in the region before
departing for the Middle East.

Offering Insights

At its heart, however, the assignment is meant to give insight into why   15
the Koran has such a strong hold on its adherents, UNC officials say. They
point out that the book also makes clear that the Koran condemns using the
term *jihad*, or struggle, as a justification for politically based battles — one

---

[2]*ACLU:* American Civil Liberties Union, a nonpartisan organization whose
mission is to preserve the individual rights guaranteed by the Constitution and laws
of the United States.

of the main differences of opinion between the September 11 terrorists and many other Muslims.

As author Sells writes: "At the day of reckoning . . . meaning and justice are brought together. The Qur'an warns those who reject the day of reckoning and who are entrenched in lives of acquisition and injustice that an accounting awaits them. Yet these warnings are not more dire or grim than the warnings the biblical Jesus gives in the parables about burning and gnashing of teeth. And in Qur'anic recitation, all Qur'anic passages on alienation between humankind and God are dominated by a tone, not of anger or wrath, but of sadness."

Such messages are important, UNC faculty and administrators say, to counter the hate-filled rhetoric put forth by Osama bin Laden and other Islamic radicals who see themselves at war with the Western world. "If Americans don't want to learn about them because of the attacks last September, we are missing an opportunity to advance ourselves and learn about who we are, as well," Ernst says. "After all, there are more Muslims in the United States than Jews."

UNC Chancellor James Moeser, who approved the committee's book choice, says, "This is Chapel Hill being Chapel Hill. People are proud of us for doing this. I had a representative from a Jewish group here tell me, 'Here I am, a Jew teaching about the Koran to Southern Baptists.' The point is, this is the front door to an exciting experience and a sample of what they will be getting at Chapel Hill."

Predictably, perhaps, students who were on campus this summer for an orientation largely criticized the assignment. Ford Williams doesn't mind being forced to study during his last official summer of childhood. His objection is more personal. A soccer standout at Broughton, he and his team were in Trinidad and Tobago on September 11. While the tourney went on, armed guards kept the team under close watch. The players found it almost impossible to concentrate. "I don't really care about learning about [Muslims] right now," he says. "I'm not in an enlightened state of mind. If anything, I want to worry about ourselves and turn to our own religion." Kevin Silva from Bedford, Massachusetts, agrees: "I feel kind of forced to do something I wouldn't normally do."

But their new friend Jon Van Assen from South River, New Jersey, takes 20 a more pragmatic view of the assignment: "It's provocative, but that's what gets people thinking," he says.

Mr. Williams adds a final assessment: "It's not like reading 'Tom Sawyer,' that's for sure."

QUESTIONS

1. This news story appeared in September 2002. What objections does it raise to requiring students to read the Koran? Who is quoted? How would you have reacted to this assignment? Explain.

2. Carl Ernst, a University of North Carolina religious studies professor, says "The question is, what's the big role of the university here?" (paragraph 6). How does he answer this question? Do you agree with him? Would his answer apply to your college or university?
3. If you have been in a class where an assigned reading was considered offensive or too controversial by one or more students who objected to reading it, how did the instructor handle the situation? What was your view of the matter?
4. Do some research into the controversy over reading the Koran at the University of North Carolina at Chapel Hill. Did the lawsuit filed by "three freshmen . . . and the Virginia-based Family Policy Network" (paragraph 10) ever come to trial, or was it dropped? Write a report of your findings.

MAKING CONNECTIONS

One of the objectors to this assignment was John Sanders, a conservative-think-tank fellow, who said, "We're at war, after all. . . . We do need to understand them, yes, but it's not the best thing to cram this down people's throats right now" (paragraph 11). Consider how you might respond to Sanders by presenting some of the information you find in Andrew Sullivan's "What's So Bad about Hate" (p. 588).

THE UNKNOWN CITIZEN

W. H. Auden

Wystan Hugh Auden (1907–1973) was born in York, England, and educated at Oxford University. He published his first volume of poems when he was twenty-three, and many of his early works, including three verse plays, reflect his ardent socialist ideals. Auden moved to the United States in 1939 (he became a U.S. citizen in 1946), and it was here he had his most important productive years as a poet. His collections include New Year Letter *(1941);* The Age of Anxiety *(1948), which earned him a Pulitzer Prize for Poetry;* The Shield of Achilles *(1956), which won the National Book Award;* About the House *(1965); and the posthumous* Thank You, Fog *(1974). His* Complete Works *was published by Princeton University Press in 1989. An opera librettist and essayist as well as a poet, Auden was one of the most versatile and influential literary figures of the twentieth century. He was a truly popular poet who often focused on moral, political, and spiritual issues that touched his readers' lives. "The Unknown Citizen" (1939) comments on a typical modern life.*

*(To JS/07/M/378
This Marble Monument
Is Erected by the State)*

He was found by the Bureau of Statistics to be
One against whom there was no official complaint,
And all the reports on his conduct agree
That, in the modern sense of an old-fashioned word, he was a saint,
For in everything he did he served the Greater Community.   5
Except for the War till the day he retired
He worked in a factory and never got fired,
But satisfied his employers, Fudge Motors Inc.
Yet he wasn't a scab or odd in his views,
For his Union reports that he paid his dues,   10
(Our report on his Union shows it was sound)
And our Social Psychology workers found
That he was popular with his mates and liked a drink.
The Press was convinced that he bought a paper every day
And that his reactions to advertisements were normal in every way.   15
Policies taken out in his name prove that he was fully insured,
And his Health-card shows he was once in hospital but left it cured.
Both Producers Research and High-Grade Living declare

He was fully sensible to the advantages of the Instalment Plan
And had everything necessary to the Modern Man,   20
A phonograph, a radio, a car and a frigidaire.
Our researchers into Public Opinion are content
That he held the proper opinions for the time of year;
When there was peace, he was for peace; when there was war, he went.
He was married and added five children to the population,   25
Which our Eugenist[1] says was the right number for a parent of his generation,
And our teachers report that he never interfered with their education.
Was he free? Was he happy? The Question is absurd:
Had anything been wrong, we should certainly have heard.

QUESTIONS

1. This poem was written during the first third of the twentieth century.
   What changes might you make were you to bring it up to date?
2. What are the implications of there being such a position as an official
   government Eugenist (line 26)?
3. There's a lot of rhyme in this poem, but it does not have the regularity
   of meter usually paired with rhyme. How does that oddity affect the way
   you hear the poem?
4. This unknown citizen is a man. In what ways would you need to alter
   or rewrite the poem for a twenty-first-century woman?

MAKING CONNECTIONS

1. This citizen is not just unknown but average. What is an average citizen?
   Read Malcolm Gladwell's "The Naked Face" (p. 438), Zoë Tracy Hardy's
   "What Did You Do in the War, Grandma? A Flashback to August 1945"
   (p. 126), or Gordon Grice's account of Joseph Paul Jernigan (p. 298), and
   write an essay on the averageness of the average citizen.
2. Read Monica M. Moore on courtship and women (p. 412) or Jane van
   Lawick-Goodall on chimpanzees (p. 237). Is it easier for them to discover the "average" in the "citizens" they observe?

---

[1]*Eugenist:* A proponent of using selective breeding to improve human beings.
Followers of the eugenics movement of the early twentieth century lobbied for legislation that would keep racial groups separate, restrict immigration from southern
and eastern Europe, and sterilize people with "bad" genes. [Eds.]

Sciences and Technologies

THE DISCUS THROWER

Richard Selzer

Richard Selzer (b. 1928) is a surgeon who has written widely, publishing articles in popular magazines as well as occasional short fiction. (See an earlier biographical note, page 135, for additional details.) In the essay reprinted here, which first appeared in Harper's magazine in 1977, Selzer reports on the visits he made to one of his patients.

I spy on my patients. Ought not a doctor to observe his patients by any means and from any stance, that he might the more fully assemble evidence? So I stand in the doorways of hospital rooms and gaze. Oh, it is not all that furtive an act. Those in bed need only look up to discover me. But they never do.

From the doorway of Room 542 the man in the bed seems deeply tanned. Blue eyes and close-cropped white hair give him the appearance of vigor and good health. But I know that his skin is not brown from the sun. It is rusted, rather, in the last stage of containing the vile repose within. And the blue eyes are frosted, looking inward like the windows of a snowbound cottage. This man is blind. This man is also legless—the right leg missing from midthigh down, the left from just below the knee. It gives him the look of a bonsai, roots and branches pruned into the dwarfed facsimile of a great tree.

Propped on pillows, he cups his right thigh in both hands. Now and then he shakes his head as though acknowledging the intensity of his suffering. In all of this he makes no sound. Is he mute as well as blind?

The room in which he dwells is empty of all possessions—no get-well cards, small, private caches of food, day-old flowers, slippers, all the usual kickshaws of the sickroom. There is only the bed, a chair, a nightstand, and a tray on wheels that can be swung across his lap for meals.

"What time is it?" he asks.   5

263

"Three o'clock."
"Morning or afternoon?"
"Afternoon."
He is silent. There is nothing else he wants to know.
"How are you?" I say.   10
"Who is it?" he asks.
"It's the doctor. How do you feel?"
He does not answer right away.
"Feel?" he says.
"I hope you feel better," I say.   15
I press the button at the side of the bed.
"Down you go," I say.
"Yes, down," he says.
He falls back upon the bed awkwardly. His stumps, unweighted by legs
and feet, rise in the air, presenting themselves. I unwrap the bandages from
the stumps, and begin to cut away the black scabs and the dead, glazed fat
with scissors and forceps. A shard of white bone comes loose. I pick it away.
I wash the wounds with disinfectant and redress the stumps. All this while,
he does not speak. What is he thinking behind those lids that do not blink?
Is he remembering a time when he was whole? Does he dream of feet? Of
when his body was not a rotting log?
He lies solid and inert. In spite of everything, he remains impressive, as   20
though he were a sailor standing athwart a slanting deck.
"Anything more I can do for you?" I ask.
For a long moment he is silent.
"Yes," he says at last and without the least irony. "You can bring me a
pair of shoes."
In the corridor, the head nurse is waiting for me.
"We have to do something about him," she says. "Every morning he   25
orders scrambled eggs for breakfast, and, instead of eating them, he picks
up the plate and throws it against the wall."
"Throws his plate?"
"Nasty. That's what he is. No wonder his family doesn't come to visit.
They probably can't stand him any more than we can."
She is waiting for me to do something.
"Well?"
"We'll see," I say.   30

The next morning I am waiting in the corridor when the kitchen delivers his breakfast. I watch the aide place the tray on the stand and swing it
across his lap. She presses the button to raise the head of the bed. Then she
leaves.
In time the man reaches to find the rim of the tray, then on to find the
dome of the covered dish. He lifts off the cover and places it on the stand.
He fingers across the plate until he probes the eggs. He lifts the plate in both
hands, sets it on the palm of his right hand, centers it, balances it. He hefts

it up and down slightly, getting the feel of it. Abruptly, he draws back his right arm as far as he can.

There is the crack of the plate breaking against the wall at the foot of his bed and the small wet sound of the scrambled eggs dropping to the floor.

And then he laughs. It is a sound you have never heard. It is something new under the sun. It could cure cancer.

Out in the corridor, the eyes of the head nurse narrow.   35

"Laughed, did he?"

She writes something down on her clipboard.

A second aide arrives, brings a second breakfast tray, puts it on the nightstand, out of his reach. She looks over at me shaking her head and making her mouth go. I see that we are to be accomplices.

"I've got to feed you," she says to the man.

"Oh, no you don't," the man says.   40

"Oh, yes I do," the aide says, "after the way you just did. Nurse says so."

"Get me my shoes," the man says.

"Here's oatmeal," the aide says. "Open." And she touches the spoon to his lower lip.

"I ordered scrambled eggs," says the man.

"That's right," the aide says.   45

I step forward.

"Is there anything I can do?" I say.

"Who are you?" the man asks.

In the evening I go once more to that ward to make my rounds. The head nurse reports to me that Room 542 is deceased. She has discovered this quite by accident, she says. No, there had been no sound. Nothing. It's a blessing, she says.

I go into his room, a spy looking for secrets. He is still there in his bed.   50
His face is relaxed, grave, dignified. After a while, I turn to leave. My gaze sweeps the wall at the foot of the bed, and I see the place where it has been repeatedly washed, where the wall looks very clean and very white.

QUESTIONS

1. Why does Selzer say, "I spy on my patients" (paragraph 1)? Don't doctors usually look in on their patients? What effect does Selzer hope to achieve by starting with such a statement?

2. Selzer uses the present tense throughout this piece. Would the past tense be just as effective? Explain your answer.

3. Selzer writes in the first person. Why might he have decided to make himself prominent in the report in this way? How would his report have come across if it had been written in the third person rather than the first person?

4. How would you describe this doctor's attitude toward his patient? How would you describe the nurse's attitude toward the patient? How does the narrator manage to characterize himself in one way and the nurse in another?

5. Is the title "The Discus Thrower" appropriate for this piece? In a slightly revised version, the title was changed to "Four Appointments with the Discus Thrower." Is this a better title?

6. What do you think Selzer's purpose was in writing this essay? Did he simply wish to shock us, or is there a message in this piece for the medical profession or for those of us who fear illness and death?

7. The essay reports on four visits to the patient by Selzer. Write a shorter version reporting on two or more visits by the head nurse. How would she react to the patient's request for shoes? How might her point of view explain some of her reactions?

8. For many of us, knowledge of hospitals is limited, perhaps to television shows in which the hospital functions as a backdrop for the romances of its staff. Write a short essay in which you present your conception of what a hospital is and in which you consider how Selzer's essay either made you revise that conception or reaffirmed what you know through experience.

MAKING CONNECTIONS

Selzer and Roy C. Selby Jr. (p. 267) write of human subjects. Jane van Lawick-Goodall (p. 237) writes of animals. Does this choice of subject seem to affect the distance that the writer maintains, achieves, or overcomes in writing his or her report? Do you find any common denominators here? How do you account for them?

A DELICATE OPERATION

Roy C. Selby Jr.

Roy C. Selby Jr. (1930–2001) graduated from Louisiana State University and the University of Arkansas Medical School, where he specialized in neurology and neurosurgery. He was the author of numerous professional articles on neurosurgery and a member of the American Association of Neurological Surgeons. "A Delicate Operation," which first appeared in Harper's *magazine in 1975, reports for a more general audience the details of a difficult brain operation.*

In the autumn of 1973 a woman in her early fifties noticed, upon closing one eye while reading, that she was unable to see clearly. Her eyesight grew slowly worse. Changing her eyeglasses did not help. She saw an ophthalmologist, who found that her vision was seriously impaired in both eyes. She then saw a neurologist, who confirmed the finding and obtained X rays of the skull and an EMI scan—a photograph of the patient's head. The latter revealed a tumor growing between the optic nerves at the base of the brain. The woman was admitted to the hospital by a neurosurgeon.

Further diagnosis, based on angiography, a detailed X-ray study of the circulatory system, showed the tumor to be about two inches in diameter and supplied by many small blood vessels. It rested beneath the brain, just above the pituitary gland, stretching the optic nerves to either side and intimately close to the major blood vessels supplying the brain. Removing it would pose many technical problems. Probably benign and slow-growing, it may have been present for several years. If left alone it would continue to grow and produce blindness and might become impossible to remove completely. Removing it, however, might not improve the patient's vision and could make it worse. A major blood vessel could be damaged, causing a stroke. Damage to the undersurface of the brain could cause impairment of memory and changes in mood and personality. The hypothalamus, a most important structure of the brain, could be injured, causing coma, high fever, bleeding from the stomach, and death.

The neurosurgeon met with the patient and her husband and discussed the various possibilities. The common decision was to operate.

The patient's hair was shampooed for two nights before surgery. She was given a cortisonelike drug to reduce the risk of damage to the brain during surgery. Five units of blood were cross-matched, as a contingency against hemorrhage. At 1:00 P.M. the operation began. After the patient was anesthetized her hair was completely clipped and shaved from the scalp. Her head was prepped with an organic iodine solution for ten minutes.

Drapes were placed over her, leaving exposed only the forehead and crown of the skull. All the routine instruments were brought up—the electro-cautery used to coagulate areas of bleeding, bipolar coagulation forceps to arrest bleeding from individual blood vessels without damaging adjacent tissues, and small suction tubes to remove blood and cerebrospinal fluid from the head, thus giving the surgeon a better view of the tumor and sur-rounding areas.

A curved incision was made behind the hairline so it would be concealed when the hair grew back. It extended almost from ear to ear. Plastic clips were applied to the cut edges of the scalp to arrest bleeding. The scalp was folded back to the level of the eyebrows. Incisions were made in the muscle of the right temple, and three sets of holes were drilled near the temple and the top of the head because the tumor had to be approached from directly in front. The drill, powered by nitrogen, was replaced with a fluted steel blade, and the holes were connected. The incised piece of skull was pried loose and held out of the way by a large sponge.

Beneath the bone is a yellowish leatherlike membrane, the dura, that surrounds the brain. Down the middle of the head the dura carries a large vein, but in the area near the nose the vein is small. At that point the vein and dura were cut, and clips made of tantalum, a hard metal, were applied to arrest and prevent bleeding. Sutures were put into the dura and tied to the scalp to keep the dura open and retracted. A malleable silver retractor, resembling the blade of a butter knife, was inserted between the brain and skull. The anesthesiologist began to administer a drug to relax the brain by removing some of its water, making it easier for the surgeon to manipulate the retractor, hold the brain back, and see the tumor. The nerve tracts for smell were cut on both sides to provide additional room. The tumor was seen approximately two-and-one-half inches behind the base of the nose. It was pink in color. On touching it, it proved to be very fibrous and tough. A special retractor was attached to the skull, enabling the other retractor blades to be held automatically and freeing the surgeon's hands. With fur-ther displacement of the frontal lobes of the brain, the tumor could be seen better, but no normal structures—the carotid arteries, their branches, and the optic nerves—were visible. The tumor obscured them.

A surgical microscope was placed above the wound. The surgeon had se-lected the lenses and focal length prior to the operation. Looking through the microscope, he could see some of the small vessels supplying the tumor and he coagulated them. He incised the tumor to attempt to remove its core and thus collapse it, but the substance of the tumor was too firm to be removed in this fashion. He then began to slowly dissect the tumor from the adjacent brain tissue and from where he believed the normal structures to be.

Using small squares of cotton, he began to separate the tumor from very loose fibrous bands connecting it to the brain and to the right side of the part of the skull where the pituitary gland lies. The right optic nerve and carotid artery came into view, both displaced considerably to the right. The optic nerve had a normal appearance. He protected these structures with cotton compresses placed between them and the tumor. He began to raise the tumor from the skull and slowly to reach the point of its origin and attachment — just in front of the pituitary gland and medial to the left optic nerve, which still could not be seen. The small blood vessels entering the tumor were cauterized. The upper portion of the tumor was gradually separated from the brain, and the branches of the carotid arteries and the branches to the tumor were coagulated. The tumor was slowly and gently lifted from its bed, and for the first time the left carotid artery and optic nerve could be seen. Part of the tumor adhered to this nerve. The bulk of the tumor was amputated, leaving a small bit attached to the nerve. Very slowly and carefully the tumor fragment was resected.

The tumor now removed, a most impressive sight came into view — the pituitary gland and its stalk of attachment to the hypothalamus, the hypothalamus itself, and the brainstem, which conveys nerve impulses between the body and the brain. As far as could be determined, no damage had been done to these structures or other vital centers, but the left optic nerve, from chronic pressure of the tumor, appeared gray and thin. Probably it would not completely recover its function.

After making certain there was no bleeding, the surgeon closed the   10
wounds and placed wire mesh over the holes in the skull to prevent dimpling of the scalp over the points that had been drilled. A gauze dressing was applied to the patient's head. She was awakened and sent to the recovery room.

Even with the microscope, damage might still have occurred to the cerebral cortex and hypothalamus. It would require at least a day to be reasonably certain there was none, and about seventy-two hours to monitor for the major postoperative dangers — swelling of the brain and blood clots forming over the surface of the brain. The surgeon explained this to the patient's husband, and both of them waited anxiously. The operation had required seven hours. A glass of orange juice had given the surgeon some additional energy during the closure of the wound. Though exhausted, he could not fall asleep until after two in the morning, momentarily expecting a call from the nurse in the intensive care unit announcing deterioration of the patient's condition.

At 8:00 A.M. the surgeon saw the patient in the intensive care unit. She was alert, oriented, and showed no sign of additional damage to the optic nerves or the brain. She appeared to be in better shape than the surgeon or her husband.

QUESTIONS

1. Why did Selby decide to operate? What could have happened if the patient chose not to have the operation? What effect does knowing this information have on the reader?
2. Although the essay is probably based on Selby's experience, it is reported in the third person. What effect does this have on the information

reported? How would the report have come across if it had been written in the first person?

3. Selby uses different methods of reporting to create the drama of "A Delicate Operation." At what point in the essay does he provide background information? How much of the essay reports events before, during, and after the operation? At what points does the writer explain terms and procedures for the reader?

4. Which passages in this essay do you find especially powerful? How did Selby create this effect?

5. Write a report of a procedure with which you are familiar. Select a procedure that calls for some expertise or sensitivity because there is the chance that something could go wrong. Proceed step-by-step, giving the reader as much information as necessary to understand and follow the procedure. At appropriate points, also include the problems you face. Possible topics are trimming a Christmas tree, carrying out a chemistry experiment, getting a child off to school, or preparing a gourmet meal.

MAKING CONNECTIONS

1. Compare Selby's essay with Richard Selzer's "The Discus Thrower" (p. 263). Whereas Selby writes in the third person, Selzer uses the first. How do those choices affect the resulting essays?

2. Rewrite several paragraphs of Selby's and Selzer's essays, changing Selby's piece from third person to first person and Selzer's piece from first person to third person. How do these changes alter the nature of the information presented and the effect of each report?

LOVE CANAL AND THE POISONING OF AMERICA

Michael Brown

Michael Brown (b. 1952) is a freelance writer whose investigations into the dumping of toxic waste, which appeared in newspaper and magazine articles, won him three Pulitzer Prize nominations and a special award from the U.S. Environmental Protection Agency. He has authored several books, including The Toxic Cloud: Poisoning of America's Air *(1988) and* Laying Waste: The Poisoning of America by Toxic Chemicals *(1980), from which this essay is taken. Now a self-proclaimed "evangelical journalist," Brown today writes chiefly about religious issues.*

Niagara Falls is a city of unmatched natural beauty; it is also a tired industrial workhorse, beaten often and with a hard hand. A magnificent river—a strait, really—connecting Lake Erie to Lake Ontario flows hurriedly north, at a pace of a half-million tons a minute, widening into a smooth expanse near the city before breaking into whitecaps and taking its famous 186-foot plunge. Then it cascades through a gorge of overhung shale and limestone to rapids higher and swifter than anywhere else on the continent.

The falls attract long lines of newlyweds and other tourists. At the same time, the river provides cheap electricity for industry; a good stretch of its shore is now filled with the spiraled pipes of distilleries, and the odors of chlorine and sulfides hang in the air.

Many who live in the city of Niagara Falls work in chemical plants, the largest of which is owned by the Hooker Chemical Company, a subsidiary of Occidental Petroleum since the 1960s. Timothy Schroeder did not. He was a cement technician by trade, dealing with the factories only if they needed a pathway poured, or a small foundation set. Tim and his wife, Karen, lived in a ranch-style home with a brick and wood exterior at 460 99th Street. One of the Schroeders' most cherished purchases was a Fiberglas pool, built into the ground and enclosed by a redwood fence.

Karen looked from a back window one morning in October 1974, noting with distress that the pool had suddenly risen two feet above the ground. She called Tim to tell him about it. Karen then had no way of knowing that this was the first sign of what would prove to be a punishing family and economic tragedy.

Mrs. Schroeder believed that the cause of the uplift was the unusual 5 groundwater flow of the area. Twenty-one years before, an abandoned hydroelectric canal directly behind their house had been backfilled with industrial rubble. The underground breaches created by this disturbance, aided by the marshland nature of the region's surficial layer, collected large volumes of rainfall and undermined the back yard. The Schroeders allowed the pool to remain in its precarious position until the following summer and then pulled it from the ground, intending to pour a new pool, cast in cement. This they were unable to do, for the gaping excavation immediately filled with what Karen called "chemical water," rancid liquids of yellow and orchid and blue. These same chemicals had mixed with the groundwater and flooded the entire yard, attacking the redwood posts with such a caustic bite that one day the fence simply collapsed. When the chemicals receded in the dry weather, they left the gardens and shrubs withered and scorched, as if by a brush fire.

How the chemicals got there was no mystery. In the late 1930s, or perhaps early 1940s, the Hooker Company, whose many processes included the manufacture of pesticides, plasticizers, and caustic soda, began using the abandoned canal as a dump for at least 20,000 tons of waste residues — "still-bottoms," in the language of the trade.

Karen Schroeder's parents had been the first to experience problems with the canal's seepage. In 1959, her mother, Aileen Voorhees, encountered a strange black sludge bleeding through the basement walls. For the next twenty years, she and her husband, Edwin, tried various methods of halting the irritating intrusion, pasting the cinder-block wall with sealants and even constructing a gutter along the walls to intercept the inflow. Nothing could stop the chemical smell from permeating the entire household, and neighborhood calls to the city for help were fruitless. One day, when Edwin punched a hole in the wall to see what was happening, quantities of black liquid poured from the block. The cinder blocks were full of the stuff.

More ominous than the Voorhees basement was an event that occurred at 11:12 P.M. on November 21, 1968, when Karen Schroeder gave birth to her third child, a seven-pound girl named Sheri. No sense of elation filled the delivery room. The child was born with a heart that beat irregularly and had a hole in it, bone blockages of the nose, partial deafness, deformed ear exteriors, and a cleft palate. Within two years, the Schroeders realized Sheri was also mentally retarded. When her teeth came in, a double row of them appeared on her lower jaw. And she developed an enlarged liver.

The Schroeders considered these health problems, as well as illnesses among their other children, as acts of capricious genes — a vicious quirk of nature. Like Mrs. Schroeder's parents, they were concerned that the chemicals were devaluing their property. The crab apple tree and evergreens in the back were dead, and even the oak in front of the home was sick; one year, the leaves had fallen off on Father's Day.

The canal had been dug with much fanfare in the late nineteenth century by a flamboyant entrepreneur named William T. Love, who wanted to construct an industrial city with ready access to water power, and major markets. The setting for Love's dream was to be a navigable power channel that would extend seven miles from the Upper Niagara before falling two hundred feet, circumventing the treacherous falls and at the same time providing cheap power. A city would be constructed near the point where the canal fed back into the river, and he promised it would accommodate half a million people.

So taken with his imagination were the state's leaders that they gave Love a free hand to condemn as much property as he liked, and to divert whatever amounts of water. Love's dream, however, proved grander than his resources, and he was eventually forced to abandon the project after a mile-long trench, ten to forty feet deep and generally twenty yards wide, had been scoured perpendicular to the Niagara River. Eventually, the trench was purchased by Hooker.

Few of those who, in 1977, lived in the numerous houses that had sprung up by the site were aware that the large and barren field behind them was a burial ground for toxic waste. Both the Niagara County Health Department and the city said it was a nuisance condition, but not a serious danger to the people. Officials of the Hooker Company refused comment, claiming only that they had no records of the chemical burials and that the problem was not their responsibility. Indeed, Hooker had deeded the land to the Niagara Falls Board of Education in 1953, for a token $1. With it the company issued no detailed warnings of the chemicals, only a brief paragraph in the quitclaim document that disclaimed company liability for any injuries or deaths which might occur at the site.

Though Hooker was undoubtedly relieved to rid itself of the contaminated land, the company was so vague about the hazards involved that one might have thought the wastes would cause harm only if touched, because they irritated the skin; otherwise, they were not of great concern. In reality, as the company must have known, the dangers of these wastes far exceeded those of acids or alkalines or inert salts. We now know that the drums Hooker had dumped in the canal contained a veritable witch's brew—compounds of truly remarkable toxicity. There were solvents that attacked the heart and liver, and residues from pesticides so dangerous that their commercial sale was shortly thereafter restricted outright by the government; some of them were already suspected of causing cancer.

Yet Hooker gave no hint of that. When the board of education, which wanted the parcel for a new school, approached Hooker, B. Kaussen, at the time Hooker's executive vice president, said in a letter to the board: "Our officers have carefully considered your request. We are very conscious of the need for new elementary schools and realize that the sites must be carefully selected. We will be willing to donate the entire strip of property which we own between Colvin Boulevard and Frontier Avenue to be used for the erection of a school at a location to be determined. . . ."

The board built the school and playground at the canal's midsection. 15 Construction progressed despite the contractor's hitting a drainage trench that gave off a strong chemical odor and the discovery of a waste pit nearby. Instead of halting the work, the authorities simply moved the school eighty feet away. Young families began to settle in increasing numbers alongside the dump, many of them having been told that the field was to be a park and recreation area for their children.

Children found the "playground" interesting, but at times painful. They sneezed, and their eyes teared. In the days when the dumping was still in progress, they swam at the opposite end of the canal, occasionally arriving home with hard pimples all over their bodies. Hooker knew children were playing on its spoils. In 1958, three children were burned by exposed residues on the canal's surface, much of which, according to residents, had been covered with nothing more than fly ash and loose dirt. Because it wished to avoid legal repercussions, the company chose not to issue a public warning of the dangers it knew were there, nor to have its chemists explain to the people that their homes would have been better placed elsewhere.

The Love Canal was simply unfit as a container for hazardous substances, poor even by the standards of the day, and now, in 1977, local authorities were belatedly finding that out. Several years of heavy snowfall and rain had filled the sparingly covered channel like a bathtub. The contents were overflowing at a frightening rate.

The city of Niagara Falls, I was assured, was planning a remedial drainage program to halt in some measure the chemical migration off the site. But no sense of urgency had been attached to the plan, and it was stalled in red tape. No one could agree on who should pay the bill—the city, Hooker, or the board of education—and engineers seemed confused over what exactly needed to be done.

Niagara Falls City Manager Donald O'Hara persisted in his view that, however displeasing to the eyes and nose, the Love Canal was not a crisis matter, mainly a question of aesthetics. O'Hara reminded me that Dr. Francis Clifford, county health commissioner, supported that opinion.

With the city, the board, and Hooker unwilling to commit themselves to a remedy, conditions degenerated in the area between 97th and 99th streets, until, by early 1978, the land was a quagmire of sludge that oozed from the canal's every pore. Melting snow drained the surface soot onto the private yards, while on the dump itself the ground had softened to the point of collapse, exposing the crushed tops of barrels. Beneath the surface, masses of sludge were finding their way out at a quickening rate, constantly forming springs of contaminated liquid. The Schroeder back yard, once featured in a local newspaper for its beauty, had reached the point where it was unfit even to walk upon. Of course, the Schroeders could not leave. No one would think of buying the property. They still owed on their mortgage and, with Tim's salary, could not afford to maintain the house while they moved into a safer setting. They and their four children were stuck.

Apprehension about large costs was not the only reason the city was reluctant to help the Schroeders and the one hundred or so other families whose properties abutted the covered trench. The city may also have feared distressing Hooker. To an economically depressed area, the company provided desperately needed employment—as many as 3000 blue-collar jobs and a substantial number of tax dollars. Hooker was speaking of building a $17 million headquarters in downtown Niagara Falls. So anxious were city officials to receive the new building that they and the state granted the company highly lucrative tax and loan incentives, and made available to the firm a prime parcel of property near the most popular tourist park on the American side.

City Manager O'Hara and other authorities were aware of the nature of Hooker's chemicals. In fact, in the privacy of his office, O'Hara, after receiving a report on the chemical tests at the canal, had informed the people at Hooker that it was an extremely serious problem. Even earlier, in 1976, the New York State Department of Environmental Conservation had been made aware that dangerous compounds were present in the basement sump pump of at least one 97th Street home, and soon after, its own testing had revealed that highly injurious halogenated hydrocarbons were flowing from the canal into adjoining sewers. Among them were the notorious PCBs; quantities as low as one part PCBs to a million parts normal water were enough to create serious environmental concerns; in the sewers of Niagara Falls, the quantities of halogenated compounds were thousands of times higher. The other materials tracked, in sump pumps or sewers, were just as toxic as PCBs, or more so. Prime among the more hazardous ones was residue from hexachlorocyclopentadiene, or C-56, which was deployed as an intermediate in the manufacture of several pesticides. In certain dosages, the chemical could damage every organ in the body.

While the mere presence of C-56 should have been cause for alarm, government remained inactive. Not until early 1978 — a full eighteen months after C-56 was first detected — was testing conducted in basements along 97th and 99th streets to see if the chemicals had vaporized off the sump pumps and walls and were present in the household air.

While the basement tests were in progress, the rains of spring arrived at the canal, further worsening the situation. Heavier fumes rose above the barrels. More than before, the residents were suffering from headaches, respiratory discomforts, and skin ailments. Many of them felt constantly fatigued and irritable, and the children had reddened eyes. In the Schroeder home, Tim developed a rash along the backs of his legs. Karen could not rid herself of throbbing pains in her head. Their daughter, Laurie, seemed to be losing some of her hair.

The EPA test revealed that benzene, a known cause of cancer in   25 humans, had been readily detected in the household air up and down the streets. A widely used solvent, benzene was known in chronic-exposure cases to cause headaches, fatigue, loss of weight, and dizziness followed by pallor, nose-bleeds, and damage to the bone marrow.

No public announcement was made of the benzene hazard. Instead, officials appeared to shield the finding until they could agree among themselves on how to present it.

Dr. Clifford, the county health commissioner, seemed unconcerned by the detection of benzene in the air. His health department refused to conduct a formal study of the people's health, despite the air-monitoring results. For this reason, and because of the resistance growing among the local authorities, I went to the southern end of 99th Street to take an informal health survey of my own. I arranged a meeting with six neighbors, all of them instructed beforehand to list the illnesses they were aware of on their block, with names and ages specified for presentation at the session.

The residents' list was startling. Though unafflicted before they moved there, many people were now plagued with ear infections, nervous disorders, rashes, and headaches. One young man, James Gizzarelli, said he had missed four months of work owing to breathing troubles. His wife was suffering epileptic-like seizures which her doctor was unable to explain. Meanwhile, freshly applied paint was inexplicably peeling from the exterior of their house. Pets too were suffering, most seriously if they had been penned in the back yards nearest to the canal, constantly breathing air that smelled like mothballs and weedkiller. They lost their fur, exhibited skin lesions, and, while still quite young, developed internal tumors. A great many cases of cancer were reported among the women, along with much deafness. On both 97th and 99th streets, traffic signs warned passing motorists to watch for deaf children playing near the road.

Evidence continued to mount that a large group of people, perhaps all of the one hundred families immediately by the canal, perhaps many more, were in imminent danger. While watching television, while gardening or doing a wash, in their sleeping hours, they were inhaling a mixture of damaging chemicals. Their hours of exposure were far longer than those of a chemical factory worker, and they wore no respirators or goggles. Nor could they simply open a door and escape. Helplessness and despair were the main responses to the blackened craters and scattered cinders behind their back yards.

But public officials often characterized the residents as hypochondriacs.   30
Every agent of government had been called on the phone or sent pleas for help, but none offered aid.

Commissioner Clifford expressed irritation at my printed reports of illness, and disagreement began to surface in the newsroom on how the stories should be printed. "There's a high rate of cancer among my friends," Dr. Clifford argued. "It doesn't mean anything."

Yet as interest in the small community increased, further revelations shook the neighborhood. In addition to benzene, eighty or more other compounds were found in the makeshift dump, ten of them potential carcinogens. The physiological effects they could cause were profound and diverse. At least fourteen of them could impact on the brain and central nervous system. Two of them, carbon tetrachloride and chlorobenzene, could readily cause narcotic and anesthetic consequences. Many others were known to cause headaches, seizures, loss of hair, anemia, or skin rashes. Together, the compounds were capable of inflicting innumerable illnesses, and no one knew what new concoctions were being formulated by their mixture underground.

Edwin and Aileen Voorhees had the most to be concerned about. When a state biophysicist analyzed the air content of their basement, he determined that the safe exposure time there was less than 2.4 minutes—the toxicity in the basement was thousands of times the acceptable limit for twenty-four-hour breathing. This did not mean they would necessarily become permanently ill, but their chances of contracting cancer, for example, had been measurably increased. In July, I visited Mrs. Voorhees for further discussion of her problems, and as we sat in the kitchen, drinking coffee, the industrial odors were apparent. Aileen, usually chipper and feisty, was visibly anxious. She stared down at the table, talking only in a lowered voice. Everything now looked different to her. The home she and Edwin had built had become their jail cell. Their yard was but a pathway through which toxicants entered the cellar walls. The field out back, that proposed "park," seemed destined to be the ruin of their lives.

On July 14 I received a call from the state health department with some shocking news. A preliminary review showed that women living at the southern end had suffered a high rate of miscarriages and had given birth to an abnormally high number of children with birth defects. In one age group, 35.3 percent had records of spontaneous abortions. That was far in excess of the norm. The odds against it happening by chance were 250 to one. These tallies, it was stressed, were "conservative" figures. Four children in one small section of the neighborhood had documentable birth defects, club feet, retardation, and deafness. Those who lived there the longest suffered the highest rates.

The data on miscarriages and birth defects, coupled with the other   35
accounts of illness, finally pushed the state's bureaucracy into motion. A meeting was scheduled for August 2, at which time the state health commissioner, Dr. Robert Whalen, would formally address the issue. The day before the meeting, Dr. Nicholas Vianna, a state epidemiologist, told me that the residents were also incurring some degree of liver damage. Blood analyses had shown hepatitislike symptoms in enzyme levels. Dozens if not hundreds of people, apparently, had been adversely affected.

In Albany, on August 2, Dr. Whalen read a lengthy statement in which he urged that pregnant women and children under two years of age leave the southern end of the dump site immediately. He declared the Love Canal an official emergency, citing it as a "great and imminent peril to the health of the general public."

When Commissioner Whalen's words hit 97th and 99th streets, by way of one of the largest banner headlines in the Niagara *Gazette*'s 125-year history, dozens of people massed on the streets, shouting into bullhorns and microphones to voice frustrations that had been accumulating for months. Many of them vowed a tax strike because their homes were rendered unmarketable and unsafe. They attacked their government for ignoring their welfare. A man of high authority, a physician with a title, had confirmed that their lives were in danger. Most wanted to leave the neighborhood immediately.

Terror and anger roiled together, exacerbated by Dr. Whalen's failure to provide a government-funded evacuation plan. His words were only a recommendation: individual families had to choose whether to risk their health and remain, or abandon their houses and, in so doing, write off a lifetime of work and savings.

On August 3, Dr. Whalen decided he should speak to the people. He arrived with Dr. David Axelrod, a deputy who had directed the state's investigation, and Thomas Frey, a key aide to Governor Hugh Carey.

At a public meeting, held in the 99th Street School auditorium, Frey   40
was given the grueling task of controlling the crowd of 500 angry and frightened people. In an attempt to calm them, he announced that a meeting between the state and the White House had been scheduled for the following week. The state would propose that Love Canal be classified a national disaster, thereby freeing federal funds. For now, however, he could promise no more. Neither could Dr. Whalen and his staff of experts. All they could say was what was already known: twenty-five organic compounds, some of them capable of causing cancer, were in their homes, and because young children were especially prone to toxic effects, they should be moved to another area.

Dr. Whalen's order had applied only to those living at the canal's southern end, on its immediate periphery. But families living across the street from the dump site, or at the northern portion, where the chemicals were not so visible at the surface, reported afflictions remarkably similar to those suffered by families whose yards abutted the southern end. Serious respiratory problems, nervous disorders, and rectal bleeding were reported by many who were not covered by the order.

Throughout the following day, residents posted signs of protest on their front fences or porch posts. "Love Canal Kills," they said, or "Give Me Liberty, I've Got Death." Emotionally exhausted and uncertain about their future, men stayed home from work, congregating on the streets or comforting their wives. By this time the board of education had announced it was closing the 99th Street School for the following year, because of its proximity to the exposed toxicants. Still, no public relief was provided for the residents.

Another meeting was held that evening, at a firehall on 102nd Street. It was unruly, but the people, who had called the session in an effort to organize themselves, managed to form an alliance, the Love Canal Homeowners Association, and to elect as president Lois Gibbs, a pretty, twenty-seven-year-old woman with jet-black hair who proved remarkably adept at dealing with experienced politicians and at keeping the matter in the news. After Mrs. Gibbs' election, Congressman John LaFalce entered the hall and announced, to wild applause, that the Federal Disaster Assistance Administration would be represented the next morning, and that the state's two senators, Daniel Patrick Moynihan and Jacob Javits, were working with him in an attempt to get funds from Congress.

With the Love Canal story now attracting attention from the national media, the Governor's office announced that Hugh Carey would be at the 99th Street School on August 7 to address the people. Decisions were being made in Albany and Washington. Hours before the Governor's arrival, a sudden burst of "urgent" reports from Washington came across the newswires. President Jimmy Carter had officially declared the Hooker dump site a national emergency.

Hugh Carey was applauded on his arrival. The Governor announced   45
that the state, through its Urban Development Corporation, planned to purchase, at fair market value, those homes rendered uninhabitable by the marauding chemicals. He spared no promises. "You will not have to make mortgage payments on homes you don't want or cannot occupy. Don't worry about the banks. The state will take care of them." By the standards of Niagara Falls, where the real estate market was depressed, the houses were in the middle-class range, worth from $20,000 to $40,000 apiece. The state would assess each house and purchase it, and also pay the costs of moving, temporary housing during the transition period, and special items not covered by the usual real estate assessment, such as installation of telephones.

First in a trickle and then, by September, in droves, the families gathered their belongings and carted them away. Moving vans crowded 97th and 99th streets. Linesmen went from house to house disconnecting the telephones and electrical wires, while carpenters pounded plywood over the windows to keep vandals away. By the following spring, 237 families were gone; 170 of them had moved into new houses. In time the state erected around a six-block residential area a green chain-link fence, eight feet in height, clearly demarcating the contamination zone.

In October 1978, the long-awaited remedial drainage program began at the south end. Trees were uprooted, fences and garages torn down, and swimming pools removed from the area. So great were residents' apprehensions that dangerous fumes would be released over the surrounding area that the state, at a cost of $500,000, placed seventy-five buses at emergency evacuation pickup spots during the months of work, in the event that outlying homes had to be vacated quickly because of an explosion. The plan was to construct drain tiles around the channel's periphery, where the back yards had been located, in order to divert leakage to seventeen-foot-deep wet wells from which contaminated groundwater could be drawn and treated by filtration through activated carbon. (Removing the chemicals themselves would have been financially prohibitive, perhaps costing as much as $100 million — and even then the materials would have to be buried elsewhere.) After the trenching was complete, and the sewers installed, the canal was to be covered by a sloping mound of clay and planted with grass. One day, city officials hoped, the wasteland would become a park.

In spite of the corrective measures and the enormous effort by the state health department, which took thousands of blood samples from past and current residents and made uncounted analyses of soil, water, and air, the full range of the effects remained unknown. In neighborhoods immediately outside the official "zone of contamination," more than 500 families were left near the desolate setting, their health still in jeopardy. The state announced it would buy no more homes.

The first public indication that chemical contamination had probably reached streets to the east and west of 97th and 99th streets, and to the north and south as well, came on August 11, 1978, when sump-pump samples I had taken from 100th and 101st streets, analyzed in a laboratory, showed the trace presence of a number of chemicals found in the canal itself, including lindane, a restricted pesticide that had been suspected of causing cancer in laboratory animals. While probing 100th Street, I knocked on the door of Patricia Pino, thirty-four, a blond divorcee with a young son and daughter. I had noticed that some of the leaves on a large tree in front of her house exhibited a black oiliness much like that on the trees and shrubs of 99th Street; she was located near what had been a drainage swale.

After I had extracted a jar of sediment from her sump pump for the   50
analysis, we conversed about her family situation and what the trauma now unfolding meant to them. Ms. Pino was extremely depressed and embittered. Both of her children had what appeared to be slight liver abnormalities, and her son had been plagued with "non-specific" allergies, teary eyes, sinus trouble, which improved markedly when he was sent away from home. Patricia told of times, during the heat of summer, when fumes were readily noticeable in her basement and sometimes even upstairs. She herself had been treated for a possibly cancerous condition of her cervix. But, like others, her family was now trapped.

On September 24, 1978, I obtained a state memorandum that said chemical infiltration of the outer regions was significant indeed. The letter, sent from the state laboratories to the U.S. Environmental Protection Agency, said, "Preliminary analysis of soil samples demonstrates extensive migration of potentially toxic materials outside the immediate canal area." There it was, in the state's own words. Not long afterward, the state medical investigator, Dr. Nicholas Vianna, reported indications that residents from 93rd to 103rd streets might also have incurred liver damage.

On October 4, a young boy, John Allen Kenny, who lived quite a distance north of the evacuation zone, died. The fatality was due to the failure of another organ that can be readily affected by toxicants, the kidney. Naturally, suspicions were raised that his death was in some way related to a creek that still flowed behind his house and carried, near an outfall, the odor of chlorinated compounds. Because the creek served as a catch basin for a portion of the Love Canal, the state studied an autopsy of the boy. No conclusions were reached. John Allen's parents, Norman, a chemist, and Luella, a medical research assistant, were unsatisfied with the state's investigation, which they felt was "superficial." Luella said, "He played in the creek all the time. There had been restrictions on the older boys, but he was the youngest and played with them when they were old enough to go to the creek. We let him do what the other boys did. He died of nephrosis. Proteins were passing through his urine. Well, in reading the literature, we discovered that chemicals can trigger this. There was no evidence of infection, which there should have been, and there was damage to his thymus and brain. He also had nosebleeds and headaches, and dry heaves. So our feeling is that chemicals probably triggered it."

The likelihood that water-carried chemicals had escaped from the canal's deteriorating bounds and were causing problems quite a distance from the site was not lost upon the Love Canal Homeowners Association and its president, Lois Gibbs, who was attempting to have additional families relocated. Because she lived on 101st Street, she was one of those left behind, with no means of moving despite persistent medical difficulties in her six-year-old son, Michael, who had been operated on twice for urethral strictures. [Mrs. Gibbs's husband, a worker at a chemical plant, brought home only $150 a week, she told me, and when they subtracted from that the $90 a week for food and other necessities, clothing costs for their two children, $125 a month for mortgage payments and taxes, utility and phone expenses, and medical bills, they had hardly enough cash to buy gas and cigarettes, let alone vacate their house.]

Assisted by two other stranded residents, Marie Pozniak and Grace McCoulf, and with the professional analysis of a Buffalo scientist named Beverly Paigen, Lois Gibbs mapped out the swale and creekbed areas, many of them long ago filled, and set about interviewing the numerous people who lived on or near formerly wet ground. The survey indicated that these people were suffering from an abnormal number of kidney and bladder aggravations and problems of the reproductive system. In a report to the state, Dr. Paigen claimed to have found, in 245 homes outside the evacuation zone, thirty-four miscarriages, eighteen birth defects, nineteen nervous breakdowns, ten cases of epilepsy, and high rates of hyperactivity and suicide.

In their roundabout way, the state health experts, after an elaborate   55 investigation, confirmed some of the homeowners' worst fears. On February 8, 1979, Dr. David Axelrod, who by then had been appointed health commissioner, and whose excellence as a scientist was widely acknowledged, issued a new order that officially extended the health emergency of the previous August, citing high incidences of birth deformities and miscarriages in the areas where creeks and swales had once flowed, or where swamps had been. With that, the state offered to evacuate temporarily those families with pregnant women or children under the age of two from the outer areas of contamination, up to 103rd Street. But no additional homes would be purchased; nor was another large-scale evacuation, temporary or otherwise, under consideration. Those who left under the new plan would have to return when their children passed the age limit.

Twenty-three families accepted the state's offer. Another seven families, ineligible under the plan but of adequate financial means to do so, simply left their homes and took the huge loss of investment. Soon boarded windows speckled the outlying neighborhoods.

The previous November and December, not long after the evacuation of 97th and 99th streets, I became interested in the possibility that Hooker might have buried in the Love Canal waste residues from the manufacture of what is known as 2,4,5-trichlorophenol. My curiosity was keen because I knew that this substance, which Hooker produced for the manufacture of the antibacterial agent hexachlorophene, and which was also used to make defoliants such as Agent Orange, the herbicide employed in Vietnam, carries with it an unwanted by-product technically called 2,3,7, 8-tetrachlorodibenzo-para-dioxin, or tetra dioxin. The potency of dioxin of this isomer is nearly beyond imagination. Although its toxicological effects are not fully known, the few experts on the subject estimate that if three ounces were evenly distributed and subsequently ingested among a million people, or perhaps more than that, all of them would die. It compares in toxicity to the botulinum toxin. On skin contact, dioxin causes a disfiguration called "chloracne," which begins as pimples, lesions, and cysts, but can lead to calamitous internal damage. Some scientists suspect that dioxin causes cancer, perhaps even malignancies that occur, in galloping fashion, within a short time of contact. At least two (some estimates went as high as eleven) pounds of dioxin were dispersed over Seveso, Italy, in 1976, after an explosion of a trichlorophenol plant: dead animals littered the streets, and more than 300 acres of land were immediately evacuated. In Vietnam, the spraying of Agent Orange, because of the dioxin contaminant, was banned in 1970, when the first effects on human beings began to surface, including dioxin's powerful teratogenic, or fetus-deforming, effects.

I posed two questions concerning trichlorophenol: Were wastes from the process buried in the canal? If so, what were the quantities?

On November 8, before Hooker answered my queries, I learned that, indeed, trichlorophenol had been found in liquids pumped from the remedial drain ditches. No dioxin had been found yet, and some officials, ever wary of more emotionalism among the people, argued that, because the compound was not soluble in water, there was little chance it had migrated off-site. Officials at Newco Chemical Waste Systems, a local waste disposal firm, at the same time claimed that if dioxin had been there, it had probably been photolytically destroyed. Its half-life, they contended, was just a few short years.

I knew from Whiteside, however, that in every known case, waste from 2,4,5-trichlorophenol carried dioxin with it. I also knew that dioxin *could* become soluble in groundwater and migrate into the neighborhood upon mixing with solvents such as benzene. Moreover, because it had been buried, sunlight would not break it down.

On Friday, November 10, I called Hooker again to urge that they answer my questions. Their spokesman, Bruce Davis, came to the phone and, in a controlled tone, gave me the answer: His firm had indeed buried trichlorophenol in the canal—200 tons of it.

Immediately I called Whiteside. His voice took on an urgent tone. According to his calculation, if 200 tons of trichlorophenol were there, in all likelihood they were accompanied by 130 pounds of tetra dioxin, an amount equaling the estimated total content of dioxin in the thousands of tons of Agent Orange rained upon Vietnamese jungles. The seriousness of the crisis had deepened, for now the Love Canal was not only a dump for highly dangerous solvents and pesticides; it was also the broken container for one of the most toxic substances ever synthesized by man.

I reckoned that the main danger was to those working on the remedial project, digging in the trenches. The literature on dioxin indicated that, even in quantities at times too small to detect, the substance possessed vicious characteristics. In one case, workers in a trichlorophenol plant had developed chloracne, although the substance could not be traced on the equipment with which they worked. The mere tracking of minuscule amounts of dioxin on a pedestrian's shoes in Seveso led to major concerns, and, according to Whiteside, a plant in Amsterdam, upon being found contaminated with dioxin, had been "dismantled, brick by brick, and the material embedded in concrete, loaded at a specially constructed dock, on ships, and dumped at sea, in deep water near the Azores." Workers in trichlorophenol plants had died of cancer or severe liver damage, or had suffered emotional and sexual disturbances.

Less than a month after the first suspicions arose, on the evening of December 9, I received a call from Dr. Axelrod. "We found it. The dioxin. In a drainage trench behind 97th Street. It was in the part-per-trillion range."

The state remained firm in its plans to continue the construction, and, despite the ominous new findings, no further evacuations were announced. During the next several weeks, small incidents of vandalism occurred along 97th and 99th streets. Tacks were spread on the road, causing numerous flat tires on the trucks. Signs of protest were hung in the school. Meetings of the Love Canal Homeowners Association became more vociferous. Christmas was near, and in the association's office at the 99th Street School, a holiday tree was decorated with bulbs arranged to spell "DIOXIN." 65

The Love Canal people chanted and cursed at meetings with the state officials, cried on the telephone, burned an effigy of the health commissioner, traveled to Albany with a makeshift child's coffin, threatened to hold officials hostage, sent letters and telegrams to the White House, held days of mourning and nights of prayer. On Mother's Day this year, they marched down the industrial corridor and waved signs denouncing Hooker, which had issued not so much as a statement of remorse. But no happy ending was in store for them. The federal government was clearly not planning to come to their rescue, and the state felt it had already done more than its share. City Hall was silent and remains silent today. Some residents still hoped that, miraculously, an agency of government would move them. All of them watched with anxiety as each newborn came to the neighborhood, and they looked at their bodies for signs of cancer.

One hundred and thirty families from the Love Canal area began leaving their homes last August and September, seeking temporary refuge in local hotel rooms under a relocation plan funded by the state which had been implemented after fumes became so strong, during remedial trenching operations, that the United Way abandoned a care center it had opened in the neighborhood.

As soon as remedial construction is complete, the people will probably be forced to return home, as the state will no longer pay for their lodging. Some have threatened to barricade themselves in the hotels. Some have mentioned violence. Anne Hillis of 102nd Street, who told reporters her first child had been born so badly decomposed that doctors could not determine its sex, was so bitter that she threw table knives and a soda can at the state's on-site coordinator.

In October, Governor Carey announced that the state probably would buy an additional 200 to 240 homes, at an expense of some $5 million. In the meantime, lawyers have prepared lawsuits totaling about $2.65 billion and have sought court action for permanent relocation. Even if the latter action is successful, and they are allowed to move, the residents' plight will not necessarily have ended. The psychological scars are bound to remain among them and their children, along with the knowledge that, because they have already been exposed, they may never fully escape the Love Canal's insidious grasp.

QUESTIONS

1. What caused the poisoning of Love Canal? Why did it take so long for both local and state officials to acknowledge the seriousness of the condition of Love Canal?
2. What kind of information does Brown provide to document the tragedy of Love Canal? What role did he play in uncovering this information?
3. Consider the introduction to this article. Why did Brown choose to tell the story of the Schroeder family in the opening paragraphs?
4. The power of this essay has much to do with the overwhelming tragedy and horror it relates. Find passages in the essay that you feel are especially effective. Explain how Brown creates this effect on the reader.
5. In this essay, Brown relies primarily on the factual data he has collected to tell the story of Love Canal. Compare this writer's approach with that found in newspapers featuring sensational headlines. Analyze one of the headlined stories. How much factual evidence is present? How would such a newspaper's treatment of the story of the Schroeder family differ from Brown's treatment?
6. Environmental calamities such as Love Canal or Three Mile Island have become a permanent part of our lives. The U.S. Environmental Protection Agency reports that in most communities the groundwater has become so laced with toxic chemicals that it is no longer safe to drink. Investigate one aspect of the environment in your community, such as the water supply or the quality of the air. Write a report based on your investigation.

MAKING CONNECTIONS

Compare Brown's position as a reporter with Barbara Tuchman's position in "'This Is the End of the World': The Black Death" (p. 217). What similarities and differences can you find in the ways that Brown and Tuchman have gathered their information? In their organization and presentation of that information? In the points of view that they have taken toward the disasters they write about? On the basis of these comparisons, what do you think is the most effective way to present stories of large-scale human disasters and similarly provocative subject matter?

JOEY: A "MECHANICAL BOY"

Bruno Bettelheim

Austrian-born psychotherapist Bruno Bettelheim (1903–1990) received his Ph.D. from the University of Vienna and was strongly influenced by the work of Sigmund Freud. Imprisoned as a Jew in Nazi concentration camps between 1938 and 1939, he wrote about these experiences after his immigration to the United States in an article titled "Individual and Mass Behavior in Extreme Situations" (1943) and later in the book The Informed Heart *(1960). From 1944 to 1973, he was director of a Chicago-based school for the rehabilitation of emotionally disturbed children, a subject he addressed in numerous works on child psychology and child rearing, including* Love Is Not Enough *(1950) and* The Empty Fortress *(1967). He was also the author of the highly influential* The Uses of Enchantment *(1976), a study of children and fairy tales. Since his suicide at the age of eighty-seven, Bettelheim has been the subject of a number of sharp attacks regarding the veracity of some of his work, and a 1997 biography by Richard Pollak was particularly damning. Still, Bettelheim continues to have his defenders, including his most recent biographer, his friend and literary agent Theron Raines. The following essay was first published in* Scientific American *in 1959.*

Joey, when we began our work with him, was a mechanical boy. He functioned as if by remote control, run by machines of his own powerfully creative fantasy. Not only did he himself believe that he was a machine, but, more remarkably, he created this impression in others. Even while he performed actions that are intrinsically human, they never appeared to be other than machine-started and executed. On the other hand, when the machine was not working, we had to concentrate on recollecting his presence, for he seemed not to exist. A human body that functions as if it were a machine and a machine that duplicates human functions are equally fascinating and frightening. Perhaps they are so uncanny because they remind us that the human body can operate without a human spirit, that body can exist without soul. And Joey was a child who had been robbed of his humanity.

Not every child who possesses a fantasy world is possessed by it. Normal children may retreat into realms of imaginary glory or magic powers, but they are easily recalled from these excursions. Disturbed children are not always able to make the return trip; they remain withdrawn, prisoners of the inner world of delusion and fantasy. In many ways Joey presented a classic example of this state of infantile autism.[1]

At the Sonia Shankman Orthogenic School of the University of Chicago, it is our function to provide a therapeutic environment in which such children may start life over again. I have previously described in this magazine[2] the rehabilitation of another of our patients. This time I shall concentrate upon the illness, rather than the treatment. In any age, when the individual has escaped into a delusional world, he has usually fashioned it from bits and pieces of the world at hand. Joey, in his time and world, chose the machine and froze himself in its image. His story has a general relevance to the understanding of emotional development in a machine age.

Joey's delusion is not uncommon among schizophrenic[3] children today. He wanted to be rid of his unbearable humanity, to become completely automatic. He so nearly succeeded in attaining this goal that he could almost convince others, as well as himself, of his mechanical character. The descriptions of autistic children in the literature take for their point of departure and comparison the normal or abnormal human being. To do justice to Joey, I would have to compare him simultaneously to a most inept infant and a highly complex piece of machinery. Often we had to force ourselves by a conscious act of will to realize that Joey was a child. Again and again his acting-out of his delusions froze our own ability to respond as human beings.

During Joey's first weeks with us, we would watch absorbedly as this at once fragile-looking and imperious nine-year-old went about his mechanical existence. Entering the dining room, for example, he would string an imaginary wire from his "energy source" — an imaginary electric outlet — to the table. There he "insulated" himself with paper napkins and finally plugged himself in. Only then could Joey eat, for he firmly believed that the "current" ran his ingestive apparatus. So skillful was the pantomime that one had to look twice to be sure there was neither wire nor outlet nor plug. Children and members of our staff spontaneously avoided stepping on the "wires" for fear of interrupting what seemed the source of his very life.

For long periods of time, when his "machinery" was idle, he would sit so quietly that he would disappear from the focus of the most conscientious observation. Yet in the next moment he might be "working" and the center of our captivated attention. Many times a day he would turn himself on and shift noisily through a sequence of higher and higher gears until he "exploded," screaming "Crash, crash!" and hurling items from his ever present

5

---

[1]*autism:* A complex developmental disability that affects an individual in the areas of social interaction and communication. [Eds.]

[2]*in this magazine:* Bruno Bettelheim, "Schizophrenic art: A case study," *Scientific American* (April 1952). [Eds.]

[3]*schizophrenic:* Relating to a severe mental disorder that is characterized by thought disorder, delusions, and hallucinations. [Eds.]

apparatus — radio tubes, light bulbs, even motors or, lacking these, any handy breakable object. (Joey had an astonishing knack for snatching bulbs and tubes unobserved.) As soon as the object thrown had shattered, he would cease his screaming and wild jumping and retire to mute, motionless nonexistence.

Our maids, inured to difficult children, were exceptionally attentive to Joey; they were apparently moved by his extreme infantile fragility, so strangely coupled with megalomaniacal superiority. Occasionally some of the apparatus he fixed to his bed to "live him" during his sleep would fall down in disarray. This machinery he contrived from masking tape, cardboard, wire, and other paraphernalia. Usually the maids would pick up such things and leave them on a table for the children to find, or disregard them entirely. But Joey's machine they carefully restored: "Joey must have the carburetor so he can breathe." Similarly they were on the alert to pick up and preserve the motors that ran him during the day and the exhaust pipes through which he exhaled.

How had Joey become a human machine? From intensive interviews with his parents we learned that the process had begun even before birth. Schizophrenia often results from parental rejection, sometimes combined ambivalently with love. Joey, on the other hand, had been completely ignored.

"I never knew I was pregnant," his mother said, meaning that she had already excluded Joey from her consciousness. His birth, she said, "did not make any difference." Joey's father, a rootless draftee in the wartime civilian army, was equally unready for parenthood. So, of course, are many young couples. Fortunately most such parents lose their indifference upon the baby's birth. But not Joey's parents. "I did not want to see or nurse him," his mother declared. "I had no feeling of actual dislike — I simply didn't want to take care of him." For the first three months of his life Joey "cried most of the time." A colicky baby, he was kept on a rigid four-hour feeding schedule, was not touched unless necessary and was never cuddled or played with. The mother, preoccupied with herself, usually left Joey alone in the crib or playpen during the day. The father discharged his frustration by punishing Joey when the child cried at night.

Soon the father left for overseas duty, and the mother took Joey, now a   10
year and a half old, to live with her at her parents' home. On his arrival the grandparents noticed that ominous changes had occurred in the child. Strong and healthy at birth, he had become frail and irritable; a responsive baby, he had become remote and inaccessible. When he began to master speech, he talked only to himself. At an early date he became preoccupied with machinery, including an old electric fan which he could take apart and put together again with surprising deftness.

Joey's mother impressed us with a fey quality that expressed her insecurity, her detachment from the world, and her low physical vitality. We were struck especially by her total indifference as she talked about Joey. This seemed much more remarkable than the actual mistakes she made in handling him. Certainly he was left to cry for hours when hungry, because she fed him on a rigid schedule; he was toilet-trained with great rigidity so that he would give no trouble. These things happen to many children. But Joey's existence never registered with his mother. In her recollections he was fused at one moment with one event or person; at another, with something or somebody else. When she told us about his birth and infancy, it was as if she were talking about some vague acquaintance, and soon her thoughts would wander off to another person or to herself.

When Joey was not yet four, his nursery school suggested that he enter a special school for disturbed children. At the new school his autism was immediately recognized. During his three years there he experienced a slow improvement. Unfortunately a subsequent two years in a parochial school destroyed this progress. He began to develop compulsive defenses, which he called his "preventions." He could not drink, for example, except through elaborate piping systems built of straws. Liquids had to be "pumped" into him, in his fantasy, or he could not suck. Eventually his behavior became so upsetting that he could not be kept in the parochial school. At home things did not improve. Three months before entering the Orthogenic School he made a serious attempt at suicide.

To us Joey's pathological behavior seemed the external expression of an overwhelming effort to remain almost nonexistent as a person. For weeks Joey's only reply when addressed was "Bam." Unless he thus neutralized whatever we said, there would be an explosion, for Joey plainly wished to close off every form of contact not mediated by machinery. Even when he was bathed he rocked back and forth with mute, engine-like regularity, flooding the bathroom. If he stopped rocking, he did this like a machine too; suddenly he went completely rigid. Only once, after months of being lifted from his bath and carried to bed, did a small expression of puzzled pleasure appear on his face as he said very softly: "They even carry you to your bed here."

For a long time after he began to talk, he would never refer to anyone by name, but only as "that person" or "the little person" or "the big person." He was unable to designate by its true name anything to which he attached feelings. Nor could he name his anxieties except through neologisms or word contaminations.[4] For a long time he spoke about "master paintings" and "a master painting room" (i.e., masturbating and masturbating room). One of his machines, the "criticizer," prevented him from "saying words which have unpleasant feelings." Yet he gave personal names to the tubes and motors in his collection of machinery. Moreover, these dead things had feelings; the tubes bled when hurt and sometimes got sick. He consistently maintained this reversal between animate and inanimate objects.

In Joey's machine world everything, on pain of instant destruction, obeyed inhibitory laws much more stringent than those of physics. When

15

---

[4]*neologisms or word contaminations:* Words that Joey made up or words that he peculiarly altered. [Eds.]

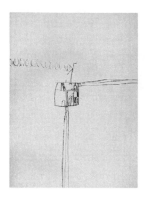  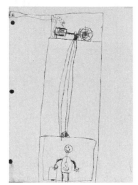

Growing self-esteem is shown in this sequence of drawings. At left Joey por-
trays himself as an electrical "papoose," completely enclosed, suspended in
empty space and operated by wireless signals. In center drawing his figure is
much larger, though still under wireless control. At right he is able to picture
the machine which controls him, and he has acquired hands with which he can
manipulate his immediate environment.

we came to know him better, it was plain that in his moments of silent
withdrawal, with his machine switched off, Joey was absorbed in pondering the compulsive laws of his private universe. His preoccupation with
machinery made it difficult to establish even practical contacts with him.
If he wanted to do something with a counselor, such as play with a toy that
had caught his vague attention, he could not do so: "I'd like this very
much, but first I have to turn off the machine." But by the time he had ful-
filled all the requirements of his preventions, he had lost interest. When a
toy was offered to him, he could not touch it because his motors and his
tubes did not leave him a hand free. Even certain colors were dangerous
and had to be strictly avoided in toys and clothing, because "some colors
turn off the current, and I can't touch them because I can't live without the
current."

Joey was convinced that machines were better than people. Once when
he bumped into one of the pipes on our jungle gym he kicked it so violently that his teacher had to restrain him to keep him from injuring himself.
When she explained that the pipe was much harder than his foot, Joey
replied: "That proves it. Machines are better than the body. They don't
break; they're much harder and stronger." If he lost or forgot something, it
merely proved that this brain ought to be thrown away and replaced by
machinery. If he spilled something, his arm should be broken and twisted
off because it did not work properly. When his head or arm failed to work
as it should, he tried to punish it by hitting it. Even Joey's feelings were
mechanical. Much later in his therapy, when he had formed a timid attachment to another child and had been rebuffed, Joey cried: "He broke my
feelings."

Gradually we began to understand what had seemed to be contradictory in Joey's behavior — why he held on to the motors and tubes, then suddenly destroyed them in a fury, then set out immediately and urgently to equip himself with new and larger tubes. Joey had created these machines to run his body and mind because it was too painful to be human. But again and again he became dissatisfied with their failure to meet his need and rebellious at the way they frustrated his will. In a recurrent frenzy he "exploded" his light bulbs and tubes, and for a moment became a human being — for one crowning instant he came alive. But as soon as he had asserted his dominance through the self-created explosion, he felt his life ebbing away. To keep on existing he had immediately to restore his machines and replenish the electricity that supplied his life energy.

What deep-seated fears and needs underlay Joey's delusional system? We were long in finding out, for Joey's preventions effectively concealed the secret of his autistic behavior. In the meantime we dealt with his peripheral problems one by one.

During his first year with us Joey's most trying problem was toilet behavior. This surprised us, for Joey's personality was not "anal" in the Freudian sense; his original personality damage had antedated the period of his toilet-training. Rigid and early toilet-training, however, had certainly contributed to his anxieties. It was our effort to help Joey with this problem that led to his first recognition of us as human beings.

Going to the toilet, like everything else in Joey's life, was surrounded by 20 elaborate preventions. We had to accompany him; he had to take off all his clothes; he could only squat, not sit, on the toilet seat; he had to touch the wall with one hand, in which he also clutched frantically the vacuum tubes that powered his elimination. He was terrified lest his whole body be sucked down.

To counteract this fear we gave him a metal wastebasket in lieu of a toilet. Eventually, when eliminating into the wastebasket, he no longer needed to take off all his clothes, nor to hold on to the wall. He still needed the tubes and motors which, he believed, moved his bowels for him. But here again the all-important machinery was itself a source of new terrors. In Joey's world the gadgets had to move their bowels, too. He was terribly concerned that they should, but since they were so much more powerful than men, he was also terrified that if his tubes moved their bowels, their feces would fill all of space and leave him no room to live. He was thus always caught in some fearful contradiction.

Our readiness to accept his toilet habits, which obviously entailed some hardship for our counselors, gave Joey the confidence to express his obsessions in drawings. Drawing these fantasies was a first step toward letting us in, however distantly, to what concerned him most deeply. It was the first step in a yearlong process of externalizing his anal preoccupations. As a result he began seeing feces everywhere; the whole world became to him a mire of excrement. At the same time he began to eliminate freely wherever he happened to be. But with this release from his infantile imprisonment in compulsive rules, the toilet and the whole process of elimination became less dangerous. Thus far it had been beyond Joey's comprehension that any-body could possibly move his bowels without mechanical aid. Now Joey took a further step forward; defecation became the first physiological process he could perform without the help of vacuum tubes. It must not be thought that he was proud of this ability. Taking pride in an achievement presupposes that one accomplishes it of one's own free will. He still did not feel himself an autonomous person who could do things on his own. To Joey defecation still seemed enslaved to some incomprehensible but utterly binding cosmic law, perhaps the law his parents had imposed on him when he was being toilet-trained.

It was not simply that his parents had subjected him to rigid, early train-ing. Many children are so trained. But in some cases the parents have a deep emotional investment in the child's performance. The child's response in turn makes training an occasion for interaction between them and for the building of genuine relationships. Joey's parents had no emotional investment in him. His obedience gave them no satisfaction and won him no affection or approval. As a toilet-trained child he saved his mother labor, just as household machines saved her labor. As a machine he was not loved for his performance, nor could he love himself.

So it had been with all other aspects of Joey's existence with his parents. Their reactions to his eating or noneating, sleeping or wakening, urinating or defecating, being dressed or undressed, washed or bathed did not flow from any unitary interest in him, deeply embedded in their personalities. By treating him mechanically his parents made him a machine. The various functions of life — even the parts of his body — bore no integrating rela-tionship to one another or to any sense of self that was acknowledged and confirmed by others. Though he had acquired mastery over some functions, such as toilet-training and speech, he had acquired them separately and kept them isolated from each other. Toilet-training had thus not gained him a pleasant feeling of body mastery; speech had not led to communication of thought or feeling. On the contrary, each achievement only steered him away from self-mastery and integration. Toilet-training had enslaved him. Speech left him talking in neologisms that obstructed his and our ability to relate to each other. In Joey's development the normal process of growth had been made to run backward. Whatever he had learned put him not at the end of his infantile development toward integration but, on the contrary, farther behind than he was at its very beginning. Had we understood this sooner, his first years with us would have been less baffling.

It is unlikely that Joey's calamity could befall a child in any time and cul-   25
ture but our own. He suffered no physical deprivation; he starved for human contact. Just to be taken care of is not enough for relating. It is a necessary but not a sufficient condition. At the extreme where utter scarcity reigns, the forming of relationships is certainly hampered. But our society of mecha-nized plenty often makes for equal difficulties in a child's learning to relate. Where parents can provide the simple creature-comforts for their children only at the cost of significant effort, it is likely that they will feel pleasure in

Elaborate sewage system in Joey's drawing of a house reflects his long preoccupation with excretion. His obsession with sewage reflected intense anxieties produced by his early toilet-training, which was not only rigid but also completely impersonal.

being able to provide for them; it is this, the parents' pleasure, that gives children a sense of personal worth and sets the process of relating in motion. But if comfort is so readily available that the parents feel no particular pleasure in winning it for their children, then the children cannot develop the feeling of being worthwhile around the satisfaction of their basic needs. Of course parent and children can and do develop relationships around other situations. But matters are then no longer so simple and direct. The child must be on the receiving end of care and concern given with pleasure and without the exaction of return if he is to feel loved and worthy of respect and consideration. This feeling gives him the ability to trust; he can entrust his well-being to persons to whom he is so important. Out of such trust the child learns to form close and stable relationships.

For Joey relationship with his parents was empty of pleasure in comfort-giving as in all other situations. His was an extreme instance of a plight that sends many schizophrenic children to our clinics and hospitals. Many months passed before he could relate to us; his despair that anybody could like him made contact impossible.

When Joey could finally trust us enough to let himself become more infantile, he began to play at being a papoose. There was a corresponding change in his fantasies. He drew endless pictures of himself as an electrical

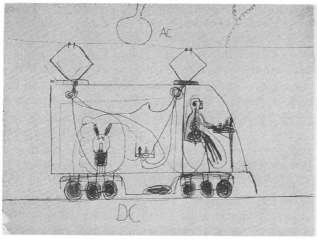

Growing autonomy is shown in Joey's drawings of the imaginary "Carr" (car) family. Top drawing shows a machine which can move but is unoccupied. Machine in center is occupied, but by a passive figure. In bottom drawing figure has gained control of machine.

papoose. Totally enclosed, suspended in empty space, he is run by unknown, unseen powers through wireless electricity.

As we eventually came to understand, the heart of Joey's delusional system was the artificial, mechanical womb he had created and into which he had locked himself. In his papoose fantasies lay the wish to be entirely reborn in a womb. His new experiences in the school suggested that life, at all, might be worth living. Now he was searching for a way to be reborn in a better way. Since machines were better than men, what was more natural than to try rebirth through them? This was the deeper meaning of this electrical papoose.

As Joey made progress, his pictures of himself became more dominant in his drawings. Though still machine-operated, he has grown in self-importance. Another great step forward is represented in the picture above. . . . Now he has acquired hands that do something, and he has had the courage to make a picture of the machine that runs him. Later still the papoose became a person, rather than a robot encased in glass.

Eventually Joey began to create an imaginary family at the school: the "Carr" family. Why the Carr family? In the car he was enclosed as he had been in his papoose, but at least the car was not stationary; it could move. More important, in a car one was not only driven but also could drive. The Carr family was Joey's way of exploring the possibility of leaving the school, of living with a good family in a safe, protecting car.

30

Gentle landscape painted by Joey after his recovery symbolizes the human emotions he had regained. At 12, having learned to express his feelings, he was no longer a machine.

Joey at last broke through his prison. In this brief account it has not been possible to trace the painfully slow process of his first true relations with other human beings. Suffice it to say that he ceased to be a mechanical boy and became a human child. This newborn child was, however, nearly 12 years old. To recover the lost time is a tremendous task. That work has occupied Joey and us ever since. Sometimes he sets to it with a will; at other times the difficulty of real life makes him regret that he ever came out of his shell. But he has never wanted to return to his mechanical life.

One last detail and this fragment of Joey's story has been told. When Joey was 12, he made a float for our Memorial Day parade. It carried the slogan: "Feelings are more important than anything under the sun." Feelings, Joey had learned, are what make for humanity; their absence, for a mechanical existence. With this knowledge Joey entered the human condition.

QUESTIONS

1. Bettelheim's task was to explain Joey's behavior as best he could. What did he and his colleagues do, what did they examine, and how did they behave as they developed their explanation of Joey?

2. Joey had come to some conclusions about himself and about the world he inhabited before Bettelheim encountered him. These explanations seem to have become fixed as interpretations, by which we mean simply that he had come to understand himself in terms of something else. In which passages does Bettelheim come closest to presenting Joey as his own interpreter? Summarize Joey's interpretation of himself — the structure or set of principles by which he understands himself.

3. To begin to be cured, Joey had to *reinterpret* his life. What were the major steps toward that reinterpretation? What changed for Joey?

4. Even to say *cured*, as we just did in question 3, involves an unexamined interpretation. What assumptions guide our use of that word? Do you find *cured* a satisfying explanation of what begins to happen to Joey?

5. The introduction to this section mentions this essay as an example of a case study — that is, a close examination of a unique person, event, or situation over time in a set of circumstances that are probably not replicable. Using this essay as your example, what else might characterize a case study? What makes a case study believable?

6. Quite a few people play roles or assume characterizations that deviate from what we think we know about them. Describe a person who does that. Offer your own limited case study. Try to indicate the extent to which the person's understanding of himself or herself is based on reality and the extent to which it isn't.

7. College can lead students to reinterpret themselves. In fact, reinterpretation traditionally has been a large part of the experience of going to

college. Write an explanation of yourself or of someone else you know well who is undergoing such a reinterpretation. What terms prevailed before college? What happened to call them into question? What kind of change has occurred, and what is at stake in this matter?

MAKING CONNECTIONS

1. If Bettelheim's essay is a kind of a case study, what other essays in this collection present something like it? Could you call Richard Selzer's "The Discus Thrower" (p. 263) a case study? Or what about one of the early pieces in "Reflections," such as essays by Maya Angelou (p. 31), Alice Walker (p. 42), or Frederick Douglass (p. 62)? Pick two or three pieces that seem close to being case studies, and describe how they are like and unlike this example by Bettelheim.

2. What does it mean to be human? Taking into account several essays besides Bettelheim's — essays by Stephen Jay Gould (p. 686), Jane van Lawick-Goodall (p. 237), Richard Selzer (p. 263), and Alice Walker (p. 42) are all possibilities — take a stab at defining our essential human nature. What if anything seems invariable within a wealth of human possibilities? Is Joey's slogan (paragraph 32) a convincing expression of what is essentially human, or would you point to something else?

SLICE OF LIFE

Gordon Grice

*Born in 1965 in rural Oklahoma, where he still resides, nature writer
and poet Gordon Grice received a bachelor's degree from Oklahoma
State University and a master's of fine arts degree from the
University of Arkansas. He has taught English and creative writing
at Seward County Community College and has been a visiting lec-
turerer at Henderson State University and CalArts, among others.
His widely anthologized essay "The Black Widow," about black
widow spiders, originally appeared in* High Plains Literary Review *in
1995 and was included in Grice's 1998 collection,* The Red
Hourglass: Lives of the Predators. *Grice also contributed an essay to
the photography book* Food Chain: Encounters between Mates,
Predators, and Prey *(2000). The following essay is from* The New
Yorker. *The* Visible Human Male *he describes here can be viewed
online at* < http://www.uchsc.edu/sm/chs/browse/browse_m.html>.

The district attorney who prosecuted Joseph Paul Jernigan called him "a
middle-of-the-road killer" — a rougher character than some he'd dealt with,
but definitely not the roughest. "I've got two other guys on death row now
who'd eat Jernigan alive," he told me. Newspapers called Jernigan a "former
mechanic"; he was also a thief, who had already done time for burglary twice
when his real troubles began.

It was 1981. Jernigan was twenty-seven. He was living with his wife
in Waco, Texas, and they needed money. Jernigan and an acquaintance, a
seventeen-year-old called Roy Lamb, decided to go to nearby Navarro
County to rob someone. They chose a farmhouse near Dawson. Though
they had been smoking marijuana and drinking, the robbery went smoothly. They took a microwave oven and a radio. But, as they drove down the
dirt road leading away from the house, they passed the man whose home
they'd just ransacked. Edward Hale was seventy-five years old and his eyesight was failing; it's unlikely that he could have identified the burglars or
their vehicle, but Jernigan didn't know that. He turned back to eliminate
the witness. At the house, Jernigan bludgeoned Hale with an ashtray,
stabbed him repeatedly, and then fired at him three times with a shotgun,
hitting him in the stomach, the heart, and, finally, the head.

A day or two later, Jernigan's wife went to the police, and Jernigan was
taken into custody, where he confessed. Roy Lamb was sentenced to thirty
years and paroled after ten; Jernigan went to death row in Huntsville. Once
he was incarcerated and free of drugs and alcohol, he started a chapter of
Alcoholics Anonymous for death-row inmates. He made jewelry and furniture

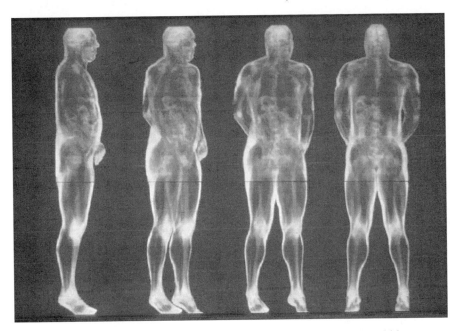

When Joseph Paul Jernigan was executed, he had no idea that his would become the most intimately known body in the world.

for friends on the outside. He wrote reflective letters. "I have no one to blame but myself," he admitted. As his first execution date approached, he told a reporter, "I'm very scared. I catch myself counting the days. It's hard for me to sleep at night." The district attorney remembers Jernigan as generally impassive in the courtroom, but when a judge told him the final date of his execution he fought his guards and had to be restrained.

On August 4, 1993, Jernigan refused to eat the last meal he had requested — cheeseburgers, fries, a salad — and just after midnight he went to the death chamber. A needle was threaded into his forearm, and he was injected with the sedative sodium thiopental, a heart-stopping dose of potassium chloride, and pancuronium bromide, a muscle relaxant meant to collapse the lungs. As a gesture of atonement, he had agreed to donate his body to medical science, but this chemical cocktail would render his organs toxic and unsuitable for transplant. He offered no last words, and was pronounced dead at 12:31 A.M.

Few people who donate their bodies to science know exactly what will   5
happen to their remains. Most often, their cadavers will be dissected by medical students learning anatomy. There would have been no way for Jernigan to guess that, even before he died, his body was coveted for a far more elaborate purpose.

After his family had taken their leave, Jernigan's body was "lightly embalmed" — that is, infused with a little formaldehyde to counteract the corrosive effect of the injections — packed into a crate, and air-freighted to Denver. There scientists contracted by a government agency called the National Library of Medicine gave the body MRIs[1] and CTs,[2] as if it were a living patient. Then they froze it solid.

Jernigan's was only one of several corpses in cold storage whose radio-logical images the scientists were comparing. They were looking for an average man, someone who fit certain parameters for size and age and health. They had had a hard time finding an appropriate cadaver; most bodies donated to science are old and emaciated or show signs of disease or trauma. Others that might have been ideal had lost their freshness by the time they became available to the scientists. Jernigan had an advantage: because he had died on a schedule, his remains had been handled according to the scientists' needs. His deficiencies were minor — a testicle and an appendix lost in operations years earlier, a missing tooth. In the end, he was chosen.

After sawing the body into four pieces, the scientists encased the chunks in blue gelatine and began to slice, milling from the feet to the head. They made 1,877 cuts. After each cut, they digitally photographed a cross-section. The process took months, because the team could work for no more than eight hours before having to put the corpse back in the freezer. By the time they were done, Jernigan's body had been reduced to ooze and ice shavings.

The scientists collated the photos with the CT scans they'd made ear-lier. They brought the resulting data to life with the three-dimensional-imaging technology used in *Star Wars*. These digital images were more detailed and realistic than the models and illustrations in traditional anato-my texts, because they were generated not from abstractions of the human form but from the thing itself, captured on camera. After months of work, the scientists emerged with fifteen gigabytes of data that constituted the Visible Human Male, the most accurate human anatomical model ever seen.

It may be hard to grasp what had become of Jernigan, but it's easy to see. His image is on thousands of Web sites. I first saw it at a computer terminal in a university library in Oklahoma. I watched Jernigan's upright body approach and pass through the plane of the computer screen, a smooth pro-gression of glistening cross-sections. When I chose another angle, I could move from head to foot, the image kaleidoscoping — a blossoming of brain, a constriction of neck, a widening into the trunk packed with organs, a sud-den bifurcation at the pelvis, and on down to the surprisingly dainty toes. I examined individual segments of his body. They resembled cuts of beef — or, given their symmetry, butterflied pork chops. They had the sleek look of   10

---

[1] *MRIs:* Magnetic resonance imaging. [Eds.]
[2] *CTs:* Computed tomography imaging. [Eds.]

something wrapped in cellophane. The cross-section of Jernigan's thighs and genitalia reminded me of a lava lamp — bubbles in a viscous liquid. Though the image would stay still as long as I liked, it seemed evanescent, on the verge of transforming into something else.

An argument at the next terminal distracted me. A thin student in a T-shirt and baggy jeans had been caught printing out photos of nude women. The librarian chastised him with remarks like "What made you think you could do something like this?" and "Didn't you realize we can monitor whatever you're looking at?" I wondered whether some hidden authority was monitoring my examination of a stranger's testicle. Would such an authority see this electronic body as an abstraction or recognize it as human flesh? Which would be worse?

At the University of Colorado Health Sciences Center, I performed my first operation. I felt my scope sliding along the bone. I was seeing structures I'd previously known only by name, from news stories about football players' knee injuries. The white pad of cartilage beneath my hand was the meniscus. The twist of fibrous tissue was the anterior cruciate ligament (the ACL). Then my scope slipped off the bone and I was floating free in the fluid at the joint. I aimed through the white architecture of bones to explore the ACL. Suddenly, without feeling any resistance, I plunged straight through the ligament, crippling my patient for life. My patient — an electronic one based on Jernigan — existed only in the memory of a computer, and the equipment that allowed me to operate worked on the same principle as a flight simulator. The palpable hardness of the bones was supplied by a robot arm pushing against me as the computer directed. I watched my progress on a monitor, just as a surgeon does when using a real scope, and, because the monitor's image was projected onto a screen beneath my hand, I could actually look down and see the knee where I felt it.

There was, of course, a reason for the extravagant treatment of Jernigan's remains. The scientists who remodelled both him and, later, a fifty-nine-year-old woman who had died of heart disease and lung disease have made the resulting sets of data freely available, and they have become a tool for an endless array of applications. They have prompted the development of surgical simulators, such as the machine I used in Colorado. They can replace cadavers in anatomy classes like one I visited in a rural nursing school in Kansas. They can be used in the designing of prosthetic limbs. Car manufacturers have taken the data in the hopes of creating virtual crash-test dummies. Lawyers have used them to illustrate injuries in court cases. Special-effects companies have adapted the data to lend verisimilitude to animation in commercials and short sequences in movies. And the Department of Defense is working toward using the models to simulate the effects of non-lethal weapons on the body. Soon, one scientist told me, doctors will combine the data with MRI or CT images of particular patients. "Your doctor will practice on a virtual you," he said, pointing emphatically to my sternum. Since such images are transmissible, doctors could also get long-distance help from specialists anywhere in the world.

We live in a time when it's possible for almost anyone to look inside the bodies of anonymous people and, occasionally, of people with names. Cable television, CD-ROMs, and the Internet have made anatomy a popular diversion. The singer Carnie Wilson's[3] stomach-reduction operation was advertised as a Web event, and it is fairly easy to witness other surgeries online, from the refurbishing of a cornea to a heart bypass. Not long ago, I watched a television documentary in which a medical examiner displayed a photograph of a murder victim's stomach, sliced open to reveal the corn and hamburger remnants that constituted a last meal and an important clue.

In this climate of public intimacy, it's hard to appreciate the depths of   15
mystery that the human form once held. Though the science of anatomy has ancient roots, most cultures have an equally ancient taboo against observing the interior of the body, except in certain highly controlled contexts. Egyptian embalming techniques, for instance, required that a corpse's belly be sliced open and the viscera removed, but the priest who performed this task was then chased out of the room and cursed, a ceremonial acknowledgment of transgression. Even the limited forms of surgery performed in ancient Greece occurred in a state of relative anatomical ignorance. Although Aristotle was able to dissect monkeys and other animals for educational purposes, the Greeks of his era found human dissection inconceivable. He was forced to deduce what he could about human anatomy by analogy and by observing emaciated people, whose veins and bones stood out well enough to be mapped.

Human dissection was first practiced in the third century B.C. in Alexandria, where the invading Greeks had fewer scruples about using the bodies of natives. Physicians like Erasistratus and Herophilus[4] cut into the corpses and occasionally, according to some sources, the living bodies of foreigners and criminals. (Executed criminals have been a source for anatomical study ever since.) The most important figure in early anatomy is, of course, Galen, a Greek physician of the second century A.D., who studied human dissection in Alexandria. After leaving Egypt, he worked on animal carcasses — lions, bears, oxen, goats, and pigs. Even better were monkeys, whose parts he found to have "an exact similarity" to those of

---

[3] *Carnie Wilson:* A singer with the group Wilson Phillips and daughter of Beach Boy Brian Wilson. Her laparoscopic gastric bypass procedure was narrated live on the Internet, but the procedure was not broadcast. [Eds.]

[4] *Erasistratus and Herophilus:* Erasistratus (c. 304–c. 250 B.C.), a Greek who practiced in Alexandria, Egypt. He continued the anatomy studies begun in Alexandria by fellow Greek physician, Herophilus (335–280 B.C.), the world's first systematic anatomist. [Eds.]

humans. He also studied the gaping wounds of gladiators, though he acknowledged that this method was not practical for most students.

After Galen, anatomical study stagnated for almost a millennium. Constrained by the Christian view that the interior of the human body was "God's province," doctors concentrated on herbal medicine and other strategies that didn't require much knowledge of anatomy. Medical procedures that necessitated physical contact between healer and patient — lancing boils, bleeding with leeches, even minor surgery — were typically handled by barbers, and medical schools taught anatomy as a theoretical subject, if at all. Then, in the thirteenth century, the legal system in Europe began to sanction autopsies to determine the causes of death, and some universities revised their curricula to include anatomical demonstrations using criminals' corpses. These demonstrations often featured a professor reading from a text while a junior academic pointed to the relevant body parts and a barber handled the cadaver. Medical students stocked the dissection rooms with rose water and incense to mask the smell. At some universities, only medical students and doctors were allowed in; elsewhere, dissections were open to anyone who could pay the admission fee. At the University of Bologna, dissections took place at carnival time, and by the seventeenth century the proceedings had come to resemble freak shows more than scientific investigations.

During the Renaissance, the Church began to shift toward the idea that understanding anatomy could enhance man's appreciation of God's handiwork. This position influenced the arts, and painters began flaying cadavers in order to study their muscles and thereby depict the body with greater accuracy. Leonardo da Vinci[5] observed such flayings and later conducted his own research. He boasted that he had whittled away "more than ten" cadavers just to diagram the circulatory system. But the most influential anatomist of the Renaissance was Andreas Vesalius.[6] His extraordinary texts are filled with innovative cross-references and illustrations — some possibly provided by Titian[7] — and they expose the weaknesses in works by Galen and others.

About two hundred years ago, dissection went back underground, or, at least, into the academy and the hospital, rarely to be observed by laymen. This change, which presaged the rise of the funeral industry, was part of a general cultural trend toward hiding the uglier facts of life, and, except for fictional glimpses of dissection — in works such as Mary Shelley's *Frankenstein* and Robert Louis Stevenson's "The Body Snatcher" — the human interior remained more or less the province of the medical establishment until the end of the twentieth century.

---

[5] *Leonardo da Vinci* (1452–1519): An Italian painter, sculptor, architect, engineer, mathematician, and scientist. [Eds.]

[6] *Andreas Vesalius* (1514–1564): A Flemish anatomist. [Eds.]

[7] *Titian* (c. 1490–1576): A Venetian painter. [Eds.]

Though it was information technology that brought about the Visible   20
Human Project, other recent innovations have reawakened public interest in
anatomy. In the late nineteen-seventies, Dr. Gunther von Hagens, an East
German refugee who was then associated with the University of Heidelberg,
developed a new method for preserving human tissue. He replaced the cell
water and soluble fat in human flesh with polymers, a process of infusion
which left the tissues almost unchanged in appearance. Such "plastinated"
organs and body sections soon turned up in medical and mortuary schools.
Skeletons had long been available for study, and organs had been pickled or
encased in plastic blocks, but von Hagens made it possible for any medical
facility to have a supply of the necessary specimens, suitable for handling.
They could be made flexible or firm, depending on the formula used in the
infusion process, and, unlike specimens preserved by other methods, von
Hagens's retained the shape and color of living organs. Von Hagens estimated
that flesh treated this way would last for at least a hundred thousand years.

Nobody objected to von Hagens's anatomical specimens as long as they
were used in a scientific setting. The trouble started when von Hagens discovered what he calls "gestalt plastination" — a method of infusing whole
bodies — and began posing corpses and displaying them in exhibitions at
science museums in Europe and Japan, where they have drawn millions of
viewers. One of his works is a man who has been skinned and split longitu-
dinally, his separate muscular halves standing a foot or so apart. His brain
and spinal column are propped between the halves, with the eyeballs and the
lungs attached in the appropriate places. The rest of the viscera have been
removed from their usual positions for clearer viewing: the man holds them
in his hands. Although it resembles sculpture, this is an actual human body.
Another is a man posed as if running, his muscles peeled open — like bou-
quets of flowers, as their creator describes the effect — to show underlying
structures. A third is a skinned woman with her womb opened to show the
five-month-old fetus she was carrying when she died. On average, at least
one spectator faints per day at von Hagens's installations. As public events,
they have more in common with Robert Mapplethorpe's[8] photography or
Damien Hirst's formaldehyde cows[9] than with the standard practice of
anatomy.

In Germany, religious leaders pressured politicians to stop the shows. "He
who styles human corpses as a so-called work of art no longer respects the
importance of death," the Catholic theologian Johannes Reiter proclaimed.
Fellow-anatomists asserted that the exhibits were too complex for laymen and
therefore could serve no educational purpose. But most of the critics, von
Hagens told me recently, had not actually seen his exhibitions. His defense of

---

[8] *Robert Mapplethorpe* (1946–1989): A New York photographer whose nudes
were considered shocking by many. [Eds.]

[9] *Damien Hirst* (b. 1965): A British artist known for experimental works
involving preserved animal parts. [Eds.]

his work took on political overtones. "It's democratic," he said. "The layman is given back what he lost two hundred years ago" — a view of human anatomy uncensored by experts. Von Hagens referred to his own past in Communist East Germany; his current work, he said, is a form of "body liberation." He described rowdy teen-agers who arrive at his exhibits looking for grotesque spectacle but then quickly fall silent: "They come to see something ugly. They find themselves anew." After seeing the exhibitions, some viewers decide to donate their own bodies, and von Hagens is generally happy to sign them up.

Both von Hagens's work and the Visible Human Project represent battles in the long war between cultural taboos and scientific advancement. "I think it's fabulous," said Victor Spitzer, the University of Colorado anatomist whose team did the work on Jernigan's body, when I asked him about von Hagens. "And if you're asking about the ethics, I still like it."

But, unlike von Hagens's subjects, Jernigan had no idea that he would become anything more than an anonymous cadaver. Instead, his body has become the most intimately known in the world. In the eyes of some observers, he has been violated on the largest scale imaginable. His lawyer and friend Mark Ticer told me that Jernigan would have been uncomfortable with the macabre fame he has achieved.

The question of privacy also came up in my conversations with Spitzer.   25 "Someday, this man is going to get up and walk away," he said of an image of Jernigan on a computer screen. The technology to make the Visible Humans move already exists, and it is only a matter of time before they can move so realistically that they could, for example, replace human actors in movies — and become even more convincing than the virtual actors in this month's *Final Fantasy*.[10] Hollywood has an incentive to advance the research in this area, and Spitzer suspects that the movie industry may overcome the remaining obstacles before science does. But this is where an unpleasant possibility arises. If the virtual bodies can be used to simulate realistic action, Spitzer said, they can also be used for pornography.

Officials at the National Library of Medicine realized that they wouldn't be able to control the use of public-domain materials, but they did want to preserve the donors' anonymity. They settled for not releasing names. The Visible Human Female remains anonymous. However, when the project was unveiled, people at the N.L.M. revealed when and where the Visible Human Male had been executed, and reporters quickly deduced his identity. The scientists regret having been so specific, and Spitzer still doesn't refer to Jernigan by name.

The research is far from complete. Spitzer hopes to slice his next cadaver much more thinly, improving the resolution by a factor of thirty. He discussed the need for cadavers of every ethnicity, body type, and age. He also

---

[10]*Final Fantasy*: An online, interactive video game. [Eds.]

showed me a virtual cadaver that hasn't received the publicity that the other two have: a human fetus. I asked Spitzer if he didn't find his line of work a little disturbing. Although he admitted that his first dissection, twelve years ago, was "traumatic," he told me that cadavers generally don't bother him. The job of dismantling Jernigan and his female counterpart was relatively easy. Most of the time, he could see only a frozen surface.

Before Spitzer and his colleagues had announced their odd and thorough dissection of a human being, they feared a backlash; they worried that their work would appear macabre, and they prepared carefully for a press conference at which they emphasized the project's scientific and medical value. A new narrative of Jernigan's afterlife began to develop, an interpretation of his continuing electronic existence as an atonement for his crime: violence redeemed by scientific progress. All of which turned out to be curiously irrelevant. Far from asking difficult questions, many reporters left the press conference early, to cover other breaking news. Those who stayed wrote about the project as a straight science story, and the public has accepted it as ethical under the umbrella of medical authority. This is the paradox of the Visible Humans: people may find them repulsive in theory, but, because they have become electronic, they don't invoke our taboo against dealing with corpses. We can handle them without the defiling touch of flesh and blood. It's as easy as watching TV.

QUESTIONS

1. The first four paragraphs of this essay present a brief history of Joseph Paul Jernigan before it reports on what was done to his corpse or how his body was transformed. Why do you think Grice presents Jernigan's history?

2. Note Grice's descriptions of what was done to Jernigan's body (paragraph 8) and how he perceives "what had become of Jernigan" (paragraphs 10–11). How would you respond to the questions that the writer raises at the end of paragraph 11 about "some hidden authority"?

3. In this essay, space is devoted to informing the reader of the scientific use of "the Visible Human Male, the most accurate human anatomical model ever seen" (paragraph 9). But is that the main topic of this essay? How is this essay organized? Make a simple outline of the areas covered to see if you can come up with a statement of the point that Grice is trying to make.

4. Grice brings up the issue of "public intimacy" (paragraph 15) and of "anatomy as a popular diversion" (paragraph 14). What surgical procedures have you seen performed on television or on the Internet? What was the purpose of their presentation? What was your reaction to what you saw?

5. Watch one or more of the reality shows on television, and write a report on the issue of public intimacy, including other reasons for these shows' appeal.

6. Visit the Visible Human Project on the Web and take a tour of a virtual body. Record your reactions to what you see as you watch, and use them as a basis for a report on what you saw and learned. Two of several possible sites are <www.nlm.nih.gov/research/visible> and <www.madsci. org/~lynn/VH>.

MAKING CONNECTIONS

This essay asks us to regard Jernigan's body as something other than what it was when alive, and it suggests that Jernigan would not be pleased at the transformation of his body into a public image. Several essays in this text deal with the perception of the body by oneself and others: Alice Walker's "Beauty: When the Other Dancer Is the Self" (p. 42); Lucy Grealy, "Mirrors" (p. 50); and Judith Ortiz Cofer, "The Story of My Body" (p. 93). Compare what these writers have to say about their bodies. You might want to tie these readings to television shows that feature people unhappy with their bodies who are made over through plastic surgery and various other means.

WHY MCDONALD'S FRIES TASTE SO GOOD

Eric Schlosser

Investigative journalist Eric Schlosser (b. 1960) graduated from Princeton University and later studied history at Oxford University in England. His journalism career began in college when he worked summers as a mailroom clerk at New York *magazine and as a fact checker at* Esquire. *After pursuing a career as a playwright with little success, Schlosser returned to journalism. Since then, his work has appeared in major national magazines, including* The Atlantic Monthly, Rolling Stone, *and* U.S. News & World Report, *and his 1994 series in* The Atlantic *about harsh prison terms for small-time marijuana users and dealers won the National Magazine Award for reporting. In 1995, Schlosser was a finalist for the same award for a report on the plight of migrant farmworkers in California. Of his work, Schlosser has said, "I did a graduate degree in history, and a lot of the stuff that I've done as a journalist is really similar to history. . . . I always start in the library. I always start with the source material. But ultimately, it's driven by, 'Oh, this is something people should know. I didn't know this either.'" Schlosser began investigating the fast-food industry for a two-part* Rolling Stone *article that appeared in 1998. The following essay is a chapter from his best-selling book on the subject,* Fast Food Nation: The Dark Side of the All-American Meal *(2001).*

The french fry was "almost sacrosanct for me," Ray Kroc, one of the founders of McDonald's, wrote in his autobiography, "its preparation a ritual to be followed religiously." During the chain's early years french fries were made from scratch every day. Russet Burbank potatoes were peeled, cut into shoestrings, and fried in McDonald's kitchens. As the chain expanded nationwide, in the mid-1960s, it sought to cut labor costs, reduce the number of suppliers, and ensure that its fries tasted the same at every restaurant. McDonald's began switching to frozen french fries in 1966 — and few customers noticed the difference. Nevertheless, the change had a profound effect on the nation's agriculture and diet. A familiar food had been transformed into a highly processed industrial commodity. McDonald's fries now come from huge manufacturing plants that can peel, slice, cook, and freeze 2 million pounds of potatoes a day. The rapid expansion of McDonald's and the popularity of its low-cost, mass-produced fries changed the way Americans eat. In 1960 Americans consumed an average of about eighty-one pounds of fresh potatoes and four pounds of frozen french fries. In 2000 they consumed an average of about fifty pounds of fresh potatoes and thirty pounds of frozen fries. Today McDonald's is the largest buyer of potatoes in the United States.

The taste of McDonald's french fries played a crucial role in the chain's success — fries are much more profitable than hamburgers — and was long praised by customers, competitors, and even food critics. James Beard[1] loved McDonald's fries. Their distinctive taste does not stem from the kind of potatoes that McDonald's buys, the technology that processes them, or the restaurant equipment that fries them: other chains use Russet Burbanks, buy their french fries from the same large processing companies, and have similar fryers in their restaurant kitchens. The taste of a french fry is largely determined by the cooking oil. For decades McDonald's cooked its french fries in a mixture of about 7 percent cottonseed oil and 93 percent beef tallow.[2] The mixture gave the fries their unique flavor — and more saturated beef fat per ounce than a McDonald's hamburger.

In 1990, amid a barrage of criticism over the amount of cholesterol in its fries, McDonald's switched to pure vegetable oil. This presented the company with a challenge: how to make fries that subtly taste like beef without cooking them in beef tallow. A look at the ingredients in McDonald's french fries suggests how the problem was solved. Toward the end of the list is a seemingly innocuous yet oddly mysterious phrase: "natural flavor." That ingredient helps to explain not only why the fries taste so good but also why most fast food — indeed, most of the food Americans eat today — tastes the way it does.

Open your refrigerator, your freezer, your kitchen cupboards, and look at the labels on your food. You'll find "natural flavor" or "artificial flavor" in just about every list of ingredients. The similarities between these two broad categories are far more significant than the differences. Both are manmade additives that give most processed food most of its taste. People usually buy a food item the first time because of its packaging or appearance. Taste usually determines whether they buy it again. About 90 percent of the money that Americans now spend on food goes to buy processed food. The canning, freezing, and dehydrating techniques used in processing destroy most of food's flavor — and so a vast industry has arisen in the United States to make processed food palatable. Without this flavor industry today's fast food would not exist. The names of the leading American fast-food chains and their best-selling menu items have become embedded in our popular culture and famous worldwide. But few people can name the companies that manufacture fast food's taste.

The flavor industry is highly secretive. Its leading companies will not   5
divulge the precise formulas of flavor compounds or the identities of clients.

---

[1]*James Beard* (1903–1985): A chef, teacher, author, speaker, and television host who has been hailed as the "Father of American Cooking." [Eds.]

[2]*Beef tallow:* Solid fat obtained from the bodies of cattle. [Eds.]

The secrecy is deemed essential for protecting the reputations of beloved brands. The fast-food chains, understandably, would like the public to believe that the flavors of the food they sell somehow originate in their restaurant kitchens, not in distant factories run by other firms. A McDonald's french fry is one of countless foods whose flavor is just a component in a complex manufacturing process. The look and the taste of what we eat now are frequently deceiving — by design.

The New Jersey Turnpike runs through the heart of the flavor industry, an industrial corridor dotted with refineries and chemical plants. International Flavors & Fragrances (IFF), the world's largest flavor company, has a manufacturing facility off Exit 8A in Dayton, New Jersey; Givaudan, the world's second largest flavor company, has a plant in East Hanover. Haarmann & Reimer, the largest German flavor company, has a plant in Teterboro, as does Takasago, the largest Japanese flavor company. Flavor Dynamics has a plant in South Plainfield; Frutarom is in North Bergen; Elan Chemical is in Newark. Dozens of companies manufacture flavors in the corridor between Teaneck and South Brunswick. Altogether the area produces about two thirds of the flavor additives sold in the United States.

The IFF plant in Dayton is a huge pale-blue building with a modern office complex attached to the front. It sits in an industrial park, not far from a BASF plastics factory, a Jolly French Toast factory, and a plant that manufactures Liz Claiborne cosmetics. Dozens of tractor-trailers were parked at the IFF loading dock the afternoon I visited, and a thin cloud of steam floated from a roof vent. Before entering the plant, I signed a nondisclosure form, promising not to reveal the brand names of foods that contain IFF flavors. The place reminded me of Willy Wonka's chocolate factory.[3] Wonderful smells drifted through the hallways, men and women in neat white lab coats cheerfully went about their work, and hundreds of little glass bottles sat on laboratory tables and shelves. The bottles contained powerful but fragile flavor chemicals, shielded from light by brown glass and round white caps shut tight. The long chemical names on the little white labels were as mystifying to me as medieval Latin. These odd-sounding things would be mixed and poured and turned into new substances, like magic potions.

I was not invited into the manufacturing areas of the IFF plant, where, it was thought, I might discover trade secrets. Instead I toured various laboratories and pilot kitchens, where the flavors of well-established brands are tested or adjusted, and where whole new flavors are created. IFF's snack-and-savory lab is responsible for the flavors of potato chips, corn chips, breads, crackers, breakfast cereals, and pet food. The confectionery lab devises flavor for ice cream, cookies, candies, toothpastes, mouthwashes,

---

[3] *Willy Wonka's chocolate factory:* The setting for the popular children's book *Charlie and the Chocolate Factory* by Roald Dahl. It was made into a popular film, retitled *Willy Wonka and the Chocolate Factory* (1971). [Eds.]

and antacids. Everywhere I looked, I saw famous, widely advertised products sitting on laboratory desks and tables. The beverage lab was full of brightly colored liquids in clear bottles. It comes up with flavors for popular soft drinks, sports drinks, bottled teas, and wine coolers, for all-natural juice drinks, organic soy drinks, beers, and malt liquors. In one pilot kitchen I saw a dapper food technologist, a middle-aged man with an elegant tie beneath his crisp lab coat, carefully preparing a batch of cookies with white frosting and pink-and-white sprinkles. In another pilot kitchen I saw a pizza oven, a grill, a milkshake machine, and a french fryer identical to those I'd seen at innumerable fast-food restaurants.

In addition to being the world's largest flavor company, IFF manufactures the smells of six of the ten best-selling fine perfumes in the United States, including Estée Lauder's Beautiful, Clinique's Happy, Lancôme's Trésor, and Calvin Klein's Eternity. It also makes the smells of household products such as deodorant, dishwashing detergent, bath soap, shampoo, furniture polish, and floor wax. All these aromas are made through essentially the same process: the manipulation of volatile chemicals. The basic science behind the scent of shaving cream is the same as that governing the flavor of your TV dinner.

Scientists now believe that human beings acquired the sense of taste as   10
a way to avoid being poisoned. Edible plants generally taste sweet, harmful ones bitter. The taste buds on our tongues can detect the presence of half a dozen or so basic tastes, including sweet, sour, bitter, salty, astringent, and umami, a taste discovered by Japanese researchers — a rich and full sense of deliciousness triggered by amino acids in foods such as meat, shellfish, mushrooms, potatoes, and seaweed. Taste buds offer a limited means of detection, however, compared with the human olfactory system, which can perceive thousands of different chemical aromas. Indeed, "flavor" is primarily the smell of gases being released by the chemicals you've just put in your mouth. The aroma of a food can be responsible for as much as 90 percent of its taste.

The act of drinking, sucking, or chewing a substance releases its volatile gases. They flow out of your mouth and up your nostrils, or up the passageway in the back of your mouth, to a thin layer of nerve cells called the olfactory epithelium, located at the base of your nose, right between your eyes. Your brain combines the complex smell signals from your olfactory epithelium with the simple taste signals from your tongue, assigns a flavor to what's in your mouth, and decides if it's something you want to eat.

A person's food preferences, like his or her personality, are formed during the first few years of life, through a process of socialization. Babies innately prefer sweet tastes and reject bitter ones; toddlers can learn to enjoy hot and spicy food, bland health food, or fast food, depending on what the people around them eat. The human sense of smell is still not fully understood. It is greatly affected by psychological factors and expectations. The mind focuses intently on some of the aromas that surround us and filters out the overwhelming majority. People can grow accustomed to bad smells or good smells; they stop noticing what once seemed overpowering. Aroma and memory are somehow inextricably linked. A smell can suddenly evoke a long-forgotten moment. The flavors of childhood foods seem to leave an indelible mark, and adults often return to them, without always knowing why. These "comfort foods" become a source of pleasure and reassurance — a fact that fast-food chains use to their advantage. Childhood memories of Happy Meals, which come with french fries, can translate into frequent adult visits to McDonald's. On average, Americans now eat about four servings of french fries every week.

The human craving for flavor has been a largely unacknowledged and unexamined force in history. For millennia royal empires have been built, unexplored lands traversed, and great religions and philosophies forever changed by the spice trade. In 1492 Christopher Columbus set sail to find seasoning. Today the influence of flavor in the world marketplace is no less decisive. The rise and fall of corporate empires — of soft-drink companies, snack-food companies, and fast-food chains — is often determined by how their products taste.

The flavor industry emerged in the mid-nineteenth century, as processed foods began to be manufactured on a large scale. Recognizing the need for flavor additives, early food processors turned to perfume companies that had long experience working with essential oils and volatile aromas. The great perfume houses of England, France, and the Netherlands produced many of the first flavor compounds. In the early part of the twentieth century Germany took the technological lead in flavor production, owing to its powerful chemical industry. Legend has it that a German scientist discovered methyl anthranilate, one of the first artificial flavors, by accident while mixing chemicals in the laboratory. Suddenly the lab was filled with the sweet smell of grapes. Methyl anthranilate later became the chief flavor compound in grape Kool-Aid. After World War II much of the perfume industry shifted from Europe to the United States, settling in New York City near the garment district and the fashion houses. The flavor industry came with it, later moving to New Jersey for greater plant capacity. Manmade flavor additives were used mostly in baked goods, candies, and sodas until the 1950s, when sales of processed food began to soar. The invention of gas chromatographs and mass spectrometers — machines capable of detecting volatile gases at low levels — vastly increased the number of flavors that could be synthesized. By the mid-1960s flavor companies were churning out compounds to supply the taste of Pop Tarts, Bac-Os, Tab, Tang, Filet-O-Fish sandwiches, and literally thousands of other new foods.

The American flavor industry now has annual revenues of about $1.4 bil-   15
lion. Approximately ten thousand new processed-food products are introduced every year in the United States. Almost all of them require flavor additives. And about nine out of ten of these products fail. The latest flavor innovations and corporate realignments are heralded in publications such as

Chemical Market Reporter, Food Chemical News, Food Engineering, and *Food Product Design*. The progress of IFF has mirrored that of the flavor industry as a whole. IFF was formed in 1958, through the merger of two small companies. Its annual revenues have grown almost fifteenfold since the early 1970s, and it currently has manufacturing facilities in twenty countries.

Today's sophisticated spectrometers, gas chromatographs, and headspace-vapor analyzers provide a detailed map of a food's flavor components, detecting chemical aromas present in amounts as low as one part per billion. The human nose, however, is even more sensitive. A nose can detect aromas present in quantities of a few parts per trillion — an amount equivalent to about 0.000000000003 percent. Complex aromas, such as those of coffee and roasted meat, are composed of volatile gases from nearly a thousand different chemicals. The smell of a strawberry arises from the interaction of about 350 chemicals that are present in minute amounts. The quality that people seek most of all in a food — flavor — is usually present in a quantity too infinitesimal to be measured in traditional culinary terms such as ounces or teaspoons. The chemical that provides the dominant flavor of bell pepper can be tasted in amounts as low as 0.02 parts per billion; one drop is sufficient to add flavor to five average-size swimming pools. The flavor additive usually comes next to last in a processed food's list of ingredients and often costs less than its packaging. Soft drinks contain a larger portion of flavor additives than most products. The flavor in a twelve-ounce can of Coke costs about half a cent.

The color additives in processed foods are usually present in even smaller amounts than the flavor compounds. Many of New Jersey's flavor companies also manufacture these color additives, which are used to make processed foods look fresh and appealing. Food coloring serves many of the same decorative purposes as lipstick, eye shadow, mascara — and is often made from the same pigments. Titanium dioxide, for example, has proved to be an especially versatile mineral. It gives many processed candies, frostings, and icings their bright white color; it is a common ingredient in women's cosmetics; and it is the pigment used in many white oil paints and house paints. At Burger King, Wendy's, and McDonald's coloring agents have been added to many of the soft drinks, salad dressings, cookies, condiments, chicken dishes, and sandwich buns.

Studies have found that the color of a food can greatly affect how its taste is perceived. Brightly colored foods frequently seem to taste better than bland-looking foods, even when the flavor compounds are identical. Foods that somehow look off color often seem to have off tastes. For thousands of years human beings have relied on visual cues to help determine what is edible. The color of fruit suggests whether it is ripe, the color of meat whether it is rancid. Flavor researchers sometimes use colored lights to modify the influence of visual cues during taste tests. During one experiment in the early 1970s people were served an oddly tinted meal of steak and french fries that appeared normal beneath colored lights. Everyone thought the meal tasted fine until the lighting was changed. Once it became apparent that the steak was actually blue and the fries were green, some people became ill.

The federal Food and Drug Administration does not require companies to disclose the ingredients of their color or flavor additives so long as all the chemicals in them are considered by the agency to be GRAS ("generally recognized as safe"). This enables companies to maintain the secrecy of their formulas. It also hides the fact that flavor compounds often contain more ingredients than the foods to which they give taste. The phrase "artificial strawberry flavor" gives little hint of the chemical wizardry and manufacturing skill that can make a highly processed food taste like strawberries.

A typical artificial strawberry flavor, like the kind found in a Burger   20
King strawberry milkshake, contains the following ingredients: amyl acetate, amyl butyrate, amyl valerate, anethol, anisyl formate, benzyl acetate, benzyl isobutyrate, butyric acid, cinnamyl isobutyrate, cinnamyl valerate, cognac essential oil, diacetyl, dipropyl ketone, ethyl acetate, ethyl amyl ketone, ethyl butyrate, ethyl cinnamate, ethyl heptanoate, ethyl heptylate, ethyl lactate, ethyl methylphenylglycidate, ethyl nitrate, ethyl propionate, ethyl valerate, heliotropin, hydroxyphenyl-2-butanone (10 percent solution in alcohol), α-ionone, isobutyl anthranilate, isobutyl butyrate, lemon essential oil, maltol, 4-methylacetophenone, methyl anthranilate, methyl benzoate, methyl cinnamate, methyl heptine carbonate, methyl naphthyl ketone, methyl salicylate, mint essential oil, neroli essential oil, nerolin, neryl isobutyrate, orris butter, phenethyl alcohol, rose, rum ether, γ-undecalactone, vanillin, and solvent.

Although flavors usually arise from a mixture of many different volatile chemicals, often a single compound supplies the dominant aroma. Smelled alone, that chemical provides an unmistakable sense of the food. Ethyl-2-methyl butyrate, for example, smells just like an apple. Many of today's highly processed foods offer a blank palette: whatever chemicals are added to them will give them specific tastes. Adding methyl-2-pyridyl ketone makes something taste like popcorn. Adding ethyl-3-hydroxy butanoate makes it taste like marshmallow. The possibilities are now almost limitless. Without affecting appearance or nutritional value, processed foods could be made with aroma chemicals such as hexanal (the smell of freshly cut grass) or 3-methyl butanoic acid (the smell of body odor).

The 1960s were the heyday of artificial flavors in the United States. The synthetic versions of flavor compounds were not subtle, but they did not have to be, given the nature of most processed food. For the past twenty years food processors have tried hard to use only "natural flavors" in their products. According to the FDA, these must be derived entirely from natural sources — from herbs, spices, fruits, vegetables, beef, chicken, yeast, bark, roots, and so forth. Consumers prefer to see natural flavors on a label, out of a belief that they are more healthful. Distinctions between artificial and natural flavors can be arbitrary and somewhat absurd, based more on how the flavor has been made than on what it actually contains.

"A natural flavor," says Terry Acree, a professor of food science at Cornell University, "is a flavor that's been derived with an out-of-date technology." Natural flavors and artificial flavors sometimes contain exactly the same chemicals, produced through different methods. Amyl acetate, for example, provides the dominant note of banana flavor. When it is distilled from bananas with a solvent, amyl acetate is a natural flavor. When it is produced by mixing vinegar with amyl alcohol and adding sulfuric acid as a catalyst, amyl acetate is an artificial flavor. Either way it smells and tastes the same. "Natural flavor" is now listed among the ingredients of everything from Health Valley Blueberry Granola Bars to Taco Bell Hot Taco Sauce.

A natural flavor is not necessarily more healthful or purer than an artificial one. When almond flavor — benzaldehyde — is derived from natural sources, such as peach and apricot pits, it contains traces of hydrogen cyanide, a deadly poison. Benzaldehyde derived by mixing oil of clove and amyl acetate does not contain any cyanide. Nevertheless, it is legally considered an artificial flavor and sells at a much lower price. Natural and artificial flavors are now manufactured at the same chemical plants, places that few people would associate with Mother Nature.

The small and elite group of scientists who create most of the flavor in 25 most of the food now consumed in the United States are called "flavorists." They draw on a number of disciplines in their work: biology, psychology, physiology, and organic chemistry. A flavorist is a chemist with a trained nose and a poetic sensibility. Flavors are created by blending scores of different chemicals in tiny amounts — a process governed by scientific principles but demanding a fair amount of art. In an age when delicate aromas and microwave ovens do not easily coexist, the job of the flavorist is to conjure illusions about processed food and, in the words of one flavor company's literature, to ensure "consumer likeability." The flavorists with whom I spoke were discreet, in keeping with the dictates of their trade. They were also charming, cosmopolitan, and ironic. They not only enjoyed fine wine but could identify the chemicals that give each grape its unique aroma. One flavorist compared his work to composing music. A well-made flavor compound will have a "top note" that is often followed by a "dry-down" and a "leveling-off," with different chemicals responsible for each stage. The taste of a food can be radically altered by minute changes in the flavoring combination. "A little odor goes a long way," one flavorist told me.

In order to give a processed food a taste that consumers will find appealing, a flavorist must always consider the food's "mouthfeel" — the unique combination of textures and chemical interactions that affect how the flavor is perceived. Mouthfeel can be adjusted through the use of various fats, gums, starches, emulsifiers, and stabilizers. The aroma chemicals in a food can be precisely analyzed, but the elements that make up mouthfeel are much harder to measure. How does one quantify a pretzel's hardness, a french fry's crispness? Food technologists are now conducting basic research in rheology, the branch of physics that examines the flow and deformation of materials. A number of companies sell sophisticated devices that attempt to measure mouthfeel. The TA.XT2i Texture Analyzer, produced by the Texture Technologies Corporation, of Scarsdale, New York, performs calculations based on data derived from as many as 250 separate probes. It is essentially a mechanical mouth. It gauges the most important rheological properties of a food — bounce, creep, breaking point, density, crunchiness, chewiness, gumminess, lumpiness, rubberiness, springiness, slipperiness, smoothness, softness, wetness, juiciness, spreadability, springback, and tackiness.

Some of the most important advances in flavor manufacturing are now occurring in the field of biotechnology. Complex flavors are being made using enzyme reactions, fermentation, and fungal and tissue cultures. All the flavors created by these methods — including the ones being synthesized by fungi — are considered natural flavors by the FDA. The new enzyme-based processes are responsible for extremely true-to-life dairy flavors. One company now offers not just butter flavor but also fresh creamy butter, cheesy butter, milky butter, savory melted butter, and super-concentrated butter flavor, in liquid or powder form. The development of new fermentation techniques, along with new techniques for heating mixtures of sugar and amino acids, have led to the creation of much more realistic meat flavors.

The McDonald's Corporation most likely drew on these advances when it eliminated beef tallow from its french fries. The company will not reveal the exact origin of the natural flavor added to its fries. In response to inquiries from *Vegetarian Journal*, however, McDonald's did acknowledge that its fries derive some of their characteristic flavor from "an animal source." Beef is the probable source, although other meats cannot be ruled out. In France, for example, fries are sometimes cooked in duck fat or horse tallow.

Other popular fast foods derive their flavor from unexpected ingredients. McDonald's Chicken McNuggets contain beef extracts, as does Wendy's Grilled Chicken Sandwich. Burger King's BK Broiler Chicken Breast Patty contains "natural smoke flavor." A firm called Red Arrow Products specializes in smoke flavor, which is added to barbecue sauces, snack foods, and processed meats. Red Arrow manufactures natural smoke flavor by charring sawdust and capturing the aroma chemicals released into the air. The smoke is captured in water and then bottled, so that other companies can sell food that seems to have been cooked over a fire.

The Vegetarian Legal Action Network recently petitioned the FDA to   30
issue new labeling requirements for foods that contain natural flavors. The group wants food processors to list the basic origins of their flavors on their labels. At the moment vegetarians often have no way of knowing whether a flavor additive contains beef, pork, poultry, or shellfish. One of the most widely used color additives — whose presence is often hidden by the phrase "color added" — violates a number of religious dietary restrictions, may cause allergic reactions in susceptible people, and comes from an unusual

source. Cochineal extract (also known as carmine or carminic acid) is made from the desiccated bodies of female *Dactylopius coccus Costa*, a small insect harvested mainly in Peru and the Canary Islands. The bug feeds on red cactus berries, and color from the berries accumulates in the females and their un-hatched larvae. The insects are collected, dried, and ground into a pigment. It takes about seventy thousand of them to produce a pound of carmine, which is used to make processed foods look pink, red, or purple. Dannon strawberry yogurt gets its color from carmine, and so do many frozen fruit bars, candies, and fruit fillings, and Ocean Spray pink-grapefruit juice drink.

In a meeting room at IFF, Brian Grainger let me sample some of the company's flavors. It was an unusual taste test — there was no food to taste. Grainger is a senior flavorist at IFF, a soft-spoken chemist with graying hair, an English accent, and a fondness for understatement. He could easily be mistaken for a British diplomat or the owner of a West End brasserie with two Michelin stars.[4] Like many in the flavor industry, he has an Old World, old-fashioned sensibility. When I suggested that IFF's policy of secrecy and discretion was out of step with our mass-marketing, brand-conscious, self-promoting age and that the company should put its own logo on the countless products that bear its flavors, instead of allowing other companies to enjoy the consumer loyalty and affection inspired by those flavors, Grainger politely disagreed, assuring me that such a thing would never be done. In the absence of public credit or acclaim, the small and secretive fraternity of flavor chemists praise one another's work. By analyzing the flavor formula of a product, Grainger can often tell which of his counterparts at a rival firm devised it. Whenever he walks down a supermarket aisle, he takes a quiet pleasure in seeing the well-known foods that contain his flavors.

Grainger had brought a dozen small glass bottles from the lab. After he opened each bottle, I dipped a fragrance-testing filter into it — a long white strip of paper designed to absorb aroma chemicals without producing off notes. Before placing each strip of paper in front of my nose, I closed my eyes. Then I inhaled deeply, and one food after another was conjured from the glass bottles. I smelled fresh cherries, black olives, sautéed onions, and shrimp. Grainger's most remarkable creation took me by surprise. After closing my eyes, I suddenly smelled a grilled hamburger. The aroma was uncanny, almost miraculous — as if someone in the room were flipping burgers on a hot grill. But when I opened my eyes, I saw just a narrow strip of white paper and a flavorist with a grin.

---

[4]*West End brasserie with two Michelin stars:* The West End is London's theater district. A brasserie is a small restaurant. Michelin publishes guidebooks that describe and rate restaurants and hotels; two stars indicates "excellent cooking, worth a detour." [Eds.]

QUESTIONS

1. How would you describe the title of this piece? Attention-getting? Misleading? Ironic?
2. Much of this article presents scientific terms, but Schlosser is writing for a general audience rather than for scientists. How does he present those scientific terms and concepts for the general reader? What is his purpose in presenting the entire list of ingredients in strawberry flavor (paragraph 20)? How do you feel about strawberry flavor after reading the list of ingredients?
3. How does Schlosser arrange his material? His tour of the IFF plant and his experiences there structure much of his report, but how much background research is present?
4. Check the ingredients on a package of your favorite processed food. Does it contain any "natural" flavors? If so, what natural flavor? Does it contain any of the chemicals mentioned in the text?
5. Schlosser claims that about 90 percent of the food we buy is processed. How much processed food is in your home right now? How much fresh food? Make lists of each, and compare your lists with your classmates' lists. Categorize the foods and beverages, and write a report on the food preferences of the class. What are the percentages of processed and of unprocessed food consumed by your class?
6. If you had some money to invest, would you consider investing it in the flavor industry? Why or why not?
7. In paragraph 12, Schlosser talks about psychological factors connected with smells and flavors. Write a report on your favorite "comfort food" and the memories connected with it. Or take the opposite approach: describe the memories that are aroused by a smell or flavor that you detest.

MAKING CONNECTIONS

Compare your approach to food memories with that of Mark Strand in his poem "Pot Roast" (p. 319).

POT ROAST

Mark Strand

Mark Strand (b. 1934) was born on Prince Edward's Island, Canada, of American parents, and was raised and educated in the United States and South America. He was educated at Antioch College and at Yale, the University of Florence, and the University of Iowa. He is the author of ten books of poems, including Blizzard of One *(1998), which won the Pulitzer Prize;* Dark Harbor *(1993);* The Continuous Life *(1990), and* Selected Poems *(1991). He has also published two books of prose, several volumes of translation, and three children's books. He has won a number of prizes and fellowships, and has served as Poet Laureate of the United States. He has taught at several universities and is currently teaching in the Committee on Social Thought at the University of Chicago. "Pot Roast," which first appeared in the collection* The Late Hour *(1978), reflects Strand's interest in memory, and his themes of absence and loss.*

I gaze upon the roast,
that is sliced and laid out
on my plate
and over it
I spoon the juices   5
of carrot and onion.
And for once I do not regret
the passage of time.

I sit by a window
that looks   10
on the soot-stained brick of buildings
and do not care that I see
no living thing — not a bird,
not a branch in bloom,
not a soul moving   15
in the rooms
behind the dark panes.
These days when there is little
to love or to praise
one could do worse   20
than yield

to the power of food.
So I bend

to inhale
the steam that rises   25
from my plate, and I think
of the first time
I tasted a roast
like this.
It was years ago   30
in Seabright,
Nova Scotia;
my mother leaned
over my dish and filled it
and when I finished   35
filled it again.
I remember the gravy,
its odor of garlic and celery,
and sopping it up
with pieces of bread.   40

And now
I taste it again.
The meat of memory.
The meat of no change.
I raise my fork   45
and I eat.

QUESTIONS

1. In the hierarchy of food, where would you locate pot roast? It's not usually found on the menus of fancy restaurants, though you might find it
   in restaurants that are rediscovering home cooking or comfort food.
2. What does Strand mean by yielding "to the power of food" (line 22)?
   What actions constitute the act of yielding here?
3. The power of food changes Strand's perception of the present and
   evokes memories of the past. How would you describe those memories?
4. Why does Strand call this pot roast "The meat of memory / The meat of
   no change" (lines 43–44)? What food has a similar power for you?
   Describe the food and the memories evoked by it.

EXPLAINING

Here in "Explaining," you will find writings by specialists from a wide range of fields who seek to account for matters as various as the color of the sky, the origin of the universe, the content of urban legends, and the art of keeping a notebook. Explanation is an essential kind of writing in every academic field and profession. Facts, after all, do not speak for themselves, nor do figures add up on their own. To make sense of a subject, we need to see it in terms of something that is related to it—the color of the sky in terms of light waves from the sun, the content of urban legends in terms of the immediate circumstances in which they are told. To understand a subject, in other words, we must examine it in terms of some relevant context that will shed light on its origin and development, its nature and design, its elements and functions, its causes and effects, or its meaning and significance. For this reason, the writers in this section draw on specific bodies of knowledge and systems of interpretation to explain the problems and subjects that they address.

This essential element of explaining can be seen in connection with the following passage from James Jeans's "Why the Sky Is Blue" (p. 467):

> We know that sunlight is a blend of lights of many colors—as we can prove for ourselves by passing it through a prism, or even through a jug of water, or as Nature demonstrates to us when she passes it through the raindrops of a summer shower and produces a rainbow. We also know that light consists of waves, and that the different colors of light are produced by waves of different lengths, red light by long waves and blue light by short waves. The mixture of waves which constitutes sunlight has to struggle through the obstacles it meets in the atmosphere, just as the mixture of waves at the seaside has to struggle past the columns of the pier. And these obstacles treat the light-waves much as the columns of the pier treat the sea-waves. The long waves which constitute red light are

hardly affected, but the short waves which constitute blue light are scattered in all directions.

Thus, the different constituents of sunlight are treated in different ways as they struggle through the earth's atmosphere. A wave of blue light may be scattered by a dust particle, and turned out of its course. After a time a second dust particle again turns it out of its course, and so on, until finally it enters our eyes by a path as zigzag as that of a flash of lightning. Consequently the blue waves of the sunlight enter our eyes from all directions. And that is why the sky looks blue. (paragraphs 3–4)

Jeans's purpose here is to explain why the sky looks blue, and beginning in his opening sentence in this passage, he systematically establishes an explanatory context by setting forth relevant information about the nature and properties of sunlight, light, and light waves. That is, he approaches the explanatory problem in terms of knowledge drawn from his specialized fields of astronomy and physics. With this knowledge in hand, he then proceeds to show how "the different constituents of sunlight are treated in different ways as they struggle through the earth's atmosphere." In this way, he develops his explanation according to the analytic framework of an astronomer and physicist who is concerned with the interaction of the atmosphere and light waves. After formulating a cause-and-effect analysis that demonstrates that blue light is scattered "in all directions," Jeans is able to conclude that "the blue waves of the sunlight enter our eyes from all directions. And that is why the sky looks blue." Thus, the information that Jeans draws on from astronomy and physics allows him to offer a knowledgeable, systematic, and instructive explanation.

To appreciate how significant an explanatory context can be, consider how knowledge from other fields might influence an understanding of why the sky looks blue. A zoologist specializing in optics, for example, might note the importance of the retinal organs known as cones, which are thought to allow animals to receive and process color. Given this crucial bit of information, a zoologist might observe that the sky looks blue to human beings because their eyes are equipped with cones, whereas it does not look blue to animals such as guinea pigs, owls, and armadillos because their eyes lack cones. An anthropologist, in turn, might note that people living in coastal and island cultures tend to develop unusually rich vocabularies for describing how the sea looks and how the sky looks. Thus, an anthropologist might conclude that people who live in maritime environments are likely to be especially discerning about the colors of the sea and sky.

Our hypothetical zoologist and anthropologist would both differ from Jeans in their explanatory approaches to the blue sky. Whereas Jeans sought to account for the source and prevalence of blue color, a zoologist and an anthropologist might take the color for granted and instead seek to account for the human ability to perceive the color or the propensity of some cultures to be especially discriminating in their perception of it. Their differing approaches would result from their differing fields of study. Each academic area, after all, involves a distinctive body of knowledge, a distinctive array of interests, and a distinctive set of methods for making sense of the subjects that its proponents study. Thus each area is likely to approach problems from different angles and arrive at different kinds of explanations. No area can lay claim to the ultimate truth about things, but, as the case of the blue sky illustrates, each field does have a special angle on the truth, particularly about subjects that fall within its area of specialization. A zoologist and an anthropologist could be as valid and as enlightening in this case as astronomer-physicist Jeans. In a broader sense, a particular subject or problem can be approached from one particular angle or from a combination of viewpoints, and each approach emerges from a corresponding body of knowledge that brings its own perspective to bear on an understanding of the subject. Relevant knowledge, quite simply, is the most essential element of explaining.

But knowledge alone is not sufficient to produce intelligible and effective explanation. Jeans's explanation, for example, depends both on a body of information (about the properties and movement of light and light waves) and also on the form and style in which the information is presented. To develop your ability to explain, you will need to develop a resourcefulness in putting your knowledge to use. One way to do this is to familiarize yourself with some of the many forms that explanatory writing can take in academic and professional situations.

The Range of Explanatory Writing

Explanatory writing serves a wide range of academic, professional, and public purposes. Rules and regulations, guidelines and instructions — these are familiar examples of explanations that tell people how to carry on many of the practical and public activities of their lives. Textbooks, such as the one you are reading right now, as well as simplified presentations of highly specialized research or theories are common examples of explanatory writing that help people understand a particular body of information and ideas. Scholarly research papers, government documents, and other highly technical presentations of data and analysis, though less familiar to the general reader, are important kinds of explanation that advance knowledge and informed decision making.

To serve the differing needs of such varied purposes and audiences, explanatory writing incorporates various styles of presentation. Jeans's piece about the sky, for example, comes from a book that he wrote as an introduction to astronomy. Thus, he uses a vocabulary that is accessible to most readers. And to make sure that beginners will understand the important concepts in his explanation, Jeans repeatedly illustrates his discussion with analogies and references to familiar experiences. In fact, if you look at the whole of Jeans's piece, you will see that he establishes his analogy of light waves to sea waves at the beginning of his discussion and then systematically uses it to organize and clarify the rest of his explanation.

For another variation in the format and style of explanatory writing, look at Oliver Sacks's "The Man Who Mistook His Wife for a Hat" (p. 475). Here Sacks, a neurologist, offers the results of a case study, which entails the close observation of an individual subject over time. Because the subject of a case study is by definition unique, the study cannot be replicated by other researchers. A case study therefore must be written in sufficient detail to document the observer's understanding of the subject and to enable other researchers to draw their own conclusions about the subject. You will find that Sacks provides a detailed description, history, and analysis of Dr. P.'s behavior. You will also find that Sacks writes on the whole in a standard rather than specialized style, as befits an audience of generally educated readers.

Explanations can vary widely in their form, involving in every case a delicate mix of adjustments to the audience, purpose, specialized field, and subject matter. As a reader of explanations, you will have to be flexible in your approach, always willing to move through unfamiliar territory on the way to understanding the subject being discussed or perhaps to recognizing that understanding may be beyond the scope of your knowledge in a particular field. As a writer of explanations, you will have to be equally flexible in choosing language and in selecting and arranging material to put your knowledge and understanding in a form that satisfies you and fulfills the complex set of conditions that you are addressing in your explanation.

Methods of Explaining

In planning a piece of explanatory writing, you should review your research materials with an eye to selecting an approach that is adjusted to all the conditions of your explanatory situation. Some methods, you will find, are inescapable, no matter what your subject, audience, or purpose. Every piece of explanation requires that ideas be clarified and demonstrated through *illustration*—that is, through the citing of specific examples, as you can see from the earlier passage by Jeans and in the following excerpt from Sacks's essay on Dr. P., the musician:

> He saw all right, but what did he see? I opened out a copy of the *National Geographic Magazine* and asked him to describe some pictures in it.
>
> His responses here were very curious. His eyes would dart from one thing to another, picking up tiny features, individual features, as they had done with my face. A striking brightness, a color, a shape would arrest his attention and elicit comment—but in no case did he get the scene-as-a-whole. He failed to see the whole, seeing only details, which he spotted like blips on a radar screen.

He never entered into relation with the picture as a whole—never faced, so to speak, *its* physiognomy. He had no sense whatever of a landscape or scene.

I showed him the cover, an unbroken expanse of Sahara dunes. "What do you see here?" I asked.

"I see a river," he said. "And a little guest-house with its terrace on the water. People are dining out on the terrace. I see colored parasols here and there." He was looking, if it was "looking," right off the cover into mid-air and confabulating nonexistent features, as if the absence of features in the actual picture had driven him to imagine the river and the terrace and the colored parasols.

I must have looked aghast, but he seemed to think he had done rather well. There was a hint of a smile on his face. He also appeared to have decided that the examination was over and started to look around for his hat. He reached out his hand and took hold of his wife's head, tried to lift it off, to put it on. He had apparently mistaken his wife for a hat! His wife looked as if she was used to such things. (paragraphs 24–29)

Sacks's obligation to illustrate and demonstrate Dr. P.'s unusual symptoms leads him here, as elsewhere in his piece, to turn to a detailed *description* and *narration* of Dr. P.'s actions. Reporting constitutes an essential element of explaining—for reasons of clarity, reliability, and credibility. If an explanation cannot be illustrated or can be only weakly documented, it is likely to be unreliable and therefore not credible to readers.

Some methods are not required in every case but are important in certain pieces of explanation. An essay that depends on the use of special terms or concepts almost certainly will call for *definitions* to ensure that the reader understands the phrases exactly as the writer intends them to be understood. In "Urban Legends: 'The Boyfriend's Death'" (p. 335), for example, Jan Harold Brunvand begins his study by defining urban legends as a subclass of folklore and by defining what is entailed in the study of folklore.

In his essay about Dr. P., Sacks proceeds in a different way. He presents the case of Dr. P., who is suffering from visual agnosia, by trying to replicate for readers his own process of uncovering the mystery lying behind Dr. P.'s unusual behavior. He shows, through description and dialogue with Dr. P. and his wife, the remarkable things Dr. P. can do (his extraordinary musical ability, for example) and the ordinary things he cannot do (such as recognize the faces of his wife and friends). At the end of this descriptive section, Sacks reveals the pathological cause of Dr. P.'s visual agnosia. But that is insufficient explanation for Sacks. He goes on to ask how Dr. P.'s inability to make cognitive judgments should be interpreted. He talks about the limitations of neurological and psychological explanations of what appear to be neuropsychological disorders when those sciences overlook "the judgmental, the particular, the personal" and rely on the "abstract and computational" alone. In so doing, Sacks defines the limits of cognitive neurology and psychology, suggesting that they, too, may suffer from "an agnosia essentially similar to Dr. P's." Definition, in other words, can be carried out in a variety of ways—by citing examples, by identifying essential qualities or characteristics, by offering synonyms, by making distinctions.

Other methods of explanation can be effective in a broad range of explanatory situations. If you are trying to explain the character, design, elements, or nature of something, you will often do best to *compare and contrast* it with something to which it is logically related. Comparison calls attention to similarities; contrast focuses on differences. Together, the methods work to clarify and emphasize important points by playing related subjects against each other. In his study of urban legends, for example, Brunvand attempts to shed light on the complex circumstances that influence the content of such folktales by comparing and contrasting several versions of the same legendary story. This method enables him to show that popular urban legends, such as "The Boyfriend's Death," retain a basically unvarying situation and plot as they travel from one storyteller and locale to another but that specific details are altered by individual storytellers to make them fit the circumstances of a particular audience. Like Brunvand's piece, some examples of comparison and contrast rely on a strategic balancing of similarities and differences. Other pieces depend largely on a sustained contrast. And still other pieces might work primarily in terms of comparison. By the same token, whenever you use comparison and contrast, your attention to similarities and differences should be adjusted to the needs of your explanatory situation.

A special form of comparison, *analogy*, can be useful in many explanatory situations. Analogies help readers understand difficult or unfamiliar ideas by putting them in tangible and familiar terms. In "Why the Sky Is Blue," for example, Jeans's analogy of light waves to sea waves helps readers to visualize a process that they could not otherwise see. As useful as analogies are, however, they rely on drawing resemblances between things that are otherwise unlike. Sea waves, after all, are not light waves, and the dimensions of the universe are not the same as anything within the range of ordinary human experience. Whenever you develop an analogy, be sure that the analogy fits your explanatory situation and that it does not involve misleading implications.

Some explanatory methods are especially suited to a particular kind of situation. If you are trying to show how to do something, how something works, or how something was done, you will use a method known as *process analysis*. In analyzing a process, your aim is to identify and describe each step or stage in the process, show how each step leads to the next, and explain how the process as a whole leads to its final result. Jeans's piece, for example, analyzes the process by which light waves from the sun make their way through the earth's atmosphere and determine human perception of the color of the sky.

A method related to process analysis is *causal analysis*. As the term suggests, this type of analysis seeks to explain the causes of things, particularly causes that are complex. Usually, a causal analysis begins with a complex outcome and then examines various explanations that might account for the situation. Sometimes, however, an analysis might begin with a particular cause and then examine the various effects that the cause has produced. Monica M. Moore follows this pattern of explanation in "Nonverbal Courtship Patterns in Women: Context and Consequences" (p. 412), in which she finds that the biological imperative of mating (the cause) produces a range of "flirting behaviors" and a range, also, of "mate relevant" responses to them. Because no two things can be identically accounted for, no set method exists for carrying out a causal analysis. Keep in mind, however, a few cautionary procedures. You should review other possible causes and other related circumstances before attempting to assert the priority of one cause or set of causes over another, and you should present enough evidence to demonstrate the reliability of your explanation. By doing so, you will avoid the temptation to oversimplify things.

As you can probably tell by now, almost any piece of writing that aims to make sense of something combines several methods of explanation. This should come as no surprise if you stop to think about the way that people usually explain even the simplest things in their day-to-day conversations with each other. Just ask someone, for example, to give you directions for getting from one place to another. The person will probably give you an overview of where the place is situated, a step-by-step set of movements to follow and places to look for, brief descriptions of prominent guideposts along the way, a review of the original directions, and possibly a remark or two about misleading spots to avoid. Similarly, when people try to explain something in writing, they want to help readers get from one place to another in a particular subject matter. Thus, in the midst of giving a process analysis or causal analysis, a writer might feel compelled to illustrate a point, define a term, or offer a telling analogy.

In the pieces in this section, you will see how writers in different fields combine various methods of explaining things. And in the next section, you will see how explaining also contributes to arguing.

Arts and Humanities

ON KEEPING A NOTEBOOK

Joan Didion

Joan Didion was born in Sacramento, California, in 1934 and graduated from the University of California at Berkeley in 1956. Until the publication of her first novel, Run River, *in 1963, she woked as an editor for* Vogue *magazine. Since then, she has written four more novels, including* Play It as It Lays *(1971) and* The Last Thing He Wanted *(1996); six books of essays, most notably* Slouching towards Bethlehem *(1968) and* The White Album *(1979); and, in collaboration with her husband, John Gregory Dunne, a number of successful screenplays. As both novelist and essayist, Didion has shown herself to be a trenchant observer and interpreter of American society and culture. Many of her essays also explore her own private life in intimate detail. The following piece appeared in* Holiday *magazine in 1966 and was collected in* Slouching towards Bethlehem.

"'That woman Estelle,'" the note reads, "'is partly the reason why George Sharp and I are separated today.' *Dirty crepe-de-Chine wrapper, hotel bar, Wilmington RR, 9:45 A.M. August Monday morning.*"

Since the note is in my notebook, it presumably has some meaning to me. I study it for a long while. At first I have only the most general notion of what I was doing on an August Monday morning in the bar of the hotel across from the Pennsylvania Railroad station in Wilmington, Delaware (waiting for a train? missing one? 1960? 1961? why Wilmington?), but I do remember being there. The woman in the dirty crepe-de-Chine wrapper had come down from her room for a beer, and the bartender had heard before the reason why George Sharp and she were separated today. "Sure," he said, and went on mopping the floor. "You told me." At the other end of the bar is a girl. She is talking, pointedly, not to the man beside her but to a cat lying in the triangle of sunlight cast through the open door. She is wearing a plaid silk dress from Peck & Peck, and the hem is coming down.

Here is what it is: the girl has been on the Eastern Shore, and now she is going back to the city, leaving the man beside her, and all she can see ahead are the viscous summer sidewalks and the 3 A.M. long-distance calls that will make her lie awake and then sleep drugged through all the steaming mornings left in August (1960? 1961?). Because she must go directly from the train to lunch in New York, she wishes that she had a safety pin for the hem of the plaid silk dress, and she also wishes that she could forget about the hem and the lunch and stay in the cool bar that smells of disinfectant and malt and make friends with the woman in the crepe-de-Chine wrapper. She is afflicted by a little self-pity, and she wants to compare Estelles. That is what that was all about.

Why did I write it down? In order to remember, of course, but exactly what was it I wanted to remember? How much of it actually happened? Did any of it? Why do I keep a notebook at all? It is easy to deceive oneself on all those scores. The impulse to write things down is a peculiarly compulsive one, inexplicable to those who do not share it, useful only accidentally, only secondarily, in the way that any compulsion tries to justify itself. I suppose that it begins or does not begin in the cradle. Although I have felt compelled to write things down since I was five years old, I doubt that my daughter ever will, for she is a singularly blessed and accepting child, delighted with life exactly as life presents itself to her, unafraid to go to sleep and unafraid to wake up. Keepers of private notebooks are a different breed altogether, lonely and resistant rearrangers of things, anxious malcontents, children afflicted apparently at birth with some presentiment of loss.

My first notebook was a Big Five tablet, given to me by my mother with the sensible suggestion that I stop whining and learn to amuse myself by writing down my thoughts. She returned the tablet to me a few years ago; the first entry is an account of a woman who believed herself to be freezing to death in the Arctic night, only to find, when day broke, that she had stumbled onto the Sahara Desert, where she would die of the heat before lunch. I have no idea what turn of a five-year-old's mind could have prompted so insistently "ironic" and exotic a story, but it does reveal a certain predilection for the extreme which has dogged me into adult life; perhaps if I were analytically inclined I would find it a truer story than any I might have told about Donald Johnson's birthday party or the day my cousin Brenda put Kitty Litter in the aquarium.

So the point of my keeping a notebook has never been, nor is it now, to have an accurate factual record of what I have been doing or thinking. That would be a different impulse entirely, an instinct for reality which I sometimes envy but do not possess. At no point have I ever been able successfully to keep a diary; my approach to daily life ranges from the grossly negligent to the merely absent, and on those few occasions when I have tried dutifully to record a day's events, boredom has so overcome me that the results are mysterious at best. What is this business about "shopping, typing piece, dinner with E, depressed"? Shopping for what? Typing what piece? Who is E? Was this "E" depressed, or was I depressed? Who cares?

In fact I have abandoned altogether that kind of pointless entry; instead I tell what some would call lies. "That's simply not true," the members of my family frequently tell me when they come up against my memory of a shared event. "The party was *not* for you, the spider was *not* a black widow, *it wasn't that way at all.*" Very likely they are right, for not only have I always had trouble distinguishing between what happened and what merely might have happened, but I remain unconvinced that the distinction, for my purposes, matters. The cracked crab that I recall having for lunch the day my father came home from Detroit in 1945 must certainly be embroidery, worked into the day's pattern to lend verisimilitude; I was ten years old and would not now remember the cracked crab. The day's events did not turn on cracked crab. And yet it is precisely that fictitious crab that makes me see the afternoon all over again, a home movie run all too often, the father bearing gifts, the child weeping, an exercise in family love and guilt. Or that is what it was to me. Similarly, perhaps it never did snow that August in Vermont; perhaps there never were flurries in the night wind, and maybe no one else felt the ground hardening and summer already dead even as we pretended to bask in it, but that was how it felt to me, and it might as well have snowed, could have snowed, did snow.

How it felt to me: that is getting closer to the truth about a notebook. I sometimes delude myself about why I keep a notebook, imagine that some thrifty virtue derives from preserving everything observed. See enough and write it down, I tell myself, and then some morning when the world seems drained of wonder, some day when I am only going through the motions of doing what I am supposed to do, which is write — on that bankrupt morning I will simply open my notebook and there it will all be, a forgotten account with accumulated interest, paid passage back to the world out there: dialogue overheard in hotels and elevators and at the hat-check counter in Pavillon (one middle-aged man shows his hat check to another and says, "That's my old football number"); impressions of Bettina Aptheker and Benjamin Sonnenberg and Teddy ("Mr. Acapulco") Stauffer; careful *aperçus* about tennis bums and failed fashion models and Greek shipping heiresses, one of whom taught me a significant lesson (a lesson I could have learned from F. Scott Fitzgerald, but perhaps we all must meet the very rich for ourselves) by asking, when I arrived to interview her in her orchid-filled sitting room on the second day of a paralyzing New York blizzard, whether it was snowing outside.

I imagine, in other words, that the notebook is about other people. But of course it is not. I have no real business with what one stranger said to another at the hat-check counter in Pavillon; in fact I suspect that the line "That's my old football number" touched not my own imagination at all, but merely some memory of something once read, probably "The Eighty-Yard Run." Nor is my concern with a woman in a dirty crepe-de-Chine wrapper in a

Wilmington bar. My stake is always, of course, in the unmentioned girl in the plaid silk dress. *Remember what it was to be me:* that is always the point.

It is a difficult point to admit. We are brought up in the ethic that oth-   10
ers, any others, all others, are by definition more interesting than ourselves;
taught to be diffident, just this side of self-effacing. ("You're the least
important person in the room and don't forget it," Jessica Mitford's gov-
erness would hiss in her ear on the advent of any social occasion; I copied
that into my notebook because it is only recently that I have been able to
enter a room without hearing some such phrase in my inner ear.) Only the
very young and the very old may recount their dreams at breakfast, dwell
upon self, interrupt with memories of beach picnics and favorite Liberty
lawn dresses and the rainbow trout in a creek near Colorado Springs. The
rest of us are expected, rightly, to affect absorption in other people's
favorite dresses, other people's trout.

And so we do. But our notebooks give us away, for however dutifully we
record what we see around us, the common denominator of all we see is
always, transparently, shamelessly, the implacable "I." We are not talking here
about the kind of notebook that is patently for public consumption, a structural conceit for binding together a series of graceful *pensées;* we are talking
about something private, about bits of the mind's string too short to use, an
indiscriminate and erratic assemblage with meaning only for its maker.

And sometimes even the maker has difficulty with the meaning. There
does not seem to be, for example, any point in my knowing for the rest of
my life that, during 1964, 720 tons of soot fell on every square mile of New
York City, yet there it is in my notebook, labeled "FACT." Nor do I really
need to remember that Ambrose Bierce liked to spell Leland Stanford's
name "£eland $tanford" or that "smart women almost always wear black
in Cuba," a fashion hint without much potential for practical application.
And does not the relevance of these notes seem marginal at best?:

> In the basement museum of the Inyo County Courthouse in
> Independence, California, sign pinned to a mandarin coat: "This
> MANDARIN COAT was often worn by Mrs. Minnie S. Brooks when
> giving lectures on her TEAPOT COLLECTION."

> Redhead getting out of car in front of Beverly Wilshire Hotel, chin-
> chilla stole, Vuitton bags with tags reading:

> > MRS LOU FOX
> > HOTEL SAHARA
> > VEGAS

Well, perhaps not entirely marginal. As a matter of fact, Mrs. Minnie
S. Brooks and her MANDARIN COAT pull me back into my own childhood,
for although I never knew Mrs. Brooks and did not visit Inyo County until

I was thirty, I grew up in just such a world, in houses cluttered with Indian relics and bits of gold ore and ambergris and the souvenirs my Aunt Mercy Farnsworth brought back from the Orient. It is a long way from that world to Mrs. Lou Fox's world, where we all live now, and is it not just as well to remember that? Might not Mrs. Minnie S. Brooks help me to remember what I am? Might not Mrs. Lou Fox help me to remember what I am not?

But sometimes the point is harder to discern. What exactly did I have in mind when I noted down that it cost the father of someone I know $650 a month to light the place on the Hudson in which he lived before the Crash? What use was I planning to make of this line by Jimmy Hoffa: "I may have my faults, but being wrong ain't one of them"? And although I think it interesting to know where the girls who travel with the Syndicate have their hair done when they find themselves on the West Coast, will I ever make suitable use of it? Might I not be better off just passing it on to John O'Hara? What is a recipe for sauerkraut doing in my notebook? What kind of magpie keeps this notebook? "*He was born the night the Titanic went down.*" That seems a nice enough line, and I even recall who said it, but is it not really a better line in life than it could ever be in fiction?

But of course that is exactly it: not that I should ever use the line, but that   15
I should remember the woman who said it and the afternoon I heard it. We were on her terrace by the sea, and we were finishing the wine left from lunch, trying to get what sun there was, a California winter sun. The woman whose husband was born the night the *Titanic* went down wanted to rent her house, wanted to go back to her children in Paris. I remember wishing that I could afford the house, which cost $1,000 a month. "Someday you will," she said lazily. "Someday it all comes." There in the sun on her terrace it seemed easy to believe in someday, but later I had a low-grade afternoon hangover and ran over a black snake on the way to the supermarket and was flooded with inexplicable fear when I heard the checkout clerk explaining to the man ahead of me why she was finally divorcing her husband. "He left me no choice," she said over and over as she punched the register. "He has a little seven-month-old baby by her, he left me no choice." I would like to believe that my dread then was for the human condition, but of course it was for me, because I wanted a baby and did not then have one and because I wanted to own the house that cost $1,000 a month to rent and because I had a hangover.

It all comes back. Perhaps it is difficult to see the value in having one's self back in that kind of mood, but I do see it; I think we are well advised to keep on nodding terms with the people we used to be, whether we find them attractive company or not. Otherwise they turn up unannounced and surprise us, come hammering on the mind's door at 4 A.M. of a bad night and demand to know who deserted them, who betrayed them, who is going to make amends. We forget all too soon the things we thought we could never forget. We forget the loves and the betrayals alike, forget what we whispered and what we screamed, forget who we were. I have already lost touch with a couple of people I used to be; one of them, a seventeen-year-old, presents little threat, although it would be of some interest to me to know again what it feels like to sit on a river levee drinking vodka-and-orange-juice and listening to Les Paul and Mary Ford and their echoes sing "How High the Moon" on the car radio. (You see I still have the scenes, but I no longer perceive myself among those present, no longer could even improvise the dialogue.) The other one, a twenty-three-year-old, bothers me more. She was always a good deal of trouble, and I suspect she will reappear when I least want to see her, skirts too long, shy to the point of aggravation, always the injured party, full of recriminations and little hurts and stories I do not want to hear again, at once saddening me and angering me with her vulnerability and ignorance, an apparition all the more insistent for being so long banished.

It is a good idea, then, to keep in touch, and I suppose that keeping in touch is what notebooks are all about. And we are all on our own when it comes to keeping those lines open to ourselves: your notebook will never help me, nor mine you. *"So what's new in the whiskey business?"* What could that possibly mean to you? To me it means a blonde in a Pucci bathing suit sitting with a couple of fat men by the pool at the Beverly Hills Hotel. Another man approaches, and they all regard one another in silence for a while. "So what's new in the whiskey business?" one of the fat men finally says by way of welcome, and the blonde stands up, arches one foot and dips it in the pool, looking all the while at the cabaña where Baby Pignatari is talking on the telephone. That is all there is to that, except that several years later I saw the blonde coming out of Saks Fifth Avenue in New York with her California complexion and a voluminous mink coat. In the harsh wind that day she looked old and irrevocably tired to me, and even the skins in the mink coat were not worked the way they were doing them that year, not the way she would have wanted them done, and there is the point of the story. For a while after that I did not like to look in the mirror, and my eyes would skim the newspapers and pick out only the deaths, the cancer victims, the premature coronaries, the suicides, and I stopped riding the Lexington Avenue IRT because I noticed for the first time that all the strangers I had seen for years—the man with the seeing-eye dog, the spinster who read the classified pages every day, the fat girl who always got off with me at Grand Central—looked older than they once had.

It all comes back. Even that recipe for sauerkraut: even that brings it back. I was on Fire Island when I first made that sauerkraut, and it was raining, and we drank a lot of bourbon and ate the sauerkraut and went to bed at ten, and I listened to the rain and the Atlantic and felt safe. I made the sauerkraut again last night and it did not make me feel any safer, but that is, as they say, another story.

QUESTIONS

1. The first paragraphs of Didion's essay present a pattern that she replicates throughout the remainder of the piece—the transcription of a passage

from her notebook, an elaboration, and an attempt to explain her original motives for taking note of this observation. She thereby reproduces her own curiosity about her writing. How many times does she quote from her notebook, and how do her responses differ (in length, emphasis, quality)? How do the responses evolve as the essay progresses?

2. Didion offers a number of tentative answers to her main question, "Why do I keep a notebook at all?" (paragraph 4). Make a list of these responses and their revisions throughout the essay. Why doesn't she simply explain at the beginning "what notebooks are all about"(paragraph 17) rather than waiting until the last paragraphs? Do you find this way of explaining to be effective? Explain why or why not.

3. Consider the title of the essay, "On Keeping a Notebook." Select a phrase from the essay that you think would serve as a better title—for example, "How it felt to me," or "the truth about a notebook" (paragraph 8)—or make up your own. How does the title of an essay (yours included) create expectations about what will be explained in the body of the text?

4. How does Didion distinguish between a diary and a notebook? Does that distinction affect her sense of the difference "between what happened and what merely might have happened" (paragraph 7)? Is Didion concerned with truth in her notebook writing?

5. Didion's style feels somewhat like a conversation with herself. Note how she begins some sentences informally with words like *so, or, and*, and *well*. In effect, she's working through a dialogue between her present and her past. Write an essay in which you quote your own writing from a different period (a notebook, journal, or even writing assignment from a previous year), and then reflect on why this was important to you at the time. What does it teach you about keeping in touch with your past selves?

6. What is the point of notebooks for you? Begin an essay with a statement from Didion with which you disagree, and then proceed to discuss what you suggest as an alternative reason for writing.

MAKING CONNECTIONS

Didion writes, "I think we are well advised to keep on nodding terms with the people we used to be, whether we find them attractive company or not" (paragraph 16). Compare how Didion, Maya Angelou in "Graduation" (p. 31), Alice Walker in "Beauty: When the Other Dancer Is the Self" (p. 42), and Nancy Mairs in "Carnal Acts" (p. 367) view events from their youth and how they connect their youthful experiences to adult knowledge.

URBAN LEGENDS
"The Boyfriend's Death"

Jan Harold Brunvand

*Trained in the study of folklore, Jan Harold Brunvand (b. 1933)
has become a leading collector and interpreter of contemporary
legends. These "urban legends" are stories told around campfires
and in college dormitories, often as true experiences that happened
to somebody other than the teller of the tale. For many years a professor at the University of Utah, Brunvand has been the editor of
the* Journal of American Folklore *and* American Folklore: An
Encyclopedia *(1996), and is the author of the standard introduction to the field,* The Study of American Folklore: An Introduction,
*fourth edition (1997). The following selection is taken from the
first of his several collections of urban legends,* The Vanishing
Hitchhiker: American Urban Legends and Their Meanings *(1981).
Here Brunvand defines* urban legend, *gives one striking example,
and offers some explanations about how and why such stories
flourish even in the midst of a highly technologized society. The
selection as reprinted is complete, except for the deletion of a few
brief references to other discussions elsewhere in Brunvand's book.*

We are not aware of our own folklore any more than we are of the
grammatical rules of our language. When we follow the ancient practice of
informally transmitting "lore"—wisdom, knowledge, or accepted modes
of behavior—by word of mouth and customary example from person to
person, we do not concentrate on the form or content of our folklore;
instead, we simply listen to information that others tell us and then pass it
on—more or less accurately—to other listeners. In this stream of unself-
conscious oral tradition the information that acquires a clear story line is
called *narrative folklore*, and those stories alleged to be true are *legends*.
This, in broad summary, is the typical process of legend formation and
transmission as it has existed from time immemorial and continues to operate today. It works about the same way whether the legendary plot concerns
a dragon in a cave or a mouse in a Coke bottle.

It might seem unlikely that legends—*urban* legends at that—would
continue to be created in an age of widespread literacy, rapid mass communications, and restless travel. While our pioneer ancestors may have
had to rely heavily on oral traditions to pass the news along about changing events and frontier dangers, surely we no longer need mere "folk"
reports of what's happening, with all their tendencies to distort the facts.

A moment's reflection, however, reminds us of the many weird, fascinating, but unverified rumors and tales that so frequently come to our ears — killers and madmen on the loose, shocking or funny personal experiences, unsafe manufactured products, and many other unexplained mysteries of daily life. Sometimes we encounter different oral versions of such stories, and on occasion we may read about similar events in newspapers or magazines; but seldom do we find, or even seek after, reliable documentation. The lack of verification in no way diminishes the appeal urban legends have for us. We enjoy them merely as stories, and we tend at least to half-believe them as possibly accurate reports. And the legends we tell, as with any folklore, reflect many of the hopes, fears, and anxieties of our time. In short, legends are definitely part of our modern folklore — legends which are as traditional, variable, and functional as those of the past.

Folklore study consists of collecting, classifying, and interpreting in their full cultural context the many products of everyday human interaction that have acquired a somewhat stable underlying form and that are passed traditionally from person to person, group to group, and generation to generation. Legend study is a most revealing area of such research because the stories that people believe to be true hold an important place in their worldview. "If it's true, it's important" is an axiom to be trusted, whether or not the lore really *is* true or not. Simply becoming aware of this modern folklore which we all possess to some degree is a revelation in itself, but going beyond this to compare the tales, isolate their consistent themes, and relate them to the rest of the culture can yield rich insights into the state of our current civilization. . . .

Urban Legends as Folklore

Folklore subsists on oral tradition, but not all oral communication is folklore. The vast amounts of human interchange, from casual daily conversations to formal discussions in business or industry, law, or teaching, rarely constitute straight oral folklore. However, all such "communicative events" (as scholars dub them) are punctuated routinely by various units of traditional material that are memorable, repeatable, and that fit recurring social situations well enough to serve in place of original remarks. "Tradition" is the key idea that links together such utterances as nicknames, proverbs, greeting and leave-taking formulas, wisecracks, anecdotes, and jokes as "folklore"; indeed, these are a few of the best known "conversational genres" of American folklore. Longer and more complex folk forms — fairy tales, epics, myths, legends, or ballads, for example — may thrive only in certain special situations of oral transmission. All true folklore ultimately depends upon continued oral dissemination, usually within fairly homogeneous "folk groups," and upon the retention through time of internal patterns and motifs that become traditional in the oral exchanges. The corollary of this rule of stability in oral tradition is that all items of folklore, while retaining a fixed central core, are constantly changing as they are transmitted, so as to create countless "variants" differing in length, detail, style, and performance technique. Folklore, in short, consists of oral tradition in variants.

Urban legends belong to the subclass of folk narratives, legends, that—unlike fairy tales—are believed, or at least believable, and that—unlike myths—are set in the recent past and involve normal human beings rather than ancient gods or demigods. Legends are folk history, or rather quasi-history. As with any folk legends, urban legends gain credibility from specific details of time and place or from references to source authorities. For instance, a popular western pioneer legend often begins something like, "My great-grandmother had this strange experience when she was a young girl on a wagon train going through Wyoming when an Indian chief wanted to adopt her. . . ." Even though hundreds of different great-grandmothers are supposed to have had the same doubtful experience (being desired by the chief because of her beautiful long blond hair), the fact seldom reaches legend-tellers; if it does, they assume that the family lore has indeed spread far and wide. This particular popular tradition, known as "Goldilocks on the Oregon Trail," interests folklorists because of the racist implications of a dark Indian savage coveting a fair young civilized woman—this legend is familiar in the *white* folklore only—and it is of little concern that the story seems to be entirely apocryphal.

In the world of modern urban legends there is usually no geographical or generational gap between teller and event. The story is *true;* it really occurred, and recently, and always to someone else who is quite close to the narrator, or at least "a friend of a friend." Urban legends are told both in the course of casual conversations and in such special situations as campfires, slumber parties, and college dormitory bull sessions. The legends' physical settings are often close by, real, and sometimes even locally renowned for other such happenings. Though the characters in the stories are usually nameless, they are true-to-life examples of the kind of people the narrators and their audience know firsthand.

One of the great mysteries of folklore research is where oral traditions originate and who invents them. One might expect that at least in modern folklore we could come up with answers to such questions, but this is seldom, if ever, the case. . . .

The Performance of Legends

Whatever the origins of urban legends, their dissemination is no mystery. The tales have traveled far and wide, and have been told and retold from person to person in the same manner that myths, fairy tales, or ballads spread in earlier cultures, with the important difference that today's legends are also disseminated by the mass media. Groups of age-mates, especially adolescents, are one important American legend channel, but other paths of transmission are among office workers and club members, as well as among religious, recreational, and regional groups. Some individuals make a point of learning every recent rumor or tale, and they can enliven any coffee break, party, or trip with the latest supposed "news." The telling of one story inspires other people to share what they have read or heard, and in a short time a lively exchange of details occurs and perhaps new variants are created.

Tellers of these legends, of course, are seldom aware of their roles as "performers of folklore." The conscious purpose of this kind of storytelling is to convey a true event, and only incidentally to entertain an audience. Nevertheless, the speaker's demeanor is carefully orchestrated, and his or her delivery is low-key and soft-sell. With subtle gestures, eye movements, and vocal inflections the stories are made dramatic, pointed, and suspenseful. But, just as with jokes, some can tell them and some can't. Passive tellers of urban legends may just report them as odd rumors, but the more active legend tellers re-create them as dramatic stories of suspense and, perhaps, humor.

"The Boyfriend's Death"

With all these points in mind — folklore's subject-matter, style, and oral performance — consider this typical version of a well-known urban legend that folklorists have named "The Boyfriend's Death," collected in 1964 (the earliest documented instance of the story) by folklorist Daniel R. Barnes from an eighteen-year-old freshman at the University of Kansas. The usual tellers of the story are adolescents, and the normal setting for the narration is a college dormitory room with fellow students sprawled on the furniture and floors. 10

> This happened just a few years ago out on the road that turns off highway 59 by the Holiday Inn. This couple were parked under a tree out on this road. Well, it got to be time for the girl to be back at the dorm, so she told her boyfriend that they should start back. But the car wouldn't start, so he told her to lock herself in the car and he would go down to the Holiday Inn and call for help. Well, he didn't come back and he didn't come back, and pretty soon she started hearing a scratching noise on the roof of the car. "Scratch, scratch . . . scratch, scratch." She got scareder and scareder, but he didn't come back. Finally, when it was almost daylight, some people came along and stopped and helped her out of the car, and she looked up and there was her boyfriend hanging from the tree, and his feet were scraping against the roof of the car. This is why the road is called "Hangman's Road."

Here is a story that has traveled rapidly to reach nationwide oral circulation, in the process becoming structured in the typical manner of folk narratives. The traditional and fairly stable elements are the parked couple, the abandoned girl, the mysterious scratching (sometimes joined by a dripping sound and ghostly shadows on the windshield), the daybreak rescue, and the horrible climax. Variable traits are the precise location, the reason for her abandonment, the nature of the rescuers, murder details, and the concluding placename explanation. While "The Boyfriend's Death" seems to have captured teenagers' imaginations as a separate legend only since the early 1960s, it is clearly related to at least two older yarns, "The Hook" and "The Roommate's Death." All three legends have been widely collected by American folklorists, although only scattered examples have been published, mostly in professional journals. Examination of some of these variations helps to make clear the status of the story as folklore and its possible meanings.

At Indiana University, a leading American center of folklore research, folk-narrative specialist Linda Dégh and her students have gathered voluminous data on urban legends, especially those popular with adolescents. Dégh's preliminary published report on "The Boyfriend's Death" concerned nineteen texts collected from IU students from 1964 to 1968. Several storytellers had heard it in high school, often at parties; others had picked it up in college dormitories or elsewhere on campus. Several students expressed some belief in the legend, supposing either that it had happened in their own hometowns, or possibly in other states, once as far distant as "a remote part of Alabama." One informant reported that "she had been sworn to that the incident actually happened," but another, who had heard some variations of the tale, felt that "it seemed too horrible to be true." Some versions had incorporated motifs from other popular teenage horror legends or local ghost stories. . . .

One of the Indiana texts, told in the state of Washington, localizes the story there near Moses Lake, "in the country on a road that leads to a dead-end right under a big weeping willow tree . . . about four or five miles from town." As in most American versions of the story, these specific local touches make believable what is essentially a traveling legend. In a detail familiar from other variants of "The Boyfriend's Death," the body—now decapitated—is left hanging upside down from a branch of the willow tree with the fingernails scraping the top of the car. Another version studied by the Indiana researcher is somewhat aberrant, perhaps because the student was told the story by a friend's parents who claimed that "it happened a long time ago, probably thirty or forty years." Here a murderer is introduced, a "crazy old lady" on whose property the couple has parked. The victim this time is skinned rather than decapitated, and his head scrapes the car as the corpse swings to and fro in the breezy night.

A developing motif in "The Boyfriend's Death" is the character and role of the rescuers, who in the 1964 Kansas version are merely "some people." The standard identification later becomes "the police," authority figures whose presence lends further credence to the story. They are either called by the missing teenagers' parents, or simply appear on the scene in the morning to check the car. In a 1969 variant from Leonardtown, Maryland, the police give a warning, "Miss, please get out of the car and walk to the police car with us, but don't look back." . . . In a version from Texas collected in 1971, set "at this lake somewhere way out in nowhere," a policeman gets an even longer line: "Young lady, we want you to get out of the car and come with us. Whatever you do, don't turn, don't turn around, just keep walking, just keep going straight and don't look back at the car." The more detailed the police instructions are, the more plausible the tale seems to become. Of course the standard rule of folk-narrative plot development now applies: the taboo must be broken (or the "interdiction violated" as some scholars put it). The girl always *does* look back, like Orpheus in the underworld, and in a number of versions her hair turns white from the shock of what she sees, as in a dozen other American legends.

In a Canadian version of "The Boyfriend's Death," told by a fourteen-year-old boy from Willowdale, Ontario, in 1973, the words of the policemen are merely summarized, but the opening scene of the legend is developed more fully, with several special details, including . . . a warning heard on the car radio. The girl's behavior when left behind is also described in more detail.   15

> A guy and his girlfriend are on the way to a party when their car starts to give them some trouble. At that same time they catch a news flash on the radio warning all people in the area that a lunatic killer has escaped from a local criminal asylum. The girl becomes very upset and at that point the car stalls completely on the highway. The boyfriend gets out and tinkers around with the engine but can't get the car to start again. He decides that he is going to have to walk on up the road to a gas station and get a tow truck but wants his girlfriend to stay behind in the car. She is frightened and pleads with him to take her, but he says that she'll be safe on the floor of the car covered with a blanket so that anyone passing will think it is an abandoned car and not bother her. Besides he can sprint along the road and get back more quickly than if she comes with him in her high-heeled shoes and evening dress. She finally agrees and he tells her not to come out unless she hears his signal of three knocks on the window. . . .

She does hear knocks on the car, but they continue eerily beyond three; the sound is later explained as the shoes of the boyfriend's corpse bumping the car as the body swings from a limb above the car.

The style in which oral narratives are told deserves attention, for the live telling that is dramatic, fluid, and often quite gripping in actual folk performance before a sympathetic audience may seem stiff, repetitious, and awkward on the printed page. Lacking in all our examples of "The Boyfriend's Death" is the essential ingredient of immediate context—the setting of the legend-telling, the storyteller's vocal and facial expression and

gestures, the audience's reaction, and the texts of other similar tales narrated at the same session. Several of the informants explained that the story
was told to them in spooky situations, late at night, near a cemetery, out
camping, or even "while on a hayride or out parked," occasionally near the
site of the supposed murder. Some students refer to such macabre legends,
therefore, as "scary stories," "screamers," or "horrors."

A widely-distributed folk legend of this kind as it travels in oral tradition acquires a good deal of its credibility and effect from the localized
details inserted by individual tellers. The highway and motel identification
in the Kansas text are good examples of this, and in a New Orleans version,
"The Boyfriend's Death" is absorbed into a local teenage tradition about
"The Grunch"—a half-sheep, half-human monster that haunts specific
local sites. One teenager there reported, "A man and lady went out by the
lake and in the morning they found 'em hanging upside down on a tree and
they said grunches did it." Finally, rumors or news stories about missing
persons or violent crimes (as mentioned in the Canadian version) can merge
with urban legends, helping to support their air of truth, or giving them
renewed circulation after a period of less frequent occurrence.

Even the bare printed texts retain some earmarks of effective oral tradition. Witness in the Kansas text the artful use of repetition (typical of folk
narrative style): "Well, he didn't come back and he didn't come
back . . . but he didn't come back." The repeated use of "well" and the
building of lengthy sentences with "and" are other hallmarks of oral style
which give the narrator complete control over his performance, tending to
squeeze out interruptions or prevent lapses in attention among the listeners.
The scene that is set for the incident—lonely road, night, a tree looming
over the car, out of gas—and the sound effects—scratches or bumps on the
car—contribute to the style, as does the dramatic part played by the policeman and the abrupt ending line: "She looked back, and she saw. . . !" Since
the typical narrators and auditors of "The Boyfriend's Death" themselves
like to "park" and may have been alarmed by rumors, strange sights and
noises, or automobile emergencies (all intensified in their effects by the
audience's knowing other parking legends), the abrupt, unresolved ending
leaves open the possibilities of what "really happened."

Urban Legends as Cultural Symbols

Legends can survive in our culture as living narrative folklore if they
contain three essential elements: a strong basic story-appeal, a foundation
in actual belief, and a meaningful message or "moral." That is, popular stories like "The Boyfriend's Death" are not only engrossing tales, but also
"true," or at least so people think, and they teach valuable lessons. Jokes
are a living part of oral tradition, despite being fictional and often silly,
because of their humor, brevity, and snappy punch lines, but legends are by
nature longer, slower, and more serious. Since more effort is needed to tell

and appreciate a legend than a joke, it needs more than just verbal art to carry it along. Jokes have significant "messages" too, but these tend to be disguised or implied. People tell jokes primarily for amusement, and they seldom sense their underlying themes. In legends the primary messages are quite clear and straightforward; often they take the form of explicit warnings or good examples of "poetic justice." Secondary messages in urban legends tend to be suggested metaphorically or symbolically; these may provide deeper criticisms of human behavior or social condition.

People still tell legends, therefore, and other folk take time to listen to them, not only because of their inherent plot interest but because they seem to convey true, worthwhile, and relevant information, albeit partly in a subconscious mode. In other words, such stories are "news" presented to us in an attractive way, with hints of larger meanings. Without this multiple appeal few legends would get a hearing in the modern world, so filled with other distractions. Legends survive by being as lively and "factual" as the television evening news, and, like the daily news broadcasts, they tend to concern deaths, injuries, kidnappings, tragedies, and scandals. Apparently the basic human need for meaningful personal contact cannot be entirely replaced by the mass media and popular culture. A portion of our interest in what is occurring in the world must be filled by some face-to-face reports from other human beings.   20

On a literal level a story like "The Boyfriend's Death" simply warns young people to avoid situations in which they may be endangered, but at a more symbolic level the story reveals society's broader fears of people, especially women and the young, being alone and among strangers in the darkened world outside the security of their own home or car. Note that the young woman in the story (characterized by "her high-heeled shoes and evening dress") is shown as especially helpless and passive, cowering under the blanket in the car until she is rescued by men. Such themes recur in various forms in many other urban legends. . . .

In order to be retained in a culture, any form of folklore must fill some genuine need, whether this be the need for an entertaining escape from reality, or a desire to validate by anecdotal examples some of the culture's ideals and institutions. For legends in general, a major function has always been the attempt to explain unusual and supernatural happenings in the natural world. To some degree this remains a purpose for urban legends, but their more common role nowadays seems to be to show that the prosaic contemporary scene is capable of producing shocking or amazing occurrences which may actually have happened to friends or to near-acquaintances but which are nevertheless explainable in some reasonably logical terms. On the one hand we want our factual lore to inspire awe, and at the same time we wish to have the most fantastic tales include at least the hint of a rational explanation and perhaps even a conclusion. Thus an escaped lunatic, a possibly *real* character, not a fantastic invader from outer space or Frankenstein's monster, is said to be responsible for the atrocities committed in the gruesome tales that teenagers tell. As sometimes happens in real life, the car radio gives warning, and the police get the situation back under control. (The policemen's role, in fact, becomes larger and more commanding as the story grows in oral tradition.) Only when the young lovers are still alone and scared are they vulnerable, but society's adults and guardians come to their rescue presently.

In common with brief unverified reports ("rumors"), to which they are often closely related, urban legends gratify our desire to know about and to try to understand bizarre, frightening, and potentially dangerous or embarrassing events that *may* have happened. (In rumors and legends there is always some element of doubt concerning where and when these things *did* occur.) These floating stories appeal to our morbid curiosity and satisfy our sensation-seeking minds that demand gratification through frequent infusions of new information, "sanitized" somewhat by the positive messages. Informal rumors and stories fill in the gaps left by professional news reporting, and these marvelous, though generally false, "true" tales may be said to be carrying the folk-news—along with some editorial matter—from person to person even in today's technological world.

QUESTIONS

1. In your own words, define *urban legend.*
2. Had you ever heard the story of "The Boyfriend's Death" before you read it here? Did you believe it was true? Can you remember the circumstances in which you first heard this legend (or a similar one)? Describe your first encounter with the tale. How does your experience compare with those described by Brunvand?
3. Below is a list of other tales collected by Brunvand. Do you know any stories that might correspond to these titles?

   The Vanishing Hitchhiker
   The Mexican Pet
   The Baby-Sitter and the Man Upstairs
   The Microwaved Pet
   The Toothbrush Story
   Alligators in the Sewers
   The Nude in the RV
   The Kidney Heist

   Briefly describe the stories you have heard. Compare the various versions produced by members of the class. What are the variables in the tale, and what seem to be the common features?
4. Do you know a story that sounds like an urban legend but is true? Can you prove it?
5. Select an urban legend that you have recently heard. Write down the best version of it that you can, and analyze what you have written as an urban legend. That is, explain the features that mark it as an urban legend, and discuss the elements that make it interesting or appealing to you.

6. Can you remember someone who told you something as a "true" story that you now recognize is an urban legend? Write an essay in which you describe that person, report on the legend that he or she told you, and explain to that person that the story he or she told is not true but is an urban legend. If you think that your explanation would not convince the person in question, try to explain why this is so. Describe the resistance you might encounter, and indicate how you might modify your explanation to make it more persuasive.

MAKING CONNECTIONS

1. Several of the pieces in "Reporting" deal with events that could provide the material for an urban legend. Richard Selzer's "The Discus Thrower" (p. 263) and Michael Brown's "Love Canal and the Poisoning of America" (p. 271) are examples. What elements of these stories qualify them as urban legends? In what ways do they not qualify as urban legends?
2. Rewrite "The Discus Thrower" (p. 263) or "Love Canal and the Poisoning of America" (p. 271) as an urban legend. Make any changes you find necessary to make it read like an urban legend. Then write a few paragraphs of explanation, discussing the changes that you made and why you made them.

WHAT HIGH SCHOOL IS

Theodore R. Sizer

Born in New Haven, Connecticut, in 1932, and educated at Yale and Harvard, Theodore R. Sizer has been headmaster at Phillips Academy in Andover, Massachusetts, dean of the Graduate School of Education at Harvard, and chair of the Education Department at Brown. He is the author of several influential books on educational reform and American secondary schools, most recently Horace's Hope: What Works for the American High School *(1996), and* The Students Are Watching: Schools and the Moral Contract *(1999, with Nancy Faust Sizer). The following selection is a chapter from an earlier book,* Horace's Compromise: The Dilemma of the American High School *(1984), which reports the results of a study of American high schools sponsored by the National Association of Independent Schools.*

Mark, sixteen and a genial eleventh-grader, rides a bus to Franklin High School, arriving at 7:25. It is an Assembly Day, so the schedule is adapted to allow for a meeting of the entire school. He hangs out with his friends, first outside school and then inside, by his locker. He carries a pile of textbooks and notebooks; in all, it weighs eight and a half pounds.

From 7:30 to 8:19, with nineteen other students, he is in Room 304 for English class. The Shakespeare play being read this year by the eleventh grade is *Romeo and Juliet*. The teacher, Ms. Viola, has various students in turn take parts and read out loud. Periodically, she interrupts the (usually halting) recitations to ask whether the thread of the conversation in the play is clear. Mark is entertained by the stumbling readings of some of his classmates. He hopes he will not be asked to be Romeo, particularly if his current steady, Sally, is Juliet. There is a good deal of giggling in class, and much attention paid to who may be called on next. Ms. Viola reminds the class of a test on this part of the play to be given next week.

The bell rings at 8:19. Mark goes to the boys' room, where he sees a classmate who he thinks is a wimp but who constantly tries to be a buddy. Mark avoids the leech by rushing off. On the way, he notices two boys engaged in some sort of transaction, probably over marijuana. He pays them no attention. 8:24. Typing class. The rows of desks that embrace big office machines are almost filled before the bell. Mark is uncomfortable here: typing class is girl country. The teacher constantly threatens what to Mark is a humiliatingly female future: "Your employer won't like these erasures." The minutes during the period are spent copying a letter from a handbook onto business stationery. Mark struggles to keep from looking at his work; the teacher wants him to watch only the material from which he is copying. Mark is frustrated, uncomfortable, and scared that he will not complete his letter by the class's end, which would be embarrassing.

Nine tenths of the students present at school that day are assembled in the auditorium by the 9:18 bell. The dilatory tenth still stumble in, running down aisles. Annoyed class deans try to get the mob settled. The curtains part; the program is a concert by a student rock group. Their electronic gear flashes under the lights, and the five boys and one girl in the group work hard at being casual. Their movements on stage are studiously at three-quarter time, and they chat with one another as though the tumultuous screaming of their schoolmates were totally inaudible. The girl balances on a stool; the boys crank up the music. It is very soft rock, the sanitized lyrics surely cleared with the assistant principal. The girl sings, holding the mike close to her mouth, but can scarcely be heard. Her light voice is tentative, and the lyrics indecipherable. The guitars, amplified, are tuneful, however, and the drums are played with energy.

The students around Mark—all juniors, since they are seated by   5
class—alternately slouch in their upholstered, hinged seats, talking to one another, or sit forward, leaning on the chair backs in front of them, watching the band. A boy near Mark shouts noisily at the microphone-fondling singer, "Bite it . . . ohhh," and the area around Mark explodes in vulgar male laughter, but quickly subsides. A teacher walks down the aisle. Songs continue, to great applause. Assembly is over at 9:46, two minutes early.

9:53 and biology class. Mark was at a different high school last year and did not take this course there as a tenth-grader. He is in it now, and all but one of his classmates are a year younger than he. He sits on the side, not taking part in the chatter that goes on after the bell. At 9:57, the public address system goes on, with the announcements of the day. After a few words from the principal ("Here's today's cheers and jeers . . ." with a cheer for the winning basketball team and a jeer for the spectators who made a ruckus at the gymnasium), the task is taken over by officers of ASB (Associated Student Bodies). There is an appeal for "bat bunnies." Carnations are for sale by the Girls' League. Miss Indian American is coming. Students are auctioning off their services (background catcalls are heard) to earn money for the prom. Nominees are needed for the ballot for school bachelor and school bachelorette. The announcements end with a "thought for the day. When you throw a little mud, you lose a little ground."

At 10:04 the biology class finally turns to science. The teacher, Mr. Robbins, has placed one of several labeled laboratory specimens—some are pinned in frames, others swim in formaldehyde—on each of the classroom's eight laboratory tables. The three or so students whose chairs circle each of these benches are to study the specimen and make notes about it or drawings of it. After a few minutes each group of three will move to another table. The teacher points out that these specimens are of organisms already studied in previous classes. He says that the period-long test set for the following day will involve observing some of these specimens—then to be without labels—and writing an identifying paragraph on each. Mr. Robbins points out that some of the printed labels ascribe the specimens names different from those given in the textbook. He explains that biologists often give several names to the same organism.

The class now falls to peering, writing, and quiet talking. Mr. Robbins comes over to Mark, and in whispered words asks him to carry a requisition form for science department materials to the business office. Mark, because of his "older" status, is usually chosen by Robbins for this kind of errand. Robbins gives Mark the form and a green hall pass to show to any teacher who might challenge him, on his way to the office, for being out of a classroom. The errand takes Mark four minutes. Meanwhile Mark's group is hard at work but gets to only three of the specimens before the bell rings at 10:42. As the students surge out, Robbins shouts a reminder about a "double" laboratory period on Thursday.

Between classes one of the seniors asks Mark whether he plans to be a candidate for schoolwide office next year. Mark says no. He starts to explain. The 10:47 bell rings, meaning that he is late for French class.

There are fifteen students in Monsieur Bates's language class. He hands out tests taken the day before: *"C'est bien fait, Etienne . . . c'est mieux, Marie . . . Tch, tch, Robert . . ."* Mark notes his C+ and peeks at the A− in front of Susanna, next to him. The class has been assigned seats by M. Bates; Mark resents sitting next to prissy, brainy Susanna. Bates starts by asking a student to read a question and give the correct answer. *"James, question un."* James haltingly reads the question and gives the answer that Bates, now speaking English, says is incomplete. In due course: *"Mark, question cinq."* Mark does his bit, and the sequence goes on, the eight quiz questions and answers filling about twenty minutes of time.

"Turn to page forty-nine. *Maintenant, lisez après moi . . ."* and Bates reads a sentence and has the class echo it. Mark is embarrassed by this and mumbles with a barely audible sound. Others, like Susanna, keep the decibel count up, so Mark can hide. This I-say-you-repeat drill is interrupted once by the public address system, with an announcement about a meeting for the cheerleaders. Bates finishes the class, almost precisely at the bell, with a homework assignment. The students are to review these sentences for a brief quiz the following day. Mark takes note of the assignment, because he knows that tomorrow will be a day of busy-work in French class. Much though he dislikes oral drills, they are better than the workbook stuff that Bates hands out. Write, write, write, for Bates to throw away, Mark thinks.

11:36. Down to the cafeteria, talking noisily, hanging, munching. Getting to room 104 by 12:17: U.S. history. The teacher is sitting cross-legged on his desk when Mark comes in, heatedly arguing with three students over the fracas that had followed the previous night's basketball game. The teacher, Mr. Suslovic, while agreeing that the spectators from their school certainly were provoked, argues that they should neither have

10

been so obviously obscene in yelling at the opposing cheerleaders nor have allowed Coke cans to be rolled out on the floor. The three students keep saying that "it isn't fair." Apparently they and some others had been assigned "Saturday mornings" (detentions) by the principal for the ruckus.

At 12:34, the argument appears to subside. The uninvolved students, including Mark, are in their seats, chatting amiably. Mr. Suslovic climbs off his desk and starts talking: "We've almost finished this unit, chapters nine and ten . . ." The students stop chattering among themselves and turn toward Suslovic. Several slouch down in their chairs. Some open notebooks. Most have the five-pound textbook on their desks.

Suslovic lectures on the cattle drives, from north Texas to railroads west of St. Louis. He breaks up this narrative with questions ("Why were the railroad lines laid largely east to west?"), directed at nobody in particular and eventually answered by Suslovic himself. Some students take notes. Mark doesn't. A student walks in the open door, hands Mr. Suslovic a list, and starts whispering with him. Suslovic turns from the class and hears out this messenger. He then asks, "Does anyone know where Maggie Sharp is?" Someone answers, "Sick at home"; someone else says, "I thought I saw her at lunch." Genial consternation. Finally Suslovic tells the messenger, "Sorry, we can't help you," and returns to the class: "Now, where were we?" He goes on for some minutes. The bell rings. Suslovic forgets to give the homework assignment.

1:11 and Algebra II. There is a commotion in the hallway: someone's   15
locker is rumored to have been opened by the assistant principal and a narcotics agent. In the five-minute passing time, Mark hears the story three times and three ways. A locker had been broken into by another student. It was Mr. Gregory and a narc. It was the cops, and they did it without Gregory's knowing. Mrs. Ames, the mathematics teacher, has not heard anything about it. Several of the nineteen students try to tell her and start arguing among themselves. "O.K., that's enough." She hands out the day's problem, one sheet to each student. Mark sees with dismay that it is a single, complicated "word" problem about some train that, while traveling at 84 mph, due west, passes a car that was going due east at 55 mph. Mark struggles: Is it $d = rt$ or $t = rd$? The class becomes quiet, writing, while Mrs. Ames writes some additional, short problems on the blackboard. "Time's up." A sigh; most students still writing. A muffled "Shit." Mrs. Ames frowns. "Come on, now." She collects papers, but it takes four minutes for her to corral them all.

"Copy down the problems from the board." A minute passes. "William, try number one." William suggests an approach. Mrs. Ames corrects and cajoles, and William finally gets it right. Mark watches two kids to his right passing notes; he tries to read them, but the handwriting is illegible from his distance. He hopes he is not called on, and he isn't. Only three students are asked to puzzle out an answer. The bell rings at 2:00. Mrs. Ames shouts a homework assignment over the resulting hubbub.

Mark leaves his books in his locker. He remembers that he has homework, but figures that he can do it during English class the next day. He knows that there will be an in-class presentation of one of the *Romeo and Juliet* scenes and that he will not be in it. The teacher will not notice his homework writing, or won't do anything about it if she does.

Mark passes various friends heading toward the gym, members of the basketball teams. Like most students, Mark isn't an active school athlete. However, he is associated with the yearbook staff. Although he is not taking "Yearbook" for credit as an English course, he is contributing photographs. Mark takes twenty minutes checking into the yearbook staff's headquarters (the classroom of its faculty adviser) and getting some assignments of pictures from his boss, the senior who is the photography editor. Mark knows that if he pleases his boss and the faculty adviser, he'll take that editor's post for the next year. He'll get English credit for his work then.

After gossiping a bit with the yearbook staff, Mark will leave school by 2:35 and go home. His grocery market bagger's job is from 4:45 to 8:00, the rush hour for the store. He'll have a snack at 4:30, and his mother will save him some supper to eat at 8:30. She will ask whether he has any homework, and he'll tell her no. Tomorrow, and virtually every other tomorrow, will be the same for Mark, save for the lack of the assembly: each period then will be five minutes longer.

Most Americans have an uncomplicated vision of what secondary education should be. Their conception of high school is remarkably uniform across the country, a striking fact, given the size and diversity of the United States and the politically decentralized character of the schools. This uniformity is of several generations' standing. It has, however, two appearances, each quite different from the other, one of words and the other of practice, a world of political rhetoric and Mark's world. 20

A California high school's general goals, set out in 1979, could serve equally well most of America's high schools, public and private. This school had as its ends:

- Fundamental scholastic achievement . . . to acquire knowledge and share in the traditionally academic fundamentals . . . to develop the ability to make decisions, to solve problems, to reason independently, and to accept responsibility for self-evaluation and continuing self-improvement.
- Career and economic competence . . .
- Citizenship and civil responsibility . . .
- Competence in human and social relations . . .
- Moral and ethical values . . .
- Self-realization and mental and physical health . . .

- Aesthetic awareness . . .
- Cultural diversity . . .[1]

In addition to its optimistic rhetoric, what distinguishes this list is its comprehensiveness. The high school is to touch most aspects of an adolescent's existence — mind, body, morals, values, career. No one of these areas is given especial prominence. School people arrogate to themselves an obligation to all.

An example of the wide acceptability of these goals is found in the courts. Forced to present a detailed definition of "thorough and efficient education," elementary as well as secondary, a West Virginia judge sampled the best of conventional wisdom and concluded that

> there are eight general elements of a thorough and efficient system of education: (a) Literacy, (b) The ability to add, subtract, multiply, and divide numbers, (c) Knowledge of government to the extent the child will be equipped as a citizen to make informed choices among persons and issues that affect his own governance, (d) Self-knowledge and knowledge of his or her total environment to allow the child to intelligently choose life work — to know his or her options, (e) Work-training and advanced academic training as the child may intelligently choose, (f) Recreational pursuits, (g) Interests in all creative arts such as music, theater, literature, and the visual arts, and (h) Social ethics, both behavioral and abstract, to facilitate compatibility with others in this society.[2]

That these eight — now powerfully part of the debate over the purpose and practice of education in West Virginia — are reminiscent of the influential list, "The Seven Cardinal Principles of Secondary Education," promulgated in 1918 by the National Education Association, is no surprise.[3] The rhetoric of high school purpose has been uniform and consistent for decades. Americans agree on the goals for their high schools.

----

[1]Shasta High School, Redding, California. An eloquent and analogous statement, "The Essentials of Education," one stressing explicitly the "interdependence of skills and content" that is implicit in the Shasta High School statement, was issued in 1980 by a coalition of educational associations, Organizations for the Essentials of Education (Urbana, Illinois).

[2]Judge Arthur M. Recht, in his order resulting from *Pauley v. Kelly,* 1979, as reprinted in *Education Week,* May 26, 1982, p. 10. See also, in *Education Week,* January 16, 1983, pp. 21, 24, Jonathan P. Sher, "The Struggle to Fulfill a Judicial Mandate: How Not to 'Reconstruct' Education in W. Va."

[3]Bureau of Education, Department of the Interior, "Cardinal Principles of Secondary Education: A Report of the Commission on the Reorganization of Secondary Education, appointed by the National Education Association," *Bulletin,* no. 35 (Washington: U.S. Government Printing Office, 1918).

That agreement is convenient, but it masks the fact that virtually all the words in these goal statements beg definition. Some schools have labored long to identify specific criteria beyond them; the result has been lists of daunting pseudospecificity and numbing earnestness. However, most leave the words undefined and let the momentum of traditional practice speak for itself. That is why analyzing how Mark spends his time is important: from watching him one uncovers the important purposes of education, the ones that shape practice. Mark's day is similar to that of other high school students across the country, as similar as the rhetoric of one goal statement to others'. Of course, there are variations, but the extent of consistency in the shape of school routine for a large and diverse adolescent population is extraordinary, indicating more graphically than any rhetoric the measure of agreement in America about what one does in high school, and, by implication, what it is for.

The basic organizing structures in schools are familiar. Above all, students are grouped by age (that is, freshman, sophomore, junior, senior), and all are expected to take precisely the same time—around 720 school days over four years, to be precise—to meet the requirements for a diploma. When one is out of his grade level, he can feel odd, as Mark did in his biology class. The goals are the same for all, and the means to achieve them are also similar.

Young males and females are treated remarkably alike; the schools'   25
goals are the same for each gender. In execution, there are differences, as those pressing sex discrimination suits have made educators intensely aware. The students in metalworking classes are mostly male; those in home economics, mostly female. But it is revealing how much less sex discrimination there is in high schools than in other American institutions. For many young women, the most liberated hours of their week are in school.

School is to be like a job: you start in the morning and end in the afternoon, five days a week. You don't get much of a lunch hour, so you go home early, unless you are an athlete or are involved in some special school or extracurricular activity. School is conceived of as the children's workplace, and it takes young people off parents' hands and out of the labor market during prime-time work hours. Not surprisingly, many students see going to school as little more than a dogged necessity. They perceive the day-to-day routine, a Minnesota study reports, as one of "boredom and lethargy." One of the students summarizes: School is "boring, restless, tiresome, puts ya to sleep, tedious, monotonous, pain in the neck."[4]

The school schedule is a series of units of time: the clock is king. The base time block is about fifty minutes in length. Some schools, on what they call modular scheduling, split that fifty-minute block into two or even three

---

[4]Diane Hedin, Paula Simon, and Michael Robin, *Minnesota Youth Poll: Youth's Views on School and School Discipline*, Minnesota Report 184 (1983), Agricultural Experiment Station, University of Minnesota, p. 13.

pieces. Most schools have double periods for laboratory work, especially in the sciences, or four-hour units for the small numbers of students involved in intensive vocational or other work-study programs. The flow of all school activity arises from or is blocked by these time units. "How much time do I have with my kids" is the teacher's key question.

Because there are many claims for those fifty-minute blocks, there is little time set aside for rest between them, usually no more than three to ten minutes, depending on how big the school is and, consequently, how far students and teachers have to walk from class to class. As a result, there is a frenetic quality to the school day, a sense of sustained restlessness. For the adolescents, there are frequent changes of room and fellow students, each change giving tempting opportunities for distraction, which are stoutly resisted by teachers. Some schools play soft music during these "passing times," to quiet the multitude, one principal told me.

Many teachers have a chance for a coffee break. Few students do. In some city schools where security is a problem, students must be in class for seven consecutive periods, interrupted by a heavily monitored twenty-minute lunch period for small groups, starting as early as 10:30 A.M. and running to after 1:00 P.M. A high premium is placed on punctuality and on "being where you're supposed to be." Obviously, a low premium is placed on reflection and repose. The students rush from class to class to collect knowledge. Savoring it, it is implied, is not to be done much in school, nor is such meditation really much admired. The picture that these familiar patterns yield is that of an academic supermarket. The purpose of going to school is to pick things up, in an organized and predictable way, the faster the better.

What is supposed to be picked up is remarkably consistent among all   30
sorts of high schools. Most schools specifically mandate three out of every five courses a student selects. Nearly all of these mandates fall into five areas — English, social studies, mathematics, science, and physical education. On the average, English is required to be taken each year, social studies and physical education three out of the four high school years, and mathematics and science one or two years. Trends indicate that in the mid-eighties there is likely to be an increase in the time allocated to these last two subjects. Most students take classes in these four major academic areas beyond the minimum requirements, sometimes in such special areas as journalism and "yearbook," offshoots of English departments.[5]

Press most adults about what high school is for, and you hear these subjects listed. *High school? That's where you learn English and math and that sort of thing.* Ask students, and you get the same answer. High school is to "teach" these "subjects."

---

[5]I am indebted to Harold F. Sizer and Lyde E. Sizer for a survey of the diploma requirements of fifty representative secondary schools, completed for *A Study of High Schools.*

What is often absent is any definition of these subjects or any rationale for them. They are just there, labels. Under those labels lie a multitude of things. A great deal of material is supposed to be "covered"; most of these courses are surveys, great sweeps of the stuff of their parent disciplines.

While there is often a sequence *within* subjects—algebra before trigonometry, "first-year" French before "second-year" French—there is rarely a coherent relationship or sequence *across* subjects. Even the most logically related matters—reading ability as a precondition for the reading of history books, and certain mathematical concepts or skills before the study of some of physics—are only loosely coordinated, if at all. There is little demand for a synthesis of it all; English, mathematics, and the rest are discrete items, to be picked up individually. The incentive for picking them up is largely through tests and, with success at these, in credits earned.

Coverage within subjects is the key priority. If some imaginative teacher makes a proposal to force the marriage of, say, mathematics and physics or to require some culminating challenges to students to use several objects in the solution of a complex problem, and if this proposal will take "time" away from other things, opposition is usually phrased in terms of what may be thus forgone. If we do that, we'll have to give up colonial history. We won't be able to get to programming. We'll not be able to read *Death of a Salesman*. There isn't time. The protesters usually win out.

The subjects come at a student like Mark in random order, a kaleido-   35
scope of worlds: algebraic formulae to poetry to French verbs to Ping-Pong to the War of the Spanish Succession, all before lunch. Pupils are to pick up these things. Tests measure whether the picking up has been successful.

The lack of connection between stated goals, such as those of the California high school cited earlier, and the goals inherent in school practice is obvious and, curiously, tolerated. Most striking is the gap between statements about "self-realization and mental and physical growth" or "moral and ethical values"—common rhetoric in school documents—and practice. Most physical education programs have neither the time nor the focus really to ensure fitness. Mental health is rarely defined. Neither are ethical values, save at the negative extremes, such as opposition to assault or dishonesty. Nothing in the regimen of a day like Mark's signals direct or implicit teaching in this area. The "school boy code" (not ratting on a fellow student) protects the marijuana pusher, and a leechlike associate is shrugged off without concern. The issue of the locker search was pushed aside, as not appropriate for class time.

Most students, like Mark, go to class in groups of twenty to twenty-seven students. The expected attendance in some schools, particularly those in low-income areas, is usually higher, often thirty-five students per class, but high absentee rates push the actual numbers down. About twenty-five per class is an average figure for expected attendance, and the actual numbers are somewhat lower. There are remarkably few students who go to class in groups much larger or smaller than twenty-five.[6]

A student such as Mark sees five or six teachers per day; their differing styles and expectations are part of his kaleidoscope. High school staffs are highly specialized: guidance counselors rarely teach mathematics, mathematics teachers rarely teach English, principals rarely do any classroom instruction. Mark, then, is known a little bit by a number of people, each of whom sees him in one specialized situation. No one may know him as a "whole person"—unless he becomes a special problem or has special needs.

Save in extracurricular or coaching situations, such as in athletics, drama, or shop classes, there is little opportunity for sustained conversation between student and teacher. The mode is a one-sentence or two-sentence exchange: *Mark, when was Grover Cleveland president?* Let's see, was 1890 . . . or something . . . wasn't he the one . . . he was elected twice, wasn't he . . . *Yes . . . Gloria, can you get the dates right?* Dialogue is strikingly absent, and as a result the opportunity of teachers to challenge students' ideas in a systematic and logical way is limited. Given the rushed, full quality of the school day, it can seldom happen. One must infer that careful probing of students' thinking is not a high priority. How one gains (to quote the California school's statement of goals again) "the ability to make decisions, to solve problems, to reason independently, and to accept responsibility for self-evaluation and continuing self-improvement" without being challenged is difficult to imagine. One certainly doesn't learn these things merely from lectures and textbooks.

Most schools are nice places. Mark and his friends enjoy being in   40
theirs. The adults who work in schools generally like adolescents. The academic pressures are limited, and the accommodations to students are substantial. For example, if many members of an English class have jobs after school, the English teacher's expectations for them are adjusted, downward. In a word, school is sensitively accommodating, as long as students are punctual, where they are supposed to be, and minimally dutiful about picking things up from the clutch of courses in which they enroll.

This characterization is not pretty, but it is accurate, and it serves to describe the vast majority of American secondary schools. "Taking subjects" in a systematized, conveyer-belt way is what one does in high school. That this process is, in substantial respects, not related to the rhetorical purposes of education is tolerated by most people, perhaps because they do not really either believe in those ill-defined goals or, in their heart of hearts, believe that schools can or should even try to achieve them. The students are happy taking subjects. The parents are happy, because that's what they

<hr />

[6]Education Research Service, Inc., *Class Size: A Summary of Research* (Arlington, Virginia, 1978); and *Class Size Research: A Critique of Recent Meta-Analyses* (Arlington, Virginia, 1980).

did in high school. The rituals, the most important of which is graduation, remain intact. The adolescents are supervised safely and constructively most of the time, during the morning and afternoon hours, and they are off the labor market. That is what high school is all about.

QUESTIONS

1. The first nineteen paragraphs of this essay are a report. What do you think of this report? Given your own experience, how accurate is it? What attitude does the report convey, or is it objective?
2. Paragraph 19 is the conclusion of the report. It ends the story of Mark's day. Does it draw or imply any conclusions from the events reported?
3. How is the explanatory section of the essay (paragraphs 20 through 41) organized? The first subtopic discussed is the goals of high school. What are the other subtopics?
4. What is the major conclusion of this explanation? To what extent do you agree with the last sentence of the essay and what it implies?
5. How does the report (paragraphs 1 through 19) function in the explanation that follows? What would be lost if the report were omitted? In considering how the two sections of the essay relate, note especially places where the explanation specifically refers to the report.
6. Your view of high school might be different than Sizer's, or perhaps your high school was different than the one he describes. Write an essay that is organized like Sizer's but that presents your own report and explanation of what school is.
7. Using the basic outline of Sizer's essay, write your own explanation of the workings of some institution — store, family, religious group, club, team, or whatever else you know well. Think of your project in terms of Sizer's title: "What X Is."

MAKING CONNECTIONS

How do you suppose Sizer got this information about Mark and "what high school is"? Compare his approach to those of Jane van Lawick-Goodall (p. 237) and Monica M. Moore (p. 412). Which one of these writers comes closest, do you think, to Sizer's method for researching his essay? Explain the resemblances and differences.

UNDERSTANDING OVATION

Roger Gilbert

Roger Gilbert (b. 1960) received his undergraduate and graduate degrees from Yale University, and he is currently a professor of English and director of graduate studies at Cornell, where he teaches American poetry. The author of many articles about poetry and popular culture, he has also published the books Walks in the World: Representation and Experience in Modern Poetry *(1991) and* The Walker's Literary Companion *(2000) and was a coeditor of* The Quotable Walker *(2000). The following essay appeared originally in* The Southwest Review *(in 2001) and was later adapted for* Harper's *magazine.*

During a partial solar eclipse some years ago, I found myself standing in a crowd of about two hundred people on the Cornell Arts quad. Dutifully heeding the experts' warnings against looking directly at the sky, we were watching an optical projection of the eclipse on a large white screen. At the moment of complete annularity, when the silhouette of the moon was fully superimposed on the sun, the thin crescent of light on the screen suddenly became a perfect ring, a breathtaking sight. And at that moment the entire crowd spontaneously burst into applause.

Whom or what were we applauding? We tend to imagine, when we applaud at a live performance, that the applause is for the performers, that its purpose is to communicate our approval to them. But this applause suggested that, in some cases at least, communication is a secondary motive, that applause is first and foremost a way of responding to the elation of a moment.

Applause is a curious and neglected phenomenon. There's something vaguely embarrassing about it, I suspect, particularly to philosophers and critics in love with the purity of abstractions. Applause is real, sweaty, a kind of bodily secretion rather than an operation of the sensibility. Moreover applause is a public ritual, governed by elaborate codes and conventions, and as such seems an unlikely source of insight into the nature of aesthetic value. Cultural, social, and economic variables all affect applause, prolonging or aborting it, changing its tone and intensity. In this country in particular, the more extreme expressions of approval—whistles, stamping feet, standing ovations—have become tediously predictable. Audiences apparently feel that without them they are all but admitting they've wasted their evening. Given these corrupting influences, it would seem foolish to claim that applause can offer anything like a reliable measure of aesthetic value. And yet there are times when applause feels real, when it feels less like a duty or a ritual than a physical need, as urgent and visceral as any other bodily appetite or compulsion.

Applause first needs to be distinguished from responses such as laughter and tears, which tend to greet particular moments within a performance or event. Overt weeping has become a rare phenomenon in our cool, post-modern audiences, but there were times when the sound of collective sobbing threatened to drown out performances of *The Drunkard* or *Uncle Tom's Cabin*. Laughter, by contrast, depends not on identification but on distance, and has therefore become a much more prevalent response in contemporary theaters. Indeed a common complaint today is that younger audiences tend to laugh nervously at moments of high pathos, as though unable to surrender to a represented emotion or regard it without irony. Whether or not these responses occur in sync with a given performance, they have a purely reflexive quality that separates them from applause, which entails at least a minimal degree of aesthetic judgment.

On the other side of applause we encounter that ever more ubiquitous   5 demonstration known as the standing ovation. Ostensibly an audience's way of making its approval visible as well as audible, the standing ovation may look like a natural extension and intensification of applause but in fact marks a fundamental shift in the dynamics of response. Whereas traditional applause is infinitely elastic, capable of registering, however subtly, thousands of individual modulations in rhythm, volume, and zeal, a standing ovation is essentially a binary code — it's either on or off, up or down. Of course it sometimes happens that one or two especially enthused spectators will leap to their feet only to find that no one is joining them. Far more common, however, is the tediously predictable and subtly tyrannical progression from a few isolated standers to scattered perpendicular patches and clumps that spread steadily outward, until finally even the most tepid of spectators feels obliged to join in the general uprightness.

Why are standing ovations so coercive? Perhaps because once they achieve a certain critical mass anyone who stays seated feels like a spoilsport. Your dissent becomes painfully obvious in a way it never does when you simply aren't clapping as loudly as everyone else. Indeed to keep one's seat in the midst of a wildfire standing ovation seems to convey a distinctly negative judgment rather than a merely less positive one. However loudly you may clap, cheer, whistle, your very failure to stand acts as the equivalent of a boo, a thumbs-down, a churlish withholding of enthusiasm. The sad truth is that standing ovations have become an audience's way of certifying its own wisdom, of collectively driving up the value of its monetary and aesthetic investment.

"The poem is the cry of its occasion," Wallace Stevens proclaimed, and the same might be said of applause. No two ovations sound exactly the same: the dynamics of applause vary broadly depending on the kind of event it greets or rewards. Indeed our assumptions about what and when to applaud turn out to be surprisingly arbitrary. As Frederick Stocken points out in an article for the *BBC Music Magazine*, "Because applause seems so natural to us, we tend to assume that its methods and conventions have remained constant throughout history." Not so; Stocken proceeds to list some of the more significant variations in the practice, beginning with Nero's insistence on being applauded by the "Alexandrian" method, a blend of hollow-handed and flat-handed clapping overlaid with loud humming. Less exotic are more recent customs such as applauding between movements of extended works, which became obsolete only in the twentieth century (though not in the opera house, where it's still kosher to applaud big arias). Stocken notes that in the eighteenth and early nineteenth centuries, it was even customary to applaud specific moments within a piece—e.g., a fortissimo passage or a brilliant cadenza. In the pious atmosphere of the modern concert hall, such behavior would be considered criminal. To applaud before the final note has sounded feels like a violation of the integrity of the Work. This assumption is no doubt as arbitrary as any other, but it reflects a basic shift in the way we understand and respond to musical performances.

Of course not all music gets the same treatment. Jazz aficionados routinely applaud after solos, reflecting not only the special recognition due improvisers but the more paratactic grammar of jazz, in which the coherence of the whole is often less compelling than the intensity of the parts. But here an interesting dilemma can arise: the more enthusiastically one applauds the last soloist, the less one hears of the next. Applause becomes a kind of feedback, entering into and distorting the performance itself, in some instances leading the soloist to play deliberately "throwaway" passages knowing that they won't be heard.

Applause often satisfies a need or appetite as profound as the appetite for the aesthetic experience that elicits it. In its simplest form the law of stimulus and response dictates that when we feel something we must do something, and applause is the place where that doing first takes on an irreducibly aesthetic form. Applauding for a good performance can itself be a pleasure of the highest order. Anticipating a trip to see the famous actress Berma, Proust's Marcel compares himself to a "battery that accumulates and stores up electricity," nicely capturing the temporal character of aesthetic experience generally. We take in stimuli and store them, letting them build in pressure until they eventually demand to be released. The sexual analogue is inescapable; if art produces a kind of pleasurable friction or excitation, then applause is the orgasmic discharge that dispels the accumulated tension. (Other forms of bodily relief may also be apposite; consider the phrase "Hold your applause," with its faint evocation of a full bladder.) Traditionally, catharsis or emotional release has been located within the bounds of the aesthetic experience proper—at the denouement of a tragedy, or in the harmonic resolution of a symphony. Yet in a real sense the process has not been completed, the gathered energy spent, until mind and body have been able to expel something commensurate with what they have absorbed. "Dazzling and tremendous, how quick the sunrise would kill me," chants Whitman, "If I could not now and always send sunrise out of me."

One reason applause can be deeply satisfying is that it confirms the deep-seated intuition that our own aesthetic responses are not simply perverse or idiosyncratic but find an answering chord in other minds. As individual handclaps merge into a homogeneous roar, so the separate responses of audience members merge into what feels like a shared judgment, a consensus. Applause is a great leveler, averaging particular responses into a single measurable quantity. What happens to the individual in the crowd? Where do his claps go? Even the applauder usually can't distinguish her own noise from that of her fellows. Yet each person claps at a slightly different rhythm, pace, pitch, volume. In this respect applause is less like a chorus singing in unison than an ensemble of instruments playing a counterpoint so dense the separate lines can't be made out. This is why the practice of synchronized clapping common at classical concerts in Europe seems profoundly wrong to me, as coercive in its way as the Great American Standing Ovation or that other spectatorial display known as The Wave. Applause may muffle individual voices, but the freedom of each spectator to make exactly the noise he or she deems fit is crucial to the ritual's legitimacy.

Much of the pleasure of applause comes from the almost miraculous sense of amplification it gives. At its most intense and spontaneous, applause verges on religious ecstasy. We feel ourselves merging into a collective body, yet we also feel that the body is ours, that we stand at the source of the storm, that the roar we hear is an emanation of our own wills. Your own paltry claps return to your ears multiplied a thousandfold.

No self-respecting clapper simply follows the crowd's lead, yet the awareness of a collective response distinct from one's own can influence the timbre and volume of one's applause in complex and subtle ways. Thus, if the general ovation seems too tepid, one may clap a little harder or faster. Conversely, if the crowd's enthusiasm seems excessive, one may dampen one's applause a bit in protest. But the relation can be more symbiotic as well, the individual's appreciation feeding on and into the group's. As thousands of separate sounds spread in ripples from each body, they create complex patterns of interference and reciprocity that swirl back around their sources and alter them, adding or subtracting volume, changing rhythm or pace, cooling or firing intensity.

In the end, other people's responses matter to us, not because we want to keep in step but because we want to feel all there is to be felt. Our sensibilities are porous, not insular; our initial judgment of a performance or work can be modified simply by the force of another person's enthusiasm or contempt. During applause these modifications are tinier and less visible, but they happen all the same. An intricate mesh of sonic filaments connects every person in the hall to every other, whether the audience numbers a dozen or three thousand. We're probably most conscious of our immediate neighbors' reactions—gasps, giggles, groans, muttered wisecracks—which may or may not echo or reinforce our own. But every member of the audience exerts a slight pull on us, and we on them. Ultimately, of course, our response to any work of art must be our own and no one else's; what applause underscores is that no response occurs in a vacuum. One of the kindest questions we can ask another person is, "How did you like it?" Applause is a way of asking and answering that question simultaneously.

QUESTIONS

1. Though Gilbert is primarily concerned with "understanding ovation," he doesn't focus explicitly and continuously on applause until midway through his essay, in paragraph 7. What is the purpose of his preceding six paragraphs? What does each of those paragraphs contribute to his explanation?
2. At the end of paragraph 2, Gilbert declares "that applause is first and foremost a way of responding to the elation of a moment." How closely does this assertion reflect your own experience of applause and applauding? Assuming that this is one of Gilbert's main points, what is the purpose of his remaining discussion?
3. Although applause is often so audible and palpable that it momentarily seems as if might be an enduring memory, it usually ends so quickly that it is often hard to remember, much less define and analyze. What specific techniques does Gilbert use in each paragraph to make this somewhat vague phenomenon more specific and explainable?
4. In paragraph 9, Gilbert compares ovation to bodily excretion and sexual orgasm. What are the grounds for these comparisons? Do you consider one comparison to be more valid? Why or why not?
5. Attend a musical performance, a theatrical production, or another event where applause is likely to take place, and immediately after the event is over, make a detailed record of your impressions. Use them as the basis for an essay agreeing or disagreeing with one or more of Gilbert's points about ovation. Or, if you prefer, use your firsthand experience and observations as the basis for an explanatory piece of your own about ovation.

MAKING CONNECTIONS

Gilbert and Elisabeth Kübler-Ross (p. 405) both seek to explain and understand a universal kind of response to a fundamental aspect of human experience. Compare and contrast the methods, evidence, and reasoning they use to explore their chosen subjects.

"LIFE, VIGOR, FIRE": THE WATERCOLORS OF WINSLOW HOMER

Joyce Carol Oates

Known primarily as a fiction writer and literary critic, Joyce Carol Oates (b. 1938) grew up in the countryside outside of Lockport, New York. A scholarship student at Syracuse University, she was valedictorian of her class and then earned a master's degree in English at the University of Wisconsin. From 1962 to 1978, Oates lived in Detroit and commuted to teach at the University of Windsor in Canada; since then she has been on the faculty at Princeton University. Her earliest literary success came when she won the Mademoiselle *fiction contest while still an undergraduate. By the time she was thirty-one, she had published two short story collections as well as four well-received novels, one of which,* them *(1969), won the National Book Award. Perhaps the country's most prolific author, Oates has published nearly seventy books of fiction, in addition to numerous poetry collections, plays, nonfiction works, and, as editor, anthologies. She also regularly contributes to periodicals ranging from the* Village Voice *to* Critical Inquiry. *The following essay was included in Oates's 1988 collection of criticism,* (Woman) Writer: Occasions and Opportunities.*

> The life that I have chosen gives me my
> full hours of enjoyment for the balance
> of my life. The Sun will not rise, or set,
> without my notice, and thanks.
> —WINSLOW HOMER, 1903

Winslow Homer's brilliant and innovative career as a watercolorist—he was to paint approximately 685 watercolors in thirty years—began in the summer of 1873 when, discouraged by unreliable sales and mixed reviews of his ambitious oil paintings, he vacationed in Gloucester, Massachusetts, and worked on a series of paintings that focused primarily on children against a seacoast background. The artist was thirty-seven years old at this turning point in his life and made his living as a free-lance illustrator for such magazines as *Harper's Weekly* ("a treadmill existence," as he called it, "a form of bondage"); he had had an early but misleading success at the age of thirty with his famous oil *Prisoners from the Front* (1866) but found, to his immense discouragement, that critics and collectors expected him to produce similar work: the chronic predicament of the artist of genius who almost at once leaves established taste behind, even as he has helped establish it. Homer's success at watercolors, however, not only allowed him to give up commercial art but freed him, for summers at least, from the concentrated labor of oil painting, which he assumed would be the primary focus of his career. It also freed him to experiment — to conceive of his art in terms of light, color, and composition, not merely in terms of subject. The artist could not have anticipated that, in a "lesser" medium to which relative failure had driven him, he would not only create an astonishing volume of exceptional work but would, in the words of the art historian Virgil Barker, remake the craft: "He invented the handling where everything depends upon a trained spontaneity. . . . No one since has added to its technical sources, and it is even unlikely that anyone can."

Just as Winslow Homer's watercolors span many years, so too do they focus upon greatly differing subjects and take up, sometimes obsessively, greatly varying themes. They are also closely identified with specific geographical settings: Gloucester, Massachusetts; Prouts Neck, Maine; the English fishing village of Cullercoats, Northumberland; the Adirondacks and the Canadian North Woods; Florida and the Caribbean. "If a man wants to be an artist," Homer said as a very young man, "he should never look at pictures." This was in fact not Homer's practice — he was too intelligent to imagine himself truly superior to the historical development of his craft — but his art even at its most visionary is always in response to the physical world. The grim North Sea of England is very different from the benign and sunlit beach at Gloucester, Maine, and draws forth a radically different art; images of nostalgia evoked by upstate New York seem hardly to belong to the same sensibility — the same *eye* — as those so brilliantly and seemingly effortlessly evoked by the Caribbean. Except for his experimentation with light, color, and composition and the mastery of his brushwork, the Winslow Homer of Prouts Neck is not the Winslow Homer of the Adirondacks. "You must not paint everything you see," Homer advised a fellow artist, "you must wait, and wait patiently, until the exceptional, the wonderful effect or aspect comes." Homer's genius was to paint the exceptional as if it were somehow ordinary; to so convincingly capture the fluidity of motion of the present moment — its "life, vigor, fire," in the words of a contemporary critic — that other paintings, by other highly regarded artists, appear static by contrast. To observe the evolution of Homer's art from its earliest beginnings to its maturity is to be witness to the development of a major artist: an American painter of world stature and significance.

Winslow Homer was born in Boston in 1836, to educated and well-to-do parents; he would die in Prouts Neck, Maine, in September 1910, having lived in relative isolation for decades. At approximately the midpoint of his career he began to withdraw from society, though he was never, strictly speaking, a recluse; he went on frequent hunting and fishing expeditions, insisted upon first-rate accommodations in his frequent travels, was even something of a dandy. He never married, though he was said by a friend to have had "the usual number of love affairs." (In the 1870s Homer repeatedly painted studies of an attractive young redheaded woman whom he seems to have loved and, according to family legend, wanted to marry. But she disappeared from his work near the end of the decade and has never been identified. See "Winslow Homer's Mystery Woman," by Henry Adams, in the November 1984 issue of *Art & Antiques*.) By adroitly resisting the advances of would-be acquaintances he acquired a reputation, only partly justified, for being rude and antisocial; he was in fact friendly enough, when he chose to be, and always remained on intimate terms with his family. Like most artists he lived more and more intensely in his art as he aged, and though he suffered periods of discouragement over poor or erratic sales there is no evidence that he ever suffered a moment's self-doubt. His extraordinary painterly genius remained with him to the very end: his last painting, an oil titled *Driftwood*, 1909, painted after he had had a stroke, is a masterly Impressionist seascape.

As a boy Homer exhibited a precocious talent for drawing and painting, but he seems to have had no formal instruction apart from that given him by his mother, the gifted amateur watercolorist Henrietta Benson Homer. His work as a free-lance illustrator provided him with an apprenticeship in his craft: such early watercolors as *Fresh Eggs* and *Rural Courtship* have the look of magazine illustrations executed by a first-rate professional. There is a delight here in closely observed detail; colors are bright and fresh; the overall impression is affable, anecdotal, warmly nostalgic. Homer began his watercolor career at a time when post–Civil War America was rapidly changing, hence the avid interest in sentimental genre art depicting "typical" Americans in "typical" activities—the most popular being mass-produced, of course, by the printmakers Currier and Ives. He found that he could execute and sell these watercolors easily (he got about $75 apiece for them), yet his professional facility was not to interfere with his instinct for experimentation.

Homer's watercolors differed significantly from those painted by the   5 majority of his American contemporaries, who worked diligently, and often prettily, in the prevailing English style. Indeed, the medium of watercolor itself was not taken very seriously at this time, being largely the province of amateurs, for whom the rigor of oils was too demanding. Homer's first exhibits drew praise from critics, who thought him original and striking; but he was also faulted for what was perceived to be his crudeness and sketchiness—his conspicuous "lack of finish." The thirty-two-year-old Henry James, reviewing an exhibit of 1875, could not have been more ambivalent in his response to Homer's work:

> He is almost barbarously simple, and, to our eye, he is horribly ugly; but there is nevertheless something one likes about him. What is it? For ourselves, it is not his subjects. We frankly confess that we detest

his subjects—his barren plank fences . . . his flat-breasted maidens, suggestive of a dish of rural doughnuts and pie. . . . He has chosen the least pictorial features of the least pictorial range of scenery and civilization; he has resolutely treated them as if they *were* pictorial, as if they were every inch as good as Capri or Tangiers; and, to reward his audacity, he has incontestably succeeded.

It may well have been that Homer himself was impatient with his American subjects or, in any case, with his mode of depicting them. In 1881 he went to live for twenty months in the fishing village of Cullercoats, Northumberland; he was in his mid-forties, no longer young, and ready for a complete break with his past. The paintings that derive from that period of isolation and intense work are like nothing he had ever done before, and represent a break too with the genteel tradition of American nature art. This is not the "English" England but the more primitive England of Shakespeare's Lear, Brontë's Heathcliff, Hardy's Tess. Homer's realistic rendering of the hardworking fisherfolk of Cullercoats—the women in particular—gives these paintings a dramatic urgency totally alien to his earlier work. His women are closely observed individuals, yet they are also monumental, heroic, mythic: they bear virtually no resemblance to women of the sort commonly depicted by Homer's American contemporaries. In *Fisherwoman, Tynemouth,* a young woman strides along the beach wind-whipped and unflinching, a study in blues and browns, seemingly one with her element; the painting is a small masterpiece of design and execution. *Watching the Tempest* and *The Wreck of the Iron Crown* are yet more ambitious compositions, remarkable for the artist's success in capturing the wildness of a storm-tossed sea and the helplessness of human beings in confronting it. This is not the Romantic vision of a nature sublime and unknowable but bound up in some mystical way with man's own emotions; it is dramatically different from the pantheism suggested by the work of Homer's contemporaries George Inness, Frederick Church, Albert Bierstadt, and the Hudson Valley painters generally. The man who would one day stun and offend critics no less than potential customers by his unjudging depiction of acts of human violence—a hunter slashing a deer's throat, for instance—had found his subject and theme by way of the impersonal violence of the North Sea; in his later work even human figures were to be eliminated in the artist's obsessive contemplation of the forms and forces of nature.

After the Cullercoats series Winslow Homer's reputation was established, though sales of his work were, as always, erratic and unpredictable. He returned to Prouts Neck, Maine, where he was to live from 1884 onward, concentrating on marine paintings—watercolors and oils; he visited the Caribbean and Florida, where the dazzling sunshine had the effect of liberating his palette and inspiring him to open-air painting of a particularly lyric sort. If the watercolor bears a relationship to any literary form it is surely to the lyric poem: a work which, in Robert Frost's words, rides on its own melting, like a piece of ice on a hot stove. The transparent luminosities and compositional brilliance of such works as *Shark Fishing* (1884–85), *The Gulf Stream* (1889), and *After the Tornado* (1898) are extraordinary. Out of wholly realistic material, charged with intense but thoroughly muted emotion, the artist renders an art that suggests abstraction—the very reverse of "genre" or narrative painting. In this sun-flooded space we contemplate a fractured world of planes, angles, gradations of light, in which the human figure is but an element in design. Homer had long been conscious of the phenomenon of light and had experimented with its possibilities for years, like his Impressionist contemporaries Monet, Pissarro, and Sisley: "You have the sky overhead giving one light; then the reflected light from whatever reflects; then the direct light of the sun; so that, in the blending and suffusing of these several illuminations, there is no such thing as a line to be seen anywhere." The elegaic *Rowing Home* (1890) might be said to be a study in the withdrawal of light—a muted evening sun presides over the subdued and seemingly melancholy action of rowers on a lake or an inlet in the North Woods; faint grays and blues wash transparently together; the human figures bleed into the stillness of impending night. In this beautiful tone poem there are no lines or outlines, only shadowy, smudged silhouettes, on the verge of dissolution.

Along with his marine studies, it is Homer's Adirondacks and North Woods paintings that most admirers know, and upon which his popular reputation rests. Certainly these are dazzling works—bold, eye-stopping, executed with the bravura of a master. So exquisite is Homer's brushwork in the large Adirondack series, so absolute his confidence in his art, the "impression" one forms in contemplating such works of the early 1890s as *Adirondack Guide, An Adirondack Lake, Old Friends,* and *The End of the Hunt* is that they are, despite their incalculable complexity, simple compositions. So too with the remarkable *Shooting the Rapids,* where a sense of vertiginous motion is conveyed by the most economic means, as two canoers plunge through tumultuous white water, gripping their oars tightly. White paper breaks through transparent washes to suggest the dim reflections of the sky; all colors are muted—browns, blues, greens, black. Here as elsewhere Homer succeeds wonderfully in communicating the fluidity of the present moment, the experience of physical action, as few other painters have done. Set beside his seemingly effortless watercolors, the experimental work of certain avant-garde artists who similarly attempted "movement"—the Italian Futurists, for instance—seems studied and artificial. It is only Homer's occasional predilection for frank sentiment, or sentimentality, and for the emotional tug of narrative, in such paintings as *Old Friends* and *The End of the Hunt,* that suggests his background in magazine illustration and his kinship with American genre artists of the nineteenth century.

But Winslow Homer was—and is—an artist to transcend all categories, as the 1986 exhibit of one hundred of his watercolors in the

National Gallery attested. It might even be argued that, had Homer worked only in watercolor, he would still be considered one of America's most original artists. "Only think of my being *alive* with a reputation," he wrote to his brother a few years before his death. And living, still, today.

QUESTIONS

1. What characteristics of Winslow Homer's paintings does Oates believe to be most extraordinary?
2. Reread the first two paragraphs of Oates's essay. Now read the third paragraph of the essay as if it were her first. Why didn't Oates begin her piece with Homer's birth and upbringing? How would the piece be different if she had? What are the benefits of beginning the piece the way she did?
3. Midway through her essay, Oates includes a long block quotation from Henry James that emphasizes all that is ugly and strange about Homer's paintings. Why do you think Oates chose to include this quotation, and how did it alter your perception of Homer? Is there a piece of artwork that you like despite its oddity or ugliness? Why?
4. In her descriptions of Homer's paintings, Oates does more than describe the colors that he used on his canvases and the figures that he represented. How else does she convey the qualities of Homer's paintings to her reader? Give examples, and explain how they help you envision his works.
5. Choose a painting in a gallery, and write an essay explaining what makes it extraordinary. Describe the visual aspects of the painting (the subject, the colors, and the brushstrokes) and also the psychological dimensions of the painting (the feelings that you get when you stand in front of it and study it). Assume that your reader has never seen the painting you are describing.

MAKING CONNECTIONS

Both Oates and Malcolm Gladwell with "The Naked Face" (p. 438) are faced with the challenge of describing the worth of one person's lifework. Oates must describe the aesthetic value of Homer's contribution to art. Gladwell faces a similar challenge in describing Ekman's scientific contributions to the understanding of emotions and facial expressions. How do these writers approach their subjects? To what extent do their descriptions of the artist and the scientist as people contribute to our understanding of their subjects' work?

CARNAL ACTS

Nancy Mairs

Nancy Mairs (b. 1943) grew up in the suburbs north of Boston and graduated from Wheaton College in Illinois. She later earned her Ph.D. from the University of Arizona, where she taught English and women's studies in the 1970s and 1980s. Her earliest publications were collections of poetry, but Plaintext: Autobiographical Essays *(1986) first brought her wide critical attention, particularly for such revealing pieces as "On Being a Cripple," which focuses on her struggle with multiple sclerosis. Subsequent books include* Remembering the Bone-House *(1989),* Ordinary Time *(1993),* Waist-High in the World: Life among the Nondisabled *(1994), and* A Troubled Guest: Life and Death Stories *(2001). Mairs has said of her work, "In my writing I aim to speak the 'unspeakable,' in defiance of polite discourse." Following is the title essay of* Carnal Acts *(1990), a collection of essays and short fiction.*

Inviting me to speak at her small liberal arts college during Women's Week, a young woman set me a task: "We would be pleased," she wrote, "if you could talk on how you cope with your MS disability, and also how you discovered your voice as a writer." Oh, Lord, I thought in dismay, how am I going to pull this one off? How can I yoke two such disparate subjects into a coherent presentation, without doing violence to one, or the other, or both, or myself? This is going to take some fancy footwork, and my feet scarcely carry out the basic steps, let alone anything elaborate.

To make matters worse, the assumption underlying each of her questions struck me as suspect. To ask *how* I cope with multiple sclerosis suggests that I *do* cope. Now, "to cope," *Webster's Third* tells me, is "to face or encounter and to find necessary expedients to overcome problems and difficulties." In these terms, I have to confess, I don't feel like much of a coper. I'm likely to deal with my problems and difficulties by squawking and flapping around like that hysterical chicken who was convinced the sky was falling. Never mind that in my case the sky really *is* falling. In response to a clonk on the head, regardless of its origin, one might comport oneself with a grace and courtesy I generally lack.

As for "finding" my voice, the implication is that it was at one time lost or missing. But I don't think it ever was. Ask my mother, who will tell you a little wearily that I was speaking full sentences by the time I was a year old and could never be silenced again. As for its being a writer's voice, it seems to have become one early on. Ask Mother again. At the age of eight

I rewrote the Trojan War, she will say, and what Nestor was about to do to Helen at the end doesn't bear discussion in polite company.

Faced with these uncertainties, I took my own teacherly advice, something, I must confess, I don't always do. "If an idea is giving you trouble," I tell my writing students, "put it on the back burner and let it simmer while you do something else. Go to the movies. Reread a stack of old love letters. Sit in your history class and take detailed notes on the Teapot Dome scandal. If you've got your idea in mind, it will go on cooking at some level no matter what else you're doing." "I've had an idea for my documented essay on the back burner," one of my students once scribbled in her journal, "and I think it's just boiled over!"

I can't claim to have reached such a flash point. But in the weeks I've   5
had the themes "disability" and "voice" sitting around in my head, they seem to have converged on their own, without my having to wrench them together and bind them with hoops of tough rhetoric. They *are* related, indeed interdependent, with an intimacy that has for some reason remained, until now, submerged below the surface of my attention. Forced to juxtapose them, I yank them out of the depths, a little startled to discover how they were intertwined down there out of sight. This kind of discovery can unnerve you at first. You feel like a giant hand that, pulling two swimmers out of the water, two separate heads bobbing on the iridescent swells, finds the two bodies below, legs coiled around each other, in an ecstasy of copulation. You don't quite know where to turn your eyes.

Perhaps the place to start illuminating this erotic connection between who I am and how I speak lies in history. I have known that I have multiple sclerosis for about seventeen years now, though the disease probably started long before. The hypothesis is that the disease process, in which the protective covering of the nerves in the brain and spinal cord is eaten away and replaced by scar tissue, "hard patches," is caused by an autoimmune reaction to a slow-acting virus. Research suggests that I was infected by this virus, which no one has ever seen and which therefore, technically, doesn't even "exist," between the ages of four and fifteen. In effect, living with this mysterious mechanism feels like having your present self, and the past selves it embodies, haunted by a capricious and meanspirited ghost, unseen except for its footprints, which trips you even when you're watching where you're going, knocks glassware out of your hand, squeezes the urine out of your bladder before you reach the bathroom, and weights your whole body with a weariness no amount of rest can relieve. An alien invader must be at work. But of course it's not. It's your own body. That is, it's you.

This, for me, has been the most difficult aspect of adjusting to a chronic incurable degenerative disease: the fact that it has rammed my "self" straight back into the body I had been trained to believe it could, through highminded acts and aspirations, rise above. The Western tradition of distinguishing the body from the mind and/or the soul is so ancient as to have become part of our collective unconscious, if one is inclined to believe in such a noumenon, or at least to have become an unquestioned element in the social instruction we impose upon infants from birth, in much the same way we inculcate, without reflection, the gender distinctions "female" and "male." I *have* a body, you are likely to say if you talk about embodiment at all; you don't say, I *am* a body. A body is a separate entity possessable by the "I"; the "I" and the body aren't, as the copula would make them, grammatically indistinguishable.

To widen the rift between the self and the body, we treat our bodies as subordinates, inferior in moral status. Open association with them shames us. In fact, we treat our bodies with very much the same distance and ambivalence women have traditionally received from men in our culture. Sometimes this treatment is benevolent, even respectful, but all too often it is tainted by outright sadism. I think of the body-building regimens that have become popular in the last decade or so, with the complicated vacillations they reflect between self-worship and self-degradation: joggers and aerobic dancers and weightlifters all beating their bodies into shape. "No pain, no gain," the saying goes. "Feel the burn." Bodies get treated like wayward women who have to be shown who's boss, even if it means slapping them around a little. I'm not for a moment opposing rugged exercise here. I'm simply questioning the spirit in which it is often undertaken.

Since, as Hélène Cixous points out in her essay on women and writing, "Sorties," thought has always worked "through dual, hierarchical oppositions,"[1] the mind/body split cannot possibly be innocent. The utterance of an "I" immediately calls into being its opposite, the "not-I," Western discourse being unequipped to conceive "that which is neither 'I' nor 'not-I,'" "that which is both 'I' and 'not-I,'" or some other permutation which language doesn't permit me to speak. The "not-I" is, by definition, other. And we've never been too fond of the other. We prefer the same. We tend to ascribe to the other those qualities we prefer not to associate with our selves: it is the hidden, the dark, the secret, the shameful. Thus, when the "I" takes possession of the body, it makes the body into an other, direct object of a transitive verb, with all the other's repudiated and potentially dangerous qualities.

At the least, then, the body had best be viewed with suspicion. And a woman's body is particularly suspect, since so much of it is in fact hidden, dark, secret, carried about on the inside where, even with the aid of a speculum, one can never perceive all of it in the plain light of day, a graspable whole. I, for one, have never understood why anyone would want to carry all that delicate stuff around on the outside. It would make you awfully anxious, I should think, put you constantly on the defensive, create a kind of siege mentality that viewed all other beings, even your own kind, as threats to be warded off with spears and guns and atomic missiles. And you'd never get to experience that inward dreaming that comes when your

10

---

[1]Hélène Cixous, "Sorties," in *The Newly Born Woman*, translated by Betsy Wing (Minneapolis: University of Minnesota Press, 1986), p.64. [Eds.]

flesh surrounds all your treasures, holding them close, like a sturdy shut-tered house. Be my personal skepticism as it may, however, as a cultural woman I bear just as much shame as any woman for my dark, enfolded secrets. Let the word for my external genitals tell the tale: my pudendum, from the Latin infinitive meaning "to be ashamed."

It's bad enough to carry your genitals like a sealed envelope bearing the cipher that, once unlocked, might loose the chaotic flood of female pleasure — *jouissance*, the French call it — upon the world-of-the-same. But I have an additional reason to feel shame for my body, less explicitly con-nected with its sexuality: it is a crippled body. Thus it is doubly other, not merely by the homo-sexual standards of patriarchal culture but by the stan-dards of physical desirability erected for every body in our world. Men, who are by definition exonerated from shame in sexual terms (this doesn't mean that an individual man might not experience sexual shame, of course; remember that I'm talking in general about discourse, not folks), may — more likely must — experience bodily shame if they are crippled. I won't presume to speak about the details of their experience, however. I don't know enough. I'll just go on telling what it's like to be a crippled woman, trusting that, since we're fellow creatures who've been living together for some thousands of years now, much of my experience will resonate with theirs.

I was never a beautiful woman, and for that reason I've spent most of my life (together with probably at least 95 percent of the female population of the United States) suffering from the shame of falling short of an un-attainable standard. The ideal woman of my generation was . . . perky, I think you'd say, rather than gorgeous. Blond hair pulled into a bouncing ponytail. Wide blue eyes, a turned-up nose with maybe a scattering of gold-en freckles across it, a small mouth with full lips over straight white teeth. Her breasts were large but well harnessed high on her chest; her tiny waist flared to hips just wide enough to give the crinolines under her circle skirt a starting outward push. In terms of personality, she was outgoing, even bubbly, not pensive or mysterious. Her milieu was the front fender of a white Corvette convertible, surrounded by teasing crewcuts, dressed in black flats, a sissy blouse, and the letter sweater of the Corvette owner. Needless to say, she never missed a prom.

Ten years or so later, when I first noticed the symptoms that would be diagnosed as MS, I was probably looking my best. Not beautiful still, but the ideal had shifted enough so that my flat chest and narrow hips gave me an elegantly attenuated shape, set off by a thick mass of long, straight, shin-ing hair. I had terrific legs, long and shapely, revealed nearly to the puden-dum by the fashionable miniskirts and hot pants I adopted with more enthusiasm than delicacy of taste. Not surprisingly, I suppose, during this time I involved myself in several pretty torrid love affairs.

The beginning of MS wasn't too bad. The first symptom, besides the pernicious fatigue that had begun to devour me, was "foot drop," the inability to raise my left foot at the ankle. As a consequence, I'd started to limp, but I could still wear high heels, and a bit of a limp might seem more intriguing than repulsive. After a few months, when the doctor suggested a cane, a crippled friend gave me quite an elegant wood-and-silver one, which I carried with a fair amount of panache. The real blow to my self-image came when I had to get a brace. As braces go, it's not bad: lightweight plastic molded to my foot and leg, fitting down into an ordinary shoe and secured around my calf by a Velcro strap. It reduces my limp and, more important, the danger of tripping and falling. But it meant the end of high heels. And it's ugly. Not as ugly as I think it is, I gather, but still pretty ugly. It signified for me, and perhaps still does, the permanence and irreversibility of my condition. The brace makes my MS concrete and forces me to wear it on the outside. As soon as I strapped the brace on, I climbed into trousers and stayed there (though not in the same trousers, of course). The idea of going around with my bare brace hanging out seemed almost as indecent as exposing my breasts. Not until 1984, soon after I won the Western States Book Award for poetry, did I put on a skirt short enough to reveal my plasticized leg. The connection between winning a writing award and baring my brace is not merely fortuitous; being affirmed as a writer really did embolden me. Since then, I've grown so accustomed to wearing skirts that I don't think about my brace any more than I think about my cane. I've incorporated them, I suppose: made them, in their necessity, insensate but fundamental parts of my body.

Meanwhile, I had to adjust to the most outward and visible sign of all,   15
a three-wheeled electric scooter called an Amigo. This lessens my fatigue and increases my range terrifically, but it also shouts out to the world, "Here is a woman who can't stand on her own two feet." At the same time, paradoxically, it renders me invisible, reducing me to the height of a seven-year-old, with a child's attendant low status. "Would she like smoking or nonsmoking?" the gate agent assigning me a seat asks the friend traveling with me. In crowds I see nothing but buttocks. I can tell you the name of every type of designer jeans ever sold. The wearers, eyes front, trip over me and fall across my handlebars into my lap. "Hey!" I want to shout to the lofty world. "Down here! There's a person down here!" But I'm not, by their standards, quite a person anymore.

My self-esteem diminishes further as age and illness strip from me the features that made me, for a brief while anyway, a good-looking, even sexy, young woman. No more long, bounding strides: I shuffle along with the timid gait I remember observing, with pity and impatience, in the little old ladies at Boston's Symphony Hall on Friday afternoons. No more lithe, girlish figure: my belly sags from the loss of muscle tone, which also creates all kinds of intestinal disruptions, hopelessly humiliating in a society in which excretory functions remain strictly unspeakable. No more sex, either, if society had its way. The sexuality of the disabled so repulses most people that you can hardly get a doctor, let alone a member of the general population, to consider the issues it raises. Cripples simply aren't supposed to Want It, much less Do It. Fortunately, I've got a husband with a strong libido and a weak sense of social propriety, or else I'd find myself perforce practicing a vow of chastity I never cared to take.

Afflicted by the general shame of having a body at all, and the specific shame of having one weakened and misshapen by disease, I ought not to be able to hold my head up in public. And yet I've gotten into the habit of holding my head up in public, sometimes under excruciating circumstances. Recently, for instance, I had to give a reading at the University of Arizona. Having smashed three of my front teeth in a fall onto the concrete floor of my screened porch, I was in the process of getting them crowned, and the temporary crowns flew out during dinner right before the reading. What to do? I wanted, of course, to rush home and hide till the dental office opened the next morning. But I couldn't very well break my word at this last moment. So, looking like Hansel and Gretel's witch, and lisping worse than the Wife of Bath, I got up on stage and read. Somehow, over the years, I've learned how to set shame aside and do what I have to do.

Here, I think, is where my "voice" comes in. Because, in spite of my demurral at the beginning, I do in fact cope with my disability at least some of the time. And I do so, I think, by speaking about it, and about the whole experience of being a body, specifically a female body, out loud, in a clear, level tone that drowns out the frantic whispers of my mother, my grand-mothers, all the other trainers of wayward childish tongues: "Sssh! Sssh! Nice girls don't talk like that. Don't mention sweat. Don't mention men-strual blood. Don't ask what your grandfather does on his business trips. Don't laugh so loud. You sound like a loon. Keep your voice down. Don't tell. Don't tell. Don't tell." Speaking out loud is an antidote to shame. I want to distinguish clearly here between "shame," as I'm using the word, and "guilt" and "embarrassment," which, though equally painful, are not similarly poisonous. Guilt arises from performing a forbidden act or failing to perform a required one. In either case, the guilty person can, through reparation, erase the offense and start fresh. Embarrassment, less opprobri-ous though not necessarily less distressing, is generally caused by acting in a socially stupid or awkward way. When I trip and sprawl in public, when I wet myself, when my front teeth fly out, I feel horribly embarrassed, but, like the pain of childbirth, the sensation blurs and dissolves in time. If it didn't, every child would be an only child, and no one would set foot in public after the onset of puberty, when embarrassment erupts like a geyser and bathes one's whole life in its bitter stream. Shame may attach itself to guilt or embarrassment, complicating their resolution, but it is not the same emotion. I feel guilt or embarrassment for something I've done; shame, for who I am. I may stop doing bad or stupid things, but I can't stop being. How then can I help but be ashamed? Of the three conditions, this is the one that cracks and stifles my voice.

I can subvert its power, I've found, by acknowledging who I am, shame and all, and, in doing so, raising what was hidden, dark, secret about my life into the plain light of shared human experience. What we aren't permitted to utter holds us, each isolated from every other, in a kind of solipsistic thrall. Without any way to check our reality against anyone else's, we assume that our fears and shortcomings are ours alone. One of the strangest consequences of publishing a collection of personal essays called *Plaintext* has been the steady trickle of letters and telephone calls saying essentially, in a tone of unmistakable relief, "Oh, me too! Me too!" It's as though the part I thought was solo has turned out to be a chorus. But none of us was singing loud enough for the others to hear.

Singing loud enough demands a particular kind of voice, I think. And   20 I was wrong to suggest, at the beginning, that I've always had my voice. I have indeed always had *a* voice, but it wasn't *this* voice, the one with which I could call up and transform my hidden self from a naughty girl into a woman talking directly to others like herself. Recently, in the process of writing a new book, a memoir entitled *Remembering the Bone House,* I've had occasion to read some of my early writing, from college, high school, even junior high. It's not an experience I recommend to anyone susceptible to shame. Not that the writing was all that bad. I was surprised at how competent a lot of it was. Here was a writer who already knew precisely how the language worked. But the voice . . . oh, the voice was all wrong: maudlin, rhapsodic, breaking here and there into little shrieks, almost, you might say, hysterical. It was a voice that had shucked off its own body, its own homely life of Cheerios for breakfast and seventy pages of Chaucer to read before the exam on Tuesday and a planter's wart growing painfully on the ball of its foot, and reeled now wraithlike through the air, seeking incarnation only as the heroine who enacts her doomed love for the tall, dark, mysterious stranger. If it didn't get that part, it wouldn't play at all.

Among all these overheated and vaporous imaginings, I must have retained some shred of sense, because I stopped writing prose entirely, except for scholarly papers, for nearly twenty years. I even forgot, not exactly that I had written prose, but at least what kind of prose it was. So when I needed to take up the process again, I could start almost fresh, using the vocal range I'd gotten used to in years of asking the waiter in the Greek restaurant for an extra anchovy on my salad, congratulating the puppy on making a puddle outside rather than inside the patio door, pondering with my daughter the vagaries of female orgasm, saying goodbye to my husband, and hello, and goodbye, and hello. This new voice—thoughtful, affectionate, often amused—was essential because what I needed to write about when I returned to prose was an attempt I'd made not long before to kill myself, and suicide simply refuses to be spoken of authentically in high-flown romantic language. It's too ugly. Too shameful. Too strictly a bodily event. And, yes, too funny as well, though people are sometimes shocked to find humor shoved up against suicide. They don't like the incongruity. But let's face it, life (real life, I mean, not the edited-for-television version) is a cacophonous affair from start to finish. I might have wanted to portray my suicidal self as a languishing maiden, too exquisitely sensitive to sustain life's wounding pressures on her soul. (I didn't want to, as a matter of fact, but I might have.) The truth remained, regardless of my desires, that when my husband lugged me into the emergency room, my hair matted, my face swollen and gray, my nightgown streaked with blood and urine, I was no frail and tender spirit. I was a body, and one in a hell of a mess.

I "should" have kept quiet about that experience. I know the rules of polite discourse. I should have kept my shame, and the nearly lethal sense of isolation and alienation it brought, to myself. And I might have, except for something the psychiatrist in the emergency room had told my husband. "You might as well take her home," he said. "If she wants to kill herself, she'll do it no matter how many precautions we take. They always do." *They* always do. I was one of "them," whoever they were. I was, in this context anyway, not singular, not aberrant, but typical. I think it was this sense of commonality with others I didn't even know, a sense of being returned somehow, in spite of my appalling act, to the human family, that urged me to write that first essay, not merely speaking out but calling out, perhaps. "Here's the way I am," it said. "How about you?" And the answer came, as I've said: "Me too! Me too!"

This has been the kind of work I've continued to do: to scrutinize the details of my own experience and to report what I see, and what I think about what I see, as lucidly and accurately as possible. But because feminine experience has been immemorially devalued and repressed, I continue to find this task terrifying. "Every woman has known the torture of beginning to speak aloud," Cixous writes, "heart beating as if to break, occasionally falling into loss of language, ground and language slipping out from under her, because for woman speaking—even just opening her mouth—in public is something rash, a transgression."[2]

The voice I summon up wants to crack, to whisper, to trail back into silence. "I'm sorry to have nothing more than this to say," it wants to apologize. "I shouldn't be taking up your time. I've never fought in a war, or even in a schoolyard free-for-all. I've never tried to see who could piss farthest up the barn wall. I've never even been to a whorehouse. All the important formative experiences have passed me by. I was raped once. I've borne two children. Milk trickling out of my breasts, blood trickling from between my legs. You don't want to hear about it. Sometimes I'm too scared to leave my house. Not scared *of* anything, just scared: mouth dry, bowels writhing. When the fear got really bad, they locked me up for six months, but that was years ago. I'm getting old now. Misshapen, too. I don't blame you if you can't get it up. No one could possibly desire a body like this. It's not your fault. It's mine. Forgive me. I didn't mean to start crying. I'm sorry . . . sorry . . . sorry. . . ."

An easy solace to the anxiety of speaking aloud: this slow subsidence   25
beneath the waves of shame, back into what Cixous calls "this body that has been worse than confiscated, a body replaced with a disturbing

---

[2]Cixous, "Sorties," p. 92. [Eds.]

stranger, sick or dead, who so often is a bad influence, the cause and place of inhibitions. By censuring the body," she goes on, "breath and speech are censored at the same time."[3] But I am not going back, not going under one more time. To do so would demonstrate a failure of nerve far worse than the depredations of MS have caused. Paradoxically, losing one sort of nerve has given me another. No one is going to take my breath away. No one is going to leave me speechless. To be silent is to comply with the standard of feminine grace. But my crippled body already violates all notions of feminine grace. What more have I got to lose? I've gone beyond shame. I'm shameless, you might say. You know, as in "shameless hussy"? A woman with her bare brace and her tongue hanging out.

I've "found" my voice, then, just where it ought to have been, in the body-warmed breath escaping my lungs and throat. Forced by the exigencies of physical disease to embrace my self in the flesh, I couldn't write bodiless prose. The voice is the creature of the body that produces it. I speak as a crippled woman. At the same time, in the utterance I redeem both "cripple" and "woman" from the shameful silences by which I have often felt surrounded, contained, set apart; I give myself permission to live openly among others, to reach out for them, stroke them with fingers and sighs. No body, no voice; no voice, no body. That's what I know in my bones.

QUESTIONS

1. Why do you think Mairs compares her struggle with multiple sclerosis to such common "problems" as having a female body and going through puberty? In what ways is her essay as much about a writer who finds her voice as a woman as it is about a woman who finds her voice as an individual with MS?

2. When asked to explain how she discovered her voice, Mairs at first proclaims that she did not need to find her voice — in that her voice was in place from the time she was speaking full sentences when she was a year old. Later in the essay, however, she takes back her statement: "I was wrong to suggest, at the beginning, that I've always had my voice. I have indeed always had *a* voice, but it wasn't *this* voice, the one with which I could call up and transform my hidden self from a naughty girl into a woman talking directly to others like herself" (paragraph 20). Why did Mairs change her mind midway through the essay? How does her revision of her own words reflect the "simmering" writing technique she describes in the fourth paragraph of her essay?

3. Toward the end of her essay, Mairs summons up her voice as if it were separate from her writing up to that point. Her voice then begins a long apology, ending with "Forgive me. I didn't mean to start crying. I'm

---

[3]Cixous, "Sorties," p. 97. [Eds.]

sorry . . . sorry . . . sorry. . . ." (paragraph 24). Why does Mairs refer to her summoned voice as "it" and set off its words with quotation marks? How do the language and tone of this passage differ from the rest of her essay? How would her essay have been different had she excluded this paragraph? Do you believe that it adds to or detracts from her explanation of multiple sclerosis?

4. Mairs concludes her essay with a powerful statement: "No body, no voice; no voice, no body. That's what I know in my bones." What is Mairs saying about the relationship between her voice and body? How did each give rise to the other?

5. What do you think Mairs means by "bodiless prose" (paragraph 26)? What would such a voice sound like?

6. When have you felt most connected or disconnected with your body? Write down your first answer to this question, and then put it on "simmer" for several days, as Mairs suggests. Write an essay comparing these two experiences (connection and disconnection with your body), including your first response and the process of revising it within your essay.

MAKING CONNECTIONS

1. For Mairs, the act of speaking and writing about her body has helped her to cope with her multiple sclerosis. Read Atul Gawande's "Crimson Tide" (p. 455), and compare the plights of Mairs and Christine Drury, who overcame her shame by "revealing her secret" about her blush-removal operation. What is powerful about giving voice to something that is secret or shameful? If Mairs had met Drury before her operation, what advice do you think Mairs might have given her? Do you believe that speaking about her blushing problem might have helped Drury enough to make the operation unnecessary?

2. Both Mairs and Lucy Grealy (p. 50) narrate their struggles with being bothered about how they appear in public. Compare and contrast their two essays. What similar points do both authors reveal about appearing different or disabled? How would you characterize the conclusions of both authors? Do you feel more strongly about one author's piece? Why?

METAPHORS

Sylvia Plath

Born in a suburb of Boston in 1932, Sylvia Plath began writing at an early age, publishing stories and poems in magazines such as Seventeen *and* Mademoiselle, *where she was a guest editor at the age of twenty-one. After graduating summa cum laude from Smith College, Plath studied at Cambridge University in England, where she met her husband, the poet Ted Hughes. They lived for a time in Massachusetts, where Plath was on the faculty at Smith for a year, and then returned to England. Plath's first collection of poetry,* The Colossus, *appeared in 1960, and she continued to write prolifically until, overcome by the personal demons that had haunted her all of her life, she committed suicide in 1963 at the age of thirty. Plath's posthumously published works include the autobiographical novel* The Bell Jar *(1963), which was an influential best-seller, as well as the poetry collections* Ariel *(1965),* Crossing the Water: Transitional Poems *(1971), and* Winter Dreams *(1971), made up of works written during her final months. Her* Collected Poems *won the 1982 Pulitzer Prize for poetry. The following poem, from* The Colossus, *was written when Plath was pregnant with her first child.*

I'm a riddle in nine syllables,
An elephant, a ponderous house,
A melon strolling on two tendrils.
O red fruit, ivory, fine timbers!
This loaf's big with its yeasty rising.   5
Money's new-minted in this fat purse.
I'm a means, a stage, a cow in calf.
I've eaten a bag of green apples,
Boarded the train there's no getting off.

QUESTIONS

1. The poetry critic Helen Vendler believes that many poems "originate in crucial moments of private life." What crucial moment of Plath's private life may have catalyzed this poem? What is the answer to the "riddle"? If you are not sure, reread the poem several times, and visualize the imagery in the poem. What lines in the poem support your answer?
2. Six of the nine lines in the poem are food or animal metaphors. What effect do these metaphors have?

3. What is the tone of the poem? How do you think Plath feels about what is happening to her? What lines in the poem support your answer?

4. Plath chose to write "Metaphors" in free verse—that is, with no set pattern of rhymes. But her poem is not completely free form. What other kind of pattern does she employ, and why do you think she chose to use it? How does it complement the meaning of her poem?

5. Reread the poem, paying special attention to the last line, "Boarded the train there's no getting off." This line gives a sense of inevitability—of an event or a state of being that is beyond the writer's control. Write a poem about something that seems inevitable in your life. Use metaphors to characterize that inevitability. Choose a strict pattern to follow in the poem, either in terms of number of lines, number of syllables per line, or rhyme.

MAKING CONNECTIONS

What do Nancy Mairs's "Carnal Acts" (p. 367) and Plath's "Metaphors" have in common? Compare the ways that Plath and Mairs use metaphors to describe their conditions. If Plath were asked to write a poem about Mairs, what do you think it would sound like? Which of Mairs's metaphors would she choose to include in her poem? Pick three of Mairs's metaphors, and write the poem that you think Plath might write.

Social Sciences and Public Affairs

SOME CONDITIONS OF OBEDIENCE AND DISOBEDIENCE TO AUTHORITY

Stanley Milgram

Stanley Milgram (1933–1984) was born in New York, went to Queens College and Harvard University, and was a professor of social psychology at the Graduate Center of the City University of New York. The following explanation of Milgram's obedience experiment first appeared in the professional journal Human Relations *in 1965 and made him famous, causing a storm of controversy over his method of experimentation and the results of his experiment. Milgram once said of his work, "As a social psychologist, I look at the world not to master it in any practical sense, but to understand it and to communicate that understanding to others."*

The situation in which one agent commands another to hurt a third turns up time and again as a significant theme in human relations.[1] It is powerfully expressed in the story of Abraham, who is commanded by God to kill his son. It is no accident that Kierkegaard,[2] seeking to orient his thought to the central themes of human experience, chose Abraham's conflict as the springboard to his philosophy.

---

[1]This research was supported by two grants from the National Science Foundation: NSF G-7916 and NSF G-24152. Exploratory studies carried out in 1960 were financed by a grant from the Higgins Funds of Yale University. I am grateful to John T. Williams, James J. McDonough, and Emil Elges for the important part they played in the project. Thanks are due also to Alan Elms, James Miller, Taketo Murata, and Stephen Stier for their aid as graduate assistants. My wife, Sasha, performed many valuable services. Finally, I owe a profound debt to the many persons in New Haven and Bridgeport who served as subjects.

[2]*Søren Kierkegaard* (1813–1855): Danish philosopher and theologian. [Eds.]

War too moves forward on the triad of an authority which commands a person to destroy the enemy, and perhaps all organized hostility may be viewed as a theme and variation on the three elements of authority, executant, and victim.[3] We describe an experimental program, recently concluded at Yale University, in which a particular expression of this conflict is studied by experimental means.

In its most general form the problem may be defined thus: if X tells Y to hurt Z, under what conditions will Y carry out the command of X and under what conditions will he refuse? In the more limited form possible in laboratory research, the question becomes: If an experimenter tells a subject to hurt another person, under what conditions will the subject go along with this instruction, and under what conditions will he refuse to obey? The laboratory problem is not so much a dilution of the general statement as one concrete expression of the many particular forms this question may assume.

One aim of the research was to study behavior in a strong situation of deep consequence to the participants, for the psychological forces operative in powerful and lifelike forms of the conflict may not be brought into play under diluted conditions.

This approach meant, first, that we had a special obligation to protect   5
the welfare and dignity of the persons who took part in the study; subjects were, of necessity, placed in a difficult predicament, and steps had to be taken to ensure their well-being before they were discharged from the laboratory. Toward this end, a careful, post-experimental treatment was devised and has been carried through for subjects in all conditions.[4]

---

[3]Consider, for example, J. P. Scott's analysis of war in his monograph on aggression:
   . . . while the actions of key individuals in a war may be explained in terms of direct stimulation to aggression, vast numbers of other people are involved simply by being part of an organized society.
   . . . For example, at the beginning of World War I an Austrian archduke was assassinated in Sarajevo. A few days later soldiers from all over Europe were marching toward each other, not because they were stimulated by the archduke's misfortune, but because they had been trained to obey orders. (Slightly rearranged from Scott (1958), *Aggression*, p. 103.)

[4]It consisted of an extended discussion with the experimenter and, of equal importance, a friendly reconciliation with the victim. It is made clear that the victim did *not* receive painful electric shocks. After the completion of the experimental series, subjects were sent a detailed report of the results and full purposes of the experimental program. A formal assessment of this procedure points to its overall effectiveness. Of the subjects, 83.7 percent indicated that they were glad to have taken part in the study; 15.1 percent reported neutral feelings; and 1.3 percent stated that they were sorry to have participated. A large number of subjects spontaneously requested that they be used in further experimentation. Four-fifths of the subjects felt that more experiments of this sort should be carried out, and 74 percent indicated that they had

Terminology

If *Y* follows the command of *X* we shall say that he has obeyed *X*; if he fails to carry out the command of *X*, we shall say that he has disobeyed *X*. The terms to *obey* and to *disobey*, as used here, refer to the subject's overt action only, and carry no implication for the motive or experiential states accompanying the action.[5]

To be sure, the everyday use of the word *obedience* is not entirely free from complexities. It refers to action within varying situations, and connotes diverse motives within those situations: a child's obedience differs from a soldier's obedience, or the love, honor, and *obey* of the marriage vow. However, a consistent behavioral relationship is indicated in most uses

---

learned something of personal importance as a result of being in the study. Furthermore, a university psychiatrist, experienced in outpatient treatment, interviewed a sample of experimental subjects with the aim of uncovering possible injurious effects resulting from participation. No such effects were in evidence. Indeed, subjects typically felt that their participation was instructive and enriching. A more detailed discussion of this question can be found in Milgram (1964).

[5]To *obey* and to *disobey* are not the only terms one could use in describing the critical action of *Y*. One could say that *Y* is cooperating with *X*, or displays conformity with regard to *X*'s commands. However, *cooperation* suggests that *X* agrees with *Y*'s ends, and understands the relationship between his own behavior and the attainment of those ends. (But the experimental procedure, and, in particular, the experimenter's command that the subject shock the victim even in the absence of a response from the victim, preclude such understanding.) Moreover, cooperation implies status parity for the co-acting agents, and neglects the asymmetrical, dominance-subordination element prominent in the laboratory relationship between experimenter and subject. *Conformity* has been used in other important contexts in social psychology, and most frequently refers to imitating the judgments or actions of others when no explicit requirement for imitation has been made. Furthermore, in the present study there are two sources of social pressure; pressure from the experimenter issuing the commands, and pressure from the victim to stop the punishment. It is the pitting of a common man (the victim) against an authority (the experimenter) that is the distinctive feature of the conflict. At a point in the experiment the victim demands that he be let free. The experimenter insists that the subject continue to administer shocks. Which act of the subject can be interpreted as conformity? The subject may conform to the wishes of his peer or to the wishes of the experimenter, and conformity in one direction means the absence of conformity in the other. Thus the word has no useful reference in this setting, for the dual and conflicting social pressures cancel out its meaning.

In the final analysis, the linguistic symbol representing the subject's action must take its meaning from the concrete context in which that action occurs; and there is probably no word in everyday language that covers the experimental situation exactly, without omissions or irrelevant connotations. It is partly for convenience, therefore, that the terms *obey* and *disobey* are used to describe the subject's actions. At the same time, our use of the words is highly congruent with dictionary meaning.

of the term: in the act of obeying, a person does what another person tells him to do. Y obeys X if he carries out the prescription for action which X has addressed to him; the term suggests, moreover, that some form of dominance-subordination, or hierarchical element, is part of the situation in which the transaction between X and Y occurs.

A subject who complies with the entire series of experimental commands will be termed an *obedient* subject; one who at any point in the command series defies the experimenter will be called a *disobedient* or *defiant* subject. As used in this report the terms refer only to the subject's performance in the experiment, and do not necessarily imply a general personality disposition to submit to or reject authority.

Subject Population

The subjects used in all experimental conditions were male adults, residing in the greater New Haven and Bridgeport areas, aged 20 to 50 years, and engaged in a wide variety of occupations. Each experimental condition described in this report employed 40 fresh subjects and was carefully balanced for age and occupational types. The occupational composition for each experiment was: workers, skilled and unskilled: 40 percent; white collar, sales, business: 40 percent; professionals: 20 percent. The occupations were intersected with three age categories (subjects in 20's, 30's, and 40's, assigned to each condition in the proportions of 20, 40, and 40 percent, respectively).

The General Laboratory Procedure[6]

The focus of the study concerns the amount of electric shock a subject   10
is willing to administer to another person when ordered by an experimenter to give the "victim" increasingly more severe punishment. The act of administering shock is set in the context of a learning experiment, ostensibly designed to study the effect of punishment on memory. Aside from the experimenter, one naïve subject and one accomplice perform in each session. On arrival each subject is paid $4.50. After a general talk by the experimenter, telling how little scientists know about the effect of punishment on memory, subjects are informed that one member of the pair will serve as teacher and one as learner. A rigged drawing is held so that the

---

[6]A more detailed account of the laboratory procedure can be found in Milgram (1963). A similar and independently evolved experimental procedure, employing a shock generator, victim, and learning task, was reported by Buss (1961). Buss used the technique for studying aggression, not obedience, and did not make use of the fundamental measure employed in the present study: breakoff points.

naïve subject is always the teacher, and the accomplice becomes the learner. The learner is taken to an adjacent room and strapped into an "electric chair."

The naïve subject is told that it is his task to teach the learner a list of paired associates, to test him on the list, and to administer punishment whenever the learner errs in the test. Punishment takes the form of electric shock, delivered to the learner by means of a shock generator controlled by the naïve subject. The teacher is instructed to increase the intensity of electric shock one step on the generator on each error. The learner, according to plan, provides many wrong answers, so that before long the naïve subject must give him the strongest shock on the generator. Increases in shock level are met by increasingly insistent demands from the learner that the experiment be stopped because of the growing discomfort to him. However, in clear terms the experimenter orders the teacher to continue with the procedure in disregard of the learner's protests. *Thus, the naïve subject must resolve a conflict between two mutually incompatible demands from the social field. He may continue to follow the orders of the experimenter and shock the learner with increasing severity, or he may refuse to follow the orders of the experimenter and heed the learner's pleas. The experimenter's authority operates not in a free field, but against ever-mounting countervailing pressure from the person being punished.*

A few technical points need to be considered before the findings of the study are described. For the purpose of delivering shock, a simulated shock generator is used, with 30 clearly marked voltage levels that range from 15 to 450 volts. (Each level is activated by one of 30 individual lever switches set in a horizontal line.) The naïve subject is given a sample shock of 45 volts to convince him of the authenticity of the instrument. The generator bears verbal designations that range from "Slight Shock" to "Danger: Severe Shock."

The responses of the victim are standardized on tape, and each protest is coordinated to a particular voltage level on the shock generator. Starting with 75 volts the learner begins to grunt and moan. At 150 volts he demands to be let out of the experiment. At 180 volts he cries out that he can no longer stand the pain. At 300 volts he refuses to provide any more answers to the memory test, insisting that he is no longer a participant in the experiment and must be freed. In response to this last tactic, the experimenter instructs the naïve subject to treat the absence of an answer as equivalent to a wrong answer, and to follow the usual shock procedure. The experimenter reinforces his demand with the statement: "You have no other choice, you must go on!" (This imperative is used whenever the naïve subject tries to break off the experiment.) If the subject refuses to give the next higher level of shock, the experiment is considered at an end. A quantitative value is assigned to the subject's performance based on the maximum-intensity shock he administered before breaking off. Thus any subject's score may range from zero (for a subject unwilling to administer the first shock level) to 30 (for a subject who proceeds to the highest voltage level on the board). For any particular subject and for any particular experimental condition, the degree to which participants have followed the experimenter's orders may be specified with a numerical value, corresponding to the metric on the shock generator.

This laboratory situation gives us a framework in which to study the subject's reactions to the principal conflict of the experiment. Again, this conflict is between the experimenter's demands that he continue to administer the electric shock, and the learner's demands, which become increasingly more insistent, that the experiment be stopped. The crux of the study is to vary systematically the factors believed to alter the degree of obedience to the experimental commands, to learn under what conditions submission to authority is most probable and under what conditions defiance is brought to the fore.

Pilot Studies

Pilot studies for the present research were completed in the winter of 1960; they differed from the regular experiments in a few details: for one, the victim was placed behind a silvered glass, with the light balance on the glass such that the victim could be dimly perceived by the subject (Milgram, 1961).   15

Though essentially qualitative in treatment, these studies pointed to several significant features of the experimental situation. At first no vocal feedback was used from the victim. It was thought that the verbal and voltage designations on the control panel would create sufficient pressure to curtail the subject's obedience. However, this was not the case. In the absence of protests from the learner, virtually all subjects, once commanded, went blithely to the end of the board, seemingly indifferent to the verbal designations ("Extreme Shock" and "Danger: Severe Shock"). This deprived us of an adequate basis for scaling obedient tendencies. A force had to be introduced that would strengthen the subject's resistance to the experimenter's commands, and reveal individual differences in terms of a distribution of break-off points.

This force took the form of protests from the victim. Initially, mild protests were used, but proved inadequate. Subsequently, more vehement protests were inserted into the experimental procedure. To our consternation, even the strongest protests from the victim did not prevent all subjects from administering the harshest punishment ordered by the experimenter; but the protests did lower the mean maximum shock somewhat and created some spread in the subject's performance; therefore, the victim's cries were standardized on tape and incorporated into the regular experimental procedure.

The situation did more than highlight the technical difficulties of finding a workable experimental procedure: It indicated that subjects would obey authority to a greater extent than we had supposed. It also pointed to the importance of feedback from the victim in controlling the subject's behavior.

One further aspect of the pilot study was that subjects frequently averted their eyes from the person they were shocking, often turning their heads in an awkward and conspicuous manner. One subject explained: "I didn't want to see the consequences of what I had done." Observers wrote:

> . . . subjects showed a reluctance to look at the victim, whom they could see through the glass in front of them. When this fact was brought to their attention they indicated that it caused them discomfort to see the victim in agony. We note, however, that although the subject refuses to look at the victim, he continues to administer shocks.

This suggested that the salience of the victim may have, in some degree, regulated the subject's performance. If, in obeying the experimenter, the subject found it necessary to avoid scrutiny of the victim, would the converse be true? If the victim were rendered increasingly more salient to the subject, would obedience diminish? The first set of regular experiments was designed to answer this question. 20

Immediacy of the Victim

This series consisted of four experimental conditions. In each condition the victim was brought "psychologically" closer to the subject giving him shocks.

In the first condition (Remote Feedback) the victim was placed in another room and could not be heard or seen by the subject, except that, at 300 volts, he pounded on the wall in protest. After 315 volts he no longer answered or was heard from.

The second condition (Voice Feedback) was identical to the first except that voice protests were introduced. As in the first condition the victim was placed in an adjacent room, but his complaints could be heard clearly through a door left slightly ajar and through the walls of the laboratory.[7]

---

[7]It is difficult to convey on the printed page the full tenor of the victim's responses, for we have no adequate notation for vocal intensity, timing, and general qualities of delivery. Yet these features are crucial to producing the effect of an increasingly severe reaction to mounting voltage levels. (They can be communicated fully only by sending interested parties the recorded tapes.) In general terms, however, the victim indicates no discomfort until the 75-volt shock is administered, at which time there is a light grunt in response to the punishment. Similar reactions follow the 90- and 105-volt shocks, and at 120 volts the victim shouts to the experimenter that the shocks are becoming painful. Painful groans are heard on administration of the 135-volt shock, and at 150 volts the victim cries out, "Experimenter, get me out of here! I won't be in the experiment any more! I refuse to go on!" Cries of this type continue with generally rising intensity, so that at 180 volts the victim

The third experimental condition (Proximity) was similar to the second, except that the victim was now placed in the same room as the subject, and 1⅜ feet from him. Thus he was visible as well as audible, and voice cues were provided.

The fourth, and final, condition of this series (Touch-Proximity) was   25
identical to the third, with this exception: The victim received a shock only when his hand rested on a shockplate. At the 150-volt level the victim again demanded to be let free and, in this condition, refused to place his hand on the shockplate. The experimenter ordered the naïve subject to force the victim's hand onto the plate. Thus obedience in this condition required that the subject have physical contact with the victim in order to give him punishment beyond the 150-volt level.

Forty adult subjects were studied in each condition. The data revealed that obedience was significantly reduced as the victim was rendered more immediate to the subject. The mean maximum shock for the conditions is shown in Figure 1.

Expressed in terms of the proportion of obedient to defiant subjects, the findings are that 34 percent of the subjects defied the experimenter in the Remote condition, 37.5 percent in Voice Feedback, 60 percent in Proximity, and 70 percent in Touch-Proximity.

How are we to account for this effect? A first conjecture might be that as the victim was brought closer the subject became more aware of the intensity of his suffering and regulated his behavior accordingly. This makes sense, but our evidence does not support the interpretation. There are no consistent differences in the attributed level of pain across the four conditions (i.e., the amount of pain experienced by the victim as estimated by the subject and

---

cries out, "I can't stand the pain," and by 270 volts his response to the shock is definitely an agonized scream. Throughout, he insists that he be let out of the experiment. At 300 volts the victim shouts in desperation that he will no longer provide answers to the memory test; and at 315 volts, after a violent scream, he reaffirms with vehemence that he is no longer a participant. From this point on, he provides no answers, but shrieks in agony whenever a shock is administered; this continues through 450 volts. Of course, many subjects will have broken off before this point.

A revised and stronger set of protests was used in all experiments outside the Proximity series. Naturally, new baseline measures were established for all comparisons using the new set of protests.

There is overwhelming evidence that the great majority of subjects, both obedient and defiant, accepted the victims' reactions as genuine. The evidence takes the form of: (a) tension created in the subjects (see discussion of tension); (b) scores on "estimated-pain" scales filled out by subjects immediately after the experiment; (c) subjects' accounts of their feelings in post-experimental interviews; and (d) quantifiable responses to questionnaires distributed to subjects several months after their participation in the experiments. This matter will be treated fully in a forthcoming monograph.

(The procedure in all experimental conditions was to have the naïve subject announce the voltage level before administering each shock, so that — independently of the victim's responses — he was continually reminded of delivering punishment of ever-increasing severity.)

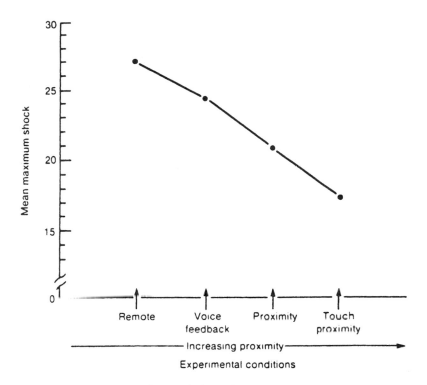

FIGURE 1 Mean maxima in proximity series.

expressed on a 14-point scale). But it is easy to speculate about alternative mechanisms:

> *Empathic cues.* In the Remote and to a lesser extent the Voice Feedback conditions, the victim's suffering possesses an abstract, remote quality for the subject. He is aware, but only in a conceptual sense, that his actions cause pain to another person; the fact is apprehended, but not felt. The phenomenon is common enough. The bombardier can reasonably suppose that his weapons will inflict suffering and death, yet this knowledge is divested of affect and does not move him to a felt, emotional response to the suffering resulting from his actions. Similar observations have been made in wartime. It is possible that the visual cues associated with the victim's suffering trigger empathic responses in the subject and provide him with a more complete grasp of the victim's experience. Or it is possible that the empathic responses are themselves unpleasant, possessing drive properties which cause the subject to terminate the arousal situation. Diminishing obedience, then, would be explained by the enrichment of empathic cues in the successive experimental conditions.

> *Denial and narrowing of the cognitive field.* The Remote condition allows a narrowing of the cognitive field so that the victim is put out of mind. The subject no longer considers the act of depressing a lever relevant to moral judgment, for it is no longer associated with the victim's suffering.

30

When the victim is close it is more difficult to exclude him phenomenologically. He necessarily intrudes on the subject's awareness since he is
continuously visible. In the Remote condition his existence and reactions
are made known only after the shock has been administered. The auditory feedback is sporadic and discontinuous. In the Proximity conditions his
inclusion in the immediate visual field renders him a continuously salient
element for the subject. The mechanism of denial can no longer be
brought into play. One subject in the Remote condition said: "It's funny
how you really begin to forget that there's a guy out there, even though
you can hear him. For a long time I just concentrated on pressing the
switches and reading the words."

Reciprocal fields. If in the Proximity condition the subject is in an
improved position to observe the victim, the reverse is also true. The
actions of the subject now come under proximal scrutiny by the victim.
Possibly, it is easier to harm a person when he is unable to observe our
actions than when he can see what we are doing. His surveillance of the
action directed against him may give rise to shame, or guilt, which may
then serve to curtail the action. Many expressions of language refer to
the discomfort or inhibitions that arise in face-to-face confrontation. It
is often said that it is easier to criticize a man "behind his back" than
to "attack him to his face." If we are in the process of lying to a person
it is reputedly difficult to "stare him in the eye." We "turn away from
others in shame" or in "embarrassment" and this action serves to
reduce our discomfort. The manifest function of allowing the victim of
a firing squad to be blindfolded is to make the occasion less stressful for
him, but it may also serve a latent function of reducing the stress of the
executioner. In short, in the Proximity conditions, the subject may sense
that he has become more salient in the victim's field of awareness.
Possibly he becomes more self-conscious, embarrassed, and inhibited in
his punishment of the victim.

Phenomenal unity of act. In the Remote condition it is more difficult
for the subject to gain a sense of *relatedness* between his own actions
and the consequences of these actions for the victim. There is a physical and spatial separation of the act and its consequences. The subject
depresses a lever in one room, and protests and cries are heard from
another. The two events are in correlation, yet they lack a compelling
phenomenological unity. The structure of a meaningful act—*I am
hurting a man*—breaks down because of the spatial arrangements, in a
manner somewhat analogous to the disappearance of phi phenomena[8]

---

[8]*phi phenomena:* Optical illusions of motion. The phi phenomenon is an illusion of apparent motion that is generated when similar stationary objects are presented one after another at a certain time interval. [Eds.]

when the blinking lights are spaced too far apart. The unity is more fully achieved in the Proximity condition as the victim is brought closer to the action that causes him pain. It is rendered complete in Touch-Proximity.

Incipient group formation. Placing the victim in another room not only takes him further from the subject, but the subject and the experimenter are drawn relatively closer. There is incipient group formation between the experimenter and the subject, from which the victim is excluded. The wall between the victim and the others deprives him of an intimacy which the experimenter and subject feel. In the Remote condition, the victim is truly an outsider, who stands alone, physically and psychologically.

When the victim is placed close to the subject, it becomes easier to form an alliance with him against the experimenter. Subjects no longer have to face the experimenter alone. They have an ally who is close at hand and eager to collaborate in a revolt against the experimenter. Thus, the changing set of spatial relations leads to a potentially shifting set of alliances over the several experimental conditions.

Acquired behavior dispositions. It is commonly observed that laboratory mice will rarely fight with their litter mates. Scott (1958) explains this in terms of passive inhibition. He writes: "By doing nothing under . . . circumstances [the animal] learns to do nothing, and this may be spoken of as passive inhibition . . . this principle has great importance in teaching an individual to be peaceful, for it means that he can learn not to fight simply by not fighting." Similarly, we may learn not to harm others simply by not harming them in everyday life. Yet this learning occurs in a context of proximal relations with others, and may not be generalized to that situation in which the person is physically removed from us. Or possibly, in the past, aggressive actions against others who were physically close resulted in retaliatory punishment which extinguished the original form of response. In contrast, aggression against others at a distance may have only sporadically led to retaliation. Thus the organism learns that it is safer to be aggressive toward others at a distance, and precarious to be so when the parties are within arm's reach. Through a pattern of rewards and punishments, he acquires a disposition to avoid aggression at close quarters, a disposition which does not extend to harming others at a distance. And this may account for experimental findings in the remote and proximal experiments.

Proximity as a variable in psychological research has received far less attention than it deserves. If men were sessile[9] it would be easy to understand

---

[9]*sessile:* Permanently attached, not moving freely. [Eds.]

this neglect. But we move about; our spatial relations shift from one situation to the next, and the fact that we are near or remote may have a powerful effect on the psychological processes that mediate our behavior toward others. In the present situation, as the victim is brought closer to the subject ordered to give him shocks, increasing numbers of subjects break off the experiment, refusing to obey. The concrete, visible, and proximal presence of the victim acts in an important way to counteract the experimenter's power to generate disobedience.[10]

Closeness of Authority

If the spatial relationship of the subject and victim is relevant to the degree of obedience, would not the relationship of subject to experimenter also play a part?

There are reasons to feel that, on arrival, the subject is oriented primarily to the experimenter rather than to the victim. He has come to the laboratory to fit into the structure that the experimenter—not the victim—would provide. He has come less to understand his behavior than to *reveal* that behavior to a competent scientist, and he is willing to display himself as the scientist's purposes require. Most subjects seem quite concerned about the appearance they are making before the experimenter, and one could argue that this preoccupation in a relatively new and strange setting makes the subject somewhat insensitive to the triadic nature of the social situation. In other words, the subject is so concerned about the show he is putting on for the experimenter that influences from other parts of the social field do not receive as much weight as they ordinarily would. This overdetermined orientation to the experimenter would account for the relative insensitivity of the subject to the victim, and would also lead us to believe that alterations in the relationship between subject and experimenter would have important consequences for obedience.

In a series of experiments we varied the physical closeness and degree of surveillance of the experimenter. In one condition the experimenter sat just a few feet away from the subject. In a second condition, after giving initial instructions, the experimenter left the laboratory and gave his orders by

---

[10]Admittedly, the terms *proximity, immediacy, closeness,* and *salience-of-the-victim* are used in a loose sense, and the experiments themselves represent a very coarse treatment of the variable. Further experiments are needed to refine the notion and tease out such diverse factors as spatial distance, visibility, audibility, barrier interposition, etc.

The Proximity and Touch-Proximity experiments were the only conditions where we were unable to use taped feedback from the victim. Instead, the victim was trained to respond in these conditions as he had in Experiment 2 (which employed taped feedback). Some improvement is possible here, for it should be technically feasible to do a proximity series using taped feedback.

telephone. In still a third condition the experimenter was never seen, providing instructions by means of a tape recording activated when the subjects entered the laboratory.

Obedience dropped sharply as the experimenter was physically removed from the laboratory. The number of obedient subjects in the first condition (Experimenter Present) was almost three times as great as in the second, where the experimenter gave his orders by telephone. Twenty-six subjects were fully obedient in the first condition, and only nine in the second (Chi square obedient vs. defiant in the two conditions, df = 14.7; $p < 0.001$). Subjects seemed able to take a far stronger stand against the experimenter when they did not have to encounter him face to face, and the experimenter's power over the subject was severely curtailed.[11]

Moreover, when the experimenter was absent, subjects displayed an interesting form of behavior that had not occurred under his surveillance. Though continuing with the experiment, several subjects administered lower shocks than were required and never informed the experimenter of their deviation from the correct procedure. (Unknown to the subjects, shock levels were automatically recorded by an Esterline-Angus event recorder wired directly into the shock generator; the instrument provided us with an objective record of the subjects' performance.) Indeed, in telephone conversations some subjects specifically assured the experimenter that they were raising the shock level according to instruction, whereas in fact they were repeatedly using the lowest shock on the board. This form of behavior is particularly interesting: although these subjects acted in a way that clearly undermined the avowed purposes of the experiment, they found it easier to handle the conflict in this manner than to precipitate an open break with authority.

Other conditions were completed in which the experimenter was absent during the first segment of the experiment, but reappeared at the point that the subject definitely refused to give higher shocks when commanded by telephone. Although he had exhausted his power via telephone, the experimenter could frequently force further obedience when he reappeared in the laboratory.

Experiments in this series show that the *physical presence* of an authority is an important force contributing to the subject's obedience or defiance. Taken together with the first experimental series on the proximity of the victim, it would appear that something akin to fields of force, diminishing in effectiveness with increasing psychological distance from their source, have a controlling effect on the subject's performance. As the victim is brought closer, the subject finds it harder to administer shocks to him. When the victim's position is held constant relative to the subject, and the authority is made more remote, the subject finds it easier to break off the

---

[11]The third condition also led to significantly lower obedience than this first situation in which the experimenter was present, but it contains technical difficulties that require extensive discussion.

experiment. This effect is substantial in both cases, but manipulation of the experimenter's position yielded the more powerful results. Obedience to destructive commands is highly dependent on the proximal relations between authority and subject.

Tensions

The description of final scores does not fully convey the character of the subjects' performance, and it would be useful to interrupt our reporting of quantitative relationships to remark on the subjects' general reaction to the situation.

One might suppose that a subject would simply break off or continue   45 as his conscience and temperament dictated. Yet this is very far from what happened. There were powerful reactions of tension and emotional strain in a substantial proportion of the participants. Persons were observed to sweat, tremble, stutter, bite their lips, and groan as they found themselves increasingly implicated in the experimental conflict. Some sense of the subjects' mood can be found in a transcript of their remarks at break-off point. Here are the remarks of two defiant subjects:

> Is he banging? . . . Is he hurt out there? Well, I don't want to be responsible for anything that happens to him. No, I can't go on with it. I don't know whether he's all right or not. I mean he may have a heart condition or something; I wouldn't feel right doing it. He's banging for help. He's evidently in trouble or he wouldn't bang . . . I don't see any sense to this—to knocking him out or something. I just can't see it.
> [*Subject refuses to administer shocks*]   [*Subject 0108*]

> The man is banging. He wants to get out . . . I'm sorry. If the man wants to get out I'd just as soon stop . . . I don't want to administer any more [extremely excited] . . . I will gladly refund the check, but I will not harm this man . . . I'm sorry, I will not give him any more if he obviously wants to get out. There is no money in the world that will make me hurt another individual.
> [*Subject 010X*]

And here is a transcript from an obedient subject. He began the experiment calmly, but became increasingly tense as the experiment proceeded. After administering the 150-volt shock, he began to address the experimenter in agitated tones:

> *150 volts delivered.* You want me to keep going?
> *165 volts delivered.* That guy is hollering in there. There's a lot of them here. He's liable to have a heart condition. You want me to go?

180 volts delivered. He can't stand it! I'm not going to kill that man in there! You hear him hollering? He's hollering. He can't stand it. What if something happens to him? . . . I'm not going to get that man sick in there. He's hollering in there. You know what I mean? I mean I refuse to take responsibility. He's getting hurt in there. He's in there hollering. Too many left here. Geez, if he gets them wrong. There's too many of them left. I mean who is going to take responsibility if anything happens to that gentleman?
[*The experimenter accepts responsibility.*] All right.
195 volts delivered. You see he's hollering. Hear that. Gee, I don't know.
[*The experimenter says: "The experiment requires that you go on."*]—I know it does, sir, but I mean—hugh—he don't know what he's in for. He's up to 195 volts.
210 volts delivered.
225 volts delivered.
240 volts delivered. Aw, no. You mean I've got to keep going up with the scale? No sir. I'm not going to kill that man! I'm not going to give him 450 volts!
[*The experimenter says: "The experiment requires that you go on."*]—I know it does, but that man is hollering there, sir . . .

Despite his numerous, agitated objections, which were constant accompaniments to his actions, the subject unfailingly obeyed the experimenter, proceeding to the highest shock level on the generator. He displayed a curious dissociation between word and action. Although at the verbal level he had resolved not to go on, his actions were fully in accord with the experimenter's commands. This subject did not want to shock the victim, and he found it an extremely disagreeable task, but he was unable to invent a response that would free him from *E*'s authority. Many subjects cannot find the specific verbal formula that would enable them to reject the role assigned to them by the experimenter. Perhaps our culture does not provide adequate models for disobedience.

One puzzling sign of tension was the regular occurrence of nervous laughing fits. In the first four conditions 71 of the 160 subjects showed definite signs of nervous laughter and smiling. The laughter seemed entirely out of place, even bizarre. Full-blown, uncontrollable seizures were observed for 15 of these subjects. On one occasion we observed a seizure so violently convulsive that it was necessary to call a halt to the experiment. In the post-experimental interviews subjects took pains to point out that they were not sadistic types and that the laughter did not mean they enjoyed shocking the victim.

In the interview following the experiment subjects were asked to indicate on a 14-point scale just how nervous or tense they felt at the point of maximum tension (Figure 2). The scale ranged from "not at all tense and nervous" to "extremely tense and nervous." Self-reports of this sort are of limited precision and at best provide only a rough indication of the subject's emotional response. Still, taking the reports for what they are worth, it can be seen that the distribution of responses spans the entire range of the scale, with the majority of subjects concentrated at the center and upper extreme. A further breakdown showed that obedient subjects reported themselves as having been slightly more tense and nervous than the defiant subjects at the point of maximum tension.

How is the occurrence of tension to be interpreted? First, it points to the presence of conflict. If a tendency to comply with authority were the only psychological force operating in the situation, all subjects would have continued to the end and there would have been no tension. Tension, it is assumed, results from the simultaneous presence of two or more incompatible response tendencies (Miller, 1944). If sympathetic concern for the victim were the exclusive force, all subjects would have calmly defied the experimenter. Instead, there were both obedient and defiant outcomes, frequently accompanied by extreme tension. A conflict develops between the deeply ingrained disposition not to harm others and the equally compelling tendency to obey others who are in authority. The subject is quickly drawn into a dilemma of a deeply dynamic character, and the presence of high tension points to the considerable strength of each of the antagonistic vectors.

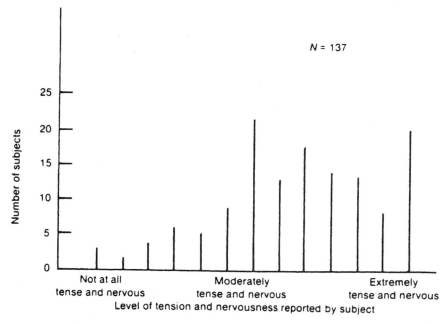

FIGURE 2 Level of tension and nervousness: the self-reports on "tension and nervousness" for 137 subjects on the Proximity experiments. Subjects were given a scale with 14 values ranging from "not at all tense and nervous" to "extremely tense and nervous." They were instructed: "Thinking back to that point in the experiment when you felt the most tense and nervous, indicate just how you felt by placing an X at the appropriate point on the scale." The results are shown in terms of midpoint values.

Moreover, tension defines the strength of the aversive state from which   50
the subject is unable to escape through disobedience. When a person is
uncomfortable, tense, or stressed, he tries to take some action that will allow
him to terminate this unpleasant state. Thus tension may serve as a drive that
leads to escape behavior. But in the present situation, even where tension is
extreme, many subjects are unable to perform the response that will bring
about relief. Therefore there must be a competing drive, tendency, or inhibition that precludes activation of the disobedient response. The strength of
this inhibiting factor must be of greater magnitude than the stress experienced, or else the terminating act would occur. Every evidence of extreme
tension is at the same time an indication of the strength of the forces that
keep the subject in the situation.

Finally, tension may be taken as evidence of the reality of the situations
for the subjects. Normal subjects do not tremble and sweat unless they are
implicated in a deep and genuinely felt predicament.

Background Authority

In psychophysics, animal learning, and other branches of psychology,
the fact that measures are obtained at one institution rather than another is
irrelevant to the interpretation of the findings, so long as the technical facilities for measurement are adequate and the operations are carried out with
competence.

But it cannot be assumed that this holds true for the present study. The
effectiveness of the experimenter's commands may depend in an important
way on the larger institutional context in which they are issued. The experiments described thus far were conducted at Yale University, an organization which most subjects regarded with respect and sometimes awe. In
post-experimental interviews several participants remarked that the locale
and sponsorship of the study gave them confidence in the integrity, competence, and benign purposes of the personnel; many indicated that they
would not have shocked the learner if the experiments had been done
elsewhere.

This issue of background authority seemed to us important for an interpretation of the results that had been obtained thus far; moreover it is highly relevant to any comprehensive theory of human obedience. Consider, for
example, how closely our compliance with the imperatives of others is tied
to particular institutions and locales in our day-to-day activities. On
request, we expose our throats to a man with a razor blade in the barber
shop, but would not do so in a shoe store; in the latter setting we willingly
follow the clerk's request to stand in our stockinged feet, but resist the command in a bank. In the laboratory of a great university, subjects may comply with a set of commands that would be resisted if given elsewhere. *One
must always question the relationship of obedience to a person's sense of
the context in which he is operating.*

To explore the problem we moved our apparatus to an office building   55
in industrial Bridgeport and replicated experimental conditions, without
any visible tie to the university.

Bridgeport subjects were invited to the experiment through a mail circular similar to the one used in the Yale study, with appropriate changes in
letterhead, etc. As in the earlier study, subjects were paid $4.50 for coming
to the laboratory. The same age and occupational distributions used at Yale
and the identical personnel were employed.

The purpose in relocating in Bridgeport was to assure a complete dissociation from Yale, and in this regard we were fully successful. On the surface,
the study appeared to be conducted by Research Associates of Bridgeport, an
organization of unknown character (the title had been concocted exclusively
for use in this study).

The experiments were conducted in a three-room office suite in a somewhat run-down commercial building located in the downtown shopping
area. The laboratory was sparsely furnished, though clean, and marginally
respectable in appearance. When subjects inquired about professional affiliations, they were informed only that we were a private firm conducting research for industry.

Some subjects displayed skepticism concerning the motives of the
Bridgeport experimenter. One gentleman gave us a written account of the
thoughts he experienced at the control board:

> . . . Should I quit this damn test? Maybe he passed out? What
> dopes we were not to check up on this deal. How do we know that
> these guys are legit? No furniture, bare walls, no telephone. We
> could of called the Police up or the Better Business Bureau. I
> learned a lesson tonight. How do I know that Mr. Williams [the
> experimenter] is telling the truth . . . I wish I knew how many volts
> a person could take before lapsing into unconsciousness . . .
>
> *[Subject 2414]*

Another subject stated:

> I questioned on my arrival my own judgment [about coming]. I had
> doubts as to the legitimacy of the operation and the consequences
> of participation. I felt it was a heartless way to conduct memory or
> learning processes on human beings and certainly dangerous with-
> out the presence of a medical doctor.   *[Subject 2440V]*

There was no noticeable reduction in tension for the Bridgeport sub-   60
jects. And the subjects' estimation of the amount of pain felt by the victim
was slightly, though not significantly, higher than in the Yale study.

A failure to obtain complete obedience in Bridgeport would indicate
that the extreme compliance found in New Haven subjects was tied closely

to the background authority of Yale University; if a large proportion of the subjects remained fully obedient, very different conclusions would be called for.

As it turned out, the level of obedience in Bridgeport, although somewhat reduced, was not significantly lower than that obtained at Yale. A large proportion of the Bridgeport subjects were fully obedient to the experimenter's commands (48 percent of the Bridgeport subjects delivered the maximum shock versus 65 percent in the corresponding condition at Yale).

How are these findings to be interpreted? It is possible that if commands of a potentially harmful or destructive sort are to be perceived as legitimate they must occur within some sort of institutional structure. But it is clear from the study that it need not be a particularly reputable or distinguished institution. The Bridgeport experiments were conducted by an unimpressive firm lacking any credentials; the laboratory was set up in a respectable office building with a title listed in the building directory. Beyond that, there was no evidence of benevolence or competence. It is possible that the *category* of institution, judged according to its professed function, rather than its qualitative position within that category, wins our compliance. Persons deposit money in elegant, but also in seedy-looking banks, without giving much thought to the differences in security they offer. Similarly, our subjects may consider one laboratory to be as competent as another, so long as it is a scientific laboratory.

It would be valuable to study the subjects' performance in other contexts which go even further than the Bridgeport study in denying institutional support to the experimenter. It is possible that, beyond a certain point, obedience disappears completely. But that point had not been reached in the Bridgeport office: almost half the subjects obeyed the experimenter fully.

Further Experiments

We may mention briefly some additional experiments undertaken in   65
the Yale series. A considerable amount of obedience and defiance in everyday life occurs in connection with groups. And we had reason to feel in light of the many group studies already done in psychology that group forces would have a profound effect on reactions to authority. A series of experiments was run to examine these effects. In all cases only one naïve subject was studied per hour, but he performed in the midst of actors who, unknown to him, were employed by the experimenter. In one experiment (Groups for Disobedience) two actors broke off in the middle of the experiment. When this happened 90 percent of the subjects followed suit and defied the experimenter. In another condition the actors followed the orders obediently; this strengthened the experimenter's power only slightly. In still a third experiment the job of pushing the switch to shock the learner was

given to one of the actors, while the naïve subject performed a subsidiary act. We wanted to see how the teacher would respond if he were involved in the situation but did not actually give the shocks. In this situation only three subjects out of forty broke off. In a final group experiment the subjects themselves determined the shock level they were going to use. Two actors suggested higher and higher shock levels; some subjects insisted, despite group pressure, that the shock level be kept low; others followed along with the group.

Further experiments were completed using women as subjects, as well as a set dealing with the effects of dual, unsanctioned, and conflicting authority. A final experiment concerned the personal relationship between victim and subject. These will have to be described elsewhere, lest the present report be extended to monographic length.

It goes without saying that future research can proceed in many different directions. What kinds of response from the victim are most effective in causing disobedience in the subject? Perhaps passive resistance is more effective than vehement protest. What conditions of entry into an authority system lead to greater or lesser obedience? What is the effect of anonymity and masking on the subject's behavior? What conditions lead to the subject's perception of responsibility for his own actions? Each of these could be a major research topic in itself, and can readily be incorporated into the general experimental procedure described here.

Levels of Obedience and Defiance

One general finding that merits attention is the high level of obedience manifested in the experimental situation. Subjects often expressed deep disapproval of shocking a man in the face of his objections, and others denounced it as senseless and stupid. Yet many subjects complied even while they protested. The proportion of obedient subjects greatly exceeded the expectations of the experimenter and his colleagues. At the outset, we had conjectured that subjects would not, in general, go above the level of "Strong Shock." In practice, many subjects were willing to administer the most extreme shocks available when commanded by the experimenter. For some subjects the experiment provided an occasion for aggressive release. And for others it demonstrated the extent to which obedient dispositions are deeply ingrained and engaged, irrespective of their consequences for others. Yet this is not the whole story. Somehow, the subject becomes implicated in a situation from which he cannot disengage himself.

The departure of the experimental results from intelligent expectation, to some extent, has been formalized. The procedure was to describe the experimental situation in concrete detail to a group of competent persons, and to ask them to predict the performance of 100 hypothetical subjects. For purposes of indicating the distribution of break-off points, judges were provided with a diagram of the shock generator and recorded their predictions before being informed of the actual results. Judges typically underestimated the amount of obedience demonstrated by subjects.

In Figure 3, we compare the predictions of forty psychiatrists at a   70
leading medical school with the actual performance of subjects in the experiment. The psychiatrists predicted that most subjects would not go beyond the tenth shock level (150 volts; at this point the victim makes his first explicit demand to be freed). They further predicted that by the twentieth shock level (300 volts; the victim refuses to answer) 3.73 percent of the subjects would still be obedient; and that only a little over one-tenth of one percent of the subjects would administer the highest shock on the board. But, as the graph indicates, the obtained behavior was very different. Sixty-two percent of the subjects obeyed the experimenter's commands fully. Between expectation and occurrence there is a whopping discrepancy.

Why did the psychiatrists underestimate the level of obedience? Possibly, because their predictions were based on an inadequate conception of the determinants of human action, a conception that focuses on motives *in vacuo*. This orientation may be entirely adequate for the repair of bruised impulses as

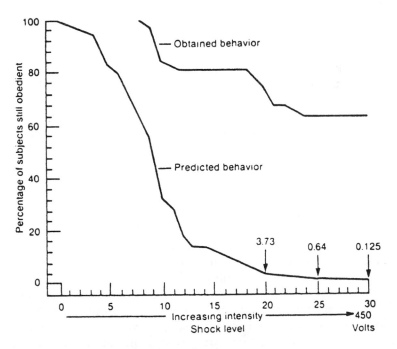

FIGURE 3 Predicted and obtained behavior in voice feedback.

revealed on the psychiatrist's couch, but as soon as our interest turns to action in larger settings, attention must be paid to the situations in which motives are expressed. A situation exerts an important press on the individual. It exercises constraints and may provide push. In certain circumstances it is not so much the kind of person a man is, as the kind of situation in which he is placed, that determines his actions.

Many people, not knowing much about the experiment, claim that subjects who go to the end of the board are sadistic. Nothing could be more foolish than an overall characterization of these persons. It is like saying that a person thrown into a swift-flowing stream is necessarily a fast swimmer, or that he has great stamina because he moves so rapidly relative to the bank. The context of action must always be considered. The individual, upon entering the laboratory, becomes integrated into a situation that carries its own momentum. The subject's problem then is how to become disengaged from a situation which is moving in an altogether ugly direction.

The fact that disengagement is so difficult testifies to the potency of the forces that keep the subject at the control board. Are these forces to be conceptualized as individual motives and expressed in the language of personality dynamics, or are they to be seen as the effects of social structure and pressures arising from the situational field?

A full understanding of the subject's action will, I feel, require that both perspectives be adopted. The person brings to the laboratory enduring dispositions toward authority and aggression, and at the same time he becomes enmeshed in a social structure that is no less an objective fact of the case. From the standpoint of personality theory one may ask: What mechanisms of personality enable a person to transfer responsibility to authority? What are the motives underlying obedient and disobedient performance? Does orientation to authority lead to a short-circuiting of the shame-guilt system? What cognitive and emotional defenses are brought into play in the case of obedient and defiant subjects?

The present experiments are not, however, directed toward an exploration of the motives engaged when the subject obeys the experimenter's commands. Instead, they examine the situational variables responsible for the elicitation of obedience. Elsewhere, we have attempted to spell out some of the structural properties of the experimental situation that account for high obedience, and this analysis need not be repeated here (Milgram, 1963). The experimental variations themselves represent our attempt to probe that structure, by systematically changing it and noting the consequences for behavior. It is clear that some situations produce greater compliance with the experimenter's commands than others. However, this does not necessarily imply an increase or decrease in the strength of any single definable motive. Situations producing the greatest obedience could do so by triggering the most powerful, yet perhaps the most idiosyncratic, of motives in each subject confronted by the setting. Or they may simply recruit a greater number and variety of motives in their service. But whatever the motives involved—and it is far from certain that they can ever be known — action may be studied as a direct function of the situation in which it occurs. This has been the approach of the present study, where we sought to plot behavioral regularities against manipulated properties of the social field. Ultimately, social psychology would like to have a compelling *theory of situations* which will, first, present a language in terms of which situations can be defined; proceed to a typology of situations; and then point to the manner in which definable properties of situations are transformed into psychological forces in the individual.[12]

Postscript

Almost a thousand adults were individually studied in the obedience research, and there were many specific conclusions regarding the variables that control obedience and disobedience to authority. Some of these have been discussed briefly in the preceding sections, and more detailed reports will be released subsequently.

There are now some other generalizations I should like to make, which do not derive in any strictly logical fashion from the experiments as carried out, but which, I feel, ought to be made. They are formulations of an intuitive sort that have been forced on me by observation of many subjects responding to the pressures of authority. The assertions represent a painful alteration in my own thinking; and since they were acquired only under the repeated impact of direct observation, I have no illusion that they will be generally accepted by persons who have not had the same experience.

With numbing regularity good people were seen to knuckle under the demands of authority and perform actions that were callous and severe. Men who are in everyday life responsible and decent were seduced by the trappings of authority, by the control of their perceptions, and by the uncritical acceptance of the experimenter's definition of the situation, into performing harsh acts.

What is the limit of such obedience? At many points we attempted to establish a boundary. Cries from the victim were inserted; not good enough. The victim claimed heart trouble; subjects still shocked him on command. The victim pleaded that he be let free, and his answers no longer registered on the signal box; subjects continued to shock him. At the outset we had not conceived that such drastic procedures would be needed to generate disobedience, and each step was added only as the ineffectiveness of the earlier techniques became clear. The final effort to establish a limit was the Touch-Proximity condition. But the very first subject in this condition subdued the victim on command, and proceeded to the highest shock level. A quarter of the subjects in this condition performed similarly.

---

[12]My thanks to Professor Howard Leventhal of Yale for strengthening the writing in this paragraph.

The results, as seen and felt in the laboratory, are to this author dis-   80
turbing. They raise the possibility that human nature or, more specifically,
the kind of character produced in American democratic society cannot be
counted on to insulate its citizens from brutality and inhumane treatment
at the direction of malevolent authority. A substantial proportion of people
do what they are told to do, irrespective of the content of the act and without limitations of conscience, so long as they perceive that the command
comes from a legitimate authority. If in this study an anonymous experimenter could successfully command adults to subdue a fifty-year-old man
and force on him painful electric shocks against his protests, one can only
wonder what government, with its vastly greater authority and prestige, can
command of its subjects. There is, of course, the extremely important question of whether malevolent political institutions could or would arise in
American society. The present research contributes nothing to this issue.

In an article titled "The Danger of Obedience," Harold J. Laski wrote:

> . . . civilization means, above all, an unwillingness to inflict
> unnecessary pain. Within the ambit of that definition, those of us
> who heedlessly accept the commands of authority cannot yet claim
> to be civilized men.
>
> . . . Our business, if we desire to live a life, not utterly devoid of
> meaning and significance, is to accept nothing which contradicts
> our basic experience merely because it comes to us from tradition or
> convention or authority. It may well be that we shall be wrong; but
> our self-expression is thwarted at the root unless the certainties we
> are asked to accept coincide with the certainties we experience.
> That is why the condition of freedom in any state is always a wide-
> spread and consistent skepticism of the canons upon which power
> insists.

References

Buss, Arnold H. 1961. *The Psychology of Aggression*. New York and London: John
    Wiley.

Kierkegaard, S. 1843. *Fear and Trembling*. English edition, Princeton: Princeton
    University Press, 1941.

Laski, Harold J. 1929. "The dangers of obedience." *Harper's Monthly Magazine*,
    15 June, 1–10.

Milgram, S. 1961. "Dynamics of obedience: experiments in social psychology."
    Mimeographed report, *National Science Foundation*, January 25.

——— 1963. "Behavioral study of obedience." *J. Abnorm. Soc. Psychol.* 67,
    371–378.

———1964. "Issues in the study of obedience: a reply to Baumrind." *Amer. Psychol.*
    1, 848–852.

Miller, N. E. 1944. "Experimental studies of conflict." In J. McV. Hunt (ed.),
    Personality and the Behavior Disorders. New York: Ronald Press.

Scott, J. P. 1958. *Aggression*. Chicago: University of Chicago Press.

QUESTIONS

1. What did Milgram want to determine by his experiment? What were his anticipated outcomes?

2. What conclusions did Milgram reach about the extent to which ordinary individuals would obey the orders of an authority figure? Under what conditions is this submission most probable? Under what conditions is defiance most likely?

3. Describe the general procedures of this experiment. Some people have questioned Milgram's methods. Do you think it is ethical to expose participants without warning to experiments that might have a lasting effect on them? What effects might this experiment have had on its participants?

4. One characteristic of this article is Milgram's willingness to consider several possible explanations of the same phenomenon. Study the interpretations in paragraphs 28 through 35. What do you make of the range of interpretation there and elsewhere in the article? How does Milgram achieve such a range?

5. A report such as Milgram's is not structured in the same way as a conventional essay. His research is really a collection of separate but related experiments, each one of which requires its own interpretation. Describe the groups into which these experiments fall. Which results seemed most surprising to you? Which were easiest to anticipate?

6. In Milgram's experiment, people who are responsible and decent in everyday life were seduced, he says, by trappings of authority. Most of us, however, like to believe that we would neither engage in brutality on our own nor obey directions of this kind. Has Milgram succeeded in getting you to question your own behavior? Would you go so far as to say that he forces you to question your own human nature?

7. In paragraph 46 Milgram comments, "Perhaps our culture does not provide adequate models for disobedience." What do you think of this hypothesis? Are there such models? Ought there to be? Have such models appeared since the experiment was conducted? Explain your stand on Milgram's statement.

8. If research in social psychology takes place in your school today, a panel of some sort probably enforces guidelines on research with human participants. Locate that board, if it exists, and find out whether this experiment could take place today. Report to your class on the rules that currently guide researchers. Do you think that those rules are wise?

9. What, in your opinion, should be the guidelines for psychological research with human subjects? List the guidelines that you think are appropriate, and compare your list with the lists of your classmates. Would your guidelines have allowed Milgram's experiment?

10. Think of a situation in which you were faced with the moral and ethical dilemma of whether to obey a figure of authority. How did you behave? Did your behavior surprise you? Describe and explain that experience.

MAKING CONNECTIONS

1. One of the conditions of valid scientific research is the replicability of its experiments. When we are persuaded that results are replicable, we are inclined to believe that they are valid. What provisions for replicability does Milgram make in his experiments? Compare his stance to that of Oliver Sacks (p. 475), whose observations are not replicable but who is also concerned with writing authoritative science.

2. Think of other essays in this collection in which ethical matters are at issue, particularly the ethics of composing some kind of story. Consider Richard Selzer's "A Mask on the Face of Death" (p. 135) and Michael Brown's "Love Canal and the Poisoning of America" (p. 271). In each of those studies, human subjects seem to be manipulated for the sake of the writer's interests. Perhaps you would prefer to offer another example. Whatever study you choose, compare it to Milgram's, and discuss the two writers' sensitivity to their human subjects. Note also the last sentence of Milgram's first footnote. What choices do the writers have in the cases that interest you most?

ON THE FEAR OF DEATH

Elisabeth Kübler-Ross

Elisabeth Kübler-Ross (b. 1926), a Swiss American psychiatrist, is one of the leaders of the movement that may help change the way Americans think about death. Born in Zurich, she received her M.D. from the University of Zurich in 1957 and came to the United States as an intern the following year. Kübler-Ross began her work with terminally ill patients while teaching psychiatry at the University of Chicago Medical School. She founded the hospice care movement in the United States and runs Shanti Nilaya (Sanskrit for "home of peace"), an organization "dedicated to the promotion of physical, emotional, and spiritual health." This selection is taken from her first and most famous book, On Death and Dying *(1969).*

> Let me not pray to be sheltered from
> dangers but to be fearless in facing them.
> Let me not beg for the stilling of my
> pain but for the heart to conquer it.
> Let me not look for allies in life's battle-
> field but to my own strength.
> Let me not crave in anxious fear to be
> saved but hope for the patience to win my
> freedom.
> Grant me that I may not be a coward,
> feeling your mercy in my success alone;
> but let me find the grasp of your hand in
> my failure.
> —RABINDRANATH TAGORE, *Fruit-Gathering*

Epidemics have taken a great toll of lives in past generations. Death in infancy and early childhood was frequent and there were few families who didn't lose a member of the family at an early age. Medicine has changed greatly in the last decades. Widespread vaccinations have practically eradicated many illnesses, at least in western Europe and the United States. The use of chemotherapy, especially the antibiotics, has contributed to an ever-decreasing number of fatalities in infectious diseases. Better child care and education have effected a low morbidity and mortality among children. The many diseases that have taken an impressive toll among the young and middle-aged have been conquered. The number of old people is on the rise, and with this fact come the number of people with malignancies and chronic diseases associated more with old age.

Pediatricians have less work with acute and life-threatening situations as they have an ever-increasing number of patients with psychosomatic disturbances and adjustment and behavior problems. Physicians have more people in their waiting rooms with emotional problems than they have ever had before, but they also have more elderly patients who not only try to live with their decreased physical abilities and limitations but who also face loneliness and isolation with all its pains and anguish. The majority of these people are not seen by a psychiatrist. Their needs have to be elicited and gratified by other professional people, for instance, chaplains and social workers. It is for them that I am trying to outline the changes that have taken place in the last few decades, changes that are ultimately responsible for the increased fear of death, the rising number of emotional problems, and the greater need for understanding of and coping with the problems of death and dying.

When we look back in time and study old cultures and people, we are impressed that death has always been distasteful to man and will probably always be. From a psychiatrist's point of view this is very understandable and can perhaps best be explained by our basic knowledge that, in our unconscious, death is never possible in regard to ourselves. It is inconceivable for our unconscious to imagine an actual ending of our own life here on earth, and if this life of ours has to end, the ending is always attributed to a malicious intervention from the outside by someone else. In simple terms, in our unconscious mind we can only be killed; it is inconceivable to die of a natural cause or of old age. Therefore death in itself is associated with a bad act, a frightening happening, something that in itself calls for retribution and punishment.

One is wise to remember these fundamental facts as they are essential in understanding some of the most important, otherwise unintelligible communications of our patients.

The second fact that we have to comprehend is that in our unconscious   5
mind we cannot distinguish between a wish and a deed. We are all aware of some of our illogical dreams in which two completely opposite statements can exist side by side—very acceptable in our dreams but unthinkable and illogical in our wakening state. Just as our unconscious mind cannot differentiate between the wish to kill somebody in anger and the act of having done so, the young child is unable to make this distinction. The child who angrily wishes his mother to drop dead for not having gratified his needs will be traumatized greatly by the actual death of his mother—even if this event is not linked closely in time with his destructive wishes. He will always take part or the whole blame for the loss of his mother. He will always say to himself—rarely to others—"I did it, I am responsible, I was bad, therefore Mommy left me." It is well to remember that the child will react in the same manner if he loses a parent by divorce, separation, or desertion. Death is often seen by a child as an impermanent thing and has therefore little distinction from a divorce in which he may have an opportunity to see a parent again.

Many a parent will remember remarks of their children such as, "I will bury my doggy now and next spring when the flowers come up again, he will get up." Maybe it was the same wish that motivated the ancient Egyptians to supply their dead with food and goods to keep them happy and the old American Indians to bury their relatives with their belongings.

When we grow older and begin to realize that our omnipotence is really not so omnipotent, that our strongest wishes are not powerful enough to make the impossible possible, the fear that we have contributed to the death of a loved one diminishes—and with it the guilt. The fear remains diminished, however, only so long as it is not challenged too strongly. Its vestiges can be seen daily in hospital corridors and in people associated with the bereaved.

A husband and wife may have been fighting for years, but when the partner dies, the survivor will pull his hair, whine and cry louder and beat his chest in regret, fear and anguish, and will hence fear his own death more than before, still believing in the law of talion—an eye for an eye, a tooth for a tooth—"I am responsible for her death, I will have to die a pitiful death in retribution."

Maybe this knowledge will help us understand many of the old customs and rituals which have lasted over the centuries and whose purpose is to diminish the anger of the gods or the people as the case may be, thus decreasing the anticipated punishment. I am thinking of the ashes, the torn clothes, the veil, the *Klage Weiber* of the old days[1]—they are all means to ask you to take pity on them, the mourners, and are expressions of sorrow, grief, and shame. If someone grieves, beats his chest, tears his hair, or refuses to eat, it is an attempt at self-punishment to avoid or reduce the anticipated punishment for the blame that he takes on the death of a loved one.

This grief, shame, and guilt are not very far removed from feelings of 10 anger and rage. The process of grief always includes some qualities of anger. Since none of us likes to admit anger at a deceased person, these emotions are often disguised or repressed and prolong the period of grief or show up in other ways. It is well to remember that it is not up to us to judge such feelings as bad or shameful but to understand their true meaning and origin as something very human. In order to illustrate this I will again use the example of the child—and the child in us. The five-year-old who loses his mother is both blaming himself for her disappearance and being angry at her for having deserted him and for no longer gratifying his needs. The dead person then turns into something the child loves and wants very much but also hates with equal intensity for this severe deprivation.

The ancient Hebrews regarded the body of a dead person as something unclean and not to be touched. The early American Indians talked about the evil spirits and shot arrows in the air to drive the spirits away. Many other

---

[1]*Klage Weiber:* Wailing women (German). [Eds.]

cultures have rituals to take care of the "bad" dead person, and they all originate in this feeling of anger which still exists in all of us, though we dislike
admitting it. The tradition of the tombstone may originate in the wish to keep
the bad spirits deep down in the ground, and the pebbles that many mourners put on the grave are leftover symbols of the same wish. Though we call
the firing of guns at military funerals a last salute, it is the same symbolic ritual as the Indian used when he shot his spears and arrows into the skies.

I give these examples to emphasize that man has not basically changed.
Death is still a fearful, frightening happening, and the fear of death is a universal fear even if we think we have mastered it on many levels.

What has changed is our way of coping and dealing with death and
dying and our dying patients.

Having been raised in a country in Europe where science is not so
advanced, where modern techniques have just started to find their way into
medicine, and where people still live as they did in this country half a century ago, I may have had an opportunity to study a part of the evolution of
mankind in a shorter period.

I remember as a child the death of a farmer. He fell from a tree and was   15
not expected to live. He asked simply to die at home, a wish that was granted without question. He called his daughters into the bedroom and spoke
with each one of them alone for a few moments. He arranged his affairs
quietly, though he was in great pain, and distributed his belongings and his
land, none of which was to be split until his wife should follow him in
death. He also asked each of his children to share in the work, duties, and
tasks that he had carried on until the time of the accident. He asked his
friends to visit him once more, to bid goodbye to them. Although I was a
small child at the time, he did not exclude me or my siblings. We were
allowed to share in the preparations of the family just as we were permitted to grieve with them until he died. When he did die, he was left at home,
in his own beloved home which he had built, and among his friends and
neighbors who went to take a last look at him where he lay in the midst of
flowers in the place he had lived in and loved so much. In that country
today there is still no make-believe slumber room, no embalming, no false
makeup to pretend sleep. Only the signs of very disfiguring illnesses are covered up with bandages and only infectious cases are removed from the
home prior to the burial.

Why do I describe such "old-fashioned" customs? I think they are an
indication of our acceptance of a fatal outcome, and they help the dying
patient as well as his family to accept the loss of a loved one. If a patient is
allowed to terminate his life in the familiar and beloved environment, it
requires less adjustment for him. His own family knows him well enough
to replace a sedative with a glass of his favorite wine; or the smell of a
home-cooked soup may give him the appetite to sip a few spoons of fluid
which, I think, is still more enjoyable than an infusion. I will not minimize
the need for sedatives and infusions and realize full well from my own experience as a country doctor that they are sometimes life-saving and often

unavoidable. But I also know that patience and familiar people and foods could replace many a bottle of intravenous fluids given for the simple reason that it fulfills the physiological need without involving too many people and/or individual nursing care.

The fact that children are allowed to stay at home where a fatality has struck and are included in the talk, discussions, and fears gives them the feeling that they are not alone in their grief and gives them the comfort of shared responsibility and shared mourning. It prepares them gradually and helps them view death as part of life, an experience which may help them grow and mature.

This is in great contrast to a society in which death is viewed as taboo, discussion of it is regarded as morbid, and children are excluded with the presumption and pretext that it would be "too much" for them. They are then sent off to relatives, often accompanied by some unconvincing lies of "Mother has gone on a long trip" or other unbelievable stories. The child senses that something is wrong, and his distrust in adults will only multiply if other relatives add new variations of the story, avoid his questions or suspicions, shower him with gifts as a meager substitute for a loss he is not permitted to deal with. Sooner or later the child will become aware of the changed family situation and, depending on the age and personality of the child, will have an unresolved grief and regard this incident as a frightening, mysterious, in any case very traumatic experience with untrustworthy grownups, which he has no way to cope with.

It is equally unwise to tell a little child who lost her brother that God loved little boys so much that he took little Johnny to heaven. When this little girl grew up to be a woman she never solved her anger at God, which resulted in a psychotic depression when she lost her own little son three decades later.

We would think that our great emancipation, our knowledge of science 20
and of man, has given us better ways and means to prepare ourselves and our families for this inevitable happening. Instead the days are gone when a man was allowed to die in peace and dignity in his own home.

The more we are making advancements in science, the more we seem to fear and deny the reality of death. How is this possible?

We use euphemisms, we make the dead look as if they were asleep, we ship the children off to protect them from the anxiety and turmoil around the house if the patient is fortunate enough to die at home, we don't allow children to visit their dying parents in the hospitals, we have long and controversial discussions about whether patients should be told the truth—a question that rarely arises when the dying person is tended by the family physician who has known him from delivery to death and who knows the weaknesses and strengths of each member of the family.

I think there are many reasons for this flight away from facing death calmly. One of the most important facts is that dying nowadays is more gruesome in many ways, namely, more lonely, mechanical, and dehumanized; at times it is even difficult to determine technically when the time of death has occurred.

Dying becomes lonely and impersonal because the patient is often taken out of his familiar environment and rushed to an emergency room. Whoever has been very sick and has required rest and comfort especially may recall his experience of being put on a stretcher and enduring the noise of the ambulance siren and hectic rush until the hospital gates open. Only those who have lived through this may appreciate the discomfort and cold necessity of such transportation which is only the beginning of a long ordeal — hard to endure when you are well, difficult to express in words when noise, light, pumps, and voices are all too much to put up with. It may well be that we might consider more the patient under the sheets and blankets and perhaps stop our well-meant efficiency and rush in order to hold the patient's hand, to smile, or to listen to a question. I include the trip to the hospital as the first episode in dying, as it is for many. I am putting it exaggeratedly in contrast to the sick man who is left at home — not to say that lives should not be saved if they can be saved by a hospitalization but to keep the focus on the patient's experience, his needs and his reactions.

When a patient is severely ill, he is often treated like a person with no   25
right to an opinion. It is often someone else who makes the decision if and when and where a patient should be hospitalized. It would take so little to remember that the sick person too has feelings, has wishes and opinions, and has — most important of all — the right to be heard.

Well, our presumed patient has now reached the emergency room. He will be surrounded by busy nurses, orderlies, interns, residents, a lab technician perhaps who will take some blood, an electrocardiogram technician who takes the cardiogram. He may be moved to X-ray and he will overhear opinions of his condition and discussions and questions to members of the family. He slowly but surely is beginning to be treated like a thing. He is no longer a person. Decisions are made often without his opinion. If he tries to rebel he will be sedated, and after hours of waiting and wondering whether he has the strength, he will be wheeled into the operating room or intensive treatment unit and become an object of great concern and great financial investment.

He may cry for rest, peace, and dignity, but he will get infusions, transfusions, a heart machine, or tracheotomy if necessary. He may want one single person to stop for one single minute so that he can ask one single question — but he will get a dozen people around the clock, all busily preoccupied with his heart rate, pulse, electrocardiogram or pulmonary functions, his secretions or excretions but not with him as a human being. He may wish to fight it all but it is going to be a useless fight since all this is done in the fight for his life, and if they can save his life they can consider the person afterwards. Those who consider the person first may lose precious time to save his life! At least this seems to be the rationale or justification behind all this — or is it? Is the reason for this increasingly mechanical, depersonalized approach our own defensiveness? Is this approach our own way to cope with and repress the anxieties that a terminally or critically ill patient evokes in us? Is our concentration on equipment, on blood pressure, our desperate attempt to deny the impending death which is so frightening and discomforting to us that we displace all our knowledge onto machines, since they are less close to us than the suffering face of another human being which would remind us once more of our lack of omnipotence, our own limits and failures, and last but not least perhaps our own mortality?

Maybe the question has to be raised: Are we becoming less human or more human? . . . It is clear that whatever the answer may be, the patient is suffering more — not physically, perhaps, but emotionally. And his needs have not changed over the centuries, only our ability to gratify them.

QUESTIONS

1. Why does Kübler-Ross describe the death of a farmer? What point is she making in explaining "such 'old-fashioned' customs" (paragraph 16)?
2. To what extent is this essay explanatory? Summarize a particular explanation of hers that you find intriguing. Is it persuasive?
3. At what point in this essay does Kübler-Ross turn from explanation to argument? Do you think that she has taken a stand on her subject? How sympathetic are you to her position?
4. In paragraphs 2 and 10, Kübler-Ross indicates a specialized audience for her writing. Who is that audience, and how do you relate to it?
5. Think of the audience that you described in question 4 as a primary audience and of yourself as a member of a secondary audience. To what extent do the two audiences overlap? How thoroughly can you divide one from the other?
6. What experiences of death have you had so far? Write of a death that you know something about, even if your relation to it is distant, perhaps only through the media. Can you locate elements of fear and anger in your own behavior or in the behavior of other people involved? Does Kübler-Ross's interpretation of those reactions help you come to terms with the experience?
7. What kind of balance do you think is best between prolonging life and allowing a person to die with dignity? What does the phrase "dying with dignity" mean?
8. If you were told you had a limited time to live, how would that news change the way you are living? Or would it? Offer an explanation for your position.

MAKING CONNECTIONS

Kübler-Ross suggests that we have significant lessons to learn from the dying and warns that we avoid thinking about death only at our own peril. Read Gary Greenberg's essay "As Good as Dead" (p. 707), and imagine a conversation between Kübler-Ross and Greenberg.

Nonverbal Courtship Patterns in Women
Context and Consequences

Monica M. Moore

Monica M. Moore (b. 1953) is a professor of psychology at Webster University in St. Louis, Missouri. Moore has conducted research on nonverbal courtship behavior in women since 1978, publishing articles in such journals as Semiotica *and the* Journal of Sex Research. *In this article, which originally appeared in the journal* Ethology and Sociobiology, *Moore applied the research methods of psychology to study the mating habits of the human female.*

[Abstract.] *There is a class of nonverbal facial expressions and gestures, exhibited by human females, that are commonly labeled "flirting behaviors." I observed more than 200 randomly selected adult female subjects in order to construct a catalog of these nonverbal solicitation behaviors. Pertinent behaviors were operationally defined through the use of consequential data; these behaviors elicited male attention. Fifty-two behaviors were described using this method. Validation of the catalog was provided through the use of contextual data. Observations were conducted on 40 randomly selected female subjects in one of four contexts: a singles' bar, a university snack bar, a university library, and at university Women's Center meetings. The results indicated that women in "mate relevant" contexts exhibited higher average frequencies of nonverbal displays directed at males. Additionally, women who signaled often were also those who were most often approached by a man; and this relationship was not context specific.*

I suggest that the observation of women in field situations may provide clues to criteria used by females in the initial selection of male partners. As much of the work surrounding human attraction has involved laboratory studies or data collected from couples in established relationships, the observation of nonverbal behavior in field settings may provide a fruitful avenue for the exploration of human female choice in the preliminary stages of male-female interaction.

Introduction

Biologically, one of the most important choices made by an organism is the selection of a mate. The evolution of traits that would assist in the identification of "superior mates" prior to the onset of mating is clearly advantageous. One legacy of anisogamy[1] is that errors in mate selection are generally more expensive to females than to males (Trivers 1972). Hence, the females of a wide variety of species may be expected to exhibit traits that would facilitate the assessment of the quality of potential suitors in respect to their inherited attributes and acquired resources. There are many examples of female selectivity in a variety of species, including elephant seals (LeBoeuf and Peterson 1969; Bertram 1975), mice (McClearn and Defries 1973), fish (Weber and Weber 1975), rats (Doty 1974), gorillas (Nadler 1975), monkeys (Beach 1976), birds (Selander 1972; Wiley 1973; Williams 1975), and a few ungulates[2] (Beuchner and Schloeth 1965; Leuthold 1966).

Very few studies in the area of human mate selection and attraction have focused on the issue of female choice. Fowler (1978) interviewed women to identify the parameters of male sexual attractiveness. The results showed that the male's value as a sexual partner correlated with the magnitude of emotional and material security he provided. Baber (1939) found that women emphasize qualities such as economic status, disposition, family religion, morals, health, and education in a prospective marriage partner, whereas men most frequently chose good looks, morals, and health as important qualities. More recent studies (Coombs and Kenkel 1966; Tavris 1977) also found women rating attributes such as physical attractiveness as less important than did men. Reiss (1960) believes that many more women than men choose "someone to look up to" and Hatkoff and Luswell (1977) presented data that indicated that women want the men with whom they fall in love to be persons whom they can respect and depend on. Daly and Wilson (1978) conclude from cross-cultural data that a male's financial status is an important determinant of his mating success.

Although these reports are valuable, it is clear that the mechanisms   5 and expression of male assessment and female choice in humans have received little attention. In addition, much of the information available regarding human female choice is derived from interviews or questionnaires. Few studies have focused on initial choice situations in field observations. There are several difficulties with a field approach. A major problem surrounds the determination that a choice situation is being observed when verbal information is unavailable. I suggest that this problem may be solved through observations of nonverbal behavior. Indeed, there appears to be a repertoire of gestures and facial expressions that are used by humans as courtship signals (Birdwhistell 1970), much as there is signaling between members of the opposite sex in other species. Even in

---

[1]*anisogamy:* The union of unlike gametes — or mates, in this case. [Eds.]
[2]*ungulates:* Hoofed, herbivorous mammals, including camels, horses, and swine. [Eds.]

humans courtship and the choice of a mate have been characterized as largely nonverbal, with the cues being so persuasive that they can, as one observer put it, "turn a comment about the weather into a seductive invitation" (Davis 1971, p. 97).

The focus of much study in the area of nonverbal communication has been description (Scheflen 1965; Birdwhistell 1970; Mehrabian 1972). The primary aim of this research has been the categorization and analysis of nonverbal behaviors. By employing frame-by-frame analysis of films, Birdwhistell and his associates have been able to provide detailed descriptions of the facial expressions and movements or gestures of subjects in a variety of contexts. Observations conducted in this fashion as well as field studies have resulted in the labeling of many nonverbal behaviors as courtship signals. For example, Givens (1978) has described five phases of courtship between unaquainted adults. Scheflen (1965) investigated flirting gestures in the context of psychotherapy, noting that both courtship behaviors and qualifiers of the courtship message were exhibited by therapists and clients. Eibl-Eibesfeldt (1971) used two approaches to describe flirting behavior in people from diverse cultural backgrounds. Employing a camera fitted with right angle lenses to film people without their knowledge, he found that an eyebrow flash combined with a smile was a common courtship behavior. Through comments made to women, Eibl-Eibesfeldt has been able to elicit the "coy glance," an expression combining a half-smile and lowered eyes. Kendon (1975) filmed a couple seated on a park bench in order to document the role of facial expression during a kissing round. He discovered that it was the female's behavior, particularly her facial expressions that functioned as a regulator in modulating the behavior of the male. Cary (1976) has shown that the female's behavior is important in initiating conversation between strangers. Both in laboratory settings and singles' bars conversation was initiated only after the female glanced at the male. These results are valuable in documenting the importance of nonverbal behavior in human courtship. But what is lacking is an ethogram[3] of female solicitation behavior.

The purpose of this study was to describe an ensemble of visual and tactile displays emitted by women during initial meetings with men. I shall argue here that these nonverbal displays are courtship signals; they serve as attractants and elicit the approach of males or ensure the continued attention of males. In order to establish the immediate function of the described behaviors as courtship displays, I employed two classes of evidence described by Hinde (1975) for use in the establishment of the immediate function of a behavior; contextual evidence and consequential evidence. The rationale behind the use of consequential data was that behavior has certain consequences and that if the consequence appears to be a "good thing" it should have relevance for the immediate function of

---

[3]*ethogram:* A pictorial catalog of behavior patterns shown by members of a species. [Eds.]

the behavior in question. It should be noted, however, that Eibl-Eibesfeldt (1970) has pointed out the danger in this approach because of interpretations of value on the part of the observer. Therefore, contextual information was provided as further documentation that the nonverbal behaviors in question were courtship signals. Hinde has noted that if certain behaviors are seen in some contexts but are absent in others their function must relate to those contexts in which they were observed. Together these two classes of information provide an indication of the immediate function of the behavior, in this case nonverbal behavior in women interacting with men. Thus, this study consisted of two parts: catalog compilation based on consequential information and validation of the catalog obtained through contextual data.

Development of the Catalog

Method

Subjects   For the initial study, more than 200 subjects were observed in order to obtain data to be used in the development of the catalog of nonverbal solicitation signals. Subjects were judged to be between the ages of 18 and 35 years. No systematic examination was made of background variables due to restrictions imposed by anonymity. All subjects were white and most were probably college students.

Procedure   Subjects were covertly observed in one social context where opportunities for male–female interaction were available, a singles' bar. Subjects were observed for 30 minutes by two trained observers. Focal subjects were randomly selected from the pool of possible subjects at the start of the observation period. We observed a woman only if she was surrounded by at least 25 other people (generally there were more than 50 others present) and if she was not accompanied by a male. In order to record all instances of the relevant behaviors, observers kept a continuous narrative account of all behaviors exhibited by a single subject and the observable consequences of those actions (Altmann 1974). The following criteria were used for identifying behaviors: a nonverbal solicitation behavior was defined as a movement of body part(s) or whole body that resulted in male attention, operationally defined, within 15 seconds following the behavior. Male attention consisted of the male performing one of the following behaviors: approaching the subject, talking to her, leaning toward her or moving closer to her, asking the subject to dance, touching her, or kissing her. Field notes were transcribed from concealed audio tape recorders. Estimates of interobserver reliability were calculated for 35 hours of observation using the formula:

$$\frac{\text{No. of agreements (A + B)}}{\text{No. of agreements (A + B) + No. seen by B only + No. seen by A only}}$$

(McGrew 1972). The range of interobserver reliability scores was 0.72–0.98, with the average score equaling .88. Low reliability scores were obtained only for behaviors difficult for an observer to catch in a darkened room, such as glancing behaviors.

Subsequently, five randomly selected subjects were observed for a peri-   10
od of at least 1 hour. Again observers kept a continuous narrative account of all nonverbal behavior exhibited by the woman.

The behaviors observed in courting women can be conceptualized in various ways: distance categories (Crook 1972), directional versus nondirectional, or on the basis of body part and movement employed in the exhibition of the nonverbal pattern (McGrew 1972). The third framework was chosen because the displays were most discretely partitioned along these dimensions.

Results

Fifty-two different behaviors were exhibited by the subjects in the present study. Nonverbal solicitation behaviors and their frequencies are summarized in Table 1 according to category. These behaviors were highly visible and most appeared very similar in form in each subject. In other words, each behavior was discrete, or distinct from all other solicitation behaviors.

Descriptions of Nonverbal Solicitation Behaviors

FACIAL AND HEAD PATTERNS. A number of different facial and head patterns were seen in the women we observed. All women performed glancing behaviors, although the particular pattern varied among the individual subjects in the duration or length of time involved in eye to eye contact.

Type I glance (the room encompassing glance) was not restricted to an identifiable recipient. It was usually exhibited early in the evening and often was not seen later in the evening, particularly if the woman made contact with a man. The woman moved her head rapidly, orienting her face around the room. This movement was followed by another head movement that reoriented the woman's face to its original position. The total duration of the glance was brief, 5–10 seconds, with the woman not making eye contact with any specific individual. In some women this pattern of behavior was exaggerated: the woman stood up as her glance swept about the room.

The glancing behavior called the *type II glance (the short darting*   15
glance) was a solicitation behavior that appeared directed at a particular man. The woman directed her gaze at the man, then quickly away (within 3 seconds). The target axis of the horizontal rotation of the head was approximately 25–45 degrees. This behavior was usually repeated in bouts, with three glances the average number per bout.

In contrast, *type III glance (gaze fixate)* consisted of prolonged (more than 3 seconds) eye contact. The subject looked directly at the man; sometimes her glance was returned. Again, this behavior was seen several times in a period of minutes in some subjects.

TABLE 1
Catalog of Nonverbal Solicitation Behaviors

Facial and Head Patterns	Frequency	Gestures	Frequency	Posture Patterns	Frequency
Type I glance (room-encompassing glance)	253	Arm flexion	10	Lean	121
		Tap	8	Brush	28
		Palm	18	Breast touch	6
Type II glance (short darting glance)	222				
Type III glance (gaze fixate)	117				
Eyebrow flash	4	Gesticulation	62	Knee touch	25
Head toss	102	Hand hold	20	Thigh touch	23
Neck presentation	58	Primp	46	Foot to foot	14
Hair flip	139	Hike skirt	4	Placement	19
Head nod	66	Object caress	56	Shoulder hug	25
Lip lick	48	Caress (face/hair)	5	Hug	11
Lipstick application	1	Caress (leg)	32	Lateral body contact	1
Pout	27	Caress (arm)	23	Frontal body contact	7
Smile	511	Caress (torso)	8	Hang	2
Coy smile	20	Caress (back)	17	Parade	41
Laugh	249	Buttock pat	8	Approach	18
Giggle	61			Request dance	12
Kiss	6			Dance (acceptance)	59
Whisper	60			Solitary dance	253
Face to face	9			Point/permission grant	62
			9	Aid solicitation	34
				Play	31

Another movement involving the eye area was an *eyebrow flash*, which consisted of an exaggerated raising of the eyebrows of both eyes, followed by a rapid lowering to the normal position. The duration of the raised eyebrow portion of the movement was approximately 2 seconds. This behavior was often combined with a smile and eye contact.

Several behaviors involved the head and neck region. In *head tossing*, the head was flipped backwards so that the face was tilted upwards briefly (less than 5 seconds). The head was then lowered to its original position. The head toss was often combined with or seen before the *hair flip*. The hair flip consisted of the woman raising one hand and pushing her fingers through her hair or running her palm along the surface of her hair. Some women made only one hand movement, while in others there were bouts of hair stroking; the woman put her hand to her hair several times within a 30-second interval. The *head nod* was seen when the woman was only a short distance from the man. Usually exhibited during conversation, the head was moved forward and backward on the neck, which resulted in the face of the subject moving up and down. Another head pattern was called *face to face*. In this behavior pattern the head and face of the woman were brought directly opposite another person's face so that the noses almost touched, a distance of approximately 5 cm. A final behavior involving the head and neck was the *neck presentation*. The woman tilted her head sideways to an angle of approximately 45 degrees. This resulted in the ear almost touching the ipsilateral[4] shoulder, thereby exposing the opposite side of the neck. Occasionally the woman stroked the exposed neck area with her fingers.

There were a number of signals that involved the lips and mouth of the observed subjects. *Lipstick application* was a rare behavior. The woman directed her gaze so that she made eye contact with a particular man. She then slowly applied lipstick to her lips. She engaged in this behavior for some time (15 seconds), repeatedly circling her lips. In contrast, the *lip lick* was seen quite often, particularly in certain subjects. The woman opened her mouth slightly and drew her tongue over her lips. Some women used a single lip lick, wetting only the upper or the lower lip, while others ran the tongue around the entire lip area. The *lip pout* was another behavior involving the mouth. The lips were placed together and protruded. Generally, the lower lip was extended somewhat farther than the upper lip, so that it was fuller in appearance.

Smiling was among the most prevalent behaviors observed in the   20
sampled women. The smile consisted of the corners of the mouth being turned upward. This resulted in partial or sometimes full exposure of the teeth. In some women the smile appeared fixed and was maintained for long periods of time. The *coy smile* differed from the smile in that the woman displaying a coy smile combined a half-smile (the teeth were often not displayed or only partially shown) with a downward gaze or eye contact

---

[4]*ipsilateral:* Situated on the same side of the body. [Eds.]

which was very brief (less than 3 seconds). In the latter case the woman's glance slid quickly away from an onlooker who had become aware that he was being looked at.

Laughing and giggling were generally responses to another person's comments or behavior and were very common. In some women the *laugh* was preceded by a head toss. *Giggling* was less intense laughter. The mouth of the woman was often closed and generally the sounds were softer.

Kissing was rather unusual in the bar context. The slightly protruded lips were brought into contact with another person's body by a forward head movement. Variations consisted of the area touched by the woman's lips. The most common targets were the lips, face, and neck of the man. The woman, however, sometimes puckered her lips and waited, as if "offering" them to the male.

Finally, the *whisper* was used by most of the subjects in the sample. The woman moved her mouth near another person's ear and soft vocalizations presumedly were produced. Sometimes body contact was made.

GESTURES. There were several nonverbal patterns that involved movement of the hands and arms. Most were directed at a particular person. Some involved touching another individual. Others functioned at a distance.

Arm flexion occurred when the arm was flexed at wrist and elbow and   25
was moved toward the body. It was often repeated two or three times in a bout. This behavior was often followed by the approach of another individual toward whom the subject gazed. If the male was in close physical proximity, the female sometimes used *tapping* instead to get his attention. The elbow or wrist was flexed repeatedly so that the woman's finger was moved vertically on an object (usually another person's arm).

Women occasionally *palmed*. Palming occurred when the hand was extended or turned so that the palm faced another person for a brief period of time, less than 5 seconds. In this study, palming was also recorded when the woman coughed or touched herself with the palm up.

In several women rapid movements of the hands and arms were seen accompanying speech. This behavior was labeled *gesticulation*. Arms and hands, while held in front of the woman's torso, were waved or extended upwards in an exaggerated, conspicuous manner. This behavior was often followed by a lean forward on the part of the man.

A hand gesture sometimes initiated by a woman was the *hand hold*. The woman grasped the man's hand so that her palm was next to the man's palm. This occurred on the dance floor as well as when the man was seated at the table with the woman. Generally, this behavior had a long duration, more than 1 minute.

There were several behaviors that appeared related to each other because they involved inanimate objects. The first of these was the *primp*. In this gesture the clothing was patted or smoothed, although to the observer it appeared in no need of adjustment. A shirt was tucked in or a skirt was pulled down. On the other hand, the *skirt hike* was performed by raising the hem of the skirt with a movement of the hand or arm so that more leg was exposed. This behavior was only performed by two women and was directed at a particular man. When another man looked the skirt was pushed rapidly into place. Instead of patting or smoothing clothing, subjects sometimes "played with" an object, called *object caress*. For example, keys or rings were often fondled. Glasses were caressed with the woman sliding her palm up and down the surface of the glass. A cigarette pack was another item frequently toyed with in an object caress.

Finally, many women touched other people in a caressing fashion. Each incidence of caressing was considered separately in terms of the part of the body that was touched, because the message, in each case, may have been quite different. In *caress (face/hair)* the woman moved her hand slowly up and down the man's face and neck area or tangled her hands in his hair. While the couple was seated, women have been observed stroking the man's thigh and inner leg, *caress (leg)*. The *buttock pat,* however, occurred while the couple was standing, often while dancing. In this gesture the woman moved her hand, palm side down, up and down the man's buttocks. Other items in this group included *caress (arm), caress (torso),* and *caress (back)*.

POSTURE PATTERNS. Compared to the two categories just presented, there were some behaviors which involved more of the body in movement. These I called posture patterns. Many of these behaviors could only be accomplished while the woman was standing or moving about the room.

Lean was a common solicitation pattern. Generally while seated, the woman moved her torso and upper body forward, which resulted in closer proximity to the man. This movement was sometimes followed by a *brush* or a *breast touch*. The brush occurred when brief body contact (less than 5 seconds) was initiated by the woman against another individual. This occurred when a woman was walking across the room; she bumped into a man. The result was often conversation between the man and the woman. The breast touch also appeared accidental; and it was difficult to tell, except by length of time of contact, whether or not the movement was purposeful. The upper torso was moved so the breast made contact with the man's body (usually his arm). Most often the contact was brief (less than 5 seconds), but sometimes women maintained this position for several minutes.

There were four other actions that were similar to the brush and breast touch in that the woman made bodily contact with the man. In the *knee touch* the legs were brought into contact with the man's legs so that the knees touched. Interactants were always facing one another while seated. If the man and woman were sitting side by side, the woman may have initiated a *thigh touch*. The leg was brought into contact with the man's upper leg. *Foot to foot* resulted in the woman moving her foot so that it rested on top of the man's foot. Finally, rather than make contact with some part of her own body, an observed woman sometimes took the man's hand and placed it on her body. I called this behavior *placement*. For example, on two occasions, a woman put a man's hand in her lap. Other targets were the thigh or arm.

There was another constellation of behaviors that appeared related to each other. All of these behaviors were variations of some contact made between the woman's upper body and her partner's upper body. These were generally behaviors of long duration, more than 1 minute. The most common of these behaviors was the *shoulder hug*. In this signal, the partially flexed arm was draped on and around another person's shoulder. In contrast, the *hug* occurred when both arms were moved forward from a widespread position and around the man, thereby encircling him. The duration of this behavior, however, was brief (less than 10 seconds). *Lateral body contact* was similar to shoulder hug except that the woman moved under the man's arm so that his arm was draped around her shoulders rather than vice versa. Similarly, *frontal body contact* occurred when the chest and thighs of the woman rested against the chest and thighs of the man. This behavior was like the hug except that there was no squeeze pressure and the arms did not necessarily encircle the other person. This posture pattern was often seen on the dance floor or when a couple was standing at the bar. *Hanging* was similar to frontal body contact except that the man was supporting the woman's weight. This behavior was initiated by the woman who placed her arms around the man's neck. She was then lifted off her feet while her torso and hips rested against the man's chest and hip. This was a behavior low in frequency and brief in duration, less than 5 seconds.

There were two behaviors that involved whole body movement. These   35 were called *parade* and *approach*. Parade consisted of the woman walking across the room, perhaps on her way to the bar or the restroom. Yet rather than maintaining a relaxed attitude, the woman exaggerated the swaying motion of her hips. Her stomach was held in and her back was arched so that her breasts were pushed out; her head was held high. In general she was able to make herself "look good." The other behavior that involved walking was approach. The woman went up to the man and stood very close to him, within 2 feet. Usually verbal interaction ensued.

Some women followed an approach with a *request dance*. This was demonstrated nonverbally by the woman pointing and/or nodding in the direction of the dance floor. Two other categories involving dancing behavior were included in the catalog. *Dance (female acceptance)* was included because by accepting a dance with the man the woman maintained his attention. Another dancing behavior was one of the most frequently seen signals. It was called the *solitary dance* because, while seated or standing, the woman moved her body in time to the music. A typical male response was to request a dance.

Just as a woman, in agreeing to dance with a man, was telling him, nonverbally, that he was acceptable for the moment she also told him so when she allowed him to sit at her table with her. Thus, *point/permission grant* was given a place in the catalog. The woman pulled out the chair for the man or pointed or nodded in the direction of the chair. There was generally a verbal component to the signal which could not be overheard.

Aid solicitation consisted of several behaviors that involved the request of help by the subject. For example, the woman handed her jacket to the man and allowed him to help her put it on. Other patterns in this category included indicating that a drink be refilled, waiting to be seated, or holding a cigarette for lighting.

The final category of solicitation behavior was also a variety of posture patterns. Called *play,* these behaviors consisted of the woman pinching the man, tickling him, sticking out her tongue at him, or approaching him from behind covering his eyes. Some women sat on the man's lap, and several women in the sample came up behind men and stole their hats. All of these behaviors were simply recorded as play behavior.

Validation of the Catalog

Method

Subjects.   Forty women were covertly observed for the second portion of the study, validation of the catalog. Subjects were judged between the ages of 18 and 35. All subjects were white. Again no systematic examination of background variables was possible.

Procedure.   To justify the claim that the nonverbal behaviors described above were courtship signals, that is, carried a message of interest to the observing man, women were covertly observed in different social contexts. The four contexts selected for study were a singles' bar, a university snack bar, a university library, and university Women's Center meetings. These contexts were chosen in order to sample a variety of situations in which nonverbal solicitation might be expected to occur as well as situations in which it was unlikely to be exhibited. The selection of contexts was based on information collected through interviews and pilot observations. If non-verbal solicitation was found in situations where male–female interaction was likely but either was not found or occurred in lower frequencies where male–female interactions were impossible, then the immediate function of nonverbal solicitation can be said to be the enhancement of male–female relationships.

The methodology employed in this section was similar to that used in the development of the catalog. Focal individual sampling was the method of choice for the 40 subjects, 10 in each of the 4 contexts. Each subject was randomly selected from those individuals present at the beginning of the observation period. Sessions were scheduled to begin at 9:00 P.M. and end at 11:00 P.M. in the bar context. This time was optimal because crowd density was at its peak. Sessions in the Women's Center context always began at noon or at 7:00 P.M. because that was the time at which programs were scheduled. Observations were randomly made in both the library and the snack bar contexts; for each context, four sessions were conducted

40

at 11:00 A.M., three at 2:00 P.M., and three at 7:00 P.M. Subjects were observed for a period of 1 hour. (Any subject who did not remain for 1 hour of observation was excluded from the analyses.) Observations were conducted using either a concealed audio recorder or, when appropriate, paper and pen. No subject evidenced awareness of being observed. Again, we observed a woman only if she was surrounded by at least 25 other people and if she was not accompanied by a male.

Data for each woman consisted of a frequency measure, the number of nonverbal solicitation behaviors, described above, that she exhibited during the hour of observation. Observers counted not only the total number of nonverbal solicitation behaviors, but also kept a tally of the specific behaviors that were used by each woman.

Results

Frequency and Categorization of Nonverbal Solicitation Behaviors. Data collected on 40 subjects and the respective frequencies of their solicitation displays are given in Table 2. The results show that the emission of the cataloged behaviors was context specific in respect to both the frequency of displays and the number of different categories of the repertoire. The subjects observed in the singles' bar emitted an average of 70.6 displays in the sampled interval, encompassing a mean number of 12.8 different categories of the catalog. In contrast, the corresponding data from the snack bar, library, and women's meetings were 18.6 and 7.5, 9.6 and 4.0, and 4.7 and 2.1, respectively. The asymmetry in display frequency was highly significant ($\chi^2 = 25.079$, df = 3, $p < 0.001$). In addition, the asymmetry in the number of categories utilized was also significant ($\chi^2 = 23.099$, df = 3, $p < 0.001$).

Rate of Display. The quartile display frequencies for the four contexts are   45
given in Figure 1. As can be seen, the display frequency accelerated over time in the singles' bar context but was relatively invariant in the other three contexts.

Frequency of Approach. If subjects are pooled across contexts in which males are present and partitioned into high- and low-display categories, where the high display category is defined as more than 35 displays per hour, the data show that the high-display subjects elicited greater than 4 approaches per hour, whereas low display subjects elicited less than 0.48 approaches per hour. The number of approaches to subjects by a male in each context is presented in Table 2. Approaches were most frequent in the singles' bar where displays were also most frequent.

For the three contexts in which males were present (the singles' bar, the snack bar, and the library), the number of approaches to the subject was compared to the number of categories employed in solicitation displays. Subjects were pooled across these contexts and divided into two groups— those who utilized less than ten categories and those who employed ten or

Table 2
Social Context: Display Frequency and Number of Approaches[a]

	Singles' Bar	Snack Bar	Library	Women's Meetings
Number of subjects	10	10	10	10
Total number of displays	706	186	96	47
Mean number of displays	70.6	18.6	9.6	4.7
Mean number of catagories utilized	12.8	7.5	4.0	2.1
Number of approaches to the subject by a male	38	4	4	0
Number of approaches to a male by the subject	11	4	1	0

[a]The tabulated data are for a 60-minute observation interval. Asymmetry in display frequency: $\chi^2 = 25.079$, df = 3, $p < 0.001$; asymmetry in number of categories utilized: $\chi^2 = 23.099$, df = 3, $p < 0.001$.

more categories. The results were highly significant ($\chi^2 = 12.881$, df = 1, $p < 0.025$): regardless of when the woman utilized a high number of categories she was more likely to be approached by a male.

Also given in Table 2 are the figures for female-to-male approaches. In both cases (female to male, and male to female), approaches were much higher in the bar context. To show that the number of male approaches correlated with frequency of female solicitation, Spearman rank correlations[5] were determined for these measures. The correlation between number of male approaches and total number of solicitations, across all three contexts, equaled 0.89 ($p < 0.05$). Clearly, those women who signaled often were also those who were most often approached by a man; and this relationship was not context specific.

Discussion

The results of this study are in no way discoveries of "new" behaviors. The behaviors cataloged here have been described as courtship behaviors by others. But there has been little firm evidence to support this claim of their function, aside from references to context. This study was the first attempt to bring all the behaviors together in catalog form and provide documentation of their function.

---

[5]*Spearman rank correlations:* Measurements of associations between two variables. This method of measuring the strength of correlations when actual values are not available was first proposed by the English psychologist Charles Spearman in 1904. [Eds.]

When we compare those behaviors contained in the catalog compiled   50
in this study to other descriptions of courtship in humans, we find many
areas of congruence. Scheflen (1965) has outlined four categories of heterosexual courtship behavior: courtship readiness, preening behavior, positional cues, and actions of appeal or invitation. Many of the behaviors
observed in courting women are similar to those seen by Scheflen during
psychotherapy sessions. For example, Scheflen's category of courtship
readiness bears resemblance to parade behavior. Preening behaviors, as
described by Scheflen, are similar to the hair flip, primp, skirt hike, and
object caress cataloged here. Positional cues are found in the catalog under
leaning, brushing, and caressing or touching signals. Finally, Scheflen's
actions of appeal or invitation are included as aid solicitation, point/per-
mission grant, request dance, palm and solitary dance. What appears to be
absent in courting women are the qualifiers of the courtship message
observed by Scheflen during psychotherapy.

There is significant continuity between the expressions and gestures
described in this study and those Givens (1978) believed to be important
during the first four phrases of courtship. According to Givens, the essence
of the first stage, the attention phase, is ambivalence. Behaviors seen by
Givens during this stage and observed in this study include primping, object
caressing, and glancing at and then away from the male. During the recognition phase Givens has observed head cocking, pouting, primping, eyebrow flashing and smiling, all of which were seen by me. During the
interaction stage, conversation is initiated and the participants appear highly animated. Indeed, women in this study, while talking to men, appeared
excited, laughing, smiling, and gesticulating frequently. Givens has indicated that in the fourth stage, the sexual arousal phase, touching gestures are
exchanged. Similarly, it was not unusual to see couples hold hands, caress,
hug, or kiss after some period of interaction.

Givens' work has indicated that it is often the female who controls interaction in these early phases. The observations of Cary (1976) seem to bear
this out and glancing behavior appears to be a significant part of the female
role. In this study glancing often took place over a period of time prior to a
male approach. As Crook (1972) has stated, males are generally hesitant to
approach without some indication of interest from the partner, and repeated
eye contact seems to demonstrate that interest. Rejection behaviors were not
cataloged here, but it is entirely possible that one way women reject suitors is
by failing to recognize their presence through eye contact.

Eibl-Eibesfeldt has also stressed importance of the eye area in two flirting gestures he has observed in several cultures. The first, a rapid raising
and lowering of the eyebrows, accompanied by a smile and a nod, was seen
rarely in this study. Raised eyebrows were sometimes seen in the bar context and when directed at a man with a quick glance to the dance floor were
often followed by a request to dance. Raised eyebrows also sometimes followed comments by a man when he had joined a woman at her table. Eibl-
Eibesfeldt (1970) has also presented pictures of women exhibiting what

he calls the coy glance. Although the coy glance was sometimes seen in this study (here called the coy smile), it was more usual for a young American woman to use direct eye contact and a full smile. Yet the fact that these behaviors were observed is significant, and later cross-cultural studies may demonstrate that there are more behaviors that share the courtship message.

It appears then that although glancing behaviors were important in signaling interest, initially, other behaviors seemed to reaffirm the woman's interest later in the observation period. Behaviors such as nodding, leaning close to the man, smiling and laughing were seen in higher frequencies after the man had made contact with the woman and was dancing with her or was seated at her table. This accounts for the rise in frequency of solicitation near the end of the observation period in the bar context. Yet it is difficult to make any firm statements about a sequential pattern in the exhibition of solicitation behavior. Although these behaviors are distinct in form, variability among subjects with regard to timing was great. Neither was it possible to determine the potency of particular behaviors. Indeed, it often appeared as though behaviors had a cumulative effect; that is, the man waited to respond to the woman until after he had observed several solicitations.

However, it is clear that there is a constellation of nonverbal behaviors   55
associated with female solicitation that has been recognized by many investigators in several contexts and with similar results (Morris 1971; Kendon and Feber 1973; Nieremberg and Calero 1973; Clore et al. 1975; Key 1975; Knapp 1978; Lockard and Adams 1980). This is strong circumstantial evidence supporting the current results that these are "real" contextually valid movements, not random behaviors. Furthermore, these expressions and gestures appear to function as attractants and advertisers of female interest.

Traditionally, women have had more control in choosing men for relationships, being able to pace the course of sexual advances and having the prerogative to accept or decline proposals (Hatkoff and Luswell 1977). Nonverbal solicitation is only one of the first steps in the sequence of behaviors beginning with mate attraction and culminating with mate selection. However, these courtship gestures and expressions appear to aid the woman in her role as discriminating chooser. Females are able to determine when and where they wish to survey mate potential by exhibiting or withholding displays. They can elicit a high number of male approaches, allowing them to choose from a number of available men. Or they may direct solicitations at a particular male.

What happens after the approach of a man then becomes increasingly important. Much of the basis of actual choice must rest on what the man says to the woman in addition to his behavior toward her and others. It seems reasonable that females would enhance their fitness by making the most informed judgment possible. Yet before interaction is initiated some initial choice is made. These initial impressions and the selection of those men deemed interesting enough to warrant further attention by a woman have been virtually ignored. If, indeed, the woman is exercising her right to choose, what sort of filter system is she using? Which men are chosen for further interaction and which are rejected? Literature cited earlier indicates that behaviors that indicate status, wealth, and dependability are attributes that women may assess in initial encounters. At present data are not available to address these issues. But I believe that hypotheses regarding the particulars of human female choice can be tested through covert observation of female invitational behavior. Information obtained through observations in field settings can be added to verbal reports. The results of such a venture may present us with a more complete picture of the levels of selection involved in human female choice.

References

Altmann, J. Observational study of behavior: sampling methods. *Behavior* 49: 227–267 (1974).

Baber, R. E. *Marriage and Family.* New York: McGraw-Hill, 1939

Beach, R. A. Sexual attractivity, proceptivity and receptivity in female mammals. *Hormones and Behavior* 7: 105–138 (1976).

Bertram, B. C. Social factors influencing reproduction in wild lions. *Journal of Zoology* 177: 463–482 (1975).

Beuchner, H. K., Schloeth, R. Ceremonial mating system in Uganda kob (*Adenota kob thomase* Neuman). *Zeitschrift fur Tierpsychologie* 22: 209–225 (1965).

Birdwhistell, R. L. *Kinesics and Context.* Philadelphia: University of Pennsylvania Press, 1970.

Cary, M. S. Talk? Do you want to talk? Negotiation for the initiation of conversation between the unacquainted. Ph.D. dissertation, University of Pennsylvania, 1976.

Clore, G. L., Wiggins, N. H., Itkin, I. Judging attraction from nonverbal behavior: the gain phenomenon. *Journal of Consulting and Clinical Pyschology* 43: 491–497 (1975).

Coombs, R. H., Kenkel, W. F. Sex differences in dating aspirations and satisfaction with computer selected partners. *Journal of Marriage and the Family* 28: 62–66 (1966).

Crook, J. H. Sexual selection, dimorphism, and social organization in primates. In *Sexual Selection and the Descent of Man 1871–1971*, B. Campbell (Ed.). Chicago: Aldine, 1972.

——— The socio-ecology of primates. In *Social Behavior in Birds and Mammals: Essays on the Social Ethology of Animals and Man*, J. H. Crook (Ed.). London: Academic, 1972.

Daly, M., Wilson, M. *Sex, Evolution, and Behavior.* North Scituate, MA: Duxbury, 1978.

Davis, F. *Inside Intuition.* New York: McGraw-Hill, 1971.

Doty, R. L. A cry for the liberation of the female rodent: Courtship and copulation in Rodentia. *Psychological Bulletin* 81: 159–172 (1974).

Eibl-Eibesfeldt, I. *Ethology: The Biology of Behavior.* New York: Holt, Rinehart, and Winston, 1970.

———*Love and Hate.* New York: Holt, Rinehart and Winston, 1971.

Fowler, H. F. Female choice: An investigation into human breeding system strategy. Paper presented to Animal Behavior Society, Seattle, June 1978.

Givens, D. The nonverbal basis of attraction: Flirtation, courtship, and seduction. *Psychiatry* 41: 346–359 (1978).

Hatkoff, T. S., Luswell, T. E. Male–female similarities and differences in conceptualizing love. In *Love and Attraction,* M. Cook, G. Wilson (Eds.). Oxford: Pergamon, 1977.

Hinde, R. A. The concept of function. In *Function and Evolution in Behavior,* S. Bariends, C. Beer, and A. Manning (Eds.). Oxford: Clarendon, 1975.

Kendon, A. Some functions of the face in a kissing round. *Semiotica* 15: 299–334 (1975).

———, Ferber, A. A description of some human greetings. In *Comparative Ecology and Behavior of Primates,* R. P. Michael and J. H. Crook (Eds.). London: Academic, 1973.

Key, M. R. *Male/Female Language.* Metuchen, NJ: Scarecrow, 1975.

Knapp, M. L. *Nonverbal Communication in Human Interaction.* New York: Holt, Rinehart, and Winston, 1978.

LeBoeuf, B. J., Peterson, R. S. Social status and mating activity in elephant seals. *Science* 163: 91–93 (1969).

Leuthold, W. Variations in territorial behavior of Uganda kob *Adenota kob thomasi* (Neumann 1896). *Behaviour* 27: 215–258 (1966).

Lockard, J. S., Adams, R. M. Courtship behaviors in public: Different age/sex roles. *Ethology and Sociobiology* 1(3): 245–253 (1980).

McClearn, G. E., Defries, J. C. *Introduction to Behavioral Genetics.* San Francisco: Freeman, 1973.

McGrew, W. C. *An Ethological Study of Children's Behavior.* New York: Academic, 1972.

Mehrabian, A. *Nonverbal Communication.* Chicago: Aldine, 1972.

Morris, D. *Intimate Behavior.* New York: Random House, 1971.

Nadler, R. D. Sexual cyclicity in captive lowland gorillas. *Science* 189: 813–814 (1975).

Nieremberg, G. I., Calero, H. H. *How to Read a Person Like a Book.* New York: Hawthorne, 1973.

Reiss, I. L. Toward a sociology of the heterosexual love relationship. *Marriage and Family Living* 22: 139–145 (1960).

Scheflen, A. E. Quasi-courtship behavior in psychotherapy. *Psychiatry* 28: 245–257 (1965).

Selander, R. K. Sexual selection and dimorphism in birds. In *Sexual Selection and the Descent of Man 1871–1971,* B. Campbell (Ed.). Chicago: Aldine, 1972.

Tavris, C. Men and women report their views on masculinity. *Psychology Today* 10: 34–42 (1977).

Trivers, R. L. Parental investment and sexual selection. In *Sexual Selection and the Descent of Man 1871–1971,* B. Campbell (Ed.). Chicago: Aldine, 1972.

Weber, P. G., Weber, S. P. The effect of female color, size, dominance and early experience upon mate selection in male convict cichlids, *cichlosoma nigrofasciatum Gunther* (pisces, cichlidae). *Behaviour* 56: 116–135 (1975).

Wiley, R. H. Territoriality and nonrandom mating in sage grouse, *Centrocerus urophasiamis. Animal Behavior Monographs* 6: 85–169 (1973).

Williams, G. C. *Sex and Evolution.* Princeton, NJ: Princeton University Press, 1975.

QUESTIONS

1. Which of Moore's observations or conclusions do you find the most interesting or unusual? Explain.
2. The interest of this piece lies in its subject—flirting—which is frequently treated in popular how-to books and on talk shows. Based on your familiarity with these popular treatments and on your knowledge of the subject through your own observations, how accurate a report do you find Moore's article to be?
3. Moore suggests that different courtship behaviors may be exhibited in other cultures. If you have knowledge of another culture's courtship rituals, explain how they compare with Moore's findings.
4. Moore concludes by suggesting that further study should be made on women's "filter system," meaning how they choose a man for further interaction. She suggests that this can be done through additional "covert observation" (paragraph 57). Do you agree? What would one look for?
5. What does Moore mean when she writes, "It seems reasonable that females would enhance their fitness by making the most informed judgment possible." (paragraph 57)? What sort of "fitness" do you think Moore means?
6. Would it be possible to replicate this experiment by studying courtship behavior in males? Write an essay in which you suggest some of the categories of male courtship behavior that such a study might reveal.

MAKING CONNECTIONS

What similarities in method or substantive findings can you find between Moore's study and Jane van Lawick-Goodall's "First Observations" (p. 237)? Note that Moore presented portions of this article before publication at a meeting of the Animal Behavior Society.

INSIDE DOPE

Marcus Laffey

Marcus Laffey is the pseudonym of Edward C. Conlon, a New York City police officer who has written essays about policing for The New Yorker *since 1997 and is currently working on a book on this subject to be published in 2001. The third generation of his family to join the force (both his father and grandfather were police officers), he is a 1987 graduate of Harvard and didn't expect to find himself in law enforcement. "It kind of took me by surprise," he told an interviewer. "I wanted to give it a shot." When the following essay was published in* The New Yorker *in 1999, the writer was a five-year veteran of the force.*

If there were ever a Super Bowl matchup of junkies versus crackheads, it would be hard to figure which team the odds would favor. Both sides would most likely disappear during halftime. The crackheads would believe that they had won, and the junkies wouldn't care. If they did manage to finish the game, the smartest money would invest in a pawnshop next to the stadium, and within hours the investors would own every Super Bowl ring, for pennies on the dollar. Winners and losers would again be indistinguishable.

The war on drugs is a game for me, no matter how urgent it is for poor neighborhoods or how grave the risks are for cops. We call dealers "players," and there are rules as in chess, percentages as in poker, and moves as in schoolyard ball. When I went from being a beat cop to working in narcotics, the change was refreshing. For one thing, you deal only with criminals. No more domestic disputes, barricaded schizophrenics, or D.O.A.s, the morass of negotiable and nonnegotiable difficulties people have with their neighbors or boyfriends or stepchildren. Patrol cops deal with the fluid whole of people's lives, but usually when the tide's going out: people who have the cops called on them aren't happy to see you; people who call the cops aren't calling when they're having a good time. Now all I do is catch sellers of crack and heroin, and catch their customers to show that they sold it. The parts of their lives unaffected by coca- or opium-based products are none of my business. Patrol is politics, but narcotics is pure technique.

My unit, which consists of half a dozen cops and a sergeant, makes arrests for "observation sales." One or two of us go to an observation post ("the OP," and if you're in it you're "doing OPs") on a rooftop or in a vacant apartment to watch a "set," or drug operation, and transmit information to the "catch car," the unmarked van used to pick up the perps. The set might be a lone teen-ager standing on a corner with one pocket full of crack and another full of cash. Or it might be an organization of such intricate subterfuge — with lookouts, managers, moneymen, steerers (to guide customers), and pitchers (for the hand-to-hand transactions) — that you'd think its purpose was to deliver Soviet microfilm to covert operatives instead of a ten-dollar bag of junk to a junkie. But we watch, and give descriptions of buyers for the catch team to pick up, a few blocks away. Sometimes the dealers send out phantom or dummy buyers — people who appear to have bought narcotics but haven't — to see if they're stopped; we wait until we have a handful of buyers, then move in on the set. Most of the spots that we hit are well established, visited by both customers and cops on a regular basis; others pop up and disappear. You might drive around to see who's out — the faces at the places, the traffic pattern of steady customers and usual suspects. Sometimes you feel like the man on the catwalks over the casino floor, scanning the tables for the sharps and card counters, looking out for luck that's too good to be true. Other times, you feel as if you were watching a nature program, some *National Geographic* special on the felony ecology of the streets.

You read the block, seeing who moves and who stands still, their reactions and relations to one another; you sift the players from the idlers, the buyers from the passersby. Most people occupy their environment blithely, with only a slack and occasional awareness of their surroundings. A store window or a noisy garbage truck might distract them in passing, and they might look around before crossing the street, but the ordinary pedestrian is a poster child for daydreams and tunnel vision. Not so in the narcotics trade, where the body language of buyer and seller alike signals a taut awareness of opportunity and threat. There are distinctive addict walks, such as that of the prowler, who might be new to the spot, or sussing out an operation that has shifted to a more favorable corner. He hovers, alert for the deal, floating like a flake of ash above a fire. The addict on a "mission walk" moves with double-quick footsteps, leaning forward, as if against a strong wind, so as not to waste an extra second of his already wasted life. A player, on the other hand, has a self-contained watchfulness, a false repose, like a cat sunning itself on a windowsill, eyes half-closed but ready to pounce.

Every street set operates through an odd combination of aggressive   5
marketing and strategic defense, needing simultaneously to broadcast and to deny its function. The young man on the park bench should look like a high-school senior from thirty yards away but has to show he's a merchant at three yards, and he has to have the drugs near enough for convenience but far enough away to be out of his "custody and control" should he be stopped. If he's holding the drugs, he has to have an escape route — through a hole in a fence, say, or into an alley, or into the building where his grandmother lives. The man on the bench is just a man on a bench, after all, until his context proves him otherwise. But, as you watch, figures emerge from the flow of street life like coördinates on a grid, like pins on a drug map.

Say you're doing OPs from a rooftop, looking down on a street that has three young guys on the corner by the bodega, a couple with a baby in a carriage by the stoop, and a group of old men with brown-bagged brandy bottles by the vacant lot. A man on a bicycle moves in a slow, lazy slalom, up and down the street. The corner boys are the obvious pick, but I have to wait. When a buyer comes, he is easier to recognize, and his arrival on the set sends a signal, a vibration, like a fly landing in the web. The buyer is the bellwether and the bait: he draws the players out and makes them work, prompts them into visible display.

The buyer walks past the old men at the lot, the family on the stoop, to the corner boys, as expected. One corner boy takes the buyer aside and palms his cash, the second stands still, watching up and down the block, and the third goes to the family on the stoop and has a word with the woman with the baby. The woman steps inside the lobby for a few seconds — Thank God, I think, it's not in the carriage — and when she returns she hands something to the third boy, who meets up with the first corner boy and the buyer and hands off the product. The buyer walks away, retracing his route. The man on the bicycle follows him slowly.

I put the buyer over the air: "Hispanic male; red cap; Tommy Hilfiger jacket, blue; bluejeans. South on Third. Be advised, you got a lookout on a bike — white T-shirt, bluejeans, black bike — tailing him to see if he gets picked up. Let him run a couple of blocks, if you can."

Now I have a three-player set, with Mama and corner boys Nos. 1 and 3 down cold. The buyer should be taken, and No. 2 only observed for now. Mama's short time in the building tells me that the stash is not in an apartment but either on her person or right in the lobby, in an unlocked mailbox or a crack in the wall. Corner boy No. 2 is the one to watch, to see if he's the manager or a lookout, up a rank from the others or down. His position will become clear as I watch the group dynamic of the trio — the choreography of who stands where, who talks and who listens, who tells the jokes and who laughs, who's the one that runs to the bodega for the chips and soda. Until he participates in the exchanges, taking money or product, he's legally safe from arrest for an observation sale. If he's a manager, he's the one we want; if he's a smart manager, touching neither cash nor stash, he's the one we're least likely to get. In a sense, everybody wants the spot to get busy: the players grow careless as they get greedy, bringing out more product, paying more heed to the customer and less to us. The manager might have to step in and lend an incriminating hand. When the spot is slow, both groups — the cops and the players — have to be patient.

Even when nothing happens, there is much to interpret. Are they out of   10
product, and will they re-up within ten minutes or an hour? Are they "raised" — afraid we're around — and, if so, is it because they saw our van (unmarked but patently obvious) or saw one of us peering over the roofline, or is it because a patrol car raced by, to a robbery three blocks away? Did they turn away another customer because he wanted credit, or because they

thought he was an undercover cop, and were they right? Is the next deal worth the wait?

The wait can be the most trying part of the operation. I've spent hours on tar rooftops, crouched down till my legs cramped, sweating, shivering, wiping the rain from my binoculars every ten seconds. There have been times when I've forgotten to look down before I knelt by the ledge, and settled in beside piles of shit, broken glass, or syringes. On one rooftop, there was an ornate Victorian birdcage, five feet tall, bell-shaped and made of brass, and chained to it, still on a rotten leather leash, was the skeleton of a pit bull. You walk up dirty stairs to a dirty roof to watch a dirty street. At night, even the light is dirty, the sodium-vapor street lights giving off a muddy yellow haze. But sometimes, when something finally does happen, you realize that your concentration is perfect: you feel the cool, neutral thrill of being completely submerged in your task. The objects of surveillance inhabit a living landscape, and you can be struck by the small, random graces of the scene even as you transmit a streak of facts over the radio: "Gray livery cab, buyer in back seat, passenger side, possible white with white sleeves, U-turning now to the left. . . ."

A soap bubble, then two, then dozens rise up in front of me, iridescent, shimmering in their uncertainty. There is a child two floors below me, as rapt with the view above as I am with the view below.

"Arright, we got one, he's beelining to the player, they just popped into the lobby. . . . Now he's out—that's fast, he must have the stash on him. Arright, buyer's walking off now—Hold on, he's just kind of idling across the street. It's not an I-got-my-rock walk. I don't think he got done. Stand by. . . ."

A man standing on another tenement roof whirls an orange flag, and makes it snap like a towel. His flock of pigeons takes flight from the coop with a whoosh like a gust of wind, spiralling out in broadening arcs—showing the smoky gray of their backs as they bank out, the silver-white of their bellies as they circle in—rising up all the while.

"Player's walking off, he sent the last two away, he's out, he's raised, I 15 don't know, but—Go! Go! Go! Hit the set!"

An incinerator chimney shoots out a lash of black smoke, which loops into a lariat before dissolving into the grimy sky.

At the other end of the OP is the catch car. You want a buyer's description, or "scrip," to have something distinctive about it—something beyond the "white T-shirt, bluejeans" of warm weather, "black jacket, bluejeans" of cold. You don't want "Male, walking three pit bulls." You're glad to hear about hot pink and lime green, or T-shirts with legible writing on them, or, even better, "Female in purple-and-yellow tracksuit, with a Cat-in-the-Hat hat, riding a tiny bicycle." For crackheads, as much as for any other species, protective coloration can be a successful evolutionary strategy.

Once you get the scrip and the buyer's direction of flight, you move in, allowing yourself some distance from the set, but not too much, or else the buyer will be home; in neighborhoods like this, people don't have to go far for hard drugs. Sometimes buyers run, and sometimes they fight, and sometimes they toss the drugs (though sometimes you can find those drugs later), and sometimes they eat them when they see you coming. There have been buyers who at the sight of me have reacted with a loss of bowel control, and control of the belly and the bladder as well. The truth is, I am the least of their problems: a night on a cell bench, with prison bologna sandwiches to eat, ranks fairly low amid the hazards of being at the bottom of the criminal food chain.

For crackheads, in particular, a stint as a model prisoner might be a career peak. While the street dealers at dope spots are often junkies themselves, crackheads can't be trusted with the stash — they can't even hold a job whose main requirements are to stand still and watch. The majority of them are figures from a famine: bone-thin and filthy. Months of that life take years from their lives, and thirty-year-olds can pass for fifty, burned out almost literally, with a red-hot core of desperation beneath a dead, charred surface. Junkies generally have a longer ride to the bottom, as the habit gradually slides from being a part of their lives to becoming the point of them. Heroin is purer now than it was in the past, and fewer than half the addicts I arrest have needles on them. They snort it instead of shooting it, which decreases the risk of disease and also seems to slow the forward momentum of addiction. But to me the terminal junkies are especially awful, because they have none of the trapped-rat frenzy of the crackhead; instead, they possess a fatal calm, as if they were keeping their eyes open while drowning. When you collar them, they can have a look of confirmed and somewhat contented self-hatred, as if the world were doing to them what they expect and deserve.

Addicts deserve pity, always, though often they inspire contempt. We   20
collared one crackhead, bumping into him by accident as he stood in a project lobby counting out a handful of vials. He was a street peddler who sold clothing, and had about eighty dollars in his pocket. He had the shrink-wrapped look that crackheads get, as if his skin were two sizes too small. He moaned and wept for his infant child, who would starve, he said, without his support. Yes, he acknowledged, the baby lived with its mother, but he was the provider. The mother and child were only about ten blocks away, at a playground, so we drove to meet them. The mother was a pretty, well-dressed woman, though her soccer-mom wholesomeness may have been artificially heightened by the presence of her handcuffed mate. We called her over, and her look of mild confusion became one of mild dismay as she saw our back-seat passenger. She didn't look surprised, and didn't ask questions. He took out his wad of cash, peeled off four dollars, and handed it to me to give to her. "You gotta be kidding me," I said. "You give me all this father-of-the-year shit, just to throw her four bucks?"

"C'mon," he said. "When you get out of Central Booking, you're hungry, you want some real McDonald's or something."

I gave him back the four dollars and took the wad for the mother. "The Number Two Special, two cheeseburgers and fries, is three-twenty-nine,"

I told him. "It's what I get, and it's all you can afford." For an addict, the priorities are never unclear.

After you've collared the buyers, it's time to move in on the dealers. When you hit a set, there is always a charge of adrenaline, arising from the jungle-war vagaries of opponent and terrain. There are elusive adversaries, explosive ones, and lots of sitting ducks. Some dealers opt for a businesslike capitulation, aware that it's the way to go through the process with the least fuss. Others, especially lobby dealers with access to an apartment upstairs, tend to make a mad dash for freedom. The bust could be a surrender as slow and dignified as Lee's at Appomattox or it could be bedlam—roiling bodies and airborne stash. When you can't count the evidence at the scene, you have to at least control it—the hundreds of dollars in small bills, the fistfuls of crack slabs, the loose decks, the bundles of dope—so you jam it in your pockets like a handful of ball bearings, and all the while there may be a crowd screaming, or perps for whom the fight-or-flight reflex is not a simple either-or proposition.

I he smarter dealers carry nothing on them, but you await information from the OP, sometimes with a distaste that verges on dread:

"It's in his sock."

"It's in the cast on his right hand—"

"It's in his cheek—sorry, guy, the other cheek. I mean, check between 'em, you copy?"

Stash can be hidden under a bottle cap or in a potato-chip bag, or strewn among heaps of noncriminal trash; it can be wedged in a light fixture in a hall or tucked inside the bumper of a car; it can be in a magnetic key case stuck to the iron bolt beneath a park bench; or it can be on a string taped to the wall and dangling down the garbage-disposal chute. A thorough search can lead to unexpected threats and rewards. Once, when I was rooting through a janitor's closet in a housing project after hitting a heroin set, I found a machine gun in the bottom of a bag of clothes. We continued to search the building and found more than a thousand dollars' worth of heroin, two more guns—a 9-mm. handgun and a .45 revolver—and also ammunition for another machine gun, an AK-47: copper-jacketed bullets more than two inches long, coming to a sharp, conical point like a dunce cap. An AK-47 can discharge bullets at a speed of more than two thousand feet per second, which would allow them to pass through my vest with barely a pause.

In the movies, there are a lot of drug-dealer villains, but those characters usually have to slap their girlfriends or kill a lot of cops to heighten the dramatic point of their bad-guyness. Because the victims of drug sales line up and pay, so to speak, for the privilege, the perpetrators don't have the forthright menace of violent felons. But most of the players I collar have a rap sheet that shows a more diversified criminal career—of earlier forays into robbery or theft—before they settled on the more lucrative and "less illegal" world of drug sales. And although some drug spots operate in a

25

fairly quiet, orderly manner, as if a man were selling newspapers on the street, or a couple were running a catalogue business out of their apartment, most are established and maintained by means of assault, murder, and many subtler thefts of human dignity.

In New York, heroin dealers stamp brand names on the little wax-paper   30
envelopes in which the drug is packaged. This practice gives a glimpse not only of a corporate structure, when the same brands appear in different sites, but also of a corporate imagination, showing what they believe their product should mean to their customers. Some convey the blandly generic aspiration of quality — "First Class," "President," "Original" — that you might find on brands of cornflakes or of detergent in some discount supermarket. Others go for a racier allure, but the gimmick is so hackneyed in conventional advertising that the genuinely illicit thrill of "Knockout" or "No Limit" suggests the mock-illicit thrill of ads for perfume or fat-free ice cream. Topical references are common, from the flat-out copyright infringement of "DKNY" or "Ford" to the movie tagline "Show Me the Money." But the best brand names are the literal ones, which announce without apology the bad things to come: "911," "25 to Life," "Undertaker," "Fuck You." There is a suicidal candor to "Lethal Injection" and "Virus," a forthright finality to "O.D." — a truth in advertising here that few products can match.

Recently, I had a talk with one of my informants, a junkie with AIDS who sleeps in an alley. A few days before, I'd obtained a search warrant for a spot he visits several times a day, and he fervently wished me luck with the warrant's execution. That my success would cause him inconvenience in supplying his own habit was a mild irony that did not trouble him. He said, "I know you're a cop and I'm — " and there was a sliver of space before his next word, enough for me to wonder what term he might use for a short-hand self-portrait. And, knowing that there would be a measure of harsh truth in it, I was still surprised, and even felt sorry for him, when he said, "And I'm a fucking scumbag." But he was equally firm in his opinion of those who had benefitted from his self-destruction: "I done time, I'm no hero, but these people are blood-suckers. Them and rapists are as bad as people get. Those people are worse than rapists. Those dealers will suck you dry. I hope you get every last one of them."

Every day, we go out and hunt people. When we do well — picking off the customers with dispatch, swooping in on the dealers, taking trophies of their product and profit — we feel skilled and lucky at once, at the top of our game. We have shut down spots, reduced robberies and shootings, made whole blocks cleaner, safer, saner places. But other spots withstand daily assaults from us with negligible losses, and I've driven home after a twenty-hour day only to recognize, with the hallucinatory clarity of the sleep-deprived, the same man, on the same mission walk, that I'd collared the night before. Typically, buyers spend a night in jail and are sentenced to a few days of community service. Players might get less, odd as that may seem, if there weren't enough transactions in open view, or if no stash was recovered. We'll all meet again, soon enough. There are breaks and interruptions, retirements and replacements, but, no matter how often the whistle blows, the game is never over.

QUESTIONS

1. The conceptual metaphor that undergirds Laffey's essay is summed up in the first words of the second paragraph: "The war on drugs is a game for me." This idea of a *game* frames the essay's beginning and end and serves as an explanatory context for some of his incidental comments throughout. For instance, "the cool, neutral thrill of being completely submerged in your task" (paragraph 11) recalls the intensity of athletic performance. What other connections to a *game* can you find in the essay? Based on your reading of the essay, does this seem to be a valid comparison to make? Explain. What does the author gain? What is the purpose of positing such a vivid metaphor?

2. How does Laffey convey the repetitive quality of his work? Does calling it a *game* rather than a *war* convey a sense of futility? Explain.

3. At the beginning of paragraph 4, Laffey says that "You read the block." How exactly does his job resemble "reading"? In your own experience, what techniques of reading could be applied in such a pursuit?

4. At some points in the essay, the telling is interrupted by almost lyrical description—for example, when the "flock of pigeons takes flight from the coop with a whoosh like a gust of wind" (paragraph 14). What effect does this have on the reader? Have you ever used this kind of descriptive interruption in your own personal essays?

5. Why do you think Laffey frequently shifts between the impersonal, hypothetical "you" ("Say you're doing OPs from a rooftop," paragraph 6) and his autobiographical "I" ("I have to wait," paragraph 6). Compose a paragraph about a typical classroom experience that begins by referring to "you" but then narrows its focus to "I" by the end.

6. Write an account of a job that you have held. Use the framework of a typical day to structure your essay. As the narrative proceeds, move beyond reporting what you do, and include moments of reflective explanation to clarify particular aspects of your job.

MAKING CONNECTIONS

Laffey offers his readers closely observed details of the narcotics beat. Look at the techniques other essayists use—Antonio R. Damasio (p. 498) or George Orwell (p. 114), for instance—to understand how writers frame their interpretations from the evidence they present.

THE NAKED FACE

Malcolm Gladwell

English-born Malcolm Gladwell (b. 1963) grew up in Canada and received an undergraduate degree in history from the University of Toronto in 1984. From 1987 to 1996, he was a reporter for the Washington Post, *first as a science writer and then as New York City bureau chief. Since 1996, he has been a staff writer for* The New Yorker, *for which he has researched and written about topics as diverse as the relationship between intelligence and achievement, SAT preparation courses, paper filing systems, disposable diapers, and the history of caffeine. His first book,* The Tipping Point: How Little Things Make a Big Difference *(2000), focused on the idea that major societal trends can be initiated by seemingly minor circumstances. The following article about facial expressions originally appeared in* The New Yorker *in 2002. Other articles by Gladwell can be accessed at <http://www.gladwell.com>.*

1.

Some years ago, John Yarbrough was working patrol for the Los Angeles County Sheriff's Department. It was about two in the morning. He and his partner were in the Willowbrook section of South Central Los Angeles, and they pulled over a sports car. "Dark, nighttime, average stop," Yarbrough recalls. "Patrol for me was like going hunting. At that time of night in the area I was working, there was a lot of criminal activity, and hardly anyone had a driver's license. Almost everyone had something intoxicating in the car. We stopped drunk drivers all the time. You're hunting for guns or lots of dope, or suspects wanted for major things. You look at someone and you get an instinctive reaction. And the longer you've been working the stronger that instinctive reaction is."

Yarbrough was driving, and in a two-man patrol car the procedure is for the driver to make the approach and the officer on the passenger side to provide backup. He opened the door and stepped out onto the street, walking toward the vehicle with his weapon drawn. Suddenly, a man jumped out of the passenger side and pointed a gun directly at him. The two of them froze, separated by no more than a few yards. "There was a tree behind him, to his right," Yarbrough recalls. "He was about seventeen. He had the gun in his right hand. He was on the curb side. I was on the other side, facing him. It was just a matter of who was going to shoot first. I remember it clear as day. But for some reason I didn't shoot him." Yarbrough is an ex-marine with close-cropped graying hair and a small mustache, and he speaks in measured tones. "Is he a danger? Sure. He's standing there with a gun, and what person in his right mind does that facing a uniformed armed policeman? If you looked at it logically, I should have shot him. But logic had nothing to do with it. Something just didn't feel right. It was a gut reaction not to shoot—a hunch that at that exact moment he was not an imminent threat to me." So Yarbrough stopped, and, sure enough, so did the kid. He pointed a gun at an armed policeman on a dark street in South Central L.A., and then backed down.

Yarbrough retired last year from the sheriff's department after almost thirty years, sixteen of which were in homicide. He now lives in western Arizona, in a small, immaculate house overlooking the Colorado River, with pictures of John Wayne, Charles Bronson, Clint Eastwood, and Dale Earnhardt on the wall. He has a policeman's watchfulness: while he listens to you, his eyes alight on your face, and then they follow your hands, if you move them, and the areas to your immediate left and right—and then back again, in a steady cycle. He grew up in an affluent household in the San Fernando Valley, the son of two doctors, and he is intensely analytical: he is the sort to take a problem and break it down, working it over slowly and patiently in his mind, and the incident in Willowbrook is one of those problems. Policemen shoot people who point guns directly at them at two in the morning. But something he saw held him back, something that ninety-nine people out of a hundred wouldn't have seen.

Many years later, Yarbrough met with a team of psychologists who were conducting training sessions for law enforcement. They sat beside him in a darkened room and showed him a series of videotapes of people who were either lying or telling the truth. He had to say who was doing what. One tape showed people talking about their views on the death penalty and on smoking in public. Another featured a series of nurses who were all talking about a nature film they were supposedly watching, even though some of them were actually watching grisly documentary footage about burn victims and amputees. It may sound as if the tests should have been easy, because we all think we can tell whether someone is lying. But these were not the obvious fibs of a child, or the prevarications of people whose habits and tendencies we know well. These were strangers who were motivated to deceive, and the task of spotting the liars turns out to be fantastically difficult. There is just too much information—words, intonation, gestures, eyes, mouth—and it is impossible to know how the various cues should be weighted, or how to put them all together, and in any case it's all happening so quickly that you can't even follow what you think you ought to follow. The tests have been given to policemen, customs officers, judges, trial lawyers, and psychotherapists, as well as to officers from the F.B.I., the C.I.A., the D.E.A., and the Bureau of Alcohol, Tobacco, and Firearms—people one would have thought would be good at spotting lies. On average, they score fifty per cent, which is to say that they would have done just as well if they hadn't watched the tapes at all and just guessed. But every now and again—roughly one time in a thousand—someone scores off the charts. A Texas Ranger named David Maxwell did extremely well, for example, as did an ex-A.T.F. agent named J. J. Newberry, a few therapists, an arbitrator, a vice cop—and John Yarbrough, which suggests that what happened in Willowbrook may have been more than a fluke or a lucky guess. Something in our faces signals whether we're going to shoot, say, or whether we're lying about the film we just saw. Most of us aren't very good at spotting it. But a handful of people are virtuosos. What do they see that we miss?

2.

All of us, a thousand times a day, read faces. When someone says "I love you," we look into that person's eyes to judge his or her sincerity. When we meet someone new, we often pick up on subtle signals, so that, even though he or she may have talked in a normal and friendly manner, afterward we say, "I don't think he liked me," or "I don't think she's very happy." We easily parse complex distinctions in facial expression. If you saw me grinning, for example, with my eyes twinkling, you'd say I was amused. But that's not the only way we interpret a smile. If you saw me nod and smile exaggeratedly, with the corners of my lips tightened, you would take it that I had been teased and was responding sarcastically. If I made eye contact with someone, gave a small smile and then looked down and averted my gaze, you would think I was flirting. If I followed a remark with an abrupt smile and then nodded, or tilted my head sideways, you might conclude that I had just said something a little harsh, and wanted to take the edge off it. You wouldn't need to hear anything I was saying in order to reach these conclusions. The face is such an extraordinarily efficient instrument of communication that there must be rules that govern the way we interpret facial expressions. But what are those rules? And are they the same for everyone?

In the nineteen-sixties, a young San Francisco psychologist named Paul Ekman began to study facial expression, and he discovered that no one knew the answers to those questions. Ekman went to see Margaret Mead, climbing the stairs to her tower office at the American Museum of Natural History. He had an idea. What if he travelled around the world to find out whether people from different cultures agreed on the meaning of different facial expressions? Mead, he recalls, "looked at me as if I were crazy." Like most social scientists of her day, she believed that expression was culturally determined—that we simply used our faces according to a set of learned social conventions. Charles Darwin had discussed the face in his later writings; in his 1872 book, *The Expression of the Emotions in Man and Animals,* he argued that all mammals show emotion reliably in their faces. But in the nineteen-sixties academic psychologists were more interested in motivation and cognition than in emotion or its expression. Ekman was undaunted; he began travelling to places like Japan, Brazil, and Argentina, carrying photographs of men and women making a variety of distinctive faces. Everywhere he went, people agreed on what those expressions meant. But what if people in the developed world had all picked up the same cultural rules from watching the same movies and television shows? So Ekman set out again, this time making his way through the jungles of Papua New Guinea, to the most remote villages, and he found that the tribesmen there had no problem interpreting the expressions, either. This may not sound like much of a breakthrough. But in the scientific climate of the time it was a revelation. Ekman had established that expressions were the universal products of evolution. There were fundamental lessons to be learned from the face, if you knew where to look.

Paul Ekman is now in his sixties. He is clean-shaven, with closely set eyes and thick, prominent eyebrows, and although he is of medium build, he seems much larger than he is: there is something stubborn and substantial in his demeanor. He grew up in Newark, the son of a pediatrician, and entered the University of Chicago at fifteen. He speaks deliberately: before he laughs, he pauses slightly, as if waiting for permission. He is the sort to make lists, and number his arguments. His academic writing has an orderly logic to it; by the end of an Ekman essay, each stray objection and problem has been gathered up and catalogued. In the mid-sixties, Ekman set up a lab in a ramshackle Victorian house at the University of California at San Francisco, where he holds a professorship. If the face was part of a physiological system, he reasoned, the system could be learned. He set out to teach himself. He treated the face as an adventurer would a foreign land, exploring its every crevice and contour. He assembled a videotape library of people's facial expressions, which soon filled three rooms in his lab, and studied them to the point where he could look at a face and pick up a flicker of emotion that might last no more than a fraction of a second. Ekman created the lying tests. He filmed the nurses talking about the movie they were watching and the movie they weren't watching. Working with Maureen O'Sullivan, a psychologist from the University of San Francisco, and other colleagues, he located people who had a reputation for being uncannily perceptive, and put them to the test, and that's how Yarbrough and the other high-scorers were identified. O'Sullivan and Ekman call this study of gifted face readers the Diogenes Project, after the Greek philosopher of antiquity who used to wander around Athens with a lantern, peering into people's faces as he searched for an honest man. Ekman has taken the most vaporous of sensations—the hunch you have about someone else—and sought to give them definition. Most of us don't trust our hunches, because we don't know where they came from. We think they can't be explained. But what if they can?

3.

Paul Ekman got his start in the face-reading business because of a man named Silvan Tomkins, and Silvan Tomkins may have been the best face reader there ever was. Tomkins was from Philadelphia, the son of a dentist from Russia. He was short, and slightly thick around the middle, with a wild mane of white hair and huge black plastic-rimmed glasses. He taught psychology at Princeton and Rutgers, and was the author of *Affect, Imagery, Consciousness*, a four-volume work so dense that its readers were evenly divided between those who understood it and thought it was brilliant and those who did not understand it and thought it was brilliant. He was a legendary talker. At the end of a cocktail party, fifteen people would sit, rapt, at Tomkins's feet, and someone would say, "One more question!" and they would all sit there for another hour and a half, as Tomkins held forth on, say, comic books, a television sitcom, the biology of emotion, his problem with Kant, and his enthusiasm for the latest fad diets, all enfolded into one extended riff. During the Depression, in the midst of his doctoral studies at Harvard, he worked as a handicapper for a horse-racing syndicate, and was so successful that he lived lavishly on Manhattan's Upper East Side. At the track, where he sat in the stands for hours, staring at the horses through binoculars, he was known as the Professor. "He had a system for predicting how a horse would do based on what horse was on either side of him, based on their emotional relationship," Ekman said. If a male horse, for instance, had lost to a mare in his first or second year, he would be ruined if he went to the gate with a mare next to him in the lineup. (Or something like that—no one really knew for certain.) Tomkins felt that emotion was the code to life, and that with enough attention to particulars the code could be cracked. He thought this about the horses, and, more important, he thought this about the human face.

Tomkins, it was said, could walk into a post office, go over to the "Wanted" posters, and, just by looking at mug shots, tell you what crimes the various fugitives had committed. "He would watch the show *To Tell the Truth*, and without fault he could always pick the person who was lying and who his confederates were," his son, Mark, recalls. "He actually wrote the producer at one point to say it was too easy, and the man invited him to come to New York, go backstage, and show his stuff." Virginia Demos, who teaches psychology at Harvard, recalls having long conversations with Tomkins. "We would sit and talk on the phone, and he would turn the sound down as Jesse Jackson was talking to Michael Dukakis, at the Democratic National Convention. And he would read the faces and give his predictions on what would happen. It was profound."

Ekman's most memorable encounter with Tomkins took place in the   10 late sixties. Ekman had just tracked down a hundred thousand feet of film that had been shot by the virologist Carleton Gajdusek in the remote jungles of Papua New Guinea. Some of the footage was of a tribe called the South Fore, who were a peaceful and friendly people. The rest was of the Kukukuku, who were hostile and murderous and who had a homosexual ritual where pre-adolescent boys were required to serve as courtesans for the male elders of the tribe. Ekman was still working on the problem of whether human facial expressions were universal, and the Gajdusek film was invaluable. For six months, Ekman and his collaborator, Wallace Friesen, sorted through the footage. They cut extraneous scenes, focussing just on closeups of the faces of the tribesmen, and when the editing was finished Ekman called in Tomkins.

The two men, protégé and mentor, sat at the back of the room, as faces flickered across the screen. Ekman had told Tomkins nothing about the tribes involved; all identifying context had been edited out. Tomkins looked on intently, peering through his glasses. At the end, he went up to the screen and pointed to the faces of the South Fore. "These are a sweet, gentle people, very indulgent, very peaceful," he said. Then he pointed to the faces of the Kukukuku. "This other group is violent, and there is lots of evidence to suggest homosexuality." Even today, a third of a century later, Ekman cannot get over what Tomkins did. "My God! I vividly remember saying, 'Silvan, how on earth are you doing that?'" Ekman recalls. "And he went up to the screen and, while we played the film backward, in slow motion, he pointed out the particular bulges and wrinkles in the face that he was using to make his judgment. That's when I realized, 'I've got to unpack the face.' It was a gold mine of information that everyone had ignored. This guy could see it, and if he could see it, maybe everyone else could, too."

Ekman and Friesen decided that they needed to create a taxonomy of facial expressions, so day after day they sat across from each other and began to make every conceivable face they could. Soon, though, they realized that their efforts weren't enough. "I met an anthropologist, Wade Seaford, told him what I was doing, and he said, 'Do you have this movement?'" — and here Ekman contracted what's called the triangularis, which is the muscle that depresses the corners of the lips, forming an arc of distaste — "and it wasn't in my system, because I had never seen it before. I had built a system not on what the face can do but on what I had seen. I was devastated. So I came back and said, 'I've got to learn the anatomy.'" Friesen and Ekman then combed through medical textbooks that outlined each of the facial muscles, and identified every distinct muscular movement that the face could make. There were forty-three such movements. Ekman and Friesen called them "action units." Then they sat across from each other again, and began manipulating each action unit in turn, first locating the muscle in their mind and then concentrating on isolating it, watching each other closely as they did, checking their movements in a mirror, making notes of how the wrinkle patterns on their faces would change with each muscle movement, and videotaping the movement for their records. On the few occasions when they couldn't make a particular movement, they went next door to the U.C.S.F. anatomy department, where a surgeon they knew would stick them with a needle and electrically stimulate the recalcitrant muscle. "That wasn't pleasant at all," Ekman recalls. When each of those action units had been mastered, Ekman and Friesen began working action units in combination, layering one movement on top of another. The entire process took seven years. "There are three hundred combinations of two muscles," Ekman says. "If you add in a third, you get over four thousand. We took it up to five muscles, which is over ten thousand visible facial configurations." Most of those ten thousand facial expressions don't mean anything, of course. They are the kind of nonsense faces that children make. But, by working through each action-unit combination, Ekman and Friesen identified about three thousand that did seem to mean something, until they had catalogued the essential repertoire of human emotion.

4.

On a recent afternoon, Ekman sat in his office at U.C.S.F., in what is known as the Human Interaction Laboratory, a standard academic's lair of books and files, with photographs of his two heroes, Tomkins and Darwin, on the wall. He leaned forward slightly, placing his hands on his knees, and began running through the action-unit configurations he had learned so long ago. "Everybody can do action unit four," he began. He lowered his brow, using his depressor glabellae, depressor supercilli, and corrugator. "Almost everyone can do A.U. nine." He wrinkled his nose, using his levator labii superioris, alaeque nasi. "Everybody can do five." He contracted his levator palpebrae superioris, raising his upper eyelid.

I was trying to follow along with him, and he looked up at me. "You've got a very good five," he said generously. "The more deeply set your eyes are, the harder it is to see the five. Then there's seven." He squinted. "Twelve." He flashed a smile, activating the zygomatic major. The inner parts of his eyebrows shot up. "That's A.U. one—distress, anguish." Then he used his frontalis, pars lateralis, to raise the outer half of his eyebrows. "That's A.U. two. It's also very hard, but it's worthless. It's not part of anything except Kabuki theatre. Twenty-three is one of my favorites. It's the narrowing of the red margin of the lips. Very reliable anger sign. It's very hard to do voluntarily." He narrowed his lips. "Moving one ear at a time is still the hardest thing to do. I have to really concentrate. It takes everything I've got." He laughed. "This is something my daughter always wanted me to do for her friends. Here we go." He wiggled his left ear, then his right ear. Ekman does not appear to have a particularly expressive face. He has the demeanor of a psychoanalyst, watchful and impassive, and his ability to transform his face so easily and quickly was astonishing. "There is one I can't do," he went on. "It's A.U. thirty-nine. Fortunately, one of my postdocs can do it. A.U. thirty-eight is dilating the nostrils. Thirty-nine is the opposite. It's the muscle that pulls them down." He shook his head and looked at me again. "Oooh! You've got a fantastic thirty-nine. That's one of the best I've ever seen. It's genetic. There should be other members of your family who have this heretofore unknown talent. You've got it, you've got it." He laughed again. "You're in a position to flash it at people. See, you should try that in a singles bar!"

Ekman then began to layer one action unit on top of another, in order to   15
compose the more complicated facial expressions that we generally recognize

as emotions. Happiness, for instance, is essentially A.U. six and twelve—contracting the muscles that raise the cheek (orbicularis oculi, pars orbitalis) in combination with the zygomatic major, which pulls up the corners of the lips. Fear is A.U. one, two and four, or, more fully, one, two, four, five, and twenty, with or without action units twenty-five, twenty-six, or twenty-seven. That is: the inner brow raiser (frontalis, pars medialis) plus the outer brow raiser (frontalis, pars lateralis) plus the brow-lowering depressor supercilli plus the levator palpebrae superioris (which raises the upper lid), plus the risorius (which stretches the lips), the parting of the lips (depressor labii), and the masseter (which drops the jaw). Disgust? That's mostly A.U. nine, the wrinkling of the nose (levator labii superioris, alaeque nasi), but it can sometimes be ten, and in either case may be combined with A.U. fifteen or sixteen or seventeen.

Ekman and Friesen ultimately assembled all these combinations—and the rules for reading and interpreting them—into the Facial Action Coding System, or FACS, and wrote them up in a five-hundred-page binder. It is a strangely riveting document, full of details like the possible movements of the lips (elongate, de-elongate, narrow, widen, flatten, protrude, tighten and stretch); the four different changes of the skin between the eyes and the cheeks (bulges, bags, pouches, and lines); or the critical distinctions between infraorbital furrows and the nasolabial furrow. Researchers have employed the system to study everything from schizophrenia to heart disease; it has even been put to use by computer animators at Pixar (*Toy Story*), and at DreamWorks (*Shrek*). FACS takes weeks to master in its entirety, and only five hundred people around the world have been certified to use it in research. But for those who have, the experience of looking at others is forever changed. They learn to read the face the way that people like John Yarbrough did intuitively. Ekman compares it to the way you start to hear a symphony once you've been trained to read music: an experience that used to wash over you becomes particularized and nuanced.

Ekman recalls the first time he saw Bill Clinton, during the 1992 Democratic primaries. "I was watching his facial expressions, and I said to my wife, 'This is Peck's Bad Boy,'" Ekman says. "This is a guy who wants to be caught with his hand in the cookie jar, and have us love him for it anyway. There was this expression that's one of his favorites. It's that hand-in-the-cookie-jar, love-me-Mommy-because-I'm-a-rascal look. It's A.U. twelve, fifteen, seventeen, and twenty-four, with an eye roll." Ekman paused, then reconstructed that particular sequence of expressions on his face. He contracted his zygomatic major, A.U. twelve, in a classic smile, then tugged the corners of his lips down with his triangularis, A.U. fifteen. He flexed the mentalis, A.U. seventeen, which raises the chin, slightly pressed his lips together in A.U. twenty-four, and finally rolled his eyes—and it was as if Slick Willie himself were suddenly in the room. "I knew someone who was on his communications staff. So I contacted him. I said, 'Look, Clinton's got this way of rolling his eyes along with a certain expression, and what it conveys is "I'm a bad boy." I don't think it's a good thing. I could teach him how not to do that in two to three hours.' And he said, 'Well, we can't take the risk that he's known to be seeing an expert on lying.' I think it's a great tragedy, because . . ." Ekman's voice trailed off. It was clear that he rather liked Clinton, and that he wanted Clinton's trademark expression to have been no more than a meaningless facial tic. Ekman shrugged. "Unfortunately, I guess, he needed to get caught—and he got caught."

5.

Early in his career, Paul Ekman filmed forty psychiatric patients, including a woman named Mary, a forty-two-year-old housewife. She had attempted suicide three times, and survived the last attempt—an overdose of pills—only because someone found her in time and rushed her to the hospital. Her children had left home and her husband was inattentive, and she was depressed. When she first went to the hospital, she simply sat and cried, but she seemed to respond well to therapy. After three weeks, she told her doctor that she was feeling much better and wanted a weekend pass to see her family. The doctor agreed, but just before Mary was to leave the hospital she confessed that the real reason she wanted to go on weekend leave was so that she could make another suicide attempt. Several years later, a group of young psychiatrists asked Ekman how they could tell when suicidal patients were lying. He didn't know, but, remembering Mary, he decided to try to find out. If the face really was a reliable guide to emotion, shouldn't he be able to look back on the film and tell that she was lying? Ekman and Friesen began to analyze the film for clues. They played it over and over for dozens of hours, examining in slow motion every gesture and expression. Finally, they saw it. As Mary's doctor asked her about her plans for the future, a look of utter despair flashed across her face so quickly that it was almost imperceptible.

Ekman calls that kind of fleeting look a "microexpression," and one cannot understand why John Yarbrough did what he did on that night in South Central without also understanding the particular role and significance of microexpressions. Many facial expressions can be made voluntarily. If I'm trying to look stern as I give you a tongue-lashing, I'll have no difficulty doing so, and you'll have no difficulty interpreting my glare. But our faces are also governed by a separate, involuntary system. We know this because stroke victims who suffer damage to what is known as the pyramidal neural system will laugh at a joke, but they cannot smile if you ask them to. At the same time, patients with damage to another part of the brain have the opposite problem. They can smile on demand, but if you tell them a joke they can't laugh. Similarly, few of us can voluntarily do A.U. one, the sadness sign. (A notable exception, Ekman points out, is Woody Allen, who uses his frontalis, pars medialis, to create his trademark look of comic distress.) Yet we raise our inner eyebrows all the time, without thinking, when we are unhappy. Watch a baby just as he or she starts to cry, and you'll often see the frontalis, pars medialis, shoot up, as if it were on a string.

Perhaps the most famous involuntary expression is what Ekman has 20
dubbed the Duchenne smile, in honor of the nineteenth-century French neurologist Guillaume Duchenne, who first attempted to document the workings of the muscles of the face with the camera. If I ask you to smile, you'll
flex your zygomatic major. By contrast, if you smile spontaneously, in the
presence of genuine emotion, you'll not only flex your zygomatic but also
tighten the orbicularis oculi, pars orbitalis, which is the muscle that encir-
cles the eye. It is almost impossible to tighten the orbicularis oculi, pars lateralis, on demand, and it is equally difficult to stop it from tightening when
we smile at something genuinely pleasurable. This kind of smile "does not
obey the will," Duchenne wrote. "Its absence unmasks the false friend."
When we experience a basic emotion, a corresponding message is automatically sent to the muscles of the face. That message may linger on the face
for just a fraction of a second, or be detectable only if you attached electrical sensors to the face, but it's always there. Silvan Tomkins once began a
lecture by bellowing, "The face is like the penis!" and this is what he
meant — that the face has, to a large extent, a mind of its own. This doesn't
mean we have no control over our faces. We can use our voluntary muscular system to try to suppress those involuntary responses. But, often, some
little part of that suppressed emotion — the sense that I'm really unhappy,
even though I deny it — leaks out. Our voluntary expressive system is the
way we intentionally signal our emotions. But our involuntary expressive
system is in many ways even more important: it is the way we have been
equipped by evolution to signal our authentic feelings.

"You must have had the experience where somebody comments on your
expression and you didn't know you were making it," Ekman says. "Somebody tells you, 'What are you getting upset about?' 'Why are you smirking?'
You can hear your voice, but you can't see your face. If we knew what was
on our face, we would be better at concealing it. But that wouldn't necessarily be a good thing. Imagine if there were a switch that all of us had, to turn
off the expressions on our face at will. If babies had that switch, we wouldn't
know what they were feeling. They'd be in trouble. You could make an argument, if you wanted to, that the system evolved so that parents would be able
to take care of kids. Or imagine if you were married to someone with a
switch? It would be impossible. I don't think mating and infatuation and
friendships and closeness would occur if our faces didn't work that way."

Ekman slipped a tape taken from the O. J. Simpson trial into the VCR.
It was of Kato Kaelin, Simpson's shaggy-haired house guest, being examined by Marcia Clark, one of the prosecutors in the case. Kaelin sits in the
witness box, with his trademark vacant look. Clark asks a hostile question.
Kaelin leans forward and answers softly. "Did you see that?" Ekman asked
me. I saw nothing, just Kato being Kato — harmless and passive. Ekman
stopped the tape, rewound it, and played it back in slow motion. On the
screen, Kaelin moved forward to answer the question, and in that fraction
of a second his face was utterly transformed. His nose wrinkled, as he
flexed his levator labii superioris, alaeque nasi. His teeth were bared, his

brows lowered. "It was almost totally A.U. nine," Ekman said. "It's disgust, with anger there as well, and the clue to that is that when your eyebrows go down, typically your eyes are not as open as they are here. The raised upper eyelid is a component of anger, not disgust. It's very quick." Ekman stopped the tape and played it again, peering at the screen. "You know, he looks like a snarling dog."

Ekman said that there was nothing magical about his ability to pick up an emotion that fleeting. It was simply a matter of practice. "I could show you forty examples, and you could pick it up. I have a training tape, and people love it. They start it, and they can't see any of these expressions. Thirty-five minutes later, they can see them all. What that says is that this is an accessible skill."

Ekman showed another clip, this one from a press conference given by Kim Philby in 1955. Philby had not yet been revealed as a Soviet spy, but two of his colleagues, Donald Maclean and Guy Burgess, had just defected to the Soviet Union. Philby is wearing a dark suit and a white shirt. His hair is straight and parted to the left. His face has the hauteur of privilege.

"Mr. Philby," he is asked. "Mr. Macmillan, the foreign secretary, said   25 there was no evidence that you were the so-called third man who allegedly tipped off Burgess and Maclean. Are you satisfied with that clearance that he gave you?"

Philby answers confidently, in the plummy tones of the English upper class. "Yes, I am."

"Well, if there was a third man, were you in fact the third man?"

"No," Philby says, just as forcefully. "I was not."

Ekman rewound the tape, and replayed it in slow motion. "Look at this," he said, pointing to the screen. "Twice, after being asked serious questions about whether he's committed treason, he's going to smirk. He looks like the cat who ate the canary." The expression was too brief to see normally. But at quarter speed it was painted on his face—the lips pressed together in a look of pure smugness. "He's enjoying himself, isn't he?" Ekman went on. "I call this—duping delight—the thrill you get from fooling other people." Ekman started the VCR up again. "There's another thing he does." On the screen, Philby was answering another question. "In the second place, the Burgess-Maclean affair has raised issues of great"—he pauses—"delicacy." Ekman went back to the pause, and froze the tape. "Here it is," he said. "A very subtle microexpression of distress or unhappiness. It's only in the eyebrows—in fact, just in one eyebrow." Sure enough, Philby's right inner eyebrow was raised in an unmistakable A.U. one. "It's very brief," Ekman said. "He's not doing it voluntarily. And it totally contradicts all his confidence and assertiveness. It comes when he's talking about Burgess and Maclean, whom he had tipped off. It's a hot spot that suggests, 'You shouldn't trust what you hear.'"

A decade ago, Ekman joined forces with J. J. Newberry—the ex-A.T.F.   30 agent who is one of the high-scorers in the Diogenes Project—to put together a program for educating law-enforcement officials around the world in the techniques of interviewing and lie detection. In recent months, they have flown to Washington, D.C., to assist the C.I.A. and the F.B.I. in counter-terrorism training. At the same time, the Defense Advanced Research Projects Agency (DARPA) has asked Ekman and his former student Mark Frank, now at Rutgers, to develop experimental scenarios for studying deception that would be relevant to counter-terrorism. The objective is to teach people to look for discrepancies between what is said and what is signalled—to pick up on the difference between Philby's crisp denials and his fleeting anguish. It's a completely different approach from the shouting cop we see on TV and in the movies, who threatens the suspect and sweeps all of the papers and coffee cups off the battered desk. The Hollywood interrogation is an exercise in intimidation, and its point is to force the suspect to tell you what you need to know. It does not take much to see the limitations of this strategy. It depends for its success on the coöperation of the suspect—when, of course, the suspect's involuntary communication may be just as critical. And it privileges the voice over the face, when the voice and the face are equally significant channels in the same system.

Ekman received his most memorable lesson in this truth when he and Friesen first began working on expressions of anger and distress. "It was weeks before one of us finally admitted feeling terrible after a session where we'd been making one of those faces all day," Friesen says. "Then the other realized that he'd been feeling poorly, too, so we began to keep track." They then went back and began monitoring their body during particular facial movements. "Say you do A.U. one, raising the inner eyebrows, and six, raising the cheeks, and fifteen, the lowering of the corner of the lips," Ekman said, and then did all three. "What we discovered is that that expression alone is sufficient to create marked changes in the autonomic nervous system. When this first occurred, we were stunned. We weren't expecting this at all. And it happened to both of us. We felt *terrible*. What we were generating was sadness, anguish. And when I lower my brows, which is four, and raise the upper eyelid, which is five, and narrow the eyelids, which is seven, and press the lips together, which is twenty-four, I'm generating anger. My heartbeat will go up ten to twelve beats. My hands will get hot. As I do it, I can't disconnect from the system. It's very unpleasant, very unpleasant."

Ekman, Friesen, and another colleague, Robert Levenson, who teaches at Berkeley, published a study of this effect in *Science*. They monitored the bodily indices of anger, sadness, and fear—heart rate and body temperature—in two groups. The first group was instructed to remember and relive a particularly stressful experience. The other was told to simply produce a series of facial movements, as instructed by Ekman—to "assume the position," as they say in acting class. The second group, the people who were pretending, showed the same physiological responses as the first. A few years later, a German team of psychologists published a similar study. They had a group of subjects look at cartoons, either while holding a pen between their lips—an action that made it impossible to contract either of the two major smiling muscles, the risorius and the zygomatic major—or while holding a pen clenched between their teeth, which had the opposite effect and forced them to smile. The people with the pen between their teeth found the cartoons much funnier. Emotion doesn't just go from the inside out. It goes from the outside in. What's more, neither the subjects "assuming the position" nor the people with pens in their teeth knew they were making expressions of emotion. In the facial-feedback system, an expression you do not even know that you have can create an emotion you did not choose to feel.

It is hard to talk to anyone who knows FACS without this point coming up again and again. Face-reading depends not just on seeing facial expressions but also on taking them seriously. One reason most of us—like the TV cop—do not closely attend to the face is that we view its evidence as secondary, as an adjunct to what we believe to be *real* emotion. But there's nothing secondary about the face, and surely this realization is what set John Yarbrough apart on the night that the boy in the sports car came at him with a gun. It's not just that he saw a microexpression that the rest of us would have missed. It's that he took what he saw so seriously that he was able to overcome every self-protective instinct in his body, and hold his fire.

6.

Yarbrough has a friend in the L.A. County Sheriff's Department, Sergeant Bob Harms, who works in narcotics in Palmdale. Harms is a member of the Diogenes Project as well, but the two men come across very differently. Harms is bigger than Yarbrough, taller and broader in the chest, with soft brown eyes and dark, thick hair. Yarbrough is restoring a Corvette and wears Rush Limbaugh ties, and he says that if he hadn't been a cop he would have liked to stay in the Marines. Harms came out of college wanting to be a commercial artist; now he plans to open a bed-and-breakfast in Vermont with his wife when he retires. On the day we met, Harms was wearing a pair of jean shorts and a short-sleeved patterned shirt. His badge was hidden inside his shirt. He takes notes not on a yellow legal pad, which he considers unnecessarily intimidating to witnesses, but on a powder-blue one. "I always get teased because I'm the touchy-feely one," Harms said. "John Yarbrough is very analytical. He thinks before he speaks. There is a lot going on inside his head. He's constantly thinking four or five steps ahead, then formulating whatever his answers are going to be. That's not how I do my interviews. I have a conversation. It's not 'Where were you on Friday night?' Because that's the way we normally communicate. I never say, 'I'm Sergeant Harms.' I always start by saying, 'I'm Bob Harms, and I'm here to talk to you about your case,' and the first thing I do is smile."

The sensation of talking to the two men, however, is surprisingly similar. Normal conversation is like a game of tennis: you talk and I listen, you listen and I talk, and we feel scrutinized by our conversational partner only when the ball is in our court. But Yarbrough and Harms never stop watching, even when they're doing the talking. Yarbrough would comment on my conversational style, noting where I held my hands as I talked, or how long I would wait out a lull in the conversation. At one point, he stood up and soundlessly moved to the door—which he could have seen only in his peripheral vision—opening it just before a visitor rang the doorbell. Harms gave the impression that he was deeply interested in me. It wasn't empathy. It was a kind of powerful curiosity. "I remember once, when I was in prison custody, I used to shake prisoners' hands," Harms said. "The deputies thought I was crazy. But I wanted to see what happened, because that's what these men are starving for, some dignity and respect."

Some of what sets Yarbrough and Harms and the other face readers apart is no doubt innate. But the fact that people can be taught so easily to recognize microexpressions, and can learn FACS, suggests that we all have at least the potential capacity for this kind of perception. Among those who do very well at face-reading, tellingly, are some aphasics, such as stroke victims who have lost the ability to understand language. Collaborating with Ekman on a paper that was recently published in *Nature,* the psychologist Nancy Etcoff, of Massachusetts General Hospital, described how a group of aphasics trounced a group of undergraduates at M.I.T. on the nurses tape. Robbed of the power to understand speech, the stroke victims had apparently been forced to become far more sensitive to the information written on people's faces. "They are compensating for the loss in one channel through these other channels," Etcoff says. "We could hypothesize that there is some kind of rewiring in the brain, but I don't think we need that explanation. They simply exercise these skills much more than we do." Ekman has also done work showing that some abused children are particularly good at reading faces as well: like the aphasics in the study, they developed "interpretive strategies"—in their case, so they could predict the behavior of their volatile parents.

What appears to be a kind of magical, effortless intuition about faces, then, may not really be effortless and magical at all. This kind of intuition is a product of desire and effort. Silvan Tomkins took a sabbatical from Princeton when his son Mark was born, and stayed in his house on the Jersey Shore, staring into his son's face, long and hard, picking up the patterns of emotion—the cycles of interest, joy, sadness, and anger—that flash across an infant's face in the first few months of life. He taught himself the logic of the furrows and the wrinkles and the creases, the subtle differences between the pre-smile and the pre-cry face. Later, he put together a library of thousands of photographs of human faces, in every conceivable expression. He developed something called the Picture Arrangement Test, which was his version of the Rorschach blot: a patient would look at a series of pictures and be asked to arrange them in a sequence and then tell a story based on what he saw. The psychologist was supposed to interpret the meaning of the story, but Tomkins would watch a videotape of the patient with the sound off, and by studying the expressions on the patient's face teach himself to predict what the story was. Face-reading, for those who have mastered it, becomes a kind of compulsion; it becomes hard to be satisfied with the level and quality of information that most of us glean from normal social encounters. "Whenever we get together," Harms says of spending time with other face readers, "we debrief each other. We're constantly talking about cases, or some of these videotapes of Ekman's, and we say, 'I missed that, did you get that?' Maybe there's an emotion attached there. We're always trying to place things, and replaying interviews in our head."

This is surely why the majority of us don't do well at reading faces: we feel no need to make that extra effort. People fail at the nurses tape, Ekman says, because they end up just listening to the words. That's why, when Tomkins was starting out in his quest to understand the face, he always watched television with the sound turned off. "We are such creatures of language that what we hear takes precedence over what is supposed to be our primary channel of communication, the visual channel," he once said. "Even though the visual channel provides such enormous information, the fact is that the voice preëmpts the individual's attention, so that he cannot really see the face while he listens." We prefer that way of dealing with the world because it does not challenge the ordinary boundaries of human relationships. Ekman, in one of his essays, writes of what he learned from the legendary sociologist Erving Goffman. Goffman said that part of what it means to be civilized is not to "steal" information that is not freely given to us. When someone picks his nose or cleans his ears, out of unthinking habit, we look away. Ekman writes that for Goffman the spoken word is "the acknowledged information, the information for which the person who states it is willing to take responsibility," and he goes on:

> When the secretary who is miserable about a fight with her husband the previous night answers, "Just fine," when her boss asks, "How are you this morning?" — that false message may be the one relevant to the boss's interactions with her. It tells him that she is going to do her job. The true message — that she is miserable — he may not care to know about at all as long as she does not intend to let it impair her job performance.

What would the boss gain by reading the subtle and contradictory microexpressions on his secretary's face? It would be an invasion of her privacy and an act of disrespect. More than that, it would entail an obligation. He would be obliged to do something, or say something, or feel something that might otherwise be avoided entirely. To see what is intended to be hidden, or, at least, what is usually missed, opens up a world of uncomfortable possibilities. This is the hard part of being a face reader. People like that have more faith in their hunches than the rest of us do. But faith is not certainty. Sometimes, on a routine traffic stop late at night, you end up finding out that your hunch was right. But at other times you'll never know.

And you can't even explain it properly, because what can you say? You did something the rest of us would never have done, based on something the rest of us would never have seen.

"I was working in West Hollywood once, in the nineteen-eighties," 40 Harms said. "I was with a partner, Scott. I was driving. I had just recently come off the prostitution team, and we spotted a man in drag. He was on Sunset, and I didn't recognize him. At that time, Sunset was normally for females. So it was kind of odd. It was a cold night in January. There was an all-night restaurant on Sunset called Ben Franks, so I asked my partner to roll down the window and ask the guy if he was going to Ben Franks—just to get a reaction. And the guy immediately keys on Scott, and he's got an overcoat on, and he's all bundled up, and he starts walking over to the car. It had been raining so much that the sewers in West Hollywood had backed up, and one of the manhole covers had been cordoned off because it was pumping out water. The guy comes over to the squad car, and he's walking right through that. He's fixated on Scott. So we asked him what he was doing. He says, 'I was out for a walk.' And then he says, 'I have something to show you.'"

Later, after the incident was over, Harms and his partner learned that the man had been going around Hollywood making serious threats, that he was unstable and had just attempted suicide, that he was in all likelihood about to erupt. A departmental inquiry into the incident would affirm that Harms and his partner had been in danger: the man was armed with a makeshift flamethrower, and what he had in mind, evidently, was to turn the inside of the squad car into an inferno. But at the time all Harms had was a hunch, a sense from the situation and the man's behavior and what he glimpsed inside the man's coat and on the man's face—something that was the opposite of whatever John Yarbrough saw in the face of the boy in Willowbrook. Harms pulled out his gun and shot the man through the open window. "Scott looked at me and was, like, 'What did you do?' because he didn't perceive any danger," Harms said. "But I did."

QUESTIONS

1. Gladwell tells the story of how emotions can be seen on the face. What does each character in his story add to his explanation of facial expressions? Why do you feel that the author chose to tell the story in this way?

2. Instead of just presenting the results of Ekman and Frisen's work, Gladwell tells the story of their work with emotions and the face from the very beginning—from their initial questions, to their making faces at each other, to their cataloguing of the facial muscles that express emotions on the face. Why does Gladwell choose this approach? What is he showing us about the way that scientific inquiry works? How would the piece have been different had he not included the step-by-step evolution of their thoughts?

3. "Disgust? That's mostly A.U. nine, the wrinkling of the nose (levator labii superioris, alaeque nasi), but it can sometimes be ten, and in either case may be combined with A.U. fifteen or sixteen or seventeen" (paragraph 15). Gladwell explains some of the facial muscle patterns represented by these numbers, but he sometimes mentions only the emotion and the action unit numbers without explaining what muscles those numbers represent. Why do you think he does this? What effect does it have on the reader?

4. What is your reaction to Ekman's distillation of the display of emotion down to numbers and the Latin medical names of facial muscles? Gladwell writes that he "catalogued the essential repertoire of human emotion" (paragraph 12). How does knowing the exact muscle patterns of each emotional expression alter your perception of emotion?

5. "Emotion doesn't just go from the inside out. It goes from the outside in" (paragraph 32). What discovery allowed Ekman, Friesen, and Levenson to make this statement? What implications can you draw from the interactive nature of the facial muscles and the feelings of emotion—that is, that they are both causes and effects of each other?

6. Gladwell begins and ends his essay with stories of men whose keen perception of facial cues and behavior may have saved lives. For those of us who are not in law enforcement, how could enhanced awareness of the way that emotions are displayed on faces affect our lives? Could such awareness have negative consequences as well?

7. Closely observe the facial expressions of a friend or roommate, and write an essay explaining that person's pattern of expressions. What facial muscles seem to be most at work? Explain which emotion in particular is displayed the most often on his or her face, and describe the facial transformation that occurs. Instead of describing only the workings of their facial muscles, write a character sketch similar to Gladwell's treatment of Yarbrough, providing your reader with details about your subject's dress, appearance, mannerisms, and behavior.

MAKING CONNECTIONS

In their essays, Gladwell, Nancy Mairs (p. 367), Stephen W. Hawking (p. 488), and Atul Gawande (p. 455), all present knowledge as a process instead of a product. Instead of summarizing the results of scientific research or personal thought, they explain to the reader how those results were achieved. Explain how each author makes the reader aware of the process behind the acquisition of knowledge. How are the reader's interest in and understanding of the material affected by this exploration of process rather than of product?

CRIMSON TIDE

Atul Gawande

Atul Gawande (b. 1965) is the son of Indian-immigrant parents, both physicians who taught at Ohio University in Athens, Ohio. A Rhodes scholar, Gawande studied politics, philosophy, and economics at Oxford and later served as a White House aide during the Clinton administration. He received his medical degree and his master's of public health from Harvard Medical School, where he currently teaches surgery. A prolific writer for popular audiences, Gawande is a staff contributor to The New Yorker. *His first book was* Complications: A Surgeon's Notes on an Imperfect Science *(2002), in which he considers the potential for error among medical personnel. As the following 2001* New Yorker *essay suggests, one of Gawande's strengths is to translate medical technicalities into lay language.*

In January of 1997, Christine Drury became the overnight anchorwoman for *Channel 13 News*, the local NBC affiliate in Indianapolis. In the realm of television news and talk shows, this is how you get your start. (David Letterman began his career by doing weekend weather at the same station.) Drury worked the 9 P.M. to 5 A.M. shift, developing stories and, after midnight, reading a thirty-second and a two-and-a-half-minute bulletin. If she was lucky and there was breaking news in the middle of the night, she could get more air-time, covering the news live, either from the newsroom or in the field. If she was very lucky—like the time a Conrail train derailed in Greencastle—she'd get to stay on for the morning show.

Drury was twenty-six years old when she got the job. From the time she was a girl growing up in Kokomo, Indiana, she had wanted to be on television, and especially to be an anchorwoman. She envied the confidence and poise of the women she saw behind the desk. One day during high school, on a shopping trip to an Indianapolis mall, she spotted Kim Hood, who was then Channel 13's prime-time anchor. "I wanted to be her," Drury says, and the encounter somehow made the goal seem attainable. In college, at Purdue University, she majored in telecommunications, and one summer she did an internship at Channel 13. A year and a half after graduating, she landed a bottom-rung job there as a production assistant. She ran the teleprompter, positioned cameras, and generally did whatever she was told. During the next two years, she worked her way up to writing news and then, finally, to the overnight anchor job. Her bosses saw her as an ideal prospect. She wrote fine news scripts, they told her, had a TV-ready voice, and, not incidentally, had "the look"—which is to say that she was pretty in a wholesome, all-American, Meg Ryan way. She had perfect white teeth, blue eyes, blond hair, and an easy smile.

During her broadcasts, however, she found that she could not stop blushing. The most inconsequential event was enough to set it off. She'd be on the set, reading the news, and then she'd stumble over a word or realize that she was talking too fast. Almost instantly, she'd redden. A sensation of electric heat would start in her chest and then surge upward into her neck, her ears, her scalp. In physiological terms, it was a mere redirection of blood flow. The face and neck have an unusual number of veins near the surface, and they can carry more blood than those of similar size elsewhere. Stimulated by certain neurological signals, they will dilate while other peripheral vessels contract: the hands will turn white and clammy even as the face flushes. For Drury, more troubling than the physical reaction was the distress that accompanied it: her mind would go blank; she'd hear herself stammer. She'd have an overwhelming urge to cover her face with her hands, to turn away from the camera, to hide.

For as long as Drury could remember, she had been a blusher, and, with her pale Irish skin, her blushes stood out. She was the sort of child who almost automatically reddened with embarrassment when called on in class or while searching for a seat in the school lunchroom. As an adult, she could be made to blush by a grocery-store cashier's holding up the line to get a price on her cornflakes, or by getting honked at while driving. It may seem odd that such a person would place herself in front of a camera. But Drury had always fought past her tendency toward embarrassment. In high school, she had been a cheerleader, played on the tennis team, and been selected for the prom-queen court. At Purdue, she had played intramural tennis, rowed crew with friends, and graduated Phi Beta Kappa. She'd worked as a waitress and as an assistant manager at a Wal-Mart, even leading the staff every morning in the Wal-Mart Cheer. Her gregariousness and social grace have always assured her a large circle of friends.

On the air, though, she was not getting past the blushing. When you look at tapes of her early broadcasts—reporting on an increase in speeding-ticket fines, a hotel food poisoning, a twelve-year-old with an I.Q. of 325 who graduated from college—the redness is clearly visible. Later, she began wearing turtlenecks and applying to her face a thick layer of Merle Norman Cover Up Green concealer. Over this she would apply MAC Studiofix foundation. Her face ended up a bit dark, but the redness became virtually unnoticeable.

Still, a viewer could tell that something wasn't right. Now when she blushed—and eventually she would blush nearly every other broadcast—you could see her stiffen, her eyes fixate, her movements become mechanical. Her voice sped up and rose in pitch. "She was a real deer in the headlights," one producer said.

Drury gave up caffeine. She tried breath-control techniques. She bought self-help books for television performers and pretended the camera was her dog, her friend, her mom. For a while, she tried holding her head a certain way, very still, while on camera. Nothing worked.

Given the hours and the extremely limited exposure, being an overnight anchor is a job without great appeal. People generally do it for about a year, perfect their skills, and move on to a better position. But Drury was going nowhere. "She was definitely not ready to be on during daylight hours," a producer at the station said. In October of 1998, almost two years into her job, she wrote in her journal, "My feelings of slipping continue. I spent the entire day crying. I'm on my way to work and I feel like I may never use enough Kleenex. I can't figure out why God would bless me with a job I can't do. I have to figure out how to do it. I'll try everything before I give up."

What is this peculiar phenomenon called blushing? A skin reaction? An emotion? A kind of vascular expression? Scientists have never been sure how to describe it. The blush is at once physiology and psychology. On the one hand, blushing is involuntary, uncontrollable, and external, like a rash. On the other hand, it requires thought and feeling at the highest order of cerebral function. "Man is the only animal that blushes," Mark Twain wrote. "Or needs to."

Observers have often assumed that blushing is simply the outward 10 manifestation of shame. Freudians, for example, viewed blushing this way, arguing that it is a displaced erection, resulting from repressed sexual desire. But, as Darwin noted and puzzled over in an 1872 essay, it is not shame but the prospect of exposure, of humiliation, that makes us blush. "A man may feel thoroughly ashamed at having told a small falsehood, without blushing," he wrote, "but if he even suspects that he is detected he will instantly blush, especially if detected by one whom he reveres."

But if it is humiliation that we are concerned about, why do we blush when we're praised? Or when people sing "Happy Birthday" to us? Or when people just look at us? Michael Lewis, a professor of psychiatry at the University of Medicine and Dentistry of New Jersey, routinely demonstrates the effect in classes. He announces that he will randomly point at a student, that the pointing is meaningless and reflects no judgment whatever about the person. Then he closes his eyes and points. Everyone looks to see who it is. And, invariably, that person is overcome by embarrassment. In an odd experiment conducted a couple of years ago, two social psychologists, Janice Templeton and Mark Leary, wired subjects with facial-temperature sensors and put them on one side of a one-way mirror. The mirror was then removed to reveal an entire audience staring at them from the other side. Half the time the audience members were wearing dark glasses, and half the time they were not. Strangely, subjects blushed only when they could see the audience's eyes.

What is perhaps most disturbing about blushing is that it produces secondary effects of its own. It is itself embarrassing, and can cause intense self-consciousness, confusion, and loss of focus. (Darwin, struggling to explain why this might be, conjectured that the greater blood flow to the face drained blood from the brain.)

Why we have such a reflex is perplexing. One theory is that the blush exists to show embarrassment, just as the smile exists to show happiness. This would explain why the reaction appears only in the visible regions of the body (the face, the neck, and the upper chest). But then why do dark-skinned people blush? Surveys find that nearly everyone blushes, regardless of skin color, despite the fact that in many people it is nearly invisible. And you don't need to turn red in order for people to recognize that you're embarrassed. Studies show that people detect embarrassment *before* you blush. Apparently, blushing takes between fifteen and twenty seconds to reach its peak, yet most people need less than five seconds to recognize that someone is embarrassed—they pick it up from the almost immediate shift in gaze, usually down and to the left, or from the sheepish, self-conscious grin that follows a half second to a second later. So there's reason to doubt that the purpose of blushing is entirely expressive.

There is, however, an alternative view held by a growing number of scientists. The effect of intensifying embarrassment may not be incidental; perhaps that is what blushing is for. The notion isn't as absurd as it sounds. People may hate being embarrassed and strive not to show it when they are, but embarrassment serves an important good. For, unlike sadness or anger or even love, it is fundamentally a moral emotion. Arising from sensitivity to what others think, embarrassment provides painful notice that one has crossed certain bounds while at the same time providing others with a kind of apology. It keeps us in good standing in the world. And if blushing serves to heighten such sensitivity this may be to one's ultimate advantage.

The puzzle, though, is how to shut it off. Embarrassment causes blush-   15 ing, and blushing causes embarrassment—so what makes the cycle stop? No one knows, but in some people the mechanism clearly goes awry. A surprisingly large number of people experience frequent, severe, uncontrollable blushing. They describe it as "intense," "random," and "mortifying." One man I talked to would blush even when he was at home by himself just watching somebody get embarrassed on TV, and he lost his job as a management consultant because his bosses thought he didn't seem "comfortable" with clients. Another man, a neuroscientist, left a career in clinical medicine for a cloistered life in research almost entirely because of his tendency to blush. And even then he could not get away from it. His work on hereditary brain disease became so successful that he found himself fending off regular invitations to give talks and to appear on TV. He once hid in an office bathroom to avoid a CNN crew. On another occasion, he was invited to present his work to fifty of the world's top scientists, including five Nobel Prize winners. Usually, he could get through a talk by turning off the lights and showing slides. But this time a member of the audience stopped him with a question first, and the neuroscientist went crimson. He stood mumbling for a moment, then retreated behind the podium and surreptitiously activated his pager. He looked down at it and announced that an emergency had come up. He was very sorry, he said, but he had to go. He spent the rest of the day at home. This is someone who makes his living

studying disorders of the brain and the nerves, yet he could not make sense
of his own condition.

There is no official name for this syndrome, though it is often called
"severe" or "pathological" blushing, and no one knows how many people
have it. One very crude estimate suggests that from one to seven per cent of
the general population is afflicted. Unlike most people, whose blushing
diminishes after their teen-age years, chronic blushers report an increase as
they age. At first, it was thought that the problem was the intensity of their
blushing. But that proved not to be the case. In one study, for example, scientists used sensors to monitor the facial color and temperature of subjects,
then made them stand before an audience and do things like sing "The Star-
Spangled Banner" or dance to a song. Chronic blushers became no redder
than others, but they proved significantly more prone to blush. Christine
Drury described the resulting vicious cycle to me: one fears blushing, blushes, and then blushes at being so embarrassed about blushing. Which came
first—the blushing or the embarrassment—she did not know. She just
wanted it to stop.

In the fall of 1998, Drury went to see an internist. "You'll grow out of
it," he told her. When she pressed, however, he agreed to let her try med-
ication. It couldn't have been obvious what to prescribe. Medical textbooks
say nothing about pathological blushing. Some doctors prescribe anxiolyt-
ics, like Valium, on the assumption that the real problem is anxiety. Some
prescribe beta-blockers, which blunt the body's stress response. Some prescribe Prozac or other antidepressants. The one therapy that has been
shown to have modest success is not a drug but a behavioral technique
known as paradoxical intention—having patients actively try to blush
instead of trying not to. Drury used beta-blockers first, then antidepressants, and finally psychotherapy. There was no improvement.

By December of 1998, her blushing had become intolerable, her on-air
performance humiliating, and her career almost unsalvageable. She wrote
in her diary that she was ready to resign. Then one day she searched the
Internet for information about facial blushing, and read about a hospital in
Sweden where doctors were performing a surgical procedure that could
stop it. The operation involved severing certain nerves in the chest where
they exit the spinal cord to travel up to the head. "I'm reading this page
about people who have the exact same problem I had, and I couldn't believe
it," she told me. "Tears were streaming down my face." The next day, she
told her father that she had decided to have the surgery. Mr. Drury seldom
questioned his daughter's choices, but this sounded to him like a bad idea.
"It shocked me, really," he recalls. "And when she told her mother it
shocked her even worse. There was basically no way her daughter was
going to Sweden and having this operation."

Drury agreed to take some time to learn more about the surgery. She
read the few articles she could find in medical journals. She spoke to the
surgeons and to former patients. After a couple of weeks, she grew only

more convinced. She told her parents that she was going to Sweden, and when it became clear that she would not be deterred her father decided to go with her.

The surgery is known as endoscopic thoracic sympathectomy, or E.T.S.   20
It involves severing fibres of a person's sympathetic nervous system, part of the involuntary, or "autonomic," nervous system, which controls breathing, heart rate, digestion, sweating, and, among the many other basic functions of life, blushing. Toward the back of your chest, running along either side of the spine like two smooth white strings, are the sympathetic trunks, the access roads that sympathetic nerves travel along before exiting to individual organs. At the beginning of the twentieth century, surgeons tried removing branches of these trunks—a thoracic sympathectomy—for all sorts of conditions: epilepsy, glaucoma, certain cases of blindness. Mostly, the experiments did more harm than good. But surgeons did find two unusual instances in which a sympathectomy helped: it stopped intractable chest pain in patients with advanced, inoperable heart disease, and it put an end to hand and facial sweating in patients with hyperhidrosis—uncontrollable sweating.

Because the operation involved open-chest surgery, it was rarely performed. In recent years, however, a few surgeons, particularly in Europe, have been doing the procedure endoscopically, using scopes inserted through small incisions. Among them was a trio in Göteborg, Sweden, who noticed that many of their hyperhidrosis patients not only stopped sweating after surgery but stopped blushing, too. In 1992, the Göteborg group accepted a handful of patients who complained of disabling blushing. When the results were reported in the press, the doctors found themselves deluged with requests. Since 1998, the surgeons have done the operation for more than three thousand patients with severe blushing.

The operation is now performed around the world, but the Göteborg surgeons are among the few to have published their results: ninety-four per cent of patients experienced a substantial reduction in blushing; in most cases it was eliminated completely. In surveys taken some eight months after the surgery, two per cent regretted the decision, because of side effects, and fifteen per cent were dissatisfied. The side effects are not life-threatening, but they are not trivial. The most serious complication, occurring in one per cent of patients, is Horner's syndrome, in which inadvertent injury of the sympathetic nerves to the eye results in a constricted pupil, a drooping eyelid, and a sunken eyeball. Less seriously, patients no longer sweat from the nipples upward, and most experience a substantial increase in lower-body sweating in compensation. (A decade after undergoing E.T.S. for hand sweating, according to one study, the proportion of patients who were satisfied with the outcome dropped from an initial ninety-six per cent to sixty-seven per cent, mainly because of compensatory sweating.) About a third of patients also notice a curious reaction known as gustatory sweating—sweating prompted by certain tastes or smells. And, because sympathetic branches to the heart are removed, patients experience about a ten-percent reduction in heart rate; some complain of impaired physical performance. For all these reasons, the operation is at best a last resort, something to be tried, according to the surgeons, only after nonsurgical methods have failed. By the time people call Göteborg, they are often desperate. As one patient who had the operation told me, "I would have gone through with it even if they told me there was a fifty-per-cent chance of death."

On January 14, 1999, Christine Drury and her father arrived in Göteborg, a four-hundred-year-old seaport on Sweden's southwest coast. She remembers the day as beautiful, cold, and snowy. The Carlanderska Medical Center was old and small, with ivy-covered walls and big, arched wooden double doors. Inside, it was dim and silent; Drury was reminded of a dungeon. Only now did she become apprehensive, wondering what she was doing here, nine thousand miles away from home, at a hospital that she knew almost nothing about. Still, she checked in, and a nurse drew her blood for routine lab tests, made sure her medical records were in order, and took her payment, which came to six thousand dollars. Drury put it on a credit card.

The hospital room was reassuringly clean and modern, with white linens and blue blankets. Christer Drott, her surgeon, came to see her early the next morning. He spoke with impeccable British-accented English and was, she said, exceedingly comforting: "He holds your hand and is so compassionate. Those doctors have seen thousands of these cases. I just loved him."

At nine-thirty that morning, an orderly came to get her for the operation.   25
"We had just done a story about a kid who died because the anesthesiologist had fallen asleep," Drury says. "So I made sure to ask the anesthesiologist not to fall asleep and let me die. He kind of laughed and said, 'O.K.'"

While Drury was unconscious, Drott, in scrubs and sterile gown, swabbed her chest and axillae (underarms) with antiseptic and laid down sterile drapes so that only her axillae were exposed. After feeling for a space between the ribs in her left axilla, he made a seven-millimetre puncture with the tip of his scalpel, then pushed a large-bore needle through the hole and into her chest. Two litres of carbon dioxide were pumped in through the needle, pushing her left lung downward and out of the way. Then Drott inserted a resectoscope, a long metal tube fitted with an eyepiece, fibre-optic illumination, and a cauterizing tip. It is actually a urological instrument, thin enough to pass through the urethra (though never thin enough, of course, for urology patients). Looking through the lens, he searched for her left sympathetic trunk, taking care to avoid injuring the main blood vessels from her heart, and found the glabrous cordlike structure lying along the heads of her ribs, where they join the spine. He cauterized the trunk at two points, over the second and third ribs, destroying all the facial branches except those that lead to the eye. Then, after making sure there was no bleeding, he pulled the instrument out, inserted a catheter to suction out the carbon dioxide and let her lung reëxpand, and sutured the quarter-inch incision. Moving to the other side of the table, he performed the same procedure on the right side of her chest. Everything went without a hitch. The operation took just twenty minutes.

What happens when you take away a person's ability to blush? Is it merely a surgical version of Merle Norman Cover Up Green—removing the redness but not the self-consciousness? Or can a few snips of peripheral nerve fibres actually affect the individual herself? I remember once, as a teen-ager, buying mirrored sunglasses. I lost them within a few weeks, but when I had them on I found myself staring at people brazenly, acting a little tougher. I felt disguised behind those glasses, less exposed, somehow freer. Would the surgery be something like this?

Almost two years after Drury's operation, I had lunch with her at a sports bar in Indianapolis. I had been wondering what her face would look like without the nerves that are meant to control its coloring—would she look ashen, blotchy, unnatural in some way? In fact, her face is clear and slightly pinkish, no different, she said, from before. Yet, since the surgery, she has not blushed. Occasionally, almost randomly, she has experienced a phantom blush: a distinct feeling that she is blushing even though she is not. I asked if her face reddens when she runs, and she said no, although it will if she stands on her head. The other physical changes seemed minor to her. The most noticeable thing, she said, was that neither her face nor her arms sweat now and her stomach, back, and legs sweat much more than they used to, though not enough to bother her. The scars, tiny to begin with, have completely disappeared.

From the first morning after the operation, Drury says, she felt transformed. An attractive male nurse came to take her blood pressure. Ordinarily, she would have blushed the instant he approached. But nothing of the sort happened. She felt, she says, as if a mask had been removed.

That day, after being discharged, she put herself to the test, asking random people on the street for directions, a situation that had invariably caused her to redden. Now, as her father confirmed, she didn't. What's more, the encounters felt easy and ordinary, without a glimmer of her old self-consciousness. At the airport, she recalls, she and her father were waiting in a long check-in line and she couldn't find her passport. "So I just dumped my purse out onto the floor and started looking for it, and it occurred to me that I was doing this—and I wasn't mortified," she says. "I looked up at my dad and just started crying."

Back home, the world seemed new. Attention now felt uncomplicated, unfrightening. Her usual internal monologue when talking to people ("Please don't blush, please don't blush, oh God I'm going to blush") vanished, and she found that she could listen to others better. She could look at them longer, too, without the urge to avert her gaze. In fact, she had to teach herself not to stare.

Five days after the surgery, Drury was back at the anchor desk. She put on almost no makeup that night. She wore a navy-blue woollen blazer, the kind of warm clothing she would never have worn before. "My attitude was, This is my début," she told me. "And it went perfectly."

30

Later, I viewed some tapes of her broadcasts from the first weeks after the surgery. I saw her report on the killing of a local pastor by a drunk driver, and on the shooting of a nineteen-year-old by a sixteen-year-old; she was, in fact, more natural than she'd ever been. One broadcast in particular struck me. It was not her regular nighttime bulletin but a public-service segment called "Read, Indiana, Read!" For six minutes of live airtime on a February morning, she was shown reading a story to a crowd of obstreperous eight-year-olds as messages encouraging parents to read to their children scrolled by. Despite the chaos of kids walking by, throwing things, putting their faces up to the camera, she persevered, remaining composed the entire time.

Drury had told no one about the operation, but people at work immediately noticed a difference in her. I spoke to a producer at her station who said, "She just told me she was going on a trip with her dad, but when she came back and I saw her on TV again, I said, 'Christine! That was unbelievable!' She looked amazingly comfortable in front of the camera. You could see the confidence coming through the TV, which was completely different from before." Within months, Drury got a job as a prime-time on-air reporter at another station.

A few snips of fibres to her face and she was changed. It's an odd 35 notion, because we think of our essential self as being distinct from such corporeal details. Who hasn't seen a photo of himself, or heard his voice on tape, and thought, That isn't me? Burn patients who see themselves in a mirror for the first time — to take an extreme example — typically feel alien from their appearance. And yet they do not merely "get used" to it; their new skin changes them. It alters how they relate to people, what they expect of others, how they see themselves in others' eyes. A burn-ward nurse once told me that the secure may become fearful and bitter, the weak jut-jawed "survivors." Similarly, Drury had experienced her trip-wire blushing as something entirely external, not unlike a burn — "the red mask," she called it. Yet it reached so deep inside her that she believed it prevented her from being the person she was meant to be. Once the mask was removed, she seemed new, bold, "completely different from before." But what of the person who all her life had blushed and feared blushing and had been made embarrassed and self-conscious at the slightest scrutiny? That person, Drury gradually discovered, was still there.

One night, she went out to dinner with a friend and decided to tell him about the operation. He was the first person outside her family whom she had told, and he was horrified. She'd had an operation to *eliminate her ability to blush?* It seemed warped, he said, and, worse, vain. "You TV people will do anything to improve your career prospects," she recalls him saying.

She went home in tears, angry but also mortified, wondering whether it *was* a freakish and weak thing to have done. In later weeks and months, she became more and more convinced that her surgical solution made her a sort of impostor. "The operation had cleared my path to be the journalist I was trained to be," she says, "but I felt incredibly ashamed over needing to remove my difficulties by such artificial means."

She became increasingly fearful that others would find out about the operation. Once, a co-worker, trying to figure out what exactly seemed different about her, asked her if she had lost weight. Smiling weakly, she told him no, and said nothing more. "I remember going to a station picnic the Saturday before the Indy 500, and thinking to myself the whole time, Please, please let me get out of here without anyone saying, 'Hey, what happened to your blushing?'" It was, she found, precisely the same embarrassment as before, only now it stemmed not from blushing but from its absence.

On television, self-consciousness began to distract her again. In June of 1999, she took up her new job, but she was not scheduled to go on the air for two months. During the hiatus, she grew uncertain about going back on TV. One day that summer, she went out with a crew that was covering storm damage in a neighboring town where trees had been uprooted. They let her practice her standup before the camera. She is sure she looked fine, but that wasn't how she felt. "I felt like I didn't belong there, didn't deserve to be there," she says. A few days later, she resigned.

More than a year has passed since then, and Drury has had to spend this time getting her life back on track. Unemployed and ashamed, she withdrew, saw no one, and spent her days watching TV from her couch, in a state of growing depression. Matters changed for her only gradually. She began, against all her instincts, admitting to friends and then former co-workers what had happened. To her surprise and relief, nearly everyone was supportive. In September, 1999, she even started an organization, the Red Mask Foundation, to spread information about chronic blushing and to provide a community for its sufferers. Revealing her secret seemed to allow her finally to move on.

That winter, she found a new job—in radio, this time, which made perfect sense. She became the assistant bureau chief for Metro Networks radio in Indianapolis. She could be heard anchoring the news every weekday morning on two radio stations, and then doing the afternoon traffic report for these and several other stations. Last spring, having regained her confidence, she began contacting television stations. The local Fox station agreed to let her be a substitute broadcaster. In early July, she was called in at the last minute to cover traffic on its three-hour morning show.

It was one of those breakfast "news" programs with two chirpy co-anchors—a man and a woman—in overstuffed chairs, cradling giant coffee mugs. Every half hour or so, they'd turn to Drury for a two-minute traffic report. She'd stand before a series of projected city maps, clicking through them and describing the various car accidents and construction roadblocks to look out for. Now and then, the co-anchors would strike up some hey-you're-not-our-usual-traffic-gal banter, which she managed comfortably, laughing and joking. It was exciting, she says, but not easy. She

40

could not help feeling a little self-conscious, wondering what people might think about her coming back after her long absence. But the feelings did not overwhelm her. She is, she says, beginning to feel comfortable in her own skin.

One wants to know whether, in the end, her troubles were physical or psychological. But it is a question as impossible to answer as whether a blush is physical or mental—or, for that matter, whether a person is. Everyone is both, inseparable even by a surgeon's blade. I have asked Drury if she has any regrets about the operation. "Not at all," she says. She even calls the surgery "my cure." At the same time, she adds, "People need to know—surgery isn't the end of it." She has now reached what she describes as a happy medium. She is free from much of the intense self-consciousness that her blushing provoked, but she accepts the fact that she will never be entirely rid of it. In October, she became a freelance part-time on-air reporter for Channel 6, the ABC affiliate in Indianapolis. She hopes the job will become full time. "You know, I don't have a face for radio," she says.

QUESTIONS

1. The first paragraphs of Gawande's essay read more like the story of the career path of a TV anchorwoman than an exploration of blushing. Why do you think Gawande refrains from mentioning blushing until the third paragraph?

2. How does Christine Drury's personal story add to Gawande's essay about blushing? What is the purpose of her personal story? How would his piece have been different without the character of Drury?

3. How has reading Gawande's explanation of the physiology of blushing altered your perception of blushing? How will you view your next blush differently? How will you view someone else's next blush?

4. Why does the author include such a detailed description of Drury's surgery? Why do we need to know exactly which nerves will be cut, where they are located, and what tools the surgeon uses? Couldn't Gawande have summed up the operation with the last two sentences of paragraph 26: "Everything went without a hitch. The operation took just twenty minutes"? Explain why Gawande might have chosen to give the reader so much detail.

5. Why were Drury's problems not solved by the deblushing surgery? Do you believe that her problems with self-consciousness were caused by many years of blushing? If a decision to speak about her operation could help her overcome her shame, do you think that a decision to change her perception of blushing could have made the operation unnecessary in the first place? Why or why not?

6. Do you agree with the friend who thought that Drury's decision to have the deblushing operation was "warped" and "vain" (paragraph 36)? Does Gawande give us any indication as to what his opinion might be?

7. Do you believe that your personality would change if your body or physical appearance were altered in some way? To what extent would you change your body to prevent embarrassment? Reread Gawande's paragraph about how he felt that his behavior changed when he wore mirrored sunglasses. Write an essay about some change you have made or would like to make to your physical appearance, describing in detail how you believe your behavior or personality was (or would be) affected.

MAKING CONNECTIONS

Is a person physical or mental? According to Gawande, "Everyone is both, inseparable even by a surgeon's blade" (paragraph 43). Compare the implicit (or explicit) ways that Nancy Mairs, "Carnal Acts" (p. 367), Malcolm Gladwell, "The Naked Face" (p. 438), and Antonio R. Damasio, "How the Brain Creates the Mind" (p. 498) answer this question. Do you think they agree or disagree with Gawande? Why?

Sciences and Technologies

WHY THE SKY IS BLUE

James Jeans

Sir James Jeans (1877–1946) was a British physicist and astronomer. Educated at Trinity College, Cambridge, he lectured there and was a professor of applied mathematics at Princeton University from 1905 to 1909. He later did research at Mount Wilson Observatory in California. Jeans won many honors for his work and wrote a number of scholarly and popular scientific books. The following selection is from The Stars in Their Courses *(1931), a written version of what began as a series of radio talks for an audience assumed to have no special knowledge of science.*

Imagine that we stand on any ordinary seaside pier, and watch the waves rolling in and striking against the iron columns of the pier. Large waves pay very little attention to the columns — they divide right and left and re-unite after passing each column, much as a regiment of soldiers would if a tree stood in their road; it is almost as though the columns had not been there. But the short waves and ripples find the columns of the pier a much more formidable obstacle. When the short waves impinge on the columns, they are reflected back and spread as new ripples in all directions. To use the technical term, they are "scattered." The obstacle provided by the iron columns hardly affects the long waves at all, but scatters the short ripples.

We have been watching a sort of working model of the way in which sunlight struggles through the earth's atmosphere. Between us on earth and outer space the atmosphere interposes innumerable obstacles in the form of molecules of air, tiny droplets of water, and small particles of dust. These are represented by the columns of the pier.

The waves of the sea represent the sunlight. We know that sunlight is a blend of lights of many colors — as we can prove for ourselves by passing it through a prism, or even through a jug of water, or as Nature demonstrates to us when she passes it through the raindrops of a summer shower and produces a rainbow. We also know that light consists of waves, and that the different colors of light are produced by waves of different lengths, red light by long waves and blue light by short waves. The mixture of waves which constitutes sunlight has to struggle through the obstacles it meets in the atmosphere, just as the mixture of waves at the seaside has to struggle past the columns of the pier. And these obstacles treat the light-waves much as the columns of the pier treat the sea-waves. The long waves which constitute red light are hardly affected, but the short waves which constitute blue light are scattered in all directions.

Thus, the different constituents of sunlight are treated in different ways as they struggle through the earth's atmosphere. A wave of blue light may be scattered by a dust particle, and turned out of its course. After a time a second dust particle again turns it out of its course, and so on, until finally it enters our eyes by a path as zigzag as that of a flash of lightning. Consequently the blue waves of the sunlight enter our eyes from all directions. And that is why the sky looks blue.

QUESTIONS

1. Analogy, the comparison of something familiar with something less familiar, occurs frequently in scientific explanation. Jeans introduces an analogy in his first paragraph. How does he develop that analogy as he develops his explanation?
2. The analogy Jeans provides enables him to explain the process by which the blue light-waves scatter throughout the sky. Hence he gives us a brief process analysis of that phenomenon. Summarize that process in your own words.
3. Try rewriting this essay without the analogy. Remove paragraph 1 and all the references to ocean waves and pier columns in paragraphs 2 and 3. How clear an explanation is left?
4. Besides the sea-waves, what other familiar examples does Jeans use in his explanation?
5. This piece opens with "Imagine that we stand. . . ." Suppose that every *we* was replaced with a *you*. How would the tone of the essay change?
6. While analogy can be effective in helping to explain difficult scientific concepts, it can be equally useful in explaining and interpreting familiar things by juxtaposing them in new ways. Suppose, for example, that you wish to explain to a friend why you dislike a course you are taking. Select one of the following ideas for an analogy (or find a better one)—a forced-labor camp, a three-ring circus, squirrels on a treadmill, a tea party, a group-therapy session. Think through the analogy to your course, and write a few paragraphs of explanation. Let Jeans's essay guide you in organizing your own.

Making Connections

1. Jeans's essay is a clear explanation of a complex phenomenon, yet it is quite short. Where else in this volume have you found clear explanations? A number of short passages in the essays by Stephen W. Hawking (p. 488) and Diane Ackerman (p. 470) could provide examples. Choose a descriptive passage that you find clear in the work of one of these writers, and compare it to Jeans's. Is an analogy central to the passage you selected? If not, what are the differences in the authors' explanations?
2. Describe the audience that Jeans seems to have in mind for his explanation. How does that sense of audience differ for Stanley Milgram (p. 379) or Malcolm Gladwell (p. 438)? Compare one of those essays with Jeans's account of "Why the Sky Is Blue," and discuss how the task of explaining shifts according to the writer's assumptions about an audience.

WHY LEAVES TURN COLOR IN THE FALL

Diane Ackerman

Poet, essayist, and naturalist Diane Ackerman was born in Waukegan, Illinois, in 1948 and received her M.F.A and Ph.D in English from Cornell University, where she teaches as a visting professor. Her earliest works, published when she was still a doctoral student, were the poetry collections The Planets *(1976) and* Wife of Life *(1978); since then she has produced several further volumes, most recently* I Praise My Destroyer *(1998) and* Origami Bridges *(2002). Ackerman's first book of prose was* Twilight of the Tenderfoot *(1980), about her experiences working on a cattle ranch in New Mexico. Her subsequent prose works have focused on a range of subjects, as suggested by some of their titles:* The Moon by Whale Light: And Other Adventures among Bats, Crocodilians, Penguins, and Whales *(1990),* The Rarest of the Rare: Vanishing Animals, Timeless Worlds *(1995),* A Natural History of Love *(1994),* Deep Play *(1999), and* Cultivating Delight: A Natural History of My Garden *(2001). All, however, are characterized by Ackerman's deeply insightful observations of the natural world, as evidenced perhaps most fully in her most popular book and the source of a highly rated public television series,* A Natural History of the Senses *(1990), where the following selection appeared. Admitting that her work is difficult to categorize, Ackerman has said, "I write about nature and human nature. And most often about that twilight zone where the two meet and have something they can teach each other."*

The stealth of autumn catches one unaware. Was that a goldfinch perching in the early September woods, or just the first turning leaf? A red-winged blackbird or a sugar maple closing up shop for the winter? Keen-eyed as leopards, we stand still and squint hard, looking for signs of movement. Early-morning frost sits heavily on the grass, and turns barbed wire into a string of stars. On a distant hill, a small square of yellow appears to be a lighted stage. At last the truth dawns on us: Fall is staggering in, right on schedule, with its baggage of chilly nights, macabre holidays, and spectacular, heart-stoppingly beautiful leaves. Soon the leaves will start cringing on the trees, and roll up in clenched fists before they actually fall off. Dry seedpods will rattle like tiny gourds. But first there will be weeks of gushing color so bright, so pastel, so confettilike, that people will travel up and down the East Coast just to stare at it—a whole season of leaves.

Where do the colors come from? Sunlight rules most living things with its golden edicts. When the days begin to shorten, soon after the summer solstice on June 21, a tree reconsiders its leaves. All summer it feeds them so they can process sunlight, but in the dog days of summer the tree begins pulling nutrients back into its trunk and roots, pares down, and gradually chokes off its leaves. A corky layer of cells forms at the leaves' slender petioles, then scars over. Undernourished, the leaves stop producing the pigment chlorophyll, and photosynthesis ceases. Animals can migrate, hibernate, or store food to prepare for winter. But where can a tree go? It survives by dropping its leaves, and by the end of autumn only a few fragile threads of fluid-carrying xylem hold leaves to their stems.

A turning leaf stays partly green at first, then reveals splotches of yellow and red as the chlorophyll gradually breaks down. Dark green seems to stay longest in the veins, outlining and defining them. During the summer, chlorophyll dissolves in the heat and light, but it is also being steadily replaced. In the fall, on the other hand, no new pigment is produced, and so we notice the other colors that were always there, right in the leaf, although chlorophyll's shocking green hid them from view. With their camouflage gone, we see these colors for the first time all year, and marvel, but they were always there, hidden like a vivid secret beneath the hot glowing greens of summer.

The most spectacular range of fall foliage occurs in the northeastern United States and in eastern China, where the leaves are robustly colored, thanks in part to a rich climate. European maples don't achieve the same flaming reds as their American relatives, which thrive on cold nights and sunny days. In Europe, the warm, humid weather turns the leaves brown or mildly yellow. Anthocyanin, the pigment that gives apples their red and turns leaves red or red-violet, is produced by sugars that remain in the leaf after the supply of nutrients dwindles. Unlike the carotenoids, which color carrots, squash, and corn, and turn leaves orange and yellow, anthocyanin varies from year to year, depending on the temperature and amount of sunlight. The fiercest colors occur in years when the fall sunlight is strongest and the nights are cool and dry (a state of grace scientists find vexing to forecast). This is also why leaves appear dizzyingly bright and clear on a sunny fall day: The anthocyanin flashes like a marquee.

Not all leaves turn the same colors. Elms, weeping willows, and the 5 ancient ginkgo all grow radiant yellow, along with hickories, aspens, bottlebrush buckeyes, cottonweeds, and tall, keening poplars. Basswood turns bronze, birches bright gold. Water-loving maples put on a symphonic display of scarlets. Sumacs turn red, too, as do flowering dogwoods, black gums, and sweet gums. Though some oaks yellow, most turn a pinkish brown. The farmlands also change color, as tepees of cornstalks and bales of shredded-wheat-textured hay stand drying in the fields. In some spots, one slope of a hill may be green and the other already in bright color, because the hillside facing south gets more sun and heat than the northern one.

An odd feature of the colors is that they don't seem to have any special purpose. We are predisposed to respond to their beauty, of course. They shimmer with the colors of sunset, spring flowers, the tawny buff of a colt's pretty rump, the shuddering pink of a blush. Animals and flowers color for a reason—adaptation to their environment—but there is no adaptive reason for leaves to color so beautifully in the fall any more than there is for the sky or ocean to be blue. It's just one of the haphazard marvels the planet bestows every year. We find the sizzling colors thrilling, and in a sense they dupe us. Colored like living things, they signal death and disintegration. In time, they will become fragile and, like the body, return to dust. They are as we hope our own fate will be when we die: Not to vanish, just to sublime from one beautiful state into another. Though leaves lose their green life, they bloom with urgent colors, as the woods grow mummified day by day, and Nature becomes more carnal, mute, and radiant.

We call the season "fall," from the Old English *feallan*, to fall, which leads back through time to the Indo-European *phol*, which also means to fall. So the word and the idea are both extremely ancient, and haven't really changed since the first of our kind needed a name for fall's leafy abundance. As we say the word, we're reminded of that other Fall, in the garden of Eden, when fig leaves never withered and scales fell from our eyes. Fall is the time when leaves fall from the trees, just as spring is when flowers spring up, summer is when we simmer, and winter is when we whine from the cold.

Children love to play in piles of leaves, hurling them into the air like confetti, leaping into soft unruly mattresses of them. For children, leaf fall is just one of the odder figments of Nature, like hailstones or snowflakes. Walk down a lane overhung with trees in the never-never land of autumn, and you will forget about time and death, lost in the sheer delicious spill of color. Adam and Eve concealed their nakedness with leaves, remember? Leaves have always hidden our awkward secrets.

But how do the colored leaves fall? As a leaf ages, the growth hormone, auxin, fades, and cells at the base of the petiole divide. Two or three rows of small cells, lying at right angles to the axis of the petiole, react with water, then come apart, leaving the petioles hanging on by only a few threads of xylem. A light breeze, and the leaves are airborne. They glide and swoop, rocking in invisible cradles. They are all wing and may flutter from yard to yard on small whirlwinds or updrafts, swiveling as they go. Firmly tethered to earth, we love to see things rise up and fly—soap bubbles, balloons, birds, fall leaves. They remind us that the end of a season is capricious, as is the end of life. We especially like the way leaves rock, careen, and swoop as they fall. Everyone knows the motion. Pilots sometimes do a maneuver called a "falling leaf," in which the plane loses altitude quickly and on purpose, by slipping first to the right, then to the left. The machine weighs a ton or more, but in one pilot's mind it is a weightless thing, a falling leaf. She has seen the motion before, in the Vermont woods where she played as a child. Below her the trees radiate gold, copper, and red. Leaves are falling, although she can't see them fall, as she falls, swooping down for a closer view.

At last the leaves leave. But first they turn color and thrill us for weeks   10
on end. Then they crunch and crackle underfoot. They *shush*, as children
drag their small feet through leaves heaped along the curb. Dark, slimy
mats of leaves cling to one's heels after a rain. A damp, stuccolike mortar
of semidecayed leaves protects the tender shoots with a roof until spring,
and makes a rich humus. An occasional bulge or ripple in the leafy mounds
signals a shrew or a field mouse tunneling out of sight. Sometimes one finds
in fossil stones the imprint of a leaf, long since disintegrated, whose outlines
remind us how detailed, vibrant, and alive are the things of this earth that
perish.

QUESTIONS

1. Where, specifically, in the essay does Ackerman explain the natural
   process that leaves undergo in changing colors and eventually dropping
   from their trees' branches? Do you find this explanation clear and
   enlightening? Now, what makes up the remainder of the essay? Based on
   this analysis, how would you describe Ackerman's purpose (or purposes)
   here?
2. In paragraph 6 Ackerman writes that we are "predisposed" to respond
   favorably to the coloring of autumn leaves. What does she mean? Do
   you tend to agree with her? Why or why not?
3. In paragraphs 6, 9, and 10, Ackerman makes a connection between
   autumn leaves and the concept of death more generally. How would you
   summarize the point she is making here? What does this idea suggest
   about her view of death?
4. In paragraph 7 and at the beginning of paragraph 10, Ackerman engages
   in some rather whimsical wordplay. Does this wordplay seem to you in
   keeping with the overall tone of the essay? Why do you respond as you
   do?
5. The structure of "Why Leaves Turn Color in the Fall" is fairly loose,
   even seemingly digressive in places. Look, in particular, at the seeming
   digressions in paragraphs 8 and 9. Considering that this essay comes
   from a book titled *A Natural History of the Senses,* how might you
   relate them to Ackerman's larger point?
6. Think of other natural phenomena that can be considered beautiful in the
   way that colorful autumn leaves are for many: the formation of clouds
   that scud across a clear sky, for example, or waves rolling over the edge
   of a beach or a rosebud forming, maturing, and blooming — anything that
   you yourself regard as, in Ackerman's word, "spectacular." Choose one
   such phenomenon, and do some research to learn about the biological,
   geological, or other natural process that produces it. Then write an essay
   in which, like Ackerman, you explain the technical aspects of the natural

process while also describing the beauty of the phenomenon and perhaps exploring some of the reasons human might respond to it as they do.

MAKING CONNECTIONS

1. Like Ackerman, Annie Dillard is another contemporary nature writer noted for her penetrating insights, lyrical and enthusiastic evocations of natural phenomena, and strong sense of the "spirit" of nature. Read her essay "Lenses" (p. 146) alongside Ackerman's "Why Leaves Turn Color in the Fall," and find specific examples of similarities—as well as differences—between the two writers.
2. The title of James Jeans's essay "Why the Sky Is Blue" (p. 467) sets up expectations similar to those that Ackerman's title does: that what follows will provide an explanation of a natural process. In fact, how similar—and how different—are the two essays? Do you feel that one provides a clearer or more effective explanation than the other does? Why or why not? Which do you respond more favorably to?

THE MAN WHO MISTOOK HIS WIFE FOR A HAT

Oliver Sacks

Oliver Sacks was born in London, England, in 1933 and educated in London and Oxford before coming to the United States to complete his education in California and New York. At present he is clinical professor of neurology at Albert Einstein College of Medicine. He is best known, however, for his extraordinary writing on matters related to his medical studies, in such books as Awakenings *(1974),* Seeing Voices: A Journey into the World of the Deaf *(1989),* An Anthropologist on Mars *(1995),* The Island of the Colorblind *(1997), and his national best-seller,* The Man Who Mistook His Wife for a Hat *(1986), from which the following selection was adapted. Interested in the art of storytelling as well as in clinical neurology, Sacks subtitled the book in which this essay appeared, "and Other Clinical Tales." He insists that his essays are not just case studies, though they are that, but also tales or fables of "heroes, victims, martyrs, warriors." In his writing, he says, "the scientific and romantic . . . come together at the intersection of fact and fable." Sacks's prose style is lyrical as well as accurate; his explanation of prosopagnosia (perception without recognition) seeks to engage our interest and emotions while it defines and illustrates a syndrome unfamiliar to many readers.*

Dr. P. was a musician of distinction, well known for many years as a singer, and then, at the local School of Music, as a teacher. It was here, in relation to his students, that certain strange problems were first observed. Sometimes a student would present himself, and Dr. P. would not recognize him; or, specifically, would not recognize his face. The moment the student spoke, he would be recognized by his voice. Such incidents multiplied, causing embarrassment, perplexity, fear — and, sometimes, comedy. For not only did Dr. P. increasingly fail to see faces, but he saw faces when there were no faces to see: genially, Magoo-like, when in the street he might pat the heads of water hydrants and parking meters, taking these to be the heads of children; he would amiably address carved knobs on the furniture and be astounded when they did not reply. At first these odd mistakes were laughed off as jokes, not least by Dr. P. himself. Had he not always had a quirky sense of humor and been given to Zen-like paradoxes and jests? His musical powers were as dazzling as ever; he did not feel ill — he had never felt better; and the mistakes were so ludicrous — and so ingenious — that they could hardly be serious or betoken anything serious. The notion of there being "something the matter" did not emerge until some three years later, when diabetes developed. Well aware that diabetes could affect his eyes, Dr. P. consulted an ophthalmologist, who took a careful history and examined his eyes closely. "There's nothing the matter with your eyes," the doctor concluded. "But there is trouble with the visual parts of your brain. You don't need my help, you must see a neurologist." And so, as a result of this referral, Dr. P. came to me.

It was obvious within a few seconds of meeting him that there was no trace of dementia in the ordinary sense. He was a man of great cultivation and charm who talked well and fluently, with imagination and humor. I couldn't think why he had been referred to our clinic.

And yet there *was* something a bit odd. He faced me as he spoke, was oriented towards me, and yet there was something the matter — it was difficult to formulate. He faced me with his *ears*, I came to think, but not with his eyes. These, instead of looking, gazing, at me, "taking me in," in the normal way, made sudden strange fixations — on my nose, on my right ear, down to my chin, up to my right eye — as if noting (even studying) these individual features, but not seeing my whole face, its changing expressions, "me," as a whole. I am not sure that I fully realized this at the time — there was just a teasing strangeness, some failure in the normal interplay of gaze and expression. He saw me, he *scanned* me, and yet . . .

"What seems to be the matter?" I asked him at length.

"Nothing that I know of," he replied with a smile, "but people seem to   5
think there's something wrong with my eyes."

"But *you* don't recognize any visual problems?"

"No, not directly, but I occasionally make mistakes."

I left the room briefly to talk to his wife. When I came back, Dr. P. was sitting placidly by the window, attentive, listening rather than looking out. "Traffic," he said, "street sounds, distant trains — they make a sort of symphony, do they not? You know Honegger's[1] *Pacific 234?*"

What a lovely man, I thought to myself. How can there be anything seriously the matter? Would he permit me to examine him?

"Yes, of course, Dr. Sacks."   10

I stilled my disquiet, his perhaps, too, in the soothing routine of a neurological exam — muscle strength, coordination, reflexes, tone. . . . It was while examining his reflexes — a trifle abnormal on the left side — that the first bizarre experience occurred. I had taken off his left shoe and scratched the sole of his foot with a key — a frivolous-seeming but essential test of a reflex — and then, excusing myself to screw my ophthalmoscope together, left him to put on the shoe himself. To my surprise, a minute later, he had not done this.

"Can I help?" I asked.

---

[1]*Arthur Honegger* (1892–1955): French composer. [Eds.]

"Help what? Help whom?"

"Help you put on your shoe."

"Ach," he said, "I had forgotten the shoe," adding, *sotto voce*, "The   15
shoe? The shoe?" He seemed baffled.

"Your shoe," I repeated. "Perhaps you'd put it on."

He continued to look downwards, though not at the shoe, with an intense but misplaced concentration. Finally his gaze settled on his foot: "That is my shoe, yes?"

Did I mis-hear? Did he mis-see?

"My eyes," he explained, and put a hand to his foot. "*This* is my shoe, no?"

"No, it is not. That is your foot. *There* is your shoe."   20

"Ah! I thought that was my foot."

Was he joking? Was he mad? Was he blind? If this was one of his "strange mistakes," it was the strangest mistake I had ever come across.

I helped him on with his shoe (his foot), to avoid further complication. Dr. P. himself seemed untroubled, indifferent, maybe amused. I resumed my examination. His visual acuity was good: he had no difficulty seeing a pin on the floor, though sometimes he missed it if it was placed to his left.

He saw all right, but what did he see? I opened out a copy of the *National Geographic Magazine* and asked him to describe some pictures in it.

His responses here were very curious. His eyes would dart from one thing   25
to another, picking up tiny features, individual features, as they had done with my face. A striking brightness, a color, a shape would arrest his attention and elicit comment — but in no case did he get the scene-as-a-whole. He failed to see the whole, seeing only details, which he spotted like blips on a radar screen. He never entered into relation with the picture as a whole — never faced, so to speak, *its* physiognomy. He had no sense whatever of a landscape or scene.

I showed him the cover, an unbroken expanse of Sahara dunes.

"What do you see here?" I asked.

"I see a river," he said. "And a little guest-house with its terrace on the water. People are dining out on the terrace. I see colored parasols here and there." He was looking, if it was "looking," right off the cover into mid-air and confabulating nonexistent features, as if the absence of features in the actual picture had driven him to imagine the river and the terrace and the colored parasols.

I must have looked aghast, but he seemed to think he had done rather well. There was a hint of a smile on his face. He also appeared to have decided that the examination was over and started to look around for his hat. He reached out his hand and took hold of his wife's head, tried to lift it off, to put it on. He had apparently mistaken his wife for a hat! His wife looked as if she was used to such things.

I could make no sense of what had occurred in terms of conventional   30
neurology (or neuropsychology). In some ways he seemed perfectly preserved, and in others absolutely, incomprehensibly devastated. How could he, on the

one hand, mistake his wife for a hat and, on the other, function, as apparently he still did, as a teacher at the Music School?

I had to think, to see him again—and to see him in his own familiar habitat, at home.

A few days later I called on Dr. P. and his wife at home, with the score of the *Dichterliebe* in my briefcase (I knew he liked Schumann),[2] and a variety of odd objects for the testing of perception. Mrs. P. showed me into a lofty apartment, which recalled fin-de-siècle Berlin. A magnificent old Bösendorfer stood in state in the center of the room, and all around it were music stands, instruments, scores. . . . There were books, there were paintings, but the music was central. Dr. P. came in, a little bowed, and, distracted, advanced with outstretched hands to the grandfather clock, but, hearing my voice, corrected himself, and shook hands with me. We exchanged greetings and chatted a little of current concerts and performances. Diffidently, I asked him if he would sing.

"The *Dichterliebe!*" he exclaimed. "But I can no longer read music. You will play them, yes?"

I said I would try. On that wonderful old piano even my playing sounded right, and Dr. P. was an aged but infinitely mellow Fischer-Dieskau,[3] combining a perfect ear and voice with the most incisive musical intelligence. It was clear that the Music School was not keeping him on out of charity.

Dr. P.'s temporal lobes were obviously intact: he had a wonderful musical cortex. What, I wondered, was going on in his parietal and occipital lobes, especially in those areas where visual processing occurred? I carry the Platonic solids in my neurological kit and decided to start with these.   35

"What is this?" I asked, drawing out the first one.

"A cube, of course."

"Now this?" I asked, brandishing another.

He asked if he might examine it, which he did swiftly and systematically: "A dodecahedron, of course. And don't bother with the others—I'll get the icosahedron, too."

Abstract shapes clearly presented no problems. What about faces? I took out a pack of cards. All of these he identified instantly, including the jacks, queens, kings, and the joker. But these, after all, are stylized designs, and it was impossible to tell whether he saw faces or merely patterns. I decided I would show him a volume of cartoons which I had in my briefcase. Here, again, for the most part, he did well. Churchill's cigar, Schnozzle's nose: as soon as he had picked out a key feature he could identify the face. But cartoons, again, are formal and schematic. It remained to be seen how he would do with real faces, realistically represented.   40

---

[2]*Robert Schumann* (1810–1856): German romantic composer. [Eds.]

[3]*Dietrich Fischer-Dieskau* (b. 1925): German baritone, noted for his interpretations of Schumann's vocal music. [Eds.]

I turned on the television, keeping the sound off, and found an early Bette Davis film. A love scene was in progress. Dr. P. failed to identify the actress—but this could have been because she had never entered his world. What was more striking was that he failed to identify the expressions on her face or her partner's, though in the course of a single torrid scene these passed from sultry yearning through passion, surprise, disgust, and fury to a melting reconciliation. Dr. P. could make nothing of any of this. He was very unclear as to what was going on, or who was who or even what sex they were. His comments on the scene were positively Martian.

It was just possible that some of his difficulties were associated with the unreality of a celluloid, Hollywood world; and it occurred to me that he might be more successful in identifying faces from his own life. On the walls of the apartment there were photographs of his family, his colleagues, his pupils, himself. I gathered a pile of these together and, with some misgivings, presented them to him. What had been funny, or farcical, in relation to the movie, was tragic in relation to real life. By and large, he recognized nobody: neither his family, nor his colleagues, nor his pupils, nor himself. He recognized a portrait of Einstein because he picked up the characteristic hair and mustache; and the same thing happened with one or two other people. "Ach, Paul!" he said, when shown a portrait of his brother. "That square jaw, those big teeth—I would know Paul anywhere!" But was it Paul he recognized, or one or two of his features, on the basis of which he could make a reasonable guess as to the subject's identity? In the absence of obvious "markers," he was utterly lost. But it was not merely the cognition, the *gnosis*, at fault; there was something radically wrong with the whole way he proceeded. For he approached these faces—even of those near and dear—as if they were abstract puzzles or tests. He did not relate to them, he did not behold. No face was familiar to him, seen as a "thou," being just identified as a set of features, an "it." Thus, there was formal, but no trace of personal, gnosis. And with this went his indifference, or blindness, to expression. A face, to us, is a person looking out —we see, as it were, the person through his *persona*, his face. But for Dr. P. there was no *persona* in this sense—no outward *persona*, and no person within.

I had stopped at a florist on my way to his apartment and bought myself an extravagant red rose for my buttonhole. Now I removed this and handed it to him. He took it like a botanist or morphologist given a specimen, not like a person given a flower.

"About six inches in length," he commented. "A convoluted red form with a linear green attachment."

"Yes," I said encouragingly, "and what do you think it *is*, Dr. P.?"   45

"Not easy to say." He seemed perplexed. "It lacks the simple symmetry of the Platonic solids, although it may have a higher symmetry of its own. . . . I think this could be an inflorescence or flower."

"Could be?" I queried.

"Could be," he confirmed.

"Smell it," I suggested, and he again looked somewhat puzzled, as if I had asked him to smell a higher symmetry. But he complied courteously, and took it to his nose. Now, suddenly, he came to life.

"Beautiful!" he exclaimed. "An early rose. What a heavenly smell!" He 50 started to hum *"Die Rose, die Lillie . . ."* Reality, it seemed, might be conveyed by smell, not by sight.

I tried one final test. It was still a cold day, in early spring, and I had thrown my coat and gloves on the sofa.

"What is this?" I asked, holding up a glove.

"May I examine it?" he asked, and, taking it from me, he proceeded to examine it as he had examined the geometrical shapes.

"A continuous surface," he announced at last, "infolded on itself. It appears to have" — he hesitated — "five outpouchings, if this is the word."

"Yes," I said cautiously. "You have given me a description. Now tell me 55 what it is."

"A container of some sort?"

"Yes," I said, "and what would it contain?"

"It would contain its contents!" said Dr. P., with a laugh. "There are many possibilities. It could be a change purse, for example, for coins of five sizes. It could . . ."

I interrupted the barmy flow. "Does it not look familiar? Do you think it might contain, might fit, a part of your body?"

No light of recognition dawned on his face.[4]   60

No child would have the power to see and speak of "a continuous surface . . . infolded on itself," but any child, any infant, would immediately know a glove as a glove, see it as familiar, as going with a hand. Dr. P. didn't. He saw nothing as familiar. Visually, he was lost in a world of lifeless abstractions. Indeed, he did not have a real visual world, as he did not have a real visual self. He could speak about things, but did not see them face-to-face. Hughlings Jackson, discussing patients with aphasia and left-hemisphere lesions, says they have lost "abstract" and "propositional" thought — and compares them with dogs (or, rather, he compares dogs to patients with aphasia). Dr. P., on the other hand, functioned precisely as a machine functions. It wasn't merely that he displayed the same indifference to the visual world as a computer but — even more strikingly — he construed the world as a computer construes it, by means of key features and schematic relationships. The scheme might be identified — in an "identi-kit" way — without the reality being grasped at all.

The testing I had done so far told me nothing about Dr. P.'s inner world. Was it possible that his visual memory and imagination were still intact? I asked him to imagine entering one of our local squares from the north side,

---

[4]Later, by accident, he got it on, and exclaimed, "My God, it's a glove!" This was reminiscent of Kurt Goldstein's patient "Lanuti," who could only recognize objects by trying to use them in action.

to walk through it, in imagination or in memory, and tell me the buildings he might pass as he walked. He listed the buildings on his right side, but none of those on his left. I then asked him to imagine entering the square from the south. Again he mentioned only those buildings that were on the right side, although these were the very buildings he had omitted before. Those he had "seen" internally before were not mentioned now; presumably, they were no longer "seen." It was evident that his difficulties with leftness, his visual field deficits, were as much internal as external, bisecting his visual memory and imagination.

What, at a higher level, of his internal visualization? Thinking of the almost hallucinatory intensity with which Tolstoy visualizes and animates his characters, I questioned Dr. P. about *Anna Karenina*. He could remember incidents without difficulty, had an undiminished grasp of the plot, but completely omitted visual characteristics, visual narrative, and scenes. He remembered the words of the characters but not their faces; and though, when asked, he could quote, with his remarkable and almost verbatim memory, the original visual descriptions, these were, it became apparent, quite empty for him and lacked sensorial, imaginal, or emotional reality. Thus, there was an internal agnosia as well.[5]

But this was only the case, it became clear, with certain sorts of visualization. The visualization of faces and scenes, of visual narrative and drama—this was profoundly impaired, almost absent. But the visualization of *schemata* was preserved, perhaps enhanced. Thus, when I engaged him in a game of mental chess, he had no difficulty visualizing the chessboard or the moves—indeed, no difficulty in beating me soundly.

Luria[6] said of Zazetsky that he had entirely lost his capacity to play games but that his "vivid imagination" was unimpaired. Zazetsky and Dr. P. lived in worlds which were mirror images of each other. But the saddest difference between them was that Zazetsky, as Luria said, "fought to regain his lost faculties with the indomitable tenacity of the damned," whereas Dr. P. was not fighting, did not know what was lost, did not indeed know that anything was lost. But who was more tragic, or who was more damned—the man who knew it, or the man who did not?

65

---

[5]I have often wondered about Helen Keller's visual descriptions, whether these, for all their eloquence, are somehow empty as well? Or whether, by the transference of images from the tactile to the visual, or, yet more extraordinarily, from the verbal and the metaphorical to the sensorial and the visual, she *did* achieve a power of visual imagery, even though her visual cortex had never been stimulated, directly, by the eyes? But in Dr. P.'s case it is precisely the cortex that was damaged, the organic prerequisite of all pictorial imagery. Interestingly and typically he no longer dreamed pictorially—the "message" of the dream being conveyed in nonvisual terms.

[6]*Alexander Luria* (1902–1977): Russian neuropsychologist who developed theories of brain function that were based, in part, on his work with people with traumatic head injuries. [Eds.]

When the examination was over, Mrs. P. called us to the table, where there was coffee and a delicious spread of little cakes. Hungrily, hummingly, Dr. P. started on the cakes. Swiftly, fluently, unthinkingly, melodiously, he pulled the plates towards him and took this and that in a great gurgling stream, an edible song of food, until, suddenly, there came an interruption: a loud, peremptory rat-tat-tat at the door. Startled, taken aback, arrested by the interruption, Dr. P. stopped eating and sat frozen, motionless, at the table, with an indifferent, blind bewilderment on his face. He saw, but no longer saw, the table; no longer perceived it as a table laden with cakes. His wife poured him some coffee: the smell titillated his nose and brought him back to reality. The melody of eating resumed.

How does he do anything? I wondered to myself. What happens when he's dressing, goes to the lavatory, has a bath? I followed his wife into the kitchen and asked her how, for instance, he managed to dress himself. "It's just like the eating," she explained. "I put his usual clothes out, in all the usual places, and he dresses without difficulty, singing to himself. He does everything singing to himself. But if he is interrupted and loses the thread, he comes to a complete stop, doesn't know his clothes—or his own body. He sings all the time—eating songs, dressing songs, bathing songs, everything. He can't do anything unless he makes it a song."

While we were talking my attention was caught by the pictures on the walls.

"Yes," Mrs. P. said, "he was a gifted painter as well as a singer. The School exhibited his pictures every year."

I strolled past them curiously—they were in chronological order. All   70
his earlier work was naturalistic and realistic, with vivid mood and atmosphere, but finely detailed and concrete. Then, years later, they became less vivid, less concrete, less realistic and naturalistic, but far more abstract, even geometrical and cubist. Finally, in the last paintings, the canvases became nonsense, or nonsense to me—mere chaotic lines and blotches of paint. I commented on this to Mrs. P.

"Ach, you doctors, you're such Philistines!"[7] she exclaimed. "Can you not see *artistic development*—how he renounced the realism of his earlier years, and advanced into abstract, nonrepresentational art?"

"No, that's not it," I said to myself (but forbore to say it to poor Mrs. P.). He had indeed moved from realism to nonrepresentation to the abstract, yet this was not the artist, but the pathology, advancing—advancing towards a profound visual agnosia, in which all powers of representation and imagery, all sense of the concrete, all sense of reality, were being destroyed. This wall of paintings was a tragic pathological exhibit, which belonged to neurology, not art.

---

[7]*Philistines:* Uncultured, materialistic people. According to the Bible, the Philistines were enemies of the Israelites. [Eds.]

And yet, I wondered, was she not partly right? For there is often a struggle, and sometimes, even more interestingly, a collusion between the powers of pathology and creation. Perhaps, in his cubist period, there might have been both artistic and pathological development, colluding to engender an original form; for as he lost the concrete, so he might have gained in the abstract, developing a greater sensitivity to all the structural elements of line, boundary, contour — an almost Picasso-like power to see, and equally depict, those abstract organizations embedded in, and normally lost in, the concrete.... Though in the final pictures, I feared, there was only chaos and agnosia.

We returned to the great music room, with the Bösendorfer in the center, and Dr. P. humming the last torte.

"Well, Dr. Sacks," he said to me. "You find me an interesting case, I   75
perceive. Can you tell me what you find wrong, make recommendations?"

"I can't tell you what I find wrong," I replied, "but I'll say what I find right. You are a wonderful musician, and music is your life. What I would prescribe, in a case such as yours, is a life which consists entirely of music. Music has been the center, now make it the whole, of your life."

This was four years ago — I never saw him again, but I often wondered about how he apprehended the world, given his strange loss of image, visuality, and the perfect preservation of a great musicality. I think that music, for him, had taken the place of image. He had no body-image, he had body-music: this is why he could move and act as fluently as he did, but came to a total confused stop if the "inner music" stopped. And equally with the outside, the world. . . .[8]

In *The World as Representation and Will,* Schopenhauer[9] speaks of music as "pure will." How fascinated he would have been by Dr. P., a man who had wholly lost the world as representation, but wholly preserved it as music or will.

And this, mercifully, held to the end — for despite the gradual advance of his disease (a massive tumor or degenerative process in the visual parts of his brain) Dr. P. lived and taught music to the last days of his life.

Postscript

How should one interpret Dr. P.'s peculiar inability to interpret, to judge,   80
a glove as a glove? Manifestly, here, he could not make a cognitive judgment, though he was prolific in the production of cognitive hypotheses. A judgment

---

[8]Thus, as I learned later from his wife, though he could not recognize his students if they sat still, if they were merely "images," he might suddenly recognize them if they *moved.* "That's Karl," he would cry. "I know his movements, his body-music."

[9]*Arthur Schopenhauer* (1788–1860): German philosopher whose work included a theory to explain the life and work of the artist. [Eds.]

is intuitive, personal, comprehensive, and concrete — we "see" how things stand, in relation to one another and oneself. It was precisely this setting, this relating, that Dr. P. lacked (though his judging, in all other spheres, was prompt and normal). Was this due to lack of visual information, or faulty processing of visual information? (This would be the explanation given by a classical, schematic neurology.) Or was there something amiss in Dr. P.'s attitude, so that he could not relate what he saw to himself?

These explanations, or modes of explanation, are not mutually exclusive — being in different modes they could coexist and both be true. And this is acknowledged, implicitly or explicitly, in classical neurology: implicitly, by Macrae, when he finds the explanation of defective schemata, or defective visual processing and integration, inadequate; explicitly, by Goldstein, when he speaks of "abstract attitude." But abstract attitude, which allows "categorization," also misses the mark with Dr. P. — and, perhaps, with the concept of "judgment" in general. For Dr. P. *had* abstract attitude — indeed, nothing else. And it was precisely this, his absurd abstractness of attitude — absurd because unleavened with anything else — which rendered him incapable of perceiving identity, or particulars, rendered him incapable of judgment.

Neurology and psychology, curiously, though they talk of everything else, almost never talk of "judgment" — and yet it is precisely the downfall of judgment . . . which constitutes the essence of so many neuropsychological disorders. Judgment and identity may be casualties — but neuropsychology never speaks of them.

And yet, whether in a philosophic sense (Kant's sense),[10] or an empirical and evolutionary sense, judgment is the most important faculty we have. An animal, or a man, may get on very well without "abstract attitude" but will speedily perish if deprived of judgment. Judgment must be the *first* faculty of higher life or mind — yet it is ignored, or misinterpreted, by classical (computational) neurology. And if we wonder how such an absurdity can arise, we find it in the assumptions, or the evolution, of neurology itself. For classical neurology (like classical physics) has always been mechanical — from Hughlings Jackson's mechanical analogies to the computer analogies of today.

Of course, the brain is a machine and a computer — everything in classical neurology is correct. But our mental processes, which constitute our being and life, are not just abstract and mechanical, but personal, as well — and, as such, involve not just classifying and categorizing, but continual judging and feeling also. If this is missing, we become computer-like, as Dr. P. was. And, by the same token, if we delete feeling and judging, the personal, from the cognitive sciences, we reduce them to something as defective as Dr. P. — and we reduce our apprehension of the concrete and real.

----

[10]*Immanuel Kant* (1724–1804): German philosopher; some of his work concerned ethics and moral judgment. [Eds.]

By a sort of comic and awful analogy, our current cognitive neurology   85
and psychology resemble nothing so much as poor Dr. P.! We need the concrete and real, as he did; and we fail to see this, as he failed to see it. Our
cognitive sciences are themselves suffering from an agnosia essentially similar to Dr. P.'s. Dr. P. may therefore serve as a warning and parable—of
what happens to a science which eschews the judgmental, the particular, the
personal, and becomes entirely abstract and computational.

It was always a matter of great regret to me that, owing to circumstances beyond my control, I was not able to follow his case further, either
in the sort of observations and investigations described, or in ascertaining
the actual disease pathology.

One always fears that a case is "unique," especially if it has such
extraordinary features as those of Dr. P. It was, therefore, with a sense of
great interest and delight, not unmixed with relief, that I found, quite by
chance—looking through the periodical *Brain* for 1956—a detailed
description of an almost comically similar case, similar (indeed identical)
neuropsychologically and phenomenologically, though the underlying
pathology (an acute head injury) and all personal circumstances were wholly different. The authors speak of their case as "unique in the documented
history of this disorder"—and evidently experienced, as I did, amazement
at their own findings.[11] The interested reader is referred to the original
paper, Macrae and Trolle (1956), of which I here subjoin a brief paraphrase, with quotations from the original.

Their patient was a young man of 32, who, following a severe automobile accident, with unconsciousness for three weeks, " . . . complained,
exclusively, of an inability to recognize faces, even those of his wife and
children." Not a single face was "familiar" to him, but there were three he
could identify; these were workmates: one with an eye-blinking tic, one
with a large mole on his cheek, and a third "because he was so tall and thin
that no one else was like him." Each of these, Macrae and Trolle bring out,
was "recognized solely by the single prominent feature mentioned." In general (like Dr. P.) he recognized familiars only by their voices.

------

[11]Only since the completion of this book have I found that there is, in fact, a
rather extensive literature on visual agnosia in general, and prosopagnosia in particular. In particular I had the great pleasure recently of meeting Dr. Andrew Kertesz,
who has himself published some extremely detailed studies of patients with such
agnosias (see, for example, his paper on visual agnosia, Kertesz 1979). Dr. Kertesz
mentioned to me a case known to him of a farmer who had developed prosopagnosia
and in consequence could no longer distinguish (the faces of) his *cows,* and of another
such patient, an attendant in a Natural History Museum, who mistook his own
reflection for the diorama of an *ape.* As with Dr. P., and as with Macrae and Trolle's
patient, it is especially the animate which is so absurdly misperceived. The most
important studies of such agnosias, and of visual processing in general, are now being
undertaken by A. R. and H. Damasio.

He had difficulty even recognizing himself in a mirror, as Macrae and Trolle describe in detail: "In the early convalescent phase he frequently, especially when shaving, questioned whether the face gazing at him was really his own, and even though he knew it could physically be none other, on several occasions grimaced or stuck out his tongue 'just to make sure.' By carefully studying his face in the mirror he slowly began to recognize it, but 'not in a flash' as in the past — he relied on the hair and facial outline, and on two small moles on his left cheek."

In general he could not recognize objects "at a glance," but would have to seek out, and guess from, one or two features — occasionally his guesses were absurdly wrong. In particular, the authors note, there was difficulty with the *animate*.   90

On the other hand, simple schematic objects — scissors, watch, key, etc. — presented no difficulties. Macrae and Trolle also note that: "His *topographical memory* was strange: the seeming paradox existed that he could find his way from home to hospital and around the hospital, but yet could not name streets *en route* [unlike Dr. P., he also had some aphasia] or appear to visualize the topography."

It was also evident that visual memories of people, even from long before the accident, were severely impaired — there was memory of conduct, or perhaps a mannerism, but not of visual appearance or face. Similarly, it appeared, when he was questioned closely, that he no longer had visual images in his *dreams*. Thus, as with Dr. P., it was not just visual perception, but visual imagination and memory, the fundamental powers of visual representation, which were essentially damaged in this patient — at least those powers insofar as they pertained to the personal, the familiar, the concrete.

A final, humorous point. Where Dr. P. might mistake his wife for a hat, Macrae's patient, also unable to recognize his wife, needed her to identify herself by a visual *marker*, by ". . . a conspicuous article of clothing, such as a large hat."

QUESTIONS

1. Summarize as clearly as you can the nature of Dr. P.'s problem. What are the symptoms? What seems to have caused them?
2. What conclusions can be drawn from the case of Dr. P. about the way our visual systems work? Using what Sacks himself says and whatever additional conclusions you yourself can draw, what does the case of Dr. P. tell us about how we see things and what it means to recognize what we see?
3. Sacks has a way of drawing readers into his case studies, of making them concerned about the individuals whose cases he presents. How does he do this? That is, considering him as a writer rather than as a doctor, what aspects of his writing arouse interest and concern? Look at the opening paragraphs of the essay in particular.

4. Is this essay to any degree a story with a plot? Most people find Sacks a compelling writer. What about his way of writing causes this response? How does he keep readers reading?

5. This essay is not only a single case history and an explanation of some curious behavior. It also contains an argument about the nature of the cognitive sciences—how they should and should not proceed. What is that argument? Do you agree or disagree with the view of cognitive science that Sacks is advocating? Write an essay in which you present his position, and develop one of your own on this matter.

6. Write an essay in which you discuss Sacks as a writer and a scientist. Consider such matters as his style of writing, his interest in the arts, his clinical procedures, and the values that he expresses or implies in his work. If your instructor wishes, you may look further into his work to write this essay.

MAKING CONNECTIONS

Compare Sacks's essay with the reports of John Hersey, "Hatsuyo Nakamura" (p. 181), and Roy C. Selby Jr., "A Delicate Operation" (p. 267). What elements of a case study do these reports contain? Are they also tales or fables similar to Sacks's essay?

OUR PICTURE OF THE UNIVERSE

Stephen W. Hawking

Stephen W. Hawking (b. 1942), the Lucasian Professor of Mathematics at Cambridge University, is one of the world's leading theoretical physicists. Carl Sagan described the moment in 1974 when he observed "an ancient rite, the investiture of new fellows into the Royal Society, one of the most ancient scholarly organizations on the planet. In the front row a young man in a wheelchair was, very slowly, signing his name in a book that bore on its earliest pages the signature of Isaac Newton. When at last he finished, there was a stirring ovation. Stephen Hawking was a legend even then." Hawking's extraordinary achievements have drawn broad popular admiration in part because he suffers from the serious physical disabilities associated with Lou Gehrig's disease. Hawking is known especially for his work on "black holes" and their implications for a unified theory of physical phenomena. His best-selling book A Brief History of Time *(1988) made his thinking available to the general reader, with over a million copies in print. (In 1992, filmmaker Erroll Morris released a fascinating documentary portrait of Hawking under the same title.) The essay reprinted below is the first chapter of that book, unchanged except for the removal of references to the book as a whole.*

A well-known scientist (some say it was Bertrand Russell) once gave a public lecture on astronomy. He described how the earth orbits around the sun and how the sun, in turn, orbits around the center of a vast collection of stars called our galaxy. At the end of the lecture, a little old lady at the back of the room got up and said: "What you have told us is rubbish. The world is really a flat plate supported on the back of a giant tortoise." The scientist gave a superior smile before replying, "What is the tortoise standing on?" "You're very clever, young man, very clever," said the old lady. "But it's turtles all the way down!"

Most people would find the picture of our universe as an infinite tower of tortoises rather ridiculous, but why do we think we know better? What do we know about the universe, and how do we know it? Where did the universe come from, and where is it going? Did the universe have a beginning, and if so, what happened *before* then? What is the nature of time? Will it ever come to an end? Recent breakthroughs in physics, made possible in part by fantastic new technologies, suggest answers to some of these longstanding questions. Someday these answers may seem as obvious to us as the earth orbiting the sun — or perhaps as ridiculous as a tower of tortoises. Only time (whatever that may be) will tell.

As long ago as 340 B.C. the Greek philosopher Aristotle, in his book *On the Heavens,* was able to put forward two good arguments for believing that the earth was a round sphere rather than a flat plate. First, he realized that eclipses of the moon were caused by the earth coming between the sun and the moon. The earth's shadow on the moon was always round, which would be true only if the earth was spherical. If the earth had been a flat disk, the shadow would have been elongated and elliptical, unless the eclipse always occurred at a time when the sun was directly under the center of the disk. Second, the Greeks knew from their travels that the North Star appeared lower in the sky when viewed in the south than it did in more northerly regions. (Since the North Star lies over the North Pole, it appears to be directly above an observer at the North Pole, but to someone looking from the equator, it appears to lie just at the horizon.) From the difference in the apparent position of the North Star in Egypt and Greece, Aristotle even quoted an estimate that the distance around the earth was 400,000 stadia. It is not known exactly what length a stadium was, but it may have been about 200 yards, which would make Aristotle's estimate about twice the currently accepted figure. The Greeks even had a third argument that the earth must be round, for why else does one first see the sails of a ship coming over the horizon, and only later see the hull?

Aristotle thought that the earth was stationary and that the sun, the moon, the planets, and the stars moved in circular orbits about the earth. He believed this because he felt, for mystical reasons, that the earth was the center of the universe, and that circular motion was the most perfect. This idea was elaborated by Ptolemy in the second century A.D. into a complete cosmological model. The earth stood at the center, surrounded by eight spheres that carried the moon, the sun, the stars, and the five planets known at the time, Mercury, Venus, Mars, Jupiter, and Saturn (Figure 1). The planets themselves moved on smaller circles attached to their respective spheres in order to account for their rather complicated observed paths in the sky. The outermost sphere carried the so-called fixed stars, which always stay in the same positions relative to each other but which rotate together across the sky. What lay beyond the last sphere was never made very clear, but it certainly was not part of mankind's observable universe.

Ptolemy's model provided a reasonably accurate system for predicting the positions of heavenly bodies in the sky. But in order to predict these positions correctly, Ptolemy had to make an assumption that the moon followed a path that sometimes brought it twice as close to the earth as at other times. And that meant that the moon ought sometimes to appear twice as big as at other times! Ptolemy recognized this flaw, but nevertheless his model was generally, although not universally, accepted. It was adopted by the Christian church as the picture of the universe that was in accordance with Scripture, for it had the great advantage that it left lots of room outside the sphere of fixed stars for heaven and hell.

A simpler model, however, was proposed in 1514 by a Polish priest, Nicholas Copernicus. (At first, perhaps for fear of being branded a heretic

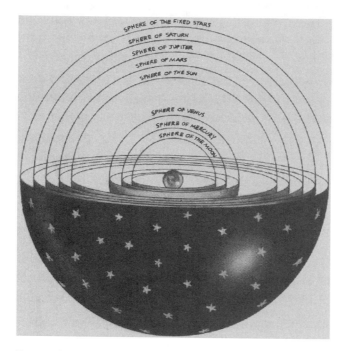

SPHERE OF THE FIXED STARS
SPHERE OF SATURN
SPHERE OF JUPITER
SPHERE OF MARS
SPHERE OF THE SUN
SPHERE OF VENUS
SPHERE OF MERCURY
SPHERE OF THE MOON

FIGURE 1

by his church, Copernicus circulated his model anonymously.) His idea was that the sun was stationary at the center and that the earth and the planets moved in circular orbits around the sun. Nearly a century passed before this idea was taken seriously. Then two astronomers—the German, Johannes Kepler, and the Italian, Galileo Galilei—started publicly to support the Copernican theory, despite the fact that the orbits it predicted did not quite match the ones observed. The death blow to the Aristotelian/Ptolemaic theory came in 1609. In that year, Galileo started observing the night sky with a telescope, which had just been invented. When he looked at the planet Jupiter, Galileo found that it was accompanied by several small satellites or moons that orbited around it. This implied that everything did *not* have to orbit directly around the earth, as Aristotle and Ptolemy had thought. (It was, of course, still possible to believe that the earth was stationary at the center of the universe and that the moons of Jupiter moved on extremely complicated paths around the earth, giving the *appearance* that they orbited Jupiter. However, Copernicus's theory was much simpler.) At the same time, Johannes Kepler had modified Copernicus's theory, suggesting that the planets moved not in circles but in ellipses (an ellipse is an elongated circle). The predictions now finally matched the observations.

As far as Kepler was concerned, elliptical orbits were merely an ad hoc hypothesis, and a rather repugnant one at that, because ellipses were clearly less perfect than circles. Having discovered almost by accident that elliptical orbits fit the observations well, he could not reconcile them with his idea that the planets were made to orbit the sun by magnetic forces. An explanation was provided only much later, in 1687, when Sir Isaac Newton published his *Philosophiae Naturalis Principia Mathematica*, probably the most important single work ever published in the physical sciences. In it Newton not only put forward a theory of how bodies move in space and time, but he also developed the complicated mathematics needed to analyse those motions. In addition, Newton postulated a law of universal gravitation according to which each body in the universe was attracted toward every other body by a force that was stronger the more massive the bodies and the closer they were to each other. It was this same force that caused objects to fall to the ground. (The story that Newton was inspired by an apple hitting his head is almost certainly apocryphal. All Newton himself ever said was that the idea of gravity came to him as he sat "in a contemplative mood" and "was occasioned by the fall of an apple.") Newton went on to show that, according to his law, gravity causes the moon to move in an elliptical orbit around the earth and causes the earth and the planets to follow elliptical paths around the sun.

The Copernican model got rid of Ptolemy's celestial spheres, and with them, the idea that the universe had a natural boundary. Since "fixed stars" did not appear to change their positions apart from a rotation across the sky caused by the earth spinning on its axis, it became natural to suppose that the fixed stars were objects like our sun but very much farther away.

Newton realized that, according to his theory of gravity, the stars should attract each other, so it seemed they could not remain essentially motionless. Would they not fall together at some point? In a letter in 1691 to Richard Bentley, another leading thinker of his day, Newton argued that this would indeed happen if there were only a finite number of stars distributed over a finite region of space. But he reasoned that if, on the other hand, there were an infinite number of stars, distributed more or less uniformly over infinite space, this would not happen, because there would not be any central point for them to fall to.

This argument is an instance of the pitfalls that you can encounter in 10 talking about infinity. In an infinite universe, every point can be regarded as the center, because every point has an infinite number of stars on each side of it. The correct approach, it was realized only much later, is to consider the finite situation, in which the stars all fall in on each other, and then to ask how things change if one adds more stars roughly uniformly distributed outside this region. According to Newton's law, the extra stars would make no difference at all to the original ones on average, so the stars would fall in just as fast. We can add as many stars as we like, but they will still always collapse in on themselves. We now know it is impossible to have an infinite static model of the universe in which gravity is always attractive.

It is an interesting reflection on the general climate of thought before the twentieth century that no one had suggested that the universe was expanding or contracting. It was generally accepted that either the universe had existed forever in an unchanging state, or that it had been created at a finite time in the past more or less as we observe it today. In part this may have been due to people's tendency to believe in eternal truths, as well as the comfort they found in the thought that even though they may grow old and die, the universe is eternal and unchanging.

Even those who realized that Newton's theory of gravity showed that the universe could not be static did not think to suggest that it might be expanding. Instead, they attempted to modify the theory by making the gravitational force repulsive at very large distances. This did not signifi-cantly affect their predictions of the motions of the planets, but it allowed an infinite distribution of stars to remain in equilibrium — with the attrac-tive forces between nearby stars balanced by the repulsive forces from those that were farther away. However, we now believe such an equilibrium would be unstable: if the stars in some region got only slightly nearer each other, the attractive forces between them would become stronger and dom-inate over the repulsive forces so that the stars would continue to fall toward each other. On the other hand, if the stars got a bit farther away from each other, the repulsive forces would dominate and drive them far-ther apart.

Another objection to an infinite static universe is normally ascribed to the German philosopher Heinrich Olbers, who wrote about this theory in 1823. In fact, various contemporaries of Newton had raised the problem, and the Olbers article was not even the first to contain plausible arguments against it. It was, however, the first to be widely noted. The difficulty is that in an infinite static universe nearly every line of sight would end on the sur-face of a star. Thus one would expect that the whole sky would be as bright as the sun, even at night. Olbers's counterargument was that the light from distant stars would be dimmed by absorption by intervening matter. However, if that happened the intervening matter would eventually heat up until it glowed as brightly as the stars. The only way of avoiding the con-clusion that the whole of the night sky should be as bright as the surface of the sun would be to assume that the stars had not been shining forever but had turned on at some finite time in the past. In that case the absorbing matter might not have heated up yet or the light from distant stars might not yet have reached us. And that brings us to the question of what could have caused the stars to have turned on in the first place.

The beginning of the universe had, of course, been discussed long before this. According to a number of early cosmologies and the Jewish/Christian /Muslim tradition, the universe started at a finite, and not very distant, time in the past. One argument for such a beginning was the feeling that it was necessary to have "First Cause" to explain the existence of the universe. (Within the universe, you always explained one event as being caused by some earlier event, but the existence of the universe itself could be explained in this way only if it had some beginning.) Another argument was put for-ward by St. Augustine in his book *The City of God*. He pointed out that civ-ilization is progressing and we remember who performed this deed or developed that technique. Thus man, and so also perhaps the universe, could not have been around all that long. St. Augustine accepted a date of about 5000 B.C. for the Creation of the universe according to the book of Genesis. (It is interesting that this is not so far from the end of the last Ice Age, about 10,000 B.C. which is when archaeologists tell us that civilization really began.)

Aristotle, and most of the other Greek philosophers, on the other hand,   15
did not like the idea of a creation because it smacked too much of divine intervention. They believed, therefore, that the human race and the world around it had existed, and would exist, forever. The ancients had already considered the argument about progress described above, and answered it by saying that there had been periodic floods or other disasters that repeatedly set the human race right back to the beginning of civilization.

The questions of whether the universe had a beginning in time and whether it is limited in space were later extensively examined by the philosopher Immanuel Kant in his monumental (and very obscure) work, *Critique of Pure Reason*, published in 1781. He called these questions antinomies (that is, contradictions) of pure reason because he felt that there were equally compelling arguments for believing the thesis, that the universe had a beginning, and the antithesis, that it had existed forever. His argument for the thesis was that if the universe did not have a beginning, there would be an infinite period of time before any event, which he considered absurd. The argument for the antithesis was that if the universe had a beginning, there would be an infinite period of time before it, so why should the universe begin at any one particular time? In fact, his cases for both the thesis and the antithesis are really the same argument. They are both based on his unspoken assumption that time continues back forever, whether or not the universe had existed forever. As we shall see, the concept of time has no meaning before the beginning of the universe. This was first pointed out by St. Augustine. When asked: What did God do before he created the universe? Augustine didn't reply: He was preparing Hell for people who asked such questions. Instead, he said that time was a property of the universe that God created, and that time did not exist before the beginning of the universe.

When most people believed in an essentially static and unchanging universe, the question of whether or not it had a beginning was really one of metaphysics or theology. One could account for what was observed equally well on the theory that the universe had existed forever or on the theory that it was set in motion at some finite time in such a manner as to look as though it had existed forever. But in 1929, Edwin Hubble made the landmark observation that wherever you look, distant galaxies are moving rapidly away from us. In other words, the universe is expanding. This means that at earlier times objects would have been closer together. In fact, it seemed that there was a time, about ten or twenty thousand million years ago, when they were all at exactly the same place and when, therefore, the density of the universe was infinite. This discovery finally brought the question of the beginning of the universe into the realm of science.

Hubble's observations suggested that there was a time, called the big bang, when the universe was infinitesimally small and infinitely dense. Under such conditions all the laws of science, and therefore all ability to predict the future, would break down. If there were events earlier than this time, then they could not affect what happens at the present time. Their existence can be ignored because it would have no observational consequences. One may say that time had a beginning at the big bang, in the sense that earlier times simply would not be defined. It should be emphasized that this beginning in time is very different from those that had been considered previously. In an unchanging universe a beginning in time is something that has to be imposed by some being outside the universe; there is no physical necessity for a beginning. One can imagine that God created the universe at literally any time in the past. On the other hand, if the universe is expanding, there may be physical reasons why there had to be a beginning. One could still imagine that God created the universe at the instant of the big bang, or even afterwards in just such a way as to make it look as though there had been a big bang, but it would be meaningless to suppose that it was created *before* the big bang. An expanding universe does not preclude a creator, but it does place limits on when he might have carried out his job!

In order to talk about the nature of the universe and to discuss questions such as whether it has a beginning or an end, you have to be clear about what a scientific theory is. I shall take the simpleminded view that a theory is just a model of the universe, or a restricted part of it, and a set of rules that relate quantities in the model to observations that we make. It exists only in our minds and does not have any other reality (whatever that might mean). A theory is a good theory if it satisfies two requirements: It must accurately describe a large class of observations on the basis of a model that contains only a few arbitrary elements, and it must make definite predictions about the results of future observations. For example, Aristotle's theory that everything was made out of four elements, earth, air, fire, and water, was simple enough to qualify, but it did not make any definite predictions. On the other hand, Newton's theory of gravity was based on an even simpler model, in which bodies attracted each other with a force that was proportional to a quantity called their mass and inversely proportional to the square of the distance between them. Yet it predicts the motions of the sun, the moon, and the planets to a high degree of accuracy.

Any physical theory is always provisional, in the sense that it is only a   20
hypothesis: you can never prove it. No matter how many times the results of experiments agree with some theory, you can never be sure that the next time the result will not contradict the theory. On the other hand, you can disprove a theory by finding even a single observation that disagrees with the predictions of the theory. As philosopher of science Karl Popper has emphasized, a good theory is characterized by the fact that it makes a number of predictions that could in principle be disproved or falsified by observation. Each time new experiments are observed to agree with the predictions the theory

survives, and our confidence in it is increased; but if ever a new observation is found to disagree, we have to abandon or modify the theory. At least that is what is supposed to happen, but you can always question the competence of the person who carried out the observation.

In practice, what often happens is that a new theory is devised that is really an extension of the previous theory. For example, very accurate observations of the planet Mercury revealed a small difference between its motion and the predictions of Newton's theory of gravity. Einstein's general theory of relativity predicted a slightly different motion from Newton's theory. The fact that Einstein's predictions matched what was seen, while Newton's did not, was one of the crucial confirmations of the new theory. However, we still use Newton's theory for all practical purposes because the difference between its predictions and those of general relativity is very small in the situations that we normally deal with. (Newton's theory also has the great advantage that it is much simpler to work with than Einstein's!)

The eventual goal of science is to provide a single theory that describes the whole universe. However, the approach most scientists actually follow is to separate the problem into two parts. First, there are the laws that tell us how the universe changes with time. (If we know what the universe is like at any one time, these physical laws tell us how it will look at any later time.) Second, there is the question of the initial state of the universe. Some people feel that science should be concerned with only the first part; they regard the question of the initial situation as a matter for metaphysics or religion. They would say that God, being omnipotent, could have started the universe off any way he wanted. That may be so, but in that case he also could have made it develop in a completely arbitrary way. Yet it appears that he chose to make it evolve in a very regular way according to certain laws. It therefore seems equally reasonable to suppose that there are also laws governing the initial state.

It turns out to be very difficult to devise a theory to describe the universe all in one go. Instead, we break the problem up into bits and invent a number of partial theories. Each of these partial theories describes and predicts a certain limited class of observations, neglecting the effects of other quantities, or representing them by simple sets of numbers. It may be that this approach is completely wrong. If everything in the universe depends on everything else in a fundamental way, it might be impossible to get close to a full solution by investigating parts of the problem in isolation. Nevertheless, it is certainly the way that we have made progress in the past. The classic example again is the Newtonian theory of gravity, which tells us that the gravitational force between two bodies depends only on one number associated with each body, its mass, but is otherwise independent of what the bodies are made of. Thus one does not need to have a theory of the structure and constitution of the sun and the planets in order to calculate their orbits.

Today scientists describe the universe in terms of two basic partial theories—the general theory of relativity and quantum mechanics. They are the great intellectual achievements of the first half of this century. The general theory of relativity describes the force of gravity and the large-scale structure of the universe, that is, the structure on scales from only a few miles to as large as a million million million million (1 with twenty-four zeros after it) miles, the size of the observable universe. Quantum mechanics, on the other hand, deals with phenomena on extremely small scales, such as a millionth of a millionth of an inch. Unfortunately, however, these two theories are known to be inconsistent with each other—they cannot both be correct. One of the major endeavors in physics today . . . is the search for a new theory that will incorporate them both—a quantum theory of gravity. We do not yet have such a theory, and we may still be a long way from having one, but we do already know many of the properties that it must have. And . . . we already know a fair amount about the predictions a quantum theory of gravity must make.

    Now, if you believe that the universe is not arbitrary, but is governed   25 by definite laws, you ultimately have to combine the partial theories into a complete unified theory that will describe everything in the universe. But there is a fundamental paradox in the search for such a complete unified theory. The ideas about scientific theories outlined above assume we are rational beings who are free to observe the universe as we want and to draw logical deductions from what we see. In such a scheme it is reasonable to suppose that we might progress even closer toward the laws that govern our universe. Yet if there really is a complete unified theory, it would also presumably determine our actions. And so the theory itself would determine the outcome of our search for it! And why should it determine that we come to the right conclusions from the evidence? Might it not equally well determine that we draw the wrong conclusion? Or no conclusion at all?

    The only answer that I can give to this problem is based on Darwin's principle of natural selection. The idea is that in any population of self-reproducing organisms, there will be variations in the genetic material and upbringing that different individuals have. These differences will mean that some individuals are better able than others to draw the right conclusions about the world around them and to act accordingly. These individuals will be more likely to survive and reproduce and so their pattern of behavior and thought will come to dominate. It has certainly been true in the past that what we call intelligence and scientific discovery has conveyed a survival advantage. It is not so clear that this is still the case: our scientific discoveries may well destroy us all, and even if they don't, a complete unified theory may not make much difference to our chances of survival. However, provided the universe has evolved in a regular way, we might expect that the reasoning abilities that natural selection has given us would be valid also in our search for a complete unified theory, and so would not lead us to the wrong conclusions.

    Because the partial theories that we already have are sufficient to make accurate predictions in all but the most extreme situations, the search for the ultimate theory of the universe seems difficult to justify on practical grounds. (It is worth noting, though, that similar arguments could have been used against both relativity and quantum mechanics, and these theories have given us both nuclear energy and the microelectronics revolution!) The discovery of a complete unified theory, therefore, may not aid the survival of our species. It may not even affect our life-style. But ever since the dawn of civilization, people have not been content to see events as unconnected and inexplicable. They have craved an understanding of the underlying order in the world. Today we still yearn to know why we are here and where we came from. Humanity's deepest desire for knowledge is justification enough for our continuing quest. And our goal is nothing less than a complete description of the universe we live in.

QUESTIONS

1. The essay has a break after paragraph 18, indicated by extra space between paragraphs. If you had to provide a subtitle for each of the two sections demarcated by that break, what would these subtitles be?
2. What is the function of the anecdote in paragraph 1? Why do you suppose Hawking begins with that story?
3. What is the function of paragraph 2? What kind of sentence structure predominates in this paragraph? Why?
4. The first date mentioned in the essay comes in paragraph 3. Make a list of all the other exact dates that are given, noting the paragraphs in which they appear. Discuss any patterns (or violations of pattern) that you note. What does this list tell you about the organization of the essay?
5. Hawking uses the word *God* with some frequency. How would you describe the notion of God generated by his text? Is it different from your own views? How important is God to Hawking's view of the universe?
6. What is the notion of science that can be derived from Hawking's use of that word? That is, with what definition or concept of science is he working? Is it the same as your own? Discuss.
7. In the latter part of his essay, Hawking takes up the philosophical question of how we can know that we know what we know. Describe and discuss the view that he presents, bringing in any other theories of knowledge that you have encountered in your studies or reading on the subject.

MAKING CONNECTIONS

Read Carl Sagan's essay, "Can We Know the Universe? Reflections on a Grain of Salt" (p. 150). Are Sagan and Hawking talking about the same universe? Note Sagan's strongest beliefs as expressed in his final paragraphs. Are Sagan and Hawking thinking along the same lines? To what extent does Hawking seem to be answering the challenge that Sagan makes?

HOW THE BRAIN CREATES THE MIND

Antonio R. Damasio

Neuroscientist Antonio Damasio was born in 1944 in Lisbon, Portugal, and received his medical degree at the University of Lisbon. He immigrated to the United States in 1974 and currently teaches medicine at the University of Iowa, where he is a professor of neurology. In 1994, he published Descartes' Error: Emotion, Reason, and the Human Brain, *which a review in* Natural History *magazine called "a clear view of how reason and emotions interact to produce our decisions, our beliefs, our plans for action." Damasio's latest book is* The Feeling of What Happens: Body and Emotion in the Making of Consciousness *(1999), and he also served as a contributor to the* Scientific American Book of the Brain *(1999). The following essay originally appeared in* Scientific American.

At the start of the new millennium, it is apparent that one question towers above all others in life sciences: How does the set of processes we call mind emerge from the activity of the organ we call brain? The question is hardly new. It has been formulated in one way or another for centuries. Once it became possible to pose the question and not be burned at the stake, it has been asked openly and insistently. Recently the question has preoccupied both the experts—neuroscientists, cognitive scientists, and philosophers—and others who wonder about the origin of the mind, specifically the conscious mind.

The question of consciousness now occupies center stage because biology in general and neuroscience in particular have been so remarkably successful at unraveling a great many of life's secrets. More may have been learned about the brain and the mind in the 1990s—the so-called decade of the brain—than during the entire previous history of psychology and neuroscience. Elucidating the neurobiological basis of the conscious mind—a version of the classic mind-body problem—has become almost a residual challenge.

Contemplation of the mind may induce timidity in the contemplator, especially when consciousness becomes the focus of the inquiry. Some thinkers, expert and amateur alike, believe the question may be unanswerable in principle. For others, the relentless and exponential increase in new knowledge may give rise to a vertiginous feeling that no problem can resist the assault of science if only the theory is right and the techniques are powerful enough. The debate is intriguing and even unexpected, as no comparable doubts have been raised over the likelihood of explaining how the brain is responsible for processes such as vision or memory, which are obvious components of the larger process of the conscious mind.

I am firmly in the confident camp: a substantial explanation for the mind's emergence from the brain will be produced and perhaps soon. The giddy feeling, however, is tempered by the acknowledgment of some sobering difficulties.

Nothing is more familiar than the mind. Yet the pilgrim in search of the   5
sources and mechanisms behind the mind embarks on a journey into a strange and exotic landscape. In no particular order, what follows are the main problems facing those who seek the biological basis for the conscious mind.

The first quandary involves the perspective one must adopt to study the conscious mind in relation to the brain in which we believe it originates. Anyone's body and brain are observable to third parties; the mind, though, is observable only to its owner. Multiple individuals confronted with the same body or brain can make the same observations of that body or brain, but no comparable direct third-person observation is possible for anyone's mind. The body and its brain are public, exposed, external and unequivocally objective entities. The mind is a private, hidden, internal, unequivocally subjective entity.

How and where then does the dependence of a first-person mind on a third-person body occur precisely? Techniques used to study the brain include refined brain scans and the measurement of patterns of activity in the brain's neurons. The naysayers argue that the exhaustive compilation of all these data adds up to *correlates* of mental states but nothing resembling an *actual mental state*. For them, detailed observation of living matter thus leads not to mind but simply to the details of living matter. The understanding of how living matter generates the sense of self that is the hallmark of a conscious mind—the sense that the images in my mind are mine and are formed in my perspective—is simply not possible. This argument, though incorrect, tends to silence most hopeful investigators of the conscious mind.

To the pessimists, the conscious-mind problem seems so intractable that it is not even possible to explain why the mind is even *about* something— why mental processes represent internal states or interactions with external objects. (Philosophers refer to this representational quality of the mind with the confusing term "intentionality.") This argument is false.

The final negative contention is the reminder that elucidating the emergence of the conscious mind depends on the existence of that same conscious mind. Conducting an investigation with the very instrument being investigated makes both the definition of the problem and the approach to a solution especially complicated. Given the conflict between observer and observed, we are told, the human intellect is unlikely to be up to the task of comprehending how mind emerges from brain. This conflict is real, but the notion that it is insurmountable is inaccurate.

In summary, the apparent uniqueness of the conscious-mind problem   10
and the difficulties that complicate ways to get at that problem generate
two effects: they frustrate those researchers committed to finding a solution
and confirm the conviction of others who intuitively believe that a solution
is beyond our reach.

Evaluating the Difficulties

Those who cite the inability of research on the living matter of the brain
to reveal the "substance of mind" assume that the current knowledge of
that living matter is sufficient to make such judgment final. This notion is
entirely unacceptable. The current description of neurobiological phenomena is quite incomplete, any way you slice it. We have yet to resolve numerous details about the function of neurons and circuits at the molecular level;
we do not yet grasp the behavior of populations of neurons within a local
brain region; and our understanding of the large-scale systems made up of
multiple brain regions is also incomplete. We are barely beginning to
address the fact that interactions among many noncontiguous brain regions
probably yield highly complex biological states that are vastly more than
the sum of their parts.

In fact, the explanation of the physics related to biological events is still
incomplete. Consequently, declaring the conscious-mind problem insoluble
because we have studied the brain to the hilt and have not found the mind
is ludicrous. We have not yet fully studied either neurobiology or its related physics. For example, at the finest level of description of mind, the swift
construction, manipulation and superposition of many sensory images
might require explanation at the quantum level. Incidentally, the notion of
a possible role for quantum physics in the elucidation of mind, an idea usually associated with mathematical physicist Roger Penrose of the University
of Oxford, is not an endorsement of his specific proposals, namely that consciousness is based on quantum-level phenomena occurring in the micro-
tubules—constituents of neurons and other cells. The quantum level of
operations might help explain how we have a mind, but I regard it as
unnecessary to explain how we *know* that we own that mind—the issue I
regard as most critical for a comprehensive account of consciousness.

The strangeness of the conscious-mind problem mostly reflects ignorance, which limits the imagination and has the curious effect of making the
possible seem impossible. Science-fiction writer Arthur C. Clarke has said,
"Any sufficiently advanced technology is indistinguishable from magic."
The "technology" of the brain is so complex as to appear magical, or at
least unknowable. The appearance of a gulf between mental states and
physical/biological phenomena comes from the large disparity between two
bodies of knowledge—the good understanding of mind we have achieved
through centuries of introspection and the efforts of cognitive science versus the incomplete neural specification we have achieved through the efforts

of neuroscience. But there is no reason to expect that neurobiology cannot bridge the gulf. Nothing indicates that we have reached the edge of an abyss that would separate, in principle, the mental from the neural.

Therefore, I contend that the biological processes now presumed to correspond to mind processes in fact *are* mind processes and will be seen to be so when understood in sufficient detail. I am not denying the existence of the mind or saying that once we know what we need to know about biology the mind ceases to exist. I simply believe that the private, personal mind, precious and unique, indeed *is* biological and will one day be described in terms both biological and mental.

The other main objection to an understanding of mind is that the real conflict between observer and observed makes the human intellect unfit to study itself. It is important, however, to point out that the brain and mind are not a monolith: they have multiple structural levels, and the highest of those levels creates instruments that permit the observation of the other levels. For example, language endowed the mind with the power to categorize and manipulate knowledge according to logical principles, and that helps us classify observations as true or false. We should be modest about the likelihood of ever observing our entire nature. But declaring defeat before we even make the attempt defies Aristotle's observation that human beings are infinitely curious about their own nature. 15

Reasons for Optimism

My proposal for a solution to the conundrum of the conscious mind requires breaking the problem into two parts. The first concern is how we generate what I call a "movie-in-the-brain." This "movie" is a metaphor for the integrated and unified composite of diverse sensory images—visual, auditory, tactile, olfactory and others—that constitutes the multimedia show we call mind. The second issue is the "self" and how we automatically generate a sense of ownership for the movie-in-the-brain. The two parts of the problem are related, with the latter nested in the former. Separating them is a useful research strategy, as each requires its own solution.

Neuroscientists have been attempting unwittingly to solve the movie-in-the-brain part of the conscious-mind problem for most of the history of the field. The endeavor of mapping the brain regions involved in constructing the movie began almost a century and a half ago, when Paul Broca and Carl Wernicke first suggested that different regions of the brain were involved in processing different aspects of language. More recently, thanks to the advent of ever more sophisticated tools, the effort has begun to reap handsome rewards.

Researchers can now directly record the activity of a single neuron or group of neurons and relate that activity to aspects of a specific mental state, such as the perception of the color red or of a curved line. Brain-imaging techniques such as PET (positron emission tomography) scans and

FMR (functional magnetic resonance) scans reveal how different brain regions in a normal, living person are engaged by a certain mental effort, such as relating a word to an object or learning a particular face. Investigators can determine how molecules within microscopic neuron circuits participate in such diverse mental tasks, and they can identify the genes necessary for the production and deployment of those molecules.

Progress in this field has been swift ever since David H. Hubel and Torsten Wiesel of Harvard University provided the first clue for how brain circuits represent the shape of a given object, by demonstrating that neurons in the primary visual cortex were selectively tuned to respond to edges oriented in varied angles. Hubel and Margaret S. Livingstone, also at Harvard, later showed that other neurons in the primary visual cortex respond selectively to color but not shape. And Semir Zeki of University College London found that brain regions that received sensory information after the primary visual cortex did were specialized for the further processing of color or movement. These results provided a counterpart to observations made in living neurological patients: damage to distinct regions of the visual cortices interferes with color perception while leaving discernment of shape and movement intact.

A large body of work, in fact, now points to the existence of a correspondence between the structure of an object as taken in by the eye and the pattern of neuron activity generated within the visual cortex of the organism seeing that object.   20

Further remarkable progress involving aspects of the movie-in-the-brain has led to increased insights related to mechanisms of learning and memory. In rapid succession, research has revealed that the brain uses discrete systems for different types of learning. The basal ganglia and cerebellum are critical for the acquisition of skills—for example, learning to ride a bicycle or play a musical instrument. The hippocampus is integral to the learning of facts pertaining to such entities as people, places or events. And once facts are learned, the long-term memory of those facts relies on multicomponent brain systems, whose key parts are located in the vast brain expanses known as cerebral cortices.

Moreover, the process by which newly learned facts are consolidated in long-term memory goes beyond properly working hippocampi and cerebral cortices. Certain processes must take place, at the level of neurons and molecules, so that the neural circuits are etched, so to speak, with the impressions of a newly learned fact. This etching depends on strengthening or weakening the contacts between neurons, known as synapses. A provocative finding by Eric R. Kandel of Columbia University and Timothy P. Tully of Cold Spring Harbor Laboratory is that etching the impression requires the synthesis of fresh proteins, which in turn relies on the engagement of specific genes within the neurons charged with supporting the consolidated memory.

These brief illustrations of progress could be expanded with other revelations from the study of language, emotion and decision making.

Whatever mental function we consider, it is possible to identify distinct parts of the brain that contribute to the production of a function by working in concert; a close correspondence exists between the appearance of a mental state or behavior and the activity of selected brain regions. And that correspondence can be established between a given macroscopically identifiable region (for example, the primary visual cortex, a language-related area or an emotion-related nucleus) and the microscopic neuron circuits that constitute the region.

Most exciting is that these impressive advances in the study of the brain are a mere beginning. New analytical techniques continuously improve the ability to study neural function at the molecular level and to investigate the highly complex large-scale phenomena arising from the whole brain. Revelations from those two areas will make possible ever finer correspondences between brain states and mental states, between brain and mind. As

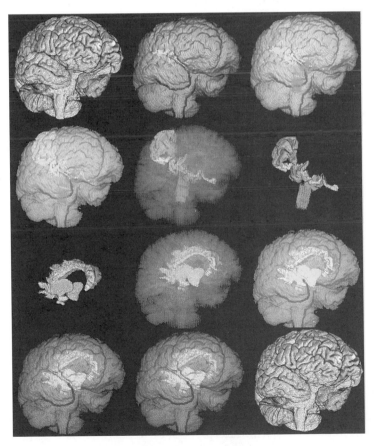

The sense of self has a seat in the core of the brain. Stripping away the external anatomy of a human brain shows a number of deep-seated regions responsible for homeostatic regulation, emotion, wakefulness, and the sense of self.

technology develops and the ingenuity of researchers grows, the fine grain of physical structures and biological activities that constitute the movie-in-the-brain will gradually come into focus.

Confronting the Self

The momentum of current research on cognitive neuroscience, and the   25
sheer accumulation of powerful facts, may well convince many doubters that the neural basis for the movie-in-the-brain can be identified. But the skeptics will still find it difficult to accept that the second part of the conscious-mind problem — the emergence of a sense of self — can be solved at all. Although I grant that solving this part of the problem is by no means obvious, a possible solution has been proposed, and a hypothesis is being tested.

The main ideas behind the hypothesis involve the unique representational ability of the brain. Cells in the kidney or liver perform their assigned functional roles and do not represent any other cells or functions. But brain cells, at every level of the nervous system, represent entities or events occurring elsewhere in the organism. Brain cells are assigned by design to be *about* other things and other doings. They are born cartographers of the geography of an organism and of the events that take place within that geography. The oft-quoted mystery of the "intentional" mind relative to the representation of external objects turns out to be no mystery at all. The philosophical despair that surrounds this "intentionality" hurdle alluded to earlier — why mental states represent internal emotions or interactions with external objects — lifts with the consideration of the brain in a Darwinian context: evolution has crafted a brain that is in the business of directly representing the organism and indirectly representing whatever the organism interacts with.

The brain's natural intentionality then takes us to another established fact: the brain possesses devices within its structure that are designed to manage the life of the organism in such a way that the internal chemical balances indispensable for survival are maintained at all times. These devices are neither hypothetical nor abstract; they are located in the brain's core, the brain stem and hypothalamus. The brain devices that regulate life also represent, of necessity, the constantly changing states of the organism as they occur. In other words, the brain has a natural means to represent the structure and state of the *whole* living organism.

But how is it possible to move from such a biological self to the sense of ownership of one's thoughts, the sense that one's thoughts are constructed in one's own perspective, without falling into the trap of invoking an all-knowing homunculus who interprets one's reality? How is it possible to know about self and surroundings? I have argued in my book *The Feeling of What Happens* that the biological foundation for the sense of self can be found in those brain devices that represent, moment by moment, the continuity of the same individual organism.

Simply put, my hypothesis suggests that the brain uses structures designed to map both the organism and external objects to create a fresh, second-order representation. This representation indicates that the organism, as mapped in the brain, is involved in interacting with an object, also mapped in the brain. The second-order representation is no abstraction; it occurs in neural structures such as the thalamus and the cingulate cortices.

Such newly minted knowledge adds important information to the   30
evolving mental process. Specifically, it *presents* within the mental process the information that the organism is the owner of the mental process. It volunteers an answer to a question never posed: To whom is this happening? The sense of a self in the act of knowing is thus created, and that forms the basis for the first-person perspective that characterizes the conscious mind.

Again from an evolutionary perspective, the imperative for a sense of self becomes clear. As Willy Loman's wife says in Arthur Miller's *Death of a Salesman*: "Attention must be paid!" Imagine a self-aware organism versus the same type of organism lacking it. A self-aware organism has an incentive to heed the alarm signals provided by the movie-in-the-brain (for instance, pain caused by a particular object) and plan the future avoidance of such an object. Evolution of self rewards awareness, which is clearly a survival advantage.

With the movie metaphor in mind, if you will, my solution to the conscious-mind problem is that the sense of self in the act of knowing emerges *within* the movie. Self-awareness is actually part of the movie and thus creates, within the same frame, the "seen" and the "seer," the "thought" and the "thinker." There is no separate spectator for the movie-in-the-brain. The idea of spectator is constructed within the movie, and no ghostly homunculus haunts the theater. Objective brain processes knit the subjectivity of the conscious mind out of the cloth of sensory mapping. And because the most fundamental sensory mapping pertains to body states and is imaged as feelings, the sense of self in the act of knowing emerges as a special kind of feeling — the feeling of what happens in an organism caught in the act of interacting with an object.

The Future

I would be foolish to make predictions about what can and cannot be discovered or about when something might be discovered and the route of a discovery. Nevertheless, it is probably safe to say that by 2050 sufficient knowledge of biological phenomena will have wiped out the traditional dualistic separations of body/brain, body/mind and brain/mind.

Some observers may fear that by pinning down its physical structure something as precious and dignified as the human mind may be downgraded or vanish entirely. But explaining the origins and workings of the mind in biological tissue will not do away with the mind, and the awe we have for it can be extended to the amazing microstructure of the organism and to the immensely complex functions that allow such a microstructure to generate the mind. By understanding the mind at a deeper level, we will see it as nature's most complex set of biological phenomena rather than as a mystery with an unknown nature. The mind will survive explanation, just as a rose's perfume, its molecular structure deduced, will still smell as sweet.

QUESTIONS

1. Damasio begins his essay by listing and rejecting three arguments for why "elucidating the neurobiological basis of the conscious mind" (paragraph 2) is impossible. What are these arguments? Why does Damasio begin his essay by dismissing them?
2. What is what Damasio calls the "movie-in-the-brain" (paragraph 16)? How does Damasio use this movie metaphor to explain the conscious mind?
3. Damasio revisits the movie metaphor at the end of his piece (paragraph 32). What has changed about it? Do you agree with Damasio's description of the mind? Why or why not?
4. Do you agree with Damasio that the mind can be both "precious and dignified" (paragraph 34) and fully explained in biological terms? What do you think of Damasio's assertion that "the mind will survive explanation, just as a rose's perfume, its molecular structure deduced, will still smell as sweet" (paragraph 34)?
5. According to Damasio, "Researchers can now directly record the activity or a single neuron or group of neurons and relate that activity to aspects of a specific mental state, such as the perception of the color red or of a curved line" (paragraph 18). Do you believe there is some aspect of the human mind that is too ethereal or mysterious to be "pinned down" biologically? If so, what is it? If not, why? Write an essay explaining your position. Begin your essay by presenting counterarguments — that is, arguments that oppose your position.

MAKING CONNECTIONS

In "Crimson Tide" (p. 455), "The Naked Face" (p. 438) and "How the Brain Creates the Mind" (p. 498), the authors give scientific explanations behind elements of the human condition — blushing, facial expressions, consciousness, and colds, respectively. Which explanation were you most surprised by? Did any detract from your idea of the mystery of the human condition? Why or why not? Did any of the explanations add to the mystery and make you feel more rather than less in awe of the human condition? Explain.

THE BEST CLOCK IN THE WORLD

Verlyn Klinkenborg

Verlyn Klinkenborg (b. 1953) received his Ph.D. from Princeton University and later taught creative writing at Harvard University for six years. His books include Making Hay *(1986), about Midwestern farm life;* The Last Fine Time *(1991), the chronicle of a neighborhood bar in Buffalo, New York; and* The Rural Life *(2002), a collection of essays. Klinkenborg has written articles on many subjects for a wide variety of publications, and he currently contributes a regular column to the* New York Times *in addition to serving as a member of its editorial board. He has said of his work, "I look for subjects that offer a clear sense of metaphorical possibility. . . . I'm as interested in the character of the language as the story itself." The following essay originally appeared in* Discover *magazine in 2000.*

In a lab off a humdrum hallway of a federal building on the western edge of Boulder, Colorado, an extraordinary instrument tosses a microscopic ball of cesium atoms up and down, up and down. I can see it happening. On a small monitor, a sudden, globular condensation of light flashes again and again as six lasers shape a cloud of cesium atoms into a tight sphere, then loft it upward into a cavity where it pauses and falls. The video feed is coming from somewhere deep within a cylindrical metal pillar in the middle of the lab. The pillar, as tall as I am, stands on a steel bench a little larger than a Ping-Pong table and perforated with holes. Mounted on the bench is a bewildering maze of lenses and mirrors designed to refine laser beams and shunt them into the pillar at various angles. The bench is shrouded in transparent plastic sheets attached to a frame of pressure-treated wooden studs—a crude dust shield. Another layer of plastic clings to the ceiling, which leaks from time to time. The contraption—bench, pillar, lenses, mirrors, plastic, studs, and all—looks like a model railroad, just waiting for track to be laid down and a train to start running through this brittle wilderness of glass and metal. A $650,000 model railroad, that is.

This device is actually a clock. In fact, NIST-F1, a cesium fountain clock housed at the National Institute of Standards and Technology, is the most precise clock in the world, a distinction it shares with a similar device at the Laboratoire Primaire du Temps et des Frequences in Paris. Despite its homemade look, F1 is accurate to 0.0000000000000015 of a second, or, as the scientists here put it, 1.5 parts in 10 to the 15th power. In other words, if it were to run for 20 million years, it would neither lose nor gain a second. Everyone who visits the Boulder lab instinctively looks at his or her wristwatch, hoping, somehow, to set it to this remarkable standard. I look at my watch, then at the fountain clock, then back at my watch. It's a naive, almost comical gesture. Ultimately, the output of the fountain clock has a bearing on the time my watch tells. But the difference between the two clocks is a story in itself, a story about the science of keeping time.

For centuries, Earth was our timekeeper. The sun rose and set, and the day was parsed into hours, minutes, and seconds based on Earth's rotation, which is why astronomical observatories, like the one in Greenwich, England, kept official time. Until the twentieth century, pendulum clocks were calibrated against the rotation of Earth by taking astronomical measurements. But as clocks grew more and more precise, they exposed the idiosyncrasies of our planet. It wobbles, it oscillates, it undergoes slight shifts in shape, all of which affect its rotation. As a standard of accuracy, the pendulum gave way in the 1940s to electrically induced vibrations in quartz crystals, which in turn gave way in the 1950s to measurements of atomic activity. And, in effect, Earth gave way to the atom as a gauge of time. Instead of using a definition of the second based on Earth's rotation, scientists began to search for one based on frequencies generated by certain atoms — particularly cesium — as they changed from one atomic state to another. Atomic frequencies, unlike the frequency of a pendulum's swing, have the virtue of being the same anywhere in the universe. In 1967, the international definition of the second shifted to an atomic standard. The Bureau International des Poids et Mesures (BIPM) near Paris now defines a second as "the duration of 9,192,631,770 periods of the radiation corresponding to the transition between the two hyperfine levels of the ground state of the cesium 133 atom."

It's one thing to define the second — to postulate its length — and something entirely different to build an instrument that can actually measure it according to that definition. Imagine the difference between defining a car and actually building one. Almost any enclosed vehicle that propels itself and carries passengers can be called a car. But the definition of a second is absolute, and what the scientists in the Time and Frequency Division at Boulder have done is build devices that come closer and closer to measuring the precise length of a real second, as defined by international convention. In the twentieth century, we have progressed from a 1921 pendulum clock, accurate to .3 second per year, to the fountain clock — 7 million times more accurate.

Gaining or losing a second here or there might not seem so important in our daily lives. But as the scientists at Boulder have chased greater and greater accuracy, industry has come to depend more and more on the increasingly precise measures of time that the Time and Frequency Division makes possible. Perhaps the best example is GPS, the Global Positioning System. Even an ordinary handheld GPS receiver determines its position by measuring the time it takes to receive signals from GPS satellites overhead. To put it simply, the precision of the coordinates your GPS receiver gives you — whether you're canoeing the Boundary Waters or surveying a new interchange on I-70—depends directly on the precision of the time signal the system uses.

One of the classic scenes in any old war movie is the moment when the platoon leader gathers his men around him and says, "Let's synchronize our watches." We take it for granted that to carry out any coordinated action—military or civil—we need to agree on the time. We've spent the last century building increasingly complicated networks of machines and systems—satellites, Internet nodes, electrical grids, landline and cell-based phone communications. For those networks to carry out coordinated actions, they, too, need to agree on the time as they communicate with one another. In order to share information, computers in a network—whether it's an office network or the Internet as a whole—need to know when to talk, when to respond, and at what rate to do so. And, in a sense, the amount of information a network can distribute is directly related to how fast that information can be transmitted and how accurately time can be synchronized across a network. Time is no longer merely the natural fourth dimension of the universe around us. It's the beat that meters the electronic motions of money and information. Its precise measurement and distribution is a subject of detailed international agreements and of a treaty, called the Convention of the Meter, that has been in force since 1875.

Before the advent of railroads in the mid-1800s, it scarcely mattered if every city and every country kept time on its own, because the rate of communication among them was usually measured in days, weeks, and months. But these days a commonly distributed, accurately calibrated pulse of time, precise down to the level of billionths of a second, is what makes synchronization—indeed, communication itself—possible. When the public clock in a town in Renaissance Europe failed, it mainly affected the repairman who was called in to fix it. If our public clock failed, the Internet would dissolve into an array of freestanding, no-longer-networked computers. Trade would abruptly cease on Wall Street, and money and shares would come to rest wherever they were. Air traffic would stagger to a halt. Scientific labs of every description would find themselves deprived of their most fundamental measure. Even a temporary desynchronizing in the twenty-first century would leave turmoil in its wake. We would see in a sudden, displeasing instant how vitally our lives are shaped by agreement on the smallest measurable part of a second.

So, here I am, standing in front of the new fountain clock in Boulder, Colorado. This is, as they say, a primary standard, as far as you can presently go toward the measurement of time as a quantity. I look at my watch, which was set to the time on my computer at home, which was set by an automated link via the Internet to the time service at the Time and Frequency Division—just one of 25 million time requests that Boulder receives daily. The question is: "Am I looking at the source of that time?"

The answer is no. A cesium fountain clock isn't a tool for measuring the flow of time as it ticks past, month by month, year by year. It's a tool for measuring the length of the second, which is a very different thing. The fountain

The cesium fountain clock in Boulder, Colorado.

clock at Boulder usually runs for only a few days at a time. Each run is a test of sorts to see if the timekeepers can nudge a little more accuracy from the instrument, the way Formula One mechanics try to nudge one more mile per hour from their race cars. Time, as generated by this instrument, is an experimental result, an effort to match, in reality, an unwavering physical description of a second. But the second that the cesium fountain clock measures is any second, not a particular second from the flow of time. And even if this clock could tell you which second was passing—could tell you the time, in other words—it would still be an ambiguous result.

Don Sullivan, who is chief of the Time and Frequency Division, explains: "If you look at a single clock, you don't know whether it's right or wrong. And if you have two clocks and they disagree, you don't know which one's right. Things are much better with three clocks, because then you have majority voting." In other words, the cesium fountain can tell you the length of the second to a stupefying degree of precision, but it cannot, by itself, tell you the time in Boulder any more accurately than my ordinary wristwatch. In fact, it can't tell you the time at all.

What matters in international timekeeping isn't a single ultra-precise clock but a global network of clocks. The time that is propagated by international agreement—Coordinated Universal Time—depends as much on the accurate comparison of time measurements as it does on the accurate measurement of time itself. To keep accurate time, as Sullivan describes it, you need at least three clocks. If they're all in one room, it's easy to compare them. But if they're in different rooms, or in different buildings, or in different countries, how do you compare them, then? How, for that matter, do you formulate an "international" time?

The Time and Frequency Division maintains an entire array of clocks, called a time scale, not just the atomic primary standard. The fountain clock provides the measure of the second against which the rate of inherently less accurate but more stable clocks is judged. In another room, Sullivan shows me five hydrogen masers—a different kind of atomic clock—or rather he shows me the large commercial incubators, the size of refrigerators, that permanently house them. "These are our best reference clocks," he says. "They're very, very stable over short to intermediate times, intermediate being out to many months." Like precision—the ability to measure the second in microscopic intervals—stability is a critical factor in good timekeeping. Several different effects cause hydrogen masers to drift. The drift is minuscule but it's also predictable, which means that when the scientists at Boulder factor the drift out, they're left with a rock-steady record of time, the standard of steadiness against which other clocks in the time scale are measured.

For accuracy over longer periods of time, the National Institute of Standards and Technology relies on a roomful of commercial cesium clocks, the kind that anyone can buy for, say, $40,000 to $60,000. In fact, the time that comes from Boulder—what Sullivan calls "our best estimate of the international time"—is an average of the output of those cesium clocks plus that of the hydrogen masers plus that of the cesium fountain clock plus that of its predecessor, with which it is still running in tandem. "When we average all the clocks together, we weight them according to their long-term and short-term stability," Sullivan says. "The masers dominate the performance of the time scale out to months, but the cesium standards then start to become more important longer term. So it's a very intelligent average. The fountain clock then calibrates this periodically." What the time scale generates is a sophisticated average—an equation of time, so to speak—to which each kind of clock contributes its strength but not its weakness. It's as though one kind of clock added the seconds, another the minutes, and still another the hours.

Sullivan leads the way into one more room with rows of racks lined with stationary batteries—car batteries, essentially, but with the life span of a seventeen-year cicada. It is here that the peculiar isolation of the Time and Frequency Division becomes apparent. It would be unwise for a source of precise timing for national and international telecommunications to depend completely on the power grid. The time service Sullivan and his colleagues provide is so vital that frequency—even electrical frequency—is actually generated at Boulder. All of the clocks in Boulder's time scale are

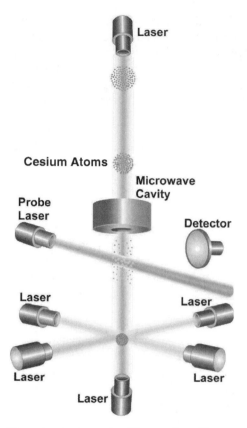

Laser

Cesium Atoms

Microwave
Cavity

Probe
Laser

Detector

Laser

Laser

Laser

Laser

Laser

How the clock works: Three pairs of inter-
secting lasers gather cesium atoms to send
up through a microwave cavity. When the
cesium cloud drifts back down through a
probe laser, a detector measures the resonance frequency of the descending atoms.

powered by this congregation of batteries, which is backed up by two gen-
erators, a reservoir of fuel, and technicians wearing pagers. "You wouldn't
even trust a switchover to batteries," says Sullivan. "You just run the clocks
on batteries and keep charging the batteries all the time. You don't want
99.999 percent reliability. You want 100 percent."

When it's noon sharp in Boulder, the Coordinated Universal Time is   15
7:00 P.M., or 6:00 P.M. during daylight-saving time. But international time
isn't just Boulder time shifted six or seven hours ahead. It's an average generated in Paris from some 220 clocks around the world, including nearly a
dozen primary standards, which are located at Boulder, the Paris
Observatory, and labs in Germany, Japan, and Canada. Just as the National
Institute of Standards and Technology time, roughly speaking, is an average
of the clocks in its time scale, international time is an average of time scales

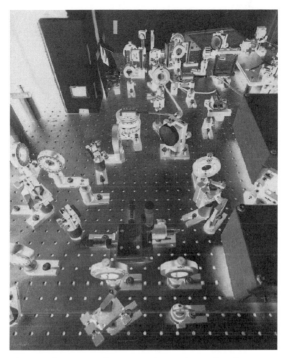

Photo of mirrors that trap the cesium cloud.

around the world. In effect, it's the result of clock-comparison on a global scale, using a global tool: GPS and its Russian counterpart. Not surprisingly, the technique for international time comparison and distribution, called GPS common-view time transfer, was invented at Boulder.

Throughout the day and night, for thirteen minutes at a time, Boulder and all the other metrology labs in the world lock on to one GPS receiver after another and compare their clocks. The data is compressed and then brought together in Paris. And this is where a search for the source of time begins to grow very strange. "Weeks and weeks after the fact," Sullivan says, "Paris sends us a notice, and they say, 'Here is where each of your clocks is relative to the average.'" Boulder then tries to steer its own time-scale average to the average generated in Paris. *Steer* is an odd word to hear in the world of timekeeping. When I ask Sullivan what he means by it, he says, "One of the axioms in modern timekeeping is that you never touch a clock once it's running. So you never go in and say, 'Well, that clock's running a little fast.'" He reaches into midair to fiddle with an imaginary dial. The atomic standards and hydrogen masers and cesium clocks stay locked away.

Instead, what the Boulder lab steers is a computerized output based on the results from Paris. Sullivan calls it a paper clock, but, in fact, one of the clocks at Boulder is adjusted to track the international average. The time computer-users get when they log on to the Time and Frequency Division time server is its most accurate estimate, which is derived from a weeks-old international average based, in part, on its own, still-older initial average. Meanwhile, the Time and Frequency Division keeps a taped record of the individual output of all the clocks in its time scale so that, as statistical methods improve, scientists there can go back through time and analyze the accuracy and drift of those clocks. Gauging the past performance of the clocks helps the scientists predict their future performance. Somewhere in the laboratories at 325 Broadway, Boulder, Colorado, is a chronicle of every second that has passed since the National Institute of Standards and Technology established the time scale in 1960.

I had thought that in the presence of the cesium fountain clock I might have come to the farthest threshold of time. But other labs at Boulder are working on the possibility of newer, more precise clocks. Another threshold in timekeeping is already in sight, although it may be years before it's crossed. In the fountain clock the cesium atoms are observed while in motion, which makes their frequencies hard to determine. "We're keen on something called stored-ion frequency standards," says Sullivan. "The fountain clock—all of our clocks—are limited by the time that we get to observe the transition and the speed of the atoms. In stored-ion clocks, rather than slow the atoms down and look at them for a second, we just stop them altogether and trap them and hold them. We can look at the atoms indefinitely. In a sense it's an ultimate kind of technology." As the clocks at Boulder grow still more precise, they will reach a point where the very noise they generate while running becomes a limiting factor. The effect of gravitation itself will weigh in. In a sense, it already does. "Our clock runs at a different rate here in Boulder than it would at sea level, and we have to correct for that when we're doing our evaluation," says Sullivan. "Curiously, if we continue with the present development rate of clocks, ten or twenty years from now we will run into a position where knowing our location in the gravitational field will be one of the key difficulties." The clocks are already so precise that the effect of relativity can be detected within a gravitational field.

But no matter how radically the standard of timekeeping changes, no matter how minutely scientists manage to divide the second or how perfectly they distribute time itself, the questions St. Augustine posed some 1,600 years ago—when the minute, not to mention the second, had not yet been invented—will still prevail. "While we are measuring it," Augustine asked, "where is it coming from, what is it passing through, and where is it going?" These questions echo in nearly everyone's experience, whether they live by the clock in this split-second world or blithely measure their days by the sun and the moon. Mankind has made a science of measuring time and distributing it, but not of using it wisely. And when it comes to Augustine's questions, science still does not have any answers.

QUESTIONS

1. Reread the first paragraph of the essay. Why does the author choose to describe the cesium contraption in such detail without giving the reader any hint about its function?
2. How does the author establish a motive for his piece—that is, the reason that readers should be interested in the precise workings of time? Why does it matter that a second is defined as "the duration of 9,192,631,770 periods of the radiation corresponding to the transition between the two hyperfine levels of the ground state of the cesium 133 atom" (paragraph 3)? If the planet we live on "wobbles, . . . oscillates, . . . [and] undergoes slight shifts in shape" (paragraph 3), why must we keep perfect time?
3. The cesium clock is not a typical clock in the sense that it does not display hours and minutes. What methods does Klinkenborg use to make the complicated workings of the cesium clock and modern time measurement accessible to the lay reader? Explain what must occur for the cesium clock to play a part in the makings of the most accurate time reading in the world.
4. What was your reaction to the news that the most accurate reading of time you can find is an average of dozens of clocks around the world and is not the output of one precise machine? How could something as seemingly straightforward as timekeeping require international cooperation?
5. Do you "live by the clock in this split-second world," or do you "blithely measure . . . [your] days by the sun and the moon" (paragraph 19)? Does your perception of the passing of time change when you wear a watch and check the time frequently? On days when you do not wear a watch, does time seem to pass at a different rate? What would you be unable to do if you had no access to a clock? Write an essay about the way that you measure time and the impact that it has on your daily routine.

MAKING CONNECTIONS

Compare the beginning paragraphs of "The Best Clock in the World" and "The Naked Face" (p. 438). Each of these pieces first appeared in magazines, whose readers have no obligation to finish the articles that they begin to read. What methods do the authors use to make readers care enough about their subjects to read on? Compare the authors' techniques, and explain which one you feel is most effective.

ARGUING

Here in "Arguing" you will find authors taking positions on a wide range of controversial subjects — from the issue of cigarette smoking to the status of black English, from the nature of hate to the practices of body management. No matter what their academic fields or professions, these authors energetically defend their stands on the issues and questions they address. But this should come as no surprise. None of us, after all, holds lightly to our beliefs and ideas about what is true or beautiful or good. Indeed, most of us get especially fired up when our views are pitted against the ideas and beliefs of others. So you will find these authors vigorously engaged in the give and take of argument. As a consequence, you will repeatedly find yourself having to weigh the merits of competing positions in a debate or disagreement about some controversial issue.

The distinctive quality of arguing can be seen in the following paragraphs from Martin Luther King Jr.'s "Letter from Birmingham Jail" (p. 617):

> I think I should indicate why I am here in Birmingham, since you have been influenced by the view which argues against "outsiders coming in." I have the honor of serving as president of the Southern Christian Leadership Conference, an organization operating in every southern state, with headquarters in Atlanta, Georgia. We have some eighty-five affiliated organizations across the South, and one of them is the Alabama Christian Movement for Human Rights. Frequently we share staff, educational, and financial resources with our affiliates. Several months ago the affiliate here in Birmingham asked us to be on call to engage in a nonviolent direct-action program if such were deemed necessary. We readily consented, and when the hour came we lived up to our promise. So I, along with several members of my staff, am here because I was invited here. I am here because I have organizational ties here.
>
> But more basically, I am in Birmingham because injustice is here. Just as the prophets of the eighth century B.C. left their villages and

carried their "thus saith the Lord" far beyond the boundaries of their home towns, and just as the Apostle Paul left his village of Tarsus and carried the gospel of Jesus Christ to the far corners of the Greco-Roman world, so am I compelled to carry the gospel of freedom beyond my own home town. Like Paul, I must constantly respond to the Macedonian call for aid.

Moreover, I am cognizant of the interrelatedness of all communities and states. I cannot sit idly by in Atlanta and not be concerned about what happens in Birmingham. Injustice anywhere is a threat to justice everywhere. We are caught in an inescapable network of mutuality, tied in a single garment of destiny. Whatever affects one directly, affects all indirectly. Never again can we afford to live with the narrow, provincial "outside agitator" idea. Anyone who lives inside the United States can never be considered an outsider anywhere within its bounds. (paragraphs 2–4)

These are the first few paragraphs of an argument that continues for several more pages. It is one of the finest statements of democratic values that our country has yet produced. Arguments usually place themselves against an opposing point of view. In this case, eight Alabama clergymen had published a statement calling King's actions "unwise and untimely." He was also accused of being an "outside agitator." King counters that accusation immediately by outlining his affiliations with the South, with Alabama, and even with Birmingham. He has ample reason, he argues, to be "here," a word he places unhesitatingly in the first sentence of the first paragraph quoted above and then three more times in the last two sentences of that paragraph.

From this point on, King's argument expands to include larger and larger ideas of appropriate affiliation and of justice. "I am in Birmingham because injustice is here," he says, opening his next paragraph by pivoting on "here," which by now has become thematic. Calling on biblical parallels to support his idea that the Christian is always "here," confronting need and injustice, King asserts first that all U.S. citizens have every right to converge on whatever "here" they identify as necessary. In the argument that follows, he expands on that idea. However local they may have been, the clergymen who had objected to his intervention had not been "here" at all—not with King, not on the side of justice. Nor had most white churchmen or sympathetic white moderates been "here." Almost everyone had displaced King's "here" to some more distant "there," distant in time as much as in place, so much so that the "shallow understanding from people of good will" distressed King almost as much as had the overt antagonism of segregationist authorities.

The Range of Argumentative Writing

Argumentative writing so pervades our lives that we may not even recognize it as such in the many brochures and leaflets that come our way, urging us to vote for one candidate rather than another or to support one cause rather than another. Argumentative writing also figures heavily in newspaper editorials, syndicated columns, and letters to the editor, which typically debate the pros and cons of one public issue or another, from local taxes to national defense policies. Argument is fundamental in the judicial process, crucial in the legislative process, and serves the basic aims of the academic world, testing ideas and theories by pitting them against each other. Argument is an important activity in the advancement of knowledge and society.

The broad range of argumentative writing can be understood by considering the kinds of issues and questions that typically give rise to disagreement and debate. The most basic sources of controversy are questions of fact—the who, what, when, and where of things, as well as how much. Intense arguments over questions of fact can develop in any academic or professional field, especially when the facts in question have a significant bearing on the explanation or judgment of a particular subject, body of material, or type of investigation.

Indeed, Barry Commoner's "Unraveling the DNA Myth: The Spurious Foundation of Genetic Engineering" (p. 693), argues that many biological researchers and "scientific entrepreneurs" (paragraph 2) are working from an obsolete theory: "DNA did not create life," he concludes, "life created DNA. When life was first formed on the earth, proteins must have appeared before DNA because" (paragraph 35), and he goes on to provide some reasons.

Even when the facts themselves are plain, arguments about how to explain the facts are likely to arise. Disagreements of this kind abound across the full range of academic and professional fields. Arguments inevitably arise out of sharply differing points of view and definitions of key terms. Pablo Picasso's "A Statement" (p. 572), for example, argues that art has nothing to do with "research," which must "evolve" over time, but that it is an expression of "discovery" that lives in a continuous present. "The idea of research has often made painting go astray" (paragraph 4), he asserts, and so:

> Arts of transition do not exist. In the chronological history of art there are periods which are more positive, more complete than others. This means that there are periods in which there are better artists than in others. (paragraph 12)

That is an argumentative position. Similarly, Cynthia Ozick (p. 562) argues that although "scholars may place the Book of Job in the age of Babylonian Exile," it is clearly a "timeless" work, the "historicity" of which "hardly matters." Despite "his peerless Hebrew speech, [the poet] is plainly not a Hebrew"; the work is conceived instead, "like almost no other primordial poem the West has inherited . . . under the aspect of the universal" (paragraph 1).

Differing viewpoints, of course, ultimately reflect differing beliefs and values. Ozick's essay stands against a view that would explain the Book of Job as an expression of the Hebrews' Babylonian exile. Similarly, Picasso argues against a view that would seek to "understand" an artist in terms of his or her "research," personal growth, and immediate social influences. The way we view any particular subject is, after all, a matter of personal choice, an outgrowth of what our experience and knowledge have led us to hold as being self-evident. In this sense, beliefs and values are always to some extent at issue in any argumentative situation, even when they remain more or less in the background. But in some cases the conflicting values themselves are so clearly at the heart of the argument that they become a central focus in the debate, as you can see in this well-known passage from the Declaration of Independence (p. 612):

> We hold these truths to be self-evident, that all men are created equal, that they are endowed by their Creator with certain unalienable Rights, that among these are Life, Liberty and the pursuit of Happiness. That to secure these rights, Governments are instituted among Men, deriving their just powers from the consent of the governed. That whenever any Form of Government becomes destructive of these ends, it is the Right of the People to alter or to abolish it, and to institute new Government, laying its foundation on such principles and organizing its powers in such form, as to them shall seem most likely to affect their Safety and Happiness. (paragraph 2)

In this crucial passage, Thomas Jefferson and his congressional colleagues directly challenged several fundamental assumptions about the rights of people and the sources of governmental power that were held by the British king and by many British people and others throughout the world. Only in this way was it possible for them to make the compelling case for their ultimate claim that the colonies should be "FREE AND INDEPENDENT STATES . . . Absolved from all Allegiance to the British Crown" (paragraph 23).

Though Jefferson and his colleagues did not outline a new system of government in the Declaration itself, the document does enable us to see that conflicts over beliefs and values can, and often do, have a decisive bearing on questions of policy and planning. For a clear-cut example of how conflicts over beliefs lead to debates over policy, you need only look at Andrew Sullivan's "What's So Bad about Hate" (p. 588). Sullivan notes that "we have created an entirely new offense in American criminal law—a 'hate crime'" (paragraph 5), but we have only "a remarkably vague idea of what [hate] actually is" (paragraph 7). President Clinton declared a hate-crime law to be "what America needs in our battle against hate" (paragraph 5). While most people would respond to the rallying cry to battle against hate, they might have some difficulty in defining just what it is they are to battle against.

Sullivan's strategy is to provide evidence to show how difficult it is to define hate. In the process, he challenges common clichés about hate, such as the belief that "the hate that comes from knowledge is always different from the hate that comes from ignorance" (paragraph 24) or that hate for a group is worse than hate for a person, a belief that prevents rape from being considered a hate crime. Part of the difficulty of defining hate as a crime is that there are many different kinds of hate. Sullivan cites an authority, psychotherapist Elisabeth Young-Bruehl, who "proposes a typology of the distinct kinds of hate: obsessive, hysterical, and narcissistic" (paragraph 26). But he concludes that each kind of hate is complicated and likely to be a combination of various types. He presents a number of different cases as evidence to underscore the difficulty of using *hate crime* as a label.

Just as his argument requires Sullivan to demonstrate the difficulty of defining *hate* and *hate crime*, so every other kind of question imposes on writers a particular set of argumentative obligations. To argue for his right to lead a protest in Birmingham, King had to outline a convincing case for a citizen's moral obligation in the face of injustice. In offering, similarly, her reading of the Book of Job, Ozick had to characterize and elaborate on her idea of the universal, of how Job speaks to us all, no matter our situations, by opening "even the sacred gates of Scripture to philosophic doubt" (paragraph 35).

A writer who aims to be persuasive cannot simply assert that something is or is not the case, for readers in general are not willing to be bullied into accepting a particular claim. But they are capable of being reached by civilized and rational methods of persuasion that are appropriate to controversial issues — by evidence, logic, and eloquence.

Methods of Arguing

In any piece of argumentative writing, your primary purpose is to bring readers around to your point of view. Some readers, of course, will agree with you in advance, but others will disagree, and still others will be undecided. So in planning a piece of argumentative writing, you should begin by examining your material with an eye to discovering the issues that have to be addressed and the points that have to be made to present your case most persuasively to readers, especially those who oppose you or are undecided. This means that you will have to deal not only with issues that you consider relevant but also with matters that have been raised by your opponents. In other words, you will have to show readers that you have considered both sides of the controversy. Again, Ozick offers an example of this consideration of opponents' points. While stressing the universal element of Job, she admits that English translations remove much of the complexity of the original language and that Eastern wisdom literature contributed much of the philosophical context for the story. Commoner, similarly, must review the claims for the uniquely creative power of DNA before he can argue for its limits as a theory given the results of the human genome project.

After you have identified the crucial points to be addressed, you should then select the methods you'll need to make a convincing case with respect to each of the points. Some methods, of course, are imperative no matter what point you are trying to prove. Every piece of argumentation requires that you offer readers evidence to support your position. To do so, you will need to gather and present specific details that bear on each of the points you are trying to make. This basic concern for providing readers with appropriate evidence will lead you inevitably into the activity of reporting. Jefferson, for example, provides a lengthy and detailed list of "injuries" that the king of Great Britain inflicted on the colonies in his attempt to demonstrate the right of the colonies "to throw off such Government." Reporting appropriate evidence constitutes the most basic means of making a persuasive case for any point under consideration. So any point for which evidence cannot be provided or for which only weak or limited evidence can be offered is likely to be much less convincing to readers than one that can be amply and vividly substantiated.

But evidence alone will not be persuasive to readers unless it is brought to bear on a point in a reasonable or logical way. In one of its most familiar forms, induction, logic involves the process of moving from bits of evidence to a generalization or a conclusion that is based on that evidence. For example, Emily Martin, in "The Egg and the Sperm: How Science Has Constructed a Romance Based on Stereotypical Male-Female Roles"(p. 669), examines in detail the imagery used in science textbooks and other scientific discourse to demonstrate the use of metaphors based on the notion that men are active and women are passive. Though recent studies show both the egg and the sperm to be active in the process of fertilization, these stereotypes persist, as does a contradicting one of "woman as a dangerous and aggressive threat" (paragraph 30). This evidence allows Martin to generalize, to make what is called an *inductive leap* — that stereotyped personalization on the level of the cell can lay the foundation for social control of the moment of fertilization.

Deduction, another form of logic, involves the movement from general assumptions or premises to particular conclusions that can be derived from them. For example, having made the general claim that "a long train of abuses" entitles people "to throw off such Government" (paragraph 2) and having cited, in turn, a long list of abuses that Great Britain had inflicted on the colonies, Jefferson is able to reach the conclusion that the colonies "are Absolved from all Allegiance to the British Crown" (paragraph 23). Given his initial assumptions about government and the rights of the people, together with his evidence about British abuse of the colonists, Jefferson's deduction seems to be a logical conclusion, as indeed it is. But as in any case of deductive logic, the conclusion is only as convincing as the premises on which it is based. Great Britain did not accept Jefferson's premises, so it did not accept his conclusions, logical though they were. Other countries of the time took a different view of the matter. So in developing an argument deductively, you need to keep in mind not only the logic of your case but also the appeal its premises are likely to have for those whom you are most interested in convincing.

As you can see from the cases of Jefferson, Sullivan, Ozick, Martin, Commoner, and other writers collected in this section, presenting evidence and using it in a logical way can take a variety of common forms, and all of these forms are likely to be present in subtle and complicated ways in virtually every piece of argumentative writing. Arguing calls on writers to be especially resourceful in developing and presenting their positions. Actually, logic is a necessary — and powerful — tool in every field and profession because it serves to fill in gaps where evidence does not exist or, as in a court case, to move beyond the accumulated evidence to conclusions that follow from it. But like any powerful tool it must be used with care. One weak link in a logical chain of reasoning can lead, after all, to a string of falsehood.

Explanatory techniques, as discussed in the introduction to "Explaining" (p. 321), also can play a role in argument, as you may already have inferred from the passages we have just been discussing. Sullivan's argument about hate is based on his interpretation of key terms, and Commoner thinks closely about cause and effect, employing a kind of causal analysis, as he seeks out the errors of genetic engineering. Any piece of argument, in other words, is likely to draw on a wide range of techniques, for argument is always attempting to achieve the complex purpose of getting at the truth about something, making that truth intelligible to readers, and persuading them to accept it as such.

No matter what particular combination of techniques a writer favors, when carrying out an argument, most save a very telling point or bit of evidence or well-turned phrase for last. Like effective storytellers or successful courtroom lawyers, writers know that a memorable detail makes for a powerful climax. In the pieces that follow in this section, you will see how different writers use the various resources of language to produce some striking and compelling pieces of argument.

Arts and Humanities

HIROSHIMA

John Berger

After beginning his career as a painter and drawing instructor, John Berger (b. 1926) became one of Britain's most influential art critics. He has achieved recognition as a screenwriter, novelist, and documentary writer. As a Marxist, he is concerned with the ideological and technological conditioning of our ways of seeing both art and the world. In Ways of Seeing *(1972), he explores the interrelation between words and images, between verbal and visual meaning. "Hiroshima" first appeared in 1981 in the journal* New Society *and later in a collection of essays,* The Sense of Sight *(1985). Berger examines how the facts of nuclear holocaust have been hidden through "a systematic, slow and thorough process of suppression and elimination . . . within the reality of politics." Images, rather than words, Berger asserts, can help us see through the "mask of innocence" that evil wears.*

The whole incredible problem begins with the need to reinsert those events of 6 August 1945 back into living consciousness.

I was shown a book last year at the Frankfurt Book Fair. The editor asked me some question about what I thought of its format. I glanced at it quickly and gave some reply. Three months ago I was sent a finished copy of the book. It lay on my desk unopened. Occasionally its title and cover picture caught my eye, but I did not respond. I didn't consider the book urgent, for I believed that I already knew about what I would find within it.

Did I not clearly remember the day — I was in the army in Belfast — when we first heard the news of the bomb dropped on Hiroshima? At how many meetings during the first nuclear disarmament movement had I and others not recalled the meaning of that bomb?

And then, one morning last week, I received a letter from America, accompanying an article written by a friend. This friend is a doctor of philosophy and a Marxist. Furthermore, she is a very generous and warm-hearted woman. The article was about the possibilities of a third world war. Vis-à-vis the Soviet Union she took, I was surprised to read, a position very close to Reagan's. She concluded by evoking the likely scale of destruction which would be caused by nuclear weapons, and then welcomed the positive possibilities that this would offer the socialist revolution in the United States.

It was on that morning that I opened and read the book on my desk. It 5
is called *Unforgettable Fire.*[1]

The book consists of drawings and paintings made by people who were in Hiroshima on the day that the bomb was dropped, thirty-six years ago today. Often the pictures are accompanied by a verbal record of what the image represents. None of them is by a professional artist. In 1974, an old man went to the television center in Hiroshima to show to whomever was interested a picture he had painted, entitled "At about 4 pm, 6th August 1945, near Yurozuyo bridge."

This prompted an idea of launching a television appeal to other survivors of that day to paint or draw their memories of it. Nearly a thousand pictures were sent in, and these were made into an exhibition. The appeal was worded: "Let us leave for posterity pictures about the atomic bomb, drawn by citizens."

Clearly, my interest in these pictures cannot be an art-critical one. One does not musically analyze screams. But after repeatedly looking at them, what began as an impression became a certainty. These were images of hell.

I am not using the word as hyperbole. Between these paintings by women and men who never painted anything else since leaving school, and who have surely, for the most part, never traveled outside Japan, between these traced memories which had to be exorcised, and the numerous representations of hell in European medieval art, there is a very close affinity.

This affinity is both stylistic and fundamental. And fundamentally it is 10
to do with the situations depicted. The affinity lies in the degree of the multiplication of pain, in the lack of appeal or aid, in the pitilessness, in the equality of wretchedness, and in the disappearance of time.

> I am 78 years old. I was living at Midorimachi on the day of the A-bomb blast. Around 9 am that morning, when I looked out of my window, I saw several women coming along the street one after another towards the Hiroshima prefectural hospital. I realized for the first time, as it is sometimes said, that when people are very much frightened hair really does stand on end. The women's hair was, in fact, standing straight up and the skin of their arms was peeled off. I suppose they were around 30 years old.

Time and again, the sober eyewitness accounts recall the surprise and horror of Dante's verses about the Inferno. The temperature at the center of the Hiroshima fireball was 300,000 degrees centigrade. The survivors are called in Japanese *hibakuska*—"those who have seen hell."

> Suddenly, one man who was stark naked came up to me and said in a quavering voice, "Please help me!" He was burned and swollen all over from the effects of the A-bomb. Since I did not recognize him as my neighbor, I asked who he was. He answered that he was Mr. Sasaki, the son of Mr. Ennosuke Sasaki, who had a lumber shop in Funairi town. That morning he had been doing volunteer labor service, evacuating the houses near the prefectural office in Kato town. He had been burned black all over and had started back to his home in Funairi. He looked miserable—burned and sore, and naked with only pieces of his gaiters trailing behind as he walked. Only the part of his hair covered by his soldier's hat was left, as if he was wearing a bowl. When I touched him, his burned skin slipped off. I did not know what to do, so I asked a passing driver to take him to Eba hospital.

Does not this evocation of hell make it easier to forget that these scenes belonged to life? Is there not something conveniently unreal about hell? The whole history of the twentieth century proves otherwise.

Very systematically in Europe the conditions of hells have been constructed. It is not even necessary to list the sites. It is not even necessary to

How survivors saw it. A painting by Kazuhiro Ishizu, aged 68.

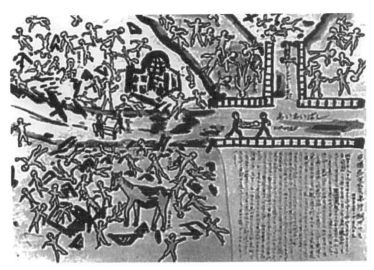

At the Aioi bridge, by Sawami Katagiri, aged 76.

repeat the calculations of the organizers. We know this, and we choose to forget it.

We find it ridiculous or shocking that most of the pages concerning, for example, Trotsky were torn out of official Soviet history. What has been torn out of our history are the pages concerning the experience of the two atom bombs dropped on Japan.

Of course, the facts are there in the textbooks. It may even be that school children learn the dates. But what these facts mean—and originally their meaning was so clear, so monstrously vivid, that every commentator in the world was shocked, and every politician was obliged to say (whilst planning differently), "Never again"—what these facts mean has now been torn out. It has been a systematic, slow and thorough process of suppression and elimination. This process has been hidden within the reality of politics.

Do not misunderstand me. I am not here using the word "reality" ironically, I am not politically naïve. I have the greatest respect for political reality, and I believe that the innocence of political idealists is often very dangerous. What we are considering is how in this case in the West—not in Japan for obvious reasons and not in the Soviet Union for different reasons—political and military realities have eliminated another reality.

The eliminated reality is both physical—

> Yokogawa bridge above Tenma river, 6th August 1945, 8:30 am.
>   People crying and moaning were running towards the city. I did not know why. Steam engines were burning at Yokogawa station.
>   Skin of cow tied to wire.
>   Skin of girl's hip was hanging down.
>   "My baby is dead, isn't she?"

and moral.

The political and military arguments have concerned such issues as deterrence, defense systems, relative strike parity, tactical nuclear weapons and—pathetically—so-called civil defense. Any movement for nuclear disarmament today has to contend with those considerations and dispute their false interpretation. To lose sight of them is to become as apocalyptic as the Bomb and all utopias. (The construction of hells on earth was accompanied in Europe by plans for heavens on earth.)

What has to be redeemed, reinserted, disclosed and never be allowed to be forgotten, is the other reality. Most of the mass means of communication are close to what has been suppressed .

These paintings were shown on Japanese television. Is it conceivable that the BBC would show these pictures on Channel One at a peak hour? Without any reference to "political" and "military" realities, under the straight title, *This Is How It Was, 6th August 1945*? I challenge them to do so.

What happened on that day was, of course, neither the beginning nor the end of the act. It began months, years before, with the planning of the action, and the eventual final decision to drop two bombs on Japan. However much the world was shocked and surprised by the bomb dropped on Hiroshima, it has to be emphasized that it was not a miscalculation, an error, or the result (as can happen in war) of a situation deteriorating so rapidly that it gets out of hand. What happened was consciously and precisely planned. Small scenes like this were part of the plan: 20

> I was walking along the Hihiyama bridge about 3 pm on 7th August. A woman, who looked like an expectant mother, was dead. At her side, a girl of about three years of age brought some water in an empty can she had found. She was trying to let her mother drink from it.
>
> As soon as I saw this miserable scene with the pitiful child, I embraced the girl close to me and cried with her, telling her that her mother was dead.

There was a preparation. And there was an aftermath. The latter included long, lingering deaths, radiation sickness, many fatal illnesses which developed later as a result of exposure to the bomb, and tragic genetical effects on generations yet to be born.

I refrain from giving the statistics: how many hundreds of thousands of dead, how many injured, how many deformed children. Just as I refrain from pointing out how comparatively "small" were the atomic bombs dropped on Japan. Such statistics tend to distract. We consider numbers instead of pain. We calculate instead of judging. We relativize instead of refusing.

It is possible today to arouse popular indignation or anger by speaking of the threat and immorality of terrorism. Indeed, this appears to be the central plank of the rhetoric of the new American foreign policy ("Moscow is the world-base of all terrorism") and of British policy towards Ireland. What is able to shock people about terrorist acts is that often their targets are unselected and innocent—a crowd in a railway station, people waiting for a bus to go home after work. The victims are chosen indiscriminately in the hope of producing a shock effect on political decision-making by their government.

The two bombs dropped on Japan were terrorist actions. The calculation was terrorist. The indiscriminacy was terrorist. The small groups of terrorists operating today are, by comparison, humane killers.

Another comparison needs to be made. Today terrorist groups mostly   25 represent small nations or groupings, who are disputing large powers in a position of strength. Whereas Hiroshima was perpetrated by the most powerful alliance in the world against an enemy who was already prepared to negotiate, and was admitting defeat.

To apply the epithet "terrorist" to the acts of bombing Hiroshima and Nagasaki is logically justifiable, and I do so because it may help to reinsert that act into living consciousness today. Yet the word changes nothing in itself.

The first-hand evidence of the victims, the reading of the pages which have been torn out, provokes a sense of outrage. This outrage has two natural faces. One is a sense of horror and pity at what happened; the other face is self-defensive and declares: *this should not happen again (here)*. For some the *here* is in brackets, for others it is not.

The face of horror, the reaction which has now been mostly suppressed, forces us to comprehend the reality of what happened. The second reaction, unfortunately, distances us from that reality. Although it begins as a straight declaration, it quickly leads into the labyrinth of defense policies, military arguments and global strategies. Finally it leads to the sordid commercial absurdity of private fall-out shelters.

This split of the sense of outrage into, on one hand, horror, and, on the other hand, expediency occurs because the concept of evil has been abandoned. Every culture, except our own in recent times, has had such a concept.

That its religious or philosophical bases vary is unimportant. The con-   30 cept of evil implies a force or forces which have to be continually struggled against so that they do not triumph over life and destroy it. One of the very first written texts from Mesopotamia, 1,500 years before Homer, speaks of this struggle, which was the first condition of human life. In public thinking nowadays, the concept of evil has been reduced to a little adjective to support an opinion or hypothesis (abortions, terrorism, ayatollahs).

Nobody can confront the reality of 6th August 1945 without being forced to acknowledge that what happened was evil. It is not a question of opinion or interpretation, but of events.

The memory of these events should be continually before our eyes. This is why the thousand citizens of Hiroshima started to draw on their little scraps of paper. We need to show their drawings everywhere. These terrible images can now release an energy for opposing evil and for the lifelong struggle of that opposition.

And from this a very old lesson may be drawn. My friend in the United States is, in a sense, innocent. She looks beyond a nuclear holocaust without considering its reality. This reality includes not only its victims but also its planners and those who support them. Evil from time immemorial has often worn a mask of innocence. One of evil's principal modes of being is *looking beyond* (with indifference) that which is before the eyes.

> August 9th: On the west embankment of a military training field was a young boy four or five years old. He was burned black, lying on his back, with his arms pointing towards heaven.

Only by looking beyond or away can one come to believe that such evil is relative, and therefore under certain conditions justifiable. In reality —the reality to which the survivors and the dead bear witness—it can never be justified.

Note

1. Edited by Japan Broadcasting Corporation, London, Wildwood House, 1981; New York, Pantheon, 1981.

QUESTIONS

1. Berger begins his essay with this powerful sentence: "The whole incredible problem begins with the need to reinsert those events of 6 August 1945 back into living consciousness." What is "the whole incredible problem" as Berger describes and defines it?
2. Berger argues that what happened on August 6, 1945, was "consciously and precisely planned" (paragraph 20). What evidence does he present to support this claim? How does this argument advance his larger purpose?
3. Berger tells his readers that he refrains from giving statistics because "statistics tend to distract" (paragraph 22). What do statistics distance us from understanding about Hiroshima?
4. The content in Berger's essay ranges from thoughts about Hiroshima, to images of hell, to political realities, to terrorist actions, to concepts of evil. How does he connect these various subjects? What is the chain of reasoning?
5. Berger offers various images from the book *Unforgettable Fire*, such as "August 9th: On the west embankment of a military training field was a young boy four or five years old. He was burned black, lying on his back, with his arms pointing towards heaven" (paragraph 33). Look at the various places in the essay where Berger presents such images from *Unforgettable Fire*. What effect does this evidence have on you? How does this evidence strengthen Berger's argument?
6. Spend some time looking at and thinking about the paintings by the survivors, Kazuhiro Ishizu and Sawami Katagiri, reprinted on pages 526

and 527. What do you *see* in these paintings? What do these images represent to you?

MAKING CONNECTIONS

1. Zoë Tracy Hardy's essay "What Did You Do in the War, Grandma?" (p. 126) reports on Hiroshima from the other side of that experience. How different are Berger's and Hardy's essays in their conclusions about the meaning of the event? Do the two essays contradict one another or reinforce one another?

2. Many of the arguments that are presented in this section are based on the definitions of words and on extending or revising the meanings that are commonly attached to a particular word or phrase. In Berger's essay (p. 524), the key words are *terror*, *terrorism*, and *evil*. In Malcolm Gladwell's "The Art of Failure" (p. 638), the key words are *choke* and *panic*. In these and in many other essays in this collection, the fit between language and the world is at stake. Consider the following statement: "The world is not neatly divided into things to which we give names but is a maze of overlapping fields that we divide into separate entities by giving them names." Drawing your illustrations from essays in this section, make an argument that either supports or challenges that statement. Among the essays that you consider, try to find a place for Gary Greenberg's "As Good as Dead" (p. 707) and Robert A. Weinberg's "Of Clones and Clowns" (p. 718).

If Black English Isn't a Language, Then Tell Me, What Is?

James Baldwin

James Baldwin (1924–1987) was born in Harlem and followed his father's vocation, becoming a preacher at the age of fourteen. At seventeen, he left the ministry and devoted himself to writing. Baldwin's most frequent subject was the relationship between blacks and whites, about which he wrote, "The color of my skin made me automatically an expert." Baldwin himself might also have added that his life's work lay in defining and legitimizing the black voice; like Orwell, Baldwin argued that language is "a political instrument, means, and proof of power." He wrote five novels, a book of stories, one play, and several collections of essays. The following essay on language and legitimacy first appeared in 1979 in the New York Times *and later was included in* The Price of the Ticket: Collected Nonfiction, 1948–1985 *(1985).*

The argument concerning the use, or the status, or the reality, of black English is rooted in American history and has absolutely nothing to do with the question the argument supposes itself to be posing. The argument has nothing to do with language itself but with the role of language. Language, incontestably, reveals the speaker. Language, also, far more dubiously, is meant to define the other—and, in this case, the other is refusing to be defined by a language that has never been able to recognize him.

People evolve a language in order to describe and thus control their circumstances or in order not to be submerged by a situation that they cannot articulate. (And if they cannot articulate it, they are submerged.) A Frenchman living in Paris speaks a subtly and crucially different language from that of the man living in Marseilles; neither sounds very much like a man living in Quebec; and they would all have great difficulty in apprehending what the man from Guadeloupe, or Martinique, is saying, to say nothing of the man from Senegal—although the "common" language of all these areas is French. But each has paid, and is paying, a different price for this "common" language, in which, as it turns out, they are not saying, and cannot be saying, the same things: They each have very different realities to articulate, or control.

What joins all languages, and all men, is the necessity to confront life, in order, not inconceivably, to outwit death: The price for this is the acceptance, and achievement, of one's temporal identity. So that, for example, though it is not taught in the schools (and this has the potential of becoming a political issue) the south of France still clings to its ancient and musical Provençal, which resists being described as a "dialect." And much of the tension in the Basque countries, and in Wales, is due to the Basque and Welsh determination not to allow their languages to be destroyed. This determination also feeds the flames in Ireland for among the many indignities the Irish have been forced to undergo at English hands is the English contempt for their language.

It goes without saying, then, that language is also a political instrument, means, and proof of power. It is the most vivid and crucial key to identity: It reveals the private identity, and connects one with, or divorces one from, the larger, public, or communal identity. There have been, and are, times and places, when to speak a certain language could be dangerous, even fatal. Or, one may speak the same language, but in such a way that one's antecedents are revealed, or (one hopes) hidden. This is true in France, and is absolutely true in England: The range (and reign) of accents on that damp little island make England coherent for the English and totally incomprehensible for everyone else. To open your mouth in England is (if I may use black English) to "put your business in the street." You have confessed your parents, your youth, your school, your salary, your self-esteem, and, alas, your future.

Now, I do not know what white Americans would sound like if there had   5
never been any black people in the United States, but they would not sound the way they sound. *Jazz*, for example, is a very specific sexual term, as in *jazz me, baby*, but white people purified it into the Jazz Age. *Suck it to me*, which means, roughly, the same thing, has been adopted by Nathaniel Hawthorne's descendants with no qualms or hesitations at all, along with *let it all hang out* and *right on! Beat to his socks*, which was once the black's most total and despairing image of poverty, was transformed into a thing called the Beat Generation, which phenomenon was, largely, composed of *uptight*, middle-class white people, imitating poverty, trying to *get down*, to *get with it*, doing their *thing*, doing their despairing best to be *funky*, which we, the blacks, never dreamed of doing—we were funky, baby, like *funk* was going out of style.

Now, no one can eat his cake, and have it, too, and it is late in the day to attempt to penalize black people for having created a language that permits the nation its only glimpse of reality, a language without which the nation would be even more *whipped* than it is.

I say that the present skirmish is rooted in American history, and it is. Black English is the creation of the black diaspora. Blacks came to the United States chained to each other, but from different tribes. Neither could speak the other's language. If two black people, at that bitter hour of the world's history, had been able to speak to each other, the institution of chattel slavery could never have lasted as long as it did. Subsequently, the slave was given, under the eye, and the gun, of his master, Congo Square, and the Bible—or, in other words, and under those conditions, the slave began the formation of the black church, and it is within this unprecedented tabernacle that black English began to be formed. This was not, merely, as in the

European example, the adoption of a foreign tongue, but an alchemy that transformed ancient elements into a new language: *A language comes into existence by means of brutal necessity, and the rules of the language are dictated by what the language must convey.*

There was a moment, in time, and in this place, when my brother, or my mother, or my father, or my sister, had to convey to me, for example, the danger in which I was standing from the white man standing just behind me, and to convey this with a speed and in a language, that the white man could not possibly understand, and that, indeed, he cannot understand, until today. He cannot afford to understand it. This understanding would reveal to him too much about himself and smash that mirror before which he has been frozen for so long.

Now, if this passion, this skill, this (to quote Toni Morrison) "sheer intelligence," this incredible music, the mighty achievement of having brought a people utterly unknown to, or despised by "history" — to have brought this people to their present, troubled, troubling, and unassailable and unanswerable place — if this absolutely unprecedented journey does not indicate that black English is a language, I am curious to know what definition of languages is to be trusted.

A people at the center of the western world, and in the midst of so hos-   10
tile a population, has not endured and transcended by means of what is patronizingly called a "dialect." We, the blacks, are in trouble, certainly, but we are not inarticulate because we are not compelled to defend a morality that we know to be a lie.

The brutal truth is that the bulk of the white people in America never had any interest in educating black people, except as this could serve white purposes. It is not the black child's language that is despised. It is his experience. A child cannot be taught by anyone who despises him, and a child cannot afford to be fooled. A child cannot be taught by anyone whose demand, essentially, is that the child repudiate his experience, and all that gives him sustenance, and enter a limbo in which he will no longer be black, and in which he knows that he can never become white. Black people have lost too many black children that way.

And, after all, finally, in a country with standards so untrustworthy, a country that makes heroes of so many criminal mediocrities, a country unable to face why so many of the nonwhite are in prison, or on the needle, or standing, futureless, in the streets — it may very well be that both the child, and his elder, have concluded that they have nothing whatever to learn from the people of a country that has managed to learn so little.

QUESTIONS

1. Baldwin begins his essay by challenging the standard argument concerning black English: "The argument has nothing to do with language itself but with the role of language" (paragraph 1). What distinctions

does Baldwin note between "language itself" and "the role of language"? Why is this distinction central to his argument?

2. Baldwin's position on black English is at odds with those who would like to deny black English status as a language. Summarize Baldwin's position. Summarize the position of Baldwin's opponents.

3. In paragraph 4, Baldwin writes, "It goes without saying, then, that language is also a political instrument, means, and proof of power." How, according to Baldwin, does language connect or divide one from "public or communal identity"? What evidence does he provide to support this claim that language is a political instrument?

4. Baldwin asks his readers, "What is language?" and thus leads them to define for themselves "what definition of languages is to be trusted" (paragraph 9). Do you find that Baldwin's definition and position are persuasive? Explain.

5. Reread Baldwin's memorable conclusion. How does he prepare you for this conclusion? What are you left to contemplate?

6. How has Baldwin's essay made you think about your own use of language and the role language plays in your identity? Baldwin makes an important distinction between *dialect* and *language*. Write an essay in which you take a position on the role of language in shaping your identity.

7. Select a dialect with which you are familiar. Analyze the features of this dialect. Write an essay in which you develop a position showing how this dialect reflects the richness of its culture.

MAKING CONNECTIONS

1. Both Baldwin and George Orwell (p. 536) are interested in understanding language as a political instrument. Write an essay in which you examine their views on the politics of language, pointing out their similarities and differences. (You may want to consider Louis Menand's essay on Orwell (p. 548) before you write about Orwell.)

2. In this section, both Baldwin and Martin Luther King Jr. (p. 617) make strong arguments about racial questions. Both of these writers are considered to be exceptional masters of English prose. What color is their English? Write an essay in which you consider them as argumentative writers. Are their styles of argument different? Do they use the same vocabulary? How would you characterize each of them as a writer? Do you prefer one style over the other? Do you find that one of their arguments is more effective than the other? Present your opinions, and make your case.

POLITICS AND THE ENGLISH LANGUAGE

George Orwell

The rise of totalitarianism in Europe led George Orwell (1903–1950) to write about its causes in his most famous novels, Animal Farm (1945) and 1984 (1949), and in essays like "Politics and the English Language." In this essay, written in 1946, Orwell tells his readers that "in our time, political speech and writing are largely the defense of the indefensible." He attacks language that consists "largely of euphemism, question begging, and sheer cloudy vagueness." Orwell, like John Berger earlier in this section, is concerned with the ways in which language is often used to conceal unpleasant and horrifying realities.

Most people who bother with the matter at all would admit that the English language is in a bad way, but it is generally assumed that we cannot by conscious action do anything about it. Our civilization is decadent and our language—so the argument runs—must inevitably share in the general collapse. It follows that any struggle against the abuse of language is a sentimental archaism, like preferring candles to electric light or hansom cabs to aeroplanes. Underneath this lies the half-conscious belief that language is a natural growth and not an instrument which we shape for our own purposes.

Now, it is clear that the decline of a language must ultimately have political and economic causes: it is not due simply to the bad influence of this or that individual writer. But an effect can become a cause, reinforcing the original cause and producing the same effect in an intensified form, and so on indefinitely. A man may take to drink because he feels himself to be a failure, and then fail all the more completely because he drinks. It is rather the same thing that is happening to the English language. It becomes ugly and inaccurate because our thoughts are foolish, but the slovenliness of our language makes it easier for us to have foolish thoughts. The point is that the process is reversible. Modern English, especially written English, is full of bad habits which spread by imitation and which can be avoided if one is willing to take the necessary trouble. If one gets rid of these habits one can think more clearly, and to think clearly is a necessary first step towards political regeneration: so that the fight against bad English is not frivolous and is not the exclusive concern of professional writers. I will come back to this presently, and I hope that by that time the meaning of what I have said here will have become clearer. Meanwhile, here are five specimens of the English language as it is now habitually written.

These five passages have not been picked out because they are especially bad—I could have quoted far worse if I had chosen—but because they illustrate various of the mental vices from which we now suffer. They are a little below the average, but are fairly representative samples. I number them so that I can refer back to them when necessary:

"(1) I am not, indeed, sure whether it is not true to say that the Milton who once seemed not unlike a seventeenth-century Shelley had not become, out of an experience ever more bitter in each year, more alien [*sic*] to the founder of that Jesuit sect which nothing could induce him to tolerate."

> Professor Harold Laski (Essay in *Freedom of Expression*)

"(2) Above all, we cannot play ducks and drakes with a native battery of idioms which prescribes such egregious collocations of vocables as the basic *put up with* for *tolerate* or *put at a loss* for *bewilder*."

> Professor Lancelot Hogben (*Interglossa*)

"(3) On the one side we have the free personality: by definition it is not neurotic, for it has neither conflict nor dream. Its desires, such as they are, are transparent, for they are just what institutional approval keeps in the forefront of consciousness; another institutional pattern would alter their number and intensity; there is little in them that is natural, irreducible, or culturally dangerous. But *on the other* side, the social bond itself is nothing but the mutual reflection of these self-secure integrities. Recall the definition of love. Is not this the very picture of a small academic? Where is there a place in this hall of mirrors for either personality or fraternity?"

> Essay on psychology in *Politics* (New York)

"(4) All the 'best people' from the gentlemen's clubs, and all the frantic fascist captains, united in common hatred of Socialism and bestial horror of the rising tide of the mass revolutionary movement, have turned to acts of provocation, to foul incendiarism, to medieval legends of poisoned wells, to legalize their own destruction of proletarian organizations, and rouse the agitated petty-bourgeoisie to chauvinistic fervour on behalf of the fight against the revolutionary way out of the crisis."

> Communist pamphlet

"(5) If a new spirit *is* to be infused into this old country, there is one thorny and contentious reform which must be tackled, and that is the humanization and galvanization of the B.B.C. Timidity here will bespeak cancer and atrophy of the soul. The heart of Britain may be sound and of strong beat, for instance, but the British lion's roar at present is like that of Bottom in Shakespeare's *Midsummer Night's*

Dream—as gentle as any sucking dove. A virile new Britain cannot continue indefinitely to be traduced in the eyes or rather ears, of the world by the effete languors of Langham Place, brazenly masquerading as 'standard English.' When the Voice of Britain is heard at nine o'clock, better far and infinitely less ludicrous to hear aitches honestly dropped than the present priggish, inflated, inhibited, school-ma'amish arch braying of blameless bashful mewing maidens!"

Letter in *Tribune*

Each of these passages has faults of its own, but, quite apart from avoidable ugliness, two qualities are common to all of them. The first is staleness of imagery: the other is lack of precision. The writer either has a meaning and cannot express it, or he inadvertently says something else, or he is almost indifferent as to whether his words mean anything or not. This mixture of vagueness and sheer incompetence is the most marked characteristic of modern English prose, and especially of any kind of political writing. As soon as certain topics are raised, the concrete melts into the abstract and no one seems able to think of turns of speech that are not hackneyed: prose consists less and less of *words* chosen for the sake of their meaning, and more and more of *phrases* tacked together like the sections of a prefabricated hen-house. I list below, with notes and examples, various of the tricks by means of which the work of prose-construction is habitually dodged:

Dying Metaphors. A newly invented metaphor assists thought by evoking   5
a visual image, while on the other hand a metaphor which is technically "dead" (e.g. *iron resolution*) has in effect reverted to being an ordinary word and can generally be used without loss of vividness. But in between these two classes there is a huge dump of worn-out metaphors which have lost all evocative power and are merely used because they save people the trouble of inventing phrases for themselves. Examples are: *Ring the changes on, take up the cudgels for, toe the line, ride roughshod over, stand shoulder to shoulder with, play into the hands of, no axe to grind, grist to the mill, fishing in troubled waters, on the order of the day, Achilles' heel, swan song, hotbed.* Many of these are used without knowledge of their meaning (what is a "rift," for instance?), and incompatible metaphors are frequently mixed, a sure sign that the writer is not interested in what he is saying. Some metaphors now current have been twisted out of their original meaning without those who use them even being aware of the fact. For example, *toe the line* is sometimes written *tow the line.* Another example is *the hammer and the anvil,* now always used with the implication that the anvil gets the worst of it. In real life it is always the anvil that breaks the hammer, never the other way about: a writer who stopped to think what he was saying would be aware of this, and would avoid perverting the original phrase.

Operators or Verbal False Limbs. These save the trouble of picking out appropriate verbs and nouns, and at the same time pad each sentence with extra syllables which give it an appearance of symmetry. Characteristic phrases are: *render inoperative, militate against, make contact with, be subjected to, give rise to, give grounds for, have the effect of, play a leading part (role) in, make itself felt, take effect, exhibit a tendency to, serve the purpose of,* etc., etc. The keynote is the elimination of simple verbs. Instead of being a single word, such as *break, stop, spoil, mend, kill,* a verb becomes a *phrase,* made up of a noun or adjective tacked on to some general-purposes verb such as *prove, serve, form, play, render.* In addition, the passive voice is wherever possible used in preference to the active, and noun constructions are used instead of gerunds (*by examination of* instead of *by examining*). The range of verbs is further cut down by means of the *-ize* and *de-* formation, and the banal statements are given an appearance of profundity by means of the *not un-* formation. Simple conjunctions and prepositions are replaced by such phrases as *with respect to, having regard to, the fact that, by dint of, in view of, in the interests of, on the hypothesis that;* and the ends of sentences are saved from anticlimax by such resounding commonplaces as *greatly to be desired, cannot be left out of account, a development to be expected in the near future, deserving of serious consideration, brought to a satisfactory conclusion,* and so on and so forth.

Pretentious Diction. Words like *phenomenon, element, individual* (as noun), *objective, categorical, effective, virtual, basic, primary, promote, constitute, exhibit, exploit, utilize, eliminate, liquidate,* are used to dress up simple statements and give an air of scientific impartiality to biased judgments. Adjectives like *epoch-making, epic, historic, unforgettable, triumphant, age-old, inevitable, inexorable, veritable,* are used to dignify the sordid processes of international politics, while writing that aims at glorifying war usually takes on an archaic color, its characteristic words being: *realm, throne, chariot, mailed fist, trident, sword, shield, buckler, banner, jackboot, clarion.* Foreign words and expressions such as *cul de sac, ancien régime, deus ex machina, mutatis mutandis, status quo, gleichschaltung, weltanschauung,* are used to give an air of culture and elegance. Except for the useful abbreviations *i.e., e.g.,* and *etc.,* there is no real need for any of the hundreds of foreign phrases now current in English. Bad writers, and especially scientific, political and sociological writers, are nearly always haunted by the notion that Latin or Greek words are grander than Saxon ones, and unnecessary words like *expedite, ameliorate, predict, extraneous, deracinated, clandestine, subaqueous* and hundreds of others constantly gain ground from their Anglo-Saxon opposite numbers.[1] The jargon peculiar to Marxist writing

---

[1]An interesting illustration of this is the way in which the English flower names which were in use till very recently are being ousted by Greek ones, *snapdragon* becoming *antirrhinum, forget-me-not* becoming *myosotis,* etc. It is hard to see any practical reason for this change of fashion: it is probably due to an instinctive turning-away from the more homely word and a vague feeling that the Greek word is scientific.

(*hyena, hangman, cannibal, petty bourgeois, these gentry, lackey, flunky, mad dog, White Guard,* etc.) consists largely of words and phrases translated from Russian, German or French; but the normal way of coining a new word is to use a Latin or Greek root with the appropriate affix and, where necessary, the *-ize* formation. It is often easier to make up words of this kind (*deregionalize, impermissible, extramarital, nonfragmentatory* and so forth) than to think up the English words that will cover one's meaning. The result, in general, is an increase in slovenliness and vagueness.

Meaningless Words.   In certain kinds of writing, particularly in art criticism and literary criticism, it is normal to come across long passages which are almost completely lacking in meaning.[2] Words like *romantic, plastic, values, human, dead, sentimental, natural, vitality,* as used in art criticism, are strictly meaningless in the sense that they not only do not point to any discoverable object, but are hardly ever expected to do so by the reader. When one critic writes, "The outstanding feature of Mr. X's work is its living quality," while another writes, "The immediately striking thing about Mr. X's work is its peculiar deadness," the reader accepts this as a simple difference of opinion. If words like *black* and *white* were involved, instead of the jargon words *dead* and *living,* he would see at once that language was being used in an improper way. Many political words are similarly abused. The word *Fascism* has now no meaning except in so far as it signifies "something not desirable." The words *democracy, socialism, freedom, patriotic, realistic, justice,* have each of them several different meanings which cannot be reconciled with one another. In the case of a word like *democracy,* not only is there no agreed definition, but the attempt to make one is resisted from all sides. It is almost universally felt that when we call a country democratic we are praising it: consequently the defenders of every kind of régime claim that it is a democracy, and fear that they might have to stop using the word if it were tied down to any one meaning. Words of this kind are often used in a consciously dishonest way. That is, the person who uses them has his own private definition, but allows his hearer to think he means something quite different. Statements like *Marshal Pétain was a true patriot, The Soviet Press is the freest in the world, The Catholic Church is opposed to persecution,* are almost always made with intent to deceive. Other words used in variable meanings, in most cases more or less dishonestly, are: *class, totalitarian, science, progressive, reactionary, bourgeois, equality.*

---

[2]Example: "Comfort's catholicity of perception and image, strangely Whitmanesque in range, almost the exact opposite in aesthetic compulsion, continues to evoke that trembling atmospheric accumulative hinting at a cruel, an inexorably serene timelessness . . . Wrey Gardiner scores by aiming at simple bull's-eyes with precision. Only they are not so simple, and through this contented sadness runs more than the surface bittersweet of resignation" (*Poetry Quarterly*).

Now that I have made this catalog of swindles and perversions, let me give another example of the kind of writing that they lead to. This time it must of its nature be an imaginary one. I am going to translate a passage of good English into modern English of the worst sort. Here is a well-known verse from *Ecclesiastes:*

"I returned and saw under the sun, that the race is not to the swift, nor the battle to the strong, neither yet bread to the wise, nor yet riches to men of understanding, nor yet favor to men of skill; but time and chance happeneth to them all."

Here it is in modern English: 10

"Objective consideration of contemporary phenomena compels the conclusion that success or failure in competitive activities exhibits no tendency to be commensurate with innate capacity, but that a considerable element of the unpredictable must invariably be taken into account."

This is a parody, but not a very gross one. Exhibit (3), above, for instance, contains several patches of the same kind of English. It will be seen that I have not made a full translation. The beginning and ending of the sentence follow the original meaning fairly closely, but in the middle the concrete illustrations—race, battle, bread—dissolve into the vague phrase "success or failure in competitive activities." This had to be so, because no modern writer of the kind I am discussing—no one capable of using phrases like "objective consideration of contemporary phenomena"—would ever tabulate his thoughts in that precise and detailed way. The whole tendency of modern prose is away from concreteness. Now analyse these two sentences a little more closely. The first contains forty-nine words but only sixty syllables, and all its words are those of everyday life. The second contains thirty-eight words of ninety syllables: eighteen of its words are from Latin roots, and one from Greek. The first sentence contains six vivid images, and only one phrase ("time and chance") that could be called vague. The second contains not a single fresh, arresting phrase, and in spite of its ninety syllables it gives only a shortened version of the meaning contained in the first. Yet without a doubt it is the second kind of sentence that is gaining ground in modern English. I do not want to exaggerate. This kind of writing is not yet universal, and outcrops of simplicity will occur here and there in the worst-written page. Still, if you or I were told to write a few lines on the uncertainty of human fortunes, we should probably come much nearer to my imaginary sentence than to the one from *Ecclesiastes.*

As I have tried to show, modern writing at its worst does not consist in picking out words for the sake of their meaning and inventing images in order to make the meaning clearer. It consists in gumming together long strips of words which have already been set in order by someone else, and making the results presentable by sheer humbug. The attraction of this way of writing is that it is easy. It is easier — even quicker, once you have the habit — to say *In my opinion it is a not unjustifiable assumption that* than to say *I think*. If you use ready-made phrases, you not only don't have to hunt about for words; you also don't have to bother with the rhythms of your sentences, since these phrases are generally so arranged as to be more or less euphonious. When you are composing in a hurry — when you are dictating to a stenographer, for instance, or making a public speech — it is natural to fall into a pretentious, Latinized style. Tags like *a consideration which we should do well to bear in mind* or *a conclusion to which all of us would readily assent* will save many a sentence from coming down with a bump. By using stale metaphors, similes and idioms, you save much mental effort, at the cost of leaving your meaning vague, not only for your reader but for yourself. This is the significance of mixed metaphors. The sole aim of a metaphor is to call up a visual image. When these images clash — as in *The Fascist octopus has sung its swan song, the jackboot is thrown into the melting pot* — it can be taken as certain that the writer is not seeing a mental image of the objects he is naming; in other words he is not really thinking. Look again at the examples I gave at the beginning of this essay. Professor Laski (1) uses five negatives in fifty-three words. One of these is superfluous, making nonsense of the whole passage, and in addition there is the slip *alien* for akin, making further nonsense, and several avoidable pieces of clumsiness which increase the general vagueness. Professor Hogben (2) plays ducks and drakes with a battery which is able to write prescriptions, and, while disapproving of the everyday phrase *put up with,* is unwilling to look *egregious* up in the dictionary and see what it means. (3), if one takes an uncharitable attitude towards it, is simply meaningless: probably one could work out its intended meaning by reading the whole of the article in which it occurs. In (4), the writer knows more or less what he wants to say, but an accumulation of stale phrases chokes him like tea leaves blocking a sink. In (5), words and meaning have almost parted company. People who write in this manner usually have a general emotional meaning — they dislike one thing and want to express solidarity with another — but they are not interested in the detail of what they are saying. A scrupulous writer, in every sentence that he writes, will ask himself at least four questions, thus: What am I trying to say? What words will express it? What image or idiom will make it clearer? Is this image fresh enough to have an effect? And he will probably ask himself two more: Could I put it more shortly? Have I said anything that is avoidably ugly? But you are not obliged to go to all this trouble. You can shirk it by simply throwing your mind open and letting the ready-made phrases come crowding in. They will construct your sentences for you — even think your thoughts for you, to a certain extent — and at need they will perform the important service of partially concealing your meaning even from yourself. It is at this point that the special connection between politics and the debasement of language becomes clear.

In our time it is broadly true that political writing is bad writing. Where it is not true, it will generally be found that the writer is some kind of rebel, expressing his private opinions and not a "party line." Orthodoxy, of whatever color, seems to demand a lifeless, imitative style. The political dialects to be found in pamphlets, leading articles, manifestos, White Papers and the speeches of under-secretaries do, of course, vary from party to party, but they are all alike in that one almost never finds in them a fresh, vivid, home-made turn of speech. When one watches some tired hack on the platform mechanically repeating the familiar phrases — *bestial atrocities, iron heel, blood-stained tyranny, free peoples of the world, stand shoulder to shoulder* — one often has a curious feeling that one is not watching a live human being but some kind of dummy: a feeling which suddenly becomes stronger at moments when the light catches the speaker's spectacles and turns them into blank discs which seem to have no eyes behind them. And this is not altogether fanciful. A speaker who uses that kind of phraseology has gone some distance towards turning himself into a machine. The appropriate noises are coming out of his larynx, but his brain is not involved as it would be if he were choosing his words for himself. If the speech he is making is one that he is accustomed to make over and over again, he may be almost unconscious of what he is saying, as one is when one utters the responses in church. And this reduced state of consciousness, if not indispensable, is at any rate favorable to political conformity.

In our time, political speech and writing are largely the defense of the indefensible. Things like the continuance of British rule in India, the Russian purges and deportations, the dropping of the atom bombs on Japan, can indeed be defended, but only by arguments which are too brutal for most people to face, and which do not square with the professed aims of political parties. Thus political language has to consist largely of euphemism, question-begging and sheer cloudy vagueness. Defenseless villages are bombarded from the air, the inhabitants driven out into the countryside, the cattle machine-gunned, the huts set on fire with incendiary bullets: this is called *pacification*. Millions of peasants are robbed of their farms and sent trudging along the roads with no more than they can carry: this is called *transfer of population* or *rectification of frontiers*. People are imprisoned for years without trial, or shot in the back of the neck or sent to die of scurvy in Arctic lumber camps: this is called *elimination of unreliable elements*. Such phraseology is needed if one wants to name things without calling up mental pictures of them. Consider for instance some comfortable English professor defending Russian totalitarianism. He cannot say outright, "I believe in killing off your opponents when you can get good results by doing so." Probably, therefore, he will say something like this:

"While freely conceding that the Soviet régime exhibits certain features   15
which the humanitarian may be inclined to deplore, we must, I think, agree
that a certain curtailment of the right to political opposition is an unavoidable concomitant of transitional periods, and that the rigors which the

Russian people have been called upon to undergo have been amply justified in the sphere of concrete achievement."

The inflated style is itself a kind of euphemism. A mass of Latin words falls upon the facts like soft snow, blurring the outlines and covering up all the details. The great enemy of clear language is insincerity. When there is a gap between one's real and one's declared aims, one turns as it were instinctively to long words and exhausted idioms, like a cuttlefish squirting out ink. In our age there is no such thing as "keeping out of politics." All issues are political issues, and politics itself is a mass of lies, evasions, folly, hatred and schizophrenia. When the general atmosphere is bad, language must suffer. I should expect to find—this is a guess which I have not sufficient knowledge to verify—that the German, Russian and Italian languages have all deteriorated in the last ten or fifteen years, as a result of dictatorship.

But if thought corrupts language, language can also corrupt thought. A bad usage can spread by tradition and imitation, even among people who should and do know better. The debased language that I have been discussing is in some ways very convenient. Phrases like *a not unjustifiable assumption, leaves much to be desired, would serve no good purpose, a consideration which we should do well to bear in mind,* are a continuous temptation, a packet of aspirins always at one's elbow. Look back through this essay, and for certain you will find that I have again and again committed the very faults I am protesting against. By this morning's post I have received a pamphlet dealing with conditions in Germany. The author tells me that he "felt impelled" to write it. I open it at random, and here is almost the first sentence that I see: "(The Allies) have an opportunity not only of achieving a radical transformation of Germany's social and political structure in such a way as to avoid a nationalistic reaction in Germany itself, but at the same time of laying the foundations of a cooperative and unified Europe." You see, he "feels impelled" to write—feels, presumably, that he has something new to say—and yet his words, like cavalry horses answering the bugle, group themselves automatically into the familiar dreary pattern. This invasion of one's mind by ready-made phrases (*lay the foundations, achieve a radical transformation*) can only be prevented if one is constantly on guard against them, and every such phrase anaesthetizes a portion of one's brain.

I said earlier that the decadence of our language is probably curable. Those who deny this would argue, if they produced an argument at all, that language merely reflects existing social conditions, and that we cannot influence its development by any direct tinkering with words and constructions. So far as the general tone or spirit of a language goes, this may be true, but it is not true in detail. Silly words and expressions have often disappeared, not through any evolutionary process but owing to the conscious action of a minority. Two recent examples were *explore every avenue* and *leave no stone unturned,* which were killed by the jeers of a few journalists. There is a long list of flyblown metaphors which could similarly be got rid of if enough people would interest themselves in the job; and it should also be possible to laugh the *not un-* formation out of existence,[3] to reduce the amount of Latin and Greek in the average sentence, to drive out foreign phrases and strayed scientific words, and, in general, to make pretentiousness unfashionable. But all these are minor points. The defense of the English language implies more than this, and perhaps it is best to start by saying what it does not imply.

To begin with it has nothing to do with archaism, with the salvaging of obsolete words and turns of speech, or with the setting up of a "standard English" which must never be departed from. On the contrary, it is especially concerned with the scrapping of every word or idiom which has outworn its usefulness. It has nothing to do with correct grammar and syntax, which are of no importance so long as one makes one's meaning clear, or with the avoidance of Americanisms, or with having what is called a "good prose style." On the other hand it is not concerned with fake simplicity and the attempt to make written English colloquial. Nor does it even imply in every case preferring the Saxon word to the Latin one, though it does imply using the fewest and shortest words that will cover one's meaning. What is above all needed is to let the meaning choose the word, and not the other way about. In prose, the worst thing one can do with words is to surrender to them. When you think of a concrete object, you think wordlessly, and then, if you want to describe the thing you have been visualizing you probably hunt about till you find the exact words that seem to fit. When you think of something abstract you are more inclined to use words from the start, and unless you make a conscious effort to prevent it, the existing dialect will come rushing in and do the job for you, at the expense of blurring or even changing your meaning. Probably it is better to put off using words as long as possible and get one's meaning as clear as one can through pictures or sensations. Afterwards one can choose—not simply *accept*—the phrases that will best cover the meaning, and then switch round and decide what impression one's words are likely to make on another person. This last effort of the mind cuts out all stale or mixed images, all prefabricated phrases, needless repetitions, and humbug and vagueness generally. But one can often be in doubt about the effect of a word or a phrase, and one needs rules that one can rely on when instinct fails. I think the following rules will cover most cases:

(i) Never use a metaphor, simile or other figure of speech which you are used to seeing in print.

(ii) Never use a long word where a short one will do.

(iii) If it is possible to cut a word out, always cut it out.

(iv) Never use the passive where you can use the active.

---

[3]One can cure oneself of the *not un-* formation by memorizing this sentence: *A not unblack dog was chasing a not unsmall rabbit across a not ungreen field.*

(v) Never use a foreign phrase, a scientific word or a jargon word
     if you can think of an everyday English equivalent.

(vi) Break any of these rules sooner than say anything outright bar-
     barous.

These rules sound elementary, and so they are, but they demand a deep
change of attitude in anyone who has grown used to writing in the style
now fashionable. One could keep all of them and still write bad English,
but one could not write the kind of stuff that I quoted in those five specimens at the beginning of this article.

I have not here been considering the literary use of language, but merely   20
language as an instrument for expressing and not for concealing or preventing thought. Stuart Chase and others have come near to claiming that all
abstract words are meaningless, and have used this as a pretext for advocating a kind of political quietism. Since you don't know what Fascism is, how
can you struggle against Fascism? One need not swallow such absurdities as
this, but one ought to recognize that the present political chaos is connected
with the decay of language, and that one can probably bring about some
improvement by starting at the verbal end. If you simplify your English, you
are freed from the worst follies of orthodoxy. You cannot speak any of the
necessary dialects, and when you make a stupid remark its stupidity will be
obvious, even to yourself. Political language — and with variations this is true
of all political parties, from Conservatives to Anarchists — is designed to
make lies sound truthful and murder respectable, and to give an appearance
of solidity to pure wind. One cannot change this all in a moment, but one can
at least change one's own habits, and from time to time one can even, if one
jeers loudly enough, send some worn-out and useless phrase — some *jackboot, Achilles' heel, hotbed, melting pot, acid test, veritable inferno* or other
lump of verbal refuse — into the dustbin where it belongs.

QUESTIONS

1. What is Orwell's position on the ways that modern writers are destroying the English language?
2. Orwell argues that "thought corrupts language," but he also argues that
   "language can also corrupt thought" (paragraph 17). What argument is
   he making? How does language corrupt thought?
3. Orwell writes in paragraph 17, "Look back through this essay, and for
   certain you will find that I have again and again committed the very
   faults I am protesting against." Does Orwell, in fact, break his own
   rules? If so, what might his purpose be in doing so?
4. What sense of himself does Orwell present to his readers? How would
   you describe his persona, his character?
5. Why do people write badly, according to Orwell? What causes does he
   identify in his essay? Do you agree with him? Explain.

6. Orwell presents guidelines for good writing in paragraph 19. Take one of your recent essays, and analyze how your writing measures up to Orwell's standards.

7. Spend one week developing a list of examples of bad writing from newspapers and popular magazines. Use this material as the basis for an essay in which you develop a thesis to argue your position on politics and language.

8. Written nearly sixty years ago, this is probably the best known of all of Orwell's essays. How insightful and current do you find it today? Take five examples from your reading, as Orwell takes from his, and use them as evidence in an argument of your own about the state of contemporary written English. Take your examples from anything you like, including this book—even this question—if you wish. Be careful to choose recent pieces of writing.

MAKING CONNECTIONS

1. Read George Orwell's essay, "Shooting an Elephant" (p. 114), in "Reflecting." What do you learn about Orwell, the essayist, from reading "Shooting an Elephant" and "Politics and the English Language" (p. 536)?

2. John Berger (p. 524) and James Baldwin (p. 532), as represented by their essays in this section, are two writers who probably were influenced by Orwell's essay "Politics and the English Language." Choose either Berger's or Baldwin's essay, and write an essay of your own explaining the connections that you find between Orwell and either Berger or Baldwin.

HONEST, DECENT, WRONG: THE INVENTION OF GEORGE ORWELL

Louis Menand

Literary and social critic Louis Menand was born in 1951 in upstate New York and grew up in Boston, where his father was the head-master of a private school. He graduated from Pomona College, attended Harvard University, and received his Ph.D in literature from Columbia University. He has taught at Columbia, Princeton University, and the University of Virginia, and he is currently on the faculty of the Graduate Center of the City University of New York. Menand is the author of several books, including Discovering Modernism: T. S. Eliot and His Context *(1987),* Pragmatism: A Reader *(1997), and* The Metaphysical Club: A History of Ideas in America *(2001), which won the Pulitzer Prize for history. His latest book is* American Studies *(2002), a collection of essays. In addition, Menand is a contributing editor for the* New York Review of Books *and a staff writer with* The New Yorker, *where the following essay originally appeared. Of his work Menand has said, "I've always written for nonacademic publications. I've hardly ever written for academic ones. It's just the way I write."*

Animal Farm, George Orwell's satire, which became the Cold War *Candide*, was finished in 1944, the high point of the Soviet-Western alliance against fascism. It was a warning against dealing with Stalin and, in the circumstances, a prescient book. Orwell had trouble finding a publisher, though, and by the time the book finally appeared, in August, 1945, the month of the Hiroshima and Nagasaki bombs, the Cold War was already on the horizon. *Animal Farm* was an instant success in England and the United States. It was a Book-of-the-Month Club selection; it was quickly translated into many languages and distributed, in some countries, by the United States government; and it made Orwell, who had spent most of his life scraping by, famous and rich. *1984*, published four years later, had even greater success. Orwell was fatally ill with pulmonary tuberculosis when he wrote it, and he died in January, 1950. He was forty-six.

The revision began almost immediately. Frances Stonor Saunders, in her fascinating study *The Cultural Cold War*, reports that right after Orwell's death the C.I.A (Howard Hunt was the agent on the case) secretly bought the film rights to *Animal Farm* from his widow, Sonia, and had an animated-film version produced in England, which it distributed throughout the world.

The book's final scene, in which the pigs (the Bolsheviks, in Orwell's allegory) can no longer be distinguished from the animals' previous exploiters, the humans (the capitalists), was omitted. A new ending was provided, in which the animals storm the farmhouse where the pigs have moved and liberate themselves all over again. The great enemy of propaganda was subjected, after his death, to the deceptions and evasions of propaganda—and by the very people, American Cold Warriors, who would canonize him as the great enemy of propaganda.

Howard Hunt at least kept the story pegged to the history of the Soviet Union, which is what Orwell intended. Virtually every detail in *Animal Farm* allegorizes some incident in that history: the Kronstadt rebellion, the five-year plan, the Moscow trials, the Molotov-Ribbentrop pact, the Tehran conference. But although Orwell didn't want Communism, he didn't want capitalism, either. This part of his thought was carefully elided, and *Animal Farm* became a warning against political change per se. It remains so today. The cover of the current Harcourt paperback glosses the contents as follows:

> As ferociously fresh as it was more than half a century ago, *Animal Farm* is a parable about would-be liberators everywhere. As we witness the rise and bloody fall of the revolutionary animals through the lens of our own history, we see the seeds of totalitarianism in the most idealistic organizations; and in our most charismatic leaders, the souls of our cruelest oppressors.

This is the opposite of what Orwell intended. But almost everything in the popular understanding of Orwell is a distortion of what he really thought and the kind of writer he was.

Writers are not entirely responsible for their admirers. It is unlikely that Jane Austen, if she were here today, would wish to become a member of the Jane Austen Society. In his lifetime, George Orwell was regarded, even by his friends, as a contrary man. It was said that the closer you got to him the colder and more critical he became. As a writer, he was often hardest on his allies. He was a middle-class intellectual who despised the middle class and was contemptuous of intellectuals, a Socialist whose abuse of Socialists— "all that dreary tribe of high-minded women and sandal-wearers and bearded fruit-juice drinkers who come flocking toward the smell of 'progress' like bluebottles to a dead cat"—was as vicious as any Tory's. He preached solidarity, but he had the habits of a dropout, and the works for which he is most celebrated, *Animal Farm, 1984*, and the essay "Politics and the English Language," were attacked by people who purported to share his political views. He was not looking to make friends. But after his death he suddenly acquired an army of fans—all middle-class intellectuals eager to suggest that a writer who approved of little would have approved of them.

Orwell's army is one of the most ideologically mixed up ever to assem- 5
ble. John Rodden, whose *George Orwell: The Politics of Literary Reputation* was published in 1989 and recently reprinted, with a new introduction, has

catalogued it exhaustively. It has included, over the years, ex-Communists, Socialists, left-wing anarchists, right-wing libertarians, liberals, conservatives, doves, hawks, the *Partisan Review* editorial board, and the John Birch Society: every group in a different uniform, but with the same button pinned to the lapel—Orwell Was Right. Irving Howe claimed Orwell, and so did Norman Podhoretz. Almost the only thing Orwell's posthumous admirers have in common, besides the button, is anti-Communism. But they all some- how found support for their particular bouquet of moral and political values in Orwell's writings, which have been universally praised as "honest," "decent," and "clear." In what sense, though, can writings that have been taken to mean so many incompatible things be called "clear"? And what, exactly, was Orwell right about?

Indifferent to his own person as Orwell genuinely was, his writing is essentially personal. He put himself at the center of all his nonfiction books and many of his essays, and he often used personal anecdotes in his political journalism to make, or reinforce, his points. He never figured himself as the hero of these stories, in part because his tendency to self-abnegation was fairly remorseless. But self-abnegation was perhaps the most seductive aspect of the persona he devised. Orwell had the rare talent for making readers feel that they were dealing not with a reporter or a columnist or a literary man— not with a writer—but with an ordinary person. His method for making people believe what he wrote was to make them believe, first of all, in him.

He was a writer, of course — he was a graphomaniac, in fact: writing was what he lived for — and there was not much that was ordinary about him. He was born, a hundred years ago, in Bengal, where his father was a sub-agent in the Opium Department of the Indian Civil Service, and he came to England when he was one, and was brought up there by his mother. (The family name was Blair, and Orwell's given name was Eric.) Orwell's father visited the family for three months in 1907, engaging in domestic life with sufficient industry to leave his wife pregnant, and did not come back until 1912. By then, Orwell was boarding as a scholarship student at St. Cyprian's, the school he wrote about, many years later, in the essay "Such, Such Were the Joys." He studied hard and won a scholarship to Eton, and it was there that he began his career in self-denial. He deliberately slacked off, finishing a hundred and thirty-eighth in a class of a hundred and sixty-seven, and then, instead of taking the exams for university, joined the Imperial Police and went to Burma, the scene of the essays "A Hanging" and "Shooting an Elephant." In 1927, after five years in Burma, while on leave in England and with no employment prospects, he resigned.

He spent the next four years as a tramp and an itinerant worker, expe- riences that became the basis for *Down and Out in Paris and London*, the first work to appear under the pen name George Orwell, in 1933. He taught school briefly, worked in a bookstore (the subject of the essay "Bookshop Memories"), and spent two months travelling around the industrial districts in the North of England gathering material for *The Road to Wigan Pier*, which came out in 1937. Orwell spent the first half of 1937 fighting with the Loyalists in Spain, where he was shot in the throat by a fascist sniper, and where he witnessed the brutal Communist suppression of the revolutionary parties in the Republican alliance. His account of these events, *Homage to Catalonia*, which appeared in 1938, was, indeed, brave and iconoclastic (though not the only work of its kind), and it established Orwell in the position that he would maintain for the rest of his life, as the leading anti-Stalinist writer of the British left.

During the war, Orwell took a job with the Indian section of the BBC's Eastern Service, where he produced and, with T. S. Eliot, William Empson, Louis MacNeice, and other distinguished writers, delivered radio talks, mostly on literary subjects, intended to rally the support of Indians for the British war effort. For the first time since 1927, he received the salary he had once enjoyed as a policeman in Burma, but he regarded the work as propaganda — he felt, he said, like "an orange that's been trodden on by a very dirty boot" — and, in 1943, he quit. He worked for a while as literary editor and as a columnist at the *Tribune*, a Socialist paper edited by Aneurin Bevan, the leader of the left wing of the Labour Party in Britain and a man Orwell admired. In 1946, after the success of *Animal Farm*, and knowing that he was desperately ill with lung disease, he removed himself to one of the dankest places in the British Isles: the island of Jura, off the coast of Scotland. When he was not too sick to type, he sat in a room all day smoking black shag tobacco, and writing *1984*. His biographers have noted that the life of Winston Smith at the Ministry of Truth in that novel is based in part on Orwell's own career (as he experienced it) at the BBC. Room 101, the torture chamber in the climactic scene, was the name of the room where the Eastern Service held compulsory committee meetings. Orwell (is it necessary to say?) hated committees.

His first wife, Eileen, with whom he adopted a son, died in 1945. He   10
proposed to several women thereafter, sometimes suggesting, as an inducement, that he would probably die soon and leave his widow with a valuable estate; but he struck out. Then, in 1949, when he really was on his deathbed, he married Sonia Brownell, a woman whose sex appeal was widely appreciated. Brownell had slept with Orwell once, in 1945, apparently from the mixed motives of pity and the desire to sleep with famous writers, one of her hobbies. The marriage was performed in a hospital room; Orwell died three months later. He ended up selling more books than any other serious writer of the twentieth century — *Animal Farm* and *1984* were together translated into more than sixty languages; in 1973, English-language editions of *1984* were still selling at a rate of 1,340 copies a *day* — and he left all his royalties to Sonia. She squandered them and died more or less in poverty, in 1980. Today Orwell's gravesite, in a churchyard in Sutton Courtenay, Oxfordshire, is tended by volunteers.

Orwell has been posthumously psychoanalyzed, but there is no great mystery behind the choices he made in his life. He explained his motive plainly and repeatedly in his writing: he wanted to de-class himself. From his days at St. Cyprian's, and possibly even earlier, he saw the class system as a system of oppression—and nothing but a system of oppression. The guilt (his term) that he felt about his position as a member of the white imperialist bourgeoisie preceded his interest in politics as such. He spent much of his time criticizing professional Socialists, particularly the leaders of the British Labour Party, because, apart from the commitment to equality, there was not much about Socialism that was important to him. His economics were rudimentary, and he had little patience for the temporizing that ordinary politics requires. In 1945, after Germany surrendered, Churchill and the Conservatives were voted out and a Labour government came in (with Bevan as Minister of Health). In less than a year, Orwell was complaining that no steps had been taken to abolish the House of Lords.

He didn't merely go on adventures in class-crossing. He turned his life into an experiment in classlessness, and the intensity of his commitment to that experiment was the main reason that his friends and colleagues found him a perverse and sometimes exasperating man. His insistence on living in uncomfortable conditions, his refusal (despite his bad lungs) to wear a hat or coat in winter, his habit of pouring his tea into the saucer and slurping it noisily (in the working-class manner) struck his friends not as colorful eccentricities but as reproaches directed at their own bourgeois addiction to comfort and decorum. Which they were. Orwell was a brilliant and cultured man, with an Eton accent and an anomalous, vaguely French mustache, who wore the same beat-up tweed jacket nearly every day, made (very badly) his own furniture, and lived, most of the time, one step up from squalor. He read Joyce and kept a goat in the back yard. He was completely authentic and completely inauthentic at the same time—a man who believed that to write honestly he needed to publish under a false name.

Orwell's writing is effortlessly compelling. He was in the tradition of writers who—as Leslie Stephen said of Defoe—understand that there is a literary fascination in a clear recitation of the facts. There is much more to Orwell than this, though. As Christopher Hitchens points out in *Why Orwell Matters*, a book more critical of Orwell than the title might suggest, *Homage to Catalonia* survives as a model of political journalism, and *Animal Farm* and *1984* belong permanently to the literature of resistance. Whatever uses they were made to serve in the West, they gave courage to people in the East. The territory that Orwell covered in *Down and Out in Paris and London* and *The Road to Wigan Pier*—the lower-class extremes—was by no means new to nonfiction prose. Engels wrote about it feelingly in *The Condition of the Working Class in England in 1844*; Jacob Rüs studied it in *How the Other Half Lives*. But Orwell discovered a tone—"generous anger" is the phrase he once used to describe Dickens, and it has been applied to him, but "cool indignation" seems a little more accurate—that has retained its freshness after seventy years.

Orwell's essays have recently been collected, with exceptional thoroughness, by John Carey. The essay on Dickens, published in 1940, is weaker criticism than Edmund Wilson's "Dickens: The Two Scrooges," which came out the same year. But Orwell's essay on Henry Miller, "Inside the Whale," which also appeared in 1940, was original and unexpected. His personal essays, especially "Shooting an Elephant" and "Such, Such Were the Joys," are models of the form. Still, his qualities as a writer are obscured by the need of his admirers to claim for his work impossible virtues.

Honesty was important to Orwell. He was certainly quick enough to   15
accuse people he disagreed with of dishonesty. But there is sometimes a confusion, when people talk about Orwell's writing, between honesty and objectivity. "He said what he believed" and "He told it like it was" refer to different virtues. One of the effects of the tone Orwell achieved—the tone of a reasonable, modest, supremely undogmatic man, hoping for the best but resigned to the worst—was the impression of transparency, something that Orwell himself, in an essay called "Why I Write," identified as the ideal of good prose. It was therefore a shock when Bernard Crick, in the first major biography of Orwell, authorized by Sonia Orwell and published the year of her death, confessed that he had found it difficult to corroborate some of the incidents in Orwell's autobiographical writings. Jeffrey Meyers, whose biography *Orwell: Wintry Conscience of a Generation* came out in 2000, concluded that Orwell sometimes "heightened reality to achieve dramatic effects."

Crick has doubts that the event Orwell recounted in remarkably fine detail in "A Hanging"—he describes the condemned man stepping aside to avoid a puddle of water on his way to the scaffold—ever happened, and Meyers notes that, during his years as a tramp, Orwell would take time off to rest and write in the homes of family and friends, something he does not mention in *Down and Out in Paris and London*, where the narrator is sometimes on the verge of death by starvation. Both Crick and Meyers suspect that "Shooting an Elephant" has fabricated elements. And everything that Orwell wrote was inflected by his predilection for the worm's-eye view. When biographers asked Orwell's contemporaries what it was really like at St. Cyprian's, or in Burma, or working at the bookshop, the usual answer was "It was bad, but it wasn't *that* bad."

The point is not that Orwell made things up. The point is that he used writing in a literary, not a documentary, way: he wrote in order to make you see what he wanted you to see, to persuade. During the war, Orwell began contributing a "London Letter" to *Partisan Review*. In one letter, he wrote that park railings in London were being torn down for scrap metal, but that only working-class neighborhoods were being plundered; parks and squares in upper-class neighborhoods, he reported, were untouched. The story, Crick says, was widely circulated. When a friend pointed out that it was untrue, Orwell is supposed to have replied that it didn't matter, "it was *essentially* true."

You need to grasp Orwell's premises, in other words, before you can start talking about the "truth" of what he writes. He is not saying, This is the way it objectively was from any possible point of view. He is saying, This is the way it looked to someone with my beliefs. Otherwise, his work can be puzzling. *Down and Out in Paris and London* is a powerful book, but you are always wondering what this obviously decent, well-read, talented person is doing washing dishes in the kitchen of a Paris hotel. In *The Road to Wigan Pier*, Orwell gave the reader some help with this problem by explaining, at length, where he came from, what his views were, and why he went to live with the miners. Orwell was not a reporter or a sociologist. He was an advocate. He had very definite political opinions, and promoting them was his reason for writing. "No book is genuinely free of political bias," he asserted in "Why I Write." "Every line of serious work that I have written since 1936 has been written, directly or indirectly, *against* totalitarianism and *for* democratic Socialism, as I understand it."

Here we arrive at the challenge presented by the "Orwell Was Right" button. Hitchens says that there were three great issues in the twentieth century, and that Orwell was right on all three: imperialism, fascism, and Stalinism. What does this mean, though? Orwell was against imperialism, fascism, and Stalinism. Excellent. Many people were against them in Orwell's time, and a great many more people have been against them since. The important question, after condemning those things, was what to do about them, and how to understand the implications for the future. On this level, Orwell was almost always wrong.

Orwell thought that any Englishman who boasted of liberty and prosperity while India was still a colony was a hypocrite. "In order that England may live in comparative comfort, a hundred million Indians must live on the verge of starvation—an evil state of affairs, but you acquiesce in it every time you step into a taxi or eat a plate of strawberries and cream," he wrote in *The Road to Wigan Pier*. Still, he did not believe that India was capable of complete independence, and was still saying so as late as 1943. At first, he had the idea that the British Empire should be turned into "a federation of Socialist states, like a looser and freer version of the Union of Soviet Republics," but eventually he arrived at another solution. In 1943, entering a controversy in the pages of the *Tribune* over the future of Burma, which had been invaded by Japan, he laid out his position. The notion of an independent Burma, he explained, was as ludicrous as the notion of an independent Lithuania or Luxembourg. To grant those countries independence would be to create a bunch of "comic opera states," he wrote. "The plain fact is that small nationalities *cannot* be independent, because they cannot defend themselves." The answer was to place "the whole main-land of southeast Asia, together with Formosa, under the guidance of China, while leaving the islands under an Anglo-American-Dutch condominium." Orwell was against colonial exploitation, in other words, but not in favor of national self-determination. If this is anti-imperialism, make the most of it.

Orwell took a particular dislike to Gandhi. He referred to him, in private correspondence, as a "bit of a charlatan"; in 1943, he wrote that "there is indeed a sort of apocalyptic truth in the statement of the German radio that

20

the teachings of Hitler and Gandhi are the same." One of his last essays was on Gandhi, written two years after India, and one year after Burma, became independent, and a year after Gandhi's assassination. It is a grudging piece of writing. The method of Satyagraha, Orwell said, might have been effective against the British, but he was doubtful about its future as a tactic for political struggle. (A few years later, Martin Luther King, Jr., would find a use for it.) He confessed to "a sort of aesthetic distaste" for Gandhi himself— Gandhi was, after all, just the sort of sandal-wearing, vegetarian mystic Orwell had always abhorred— and he attributed the success of the Indian independence movement as much to the election of a Labour government in Britain as to Gandhi's efforts. "I have never been able to feel much liking for Gandhi, but I do not feel sure that as a political thinker he was wrong in the main, nor do I believe that his life was a failure" was the most that he could bring himself to say.

Hitler, on the other hand, Orwell did find personally appealing. "I have never been able to dislike Hitler," he admitted, in 1940. Hitler, it seems, "grasped the falsity of the hedonistic attitude to life," which Orwell called the attitude of "nearly all Western thought since the last war, certainly all 'progressive' thought." This response— the idea that fascism, whatever might be wrong with it, is at least about the necessity of struggle and self-sacrifice— is not that far from the response of the relatively few people in England (there were more in France) who actively endorsed fascism.

Orwell was opposed to Nazi Germany. But he thought that Britain, as an imperial power, had no moral right to go to war against Hitler, and he was sure that a war would make Britain fascist. This is a theme in his novel *Coming Up for Air*, which was published in 1939, and that winter he was urging friends to begin planning "illegal anti-war activities." He thought that it would be a good idea to set up an underground antiwar organization, in anticipation of what he called the "pre-war fascising processes," and predicted that he would end up in a British concentration camp because of his views. He kept up his antiwar agitation until August, 1939. Then, with the Nazi-Soviet non-aggression pact, he flipped completely. In *The Lion and the Unicorn*, in 1941, he accused British antiwar intellectuals of "sabotage." They had become "Europeanized"; they sneered at patriotism. (This from a man who, two years earlier, had been proposing an illegal campaign against government policy.) They had weakened the morale of the English people, "so that the Fascist nations judged that they were 'decadent' and that it was safe to plunge into war. . . . Ten years of systematic Blimp-baiting affected even the Blimps themselves and made it harder than it had been before to get intelligent young men to enter the armed forces." The prediction of a fascist Britain had evidently been forgotten.

What were Orwell's political opinions? Orwell was a revolutionary Socialist. That is, he hoped that there would be a Socialist revolution in England, and, as he said more than once, if violence was necessary, violence there should be. "I dare say the London gutters will have to run with blood," he wrote in "My Country Right or Left," in 1940. And a year later, in "The Lion and the Unicorn," "It is only by revolution that the native genius of the English people can be set free. . . . Whether it happens with or without bloodshed is largely an accident of time and place." Orwell had concluded long before that capitalism had failed unambiguously, and he never changed his opinion. He thought that Hitler's military success on the Continent proved once and for all the superiority of a planned economy. "It is not certain that Socialism is in all ways superior to capitalism, but it is certain that, unlike capitalism, it can solve the problems of production and consumption," he wrote. "The State simply calculates what goods will be needed and does its best to produce them."

A Socialist England, as Orwell described it, would be a classless society   25
with virtually no private property. The State would own everything, and would require "that nobody shall live without working." Orwell thought that perhaps fifteen acres of land, "at the very most," might be permitted, presumably to allow subsistence farming, but that there would be no ownership of land in town areas. Incomes would be equalized, so that the highest income would never be greater than ten times the lowest. Above that, the tax rate should be a hundred per cent. The House of Lords would be abolished, though Orwell thought that the monarchy might be preserved. (Everybody would drink at the same pub, presumably, but one of the blokes would get to wear a crown.) As for its foreign policy: a Socialist state "will not have the smallest scruple about attacking hostile neutrals or stirring up native rebellions in enemy colonies."

Orwell was not a cultural radical. Democracy and moral decency (once the blood was cleaned off the pavement, anyway) were central to his vision of Socialism. His admirers remembered the democracy and the decency, and managed to forget most of the rest. When *Homage to Catalonia* was finally published in the United States, in 1952, Lionel Trilling wrote an introduction, which Jeffrey Meyers has called "probably the most influential essay on Orwell." It is a work of short fiction. "Orwell clung with a kind of wry, grim pride to the old ways of the last class that had ruled the old order," Trilling wrote; he exemplified the meaning of the phrase "my station and its duties," and respected "the old bourgeois virtues." He even "came to love things, material possessions." A fully housebroken anti-Communist. It is amusing to imagine Orwell slurping his tea at the Columbia Faculty House.

Understanding Orwell's politics helps to explain that largely inaccurate prediction about postwar life, *1984*. There was, Hitchens points out, an enormous blind spot in Orwell's view of the world: the United States. Orwell never visited the United States and, as Hitchens says, showed little curiosity about what went on there. To the extent that he gave it any attention, he tended to regard the United States as vulgar, materialistic, and a threat to the English language. ("Many Americans pronounce . . . *water* as though it had no *t* in it, or even as though it had no consonant in it at all, except the *w*," he claimed. "On the whole we are justified in regarding the

American language with suspicion.") He thought that, all things considered, Britain was better off as a client-state of Washington than as a client-state of Moscow, but he did not look on an increased American role in the world with hope. Since Orwell was certain that capitalism was doomed, the only future he could imagine for the United States was as some sort of totalitarian regime.

He laid out his view in 1947, in the pages of *Partisan Review.* There were, he explained, three possible futures in a nuclear world: a preëmptive nuclear strike by the United States against the Soviet Union; a nuclear war between the United States and the Soviet Union, wiping out most of the race and returning life to the Bronze Age; and a stalemate created by the fear of actually using atomic bombs and other weapons of mass destruction — what would be known as the policy of mutually assured destruction. This third possibility, Orwell argued, was the worst of all:

> It would mean the division of the world among two or three vast superstates, unable to conquer one another and unable to be overthrown by any internal rebellion. In all probability their structure would be hierarchic, with a semi-divine caste at the top and outright slavery at the bottom, and the crushing out of liberty would exceed anything that the world has yet seen. Within each state the necessary psychological atmosphere would be kept up by complete severance from the outer world, and by a continuous phony war against rival states. Civilizations of this type might remain static for thousands of years.

Orwell's third possibility was, of course, the path that history took. Mutually assured destruction was the guiding policy of the arms race and the Cold War. Orwell himself coined the term "Cold War," and after his death he became a hero to Cold Warriors, liberal and conservative alike. But he hated the idea of a Cold War — he preferred being bombed back to the Bronze Age — because it seems never to have entered his mind that the United States would be a force for liberty and democracy. *1984* is, precisely, Orwell's vision of what the Cold War might be like: a mindless and interminable struggle among totalitarian monsters. Was he right?

Some people in 1949 received *1984* as an attack on the Labour Party (in the book, the regime of Big Brother is said to have derived from the principles of "Ingsoc"; that is, English Socialism), and Orwell was compelled to issue, through his publisher, a statement clarifying his intentions. He was a supporter of the Labour Party, he said. "I do not believe that the kind of society I describe necessarily *will* arrive," he continued, "but I believe (allowing of course for the fact that the book is satire) that something resembling it *could* arrive. I believe also that totalitarian ideas have taken root in the minds of intellectuals everywhere, and I have tried to draw these ideas out to their logical consequences."

The attitude behind this last sentence seems to me the regrettable part of   30
Orwell's legacy. If ideas were to stand or fall on the basis of their logically
possible consequences, we would have no ideas, because the ultimate conceivable consequence of every idea is an absurdity—is, in some way, "against
life." We don't live just by ideas. Ideas are part of the mixture of customs and
practices, intuitions and instincts that make human life a conscious activity
susceptible to improvement or debasement. A radical idea may be healthy as
a provocation; a temperate idea may be stultifying. It depends on the circumstances. One of the most tiresome arguments against ideas is that their
"tendency" is to some dire condition—to totalitarianism, or to moral rela-
tivism, or to a war of all against all. Orwell did not invent this kind of argument, but he provided, in *1984*, a vocabulary for its deployment.

"Big Brother" and "doublethink" and "thought police" are frequently cited
as contributions to the language. They are, but they belong to the same category as "liar" and "pervert" and "madman." They are conversation-stoppers.
When a court allows videotape from a hidden camera to be used in a trial,
people shout "Big Brother." When a politician refers to his proposal to permit
logging on national land as "environmentally friendly," he is charged with
"doublethink." When a critic finds sexism in a poem, she is accused of being a
member of the "thought police." The terms can be used to discredit virtually
any position, which is one of the reasons that Orwell became everyone's
favorite political thinker. People learned to make any deviation from their own
platform seem the first step on the slippery slope to *1984*.

There are Big Brothers and thought police in the world, just as there are
liars and madmen. *1984* may have been intended to expose the true character of Soviet Communism, but, because it describes a world in which
there are no moral distinctions among the three fictional regimes that dominate the globe, it ended up encouraging people to see totalitarian "tendencies" everywhere. There was visible totalitarianism, in Russia and in Eastern
Europe; but there was also the invisible totalitarianism of the so-called "free
world." When people talk about Big Brother, they generally mean a system
of covert surveillance and manipulation, oppression in democratic disguise
(unlike the system in Orwell's book, which is so overt that it is advertised).
1984 taught people to imagine government as a conspiracy against liberty.
This is why the John Birch Society used 1984 as the last four digits in the
phone number of its Washington office.

Orwell himself was a sniffer of tendencies. He, too, could blur moral
distinctions among the things he disliked, between the BBC and the Ministry
of Love, for instance; he apparently thought of the Ministry of Love as the
logical consequence of the mass media's "tendency" to thought control. His
most celebrated conflation of dislikes is the essay, for many years a staple of
the freshman-composition syllabus, "Politics and the English Language."

Orwell wrote many strong essays, but "Politics and the English
Language," published in 1946, is not one of them. Half of the essay is an
attack on bad prose. Orwell is against abstractions, mixed metaphors,
Latinate roots, polysyllabic words, clichés, and most of the other stylistic

vices identified in Fowler's *Modern English Usage* (in its fourth printing in 1946). The other half is an attack on political dishonesty. Certain political terms, Orwell argues,

> are often used in a consciously dishonest way. That is, the person who uses them has his own private definition, but allows his hearer to think he means something quite different. Statements like *Marshal Pétain was a true patriot, The Soviet Press is the freest in the world, The Catholic Church is opposed to persecution,* are almost always made with intent to deceive.

Fowler would have found nothing to complain about, though, in the sentences Orwell objects to. They are as clear as can be. Somehow, Orwell has run together his distaste for flowery, stale prose with his distaste for fascism, Stalinism, and Roman Catholicism. He makes it seem that the problem with fascism (and the rest) is, at bottom, a problem of style. They're bad, we are encouraged to feel, because their language is bad, because they're ugly.   35

This is not an isolated instance of this way of thinking in Orwell. From his earliest work, he was obsessed with body odor, and olfactory metaphors are probably the most consistent figure in his prose, right to the end of his life, when he congratulated Gandhi for leaving a clean smell when he died. But Orwell didn't think of the relation between smell and virtue as only metaphorical. He took quite seriously the question of whether it was ever possible to feel true solidarity with a man who smelled. Many pages in *The Road to Wigan Pier* are devoted to the problem. In his fiction, a bad character is, often, an ugly, sweaty, smelly character.

Smell has no relation to virtue, however. Ugliness has no relation to insincerity or evil, and short words with Anglo-Saxon roots have no relation to truth or goodness. Political speech, like etiquette, has its codes and its euphemisms, and Orwell is right to insist that it is important to be able to decipher them. He says that if what he calls political speech—by which he appears to mean political clichés—were translated into plain, everyday speech, confusion and insincerity would begin to evaporate. It is a worthy, if unrealistic, hope. But he does not stop there. All politics, he writes, "is a mass of lies, evasions, folly, hatred and schizophrenia." And by the end of the essay he has damned the whole discourse: "Political language—and with variations this is true of all political parties, from Conservatives to Anarchists—is designed to make lies sound truthful and murder respectable." *All* political parties? Orwell had sniffed out a tendency.

Orwell's prose was so effective that it seduced many readers into imagining, mistakenly, that he was saying what they wanted him to say, and what they themselves thought. Orwell was not clairvoyant; he was not infallible; he was not even consistent. He changed his mind about things, as most writers do. He dramatized out of a desire to make the world more the

way he wished it to be, as most writers do. He also said what he thought
without hedging or trimming, as few writers do all the time. It is strange
how selectively he was heard. It is no tribute to him to turn his books into
anthems to a status quo he hated. Orwell is admired for being a paragon
when he was, self-consciously, a naysayer and a misfit. If he is going to be
welcomed into the pantheon of right-thinking liberals, he should at least be
allowed to bring along his goat.

QUESTIONS

1. What point or points is Menand arguing here? You can start to answer
   this question by comparing the title of his essay with the last sentences
   of the first section (in paragraph 5).
2. Consider each of the three words in the expression "honest, decent, and
   right." The title of the essay only reverses one of the three but authors
   of pieces in newspapers and magazines do not necessarily compose their
   own titles. Often an editor does that. So, does Menand's argument only
   pertain to the right/wrong question, or does he have arguments to make
   about "honest" and "decent" as well? Obviously, he could either affirm
   or dispute either of those descriptions of Orwell and his work. What, in
   fact, does he do about those terms?
3. Menand points out that George Orwell is not this writer's given name.
   What difference does this make? What difference does Menand think
   that it makes?
4. Did you come to this essay with a previous experience of Orwell or a
   previous opinion about him? If so, what was it? What had you heard
   about him? How does Menand's essay connect with what you "knew"
   before you read it?
5. How important is the life of a writer for the readers of that writer?
   Should a work be judged on its own merits, or should the work and the
   author's life be treated as one thing? Does the importance of the writer's
   life vary depending on the kind of writing that is being examined? In the
   case of Orwell, is it important to connect his life to his work? Why or
   why not? Take a stand on these matters, and argue your case.

MAKING CONNECTIONS

1. If Menand is right, the editors of this book may have made a serious
   error in including "Politics and the English Language" (p. 536) for
   impressionistic young students to read. Did they? (Are you an impressionistic young student?) Present an argument on this issue. That is,
   make an argument about the rightness or wrongness of including
   Orwell's essay in this book.

2. Taking the two essays together—Orwell's and Menand's—and referring to any others in this section, write an essay in which you discuss "honesty" in argument. Consider both how honesty is achieved (or how the impression of honesty is conveyed) and whether honesty in writing is important. Offer examples of honest and dishonest writing (or the appearance of this) to support your case.

3. Menand mentions another George Orwell essay included in this book, "Shooting an Elephant" (p. 114). Does Menand's essay change the way you read that other Orwell essay? If so, how? If not, why not?

THE IMPIOUS IMPATIENCE OF JOB

Cynthia Ozick

One of the country's foremost fiction writers, Cynthia Ozick (b. 1927) grew up in New York City, graduated from New York University, and later received her Ph.D. from Ohio State University. Her novels include Trust *(1966),* The Cannibal Galaxy *(1983), and* The Puttermesser Papers *(1997), and she has also published several collections of short stories and essays. Much of Ozick's writing focuses on Jewish culture and tradition, and she has written movingly about the effects of the Holocaust. A visiting lecturer at numerous colleges, she is an articulate literary critic, as the following analysis of the Bible's Book of Job illustrates.*

The riddles of God are more satisfying than the solutions of men.
—G. K. CHESTERTON

Twenty-five centuries ago (or perhaps twenty-four or twenty-three), an unnamed Hebrew poet took up an old folktale and transformed it into a sacred hymn so sublime—and yet so shocking to conventional religion—that it agitates and exalts us even now. Scholars may place the Book of Job in the age of the Babylonian Exile, following the conquest of Jerusalem by Nebuchadnezzar—but to readers of our own time, or of any time, the historicity of this timeless poem hardly matters. It is timeless because its author intended it so; it is timeless the way Lear on the heath is timeless (and Lear may owe much to Job). Job is a man who belongs to no known nation; despite his peerless Hebrew speech, he is plainly not a Hebrew. His religious customs are unfamiliar, yet he is no pagan: he addresses the One God of monotheism. Because he is unidentified by period or place, nothing in his situation is foreign or obsolete; his story cannot blunder into anachronism or archaism. Like almost no other primordial poem the West has inherited, the Book of Job is conceived under the aspect of the universal—if the universal is understood to be a questioning so organic to our nature that no creed or philosophy can elude it.

That is why the striking discoveries of scholars—whether through philological evidence or through the detection of infusions from surrounding ancient cultures—will not deeply unsettle the common reader. We are driven—we common readers—to approach Job's story with tremulous palms held upward and unladen. Not for us the burden of historical linguistics, or the torrent of clerical commentary that sweeps through the centuries, or the dusty overlay of partisan interpretation. Such a refusal of context, historical and theological, is least of all the work of willed ignorance; if we choose to turn from received instruction, it is rather because of an intrinsic knowledge — the terror, in fact, of self-knowledge. Who among us has not been tempted to ask Job's questions? Which of us has not doubted God's justice? What human creature ever lived in the absence of suffering? If we, ordinary clay that we are, are not equal to Job in the wild intelligence of his cries, or in the unintelligible wilderness of his anguish, we are, all the same, privy to his conundrums.

Yet what captivates the scholars may also captivate us. A faithful English translation, for instance, names God as "God," "the Lord," "the Holy One," "the Almighty" — terms reverential, familiar, and nearly interchangeable in their capacity to evoke an ultimate Presence. But the author of Job, while aiming for the same effect of incalculable awe, has another resonance in mind as well: the dim tolling of some indefinable aboriginal chime, a suggestion of immeasurable antiquity. To achieve this, he is altogether sparing in his inclusion of the Tetragrammaton, the unvocalized YHVH — the root of which is "to be," rendered as "I am that I am" — which chiefly delineates God in the Hebrew Bible (and was later approximately transliterated as Yahweh or Jehovah). Instead, he sprinkles his poem, cannily and profusely, with pre-Israelite God-names: El, Eloah, Shaddai — names so lost in the long-ago, so unembedded in usage, that the poem is inevitably swept clean of traditional pieties. Translation veils the presence   and the intent — of these old names; and the necessary seamlessness of translation will perforce paper over the multitude of words and passages that are obscure in the original, subject to philological guesswork. Here English allows the common reader to remain untroubled by scholarly puzzles and tangles.

But how arresting to learn that Satan appears in the story of Job not as that demonic figure of later traditions whom we meet in our translation but as *ha-Satan*, with the definite article attached, meaning "the Adversary" — the counter-arguer among the angels, who is himself one of "the sons of God." Satan's arrival in the tale helps date its composition. It is under Persian influence that he turns up — via Zoroastrian duality, which pits, as equal contenders, a supernatural power for Good against a supernatural power for Evil. In the Book of Job, the scholars tell us, Satan enters Scripture for the first time as a distinct personality and as an emblem of destructive forces. But note: when the tale moves out of the prose of its fablelike frame into the sovereign grandeur of its poetry, Satan evaporates; the poet, an uncompromising monotheist, recognizes no alternative to the Creator, and no opposing might. Nor does the poet acknowledge any concept of afterlife, though Pharisaic thought in the period of his writing is just beginning to introduce that idea into normative faith.

There is much more that textual scholarship discloses in its search for   5 the Job-poet's historical surround: for example, the abundance of words and phrases in Aramaic, a northwestern Semitic tongue closely related to Hebrew, which was rapidly becoming the lingua franca of the ancient Near East. Aramaic is significantly present in other biblical books as well: in the later Psalms, in Ecclesiastes, Esther, and Chronicles—and, notably, in the Dead Sea Scrolls. The Babylonian Talmud is written in Aramaic; it is the language that Jesus speaks. Possibly the Job-poet's everyday speech is Aramaic—this may account for his many Aramaisms—but clearly, for the literary heightening of poetry, he is drawn to the spare beauty and noble diction of classical Hebrew (much as Milton, say, in constructing his poems of Paradise, invokes the cadences of classical Latin).

And beyond the question of language, the scholars lead us to still another enchanted garden of context and allusion: the flowering, all over the Levant, of a form known as "wisdom literature." A kind of folk-philosophy linking virtue to prudence, and pragmatically geared to the individual's worldly success, it intends instruction in levelheaded judgment and in the achievement of rational contentment. The biblical Proverbs belong to this genre, and, in a more profoundly reflective mode, so do Ecclesiastes and portions of Job; but wisdom literature can also be found in Egyptian, Babylonian, Ugaritic, and Hellenistic sources. It has no overriding national roots and deals with personal rather than collective conduct, and with a commonsensical morality guided by principles of resourcefulness and discretion. A great part of the Book of Job finds its ancestry in the region's pervasive wisdom literature (and its descendants in today's self-improvement bestsellers). But what genuinely seizes the heart are those revolutionary passages in Job that violently contradict what all the world, yesterday and today, takes for ordinary wisdom.

However seductive they are in their insight and learning, all these scholarly excavations need not determine or deter our own reading. We, after all, have in our hands neither the Hebrew original nor a linguistic concordance. What we do have—and it is electrifying enough—is the Book of Job as we readers of English encounter it. And if we are excluded from the sound and texture of an elevated poetry in a tongue not ours, we are also shielded from problems of structure and chronology, and from a confrontation with certain endemic philological riddles. There is riddle enough remaining—a riddle that is, besides, an elemental quest, the appeal for an answer to humankind's primal inquiry.

So there is something to be said for novice readers who come to Job's demands and plaints unaccoutered: we will perceive God's world exactly as Job himself perceives it. Or put it that Job's bewilderment will be ours, and our kinship to his travail fully unveiled, only if we are willing to absent ourselves from the accretion of centuries of metaphysics, exegesis, theological polemics. Of the classical Jewish and Christian theologians (Saadia Gaon, Rashi, ibn Ezra, Maimonides, Gersonides, Gregory, Aquinas, Calvin), each wrote from a viewpoint dictated by his particular religious perspective. But for us to be as (philosophically) naked as Job will mean to be naked of bias, dogma, tradition. It will mean to imagine Job solely as he is set forth by his own words in his own story.

His story, because it is mostly in dialogue, reads as a kind of drama. There is no proscenium; there is no scenery. But there is the dazzling spiral of words—extraordinary words, Shakespearean words; and there are the six players, who alternately cajole, console, contradict, contend, satirize, fulminate, remonstrate, accuse, deny, trumpet, succumb. Sometimes we are reminded of *Antigone*, sometimes of *Oedipus* (Greek plays that are contemporaneous with Job), sometimes of *Othello*. The subject is innocence and power; virtue and injustice; the Creator and His Creation; or what philosophy has long designated as theodicy, the Problem of Evil. And the more we throw off sectarian sophistries—the more we attend humbly to the drama as it plays itself out—the more clearly we will see Job as he emerges from the venerable thicket of theodicy into the heat of our own urgency. Or call it our daily breath.

Job's story—his fate, his sentence—begins in heaven, with Satan as   10
prosecuting attorney. Job, Satan presses, must be put to trial. Look at him: a man of high estate, an aristocrat, robust and in his prime, the father of sons and daughters, respected, affluent, conscientious, charitable, virtuous, God-fearing. God-fearing? How effortless to be always praising God when you are living in such ease! Look at him: how he worries about his lucky children and their feasting, days at a time—was there too much wine, did they slide into blasphemy? On their account he brings sacred offerings in propitiation. His possessions are lordly, but he succors the poor and turns no one away; his hand is lavish. Yet look at him—how easy to be righteous when you are carefree and rich! Strip him of his wealth, wipe out his family, afflict him with disease, and *then* see what becomes of his virtue and his piety!
So God is persuaded to test Job. Invasion, fire, tornado, destruction, and the cruelest loss of all: the death of his children. Nothing is left. Odious lesions creep over every patch of Job's skin. Tormented, he sits in the embers of what was once his domain and scratches himself with a bit of shattered bowl. His wife despairs: after all this, he still declines to curse God! She means for him to dismiss God as worthless to his life, and to dismiss his ruined life as worthless. But now a trio of gentlemen from neighboring lands arrives—a condolence call from Eliphaz, Bildad, and Zophar, Job's distinguished old friends. The three weep and are mute. Job's broken figure appalls: pitiable, desolate, dusted with ash, scraped, torn.
All the foregoing is told in the plain prose of a folktale: a blameless man's undoing through the conniving of a mischievous sprite. A prose epilogue will ultimately restore Job to his good fortune, and, in the arbitrary style of a fable, will even double it; but between the two halves of this simple narrative of loss and restitution the coloration of legend falls away, and a majesty of outcry floods speech after speech. And then Job's rage ascends—a rage against the loathsomeness of "wisdom."
When the horrified visitors regain their voices, it is they who appear to embody reasonableness, logic, and prudence, while Job—introduced in the prologue as a man of steadfast faith who will never affront the Almighty—rails like a blasphemer against an unjust God. The three listen courteously

as Job bewails the day he was born, a day that "did not shut the doors of my mother's womb, nor hide trouble from my eyes." In response to which Eliphaz begins his first attempt at solace: "Can mortal man be righteous before God? Can a man be pure before his Maker? . . . Behold, happy is the man whom God reproves; therefore despise not the chastening of the Almighty." Here is an early and not altogether brutal hint of what awaits Job in the severer discourse of his consolers: the logic of punishment, the dogma of requital. If a man suffers, it must be because of some impiety he has committed. Can Job claim that he is utterly without sin? And is not God a merciful God, "for He wounds, but binds up; He smites, but His hands heal?" In the end (Eliphaz reassures Job), all will be well.

Job is not comforted; he is made furious. He has been accused, however obliquely, of having sinned, and he knows with his whole soul that he has not. His friends show themselves to be as inconstant as a torrential river, icy in winter, vanishing away in the heat. Rather than condole, they defame. They root amelioration in besmirchment. But if Job's friends are no friends, then what of God? The poet, remembering the psalm—"What is man that thou are mindful of him?"—has Job echo the very words. "What is man," Job charges God, that "thou dost set thy mind upon him, dost visit him every morning, and test him every moment? . . . If I sin, what do I do to thee, thou watcher of men?" And he dreams of escaping God in death: "For now I shall lie in the earth; thou wilt seek me, but I shall not be."

Three rounds of increasingly tumultuous debate follow, with Eliphaz, 15 Bildad, and Zophar each having a turn, and Job replying. Wilder and wilder grow the visitors' accusations; wilder and wilder grow Job's rebuttals, until they are pitched into an abyss of bitterness. Job's would-be comforters have become his harriers; men of standing themselves, they reason from the conventional doctrines of orthodox religion, wherein conduct and consequence are morally linked: goodness rewarded, wickedness punished. No matter how hotly Job denies and protests, what greater proof of Job's impiety can there be than his deadly ordeal? God is just; he metes out just deserts. Is this not the grand principle on which the world rests?

Job's own experience refutes these arguments; and his feverish condemnation of God's injustice refutes religion itself. "I am blameless!" he cries yet again, and grimly concludes: "It is all one: therefore I say, He destroys both the blameless and the wicked. When disaster brings sudden death, He mocks the calamity of the innocent. The earth is given into the hand of the wicked; He covers the face of its judges." Here Job, remarkably, is both believer and atheist. God's presence is incontrovertible; God's moral integrity is nil. And how strange: in the heart of Scripture, a righteous man impugning God! Genesis, to be sure, records what appears to be a precedent. "Wilt thou destroy the righteous with the wicked?" Abraham asks God when Sodom's fate is at stake; but that is more plea than indictment, and anyhow there is no innocence in Sodom. Yet how distant Job is from the Psalmist who sings "The Lord is upright . . . there is no unrighteousness in Him," who pledges that "the righteous shall flourish like the palm tree" and "the workers of iniquity shall be destroyed forever." The Psalmist's is the voice of faith. Job's is the voice of a wounded lover, betrayed.

Like a wounded lover, he envisions, fleetingly, a forgiving afterlife, the way a tree, cut down to a stump, can send forth new shoots and live again — while man, by contrast, "lies down and rises not again." Or he imagines the workings of true justice: on the one hand, he wishes he might bring God Himself to trial; on the other, he ponders man-made law and its courts and declares that the transcript of his testimony ought to be inscribed permanently in stone, so that some future clansman might one day come as a vindicator, to proclaim the probity of Job's case. (Our translation famously renders the latter as "I know that my Redeemer lives," a phrase that has, of course, been fully integrated into Christian hermeneutics.) Throughout, there is a thundering of discord and clangor. "Miserable comforters are you all!" Job groans. "Surely there are mockers about me" — while Eliphaz, Bildad, and Zophar press on, from pious apologies to uncontrolled denunciation. You, Job, they accuse, you who stripped the naked of their clothing, gave no water to the weary, withheld bread from the hungry!

And Job sees how the tenets of rectitude, in the mouths of the zealous, are perverted to lies.

But now, abruptly, a new voice is heard: a fifth and so far undisclosed player strides onstage. He is young, intellectually ingenious, confident, a bit brash. Unlike the others, he bears a name with a Hebrew ring to it: Elihu. "I also will declare my opinion," he announces. He arrives as a supplanter, to replace stale wisdom with fresh, and begins by rebuking Job's haranguers for their dogma of mechanical tit for tat. As for Job: in his recalcitrance, in his litanies of injured innocence, in his prideful denials, he has been blind to the *uses* of suffering; and doesn't he recognize that God manifests Himself in night visions and dreams? Suffering educates and purifies; it humbles pride, tames the rebel, corrects the scoffer. "What man is like Job, who drinks up scoffing like water?" Elihu points out — but here the reader detects a logical snag. Job has become a scoffer only as a result of gratuitous suffering: then how is such suffering a "correction" of scoffing that never was? Determined though he is to shake Job's obstinacy, Elihu is no wiser than his elders. Job's refusal of meaningless chastisement stands.

So Elihu, too, fails as comforter. Yet as he leaves off suasion, his speech   20 metamorphoses into a hymn in praise of God's dominion. "Hear this, O Job," Elihu calls, "stop and consider the wondrous work of God" — wind, cloud, sky, snow, lightning, ice! Elihu's sumptuous limning of God's power in nature is a fore-echo of the sublime climax to come.

Job, gargantuan figure in the human imagination that he is, is not counted among the prophets. He is not the first to be reluctant to accept God's authority: Jonah rebelled against sailing to Nineveh in order to prophesy; yet he did go, and his going was salvational for a people not his own. But the true prophets are self-starters, spontaneous fulminators against social inequity, and far from reluctant. Job, then, has much in common with Isaiah,

Jeremiah, Micah, and Amos: he is wrathful that the wicked go unpunished, that the widow and the orphan go unsuccored, that the world is not clothed in righteousness. Like the noblest of the prophets, he assails injustice; and still he is unlike them. They accuse the men and women who do evil; their targets are made of flesh and blood. It is human transgression they hope to mend. Job seeks to rectify God. His is an ambition higher, deeper, vaster, grander than theirs; he is possessed by a righteousness more frenzied than theirs; the scale of his justice-hunger exceeds all that precedes him, all that was ever conceived; he can be said to be the consummate prophet. And at the same time he is the consummate violator. If we are to understand him at all, if we are rightly to enter into his passions at their pinnacle, then we ought to name him prophet; but we may not. Call him, instead, anti-prophet. His teaching, after all, verges on atheism: the rejection of God's power. His thesis is revolution.

Eliphaz, Bildad, and Zophar are silenced. Elihu will not strut these boards again. Job's revolution may be vanity of vanities, but his adversaries have lost confidence and are scattered. Except for Job, the stage is emptied.

Then God enters—not in a dream, as Elihu theorized, not as a vision or incarnation, but as an irresistible Eloquence.

Here I am obliged to remark on the obvious. In recapitulating certain passages, I have reduced an exalted poem to ordinary spoken sentences. But the ideas that buttress Job are not merely "expressed in," as we say, language of high beauty; they are inseparable from an artistry so far beyond the grasp of mind and tongue that one can hardly imagine their origin. We think of the Greek plays; we think of Shakespeare; and still that is not marvel enough. Is it that the poet is permitted to sojourn, for the poem's brief life, in the magisterial Eye of God? Or is it God who allows Himself to peer through the poet's glass, as through a gorgeously crafted kaleidoscope? The words of the poem are preternatural, unearthly. They may belong to a rhapsodic endowment so rare as to appear among mortals only once in three thousand years. Or they may belong to the Voice that hurls itself from the whirlwind.

God has granted Job's demand: "Let the Almighty answer me!" Now   25
here at last is Job's longed-for encounter with that Being he conceives to be his persecutor. What is most extraordinary in this visitation is that it appears to be set apart from everything that has gone before. What is the Book of Job *about*? It is about gratuitous affliction. It is about the wicked who escape whipping. It is about the suffering of the righteous. God addresses none of this. It is as if He has belatedly stepped into the drama without having consulted the script—none of it: not even so much as the prologue. He does not remember Satan's mischief. He does not remember Job's calamities. He does not remember Job's righteousness.

As to the last: Job will hardly appeal for an accounting from God without first offering one of his own. He has his own credibility to defend, his own probity. "Let me be weighed in a just balance," he insists, "and let God know my integrity!" The case for his integrity takes the form of a bill of particulars that is unsurpassed as a compendium of compassionate human conduct: no conceivable ethical nuance is omitted. It is as if all the world's moral fervor, distilled from all the world's religions, and touching on all the world's pain, is assembled in Job's roster of loving-kindness. Job in his confession of integrity is both a protector and a lover of God's world.

But God seems alarmingly impatient; His mind is elsewhere. Is this the Lord whom Job once defined as a "watcher of men?" God's answer, a fiery challenge, roils out of the whirlwind. "Where were *you*," the Almighty roars, in supernal strophes that blaze through the millennia, "when I laid the foundation of the earth?" And what comes crashing and tumbling out of the gale is an exuberant ode to the grandeur of the elements, to the fecundity of nature: the sea and the stars, the rain and the dew, the constellations in their courses, the lightning, the lion, the raven, the ass, the goat, the ostrich, the horse, the hawk— and more, more, more! The lavishness, the extravagance, the infinitude! An infinitude of power; an infinitude of joy; an infinitude of love, even for the ugly hippopotamus, even for the crocodile with his terrifying teeth, even for creatures made mythical through ancient lore. Even for Leviathan! Nothing in the universe is left unpraised in these glorious stanzas—and one thinks: had the poet access to the electrons, had he an inkling of supernovas, had he parsed the chains of DNA, God's ode to Creation could not be richer. Turn it and turn it—God's ode: everything is in it.

Everything but the answer to the question that eats at Job's soul: why God permits injustice in the fabric of a world so resplendently woven. Job is conventionally judged to be a moral violator because he judges God Himself to be a moral violator. Yet is there any idea in the history of human thought more exquisitely tangled, more furiously daring, more heroically courageous, more rooted in spirit and conscience than Job's question? Why does God not praise the marrow of such a man as Job at least as much as He praises the intricacy of the crocodile's scales? God made the crocodile; He also made Job.

God's answer to Job lies precisely in His not answering; and Job, with lightning insight, comprehends. "I have uttered what I did not understand," he acknowledges, "things too wonderful for me, which I did not know."

His new knowledge is this: that a transcendent God denies us a god of   30 our own devising, a god that we would create out of our own malaise, or complaint, or desire, or hope, or imagining; or would manufacture according to the satisfaction of our own design. We are part of God's design: can the web manufacture the spider? The Voice out of the whirlwind warns against god-manufacture—against the degradation of a golden calf surely, but also against god-manufacture even in the form of the loftiest visions. Whose visions are they? Beware: they are not God's; they are ours. The ways of the true God cannot be penetrated. The false comforters cannot decipher them. Job cannot uncover them. "The secret things belong to the Lord our God," Job's poet learned long ago, reading Deuteronomy. But now: see how Job cannot draw Leviathan out with a hook—how much less can he draw out God's nature, and His purpose!

So the poet, through the whirlwind's answer, stills Job.

But can the poet still the Job who lives in us? God's majesty is eternal, manifest in cell and star. Yet Job's questions toil on, manifest in death camp and hatred, in tyranny and anthrax, in bomb and bloodshed. Why do the wicked thrive? Why do the innocent suffer? In brutal times, the whirlwind's answer tempts, if not atheism, then the sorrowing conviction of God's indifference.

And if we are to take the close of the tale as given, it is not only Job's protests that are stilled; it is also his inmost moral urge. What has become of raging conscience? What has become of loving-kindness? Prosperity is restored; the dead children are replaced by twice the number of boys, and by girls exceedingly comely. But where now is the father's bitter grief over the loss of those earlier sons and daughters, on whose account he once indicted God? Cushioned again by good fortune, does Job remember nothing, feel nothing, see nothing beyond his own renewed honor? Is Job's lesson from the whirlwind finally no more than the learning of indifference?

So much for the naked text. Perhaps this is why—century after century—we common readers go on clinging to the spiritualizing mentors of traditional faith, who clothe in comforting theologies this God-wrestling and comfortless Book.

Yet how astoundingly up to date they are, those ancient sages—redactors   35
and compilers—who opened even the sacred gates of Scripture to philosophic doubt!

QUESTIONS

1. This essay presents itself as a reading, an interpretation, of a famous Biblical text. What makes it an argument? Are all interpretations arguments?

2. Ozick's interpretation suggests that the Book of Job is itself an argument—not just an argument between Job and his comforters, but an argument with other parts of the Bible, an argument about the nature of God. Without worrying about whether Ozick is right or not, summarize the claim she makes about the argument of the Book of Job.

3. Ozick herself is making an argument about the nature of religious belief. What is that argument? And what, if anything, does the epigraph from G. K. Chesterton have to do with Ozick's argument?

4. You may have encountered other ways of reading the Book of Job in your reading or religious teaching. If not, you should be able to find one or more different interpretations of this text. Select an interpretation that differs from Ozick's and discuss the differences between them.

5. Construct your own argument about Ozick's reading. You may argue that she has got it right or got it wrong. You will certainly have to look at the biblical text to do this, and you may wish to look at other interpretations as well.

MAKING CONNECTIONS

Suffering is described in other essays in this collection—for example, John Berger's "Hiroshima," (p. 524), John Hersey's "Hatsuyo Nakamura" (p. 181), N. Scott Momaday's "The Way to Rainy Mountain" (p. 86), and Barbara Tuchman's "This Is the End of the World: The Black Death" (p. 217). What do these various considerations of suffering have in common? Is there one thing, suffering, that is the same always and everywhere? Or is every instance of suffering different? Does the scale of suffering matter? Does its intensity matter more? Do different causes change the nature of suffering? Write an essay in which you consider these or similar questions about the nature and significance of suffering.

A Statement

Pablo Picasso

Perhaps the most influential artist of the twentieth century, Pablo Ruiz Picasso (1881–1973) was born in Malaga, Spain, and began advanced studies at the Royal Academy of Art in Barcelona when he was fifteen. By the age of nineteen, he was living in Paris and painting in earnest. His early works were influenced by his immediate artistic predecessors, such as Henri Toulouse-Lautrec, but in 1907, he produced his landmark Les Demoiselles d'Avignon, *a revolutionary painting that ushered in the cubist movement as well as the beginnings of the idea of abstraction in art — that is, that works of art may exist on their own without any attempt to represent reality. Throughout his long career, Picasso continued to refine and develop his ideas in painted works as well as in sculptures, collages, etchings, and drawings. The following statement was delivered orally in Spanish in 1923 to the Mexican-born American artist Marius de Zayas, another pioneer of abstraction. Picasso approved de Zayas's transcription before it was translated into English for publication in the periodical* The Arts.

I can hardly understand the importance given to the word *research* in connection with modern painting. In my opinion to search means nothing in painting. To find, is the thing. Nobody is interested in following a man who, with his eyes fixed on the ground, spends his life looking for the pocketbook that fortune should put in his path. The one who finds something no matter what it might be, even if his intention were not to search for it, at least arouses our curiosity, if not our admiration.

Among the several sins that I have been accused of committing, none is more false than the one that I have, as the principal objective in my work, the spirit of research. When I paint my object is to show what I have found and not what I am looking for. In art intentions are not sufficient and, as we say in Spanish: love must be proved by facts and not by reasons. What one does is what counts and not what one had the intention of doing.

We all know that Art is not truth. Art is a lie that makes us realize truth, at least the truth that is given us to understand. The artist must know the manner whereby to convince others of the truthfulness of his lies. If he only shows in his work that he has searched, and researched, for the way to put over lies, he would never accomplish anything.

The idea of research has often made painting go astray, and made the artist lose himself in mental lucubrations. Perhaps this has been the principal fault of modern art. The spirit of research has poisoned those who have not

Unknown photographer, Photograph of Pablo Picasso (ca. 1912)

fully understood all the positive and conclusive elements in modern art and has made them attempt to paint the invisible and, therefore, the unpaintable.

They speak of naturalism in opposition to modern painting. I would like   5
to know if anyone has ever seen a natural work of art. Nature and art, being two different things, cannot be the same thing. Through art we express our conception of what nature is not.

Velázquez[1] left us his idea of the people of his epoch. Undoubtedly they were different from what he painted them, but we cannot conceive a Philip IV in any other way than the one Velázquez painted. Rubens[2] also made a

---

[1]*Diego Velázquez* (1599–1660): Spain's greatest painter. He served as court painter to Philip IV of Spain. [Eds.]

[2]*Peter Paul Rubens* (1577–1640): A Flemish painter who was the best-known northern European artist of his day. [Eds.]

portrait of the same king and in Rubens' portrait he seems to be quite another person. We believe in the one painted by Velázquez, for he convinces us by his right of might.

From the painters of the origins, the primitives, whose work is obviously different from nature, down to those artists who, like David,[3] Ingres[4] and even Bouguereau,[5] believed in painting nature as it is, art has always been art and not nature. And from the point of view of art there are no concrete or abstract forms, but only forms which are more or less convincing lies. That those lies are necessary to our mental selves is beyond any doubt, as it is through them that we form our aesthetic point of view of life.

Cubism is no different from any other school of painting. The same principles and the same elements are common to all. The fact that for a long time cubism has not been understood and that even today there are people who cannot see anything in it, means nothing. I do not read English, an English book is a blank book to me. This does not mean that the English language does not exist, and why should I blame anybody else but myself if I cannot understand what I know nothing about?

I also often hear the word *evolution*. Repeatedly I am asked to explain how my painting evolved. To me there is no past or future in art. If a work of art cannot live always in the present it must not be considered at all. The art of the Greeks, of the Egyptians, of the great painters who lived in other times, is not an art of the past; perhaps it is more alive today than it ever was. Art does not evolve by itself, the ideas of people change and with them their mode of expression. When I hear people speak of the evolution of an artist, it seems to me that they are considering him standing between two mirrors that face each other and reproduce his image an infinite number of times, and that they contemplate the successive images of one mirror as his past, and the images of the other mirror as his future, while his real image is taken as his present. They do not consider that they all are the same images in different planes.

Variation does not mean evolution. If an artist varies his mode of   10
expression this only means that he has changed his manner of thinking, and in changing, it might be for the better or it might be for the worse.

The several manners I have used in my art must not be considered as an evolution, or as steps toward an unknown ideal of painting. All I have ever made was made for the present and with the hope that it will always remain in the present. I have never taken into consideration the spirit of research. When I have found something to express, I have done it without

[3]*Jacques-Louis David* (1748–1825): A French painter who introduced the neoclassical style in France. [Eds.]

[4]*Jean August Dominique Ingres* (1780–1867): One of the major French painters of the first half of the nineteenth century. He was a student in Jacques-Louis David's studio. [Eds.]

[5]*William Bouguereau* (1825–1905): A French painter who painted in the traditional academic style despite the advent of impressionism. [Eds.]

thinking of the past or of the future. I do not believe I have used radically different elements in the different manners I have used in painting. If the subjects I have wanted to express have suggested different ways of expression I have never hesitated to adopt them. I have never made trials nor experiments. Whenever I had something to say, I have said it in the manner in which I have felt it ought to be said. Different motives inevitably require different methods of expression. This does not imply either evolution or progress, but an adaptation of the idea one wants to express and the means to express that idea.

Arts of transition do not exist. In the chronological history of art there are periods which are more positive, more complete than others. This means that there are periods in which there are better artists than in others. If the history of art could be graphically represented, as in a chart used by a nurse to mark the changes of temperature of her patient, the same silhouettes of mountains would be shown, proving that in art there is no ascendant progress, but that it follows certain ups and downs that might occur at any time. The same occurs with the work of an individual artist.

Juan Gris, Portrait of Pablo Picasso (1912)

Pablo Picasso, Self-Portrait (1907)

Many think that cubism is an art of transition, an experiment which is to bring ulterior results. Those who think that way have not understood it. Cubism is not either a seed or a foetus, but an art dealing primarily with forms, and when a form is realized it is there to live its own life. A mineral substance, having geometric formation, is not made so for transitory purposes, it is to remain what it is and will always have its own form. But if we are to apply the law of evolution and transformation to art, then we have to admit that all art is transitory. On the contrary, art does not enter into these philosophic absolutisms. If cubism is an art of transition I am sure that the only thing that will come out of it is another form of cubism.

Mathematics, trigonometry, chemistry, psychoanalysis, music and whatnot have been related to cubism to give it an easier interpretation. All this has been pure literature, not to say nonsense, which brought bad results, blinding people with theories.

Cubism has kept itself within the limits and limitations of painting, never pretending to go beyond it. Drawing, design and color are understood and practiced in cubism in the spirit and manner that they are understood and practiced in all other schools. Our subjects might be different, as we have introduced into painting objects and forms that were formerly ignored. We have kept our eyes open to our surroundings, and also our brains.

We give to form and color all their individual significance, as far as we can see it; in our subjects, we keep the joy of discovery, the pleasure of the unexpected; our subject itself must be a source of interest. But of what use is it to say what we do when everybody can see it if he wants to?

QUESTIONS

1. This statement might be described as an antiargument. In what ways does it refuse or reject the normal methods of argument?
2. Picasso makes a number of provocative assertions in this statement. What is the relation between asserting and arguing? Is there a difference between them?
3. Make a short list of the most provocative assertions in this statement. For each assertion, decide what supports it, whether you agree or disagree with it, and why you take the position you do.
4. Picasso considers some theories of art other than his own. What are they? How are they used in his argument?
5. The relationship of art to truth is a major question taken up in this statement. How would you summarize Picasso's position on the matter? In formulating your response, try to consider every use of the word *truth* in the statement.
6. What would a counterstatement to Picasso's look like? Try to produce a persuasive version of such a response to Picasso.
7. Picasso says that art is a lie that makes us realize the truth. Is this statement a lie? Is it art? Is everything an artist says or does art?

MAKING CONNECTIONS

1. Picasso says that art is a lie that leads us to the truth. Assuming that he may be right about this, consider how this statement may or may not apply to other works in this volume. You first should look at those works that make an obvious claim to be art, such as the poems and the images in John Berger's "Hiroshima" (p. 524). But what about the essays? Do they present arguments that function in an artistic way?
2. Consider Picasso's statement about art, lies, and truth in connection with the three portraits of Picasso presented with this statement. Is the photograph the truth, and are the two paintings lies? Are the paintings art, and is the photograph something else? Consider each of the three images in relation to Picasso's statement, and write an essay based on your consideration. (You may wish to see color reproductions of the paintings, which are available on the Web.) Your argument can explore the truth value of any one of the three images or all three of them or can make a more general inquiry into the truth and falsehood of representational images. Be sure to discuss all three portraits in your essay. You may also wish to argue about the truth or falsehood of Picasso's statement.

WHY WE HATE TEACHERS

Garret Keizer

A graduate of the University of Vermont, Garret Keizer (b. 1954) worked as a high school English teacher for fifteeen years, an experience that provided the basis for his first book, No Place but Here: A Teacher's Vocation in a Rural Community *(1988). He went on to become an Episcopal minister, a transition he chronicled in* A Dresser of Sycamore Trees: The Finding of a Ministry *(1991). A prolific essayist, Keizer has also published* The Enigma of Anger: Essays on a Sometimes Deadly Sin *(2002) and a young adult novel,* God of Beer *(2002). The following essay appeared in a 2001 issue of* Harper's *magazine devoted to contemporary American education.*

Glory, glory, alleluia.
Teacher hit me with a ruler.
I knocked her on the bean
With a rotten tangerine,
And she ain't gonna teach no more.
    — "Mine Eyes Have Seen
      the Glory of the
     Burning of the School"
       (Traditional)

As soon as I entered first grade, I began throwing up my breakfast every day, Monday through Friday, usually two or three minutes before the school bus came. I do not recall having what are nowadays referred to as "academic difficulties." In fact, I was already the good student I would continue to be right through graduate school. Nor do I recall being picked on in any particular way; that would come later. What I recall is being struck at about the same time as my mother handed me my lunch with an irresistible urge to vomit my breakfast — that, and the sight of my mother on her knees again, wiping up my mess.

I have long since marveled at the way in which my parents, without benefit of formal courses in psychology or any thought of sending me to a psychologist (this was 1959), set about trying to cure me by a psychological stratagem at once desperate, risky, and ingenious. It amounted to the contrivance of an epiphany. One evening they announced that the next day I would not be going to school. Instead, my mother and I would be taking a trip "up country" to see Aunt Em and have a picnic. Aunt Em and her husband were caretakers of a sprawling rural cemetery in which I delighted to play and explore. They lived in a house "as old as George Washington."

Propped against one of their porch pillars was an enormous Chiclet-shaped rock, an object of great fascination for me, which they claimed was a petrified dinosaur tooth. There were few places on earth I would rather have gone.

The next morning arrived like an early Christmas. I watched impatiently as my mother packed a lunch for our adventure. Then, just at the time when the school bus would have picked me up, she turned to me and in a tone of poignant resignation said, "Now, you see, Gary, there is nothing wrong with your stomach. You get sick because you don't want to go to school." She handed me my lunch and told me that we were not going to Aunt Em's that day. I did not throw up. I forget whether or not I cried. But, for the most part, I was cured.

I say for the most part because even now, at the age of forty-eight, I am rarely able to walk into any school without feeling something of the same duodenal ominousness that haunted my first days as a student. I doubt I am unique in this, though it does seem like an odd symptom for someone who went to school for almost twenty years, who taught high school for fifteen years after that, who saw his wife through graduate school after she had done the same for him, and who will be in his mid-fifties by the time he has seen his daughter through college. I have spent most of my life "in school," doing homework or correcting it, which means that for much of my life I have either skipped breakfast or eaten it as an act of faith.

And I still catch myself thinking of that aborted trip to Aunt Em's. I pic- 5
ture myself running over the mown graves, past generations of polished monuments, with a cool breeze at my back and the clouds unfolding like angel wings above me. It amounts to a waking dream, with a dream's psychic symbolism, and what I think it means is that I have reconciled myself to death by imagining it as the most sublime form of hooky: the blessed stage at which no one will ever again, in any form whatsoever, make me go to school.

I do not have frightful memories of my first-grade teacher, though my parents have told me she was "stern." I remember her punishing a boy who'd meandered into the girls' bathroom by forcing him to wear a cardboard sign that read I AM A GIRL TODAY. I remember another boy, a budding Leonardo da Vinci, whose crammed, cluttered desk she would from time to time dump over onto the floor, like an unfaithful wife's wardrobe tossed onto the street. I can still see him kneeling among his precocious drawings and playground-excavated fossils, straightening things up as best as he could, while the rest of us looked on with the dumbstruck fascination of smaller-brained primates. I can see these things clearly, but I do not remember the teacher herself as an ogre. As for the memories of my two classmates, the first of whom would eventually become an outlaw biker and the second of whom probably went on through a long progression of larger and even messier desks, I am not so sure.

Such stories of cruel and unusual punishment probably account at least partially for that hideous strain of American folk humor, with a pedigree that runs from Washington Irving to Garrison Keillor: the Tale of the Teacher We Drove Nuts. I used to know a man who would tell me, in the tone of someone bragging about his first sexual experience, how he and his friends had driven a nun at his Catholic school to a nervous breakdown. "Let's put it this way: She didn't come back the next year." It so happens that I was working as a teacher when I first heard the story. So was the man who told it to me.

It's hard to imagine a parallel from another profession, perhaps some folksy yarn about an undertaker driven to tears by a repeated switcheroo of his embalming fluid and his coffee, a cashier who fell down foaming at the mouth after making change for one too many ten-pound bags of dimes. It's simplistic to say that we see these tales as innocuous because their protagonists are only children. We also see them as innocuous because their victims are only teachers (and usually women). We like to tell these stories, I think, because they requite some primal — as in "primary" school — pain within us.

For many children, going to school amounts to a fall from grace. I have long sensed a mystical connection between the iconic apple on the teacher's desk and the apple Adam ate from the forbidden tree; I am tempted to take them for the same apple. Perhaps the New England Puritans who taught their children the alphabet starting with the A in "Adam's Fall" were playing with the same idea. Although teachers may figure variously in the myth as Eve, the Serpent, or God, they are almost always the flaming cherubim who bar our return to the innocence of early childhood. For better or for worse, a teacher was our first surrogate mother. The wicked stepmother and the fairy godmother are *mothers*, after all, and in the fairy tales of personal history they both tend to have teaching licenses. In other words, the story of our first encounter with school is either the tale of how we betrayed our mothers for a princess or the tale of how they abandoned us to a witch.

And the last chapter mirrors the first: the teacher who took us from our   10
mothers appears in another guise to take our children from us later on. The teacher who is a boy's first crush is also his mother's first rival. Furthermore, in an era when mothers frequently work outside the home, a teacher with the benefit of a shorter day and a longer summer vacation not only spends the best hours of the day with our children; she spends the brightest days of the year with her own. I believe this accounts for much of the disdain for teachers, particularly in working-class communities like mine. If someone gave me the power and the money to make one change that might improve the public perception of teachers, I would give working parents more time with their kids. At the very least, that would remind them to be grateful for the hours their kids are in school.

There are, of course, other ways in which schools represent a psychic fall; and teachers, the guardian angels of its trajectory. Although schools in a democracy purport to exist for the creation of "a level playing field," it does not take us long to discover that level playing fields exist mainly to sort out winners from losers. Unless we came from a large family with parents who went out of their way to play favorites, school was our first introduction to the idea of relative merit. It is not an idea with as much application to the so-called real world as we might think. Neither are any number of schoolhouse rigors justified in that name. Certainly we encounter relative merit in the world. My work as an adult is evaluated and rewarded, and I must face the fact that others are going to be better at it than I am.

But that oppressive sense of minute gradation, of success not as a mansion of many rooms but as a ladder of infinite rungs — where does that exist but in a classroom, or in the imagination of the adult who still sits there? To be a kid again, I must walk to my assigned place in a room ranked with little desks, each occupied by a writer my age, or as he was at my age. And the Updike kid always has his hand up first, and the teacher can't seem to get enough of his stories about rabbits, whereas my poems about turtles always seem to lag behind in her esteem. "Taking your degree" is the most precise phrase in all of education: that is what we take from our first day in kindergarten, our *degree* of relative worth. The educational apple of Adam's Fall, by which the first American primer said "we sinnéd all," did not give us the knowledge of good and evil but of good, better, and best, world without end.

Another way in which our teachers took us out of the Garden was by taking us out of the moment. It was in school that the future first began its incessant bullying of the present and the past. The watchword was "preparation," and, considered only by the criterion of effective pedagogy, the watchword could hardly be called progressive. Ask a random sample of parents if and when school began to grow sour for their kids, and they will usually say "sometime around fourth or fifth grade"; that is, when teachers began working with a more intentional zeal to "get kids ready for high school," a process that might be likened to getting Sir John Gielgud ready to do a Pepsi commercial. Diminishment follows diminishment, until we reach graduate school, where the ability and certainly the desire to teach are not only rare but generally held in contempt. Few can go that far without developing grave suspicions about the future — perhaps one reason why so many people end up stalled in graduate school. The Serpent promised that we would become "as gods," though it seems that what he really meant is that with the right amount of training and gumption we could become as serpents.

For some of us that meant we could become teachers. We could bring the process of preparation full circle, like the myth of the serpent that devours its own tail. That is, admittedly, a paradoxical image. To be a teacher in America is to embody any number of seeming contradictions, some peculiar to the profession and others intrinsic to the nature of democracy itself.

For one thing, teachers can find themselves an embarrassing exception to   15
the first article of their own creed: that education prepares one to be privileged and prosperous. Of the professional classes, theirs is probably one of the least esteemed; it is certainly one of the least paid. Teaching has traditionally been a port of entry, the Ellis Island by which the children of blue-collar workers entered the professional classes. I seldom see a first-year teacher with

her tote bag or briefcase without conjuring up the image of an immigrant and his duffel bag of worldly belongings — so full of faith, so free of cynicism, so ripe for exploitation. And such an easy target for prejudice.

Occupying a no-man's-land between the union hall and the reserved parking space, able in some cases to take a sabbatical but in many cases unable to get to a toilet, teachers sometimes find themselves caught in a cross-fire of contradictory resentments. On the one hand, the public expects teachers to have some of the same expertise and even some of the same polish as physicians, though no teacher of my acquaintance has ever had the opportunity of hiring his own nurse in the form of a classroom aide — assuming he even had one. On the other hand, those who see teachers as no more than a highly specialized class of clock-punchers are prone to ask what truck driver ever had a nine-week vacation, or what waitress ever had a pension fund.

It almost goes without saying that a teacher's perceived status will vary with the status of the perceiver. So to the svelte mom in the Volvo, Ms. Hart is an air-headed twit without a creative bone in her body, who probably had to write crib notes all over her chubby little hand just to get through Hohum State College with a C. To the burly dad in the rusty pickup truck, Ms. Hart is a book-addled flake without a practical bone in her body but with plenty of good teeth in her head thanks to a dental plan that comes out of said dad's property taxes. In Shakespeare's *King Henry VI*, a common rebel known as Dick the Butcher says, "The first thing we do, let's kill all the lawyers," but to honor the sentiments inside as well as outside the palace Ms. Hart has to die first.

Of course there are any number of parents, in Volvos, old Fords, and on Harley-Davidsons, who will see Ms. Hart as an angel. And of those who see otherwise, might at least a few be responding to her pedagogical competence rather than to her professional status? Undoubtedly so. Teachers probably provide some of the most and least inspiring examples we have of human beings in the act of work. A friend of mine remarked to me recently, "No one, not even a farmer, works harder than a hardworking teacher. But there is nothing on this earth lazier than a lazy teacher." Having taught school for a good part of my adult life, I tend to agree. I wouldn't say that extremes of this kind are unique to teachers, however. I would propose that the same extremes can be found in any occupation that shares the following characteristics: a notable degree of specialized training, a mission to help other human beings, a duty to help them irrespective of their ability to pay, and a measure of authority that comes from all of the above. In short, the extremes of character and performance that exist among teachers also exist among doctors and police. But most of us, even if we grow up to be invalids or criminals, will have spent more time with teachers than with either of their counterparts.

What also sets teachers apart is the milder consequences of their extremes. Doctors and cops can kill somebody or save her life; teachers at their worst or best can usually do no more than to ruin or to improve it. Because the extremes of benefit and detriment are less, the mystique may be less also. But because those extremes do exist and are so noticeable, the mediocre quality of the mediocre teacher tends to be noticeable as well. An average guy seldom looks more average than in front of a classroom.

In a society that touts both "excellence" and "equality," teachers are per- 20 haps our best example of the complex interplay of those two values — both in the evaluative nature of their work and in their own status as workers. We put them down in the clichés of populist rhetoric and we put them up in the titanium shrines of space shuttles, but the truth is, taken as a whole, they're probably more representative of "ordinary Americans" than any single occupational group. If I were Arthur Miller, I would not have made Willy Loman a salesman; I would have made him a teacher. In the lines in which Willy calls the Chevrolet "the greatest car ever built" and then, several pages later, says, "That goddamn Chevrolet, they ought to prohibit the manufacture of that car!" I would have him talking about the American public school.

Yet another way in which the conflicting currents of our democracy affect our resentment of teachers has to do with how we conceive of service, which is not much different from how Süleyman the Magnificent conceived of service. In aristocratic societies, service is the butler who appears when the master pulls the velvet bell rope. In a society like ours, service is the desk clerk who's supposed to come running (with a smile) whenever any tourist slaps the bell. Our version may be the more "democratic," but like the Greeks, whose democracies preceded our own, we always seem to need a few slaves in order to feel truly emancipated.

It would be foolish to suggest that teachers are a kind of slave. It would be equally foolish to forget that not so long ago they were virtually a kind of indentured servant. That they have advanced beyond servitude is not always regarded as a cause for celebration. Add teachers to that list of groups and persons who eventually "got so uppity" that they threatened to diminish the status that came of having them under our thumbs. Here again I must be careful not to overstate my case. One of my favorite school stories has to do with a principal who told a friend of mine that although he understood his frustration when his son's teacher consistently failed to return his phone calls, he should understand that "returning calls has never been Mrs. Van Winkle's strength."

Still, even when one allows for the maddening imperviousness — and equally maddening impunity — of certain teachers, one is still struck from time to time by the popular assumption that public schools, like Third World bazaars and Atlantic City casinos, ought to be places where the almighty spender can throw his weight around like Almighty God. Whenever one hears that dearly beloved phrase "local control," and one hears it in my corner of New England about once a day, the accent is usually on *control*; and the control, firmly on the teachers. Of course this is also true beyond the local level, most recently in proposals to fingerprint teachers in order to "protect children." What politician as keen on protecting his or her career as on protecting children would ever propose fingerprinting clergy, orthodontists, or live-in boyfriends? Not to forget every legislator employing a page.

For the most part, though, I do not hear teachers criticized for having slipped their leashes so much as for having dropped their halos. "Teachers are not supposed to be in it for the money; they're supposed to be in it for the children" — a sentiment that sounds reasonable enough until we remember that even the most altruistic teachers have been known to produce children, and that teachers' children have been known to eat. Still, one can almost hear the aggrieved tones of unrequited love in the voices of those who wistfully recall the days "when a teacher was respected" and wouldn't have known what to do with anything so crass as a dollar bill, not if you taped it to her nose.

Once again there's a contradiction lurking under the rhetoric, which   25
reveals a cultural contradiction as well. Teachers are also resented *for* their altruism, and one does not have to look too far for examples of the resentment. I remember sitting next to a father at Town Meeting who in his litany of grievances against teachers closed with this: "They teach kids not to work." It was a hardworking man who said this. What I think he meant was: "They teach kids that there are other things in life *besides* work, that is, besides work done for money." I recall another father, also hardworking but with the added perspective of being a teacher's husband, who gave as his explanation for the bitter controversy surrounding a guidance counselor at his school: "I think people resent her goodness."

It was a remark that struck home, in part because home for me is a hard-scrabble place where many people have led very hard lives. In their eyes, teachers make children unfit to live in a world where survival belongs to the toughest. Special education, cooperative learning, second chances — even art and music — are "fine for some," but what have such things to do with real life as these people have known it? And if all this coddling is indeed valuable, does that mean that a hard life is not? I'm told there's a Sicilian proverb that says, "It's a foolish man who educates his children so they can despise him." It's a foolish man who doesn't see that fear at the root of nearly everything we might call reactionary.

People are said to hate change, even though in our society political change, at least, is supposed to come about by the will of the people. I imagine that for many of them hating teachers comes down to the same thing. Whenever our society changes, or wishes to change, or pretends that it wishes to change, schools and teachers are enlisted in the cause. If we decide that cyberspace is the place to go, we start by sending the second grade. If we come to fear that morality is going to hell in a handbasket, we draw up a curriculum of "values-based" education. No teacher can hear the phrase "launching a new initiative" without knowing that the launching pad is going to be located on top of his desk.

If we oppose a given change, we may be inclined to disdain the teacher who carries it forward, though in many cases this amounts to hearing bad news and killing the messenger. Our chagrin can come not only from the change itself but from the sense of having to subsidize our own obsolescence. We shall never require a sign outside a school building that reads YOUR TAX

DOLLARS AT WORK: people feel them at work, no less than the workings of their own bowels, which is why, in times of unsettling social change and political insecurity, citizens will sometimes descend with merciless indignation on a school budget. The first thing we do, let's kill all the special programs. I have even heard people say, "It's the one thing left that I have some control over."

But schools have not only been placed in the vanguard of change; they have in many ways been used to contain and minimize change. So if, for instance, we want to continue to practice de facto racial segregation, we can pretend otherwise by busing children between racially homogeneous schools. If we are content to see the gap between rich and poor grow wider every year, but wish to seem more "compassionate," we can try to establish some semblance of equity in the funding of public education. Ostensibly, our guiding principle here is that the first step in changing society for the better is changing schools.

That is a fairly sound guiding principle — provided that the *first* step   30
doesn't wind up being the *only* step. Schools can indeed be better places than the communities that sustain them, but never much better, and never better for long. In the end, we can only change the world by changing the world. When something happens in a schoolyard to remind us of this, something awful and sad, we lash out at "the teachers" and "the schools." They were supposed to be making the world a better place, or at least maintaining the illusion that we wanted them to.

Public schools embody our democratic principles and contradictions better than any other institution we know. In schools we behold our own spitting image as a people who value equality but crave excellence, who live for the moment but bet on the future, who espouse altruism but esteem self-reliance, who sincerely believe in change but just as sincerely doubt that change will do them any good. Whether we call these contradictions schizophrenia or creative tension, beauty or ugliness, will depend on the eye of the beholder. Public-school teachers themselves are no less an embodiment of the same contradictions, just as in the broadest sense all teachers embody the subjects that they teach. At least the more memorable ones do. Think of it sometime: lean Mr. Silverstein didn't teach you math; he *was* math, fleshed out in its angular glory. All of this is to say that the best teaching is incarnational. Teaching is the *word* — the music, the formula, and even the Constitution of the United States — made flesh and dwelling among us.

The forty-odd years that I have spent in school are not unlike the forty-eight years I have spent in my body, a mix of pain and pleasure in which the pain has perhaps been more intense but the pleasure more constant, more influential, and, in some way I can't entirely explain, more true. At some level it was most fitting that my mother sent me off to school that morning, and every morning, by handing me my lunch, as if to say that the part of me that learns is one with the part that eats, even if on certain mornings it was also one with the part that pukes. In contrast, the daydream of the boy

I was at six, playing among the tombstones when he ought to have been at school, amounts to a wish for disembodiment. It is the vision of a gnostic heaven, in which the emancipated spirits of the elect rise from the complications of the flesh, not in a new body but in no body at all.

The same can be said for many of the present initiatives to diminish radically the scope of public education in America, if not to abolish it altogether. The utopian school, the cyber-school, the voucher-subsidized school, the school of "school choice," all reduce to a fantasy of social and political transcendence — an attempt to sidestep the contradictions of democracy, the cruel jokes of genetics, the crueler jokes of class, and the darker side of diversity. If we can but find the right gnosis, you see, the secret path to educational enlightenment, we shall at last be able to shed the blemished, prickly skin of the body politic and live as unencumbered spirits with harps and cornets or whichever golden instrument best accompanies the appropriate lifestyle choice. It may sound like a return to Eden, like the miraculous reversal of some irreversible fall, but make no mistake; it is the equivalent of a wish for death.

QUESTIONS

1. This essay is about teachers and includes an explanation of why we feel emotionally about them, but it is finally an argument about schools and what we should and shouldn't expect of them. Summarize this argument.
2. Consider Keizer's explanation of why we feel strongly about teachers, particularly the comparison to the wicked stepmothers and fairy godmothers of folk tales. How persuasive are these and similar explanatory passages in this essay? That is, do they work for you? Why or why not?
3. One element of argument is establishing the authority of the speaker for the statements that he or she makes. How does Keizer attempt to do this?
4. A good argument presents counterarguments and deals with them. Can you find examples of this process in Keizer's essay?
5. Long essays, like this one, need to repeat ideas, phrases, and images throughout the text. Can you find examples of this kind of repetition in Keizer's essay?
6. This essay mixes personal experiences with a generalized argument. Consider some examples of Keizer's use of personal experiences. How effectively does he move from the personal level to a general level?
7. You know a lot about schools and teachers. Take Keizer's title (or a variant on it), and produce an essay of your own on that topic.

MAKING CONNECTIONS

Look at other essays about education in this collection — by Theodore R. Sizer (p. 345), Frederick Douglass (p. 62), and Phillip Richards (p. 632).

Write an essay in which you consider what education is — and what teaching and learning are and should be. Draw on these essays and your own experiences to make an argument about current and ideal teaching and learning. As in the case of many of the essays you are reading, you may find that you need to develop your own definitions of the key terms.

Social Sciences and Public Affairs

WHAT'S SO BAD ABOUT HATE

Andrew Sullivan

Born in Godstone, England, in 1963, Andrew Sullivan attended Oxford University and afterward came to the United States to pursue his M.A. and Ph.D. at Harvard. He worked for many years as a staff writer and editor for The New Republic *and is currently a contributing writer for various publications. He has also written two provocative books:* Virtually Normal: An Argument about Homosexuality *(1995), in which he argues in favor of full gay rights, including same-sex marriages; and* Love Undetectable: Notes on Friendship, Sex, and Survival *(1998), in which he reflects on his own status as an HIV-positive gay man. Paradoxically, Sullivan most often casts himself as a political and social conservative, as suggested by the following essay, which originally appeared in* The New York Times Magazine *in 1999.*

I

I wonder what was going on in John William King's head two years ago when he tied James Byrd Jr.'s feet to the back of a pickup truck and dragged him three miles down a road in rural Texas. King and two friends had picked up Byrd, who was black, when he was walking home, half-drunk, from a party. As part of a bonding ritual in their fledgling white supremacist group, the three men took Byrd to a remote part of town, beat him and chained his legs together before attaching them to the truck. Pathologists at King's trial testified that Byrd was probably alive and conscious until his body finally hit a culvert and split in two. When King was offered a chance to say something to Byrd's family at the trial, he smirked and uttered an obscenity.

We know all these details now, many months later. We know quite a large amount about what happened before and after. But I am still drawn, again and again, to the flash of ignition, the moment when fear and loathing became hate, the instant of transformation when King became hunter and Byrd became prey.

What was that? And what was it when Buford Furrow Jr., longtime member of the Aryan Nations,[1] calmly walked up to a Filipino-American mailman he happened to spot, asked him to mail a letter and then shot him at point-blank range? Or when Russell Henderson beat Matthew Shepard, a young gay man, to a pulp, removed his shoes and then, with the help of a friend, tied him to a post, like a dead coyote, to warn off others?

For all our documentation of these crimes and others, our political and moral disgust at them, our morbid fascination with them, our sensitivity to their social meaning, we seem at times to have no better idea now than we ever had of what exactly they were about. About what that moment means when, for some reason or other, one human being asserts absolute, immutable superiority over another. About not the violence, but what the violence expresses. About what—exactly—hate is. And what our own part in it may be.

I find myself wondering what hate actually is in part because we have created an entirely new offense in American criminal law—a "hate crime"—to combat it. And barely a day goes by without someone somewhere declaring war against it. Last month President Clinton called for an expansion of hate-crime laws as "what America needs in our battle against hate." A couple of weeks later, Senator John McCain used a campaign speech to denounce the "hate" he said poisoned the land. New York's Mayor, Rudolph Giuliani, recently tried to stop the Million Youth March in Harlem on the grounds that the event was organized by people "involved in hate marches and hate rhetoric."

The media concurs in its emphasis. In 1985, there were 11 mentions of "hate crimes" in the national media database Nexis. By 1990, there were more than a thousand. In the first six months of 1999, there were 7,000. "Sexy fun is one thing," wrote a *New York Times* reporter about sexual assaults in Woodstock '99's mosh pit. "But this was an orgy of lewdness tinged with hate." And when Benjamin Smith marked the Fourth of July this year by targeting blacks, Asians and Jews for murder in Indiana and Illinois, the story wasn't merely about a twisted young man who had emerged on the scene. As the *Times* put it, "Hate arrived in the neighborhoods of Indiana University, in Bloomington, in the early-morning darkness."

But what exactly was this thing that arrived in the early-morning darkness? For all our zeal to attack hate, we still have a remarkably vague idea of what it actually is. A single word, after all, tells us less, not more. For all its emotional punch, "hate" is far less nuanced an idea than prejudice, or

---

[1] *Aryan Nations:* A paramilitary, pseudo-theological hate group that advocates anti-Semitism and the establishment of a white racist state.

bigotry, or bias, or anger, or even mere aversion to others. Is it to stand in for all these varieties of human experience—and everything in between? If so, then the war against it will be so vast as to be quixotic. Or is "hate" to stand for a very specific idea or belief, or set of beliefs, with a very specific object or group of objects? Then waging war against it is almost certainly unconstitutional. Perhaps these kinds of questions are of no concern to those waging war on hate. Perhaps it is enough for them that they share a sentiment that there is too much hate and never enough vigilance in combating it. But sentiment is a poor basis for law, and a dangerous tool in politics. It is better to leave some unwinnable wars unfought.

II

Hate is everywhere. Human beings generalize all the time, ahead of time, about everyone and everything. A large part of it may even be hard-wired. At some point in our evolution, being able to know beforehand who was friend or foe was not merely a matter of philosophical reflection. It was a matter of survival. And even today it seems impossible to feel a loyalty without also feeling a disloyalty, a sense of belonging without an equal sense of unbelonging. We're social beings. We associate. Therefore we disassociate. And although it would be comforting to think that the one could happen without the other, we know in reality that it doesn't. How many patriots are there who have never felt a twinge of xenophobia?

Of course by hate, we mean something graver and darker than this kind of lazy prejudice. But the closer you look at this distinction, the fuzzier it gets. Much of the time, we harbor little or no malice toward people of other backgrounds or places or ethnicities or ways of life. But then a car cuts you off at an intersection and you find yourself noticing immediately that the driver is a woman, or black, or old, or fat, or white, or male. Or you are walking down a city street at night and hear footsteps quickening behind you. You look around and see that it is a white woman and not a black man, and you are instantly relieved. These impulses are so spontaneous they are almost involuntary. But where did they come from? The mindless need to be mad at someone—anyone—or the unconscious eruption of a darker prejudice festering within?

In 1993, in San Jose, Calif., two neighbors—one heterosexual, one   10
homosexual—were engaged in a protracted squabble over grass clippings. (The full case is recounted in *Hate Crimes*, by James B. Jacobs and Kimberly Potter.) The gay man regularly mowed his lawn without a grass catcher, which prompted his neighbor to complain on many occasions that grass clippings spilled over onto his driveway. Tensions grew until one day, the gay man mowed his front yard, spilling clippings onto his neighbor's driveway, prompting the straight man to yell an obscene and common anti-gay insult. The wrangling escalated. At one point, the gay man agreed to collect the clippings from his neighbor's driveway but then later found them dumped

on his own porch. A fracas ensued with the gay man spraying the straight man's son with a garden hose, and the son hitting and kicking the gay man several times, yelling anti-gay slurs. The police were called, and the son was eventually convicted of a hate-motivated assault, a felony. But what was the nature of the hate: anti-gay bias, or suburban property-owner madness?

Or take the Labor Day parade last year in Broad Channel, a small island in Jamaica Bay, Queens. Almost everyone there is white, and in recent years a group of local volunteer firefighters has taken to decorating a pickup truck for the parade in order to win the prize for "funniest float." Their themes have tended toward the outrageously provocative. Beginning in 1995, they won prizes for floats depicting "Hasidic Park," "Gooks of Hazzard" and "Happy Gays." Last year, they called their float "Black to the Future, Broad Channel 2098." They imagined their community a century hence as a largely black enclave, with every stereotype imaginable: watermelons, basketballs and so on. At one point during the parade, one of them mimicked the dragging death of James Byrd. It was caught on videotape, and before long the entire community was depicted as a caldron of hate.

It's an interesting case, because the float was indisputably in bad taste and the improvisation on the Byrd killing was grotesque. But was it hate? The men on the float were local heroes for their volunteer work; they had no record of bigoted activity, and were not members of any racist organizations. In previous years, they had made fun of many other groups and saw themselves more as provocateurs than bigots. When they were described as racists, it came as a shock to them. They apologized for poor taste but refused to confess to bigotry. "The people involved aren't horrible people," protested a local woman. "Was it a racist act? I don't know. Are they racists? I don't think so."

If hate is a self-conscious activity, she has a point. The men were primarily motivated by the desire to shock and to reflect what they thought was their community's culture. Their display was not aimed at any particular black people, or at any blacks who lived in Broad Channel—almost none do. But if hate is primarily an unconscious activity, then the matter is obviously murkier. And by taking the horrific lynching of a black man as a spontaneous object of humor, the men were clearly advocating indifference to it. Was this an aberrant excess? Or the real truth about the men's feelings toward African-Americans? Hate or tastelessness? And how on earth is anyone, even perhaps the firefighters themselves, going to know for sure?

Or recall H. L. Mencken.[2] He shared in the anti-Semitism of his time with more alacrity than most and was an indefatigable racist. "It is impossible," he wrote in his diary, "to talk anything resembling discretion or judgment into a colored woman. They are all essentially childlike, and even hard experience does not teach them anything." He wrote at another time of the "psychological stigmata" of the "Afro-American race." But it is also

---

[2]*H. L. Mencken* (1880–1956): An American writer, editor, and critic. [Eds.]

true that, during much of his life, day to day, Mencken conducted himself with no regard to race, and supported a politics that was clearly integrationist. As the editor of his diary has pointed out, Mencken published many black authors in his magazine, *The Mercury*, and lobbied on their behalf with his publisher, Alfred A. Knopf. The last thing Mencken ever wrote was a diatribe against racial segregation in Baltimore's public parks. He was good friends with leading black writers and journalists, including James Weldon Johnson, Walter White and George S. Schuyler, and played an underappreciated role in promoting the Harlem Renaissance.

What would our modern view of hate do with Mencken? Probably   15 ignore him, or change the subject. But, with regard to hate, I know lots of people like Mencken. He reminds me of conservative friends who oppose almost every measure for homosexual equality yet genuinely delight in the company of their gay friends. It would be easier for me to think of them as haters, and on paper, perhaps, there is a good case that they are. But in real life, I know they are not. Some of them clearly harbor no real malice toward me or other homosexuals whatsoever.

They are as hard to figure out as those liberal friends who support every gay rights measure they have ever heard of but do anything to avoid going into a gay bar with me. I have to ask myself in the same, frustrating kind of way: are they liberal bigots or bigoted liberals? Or are they neither bigots nor liberals, but merely people?

III

Hate used to be easier to understand. When Sartre[3] described anti-Semitism in his 1946 essay "Anti-Semite and Jew," he meant a very specific array of firmly held prejudices, with a history, an ideology and even a pseudo-science to back them up. He meant a systematic attempt to demonize and eradicate an entire race. If you go to the Web site of the World Church of the Creator, the organization that inspired young Benjamin Smith to murder in Illinois earlier this year, you will find a similarly bizarre, pseudorational ideology. The kind of literature read by Buford Furrow before he rained terror on a Jewish kindergarten last month and then killed a mailman because of his color is full of the same paranoid loopiness. And when we talk about hate, we often mean this kind of phenomenon.

But this brand of hatred is mercifully rare in the United States. These professional maniacs are to hate what serial killers are to murder. They should certainly not be ignored; but they represent what Harold Meyerson, writing in *Salon*, called "niche haters": cold-blooded, somewhat deranged, often poorly socialized psychopaths. In a free society with relatively easy access to guns, they will always pose a menace.

---

[3]*Jean-Paul Sartre* (1905–1980): A French philosopher and writer. [Eds.]

But their menace is a limited one, and their hatred is hardly typical of anything very widespread. Take Buford Furrow. He famously issued a "wake-up call" to "kill Jews" in Los Angeles, before he peppered a Jewish community center with gunfire. He did this in a state with two Jewish female Senators, in a city with a large, prosperous Jewish population, in a country where out of several million Jewish Americans, a total of 66 were reported by the F.B.I. as the targets of hate-crime assaults in 1997. However despicable Furrow's actions were, it would require a very large stretch to describe them as representative of anything but the deranged fringe of an American subculture.

Most hate is more common and more complicated, with as many vari-   20 eties as there are varieties of love. Just as there is possessive love and needy love; family love and friendship; romantic love and unrequited love; passion and respect, affection and obsession, so hatred has its shadings. There is hate that fears, and hate that merely feels contempt; there is hate that expresses power, and hate that comes from powerlessness; there is revenge, and there is hate that comes from envy. There is hate that was love, and hate that is a curious expression of love. There is hate of the other, and hate of something that reminds us too much of ourselves. There is the oppressor's hate, and the victim's hate. There is hate that burns slowly, and hate that fades. And there is hate that explodes, and hate that never catches fire.

The modern words that we have created to describe the varieties of hate — "sexism," "racism," "anti-Semitism," "homophobia" — tell us very little about any of this. They tell us merely the identities of the victims; they don't reveal the identities of the perpetrators, or what they think, or how they feel. They don't even tell us how the victims feel. And this simplicity is no accident. Coming from the theories of Marxist and post-Marxist academics, these "isms" are far better at alleging structures of power than at delineating the workings of the individual heart or mind. In fact, these "isms" can exist without mentioning individuals at all.

We speak of institutional racism, for example, as if an institution can feel anything. We talk of "hate" as an impersonal noun, with no hater specified. But when these abstractions are actually incarnated, when someone feels something as a result of them, when a hater actually interacts with a victim, the picture changes. We find that hates are often very different phenomena one from another, that they have very different psychological dynamics, that they might even be better understood by not seeing them as varieties of the same thing at all.

There is, for example, the now unfashionable distinction between reasonable hate and unreasonable hate. In recent years, we have become accustomed to talking about hates as if they were all equally indefensible, as if it could never be the case that some hates might be legitimate, even necessary. But when some 800,000 Tutsis are murdered under the auspices of a Hutu regime in Rwanda, and when a few thousand Hutus are killed in revenge, the hates are not commensurate. Genocide is not an event like a hurricane, in which damage is random and universal; it is a planned and often merciless attack of one group upon another. The hate of the perpetrators is a monstrosity. The hate of the victims, and their survivors, is justified. What else, one wonders, were surviving Jews supposed to feel toward Germans after the Holocaust? Or, to a different degree, South African blacks after apartheid? If the victims overcome this hate, it is a supreme moral achievement. But if they don't, the victims are not as culpable as the perpetrators. So the hatred of Serbs for Kosovars today can never be equated with the hatred of Kosovars for Serbs.

Hate, like much of human feeling, is not rational, but it usually has its reasons. And it cannot be understood, let alone condemned, without knowing them. Similarly, the hate that comes from knowledge is always different from the hate that comes from ignorance. It is one of the most foolish clichés of our time that prejudice is always rooted in ignorance, and can usually be overcome by familiarity with the objects of our loathing. The racism of many Southern whites under segregation was not appeased by familiarity with Southern blacks; the virulent loathing of Tutsis by many Hutus was not undermined by living next door to them for centuries. Theirs was a hatred that sprang, for whatever reasons, from experience. It cannot easily be compared with, for example, the resilience of anti-Semitism in Japan, or hostility to immigration in areas where immigrants are unknown, or fear of homosexuals by people who have never knowingly met one.

The same familiarity is an integral part of what has become known as   25
"sexism." Sexism isn't, properly speaking, a prejudice at all. Few men live without knowledge or constant awareness of women. Every single sexist man was born of a woman, and is likely to be sexually attracted to women. His hostility is going to be very different than that of, say, a reclusive member of the Aryan Nations toward Jews he has never met.

In her book *The Anatomy of Prejudices*, the psychotherapist Elisabeth Young-Bruehl proposes a typology of three distinct kinds of hate: obsessive, hysterical and narcissistic. It's not an exhaustive analysis, but it's a beginning in any serious attempt to understand hate rather than merely declaring war on it. The obsessives, for Young-Bruehl, are those, like the Nazis or Hutus, who fantasize a threat from a minority, and obsessively try to rid themselves of it. For them, the very existence of the hated group is threatening. They often describe their loathing in almost physical terms: they experience what Patrick Buchanan, in reference to homosexuals, once described as a "visceral recoil" from the objects of their detestation. They often describe those they hate as diseased or sick, in need of a cure. Or they talk of "cleansing" them, as the Hutus talked of the Tutsis, or call them "cockroaches," as Yitzhak Shamir[4] called the Palestinians. If you read material from the Family Research Council, it is clear that the group regards homosexuals as similar contaminants. A recent posting on its Web site about syphilis among gay men was headlined, "Unclean."

---

[4]*Yitzhak Shamir* (b. 1915): A former Israeli prime minister. [Eds.]

Hysterical haters have a more complicated relationship with the objects of their aversion. In Young-Bruehl's words, hysterical prejudice is a prejudice that "a person uses unconsciously to appoint a group to act out in the world forbidden sexual and sexually aggressive desires that the person has repressed." Certain kinds of racists fit this pattern. White loathing of blacks is, for some people, at least partly about sexual and physical envy. A certain kind of white racist sees in black America all those impulses he wishes most to express himself but cannot. He idealizes in "blackness" a sexual freedom, a physical power, a Dionysian[5] release that he detests but also longs for. His fantasy may not have any basis in reality, but it is powerful nonetheless. It is a form of love-hate, and it is impossible to understand the nuances of racism in, say, the American South, or in British Imperial India, without it.

Unlike the obsessives, the hysterical haters do not want to eradicate the objects of their loathing; rather they want to keep them in some kind of permanent and safe subjugation in order to indulge the attraction of their repulsion. A recent study, for example, found that the men most likely to be opposed to equal rights for homosexuals were those most likely to be aroused by homoerotic imagery. This makes little rational sense, but it has a certain psychological plausibility. If homosexuals were granted equality, then the hysterical gay-hater might panic that his repressed passions would run out of control, overwhelming him and the world he inhabits.

A narcissistic hate, according to Young-Bruehl's definition, is sexism. In its most common form, it is rooted in many men's inability even to imagine what it is to be a woman, a failing rarely challenged by men's control of our most powerful public social institutions. Women are not so much hated by most men as simply ignored in nonsexual contexts, or never conceived of as true equals. The implicit condescension is mixed, in many cases, with repressed and sublimated erotic desire. So the unawareness of women is sometimes commingled with a deep longing or contempt for them.

Each hate, of course, is more complicated than this, and in any one person hate can assume a uniquely configured combination of these types. So there are hysterical sexists who hate women because they need them so much, and narcissistic sexists who hardly notice that women exist, and sexists who oscillate between one of these positions and another. And there are gay-bashers who are threatened by masculine gay men and gay-haters who feel repulsed by effeminate ones. The soldier who beat his fellow soldier Barry Winchell to death with a baseball bat in July had earlier lost a fight to him. It was the image of a macho gay man—and the shame of being bested by him—that the vengeful soldier had to obliterate, even if he needed a gang of accomplices and a weapon to do so. But the murderers of Matthew Shepard seem to have had a different impulse: a visceral disgust at the thought of any sexual contact with an effeminate homosexual. Their

30

---

[5]*Dionysian:* Ecstatic, orgiastic. Dionysus was the Greek god of wine and a fertility cult that celebrated nature. [Eds.]

anger was mixed with mockery, as the cruel spectacle at the side of the road suggested.

In the same way, the pathological anti-Semitism of Nazi Germany was obsessive, inasmuch as it tried to cleanse the world of Jews; but also, as Daniel Jonah Goldhagen shows in his book, *Hitler's Willing Executioners*, hysterical. The Germans were mysteriously compelled as well as repelled by Jews, devising elaborate ways, like death camps and death marches, to keep them alive even as they killed them. And the early Nazi phobia of interracial sex suggests as well a lingering erotic quality to the relationship, partaking of exactly the kind of sexual panic that persists among some homosexual-haters and anti-miscegenation racists. So the concept of "homophobia," like that of "sexism" and "racism," is often a crude one. All three are essentially cookie-cutter formulas that try to understand human impulses merely through the one-dimensional identity of the victims, rather than through the thoughts and feelings of the haters and hated.

This is deliberate. The theorists behind these "isms" want to ascribe all blame to one group in society—the "oppressors"—and render specific others—the "victims"—completely blameless. And they want to do this in order in part to side unequivocally with the underdog. But it doesn't take a genius to see how this approach, too, can generate its own form of bias. It can justify blanket condemnations of whole groups of people—white straight males for example—purely because of the color of their skin or the nature of their sexual orientation. And it can condescendingly ascribe innocence to whole groups of others. It does exactly what hate does: it hammers the uniqueness of each individual into the anvil of group identity. And it postures morally over the result.

In reality, human beings and human acts are far more complex, which is why these "isms" and the laws they have fomented are continually coming under strain and challenge. Once again, hate wriggles free of its definers. It knows no monolithic groups of haters and hated. Like a river, it has many eddies, backwaters and rapids. So there are anti-Semites who actually admire what they think of as Jewish power, and there are gay-haters who look up to homosexuals and some who want to sleep with them. And there are black racists, racist Jews, sexist women and anti-Semitic homosexuals. Of course there are.

IV

Once you start thinking of these phenomena less as the "isms" of sexism, racism and "homophobia," once you think of them as independent psychological responses, it's also possible to see how they can work in a bewildering variety of ways in a bewildering number of people. To take one obvious and sad oddity: people who are demeaned and objectified in society may develop an aversion to their tormentors that is more hateful in its expression than the prejudice they have been subjected to. The F.B.I. statistics on hate crimes throws up an interesting point. In America in the 1990's, blacks were up to three times as likely as whites to commit a hate crime, to express their hate by physically attacking their targets or their property. Just as sexual abusers have often been victims of sexual abuse, and wife-beaters often grew up in violent households, so hate criminals may often be members of hated groups.

Even the Columbine murderers were in some sense victims of hate before   35
they were purveyors of it. Their classmates later admitted that Dylan Klebold and Eric Harris were regularly called "faggots" in the corridors and classrooms of Columbine High and that nothing was done to prevent or stop the harassment. This climate of hostility doesn't excuse the actions of Klebold and Harris, but it does provide a more plausible context. If they had been black, had routinely been called "nigger" in the school and had then exploded into a shooting spree against white students, the response to the matter might well have been different. But the hate would have been the same. In other words, hate-victims are often hate-victimizers as well. This doesn't mean that all hates are equivalent, or that some are not more justified than others. It means merely that hate goes both ways; and if you try to regulate it among some, you will find yourself forced to regulate it among others.

It is no secret, for example, that some of the most vicious anti-Semites in America are black, and that some of the most virulent anti-Catholic bigots in America are gay. At what point, we are increasingly forced to ask, do these phenomena become as indefensible as white racism or religious toleration of anti-gay bigotry? That question becomes all the more difficult when we notice that it is often minorities who commit some of the most hate-filled offenses against what they see as their oppressors. It was the mainly gay AIDS activist group Act Up that perpetrated the hateful act of desecrating Communion hosts at a Mass at St. Patrick's Cathedral in New York. And here is the playwright Tony Kushner, who is gay, responding to the Matthew Shepard beating in *The Nation* magazine: "Pope John Paul II endorses murder. He, too, knows the price of discrimination, having declared anti-Semitism a sin. . . . He knows that discrimination kills. But when the Pope heard the news about Matthew Shepard, he, too, worried about spin. And so, on the subject of gay-bashing, the Pope and his cardinals and his bishops and priests maintain their cynical political silence. . . . To remain silent is to endorse murder." Kushner went on to describe the Pope as a "homicidal liar."

Maybe the passion behind these words is justified. But it seems clear enough to me that Kushner is expressing hate toward the institution of the Catholic Church, and all those who perpetuate its doctrines. How else to interpret the way in which he accuses the Pope of cynicism, lying and murder? And how else either to understand the brutal parody of religious vocations expressed by the Sisters of Perpetual Indulgence, a group of gay men who dress in drag as nuns and engage in sexually explicit performances in public? Or T-shirts with the words "Recovering Catholic" on them, hot items among some gay and lesbian activists? The implication that someone's religious faith is a mental illness is clearly an expression of contempt. If that isn't covered under the definition of hate speech, what is?

Or take the following sentence: "The act male homosexuals commit is ugly and repugnant and afterwards they are disgusted with themselves. They drink and take drugs to palliate this, but they are disgusted with the act and they are always changing partners and cannot be really happy." The thoughts of Pat Robertson or Patrick Buchanan? Actually that sentence was written by Gertrude Stein,[6] one of the century's most notable lesbians. Or take the following, about how beating up "black boys like that made us feel *good* inside. . . . Every time I drove my foot into his [expletive], I felt better." It was written to describe the brutal assault of an innocent bystander for the sole reason of his race. By the end of the attack, the victim had blood gushing from his mouth as his attackers stomped on his genitals. Are we less appalled when we learn that the actual sentence was how beating up "white boys like that made us feel *good* inside. . . . Every time I drove my foot into his [expletive], I felt better?" It was written by Nathan McCall, an African-American who later in life became a successful journalist at the *Washington Post* and published his memoir of this "hate crime" to much acclaim.

In fact, one of the stranger aspects of hate is that the prejudice expressed by a group in power may often be milder in expression than the prejudice felt by the marginalized. After all, if you already enjoy privilege, you may not feel the anger that turns bias into hate. You may not need to. For this reason, most white racism may be more influential in society than most black racism—but also more calmly expressed.

So may other forms of minority loathing—especially hatred within   40
minorities. I'm sure that black conservatives like Clarence Thomas or Thomas Sowell have experienced their fair share of white racism. But I wonder whether it has ever reached the level of intensity of the hatred directed toward them by other blacks? In several years of being an openly gay writer and editor, I have experienced the gamut of responses to my sexual orientation. But I have only directly experienced articulated, passionate hate from other homosexuals. I have been accused over the years by other homosexuals of being a sellout, a hypocrite, a traitor, a sexist, a racist, a narcissist, a snob. I've been called selfish, callous, hateful, self-hating and malevolent. At a reading, a group of lesbian activists portrayed my face on a poster within the crossfires of a gun. Nothing from the religious right has come close to such vehemence.

I am not complaining. No harm has ever come to me or my property, and much of the criticism is rooted in the legitimate expression of political differences. But the visceral tone and style of the gay criticism can only be described as hateful. It is designed to wound personally, and it often does. But its intensity comes in part, one senses, from the pain of being excluded for so long, of anger long restrained bubbling up and directing itself more aggressively toward an alleged traitor than an alleged enemy. It is the hate of

---

[6]These words were not written by Gertrude Stein. Ernest Hemingway wrote them and attributed them to Stein in *A Moveable Feast* (1964). [Eds.]

the hated. And it can be the most hateful hate of all. For this reason, hate-crime laws may themselves be an oddly biased category — biased against the victims of hate. Racism is everywhere, but the already victimized might be more desperate, more willing to express it violently. And so more prone to come under the suspicious eye of the law.

V

And why is hate for a group worse than hate for a person? In Laramie, Wyo., the now-famous epicenter of "homophobia," where Matthew Shepard was brutally beaten to death, vicious murders are not unknown. In the previous 12 months, a 15-year-old pregnant girl was found east of the town with 17 stab wounds. Her 38-year-old boyfriend was apparently angry that she had refused an abortion and left her in the Wyoming foothills to bleed to death. In the summer of 1998, an 8-year-old Laramie girl was abducted, raped and murdered by a pedophile, who disposed of her young body in a garbage dump. Neither of these killings was deemed a hate crime, and neither would be designated as such under any existing hate-crime law. Perhaps because of this, one crime is an international legend; the other two are virtually unheard of.

But which crime was more filled with hate? Once you ask the question, you realize how difficult it is to answer. Is it more hateful to kill a stranger or a lover? Is it more hateful to kill a child than an adult? Is it more hateful to kill your own child than another's? Under the law before the invention of hate crimes, these decisions didn't have to be taken. But under the law after hate crimes, a decision is essential. A decade ago, a murder was a murder. Now, in the era when group hate has emerged as our cardinal social sin, it all depends.

The supporters of laws against hate crimes argue that such crimes should be disproportionately punished because they victimize more than the victim. Such crimes, these advocates argue, spread fear, hatred and panic among whole populations, and therefore merit more concern. But, of course, all crimes victimize more than the victim, and spread alarm in the society at large. Just think of the terrifying church shooting in Texas only two weeks ago.[7] In fact, a purely random murder may be even more terrifying than a targeted one, since the entire community, and not just a part of it, feels threatened. High rates of murder, robbery, assault and burglary victimize everyone, by spreading fear, suspicion and distress everywhere. Which crime was more frightening to more people this summer: the mentally ill Buford Furrow's crazed attacks in Los Angeles, killing one, or Mark Barton's murder of his own family and several random day-traders in Atlanta, killing 12? Almost certainly the latter. But only Furrow was guilty of "hate."

---

[7]*Church shooting:* On September 15, 1999, Larry Gene Ashbrook fired into an evening youth service at Wedgwood Baptist Church in Fort Worth, Texas, killing six people before taking his own life. [Eds.]

One response to this objection is that certain groups feel fear more   45
intensely than others because of a history of persecution or intimidation.
But doesn't this smack of a certain condescension toward minorities? Why,
after all, should it be assumed that gay men or black women or Jews, for
example, are as a group more easily intimidated than others? Surely in any
of these communities there will be a vast range of responses, from panic to
concern to complete indifference. The assumption otherwise is the kind of
crude generalization the law is supposed to uproot in the first place. And
among these groups, there are also likely to be vast differences. To equate a
population once subjected to slavery with a population of Mexican immigrants or third-generation Holocaust survivors is to equate the unequat-
able. In fact, it is to set up a contest of vulnerability in which one group vies
with another to establish its particular variety of suffering, a contest that
can have no dignified solution.

Rape, for example, is not classified as a "hate crime" under most existing laws, pitting feminists against ethnic groups in a battle for recognition. If,
as a solution to this problem, everyone, except the white straight able-bodied
male, is regarded as a possible victim of a hate crime, then we have simply
created a two-tier system of justice in which racial profiling is reversed, and
white straight men are presumed guilty before being proven innocent, and
members of minorities are free to hate them as gleefully as they like. But if we
include the white straight male in the litany of potential victims, then we have
effectively abolished the notion of a hate crime altogether. For if every crime
is possibly a hate crime, then it is simply another name for crime. All we will
have done is widened the search for possible bigotry, ratcheted up the sentences for everyone and filled the jails up even further.

Hate-crime-law advocates counter that extra penalties should be
imposed on hate crimes because our society is experiencing an "epidemic" of
such crimes. Mercifully, there is no hard evidence to support this notion. The
Federal Government has only been recording the incidence of hate crimes in
this decade, and the statistics tell a simple story. In 1992, there were 6,623
hate-crime incidents reported to the F.B.I. by a total of 6,181 agencies, covering 51 percent of the population. In 1996, there were 8,734 incidents
reported by 11,355 agencies, covering 84 percent of the population. That
number dropped to 8,049 in 1997. These numbers are, of course, hazardous.
They probably underreport the incidence of such crimes, but they are the only
reliable figures we have. Yet even if they are faulty as an absolute number,
they do not show an epidemic of "hate crimes" in the 1990's.

Is there evidence that the crimes themselves are becoming more vicious?
None. More than 60 percent of recorded hate crimes in America involve no
violent, physical assault against another human being at all, and, again,
according to the F.B.I., that proportion has not budged much in the 1990's.
These impersonal attacks are crimes against property or crimes of "intimidation." Murder, which dominates media coverage of hate crimes, is a tiny
proportion of the total. Of the 8,049 hate crimes reported to the F.B.I. in
1997, a total of eight were murders. Eight. The number of hate crimes that

were aggravated assaults (generally involving a weapon) in 1997 is less than 15 percent of the total. That's 1,237 assaults too many, of course, but to put it in perspective, compare it with a reported 1,022,492 "equal opportunity" aggravated assaults in America in the same year. The number of hate crimes that were physical assaults is half the total. That's 4,000 assaults too many, of course, but to put it in perspective, it compares with around 3.8 million "equal opportunity" assaults in America annually.

The truth is, the distinction between a crime filled with personal hate and a crime filled with group hate is an essentially arbitrary one. It tells us nothing interesting about the psychological contours of the specific actor or his specific victim. It is a function primarily of politics, of special interest groups carving out particular protections for themselves, rather than a serious response to a serious criminal concern. In such an endeavor, hate-crime-law advocates cram an entire world of human motivations into an immutable, tiny box called hate, and hope to have solved a problem. But nothing has been solved; and some harm may even have been done.

In an attempt to repudiate a past that treated people differently because 50 of the color of their skin, or their sex, or religion or sexual orientation, we may merely create a future that permanently treats people differently because of the color of their skin, or their sex, religion or sexual orientation. This notion of a hate crime, and the concept of hate that lies behind it, takes a psychological mystery and turns it into a facile political artifact. Rather than compounding this error and extending it even further, we should seriously consider repealing the concept altogether.

To put it another way: Violence can and should be stopped by the government. In a free society, hate can't and shouldn't be. The boundaries between hate and prejudice and between prejudice and opinion and between opinion and truth are so complicated and blurred that any attempt to construct legal and political fire walls is a doomed and illiberal venture. We know by now that hate will never disappear from human consciousness; in fact, it is probably, at some level, definitive of it. We know after decades of education measures that hate is not caused merely by ignorance; and after decades of legislation, that it isn't caused entirely by law.

To be sure, we have made much progress. Anyone who argues that America is as inhospitable to minorities and to women today as it has been in the past has not read much history. And we should, of course, be vigilant that our most powerful institutions, most notably the government, do not actively or formally propagate hatred; and insure that the violent expression of hate is curtailed by the same rules that punish all violent expression.

But after that, in an increasingly diverse culture, it is crazy to expect that hate, in all its variety, can be eradicated. A free country will always mean a hateful country. This may not be fair, or perfect, or admirable, but it is reality, and while we need not endorse it, we should not delude ourselves into thinking we can prevent it. That is surely the distinction between toleration and tolerance. Tolerance is the eradication of hate; toleration is co-existence despite it. We might do better as a culture and as a polity if we concentrated more on achieving the latter rather than the former. We would certainly be less frustrated.

And by aiming lower, we might actually reach higher. In some ways, some expression of prejudice serves a useful social purpose. It lets off steam; it allows natural tensions to express themselves incrementally; it can siphon off conflict through words, rather than actions. Anyone who has lived in the ethnic shouting match that is New York City knows exactly what I mean. If New Yorkers disliked each other less, they wouldn't be able to get on so well. We may not all be able to pull off a Mencken—bigoted in words, egalitarian in action—but we might achieve a lesser form of virtue: a human acceptance of our need for differentiation, without a total capitulation to it.

Do we not owe something more to the victims of hate? Perhaps we do.   55
But it is also true that there is nothing that government can do for the hated that the hated cannot better do for themselves. After all, most bigots are not foiled when they are punished specifically for their beliefs. In fact, many of the worst haters crave such attention and find vindication in such rebukes. Indeed, our media's obsession with "hate," our elevation of it above other social misdemeanors and crimes, may even play into the hands of the pathetic and the evil, may breathe air into the smoldering embers of their paranoid loathing. Sure, we can help create a climate in which such hate is disapproved of—and we should. But there is a danger that if we go too far, if we punish it too much, if we try to abolish it altogether, we may merely increase its mystique, and entrench the very categories of human difference that we are trying to erase.

For hate is only foiled not when the haters are punished but when the hated are immune to the bigot's power. A hater cannot psychologically wound if a victim cannot psychologically be wounded. And that immunity to hurt can never be given; it can merely be achieved. The racial epithet only strikes at someone's core if he lets it, if he allows the bigot's definition of him to be the final description of his life and his person—if somewhere in his heart of hearts, he believes the hateful slur to be true. The only final answer to this form of racism, then, is not majority persecution of it, but minority indifference to it. The only permanent rebuke to homophobia is not the enforcement of tolerance, but gay equanimity in the face of prejudice. The only effective answer to sexism is not a morass of legal proscriptions, but the simple fact of female success. In this, as in so many other things, there is no solution to the problem. There is only a transcendence of it. For all our rhetoric, hate will never be destroyed. Hate, as our predecessors knew better, can merely be overcome.

Questions

1. Sullivan's argument begins with his title, which contains the premise "hate *is* so bad." Suppose the title ended with a question mark. How might a question affect your reading of the text?

2. In many arguments, the writer begins by defining terms. What problems does Sullivan run into when defining *hate*?
3. Why does Sullivan call the hate-crime law a "facile political artifact" (paragraph 50)? Do you agree with him? Explain.
4. What does Sullivan mean by "A free country will always mean a hateful country" (paragraph 53)?
5. Sullivan concludes that "hate will never be destroyed. . . . [It] can merely be overcome" (paragraph 56). He suggests that we concentrate on achieving "toleration" rather than "tolerance" (paragraph 53). What do you think of this conclusion? Does the evidence that he presents substantiate his opening premise? Explain.
6. Find a newspaper or newsmagazine account of a recent crime of violence that has been characterized as a hate crime, and, using some of Sullivan's terms and issues, argue whether the crime may or may not be defined that way.

MAKING CONNECTIONS

For a long essay, do some research like that suggested in item 6 above. Assemble a group of news stories detailing violent crimes, and analyze the answers given to the question that is always asked: Why did he/she/they do it? Use your material as the basis for an argument. You may wish to take up Sullivan's questioning of the hate crime law, or you may find that your material leads you toward a different thesis.

A MODEST PROPOSAL

Jonathan Swift

Jonathan Swift (1667–1745) was born in Dublin, Ireland, of English parents and was educated in Irish schools. A graduate of Trinity College, Dublin, he received a master's degree from Oxford and was ordained as a priest in the Church of England in 1695. He was active in politics as well as religion, becoming an editor and pamphlet writer for the Tory party in 1710. After becoming Dean of St. Patrick's Cathedral, Dublin, in 1713, he settled in Ireland and began to take an interest in the English economic exploitation of Ireland, gradually becoming a fierce Irish patriot. By 1724, the English were offering a reward for the discovery of the writer of the Drapier's Letters, *a series of pamphlets that were secretly written by Swift and attacked the British for their treatment of Ireland. In 1726, Swift produced the first volume of a more universal satire, known to modern readers as* Gulliver's Travels, *which has kept his name alive for 250 years. "A Modest Proposal," his best-known essay on Irish affairs, appeared in 1729.*

A Modest Proposal
for Preventing the Children of Poor People in Ireland
from Being a Burden to Their Parents or Country,
and for Making Them Beneficial to the Public

It is a melancholy object to those who walk through this great town,[1] or travel in the country, when they see the streets, the roads and cabin-doors crowded with beggars of the female sex, followed by three, four, or six children, all in rags, and importuning every passenger for an alms. These mothers, instead of being able to work for their honest livelihood, are forced to employ all their time in strolling, to beg sustenance for their helpless infants, who, as they grow up, either turn thieves for want of work, or leave their dear native country to fight for the Pretender in Spain,[2] or sell themselves to the Barbadoes.[3]

---

[1] *this great town:* Dublin. [Eds.]

[2] *Pretender in Spain:* A Catholic descendant of the British royal family (James I, Charles I, Charles II, and James II) of Stuart. Exiled to France and Spain so that England could be governed by Protestant rulers, the Stuarts prepared various disastrous schemes for regaining the throne. [Eds.]

[3] *sell themselves to the Barbadoes:* Sell themselves as indentured servants, a sort of temporary slavery, to the sugar merchants of the British Caribbean islands. [Eds.]

I think it is agreed by all parties that this prodigious number of children, in the arms, or on the backs, or at the heels of their mothers, and frequently of their fathers, is in the present deplorable state of the kingdom a very great additional grievance; and therefore whoever could find out a fair, cheap, and easy method of making these children sound and useful members of the commonwealth would deserve so well of the public as to have his statue set up for a preserver of the nation.

But my intention is very far from being confined to provide only for the children of professed beggars; it is of a much greater extent, and shall take in the whole number of infants at a certain age who are born of parents in effect as little able to support them as those who demand our charity in the streets.

As to my own part, having turned my thoughts for many years upon this important subject, and maturely weighed the several schemes of other projectors, I have always found them grossly mistaken in their computation. It is true a child just dropped from its dam may be supported by her milk for a solar year with little other nourishment, at most not above the value of two shillings,[4] which the mother may certainly get, or the value in scraps, by her lawful occupation of begging, and it is exactly at one year old that I propose to provide for them, in such a manner as, instead of being a charge upon their parents, or the parish, or wanting food and raiment for the rest of their lives, they shall, on the contrary, contribute to the feeding and partly to the clothing of many thousands.

There is likewise another great advantage to my scheme, that it will prevent those voluntary abortions, and that horrid practice of women murdering their bastard children, alas, too frequent among us, sacrificing the poor innocent babes, I doubt, more to avoid the expense than the shame, which would move tears and pity in the most savage and inhuman breast.

The number of souls in Ireland being usually reckoned one million and a half, of these I calculate there may be about two hundred thousand couples whose wives are breeders, from which number I subtract thirty thousand couples who are able to maintain their own children, although I apprehend there cannot be so many under the present distresses of the kingdom, but this being granted, there will remain an hundred and seventy thousand breeders. I again subtract fifty thousand for those women who miscarry, or whose children die by accident or disease within the year. There only remain an hundred and twenty thousand children of poor parents annually born: the question therefore is, how this number shall be reared, and provided for, which as I have already said, under the present situation of affairs is utterly impossible by all the methods hitherto proposed, for we can neither employ them in handicraft or agriculture; we neither build houses (I mean in the country), nor cultivate land: they can very seldom

---

[4]*shillings:* A shilling used to be worth about one day's labor. [Eds.]

pick up a livelihood by stealing until they arrive at six years old, except where they are of towardly parts, although I confess they learn the rudiments much earlier, during which time they can however be properly looked upon only as probationers, as I have been informed by a principal gentleman in the County of Cavan, who protested to me that he never knew above one or two instances under the age of six, even in a part of the kingdom so renowned for the quickest proficiency in that art.

I am assured by our merchants that a boy or girl before twelve years old, is no saleable commodity, and even when they come to this age, they will not yield above three pounds, or three pounds and half-a-crown at most on the Exchange, which cannot turn to account either to the parents or the kingdom, the charge of nutriment and rags having been at least four times that value.

I shall now therefore humbly propose my own thoughts, which I hope will not be liable to the least objection.

I have been assured by a very knowing American of my acquaintance in London, that a young healthy child well nursed is at a year old a most delicious, nourishing and wholesome food, whether stewed, roasted, baked, or boiled, and I make no doubt that it will equally serve in a fricassee, or a ragout.

I do therefore humbly offer it to public consideration, that of the hundred and twenty thousand children already computed, twenty thousand may be reserved for breed, whereof only one fourth part to be males, which is more than we allow to sheep, black-cattle, or swine, and my reason is that these children are seldom the fruits of marriage, a circumstance not much regarded by our savages, therefore one male will be sufficient to serve four females. That the remaining hundred thousand may at a year old be offered in sale to the persons of quality, and fortune, through the kingdom, always advising the mother to let them suck plentifully in the last month, so as to render them plump, and fat for a good table. A child will make two dishes at an entertainment for friends, and when the family dines alone, the fore or hind quarters will make a reasonable dish, and seasoned with a little pepper or salt will be very good boiled on the fourth day, especially in winter.

10

I have reckoned upon a medium, that a child just born will weigh twelve pounds, and in a solar year if tolerably nursed increaseth to twenty-eight pounds.

I grant this food will be somewhat dear, and therefore very proper for landlords, who, as they have already devoured most of the parents, seem to have the best title to the children.

Infant's flesh will be in season throughout the year, but more plentiful in March, and a little before and after, for we are told by a grave author, an eminent French physician,[5] that fish being a prolific diet, there

---

[5]*French physician*: François Rabelais (1494?–1553), a French physician and satirist who is known for his novel, *Gargantua and Pantagruel*. [Eds.]

are more children born in Roman Catholic countries about nine months after Lent than at any other season; therefore reckoning a year after Lent, the markets will be more glutted than usual, because the number of Popish infants is at least three to one in this kingdom, and therefore it will have one other collateral advantage by lessening the number of Papists among us.

I have already computed the charge of nursing a beggar's child (in which list I reckon all cottagers, laborers, and four-fifths of the farmers) to be about two shillings *per annum*, rags included, and I believe no gentleman would repine to give ten shillings for the carcass of a good fat child, which, as I have said, will make four dishes of excellent nutritive meat, when he hath only some particular friend of his own family to dine with him. Thus the Squire will learn to be a good landlord and grow popular among his tenants, the mother will have eight shillings net profit, and be fit for work until she produces another child.

Those who are more thrifty (as I must confess the times require) may flay the carcass; the skin of which artificially dressed, will make admirable gloves for ladies, and summer boots for fine gentlemen.   15

As to our city of Dublin, shambles[6] may be appointed for this purpose, in the most convenient parts of it, and butchers we may be assured will not be wanting, although I rather recommend buying the children alive, and dressing them hot from the knife, as we do roasting pigs.

A very worthy person, a true lover of his country, and whose virtues I highly esteem was lately pleased, in discoursing on this matter to offer a refinement upon my scheme. He said that many gentlemen of this kingdom, having of late destroyed their deer, he conceived that the want of venison might be well supplied by the bodies of young lads and maidens, not exceeding fourteen years of age, nor under twelve, so great a number of both sexes in every county being now ready to starve, for want of work and service: and these to be disposed of by their parents if alive, or otherwise by their nearest relations. But with due deference to so excellent a friend, and so deserving a patriot, I cannot be altogether in his sentiments. For as to the males, my American acquaintance assured me from frequent experience that their flesh was generally tough and lean, like that of our schoolboys, by continual exercise, and their taste disagreeable, and to fatten them would not answer the charge. Then as to the females, it would, I think with humble submission, be a loss to the public, because they soon would become breeders themselves: and besides, it is not improbable that some scrupulous people might be apt to censure such a practice (although indeed very unjustly) as a little bordering upon cruelty, which I confess, hath always been with me the strongest objection against any project, howsoever well intended.

---

[6]*shambles:* Slaughterhouses. [Eds.]

But in order to justify my friend, he confessed that this expedient was put into his head by the famous Psalmanazar, a native of the island Formosa, who came from thence to London, above twenty years ago, and in conversation told my friend that in his country when any young person happened to be put to death, the executioner sold the carcass to persons of quality, as a prime dainty, and that, in his time, the body of a plump girl of fifteen, who was crucified for an attempt to poison the emperor, was sold to his Imperial Majesty's Prime Minister of State, and other great Mandarins of the Court, in joints from the gibbet, at four hundred crowns. Neither indeed can I deny that if the same use were made of several plump young girls in this town who, without one single groat to their fortunes, cannot stir abroad without a chair, and appear at the playhouse and assemblies in foreign fineries, which they never will pay for, the kingdom would not be the worse.

Some persons of a desponding spirit are in great concern about that vast number of poor people, who are aged, diseased, or maimed, and I have been desired to employ my thoughts what course may be taken to ease the nation of so grievous an encumbrance. But I am not in the least pain upon that matter, because it is very well known that they are every day dying, and rotting, by cold, and famine, and filth, and vermin, as fast as can be reasonably expected. And as to the younger laborers they are now in almost as hopeful a condition. They cannot get work, and consequently pine away from want of nourishment, to a degree that if at any time they are accidentally hired to common labor, they have not strength to perform it; and thus the country and themselves are in a fair way of being soon delivered from the evils to come.

I have too long digressed, and therefore shall return to my subject. I   20
think the advantages by the proposal which I have made are obvious and many, as well as of the highest importance.

For first, as I have already observed, it would greatly lessen the number of Papists, with whom we are yearly over-run, being the principal breeders of the nation, as well as our most dangerous enemies, and who stay at home on purpose with a design to deliver the kingdom to the Pretender, hoping to take their advantage by the absence of so many good Protestants, who have chosen rather to leave their country than stay at home and pay tithes against their conscience to an idolatrous Episcopal curate.

Secondly, the poorer tenants will have something valuable of their own, which by law may be made liable to distress, and help to pay their landlord's rent, their corn and cattle being already seized, and money a thing unknown.

Thirdly, whereas the maintenance of an hundred thousand children, from two years old, and upwards, cannot be computed at less than ten shillings a piece *per annum*, the nation's stock will be thereby increased fifty thousand pounds *per annum*, besides the profit of a new dish, introduced to the tables of all gentlemen of fortune in the kingdom, who have any refinement in taste, and the money will circulate among ourselves, the goods being entirely of our own growth and manufacture.

Fourthly, the constant breeders, besides the gain of eight shillings sterling *per annum*, by the sale of their children, will be rid of the charge of maintaining them after the first year.

Fifthly, this food would likewise bring great custom to taverns, where   25
the vintners will certainly be so prudent as to procure the best receipts for dressing it to perfection, and consequently have their houses frequented by all the fine gentlemen, who justly value themselves upon their knowledge in good eating; and a skillful cook, who understands how to oblige his guests, will contrive to make it as expensive as they please.

Sixthly, this would be a great inducement to marriage, which all wise nations have either encouraged by rewards, or enforced by laws and penalties. It would increase the care and tenderness of mothers towards their children, when they were sure of a settlement for life, to the poor babes, provided in some sort by the public to their annual profit instead of expense. We should soon see an honest emulation among the married women, which of them could bring the fattest child to the market. Men would become as fond of their wives, during the time of their pregnancy, as they are now of their mares in foal, their cows in calf, or sows when they are ready to farrow, nor offer to beat or kick them (as it is too frequent a practice) for fear of a miscarriage.

Many other advantages might be enumerated. For instance, the addition of some thousand carcasses in our exportation of barreled beef; the propagation of swine's flesh, and improvement in the art of making good bacon, so much wanted among us by the great destruction of pigs, too frequent at our tables, are no way comparable in taste or magnificence to a well-grown, fat yearling child, which roasted whole will make a considerable figure at a Lord Mayor's feast, or any other public entertainment. But this and many others I omit, being studious of brevity.

Supposing that one thousand families in this city would be constant customers for infants' flesh, besides others who might have it at merry meetings, particularly weddings and christenings; I compute that Dublin would take off annually about twenty thousand carcasses, and the rest of the kingdom (where probably they will be sold somewhat cheaper) the remaining eighty thousand.

I can think of no one objection that will possibly be raised against this proposal, unless it should be urged that the number of people will be thereby much lessened in the kingdom. This I freely own, and it was indeed one principal design in offering it to the world. I desire the reader will observe, that I calculate my remedy *for this one individual Kingdom of* Ireland, *and for no other that ever was, is, or, I think, ever can be upon earth.* Therefore let no man talk to me of other expedients: *Of taxing our absentees at five shillings a pound: Of using neither clothes, nor household furniture, except what is of our own growth and manufacture: Of utterly rejecting the materials and instruments that promote foreign luxury: Of curing the expensiveness of pride, vanity, idleness, and gaming in our women: Of introducing a vein of parsimony, prudence, and temperance: Of learning to love our country, wherein we differ even from* Laplanders, *and the inhabitants of*

Topinamboo: *Of quitting our animosities and factions, nor act any longer like the* Jews, *who were murdering one another at the very moment their city was taken: Of being a little cautious not to sell our country and consciences for nothing: Of teaching landlords to have at least one degree of mercy towards their tenants.* Lastly, *of putting a spirit of honesty, industry, and skill into our shopkeepers, who, if a resolution could now be taken to buy only our native goods, would immediately unite to cheat and exact upon us in the price, the measure and the goodness, nor could ever yet be brought to make one fair proposal of just dealing, though often and earnestly invited to it.*

Therefore I repeat, let no man talk to me of these and the like expedi-   30
ents, till he hath at least a glimpse of hope that there will ever be some hearty and sincere attempt to put them in practice.

But as to myself, having been wearied out for many years with offering vain, idle, visionary thoughts, and at length utterly despairing of success, I fortunately fell upon this proposal, which as it is wholly new, so it hath something solid and real, of no expense and little trouble, full in our own power, and whereby we can incur no danger in disobliging England. For this kind of commodity will not bear exportation, the flesh being of too tender a consistence to admit a long continuance in salt, *although perhaps I could name a country which would be glad to eat up our whole nation without it.*

After all I am not so violently bent upon my own opinion as to reject any offer, proposed by wise men, which shall be found equally innocent, cheap, easy and effectual. But before some thing of that kind shall be advanced in contradiction to my scheme, and offering a better, I desire the author, or authors, will be pleased maturely to consider two points. First, as things now stand, how they will be able to find food and raiment for a hundred thousand useless mouths and backs? And secondly, there being a round million of creatures in human figure, throughout this kingdom, whose whole subsistence put into a common stock would leave them in debt two millions of pounds sterling; adding those who are beggars by profession, to the bulk of farmers, cottagers, and laborers with their wives and children, who are beggars in effect; I desire those politicians who dislike my overture, and may perhaps be so bold to attempt an answer, that they will first ask the parents of these mortals whether they would not at this day think it a great happiness to have been sold for food at a year old, in the manner I prescribe, and thereby have avoided such a perpetual scene of misfortunes as they have since gone through, by the oppression of landlords, the impossibility of paying rent without money or trade, the want of common sustenance, with neither house nor clothes to cover them from the inclemencies of weather, and the most inevitable prospect of entailing the like, or greater miseries upon their breed for ever.

I profess in the sincerity of my heart that I have not the least personal interest in endeavoring to promote this necessary work, having no other motive than the *public good of my country, by advancing our trade, providing for infants, relieving the poor, and giving some pleasure to the rich.* I have no children by which I can propose to get a single penny; the youngest being nine years old, and my wife past child-bearing.

QUESTIONS

1. A proposal always involves a proposer. What is the character of the proposer here? Do we perceive his character to be the same throughout the essay? Compare, for example, paragraphs 21, 26, and 33.
2. When does the proposer actually offer his proposal? What does he do before making his proposal? What does he do after making his proposal? How does the order in which he does things affect our impression of him and of his proposal?
3. What kinds of counterarguments to his own proposal does this proposer anticipate? How does he answer and refute proposals that might be considered alternatives to his?
4. In reading this essay, most people are certain that the author, Swift, does not endorse the proposer's idea. How do we distinguish between the author and the proposer? What details of style help us make this distinction?
5. Consider the proposer, the counterarguments that he acknowledges and refutes, and Swift himself, who presumably does not endorse the proposal. To what extent is Swift's position essentially the one that his proposer refutes? To what extent is it still a somewhat different position?
6. To what extent does an ironic essay like this depend on shared values that are held by both the author and reader without question or reservation? Can you discover any such values explicitly or implicitly present in Swift's essay?
7. Use Swift's technique to write a "modest proposal" of your own about a contemporary situation. That is, use some outlandish proposal as a way of drawing attention to a situation that needs correcting. Consider carefully the character that you intend to project for your proposer and the way that you intend to make your own view distinguishable from hers or his.

MAKING CONNECTIONS

In "A Statement" (p. 572), Pablo Picasso says that "art is a lie that makes us realize truth." Consider the way that this applies to Swift's essay. Is it a lie? What truth can it be said to make us realize? Consider some of the other works in this volume that might be called art, especially the poems by Emily Dickinson (p. 84), W. H. Auden (p. 261), Randall Jarrell (p. 665), and Gwendolyn Brooks (p. 667). What do they have in common with Swift's essay? Does Picasso's statement apply to all of them? In considering them, be as precise as possible about both the lie part and the truth part of the equation.

THE DECLARATION OF INDEPENDENCE

Thomas Jefferson

Thomas Jefferson (1743–1826) was born in Shadwell, Virginia, attended the College of William and Mary, and became a lawyer. He was elected to the Virginia House of Burgesses in 1769 and was a delegate to the Continental Congress in 1776. When the Congress voted in favor of Richard Henry Lee's resolution that the colonies "ought to be free and independent states," a committee of five members, including John Adams, Benjamin Franklin, and Jefferson, was appointed to draw up a declaration. Jefferson, because of his eloquence as a writer, was asked by this committee to draw up a first draft. Jefferson's text, with a few changes suggested by Franklin and Adams, was presented to the Congress. After a debate in which further changes were made, including striking out a passage condemning the slave trade, the Declaration was approved on July 4, 1776. Jefferson said of it, "Neither aiming at originality of principles or sentiments, nor yet copied from any particular and previous writing, it was intended to be an expression of the American mind."

In Congress, July 4, 1776
The unanimous Declaration of the
thirteen united States of America

When in the Course of human events it becomes necessary for one people to dissolve the political bands which have connected them with another, and to assume among the powers of the earth, the separate and equal station to which the Laws of Nature and of Nature's God entitle them, a decent respect to the opinions of mankind requires that they should declare the causes which impel them to the separation.

We hold these truths to be self-evident, that all men are created equal, that they are endowed by their Creator with certain unalienable Rights, that among these are Life, Liberty and the pursuit of Happiness. That to secure these rights, Governments are instituted among Men, deriving their just powers from the consent of the governed. That whenever any Form of Government becomes destructive of these ends, it is the Right of the People to alter or to abolish it, and to institute new Government, laying its foundation on such principles and organizing its powers in such form, as to them shall seem most likely to affect their Safety and Happiness. Prudence, indeed, will dictate that Governments long established should not be changed for light and transient causes; and accordingly all experience hath shewn that mankind are more disposed to suffer, while evils are sufferable, than to right themselves by abolishing the forms to which they are accustomed. But when a long train of abuses and usurpations, pursuing invariably the same Object evinces a design to reduce them under absolute Despotism, it is their right, it is their duty, to throw off such Government, and to provide new Guards for their future security. Such has been the patient sufferance of these Colonies; and such is now the necessity which constrains them to alter their former Systems of Government. The history of the present King of Great Britain is a history of repeated injuries and usurpations, all having in direct object the establishment of an absolute Tyranny over these States. To prove this, let Facts be submitted to a candid world.

He has refused his Assent to Laws, the most wholesome and necessary for the public good.

He has forbidden his Governors to pass laws of immediate and pressing importance, unless suspended in their operation till his Assent should be obtained; and when so suspended, he has utterly neglected to attend to them.

He has refused to pass other Laws for the accommodation of large districts of people, unless those people would relinquish the right of Representation in the Legislature, a right inestimable to them and formidable to tyrants only.   5

He has called together legislative bodies at places unusual, uncomfortable, and distant from the depository of their Public Records, for the sole purpose of fatiguing them into compliance with his measures.

He has dissolved Representative Houses repeatedly, for opposing with manly firmness his invasions on the rights of the people.

He has refused for a long time, after such dissolutions, to cause others to be elected; whereby the Legislative Powers, incapable of Annihilation, have returned to the People at large for their exercise; the State remaining in the mean time exposed to all the dangers of invasion from without, and convulsions within.

He has endeavored to prevent the population of these States; for that purpose obstructing the Laws for Naturalization of Foreigners; refusing to pass others to encourage their migration hither, and raising the conditions of new Appropriations of Lands.

He has obstructed the Administration of Justice, by refusing his Assent to Laws for Establishing Judiciary Powers.   10

He has made Judges dependent on his Will alone, for the tenure of their offices, and the amount and payment of their salaries.

He has erected a multitude of New Offices, and sent hither swarms of Officers to harass our people, and eat out their substance.

He has kept among us, in times of peace, Standing Armies without the Consent of our legislatures.

He has affected to render the Military independent of and superior to the Civil Power.

He has combined with others to subject us to a jurisdiction foreign to   15
our constitution, and unacknowledged by our laws; giving his Assent to the
Acts of pretended Legislation: For quartering large bodies of armed troops
among us: For protecting them, by a mock Trial, from punishment for any
Murders which they should commit on the Inhabitants of these States: For
cutting off our Trade with all parts of the world: For imposing Taxes on us
without our Consent: For depriving us in many cases, of the benefits of
Trial by Jury: For Transporting us beyond Seas to be tried for pretended
offenses: For abolishing the free System of English Laws in a neighboring
Province, establishing therein an Arbitrary government, and enlarging its
Boundaries so as to render it at once an example and fit instrument for
introducing the same absolute rule into these Colonies: For taking away our
Charters, abolishing our most valuable Laws and altering fundamentally
the Forms of our Governments: For suspending our own Legislatures, and
declaring themselves invested with power to legislate for us in all cases
whatsoever.

He has abdicated Government here, by declaring us out of his Protection and waging War against us.

He has plundered our seas, ravaged our Coasts, burnt our towns, and
destroyed the lives of our people.

He is at this time transporting large Armies of foreign Mercenaries to
complete the works of death, desolation and tyranny, already begun with
circumstances of Cruelty & Perfidy scarcely paralleled in the most bar-
barous ages, and totally unworthy the Head of a civilized nation.

He has constrained our fellow Citizens taken Captive on the high Seas
to bear Arms against their Country, to become the executioners of their
friends and Brethren, or to fall themselves by their Hands.

He has excited domestic insurrections amongst us, and has endeavored   20
to bring on the inhabitants of our frontiers, the merciless Indian Savages,
whose known rule of warfare is an undistinguished destruction of all ages,
sexes, and conditions.

In every stage of these Oppressions We have Petitioned for Redress in
the most humble terms: Our repeated petitions have been answered only by
repeated injury. A Prince, whose character is thus marked by every act which
may define a Tyrant, is unfit to be the ruler of a free people.

Nor have we been wanting in attention to our British brethren. We have
warned them from time to time of attempts by their legislature to extend an
unwarrantable jurisdiction over us. We have reminded them of the circumstances of our emigration and settlement here. We have appealed to their
native justice and magnanimity, and we have conjured them by the ties of
our common kindred to disavow these usurpations, which would inevitably
interrupt our connections and correspondence. They too have been deaf to
the voice of justice and of consanguinity. We must, therefore, acquiesce in the
necessity, which denounces our Separation, and hold them, as we hold the rest
of mankind, Enemies in War, in Peace Friends.

We, THEREFORE, the Representatives of the UNITED STATES OF AMERICA, in General Congress, Assembled, appealing to the Supreme Judge of the world for the rectitude of our intentions, do, in the Name, and by Authority of the good People of these Colonies, solemnly publish and declare, That these United Colonies are, and of Right ought to be FREE AND INDEPENDENT STATES; that they are Absolved from all Allegiance to the British Crown, and that all political connection between them and the State of Great Britain, is and ought to be totally dissolved; and that as Free and Independent States; they have full Power to levy War, conclude Peace, contract Alliances, establish Commerce, and to do all the Acts and Things which Independent States may of right do. And for the support of this Declaration, with a firm reliance on the protection of Divine Providence, we mutually pledge to each other our Lives, our Fortunes, and our sacred Honor.

QUESTIONS

1. The Declaration of Independence is frequently cited as a classic deductive argument. A deductive argument is based on a general statement, or premise, that is assumed to be true. What does this document assume that the American colonists are entitled to, and on what is this assumption based? Look at the reasoning in paragraph 2. What truths are considered self-evident? What does *self-evident* mean?
2. What accusations against the king of Great Britain are the Declaration's facts meant to substantiate? If you were the British king who was presented with this document, how might you reply to it? Would you attack its premise or reply to its accusations? Or would you do both? (How did George III respond?)
3. To what extent is the audience of the Declaration intended to be the king and people of Great Britain?
4. What other audiences were intended for this document? Define at least two other audiences, and describe how each might be expected to respond.
5. Although this declaration could have been expected to lead to war and all the horrors thereof, it is a civilized document, showing great respect throughout for certain standards of civility among people and among nations. Define the civilized standards that the Declaration assumes. Write an essay that identifies and characterizes the nature and variety of those expectations.
6. Write a declaration of your own, announcing your separation from some injurious situation (an incompatible roommate, a noisy sorority or fraternity house, an awful job, or whatever). Start with a premise, give reasons to substantiate it, provide facts that illustrate the injurious conditions, and conclude with a statement of what your new condition will mean to you and to other oppressed people.

MAKING CONNECTIONS

What if, rather than writing the Declaration of Independence, Jefferson had offered "a modest proposal" to the British king? What do you suppose he would have said? How would he have formulated his argument? Write your own "modest proposal" to the king, addressing him more or less in the manner of Jonathan Swift (p. 604) but drawing on the evidence that Jefferson provides in the Declaration.

LETTER FROM BIRMINGHAM JAIL

Martin Luther King Jr.

The son of an Atlanta, Georgia, minister, civil rights leader Martin Luther King Jr. (1929–1968) graduated from Morehouse College and Crozier Theological Seminary before receiving a Ph.D. in theology from Boston University in 1955. He became pastor of Dexter Avenue Baptist Church in Montgomery, Alabama, in 1954 and the next year led a boycott of the city's segregated bus system that brought him national attention when the system began to be integrated in 1956. He organized the Southern Christian Leadership Conference to pursue civil rights gains through nonviolent resistence, and his participation in nonviolent protests led to several arrests. In 1963, King helped plan a massive march on Washington, D.C., where he delivered his famous "I Have a Dream" speech, calling for racial justice. The next year he was awarded the Nobel Prize for peace. He was assassinated in Memphis, Tennessee, at the age of thirty-nine. King wrote the following letter while serving an eight-day jail sentence for participating in protests against segregated businesses in Birmingham, Alabama. In the introduction to its published version, King noted, "This response to a published statement by eight fellow clergymen from Alabama . . . was composed under somewhat constricting circumstance. Begun on the margins of the newspaper in which the statement appeared while I was in jail, the letter was continued on scraps of writing paper supplied by a friendly Negro trusty, and concluded on a pad my attorneys were eventually permitted to leave me. Although the text remains in substance unaltered, I have indulged in the author's prerogative of polishing it for publication."

April 16, 1963

My Dear Fellow Clergymen:

While confined here in the Birmingham city jail, I came across your recent statement calling my present activities "unwise and untimely." Seldom do I pause to answer criticism of my work and ideas. If I sought to answer all the criticisms that cross my desk, my secretaries would have little time for anything other than such correspondence in the course of the day, and I would have no time for constructive work. But since I feel that you are men of genuine good will and that your criticisms are sincerely set forth, I want to try to answer your statement in what I hope will be patient and reasonable terms.

I think I should indicate why I am here in Birmingham, since you have been influenced by the view which argues against "outsiders coming in." I have the honor of serving as president of the Southern Christian Leadership Conference, an organization operating in every southern state, with headquarters in Atlanta, Georgia. We have some eighty-five affiliated organizations across the South, and one of them is the Alabama Christian Movement for Human Rights. Frequently we share staff, educational, and financial resources with our affiliates. Several months ago the affiliate here in Birmingham asked us to be on call to engage in a nonviolent direct-action program if such were deemed necessary. We readily consented, and when the hour came we lived up to our promise. So I, along with several members of my staff, am here because I was invited here. I am here because I have organizational ties here.

But more basically, I am in Birmingham because injustice is here. Just as the prophets of the eighth century B.C. left their villages and carried their "thus saith the Lord" far beyond the boundaries of their home towns, and just as the Apostle Paul left his village of Tarsus and carried the gospel of Jesus Christ to the far corners of the Greco-Roman world, so am I compelled to carry the gospel of freedom beyond my own home town. Like Paul, I must constantly respond to the Macedonian call for aid.[1]

Moreover, I am cognizant of the interrelatedness of all communities and states. I cannot sit idly by in Atlanta and not be concerned about what happens in Birmingham. Injustice anywhere is a threat to justice everywhere. We are caught in an inescapable network of mutuality, tied in a single garment of destiny. Whatever affects one directly, affects all indirectly. Never again can we afford to live with the narrow, provincial, "outside agitator" idea. Anyone who lives inside the United States can never be considered an outsider anywhere within its bounds.

You deplore the demonstrations taking place in Birmingham. But your   5
statement, I am sorry to say, fails to express a similar concern for the conditions that brought about the demonstrations. I am sure that none of you would want to rest content with the superficial kind of social analysis that deals merely with effects and does not grapple with underlying causes. It is unfortunate that demonstrations are taking place in Birmingham, but it is even more unfortunate that the city's white power structure left the Negro community with no alternative.

In any nonviolent campaign there are four basic steps: collection of the facts to determine whether injustices exist; negotiation; self-purification; and direct action. We have gone through all these steps in Birmingham. There can be no gainsaying the fact that racial injustice engulfs this community.

---

[1]*Macedonian call for aid:* A reference to Paul's vision of a Macedonian man requesting help (see Acts 16:9–10). [Eds.]

Birmingham is probably the most thoroughly segregated city in the United States. Its ugly record of brutality is widely known. Negroes have experienced grossly unjust treatment in the courts. There have been more unsolved bombings of Negro homes and churches in Birmingham than in any other city in the nation. These are the hard brutal facts of the case. On the basis of these conditions, Negro leaders sought to negotiate with the city fathers. But the latter consistently refused to engage in good-faith negotiation.

Then, last September, came the opportunity to talk with leaders of Birmingham's economic community. In the course of the negotiations, certain promises were made by the merchants — for example, to remove the stores' humiliating racial signs. On the basis of these promises, the Reverend Fred Shuttlesworth and the leaders of the Alabama Christian Movement for Human Rights agreed to a moratorium on all demonstrations. As the weeks and months went by, we realized that we were the victims of a broken promise. A few signs, briefly removed, returned; the others remained.

As in so many past experiences, our hopes had been blasted, and the shadow of deep disappointment settled upon us. We had no alternative except to prepare for direct action, whereby we would present our very bodies as a means of laying our case before the conscience of the local and the national community. Mindful of the difficulties involved, we decided to undertake a process of self-purification. We began a series of workshops on nonviolence, and we repeatedly asked ourselves: "Are you able to accept blows without retaliating?" "Are you able to endure the ordeal of jail?" We decided to schedule our direct action program for the Easter season, realizing that except for Christmas, this is the main shopping period of the year. Knowing that a strong economic-withdrawal program would be the by-product of direct action, we felt that this would be the best time to bring pressure to bear on the merchants for the needed change.

Then it occurred to us that Birmingham's mayoral election was coming up in March, and we speedily decided to postpone action until after election day. When we discovered that the Commissioner of Public Safety, Eugene "Bull" Connor, had piled up enough votes to be in the run-off, we decided again to postpone action until the day after the run-off so that the demonstrations could not be used to cloud the issues. Like many others, we waited to see Mr. Connor defeated, and to this end we endured postponement after postponement. Having aided in this community need, we felt that our direct-action program could be delayed no longer.

You may well ask, "Why direct action? Why sit-ins, marches, and so 10 forth? Isn't negotiation a better path?" You are quite right in calling for negotiation. Indeed, this is the very purpose of direct action. Nonviolent direct action seeks to create such a crisis and foster such a tension that a community which has constantly refused to negotiate is forced to confront the issue. It seeks so to dramatize the issue that it can no longer be ignored. My citing the creation of tension as part of the work of the nonviolent resister may sound rather shocking. But I must confess that I am not afraid of the word "tension." I have earnestly opposed violent tension, but there is a type of constructive, nonviolent tension which is necessary for growth. Just as Socrates felt that it was necessary to create a tension in the mind so that individuals could rise from the bondage of myths and half truths to the unfettered realm of creative analysis and objective appraisal, so must we see the need for nonviolent gadflies to create the kind of tension in society that will help men rise from the dark depths of prejudice and racism to the majestic heights of understanding and brotherhood.

The purpose of our direct-action program is to create a situation so crisis-packed that it will inevitably open the door to negotiation. I therefore concur with you in your call for negotiation. Too long has our beloved Southland been bogged down in a tragic effort to live in monologue rather than dialogue.

One of the basic points in your statement is that the action that I and my associates have taken in Birmingham is untimely. Some have asked: "Why didn't you give the new city administration time to act?" The only answer that I can give to this query is that the new Birmingham administration must be prodded about as much as the outgoing one, before it will act. We are sadly mistaken if we feel that the election of Albert Boutwell as mayor will bring the millennium[2] to Birmingham. While Mr. Boutwell is a much more gentle person than Mr. Connor, they are both segregationists, dedicated to maintenance of the status quo. I have hoped that Mr. Boutwell will be reasonable enough to see the futility of massive resistance to desegregation. But he will not see this without pressure from devotees of civil rights. My friends, I must say to you that we have not made a single gain in civil rights without determined legal and nonviolent pressure. Lamentably, it is an historical fact that privileged groups seldom give up their privileges voluntarily. Individuals may see the moral light and voluntarily give up their unjust posture; but, as Reinhold Niebuhr[3] has reminded us, groups tend to be more immoral than individuals.

We know through painful experience that freedom is never voluntarily given by the oppressor; it must be demanded by the oppressed. Frankly, I have yet to engage in a direct-action campaign that was "well timed" in the view of those who have not suffered unduly from the disease of segregation. For years now I have heard the word "Wait!" It rings in the ear of every Negro with piercing familiarity. This "Wait" has almost always meant "Never." We must come to see, with one of our distinguished jurists, that "justice too long delayed is justice denied."[4]

We have waited for more than 340 years for our constitutional and God-given rights. The nations of Asia and Africa are moving with jet-like

---

[2]*the millennium:* A reference to the second coming of Christ, which the Book of Revelation says will be followed by a thousand years of peace. [Eds.]

[3]*Reinhold Niebuhr* (1892–1971): A Protestant philosopher who urged church members to put their beliefs into action against social injustice. [Eds.]

[4]*"justice too long delayed is justice denied":* A statement made by U.S. Supreme Court Chief Justice Earl Warren. It was inspired by English writer Walter Savage Landor's statement that "Justice delayed is justice denied." [Eds.]

speed toward gaining political independence, but we still creep at horse-and-buggy pace toward gaining a cup of coffee at a lunch counter. Perhaps it is easy for those who have never felt the stinging darts of segregation to say, "Wait." But when you have seen vicious mobs lynch your mothers and fathers at will and drown your sisters and brothers at whim; when you have seen hate-filled policemen curse, kick, and even kill your black brothers and sisters; when you see the vast majority of your twenty million Negro brothers smothering in an airtight cage of poverty in the midst of an affluent society; when you suddenly find your tongue twisted and your speech stammering as you seek to explain to your six-year-old daughter why she can't go to the public amusement park that has just been advertised on television, and see tears welling up in her eyes when she is told that Funtown is closed to colored children, and see ominous clouds of inferiority beginning to form in her little mental sky, and see her beginning to distort her personality by developing an unconscious bitterness toward white people; when you have to concoct an answer for a five-year-old son who is asking, "Daddy, why do white people treat colored people so mean?"; when you take a cross-country drive and find it necessary to sleep night after night in the uncomfortable corners of your automobile because no motel will accept you; when you are humiliated day in and day out by nagging signs reading "white" and "colored"; when your first name becomes "nigger," your middle name becomes "boy" (however old you are) and your last name becomes "John," and your wife and mother are never given the respected title "Mrs."; when you are harried by day and haunted by night by the fact that you are a Negro, living constantly at tiptoe stance, never quite knowing what to expect next, and are plagued with inner fears and outer resentments; when you are forever fighting a degenerating sense of "nobodiness" — then you will understand why we find it difficult to wait. There comes a time when the cup of endurance runs over, and men are no longer willing to be plunged into the abyss of despair. I hope, sirs, you can understand our legitimate and unavoidable impatience.

You express a great deal of anxiety over our willingness to break laws. 15 This is certainly a legitimate concern. Since we so diligently urge people to obey the Supreme Court's decision of 1954 outlawing segregation in the public schools, at first glance it may seem rather paradoxical for us consciously to break laws. One may then ask: "How can you advocate breaking some laws and obeying others?" The answer lies in the fact that there are two types of laws: just and unjust. I would be the first to advocate obeying just laws. One has not only a legal but a moral responsibility to obey just laws. Conversely, one has a moral responsibility to disobey unjust laws. I would agree with St. Augustine that "an unjust law is no law at all."

Now, what is the difference between the two? How does one determine whether a law is just or unjust? A just law is a manmade code that squares with the moral law or the law of God. An unjust law is a code that is out of harmony with the moral law. To put it in the terms of St. Thomas

Aquinas: An unjust law is a human law that is not rooted in eternal law and natural law. Any law that uplifts human personality is just. Any law that degrades human personality is unjust. All segregation statutes are unjust because segregation distorts the soul and damages the personality. It gives the segregator a false sense of superiority and the segregated a false sense of inferiority. Segregation, to use the terminology of the Jewish philosopher Martin Buber, substitutes an "I-it" relationship for an "I-thou" relationship and ends up relegating persons to the status of things. Hence segregation is not only politically, economically, and sociologically unsound, it is morally wrong and sinful. Paul Tillich has said that sin is separation. Is not segregation an existential expression of man's tragic separation, his awful estrangement, his terrible sinfulness? Thus it is that I can urge men to obey the 1954 decision of the Supreme Court, for it is morally right; and I can urge them to disobey segregation ordinances, for they are morally wrong.

Let us consider a more concrete example of just and unjust laws. An unjust law is a code that a numerical or power majority group compels a minority group to obey but does not make binding on itself. This is *difference* made legal. By the same token, a just law is a code that a majority compels a minority to follow and that it is willing to follow itself. This is *sameness* made legal.

Let me give another explanation. A law is unjust if it is inflicted on a minority that, as a result of being denied the right to vote, had no part in enacting or devising the law. Who can say that the legislature of Alabama which set up that state's segregation laws was democratically elected? Throughout Alabama all sorts of devious methods are used to prevent Negroes from becoming registered voters, and there are some counties in which, even though Negroes constitute a majority of the population, not a single Negro is registered. Can any law enacted under such circumstances be considered democratically structured?

Sometimes a law is just on its face and unjust in its application. For instance, I have been arrested on a charge of parading without a permit. Now, there is nothing wrong in having an ordinance which requires a permit for a parade. But such an ordinance becomes unjust when it is used to maintain segregation and to deny citizens the First Amendment privilege of peaceful assembly and protest.

I hope you are able to see the distinction I am trying to point out. In no sense do I advocate evading or defying the law, as would the rabid segregationist. That would lead to anarchy. One who breaks an unjust law must do so openly, lovingly, and with a willingness to accept the penalty. I submit that an individual who breaks a law that conscience tells him is unjust, and who willingly accepts the penalty of imprisonment in order to arouse the conscience of the community over its injustice, is in reality expressing the highest respect for law.

Of course, there is nothing new about this kind of civil disobedience. It was evidenced subliminally in the refusal of Shadrach, Meshach, and

Abednego to obey the laws of Nebuchadnezzar,[5] on the ground that a higher moral law was at stake. It was practiced superbly by the early Christians, who were willing to face hungry lions and the excruciating pain of chopping blocks rather than submit to certain unjust laws of the Roman Empire. To a degree, academic freedom is a reality today because Socrates practiced civil disobedience. In our own nation, the Boston Tea Party represented a massive act of civil disobedience.

We should never forget that everything Adolf Hitler did in Germany was "legal" and everything the Hungarian freedom fighters did in Hungary was "illegal." It was "illegal" to aid and comfort a Jew in Hitler's Germany. Even so, I am sure that, had I lived in Germany at the time, I would have aided and comforted my Jewish brothers. If today I lived in a Communist country where certain principles dear to the Christian faith are suppressed, I would openly advocate disobeying that country's antireligious laws.

I must make two honest confessions to you, my Christian and Jewish brothers. First, I must confess that over the past few years I have been gravely disappointed with the white moderate. I have almost reached the regrettable conclusion that the Negro's great stumbling block in his stride toward freedom is not the White Citizen's Counciler[6] or the Ku Klux Klanner, but the white moderate, who is more devoted to "order" than to justice; who prefers a negative peace which is the absence of tension to a positive peace which is the presence of justice; who constantly says, "I agree with you in the goal you seek, but I cannot agree with your methods of direct action"; who paternalistically believes he can set the timetable for another man's freedom; who lives by a mythical concept of time and who constantly advises the Negro to wait for a "more convenient season." Shallow understanding from people of good will is more frustrating than absolute misunderstanding from people of ill will. Lukewarm acceptance is much more bewildering than outright rejection.

I had hoped that the white moderate would understand that law and order exist for the purpose of establishing justice and that when they fail in this purpose they become the dangerously structured dams that block the flow of social progress. I had hoped that the white moderate would understand that the present tension in the South is a necessary phase of the transition from an obnoxious negative peace, in which the Negro passively accepted his unjust plight, to a substantive and positive peace, in which all men will respect the dignity and worth of human personality. Actually, we

---

[5]*"the refusal of Shadrach . . . Nebuchadnezzar":* According to the Book of Daniel 1:7–3:30, Nebuchadnezzar (c. 630 B.C.–c. 562 B.C.), king of the Chaldean empire, ordered, Shadrach, Meschach, and Abednego to worship a golden image. When they refused, they were cast into a fiery furnace but remained unharmed. [Eds.]

[6]*White Citizen's Counciler:* A member of an organization that was formed after the U.S. Supreme Court's 1954 *Brown v. Board of Education* decision. Its purpose was to maintain segregation. [Eds.]

who engage in nonviolent direct action are not the creators of tension. We merely bring to the surface the hidden tension that is already alive. We bring it out in the open, where it can be seen and dealt with. Like a boil that can never be cured so long as it is covered up but must be opened with all its ugliness to the natural medicines of air and light, injustice must be exposed, with all the tension its exposure creates, to the light of human conscience and the air of national opinion, before it can be cured.

In your statement you assert that our actions, even though peaceful,   25 must be condemned because they precipitate violence. But is this a logical assertion? Isn't this like condemning a robbed man because his possession of money precipitated the evil act of robbery? Isn't this like condemning Socrates because his unswerving commitment to truth and his philosophical inquiries precipitated the act by the misguided populace in which they made him drink hemlock? Isn't this like condemning Jesus because his unique God-consciousness and never-ceasing devotion to God's will precipitated the evil act of crucifixion? We must come to see that, as the federal courts have consistently affirmed, it is wrong to urge an individual to cease his efforts to gain his basic constitutional rights because the quest may precipitate violence. Society must protect the robbed and punish the robber.

I had also hoped that the white moderate would reject the myth concerning time in relation to the struggle for freedom. I have just received a letter from a white brother in Texas. He writes: "All Christians know that the colored people will receive equal rights eventually, but it is possible that you are in too great a religious hurry. It has taken Christianity almost two thousand years to accomplish what it has. The teachings of Christ take time to come to earth." Such an attitude stems from a tragic misconception of time, from the strangely irrational notion that there is something in the very flow of time that will inevitably cure all ills. Actually, time itself is neutral; it can be used either destructively or constructively. More and more I feel that the people of ill will have used time much more effectively than have the people of good will. We will have to repent in this generation not merely for the hateful words and actions of the bad people, but for the appalling silence of the good people. Human progress never rolls in on wheels of inevitability; it comes through the tireless efforts of men willing to be co-workers with God, and without this hard work, time itself becomes an ally of the forces of social stagnation. We must use time creatively, in the knowledge that the time is always ripe to do right. Now is the time to make real the promise of democracy and transform our pending national elegy into a creative psalm of brotherhood. Now is the time to lift our national policy from the quicksand of racial injustice to the solid rock of human dignity.

You speak of our activity in Birmingham as extreme. At first I was rather disappointed that fellow clergymen would see my nonviolent efforts as those of an extremist. I began thinking about the fact that I stand in the middle of two opposing forces in the Negro community. One is a force of complacency, made up in part of Negroes who, as a result of long years of oppression, are so drained of self-respect and a sense of "somebodiness" that they have adjusted to segregation; and in part of a few middle-class Negroes who, because of a degree of academic and economic security and because in some ways they profit by segregation, have become insensitive to the problems of the masses. The other force is one of bitterness and hatred, and it comes perilously close to advocating violence. It is expressed in the various black nationalist groups that are springing up across the nation, the largest and best known being Elijah Muhammad's Muslim movement. Nourished by the Negro's frustration over the continued existence of racial discrimination, this movement is made up of people who have lost faith in America, who have absolutely repudiated Christianity, and who have concluded that the white man is an incorrigible "devil."

I have tried to stand between these two forces, saying that we need emulate neither the "do-nothingism" of the complacent nor the hatred and despair of the black nationalist. For there is the more excellent way of love and nonviolent protest. I am grateful to God that, through the influence of the Negro church, the way of nonviolence became an integral part of our struggle.

If this philosophy had not emerged, by now many streets of the South would, I am convinced, be flowing with blood. And I am further convinced that if our white brothers dismiss as "rabble-rousers" and "outside agitators" those of us who employ nonviolent direct action, and if they refuse to support our nonviolent efforts, millions of Negroes will, out of frustration and despair, seek solace and security in black nationalist ideologies — a development that would inevitably lead to a frightening racial nightmare.

Oppressed people cannot remain oppressed forever. The yearning for   30
freedom eventually manifests itself, and that is what has happened to the American Negro. Something within has reminded him of his birthright of freedom, and something without has reminded him that it can be gained. Consciously or unconsciously, he has been caught up by the *Zeitgeist*,[7] and with his black brothers of Africa and his brown and yellow brothers of Asia, South America, and the Caribbean, the United States Negro is moving with a sense of great urgency toward the promised land of racial justice. If one recognizes this vital urge that has engulfed the Negro community, one should readily understand why public demonstrations are taking place. The Negro has many pent-up resentments and latent frustrations, and he must release them. So let him march; let him make prayer pilgrimages to the city hall; let him go on freedom rides[8] — and try to understand why he must do so. If his repressed emotions are not released in nonviolent ways, they will seek expression through violence; this is not a threat but a fact of history. So I have not said to my people, "Get rid of your discontent." Rather, I have tried to say that this normal and healthy discontent can be channeled into

---

[7]*Zeitgeist*: The intellectual, moral, and cultural spirit of the times (German). [Eds.]

[8]*freedom rides*: The bus and train rides that black and white protesters took in the early 1960s to protest segregation. [Eds.]

the creative outlet of nonviolent direct action. And now this approach is being termed extremist.

But though I was initially disappointed at being categorized as an extremist, as I continued to think about the matter I gradually gained a measure of satisfaction from the label. Was not Jesus an extremist for love: "Love your enemies, bless them that curse you, do good to them that hate you, and pray for them which despitefully use you, and persecute you." Was not Amos an extremist for justice: "Let justice roll down like waters and righteousness like an everflowing stream." Was not Paul an extremist for the Christian gospel: "I bear in my body the marks of the Lord Jesus." Was not Martin Luther an extremist: "Here I stand; I cannot do otherwise, so help me God." And John Bunyan: "I will stay in jail to the end of my days before I make a butchery of my conscience." And Abraham Lincoln: "This nation cannot survive half slave and half free." And Thomas Jefferson: "We hold these truths to be self-evident, that all men are created equal . . ." So the question is not whether we will be extremists, but what kind of extremists we will be. Will we be extremists for hate or for love? Will we be extremists for the preservation of injustice or for the extension of justice? In that dramatic scene on Calvary's hill three men were crucified. We must never forget that all three were crucified for the same crime — the crime of extremism. Two were extremists for immorality, and thus fell below their environment. The other, Jesus Christ, was an extremist for love, truth, and goodness, and thereby rose above his environment. Perhaps the South, the nation, and the world are in dire need of creative extremists.

I had hoped that the white moderate would see this need. Perhaps I was too optimistic; perhaps I expected too much. I suppose I should have realized that few members of the oppressor race can understand the deep groans and passionate yearnings of the oppressed race, and still fewer have the vision, to see that injustice must be rooted out by strong, persistent, and determined action. I am thankful, however, that some of our white brothers in the South have grasped the meaning of this social revolution and committed themselves to it. They are still all too few in quantity, but they are big in quality. Some — such as Ralph McGill, Lillian Smith, Harry Golden, James McBride Dabbs, Ann Braden, and Sarah Patton Boyle — have written about our struggle in eloquent and prophetic terms. Others have marched with us down nameless streets of the South. They have languished in filthy, roach-infested jails, suffering the abuse and brutality of policemen who view them as "dirty nigger-lovers." Unlike so many of their moderate brothers and sisters, they have recognized the urgency of the moment and sensed the need for powerful "action" antidotes to combat the disease of segregation.

Let me take note of my other major disappointment. I have been so greatly disappointed with the white church and its leadership. Of course, there are some notable exceptions. I am not unmindful of the fact that each of you has taken some significant stands on this issue. I commend you, Reverend Stallings, for your Christian stand on this past Sunday, in welcoming

Negroes to your worship service on a nonsegregated basis. I commend the Catholic leaders of this state for integrating Spring Hill College several years ago.

But despite these notable exceptions, I must honestly reiterate that I have been disappointed with the church. I do not say this as one of those negative critics who can always find something wrong with the church. I say this as a minister of the gospel, who loves the church; who was nurtured in its bosom; who has been sustained by its spiritual blessings and who will remain true to it as long as the cord of life shall lengthen.

When I was suddenly catapulted into the leadership of the bus protest   35 in Montgomery, Alabama, a few years ago, I felt we would be supported by the white church. I felt that the white ministers, priests, and rabbis of the South would be among our strongest allies. Instead, some have been outright opponents, refusing to understand the freedom movement and misrepresenting its leaders; all too many others have been more cautious than courageous and have remained silent behind the anesthetizing security of stained-glass windows.

In spite of my shattered dreams, I came to Birmingham with the hope that the white religious leadership of this community would see the justice of our cause and, with deep moral concern, would serve as the channel through which our just grievances could reach the power structure. I had hoped that each of you would understand. But again I have been disappointed. . . .

There was a time when the church was very powerful — in the time when the early Christians rejoiced at being deemed worthy to suffer for what they believed. In those days the church was not merely a thermometer that recorded the ideas and principles of popular opinion; it was a thermostat that transformed the mores of society. Whenever the early Christians entered a town, the people in power became disturbed and immediately sought to convict the Christians for being "disturbers of the peace" and "outside agitators." But the Christians pressed on, in the conviction that they were "a colony of heaven," called to obey God rather than man. Small in number, they were big in commitment. They were too God-intoxicated to be "astronomically intimidated." By their effort and example they brought an end to such ancient evils as infanticide and gladiatorial contests.

Things are different now. So often the contemporary church is a weak, ineffectual voice with an uncertain sound. So often it is an archdefender of the status quo. Far from being disturbed by the presence of the church, the powerful structure of the average community is consoled by the church's silent — and often even vocal — sanction of things as they are.

But the judgment of God is upon the church as never before. If today's church does not recapture the sacrificial spirit of the early church, it will lose its authenticity, forfeit the loyalty of millions, and be dismissed as an irrelevant social club with no meaning for the twentieth century. Every day I meet young people whose disappointment with the church has turned into outright disgust.

Perhaps I have once again been too optimistic. Is organized religion too   40
inextricably bound to the status quo to save our nation and the world?
Perhaps I must turn my faith to the inner spiritual church, the church within
the church, as the true *ekklesia*[9] and the hope of the world. But again I am
thankful to God that some noble souls from the ranks of organized religion
have broken loose from the paralyzing chains of conformity and joined us as
active partners in the struggle for freedom. They have left their secure con-
gregations and walked the streets of Albany, Georgia, with us. They have
gone down the highways of the South on torturous rides for freedom. Yes,
they have gone to jail with us. Some have been dismissed from their churches,
have lost the support of their bishops and fellow ministers. But they have
acted in the faith that right defeated is stronger than evil triumphant. Their
witness has been the spiritual salt that has preserved the true meaning of the
gospel in these troubled times. They have carved a tunnel of hope through the
dark mountain of disappointment.

I hope the church as a whole will meet the challenge of this decisive
hour. But even if the church does not come to the aid of justice, I have no
despair about the future. I have no fear about the outcome of our struggle
in Birmingham, even if our motives are at present misunderstood. We will
reach the goal of freedom in Birmingham and all over the nation, because
the goal of America is freedom. Abused and scorned though we may be, our
destiny is tied up with America's destiny. Before the pilgrims landed at
Plymouth, we were here. Before the pen of Jefferson etched the majestic
words of the Declaration of Independence across the pages of history, we
were here. For more than two centuries our forebears labored in this country without wages; they made cotton king; they built the homes of their masters while suffering gross injustice and shameful humiliation — and yet out
of a bottomless vitality they continued to thrive and develop. If the inexpressible cruelties of slavery could not stop us, the opposition we now face
will surely fail. We will win our freedom because the sacred heritage of our
nation and the eternal will of God are embodied in our echoing demands.

Before closing I feel impelled to mention one other point in your statement that has troubled me profoundly. You warmly commended the Birmingham police force for keeping "order" and "preventing violence." I doubt
that you would have so warmly commended the police force if you had seen
its dogs sinking their teeth into unarmed, nonviolent Negroes. I doubt that
you would so quickly commend the policemen if you were to observe their
ugly and inhumane treatment of Negroes here in the city jail; if you were to
watch them push and curse old Negro women and young Negro girls; if you
were to see them slap and kick old Negro men and young boys; if you were
to observe them, as they did on two occasions, refuse to give us food
because we wanted to sing our grace together. I cannot join you in your
praise of the Birmingham police department.

----

[9]*ekklesia:* The church (Greek). It means the spirit of the church. [Eds].

It is true that the police have exercised a degree of discipline in handling the demonstrators. In this sense they have conducted themselves rather "nonviolently" in public. But for what purpose? To preserve the evil system of segregation. Over the past few years I have consistently preached that nonviolence demands that the means we use must be as pure as the ends we seek. I have tried to make clear that it is wrong to use immoral means to attain moral ends. But now I must affirm that it is just as wrong, or perhaps even more so, to use moral means to preserve immoral ends. Perhaps Mr. Connor and his policemen have been rather nonviolent in public, as was Chief Pritchett in Albany, Georgia, but they have used the moral means of nonviolence to maintain the immoral end of racial injustice. As T. S. Eliot has said, "The last temptation is the greatest treason: To do the right deed for the wrong reason."

I wish you had commended the Negro sit-inners and demonstrators of Birmingham for their sublime courage, their willingness to suffer, and their amazing discipline in the midst of great provocation. One day the South will recognize its real heroes. They will be the James Merediths,[10] with the noble sense of purpose that enables them to face jeering and hostile mobs, and with the agonizing loneliness that characterizes the life of the pioneer. They will be old, oppressed, battered Negro women, symbolized in a seventy-two-year-old woman in Montgomery, Alabama, who rose up with a sense of dignity and with her people decided not to ride segregated buses and who responded with ungrammatical profundity to one who inquired about her weariness: "My feets is tired, but my soul is at rest." They will be the young high school and college students, the young ministers of the gospel and a host of their elders, courageously and nonviolently sitting in at lunch counters and willingly going to jail for conscience' sake. One day the South will know that when these disinherited children of God sat down at lunch counters, they were in reality standing up for what is best in the American dream and for the most sacred values in our Judaeo-Christian heritage, thereby bringing our nation back to those great wells of democracy which were dug deep by the founding fathers in their formulation of the Constitution and the Declaration of Independence.

Never before have I written so long a letter. I'm afraid it is much too long to take your precious time. I can assure you that it would have been much shorter if I had been writing from a comfortable desk, but what else can one do when he is alone in a narrow jail cell, other than write long letters, think long thoughts, and pray long prayers? 45

If I have said anything in this letter that overstates the truth and indicates an unreasonable impatience, I beg you to forgive me. If I have said anything that understates the truth and indicates my having a patience that allows me to settle for anything less than brotherhood, I beg God to forgive me.

---

[10]*James Meredith* (b. 1933): In 1962, the first African American to become a student at the University of Mississippi. [Eds.]

I hope this letter finds you strong in the faith. I also hope that circumstances will soon make it possible for me to meet each of you, not as an integrationist or a civil rights leader but as a fellow clergyman and a Christian brother. Let us all hope that the dark clouds of racial prejudice will soon pass away and the deep fog of misunderstanding will be lifted from our fear-drenched communities, and in some not too distant tomorrow the radiant stars of love and brotherhood will shine over our great nation with all their scintillating beauty.

> *Yours in the cause of*
> *Peace and Brotherhood,*
> *Martin Luther King, Jr.*

QUESTIONS

1. This justly famous argument is cast in the form of a letter. What advantages did King derive from using the letter format for his argument? Can principles of argumentation be learned from this format?
2. This large argument contains other arguments. The main argument is a justification of the specific actions that landed King in jail. A more general argument is about the injustice of segregation and the proper means to address that injustice. Within these two arguments that run throughout the letter are sections that argue specific subissues within the general topics. To understand how King constructed his essay, begin by locating these separate sections and their subarguments.
3. King is always aware of the positions against which he is arguing and the counterarguments that are offered by those who hold those positions. How does he represent those positions, and how does he deal with them? Base your response on specific instances in which he mentions such positions and responds to them.
4. What is the tone of King's essay? How does the tone relate to the position that he is arguing?
5. What kinds of authority does King invoke to support his right to speak on these issues and lend gravity to his words? How do his writing style and the texts and figures that he cites contribute to his argument?
6. At times, King's language verges on the poetical. His prose is full of images and metaphors. Locate some of these, and discuss their effects.
7. Imagine that you are one of the clergymen to whom this letter was addressed. Write your reply.

MAKING CONNECTIONS

King quotes Thomas Jefferson as the last person in his list of his fellow "extremists." The text of Jefferson's statement (the Declaration of

Independence, p. 612) comes just before King's in this volume. Examine these two texts together. In what ways can they be said to be extreme? In what ways are they not extreme? Some would say that King was quoting Jefferson without regard for his intentions — namely, that Jefferson did not mean to include African Americans in his statement that "all men are created equal." This raises an important question about the interpretation of texts, which applies to documents like the Declaration of Independence and to literary texts. Are such texts to be interpreted only in the light of their authors' intentions, or do readers have the right to their own interpretations? Make an argument about that issue, using texts in this volume for your illustrative material, and apply your argument specifically to King's use of Jefferson. In your argument, consider how we might determine Jefferson's intention in this case. Your research into Jefferson's views on race may well take you beyond this volume. Try putting "Thomas Jefferson and race" into a major online search engine. You will find hundreds of thousands of hits, but remember to return to and focus on the issue of interpretation and the rights of author and reader in such matters.

THERE'S NO ROOM FOR YOU THERE: BLACK STUDENTS AND PRESTIGIOUS COLLEGES

Phillip Richards

Born in Cleveland, Ohio, in 1950, Phillip Richards received his bachelor's degree from Yale University in 1972 and later earned his master's degree and Ph.D. in American literature from the University of Chicago. He has taught at Howard University, Western Michigan University, and the University of North Carolina and since 1988 has been on the faculty at Colgate University, where he is a professor of English and African studies. He has published numerous articles in periodicals and scholarly journals, and his books include Coming of Age in Michigan: An Autobiography *(1998) and* Best Literature by and about Blacks *(2000), of which he was a coeditor. Richards is a fellow with the Institute for Race and Social Division at Boston University, and he serves as a member of the Modern Language Association's Executive Board Committee for the Study of American Literature from 1800. He wrote the following for* The Chronicle of Higher Education.

When I came to teach at Colgate University, in 1988, the white proprietor of a local store pointed to the hill on which the college sits and told me, "There is no room for you there." He meant that it was unlikely that I, a black person, would stay at that very conservative institution located in an isolated section of central New York. Over the years in Hamilton, a tiny town of a little more than 2,000 people, the storekeeper had seen a number of black professors and administrators go almost as quickly as they had come, along with countless cycles of black students who rarely returned with their white classmates for reunions.

His comment was telling, because it would never have been made on the campus itself. At Colgate — like other small, competitive liberal-arts colleges with overwhelmingly white, suburban cultures — the truth of its racial exclusivity, so basic to its social life, is rarely mentioned overtly. Yet colleges like mine seem to reproduce the inequalities of American society in ways that they can't avoid, despite their best intentions. Perhaps it's time to stop pretending otherwise and deceiving minority applicants into thinking that they will achieve the same academic and social success as their white counterparts — or even be held to similar standards.

Last fall, an unexpected incident shattered that pretense at Colgate. That the incident received significant public interest, including extensive national media coverage, has reinforced my belief that it raised issues of concern far beyond the walls of my college. It also suggests that what occurred is relevant to many other institutions.

The uproar began when Barry Shain, a tenured white political scientist at Colgate, wrote in an e-mail message to a female black student that minority students were often seduced into unchallenging courses where liberal professors, who were "sensitive" to their needs, gave them inflated grades. That practice, Shain continued, harmed black students, who were generally less well prepared academically than their white peers. He further complained that a growing number of courses encouraged students to examine their feelings as a way to explore racial issues. The message was widely disseminated to other students without his knowledge.

The specific charges in Shain's message created less of a stir than his　5 breach of the university's racial etiquette. He had publicly exposed the tacit assumption that black students hold a subordinate academic status at Colgate. The violation of that silent code predictably upset many black students, who resented the attack on their academic credentials. The claim that liberal professors gave them inflated grades distressed them much less than the implication that their teachers saw them as academically inferior.

At a campus meeting about the incident, black students broke down and cried. During a collegewide panel discussion on diversity, a male black student, incoherent with rage, publicly denounced Shain. Angry black students began a sit-in in the main administration building.

Some black students told me that the incident had intensified the academic and social anxieties that they had already experienced at Colgate. They observed that few, if any, Colgate faculty members had stood up to contest Shain's assertion that black students were less well prepared and educated than their white counterparts. The most thoughtful black students remarked, however, that Shain had simply aired a long-hidden truth about life at the college, that they were just being confronted with the reality of their stigma as black students at Colgate and in a predominantly white society.

Unfortunately, I had to agree with them. As one of the only tenured black professors who has lived in Hamilton and taught at Colgate for more than a few years, I have found that it is difficult to avoid the fact of African-American marginality at Colgate, where the tone is set by an upper-class white culture. A little less than 4 percent of the student body is African-American. And although the college doesn't keep records on the socioeconomic status of its students as a whole, my perception and the broad consensus of other professors with whom I've spoken are that the majority of black students are lower-middle-class and lower-class students.

The black students whom I encounter tend to arrive less well prepared than their classmates, and only a few go on to perform at the level of the best white and Asian students. Although the black students have ranked highly in their secondary-school classes, they now must measure themselves against students from the top 10 percent of the nation's most competitive schools. With the exception of a few high-performers — often women from the West Indies or Africa — most black students do not achieve academic distinction. That experience is clearly not unusual. The U.S. Department of Education recently released a report documenting that black students arrive on campuses with less preparation for college-level work than other groups, and that almost half of black undergraduates get C's or lower.

Over the years, colleagues have often told me that they have acquired   10 a different set of academic expectations, whatever their formal evaluations, for disadvantaged minority students. That academic stigma, which marks black Colgate students, is no doubt related to what appears to be their inadequate performance in the classroom. I myself noticed that high-performing West Indian women in my literature classes had dropped out of the pre-med program. Like many faculty members at the college, including other minority professors, I too have casually assumed that black students do poorly or fail in the sciences or in any subject that demands high levels of analytic thought, like foreign languages. The assumption of that inadequacy may create a self-fulfilling prophecy, leading to slackened standards and lowered demands for minority-student achievement.

Colleagues have told me of the exceptional accomplishments of individual minority students whom sympathetic and demanding teachers have taken by the hand and pushed to the heights that Colgate expects of its best students. Those students are exceptions, however, in an excellent liberal-arts college where white students routinely tell me of the impact of remarkable faculty members on their intellectual lives. The black students don't discuss teachers who stimulate them intellectually as much as those who give them the attention and help they need to compete respectably at the college.

The double standard leaves its mark on black students long after graduation. Whenever I read the alumni magazine, for example, I notice the dearth of black students who announce their entrance into high-level positions in law, medicine, finance, corporate life, advertising, education, and publishing — positions to which many white Colgate students aspire and in which they often succeed.

Colgate's separate tracks of expectation, performance, and success for black students have been the most disheartening aspect of my experience here — especially as those disparities have persisted over the years. Although every professor I know has observed it, the institution has done little to deal openly with the problem within the faculty as a whole. Public discussion focuses on multiculturalism and diversity — not the problem of inadequate black intellectual achievement at a prestigious academic institution.

The silence surrounding such a serious problem is, in and of itself, important. My college, like others of its type, prides itself for educating students in an environment that promotes excellent teaching, individual attention, and high student motivation and accomplishment. The visible disparity between the performance of black and white students calls many of those values into question. What does the sustained failure of black students in the sciences say about the quality of teaching and the individual attention that black students are receiving? What does it say about the institution's commitment to intellectual excellence? It is far easier for the faculty and administration to brand black students with a silent stigma.

Most upper-class white students come to Colgate expecting to gain the 15 social and academic skills they need to move into the same upper-middle-class or upper-class world as their parents — which they usually do. But can, or will, the academic culture of the college — with its economic, social, and academic divisions — educate and socialize black students for the elite levels of American life in the same way?

That is, in fact, the most important question that Shain's allegations raise concerning Colgate's commitment to the fullest education of its black students. Simply asking that question comes as a great shock to black students as well as white faculty members and administrators, who appear to optimistically assume the necessary connection between a Colgate education and social mobility, especially for poor and working-class students. And it doesn't have easy answers.

The unspoken factors that encourage a two-tiered racial system at Colgate and similar institutions will not soon disappear. My college is an oasis of genteel upper-class values in an increasingly democratic multicultural world. At the heart of this retreat are not only classes and courses but the intimate extracurricular sphere of campus life: the exclusive fraternities, sororities, and other clubs and organizations in which important information is shared, professional connections are forged, and socialization for the upper-class life of corporate America is carried out. That social life is ruthlessly segregated, and its dominance only further distances disadvantaged black students from the college's centers of life. In a system of seven fraternities, four sororities, and more than 900 students, there are only four black members: three black men and one black woman. No black Greek organizations exist.

At the very least, colleges like Colgate should no longer recruit black students without alerting them to the nature of life in an academically competitive, rigorously white upper-class environment. Black students should understand such institutions' academic and social milieu from the beginning. High-school students who visit the campuses should not be sold a bill of goods: that they will live in a world of close social and intellectual relationships between students of different classes and racial backgrounds.

That's not to say that such relationships can't develop, but few should come here expecting them. Visiting days, in which minority applicants are exposed to an unrepresentative sampling of minority students, should be either stopped or balanced with true accounts of interactions between the races. Black students, like their white counterparts, should be aware of the day-to-day realities of the still-segregated racial life at colleges like Colgate.

Those colleges may also be able to solve some of the problem by recruit- 20 ing black students who have already succeeded in the integrated social and academic worlds of prep schools or elite suburban high schools. At such schools, the colleges would find students whose parents are committed to placing their children in the still predominantly white world of America's corporate, professional, and educational elites. Those students would be either prepared for the academic rigors or ready to benefit from the relatively minimal remedial help that colleges like Colgate can offer. I suspect that student organizations would also welcome such black students, eager to make their way in literary, journalistic, theatrical, entrepreneurial, or political extracurricular activities.

Black students who immerse themselves in that culture would gain both the intellectual and the interpersonal skills that white students traditionally bring to their professional lives. In short, black students would enjoy the success that colleges like Colgate offer their white students, and they would feel — and be — an integral part of those institutions.

QUESTIONS

1. This short essay is more complicated than it may appear on a first reading. It is complicated because of the arguments that it makes and does not make. It has the following structure: (1) identify a problem and (2) suggest solutions. What, exactly, is the problem? Based on your own experiences and on what you have heard from other students, has Richards accurately identified a real problem?
2. If you feel that Richards has got it wrong, do you see no problem in campus race relations, or do you feel that he hasn't described the problem accurately?
3. Richards aims his argument at elite private colleges and universities. Does it have any bearing on other kinds of colleges and universities? How does it relate to the school that you are presently attending?
4. The solutions that Richards offers take the form of recommendations for colleges like Colgate and for black students who are thinking of attending such colleges. What are these recommendations, and how would you evaluate them? Are they appropriate? Practical? Reasonable?
5. Are problems in race relations evident at your own school? If so, present your own diagnosis of the problems and your recommendations for solutions. If not, explain what is going right, and make an argument that puts forth the causes of this racial harmony.

MAKING CONNECTIONS

There are a number of texts in this volume that deal with education, schooling, and African Americans. In addition to this essay by Richards, there are works by Maya Angelou (p. 31), Alice Walker (p. 42), Frederick Douglass (p. 62), Langston Hughes (p. 103), James Baldwin (p. 532), and Gwendolyn Brooks (p. 667). Drawing on these and any other texts or experiences that you find appropriate, write an essay in which you make an argument about these matters or about the ways in which various writers have represented them. You might consider the matter historically — from Douglass to Richards — and make a case about progress or the lack of it in educational opportunities for African Americans. Or you may wish to argue about present problems and solutions. But do not turn this into a recycled (or worse, plagiarized) essay on affirmative action. If you do take up that subject, ground your paper in the essays in the present collection that bear on the topic. This will reassure your teacher about the freshness of your approach.

THE ART OF FAILURE

Malcolm Gladwell

Biographical information for New Yorker *staff writer Malcolm Gladwell can be found on page 438. In the following article from* The New Yorker, *Gladwell considers two different ways that people fail in moments of stress.*

There was a moment, in the third and deciding set of the 1993 Wimbledon final, when Jana Novotna seemed invincible. She was leading 4–1 and serving at 40–30, meaning that she was one point from winning the game, and just five points from the most coveted championship in tennis. She had just hit a backhand to her opponent, Steffi Graf, that skimmed the net and landed so abruptly on the far side of the court that Graf could only watch, in flat-footed frustration. The stands at Center Court were packed. The Duke and Duchess of Kent were in their customary place in the royal box. Novotna was in white, poised and confident, her blond hair held back with a head-band — and then something happened. She served the ball straight into the net. She stopped and steadied herself for the second serve — the toss, the arch of the back — but this time it was worse. Her swing seemed halfhearted, all arm and no legs and torso. Double fault. On the next point, she was slow to react to a high shot by Graf, and badly missed on a forehand volley. At game point, she hit an overhead straight into the net. Instead of 5–1, it was now 4–2. Graf to serve: an easy victory, 4–3. Novotna to serve. She wasn't tossing the ball high enough. Her head was down. Her movements had slowed markedly. She double-faulted once, twice, three times. Pulled wide by a Graf forehand, Novotna inexplicably hit a low, flat shot directly at Graf, instead of a high crosscourt forehand that would have given her time to get back into position: 4–4. Did she suddenly realize how terrifyingly close she was to victory? Did she remember that she had never won a major tournament before? Did she look across the net and see Steffi Graf — Steffi Graf! — the greatest player of her generation?

On the baseline, awaiting Graf's serve, Novotna was now visibly agitated, rocking back and forth, jumping up and down. She talked to herself under her breath. Her eyes darted around the court. Graf took the game at love; Novotna, moving as if in slow motion, did not win a single point: 5–4, Graf. On the sidelines, Novotna wiped her racquet and her face with a towel, and then each finger individually. It was her turn to serve. She missed a routine volley wide, shook her head, talked to herself. She missed her first serve, made the second, then, in the resulting rally, mis-hit a backhand so badly that it sailed off her racquet as if launched into flight. Novotna was unrecognizable, not an élite tennis player but a beginner again. She was crumbling under pressure, but exactly why was as baffling to her as it was to all those looking on. Isn't pressure supposed to bring out the best in us? We try harder. We concentrate harder. We get a boost of adrenaline. We care more about how well we perform. So what was happening to her?

At championship point, Novotna hit a low, cautious, and shallow lob to Graf. Graf answered with an unreturnable overhead smash, and, mercifully, it was over. Stunned, Novotna moved to the net. Graf kissed her twice. At the awards ceremony, the Duchess of Kent handed Novotna the runner-up's trophy, a small silver plate, and whispered something in her ear, and what Novotna had done finally caught up with her. There she was, sweaty and exhausted, looming over the delicate white-haired Duchess in her pearl necklace. The Duchess reached up and pulled her head down onto her shoulder, and Novotna started to sob.

Human beings sometimes falter under pressure. Pilots crash and divers drown. Under the glare of competition, basketball players cannot find the basket and golfers cannot find the pin. When that happens, we say variously that people have "panicked" or, to use the sports colloquialism, "choked." But what do those words mean? Both are pejoratives. To choke or panic is considered to be as bad as to quit. But are all forms of failure equal? And what do the forms in which we fail say about who we are and how we think? We live in an age obsessed with success, with documenting the myriad ways by which talented people overcome challenges and obstacles. There is as much to be learned, though, from documenting the myriad ways in which talented people sometimes fail.

"Choking" sounds like a vague and all-encompassing term, yet it   5 describes a very specific kind of failure. For example, psychologists often use a primitive video game to test motor skills. They'll sit you in front of a computer with a screen that shows four boxes in a row, and a keyboard that has four corresponding buttons in a row. One at a time, x's start to appear in the boxes on the screen, and you are told that every time this happens you are to push the key corresponding to the box. According to Daniel Willingham, a psychologist at the University of Virginia, if you're told ahead of time about the pattern in which those x's will appear, your reaction time in hitting the right key will improve dramatically. You'll play the game very carefully for a few rounds, until you've learned the sequence, and then you'll get faster and faster. Willingham calls this "explicit learning." But suppose you're not told that the x's appear in a regular sequence, and even after playing the game for a while you're not aware that there is a pattern. You'll *still* get faster: you'll learn the sequence unconsciously. Willingham calls that "implicit learning" — learning that takes place outside of awareness. These two learning systems are quite separate, based in different parts of the brain. Willingham says that when you are first taught something — say, how to hit a backhand or an overhead forehand — you think it through in a very deliberate, mechanical manner. But as you get better the implicit system takes over: you start to hit a backhand fluidly, without thinking. The basal ganglia, where implicit learning partially resides, are concerned with force and timing, and when that system kicks in you begin to develop touch and accuracy, the ability to hit a drop shot or place a serve at a hundred miles per hour. "This is something that is going to happen gradually," Willingham says. "You hit several thousand forehands, after a while you may still be attending to it. But not very much. In the end, you don't really notice what your hand is doing at all."

Under conditions of stress, however, the explicit system sometimes takes over. That's what it means to choke. When Jana Novotna faltered at Wimbledon, it was because she began thinking about her shots again. She lost her fluidity, her touch. She double-faulted on her serves and mis-hit her overheads, the shots that demand the greatest sensitivity in force and timing. She seemed like a different person — playing with the slow, cautious deliberation of a beginner — because, in a sense, she *was* a beginner again: she was relying on a learning system that she hadn't used to hit serves and overhead forehands and volleys since she was first taught tennis, as a child. The same thing has happened to Chuck Knoblauch, the New York Yankees' second baseman, who inexplicably has had trouble throwing the ball to first base. Under the stress of playing in front of forty thousand fans at Yankee Stadium, Knoblauch finds himself reverting to explicit mode, throwing like a Little Leaguer again.

Panic is something else altogether. Consider the following account of a scuba-diving accident, recounted to me by Ephimia Morphew, a human-factors specialist at NASA: "It was an open-water certification dive, Monterey Bay, California, about ten years ago. I was nineteen. I'd been diving for two weeks. This was my first time in the open ocean without the instructor. Just my buddy and I. We had to go about forty feet down, to the bottom of the ocean, and do an exercise where we took our regulators out of our mouth, picked up a spare one that we had on our vest, and practiced breathing out of the spare. My buddy did hers. Then it was my turn. I removed my regulator. I lifted up my secondary regulator. I put it in my mouth, exhaled, to clear the lines, and then I inhaled, and, to my surprise, it was water. I inhaled water. Then the hose that connected that mouthpiece to my tank, my air source, came unlatched and air from the hose came exploding into my face.

"Right away, my hand reached out for my partner's air supply, as if I was going to rip it out. It was without thought. It was a physiological response. My eyes are seeing my hand do something irresponsible. I'm fighting with myself. *Don't do it.* Then I searched my mind for what I could do. And nothing came to mind. All I could remember was one thing: If you can't take care of yourself, let your buddy take care of you. I let my hand fall back to my side, and I just stood there."

This is a textbook example of panic. In that moment, Morphew stopped thinking. She forgot that she had another source of air, one that worked perfectly well and that, moments before, she had taken out of her mouth. She forgot that her partner had a working air supply as well, which could easily be shared, and she forgot that grabbing her partner's regulator would imperil both of them. All she had was her most basic instinct: *get air*. Stress wipes out short-term memory. People with lots of experience tend not to panic, because when the stress suppresses their short-term memory they still have some residue of experience to draw on. But what did a novice like Morphew have? *I searched my mind for what I could do. And nothing came to mind.*

Panic also causes what psychologists call perceptual narrowing. In one study, from the early seventies, a group of subjects were asked to perform a visual-acuity task while undergoing what they thought was a sixty-foot dive in a pressure chamber. At the same time, they were asked to push a button whenever they saw a small light flash on and off in their peripheral vision. The subjects in the pressure chamber had much higher heart rates than the control group, indicating that they were under stress. That stress didn't affect their accuracy at the visual-acuity task, but they were only half as good as the control group at picking up the peripheral light. "You tend to focus or obsess on one thing," Morphew says. "There's a famous airplane example, where the landing light went off, and the pilots had no way of knowing if the landing gear was down. The pilots were so focussed on that light that no one noticed the autopilot had been disengaged, and they crashed the plane." Morphew reached for her buddy's air supply because it was the only air supply she could see.

Panic, in this sense, is the opposite of choking. Choking is about thinking too much. Panic is about thinking too little. Choking is about loss of instinct. Panic is reversion to instinct. They may look the same, but they are worlds apart. Why does this distinction matter? In some instances, it doesn't much. If you lose a close tennis match, it's of little moment whether you choked or panicked; either way, you lost. But there are clearly cases when how failure happens is central to understanding why failure happens.

Take the plane crash in which John F. Kennedy, Jr., was killed last summer. The details of the flight are well known. On a Friday evening last July, Kennedy took off with his wife and sister-in-law for Martha's Vineyard. The night was hazy, and Kennedy flew along the Connecticut coastline, using the trail of lights below him as a guide. At Westerly, Rhode Island, he left the shoreline, heading straight out over Rhode Island Sound, and at that point, apparently disoriented by the darkness and haze, he began a series of curious maneuvers: He banked his plane to the right, farther out into the ocean, and then to the left. He climbed and descended. He sped up and slowed down. Just a few miles from his destination, Kennedy lost control of the plane, and it crashed into the ocean.

Kennedy's mistake, in technical terms, was that he failed to keep his wings level. That was critical, because when a plane banks to one side it begins to turn and its wings lose some of their vertical lift. Left unchecked, this process accelerates. The angle of the bank increases, the turn gets sharper and sharper, and the plane starts to dive toward the ground in an ever-narrowing corkscrew. Pilots call this the "graveyard spiral." And why didn't Kennedy stop the dive? Because, in times of low visibility and high stress, keeping your

10

wings level — indeed, even knowing whether you are in a graveyard spiral — turns out to be surprisingly difficult. Kennedy failed under pressure.

Had Kennedy been flying during the day or with a clear moon, he would have been fine. If you are the pilot, looking straight ahead from the cockpit, the angle of your wings will be obvious from the straight line of the horizon in front of you. But when it's dark outside the horizon disappears. There is no external measure of the plane's bank. On the ground, we know whether we are level even when it's dark, because of the motion-sensing mechanisms in the inner ear. In a spiral dive, though, the effect of the plane's G-force on the inner ear means that the pilot *feels* perfectly level even if his plane is not. Similarly, when you are in a jetliner that is banking at thirty degrees after takeoff, the book on your neighbor's lap does not slide into your lap, nor will a pen on the floor roll toward the "down" side of the plane. The physics of flying is such that an airplane in the midst of a turn always feels perfectly level to someone inside the cabin.

This is a difficult notion, and to understand it I went flying with William   15
Langewiesche, the author of a superb book on flying, *Inside the Sky*. We met at San Jose Airport, in the jet center where the Silicon Valley billionaires keep their private planes. Langewiesche is a rugged man in his forties, deeply tanned, and handsome in the way that pilots (at least since the movie "The Right Stuff") are supposed to be. We took off at dusk, heading out toward Monterey Bay, until we had left the lights of the coast behind and night had erased the horizon. Langewiesche let the plane bank gently to the left. He took his hands off the stick. The sky told me nothing now, so I concentrated on the instruments. The nose of the plane was dropping. The gyroscope told me that we were banking, first fifteen, then thirty, then forty-five degrees. "We're in a spiral dive," Langewiesche said calmly. Our airspeed was steadily accelerating, from a hundred and eighty to a hundred and ninety to two hundred knots. The needle on the altimeter was moving down. The plane was dropping like a stone, at three thousand feet per minute. I could hear, faintly, a slight increase in the hum of the engine, and the wind noise as we picked up speed. But if Langewiesche and I had been talking I would have caught none of that. Had the cabin been unpressurized, my ears might have popped, particularly as we went into the steep part of the dive. But beyond that? Nothing at all. In a spiral dive, the G-load — the force of inertia — is normal. As Langewiesche puts it, the plane *likes* to spiral-dive. The total time elapsed since we started diving was no more than six or seven seconds. Suddenly, Langewiesche straightened the wings and pulled back on the stick to get the nose of the plane up, breaking out of the dive. Only now did I feel the full force of the G-load, pushing me back in my seat. "You feel no G-load in a bank," Langewiesche said. "There's nothing more confusing for the uninitiated."

I asked Langewiesche how much longer we could have fallen. "Within five seconds, we would have exceeded the limits of the airplane," he replied, by which he meant that the force of trying to pull out of the dive would have broken the plane into pieces. I looked away from the instruments and asked Langewiesche to spiral-dive again, this time without telling me. I sat and waited. I was about to tell Langewiesche that he could start diving anytime, when, suddenly, I was thrown back in my chair. "We just lost a thousand feet," he said.

This inability to sense, experientially, what your plane is doing is what makes night flying so stressful. And this was the stress that Kennedy must have felt when he turned out across the water at Westerly, leaving the guiding lights of the Connecticut coastline behind him. A pilot who flew into Nantucket that night told the National Transportation Safety Board that when he descended over Martha's Vineyard he looked down and there was "nothing to see. There was no horizon and no light. . . . I thought the island might [have] suffered a power failure." Kennedy was now blind, in every sense, and he must have known the danger he was in. He had very little experience in flying strictly by instruments. Most of the time when he had flown up to the Vineyard the horizon or lights had still been visible. That strange, final sequence of maneuvers was Kennedy's frantic search for a clearing in the haze. He was trying to pick up the lights of Martha's Vineyard, to restore the lost horizon. Between the lines of the National Transportation Safety Board's report on the crash, you can almost feel his desperation:

> About 2138 the target began a right turn in a southerly direction. About 30 seconds later, the target stopped its descent at 2200 feet and began a climb that lasted another 30 seconds. During this period of time, the target stopped the turn, and the airspeed decreased to about 153 KIAS. About 2139, the target leveled off at 2500 feet and flew in a south-easterly direction. About 50 seconds later, the target entered a left turn and climbed to 2600 feet. As the target continued in the left turn, it began a descent that reached a rate of about 900 fpm.

But was he choking or panicking? Here the distinction between those two states is critical. Had he choked, he would have reverted to the mode of explicit learning. His movements in the cockpit would have become markedly slower and less fluid. He would have gone back to the mechanical, self-conscious application of the lessons he had first received as a pilot — and that might have been a good thing. Kennedy *needed* to think, to concentrate on his instruments, to break away from the instinctive flying that served him when he had a visible horizon.

But instead, from all appearances, he panicked. At the moment when he needed to remember the lessons he had been taught about instrument flying, his mind — like Morphew's when she was underwater — must have gone blank. Instead of reviewing the instruments, he seems to have been focussed on one question: Where are the lights of Martha's Vineyard? His gyroscope and his other instruments may well have become as invisible as the peripheral lights in the underwater-panic experiments. He had fallen back on his instincts — on the way the plane *felt* — and in the dark, of course, instinct can tell you nothing. The N.T.S.B. report says that the last time the Piper's wings were level was seven seconds past 9:40, and the plane hit the water at about 9:41, so the critical period here was less than sixty seconds. At twenty-five seconds past the minute, the plane was tilted at an angle greater than forty-five degrees. Inside the cockpit it would have felt normal. At some point, Kennedy must have heard the rising wind outside, or the roar of the engine as it picked up speed. Again, relying on instinct, he might have pulled back on the stick, trying to raise the nose of the plane. But pulling back on the stick without first levelling the wings only makes the spiral tighter and the problem worse. It's also possible that Kennedy did nothing at all, and that he was frozen at the controls, still frantically searching for the lights of the Vineyard, when his plane hit the water. Sometimes pilots don't even try to make it out of a spiral dive. Langewiesche calls that "one G all the way down."

What happened to Kennedy that night illustrates a second major differ-   20
ence between panicking and choking. Panicking is conventional failure, of the sort we tacitly understand. Kennedy panicked because he didn't know enough about instrument flying. If he'd had another year in the air, he might not have panicked, and that fits with what we believe — that performance ought to improve with experience, and that pressure is an obstacle that the diligent can overcome. But choking makes little intuitive sense. Novotna's problem wasn't lack of diligence; she was as superbly conditioned and schooled as anyone on the tennis tour. And what did experience do for her? In 1995, in the third round of the French Open, Novotna choked even more spectacularly than she had against Graf, losing to Chanda Rubin after surrendering a 5–0 lead in the third set. There seems little doubt that part of the reason for her collapse against Rubin was her collapse against Graf — that the second failure built on the first, making it possible for her to be up 5–0 in the third set and yet entertain the thought *I can still lose.* If panicking is conventional failure, choking is paradoxical failure.

Claude Steele, a psychologist at Stanford University, and his colleagues have done a number of experiments in recent years looking at how certain groups perform under pressure, and their findings go to the heart of what is so strange about choking. Steele and Joshua Aronson found that when they gave a group of Stanford undergraduates a standardized test and told them that it was a measure of their intellectual ability, the white students did much better than their black counterparts. But when the same test was presented simply as an abstract laboratory tool, with no relevance to ability, the scores of blacks and whites were virtually identical. Steele and Aronson attribute this disparity to what they call "stereotype threat": when black students are put into a situation where they are directly confronted with a stereotype about their group — in this case, one having to do with intelligence — the resulting pressure causes their performance to suffer.

Steele and others have found stereotype threat at work in any situation where groups are depicted in negative ways. Give a group of qualified women a math test and tell them it will measure their quantitative ability and they'll do much worse than equally skilled men will; present the same test simply as a research tool and they'll do just as well as the men. Or consider a handful of experiments conducted by one of Steele's former graduate students, Julio Garcia, a professor at Tufts University. Garcia gathered together a group of white, athletic students and had a white instructor lead them through a series of physical tests: to jump as high as they could, to do a standing broad jump, and to see how many pushups they could do in twenty seconds. The instructor then asked them to do the tests a second time, and, as you'd expect, Garcia found that the students did a little better on each of the tasks the second time around. Then Garcia ran a second group of students through the tests, this time replacing the instructor between the first and second trials with an African-American. Now the white students ceased to improve on their vertical leaps. He did the experiment again, only this time he replaced the white instructor with a black instructor who was much taller and heavier than the previous black instructor. In this trial, the white students actually jumped less high than they had the first time around. Their performance on the pushups, though, was unchanged in each of the conditions. There is no stereotype, after all, that suggests that whites can't do as many pushups as blacks. The task that was affected was the vertical leap, because of what our culture says: *white men can't jump.*

It doesn't come as news, of course, that black students aren't as good at test-taking as white students, or that white students aren't as good at jumping as black students. The problem is that we've always assumed that this kind of failure under pressure is panic. What is it we tell underperforming athletes and students? The same thing we tell novice pilots or scuba divers: to work harder, to buckle down, to take the tests of their ability more seriously. But Steele says that when you look at the way black or female students perform under stereotype threat you don't see the wild guessing of a panicked test taker. "What you tend to see is carefulness and second-guessing," he explains. "When you go and interview them, you have the sense that when they are in the stereotype-threat condition they say to themselves, 'Look, I'm going to be careful here. I'm not going to mess things up.' Then, after having decided to take that strategy, they calm down and go through the test. But that's not the way to succeed on a standardized test. The more you do that, the more you will get away from the intuitions that help you, the quick processing. They think they did well, and they are trying to do well. But they are not." This is choking, not panicking. Garcia's athletes and Steele's students are like Novotna, not Kennedy. They failed because they were good at what they did: only those who care about how well they perform ever feel the pressure of stereotype threat. The usual prescription for failure — to work harder and take the test more seriously — would only make their problems worse.

That is a hard lesson to grasp, but harder still is the fact that choking requires us to concern ourselves less with the performer and more with the situation in which the performance occurs. Novotna herself could do nothing to prevent her collapse against Graf. The only thing that could have saved her is if — at that critical moment in the third set — the television cameras had been turned off, the Duke and Duchess had gone home, and the spectators had been told to wait outside. In sports, of course, you can't do that. Choking is a central part of the drama of athletic competition, because the spectators *have* to be there — and the ability to overcome the pressure of the spectators is part of what it means to be a champion. But the same ruthless inflexibility need not govern the rest of our lives. We have to learn that sometimes a poor performance reflects not the innate ability of the performer but the complexion of the audience; and that sometimes a poor test score is the sign not of a poor student but of a good one.

Through the first three rounds of the 1996 Masters golf tournament, Greg Norman held a seemingly insurmountable lead over his nearest rival, the Englishman Nick Faldo. He was the best player in the world. His nickname was the Shark. He didn't saunter down the fairways; he stalked the course, blond and broad-shouldered, his caddy behind him, struggling to keep up. But then came the ninth hole on the tournament's final day. Norman was paired with Faldo, and the two hit their first shots well. They were now facing the green. In front of the pin, there was a steep slope, so that any ball hit short would come rolling back down the hill into oblivion. Faldo shot first, and the ball landed safely long, well past the cup.

Norman was next. He stood over the ball. "The one thing you guard against here is short," the announcer said, stating the obvious. Norman swung and then froze, his club in midair, following the ball in flight. It was short. Norman watched, stone-faced, as the ball rolled thirty yards back down the hill, and with that error something inside of him broke.

At the tenth hole, he hooked the ball to the left, hit his third shot well past the cup, and missed a makable putt. At eleven, Norman had a three-and-a-half-foot putt for par — the kind he had been making all week. He shook out his hands and legs before grasping the club, trying to relax. He missed: his third straight bogey. At twelve, Norman hit the ball straight into the water. At thirteen, he hit it into a patch of pine needles. At sixteen, his movements were so mechanical and out of synch that, when he swung, his hips spun out ahead of his body and the ball sailed into another pond. At that, he took his club and made a frustrated scythelike motion through the grass, because what had been obvious for twenty minutes was now official: he had fumbled away the chance of a lifetime.

Faldo had begun the day six strokes behind Norman. By the time the two started their slow walk to the eighteenth hole, through the throng of spectators, Faldo had a four-stroke lead. But he took those final steps quietly, giving only the smallest of nods, keeping his head low. He understood what had happened on the greens and fairways that day. And he was bound by the particular etiquette of choking, the understanding that what he had earned was something less than a victory and what Norman had suffered was something less than a defeat.

When it was all over, Faldo wrapped his arms around Norman. "I don't know what to say — I just want to give you a hug," he whispered, and then

25

he said the only thing you can say to a choker. "I feel horrible about what happened. I'm so sorry." With that, the two men began to cry.

QUESTIONS

1. This argument begins and ends with stories about sports. Are they versions of the same story? How do they contribute to the argument?
2. The argument is a subtle one, most plainly stated in the paragraph after the story about Novotna. In that paragraph, Gladwell says that people tend to regard all forms of failure as equal. His argument is constructed to show that there are different forms of failure. What are they, and what makes them different?
3. This essay is clearly divided into units. Stories or anecdotes are one kind of unit. What other kinds are there? Go through the essay, noting its different units. Discuss the form and function of each unit.
4. Gladwell is talking about kinds of failure. Do you agree with his definition of the different kinds? If not, make a counterargument.
5. Are there different kinds of success? Can you find anecdotes about sporting events in which neither player failed but one succeeded? Define *success*, and argue the case for your definition.

MAKING CONNECTIONS

1. Can you find other accounts of the Kennedy plane crash? If you can, compare one or more of them to Gladwell's account. Which account is more satisfying? Why?
2. Gladwell's essay is organized around the definitions of the key words *choke* and *panic*. A number of other essays in this section are also based on the definition or redefinition of words. For example, Robert A. Weinberg's "Of Clones and Clowns" (p. 718) is about the different meanings of cloning and their implications, and Gary Greenberg's "As Good as Dead" (p. 707) is about how we decide when life is over — what death is. Go back over the texts in this volume that you have already read, and note the ones in which definitions (and especially redefinitions) play a central role. Is there a pattern here? Does this happen more often in arguing than in other modes of expression? Are some uses of redefinition more successful than others? Select the example that you take to be the most successful, and analyze the reasons for this success. Use this as part of an essay on the function of definition in writing.

SIFTING THE ASHES

Jonathan Franzen

Jonathan Franzen (b. 1959) grew up in a suburb of St. Louis, Missouri. A graduate of Swarthmore College, he studied in Germany as a Fulbright scholar and later worked in the seismology laboratory at Harvard's Department of Earth and Planetary Sciences. He published his first novel, The Twenty-Seventh City, *in 1988, followed by* Strong Motion *in 1992, both called "intellectual thrillers." It was his much anticipated* The Corrections *(2001), however, that catapulted him into the public spotlight, in part because of the critical acclaim that the novel received and in part because of Franzen's notorious reluctance to allow the book to be included as a choice for Oprah Winfrey's celebrated book club. Despite the controversy,* The Corrections *went on to win the National Book Award. Franzen's most recent book is the essay collection* How to Be Alone *(2002). The following essay first appeared in* The New Yorker *in 1996 with the subtitle "Confessions of a Conscientious Objector in the Cigarette Wars."*

Cigarettes are the last thing in the world I want to think about. I don't consider myself a smoker, don't identify with the forty-six million Americans who have the habit. I dislike the smell of smoke and the invasion of nasal privacy it represents. Bars and restaurants with a stylish profile—with a clientele whose exclusivity depends in part on the toxic clouds with which it shields itself—have started to disgust me. I've been gassed in hotel rooms where smokers stayed the night before and in public bathrooms where men use the nasty, body-odorish Winston as a laxative. ("Winston tastes bad / Like the one I just had" runs the grammatically unimpeachable parody from my childhood.) Some days in New York it seems as if two-thirds of the people on the sidewalk, in the swirls of car exhaust, are carrying lighted cigarettes; I maneuver constantly to stay upwind. The first casino I ever went to, in Nevada, was a vision of damnation: row upon row of middle-aged women with foot-long faces puffing on foot-long Kents and compulsively feeding silver dollars to the slots. When someone tells me that cigarettes are sexy, I think of Nevada. When I see an actress or an actor drag deeply in a movie, I imagine the pyrenes and phenols ravaging the tender epithelial cells and hardworking cilia of their bronchi, the carbon monoxide and cyanide binding to their hemoglobin, the heaving and straining of their chemically panicked hearts. Cigarettes are a distillation of a more general paranoia that besets our culture, the awful knowledge of our bodies' fragility in a world of molecular hazards. They scare the hell out of me.

Because I'm capable of hating almost every attribute of cigarettes (let's not even talk about cigars), and because I smoked what I believed was my last cigarette five years ago and have never owned an ashtray, it's easy for me to think of myself as nicotine-free. But if the man who bears my name is not a smoker, then why is there again a box fan for exhaust purposes in his living-room window? Why at the end of every workday is there a small collection of cigarette butts in the saucer on the table by this fan?

Cigarettes were the ultimate taboo in the culturally conservative household I grew up in — more fraught, even, than sex or drugs. The year before I was born, my mother's father died of lung cancer. He'd taken up cigarettes as a soldier in the First World War and smoked heavily all his life. Everyone who met my grandfather seems to have loved him, and, much as I may sneer at our country's obsession with health — at the elevation of fitness to godliness and of sheer longevity to a mark of divine favor — the fact remains that if my grandfather hadn't smoked I might have had the chance to know him.

My mother still speaks of cigarettes with loathing. I secretly started smoking them myself in college, perhaps in part because she hated them, and as the years went by I developed a fear of exposure very similar, I'm convinced, to a gay man's fear of coming out to his parents. My mother had created my body out of hers, after all. What rejection of parentage could be more extreme than deliberately poisoning that body? To come out is to announce: this is who I am, this is my identity. The curious thing about "smoker" as a label of identity, though, is its mutability. I could decide tomorrow not to be one anymore. So why not pretend not to be one today? To take control of their lives, people tell themselves stories about the person they want to be. It's the special privilege of the smoker, who at times feels so strongly the resolve to quit that it's as if he'd quit already, to be given irrefutable evidence that these stories aren't necessarily true: here are the butts in the ashtray, here is the smell in the hair.

As a smoker, then, I've come to distrust not only my stories about myself   5
but *all* narratives that pretend to unambiguous moral significance. And it happens that . . . Americans have been subjected to just such a narrative in the daily press, as "secret" documents shed light on the machinations of Big Tobacco, industry scientists step forward to indict their former employers, nine states and a consortium of sixty law firms launch massive liability suits, and the Food and Drug Administration undertakes to regulate cigarettes as nicotine-delivery devices. The prevailing liberal view that Big Tobacco is Evil with a capital "E" is summed up in the *Times'* review of Richard Kluger's excellent new history of the tobacco industry, *Ashes to Ashes*. Chiding Kluger for (of all things) his "objectivity" and "impartiality," Christopher Lehmann-Haupt suggests that the cigarette business is on a moral par with slavery and the Holocaust. Kluger himself, impartial or not, repeatedly links the word "angels" with anti-smoking activists. In the introduction to his book he offers a stark pair of options: either cigarette manufacturers are "businessmen basically like any other" or they're "moral lepers preying on the ignorant, the miserable, the emotionally vulnerable, and the genetically susceptible."

My discomfort with these dichotomies may reflect the fact that, unlike Lehmann-Haupt, I have yet to kick the habit. But in no national debate do I feel more out of synch with the mainstream. For all that I distrust American industry, and especially an industry that is vigorously engaged in buying congressmen, some part of me insists on rooting for tobacco. I flinch as I force myself to read the latest health news: SMOKERS MORE LIKELY TO BEAR RETARDED BABIES, STUDY SAYS. I pounce on particularly choice collisions of metaphor and melodrama, such as this one from the *Times:* "The affidavits are the latest in a string of blows that have undermined the air of invincibility that once cloaked the $45 billion tobacco industry, which faces a deluge of lawsuits." My sympathy with cohorts who smoke disproportionately— blue-collar workers, African-Americans, writers and artists, alienated teens, the mentally ill—expands to include the companies that supply them with cigarettes. I think, We're all underdogs now. Wartime is a time of lies, I tell myself, and the biggest lie of the cigarette wars is that the moral equation can be reduced to ones and zeroes. Or have I, too, been corrupted by the weed?

I took up smoking as a student in Germany in the dark years of the early eighties. Ronald Reagan had recently made his "evil empire" speech, and Jonathan Schell was publishing "The Fate of the Earth." The word in Berlin was that if you woke up to an undestroyed world on Saturday morning you were safe for another week; the assumption was that NATO was at its sleepiest late on Friday nights, that Warsaw Pact forces would choose those hours to come pouring through the Fulda Gap, and that NATO would have to go ballistic to repel them. Since I rated my chances of surviving the decade at fifty-fifty, the additional risk posed by smoking seemed negligible. Indeed, there was something invitingly apocalyptic about cigarettes. The nightmare of nuclear proliferation had a counterpart in the way cigarettes—anonymous, death-bearing, missilelike cylinders—proliferated in my life. Cigarettes are a fixture of modern warfare, the soldier's best friend, and, at a time when a likely theater of war was my own living room, smoking became a symbol of my helpless civilian participation in the Cold War.

Among the anxieties best suited to containment by cigarettes is, paradoxically, the fear of dying. What serious smoker hasn't felt the surge of panic at the thought of lung cancer and immediately lighted up to beat the panic down? (It's a Cold War logic: we're afraid of nuclear weapons, so let's build even more of them.) Death is a severing of the connection between self and world, and, since the self can't imagine not existing, perhaps what's really scary about the prospect of dying is not the extinguishment of my consciousness but the extinguishment of the world. The potential deadliness of cigarettes was comforting because it allowed me, in effect, to become familiar with apocalypse, to acquaint myself with the contours of its terrors, to make the world's potential death less strange and so a little less threatening. Time stops for the duration of a cigarette: when you're smoking, you're acutely present to yourself; you step outside the unconscious forward rush of life. This is why the condemned are allowed a final cigarette, this is why (or so the story goes) gentlemen in evening dress stood puffing at the rail as the Titanic went down: it's a lot easier to leave the world if you're certain you've really been in it. As Goethe[1] writes in *Faust,* "Presence is our duty, be it only a moment."

The cigarette is famously the herald of the modern, the boon companion of industrial capitalism and high-density urbanism. Crowds, hyperkinesis, mass production, numbingly boring labor, and social upheaval all have correlatives in the cigarette. The sheer number of individual units consumed surely dwarfs that of any other manufactured consumer product. "Short, snappy, easily attempted, easily completed or just as easily discarded before completion," the *Times* wrote in a 1925 editorial that Richard Kluger quotes, "the cigarette is the symbol of a machine age in which the ultimate cogs and wheels and levers are human nerves." Itself the product of a mechanical roller called the Bonsack machine, the cigarette served as an opiate for assembly-line workers, breaking up into manageable units long days of grinding sameness. For women, the *Atlantic Monthly* noted in 1916, the cigarette was "the symbol of emancipation, the temporary substitute for the ballot." Altogether, it's impossible to imagine the twentieth century without cigarettes. They show up with Zelig-like[2] ubiquity in old photographs and newsreels, so devoid of individuality as to be hardly noticeable and yet, once noticed, utterly strange.

Kluger's history of the cigarette business reads like a history of American business in general. An industry that in the early eighteen-eighties was splintered into hundreds of small, family-owned concerns had by the turn of the century come under the control of one man, James Buchanan Duke, who by pioneering the use of the Bonsack roller and reinvesting a huge portion of his revenues in advertising, and then by alternately employing the stick of price wars and the carrot of attractive buyout offers, built his American Tobacco Company into the equivalent of Standard Oil or Carnegie Steel. Like his fellow-monopolists, Duke eventually ran afoul of the trust-busters, and in 1911 the Supreme Court ordered the breakup of American. The resulting oligopoly immediately brought out new brands— Camel, Lucky Strike, and Chesterfield—that have vied for market share ever since. To American retailers, the cigarette was the perfect commodity, a staple that generated large profits on a small investment in shelf space and inventory; cigarettes, Kluger notes, "were lightweight and durably packed, rarely spoiled, were hard to steal since they were usually sold from behind the counter, underwent few price changes, and required almost no selling effort."

10

---

[1]*Johann Wolfgang Goethe* (1749–1832): A German author and scientist, author of the dramatic poem *Faust.* [Eds.]

[2]*Zelig:* The protagonist of Woody Allen's 1982 film *Zelig,* a pseudo-documentary film about Leonard Zelig a man who has the ability to turn into the kind of people who are around him. [Eds.]

Since every brand tasted pretty much the same, tobacco companies learned early to situate themselves at the cutting edge of advertising. In the twenties, American Tobacco offered five free cartons of Lucky Strike ("it's toasted") to any doctor who would endorse it, and then launched a campaign that claimed, "20,679 Physicians Say Luckies Are Less Irritating"; American was also the first company to target weight-conscious women ("When tempted to over-indulge, reach for a Lucky instead"). The industry pioneered the celebrity endorsement (the tennis star Bill Tilden: "I've smoked Camels for years, and I never tire of their smooth, rich taste"), radio sponsorship (Arthur Godfrey: "I smoked two or three packs of these things [Chesterfields] every day—I feel pretty good"), assaultive outdoor advertising (the most famous was the "I'd Walk a Mile for a Camel" billboard in Times Square, which for twenty-five years blew giant smoke rings), and, finally, the sponsorship of television shows like "Candid Camera" and "I Love Lucy." The brilliant TV commercials made for Philip Morris—Benson & Hedges smokers whose hundred-millimeter cigarettes were crushed by elevator doors; faux-hand-cranked footage of chambermaids sneaking smokes to the tune of "You've got your own cigarette now, baby"—were vital entertainments of my childhood. I remember, too, the chanted words "Silva Thins, Silva Thins," the mantra for a short-lived American Tobacco product that wooed the female demographic with such appalling copy as "Cigarettes are like girls, the best ones are thin and rich."

The most successful campaign of all, of course, was for Marlboro, an upscale cigarette for ladies which Philip Morris reintroduced in 1954 in a filtered version for the mainstream. Like all modern products, the new Marlboro was designed with great care. The tobacco blend was strengthened so as to survive the muting of a filter, the "flip-top" box was introduced to the national vocabulary, the color red was chosen to signal strong flavor, and the graphics underwent endless tinkering before the final look, including a fake heraldic crest with the motto "*Veni, vidi, vici*,"[3] was settled on; there was even market-testing in four cities to decide the color of the filter. It was in Leo Burnett's ad campaign for Marlboro, however, that the real genius lay. The key to its success was its transparency. Place a lone ranch hand against a backdrop of buttes at sunset, and just about every positive association a cigarette can carry is in the picture: rugged individualism, masculine sexuality, escape from an urban modernity, strong flavors, the living of life intensely. The Marlboro marks our commercial culture's passage from an age of promises to an age of pleasant empty dreams.

It's no great surprise that a company smart enough to advertise as well as this ascended, in just three decades, to a position of hegemony in the industry. Kluger's account of the triumph of Philip Morris is the kind of

---

[3] "*Veni, vidi, vici*": "I came, I saw, I conquered" (Latin). These are the words that Julius Caesar used to describe his swift conquest of Asia Minor in 48 B.C. [Eds.]

thing that business schools have their students read for edification and inspiration: to succeed as an American corporation, the lesson might be, do exactly what Philip Morris did. Concentrate on products with the highest profit margin. Design new products carefully, then get behind them and push *hard.* Use your excess cash to diversify into businesses that are structurally similar to your own. Be a meritocracy. Avoid crippling debt. Patiently build your overseas markets. Never scruple to gouge your customers when you see the opportunity. Let your lawyers attack your critics. Be classy—sponsor "The Mahabharata." Defy conventional morality. Never forget that your primary fealty is to your stockholders.

While its chief competitor, R. J. Reynolds, was growing logy and inbred down in Winston-Salem—sinking into the low-margin discount-cigarette business, diversifying disastrously, and nearly drowning in debt after its leveraged buyout by Kohlberg Kravis Roberts & Company—Philip Morris was becoming the global leader in the cigarette industry and one of the most profitable corporations in the world. By the early nineties, its share of the domestic nondiscount-cigarette market had risen to eighty percent. One share of Philip Morris stock bought in 1966 was worth a hundred and ninety-two shares in 1989 dollars. Healthy, wealthy, and wise the man who quit smoking in '64 and put his cigarette money into Philip Morris common.

The company's spectacular success is all the more remarkable for having occurred in the decades when the scientific case against cigarettes was becoming overwhelming. With the possible exception of the hydrogen bomb, nothing in modernity is more generative of paradox than cigarettes. Thus, in 1955, when the Federal Trade Commission sought to curb misleading advertising by banning the publication of tar and nicotine levels, the ruling proved to be a boon to the industry, by enabling it to advertise filter cigarettes for their implicit safety even as it raised the toxic yields to compensate for the filters. So it went with the 1965 law requiring warning labels on cigarette packs, which preempted potentially more stringent state and local regulations and provided a priceless shield against future liability suits. So it went, too, with the 1971 congressional ban on broadcast cigarette advertising, which saved the industry millions of dollars, effectively froze out potential new competitors by denying them the broadcast platform, and put an end to the devastating anti-smoking ads then being broadcast under the fairness doctrine. Even such left-handed regulation as the 1982 increase in the federal excise tax benefited the industry, which used the tax as a screen for a series of price increases, doubling the price per pack in a decade, and invested the windfall in diversification. Every forward step taken by government to regulate smoking—the broadcast ban, the ban on in-flight smoking, the welter of local bans on smoking in public places—has moved cigarettes a step further back from the consciousness of nonsmoking voters. The result, given the political power of tobacco-growing states, has been the specific exemption of cigarettes from the Fair Labeling and Packaging Act of 1966, the Controlled Substances Act of 1970, the Consumer Product Safety Act of 1972, and the Toxic Substances Act of

15

1976. In the industry's defense in liability suits, the paradox can be seen in its purest form: because no plaintiff can claim ignorance of tobacco's hazards — i.e., precisely *because* the cigarette is the most notoriously lethal product in America — its manufacturers cannot be held negligent for selling it. Small wonder that until the Liggett Group broke ranks . . . no cigarette maker had ever paid a penny in civil damages.

Now, however, the age of paradox may be coming to an end. As the nation dismantles its missiles, its attention turns to cigarettes. The wall of secrecy that protected the industry is coming down as surely as the Berlin Wall did. The Third Wave is upon us, threatening to extinguish all that is quintessentially modern. It hardly seems an accident that the United States, which is leading the way into the information age, is also in the forefront of the war on cigarettes. Unlike the nations of Europe, which have taken a more pragmatic approach to the smoking problem, taxing cigarettes at rates as high as five dollars a pack, the anti-smoking forces in this country bring to the battle a puritanical zeal. We need a new Evil Empire, and Big Tobacco fills the bill.

The argument for equating the tobacco industry with slave traders and the Third Reich goes like this: because nearly half a million Americans a year die prematurely as a direct consequence of smoking, the makers of cigarettes are guilty of mass murder. The obvious difficulty with the argument is that the tobacco industry has never physically forced anyone to smoke a cigarette. To speak of its "killing" people, therefore, one has to posit more subtle forms of coercion. These fall into three categories. First, by publicly denying a truth well known to its scientists, which was that smokers were in mortal peril, the industry conspired to perpetrate a vast and deadly fraud. Second, by luring impressionable children into a habit very difficult to break, the industry effectively "forced" its products on people before they had developed full adult powers of resistance. Finally, by making available and attractive a product that it knew to be addictive, and by manipulating nicotine levels, the industry willfully exposed the public to a force (addiction) with the power to kill.

A "shocking" collection of "secret" industry documents which was express-mailed by a disgruntled employee of Brown & Williamson to the anti-smoking crusader Stanton A. Glantz, and has now been published by the University of California Press as "The Cigarette Papers," makes it clear that Big Tobacco has known for decades that cigarettes are lethal and addictive and has done everything in its power to suppress and deny that knowledge. "The Cigarette Papers" and other recent disclosures have prompted the Justice Department to pursue perjury charges against various industry executives, and may provide the plaintiffs now suing the industry with positive proof of tortious fraud. In no way, though, are the disclosures shocking. How could anyone who noticed that different cigarette brands have different (but consistent) nicotine levels fail to conclude that the industry can and does control the dosage? What reasonable person could have believed that the industry's public avowals of "doubt" about the deadliness of its products were anything but obligatory, ceremonial lies? If researchers unearthed a secret document proving that Bill Clinton inhaled, would we be shocked? When industry spokesmen impugn the integrity of the Surgeon General and persist in denying the undeniable, they're guilty not so much of fraud as of sounding (to borrow the word of one executive quoted by Kluger) "Neanderthal."

"The simple truth," Kluger writes, "was that the cigarette makers were getting richer and richer as the scientific findings against them piled higher and higher, and before anyone fully grasped the situation, the choice seemed to have narrowed to abject confession and surrender to the health advocates or steadfast denial and rationalization." In the early fifties, when epidemiological studies first demonstrated the link between smoking and lung cancer, cigarette executives did indeed have the option of simply liquidating their businesses and finding other work. But many of these executives came from families that had been respectably trading in tobacco for decades, and most of them appear to have been heavy smokers themselves: unlike the typical heroin wholesaler, they willingly ran the same risks they imposed on their customers. Because they were corporate officers, moreover, their ultimate allegiance was to their stockholders. If having simply stayed in business constitutes guilt, then the circle of those who share this guilt must be expanded to include every individual who held stock in a tobacco company after 1964, either directly or through a pension fund, a mutual fund, or a university endowment. We might also toss in every drugstore and supermarket that sold cigarettes and every publication that carried ads for them, since the Surgeon General's warning, after all, was there for everyone to see.

Once the companies made the decision to stay in business, it was only a matter of time before the lawyers took over. Nothing emerges from *Ashes to Ashes* more clearly than the deforming influence of legal counsel on the actions of the industry. Many industry scientists and some executives appear to have genuinely wished both to produce a safer cigarette and to acknowledge frankly the known risks of smoking. But the industry's attempts to do good were no less paradoxically self-defeating than the government's attempts at regulation. When executives in R. & D. proposed that filtered cigarettes and reduced tar and nicotine yields be marketed as a potential benefit to public health, in-house lawyers objected that calling one brand "safe" or "safer" constituted an admission that other brands were hazardous and thus exposed the maker to liability claims. Likewise, after Liggett had spent millions of dollars developing a substantially less carcinogenic "palladium cigarette" in the seventies, it was treated like contagion by the company's lawyers. Marketing it was bad from a liability standpoint, and developing it and then not marketing it was even worse, because in that case the company could be sued for negligently failing to introduce it. Epic, as the new cigarette was called, was ultimately smothered in legal paper.

Kluger describes an industry in which lawyerly paranoia quickly metastasized into every vital organ. Lawyers coached the executives appearing

20

before congressional committees, oversaw the woefully self-serving "independent" research that the industry sponsored, and made sure that all paperwork connected with studies of addiction or cancer was funneled through outside counsel so that it could be protected under the attorney-client privilege. The result was a weird replication of the dual contradictory narratives with which I, as a smoker, explain my life: a true story submerged beneath a utilitarian fiction. One longtime Philip Morris executive quoted by Kluger sums it up like this:

> There was a conflict in the company between science and the law that's never been resolved . . . and so we go through this ritual dance—what's "proven" and what isn't, what's causal and what's just an association—and the lawyers' answer is, "Let's stonewall." . . . If Helmut Wakeham [head of R. & D.] had run things, I think there would have been some admissions. But he was outflanked by the lawyers . . . who . . . were saying, in effect, "My God, you can't make that admission" without risking liability actions against the company. So there was no cohesive plan—when critics of the industry speak of a "conspiracy," they give the companies far too much credit.

In the inverted moral universe of a tobacco-liability trial, every honest or anguished statement by an executive is used to prove the defendants' guilt, while every calculated dodge is used to support their innocence. There's something very wrong here; but absent a demonstration that Americans actually swallowed the industry's lies it's far from clear that this something qualifies as murder.

More damning are recent reports of the industry's recruitment of underage smokers. Lorillard representatives have been observed handing out free Newports to kids in Washington, D.C.; Philip J. Hilts, in his new book, *Smoke Screen*, presents evidence that R. J. Reynolds deliberately placed special promotional displays in stores and kiosks known to be high-school hangouts; and the cuddly, penis-faced Joe Camel must rank as one of the most disgusting apparitions ever to appear in our cultural landscape. Tobacco companies claim that they are merely vying for market share in the vital eighteen-to-twenty-four age group, but internal industry documents described by Hilts suggest that at least one Canadian company has in fact studied how to target entry-level smokers as young as twelve. (According to Hilts, studies have shown that eighty-nine percent of today's adult smokers picked up the habit before the age of nineteen.) In the opinion of anti-tobacco activists, cigarette advertising hooks young customers by proffering images of carefree, attractive adult smokers while failing to hint at the havoc that smoking wreaks. By the time young smokers are old enough to appreciate the fact of mortality, they're hopelessly addicted.

Although the idea that a manufacturer might willingly stress the downside of its products is absurd, I have no doubt that the industry aims its ads at young Americans. I do doubt, though, whether these ads cause an appreciable number of children to start smoking. The insecure or alienated teen who lights up for the first time is responding to peer pressure or to the example of grownup role models—movie villains, rock stars, supermodels. At most, the industry's ads function as an assurance that smoking is a socially acceptable grownup activity. For that reason alone, they should probably be banned or more tightly controlled, just as cigarette-vending machines should be outlawed. Most people who start smoking end up regretting it, so any policy that reduces the number of starters is laudable.

That cigarettes innately appeal to teen-agers, however, is hardly the fault   25
of the manufacturers. In recent weeks, I've noticed several anti-tobacco newspaper ads that offer, evidently for its shock value, the image of a preadolescent girl holding a cigarette. The models are obviously not real smokers, yet, despite their phoniness, they're utterly sexualized by their cigarettes. The horror of underage smoking veils a horror of teen and preteen sexuality, and one of the biggest pleasant empty dreams being pushed these days by Madison Avenue is that a child is innocent until his or her eighteenth birthday. The truth is that without firm parental guidance teen-agers make all sorts of irrevocable decisions before they're old enough to appreciate the consequences—they drop out of school, they get pregnant, they major in sociology. What they want most of all is to sample the pleasures of adulthood, like sex or booze or cigarettes. To impute to cigarette advertising a "predatory" power is to admit that parents now have less control over the moral education of their children than the commercial culture has. Here, again, I suspect that the tobacco industry is being scapegoated—made to bear the brunt of a more general societal rage at the displacement of the family by the corporation.

The final argument for the moral culpability of Big Tobacco is that addiction is a form of coercion. Nicotine is a toxin whose ingestion causes the smoker's brain to change its chemistry in defense. Once those changes have occurred, the smoker must continue to consume nicotine on a regular schedule in order to maintain the new chemical balance. Tobacco companies are well aware of this, and an attorney cited by Kluger summarizes the legal case for coercion as follows: "You addicted me, and you knew it was addicting, and now you say it's my fault." As Kluger goes on to point out, though, the argument has many flaws. Older even than the common knowledge that smoking causes cancer, for example, is the knowledge that smoking is a tough habit to break. Human tolerance of nicotine varies widely, moreover, and the industry has long offered an array of brands with ultralow doses. Finally, no addiction is unconquerable: millions of Americans quit every year. When a smoker says he wants to quit but can't, what he's really saying is "I want to quit, but I want even more not to suffer the agony of withdrawal." To argue otherwise is to jettison any lingering notion of personal responsibility.

If nicotine addiction were purely physical, quitting would be relatively easy, because the acute withdrawal symptoms, the physical cravings, rarely last more than a few weeks. At the time I myself quit, six years ago, I was able to stay nicotine-free for weeks at a time, and even when I was working I seldom smoked more than a few ultralights a day. But on the day I decided that the cigarette I'd had the day before was my last, I was absolutely flattened. A month passed in which I was too agitated to read a book, too fuzzy-headed even to focus on a newspaper. If I'd had a job at the time, or a family to take care of, I might have hardly noticed the psychological withdrawal. But as it happened nothing much was going on in my life. "Do you smoke?" Lady Bracknell asks Jack Worthing in *The Importance of Being Earnest*, and when he admits that he does she replies, "I am glad to hear it. A man should always have an occupation of some kind."

There's no simple, universal reason that people smoke, but of one thing I'm convinced: they don't do it because they're slaves to nicotine. My best guess about my own attraction to the habit is that I belong to a class of people whose lives are insufficiently structured. The mentally ill and the indigent are also members of this class. We embrace a toxin as deadly as nicotine, suspended in an aerosol of hydrocarbons and nitrosamines, because we have not yet found pleasures or routines that can replace the comforting, structure-bringing rhythm of need and gratification that the cigarette habit offers. One word for this structuring might be "self-medication"; another might be "coping." But there are very few serious smokers over thirty, perhaps none at all, who don't feel guilty about the harm they inflict on themselves. Even Rose Cipollone, the New Jersey woman whose heirs in the early eighties nearly sustained a liability judgment against the industry, had to be recruited by an activist. The sixty law firms that have pooled their assets for a class-action suit on behalf of all American smokers do not seem to me substantially less predatory than the suit's corporate defendants. I've never met a smoker who blamed the habit on someone else.

The United States as a whole resembles an addicted individual, with the corporated id going about its dirty business while the conflicted political ego frets and dithers. What's clear is that the tobacco industry would not still be flourishing, thirty years after the first Surgeon General's report, if our legislatures weren't purchasable, if the concepts of honor and personal responsibility hadn't largely given way to the power of litigation and the dollar, and if the country didn't generally endorse the idea of corporations whose ultimate responsibility is not to society but to the bottom line. There's no doubt that some tobacco executives have behaved despicably, and for public-health advocates to hate these executives, as the nicotine addict comes eventually to hate his cigarettes, is natural. But to cast them as moral monsters — a point source of evil — is just another form of prime-time entertainment.

By selling its soul to its legal advisers, Big Tobacco long ago made clear   30
its expectation that the country's smoking problem would eventually be resolved in court. The industry may soon suffer such a devastating loss in a liability suit that thereafter only foreign cigarette makers will be able to

afford to do business here. Or perhaps a federal court will undertake to leg-islate a solution to a problem that the political process has clearly proved itself unequal to, and the Supreme Court will issue an opinion that does for the smoking issue what *Brown v. Board of Education* did for racial segre-gation and *Roe v. Wade* for abortion. "Businessmen are combatants, not healers," Kluger writes in *Ashes to Ashes*, "and when they press against or exceed the bounds of decency in their quest for gain, unhesitant to profit from the folly of others, should the exploited clientele and victimized soci-ety expect the perpetrators to restrain themselves out of some sudden divine visitation of conscience? Or must human nature be forcibly corrected when it goes awry?"

Liggett's recent defection notwithstanding, the Medicare suits filed by nine states seem unlikely to succeed as a forcible correction. Kluger notes that these cases arguably amount to "personal injury claims in disguise," and that the Supreme Court has ruled that federal cigarette-labeling laws are an effective shield against such claims. Logically, in other words, the states ought to be suing smokers, not cigarette makers. And perhaps smok-ers, in turn, ought to be suing Social Security and private pension funds for all the money they'll save by dying early. The best estimates of the nation-wide dollar "cost" of smoking, including savings from premature death and income from excise taxes, are negative numbers. If the country's health is to be measured fiscally, an economist quoted by Kluger jokes, "cigarette smoking should be subsidized rather than taxed."

The giant class-action suit filed in New Orleans in March of 1994 rep-resents a more serious threat to Big Tobacco. If a judge concludes that smoking constitutes a social ill on a par with racial segregation, he or she is unlikely to deny standing to the forty-six-million-member "class" repre-sented by the consortium of law firms, and once plaintiffs in a class-action suit are granted standing they almost never lose. The case for regulation of tobacco by the F.D.A is likewise excellent. The modern cigarette is a heav-ily engineered product, bolstered with a long list of additives, and its nico-tine content is manipulable at will. Tobacco companies insist that cigarettes, because no health claims are made for them by the companies, should not be considered a drug. But if nicotine is universally understood to be habit-forming—a central tenet of the industry's liability defense—then the absence of explicit health claims is meaningless. Whether Congress, in its various wafflings, intended cigarettes to be immune from F.D.A. regulation in the first place is, again, a matter that will be decided in court, but a demonstrable history of lies and distortion is sure to weaken the industry's defense.

Ultimately, the belief that the country's century-long love affair with the cigarette can be ended rationally and amicably seems as fond as the belief that there's a painless way to kick nicotine. The first time I quit, I stayed clean for nearly three years. I found I was able to work *more* productively without the distraction and cumulative unpleasantness of cigarettes, and I was happy finally to be the nonsmoker that my family had always taken me to be. Eventually, though, in a season of great personal loss, I came to resent having quit for other people rather than for myself. I was hanging out with smokers, and I drifted back into the habit. Smoking may not look sexy to me anymore, but it still *feels* sexy. The pleasure of carrying the drug, of surrendering to its imperatives and relaxing behind a veil of smoke, is thoroughly licentious. If longevity were the highest good that I could imagine, I might succeed now in scaring myself into quitting. But to the fatalist who values the present more than the future, the nagging voice of conscience — of society, of family — becomes just another factor in the mental equilibrium that sustains the habit. "Perhaps," Richard Klein writes in *Cigarettes Are Sublime*, "one stops smoking only when one starts to love cigarettes, becoming so enamored of their charms and so grateful for their benefits that one at last begins to grasp how much is lost by giving them up, how urgent it is to find substitutes for some of the seductions and powers that cigarettes so magnificently combine." To live with uncontaminated lungs and an unracing heart is a pleasure that I hope someday soon to prefer to the pleasure of a cigarette. For myself, then, I'm cautiously optimistic. For the body politic, rhetorically torn between shrill condemnation and Neanderthal denial, and habituated to the poison of tobacco money in its legal system, its legislatures, its financial markets, and its balance of foreign trade, I'm considerably less so.

A few weeks ago in Tribeca, in a Magritte-like twilight,[4] I saw a woman in a lighted window on a high floor of a loft apartment building. She was standing on a chair and lowering the window's upper sash. She tossed her hair and did something complicated with her arms which I recognized as the lighting of a cigarette. Then she leaned her elbow and her chin on the sash and blew smoke into the humid air outside. I fell in love at first sight as she stood there, both inside and outside, inhaling contradiction and breathing out ambivalence.

QUESTIONS

1. In publishing this essay with the subtitle "Confessions of a Conscientious Objector in the Cigarette Wars," *The New Yorker* sets it up as confessional, yet we have placed it in the "Arguing" section of this book. How would you categorize this essay? Is Franzen confessing or arguing or both? Give examples to support your opinion.

2. How does Franzen answer the questions of why he started smoking, why he gave it up, and why he started again? Note how he uses the first question as a frame, returning to it in paragraph 28 to link his own addiction to a national addiction.

---

[4]*René Magritte* (1898–1967): A French surrealist artist whose twilight skies were sometimes full of hats or umbrellas. [Eds.]

3. Consider the symbolic values given the cigarette and cigarette smoking. If giving up cigarettes means, as Richard Klein says, finding "substitutes for some of the seductions and powers that cigarettes so magnificently combine" (paragraph 33), what would you suggest as some possible substitutes?

4. The central section of Franzen's essay presents some of the evidence that has been gathered against "Big Tobacco" and its attempts to squelch evidence of how harmful cigarette smoking is. "The argument for equating the tobacco industry with slave traders and the Third Reich" starts in paragraph 17. What does Franzen mean by this comparison?

5. How strong is the evidence Franzen presents for his argument? In what order does he place his evidence? Why do you think he organizes his evidence in this way?

6. Since this article was published, the Food and Drug Administration has decided to regulate tobacco. Do some research on this issue, and report on the implications of such regulation, as well as the issues Franzen raises in paragraph 32.

MAKING CONNECTIONS

Compare Franzen's argument with Andrew Sullivan's in "What's So Bad about Hate" (p. 588). In what ways do the two writers each use personal experience?

MENDING WALL

Robert Frost

Perhaps the most popular and widely acclaimed American poet of the twentieth century, Robert Frost (1874–1963) grew up in Lawrence, Massachusetts. He dropped out of Dartmouth College after less than a semester and later attended Harvard University. For a time an instructor at a private boys' school while living on a farm in New Hampshire, Frost moved his large family to London in 1911, where his first collection of poems, A Boy's Will, was published in 1913. Its success there led to a growing reputation at home, and Frost returned to the United States in 1915, joining the faculty of Amherst College in 1917. He would go on to win an unprecedented four Pulitzer Prizes for his poetry and to reach a broad audience, both through his published collections and through his lectures and public readings. Frost wrote frequently on the nature and craft of poetry. Among his observations: "There are many other things I have found myself saying about poetry, but the chiefest of these is that it is metaphor, saying one thing and meaning another, saying one thing in terms of another, the pleasure of ulteriority. Poetry is simply made of metaphor."

Something there is that doesn't love a wall,
That sends the frozen-ground-swell under it,
And spills the upper boulders in the sun;
And makes gaps even two can pass abreast.
The work of hunters is another thing: 5
I have come after them and made repair
Where they have left not one stone on a stone,
But they would have the rabbit out of hiding,
To please the yelping dogs. The gaps I mean,
No one has seen them made or heard them made,   10
But at spring mending-time we find them there.
I let my neighbor know beyond the hill;
And on a day we meet to walk the line
And set the wall between us once again.
We keep the wall between us as we go.   15
To each the boulders that have fallen to each.
And some are loaves and some so nearly balls
We have to use a spell to make them balance:
"Stay where you are until our backs are turned!"
We wear our fingers rough with handling them.   20

Oh, just another kind of outdoor game,
One on a side. It comes to little more:
There where it is we do not need the wall:
He is all pine and I am apple orchard.
My apple trees will never get across   25
And eat the cones under his pines, I tell him.
He only says, "Good fences make good neighbors."
Spring is the mischief in me, and I wonder
If I could put a notion in his head:
"*Why* do they make good neighbors? Isn't it   30
Where there are cows? But here there are no cows.
Before I built a wall I'd ask to know
What I was walling in or walling out,
And to whom I was like to give offense.
Something there is that doesn't love a wall,   35
That wants it down." I could say "Elves" to him,
But it's not elves exactly, and I'd rather
He said it for himself. I see him there
Bringing a stone grasped firmly by the top
In each hand, like an old-stone savage armed.   40
He moves in darkness as it seems to me,
Not of woods only and the shade of trees.
He will not go behind his father's saying,
And he likes having thought of it so well
He says again, "Good fences make good neighbors."   45

QUESTIONS

1. This poem is a reflection with a report inside it and an argument inside it. It is a reflection on the function and meaning of walls, with a report on two neighbors mending their communal wall inside that. Motivated by "Spring," the speaker offers an argument against this particular wall. Is it an argument against walls in general? Explain.

2. Summarize the speaker's argument to his neighbor. Summarize his neighbor's reply. Are the arguments equally simple? Whom do you sympathize with the most? Why?

3. What is the "Something" that doesn't love a wall—nature? entropy? frost? chaos? God? Satan? Discuss your choice.

4. The speaker says mending the wall is a game. Explain what you think he means by that.

5. What does "Good fences make good neighbors" actually mean? Does this apply on a larger scale, to nations as well as to growers of pine and apple trees? Explain why or why not.

6. Discuss walls you know or have heard or read about (China, Berlin, playground, pigpen). Try to develop a theory of the function of walls.

MAKING CONNECTIONS

The speaker in this poem says that his neighbor "will not go behind his father's saying" (line 43). What does it mean to "go behind" a saying? This seems to be a frequent method used in constructing arguments. Why do you suppose that this is the case? Consider some of the other essays in this section in discussing these questions.

The Death of the Ball Turret Gunner

Randall Jarrell

Randall Jarrell (1914–1965) was born in Nashville, Tennessee, and earned his B.A. and M.A. from Vanderbilt University. His sensitive though somewhat bleak view of existence was evident from his first collection of poems, Blood for a Stranger, *in 1942, the year that he enlisted in the army. He served as a control tower operator, and his wartime experiences provided the subject of his second collection,* Little Friend, Little Friend (1945), *which focuses on the fears and struggles of young soldiers. Later collections include* The Seven-League Crutches (1951) *and* The Woman at the Washington Zoo (1960). *A highly influential poetry critic, Jarrell taught at the Woman's College of the University of North Carolina, Greensboro, from the end of World War II until his death in an auto accident. "The Death of the Ball Turret Gunner" originally appeared in* Little Friend, Little Friend.

From my mother's sleep I fell into the State
And I hunched in its belly till my wet fur froze.
Six miles from earth, loosed from its dream of life,
I woke to black flak and the nightmare fighters.
When I died they washed me out of the turret with a hose.   5

Questions

1. A ball turret was a ball-shaped plastic bubble on the underside of large bombing aircraft during World War II. It was equipped with a machine gun, which the gunner was supposed to use to shoot down enemy fighter planes before they shot down the bomber itself. It was a vulnerable position. The dead gunner tells us about his death and the way that his remains were treated. He also tells us, in a compressed, metaphorical way, about his life. Can you unpack those metaphors used in the first two or three lines and give a prose account of his life? Try to deal with such expressions as "mother's sleep," "fell into the State," "its belly," "my wet fur," and "dream of life."
2. The speaker tells the story of his life and death. He is not making an argument. But the poet may be making one. What argument might he be making? You will have to answer question 1 before tackling this one.

3. Why do you suppose that the poet elected to put these words in the mouth of the dead gunner? Try rewriting the poem in the third person (putting *he* for *I*, and so on), and then compare the two versions. Is there any significant difference between the two?

MAKING CONNECTIONS

1. Choosing a speaker from beyond the grave is fairly common in poetry. Emily Dickinson did it in "Because I Could Not Stop for Death" (p. 84). Compare these two voices from the beyond. Do they have the same attitudes toward death and dying?
2. W. H. Auden's "The Unknown Citizen" (p. 261) shares some concerns with Jarrell's poem. They both have something to do with citizenship and the relationship between the individual and the nation. And both the poems tell or imply stories about particular characters. Compare the values, methods, and effects of the two poems.

WE REAL COOL

Gwendolyn Brooks

Poet Gwendolyn Brooks (1917–2000) was born in Topeka, Kansas, but raised in the African American Chicago community known as Bronzeville. A precocious writer, she published one of her earliest poems in a children's magazine when she was ten, and by her teens her work had begun to appear in the Chicago Defender, *a black weekly newspaper with a national circulation. Championed by established poets like Langston Hughes and James Weldon Johnson, she published her first collection,* A Street in Bronzeville, *in 1945, followed by* Annie Allen *(1949), for which she won the Pulitzer Prize, the first African American woman to do so. Some twenty collections followed, as well as a novel and a memoir. Throughout her life, Brooks was particularly interested in cultural and intellectual opportunities for young people.*

The Pool Players.
Seven at the Golden Shovel.

We real cool. We
Left school. We

Lurk late. We   5
Strike straight. We

Sing sin. We
Thin gin. We

Jazz June. We
Die soon.   10

QUESTIONS

1. Who is speaking in this poem?
2. This poem has eight lines, and eight sentences — all with the same structure. Look at the verbs. Are they all in the same tense? Is that significant? Explain your answers.
3. At what point in life are these words presumed to be uttered? How do you know?
4. The speaker is not arguing, but the poet might be. (Poets are sneaky, right?) Assuming that the poet is arguing, what is her argument?

5. Using this structure ("We did this, we do that," and so on), produce an eight-line poem of your own about some collective destiny.

MAKING CONNECTIONS

Imagine that you are Frederick Douglass (p. 62), gazing down on modern America and reading this poem. Using his language, write your response to the poem and the situation that it presents.

Sciences and Technologies

THE EGG AND THE SPERM
How Science Has Constructed a Romance Based on Stereotypical Male-Female Roles

Emily Martin

Emily Martin (b. 1944) is a professor of anthropology at Johns Hopkins University. She has written The Woman in the Body: A Cultural Analysis of Reproduction *(1987) and* Flexible Bodies: Tracking Immunity in American Culture — From the Days of Polio to the Age of AIDS *(1994). In the following article, which originally appeared in the journal* Signs *(1991), Martin's intent is to expose the cultural stereotypes operative in the so-called scientific language surrounding human reproduction.*

The theory of the human body is always a part of a world-picture. . . .
The theory of the human body is always a part of a fantasy.
— [JAMES HILLMAN, *The Myth of Analysis*][1]

Portions of this article were presented as the 1987 Becker Lecture, Cornell University. I am grateful for the many suggestions and ideas I received on this occasion. For especially pertinent help with my arguments and data I thank Richard Cone, Kevin Whaley, Sharon Stephens, Barbara Duden, Susanne Kuechler, Lorna Rhodes, and Scott Gilbert. The article was strengthened and clarified by the comments of the anonymous *Signs* reviewers as well as the superb editorial skills of Amy Gage.
    [1]James Hillman, *The Myth of Analysis* (Evanston, Ill.: Northwestern University Press, 1972), 220.

As an anthropologist, I am intrigued by the possibility that culture shapes how biological scientists describe what they discover about the natural world. If this were so, we would be learning about more than the natural world in high school biology class; we would be learning about cultural beliefs and practices as if they were part of nature. In the course of my research I realized that the picture of egg and sperm drawn in popular as well as scientific accounts of reproductive biology relies on stereotypes central to our cultural definitions of male and female. The stereotypes imply not only that female biological processes are less worthy than their male counterparts but also that women are less worthy than men. Part of my goal in writing this article is to shine a bright light on the gender stereotypes hidden within the scientific language of biology. Exposed in such a light, I hope they will lose much of their power to harm us.

Egg and Sperm: A Scientific Fairy Tale

At a fundamental level, all major scientific textbooks depict male and female reproductive organs as systems for the production of valuable substances, such as eggs and sperm.[2] In the case of women, the monthly cycle is described as being designed to produce eggs and prepare a suitable place for them to be fertilized and grown—all to the end of making babies. But the enthusiasm ends there. By extolling the female cycle as a productive enterprise, menstruation must necessarily be viewed as a failure. Medical texts describe menstruation as the "debris" of the uterine lining, the result of necrosis, or death of tissue. The descriptions imply that a system has gone awry, making products of no use, not to specification, unsalable, wasted, scrap. An illustration in a widely used medical text shows menstruation as a chaotic disintegration of form, complementing the many texts that describe it as "ceasing," "dying," "losing," "denuding," "expelling."[3]

Male reproductive physiology is evaluated quite differently. One of the texts that sees menstruation as failed production employs a sort of breathless prose when it describes the maturation of sperm: "The mechanisms which guide the remarkable cellular transformation from spermatid to mature sperm remain uncertain. . . . Perhaps the most amazing characteristic of spermatogenesis is its sheer magnitude: the normal human male may manufacture several hundred million sperm per day."[4] In the classic text

---

[2] The textbooks I consulted are the main ones used in classes for undergraduate premedical students or medical students (or those held on reserve in the library for these classes) during the past few years at Johns Hopkins University. These texts are widely used at other universities in the country as well.

[3] Arthur C. Guyton, *Physiology of the Human Body*, 6th ed. (Philadelphia: Saunders College Publishing, 1984), 624.

[4] Arthur J. Vander, James H. Sherman, and Dorothy S. Luciano, *Human Physiology: The Mechanisms of Body Function*, 3d ed. (New York: McGraw Hill, 1980), 483–84.

Medical Physiology, edited by Vernon Mountcastle, the male/female, productive/destructive comparison is more explicit: "Whereas the female *sheds* only a single gamete each month, the seminiferous tubules *produce* hundreds of millions of sperm each day" (emphasis mine).[5] The female author of another text marvels at the length of the microscopic seminiferous tubules, which, if uncoiled and placed end to end, "would span almost one-third of a mile!" She writes, "In an adult male these structures produce millions of sperm cells each day." Later she asks, "How is this feat accomplished?"[6] None of these texts expresses such intense enthusiasm for any female processes. It is surely no accident that the "remarkable" process of making sperm involves precisely what, in the medical view, menstruation does not: production of something deemed valuable.[7]

One could argue that menstruation and spermatogenesis are not analogous processes and, therefore, should not be expected to elicit the same kind of response. The proper female analogy to spermatogenesis, biologically, is ovulation. Yet ovulation does not merit enthusiasm in these texts either. Textbook descriptions stress that all of the ovarian follicles containing ova are already present at birth. Far from being *produced*, as sperm are, they merely sit on the shelf, slowly degenerating and aging like overstocked inventory: "At birth, normal human ovaries contain an estimated one million follicles [each], and no new ones appear after birth. Thus, in marked contrast to the male, the newborn female already has all the germ cells she will ever have. Only a few, perhaps 400, are destined to reach full maturity during her active productive life. All the others degenerate at some point in their development so that few, if any, remain by the time she reaches menopause at approximately 50 years of age."[8] Note the "marked contrast" that this description sets up between male and female: the male, who continuously produces fresh germ cells, and the female, who has stockpiled germ cells by birth and is faced with their degeneration.

Nor are the female organs spared such vivid descriptions. One scientist   5 writes in a newspaper article that a woman's ovaries become old and worn out from ripening eggs every month, even though the woman herself is still relatively young: "When you look through a laparoscope . . . at an ovary that has been through hundreds of cycles, even in a superbly healthy American female, you see a scarred, battered organ."[9]

---

[5]Vernon B. Mountcastle, *Medical Physiology*, 14th ed. (London: Mosby, 1980), 2:1624.

[6]Eldra Pearl Solomon, *Human Anatomy and Physiology* (New York: CBS College Publishing, 1983), 678.

[7]For elaboration, see Emily Martin, *The Woman in the Body: A Cultural Analysis of Reproduction* (Boston: Beacon, 1987), 27–53.

[8]Vander, Sherman, and Luciano, 568.

[9]Melvin Konner, "Childbearing and Age," *New York Times Magazine* (December 27, 1987), 22–23, esp. 22.

To avoid the negative connotations that some people associate with the female reproductive system, scientists could begin to describe male and female processes as homologous. They might credit females with "producing" mature ova one at a time, as they're needed each month, and describe males as having to face problems of degenerating germ cells. This degeneration would occur throughout life among spermatogonia, the undifferentiated germ cells in the testes that are the long-lived, dormant precursors of sperm.

But the texts have an almost dogged insistence on casting female processes in a negative light. The texts celebrate sperm production because it is continuous from puberty to senescence, while they portray egg production as inferior because it is finished at birth. This makes the female seem unproductive, but some texts will also insist that it is she who is wasteful.[10] In a section heading for *Molecular Biology of the Cell,* a best-selling text, we are told that "Oogenesis is wasteful." The text goes on to emphasize that of the seven million oogonia, or egg germ cells, in the female embryo, most degenerate in the ovary. Of those that do go on to become oocytes, or eggs, many also degenerate, so that at birth only two million eggs remain in the ovaries. Degeneration continues throughout a woman's life: by puberty 300,000 eggs remain, and only a few are present by menopause. "During the 40 or so years of a woman's reproductive life, only 400 to 500 eggs will have been released," the authors write. "All the rest will have degenerated. It is still a mystery why so many eggs are formed only to die in the ovaries."[11]

The real mystery is why the male's vast production of sperm is not seen as wasteful.[12] Assuming that a man "produces" 100 million (10^8) sperm per day (a conservative estimate) during an average reproductive life of sixty

---

[10]I have found but one exception to the opinion that the female is wasteful: "Smallpox being the nasty disease it is, one might expect nature to have designed antibody molecules with combining sites that specifically recognize the epitopes on smallpox virus. Nature differs from technology, however: it thinks nothing of wastefulness. (For example, rather than improving the chance that a spermatozoon will meet an egg cell, nature finds it easier to produce millions of spermatozoa.)" (Niels Kaj Jerne, "The Immune System," *Scientific American* 229, no. 1 [July 1973]: 53.) Thanks to a *Signs* reviewer for bringing this reference to my attention.

[11]Bruce Alberts et al., *Molecular Biology of the Cell* (New York: Garland, 1983), 795.

[12]In her essay "Have Only Men Evolved?" (in *Discovering Reality: Feminist Perspectives on Epistemology, Metaphysics, Methodology, and Philosophy of Science,* ed. Sandra Harding and Merrill B. Hintikka [Dordrecht, The Netherlands: Reidel, 1983], 45–69, esp. 60–61), Ruth Hubbard points out that sociobiologists have said the female invests more energy than the male in the production of her large gametes, claiming that this explains why the female provides parental care. Hubbard questions whether it "really takes more 'energy' to generate the one or relatively few eggs than the large excess of sperms required to achieve fertilization." For further critique of how the greater size of eggs is interpreted in sociobiology, see

years, he would produce well over two trillion sperm in his lifetime. Assuming that a woman "ripens" one egg per lunar month, or thirteen per year, over the course of her forty-year reproductive life, she would total five hundred eggs in her lifetime. But the word "waste" implies an excess, too much produced. Assuming two or three offspring, for every baby a woman produces, she wastes only around two hundred eggs. For every baby a man produces, he wastes more than one trillion (10^{12}) sperm.

How is it that positive images are denied to the bodies of women? A look at language—in this case, scientific language—provides the first clue. Take the egg and the sperm.[13] It is remarkable how "femininely" the egg behaves and how "masculinely" the sperm.[14] The egg is seen as large and passive.[15] It does not *move* or *journey*, but passively "is transported," "is swept,"[16] or even "drifts"[17] along the fallopian tube. In utter contrast, sperm are small, "streamlined,"[18] and invariably active. They "deliver" their genes to the egg, "activate the developmental program of the egg,"[19] and have a "velocity" that is often remarked upon.[20] Their tails are "strong" and efficiently powered.[21] Together with the forces of ejaculation, they can "propel the semen into the deepest recesses of the vagina."[22] For this they need "energy," "fuel,"[23] so that

---

Donna Haraway, "Investment Strategies for the Evolving Portfolio of Primate Females," in *Body/Politics,* ed. Mary Jacobus, Evelyn Fox Keller, and Sally Shuttleworth (New York: Routledge, 1990), 155–56.

[13]The sources I used for this article provide compelling information on interactions among sperm. Lack of space prevents me from taking up this theme here, but the elements include competition, hierarchy, and sacrifice. For a newspaper report, see Malcolm W. Browne, "Some Thoughts on Self Sacrifice," *New York Times* (July 5, 1988), C6. For a literary rendition, see John Barth, "Night-Sea Journey," in his *Lost in the Funhouse* (Garden City, N.Y.: Doubleday, 1968), 3–13.

[14]See Carol Delaney, "The Meaning of Paternity and the Virgin Birth Debate," *Man* 21, no. 3 (September 1986): 494–513. She discusses the difference between this scientific view that women contribute genetic material to the fetus and the claim of long-standing Western folk theories that the origin and identity of the fetus comes from the male, as in the metaphor of planting a seed in soil.

[15]For a suggested direct link between human behavior and purportedly passive eggs and active sperm, see Erik H. Erikson, "Inner and Outer Space: Reflections on Womanhood," *Daedalus* 93, no. 2 (Spring 1964): 582–606, esp. 591.

[16]Guyton (n. 3), 619; and Mountcastle (n. 5), 1609.

[17]Jonathan Miller and David Pelham, *The Facts of Life* (New York: Viking Penguin, 1984), 5.

[18]Alberts et al., 796.

[19]Ibid., 796.

[20]See, e.g., William F. Ganong, *Review of Medical Physiology,* 7th ed. (Los Altos, Calif.: Lange Medical Publications, 1975), 322.

[21]Alberts et al. (n. 11), 796.

[22]Guyton, 615.

[23]Solomon (n. 6), 683.

with a "whiplashlike motion and strong lurches"[24] they can "burrow through the egg coat"[25] and "penetrate" it.[26]

At its extreme, the age-old relationship of the egg and the sperm takes on   10
a royal or religious patina. The egg coat, its protective barrier, is sometimes
called its "vestments," a term usually reserved for sacred, religious dress. The
egg is said to have a "corona,"[27] a crown, and to be accompanied by "attendant cells."[28] It is holy, set apart and above, the queen to the sperm's king. The
egg is also passive, which means it must depend on sperm for rescue. Gerald
Schatten and Helen Schatten liken the egg's role to that of Sleeping Beauty: "a
dormant bride awaiting her mate's magic kiss, which instills the spirit that
brings her to life."[29] Sperm, by contrast, have a "mission,"[30] which is to
"move through the female genital tract in quest of the ovum."[31] One popular
account has it that the sperm carry out a "perilous journey" into the "warm
darkness," where some fall away "exhausted." "Survivors" "assault" the egg,
the successful candidates "surrounding the prize."[32] Part of the urgency of this
journey, in more scientific terms, is that "once released from the supportive
environment of the ovary, an egg will die within hours unless rescued by a
sperm."[33] The wording stresses the fragility and dependency of the egg, even
though the same text acknowledges elsewhere that sperm also live for only a
few hours.[34]

In 1948, in a book remarkable for its early insights into these matters,
Ruth Herschberger argued that female reproductive organs are seen as biologically interdependent, while male organs are viewed as autonomous,
operating independently and in isolation:

> At present the functional is stressed only in connection with women:
> it is in them that ovaries, tubes, uterus, and vagina have endless
> interdependence. In the male, reproduction would seem to involve
> "organs" only.
>
>   Yet the sperm, just as much as the egg, is dependent on a great
> many related processes. There are secretions which mitigate the
> urine in the urethra before ejaculation, to protect the sperm. There

---

[24]Vander, Sherman, and Luciano (n. 4), 4th ed. (1985), 580.

[25]Alberts et al., 796.

[26]All biology texts quoted use the word "penetrate."

[27]Solomon, 700.

[28]A. Beldecos et al., "The Importance of Feminist Critique for Contemporary
Cell Biology," *Hypatia* 3, no. 1 (Spring 1988): 61–76.

[29]Gerald Schatten and Helen Schatten, "The Energetic Egg," *Medical World
News* 23 (January 23, 1984): 51–53, esp. 51.

[30]Alberts et al., 796.

[31]Guyton (n. 3), 613.

[32]Miller and Pelham (n. 17), 7.

[33]Alberts et al. (n. 11), 804.

[34]Ibid., 801.

is the reflex shutting off of the bladder connection, the provision of prostatic secretions, and various types of muscular propulsion. The sperm is no more independent of its milieu than the egg, and yet from a wish that it were, biologists have lent their support to the notion that the human female, beginning with the egg, is congenitally more dependent than the male.[35]

Bringing out another aspect of the sperm's autonomy, an article in the journal *Cell* has the sperm making an "existential decision" to penetrate the egg: "Sperm are cells with a limited behavioral repertoire, one that is directed toward fertilizing eggs. To execute the decision to abandon the haploid state, sperm swim to an egg and there acquire the ability to effect membrane fusion."[36] Is this a corporate manager's version of the sperm's activities — "executing decisions" while fraught with dismay over difficult options that bring with them very high risk?

There is another way that sperm, despite their small size, can be made to loom in importance over the egg. In a collection of scientific papers, an electron micrograph of an enormous egg and tiny sperm is titled "A Portrait of the Sperm."[37] This is a little like showing a photo of a dog and calling it a picture of the fleas. Granted, microscopic sperm are harder to photograph than eggs, which are just large enough to see with the naked eye. But surely the use of the term "portrait," a word associated with the powerful and wealthy, is significant. Eggs have only micrographs or pictures, not portraits.

One depiction of sperm as weak and timid, instead of strong and powerful — the only such representation in Western civilization, so far as I know — occurs in Woody Allen's movie *Everything You Always Wanted to Know about Sex* *But Were Afraid to Ask*. Allen, playing the part of an apprehensive sperm inside a man's testicles, is scared of the man's approaching orgasm. He is reluctant to launch himself into the darkness, afraid of contraceptive devices, afraid of winding up on the ceiling if the man masturbates.

The more common picture — egg as damsel in distress, shielded only by her sacred garments; sperm as heroic warrior to the rescue — cannot be proved to be dictated by the biology of these events. While the "facts" of biology may not *always* be constructed in cultural terms, I would argue that in this case they are. The degree of metaphorical content in these descriptions, the extent to which differences between egg and sperm are emphasized, and the parallels between cultural stereotypes of male and female behavior and the character of egg and sperm all point to this conclusion. 15

---

[35]Ruth Herschberger, *Adam's Rib* (New York: Pelligrini & Cudahy, 1948), esp. 84. I am indebted to Ruth Hubbard for telling me about Herschberger's work, although at a point when this paper was already in draft form.

[36]Bennett M. Shapiro, "The Existential Decision of a Sperm," *Cell* 49, no. 3 (May 1987): 293–94, esp. 293.

[37]Lennart Nilsson, "A Portrait of the Sperm," in *The Functional Anatomy of the Spermatozoan*, ed. Bjorn A. Afzelius (New York: Pergamon, 1975), 79–82.

New Research, Old Imagery

As new understandings of egg and sperm emerge, textbook gender imagery is being revised. But the new research, far from escaping the stereo-typical representations of egg and sperm, simply replicates elements of text-book gender imagery in a different form. The persistence of this imagery calls to mind what Ludwik Fleck termed "the self-contained" nature of sci-entific thought. As he described it, "the interaction between what is already known, what remains to be learned, and those who are to apprehend it, go to ensure harmony within the system. But at the same time they also pre-serve the harmony of illusions, which is quite secure within the confines of a given thought style."[38] We need to understand the way in which the cul-tural content in scientific descriptions changes as biological discoveries unfold, and whether that cultural content is solidly entrenched or easily changed.

In all of the texts quoted above, sperm are described as penetrating the egg, and specific substances on a sperm's head are described as binding to the egg. Recently, this description of events was rewritten in a biophysics lab at Johns Hopkins University—transforming the egg from the passive to the active party.[39]

Prior to this research, it was thought that the zona, the inner vestments of the egg, formed an impenetrable barrier. Sperm overcame the barrier by mechanically burrowing through, thrashing their tails and slowly working their way along. Later research showed that the sperm released digestive enzymes that chemically broke down the zona; thus, scientists presumed that the sperm used mechanical *and* chemical means to get through to the egg.

In this recent investigation, the researchers began to ask questions about the mechanical force of the sperm's tail. (The lab's goal was to devel-op a contraceptive that worked topically on sperm.) They discovered, to their great surprise, that the forward thrust of sperm is extremely weak, which contradicts the assumption that sperm are forceful penetrators.[40] Rather than thrusting forward, the sperm's head was now seen to move mostly back and forth. The sideways motion of the sperm's tail makes the

---

[38]Ludwik Fleck, *Genesis and Development of a Scientific Fact,* ed. Thaddeus J. Trenn and Robert K. Merton (Chicago: University of Chicago Press, 1979), 38.

[39]Jay M. Baltz carried out the research I describe when he was a graduate student in the Thomas C. Jenkins Department of Biophysics at Johns Hopkins University.

[40]Far less is known about the physiology of sperm than comparable female sub-stances, which some feminists claim is no accident. Greater scientific scrutiny of female reproduction has long enabled the burden of birth control to be placed on women. In this case, the researchers' discovery did not depend on development of any new technology. The experiments made use of glass pipettes, a manometer, and a simple microscope, all of which have been available for more than one hundred years.

head move sideways with a force that is ten times stronger than its forward movement. So even if the overall force of the sperm were strong enough to mechanically break the zona, most of its force would be directed sideways rather than forward. In fact, its strongest tendency, by tenfold, is to escape by attempting to pry itself off the egg. Sperm, then, must be exceptionally efficient at *escaping* from any cell surface they contact. And the surface of the egg must be designed to trap the sperm and prevent their escape. Otherwise, few if any sperm would reach the egg.

The researchers at Johns Hopkins concluded that the sperm and egg 20 stick together because of adhesive molecules on the surfaces of each. The egg traps the sperm and adheres to it so tightly that the sperm's head is forced to lie flat against the surface of the zona, a little bit, they told me, "like Br'er Rabbit getting more and more stuck to tar baby the more he wriggles." The trapped sperm continues to wiggle ineffectually side to side. The mechanical force of its tail is so weak that a sperm cannot break even one chemical bond. This is where the digestive enzymes released by the sperm come in. If they start to soften the zona just at the tip of the sperm and the sides remain stuck, then the weak, flailing sperm can get oriented in the right direction and make it through the zona—provided that its bonds to the zona dissolve as it moves in.

Although this new version of the saga of the egg and the sperm broke through cultural expectations, the researchers who made the discovery continued to write papers and abstracts as if the sperm were the active party who attacks, binds, penetrates, and enters the egg. The only difference was that sperm were now seen as performing these actions weakly.[41] Not until August 1987, more than three years after the findings described above, did these researchers reconceptualize the process to give the egg a more active role. They began to describe the zona as an aggressive sperm catcher, covered with adhesive molecules that can capture a sperm with a single bond and clasp it to the zona's surface.[42] In the words of their published account:

---

[41]Jay Baltz and Richard A. Cone, "What Force Is Needed to Tether a Sperm?" (abstract for Society for the Study of Reproduction, 1985), and "Flagellar Torque on the Head Determines the Force Needed to Tether a Sperm" (abstract for Biophysical Society, 1986).

[42]Jay M. Baltz, David F. Katz, and Richard A. Cone, "The Mechanics of the Sperm-Egg Interaction at the Zona Pellucida," *Biophysical Journal* 54, no. 4 (October 1988): 643–54. Lab members were somewhat familiar with work on metaphors in the biology of female reproduction. Richard Cone, who runs the lab, is my husband, and he talked with them about my earlier research on the subject from time to time. Even though my current research focuses on biological imagery and I heard about the lab's work from my husband every day, I myself did not recognize the role of imagery in the sperm research until many weeks after the period of research and writing I describe. Therefore, I assume that any awareness the lab members may have had about how underlying metaphor might be guiding this particular research was fairly inchoate.

"The innermost vestment, the *zona pellucida,* is a glyco-protein shell, which captures and tethers the sperm before they penetrate it. . . . The sperm is captured at the initial contact between the sperm tip and the *zona.* . . . Since the thrust [of the sperm] is much smaller than the force needed to break a single affinity bond, the first bond made upon the tip-first meeting of the sperm and *zona* can result in the capture of the sperm."[43]

Experiments in another lab reveal similar patterns of data interpretation. Gerald Schatten and Helen Schatten set out to show that, contrary to conventional wisdom, the "egg is not merely a large, yolk-filled sphere into which the sperm burrows to endow new life. Rather, recent research suggests the almost heretical view that sperm and egg are mutually active partners."[44] This sounds like a departure from the stereotypical textbook view, but further reading reveals Schatten and Schatten's conformity to the aggressive-sperm metaphor. They describe how "the sperm and egg first touch when, from the tip of the sperm's triangular head, a long, thin filament shoots out and harpoons the egg." Then we learn that "remarkably, the harpoon is not so much fired as assembled at great speed, molecule by molecule, from a pool of protein stored in a specialized region called the acrosome. The filament may grow as much as twenty times longer than the sperm head itself before its tip reaches the egg and sticks."[45] Why not call this "making a bridge" or "throwing out a line" rather than firing a harpoon? Harpoons pierce prey and injure or kill them, while this filament only sticks. And why not focus, as the Hopkins lab did, on the stickiness of the egg, rather than the stickiness of the sperm?[46] Later in the article, the Schattens replicate the common view of the sperm's perilous journey into the warm darkness of the vagina, this time for the purpose of explaining its journey into the egg itself: "[The sperm] still has an arduous journey ahead. It must penetrate farther into the egg's huge sphere of cytoplasm and somehow locate the nucleus, so that the two cells' chromosomes can fuse. The sperm dives down into the cytoplasm, its tail beating. But it is soon interrupted by the sudden and swift migration of the egg nucleus, which rushes toward the sperm with a velocity triple that of the movement of chromosomes during cell division, crossing the entire egg in about a minute."[47]

Like Schatten and Schatten and the biophysicists at Johns Hopkins, another researcher has recently made discoveries that seem to point to a more interactive view of the relationship of egg and sperm. This work,

---

[43]Ibid., 643, 650.

[44]Schatten and Schatten (n. 29), 51.

[45]Ibid., 52.

[46]Surprisingly, in an article intended for a general audience, the authors do not point out that these are sea urchin sperm and note that human sperm do not shoot out filaments at all.

[47]Schatten and Schatten, 53.

which Paul Wassarman conducted on the sperm and eggs of mice, focuses on identifying the specific molecules in the egg coat (the zona pellucida) that are involved in egg-sperm interaction. At first glance, his descriptions seem to fit the model of an egalitarian relationship. Male and female gametes "recognize one another," and "interactions . . . take place between sperm and egg."[48] But the article in *Scientific American* in which those descriptions appear begins with a vignette that presages the dominant motif of their presentation: "It has been more than a century since Hermann Fol, a Swiss zoologist, peered into his microscope and became the first person to see a sperm penetrate an egg, fertilize it and form the first cell of a new embryo."[49] This portrayal of the sperm as the active party—the one that *penetrates* and *fertilizes* the egg and *produces* the embryo—is not cited as an example of an earlier, now outmoded view. In fact, the author reiterates the point later in the article: "Many sperm can bind to and penetrate the zona pellucida, or outer coat, of an unfertilized mouse egg, but only one sperm will eventually fuse with the thin plasma membrane surrounding the egg proper (*inner sphere*), fertilizing the egg and giving rise to a new embryo."[50]

The imagery of sperm as aggressor is particularly startling in this case: the main discovery being reported is isolation of a particular molecule *on the egg coat* that plays an important role in fertilization! Wassarman's choice of language sustains the picture. He calls the molecule that has been isolated, ZP3, a "sperm receptor." By allocating the passive, waiting role to the egg, Wassarman can continue to describe the sperm as the actor, the one that makes it all happen: "The basic process begins when many sperm first attach loosely and then bind tenaciously to receptors on the surface of the egg's thick outer coat, the zona pellucida. Each sperm, which has a large number of egg-binding proteins on its surface, binds to many sperm receptors on the egg. More specifically, a site on each of the egg-binding proteins fits a complementary site on a sperm receptor, much as a key fits a lock."[51] With the sperm designated as the "key" and the egg the "lock," it is obvious which one acts and which one is acted upon. Could this imagery not be reversed, letting the sperm (the lock) wait until the egg produces the key? Or could we speak of two halves of a locket matching, and regard the matching itself as the action that initiates the fertilization?

It is as if Wassarman were determined to make the egg the receiving partner. Usually in biological research, the *protein* member of the pair of binding molecules is called the receptor, and physically it has a pocket in it rather like a lock. As the diagrams that illustrate Wassarman's article show,

25

---

[48]Paul M. Wassarman, "Fertilization in Mammals," *Scientific American* 259, no. 6 (December 1988): 78–84, esp. 78, 84.

[49]Ibid., 78.

[50]Ibid., 79.

[51]Ibid., 78.

the molecules on the sperm are proteins and have "pockets." The small, mobile molecules that fit into these pockets are called ligands. As shown in the diagrams, ZP3 on the egg is a polymer of "keys"; many small knobs stick out. Typically, molecules on the sperm would be called receptors and molecules on the egg would be called ligands. But Wassarman chose to name ZP3 on the egg the receptor and to create a new term, "the egg-binding protein," for the molecule on the sperm that otherwise would have been called the receptor.[52]

Wassarman does credit the egg coat with having more functions than those of a sperm receptor. While he notes that "the zona pellucida has at times been viewed by investigators as a nuisance, a barrier to sperm and hence an impediment to fertilization," his new research reveals that the egg coat "serves as a sophisticated biological security system that screens incoming sperm, selects only those compatible with fertilization and development, prepares sperm for fusion with the egg and later protects the resulting embryo from polyspermy [a lethal condition caused by fusion of more than one sperm with a single egg]."[53] Although this description gives the egg an active role, that role is drawn in stereotypically feminine terms. The egg *selects* an appropriate mate, *prepares* him for fusion, and then *protects* the resulting offspring from harm. This is courtship and mating behavior as seen through the eyes of a sociobiologist: woman as the hard-to-get prize, who, following union with the chosen one, becomes woman as servant and mother.

And Wassarman does not quit there. In a review article for *Science,* he outlines the "chronology of fertilization."[54] Near the end of the article are two subject headings. One is "Sperm Penetration," in which Wassarman describes how the chemical dissolving of the zona pellucida combines with the "substantial propulsive force generated by sperm." The next heading is "Sperm-Egg Fusion." This section details what happens inside the zona after a sperm "penetrates" it. Sperm "can make contact with, adhere to, and fuse with (that is, fertilize) an egg."[55] Wassarman's word choice, again, is astonishingly skewed in favor of the sperm's activity, for in the next breath he says that sperm *lose* all motility upon fusion with the egg's surface. In mouse and sea urchin eggs, the sperm enters at the *egg's* volition, according to Wassarman's description: "Once fused with egg plasma membrane [the surface of the egg], how does a sperm enter the egg? The surface

---

[52]Since receptor molecules are relatively immotile and the ligands that bind to them relatively motile, one might imagine the egg being called the receptor and the sperm the ligand. But the molecules in question on egg and sperm are immotile molecules. It is the sperm as a cell that has motility, and the egg as a cell that has relative immotility.

[53]Wassarman, 78–79.

[54]Paul M. Wassarman, "The Biology and Chemistry of Fertilization," *Science* 235, no. 4788 (January 30, 1987): 553–60, esp. 554.

[55]Ibid., 557.

of both mouse and sea urchin eggs is covered with thousands of plasma membrane-bound projections, called microvilli [tiny "hairs"]. Evidence in sea urchins suggests that, after membrane fusion, a group of elongated microvilli cluster tightly around and interdigitate over the sperm head. As these microvilli are resorbed, the sperm is drawn into the egg. Therefore, sperm motility, which ceases at the time of fusion in both sea urchins and mice, is not required for sperm entry."[56] The section called "Sperm Penetration" more logically would be followed by a section called "The Egg Envelops," rather than "Sperm-Egg Fusion." This would give a parallel — and more accurate — sense that both the egg and the sperm initiate action.

Another way that Wassarman makes less of the egg's activity is by describing components of the egg but referring to the sperm as a whole entity. Deborah Gordon has described such an approach as "atomism" ("the part is independent of and primordial to the whole") and identified it as one of the "tenacious assumptions" of Western science and medicine.[57] Wassarman employs atomism to his advantage. When he refers to processing going on within sperm, he consistently returns to descriptions that remind us from whence these activities came: they are part of sperm that penetrate an egg or generate propulsive force. When he refers to processes going on within eggs, he stops there. As a result, any active role he grants them appears to be assigned to the parts of the egg, and not to the egg itself. In the quote above, it is the microvilli that actively cluster around the sperm. In another example, "the driving force for engulfment of a fused sperm comes from a region of cytoplasm just beneath an egg's plasma membrane."[58]

Social Implications: Thinking Beyond

All three of these revisionist accounts of egg and sperm cannot seem to escape the hierarchical imagery of older accounts. Even though each new account gives the egg a larger and more active role, taken together they bring into play another cultural stereotype: woman as a dangerous and aggressive threat. In the Johns Hopkins lab's revised model, the egg ends up as the female aggressor who "captures and tethers" the sperm with her sticky zona, rather like a spider lying in wait in her web.[59] The Schatten lab has the egg's nucleus "interrupt" the sperm's dive with a "sudden and swift" rush by which she "clasps the sperm and guides its nucleus to the

---

[56]Ibid., 557–58. This finding throws into question Schatten and Schatten's description (n. 29 above) of the sperm, its tail beating, diving down into the egg.

[57]Deborah R. Gordon, "Tenacious Assumptions in Western Medicine," in *Biomedicine Examined,* ed. Margaret Lock and Deborah Gordon (Dordrecht, The Netherlands: Kluwer, 1988), 19–56, esp. 26.

[58]Wassarman, "The Biology and Chemistry of Fertilization," 558.

[59]Baltz, Katz, and Cone (n. 42 above), 643, 650.

center."[60] Wassarman's description of the surface of the egg "covered with thousands of plasma membrane-bound projections, called microvilli" that reach out and clasp the sperm adds to the spiderlike imagery.[61]

These images grant the egg an active role but at the cost of appearing   30 disturbingly aggressive. Images of woman as dangerous and aggressive, the femme fatale who victimizes men, are widespread in Western literature and culture.[62] More specific is the connection of spider imagery with the idea of an engulfing, devouring mother.[63] New data did not lead scientists to eliminate gender stereotypes in their descriptions of egg and sperm. Instead, scientists simply began to describe egg and sperm in different, but no less damaging, terms.

Can we envision a less stereotypical view? Biology itself provides another model that could be applied to the egg and the sperm. The cybernetic model—with its feedback loops, flexible adaptation to change, coordination of the parts within a whole, evolution over time, and changing response to the environment—is common in genetics, endocrinology, and ecology and has a growing influence in medicine in general.[64] This model has the potential to shift our imagery from the negative, in which the female reproductive system is castigated both for not producing eggs after birth and for producing (and thus wasting) too many eggs overall, to something more positive. The female reproductive system could be seen as responding to the environment (pregnancy or menopause), adjusting to monthly changes (menstruation), and flexibly changing from reproductivity after puberty to nonreproductivity later in life. The sperm and egg's interaction could also be described in cybernetic terms. J. F. Hartman's research in reproductive biology demonstrated fifteen years ago that if an egg is killed by being pricked with a needle, live sperm cannot get through the zona.[65] Clearly, this evidence shows that the egg and sperm *do* interact on more mutual terms, making biology's refusal to portray them that way all the more disturbing.

We would do well to be aware, however, that cybernetic imagery is hardly neutral. In the past, cybernetic models have played an important part in the imposition of social control. These models inherently provide a way

---

[60]Schatten and Schatten, 53.

[61]Wassarman, "The Biology and Chemistry of Fertilization," 557.

[62]Mary Ellman, *Thinking about Women* (New York: Harcourt Brace Jovanovich, 1968), 140; Nina Auerbach, *Woman and the Demon* (Cambridge, Mass.: Harvard University Press, 1982), esp. 186.

[63]Kenneth Alan Adams, "Arachnophobia: Love American Style," *Journal of Psychoanalytic Anthropology* 4, no. 2 (1981): 157–97.

[64]William Ray Arney and Bernard Bergen, *Medicine and the Management of Living* (Chicago: University of Chicago Press, 1984).

[65]J. F. Hartman, R. B. Gwatkin, and C. F. Hutchison, "Early Contact Interactions between Mammalian Gametes *In Vitro*," *Proceedings of the National Academy of Sciences (U.S.)* 69, no. 10 (1972): 2767–69.

of thinking about a "field" of interacting components. Once the field can be seen, it can become the object of new forms of knowledge, which in turn can allow new forms of social control to be exerted over the components of the field. During the 1950s, for example, medicine began to recognize the psychosocial *environment* of the patient: the patient's family and its psychodynamics. Professions such as social work began to focus on this new environment, and the resulting knowledge became one way to further control the patient. Patients began to be seen not as isolated, individual bodies, but as psychosocial entities located in an "ecological" system: management of "the patient's psychology was a new entrée to patient control."[66]

The models that biologists use to describe their data can have important social effects. During the nineteenth century, the social and natural sciences strongly influenced each other: the social ideas of Malthus about how to avoid the natural increase of the poor inspired Darwin's *Origin of Species*.[67] Once the *Origin* stood as a description of the natural world, complete with competition and market struggles, it could be reimported into social science as social Darwinism, in order to justify the social order of the time. What we are seeing now is similar: the importation of cultural ideas about passive females and heroic males into the "personalities" of gametes. This amounts to the "implanting of social imagery on representations of nature so as to lay a firm basis for reimporting exactly that same imagery as natural explanations of social phenomena."[68]

Further research would show us exactly what social effects are being wrought from the biological imagery of egg and sperm. At the very least, the imagery keeps alive some of the hoariest old stereotypes about weak damsels in distress and their strong male rescuers. That these stereotypes are now being written in at the level of the *cell* constitutes a powerful move to make them seem so natural as to be beyond alteration.

The stereotypical imagery might also encourage people to imagine that 35 what results from the interaction of egg and sperm—a fertilized egg—is the result of deliberate "human" action at the cellular level. Whatever the intentions of the human couple, in this microscope "culture" a cellular "bride" (or femme fatale) and a cellular "groom" (her victim) make a cellular baby. Rosalind Petchesky points out that through visual representations such as sonograms, we are given "*images* of younger and younger, and tinier and tinier, fetuses being 'saved.'" This leads to "the point of viability being 'pushed back' *indefinitely*."[69] Endowing egg and sperm with intentional action, a key aspect of personhood in our culture, lays the foundation for the point of viability being pushed back to the moment of

[66]Arney and Bergen, 68.

[67]Ruth Hubbard, "Have Only Men Evolved?" (n. 12 above), 51–52.

[68]David Harvey, personal communication, November 1989.

[69]Rosalind Petchesky, "Fetal Images: The Power of Visual Culture in the Politics of Reproduction," *Feminist Studies* 13, no. 2 (Summer 1987): 263–92, esp. 272.

fertilization. This will likely lead to greater acceptance of technological developments and new forms of scrutiny and manipulation, for the benefit of these inner "persons": court-ordered restrictions on a pregnant woman's activities in order to protect her fetus, fetal surgery, amniocentesis, and rescinding of abortion rights, to name but a few examples.[70]

Even if we succeed in substituting more egalitarian, interactive metaphors to describe the activities of egg and sperm, and manage to avoid the pitfalls of cybernetic models, we would still be guilty of endowing cellular entities with personhood. More crucial, then, than what *kinds* of personalities we bestow on cells is the very fact that we are doing it at all. This process could ultimately have the most disturbing social consequences.

One clear feminist challenge is to wake up sleeping metaphors in science, particularly those involved in descriptions of the egg and the sperm. Although the literary convention is to call such metaphors "dead," they are not so much dead as sleeping, hidden within the scientific content of texts — and all the more powerful for it.[71] Waking up such metaphors, by becoming aware of when we are projecting cultural imagery onto what we study, will improve our ability to investigate and understand nature. Waking up such metaphors, by becoming aware of their implications, will rob them of their power to naturalize our social conventions about gender.

QUESTIONS

1. Summarize Martin's argument. How has she structured it?
2. The first subheading in the essay is "Egg and Sperm: A Scientific Fairy Tale." The implications are that the actions of the egg and sperm constitute a story written by scientists. Why does Martin call it a fairy tale? What fairy tales does it resemble? In the process of your sexual education, what stories were you told?
3. Martin's argument raises the issue of scientific objectivity. Do you think there can be such a thing as a "pure" fact? Or can we only say that one fact is less encumbered by cultural baggage than another fact? What does Martin suggest as the best approach in presenting reproductive facts?
4. Look at some biology textbooks. How is reproduction presented? Are the same or similar "sleeping metaphors" that Martin discusses present

---

[70]Rita Arditti, Renate Klein, and Shelley Minden, *Test-Tube Women* (London: Pandora, 1984); Ellen Goodman, "Whose Right to Life?" *Baltimore Sun* (November 17, 1987); Tamar Lewin, "Courts Acting to Force Care of the Unborn," *New York Times* (November 23, 1987), A1 and B10; Susan Irwin and Brigitte Jordan, "Knowledge, Practice, and Power: Court Ordered Cesarean Sections," *Medical Anthropology Quarterly* 1, no. 3 (September 1987): 319–34.

[71]Thanks to Elizabeth Fee and David Spain, who in February 1989 and April 1989, respectively, made points related to this.

in the discussion? What about other bodily processes and functions? Is the male body used as the sole example in discussions of the heart, blood pressure, digestion, or AIDS, for instance?

5. Using the biological information in Martin's essay, write a nonsexist description of the reproductive functions. In your conclusion, reflect on any difficulties you encountered in keeping your cellular entities free of personhood. Switch papers with a classmate to check one another for "sleeping metaphors."

6. Look at a sampling of sex education texts and materials designed for elementary or secondary school students to see if the cultural stereotypes that Martin warns against are present. What analogies and metaphors do you find being used? Write up your discussion as an argument either for or against the revision of those texts.

MAKING CONNECTIONS

Martin warns us to be on the alert for "sleeping metaphors." Sylvia Plath gives us nine metaphors about the female body in her poem "Metaphors" (p. 377). Were those metaphors sleeping? Did Plath wake them up? Consider the way that metaphors are used in some of the argumentative essays in this section. If we assume that sleeping metaphors are used without the full awareness of the writer, then they may be a good place to begin a counterargument. Can you find essays that work by waking the sleeping metaphors of others? Can you find sleeping metaphors in one of these essays and use them for an argument of your own? Write an essay in which you do one or both of these things.

WOMEN'S BRAINS

Stephen Jay Gould

Stephen Jay Gould (b. 1941) is a professor of biology, geology, and the history of science at Harvard University. He is also a base-ball fan and a prolific essayist. In 1974, he began writing "This View of Life," a monthly column for Natural History, *where he has not only explained and defended Darwinian ideas of evolution but also exposed abuses and misunderstandings of scientific con-cepts and methods. The latest of his many publications is* The Lying Stones of Marrakech: Penultimate Reflections in Natural History *(2000). The following essay appeared in* Natural History *in 1992.*

In the prelude to *Middlemarch*, George Eliot[1] lamented the unfulfilled lives of talented women:

> Some have felt that these blundering lives are due to the inconve-nient indefiniteness with which the Supreme Power has fashioned the natures of women: if there were one level of feminine incompe-tence as strict as the ability to count three and no more, the social lot of women might be treated with scientific certitude.

Eliot goes on to discount the idea of innate limitation, but while she wrote in 1872, the leaders of European anthropometry were trying to mea-sure "with scientific certitude" the inferiority of women. Anthropometry, or measurement of the human body, is not so fashionable a field these days, but it dominated the human sciences for much of the nineteenth century and remained popular until intelligence testing replaced skull measurement as a favored device for making invidious comparisons among races, classes, and sexes. Craniometry, or measurement of the skull, commanded the most attention and respect. Its unquestioned leader, Paul Broca (1824–80), pro-fessor of clinical surgery at the Faculty of Medicine in Paris, gathered a school of disciples and imitators around himself. Their work, so meticulous and apparently irrefutable, exerted great influence and won high esteem as a jewel of nineteenth-century science.

Broca's work seemed particularly invulnerable to refutation. Had he not measured with the most scrupulous care and accuracy? (Indeed, he had.

---

[1]*George Eliot:* The pen name of Marianne Evans (1819–1880), British novel-ist. *Middlemarch* (1871–1872) is considered her greatest work. [Eds.]

I have the greatest respect for Broca's meticulous procedure. His numbers are sound. But science is an inferential exercise, not a catalog of facts. Numbers, by themselves, specify nothing. All depends upon what you do with them.) Broca depicted himself as an apostle of objectivity, a man who bowed before facts and cast aside superstition and sentimentality. He declared that "there is no faith, however respectable, no interest, however legitimate, which must not accommodate itself to the progress of human knowledge and bend before truth." Women, like it or not, had smaller brains than men and, therefore, could not equal them in intelligence. This fact, Broca argued, may reinforce a common prejudice in male society, but it is also a scientific truth. L. Manouvrier, a black sheep in Broca's fold, rejected the inferiority of women and wrote with feeling about the burden imposed upon them by Broca's numbers:

> Women displayed their talents and their diplomas. They also invoked philosophical authorities. But they were opposed by *numbers* unknown to Condorcet[2] or to John Stuart Mill.[3] These numbers fell upon poor women like a sledge hammer, and they were accompanied by commentaries and sarcasms more ferocious than the most misogynist imprecations of certain church fathers. The theologians had asked if women had a soul. Several centuries later, some scientists were ready to refuse them a human intelligence.

Broca's argument rested upon two sets of data: the larger brains of men in modern societies, and a supposed increase in male superiority through time. His most extensive data came from autopsies performed personally in four Parisian hospitals. For 292 male brains, he calculated an average weight of 1,325 grams; 140 female brains averaged 1,144 grams for a difference of 181 grams, or 14 percent of the male weight. Broca understood, of course, that part of this difference could be attributed to the greater height of males. Yet he made no attempt to measure the effect of size alone and actually stated that it cannot account for the entire difference because we know, a priori, that women are not as intelligent as men (a premise that the data were supposed to test, not rest upon):

> We might ask if the small size of the female brain depends exclusively upon the small size of her body. Tiedemann has proposed this explanation. But we must not forget that women are, on the average, a little less intelligent than men, a difference which we should not exaggerate but which is, nonetheless, real. We are therefore

---

[2]*Marquis de Condorcet* (1743–1794): A French mathematician and revolutionary. [Eds.]

[3]*John Stuart Mill* (1806–1873): A British economist and philosopher. [Eds.]

permitted to suppose that the relatively small size of the female brain depends in part upon her physical inferiority and in part upon her intellectual inferiority.

In 1873, the year after Eliot published *Middlemarch,* Broca measured   5
the cranial capacities of prehistoric skulls from L'Homme Mort cave. Here he found a difference of only 99.5 cubic centimeters between males and females, while modern populations range from 129.5 to 220.7. Topinard, Broca's chief disciple, explained the increasing discrepancy through time as a result of differing evolutionary pressures upon dominant men and passive women:

> The man who fights for two or more in the struggle for existence, who has all the responsibility and the cares of tomorrow, who is constantly active in combating the environment and human rivals, needs more brain than the woman whom he must protect and nourish, the sedentary woman, lacking any interior occupations, whose role is to raise children, love, and be passive.

In 1879, Gustave Le Bon, chief misogynist of Broca's school, used these data to publish what must be the most vicious attack upon women in modern scientific literature (no one can top Aristotle). I do not claim his views were representative of Broca's school, but they were published in France's most respected anthropological journal. Le Bon concluded:

> In the most intelligent races, as among the Parisians, there are a large number of women whose brains are closer in size to those of gorillas than to the most developed male brains. This inferiority is so obvious that no one can contest it for a moment; only its degree is worth discussion. All psychologists who have studied the intelligence of women, as well as poets and novelists, recognize today that they represent the most inferior forms of human evolution and that they are closer to children and savages than to an adult, civilized man. They excel in fickleness, inconstancy, absence of thought and logic, and incapacity to reason. Without doubt there exist some distinguished women, very superior to the average man, but they are as exceptional as the birth of any monstrosity, as, for example, of a gorilla with two heads; consequently, we may neglect them entirely.

Nor did Le Bon shrink from the social implications of his views. He was horrified by the proposal of some American reformers to grant women higher education on the same basis as men:

> A desire to give them the same education, and, as a consequence, to propose the same goals for them, is a dangerous chimera. . . . The day when, misunderstanding the inferior occupations which

nature has given her, women leave the home and take part in our battles; on this day a social revolution will begin, and everything that maintains the sacred ties of the family will disappear.

Sound familiar?[4]

I have reexamined Broca's data, the basis for all this derivative pronouncement, and I find his numbers sound but his interpretation ill-founded, to say the least. The data supporting his claim for increased difference through time can be easily dismissed. Broca based his contention on the samples from L'Homme Mort alone—only seven male and six female skulls in all. Never have so little data yielded such far ranging conclusions.

In 1988, Topinard published Broca's more extensive data on the Parisian hospitals. Since Broca recorded height and age as well as brain size, we may use modern statistics to remove their effect. Brain weight decreases with age, and Broca's women were, on average, considerably older than his men. Brain weight increases with height, and his average man was almost half a foot taller than his average woman. I used multiple regression, a technique that allowed me to assess simultaneously the influence of height and age upon brain size. In an analysis of the data for women, I found that, at average male height and age, a woman's brain would weigh 1,212 grams. Correction for height and age reduces Broca's measured difference of 181 grams by more than a third, to 113 grams.

I don't know what to make of this remaining difference because I cannot   10
assess other factors known to influence brain size in a major way. Cause of death has an important effect: degenerative disease often entails a substantial diminution of brain size. (This effect is separate from the decrease attributed to age alone.) Eugene Schreider, also working with Broca's data, found that men killed in accidents had brains weighing, on average, 60 grams more than men dying of infectious diseases. The best modern data I can find (from American hospitals) records a full 100-gram difference between death by degenerative arteriosclerosis and by violence or accident. Since so many of Broca's subjects were elderly women, we may assume that lengthy degenerative disease was more common among them than among the men.

More importantly, modern students of brain size still have not agreed on a proper measure for eliminating the powerful effect of body size. Height is partly adequate, but men and women of the same height do not share the same body build. Weight is even worse than height, because most of its variation reflects nutrition rather than intrinsic size—fat versus skinny exerts little influence upon the brain. Manouvrier took up this subject in the 1880s and argued that muscular mass and force should be used. He tried to measure

---

[4]When I wrote this essay, I assumed that Le Bon was a marginal, if colorful, figure. I have since learned that he was a leading scientist, one of the founders of social psychology, and best known for a seminal study on crowd behavior, still cited today (*La psychologie des foules,* 1895), and for his work on unconscious motivation.

this elusive property in various ways and found a marked difference in favor of men, even in men and women of the same height. When he corrected for what he called "sexual mass," women actually came out slightly ahead in brain size.

Thus, the corrected 113-gram difference is surely too large; the true figure is probably close to zero and may as well favor women as men. And 113 grams, by the way, is exactly the average difference between a 5 foot 4 inch and a 6 foot 4 inch male in Broca's data. We would not (especially us short folks) want to ascribe greater intelligence to tall men. In short, who knows what to do with Broca's data? They certainly don't permit any confident claim that men have bigger brains than women.

To appreciate the social role of Broca and his school, we must recognize that his statements about the brains of women do not reflect an isolated prejudice toward a single disadvantaged group. They must be weighed in the context of a general theory that supported contemporary social distinctions as biologically ordained. Women, blacks, and poor people suffered the same disparagement, but women bore the brunt of Broca's argument because he had easier access to data on women's brains. Women were singularly denigrated but they also stood as surrogates for other disenfranchised groups. As one of Broca's disciples wrote in 1881: "Men of the black races have a brain scarcely heavier than that of white women." This juxtaposition extended into many other realms of anthropological argument, particularly to claims that, anatomically and emotionally, both women and blacks were like white children—and that white children, by the theory of recapitulation, represented an ancestral (primitive) adult stage of human evolution. I do not regard as empty rhetoric the claim that women's battles are for all of us.

Maria Montessori did not confine her activities to educational reform for young children. She lectured on anthropology for several years at the University of Rome, and wrote an influential book entitled *Pedagogical Anthropology* (English edition, 1913). Montessori was no egalitarian. She supported most of Broca's work and the theory of innate criminality proposed by her compatriot Cesare Lombroso. She measured the circumference of children's heads in her schools and inferred that the best prospects had bigger brains. But she had no use for Broca's conclusions about women. She discussed Manouvrier's work at length and made much of his tentative claim that women, after proper correction of the data, had slightly larger brains than men. Women, she concluded, were intellectually superior, but men had prevailed heretofore by dint of physical force. Since technology has abolished force as an instrument of power, the era of women may soon be upon us: "In such an epoch there will really be superior human beings, there will really be men strong in morality and in sentiment. Perhaps in this way the reign of women is approaching, when the enigma of her anthropological superiority will be deciphered. Woman was always the custodian of human sentiment, morality and honor."

This represents one possible antidote to "scientific" claims for the consti-   15
tutional inferiority of certain groups. One may affirm the validity of biological distinctions but argue that the data have been misinterpreted by prejudiced
men with a stake in the outcome, and that disadvantaged groups are truly
superior. In recent years, Elaine Morgan has followed this strategy in her
Descent of Woman, a speculative reconstruction of human prehistory from the
woman's point of view—and as farcical as more famous tall tales by and for
men.

I prefer another strategy. Montessori and Morgan followed Broca's
philosophy to reach a more congenial conclusion. I would rather label the
whole enterprise of setting a biological value upon groups for what it is:
irrelevant and highly injurious. George Eliot well appreciated the special
tragedy that biological labeling imposed upon members of disadvantaged
groups. She expressed it for people like herself—women of extraordinary
talent. I would apply it more widely—not only to those whose dreams are
flouted but also to those who never realize that they may dream—but I
cannot match her prose. In conclusion, then, the rest of Eliot's prelude to
Middlemarch:

> The limits of variation are really much wider than anyone would
> imagine from the sameness of women's coiffure and the favorite
> love stories in prose and verse. Here and there a cygnet is reared
> uneasily among the ducklings in the brown pond, and never finds
> the living stream in fellowship with its own oary-footed kind. Here
> and there is born a Saint Theresa, foundress of nothing, whose lov-
> ing heartbeats and sobs after an unattained goodness tremble off
> and are dispersed among hindrances instead of centering in some
> long-recognizable deed.

QUESTIONS

1. In paragraph 3, Gould claims, "Numbers, by themselves, specify nothing. All depends upon what you do with them." What exactly does
   Gould do with numbers?
2. How does Gould's use of numbers differ from what Broca and his followers did with numbers? Specifically, what distinguishes Gould's and
   Broca's methods of calculating and interpreting the facts about women's
   brains?
3. It might also be said, "Quotations, by themselves, specify nothing. All
   depends upon what you do with them." What does Gould do with quotations in this essay?
4. Why do you suppose Gould begins and ends his piece with passages by
   George Eliot?

5. Why does Gould quote so extensively from Broca and his followers, particularly from Le Bon? What purpose do all of these quotations serve in connection with the points that Gould is trying to make about women's brains and "biological labeling"?

6. Using Gould's essay as a model, write an essay on a subject with which you are familiar, showing how different ways of gathering, calculating, and interpreting numbers have produced significantly different understandings of the subject in question.

MAKING CONNECTIONS

Compare the stereotyping of women's reproductive functions, as presented by Emily Martin in "The Egg and the Sperm: How Science Has Constructed a Romance Based on Stereotypical Male-Female Roles" (p. 669), with the stereotyping that Gould presents in this essay. What similarities do you find?

UNRAVELING THE DNA MYTH
The Spurious Foundation of Genetic Engineering

Barry Commoner

Botanist, biologist, and environmental scientist Barry Commoner was born in Brooklyn, New York, in 1917 and received degrees from Columbia and Harvard. He began his teaching career at Washington University and then taught for a number of years at Queens College of the City University of New York, from which he retired in 1987. Among his many books are Science and Survival *(1966),* The Closing Circle: Nature, Man, and Technology *(1971),* The Politics of Energy *(1979), and* Making Peace with the Planet *(1990). A longtime social activist, Commoner led protests against nuclear testing in the 1950s, has since the 1960s lobbied for a variety of environmental issues, and ran a controversial campaign for president in 1980. "Unraveling the DNA Myth: The Spurious Foundation of Genetic Engineering" was first published in* Harper's *in February 2002.*

Biology once was regarded as a languid, largely descriptive discipline, a passive science that was content, for much of its history, merely to observe the natural world rather than change it. No longer. Today biology, armed with the power of genetics, has replaced physics as the activist Science of the Century, and it stands poised to assume godlike powers of creation, calling forth artificial forms of life rather than undiscovered elements and subatomic particles. The initial steps toward this new Genesis have been widely touted in the press. It wasn't so long ago that Scottish scientists stunned the world with Dolly, the fatherless sheep cloned directly from her mother's cells; these techniques have now been applied, unsuccessfully, to human cells. ANDi, a photogenic rhesus monkey, recently was born carrying the gene of a luminescent jellyfish. Pigs now carry a gene for bovine growth hormone and show significant improvement in weight gain, feed efficiency, and reduced fat. Most soybean plants grown in the United States have been genetically engineered to survive the application of powerful herbicides. Corn plants now contain a bacterial gene that produces an insecticidal protein rendering them poisonous to earworms.

Our leading scientists and scientific entrepreneurs (two labels that are increasingly interchangeable) assure us that these feats of technological prowess, though marvelous and complex, are nonetheless safe and reliable.

Glossary of Terms

Alternative splicing   Reshuffling of the RNA transcription of a gene's nucleotide sequence that generates multiple proteins.

Cell   The fundamental, irreducible unit of life.

Central dogma   A theory concerning the relation among DNA, RNA, and protein in which the nucleotide sequence of DNA exclusively governs its own replication and engenders a specific genetic trait.

Chaperone protein   Folds new strung-out proteins into the ball-like structure that specifies their biochemical activity.

Gene   A term applied to segments of DNA that encode specific proteins that give rise to inherited traits. Human DNA contains about 30,000 genes. The term's meaning has become increasingly uncertain.

DNA   Deoxyribonucleic acid. A large molecule composed of a specific sequence of four kinds of nucleotides found in the nucleus of living cells.

Nucleotide   The four kinds of subunits of which nucleic acid is constructed.

RNA   Ribonucleic acid. Its various forms transmit genetic information from DNA to protein.

Spliceosome   A specialized group of proteins and ribonucleic acids that carries out alternative splicing.

We are told that everything is under control. Conveniently ignored, forgotten, or in some instances simply suppressed, are the caveats, the fine print, the flaws and spontaneous abortions. Most clones exhibit developmental failure before or soon after birth, and even apparently normal clones often suffer from kidney or brain malformations. ANDi, perversely, has failed to glow like a jellyfish. Genetically modified pigs have a high incidence of gastric ulcers, arthritis, cardiomegaly (enlarged heart), dermatitis, and renal disease. Despite the biotechnology industry's assurances that genetically engineered soybeans have been altered only by the presence of the alien gene, as a matter of fact the plant's own genetic system has been unwittingly altered as well, with potentially dangerous consequences. The list of malfunctions gets little notice; biotechnology companies are not in the habit of publicizing studies that question the efficacy of their miraculous products or suggest the presence of a serpent in the biotech garden.

The mistakes might be dismissed as the necessary errors that characterize scientific progress. But behind them lurks a more profound failure. The wonders of genetic science are all founded on the discovery of the DNA double helix — by Francis Crick and James Watson in 1953 — and they proceed from the premise that this molecular structure is the exclusive agent of inheritance in all living things: in the kingdom of molecular genetics, the DNA gene is absolute monarch. Known to molecular biologists as the "central dogma," the premise assumes that an organism's genome — its total complement of

DNA genes — should fully account for its characteristic assemblage of inherited traits. The premise, unhappily, is false. Tested between 1990 and 2001 in one of the largest and most highly publicized scientific undertakings of our time, the Human Genome Project, the theory collapsed under the weight of fact. There are far too few human genes to account for the complexity of our inherited traits or for the vast inherited differences between plants, say, and people. By any reasonable measure, the finding (published last February) signaled the downfall of the central dogma; it also destroyed the scientific foundation of genetic engineering and the validity of the biotechnology industry's widely advertised claim that its methods of genetically modifying food crops are "specific, precise, and predictable" and therefore safe. In short, the most dramatic achievement to date of the $3 billion Human Genome Project is the refutation of its own scientific rationale.

Since Crick first proposed it forty-four years ago, the central dogma has come to dominate biomedical research. Simple, elegant, and easily summarized, it seeks to reduce inheritance, a property that only living things possess, to molecular dimensions: The molecular agent of inheritance is DNA, deoxyribonucleic acid, a very long, linear molecule tightly coiled within each cell's nucleus. DNA is made up of four different kinds of nucleotides, strung together in each gene in a particular linear order or sequence. Segments of DNA comprise the genes that, through a series of molecular processes, give rise to each of our inherited traits.

Guided by Crick's theory, the Human Genome Project was intended to identify and enumerate all of the genes in the human body by working out the sequence of the three billion nucleotides in human DNA. In 1990, James Watson described the Human Genome Project as "the ultimate description of life." It will yield, he claimed, the information "that determines if you have life as a fly, a carrot, or a man." Walter Gilbert, one of the project's earliest proponents, famously observed that the three billion nucleotides found in human DNA would easily fit on a compact disc, to which one could point and say, "Here is a human being; it's me!" President Bill Clinton described the human genome as "the language in which God created life." How could the minute dissection of human DNA into a sequence of three billion nucleotides support such hyperbolic claims? Crick's crisply stated theory attempts to answer that question. It hypothesizes a clear-cut chain of molecular processes that leads from a single DNA gene to the appearance of a particular inherited trait. The explanatory power of the theory is based on an extravagant proposition: that the DNA genes have unique, absolute, and universal control over the totality of inheritance in all forms of life.

In order to control inheritance, Crick reasoned, genes would need to govern the synthesis of protein, since proteins form the cell's internal structures and, as enzymes, catalyze the chemical events that produce specific inherited traits. The ability of DNA to govern the synthesis of protein is facilitated by their similar structures — both are linear molecules composed of specific sequences of subunits. A particular gene is distinguished from another by the precise linear order (sequence) in which the four different nucleotides appear in its DNA. In the same way, a particular protein is distinguished from another by the specific sequence of the twenty different kinds of amino acids of which it is made. The four kinds of nucleotides can be arranged in numerous possible sequences, and the choice of any one of them in the makeup of a particular gene represents its "genetic information" in the same sense that, in poker, the order of a hand of cards informs the player whether to bet high on a straight or drop out with a meaningless set of random numbers.

Crick's "sequence hypothesis" neatly links the gene to the protein: the sequence of the nucleotides in a gene "is a simple code for the amino acid sequence of a particular protein." This is shorthand for a series of well-documented molecular processes that transcribe the gene's DNA nucleotide sequence into a complementary sequence of ribonucleic acid (RNA) nucleotides that, in turn, delivers the gene's code to the site of protein formation, where it determines the sequential order in which the different amino acids are linked to form the protein. It follows that in each living thing there should be a one-to-one correspondence between the total number of genes and the total number of proteins. The entire array of human genes — that is, the genome — must therefore represent the whole of a person's inheritance, which distinguishes a person from a fly, or Walter Gilbert from anyone else. Finally, because DNA is made of the same four nucleotides in every living thing, the genetic code is universal, which means that a gene should be capable of producing its particular protein wherever it happens to find itself, even in a different species.

Crick's theory includes a second doctrine, which he originally called the "central dogma" (though this term is now generally used to identify his theory as a whole). The hypothesis is typical Crick: simple, precise, and magisterial. "Once (sequential) information has passed into protein it cannot get out again." This means that genetic information originates in the DNA nucleotide sequence and terminates, unchanged, in the protein amino acid sequence. The pronouncement is crucial to the explanatory power of the theory because it endows the gene with undiluted control over the identity of the protein and the inherited trait that the protein creates. To stress the importance of this genetic taboo, Crick bet the future of the entire enterprise on it, asserting that "the discovery of just one type of present-day cell" in which genetic information passed from protein to nucleic acid or from protein to protein "would shake the whole intellectual basis of molecular biology."

Crick was aware of the brashness of his bet, for it was known that in living cells proteins come into promiscuous molecular contact with numerous other proteins and with molecules of DNA and RNA. His insistence that these interactions are genetically chaste was designed to protect the DNA's genetic message — the gene's nucleotide sequence — from molecular intruders that might change the sequence or add new ones as it was transferred, step by step, from gene to protein and thus destroy the theory's elegant simplicity.

Last February, Crick's gamble suffered a spectacular loss. In the journals *Nature* and *Science*, and at joint press conferences and television   10 appearances, the two genome research teams reported their results. The major result was "unexpected." Instead of the 100,000 or more genes predicted by the estimated number of human proteins, the gene count was only about 30,000. By this measure, people are only about as gene-rich as a mustardlike weed (which has 26,000 genes) and about twice as genetically endowed as a fruit fly or a primitive worm — hardly an adequate basis for distinguishing among "life as a fly, a carrot, or a man." In fact, an inattentive reader of genomic CDs might easily mistake Walter Gilbert for a mouse, 99 percent of whose genes have human counterparts.

The surprising results contradicted the scientific premise on which the genome project was undertaken and dethroned its guiding theory, the central dogma. After all, if the human gene count is too low to match the number of proteins and the numerous inherited traits that they engender, and if it cannot explain the vast inherited difference between a weed and a person, there must be much more to the "ultimate description of life" than the genes, on their own, can tell us.

Scientists and journalists somehow failed to notice what had happened. The discovery that the human genome is not much different from the roundworm's led Dr. Eric Lander, one of the leaders of the project, to declare that humanity should learn "a lesson in humility." In the *New York Times*, Nicholas Wade merely observed that the project's surprising results will have an "impact on human pride" and that "human self-esteem may be in for further blows" from future genome analyses, which had already found that the genes of mice and men are very similar.

The project's scientific reports offered little to explain the shortfall in the gene count. One of the possible explanations for why the gene count is "so discordant with our predictions" was described, in full, last February in *Science* as follows: "nearly 40% of human genes are alternatively spliced." Properly understood, this modest, if esoteric, account fulfills Crick's dire prophecy: it "shakes the whole intellectual basis of molecular biology" and undermines the scientific validity of its application to genetic engineering.

Alternative splicing is a startling departure from the orderly design of the central dogma, in which the distinctive nucleotide sequence of a single gene encodes the amino acid sequence of a single protein. According to Crick's sequence hypothesis, the gene's nucleotide sequence (i.e., its "genetic information") is transmitted, altered in form but not in content, through RNA intermediaries, to the distinctive amino acid sequence of a particular protein. In alternative splicing, however, the gene's original nucleotide sequence is split into fragments that are then recombined in different ways to encode a multiplicity of proteins, each of them different in their amino acid sequence from each other and from the sequence that the original gene, if left intact, would encode.

The molecular events that accomplish this genetic reshuffling are 15 focused on a particular stage in the overall DNA-RNA-protein progression. It occurs when the DNA gene's nucleotide sequence is transferred to the next genetic carrier — messenger RNA. A specialized group of fifty to sixty proteins, together with five small molecules of RNA — known as a "spliceosome" — assembles at sites along the length of the messenger RNA, where it cuts apart various segments of the messenger RNA. Certain of these fragments are spliced together into a number of alternative combinations, which then have nucleotide sequences that differ from the gene's original one. These numerous, redesigned messenger RNAs govern the production of an equal number of proteins that differ in their amino acid sequence and hence in the inherited traits that they engender. For example, when the word TIME is rearranged to read MITE, EMIT, and ITEM, three alternative units of information are created from an original one. Although the original word (the unspliced messenger RNA nucleotide sequence) is essential to the process, so is the agent that performs the rearrangement (the spliceosome).

Alternative splicing can have an extraordinary impact on the gene/protein ratio. We now know that a single gene originally believed to encode a single protein that occurs in cells of the inner ear of chicks (and of humans) gives rise to 576 variant proteins, differing in their amino acid sequences. The current record for the number of different proteins produced from a single gene by alternative splicing is held by the fruit fly, in which one gene generates up to 38,016 variant protein molecules.

Alternative splicing thus has a devastating impact on Crick's theory: it breaks open the hypothesized isolation of the molecular system that transfers genetic information from a single gene to a single protein. By rearranging the single gene's nucleotide sequence into a multiplicity of new messenger RNA sequences, each of them different from the unspliced original, alternative splicing can be said to generate *new* genetic information. Certain of the spliceosome's proteins and RNA components have an affinity for particular sites and, binding to them, form an active catalyst that cuts the messenger RNA and then rejoins the resulting fragments. The spliceosome proteins thus contribute to the added genetic information that alternative splicing creates. But this conclusion conflicts with Crick's second hypothesis — that proteins cannot transmit genetic information to nucleic acid (in this case, messenger RNA) — and shatters the elegant logic of Crick's interlocking duo of genetic hypotheses.

The discovery of alternative splicing also bluntly contradicts the precept that motivated the genome project. It nullifies the exclusiveness of the gene's hold on the molecular process of inheritance and disproves the notion that by counting genes one can specify the array of proteins that define the scope of human inheritance. The gene's effect on inheritance thus cannot be predicted simply from its nucleotide sequence — the determination of which is one of the main purposes of the Human Genome Project. Perhaps this is why the crucial role of alternative splicing seems to have been ignored in the planning of the project and has been obscured by the cunning manner in which its chief result has been reported. Although the genome reports do not mention it, alternative splicing was discovered well before the genome project was even planned — in 1978 in virus replication, and in 1981 in human cells. By 1989, when the Human Genome Project was still being debated among molecular biologists, its champions were surely aware that more than 200 scientific papers on alternative splicing of human genes had already been published. Thus, the shortfall in the human gene count could — indeed should — have been predicted. It is difficult to avoid the conclusion — troublesome as it is — that the project's planners knew in advance that the mismatch between the numbers of genes and proteins in the human genome was to be expected, and that the $3 billion project could not be justified by the extravagant claims that the genome — or perhaps God speaking through it — would tell us who we are.

Alternative splicing is not the only discovery over the last forty years that has contradicted basic precepts of the central dogma. Other research has tended to erode the centrality of the DNA double helix itself, the theory's ubiquitous icon. In their original description of the discovery of DNA, Watson and Crick commented that the helix's structure "immediately suggests a possible copying mechanism for the genetic material." Such self-duplication is the crucial feature of life, and in ascribing it to DNA, Watson and Crick concluded, a bit prematurely, that they had discovered life's magic molecular key.

Biological replication does include the precise duplication of DNA, but this is accomplished by the living cell, not by the DNA molecule alone. In the development of a person from a single fertilized egg, the egg cell and the multitude of succeeding cells divide in two. Each such division is preceded by a doubling of the cell's DNA; two new DNA strands are produced by attaching the necessary nucleotides (freely available in the cell), in the proper order, to each of the two DNA strands entwined in the double helix. As the single fertilized egg cell grows into an adult, the genome is replicated many billions of times, its precise sequence of three billion nucleotides retained with extraordinary fidelity. The rate of error — that is, the insertion into the newly made DNA sequence of a nucleotide out of its proper order — is about one in 10 billion nucleotides. But on its own, DNA is incapable of such faithful replication; in a test-tube experiment, a DNA strand, provided with a mixture of its four constituent nucleotides, will line them up with about one in a hundred of them out of its proper place. On the other hand, when the appropriate protein enzymes are added to the test tube, the fidelity with which nucleotides are incorporated in the newly made DNA strand is greatly improved, reducing the error rate to one in 10 million. These remaining errors are finally reduced to one in 10 billion by a set of "repair" enzymes (also proteins) that detect and remove mismatched nucleotides from the newly synthesized DNA.

Thus, in the living cell the gene's nucleotide code can be replicated faithfully only because an array of specialized proteins intervenes to prevent most of the errors — which DNA by itself is prone to make — and to repair the few remaining ones. Moreover, it has been known since the 1960s that the enzymes that synthesize DNA influence its nucleotide sequence. In this sense,

20

genetic information arises not from DNA alone but through its essential collaboration with protein enzymes — a contradiction of the central dogma's precept that inheritance is uniquely governed by the self-replication of the DNA double helix.

Another important divergent observation is the following: in order to become biochemically active and actually generate the inherited trait, the newly made protein, a strung-out ribbon of a molecule, must be folded up into a precisely organized ball-like structure. The biochemical events that give rise to genetic traits — for example, enzyme action that synthesizes a particular eye-color pigment — take place at specific locations on the outer surface of the three-dimensional protein, which is created by the particular way in which the molecule is folded into that structure. To preserve the simplicity of the central dogma, Crick was required to assume, without any supporting evidence, that the nascent protein — a linear molecule — always folded itself up in the right way once its amino acid sequence had been determined. In the 1980s, however, it was discovered that some nascent proteins are on their own likely to become misfolded — and therefore remain biochemically inactive — unless they come in contact with a special type of "chaperone" protein that properly folds them.

The importance of these chaperones has been underlined in recent years by research on degenerative brain diseases that are caused by "prions," research that has produced some of the most disturbing evidence that the central dogma is dangerously misconceived. Crick's theory holds that biological replication, which is essential to an organism's ability to infect another organism, cannot occur without nucleic acid. Yet when scrapie, the earliest known such disease, was analyzed biochemically, no nucleic acid — neither DNA nor RNA — could be found in the infectious material that transmitted the disease. In the 1980s, Stanley Prusiner confirmed that the infectious agents that cause scrapie, mad cow disease, and similar very rare but invariably fatal human diseases are indeed nucleic-acid-free proteins (he named them prions), which replicate in an entirely unprecedented way. Invading the brain, the prion encounters a normal brain protein, which it then refolds to match the prion's distinctive three-dimensional shape. The newly refolded protein itself becomes infectious and, acting on another molecule of the normal protein, sets up a chain reaction that propagates the disease to its fatal end.

The prion's unusual behavior raises important questions about the connection between a protein's amino acid sequence and its biochemically active, folded-up structure. Crick assumed that the protein's active structure is automatically determined by its amino acid sequence (which is, after all, the sign of its genetic specificity), so that two proteins with the same sequence ought to be identical in their activity. The prion violates this rule. In a scrapie-infected sheep, the prion and the brain protein that it refolds have the same amino acid sequence, but one is a normal cellular component and the other is a fatal infectious agent. This suggests that the protein's folded-up configuration is, to some degree, independent of its amino acid sequence and therefore determined, in part, by something other than the

DNA gene that governed the synthesis of that sequence. And since the prion protein's three-dimensional shape is endowed with transmissible genetic information, it violates another fundamental Crick precept as well — the forbidden passage of genetic information from one protein to another.[1] Thus, what is known about the prion is a somber warning that processes far removed from the conceptual constraints of the central dogma are at work in molecular genetics and can lead to fatal disease.[2]

By the mid 1980s, therefore, long before the $3 billion Human Genome Project was funded, and long before genetically modified crops began to appear in our fields, a series of protein-based processes had already intruded on the DNA gene's exclusive genetic franchise. An array of protein enzymes must repair the all-too-frequent mistakes in gene replication and in the transmission of the genetic code to proteins as well. Certain proteins, assembled in spliceosomes, can reshuffle the RNA transcripts, creating hundreds and even thousands of different proteins from a single gene. A family of chaperones, proteins that facilitate the proper folding — and therefore the biochemical activity — of newly made proteins, form an essential part of the gene-to-protein process. By any reasonable measure, these results contradict the central dogma's cardinal maxim: that a DNA gene exclusively governs the molecular processes that give rise to a particular inherited trait. The DNA gene clearly exerts an important influence on inheritance, but it is not unique in that respect and acts only in collaboration with a multitude of protein-based processes that prevent and repair incorrect sequences, transform the nascent protein into its folded, active form, and provide crucial added genetic information well beyond that originating in the gene itself. The net outcome is that no single DNA gene is the sole source of a given protein's genetic information and therefore of the inherited trait.

The credibility of the Human Genome Project is not the only casualty of the scientific community's stubborn resistance to experimental results that contradict the central dogma. Nor is it the most significant casualty. The fact that one gene can give rise to multiple proteins also destroys the theoretical foundation of a multibillion-dollar industry, the genetic engineering of food crops. In genetic engineering it is assumed, without adequate experimental

---

    [1]Although Crick localizes the protein's genetic information in its amino acid sequence, it must also be found in the protein's three-dimensional folded structure, on the surface of which the highly specific biochemical activity that generates the inherited trait takes place.

    [2]In 1997, when Prusiner was awarded the Nobel Prize, several scientists publicly denounced the decision because his finding that the prion, though infectious, is a nucleic-acid-free protein contradicted the central dogma and was too controversial to warrant the award. This bias impeded not only scientific progress but human health as well. Although Prusiner's results explained why the prion's unique structure resists them, conventional sterilization procedures were nevertheless relied on to fight mad cow disease in Britain, with fatal results.

proof, that a bacterial gene for an insecticidal protein, for example, transferred to a corn plant, will produce precisely that protein and nothing else. Yet in that alien genetic environment, alternative splicing of the bacterial gene might give rise to multiple variants of the intended protein — or even to proteins bearing little structural relationship to the original one, with unpredictable effects on ecosystems and human health.

The delay in dethroning the all-powerful gene led in the 1990s to a massive invasion of genetic engineering into American agriculture, though its scientific justification had already been compromised a decade or more earlier. Nevertheless, ignoring the profound fact that in nature the normal exchange of genetic material occurs exclusively within a single species, biotech-industry executives have repeatedly boasted that, in comparison, moving a gene from one species to another is not only normal but also *more* specific, precise, and predictable. In only the last five years such transgenic crops have taken over 68 percent of the U.S. soybean acreage, 26 percent of the corn acreage, and more than 69 percent of the cotton acreage.

That the industry is guided by the central dogma was made explicit by Ralph W. F. Hardy, president of the National Agricultural Biotechnology Council and formerly director of life sciences at DuPont, a major producer of genetically engineered seeds. In 1999, in Senate testimony, he succinctly described the industry's guiding theory this way: "DNA (top management molecules) directs RNA formation (middle management molecules) directs protein formation (worker molecules)." The outcome of transferring a bacterial gene into a corn plant is expected to be as predictable as the result of a corporate takeover: what the workers do will be determined precisely by what the new top management tells them to do. This Reaganesque version of the central dogma is the scientific foundation upon which each year billions of transgenic plants of soybeans, corn, and cotton are grown with the expectation that the particular alien gene in each of them will be faithfully replicated in each of the billions of cell divisions that occur as each plant develops; that in each of the resultant cells the alien gene will encode only a protein with precisely the amino acid sequence that it encodes in its original organism; and that throughout this biological saga, despite the alien presence, the plant's natural complement of DNA will itself be properly replicated with no abnormal changes in composition.

In an ordinary unmodified plant the reliability of this natural genetic process results from the compatibility between its gene system and its equally necessary protein-mediated systems. The harmonious relation between the two systems develops during their cohabitation, in the same species, over very long evolutionary periods, in which natural selection eliminates incompatible variants. In other words, within a single species the reliability of the successful outcome of the complex molecular process that gives rise to the inheritance of particular traits is guaranteed by many thousands of years of testing, in nature.

In a genetically engineered transgenic plant, however, the alien transplanted bacterial gene must properly interact with the *plant's* protein-mediated systems. Higher plants, such as corn, soybeans, and cotton, are   30

known to possess proteins that repair DNA miscoding; proteins that alternatively splice messenger RNA and thereby produce a multiplicity of different proteins from a single gene; and proteins that chaperone the proper
folding of other, nascent proteins. But the plant systems' evolutionary history is very different from the bacterial gene's. As a result, in the transgenic
plant the harmonious interdependence of the alien gene and the new host's
protein-mediated systems is likely to be disrupted in unspecified, imprecise,
and inherently unpredictable ways. In practice, these disruptions are
revealed by the numerous experimental failures that occur before a transgenic organism is actually produced and by unexpected genetic changes that
occur even when the gene has been successfully transferred.

   Most alarming is the recent evidence that in a widely grown genetically
modified food crop — soybeans containing an alien gene for herbicide
resistance — the transgenic host plant's genome has itself been unwittingly
altered. The Monsanto Company admitted in 2000 that its soybeans contained some extra fragments of the transferred gene, but nevertheless concluded that "no new proteins were expected or observed to be produced."
A year later, Belgian researchers discovered that a segment of the plant's
own DNA had been scrambled. The abnormal DNA was large enough to
produce a new protein, a potentially harmful protein.

   One way that such mystery DNA might arise is suggested by a recent
study showing that in some plants carrying a bacterial gene, the plant's
enzymes that correct DNA replication errors rearrange the alien gene's
nucleotide sequence. The consequences of such changes cannot be foreseen.
The likelihood in genetically engineered crops of even exceedingly rare,
disruptive effects of gene transfer is greatly amplified by the billions of
individual transgenic plants already being grown annually in the United
States.

   The degree to which such disruptions do occur in genetically modified
crops is not known at present, because the biotechnology industry is not
required to provide even the most basic information about the actual composition of the transgenic plants to the regulatory agencies. No tests, for
example, are required to show that the plant actually produces a protein
with the same amino acid sequence as the original bacterial protein. Yet this
information is the only way to confirm that the transferred gene does in fact
yield the theory-predicted product. Moreover, there are no required studies
based on detailed analysis of the molecular structure and biochemical activity of the alien gene and its protein product in the transgenic commercial
crop. Given that some unexpected effects may develop very slowly, crop
plants should be monitored in successive generations as well. None of these
essential tests are being performed, and billions of transgenic plants are now
being grown with only the most rudimentary knowledge about the resulting
changes in their composition. Without detailed, ongoing analyses of the
transgenic crops, there is no way of knowing if hazardous consequences
might arise. Given the failure of the central dogma, there is no assurance that
they will not. The genetically engineered crops now being grown represent a

massive uncontrolled experiment whose outcome is inherently unpredictable. The results could be catastrophic.

Crick's central dogma has played a powerful role in creating both the Human Genome Project and the unregulated spread of genetically engineered food crops. Yet as evidence that contradicts this governing theory has accumulated, it has had no effect on the decisions that brought both of these monumental undertakings into being. It is true that most of the experimental results generated by the theory confirmed the concept that genetic information, in the form of DNA nucleotide sequences, is transmitted from DNA via RNA to protein. But other observations have contradicted the one-to-one correspondence of gene to protein and have broken the DNA gene's exclusive franchise on the molecular explanation of heredity. In the ordinary course of science, such new facts would be woven into the theory, adding to its complexity, redefining its meaning, or, as necessary, challenging its basic premise. Scientific theories are meant to be falsifiable; this is precisely what makes them scientific theories. The central dogma has been immune to this process. Divergent evidence is duly reported and, often enough, generates intense research, but its clash with the governing theory is almost never noted.

Because of their commitment to an obsolete theory, most molecular biol- 35 ogists operate under the assumption that DNA is the secret of life, whereas the careful observation of the hierarchy of living processes strongly suggests that it is the other way around: DNA did not create life; life created DNA. When life was first formed on the earth, proteins must have appeared before DNA because, unlike DNA, proteins have the catalytic ability to generate the chemical energy needed to assemble small ambient molecules into larger ones such as DNA. DNA is a mechanism created by the cell to store information produced by the cell. Early life survived because it grew, building up its characteristic array of complex molecules. It must have been a sloppy kind of growth; what was newly made did not exactly replicate what was already there. But once produced by the primitive cell, DNA could become a stable place to store structural information about the cell's chaotic chemistry, something like the minutes taken by a secretary at a noisy committee meeting. There can be no doubt that the emergence of DNA was a crucial stage in the development of life, but we must avoid the mistake of reducing life to a master molecule in order to satisfy our emotional need for unambiguous simplicity. The experimental data, shorn of dogmatic theories, points to the irreducibility of the living cell, the inherent complexity of which suggests that any artificially altered genetic system, given the magnitude of our ignorance, must sooner or later give rise to unintended, potentially disastrous, consequences. We must be willing to recognize how little we truly understand about the secrets of the cell, the fundamental unit of life.

Why, then, has the central dogma continued to stand? To some degree the theory has been protected from criticism by a device more common to religion than science: dissent, or merely the discovery of a discordant fact, is a punishable offense, a heresy that might easily lead to professional ostracism. Much of this bias can be attributed to institutional inertia, a failure of rigor, but there are other, more insidious, reasons why molecular geneticists might be satisfied with the status quo; the central dogma has given them such a satisfying, seductively simplistic explanation of heredity that it seemed sacrilegious to entertain doubts. The central dogma was simply too good not to be true.

As a result, funding for molecular genetics has rapidly increased over the last twenty years; new academic institutions, many of them "genomic" variants of more mundane professions, such as public health, have proliferated. At Harvard and other universities, the biology curriculum has become centered on the genome. But beyond the traditional scientific economy of prestige and the generous funding that follows it as night follows day, money has distorted the scientific process as a once purely academic pursuit has been commercialized to an astonishing degree by the researchers themselves. Biology has become a glittering target for venture capital; each new discovery brings new patents, new partnerships, new corporate affiliations. But as the growing opposition to transgenic crops clearly shows, there is persistent public concern not only with the safety of genetically engineered foods but also with the inherent dangers in arbitrarily overriding patterns of inheritance that are embedded in the natural world through long evolutionary experience. Too often those concerns have been derided by industry scientists as the "irrational" fears of an uneducated public. The irony, of course, is that the biotechnology industry is based on science that is forty years old and conveniently devoid of more recent results, which show that there are strong reasons to fear the potential consequences of transferring a DNA gene between species. What the public fears is not the experimental science but the fundamentally irrational decision to let it out of the laboratory into the real world before we truly understand it.

QUESTIONS

The title and subtitle of this essay make the overall point of the argument very clear, through the use of those very unscientific words, *myth* and *spurious*. DNA, the author is apparently going to argue, is a myth, and genetic engineering is based on a spurious foundation. This will be a major attack, then, on a very deeply entrenched position in biology, which means that it will require a long and detailed argument. In the following questions, we will be encouraging you to examine this argument in some detail, looking at its structure, its language, and its use of evidence. This will only work if you have read the piece with close attention.

1. The first paragraph, like the title, combines scientific information with unscientific terms. What unscientific notions do you find in this paragraph? What function do they serve in the argument?
2. In the second paragraph, Commoner uses the phrase "scientists and scientific entrepreneurs." What does he mean by this, and why does he connect the two?

3. At the end of the third paragraph, Commoner makes his charge more specific — and more scientific. What, exactly, is he promising to demonstrate?

4. A complex essay like this one must be broken up into smaller units to allow readers some resting places and to keep its structure clear in the minds of those readers. What are the divisions of Commoner's essay? Try to say how each unit contributes to the larger argument.

5. An essay that is written on a scientific topic but is aimed at general readers must succeed in making complex scientific issues clear to those readers. Commoner has a reputation for being good at doing this. Examine some of his explanations, and discuss his methods for making abstract ideas concrete for his readers. Take one example of this, and discuss the way that it works. Are some of his examples more effective than others? Which ones, and why?

6. Commoner himself discusses the language that other scientists use to make their ideas clear to laypeople, as in the example of Ralph W. F. Hardy testifying before the Senate. Locate and consider this example. What do you think of Hardy's illustration? What does Commoner think of it?

7. After making his case against the "central dogma" of genetic engineering, Commoner goes on to make a further charge about the way that scientists have reacted to the sort of evidence that he has just discussed. He claims that evidence is being disregarded in a way that is unscientific, and he asks why this is so. Examine the last two paragraphs of his argument. Consider his claims, his reasoning, and the language that he uses to make it. How, for example, does the word *sacrilegious* function here, and how does it connect to the argument of the opening paragraphs of the essay?

MAKING CONNECTIONS

This essay, like the two immediately preceding it in this section, exposes an unscientific element in science, called "myth" in this case. Looking at all three essays, write an essay about the ideals of science and the practice of science. Consider such things as the sources of problems, the ways in which assumptions and motivations affect research, and the ways in which these authors define and evaluate science and nonscience. Investigate the following questions: Do Emily Martin (p. 669) and Stephen Jay Gould (p. 686) have equivalent terms for Commoner's "myth"? Are these authors attacking science or defending it? What is science? What is "myth"? Are there alternatives to science that are not "mythic"? Try to put all this together in a coherent essay about the values and practices of the life sciences.

AS GOOD AS DEAD

Gary Greenberg

*Gary Greenberg (b. 1957) is a New London, Connecticut, psy-
chotherapist and freelance journalist interested in what he sees as
the misuses of psychiatry. He is the author of* The Self on a Shelf:
Recovery Books and the Good Life *(1993) and began his career as
a journalist with an article in* McSweeny's *about his correspondence with Unabomber Theodore Kacznski. Since then he has published articles in* Rolling Stone *and* Discover, *among other popular
magazines. Greenberg also teaches in the psychology department at
Connecticut College. The following essay originally appeared in*
The New Yorker *and was collected in* The Best Science and Nature
Writing of 2001.

Just after a fourteen-year-old boy named Nicholas Breach learned that a
tumor on his brain stem would be fatal, he told his parents, Rick and Kim
Breach, that he wanted to be an organ donor. They respected his decision,
and so did the boy's medical team at the Children's Hospital of Philadelphia.
Bernadette Foley, Nick's social worker there, said that the decision reflected
a "maturity and sensitivity" and a wish to help others — something Nick
had shown throughout his eight-year battle with recurrent tumors. "I've
never been to a meeting like this one," Foley said. "The peace that came over
the family and Nick was remarkable, and once it was out that this was the
end, and the decision was made about organ donation, Nick said he was
happy. They all seemed to be happy." The decision was redemptive, she said.
"In a way, it gave some meaning to his life."

By the time I met Nick, he was confined to a hospital bed that had been
set up in the living room of the Breaches' house, a brick bungalow outside
Harrisburg. It was difficult for him to speak, and we chatted only briefly —
about his dog, Sarah; his brother, Nathan; and his hope that his heart,
lungs, liver, kidneys, and pancreas might enable other people to live — and
then he dozed off.

As Nick slept, his parents told me that, amid their other worries, they
had run into unexpected problems with the donation. Nick had wanted to
die at home, with only palliative care, but organ donation is a high-tech
affair. In most cases, the donor is someone with brain damage so severe that
he requires a respirator to breathe, even though his heart continues to work
on its own. A neurologist determines that the patient's brain has been irre-
versibly and totally destroyed, and on this basis pronounces him dead. This
condition is known as brain death. If the patient's family has consented to
donation, he is left on the respirator, which, along with his still-beating

heart, keeps his organs viable for transplant until they can be harvested. The Breaches accepted that Nick would now have to be hospitalized at the very end, but their insurance company balked at the change in plan — and the added expense — reminding them that they had already elected basic hospice care. Only after the family's state legislator and the regional organ-procurement organization got involved did the insurance company agree to pay. A plan was devised to keep Nick at home until the last possible moment and then to transport him to a hospital, where an informal protocol had been set up to help him become an organ donor.

Even with the logistical and financial arrangements in place, there was no guarantee that Nick would meet the criteria for brain death. Because the tumor was on his brain stem, which controls core physiological processes like breathing and body temperature, it was very likely that Nick's higher brain — the thinking part — would remain active until he died from respiratory or organ failure. (His oncologist told me, "In his condition, what happens is the body goes. He's a consciousness trapped inside.") This would probably rule him out as a donor.

When I spoke to Nick's parents, they still had trouble with the notion   5
that, to become a donor, it was not enough for their son to die with his body more or less intact. He would have to have the right kind of death, with the systems in his body shutting down in a particular order. "I'm so confused about this part of it," his mother said. "I don't understand why, if his heart stops beating, they can't put him back on a respirator." Rick, too, was confused about the moment at which "the plug will be pulled." In reality there is no moment when the plug is pulled; to keep the organs viable, the respirator is left operating — and the heart keeps beating — until the surgeon removes the organs.

Confusion about the concept of brain death is not unusual, even among the transplant professionals, surgeons, neurologists, and bioethicists who grapple with it regularly. Brain death is confusing because it's an artificial distinction constructed, more than thirty years ago, on a conceptual foundation that is unsound. Recently, some physicians have begun to suggest that brain-dead patients aren't really dead at all — that the concept is just the medical profession's way of dodging ethical questions about a practice that saves more than fifteen thousand lives a year.

From the beginning, transplant practice has been governed by a simple, unwritten rule: no matter how extreme the circumstances, no matter how ill or injured the potential donor, he must die of some other cause before his vital organs can be removed; it would never be acceptable to kill someone for his organs. But, ideally, a donor would be alive at the time his organs were harvested, because as soon as the flow of oxygenated blood stops, a process called warm ischemia quickly begins to ruin them. By the nineteen-sixties, as doctors began to perfect techniques for transplanting livers and hearts, the medical establishment faced a paradox: the need for both a living body and a dead donor.

The profession was also struggling with questions posed by another new technology: respirators. These machines had become a fixture in hospitals in the nineteen-fifties, and at first their main purpose was to help children with polio breathe until they regained their strength. Doctors began to use them for patients with devastating brain injuries — the kind brought on by severe trauma or loss of oxygen as a result of stroke or cardiac arrest. Some of these people recovered sufficiently to be removed from the machines, but others lingered, unable to breathe on their own, inert and unresponsive even to the most noxious stimulus, and without any detectable electrical brain activity, until their hearts gave out — often a matter of hours, but sometimes of days or even weeks.

Physicians wondered what to do with these patients, whether removing the machines would be murder or mercy killing or simply a matter of letting nature take its course. At the same time, some noticed that the patients were perfect sources of viable organs for transplant, at least as long as their hearts kept beating. And then, in 1967, a Harvard anesthesiologist named Henry K. Beecher asked the dean of the medical school to form a committee to explore the issues of artificial life support and organ donation, which he believed were related. The Harvard committee, which Beecher chaired, included ten physicians, a lawyer, and a historian, and its report was published the following year in the *Journal of the American Medical Association*. "Responsible medical opinion," it announced, "is ready to adopt new criteria for pronouncing death to have occurred in an individual sustaining irreversible coma as a result of permanent brain damage." Heartbeat or no, the committee declared, patients whose brains no longer functioned and who had no prospect of recovering were not lingering but were already dead — brain dead.

This physician-assisted redefinition of death meant that removing life-support machinery from these patients was no longer ethically suspect. And, by creating a class of dead people whose hearts were still beating, the Harvard committee gave transplant surgeons a new potential supply of organs. In the nineteen-seventies, however, only twenty-seven states adopted brain death as a legal definition of death. Theoretically, this meant that someone who had been declared dead in North Carolina could be resurrected by transferring him to a hospital in South Carolina. Practically, it meant that a doctor procuring organs from a brain-dead person was not equally protected in all jurisdictions from the charge that he was killing his patient.

In 1980, a commission appointed by President Carter began to look at medical ethical questions, which included finding a definition of death that could serve as a model for state laws. The commission recommended that doctors be given the power to declare people dead based on the neurological criteria suggested by the Harvard committee. Eventually, this recommendation was accepted in all fifty states.

The commission also wanted to convince the public that brain death was not just a legal fiction but the description of a biological truth. Two

10

rationales were considered. In one, called the "higher-brain" formulation, a brain-dead person is alleged to be dead because his neocortex, the seat of consciousness, has been destroyed. He has thus lost the ability to think and feel — the capacity for personhood — that makes us who we are, and our lives worth living. But such "quality of life" criteria, the commission noted, raised uncomfortable ethical and political questions about the treatment of senile patients and how society valued the lives of the mentally impaired.

Instead, the commission chose to rely on what it called the "whole-brain" formulation. The brain, it was argued, directed and gave order and purpose to the different mechanical functions of our bodies. If both the neocortex and the brain stem (which regulates core physiological processes, such as breathing) stopped working, a person could be pronounced dead — not just because consciousness has disappeared but because, without the brain, nothing connects: there is no internal harmony, and the body no longer exists as an integrated whole.

When Nick Breach decided to become a donor, one of his first questions was whether he would be dead when his organs were taken. His parents told him that he would be, and, in a way, they saw this as one of the few things they could be sure about. Rick and Kim were more troubled by their son's next concern, that he might be taken from them prematurely. They began a vigil that took on a strange dual nature: keeping Nick company, making him comfortable, spending as much time as possible with him, and, at the same time, monitoring him for the signs — whatever they might be — that death had come so close that it was time to get him to the hospital so that he could become an organ donor.

The organ-procurement agency that worked with the Breaches during those months was called Gift of Life. In 2000, Gift of Life, which is based in Philadelphia and has a staff of a hundred, helped manage more than eight hundred organ donations at a hundred and sixty-two member hospitals in Pennsylvania, New Jersey, and Delaware — five per cent of the total organs removed in the country.

The agency's mission is to "positively predispose all members of the   15 community to organ and tissue donation so that donation is viewed as a fundamental human responsibility." Public-service ads, a pamphlet featuring Michael Jordan, and bumper stickers that say "Don't take your organs to Heaven — Heaven knows we need them here" are all promoting an attitude about how, as Howard M. Nathan, the bearded, energetic forty-seven-year-old who heads Gift of Life, put it, "society should feel about this subject." Because of the drama and human interest of Nick Breach's case, the agency was naturally eager to publicize it: "Here's a young man who is awake and aware, contemplating his death, and he becomes a donor," Kevin Sparkman, the agency's director of community relations, explained. "What a great example of what we want families to do!"

When a person is identified as a potential organ donor — generally, when he is about to be pronounced brain dead — Gift of Life dispatches a transplant coördinator to the hospital to try to obtain the family's consent. (An organ-donor card is merely an indication of a patient's wishes; the family has the final word.) "The first thing we do is insure that the family understands and acknowledges that their loved one is dead," Linda Herzog, a senior hospital-services coördinator, told me.

Consent rates are tied directly to knowledge of brain death: families who think that donation is actually going to kill the patient refuse more often than families who believe that their relative is already dead. This is not as straightforward as it may seem, largely because of the lifelike appearance of the brain dead, whose skin is still warm to the touch and who are known within the industry as "heart-beating cadavers." Gift of Life has developed a program that trains hospital staffs to explain the phenomenon to families. I watched in a darkened conference room as Herzog reviewed the program for two transplant coördinators, who were scheduled to present it later that afternoon in a Philadelphia hospital.

Using slides, Herzog ran through the process by which brain death is established. A neurologist performs a series of tests at the bedside — checking for such things as pupillary reflexes, response to pain, and the ability to breathe spontaneously. (If the patient is entirely unresponsive during two such examinations, the doctor concludes that his whole brain — cortex and brain stem — has been destroyed.) This is not a terribly sophisticated procedure, but it's far more complicated than, say, ascertaining that a person has no pulse, and far less self-evident. Even when the tests are conducted or reënacted in front of family members, they often rely on their intuitions and insist that the patient is still alive. This failure to accept the truth is a function of denial, Herzog said, and she went on to note, with some dismay, that even highly trained professionals who fully accept the concept sometimes talk to brain-dead patients.

"It took us years to get the public to understand what brain death was," Nathan said. "We had to train people in how to talk about it. Not that they're brain dead, but they're dead: 'What you see is the machine artificially keeping the body alive. . . .'" He stopped and pointed to my notebook. "No, don't even use that. Say 'keeping the organs functioning.'"

Virtually every expert I spoke with about brain death was tripped up by its semantic trickiness. "Even I get this wrong," said one physician and bioethicist who has written extensively on the subject, after making a similar slip. Stuart Youngner, the director of the Center for Biomedical Ethics at Case Western Reserve University, thinks that the need for linguistic vigilance indicates a problem with the concept itself. "The organ-procurement people and transplant activists say you've got to stop saying things like that because that promulgates the idea that the patients are not really dead. The language is a symptom not of stupidity but of how people experience these 'dead' people — as not exactly dead."

Last year, I went to Havana for the Third International Symposium on Coma and Death, a conference held every four years and attended primarily by neurologists and bioethicists, joined by lawyers, anthropologists, and members of the clergy. At one session, I watched as a videotape of a recumbent adolescent boy, his feet toward the camera, his legs bowed, almost froglike, played on a television monitor in a corner of the room. He wore shorts, and there were two tubes entering his body, one in his abdomen, the other in his throat. The boy's chest rose and fell to the whir and click of the respirator, but otherwise he was perfectly still.

On the tape, a trim, balding man named Alan Shewmon, a pediatric neurologist at U.C.L.A., stood near the bed and conducted a medical examination. He looked into the boy's eyes, shook maracas next to his head, inserted a swab in a nostril, dropped cold water into the ears and lemon on the tongue, pinched and palpated and inspected. None of these actions drew a response from the boy, whom I will call Matthew.

Shewmon was also standing next to the monitor in Havana, offering additional commentary. He has been thinking about death for most of his career. A practicing Catholic, he has made contesting the concept of brain death a specialty, and has served on a Pontifical Academy of Sciences task force on the subject. Shewmon's inquiry has led him from the higher-brain rationale through the whole-brain rationale to his current position: a strong conviction that brain death, while a severe disability, even severe enough to warrant discontinuing life support, is not truly death.

Although Matthew didn't seem dead, it was hard to think of him as   25
alive. On the monitor, a nurse removed the upper tube, suctioned the small hole in the boy's throat, noted that he did not cough, and continued the routine of the exam. Then something different happened: some ice water trickled onto the boy's shoulder, and it twitched. And though the screen was too small to see this, Shewmon told us that Matthew sprouted goose bumps, that his flesh was mottling and flushing with the stress of the exam. He was showing signs, that is, of precisely the kind of systemic functioning that the brain dead would generally be expected to lack.

In the video, Shewmon lifted Matthew's arm by the wrist, and the hand sprang to life with a small spasm. A woman's voice — Matthew's mother, we learned — said, "When he knows what you're going to do, he stops that." Shewmon described what was going on in medical terms — clonus, an involuntary contraction and release of nerves. He was making his main point: that this boy — who at age four was struck with meningitis that swelled his brain and split his skull, who would probably have been pronounced brain dead had he not been too young under the statutes of the time, whose mother refused to discontinue life support and ultimately took her son home on a ventilator and a feeding tube, who had persisted in this twilight condition for thirteen years, healing from wounds and illness, growing — was alive. Not by virtue of intention or will, as his mother has implied, but because he had maintained a somatic integrated unity — the internal harmony, and the overarching coördination of his body's functions — which, if the whole-brain rationale is correct, he simply should not have been able to do.

After the presentation ended, I spoke to Ronald Cranford, a professor of neurology and bioethics at the University of Minnesota, who is one of Shewmon's critics. He argued that Matthew's case was only an unusually prolonged example of the normal course brain death takes. "Any patient you keep alive, or dead, longer than a few days will develop spinal-cord reflexes," he said, recalling a case in which the doctor said, "Yes, she's been getting better ever since she died."

In a question-and-answer session with Shewmon the next day, after an address in which he drew parallels between the brain dead and people who are conscious but have been paralyzed by injuries to the upper spinal cord, no one really took issue with his science. At the same time, none of the physicians would accept what Shewmon was really saying: that the brain dead are not dead. "The main philosophical question is, Is this a body or is this a person?" said Calixto Machado, the Cuban neurologist who organized the symposium. Fred Plum, the chairman emeritus of the Department of Neurology at Cornell University's Weill Medical College, had positioned himself directly in front of the podium for the talk, and shot his hand in the air as soon as Shewmon was finished. "This is anti-Darwinism," Plum said. "The brain is the person, the evolved person, not the machine person. Consciousness is the ultimate. We are not one living cell. We are the evolution of a very large group of systems into the awareness of self and the environment, and that is the production of the civilization in which any of us lives."

Shewmon had laid a trap for his audience, he later told me. He had hoped to break down the pretense that anyone subscribed to the whole-brain rationale. He wanted to show that the higher-brain rationale, which holds that living without consciousness is not really living — and which the President's commission rejected because it raised questions about quality of life which science can never settle — was the sub-rosa justification for deciding to call a brain-dead person dead. He wanted to make it clear that these doctors were not making a straightforward medical judgment but, rather, a moral judgment that people like Matthew were so devastated that they had lost their claim on existence. And, at least in his own view, the comments he'd provoked meant that he had succeeded.

The neurologist James Bernat, a professor at Dartmouth Medical School   30 and the author of the chapters on brain death in several neurology textbooks, is one of the defenders of the whole-brain concept. Like Shewmon, Bernat served on the Pontifical Academy of Sciences task force. And, last August, his position appeared to prevail when Pope John Paul II, speaking before an international transplantation congress, said that "the complete and irreversible cessation of all brain activity, if rigorously applied," along with the family's consent, gave a "moral right" to remove organs for transplant — thus resolving an ambiguity in the Church as to whether Catholics should become donors. (Orthodox Jewish and other theologians continue to debate whether a brain-dead person is truly dead.) But even Bernat sees the problem he's up against. "Brain death was accepted before it was conceptually sound," he told me on the telephone from his office in New Hampshire. He readily admits that no one has yet explained scientifically why the destruction of the brain is the death of the person, rather than an extreme injury. "I'm being driven by an intuition that the brain-centered concept of death is sound," he said. "Death is a biological function. Death is an event."

Stuart Youngner, of Case Western, however, rails against what he sees as bad faith in the way brain death came to be defined. Youngner, a white-bearded, avuncular fifty-six-year-old, calls the Harvard committee's work "conceptual gerrymandering," a redrawing of the line between life and death which was determined by something other than science. "What if the Harvard committee, instead of saying, 'Let's call them dead,' had said, 'Let's have a discussion in our society about whether there are circumstances in which people's organs can be taken without sacrificing freedom, without harming people.' Would it be better?"

The problem, as Youngner sees it, is that the veneer of scientific truth attached to the concept of brain death conceals the fact that the lives of brain-dead people have ended only by virtue of what amounts to a social agreement. According to Youngner, this means that the brain dead are really just "as good as dead," but, he is quick to add, this doesn't mean that they shouldn't be organ donors. Instead, he suggests that "as good as dead" be recognized as a special status, one that many people, brain dead or not, may achieve at the end of life. "I'm willing to point out the ambiguities and inconsistencies in the notion, and I actually think that acknowledging them may in the long run be better," he told me.

During the last decade, Youngner and other doctors and ethicists have developed protocols to allow critically ill or injured people who have no hope of recovery, but who are unlikely to become brain dead, to donate their organs after they have been declared dead by the traditional cardiopulmonary criteria. This procedure, which is known as non-heart-beating-cadaver donation and requires extremely rapid intervention and newly developed techniques, may make it possible to salvage viable organs in a wider range of cases.

As it happened, Nick Breach was a candidate for this procedure. If he was brought to the hospital, placed on a respirator, and then languished, without ever meeting the criteria for brain death — a likely scenario, given the course of his disease — only a tight orchestration of his death could conceivably give him a chance of becoming a donor. According to Gift of Life's protocol, Nick's parents would first have to decide to remove life support. Nick would then be taken to an operating room, where he would be taken off the ventilator, and the doctors would wait for his heart to stop. If that took more than an hour, warm ischemia would set in (as his breathing would be too compromised to supply oxygen to his organs), the donation would be aborted, and Nick would be returned to a hospital room to die. But if cardiac arrest came in time, a five-minute count would begin, at the end of which Nick would be declared dead. A transplant team standing by in an anteroom would immediately harvest his organs and rush them to their recipients.

(Even with this alternative, the window for success was fairly narrow. "All we're trying to do," Howard Nathan acknowledged, "is give it a shot.")

Non-heart-beating protocols have the potential to increase donation by as much as twenty-five per cent. But, as Youngner points out, the five-minute waiting period (it ranges from two minutes in some protocols to ten minutes in others) is really just a decent interval, a more or less arbitrary marker of the passage from life to death, whose significance is far more symbolic than scientific.

Robert Truog, a professor of medical ethics and anesthesiology at Harvard Medical School, is even more critical of the protocol. "Non-heart-beating protocols are a dance we do so that people can comply with the dead-donor rule," he told me. "It seems silly that we hang on to this facade. It's a bizarre way of practice, to be unwilling to say what you are doing" — that is, identifying a person as an organ donor when he is still alive and then declaring him dead by a process tailored to keep up appearances and which, in the bargain, might not best meet the requirements of transplant. In Truog's view, a better approach would be to remove these patients' organs while they are still on life support, as is done with brain-dead donors. "If they have detectable brain activity, then they should be given anesthetic," he said, but there is no reason to continue to conceal what is happening by waiting for their hearts to stop beating.

Abandoning the dead-donor convention — which is an inevitable consequence of Youngner's and Truog's positions — may, however, cause other problems. It awakens the same sort of fears that Nick Breach himself had about the premature removal of his organs. It raises vexing legal questions, because, as Truog bluntly told me, without the rule "taking organs is a form of killing" — killing that he thinks is justified, and that Youngner and others would argue is already happening. He added that repealing the rule risks "making physicians seem like a bunch of vultures."

In return, Truog points out, patients would gain more control over the end of their lives: they would no longer have to wait until they crossed over that gerrymandered border and, instead, could specify at what point they would like to be declared dead so that they could donate their organs. This, however, might not be adequate consolation for those who fear that the need for organs might create a perverse incentive for doctors to give up on them, after weighing their lives against those of others who may be more worthy or less damaged. Youngner expressed reservations about how his position would sound to other doctors and, most important, to potential donors. "I think that stridently advocating the abandonment of the dead-donor rule would be a mistake," he said. He worried, he told me, that religious conservatives and others might "seize on it as a violation of the right to life," thus turning transplant into another medical practice — like abortion or fetal stem-cell research — that's bogged down in intractable political wrangling.

As Nick Breach thought about his death, he made some additional last wishes that were easier to satisfy than his desire to become a donor: Ronald

McDonald came to visit; so did Weird Al Yankovic, one of Nick's idols. When Yankovic pulled up to the Breaches' house in a bus, the neighbors moved their cars to accommodate him. Yankovic came inside and sat for a while with Nick, who was bedridden by then. Nick told him, "I really love all your CDs, Weird Al."

Six days later, at 11:45 P.M., Nick stopped breathing. Rick, who was   40
taking his turn by the bedside, summoned Kim, who called an ambulance and began to administer CPR. The plan was to revive Nick so that he could be brought to a hospital and placed on a ventilator. But his mother's efforts, and those of the paramedics in the ambulance and the staff in the emergency room, failed. Nick's heart had stopped too soon, and ischemia had set in. In the end, the only organs he was able to donate were his eyes.

It is tempting to wish that death weren't so complicated. Had Nick and his parents realized how alive he still needed to be in order to donate his vital organs successfully, they could have been given an honest choice between having Nick remain at home until the end and giving up on his goal of becoming a donor, and going to the hospital much earlier and staying until he could be declared "as good as dead."

Over and over again at the conference in Havana, I heard ambivalence and anxiety about "the public" knowing what doctors already know. "These things ought to be worked out in the medical profession, to some extent, before you go to the public," Shewmon told me. "Because if you go public right away, it could just put the kibosh on the whole thing, because people get hysterical and misunderstand things." He paused and looked at me. "These are complex issues. You can't expect the public to understand these things in sound bites, which is what they usually get. So I'm reluctant to talk to reporters about this stuff."

During a break between sessions, I got into a conversation with a philosopher. He told me that he had been talking about this subject with a colleague, and that they'd found themselves calling brain death a "noble lie." Later, as the conference reconvened, I asked him if we could talk some more about that idea. He was visibly upset. "Listen, I'm not sure about that comment," he said. "It's inflammatory. It's too strong." Among his concerns, he explained, was the possibility that his words might discourage people from becoming organ donors.

It may be too much to say that the concept of brain death is an outright lie, but it is certainly less than the truth. Like many of technology's sublime achievements, organ transplant, for all its promise, also has an unavoidable aspect of horror — the horror of rendering a human being into raw materials, of turning death into life, of harvesting organs from an undead boy. Should a practice, however noble, be able to hold truth hostage? Perhaps the medical profession should embrace the obvious: to be an organ donor is to choose a particular way to finish our dying, at the hands of a surgeon, after some uncertain border has been crossed — a line that will change with time and circumstance, and one that science will never be able to draw with precision.

QUESTIONS

1. This is a complex and subtle argument. It is partly about concepts and definitions. How would you summarize what is being argued here?
2. Stories about two dying boys — Nicholas Breach and a boy called "Matthew" — are used in this essay. How does Greenberg use these two stories? Do they have the same function in his argument?
3. What is the function of the "Weird Al" Yankovic anecdote in this essay?
4. Greenberg's argument involves a good deal of reporting on what he saw and what various people said about the issues that he is considering. Sometimes the people that he quotes asked him not to use one form of words they had uttered but to substitute another. But he doesn't comply; he gives us both versions. Why do you suppose that he does this?
5. This essay touches on the problems of the way that issues like those considered here are reported in the media. What are the problems? Can the media — especially television — deal with complex questions without distorting them? Take a position on this issue, and argue your case.

MAKING CONNECTIONS

Some texts in this book deal with death and dying, such as Emily Dickinson's "Because I Could Not Stop for Death" (p. 84), Richard Selzer's "A Mask on the Face of Death" (p. 135), Elisabeth Kübler-Ross's "On the Fear of Death" (p. 405), and Randall Jarrell's "The Death of the Ball Turret Gunner" (p. 665). Using them and any others that you find suitable, write an essay in which you discuss what death is and how we should deal with it.

OF CLONES AND CLOWNS

Robert A. Weinberg

A Pittsburgh native, Robert A. Weinberg (b. 1942) received his B.S. and Ph.D. in biology from the Massachusetts Institute of Technology, where he began teaching in 1970. A pioneer in cancer research, he was awarded the Discover Magazine *Scientist of the Year award in 1982, the Bristol-Myers Award for Distinguished Achievement in Cancer Research in 1984, and the National Medal of Science in 1997. Weinberg, who discovered the first human oncogene and the first tumor suppressor gene, is also a founding member of the Whitehead Institute for Biomedical Research. Today, much of his research focuses on new models of breast cancer development and studies of telomerase, a key target for cancer therapy. The following essay originally appeared in* The Atlantic Monthly *in June 2002.*

Biologists have been rather silent on the subject of human cloning. Some others would accuse us, as they have with predictable regularity in the recent past, of insensitivity to the societal consequences of our research. If not insensitivity, then moral obtuseness, and if not that, then arrogance — an accusation that can never be disproved.

The truth is that most of us have remained quiet for quite another reason. Most of us regard reproductive cloning — a procedure used to produce an entire new organism from one cell of an adult — as a technology riddled with problems. Why should we waste time agonizing about something that is far removed from practical utility, and may forever remain so?

The nature and magnitude of the problems were suggested by the Scottish scientist Ian Wilmut's initial report, five years ago, on the cloning of Dolly the sheep. Dolly represented one success among 277 attempts to produce a viable, healthy newborn. Most attempts at cloning other animal species — to date cloning has succeeded with sheep, mice, cattle, goats, cats, and pigs — have not fared much better.

Even the successes come with problems. The placentas of cloned fetuses are routinely two or three times larger than normal. The offspring are usually larger than normal as well. Several months after birth one group of cloned mice weighed 72 percent more than mice created through normal reproduction. In many species cloned fetuses must be delivered by cesarean section because of their size. This abnormality, the reasons for which no one understands, is so common that it now has its own name — Large Offspring Syndrome. Dolly (who was of normal size at birth) was briefly overweight in her young years and suffers from early-onset arthritis of unknown cause. Two recent reports indicate that cloned mice suffer early-onset obesity and early death.

Arguably the most successful reproductive-cloning experiment was 5 reported last year by Advanced Cell Technology, a small biotech company in Worcester, Massachusetts. Working with cows, ACT produced 496 embryos by injecting nuclei from adult cells into eggs that had been stripped of their own nuclei. Implanting the embryos into the uteruses of cows led to 110 established pregnancies, thirty of which went to term. Five of the newborns died shortly after birth, and a sixth died several months later. The twenty-four surviving calves developed into cows that were healthy by all criteria examined. But most, if not all, had enlarged placentas, and as newborns some of them suffered from the respiratory distress typical of Large Offspring Syndrome.

The success rate of the procedure, roughly five percent, was much higher than the rates achieved with other mammalian species, and the experiment was considered a great success. Some of the cows have grown up, been artificially inseminated, and given birth to normal offspring. Whether they are affected by any of the symptoms associated with Large Offspring Syndrome later in life is not apparent from the published data. No matter: for $20,000 ACT will clone your favorite cow.

Imagine the application of this technology to human beings. Suppose that 100 adult nuclei are obtained, each of which is injected into a human egg whose own nucleus has been removed. Imagine then that only five of the 100 embryos thus created result in well-formed, viable newborns; the other ninety-five spontaneously abort at various stages of development or, if cloning experiments with mammals other than cows are any guide, yield grossly malformed babies. The five viable babies have a reasonable likelihood of suffering from Large Offspring Syndrome. How they will develop, physically and cognitively, is anyone's guess. It seems unlikely that even the richest and most egomaniacal among us, intent on recreating themselves exactly, will swarm to this technology.

Biological systems are extraordinarily complex, and there are myriad ways in which experiments can go awry or their results can be misinterpreted. Still, perhaps 95 percent of what biologists read in this year's research journals will be considered valid (if perhaps not very interesting) a century from now. Much of scientists' trust in the existing knowledge base derives from the system constructed over the past century to validate new research findings and the conclusions derived from them. Research journals impose quality controls to ensure that scientific observations and conclusions are solid and credible. They sift the scientific wheat from the chaff.

The system works like this: A biologist sends a manuscript describing his experiment to a journal. The editor of the journal recruits several experts, who remain anonymous to the researcher, to vet the manuscript. A month or two later the researcher receives a thumbs-up, a thumbs-down, or a request for revisions and more data. The system works reasonably well, which is why many of us invest large amounts of time in serving as the anonymous reviewers of one another's work. Without such rigorously imposed quality control, our subfields of research would rapidly descend into chaos, because no publicly announced result would carry the imprimatur of having been critiqued by experts.

We participate in the peer-review process not only to create a sound edifice of ideas and results for ourselves; we do it for the outside world as well — for all those who are unfamiliar with the arcane details of our field. Without the trial-by-fire of peer review, how can journalists and the public possibly know which discoveries are credible, which are nothing more than acts of self-promotion by ambitious researchers, and which smack of the delusional?   10

The hype about cloning has made a shambles of this system, creating something of a circus. Many of us have the queasy feeling that our carefully constructed world of science is under siege. The clowns — those who think that making money, lots of it, is more important than doing serious science — have invaded our sanctuary.

The cloning circus opened soon after Wilmut, a careful and well-respected scientist, reported his success with Dolly. First in the ring was Richard Seed, an elderly Chicago physicist, who in late 1997 announced his intention of cloning a human being within two years. Soon members of an international religious cult, the Raëlians (followers of Claude Vorilhon, a French-born mystic who says that he was given the name Raël by four-foot-high extraterrestrials, and who preaches that human beings were originally created by these aliens), revealed an even more grandiose vision of human cloning. To the Raëlians, biomedical science is a sacrament to be used for achieving immortality: their ultimate goal is to use cloning to create empty shells into which people's souls can be transferred. As a sideline, the Raëlian-affiliated company Clonaid hopes to offer its services to couples who would like to create a child through reproductive cloning, for $200,000 per child.

Neither Seed nor the Raëlians made any pretense of subjecting their plans to review by knowledgeable scientists; they went straight to the popular press. Still, this wasn't so bad. Few science journalists took them seriously (although they did oblige them with extensive coverage). Biologists were also unmoved. Wasn't it obvious that Seed and the Raëlians were unqualified to undertake even the beginnings of the series of technical steps required for reproductive cloning? Why dignify them with a response?

The next wave of would-be cloners likewise went straight to the mainstream press — but they were not so easily dismissed. In March of last year, at a widely covered press conference in Rome, an Italian and a U.S. physician announced plans to undertake human reproductive cloning outside the United States. The Italian member of the team was Severino Antinori, a ecologist notorious for having used donor eggs and *in vitro* fertilization ake a sixty-two-year-old woman pregnant in 1994. Now he was mov- Why, he asked, did the desires of infertile couples (he claimed to have 600 on a waiting list) not outweigh the concerns about human cloning? He repeatedly shouted down reporters and visiting researchers who had the temerity to voice questions about the biological and ethical problems associated with reproductive cloning.

The American member of the team was Panayiotis Zavos, a reproduc-   15 tive physiologist and an *in vitro* fertilization expert at the Andrology Institute of America, in Lexington, Kentucky. "The genie is out of the bottle," he told reporters. "Dolly is here, and we are next." Antinori and Zavos announced their intention of starting a human cloning project in an undisclosed Mediterranean country. Next up was Avi Ben-Abraham, an Israeli-American biotechnologist with thwarted political ambitions (he ran unsuccessfully for the Knesset) and no reputable scientific credentials, who attempted to attach himself to the project. Ben-Abraham hinted that the work would be done either in Israel or in an Arab country, because "the climate is more [receptive to human cloning research] within Judaism and Islam." He told the German magazine *Der Spiegel*, "We were all created by the Almighty, but now we will become the creators."

Both Antinori and Zavos glossed over the large gap between expertise with established infertility procedures and the technical skills required for reproductive cloning. Confronted with the prospect of high rates of aborted or malformed cloned embryos, they claimed to be able to weed out any defective embryos at an early stage of gestation. "We have a great deal of knowledge," Zavos announced to the press. "We can grade embryos. We can do genetic screening. We can do [genetic] quality control." This was possible, he said, because of highly sensitive diagnostic tests that can determine whether or not development is proceeding normally.

The fact is that no such tests exist; they have eluded even the most expert biologists in the field, and there is no hope that they will be devised anytime soon — if ever. No one knows how to determine with precision whether the repertoire of genes expressed at various stages of embryonic development is being "read" properly in each cell type within an embryo. Without such information, no one can know whether the developmental program is proceeding normally in the womb. (The prenatal tests currently done for Down syndrome and several other genetic disorders can detect only a few of the thousands of things that can go wrong during embryonic development.)

Rudolf Jaenisch, a colleague of mine with extensive experience in mouse reproductive cloning, was sufficiently exercised to say to a reporter at the *Chicago Tribune*, "[Zavos and Antinori] will produce clones, and most of these will die in utero . . . Those will be the lucky ones. Many of those that survive will have [obvious or more subtle] abnormalities." The rest of us biologists remained quiet. To us, Antinori, Zavos, and Ben-Abraham were so clearly inept that comment seemed gratuitous. In this instance we have, as on other occasions, misjudged the situation: many people seem to take these three and their plans very seriously indeed. And, in fact, this past April, Antinori claimed, somewhat dubiously, that a woman under his care was eight weeks pregnant with a cloned embryo.

In the meantime, the biotechnology industry, led by ACT, has been moving ahead aggressively with human cloning but of a different sort. The young companies in this sector have sensed, probably correctly, the enormous potential of therapeutic (rather than reproductive) cloning as a strategy for treating a host of common human degenerative diseases.

The initial steps of therapeutic cloning are identical to those of repro-   20
ductive cloning: cells are prepared from an adult tissue, their nuclei are extracted, and each nucleus is introduced into a human egg, which is allowed to develop. However, in therapeutic cloning embryonic development is halted at a very early stage — when the embryo is a blastocyst, consisting of perhaps 150 cells — and the inner cells are harvested and cultured. These cells, often termed embryonic stem cells, are still very primitive and thus have retained the ability to develop into any type of cell in the body (except those of the placenta).

Mouse and human embryonic stem cells can be propagated in a petri dish and induced to form precursors of blood-forming cells, or of the insulin-producing cells of the pancreas, or of cardiac muscle or nerve tissue. These precursor cells (tissue-specific stem cells) might then be introduced into a tissue that has grown weak from the loss of too many of its differentiated worker cells. When the ranks of the workers are replenished, the course of disease may be dramatically reversed. At least, that is the current theory. In recent months one version of the technique has been successfully applied to mice.

Therapeutic cloning has the potential to revolutionize the treatment of a number of currently untreatable degenerative diseases, but it is only a potential. Considerable research will be required to determine the technology's possibilities and limitations for treating human patients.

Some worry that therapeutic-cloning research will never get off the ground in this country. Its proponents — and there are many among the community of biomedical researchers — fear that the two very different kinds of cloning, therapeutic and reproductive, have merged in the public's mind. Three leaders of the community wrote a broadside early this year in *Science*, titled "Please Don't Call It Cloning!" Call therapeutic cloning anything else — call it "nuclear transplantation" or "stem cell research." The scientific community has finally awakened to the damage that the clowns have done.

This is where the newest acts of the circus begin. President George Bush and many pro-life activists are in one ring. A number of disease-specific advocacy groups that view therapeutic cloning as the only real prospect for treating long-resistant maladies are in another. In a third ring are several biotech companies that are flogging their wares, often in ways that make many biologists shudder.

Yielding to pressure from religious conservatives, Bush announced last   25
August that no new human embryonic stem cells could be produced from early human embryos that had been created during the course of research sponsored by the federal government; any research on the potential applications of

human embryonic stem cells, he said, would have to be conducted with the existing repertoire of sixty-odd lines. The number of available, usable cell lines actually appears to be closer to a dozen or two. And like all biological reagents, these cells tend to deteriorate with time in culture; new ones will have to be derived if research is to continue. What if experiments with the existing embryonic-stem-cell lines show enormous promise? Such an outcome would produce an almost irresistible pressure to move ahead with the derivation of new embryonic stem cells and to rapidly expand this avenue of research.

How will we learn whether human embryonic stem cells are truly useful for new types of therapy? This question brings us directly to another pitfall: much of the research on human embryonic stem cells is already being conducted by biotech companies, rather than in universities. Bush's edict will only exacerbate this situation. (In the 1970s a federal decision effectively banning government funding of *in vitro* fertilization had a similar effect, driving such research into private clinics.)

Evaluating the science coming from the labs of the biotech industry is often tricky. Those who run these companies are generally motivated more by a need to please stock analysts and venture capitalists than to convince scientific peers. For many biotech companies the peer-review process conducted by scientific journals is simply an inconvenient, time-wasting impediment. So some of the companies routinely bypass peer review and go straight to the mainstream press. Science journalists, always eager for scoops, don't necessarily feel compelled to consult experts about the credibility of industry press releases. And when experts are consulted about the contents of a press release, they are often hampered by spotty descriptions of the claimed breakthrough and thus limited to mumbling platitudes.

ACT, the company that conducted the successful cow-cloning experiment and has now taken the lead in researching human therapeutic cloning, has danced back and forth between publishing in respectable peer-reviewed journals and going directly to the popular press — and recently tried to find a middle ground. Last fall, with vast ambitions, ACT reported that it had conducted the first successful human-cloning experiment. In truth, however, embryonic development went only as far as six cells — far short of the 150-cell blastocyst that represents the first essential step of therapeutic cloning. Wishing to cloak its work in scientific respectability, ACT reported these results in a fledgling electronic research journal named *e-biomed: The Journal of Regenerative Medicine*. Perhaps ACT felt especially welcome in a journal that, according to its editor in chief, William A. Haseltine, a widely known biotech tycoon, "is prepared to publish work of a more preliminary nature." It may also have been encouraged by Haseltine's stance toward cloning, as revealed in his remarks when the journal was founded. "As we understand the body's repair process at the genetic level, we will be able to advance the goal of maintaining our bodies in normal function, perhaps perpetually," he said.

Electronic publishing is still in its infancy, and the publication of ACT's research report will do little to enhance its reputation. By the usual standards of scientific achievement, the experiments ACT published would be considered abject failures. Knowledgeable readers of the report were unable to tell whether the clump of six cells represented the beginning of a human embryo or simply an unformed aggregate of dying cells.

One prominent member of the *e-biomed* editorial board, a specialist in 30 the type of embryology used in cloning, asked Haseltine how the ACT manuscript had been vetted before its publication. Haseltine assured his board member that the paper had been seen by two competent reviewers, but he refused to provide more details. The board member promptly resigned. Two others on the editorial board, also respected embryologists, soon followed suit. (Among the scientists left on the board are two representatives of ACT — indeed, both were authors of the paper.) Mary Ann Liebert, the publisher of the journal, interpreted this exodus as a sign that "clearly some noses were out of joint." The entire publication process subverted the potentially adversarial but necessary dynamic between journal-based peer review and the research scientist.

No one yet knows precisely how to make therapeutic cloning work, or which of its many claimed potential applications will pan out and which will not. And an obstacle other than experimental problems confronts those pushing therapeutic cloning. In the wake of the cloning revolution a second revolution has taken place — quieter but no less consequential. It, too, concerns tissue-specific stem cells — but ones found in the tissues of adults. These adult stem cells may one day prove to be at least as useful as those generated by therapeutic cloning.

Many of our tissues are continually jettisoning old, worn-out cells and replacing them with freshly minted ones. The process depends on a cadre of stem cells residing in each type of tissue and specific to that type of tissue. When an adult stem cell divides, one of its two daughters becomes a precursor of a specialized worker cell, able to help replenish the pool of worker cells that may have been damaged through injury or long-term use. The other remains a stem cell like its mother, thus ensuring that the population of stem cells in the tissue is never depleted.

Until two years ago the dogma among biologists was that stem cells in the bone marrow spawned only blood, those in the liver spawned only hepatocytes, and those in the brain spawned only neurons — in other words, each of our tissues had only its own cadre of stem cells for upkeep. Once again we appear to have been wrong. There is mounting evidence that the body contains some rather unspecialized stem cells, which wander around ready to help many sorts of tissue regenerate their worker cells.

Whether these newly discovered, multi-talented adult stem cells present a viable alternative to therapeutic cloning remains to be proved. Many of the claims about their capabilities have yet to be subjected to rigorous testing. Perhaps not surprisingly, some of these claims have also reached the public without careful vetting by peers. Senator Sam Brownback, of Kansas, an ardent foe of all kinds of cloning, has based much of his case in favor of adult stem cells (and against therapeutic cloning) on these essentially unsubstantiated scientific claims. Adult stem cells provide a convenient escape hatch for Brownback. Their use placates religious conservatives, who are against all cloning, while throwing a bone to groups lobbying for new stem-cell-based therapies to treat degenerative diseases.

Brownback would have biologists shut down therapeutic-cloning 35 research and focus their energies exclusively on adult stem-cell research. But no one can know at present which of those two strategies is more likely to work. It will take a decade or more to find out. Many biologists are understandably reluctant to set aside therapeutic-cloning research in the meantime; they argue that the two technologies should be explored simultaneously.

Precisely this issue was debated recently by advisory committees in the United States and Germany. The U.S. committee was convened by Bruce Alberts, the president of the National Academy of Sciences and a highly accomplished cell biologist and scientific educator. Quite naturally, it included a number of experts who are actively involved in exploring the advantages and disadvantages of stem-cell therapies. The committee, which announced its findings in January, concluded that therapeutic cloning should be explored in parallel with alternative strategies.

For their trouble, the scientists were accused of financial self-interest by Steven Milloy of Fox News, who said, "Enron and Arthur Andersen have nothing over the National Academy of Sciences when it comes to deceiving the public. . . . Enter Bruce Alberts, the Wizard of Oz-like president of the NAS. . . . On his own initiative, Alberts put together a special panel, stacked with embryonic-stem-cell research proponents and researchers already on the taxpayer dole . . . Breast-feeding off taxpayers is as natural to the NAS panel members as breathing."

The German committee, which reached a similar conclusion, was assembled by Ernst-Ludwig Winnacker, the head of his country's national science foundation. Winnacker and his colleagues were labeled "cannibals" by the Cardinal of Cologne. Remarks like the ones from Steven Milloy and the cardinal seem calculated to make public service at the interface between science and society as unappealing as possible.

President Bush, apparently anticipating the NAS panel's conclusion, has appointed an advisory committee all but guaranteed to produce a report much more to his liking. Its chairman, Leon Kass, has gone on record as being against all forms of cloning. (Earlier in his career Kass helped to launch an attack on *in vitro* fertilization.)

Meanwhile, a coalition of a hundred people and organizations recently 40 sent a letter to Congress expressing their opposition to therapeutic cloning — among them Friends of the Earth, Greenpeace, the Sierra Club, the head of the National Latina Health Organization, and the perennial naysayer Jeremy Rifkin. "The problem with therapeutic cloning," Rifkin has said, "is that it introduces commercial eugenics from the get-go." Powerful words indeed. Few of those galvanized by Rifkin would know that therapeutic cloning has nothing whatsoever to do with eugenics.

Usually progress in biology is held back by experimental difficulties, inadequate instruments, poorly planned research protocols, inadequate funding, or plain sloppiness. But in this case the future of research may have little connection with these factors or with the scientific pros and cons being debated earnestly by members of the research community. The other, more public debates will surely be the decisive ones.

The clashes about human therapeutic cloning that have taken place in the media and in Congress are invariably built around weighty moral and ethical principles. But none of us needs a degree in bioethics to find the bottom line in the arguments. They all ultimately converge on a single question: When does human life begin? Some say it is when sperm and egg meet, others when the embryo implants in the womb, others when the fetus quickens, and yet others when the fetus can survive outside the womb. This is a question that we scientists are neither more nor less equipped to decide than the average man or woman in the street, than a senator from Kansas or a cardinal in Cologne. (Because Dolly and the other cloned animals show that a complete embryo can be produced from a single adult cell, some biologists have proposed, tongue in cheek, that a human life exists in each one of our cells.) Take your pick of the possible answers and erect your own moral scaffolding above your choice.

In the end, politics will settle the debate in this country about whether human therapeutic cloning is allowed to proceed. If the decision is yes, then we will continue to lead the world in a crucial, cutting-edge area of biomedical research. If it is no, U.S. biologists will need to undertake hegiras to laboratories in Australia, Japan, Israel, and certain countries in Europe — an outcome that would leave American science greatly diminished.

QUESTIONS

1. This essay has several strands of argument: one is about science and reproductive cloning, another is about science and the media, another is about science and therapeutic cloning, and another is about science and politics. Discuss Weinberg's position on each of these issues.
2. What does the clown metaphor contribute to Weinberg's essay? How important is it? How much use does he make of it?
3. How does Weinberg see the future of biological research? What factors does he expect will affect that future?
4. Do you agree with Weinberg's argument about the proper government position on therapeutic cloning? If not, argue your case.
5. In his next to last paragraph, Weinberg proposes an assignment for writing: say when human life begins, and "erect your own moral scaffolding above your choice." Sounds like a good assignment to us. Give it a try.

MAKING CONNECTIONS

1. This essay, like the others in this section that deal with biological science, raises questions about the definition of terms, about public policy, and about media coverage of science. These issues, in the life sciences, seem to be most acute with respect to the beginning and the end of life. Using these and any other relevant materials, write an essay in which you discuss the ways in which definitions — words and concepts — function in our debates about the beginning and the end of life.

2. Weinberg's arguments and those of Barry Commoner (p. 693) touch or overlap at many points. Discuss the two essays as views of the present state of research in biology. What common problems do they identify? What do they share in the way of assumptions, values, and conclusions? Where do they differ in their views or in the way that they argue their cases? For example, they both discuss the way that economic issues impinge on biological science. Do they agree or disagree about these matters?

CASEBOOK

In one of the essays in this casebook, Vivian Gornick remembers a rite of passage for many college students — working as a waitress during summer break. In another reading, Barbara Ehrenreich leaves her comfortable middle-class life and takes a full-time job as a waitress to see if she can survive in the world of the working poor after welfare reform. In both readings, a waitperson is enduring hardships and trying to satisfy customers, but the selections have notable differences that can be compared and contrasted. You could even ask which presents a more powerful portrait of work — Gornick's personal reflections or Ehrenreich's present-day investigation. And what do both say about the nature of work?

Unlike the other sections of this book, which focus on a single type of writing, the five readings in this casebook focus on a single topic: working. In addition to Gornick and Ehrenreich, noted social thinker C. Wright Mills explains the history and social forces behind white-collar work, Eric Schlosser and award-winning photographer Jon Lowenstein report on the hardships that illegal immigrant laborers face, and poet Philip Levine makes a case for "what work is."

By placing these readings in a separate casebook, we intend to emphasize how readings on a single topic can relate to one another. You can enter the discussion by answering the questions that follow each reading or by responding to the "Making Connections" prompts that examine similar ideas between the readings. You could also use one, a few, or all of the readings as the basis for a large research project on the topic of work.

These readings are only a small selection of the many essays and books that have been written on the topic of work. As you respond to the questions following the readings, you will be asked to explore other ideas about work and to do so by drawing on your own experiences and on other sources that you research. Of course, you should ask some general questions as you read through the casebook: What is work? What is its function? More specifically, is your education work? How are education and work related? These are the types of questions that we hope this casebook will inspire you to explore.

WHITE-COLLAR WORK

C. Wright Mills

Sociologist Charles Wright Mills (1916–1962) was born to middle-class parents in Waco, Texas, graduated from the University of Texas at Austin, and later received his Ph.D. at the University of Wisconsin. He joined the faculty at Columbia University in 1946. A controversial and larger-than-life figure, Mills was early associated with Marxist theories and vocally committed to social change in the United States. He was critical of social scientists who saw themselves as passive observers and believed that intellectuals were in the best position to spearhead a "good society." In books such as The New Men of Power: America's Labor Leaders *(1948),* White Collar: The American Middle Classes *(1951),* The Power Elite *(1956), and* The Sociological Imagination *(1959), Mills focused on issues of economic determinism, class, status, power, and oppression. Following his untimely death from a heart attack at the age of forty-five, he was immediately lionized by radical thinkers as the founder of the New Left. The following essay is a chapter from* White Collar.

Work may be a mere source of livelihood, or the most significant part of one's inner life; it may be experienced as expiation, or as exuberant expression of self; as bounden duty, or as the development of man's universal nature. Neither love nor hatred of work is inherent in man, or inherent in any given line of work. For work has no intrinsic meaning.

No adequate history of the meanings of work has been written. One can, however, trace the influences of various philosophies of work, which have filtered down to modern workers and which deeply modify their work as well as their leisure.

While the modern white-collar worker has no articulate philosophy of work, his feelings about it and his experiences of it influence his satisfactions and frustrations, the whole tone of his life. Whatever the effects of his work, known to him or not, they are the net result of the work as an activity, plus the meanings he brings to it, plus the views that others hold of it.

1. Meanings of Work

To the ancient Greeks, in whose society mechanical labor was done by slaves, work brutalized the mind, made man unfit for the practice of virtue.* It was a necessary material evil, which the elite, in their search for changeless vision, should avoid. The Hebrews also looked upon work as 'painful drudgery,' to which, they added, man is condemned by sin. In so far as work atoned for sin, however, it was worth while, yet Ecclesiastes,[1] for example, asserts that 'The labor of man does not satisfy the soul.' Later, Rabbinism[2] dignified work somewhat, viewing it as worthy exercise rather than scourge of the soul, but still said that the kingdom to come would be a kingdom of blessed idleness.

In primitive Christianity, work was seen as punishment for sin but also   5 as serving the ulterior ends of charity, health of body and soul, warding off the evil thoughts of idleness. But work, being of this world, was of no worth in itself. St. Augustine,[3] when pressed by organizational problems of the church, carried the issue further: for monks, work is obligatory, although it should alternate with prayer, and should engage them only enough to supply the real needs of the establishment. The church fathers placed pure meditation on divine matters above even the intellectual work of reading and copying in the monastery. The heretical sects that roved around Europe from the eleventh to the fourteenth century demanded work of man, but again for an ulterior reason: work, being painful and humiliating, should be pursued zealously as a 'scourge for the pride of the flesh.'

With Luther,[4] work was first established in the modern mind as 'the base and key to life.' While continuing to say that work is natural to fallen man, Luther, echoing Paul,[5] added that all who can work should do so. Idleness is an unnatural and evil evasion. To maintain oneself by work is a way of serving God. With this, the great split between religious piety and worldly activity is resolved; profession becomes 'calling,' and work is valued as a religious path to salvation.

---

*In this historical sketch of philosophies of work I have drawn upon Adriano Tilgher's *Work: What It Has Meant to Men through the Ages* (New York: Harcourt, Brace, 1930).

[1]*Ecclesiastes:* Preacher (Greek). It is the title of the book that follows Proverbs in the Hebrew Scriptures. [Eds.]

[2]*Rabbinism:* The philosophy of the Hebrew teachers of the law (rabbis) after the Jewish dispersion from Palestine. The accumulated oral teachings about Jewish law are now known as the Talmud. [Eds.]

[3]*St. Augustine* (354–430): An early Christian philosopher. He lived in Roman-controlled northern Africa and wrote extensively on issues of faith, including his own doubts and experiments with various belief systems. [Eds.]

[4]*Martin Luther* (1483–1546): A German monk who was a founder of Protestantism. [Eds.]

[5]*Paul* (5?–67?): An early interpreter of the teachings of Jesus. He is the author of several books of the Christian bible, including several letters to early churches in the Mediterranean region. [Eds.]

Calvin's[6] idea of predestination, far from leading in practice to idle apathy, prodded man further into the rhythm of modern work. It was necessary to act in the world rationally and methodically and continuously and hard, as if one were certain of being among those elected. It is God's will that everyone must work, but it is not God's will that one should lust after the fruits even of one's own labor; they must be reinvested to allow and to spur still more labor. Not contemplation, but strong-willed, austere, untiring work, based on religious conviction, will ease guilt and lead to the good and pious life.

The 'this-worldly asceticism' of early Protestantism placed a premium upon and justified the styles of conduct and feeling required in its agents by modern capitalism. The Protestant sects encouraged and justified the social development of a type of man capable of ceaseless, methodical labor. The psychology of the religious man and of the economic man thus coincided, as Max Weber[7] has shown, and at their point of coincidence the sober bourgeois entrepreneur lived in and through his work.

Locke's[8] notion that labor was the origin of individual ownership and the source of all economic value, as elaborated by Adam Smith,[9] became a keystone of the liberal economic system: work was now a controlling factor in the wealth of nations, but it was a soulless business, a harsh justification for the toiling grind of nineteenth-century populations, and for the economic man, who was motivated in work by the money he earned.

But there was another concept of work which evolved in the Renaissance; some men of that exuberant time saw work as a spur rather than a drag on man's development as man. By his own activity, man could accomplish anything; through work, man became creator. How better could he fill his hours? Leonardo da Vinci[10] rejoiced in creative labor; Bruno[11] glorified work as an arm against adversity and a tool of conquest.   10

During the nineteenth century there began to be reactions against the Utilitarian[12] meaning assigned to work by classical economics, reactions

---

[6]*John Calvin* (1509–1564): A French religious thinker (his original name is Jean Caulvin) who emphasized human sinfulness and salvation by God's grace. Calvinists felt that good deeds could not guarantee a place in heaven but that wealth was a sign of God's favor. [Eds.]

[7]*Max Weber* (1864–1920): One of the founders of sociology. One of his best-known works is *The Protestant Ethic and the Spirit of Capitalism*. [Eds.]

[8]*John Locke* (1632–1704): An English philosopher. [Eds.]

[9]*Adam Smith*(1723–1790): A Scottish philosopher and economist. [Eds.]

[10]*Leonardo da Vinci* (1452–1519): An Italian artist and inventor. [Eds.]

[11]*Giordano Bruno* (1548?–1600): An Italian philosopher. [Eds.]

[12]*Utilitarian*: Relating to the nineteenth-century philosophy that an action's usefulness should determine its goodness. Followers of utilitarianism felt that all actions should lead to the greatest good for the greatest number of people. [Eds.]

that drew upon this Renaissance exuberance. Men, such as Tolstoy,[13] Carlyle,[14] Ruskin,[15] and William Morris,[16] turned backward; others, such as Marx[17] and Engels,[18] looked forward. But both groups drew upon the Renaissance view of man as tool user. The division of labor and the distribution of its product, as well as the intrinsic meaning of work as purposive human activity, are at issue in these nineteenth-century speculations. Ruskin's ideal, set against the capitalist organization of work, rested on a pre-capitalist society of free artisans whose work is at once a necessity for livelihood and an act of art that brings inner calm. He glorified what he supposed was in the work of the medieval artisan; he believed that the total product of work should go to the worker. Profit on capital is an injustice and, moreover, to strive for profit for its own sake blights the soul and puts man into a frenzy.

In Marx we encounter a full-scale analysis of the meaning of work in human development as well as of the distortions of this development in capitalist society. Here the essence of the human being rests upon his work: 'What [individuals] . . . are . . . coincides with their production, both with *what* they produce and with *how* they produce. The nature of individuals thus depends on the material conditions determining their production.' Capitalist production, thought Marx, who accepted the humanist ideal of classic German idealism of the all-round personality, has twisted men into alien and specialized animal-like and depersonalized creatures.

Historically, most views of work have ascribed to it an extrinsic meaning. R. H. Tawney[19] refers to 'the distinction made by the philosophers of classical antiquity between liberal and servile occupations, the medieval insistence that riches exist for man, not man for riches. Ruskin's famous outburst, "there is no wealth but life," the argument of the Socialist who urges that production should be organized for service, not for profit, are but different attempts to emphasize the instrumental character of economic activities by reference to an ideal which is held to express the true nature of man.'

---

[13]*Leo Tolstoy* (1828–1910): Russia's greatest philosopher and writer. His best-known novel is *War and Peace.* [Eds.]

[14]*Thomas Carlyle* (1795–1881): An English historian. [Eds.]

[15]*John Ruskin* (1819–1900): An English art critic. [Eds.]

[16]*William Morris* (1834–1896): An English artist and craftsman. [Eds.]

[17]*Karl Marx* (1818–1883): A German political philosopher. His best-known work is *Manifesto of the Communist Party,* which is coauthored with Friedrich Engels. [Eds.]

[18]*Friedrich Engels* (1820–1895): A German socialist writer who is best known for collaborating with Karl Marx. [Eds.]

[19]*Richard Henry Tawney* (1880–1962): An English socialist and educator with a strong belief in fellowship. [Eds.]

But there are also whose who ascribe to work an intrinsic worth. All philosophies of work may be divided into these two views, although in a curious way Carlyle managed to combine the two.

I. The various forms of Protestantism, which (along with classical economics) have been the most influential doctrines in modern times, see work activity as ulterior to religious sanctions; gratifications from work are not intrinsic to the activity and experience, but are religious rewards. By work one gains a religious status and assures oneself of being among the elect. If work is compulsive it is due to the painful guilt that arises when one does not work.

II. The Renaissance view of work, which sees it as intrinsically mean- 15
ingful, is centered in the technical craftsmanship — the manual and mental operations — of the work process itself; it sees the reasons for work in the work itself and not in any ulterior realm or consequence. Not income, not way of salvation, not status, not power over other people, but the technical processes themselves are gratifying.

Neither of these views, however — the secularized gospel of work as compulsion, nor the humanist view of work as craftsmanship — now has great influence among modern populations. For most employees, work has a generally unpleasant quality. If there is little Calvinist compulsion to work among propertyless factory workers and file clerks, there is also little Renaissance exuberance in the work of the insurance clerk, freight handler, or department-store saleslady. If the shoe salesman or the textile executive gives little thought to the religious meaning of his labor, certainly few telephone operators or receptionists or schoolteachers experience from their work any Ruskinesque inner calm. Such joy as creative work may carry is more and more limited to a small minority. For the white-collar masses, as for wage earners generally, work seems to serve neither God nor whatever they may experience as divine in themselves. In them there is no taut will-to-work, and few positive gratifications from their daily round.

The gospel of work has been central to the historic tradition of America, to its image of itself, and to the images the rest of the world has of America. The crisis and decline of that gospel are of wide and deep meaning. On every hand, we hear, in the words of Wade Shortleft for example, that 'the aggressiveness and enthusiasm which marked other generations is withering, and in its stead we find the philosophy that attaining and holding a job is not a challenge but a necessary evil. When work becomes just work, activity undertaken only for reason of subsistence, the spirit which fired our nation to its present greatness has died to a spark. An ominous apathy cloaks the smoldering discontent and restlessness of the management men of tomorrow.'

To understand the significance of this gospel and its decline, we must understand the very spirit of twentieth-century America. That the historical work ethic of the old middle-class entrepreneurs has not deeply gripped the people of the new society is one of the most crucial psychological implications of the structural decline of the old middle classes. The new middle class, despite the old middle-class origin of many of its members, has never been deeply involved in the older work ethic, and on this point has been from the beginning non-bourgeois in mentality.

At the same time, the second historically important model of meaningful work and gratification — craftsmanship — has never belonged to the new middle classes, either by tradition or by the nature of their work. Nevertheless, the model of craftsmanship lies, however vaguely, back of most serious studies of worker dissatisfaction today, of most positive statements of worker gratification, from Ruskin and Tolstoy to Bergson[20] and Sorel.[21] Therefore, it is worth considering in some detail, in order that we may then gauge in just what respects its realization is impossible for the modern white-collar worker.

2. The Ideal of Craftsmanship

Craftsmanship as a fully idealized model of work gratification involves six major features: There is no ulterior motive in work other than the product being made and the processes of its creation. The details of daily work are meaningful because they are not detached in the worker's mind from the product of the work. The worker is free to control his own working action. The craftsman is thus able to learn from his work; and to use and develop his capacities and skills in its prosecution. There is no split of work and play, or work and culture. The craftsman's way of livelihood determines and infuses his entire mode of living.

I. The hope in good work, William Morris remarked, is hope of product and hope of pleasure in the work itself; the supreme concern, the whole attention, is with the quality of the product and the skill of its making. There is an inner relation between the craftsman and the thing he makes, from the image he first forms of it through its completion, which goes beyond the mere legal relations of property and makes the craftsman's will-to-work spontaneous and even exuberant.

---

[20]*Henri Bergson* (1859–1941): French philosopher who received the Nobel Prize for literature in 1927. He is best known for his studies of consciousness and intuition. [Eds.]

[21]*Georges Sorel* (1847–1922): A French engineer who advocated widespread worker strikes to bring about worker control of factories. His belief that workers needed a myth to motivate them was later adopted by fascist and communist groups. [Eds.]

Other motives and results — money or reputation or salvation — are subordinate. It is not essential to the practice of the craft ethic that one necessarily improves one's status either in the religious community or in the community in general. Work gratification is such that a man may live in a kind of quiet passion 'for his work alone.'

II. In most statements of craftsmanship, there is a confusion between its technical and aesthetic conditions and the legal (property) organization of the worker and the product. What is actually necessary for work-as-craftsmanship, however, is that the tie between the product and the producer be psychologically possible; if the producer does not legally own the product he must own it psychologically in the sense that he knows what goes into it by way of skill, sweat, and material and that his own skill and sweat are visible to him. Of course, if legal conditions are such that the tie between the work and the worker's material advantage is transparent, this is a further gratification, but it is subordinate to that workmanship which would continue of its own will even if not paid for.

The craftsman has an image of the completed product, and even though he does not make it all, he sees the place of his part in the whole, and thus understands the meaning of his exertion in terms of that whole. The satisfaction he has in the result infuses the means of achieving it, and in this way his work is not only meaningful to him but also partakes of the consummatory satisfaction he has in the product. If work, in some of its phases, has the taint of travail and vexation and mechanical drudgery, still the craftsman is carried over these junctures by keen anticipation. He may even gain positive satisfaction from encountering a resistance and conquering it, feeling his work and will as powerfully victorious over the recalcitrance of materials and the malice of things. Indeed, without this resistance he would gain less satisfaction in being finally victorious over that which at first obstinately resists his will.

George Mead[22] has stated this kind of aesthetic experience as 25 involving the power 'to catch the enjoyment that belongs to the consummation, the outcome, of an undertaking and to give to the implements, the objects that are instrumental in the undertaking, and to the acts that compose it something of the joy and satisfaction that suffuse its successful accomplishment.'

III. The workman is free to begin his work according to his own plan and, during the activity by which it is shaped, he is free to modify its form

---

[22]*George Herbert Mead* (1863–1931): An American philosopher whose social theories led him to become a founder of pragmatism. [Eds.]

and the manner of its creation. In both these senses, Henri De Man[23] observed, 'plan and performance are one,' and the craftsman is master of the activity and of himself in the process. This continual joining of plan and activity brings even more firmly together the consummation of work and its instrumental activities, infusing the latter with the joy of the former. It also means that his sphere of independent action is large and rational to him. He is responsible for its outcome and free to assume that responsibility. His problems and difficulties must be solved by him, in terms of the shape he wants the final outcome to assume.

IV. The craftsman's work is thus a means of developing his skill, as well as a means of developing himself as a man. It is not that self-development is an ulterior goal, but that such development is the cumulative result obtained by devotion to and practice of his skills. As he gives it the quality of his own mind and skill, he is also further developing his own nature; in this simple sense, he lives in and through his work, which confesses and reveals him to the world.

V. In the craftsman pattern there is no split of work and play, of work and culture. If play is supposed to be an activity, exercised for its own sake, having no aim other than gratifying the actor, then work is supposed to be an activity performed to create economic value or for some other ulterior result. Play is something you do to be happily occupied, but if work occupies you happily, it is also play, although it is also serious, just as play is to the child. 'Really free work, the work of a composer, for example,' Marx once wrote of Fourier's[24] notions of work and play, 'is damned serious work, intense strain.' The simple self-expression of play and the creation of ulterior value of work are combined in work-as-craftsmanship. The craftsman or artist expresses himself at the same time and in the same act as he creates value. His work is a poem in action. He is at work and at play in the same act.

'Work' and 'culture' are not, as Gentile[25] has held, separate spheres, the first dealing with means, the second with ends in themselves; as Tilgher,[26] Sorel, and others have indicated, either work or culture may be an end in itself, a means, or may contain segments of both ends and means.

---

[23]*Henri De Man* (1885–1953): A Belgian politician and socialist who advocated an alliance between blue-collar and middle-class workers. [Eds.]

[24]*Jean Baptiste Joseph Fourier* (1768–1830): A French mathematician whose work led to advances in trigonometry. [Eds.]

[25]*Giovanni Gentile* (1906–1942): An Italian physics professor and theoretician. [Eds.]

[26]*Adriano Tilgher* (1887–1941): An Italian writer whose 1930 *Work: What It Has Meant to Men through the Ages* suggested that secularization increased as attitudes toward work evolved. [Eds.]

In the craft model of activity, 'consumption' and 'production' are blended in the same act; active craftsmanship, which is both play and work, is the medium of culture; and for the craftsman there is no split between the worlds of culture and work.

VI. The craftsman's work is the mainspring of the only life he knows; 30 he does not flee from work into a separate sphere of leisure; he brings to his non-working hours the values and qualities developed and employed in his working time. His idle conversation is shop talk; his friends follow the same lines of work as he, and share a kinship of feeling and thought. The leisure William Morris called for was 'leisure to think about our work, that faithful daily companion. . . .'

In order to give his work the freshness of creativity, the craftsman must at times open himself up to those influences that only affect us when our attentions are relaxed. Thus for the craftsman, apart from mere animal rest, leisure may occur in such intermittent periods as are necessary for individuality in his work. As he brings to his leisure the capacity and problems of his work, so he brings back into work those sensitivities he would not gain in periods of high, sustained tension necessary for solid work.

'The world of art,' wrote Paul Bourget,[27] speaking of America, 'requires less self-consciousness — an impulse of life which forgets itself, the alternation of dreamy idleness with fervid execution.' The same point is made by Henry James,[28] in his essay on Balzac,[29] who remarks that we have practically lost the faculty of attention, meaning . . . 'that unstrenuous, brooding sort of attention required to produce or appreciate works of art.' Even rest, which is not so directly connected with work itself as a condition of creativity, is animal rest, made secure and freed from anxiety by virtue of work done — in Tilgher's words, 'a sense of peace and calm which flows from all well-regulated, disciplined work done with a quiet and contented mind.'

In constructing this model of craftsmanship, we do not mean to imply that there ever was a community in which work carried all these meanings. Whether the medieval artisan approximated the model as closely as some writers seem to assume, we do not know; but we entertain serious doubts that this is so; we lack enough psychological knowledge of medieval populations properly to judge. At any rate, for our purposes it is enough to know that at different times and in different occupations, the work men do has carried one or more features of craftsmanship.

With such a model in mind, a glance at the occupational world of the modern worker is enough to make clear that practically none of these aspects

---

[27]*Paul Bourget* (1852–1935): A French novelist, poet, and playwright. [Eds.]

[28]*Henry James* (1843–1916): An American novelist who lived and worked in England. [Eds.]

[29]*Honoré de Balzac* (1799–1850): A French novelist and story writer. [Eds.]

are now relevant to modern work experience. The model of craftsmanship has become an anachronism. We use the model as an explicit ideal in terms of which we can summarize the working conditions and the personal meaning work has in modern work-worlds, and especially to white-collar people.

3. The Conditions of Modern Work

As practice, craftsmanship has largely been trivialized into 'hobbies,' 35 part of leisure not of work; or if work — a marketable activity — it is the work of scattered mechanics in handicraft trades, and of professionals who manage to remain free. As ethic, craftsmanship is confined to minuscule groups of privileged professionals and intellectuals.

The entire shift from the rural world of the small entrepreneur to the urban society of the dependent employee has instituted the property conditions of alienation from product and processes of work. Of course, dependent occupations vary in the extent of initiative they allow and invite, and many self-employed enterprisers are neither as independent nor as enterprising as commonly supposed. Nevertheless, in almost any job, the employee sells a degree of his independence; his working life is within the domain of others; the level of his skills that are used and the areas in which he may exercise independent decisions are subject to management by others. Probably at least ten or twelve million people worked during the 'thirties at tasks below the skill level of which they were easily capable; and, as school attendance increases and more jobs are routinized, the number of people who must work below their capacities will increase.

There is considerable truth in the statement that those who find free expression of self in their work are those who securely own the property with which they work, or those whose work-freedom does not entail the ownership of property. 'Those who have no money work sloppily under the name of sabotage,' writes Charles Péguy,[30] 'and those who have money work sloppily, a counter and different sloppiness, under the name of luxury. And thus culture no longer has any medium through which it might infiltrate. There no longer exists that marvelous unity true of all ancient societies, where he who produced and he who bought equally loved and knew culture.'

The objective alienation of man from the product and the process of work is entailed by the legal framework of modern capitalism and the modern division of labor. The worker does not own the product or the tools of his production. In the labor contract he sells his time, energy, and skill into the power of others. To understand self-alienation we need not accept the metaphysical view that man's self is most crucially expressed in work-activity. In all work

---

[30]*Charles Péguy* (1873–1914): A French philosopher and poet. [Eds.]

involving the personality market, as we have seen, one's personality and personal traits become part of the means of production. In this sense a person instrumentalizes and externalizes intimate features of his person and disposition. In certain white-collar areas, the rise of personality markets has carried self and social alienation to explicit extremes.

Thoreau,[31] who spoke for the small entrepreneur, objected, in the middle of the nineteenth century, 'to the division of labor since it divided the worker, not merely the work, reduced him from a man to an operative, and enriched the few at the expense of the many.' 'It destroyed,' wrote F. O. Matthiessen,[32] 'the potential balance of his [Thoreau's] agrarian world, one of the main ideals of which was the union of labor and culture.'

The detailed division of labor means, of course, that the individual does not carry through the whole process of work to its final product; but it also means that under many modern conditions the process itself is invisible to him. The product as the goal of his work is legally and psychologically detached from him, and this detachment cuts the nerve of meaning which work might otherwise gain from its technical processes. Even on the professional levels of white-collar work, not to speak of wage-work and the lower white-collar tasks, the chance to develop and use individual rationality is often destroyed by the centralization of decision and the formal rationality that bureaucracy entails. The expropriation which modern work organization has carried through thus goes far beyond the expropriation of ownership; rationality itself has been expropriated from work and any total view and understanding of its process. No longer free to plan his work, much less to modify the plan to which he is subordinated, the individual is to a great extent managed and manipulated in his work.

The world market, of which Marx spoke as the alien power over men, has in many areas been replaced by the bureaucratized enterprise. Not the market as such but centralized administrative decisions determine when men work and how fast. Yet the more and the harder men work, the more they build up that which dominates their work as an alien force, the commodity; so also, the more and the harder the white-collar man works, the more he builds up the enterprise outside himself, which is, as we have seen, duly made a fetish and thus indirectly justified. The enterprise is not the institutional shadow of great men, as perhaps it seemed under the old captain of industry; nor is it the instrument through which men realize themselves in work, as in small-scale production. The enterprise is an impersonal and alien Name, and the more that is placed in it, the less is placed in man.

As tool becomes machine, man is estranged from the intellectual potentialities and aspects of work; and each individual is routinized in the name

40

---

[31]*Henry David Thoreau* (1817–1862): An American essayist and poet best known for his advocacy of nature and individualism. [Eds.]

[32]*Francis Otto Matthiessen* (1902–1950): An American scholar of literature who was a committed Christian and socialist. [Eds.]

of increased and cheaper per unit productivity. The whole unit and meaning of time is modified; man's 'life-time,' wrote Marx, is transformed into 'working-time.' In tying down individuals to particular tasks and jobs, the division of labor 'lays the foundation of that all-engrossing system of specializing and sorting men, that development in a man of one single faculty at the expense of all other faculties, which caused A. Ferguson, the master of Adam Smith, to exclaim: "We make a nation of Helots,[33] and have no free citizens."'

The introduction of office machinery and sales devices has been mechanizing the office and the salesroom, the two big locales of white-collar work. Since the 'twenties it has increased the division of white-collar labor, recomposed personnel, and lowered skill levels. Routine operations in minutely subdivided organizations have replaced the bustling interest of work in well-known groups. Even on managerial and professional levels, the growth of rational bureaucracies has made work more like factory production. The managerial demiurge is constantly furthering all these trends: mechanization, more minute division of labor, the use of less skilled and less expensive workers.

In its early stages, a new division of labor may specialize men in such a way as to increase their levels of skill; but later, especially when whole operations are split and mechanized, such division develops certain faculties at the expense of others and narrows all of them. And as it comes more fully under mechanization and centralized management, it levels men off again as automatons. Then there are a few specialists and a mass of automatons; both integrated by the authority which makes them interdependent and keeps each in his own routine. Thus, in the division of labor, the open development and free exercise of skills are managed and closed.

The alienating conditions of modern work now include the salaried 45 employees as well as the wage-workers. There are few, if any, features of wage-work (except heavy toil — which is decreasingly a factor in wage-work) that do not also characterize at least some white-collar work. For here, too, the human traits of the individual, from his physique to his psychic disposition, become units in the functionally rational calculation of managers. None of the features of work as craftsmanship is prevalent in office and salesroom, and, in addition, some features of white-collar work, such as the personality market, go well beyond the alienating conditions of wage-work.

Yet, as Henri De Man has pointed out, we cannot assume that the employee makes comparisons between the ideal of work as craftsmanship and his own working experience. We cannot compare the idealized portrait of the craftsman with that of the auto worker and on that basis impute any psychological state to the auto worker. We cannot fruitfully compare the

---

[33]*Helots:* Serfs in the ancient Greek city-state of Sparta. Members of this class were neither slaves nor citizens. [Eds.]

psychological condition of the old merchant's assistant with the modern saleslady, or the old-fashioned bookkeeper with the IBM machine attendant. For the historical destruction of craftsmanship and of the old office does not enter the consciousness of the modern wage-worker or white-collar employee; much less is their absence felt by him as a crisis, as it might have been if, in the course of the last generation, his father or mother had been in the craft condition — but, statistically speaking, they have not been. It is slow historical fact, long gone by in any dramatic consequence and not of psychological relevance to the present generation. Only the psychological imagination of the historian makes it possible to write of such comparisons as if they were of psychological import. The craft life would be immediately available as a fact of their consciousness only if in the lifetime of the modern employees they had experienced a shift from the one condition to the other, which they have not; or if they had grasped it as an ideal meaning of work, which they have not.

But if the work white-collar people do is not connected with its resultant product, and if there is no intrinsic connection between work and the rest of their life, then they must accept their work as meaningless in itself, perform it with more or less disgruntlement, and seek meanings elsewhere. Of their work, as of all of our lives, it can truly be said, in Henri Bergson's words, that: 'The greater part of our time we live outside ourselves, hardly perceiving anything of ourselves but our own ghost, a colourless shadow. . . . Hence we live for the external world rather than for ourselves; we speak rather than think; we are acted rather than act ourselves. To act freely is to recover possession of oneself. . . .'

If white-collar people are not free to control their working actions they, in time, habitually submit to the orders of others and, in so far as they try to act freely, do so in other spheres. If they do not learn from their work or develop themselves in doing it, in time, they cease trying to do so, often having no interest in self-development even in other areas. If there is a split between their work and play, and their work and culture, they admit that split as a common-sense fact of existence. If their way of earning a living does not infuse their mode of living, they try to build their real life outside their work. Work becomes a sacrifice of time, necessary to building a life outside of it.

4. Frames of Acceptance

Underneath virtually all experience of work today, there is a fatalistic feeling that work *per se* is unpleasant. One type of work, or one particular job, is contrasted with another type, experienced or imagined, within the present world of work; judgments are rarely made about the world of work as presently organized as against some other way of organizing it; so also, satisfaction from work is felt in comparison with the satisfactions of other jobs.

We do not know what proportions of the U.S. white-collar strata are   50
'satisfied' by their work and, more important, we do not know what being
satisfied means to them. But it is possible to speculate fruitfully about such
questions.

We do have the results of some questions, necessarily crude, regarding
feelings about present jobs. As in almost every other area, when sponge
questions are asked of a national cross-section, white-collar people, meaning here clerical and sales employees, are in the middle zones. They stand
close to the national average (64 per cent asserting they find their work interesting and enjoyable 'all the time'), while more of the professionals and
executives claim interest and enjoyment (85 per cent), and fewer of the factory workers (41 per cent) do so.

Within the white-collar hierarchy, job satisfaction seems to follow the
hierarchical levels; in one study, for example, 86 per cent of the professionals, 74 per cent of the managerial, 42 per cent of the commercial employees,
stated general satisfaction. This is also true of wage-worker levels of skill: 56
per cent of the skilled, but 48 per cent of the semi-skilled, are satisfied.

Such figures tell us very little, since we do not know what the questions
mean to the people who answer them, or whether they mean the same thing
to different strata. However, work satisfaction is related to income and, if
we had measures, we might find that it is also related to status as well as to
power. What such questions probably measure are invidious judgments of
the individual's standing with reference to other individuals. And the aspects of work, the terms of such comparisons, must be made clear.

Under modern conditions, the direct technical processes of work have
been declining in meaning for the mass of employees, but other features of
work — income, power, status — have come to the fore. Apart from the
technical operations and the skills involved, work is a source of income; the
amount, level, and security of pay, and what one's income history has been
are part of work's meaning. Work is also a means of gaining status, at the
place of work, and in the general community. Different types of work and
different occupational levels carry differential status values. These again are
part of the meaning of the job. And also work carries various sorts of
power, over materials and tools and machines, but, more crucially now,
over other people.

I. *Income:* The economic motives for work are now its only firm ration-   55
ale. Work now has no other legitimating symbols, although certainly other
gratifications and discontents are associated with it. The division of labor and
the routinization of many job areas are reducing work to a commodity, of
which money has become the only common denominator. To the worker who
cannot receive technical gratifications from his work, its market value is all
there is to it. The only significant occupational movement in the United
States, the trade unions, have the pure and simple ideology of alienated work:
more and more money for less and less work. There are, of course, other
demands, but they can be only 'fixed up' to lessen the cry for more money.

The sharp focus upon money is part and parcel of the lack of intrinsic meaning that work has come to have.

Underlying the modern approach to work there seems to be some vague feeling that 'one should earn one's own living,' a kind of Protestant undertow, attenuated into a secular convention. 'When work goes,' as H. A. Overstreet,[34] a job psychologist writing of the slump, puts it, 'we know that the tragedy is more than economic. It is psychological. It strikes at the center of our personality. It takes from us something that rightly belongs to every self-respecting human being.' But income security — the fear of unemployment or under employment — is more important. An undertow of anxiety about sickness, accident, or old age must support eagerness for work, and gratification may be based on the compulsion to relieve anxiety by working hard. Widespread unemployment, or fear of it, may even make an employee happily thankful for any job, contented to be at any kind of work when all around there are many workless, worried people. If satisfaction rests on relative status, there is here an invidious element that increases it. It is across this ground tone of convention and fear, built around work as a source of income, that other motives to work and other factors of satisfaction are available.

II. *Status:* Income and income security lead to other things, among them, status. With the decline of technical gratification, the employee often tries to center such meaning as he finds in work on other features of the job. Satisfaction in work often rests upon status satisfactions from work associations. As a social role played in relation to other people, work may become a source of self-esteem, on the job, among co-workers, superiors, subordinates, and customers, if any; and off the job, among friends, family, and community at large. The fact of doing one kind of job rather than another and doing one's job with skill and dispatch may be a source of self-esteem. For the man or woman lonely in the city, the mere fact of meeting people at the place of work may be a positive thing. Even anonymous work contacts in large enterprises may be highly esteemed by those who feel too closely bound by family and neighborhood. There is a gratification from working downtown in the city, uptown in the smaller urban center; there is the glamour of being attached to certain firms.

It is the status conferred on the exercise of given skills and on given income levels that is often the prime source of gratification or humiliation. The psychological effect of a detailed division of labor depends upon whether or not the worker has been downgraded, and upon whether or not his associates have also been downgraded. Pride in skill is relative to the skills he has exercised in the past and to the skills others exercise, and thus to the evaluation of his skills by other people whose opinions count. In like

---

[34]*Harry Allen Overstreet* (1875–1970): An American social psychologist who advocated citizen education. [Eds.]

manner, the amount of money he receives may be seen by the employee and by others as the best gauge of his worth.

This may be all the more true when relations are increasingly 'objectified' and do not require intimate knowledge. For then there may be anxiety to keep secret the amount of money earned, and even to suggest to others that one earns more. 'Who earns the most?' asks Erich Engelhard.[35] 'That is the important question, that is the gauge of all differentiations and the yardstick of the moneyed classes. We do not wish to show how we work, for in most cases others will soon have learned our tricks. This explains all the bragging. "The work I have to do!" exclaims one employee when he has only three letters to write. . . . This boastfulness can be explained by a drive which impels certain people to evaluate their occupations very low in comparison with their intellectual aspirations but very high compared with the occupations of others.'

III. *Power:* Power over the technical aspects of work has been stripped from the individual, first, by the development of the market, which determines how and when he works, and second, by the bureaucratization of the work sphere, which subjects work operations to discipline. By virtue of these two alien forces the individual has lost power over the technical operations of his own work life.

But the exercise of power over other people has been elaborated. In so far as modern organizations of work are large scale, they are hierarchies of power, into which various occupations are fitted. The fact that one takes orders as well as gives them does not necessarily decrease the positive gratification achieved through the exercise of power on the job.

Status and power, as features of work gratification, are often blended; self-esteem may be based on the social power exercised in the course of work; victory over the will of another may greatly expand one's self-estimation. But the very opposite may also be true: in an almost masochistic way, people may be gratified by subordination on the job. We have already seen how office women in lower positions of authority are liable to identify with men in higher authority, transferring from prior family connections or projecting to future family relations.

All four aspects of occupation — skill, power, income, and status — must be taken into account to understand the meaning of work and the sources of its gratification. Any one of them may become the foremost aspect of the job, and in various combinations each is usually in the consciousness of the employee. To achieve and to exercise the power and status that higher income entails may be the very definition of satisfaction in

60

[35]*Erich Engelhard*: A German sociologist, who wrote the article "The Salaried Employee" ("Die Angestellten") that Mills references here. [Eds.]

work, and this satisfaction may have nothing whatsoever to do with the craft experience as the inherent need and full development of human activity.

5. The Morale of the Cheerful Robots

The institutions in which modern work is organized have come about by drift — many little schemes adding up to unexpected results — and by plan — efforts paying off as expected. The alienation of the individual from the product and the process of his work came about, in the first instance, as a result of the drift of modern capitalism. Then, Frederick Taylor,[36] and other scientific managers, raised the division of labor to the level of planful management. By centralizing plans, as well as introducing further divisions of skill, they further routinized work; by consciously building upon the drift, in factory and in office, they have carried further certain of its efficient features.

Twenty years ago, H. Dubreuil,[37] a foreign observer of U.S. industry, could write that Taylor's 'insufficiency' shows up when he comes to approach 'the inner forces contained in the worker's soul. . . .' That is no longer true. The new (social) scientific management begins precisely where Taylor left off or was incomplete; students of 'human relations in industry' have studied not lighting and clean toilets, but social cliques and good morale. For in so far as human factors are involved in efficient and untroubled production, the managerial demiurge must bring them under control. So, in factory and in office, the world to be managed increasingly includes the social setting, the human affairs, and the personality of man as a worker.

Management effort to create job enthusiasm reflects the unhappy unwillingness of employees to work spontaneously at their routinized tasks; it indicates recognition of the lack of spontaneous will to work for the ulterior ends available; it also indicates that it is more difficult to have happy employees when the chances to climb the skill and social hierarchies are slim. These are underlying reasons why the Protestant ethic, a work compulsion, is replaced by the conscious efforts of Personnel Departments to create morale. But the present-day concern with employee morale and work enthusiasm has other sources than the meaningless character of much modern work. It is also a response to several decisive shifts in American society, particularly in its higher business circles: the enormous scale and

65

---

[36]*Frederick Taylor* (1856–1915): An American proponent of scientific management, whose time-and-motion studies revolutionized industry. [Eds.]

[37]*Hyacinthe Dubreuil*: A French author, who wrote *Robots or Men?: A French Workman's Experience in American Industry* in 1929. [Eds.]

complexity of modern business, its obviously vast and concentrated power; the rise of successfully competing centers of loyalty — the unions — over the past dozen years, with their inevitable focus upon power relations on the job; the enlargement of the liberal administrative state at the hands of politically successful New and Fair Deals; and the hostile atmosphere surrounding business during the big slump.

These developments have caused a shift in the outlook of certain sections of the business world, which in *The New Men of Power* I have called the shift from practical to sophisticated conservatism. The need to develop new justifications, and the fact that increased power has not yet been publicly justified, give rise to a groping for more telling symbols of justification among the more sophisticated business spokesmen, who have felt themselves to be a small island in a politically hostile sea of propertyless employees. Studies of 'human relations in industry' are an ideological part of this groping. The managers are interested in such studies because of the hope of lowering production costs, of easing tensions inside their plants, of finding new symbols to justify the concentrated power they exercise in modern society.

To secure and increase the will to work, a new ethic that endows work with more than an economic incentive is needed. During war, managers have appealed to nationalism; they have appealed in the name of the firm or branch of the office or factory, seeking to tap the animistic identifications of worker with work-place and tools in an effort to strengthen his identification with the company. They have repeatedly written that 'job enthusiasm is good business,' that 'job enthusiasm is a hallmark of the American Way.' But they have not yet found a really sound ideology.

What they are after is 'something in the employee' outwardly manifested in a 'mail must go through' attitude, 'the "we" attitude,' 'spontaneous discipline,' 'employees smiling and cheerful.' They want, for example, to point out to banking employees 'their importance to banking and banking's importance to the general economy.' In conferences of management associations (1947) one hears: 'There is one thing more that is wonderful about the human body. Make the chemical in the vial a little different and you have a person who is loyal. He likes you, and when mishaps come he takes a lot from you and the company, because you have been so good to him; you have changed the structure of his blood. You have to put into his work and environment the things that change the chemical that stimulates the action, so that he is loyal and productive. . . . Somebody working under us won't know why, but . . . when they are asked where they work and why, they say "I work with this company. I like it there and my boss is really one to work with."'

The over-all formula of advice that the new ideology of 'human relations in business' contains runs to this effect: to make the worker happy, efficient, and co-operative, you must make the managers intelligent, rational, knowledgeable. It is the perspective of a managerial elite, disguised in the pseudo-objective language of engineers. It is advice to the personnel manager to

70

relax his authoritative manner and widen his manipulative grip over the employees by understanding them better and countering their informal solidarities against management and exploiting these solidarities for smoother and less troublesome managerial efficiency.

Current managerial attempts to create job enthusiasm, to paraphrase Marx's comment on Proudhon,[38] are attempts to conquer work alienation within the bounds of work alienation. In the meantime, whatever satisfaction alienated men gain from work occurs within the framework of alienation; whatever satisfaction they gain from life occurs outside the boundaries of work; work and life are sharply split.

6. The Big Split

Only in the last half century has leisure been widely available to the weary masses of the big city. Before then, there was leisure only for those few who were socially trained to use and enjoy it; the rest of the populace was left on lower and bleaker levels of sensibility, taste, and feeling. Then as the sphere of leisure was won for more and more of the people, the techniques of mass production were applied to amusement as they had been to the sphere of work. The most ostensible feature of American social life today, and one of the most frenzied, is its mass leisure activities. The most important characteristic of all these activities is that they astonish, excite, and distract but they do not enlarge reason or feeling, or allow spontaneous dispositions to unfold creatively.

What is psychologically important in this shift to mass leisure is that the old middle-class work ethic — the gospel of work — has been replaced in the society of employees by a leisure ethic, and this replacement has involved a sharp, almost absolute split between work and leisure. Now work itself is judged in terms of leisure values. The sphere of leisure provides the standards by which work is judged; it lends to work such meanings as work has.

Alienation in work means that the most alert hours of one's life are sacrificed to the making of money with which to 'live.' Alienation means boredom and the frustration of potentially creative effort, of the productive sides of personality. It means that while men must seek all values that matter to them outside of work, they must be serious during work: they may not laugh or sing or even talk, they must follow the rules and not violate the fetish of 'the enterprise.' In short, they must be serious and steady about something that does not mean anything to them, and moreover during the best hours of their day, the best hours of their life. Leisure time thus comes to mean an unserious freedom from the authoritarian seriousness of the job.

---

[38]*Pierre Joseph Proudhon* (1809–1865): A French utopian socialist. [Eds.]

The split of work from leisure and the greater importance of leisure in the   75
striving consciousness of modern man run through the whole fabric of twentieth-
century America, affect the meaningful experiences of work, and set popular
goals and day-dreams. Over the last forty years, Leo Lowenthal[39] has shown, as
the 'idols of work' have declined, the 'idols of leisure' have arisen. Now the selection of heroes for popular biography appearing in mass magazines has shifted
from business, professional, and political figures — successful in the sphere of
production — to those successful in entertainment, leisure, and consumption.
The movie star and the baseball player have replaced the industrial magnate and
the political man. Today, the displayed characteristics of popular idols 'can all be
integrated around the concept of the consumer.' And the faculties of reflection,
imagination, dream, and desire, so far as they exist, do not now move in the
sphere of concrete, practical work experience.

Work is split from the rest of life, especially from the spheres of conscious enjoyment; nevertheless, most men and many women must work. So
work is an unsatisfactory means to ulterior ends lying somewhere in the
sphere of leisure. The necessity to work and the alienation from it make up
its grind, and the more grind there is, the more need to find relief in the
jumpy or dreamy models available in modern leisure. Leisure contains all
good things and all goals dreamed of and actively pursued. The dreariest
part of life, R. H. Tawney remarks, is where and when you work, the gayest
where and when you consume.

Each day men sell little pieces of themselves in order to try to buy
them back each night and week end with the coin of 'fun.' With amusement, with love, with movies, with vicarious intimacy, they pull themselves
into some sort of whole again, and now they are different men. Thus, the
cycle of work and leisure gives rise to two quite different images of self: the
everyday image, based upon work, and the holiday image, based upon
leisure. The holiday image is often heavily tinged with aspired-to and
dreamed-of features and is, of course, fed by mass-media personalities and
happenings. 'The rhythm of the week end, with its birth, its planned gai-
eties, and its announced end,' Scott Fitzgerald[40] wrote, 'followed the
rhythm of life and was a substitute for it.' The week end, having nothing in
common with the working week, lifts men and women out of the gray level
tone of everyday work life, and forms a standard with which the working
life is contrasted.

As the work sphere declines in meaning and gives no inner direction
and rhythm to life, so have community and kinship circles declined as ways
of 'fixing man into society.' In the old craft model, work sphere and family
coincided; before the Industrial Revolution, the home and the workshop

---

[39]*Leo Lowenthal* (1900–1993): A German-born American pioneer in the critical sociology of literature and culture. [Eds.]
   [40]*F. Scott Fitzgerald* (1896–1940): An American novelist and story writer who
is identified with the Jazz Age and was author of *The Great Gatsby*. [Eds.]

were one. Today, this is so only in certain smaller-bourgeois families, and there it is often seen by the young as repression. One result of the division of labor is to take the breadwinner out of the home, segregating work life and home life. This has often meant that work becomes the means for the maintenance of the home, and the home the means for refitting the worker to go back to work. But with the decline of the home as the center of psychological life and the lowering of the hours of work, the sphere of leisure and amusement takes over the home's functions.

No longer is the framework within which a man lives fixed by traditional institutions. Mass communications replace tradition as a framework of life. Being thus afloat, the metropolitan man finds a new anchorage in the spectator sports, the idols of the mass media, and other machineries of amusement.

So the leisure sphere — and the machinery of amusement in terms of which it is now organized — becomes the center of character-forming influences, of identification models: it is what one man has in common with another; it is a continuous interest. The machinery of amusement, Henry Durant[41] remarks, focuses attention and desires upon 'those aspects of our life which are divorced from work and on people who are significant, not in terms of what they have achieved, but in terms of having money and time to spend.'   80

The amusement of hollow people rests on their own hollowness and does not fill it up; it does not calm or relax them, as old middle-class frolics and jollification may have done; it does not re-create their spontaneity in work, as in the craftsman model. Their leisure diverts them from the restless grind of their work by the absorbing grind of passive enjoyment of glamour and thrills. To modern man leisure is the way to spend money, work is the way to make it. When the two compete, leisure wins hands down.

QUESTIONS

1. Describe the work that one of your parents (or someone else whom you know) does. Which of Mills's categories describes it best: Protestant, Renaissance, craft-oriented, the activity of cheerful robots, or something else? Support your conclusion.
2. How do you think that the person whom you describe in question 1 would react if you applied Mills's terms to his or her work? Why?
3. Describe a job that you either have or had at some time in your life. Which one of Mills's categories best describes it? Did you like that job? What were its satisfactions for you? How do those satisfactions compare

---

[41]*Henry Durant* (1902–1982): An English economist and social researcher, who wrote *The Problem of Leisure* in 1938. [Eds.]

with the picture of modern work that Mills depicts? Compare your satisfactions to those that Mills describes in paragraphs 54–64.

4. What work would you like to imagine for yourself as a career? Which of Mills's categories best suits the work that you imagine? How do they help you to understand why you would like to invest yourself in that particular work? How does Mills's description of modern work in the second half of his essay raise troubling issues about your relationship with work?

5. Mills wrote this piece on work over fifty years ago. Are his ideas still relevant? Think of the changes that have happened in the workforce over the last fifty years. You will probably need to research many of the changes. Do any changes seem to refute Mills's ideas on work? Do any changes support his ideas? Write an essay in which you apply Mills's ideas to the contemporary workplace, noting which ideas are still applicable and which are not.

6. Mills begins in paragraphs 1–19 with a history of work from the ancient Greeks and early Christians through Protestant times and the Renaissance and into modern times. What effect does this history have on his ideas? Does the history limit his ideas to cultures that have gone through similar histories? Research the work habits of a non-Western culture, and see how those attitudes compare with the ones that Mills describes in the second half of his essay.

7. As mentioned in the headnote, Mills is an influential thinker for political radicals on the left. What would political radicals on the right think of his ideas? Write an essay from a radically conservative point of view that criticizes (or supports) Mills's ideas. Or write an essay from a radically liberal point of view that updates Mills's ideas and anticipates the criticisms of conservatives.

MAKING CONNECTIONS

1. Read Philip Levine's poem "What Work Is" (p. 781). Mills's classic study was first published when Levine was in his early twenties. Levine may have read and learned from Mills. Do you think he did? When Levine asserts at the very end of his poem that "you don't know what work is," do you find that he and Mills share a similar understanding of work?

2. This Mills selection comes from his book *White Collar: The American Middle Classes*. Barbara Ehrenreich's essay "Nickel and Dimed: On (Not) Getting by in America" (p. 760) comes from her recent study of the lower-income working class in America. Do any of Mills's descriptions of the middle class apply to the lives of the lower-income class that Ehrenreich describes? Compare and contrast the two, noting which contrasts are due to differences in class and which could be due to differences in epoch.

WORKING IN THE CATSKILLS

Vivian Gornick

Vivian Gornick (b. 1935) grew up in New York City, where she re-ceived her bachelor's degree from the City College of New York and her master's degree from New York University. After teaching English at Hunter College for several years, she served on the staff of the Village Voice *from 1969 to 1977. Gornick's books include* The Romance of American Communism *(1977),* Essays in Feminism *(1978),* Fierce Attachments: A Memoir *(1987), and a volume of literary criticism,* The End of the Novel of Love: Critical Essays *(1997). Also the author of* The Situation and the Story: The Art of Personal Narrative *(2001), Gornick has been teaching non-fiction writing in fine arts graduate programs for more than fifteen years. This selection first appeared in* Approaching Eye Level: Personal Essays *(1996).*

For me, a college student waitressing in the late fifties, the Catskills was a wild place, dangerous and exciting, where all the beasts were predatory, none pacific. The years I spent working in those hotels were my intro-duction to the brutishness of function, the murderousness of fantasy, the isolation inflicted on all those living inside a world organized to provide pleasure. It's the isolation I've been thinking about lately — how remark-ably present it was, crude and vibrant, there from the first moment of contact.

I walked into Stella Mercury's employment agency one afternoon in the winter of my freshman year at City College. Four men sat playing cards with a greasy deck, chewing gum methodically, never looking up once. The woman at the desk, fat and lumpy with hard eyes and a voiceful of cigarette wheeze, said to me, "Where ya been?" and I rattled off a string of hotels. "Ya worked all those places," she said calmly. "Ain't the human body a mah-h-vellous thing, ya don't look old enough to have worked half of 'em." I stood there, ill with fear that on the one hand she'd throw me out and on the other she'd give me a job, and assured her that I had. She knew I was lying, and I knew that she knew I was lying, but she wrote out a job ticket anyway. Suddenly I felt lonely inside the lie, and I begged her with my eyes to acknowledge the truth between us. She didn't like that at all. Her own eyes grew even harder, and she refused me more than she had when I'd not revealed open need. She drew back with the ticket still in her hand. I snatched at it. She laughed a nasty laugh. And that was it, all of it, right there, two flights above Times Square, I was in the mountains.

That first weekend in a large glittering hotel filled with garment district salesmen and midtown secretaries, weaving clumsily in and out of the vast kitchen all heat and acrimony (food flying, trays crashing, waiters cursing), I gripped the tray so hard all ten knuckles were white for days afterward, and every time I looked at them I recalled the astonishment I'd felt when a busboy at the station next to mine stuck out his fist to a guest who'd eaten three main dishes and said, "Want a knuckle sandwich?" But on Sunday night when I flung fifty single dollar bills on the kitchen table before my open-mouthed mother there was soft exultancy, and I knew I'd go back. Rising up inside this brash, moralistic, working-class girl was the unexpected excitement of the first opportunity for greed.

I was eighteen years old, moving blind through hungers whose force I could not grasp. Unable to grasp what drove me, I walked around feeling stupid. Feeling stupid I became inept. Secretly, I welcomed going to the mountains. I knew I could do this hard but simple thing. I could enter that pig-eyed glitter and snatch from it the soft, gorgeous, fleshy excitement of quick money. This I could master. This, I thought, had only to do with endurance; inexhaustible energy; and that I was burning up with.

The summer of my initiation I'd get a job, work two weeks, get fired.   5 "You're a waitress? I thought you said you were a waitress. What kinda waitress sets a table like that? Who you think you're kidding, girlie?" But by Labor Day I *was* a waitress and a veteran of the first year. I had been inducted into an underclass elite, a world of self-selected Orwellian pariahs for whom survival was the only value.

At the first hotel an experienced waiter, attracted by my innocence, took me under his wing. In the mountains, regardless of age or actual history, your first year you were a virgin and in every hotel there was always someone, sentimental as a gangster, to love a virgin. My patron in this instance was a twenty-nine-year-old man who worked in the post office in winter and at this hotel in summer. He was a handsome vagrant, a cunning hustler, what I would come by the end of the summer to recognize as a "mountain rat."

One night a shot rang out in the sleeping darkness. Waiters and waitresses leaped up in the little barracks building we shared at the edge of the hotel grounds. Across the wide lawn, light filled the open doorway of one of the distant guest cottages. A man stood framed in the light, naked except for a jockstrap. Inside the barracks people began to laugh. It was my handsome protector. He'd been sleeping with a woman whose gambler husband had appeared unexpectedly on a Thursday night.

The next day he was fired. We took a final walk together. I fumbled for words. Why? I wanted to know. I knew he didn't like the woman, a diet-thin blonde twenty years older than himself. "Ah-h-h," my friend said wearily. "Doncha know nothing, kid? Doncha know what I am? I mean, whaddaya think I am?"

At the second hotel the headwaiter, a tall sweating man, began all his staff meetings with, "Boys and girls, the first thing to understand is, we are dealing here with animals." He stood in the dining room doorway every morning holding what I took to be a glass of apple juice until I was told it was whiskey neat. "Good morning, Mrs. Levine," he'd nod affably, then turn to a busboy and mutter, "That Holland Tunnel whore." He rubbed my arm between his thumb and his forefinger when he hired me and said, "We'll take care of each other, right, kid?" I nodded, thinking it was his way of asking me to be a responsible worker. My obtuseness derailed him. When he fired me and my friend Marilyn because he caught us eating chocolate tarts behind an alcove in the dining room he thundered at us, his voice hoarse with relief, "You are not now waitresses, you never were waitresses, you'll never *be* waitresses."

At the third hotel I had fifty dollars stolen from me at the end of a holiday weekend. Fifty dollars wasn't fifty dollars in the mountains, it was blood money. My room was crowded with fellow workers, all silent as pallbearers. The door racketed open and Kennie, a busboy who was always late, burst into the room. "I heard you had money stolen!" he cried, his face stricken. I nodded wordlessly. Kennie turned, pulled the door shut, twisted his body about, raised his arm and banged his fist, sobbing, against the door. When I said, "What are *you* getting so excited about?" he shrieked at me, "Because you're a waitress and a human being! And I'm a busboy and a human being!" At the end of the summer, four more robberies having taken place, the thief was caught. It was Kennie. 10

At the fourth hotel the children's waiter was a dedicated womanizer. A flirtatious guest held out on him longer than usual, and one morning I saw this waiter urinate into a glass of orange juice, then serve it to the woman's child with the crooning injunction to drink it all up because it was so-o-o good.

At the fifth hotel I served a woman who was all bosom from neck to knee, tiny feet daintily shod, smooth plump hands beautifully manicured, childish eyes in a painted face. When I brought her exactly-three-minute eggs to the table she said to me, "Open them for me, dear. The shells burn my hands." I turned away, to the station table against the wall, to perform in appropriate secrecy a task that told me for the first but certainly not the last time that here I was only an extension of my function. It was the Catskills, not early socialist teachings at my father's knee, that made me a Marxist.

One winter I worked weekends and Christmas at a famous hotel. This hotel had an enormous tiered dining room and was run by one of the most feared headwaiters in the mountains. The system here was that all newcomers began at the back of the dining room on the tier farthest from the kitchen. If your work met with favor you were moved steadily toward the center, closer to the kitchen doors and to the largest tips which came not from the singles who were invariably placed in the back of the room but from the middle-aged manufacturers, club owners, and gangsters who occupied the tables in the central tiers, cutting a wide swath as though across a huge belly between the upper and lower ends of the dining room.

As the autumn wore on I advanced down the tiers. By Christmas I was nearly in the center of the room, at one of the best stations in the house. This meant my guests were now middle-aged married couples whose general appearance was characterized by blond bouffants, mink stoles, midnight-blue suits, and half-smoked cigars. These people ate prodigiously and tipped well.

That Christmas the hotel was packed and we worked twelve hours a 15 day. The meals went on forever. By the end of the week we were dead on our feet but still running. On New Year's Eve at midnight we were to serve a full meal, the fourth of the day, but this was to be a banquet dinner — that is, a series of house-chosen dishes simply hauled out, course by course — and we looked forward to it. It signaled the end of the holiday. The next morning the guests checked out and that night we'd all be home in our Bronx or Brooklyn apartments, our hard-earned cash piled on the kitchen table.

But a threatening atmosphere prevailed at that midnight meal from the moment the dining room doors were flung open. I remember sky blue sequined dresses and tight mouths, satin cummerbunds and hard-edged laughter, a lot of drunks on the vomitous verge. People darted everywhere and all at once, pushing to get at the central tables (no assigned seats tonight), as though, driven from one failed part of the evening to another here, at last, they were going to get what *should* come through for them: a good table in the famous dining room during its New Year's Eve meal.

The kitchen was instantly affected: it picked up on atmosphere like an animal whose only survival equipment is hyperalertness. A kind of panicky aggression seemed to overtake the entire staff. The orderly lines that had begun to form for the first appetizer broke almost immediately. People who had grown friendly, working together over these long winter weekends, now climbed over each other's backs to break into the line and grab at the small round dishes piled up on the huge steel tables.

I made my first trip into the kitchen, took in the scene before me, and froze. Then I took a deep breath, inserted myself into a line, held my own against hands and elbows pushing into my back and ribs, and got my tray loaded and myself out the kitchen doors. I served the fruit cup quickly and, depending on my busboy to get the empties off the tables in time, made my anxious way back into the kitchen for the next course which, I'll not forget as long as I live, was chow mein. This time I thought violence was about to break out. All those people, trays, curses being flung about! And now I couldn't seem to take a deep breath: I remained motionless just inside the kitchen doors. Another waitress, a classmate from City College, grabbed my arm and whispered in my ear, "Skip the chow mein, they'll never know the difference. Go on to the next course, there's nobody on the line over there." My heart lifted, the darkness receded. I stared at her. Did we dare? Yes, she nodded grimly, and walked away. It didn't occur to either of us to consider that she, as it happened, had only drunken singles at her tables who of course wouldn't know the difference, but I had married couples who wanted everything that was coming to them.

I made my first mistake. I followed my classmate to the table with no line in front of it, loaded up on the cold fish, and fought my way out the nearest kitchen door. Rapidly, I dealt out the little dishes to the men and women at my tables. When I had finished and was moving back to my station table and its now empty tray, a set of long red fingernails plucked at my upper arm. I looked down at a woman with coarse blond hair, blue eyelids surrounded by lines so deep they seemed carved, and a thin red mouth. "We didn't get the chow mein," she said to me.

My second mistake. "Chow mein?" I said. "What chow mein?" Still   20 holding me, she pointed to the next table where chow mein was being finished and the cold fish just beginning to be served. I looked at her. Words would not come. I broke loose, grabbed my tray, and dived into the kitchen.

I must have known I was in trouble because I let myself be kicked about in the kitchen madness, wasting all sorts of time being climbed over before I got the next dish loaded onto my tray and inched myself, crablike, through the swinging doors. As I approached my station I saw, standing beside the blond woman, the headwaiter, chewing a dead cigar and staring glumly in my direction. He beckoned me with one raised index finger.

I lowered my tray onto the station table and walked over to him. "Where's the chow mein?" he asked quietly, jerking his thumb back at my tables, across the head of the woman whose blue-lidded eyes never left his face. Her mouth was a slash of narrow red. Despair made me simple.

"I couldn't get to it," I said. "The kitchen is a madhouse. The line was impossible."

The headwaiter dropped his lower lip. His black eyes flickered into dangerous life and his hand came up slowly to remove the cigar stub from between his teeth. "You couldn't *get* to it?" he said. "Did I hear you right? You said you couldn't get to it?" A few people at neighboring tables looked up.

"That's right," I said miserably.   25

And then he was yelling at me, "And you call yourself a waitress?"

A dozen heads swung around. The headwaiter quickly shut his mouth. He stared coldly at me, in his eyes the most extraordinary mixture of anger, excitement, and fear. Yes, fear. Frightened as I was, I saw that he too was afraid. Afraid of the blond woman who sat in her chair like a queen with the power of life and death in her, watching a minister do her awful bidding. His eyes kept darting toward her, as though to ask, All right? Enough? Will this do?

No, the unyielding face answered. Not enough. Not nearly enough.

"You're fired," the headwaiter said to me. "Serve your morning meal and clear out."

The blood seemed to leave my body in a single rush. For a moment   30 I thought I was going to faint. Then I realized that tomorrow morning my regular guests would be back in these seats, most of them leaving after breakfast, and I, of course, would receive my full tips exactly as though none of this had happened. The headwaiter was not really punishing me. He knew it, and now I knew it. Only the blond woman didn't know it. She required my dismissal for the appeasement of her lousy life — her lined face, her hated husband, her disappointed New Year's Eve — and he, the headwaiter, was required to deliver it up to her.

For the first time I understood something about power. I stared into the degraded face of the headwaiter and saw that he was as trapped as I, caught up in a working life that required *someone's* humiliation at all times.

QUESTIONS

1. Although Gornick's essay is supposedly concerned with the nature of her work as a waitress, she doesn't give a detailed description and example of her work until the second half of her piece, beginning in paragraph 15. Why do you suppose that she waits so long to focus on a detailed example of her work? How do paragraphs 1–14 contribute to an understanding of her work?

2. The New Year's Eve banquet dinner that Gornick describes in paragraphs 15–30 was an atypical event that entailed work that was unlike her normal waitressing chores. Note the specific ways in which the banquet was different from typical dinners, and then consider why Gornick gives so much attention to such an unrepresentative working experience. How does that evening contribute to an understanding of her work as a waitress?

3. Near the beginning of the essay, Gornick reveals that she lied to the woman at the employment agency (paragraph 2). Later in the essay, she admits to having lied to one of the women she was serving at the hotel (paragraph 20), and a bit later (paragraph 23), she shows herself lying to the headwaiter. How does she come across as a result of telling about these lies? What were her motives for lying in each case? Why do you think that she acknowledges these lies?

4. What does Gornick mean by her assertion in paragraph 12 that "here I was only an extension of my function"? To what extent are any workers — waitresses, bricklayers, bankers, professors — something other than extensions of their work? Why is Gornick so upset by this state of affairs?

5. In the final paragraph of her essay, Gornick claims that the headwaiter "was as trapped as I, caught up in a working life that required *someone's* humiliation at all times." To what extent do you believe that work involves a kind of entrapment? To what extent do you believe that a working life subjects people to humiliation?

6. Using Gornick's essay as a model, write an essay about a job that you've done. Describe the working conditions, tell about a memorable experience at work, and reflect on the thoughts about work that you developed as a result of that job.

MAKING CONNECTIONS

1. Compare and contrast Gornick's working experiences with Barbara Ehrenreich's experiences in "Nickle and Dimed: On (Not) Getting by in America" (p. 760). What are the most notable similarities in their experiences? What are the most notable differences? What are the most notable similarities in their thoughts about work? What are the most notable differences?

2. Consider Gornick's experiences in the context of C. Wright Mills's article "White-Collar Work" (p. 731). In what ways does his overview of work help you to understand Gornick's experiences and your own experiences of work?

NICKEL AND DIMED: ON (NOT) GETTING BY IN AMERICA

Barbara Ehrenreich

A native of Butte, Montana, Barbara Ehrenreich (b. 1941) is one of the country's most outspoken social critics. After graduating from Reed College, Ehrenreich earned her Ph.D. in biology from Roosevelt University in Chicago. Instead of becoming a research scientist, though, she decided to pursue liberal political activism. As she began working on leaflets and newsletters, she has said, writing "crept up on" her. She was soon a regular contributor to Ms. *magazine and has since written for* The New Republic, Mother Jones, *and* Time, *among many other periodicals. Ehrenreich's books include* Complaints and Disorders: The Sexual Politics of Sickness *(1973),* Fear of Falling: The Inner Life of the Middle Class *(1989),* The Worst Years of Our Lives: Irreverent Notes from the Decade of Greed *(1990),* The Snarling Citizen: Collected Essays *(1995), and* Blood Rites: Origins and History of the Passions of War *(1997). The recipient of a Guggenheim fellowship and a MacArthur grant, Ehrenreich contributed the following essay, which provided the basis for her 2001 book of the same title, to* The Atlantic *in 1999. As she later told an interviewer, it began in a meeting with the editor of the magazine when "the conversation drifted to talking about welfare reform and the assumption that these single moms could just get out there in the workforce and get a job and then everything would be okay. They'd be lifted out of poverty. We were both agreeing that nobody seems to see that the math doesn't work. That's when I made this, perhaps disastrous, suggestion that somebody should go out there and do the old-fashioned kind of journalism, just try it for themselves and write about it. I did not expect him to say, 'Yeah, great idea. It should be you.'"*

At the beginning of June 1998 I leave behind everything that normally soothes the ego and sustains the body — home, career, companion, reputation, ATM card — for a plunge into the low-wage workforce. There, I become another, occupationally much diminished "Barbara Ehrenreich" — depicted on job-application forms as a divorced homemaker whose sole work experience consists of housekeeping in a few private homes. I am terrified, at the beginning, of being unmasked for what I am: a middle-class journalist setting out to explore the world that welfare mothers are entering, at the rate of approximately 50,000 a month, as welfare reform kicks in.

Happily, though, my fears turn out to be entirely unwarranted: during a month of poverty and toil, my name goes unnoticed and for the most part unuttered. In this parallel universe where my father never got out of the mines and I never got through college, I am "baby," "honey," "blondie," and, most commonly, "girl."

My first task is to find a place to live. I figure that if I can earn $7 an hour — which, from the want ads, seems doable — I can afford to spend $500 on rent, or maybe, with severe economies, $600. In the Key West area, where I live, this pretty much confines me to flophouses and trailer homes — like the one, a pleasing fifteen-minute drive from town, that has no air-conditioning, no screens, no fans, no television, and, by way of diversion, only the challenge of evading the landlord's Doberman pinscher. The big problem with this place, though, is the rent, which at $675 a month is well beyond my reach. All right, Key West is expensive. But so is New York City, or the Bay Area, or Jackson Hole, or Telluride, or Boston, or any other place where tourists and the wealthy compete for living space with the people who clean their toilets and fry their hash browns.[1] Still, it is a shock to realize that "trailer trash" has become, for me, a demographic category to aspire to.

So I decide to make the common trade-off between affordability and convenience, and go for a $500-a-month efficiency thirty miles up a two-lane highway from the employment opportunities of Key West, meaning forty-five minutes if there's no road construction and I don't get caught behind some sun-dazed Canadian tourists. I hate the drive, along a roadside studded with white crosses commemorating the more effective head-on collisions, but it's a sweet little place — a cabin, more or less, set in the swampy back yard of the converted mobile home where my landlord, an affable TV repairman, lives with his bartender girlfriend. Anthropologically speaking, a bustling trailer park would be preferable, but here I have a gleaming white floor and a firm mattress, and the few resident bugs are easily vanquished.

Besides, I am not doing this for the anthropology. My aim is nothing so mistily subjective as to "experience poverty" or find out how it "really feels" to be a long-term low-wage worker. I've had enough unchosen encounters with poverty and the world of low-wage work to know it's not a place you want to visit for touristic purposes; it just smells too much like fear. And with all my real-life assets — bank account, IRA, health insurance, multiroom home — waiting indulgently in the background, I am, of course, thoroughly insulated from the terrors that afflict the genuinely poor.

---

[1]According to the Department of Housing and Urban Development, the "fair-market rent" for an efficiency is $551 here in Monroe County, Florida. A comparable rent in the five boroughs of New York City is $704; in San Francisco, $713; and in the heart of Silicon Valley, $808. The fair-market rent for an area is defined as the amount that would be needed to pay rent plus utilities for "privately owned, decent, safe, and sanitary rental housing of a modest (non-luxury) nature with suitable amenities."

No, this is a purely objective, scientific sort of mission. The humani-   5
tarian rationale for welfare reform — as opposed to the more punitive and
stingy impulses that may actually have motivated it — is that work will lift
poor women out of poverty while simultaneously inflating their self-esteem
and hence their future value in the labor market. Thus, whatever the
hassles involved in finding child care, transportation, etc., the transition
from welfare to work will end happily, in greater prosperity for all. Now
there are many problems with this comforting prediction, such as the
fact that the economy will inevitably undergo a downturn, eliminating
many jobs. Even without a downturn, the influx of a million former welfare recipients into the low-wage labor market could depress wages by as
much as 11.9 percent, according to the Economic Policy Institute (EPI) in
Washington, D.C.

But is it really possible to make a living on the kinds of jobs currently
available to unskilled people? Mathematically, the answer is no, as can be
shown by taking $6 to $7 an hour, perhaps subtracting a dollar or two an
hour for child care, multiplying by 160 hours a month, and comparing the
result to the prevailing rents. According to the National Coalition for the
Homeless, for example, in 1998 it took, on average nationwide, an hourly
wage of $8.89 to afford a one-bedroom apartment, and the Preamble
Center for Public Policy estimates that the odds against a typical welfare recipient's landing a job at such a "living wage" are about 97 to 1. If these
numbers are right, low-wage work is not a solution to poverty and possibly
not even to homelessness.

It may seem excessive to put this proposition to an experimental test.
As certain family members keep unhelpfully reminding me, the viability of
low-wage work could be tested, after a fashion, without ever leaving my
study. I could just pay myself $7 an hour for eight hours a day, charge
myself for room and board, and total up the numbers after a month. Why
leave the people and work that I love? But I am an experimental scientist by
training. In that business, you don't just sit at a desk and theorize; you
plunge into the everyday chaos of nature, where surprises lurk in the most
mundane measurements. Maybe, when I got into it, I would discover some
hidden economies in the world of the low-wage worker. After all, if 30 percent of the workforce toils for less than $8 an hour, according to the EPI,
they may have found some tricks as yet unknown to me. Maybe — who
knows? — I would even be able to detect in myself the bracing psychological effects of getting out of the house, as promised by the welfare wonks
at places like the Heritage Foundation. Or, on the other hand, maybe there
would be unexpected costs — physical, mental, or financial — to throw
off all my calculations. Ideally, I should do this with two small children in
tow, that being the welfare average, but mine are grown and no one is
willing to lend me theirs for a month-long vacation in penury. So this is not
the perfect experiment, just a test of the best possible case: an unencumbered woman, smart and even strong, attempting to live more or less off
the land.

On the morning of my first full day of job searching, I take a red pen to the want ads, which are auspiciously numerous. Everyone in Key West's booming "hospitality industry" seems to be looking for someone like me — trainable, flexible, and with suitably humble expectations as to pay. I know I possess certain traits that might be advantageous — I'm white and, I like to think, well-spoken and poised — but I decide on two rules: One, I cannot use any skills derived from my education or usual work — not that there are a lot of want ads for satirical essayists anyway. Two, I have to take the best-paid job that is offered me and of course do my best to hold it; no Marxist rants or sneaking off to read novels in the ladies' room. In addition, I rule out various occupations for one reason or another: Hotel front-desk clerk, for example, which to my surprise is regarded as unskilled and pays around $7 an hour, gets eliminated because it involves standing in one spot for eight hours a day. Waitressing is similarly something I'd like to avoid, because I remember it leaving me bone tired when I was eighteen, and I'm decades of varicosities and back pain beyond that now. Telemarketing, one of the first refuges of the suddenly indigent, can be dismissed on grounds of personality. This leaves certain supermarket jobs, such as deli clerk, or housekeeping in Key West's thousands of hotel and guest rooms. Housekeeping is especially appealing, for reasons both atavistic and practical: it's what my mother did before I came along, and it can't be too different from what I've been doing part-time, in my own home, all my life.

So I put on what I take to be a respectful-looking outfit of ironed Bermuda shorts and scooped-neck T-shirt and set out for a tour of the local hotels and supermarkets. Best Western, Econo Lodge, and HoJo's all let me fill out application forms, and these are, to my relief, interested in little more than whether I am a legal resident of the United States and have committed any felonies. My next stop is Winn-Dixie, the supermarket, which turns out to have a particularly onerous application process, featuring a fifteen-minute "interview" by computer since, apparently, no human on the premises is deemed capable of representing the corporate point of view. I am conducted to a large room decorated with posters illustrating how to look "professional" (it helps to be white and, if female, permed) and warning of the slick promises that union organizers might try to tempt me with. The interview is multiple choice: Do I have anything, such as child-care problems, that might make it hard for me to get to work on time? Do I think safety on the job is the responsibility of management? Then, popping up cunningly out of the blue: How many dollars' worth of stolen goods have I purchased in the last year? Would I turn in a fellow employee if I caught him stealing? Finally, "Are you an honest person?"

Apparently, I ace the interview, because I am told that all I have to do   10
is show up in some doctor's office tomorrow for a urine test. This seems to be a fairly general rule: if you want to stack Cheerio boxes or vacuum hotel rooms in chemically fascist America, you have to be willing to squat down and pee in front of some health worker (who has no doubt had to do the same thing herself). The wages Winn-Dixie is offering — $6 and a couple

of dimes to start with — are not enough, I decide, to compensate for this indignity.[2]

I lunch at Wendy's, where $4.99 gets you unlimited refills at the Mexican part of the Super-bar, a comforting surfeit of refried beans and "cheese sauce." A teenage employee, seeing me studying the want ads, kindly offers me an application form, which I fill out, though here, too, the pay is just $6 and change an hour. Then it's off for a round of the locally owned inns and guesthouses. At "The Palms," let's call it, a bouncy manager actually takes me around to see the rooms and meet the existing housekeepers, who, I note with satisfaction, look pretty much like me — faded ex-hippie types in shorts with long hair pulled back in braids. Mostly, though, no one speaks to me or even looks at me except to proffer an application form. At my last stop, a palatial B&B, I wait twenty minutes to meet "Max," only to be told that there are no jobs now but there should be one soon, since "nobody lasts more than a couple weeks." (Because none of the people I talked to knew I was a reporter, I have changed their names to protect their privacy and, in some cases perhaps, their jobs.)

Three days go by like this, and, to my chagrin, no one out of the approximately twenty places I've applied calls me for an interview. I had been vain enough to worry about coming across as too educated for the jobs I sought, but no one even seems interested in finding out how overqualified I am. Only later will I realize that the want ads are not a reliable measure of the actual jobs available at any particular time. They are, as I should have guessed from Max's comment, the employers' insurance policy against the relentless turnover of the low-wage workforce. Most of the big hotels run ads almost continually, just to build a supply of applicants to replace the current workers as they drift away or are fired, so finding a job is just a matter of being at the right place at the right time and flexible enough to take whatever is being offered that day. This finally happens to me at one of the big discount hotel chains, where I go, as usual, for housekeeping and am sent, instead, to try out as a waitress at the attached "family restaurant," a dismal spot with a counter and about thirty tables that looks out on a parking garage and features such tempting fare as "Pollish [sic] sausage and BBQ sauce" on 95-degree days. Phillip, the dapper young West Indian who introduces himself as the manager, interviews me with about as much enthusiasm as if he were a

[2]According to the *Monthly Labor Review* (November 1996), 28 percent of work sites surveyed in the service industry conduct drug tests (corporate workplaces have much higher rates), and the incidence of testing has risen markedly since the Eighties. The rate of testing is highest in the South (56 percent of work sites polled), with the Midwest in second place (50 percent). The drug most likely to be detected — marijuana, which can be detected in urine for weeks — is also the most innocuous, while heroin and cocaine are generally undetectable three days after use. Prospective employees sometimes try to cheat the tests by consuming excessive amounts of liquids and taking diuretics and even masking substances available through the Internet.

clerk processing me for Medicare, the principal questions being what shifts can I work and when can I start. I mutter something about being woefully out of practice as a waitress, but he's already on to the uniform: I'm to show up tomorrow wearing black slacks and black shoes; he'll provide the rust-colored polo shirt with HEARTHSIDE embroidered on it, though I might want to wear my own shirt to get to work, ha ha. At the word "tomorrow," something between fear and indignation rises in my chest. I want to say, "Thank you for your time, sir, but this is just an experiment, you know, not my actual life."

So begins my career at the Hearthside, I shall call it, one small profit center within a global discount hotel chain, where for two weeks I work from 2:00 till 10:00 P.M. for $2.43 an hour plus tips.[3] In some futile bid for gentility, the management has barred employees from using the front door, so my first day I enter through the kitchen, where a red-faced man with shoulder-length blond hair is throwing frozen steaks against the wall and yelling, "Fuck this shit!" "That's just Jack," explains Gail, the wiry middle-aged waitress who is assigned to train me. "He's on the rag again" — a condition occasioned, in this instance, by the fact that the cook on the morning shift had forgotten to thaw out the steaks. For the next eight hours, I run after the agile Gail, absorbing bits of instruction along with fragments of personal tragedy. All food must be trayed, and the reason she's so tired today is that she woke up in a cold sweat thinking of her boyfriend, who killed himself recently in an upstate prison. No refills on lemonade. And the reason he was in prison is that a few DUIs caught up with him, that's all, could have happened to anyone. Carry the creamers to the table in a monkey bowl, never in your hand. And after he was gone she spent several months living in her truck, peeing in a plastic pee bottle and reading by candlelight at night, but you can't live in a truck in the summer, since you need to have the windows down, which means anything can get in, from mosquitoes on up.

At least Gail puts to rest any fears I had of appearing overqualified. From the first day on, I find that of all the things I have left behind, such as home and identity, what I miss the most is competence. Not that I have ever felt utterly competent in the writing business, in which one day's success augurs nothing at all for the next. But in my writing life, I at least have some notion of procedure: do the research, make the outline, rough out a draft, etc. As a server, though, I am beset by requests like bees: more iced tea here,

---

[3]According to the Fair Labor Standards Act, employers are not required to pay "tipped employees," such as restaurant servers, more than $2.13 an hour in direct wages. However, if the sum of tips plus $2.13 an hour falls below the minimum wage, or $5.15 an hour, the employer is required to make up the difference. This fact was not mentioned by managers or otherwise publicized at either of the restaurants where I worked.

ketchup over there, a to-go box for table fourteen, and where are the high chairs, anyway? Of the twenty-seven tables, up to six are usually mine at any time, though on slow afternoons or if Gail is off, I sometimes have the whole place to myself. There is the touch-screen computer-ordering system to master, which is, I suppose, meant to minimize server-cook contact, but in practice requires constant verbal fine-tuning: "That's gravy on the mashed, okay? None on the meatloaf," and so forth — while the cook scowls as if I were inventing these refinements just to torment him. Plus, something I had forgotten in the years since I was eighteen: about a third of a server's job is "side work" that's invisible to customers — sweeping, scrubbing, slicing, refilling, and restocking. If it isn't all done, every little bit of it, you're going to face the 6:00 P.M. dinner rush defenseless and probably go down in flames. I screw up dozens of times at the beginning, sustained in my shame entirely by Gail's support — "It's okay, baby, everyone does that sometime" — because, to my total surprise and despite the scientific detachment I am doing my best to maintain, I care.

15 The whole thing would be a lot easier if I could just skate through it as Lily Tomlin in one of her waitress skits, but I was raised by the absurd Booker T. Washingtonian precept that says: If you're going to do something, do it well. In fact, "well" isn't good enough by half. Do it better than anyone has ever done it before. Or so said my father, who must have known what he was talking about because he managed to pull himself, and us with him, up from the mile-deep copper mines of Butte to the leafy suburbs of the Northeast, ascending from boilermakers to martinis before booze beat out ambition. As in most endeavors I have encountered in my life, doing it "better than anyone" is not a reasonable goal. Still, when I wake up at 4:00 A.M. in my own cold sweat, I am not thinking about the writing deadlines I'm neglecting; I'm thinking about the table whose order I screwed up so that one of the boys didn't get his kiddie meal until the rest of the family had moved on to their Key Lime pies. That's the other powerful motivation I hadn't expected — the customers, or "patients," as I can't help thinking of them on account of the mysterious vulnerability that seems to have left them temporarily unable to feed themselves. After a few days at the Hearthside, I feel the service ethic kick in like a shot of oxytocin, the nurturance hormone. The plurality of my customers are hard-working locals — truck drivers, construction workers, even house-keepers from the attached hotel — and I want them to have the closest to a "fine dining" experience that the grubby circumstances will allow. No "you guys" for me; everyone over twelve is "sir" or "ma'am." I ply them with iced tea and coffee refills; I return, mid-meal, to inquire how everything is; I doll up their salads with chopped raw mushrooms, summer squash slices, or whatever bits of produce I can find that have survived their sojourn in the cold-storage room mold-free.

There is Benny, for example, a short, tight-muscled sewer repairman, who cannot even think of eating until he has absorbed a half hour of air-conditioning and ice water. We chat about hyperthermia and electrolytes until he is ready to order some finicky combination like soup of the day, garden salad, and a side of grits. There are the German tourists who are so touched by my pidgin "Willkommen" and "Ist alles gut?" that they actually tip. (Europeans, spoiled by their trade-union-ridden, high-wage welfare states, generally do not know that they are supposed to tip. Some restaurants, the Hearthside included, allow servers to "grat" their foreign customers, or add a tip to the bill. Since this amount is added before the customers have a chance to tip or not tip, the practice amounts to an automatic penalty for imperfect English.) There are the two dirt-smudged lesbians, just off their construction shift, who are impressed enough by my suave handling of the fly in the piña colada that they take the time to praise me to Stu, the assistant manager. There's Sam, the kindly retired cop, who has to plug up his tracheotomy hole with one finger in order to force the cigarette smoke into his lungs.

Sometimes I play with the fantasy that I am a princess who, in penance for some tiny transgression, has undertaken to feed each of her subjects by hand. But the non-princesses working with me are just as indulgent, even when this means flouting management rules — concerning, for example, the number of croutons that can go on a salad (six). "Put on all you want," Gail whispers, "as long as Stu isn't looking." She dips into her own tip money to buy biscuits and gravy for an out-of-work mechanic who's used up all his money on dental surgery, inspiring me to pick up the tab for his milk and pie. Maybe the same high levels of agape can be found throughout the "hospitality industry." I remember the poster decorating one of the apartments I looked at, which said "If you seek happiness for yourself you will never find it. Only when you seek happiness for others will it come to you," or words to that effect — an odd sentiment, it seemed to me at the time, to find in the dank one-room basement apartment of a bellhop at the Best Western. At the Hearthside, we utilize whatever bits of autonomy we have to ply our customers with the illicit calories that signal our love. It is our job as servers to assemble the salads and desserts, pouring the dressings and squirting the whipped cream. We also control the number of butter patties our customers get and the amount of sour cream on their baked potatoes. So if you wonder why Americans are so obese, consider the fact that waitresses both express their humanity and earn their tips through the covert distribution of fats.

Ten days into it, this is beginning to look like a livable lifestyle. I like Gail, who is "looking at fifty" but moves so fast she can alight in one place and then another without apparently being anywhere between them. I clown around with Lionel, the teenage Haitian busboy, and catch a few fragments of conversation with Joan, the svelte fortyish hostess and militant feminist who is the only one of us who dares to tell Jack to shut the fuck up. I even warm up to Jack when, on a slow night and to make up for a particularly unwarranted attack on my abilities, or so I imagine, he tells me about his glory days as a young man at "coronary school" — or do you say "culinary"? — in Brooklyn, where he dated a knock-out Puerto Rican chick and learned everything there is to know about food. I finish up at 10:00 or

10:30, depending on how much side work I've been able to get done during the shift, and cruise home to the tapes I snatched up at random when I left my real home — Marianne Faithfull, Tracy Chapman, Enigma, King Sunny Ade, the Violent Femmes — just drained enough for the music to set my cranium resonating but hardly dead. Midnight snack is Wheat Thins and Monterey Jack, accompanied by cheap white wine on ice and whatever AMC has to offer. To bed by 1:30 or 2:00, up at 9:00 or 10:00, read for an hour while my uniform whirls around in the landlord's washing machine, and then it's another eight hours spent following Mao's central instruction, as laid out in the Little Red Book, which was: Serve the people.

I could drift along like this, in some dreamy proletarian idyll, except for two things. One is management. If I have kept this subject on the margins thus far it is because I still flinch to think that I spent all those weeks under the surveillance of men (and later women) whose job it was to monitor my behavior for signs of sloth, theft, drug abuse, or worse. Not that managers and especially "assistant managers" in low-wage settings like this are exactly the class enemy. In the restaurant business, they are mostly former cooks or servers, still capable of pinch-hitting in the kitchen or on the floor, just as in hotels they are likely to be former clerks, and paid a salary of only about $400 a week. But everyone knows they have crossed over to the other side, which is, crudely put, corporate as opposed to human. Cooks want to prepare tasty meals; servers want to serve them graciously; but managers are there for only one reason — to make sure that money is made for some theoretical entity that exists far away in Chicago or New York, if a corporation can be said to have a physical existence at all. Reflecting on her career, Gail tells me ruefully that she had sworn, years ago, never to work for a corporation again. "They don't cut you no slack. You give and you give, and they take."

Managers can sit — for hours at a time if they want — but it's their job   20
to see that no one else ever does, even when there's nothing to do, and this is why, for servers, slow times can be as exhausting as rushes. You start dragging out each little chore, because if the manager on duty catches you in an idle moment, he will give you something far nastier to do. So I wipe, I clean, I consolidate ketchup bottles and recheck the cheesecake supply, even tour the tables to make sure the customer evaluation forms are all standing perkily in their places — wondering all the time how many calories I burn in these strictly theatrical exercises. When, on a particularly dead afternoon, Stu finds me glancing at a USA Today a customer has left behind, he assigns me to vacuum the entire floor with the broken vacuum cleaner that has a handle only two feet long, and the only way to do that without incurring orthopedic damage is to proceed from spot to spot on your knees.

On my first Friday at the Hearthside there is a "mandatory meeting for all restaurant employees," which I attend, eager for insight into our overall marketing strategy and the niche (your basic Ohio cuisine with a tropical twist?) we aim to inhabit. But there is no "we" at this meeting. Phillip, our top manager except for an occasional "consultant" sent out by corporate headquarters, opens it with a sneer: "The break room — it's disgusting. Butts in the ashtrays, newspapers lying around, crumbs." This windowless little room, which also houses the time clock for the entire hotel, is where we stash our bags and civilian clothes and take our half-hour meal breaks. But a break room is not a right, he tells us. It can be taken away. We should also know that the lockers in the break room and whatever is in them can be searched at any time. Then comes gossip; there has been gossip; gossip (which seems to mean employees talking among themselves) must stop. Off-duty employees are henceforth barred from eating at the restaurant, because "other servers gather around them and gossip." When Phillip has exhausted his agenda of rebukes, Joan complains about the condition of the ladies' room and I throw in my two bits about the vacuum cleaner. But I don't see any backup coming from my fellow servers, each of whom has subsided into her own personal funk; Gail, my role model, stares sorrowfully at a point six inches from her nose. The meeting ends when Andy, one of the cooks, gets up, muttering about breaking up his day off for this almighty bullshit.

Just four days later we are suddenly summoned into the kitchen at 3:30 P.M., even though there are live tables on the floor. We all — about ten of us — stand around Phillip, who announces grimly that there has been a report of some "drug activity" on the night shift and that, as a result, we are now to be a "drug-free" workplace, meaning that all new hires will be tested, as will possibly current employees on a random basis. I am glad that this part of the kitchen is so dark, because I find myself blushing as hard as if I had been caught toking up in the ladies' room myself: I haven't been treated this way — lined up in the corridor, threatened with locker searches, peppered with carelessly aimed accusations — since junior high school. Back on the floor, Joan cracks, "Next they'll be telling us we can't have sex on the job." When I ask Stu what happened to inspire the crackdown, he just mutters about "management decisions" and takes the opportunity to upbraid Gail and me for being too generous with the rolls. From now on there's to be only one per customer, and it goes out with the dinner, not with the salad. He's also been riding the cooks, prompting Andy to come out of the kitchen and observe — with the serenity of a man whose customary implement is a butcher knife — that "Stu has a death wish today."

Later in the evening, the gossip crystallizes around the theory that Stu is himself the drug culprit, that he uses the restaurant phone to order up marijuana and sends one of the late servers out to fetch it for him. The server was caught, and she may have ratted Stu out or at least said enough to cast some suspicion on him, thus accounting for his pissy behavior. Who knows? Lionel, the busboy, entertains us for the rest of the shift by standing just behind Stu's back and sucking deliriously on an imaginary joint.

The other problem, in addition to the less-than-nurturing management style, is that this job shows no sign of being financially viable. You might imagine, from a comfortable distance, that people who live, year in and year out, on $6 to $10 an hour have discovered some survival stratagems unknown to the middle class. But no. It's not hard to get my co-workers to talk about their living situations, because housing, in almost every case, is the principal source of disruption in their lives, the first thing they fill you in on when they arrive for their shifts. After a week, I have compiled the following survey:

- Gail is sharing a room in a well-known downtown flophouse for which she and a roommate pay about $250 a week. Her roommate, a male friend, has begun hitting on her, driving her nuts, but the rent would be impossible alone.
- Claude, the Haitian cook, is desperate to get out of the two-room apartment he shares with his girlfriend and two other, unrelated, people. As far as I can determine, the other Haitian men (most of whom only speak Creole) live in similarly crowded situations.
- Annette, a twenty-year-old server who is six months pregnant and has been abandoned by her boyfriend, lives with her mother, a postal clerk.
- Marianne and her boyfriend are paying $170 a week for a one-person trailer.
- Jack, who is, at $10 an hour, the wealthiest of us, lives in the trailer he owns, paying only the $400-a-month lot fee.
- The other white cook, Andy, lives on his dry-docked boat, which, as far as I can tell from his loving descriptions, can't be more than twenty feet long. He offers to take me out on it, once it's repaired, but the offer comes with inquiries as to my marital status, so I do not follow up on it.
- Tina and her husband are paying $60 a night for a double room in a Days Inn. This is because they have no car and the Days Inn is within walking distance of the Hearthside. When Marianne, one of the breakfast servers, is tossed out of her trailer for subletting (which is against the trailer-park rules), she leaves her boyfriend and moves in with Tina and her husband.
- Joan, who had fooled me with her numerous and tasteful outfits (hostesses wear their own clothes), lives in a van she parks behind a shopping center at night and showers in Tina's motel room. The clothes are from thrift shops.[4]

It strikes me, in my middle-class solipsism, that there is gross improvidence   25
in some of these arrangements. When Gail and I are wrapping silverware

---

[4]I could find no statistics on the number of employed people living in cars or vans, but according to the National Coalition for the Homeless's 1997 report "Myths and Facts About Homelessness," nearly one in five homeless people (in twenty-nine cities across the nation) is employed in a full- or part-time job.

in napkins — the only task for which we are permitted to sit — she tells me she is thinking of escaping from her roommate by moving into the Days Inn herself. I am astounded: How can she even think of paying between $40 and $60 a day? But if I was afraid of sounding like a social worker, I come out just sounding like a fool. She squints at me in disbelief, "And where am I supposed to get a month's rent and a month's deposit for an apartment?" I'd been feeling pretty smug about my $500 efficiency, but of course it was made possible only by the $1,300 I had allotted myself for start-up costs when I began my low-wage life: $1,000 for the first month's rent and deposit, $100 for initial groceries and cash in my pocket, $200 stuffed away for emergencies. In poverty, as in certain propositions in physics, starting conditions are everything.

There are no secret economies that nourish the poor; on the contrary, there are a host of special costs. If you can't put up the two months' rent you need to secure an apartment, you end up paying through the nose for a room by the week. If you have only a room, with a hot plate at best, you can't save by cooking up huge lentil stews that can be frozen for the week ahead. You eat fast food, or the hot dogs and styrofoam cups of soup that can be microwaved in a convenience store. If you have no money for health insurance — and the Hearthside's niggardly plan kicks in only after three months — you go without routine care or prescription drugs and end up paying the price. Gail, for example, was fine until she ran out of money for estrogen pills. She is supposed to be on the company plan by now, but they claim to have lost her application form and need to begin the paperwork all over again. So she spends $9 per migraine pill to control the headaches she wouldn't have, she insists, if her estrogen supplements were covered. Similarly, Marianne's boyfriend lost his job as a roofer because he missed so much time after getting a cut on his foot for which he couldn't afford the prescribed antibiotic.

My own situation, when I sit down to assess it after two weeks of work, would not be much better if this were my actual life. The seductive thing about waitressing is that you don't have to wait for payday to feel a few bills in your pocket, and my tips usually cover meals and gas, plus something left over to stuff into the kitchen drawer I use as a bank. But as the tourist business slows in the summer heat, I sometimes leave work with only $20 in tips (the gross is higher, but servers share about 15 percent of their tips with the busboys and bartenders). With wages included, this amounts to about the minimum wage of $5.15 an hour. Although the sum in the drawer is piling up, at the present rate of accumulation it will be more than a hundred dollars short of my rent when the end of the month comes around. Nor can I see any expenses to cut. True, I haven't gone the lentil-stew route yet, but that's because I don't have a large cooking pot, pot holders, or a ladle to stir with (which cost about $30 at Kmart, less at thrift stores), not to mention onions, carrots, and the indispensable bay leaf. I do make my lunch almost every day — usually some slow-burning, high-protein combo like frozen chicken patties with melted cheese on top and canned pinto beans on the side. Dinner is at the Hearthside, which offers its employees a choice of BLT, fish sandwich, or hamburger for only $2. The burger lasts longest, especially if it's heaped with gut-puckering jalapeños, but my midnight my stomach is growling again. . . .

When I moved out of the trailer park, I gave the key to number 46 to Gail and arranged for my deposit to be transferred to her. She told me that Joan is still living in her van and that Stu had been fired from the Hearthside. . . .

In one month, I had earned approximately $1,040 and spent $517 on food, gas, toiletries, laundry, phone, and utilities. If I had remained in my $500 efficiency, I would have been able to pay the rent and have $22 left over (which is $78 less than the cash I had in my pocket at the start of the month). During this time I bought no clothing except for the required slacks and no prescription drugs or medical care (I did finally buy some vitamin B to compensate for the lack of vegetables in my diet). Perhaps I could have saved a little on food if I had gotten to a supermarket more often, instead of convenience stores, but it should be noted that I lost almost four pounds in four weeks, on a diet weighted heavily toward burgers and fries.

How former welfare recipients and single mothers will (and do) survive   30
in the low-wage workforce, I cannot imagine. Maybe they will figure out how to condense their lives — including child-raising, laundry, romance, and meals — into the couple of hours between full-time jobs. Maybe they will take up residence in their vehicles, if they have one. All I know is that I couldn't hold two jobs and I couldn't make enough money to live on with one. And I had advantages unthinkable to many of the long-term poor — health, stamina, a working car, and no children to care for and support. Certainly nothing in my experience contradicts the conclusion of Kathryn Edin and Laura Lein, in their recent book *Making Ends Meet: How Single Mothers Survive Welfare and Low-Wage Work*, that low-wage work actually involves more hardship and deprivation than life at the mercy of the welfare state. In the coming months and years, economic conditions for the working poor are bound to worsen, even without the almost inevitable recession. As mentioned earlier, the influx of former welfare recipients into the low-skilled workforce will have a depressing effect on both wages and the number of jobs available. A general economic downturn will only enhance these effects, and the working poor will of course be facing it without the slight, but nonetheless often saving, protection of welfare as a backup.

The thinking behind welfare reform was that even the humblest jobs are morally uplifting and psychologically buoying. In reality they are likely to be fraught with insult and stress. But I did discover one redeeming feature of the most abject low-wage work — the camaraderie of people who are, in almost all cases, far too smart and funny and caring for the work they do and the wages they're paid. The hope, of course, is that someday these people will come to know what they're worth, and take appropriate action.

QUESTIONS

1. Ehrenreich tells us in the first paragraph who she is and what she wants to uncover: "I am . . . a middle-class journalist setting out to explore the world that welfare mothers are entering, at the rate of approximately 50,000 a month, as welfare reform kicks in." What questions does Ehrenreich ask about this world? How does she make you, her reader, care about these questions?
2. According to Ehrenreich, what is the rationale for welfare reform? Why does she distrust this rationale?
3. Ehrenreich plunges us into the middle of her work life at the Hearthside. Identify the details and images that you find most compelling and memorable. How do these details help her to establish her credibility?
4. Ehrenreich tells us that she spent "weeks under the surveillance of men (and later women) whose job it was to monitor my behavior for signs of sloth, theft, drug abuse, or worse" (paragraph 19). What role do these supervisors play in Ehrenreich's work life?
5. Ehrenreich points to housing as "the principal source of disruption" (paragraph 24) in her coworkers' lives. Look at her survey of where and how her coworkers live. What does this survey suggest about the difficulties of "(not) getting by in America"?
6. At the end of the essay, Ehrenreich calculates how much money she earned and how much she spent during her month as a waitress. What conclusions does she draw from her budget?
7. What questions are you asking about work? Keep a journal in which you ask yourself questions about your current job or former jobs.
8. Go to the library, and research the federal Welfare Reform Act of 1996. What main arguments did members of Congress offer for and against welfare reform during the debates that preceded their vote on the act? Research the consequences of welfare reform within your region or state.
9. Ehrenreich tells us at the end of her essay that the one redeeming feature of her job was "the camaraderie of people who are, in almost all cases, far too smart and funny and caring for the work they do and the wages they're paid" (paragraph 31). What redeeming features of work are portrayed in the various readings in this unit? What continuities or contradictions do you see between these images?

MAKING CONNECTIONS

1. Compare the situation of Ehrenreich's coworkers to that of the immigrant laborers in the photo essay by Eric Schlosser and Jon Lowenstein (p. 775). What similarities and differences do you notice? Is either situation better than the other?

2. Compare Ehrenreich's experience to Vivian Gornick's experience in "The Catskills Remembered" (p. 753). What are the most notable similarities in their experiences? What are the most notable differences? What are the most notable similarities in their thoughts about work? What are the most notable differences?

MAKING IT WORK

Eric Schlosser and Jon Lowenstein

*Biographical notes for journalist Eric Schlosser can be found on
p. 308. His most recent book,* Reefer Madness: Sex, Drugs, and
Cheap Labor in the American Black Market, *examines various un-
derground economies, including the market for migrant labor. Jon
Lowenstein was born in Brookline, Massachusetts, attended the
University of Iowa, and has been a faculty member at Western
Kentucky's Mountain Workshop and the Southern Short Course.
Lowenstein's photos have appeared in* Mother Jones, Time, U.S.
News and World Report, Fortune, Elle, Ladies' Home Journal,
Kiplinger's Business Journal, *the* New York Times, *and* Chicago
Magazine, *among others. He has won many awards, including the
2003 Nikon Sabbatical Grant. In December 1999, he was one of
eight staff photographers who were selected for the CITY 2000
(Chicago in the Year 2000) project, during which time he focused
on Mexican day laborers in Chicago. He recently published* Feel
Our Freedom: Communities and Connections for People with
Developmental Disabilities *(2002). He currently teaches photography at Northwestern University's Medill School of Journalism and
the Paul Revere Elementary School on Chicago's South Side. This
photo essay originally appeared in the September/October 2002
issue of* Mother Jones.

Roofing, painting, wiring, plumbing, laying carpet, building a house;
weeding, planting, watering, pruning, digging a ditch; moving boxes and removing asbestos; working in a soap factory, a sweatshop, a meatpacking
plant; washing dishes, flipping burgers, sweeping the floor — when you're a
day laborer, you never know what a day's work will be. It could be 12 hours
of construction work for $100, four hours of yardwork at minimum wage,
or no work at all.

Early in the morning, *los jornaleros,* Mexican slang for "day laborers,"
stand on sidewalks and at busy intersections, outside paint stores and
Home Depots, waiting. When a van or a pickup appears, they rush toward
it, surround it, declaring their skills in broken English. A few get hired,
climb in, and drive off. The rest wait for the next one. Day labor is work at
its most elemental: no benefits, no job security, no overtime, and payment
in cash. The employers get cheap labor, tax-free. And the workers get work.

Until recently los jornaleros were a common sight only in California
and the Southwest. Today, you can find them at the intersection of
Lawrence and Springfield in northwest Chicago, — which is known as

Day laborers negotiate their fee through the window of a contractor's van.

la parada ("the stop") — and on street corners across the United States. They have become the urban and suburban equivalent of migrant farmworkers. In his writings on day laborers, UCLA professor Abel Valenzuela Jr. offers a portrait of working life at the bottom. Day laborers are overwhelmingly male and Latino (though Latinas can find day work in factories or as domestics). One survey found that more than 80 percent are illegal immigrants and more than half never made it past sixth grade. Most speak little English. Their marginal legal status and lack of education make them vulnerable to unscrupulous smugglers, landlords, and employers.

Sometimes day laborers work all day but never get paid. Or they get paid less than what was promised. They handle toxic materials without proper safety equipment, perform dangerous work without health insurance, suffer injuries on the job, and then get fired. Anti-immigrant groups blame them for all kinds of social problems. More than 30 cities and towns have passed laws to keep day laborers off the streets. But the new laws rarely target the contractors, home owners, and factory managers who profit most from this unregulated, illegal work.

In Chicago, many jornaleros find jobs through the temporary employ- 5
ment agencies that have sprung up in Latino neighborhoods on the city's West and South sides, as well as in suburban towns such as Villa Park, West Chicago, and Bensenville. Such private firms give day labor a rudimentary structure, maintaining relationships with employers, requiring Social Security numbers from workers (authentic or not), paying wages by check, and charging workers for these services (see "Street Corner, Incorporated,"

Angelo Ojeda was promised $60 to dig this ditch but worries that the contractor won't pay him.

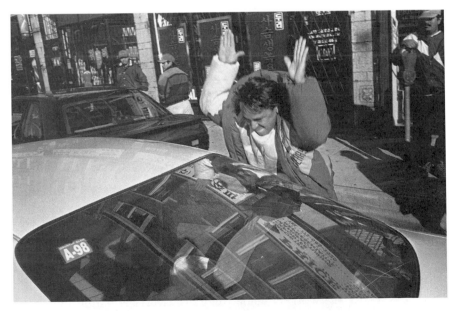

Frustration boils over after a worker is offered less than minimum wage.

The building owner refused to pay the contractor, so the contractor refused to pay the laborers, including Antonio Velazquez, who complains to police. Velazquez says that living in the United States is difficult and he often feels like "doing something crazy."

Mother Jones, March/April 2002). Most of the agencies are legitimate, but some rip off day laborers as efficiently as any crooked employer. The jobs they provide are often located in the factories and industrial parks where Chicago's stockyards once stood. In the neighborhood known as Back of the Yards, in the same small houses where Eastern European meatpackers lived for generations, Mexican day laborers now sleep half a dozen to a room.

Activists across the country recently formed the National Day Labor Organizing Network. And church groups and nonprofits have opened about 75 day-labor centers that offer a variety of services to poor immigrant workers. But most of America's jornaleros must look after themselves. The one trait that their job requires, more than any other, is self-reliance. They come to the United States at great risk, operate outside any formal hierarchy, rely solely on their own skills, work hard, send money home, save money to bring relatives north, and usually succeed at raising the income of their families. They possess the very qualities that our business schools celebrate. The great irony of day laborers is that they embody the American dream, yet are widely used, abused, and despised. Some of the strongest animosity is felt by the workers whom they displace. The nation's poor are now being forced to compete with the even poorer. It's the latest chapter of an old story, unfolding on a street corner near you.

Exhausted from long days in a Chicago factory, a Mexican woman counts out the $4,500 her family is sending to a "coyote" to smuggle three relatives across the border to Phoenix.

QUESTIONS

1. In this article, a visual text and a written text are meant to be read together. The first thing to consider is how they work together. How does one text complement the other?

2. Read the article two ways. First make a list of the main points that are made in the written text. Then read the photographs and their captions to see which points they illustrate. Return to the written text to see whether those same points are made there. Do you find one text more informative or effective than the other? In what ways do they differ?

3. Describe the conditions of a typical working day for one of these laborers. How do the photographs want us to evaluate those conditions? Why do you think Loewenstein, the photographer, chose to use black-and-white film for this photo essay?

4. In the fourth paragraph, Schlosser describes the problems that the jornaleros encounter at work, with anti-immigrant groups, and with community laws to keep them off the streets. What solutions can you suggest that might alleviate some of their problems? Do you think that those who hire these workers should be held to the same fair labor practices that protect other American workers?

5. The article refers to the work of Abel Valenzuela Jr. of the University of California at Los Angeles (paragraph 3) and to an article that appeared in

the March/April 2002 issue of *Mother Jones* (paragraph 5). Consult these two sources and at least two others to add to the information provided by this article. If day workers are active in your own community, how are they treated? Do some research in your local newspaper, and write a report of what you find to add to the national information you've come across.

MAKING CONNECTIONS

1. Michael Kamber's "Toil and Temptation" (p. 205) reports on Mexican workers in New York City. What similarities and differences do you find between the workers in New York City and the workers in Chicago?
2. Compare the experiences of the immigrant workers that Schlosser and Lowenstein depict to the ideas of C. Wright Mills in "White-Collar Work" (p. 731). Although Mills is writing about the American middle class of the 1950s, do any of his ideas apply to immigrant workers? How do you think that Mills would describe the working situation for the immigrants?

WHAT WORK IS

Philip Levine

Poet Philip Levine (b. 1928) grew up in Detroit, Michigan, the son of Russian Jewish immigrants. He graduated from what is now Wayne State University and later earned an M.F.A. degree at the University of Iowa. He has been a member of the faculty at the University of Iowa, California State University at Fresno, and Tufts University, and from 1984 to 1985, he was chair of the literature board of the National Endowment for the Arts. Levine published his first collection of poetry in 1963 and since then has published more than twenty volumes, including Ashes: Poems New and Old *(1979) and* What Work Is *(1991), both of which won the National Book Award, and* The Simple Truth: Poems *(1994), which won the Pulitzer Prize. He is also author of the memoir* The Bread of Time *(1994). As a young man, Levine was a factory worker in auto plants in the Detroit area, where he determined "to find a voice for the voiceless . . . the people I was working with."*

We stand in the rain in a long line
waiting at Ford Highland Park. For work.
You know what work is — if you're
old enough to read this you know what
work is, although you may not do it.   5
Forget you. This is about waiting,
shifting from one foot to another.
Feeling the light rain falling like mist
into your hair, blurring your vision
until you think you see your own brother   10
ahead of you maybe ten places.
You rub your glasses with your fingers,
and of course it's someone else's brother,
narrower across the shoulders than
yours but with the same sad slouch, the grip   15
that does not hide the stubbornness,
the sad refusal to give in to
rain, to the hours wasted waiting,
to the knowledge that somewhere ahead
a man is waiting who will say, "No,   20
we're not hiring today," for any
reason he wants. You love your brother,
now suddenly you can hardly stand

the love flooding you for your brother,
who's not beside you or behind or   25
ahead because he's home trying to
sleep off a miserable night shift
at Cadillac so he can get up
before noon to study his German.
Works eight hours a night so he can sing   30
Wagner, the opera you hate most,
the worst music ever invented.
How long has it been since you told him
you loved him, held his wide shoulders,
opened your eyes wide and said those words,   35
and maybe kissed his cheek? You've never
done something so simple, so obvious,
not because you're too young or too dumb,
not because you're jealous or even mean
or incapable of crying in   40
the presence of another man, no,
just because you don't know what work is.

QUESTIONS

1. Start with your general response to the poem. What do you think that
   Levine is saying about work, working, and workers? What *is* work, according to this poem? Discuss this with others, and try to reach a consensus on the case that's being made here.
2. The word "you" — a harmless pronoun — appears several times in the
   poem. Does every "you" refer to the same you? How do you read the
   expression "Forget you"?
3. If you were going to stage this poem as a very short play, how would you
   begin? How many actors would you need? How many locations? Who
   would speak the words? Discuss your options, your problems, and your
   choices.
4. Take question 3 and run with it. That is, organize a performance of the
   poem, and perform it. You might even perform it in more than one way
   to explore the options or problems that the poem presents as a vehicle
   for the stage.
5. What is the function of Wagner in the poem? What does it mean to "sing
   Wagner" (lines 30–31), and why do you suppose that "you" hates the
   composer so much? What can you find out about Richard Wagner and
   about the people who love or hate his music? Try putting "Richard
   Wagner" and "Nazi" together in a Web search, and see what you get.
   After that, consider again what Wagner is doing in the poem. Does
   Wagner's history influence his function in this poem?

6. What's love got to do with it? That is, what's love got to do with work? Can you make a statement that sums up what the poem is about, using the words *love* and *work* prominently? Compare your answers to these questions with the answers that are prepared by others in your class.

7. Come back to the question of "you." Consider it again, now that you have done more thinking about the poem. To what extent would you consider that you — the reader — are the "you" that is being addressed?

MAKING CONNECTIONS

How does Levine's idea of what work is compare with the ideas that are presented in the other readings in this section? What similarities can you find among Levine, C. Wright Mills (p. 731), Vivian Gornick (p. 753), Barbara Ehrenreich (p. 760), and Eric Schlosser and Jon Lowenstein (p. 775)? How would you characterize each writer's definition of what work is (or could be)? Are there other aspects of work that these readings leave unconsidered? Research the question, or use your own experiences to write an essay that defines what work is.

Acknowledgments

Diane Ackerman. "Why Leaves Turn Color in the Fall." From *A Natural History of the Senses* by Diane Ackerman. Copyright © 1990 by Diane Ackerman. Reprinted with the permission of Random House, Inc.

Maya Angelou. "Graduation." From *I Know Why a Caged Bird Sings* by Maya Angelou. Copyright © 1969 by Maya Angelou. Reprinted with the permission of Random House, Inc.

W. H. Auden. "The Unknown Citizen." From *W.H. Auden Collected Poems* edited by Edward Mendelson. Copyright © 1940 and renewed 1968 by W. H. Auden. Reprinted with the permission of Random House, Inc.

James Baldwin. "If Black English Isn't a Language, Then Tell Me What Is." From *The New York Times*, July 29, 1979, Op-Ed page. Copyright © 1979 by The New York Times Company. Reprinted with permission.

John Berger. "Hiroshima." From *The Sense of Sight* by John Berger. Copyright © 1985 by John Berger. Reprinted with the permission of Pantheon Books, a division of Random House, Inc.

Bruno Bettelhiem. "Joey: A 'Mechanical Boy." From *Scientific American*, Vol. 200 (1959). Copyright © 1959 by Scientific American. All rights reserved.

Christina Boufis. "Teaching Literature at the County Jail." Originally published in *The Common Review* 1, No. 1. Copyright © 1920. Reprinted with the permission of the author.

Gwendolyn Brooks. "We Real Cool." From *Blacks* by Gwendolyn Brooks. Copyright © 1991 by Third World Press. Reprinted with the permission of Brooks Permissions.

Michael H. Brown. "Love Canal and the Poisoning of America." From *Laying Waste: Love Canal and the Poisoning of America* by Michael H. Brown. Copyright © 1979, 1980 by Michael H. Brown. Reprinted with the permission of Pantheon Books, a division of Random House, Inc.

Jan Harold Brunvand. "Urban Legends: The Boyfriend's Death." From *The Vanishing Hitchhiker: American Urban Legends and Their Meaning* by Jan Harold Brunvand. Copyright © 1981 by Jan Harold Brunvand. Reprinted with the permission of W.W. Norton & Company, Inc.

Judith Ortiz Cofer. "The Story of My Body." From *The Latin Deli: Prose & Poetry* by Judith Ortiz Cofer. Copyright © 1993 by Judith Ortiz Cofer. Reprinted with the permission of University of Georgia Press.

Barry Commoner. "Unraveling the DNA Myth." From the February 2002 issue of *Harper's Magazine*. Copyright © 2002 by Harper's Magazine Reprinted by special permission. All rights reserved.

Amanda Coyne. "The Long Goodbye: Mother's Day in Federal Prison." From the May 1997 issue of *Harper's Magazine*. Copyright © 1997 by Harper's Magazine. Reprinted by special permission. All rights reserved.

Antonio Damasio. "How the Brain Creates the Mind." From *Scientific American* 12, No. 1, August 2002. Copyright © 2002 by Scientific American, Inc. All rights reserved.

Emily Dickinson. "Because I could not stop for Death." From *The Complete Works of Emily Dickinson* edited by Thomas Johnson. Copyright © 1951, 1955, 1979 by the Presidents and Fellows of Harvard College. Reprinted with the permission of The Belknap Press of Harvard University Press.

Joan Didion. "On Keeping a Notebook." From *Slouching Toward Bethlehem* by Joan Didion. Copyright © 1966, 1968 by Joan Didion. Reprinted with the permission of Farrar, Straus & Giroux, LLC.

Annie Dillard. "Lenses." From *Teaching a Stone to Talk* by Annie Dillard. Copyright © 1982 by Annie Dillard. Reprinted with the permission of HarperCollins Publishers, Inc.

Barbara Ehrenreich. Excerpt from *Nickel and Dimed: On (Not) Getting By in America* by Barbara Ehrenreich. Copyright © 1999 by Barbara Ehrenreich. Reprinted with the permission of International Creative Management, Inc.

Anne Frank. "At Home, At School, In Hiding." From *The Diary of a Young Girl: The Definitive Edition*, edited by Otto M. Frank and Murjam Pressler and translated by Susan Massotty. Translation © 1995 by Doubleday. Reprinted with the permission of Doubleday, a division of Random House, Inc.

Jonathan Franzen. "Sifting the Ashes." From *The New Yorker*, May 13, 1996, pp. 40–48. Copyright © 1996 by Jonathan Franzen. Reprinted with the permission of the author.

Robert Frost. "Mending Wall." From *The Poetry of Robert Frost*, edited by Edward Connery Lathem. Copyright © 1923, 1928 by Henry Holt and Company, Inc. Renewed © 1951, 1956 by Robert Frost. Reprinted with the permission of Henry Holt and Company LLC.

Atul Gawande. "The Crimson Tide." From *The New Yorker*, February 12, 2001. Copyright © 2001 by Atul Gawande. Reprinted by permission of the author.

Robert Gilbert. "Understanding Ovation." Originally published by *Harper's Magazine*, October 2001. Copyright © 2001 by the author. Reprinted by permission of the author.

Malcolm Gladwell. "The Naked Face." From *The New Yorker*, August 5, 2002. Copyright © 2002 by Malcolm Gladwell. "The Art of Failure." From *The New Yorker*, August 21/28, 2000. Copyright © 2000 by Malcolm Gladwell. Both reprinted with the permission of the author.

Jane Goodall. "First Observations." From *In the Shadow of Man* by Jane Goodall. Copyright © 1971 by Hugo and Jane Van Lawick-Goodall. Reprinted with the permission of Houghton Mifflin Company. All rights reserved.

Adam Gopnik. "The City and the Pillars." From *The New Yorker*, September 24, 2001. Copyright © 2001 by Adam Gopnik. Reprinted with permission of The Wylie Agency, Inc.

Vivian Gornick. "A Narrator Leaps Past Journalism." From *The New York Times*, May 6, 2002. Copyright © 2002 by The New York Times Company. Reprinted with permission. "The Catskills Remembered." From *Approaching Eye Level* by Vivian Gornick. Copyright © 1996 by Vivian Gornick. Reprinted with the permission of Beacon Press, Boston.

Stephen Jay Gould. "Women's Brains." From *The Panda's Thumb: More Reflections in Natural History* by Stephen Jay Gould. Copyright © 1980 by Stephen Jay Gould. Reprinted with the permission of W.W. Norton & Company, Inc.

Lucy Grealy. "Mirrorings." From *Harper's Magazine*, February 1993. Copyright © 1993 by Harper's Magazine. Reprinted by special permission. All rights reserved.

Gary Greenberg. "As Good as Dead." From *The New Yorker*, August 13, 2001, pp. 36–41. Copyright © 2001 by Gary Greenberg. Reprinted with the permission of the author.

Gordon Grice. "A Slice of Life." Originally published in *The New Yorker*, July 30, 2001, pp. 36–41. Copyright © 2001 by Gordon Grice. Reprinted with permission of the author.

Patricia Hampl. "Review of *The Diary of Anne Frank*." Copyright © 1995 by Patricia Hampl. "Reviewing Anne Frank." Copyright © 1997 by Patricia Hampl. Reprinted by permission of the author and Marly Rusoff & Associates, Inc.

Zoë Tracy Hardy. "What Did You Do In the War, Daddy? A Flashback to August 1945." Originally published in *Ms.*, August 1985.

Stephen W. Hawking. "Our Picture of the Universe." From *A Brief History of Time* by Stephen W. Hawking. Copyright © 1988 by Stephen W. Hawking. Reprinted with the permission of Bantam Books, a division of Random House, Inc.

John Hersey. "Hatsuyo Nakamura" from *Hiroshima* by John Hersey. Copyright © 1946, 1985 by John Hersey. Copyright © renewed 1973 by John Hersey. Reprinted with the permission of Alfred A. Knopf, a division of Random House, Inc.

Langston Hughes. "Theme for English B." From *The Collected Poems of Langston Hughes* by Arnold Rampersad and David Rossel. Copyright © 1994 by the Estate of Langston Hughes. Reprinted with the permission of Alfred A. Knopf, a division of Random House, Inc.

Randall Jarrell. "The Death of the Ball Turret Gunner." From *The Complete Poems* by Randall Jarrell. Copyright © 1945, 1969 by Mrs. Randall Jarrell. Reprinted with the permission of Farrar, Straus & Giroux, LLC.

James Jeans. "Why the Sky Is Blue." From *The Stars in Their Courses* by James Jeans. Copyright © 1931 by James Jeans. Reprinted with the permission of Cambridge University Press.

Patrik Jonsson. "Edgy First College Assignment: Study the Koran." From *The Christian Science Monitor*, July 30, 2002. Copyright © 2002 by Patrik Jonsson. Reprinted with the permission of the author.

Michael Kamber. "Toil and Temptation." Originally published in *The Village Voice*, April 24, 2001. Copyright © 2001 by Michael Kamber. Reprinted with permission of the author.

Garrett Keizer. "Why We Hate Teachers." From *Harper's Magazine*, September 2001. Copyright © 2001 by Garrett Keizer. Reprinted with permission of Sterling Lord Literistic, Inc.

Martin Luther King Jr. "Pilgrimage to Nonviolence." From *Fellowship*, September 1, 1958 by Martin Luther King Jr. Copyright © 1958 by Martin Luther King Jr. Copyright renewed 1986 by Coretta Scott King. "A Letter from Birmingham Jail." Copyright © 1963 by Martin Luther King Jr. Copyright renewed 1991 by Coretta Scott King. Reprinted with the permission of The Heirs to the Estate of Martin Luther King Jr., c/o Writers House, Inc., as agents for the proprietors.

Verlyn Klinkenberg. "The Best Clock in the World." From *Discover*, June 2000 21, No. 6. Copyright © 2000 by Verlyn Klinkenberg. Reprinted with the permission of the author.

Elizabeth Kubler-Ross. "On the Fear of Death." From *On Death and Dying* by Elizabeth Kubler-Ross. Copyright © 1969 by Elizabeth Kubler-Ross. Reprinted with the permission of Scribner, an imprint of Simon & Schuster Adult Publishing Group.

Marcus Laffey. "Inside Dope." From *Blue Blood*. Originally from *The New Yorker*, February 1, 1999, pp. 29–32. Copyright © 2003 by Marcus Laffey. Reprinted with the permission of Riverhead Books, a division of Penguin Group (USA) Inc.

William L. Laurence. "Atomic Bombing of Nagasaki Told by a Flight Member." From *The New York Times*, September 9, 1945. Copyright © 1945 by The New York Times Company. Reprinted with permission.

Philip Levine. "What Work Is." From *What Work Is: Poems* by Philip Levine. Copyright © 1992 by Philip Levine. Reprinted with the permission of Alfred A. Knopf, a division of Random House, Inc.

Nancy Mairs. Excerpt from *Carnal Acts* by Nancy Mairs. Copyright © 1990 by Nancy Mairs. Reprinted with the permission of Beacon Press, Boston.

Emily Martin. "The Egg and the Sperm: How Science Has Constructed a Romance Based on Stereotypical Male-Female Roles." From *Signs: Journal of Women in Culture and Society* 16, no. 3, p. 501. Copyright © 1991 by The University of Chicago Press. Reprinted with the permission of the publisher and the author.

Louis Menand. "Honest, Decent, Wrong." From *The New Yorker*, January 27, 2003. Copyright © 2003 by Louis Menand. Reprinted with the permission of The Wylie Agency, Inc.

Stanley Milgram. "Some Conditions of Obedience and Disobedience to Authority." From *Human Relations* 18, No. 1 (1965). Copyright © 1972 by Stanley Milgram. Reprinted with permission. All rights controlled by Alexandra Milgram, Literary Executor.

C. Wright Mills. "A White Collar Works." (Chapter 10, pp. 215–238) from *White Collar: The American Middle Classes* by C. Wright Mills. Copyright © 1951 by C. Wright Mills. Reprinted with the permission of Oxford University Press, Inc.

N. Scott Momaday. "The Way to Rainy Mountain." From *The Way to Rainy Mountain* by N. Scott Momaday. Originally published in *The Reporter*, January 26, 1967. Copyright © 1969 by N. Scott Momaday. Reprinted with the permission of The University of New Mexico Press.

Monica M. Moore. "Nonverbal Courtship in Women: Context and Consequences" from *Ethology and Sociobiology* 6, No. 4 (1995). Copyright © 1995 by Monica M. Moore. Reprinted with the permission of the author.

Joyce Carol Oates. "Life, Vigor, Fire: The Watercolors of Winslow Homer." From *Woman Writer* by Joyce Carol Oates. Copyright © 1988 by Joyce Carol Oates. Reprinted with the permission of Dutton, a division of Penguin Group (USA) Inc.

George Orwell. "Shooting an Elephant" and "Politics and the English Language." From *Shooting an Elephant and Other Stories* by George Orwell. Copyright © 1950 by Sonia Brownell Orwell and renewed © 1978 by Sonia Pitt-Rivers. Reprinted with the permission of Harcourt, Inc. and Bill Hamilton as the Literary Executor of the Estate of the Late Sonia Brownell Orwell and Secker & Warburg Limited.

Cynthia Ozick. "The Impious Impatience of Job." From *Quarrel and Quandary* by Cynthia Ozick. Copyright © 2000 by Cynthia Ozick. Originally published in *The American Scholar* 67 (1998). Reprinted with the permission of Alfred A. Knopf, a division of Random House, Inc.

Pablo Picasso. "A Statement by Picasso." From *Picasso On Art*, by Alfred J. Barr, Jr. Copyright © 1974 by The Museum of Modern Art, New York. Reprinted by permission.

Sylvia Plath. "Metaphors." From *The Collected Poems of Sylvia Plath*, edited by Ted Hughes. Copyright © 1957 by Ted Hughes. Reprinted with the permission of HarperCollins Publishers, Inc. and Faber and Faber Ltd.

Phillip Richards. "There's No Room for You There: Black Students and Prestigious Colleges." Originally titled "Facing Races" from *The Chronicle Review*, September 13, 2002. Copyright © 2002 by Phillip Richards. Reprinted with the permission of the author.

Phyllis Rose. "Tools of Torture: An Essay on Beauty and Pain." From *The Atlantic Monthly*, October 1986. Copyright © 1986 by Phyllis Rose. Reprinted with the permission of The Wylie Agency, Inc.

Oliver Sacks. Excerpt from *The Man Who Mistook His Wife for a Hat* by Oliver Sacks. Copyright © 1970, 1981, 1983, 1984, 1985 by Oliver Sacks. Reprinted with the permission of Simon & Schuster Adult Publishing Group.

Carl Sagan. "Can We Know the Universe? Reflections on a Grain of Salt." From *Broca's Brain: Reflections on the Romance of Science* by Carol Sagan. Copyright © 1979 by Carl Sagan. Reprinted with the permission of the Estate of Carl Sagan.

Scott Russell Sanders. "Earth, Air, Fire, and Water." From *Writing from the Center* by Scott Russell Sanders. Copyright © 1995 by Scott Russell Sanders. Reprinted with the permission of Scott Russell Sanders.

Eric Schlosser. "Why McDonald's Fries Taste So Good." From *Fast Food Nation* by Eric Schlosser. Originally published in *The Atlantic Monthly*, January 2001. Excerpted and reprinted with the permission of Houghton Mifflin Company. All rights reserved.

Eric Schlosser and Jon Lowenstein. "Making It Work." From *Mother Jones*, September/October 2002, pp. 68–73. Copyright © 2002 by Eric Schlosser. Reprinted with the permission of Eric Schlosser.

Serge Schmemann. "U.S. Attacked; Hijacked Jets Destroy Twin Towers and Hit Pentagon in Day of Terror: President Vows to Exact Punishment for Evil." From *The New York Times*, September 12, 2001, A-1. Copyright © 2001 by The New York Times Company. Reprinted with permission.

Roy C. Selby, Jr. "A Delicate Operation." From the December 1975 issue of *Harper's Magazine*. Copyright © 1975 by Harper's Magazine. Reprinted by special permission. All rights reserved.

Richard Selzer. "The Discus Thrower." From *Confessions of a Knife* by Richard Selzer. Copyright © 1979 by David Goldman and Janet Selzer, Trustees. "A Mask on the Face of Death." From *Life*, 1988, Copyright © 1987 by Richard Selzer. Reprinted with the permission of Georges Borchardt, Inc. Literary Agency.

Theodore R. Sizer. "What High School Is." From *Horace's Compromise* by Theodore R. Sizer. Copyright © 1984 by Theodore R. Sizer. Reprinted with the permission of Houghton Mifflin Company. All rights reserved.

Mark Strand. "Pot Roast." From *Selected Poems* by Mark Strand. Copyright © 1979, 1980 by Mark Strand. Reprinted with the permission of Alfred A. Knopf, a division of Random House, Inc.

Andrew Sullivan. "What's So Bad About Hate?" From the *New York Times Magazine*, September 26, 1999. Copyright © 1999, 2000 by Andrew Sullivan. Reprinted with the permission of The Wylie Agency, Inc.

Amy Tan. "Mother Tongue." Originally published as "Under Western Eyes." From *The Threepenny Review*, 1990. Copyright © 1990 by Amy Tan. Reprinted with the permission of the author and Sandra Dijkstra Literary Agency.

Barbara Tuchman. "This is the End of the World: The Black Death." From *A Distant Mirror* by Barbara Tuchman. Copyright © 1978 by Barbara W. Tuchman. Reprinted with the permission of Alfred A. Knopf, a division of Random House, Inc.

Alice Walker. "Beauty: When the Other Dancer Is the Self." From *In Search of Our Mothers' Gardens: Womanist Prose* by Alice Walker. Copyright © 1983 by Alice Walker. Reprinted with the permission of Harcourt, Inc.

Robert A. Weinberg. "Of Clones and Clowns." Originally published in *Atlantic Monthly*, June 2002, pp. 54–59. Copyright © 2002 by Robert A. Weinberg. Reprinted with the permission of the author.

Picture Credits

Page 89: Illustration by Al Momaday, from *The Way to Rainy Mountain* by N. Scott Momaday, University of New Mexico Press, 1969. © N. Scott Momaday, Photo: General Research Division, The New York Public Library.

Page 190: © Tim Zielenbach/Contact Press Images.

Page 219: Alinari/Art Resource.

Page 221: Bibliothèque Royale Albert I, Brussels. Giraudon/Art Resource, NY.

Page 234: AP/Wide World Photos.

Pages 238, 239, 244: Photographs and line drawings from *In The Shadow of Man* by Jane Goodall. Photographs by Hugo van Lawick; line drawings by David Bygott. Copyright © 1971 by Hugo and Jane van Lawick-Goodall. Reprinted by permission of Houghton Mifflin Company. All rights reserved.

Page 248: Copyright © 2001 by "The New York Times Company."

Pages 290, 293, 294, 295: First published in *Scientific American*, March 1959, © Scientific American. Drawings on pages 290, 293, 294 and 295 were subsequently reprinted with permission in *The Empty Fortress* by Bruno Bettelheim, The Free Press, NY, 1967. Photos: General Research Division, The New York Public Library. Drawings on page 295 from *Scientific American*, March 1959. Photos: Science, Industry & Business Library, The New York Public Library.

Page 299: Courtesy National Library of Medicine.

Page 490: Illustration by Ron Miller, copyright © 1988 by Ron Miller, from *A Brief History of Time* by Stephen W. Hawking. Used by permission of Bantam Books, a division of Random House, Inc. Photo: General Research Division, The New York Public Library.

Page 503: Courtesy Hanna Damasio, University of Iowa.

Pages 510, 513: Photographs by Bernd Auers.

Page 512: National Institute of Standards and Technology.

Pages 526, 527: From *Unforgettable Fire: Pictures Drawn by Atomic Bomb Survivors*, edited by The Japan Broadcasting Association, Copyright © 1977 by NHK. Used by permission of Pantheon Books, a division of Random House, Inc. Photo: General Research Division, The New York Public Library. Courtesy Hiroshima Peace Memorial Museum.

Page 573: Photograph of Pablo Picasso: Beinecke Rare Book and Manuscript Library, Yale University. Painting in background: "Ma Jolie" by Pablo Picasso © 2003. Estate of Pablo Picasso/Artists Rights Society (ARS).

Page 575: Portrait of Pablo Picasso by Juan Gris (Spanish 1887–1927). Oil on canvas, 93.3x74.3 cm. Gift of Leigh B. Block, 1958.525. The Art Institute of Chicago. © 2003 Artists Rights Society (ARS), New York/ ADAGP, Paris.

Page 576: Self-Portrait of Pablo Picasso. Oil on canvas, 56x45 cm. National Gallery, Prague. Nimatallah/Art Resource, NY. © 2003 Estate of Pablo Picasso/Artists Rights Society (ARS), New York.

Pages 776–779: Photographs by Jon Lowenstein.

Rhetorical Index

Author and Title Index